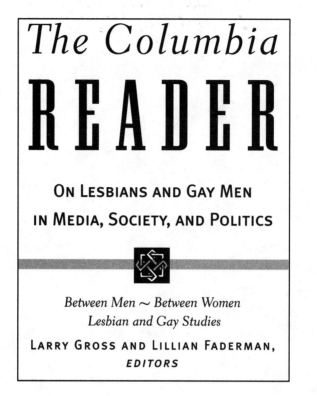

# The Columbia

# READER

## ON LESBIANS AND GAY MEN
## IN MEDIA, SOCIETY, AND POLITICS

*Between Men ~ Between Women*
*Lesbian and Gay Studies*

LARRY GROSS AND LILLIAN FADERMAN,
*EDITORS*

# The Columbia
# READER

## ON LESBIANS AND GAY MEN
## IN MEDIA, SOCIETY, AND POLITICS

*Edited and with an introduction by*

## LARRY GROSS AND JAMES D. WOODS

NEW YORK
COLUMBIA UNIVERSITY PRESS

Columbia University Press
Publishers Since 1893
New York    Chichester, West Sussex
Copyright © 1999 Columbia University Press
All rights reserved

Library of Congress Cataloging-in-Publication Data
The Columbia Reader on lesbians and gay men in media, society, and politics  /  edited and with
an introduction by Larry Gross and James D. Woods.
Includes bibliographical references.
ISBN  0-231-10446-4.   ISBN  0-231-10447-2 (pbk.)
1. Gay men in mass media.   2. Lesbians in mass media.
3. Mass media—United States.   4. Gay men—United States.
5. Lesbians—United States.   6. United States—Social conditions—1980.
I. Gross, Larry , 1942–   .   II. Woods, James D.   III. Series.
P96.H632U63      1999      98-36595
302.23'08664—dc21    CIP

Casebound editions of Columbia University Press books are printed on permanent and durable
acid-free paper.

Printed in the United States of America

c 10 9 8 7 6 5 4 3 2 1
p 10 9 8 7 6 5 4 3 2 1

# CONTENTS

Preface,   xvii

Introduction: Being Gay in American Media and Society
*Larry Gross and James D. Woods,*   3

## ONE   IDENTITY: THE MODERN HOMOSEXUAL

### A. *Other Times, Other Customs,*   25

1. A Matter of Difference
   *Martin Duberman,*   31

2. ``Intimate Friendships''
   *Erica E. Goode, with Betsy Wagner,*   33

3. Categories, Experience, and Sexuality
   *John Boswell,*   36

4. Capitalism and Gay Identity
   *John D'Emilio,*   48

5. A Worm in the Bud: The Early Sexologists and Love Between Women
   *Lillian Faderman,*   56

6. The Bowery as Haven and Spectacle
   *George Chauncey,*   67

### B. *Who's a Queer? Identities in Question,*   75

7. Making Ourselves from Scratch
   *Joseph Beam,*   79

8. Becoming Lesbian: Identity Work and the Performance of Sexuality
   *Arlene Stein,* 81

9. Gay Men, Lesbians, and Sex: Doing It Together
   *Pat Califia,* 92

10. Maiden Voyage: Excursion Into Sexuality and Identity Politics
    in Asian America
    *Dana Y. Takagi,* 96

11. Strangers at Home: Bisexuals in the Queer Movement
    *Carol Queen,* 105

12. Just Add Water: Searching for the Bisexual Politic
    *Ara Wilson,* 108

13. To Be or Not to Be
    *Leslie Feinberg,* 112

## Two   Institutions and Opinion Makers

### A. *Inventing Sin: Religion and the Church,*   *119*

14. The Abominable Sin: The Spanish Campaign Against ``Sodomy,'' and Its Results
    in Modern Latin America
    *Walter Williams,* 125

15. Letter to the Bishops of the Catholic Church on the Pastoral Care
    of Homosexual Persons
    *Joseph Cardinal Ratzinger, Congregation for the Doctrine of the Faith,* 135

16. Homophobic? Re-Read Your Bible
    *Peter J. Gomes,* 138

17. Biblical Verse: Is It a Reason or an Excuse?
    *Deb Price,* 140

18. The Homosexual Movement:
    A Response by the Ramsey Colloquium
    *Ramsey Colloquium,* 141

19. In God's Image: Coming to Terms with Leviticus
   *Rebecca T. Alpert*,   147


**B. Making Us Sick: The Medical and Psychological Establishment,   153**

20. The Product Conversion—From Heresy to Illness
   *Thomas Szasz*,   157

21. Homosexuals in Uniform
   Newsweek,   163

22. I Was Raising a Homosexual Child
   *Flora Rheta Schreiber*,   164

23. The Psychologist—Dr. Evelyn Hooker
   *Eric Marcus*,   169

24. A Symposium: Should Homosexuality Be
   in the APA Nomenclature?
   *Judd Marmor, Irving Bieber, Ronald Gold*,   175

25. If Freud Had Been a Neurotic Colored Woman:
   Reading Dr. Frances Cress Welsing
   *Essex Hemphill*,   180


**C. Causes and Cures: The Etiology Debate,   185**

26. Boys Will Be Girls: Sexology and Homosexuality
   *Janice Irvine*,   191

27. How to Bring Your Kids Up Gay: The War
   on Effeminate Boys
   *Eve Kosofsky Sedgwick*,   201

28. Studying the Biology of Sexual Orientation Has Political Fallout
   *David J. Jefferson*,   207

29. Are Gay Men Born That Way?
   *Kay Diaz*,   211

# Contents

## D. Creating Criminals: Government and the Legal System, 219

30. Crime Story
    *Sten Russell,* 223

31. Public Policy and Private Prejudice: Psychology and Law
    on Gay Rights
    *Gary B. Melton,* 225

32. Crimes of Lesbian Sex
    *Ruthann Robson,* 228

## E. Denial and Erasure: Education and Culture, 235

33. Who Hid Lesbian History?
    *Lillian Faderman,* 241

34. Stolen Goods
    *Michael Bronski,* 245

35. Remembering Lenny: Parting Notes on a Friend
    Who Never Quite Came Out
    *Paul Moor,* 251

36. Willa Cather
    *Sharon O'Brien,* 253

37. Closets in the Museum: Homophobia and Art History
    *James Saslow,* 256

38. Imagine a Lesbian, a Black Lesbian
    *Jewelle Gomez,* 262

39. Too Queer for College: Notes on Homophobia
    *Esther Newton,* 270

40. The Gay and Lesbian Publishing Boom
    *William J. Mann,* 273

41. A Lesson in Tolerance
    *David Ruenzel,* 278

# CONTENTS

42. Gay Teachers Make Their Lives Whole Again
   *Deb Price,*   285

43. Pop Tune Can Comfort Teens Unsure of Their Sexuality
   *Victoria Brownworth,*   286

## THREE   MAINSTREAM MEDIA

### A. *Up From Invisibility: Film and Television,*   291

44. Stereotyping
   *Richard Dyer,*   297

45. Lesbians and Film: Some Thoughts
   *Caroline Sheldon,*   301

46. Where Is the Life That Late He Led? Hollywood's Construction of Sexuality in
   the Life of Cole Porter
   *George F. Custen,*   306

47. Old Strategies for New Texts: How American Television Is Creating and Treating
   Lesbian Characters
   *Marguerite J. Moritz,*   316

48. Culture Stays Screen-Shy of Showing the Gay Kiss
   *Frank Bruni,*   327

49. Do Ask, Do Tell: Freak Talk on TV
   *Joshua Gamson,*   329

50. More Than Friends
   *David Ehrenstein,*   335

51. Anything But Idyllic: Lesbian Filmmaking in the 1980s and 1990s
   *Liz Kotz,*   341

### B. *Fit to Print? Journalism,*   349

52. Perverts Called Government Peril
   New York Times,   354

53. The Homosexual in America
   Time,   355

54. A Rebuke for TIME's Pernicious Prejudice
   *Kay Tobin*,   358

55. A Minority's Plea: U.S. Homosexuals Gain in Trying to Persuade Society to Accept Them
   *Charles Alverson*,   360

56. Homo Nest Raided! Queen Bees Are Stinging Mad
   *Jerry Lisker*,   363

57. The ``Gay'' People Demand Their Rights
   *Lacey Fosburgh*,   365

58. The Lesbian Issue and Women's Lib
   *Judy Klemesrud*,   366

59. Uptight on Gay News: Can the Straight Press Get the Gay Story Straight?
   *Ransdell Pierson*,   368

60. Out at the New York Times
   *Michelangelo Signorile*,   375

C. *Cries and Whispers: AIDS and the Media*,   387

61. Illness and Deviance: The Response of the Press to AIDS
   *Edward Albert*,   393

62. The Second Wave
   *James Kinsella*,   402

63. A Test of Who We Are As a People
   *Vito Russo*,   408

64. More to the Shilts Story
   *Jessea Greenman*,   410

65. Big Science: What Ever Happened to Safer Sex?
   *Richard Goldstein*,   412

## D. Naming Names: Outing, 417

66. Contested Closets: The Politics and Ethics of Outing
    *Larry Gross,* 421

67. How I Brought Out Malcom Forbes and the Media Flinched
    *Michelangelo Signorile,* 429

68. Why Outing Must Stop
    *C. Carr,* 431

69. The Inning of Outing
    *Gabriel Rotello,* 433

# FOUR   LESBIAN AND GAY MEDIA

## A. In Our Own Voices: The Lesbian and Gay Press, 437

70. "Gay Gal"—Lisa Ben
    *Eric Marcus,* 443

71. "News Hound"—Jim Kepner
    *Eric Marcus,* 446

72. *The Advocate*: Setting the Standard for the Gay Liberation Press
    *Rodger Streitmatter,* 450

73. Representation, Liberation, and the Queer Press
    *Polly Thistlethwaite,* 460

74. Flaunting It! A Decade of Gay Journalism from *The Body Politic*
    *Ed Jackson,* 461

75. I Want My Gay TV
    *Larry Closs,* 466

## B. The Good Parts: Pornography, 475

76. Coming to Terms: Gay Pornography
    *Richard Dyer,* 479

77. Gender, Fucking, and Utopia: An Essay in Response to John Stoltenberg's *Refusing to Be a Man*
    *Scott Tucker,* 486

78. Free Speech or Hate Speech: Pornography and Its Means of Production
    *Charles I. Nero,* 497

79. My History with Censorship
    *Joan Nestle,* 502

80. My Mother Liked to Fuck
    *Joan Nestle,* 505

81. Lesbian Pornography: Cultural Transgression and Sexual Demystification
    *Lisa Henderson,* 506

82. Looking for My Penis: The Eroticized Asian in Gay Video Porn
    *Richard Fung,* 517

C. *Queers in Cyberspace,* 527

83. Notes on Queer 'N Asian Virtual Sex
    *Daniel C. Tsang,* 531

84. We're Teen, We're Queer, and We've Got E-mail
    *Steve Silberman,* 537

85. Logging On, Coming Out
    *Jeff Walsh,* 540

## FIVE COMMUNITY PROSPECTS AND TACTICS

A. *Queer Positions and Perspectives,* 545

86. With Downcast Gays: Aspects of Homosexual Self-Oppression
    *Andrew Hodges and David Hutter,* 551

87. The Woman-Identified Woman
    *Radicalesbians,* 562

88. Lesbianism: An Act of Resistance
    *Cheryl Clarke,* 565

89. I Paid Very Hard for My Immigrant Ignorance
    *Mirtha Quintanales,* 571

90. Our Right to the World: Beyond the Right to Privacy
    *Scott Tucker,* 575

91. Chasing the Crossover Audience and Other Self-Defeating Strategies
    *Michael Denneny,* 583

92. Queers Read This: I Hate Straights
    *Anonymous Queers,* 588

**B. The New Right = The Old Wrongs?** 595

93. The Boys on the Beach
    *Midge Decter,* 601

94. Straight Talk About Gays
    *E. L. Pattullo,* 611

95. In God's Country
    *John Weir,* 616

**C. A Place at Which Table?** 625

96. Here Comes the Groom: A (Conservative) Case for Gay Marriage
    *Andrew Sullivan,* 631

97. Why Gay People Should Seek the Right to Marry
    *Thomas B. Stoddard,* 633

98. Since When Is Marriage a Path to Liberation?
    *Paula L. Ettelbrick,* 637

99. Homocons
    *Matthew Rees,* 640

100. The Naked Truth
*Candace Chellew,*   643

101. Out of Asia
*Jeff Yang,*   644

102. Backlash?
*Henry Louis Gates, Jr.,*   647

103. Blacks and Gays: Healing the Great Divide
*Barbara Smith,*   649

**D. Parting Glances,**   653

104. Why I'm Not a Revolutionary
*Sarah Schulman,*   655

105. In an Afternoon Light
*Essex Hemphill,*   658


Credits,   661

# PREFACE

In the fall of 1980, when I began teaching the first lesbian and gay studies course at the University of Pennsylvania, the field of lesbian and gay studies was in its infancy. Despite such pioneering work as Laud Humphrey's 1970 *Tearoom Trade*, Esther Newton's *Mother Camp*, Parker Tyler's *Screening the Sexes: Homosexuality in the Movies*, and Karla Jay and Allen Young's *Out of the Closets: Voice of Gay Liberation*, published in 1972, few scholars took such risks. In the course of the post-Stonewall decade, however, this trickle of original work became a stream crossing the boundaries of several disciplines, mostly through the efforts of independent scholars and activists. The Gay Academic Union was founded in 1973 and the following year the *Journal of Homosexuality* was launched. In 1975 Carroll Smith-Rosenberg published "The Female World of Love and Ritual." Jonathan Ned Katz's landmark *Gay American History* was published in 1976; Richard Dyer's collection, *Gays and Film*, and Jeffrey Weeks's *Coming Out: Homosexual Politics in Britain from the Nineteenth Century to the Present* were published in 1977. Gay studies' first best-seller, John Boswell's *Christianity, Social Tolerance, and Homosexuality*, appeared just months before I began teaching the course, and both Lillian Faderman's *Surpassing the Love of Men* and Vito Russo's *The Celluloid Closet* followed shortly after, in 1981.

The pace of publication and presentation picked up as international conferences were held in the early 1980s in Toronto and Amsterdam, bringing together scholars (and activists) from North America and Europe (as well as some from Latin America and Asia), at that time mostly historians and social scientists. In the 1980s the scope of lesbian and gay studies began to include more contributors from literary and cultural theory perspectives, many adding a Lacanian twist to the Foucauldian French accents of the social constructionist school.

By the early 1990s, after the first U.S.-based large-scale lesbian and gay studies conferences were held, at Yale and later at Harvard, Rutgers, and Iowa (along with the OutWrite conferences in San Francisco and Boston), the realm of lesbian and gay studies and the overlapping territory of queer theory seemed to be expanding exponentially. Book series, special issues, and new journals are devoted to lesbian and gay studies and queer theory.

▼ ▼ ▼

James Woods assisted me in my course while in graduate school, and in 1991 began teaching "Sexual Minorities in Film and Popular Culture" at the College of Staten Island/CUNY and the CUNY Graduate Center. Around that time we began discussing the need for a comprehensive and accessible Reader for courses in lesbian and gay studies. We wanted a Reader with a broad frame of reference, while devoting a greater degree of attention to the role of mass media in both reflecting and shaping images of lesbians and gay men held by society and by lesbian and gay people themselves.

The Reader opens with an introduction that establishes a general framework for understanding the role of cultural forces, and the mass media in particular, in shaping the experiences and images of lesbian and gay people in America. Following the introduction, the Reader is divided into five parts, within which each section opens with a short introductory essay by the editors. These introductions form an expository spine that runs through the body of the Reader.

The first section introduces historical and cross-cultural dimensions that are necessary to ground any discussion of sexuality, let alone an understanding of the contemporary views of homosexuality identity. The next section illustrates the complexities involved in defining and adopting sexual minority identities, noting the experiences of racial/ethnic minorities as well as bisexual and transgendered persons. Following these opening sections are sections focusing on central institutions that have claimed (and held) the authority to define and control sexuality in Western societies: medicine (psychiatry in particular), religion, and law. While these sections emphasize the "bad old days" of these institutions (and these days are not necessarily over!), material is included to reflect the more forward thinking in medicine and religion. The section that follows the one on psychiatry addresses the currently hot area of scientific research on the "causes" of sexual orientation.

The final section in this part includes material on the realms of culture that are represented in the "formal curricula" of American society—K-12 schools and higher education. The articles in this section illustrate the erasure and denial mechanisms adopted in mainstream culture's handling of lesbian and gay creators and performers.

The next part includes four sections that focus on the mass media—the "informal curriculum" of American society. The first addresses the fictional media of movies and television, and the story is one that mixes a history of stereotyping with some evidence of growth and progress. The next section concerns the press and goes beyond the story of media failure to chronicle the dramatic transformation that has occurred in journalistic treatment of lesbian and gay issues in the past few years (with the *New York Times* as the prime case in point). The final two sections in this part deal with topical issues: the AIDS epidemic has left its mark on every aspect of lesbian and gay existence, and in the context of this reader it seems particularly appropriate to attend to the central role of the media in shaping the tragic course of the crisis. The controversy over outing raised basic questions about the norms of secretiveness that generations of gay people had accepted without serious questioning, and challenged journalists to abandon a double standard that defined homosexuality as the dirtiest of dirty secrets.

In the next part we turn our attention from the outside world to the inside realm of the lesbian and gay community, beginning with the gay press that catalyzed the emergence of gay community and politics as well as lesbian and gay studies. The debates about the politics of pornography were not primarily concerned with lesbian and gay people, yet many of the most engaged on all sides of the "porn" or "sex wars" were in fact lesbian women and gay men, and it is important to pay attention to the particular ways in which sexual representations have helped shape the nature of lesbian and gay identity in an erotophobic and heterosexist culture. The final section highlights the rapidly expanding realm of cyberspace, the explosive growth of the internet on which lesbian and gay people are disproportionately represented.

The final part includes three sections that focus most directly on the transformations, from oppression to fighting for liberation that occurred around the time of Stonewall and continue even today, and take up issues of strategy and political analysis that animate the politics of the contemporary movement. The first of these presents a range of what might be called identity-oriented, even separatist positions. The next section illustrates antigay bigotry, with two unabashed attacks on gay people's lives, and a journalistic account of the fundamentalist antigay movement. The next section offers a variety of contemporary perspectives on same-sex marriage, the growing conservative wing of the gay movement, and the tensions between sexual and racial minorities and identities.

The Reader concludes with two brief essays that allow us to leave on a poetic and even elegiac note.

▼ ▼ ▼

Beginning with the first offering in 1980, the first assignment I give in my course has asked each student to

> Imagine that you are a fifteen year old and are beginning to have questions about your sexuality. Specifically, you have heard of homosexuality and wonder whether this might have something to do with you. You want to find out more about homosexuality and you do not feel that you can ask anyone you know, so you look for printed information. You go to a public library.
> Your task is to go to such a library and play the role of a 15-year-old explorer: what can you find in the library that will "explain" homosexuality to you, and what is the "message"?

Over the many years I have been assigning this paper there has been a remarkable and gratifying improvement in the quantity and the quality of the books my students find on the shelves of public libraries in Philadelphia and its suburbs, although the picture is not without its flaws: many books are housed in locked sections, so that readers must go to the desk and ask for them by name; many outdated and bigoted works remain on library shelves; many items listed in the catalogue have been lost or stolen. Even more striking is the expansion of other sources of image and information for curious and questioning young people. If a fifteen year old in 1980 might have seen or read little about homosexuality (and many of my students attested to this from their own recent experiences), in 1998 they have lived in a very different world. For today's teens the existence of gay people is a fact of life reflected in the news, in film and television, and in popular music. Many of them have known about or belonged to lesbian/gay groups in high school, and even more of them have found friendly and supportive communities on the internet.

In the summer of 1997 Melissa Gurley, a seventeen-year-old high school senior in Burlington, Wisconsin, responded to Ellen DeGeneres's coming out on the cover of *Time*, the Oprah Winfrey Show, and nearly every other media forum, by writing a column for *Oasis*, an "online magazine for lesbian, gay, bisexual, transgender, and questioning youth," in which she proclaimed her intention of living her life honestly, "because I have nothing to hide."

Yet, despite all these signs of rapid cultural change, growing up queer in America is never easy and is often unbearable. In November of 1997 James Wheeler, a talented eighteen-year-old artist and poet who had been harassed by high school classmates in Lebanon, Pennsylvania, added his name to the long list of teenage lesbian and gay suicides. Such tragedies remind me why I first began to conduct and teach lesbian and gay studies, and why the work begun in the heady days of gay liberation is still not complete.

▼ ▼ ▼

Many people contributed to the work that went into creating the courses on which this reader is based, and to the often frustrating task of assembling the Reader itself.

Much of the initial inspiration for the course was provided by Sean O'Neil, then a graduate student in communications, who urged me to develop the course and served as my first teaching assistant. Sean's master's thesis, on the role of media in the formation of gay identity, was itself a worthy contribution to the largely uncharted field we were helping launch. Sean's death from AIDS in 1986 was unfortunately only the first time the epidemic reached into that classroom.

Following Sean O'Neil, I have been blessed with many skillful and sensitive assistants in teaching this course, each of whom has taught me as well as the students: Paul Carlson, Deb Conry, David Gleason, Lisa Henderson, Steven Hocker, Judy Kisor, David Phillips, Connie Ruzich, Danny Tate, and James Woods. Since 1980 nearly six hundred students have taken "Communications, Culture and Sexual Minorities." I have been challenged, moved, and enriched by the experience.

Research and technical assistance has been provided by Annenberg School librarians Sandra Grilikhes and Susan Williamson and computer wizards David Graper, Timothy Blake, and Rich Cardona. I have been fortunate in having the assistance of graduate students Tina Anderson, Denine Benedetto, Heather Rule, and Jo Stryker; Tracy Morgan provided assistance to Jim Woods in New York. As usual, I have benefited from Geoff Falen's varied talents and invariable good humor. The Annenberg School, under Deans George Gerbner and Kathleen Hall Jamieson, has supported my teaching of the course on which this Reader is based.

Colleagues and friends, both mine and Jim's, helped shape the form and content of the course and reader with their suggestions and criticisms. Particular thanks to George Custen, Richard Dyer, Lisa Henderson, Carolyn Marvin, Nancy Morris, Esther Newton, Vito Russo, Joyce Seltzer, Joseph Turow, Barbie Zelizer, and six anonymous reviewers. Ann Miller at Columbia University Press has combined patience and urgency as needed, and Susan Pensak has provided sympathetic and insightful editing.

Scott Tucker's contributions to this reader far exceed the eloquence and intelligence of his writing, though readers will appreciate those. For the past twenty-two years my life and work have been enriched by his love and companionship, and his fingerprints can be found throughout my teaching and writing. James Woods spent the last few years of his life in a loving and rewarding relationship with Paul Young. The image of Jim and Paul, surrounded by family and friends at their commitment celebration in the fall of 1994, will remain among my fondest memories.

Writing a preface is always a bittersweet task, coming at the end of a long project, mixing the pleasure of completion with the pang of separation. In this instance, however, the pain is especially sharp as the experience of working on the Reader is entwined with the joys of my decade-long friendship with Jim Woods and the still palpable grief at his death.

James Woods died of AIDS complications in November 1995, shortly past his thirty-second birthday. I first knew Jim as a graduate student and advisee, but we quickly became friends and collaborators. I was pleased when he undertook dissertation research on the professional lives of gay men—still a risky topic for a graduate student—and thrilled when the work was snapped up for publication before the ink was dry. *The Corporate Closet* (Free Press, 1993) was designated the "Outstanding Book on Human Rights" by the Gustavus Myers Center for the Study of Human Rights. Jim began teaching at the College of Staten Island/CUNY and then became one of the few nontenured faculty members to receive an appointment at CUNY's Graduate Center. As he started teaching courses similar to mine, we began to plan the reader. For the next few years we phoned, faxed, and e-mailed back and forth, sending articles, clippings, drafts of the section introductions, and endless iterations of the table of contents. Even as Jim's health deteriorated he continued to work on the project, and when I visited him in the hospital we would discuss possible additions and subtractions. Those who knew Jim will always remember his warmth, beauty, and brilliance, and I hope we will carry on his fighting spirit.

**Larry Gross**
*Philadelphia*
*April 1998*

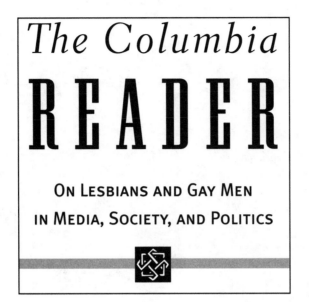

*The Columbia*

# READER

ON LESBIANS AND GAY MEN
IN MEDIA, SOCIETY, AND POLITICS

# Introduction:
# Being Gay in American Media and Society

## LARRY GROSS AND JAMES D. WOODS

Ryan, the only person in this world I can relate to is your character Billy Douglas on One Life to Live. Ryan, I'm so scared. I don't know what to do and I'm afraid of what I might do. You, God, and I are the only ones that know! Ryan, *please* help!

— LETTER FROM A SIXTEEN-YEAR-OLD GAY MALE

I'll begin this letter by being blunt and upfront. I am a twenty-two-year-old homosexual male. . . . Life has been so hard for me: I've tried suicide. I was threatened with expulsion from my high school. I ran away and was nearly stabbed by some people at my college. Your storyline may be fiction, but mine was not. It was an ugly reality.

— LETTER FROM A TWENTY-TWO-YEAR-OLD

I can relate so much to the situations Billy is experiencing on the show—the lying, hiding, etc. My family and friends consider homosexuality "not human." This really makes me hate what I see in the mirror sometimes. . . . I thank you and the producers of One Life to Live for helping me to hate what I am a little less.

— UNSIGNED LETTER

When we were growing up, we had no role model to look up to. However, the gay teens in the country today have you. They have someone in the exact same situations they are in. In some cases, you may be their only friend.

— LETTER FROM A 25-YEAR-OLD MALE

The letters above, culled from more than two thousand received by the heterosexual actor Ryan Phillipe, seem to make a common appeal: Tell me I'm not alone. The writers who composed them have all reached out to a potential role model—in this case, an actor playing the fictional gay teenager Billy Douglas on the daytime drama One Life to Live in the summer of 1992—for guidance on how to view themselves, how to function in society, what to think. Many claim to have no other friends in whom they can confide their terrible secret; one even invites Ryan to visit Nebraska for a week, "so I'd have someone to talk to." While these contacts between audience and performer are clearly "parasocial" (Horton and

Wohl 1956) in nature, at least one writer speculates that, for some viewers, Billy Douglas "may be their only friend."

For lesbians and gay men the scenario is a familiar one. As they approach adolescence and face the distressing realization that they are somehow *different* from their peers, where do they turn to nurture a sense of sexual identity and self-worth? In groups distinguished by gender, race, creed, ethnicity, or national origin individuals can simply observe the people around them and the choices, opportunities, and fates that befall others who are similarly female, African American, Mormon, Jewish, and so forth.

In many cases they can also observe their

respective social group(s) through the lens of the media. True, the media selectively feature and reinforce certain characteristics and images of all these groups—in other words, they routinely use stereotypes—but viewers can at least evaluate these images in light of actual first-hand experiences; whatever distortions the media promote about a particular social group, their influence is constrained by real-world experiences that may contradict, discredit, or challenge these distortions. The media are only one part of the mix.

Sexual minorities differ from "traditional" minorities in several significant respects. In many ways we have more in common with "fringe" political, religious, or ideological groups. Like other social groups defined by forbidden thoughts or deeds, we are rarely born into minority communities or families in which parents or siblings share our minority status. Rather, lesbians and gay men are a self-identifying minority and rarely recognize or announce our status before adolescence. Up until that point society simply presumes us to be heterosexual and treats us as such. (The "obvious" exceptions, the "effeminate" man or "masculine" woman, may well be heterosexual). Like unwitting spies, we spend our formative years tucked away in the homes of people who assume we are like them, who school us in traditions that will ultimately exclude us, and who teach us, quite often, to despise the people we will become. Little wonder, then, that at the hour of sexual awakening gay and lesbian youth often feel they are alone in the world, with no sense that they belong to a people or to a past, with no public heroes to call their own.

But of course we *do* have the mass media. As they realize that their sexual impulses or self-concepts do not conform to the heterosexual standard, that their desires don't fit the prescribed pattern, lesbian and gay youth have little else from which to shape a sense of self. They can draw on the stereotypes familiar to any adolescent (queer, faggot, dyke) and may already have direct contact with local eccentrics such as the tweedy librarian or the tomboyish gym teacher, the ones their peers routinely mock on the playground or at the lunch table. But their primary source of information is ultimately the mass media, which depict them as victims and villains, inconsequential sidekicks and bit players, sources of comic relief—or simply as nonexistent, not part of the "normal" social landscape. Thus, from an inchoate sense of sexual difference and whatever scraps of (mis)information they have accumulated along the way, lesbian and gay adolescents must fashion a sexual identity.

Media representations of sexual minorities (or the lack thereof) are thus the product of our social invisibility and the opportunities it creates for the stereotyping and stigmatization of lesbians and gay men. What effect do media depictions of lesbians and gay men have on the images society holds of such groups? And what effect do they have on lesbians and gay men themselves? Put more generally: in a society dominated by centralized sources of information and imagery—the film studios, news and entertainment media, newspaper and magazine publishers, and their shrinking conglomeration of owners—what is the fate of cultural groups that, for one reason or another, find themselves outside the cultural mainstream?

As we shall see, groups that exist outside the shifting borders of this mediated mainstream share a common fate: media invisibility, stereotyping, and confinement in restricted secondary roles that ultimately serve only to justify their status as outsiders. Sexual minorities in particular have long been invisible on screen and in print. While in recent years lesbians, gay men, and bisexuals have become more frequent figures in the media lineup, they are still found in limited, and often demeaning, or negative roles.

Before returning to our initial questions, then, we will explore the social function of the mass media in broader terms. We will also respond to an objection raised by many newcomers to the field of media studies (including our own students and peers): Why focus on the media? Given that cultural attitudes toward sexual variation are shaped by countless other influences, is there reason to believe that the mass media play an especially central role in this process? It is to this question that we turn first.

## ENVISIONING OUTLAWS

All societies invent classes of outlaws, whether they are classified by their backgrounds, skin color, belief systems, ways of experiencing desire, or some other personal characteristic. Indeed, history is a virtual parade of social types who have at one time or another been viewed as threats to the prevailing social order: heretics, witches, political radicals, homosexuals, and so forth. The particular names and behaviors change, but the social function of such deviants remains constant over time.

One function of the deviant is to help define for others that which is *not* deviant. In an important sense a society cannot judge some of its members good, polite, or moral without simultaneously offering contrasting figures who can be deemed bad, rude, or immoral. The definitions are inherently *relational*, with goodness defined in contrast to badness such that each definition depends upon the other for its meaning. Consequently, as labeling theorists have argued, deviance is not the failure of society to maintain control, something to be strictly patrolled or eradicated. Rather, it is the result of the complex process by which society affixes labels to particular acts or people; until someone else has successfully labeled them so, neither is inherently normal or abnormal. As Erikson (1966) suggests:

> Social groups create deviance by making the rules whose infraction constitutes deviance, and by applying those rules to particular people and labeling them as outsiders. From this point of view, deviance is not a quality of the act the person commits, but rather a consequence of the application by others of rules and sanctions to an "offender." The deviant is the one to whom that label has been successfully applied; deviant behavior is behavior that people so label. (9)

In order to understand deviance, we must look beyond the deviant behaviors themselves to the interaction between act and society, between labeled individuals and those who do the labeling.

Enforcing rules about what constitutes acceptable behavior—in part, by labeling and stigmatizing behaviors considered unacceptable—is a central project of any society. As Erikson has argued, all societies are "centripetal" in the sense that they draw the behavior of actors toward those centers in social space where the core values of the group are figuratively located, bringing them within range of basic norms (1966). Conduct not drawn toward this imaginary core by rewards (or forced toward it by social pressures) activates the machinery of social control: punishment, stigmatization, excommunication. Indeed, it is precisely these attempts at social control—whether made by police, psychiatrists, priests, parents, or peers—that constitute an individual's principal source of information about the normative outlines of the community.

Demarcating and punishing deviance are thus forms of "border control." Witches, demons, communists, homosexuals, and other deviants are socially useful in the sense that they give human form to deviance and the various guises it can assume. They come to personify evil, danger, immorality, a lack of patriotism, or some other negative trait. But far from actually threatening society or being alien to it, these deviants are a resource that helps affirm its contours:

> The deviant act, then, creates a sense of mutuality among the people of a community by supplying a focus for group feeling. Like a war, a flood, or some other emergency, deviance makes people more alert to the interests they share in common and draws attention to those values which constitute the "collective conscience" of the community. Unless the rhythm of group life is punctuated by occasional moments of deviant behavior, presumably, social organization would be impossible. (Erikson 1966:4)

By punishing or stigmatizing deviants, society is simply reminding its membership where the group begins and ends, behaviorally speaking. Indeed, without this ongoing drama at the outer edges of group space, the community would have no inner feeling of cohesion, no sense of what makes it a unique place in the larger world. It is for this reason that the punishment of deviance must be *public* if it is to impact communal notions of right and wrong, good and evil, proper and improper behavior.

The media play a central role in this process by propagating stories and images of cultural deviants—or, more precisely, by "envisioning" them for others. In earlier times the trial and punishment of deviants was publicized in other ways; societies once paraded their drunkards, thieves, or heretics through the public square, inviting the populace to observe the offenders being whipped, hanged, stoned, or placed in the stocks. The disappearance of such practices coincides historically with the rise of the mass media. Today, rather than disgrace a politician with tar, feathers, and a procession through town, we subject him or her to their media equivalent on *Sixty Minutes*, in *Time* magazine, or in some other public arena.

Indeed, most contemporary media fare can be seen as variations on familiar, archetypal moral dramas. Tune in to prime-time television, for example, and you will see a succession of minidramas in which "bad" people (criminals, liars, unfaithful lovers) are symbolically punished with death, arrest, sorrow, the loss of love, or whatever fate befalls them by the show's end. Similarly, television talk shows are often little more than public trials in which the audience is called upon to pass judgment on the guests. Likewise, such programs carry implicit lessons about particular social groups, insofar as the unhappy endings are not meted out in a random way. Different races, genders, and sexual groups vary widely in the degree to which they turn up as television villains, victims, and heroes. Others are largely invisible, a phenomenon Gerbner and Gross (1976:182) have termed "symbolic annihilation."

The central question then becomes: Who wields the power to label others as deviant and control the ways they are represented in the mass media, and what are the consequences for individuals so labeled? Historically, in the case of lesbians and gay men, our status as a self-identifying minority has encouraged us to mask ourselves as heterosexuals and remain silent, even as we were vilified and demonized in the media—and, before them, by organized religion, medicine, law, and other powerful social institutions. As a result, while lesbians and gay men are often spoken *about* on television and in the press, until recently we weren't doing the talking. Afraid or (understandably) unwilling to speak for ourselves, we have played the role played by all cultural outlaws: personifying our society's vision of evil, visibly suffering for it, and thus issuing a warning to others.

## THE MEDIA AS THE MAINSTREAM

How did the media, and television in particular, acquire such power in a society of over 250 million people? Are they really such definitive arbiters of good and evil? Put another way, given the numerous channels through which individuals receive information about their society—peers, parents, teachers, and formal authorities of various sorts—how is it that the mass media have become such influential agents of socialization?

The answer lies in the centrality of the media to our lives. The world is becoming a Leviathan, like it or not, and its nervous system is telecommunications; as modern industrial society becomes more integrated and homogeneous, little room is left for autonomous communities or individuals. Consequently, our knowledge of the "wide world" is largely what this nervous system transmits to us. The mass media have become, in effect, our common ground with countless other groups that make up the larger national and inter-national community. Never before have all classes, groups, and ages shared so much of the same culture and perspectives while having so little to do with their creation.

Indeed, for most of human history the stories, songs, and images we encountered were crafted by members of our own community, with whom we shared the basic conditions of life. In contrast, in the present mass-media dominated era we find ourselves confronted by cultural products provided by people with whom we may have nothing in common and whose motives for producing and distributing these products are not likely to include our well-being. In stark contrast to life in preindustrial societies, in which music, stories, dance, and ritual were limited to what the group itself could produce, we are now faced with endless competing choices, twenty-four hours a day, produced by industrial corporations with which we may have no social contact whatsoever. Remember: this cornucopia of options is not there because anyone actually *asked* for these particular images, songs, or stories. Rather, they exist because someone, somewhere, has a commercial interest in selling us a product—or, more precisely, in attracting our attention so that we can be sold as "audiences" to advertisers who do.

The corporations that create media fare also control the way particular social groups are represented in it. Indeed, representation in this mediated "reality" is in itself a kind of power; certainly media invisibility helps maintain the powerlessness of groups that lack significant material or political resources. While the holders of real power—the ruling corporate elites—may not require or seek mediated visibility, those at the bottom of the various power hierarchies are kept in their place in part through their invisibility. As a result, not all interests or viewpoints are treated equal, and judgments are routinely made by journalists, writers, and editors about what to exclude or include (Gans 1979). These judgments in turn can either broaden or narrow (usually narrow) the spectrum of views presented. Whatever the motives of preindustrial storytellers, in our commercially based mass media those who determine the content of our news and entertainment programming live and die by the bottom line. In such circumstances their decisions are inevitably weighted toward the safe and predictable, toward formulae that have worked in the past, and their goal is to attract the largest possible audience of individuals whose spending power appeals to potential advertisers (who ultimately foot the bill by purchasing media time or space). It is far safer under these conditions to repeat previous successes—in the form of sequels, spin-offs, and imitations—than to introduce innovations that push the envelope too far or too quickly.

Thus, when groups or perspectives *do* attain visibility, the manner of their representation will itself reflect the particular biases and interests of the elites who define the public agenda. And these elites are (mostly) white, (mostly) middle-aged, (mostly) male, (mostly) middle and upper-middle class, and entirely heterosexual (at least in public). As we near the end of the twentieth century the television networks and major film studios, with virtually no exceptions, still are run by men who fit this demographic profile. While a woman has occasionally broken into the white boys club of the studio complex, she has rarely lasted long. In a closed world of writers, directors, producers, etc., who read, watch, and listen to the same media fare we can only expect that shared assumptions would be reinforced. The images of women, the elderly, and minorities that do appear on the country's big and little screens will be those that make sense to these decision makers— the ones that fit their own worldview or have succeeded in the past. Innovations tend to appear only when nurtured by particularly powerful producers, when "focus groups" or other forms of audience research make them seem viable, or when an "oddball" production achieves unexpected success—itself becoming a model for future emulation.

As we've noted, those who own and operate media companies cannot escape the crushing imperative of the bottom line. Above all, a television network or a media conglomerate is a public corporation and must return a profit to its owners. That means that whatever else they do in terms of providing information or entertainment, the media's cultivation of advertisers is necessarily a top priority. In the logic of the media ratings game this often means that it is more profitable to serve only a fraction of the total possible audience— namely those with the most spending power, the right "psychographics," socially approved values, and whatever other attributes make them attractive to those who market laundry detergent, automobiles, or clothing. Certain classes and social groups have (and spend) less money than others and are thus of less interest to advertisers. A similar point, though one with more exceptions, can be made about mainstream newspapers, maga-

zines, radio programs, and books.

Ironically, these same demographic concerns have fueled a boom in marketing to the gay (male) community, which has recently been recognized by market researchers and ad agencies as a viable "niche" market. Emboldened by surveys showing that upper-middle-class white gay men earn slightly more than their heterosexual counterparts (especially in two-income households) a growing number of marketers have reached out with advertising that specifically targets the gay community. On television a 1994 Ikea ad featured two men (who were clearly more than friends) discussing plans for decorating their new home. And in gay and lesbian magazines the list of advertisers now includes Absolut Vodka, American Express, Apple Computers, Coors Beer, Naya Water, Subaru, Volvo, and a growing list of others.

While it is conventional to acknowledge a distinction between advertising and programming (or print ads and news copy), we should avoid overstating these differences, especially in the case of television. News, drama, quiz shows, sports programs, and commercials share underlying similarities of theme, emphasis, and value. Even the most widely accepted distinctions (i.e., between news programs, soap operas, and commercials) are easily blurred. In Sarah Kozloff's nice phrase, "American television is as saturated in narrative as a sponge in a swimming pool. . . . Forms that are not ostensibly fictional entertainments, but rather have other goals—description, education, persuasion, exhortation, and so on— covertly tend to use narrative as a means to their ends" (1987:43). In 1963 NBC news executive producer (and later president) Reuven Frank advised journalists that "every news story should, without sacrifice of probity or responsibility, display the attributes of fiction, of drama. It should have structure and conflict, problem and denouement, rising action and falling action, a beginning, a middle, and an end" (quoted in Epstein 1974:4).

Likewise, the polished minidramas of most commercials reveal a mastery of fictional conventions. Consider the compressed thirty- or fifteen-second narrative structure of a typical commercial: conflict (dirty laundry, headache, romantic difficulties), followed by plot development (use of the product), and, ultimately, resolution (clean socks, relief, and implied romantic or sexual success).

With the arrival of the infomercial and so-called reality-based television (which often blends staged and documentary footage), it has become even more difficult to distinguish programming from outright peddling. Each activity supports the other by using identical narrative structures and visual styles, and by dramatizing congruent values regarding consumerism and "the good life." In short, commercials and programming generally look and sound alike and teach complementary lessons about consumption, materialism, and morality. Programs that fail to reinforce these "mainstream values" often find themselves unable to attract advertisers—landing them, ultimately, in the vast graveyard of canceled programs.

Commercials and programs also share the dominant formal conventions of the mass media: namely, realism and psychologically grounded naturalism. Despite a limited degree of reflexivity—in which a program deliberately calls attention to its own artifice—mainstream films and television programs are usually presented as transparent windows on reality that show us how people and places look, how institutions operate—in short, "the way it is." Even "backstage" dramas about the media themselves, such as *Murphy Brown* and *Frasier*, are highly stylized and unrealistic and conform thoroughly to the contours of other network fare. Even so, for many viewers they constitute their only source of information about the inner workings of a newsroom or radio station.

These depictions of how the world works, and why, are personified through dramatic plots and characterizations that take us into situations and places we might otherwise never see: the hidden gyrations of personal motivation, organizational performance, and subcultural life. Normal adult viewers, to be sure, are aware of the fictiveness of media drama; no one calls the police when a television character is shot. But there are reasons to question how often and how completely viewers actually suspend their disbelief in the seductive realism of the media's fictional worlds. Indeed, even the most sophisticated among us can find components of our "knowledge" that derive wholly or in part from fictional representations. Few of us have been in an operating room or a judge's private chambers; fewer still have been in jail or a corporate boardroom. Yet we all possess images of, and information about, such places that, upon examination, are patched together from our media forays into them. Through the

media, we can take part in, or at least witness, open-heart surgery, high-level corporate deliberations, or the plottings of mafia kingpins. Likewise, most heterosexuals, if asked to describe a "gay bar," would probably rely on episodes of *Coach*, *Murphy Brown*, *Roseanne* or (worse yet) films such as *Cruising* or *The Birdcage*.

As noted above, the mass media are likely to be especially powerful in cultivating images of groups and events about which there is little first-hand opportunity for learning. By definition, most minority groups and "deviants" of various sorts will be relatively distant from the daily experience of viewers. Lacking other sources of information, it is easy for most people to accept even the most inaccurate or derogatory information about a particular group or event. In effect, the media appear to have a monopoly on the "truth."

Television in particular has become a key source of (mis)information about the world, thus helping to create and maintain a common set of values and perspectives among its viewers. In fact, given that the average American adult spends several hours each day with television, and children spend even more time immersed in its fictional reality, the media have become central agents of enculturation. Expanding this observation, the Cultural Indicators research conducted by George Gerbner, Larry Gross, and their colleagues in the 1970s and 1980s (Gerbner et al. 1994) used the term *cultivation* to describe the resulting influence of television on viewers' conceptions of social reality. On issue after issue the assumptions, beliefs, and values of heavy television viewers were found to differ systematically from those of light viewers in the same demographic groups. Put another way, those who watch more television are more likely—whatever their previous background—to give "television answers" to questions about the world, its people, and how they function.

The researchers ultimately isolated a pattern that they termed mainstreaming (Gerbner et al. 1980, 1982, 1986, 1994). The mainstream can be thought of as a commonality of viewpoints and values that television tends to cultivate in its viewers. While light viewers in any particular demographic group may exhibit relatively divergent positions on a given topic, heavy viewers are more likely to agree with the viewpoint proffered by television. In other words, differences explained by the viewers' divergent backgrounds and life situations—differences that are readily apparent in the answers given by light viewers—tend to diminish or even disappear when heavy viewers in the same groups are compared. Heavy television use is thus associated with a convergence of outlooks, a mainstreaming of opinion.

Integral to this cultural and political mainstream is the pattern of roles associated with sexual identity: our conceptions of masculinity and femininity, of the "normal" and "natural" sexual attributes and responsibilities of men and women. And, as with other pillars of our moral order, these definitions of what is normal and natural serve to support the existing social structure. The maintenance of the "normal" gender hierarchy requires that children be socialized into—and adults be discouraged from toppling—a set of expectations that channel their beliefs about what is possible and proper for men and for women. The firestorm of opposition that prevented President Clinton from keeping his promise to end the military's unfair treatment of lesbians and gay men exemplifies our society's dedication to traditional definitions of male and female behavior.

The gender hierarchy is supported, in turn, by the mass media's treatment of sexual minorities. Lesbians and gay men are usually ignored altogether, but when they *do* appear, it is in roles that *support* the natural order and are thus narrowly and negatively stereotyped. Sexual minorities are not unique in this regard, of course, but our cultural invisibility makes us especially vulnerable to the power of the mass media. Of all social groups we are probably the least permitted to speak for ourselves in the mass media. Until "Ellen Morgan" (and Ellen DeGeneres) came out in April 1997 no major network program had a lesbian or gay lead character (or star). Openly lesbian and gay reporters are also absent from the news programs inhabited by the likes of Tom Brokaw, Bernard Shaw, Carole Simpson, and Barbara Walters. While we are certainly present in the newsrooms and story conferences in which such programs are assembled, our speech is both censored and self-censored. We are also the only group (except perhaps for Arab "terrorists" and Latin American "drug dealers") whose enemies are generally uninhibited by the notions of "good taste" that usually shield other minorities from open public displays of bigotry.

The reason for this vulnerability lies, once again, in our frequent isolation and invisibility. From the moment of birth, a baby is immediately classified as male or female, white or black, and treated accordingly. The baby is also invariably defined as heterosexual and is thereafter expected to follow the "normal" heterosexual trajectory: grow up, marry, have children, and live in nuclear familial bliss, sanctified by religion, licensed by the state, and paid homage in the media. To live otherwise, lesbians and gay men must swim upstream. Thus while women are surrounded by other women, Latinos by other Latinos, and so forth, lesbians and gay men generally have little first-hand experience with anything resembling a community or peer group. Into this informational void step the mass media, leaving most viewers—gay or straight—little choice but to accept media stereotypes they imagine must be typical of all lesbians and gay men.

As the lesbian and gay liberation movement gained momentum in the late 1960s, spurred by the example of the civil rights, antiwar, and feminist movements, media attention to gay people and issues increased dramatically. Compared to earlier depictions and discussions of gay issues, much of it was relatively positive, culminating with coverage of the 1973 decision by the American Psychiatric Association to delete homosexuality from its official menu of mental disorders, the *Diagnostic and Statistical Manual*. Publications such as *Time* and *Newsweek*, which had previously used the words *homosexual*, *pansy*, and *pervert* interchangeably, now featured cover stories about a "new minority group" that was demanding its civil rights.

By the mid-1970s, however, a backlash against even these modest gains could already be felt around the country, gaining national attention in such campaigns as Anita Bryant's 1977 "Save the Children" crusade, which succeeded in repealing a Dade County nondiscrimination clause, and California's infamous 1978 "Briggs Initiative," which would have mandated the firing of all gay and lesbian school teachers. These same years produced virulent antigay essays in magazines such as *Harper's* and *Commentary* (see Decter, this volume). Since that time the lesbian and gay movement and its adversaries, primarily the so-called new right and its theocratic successor, the Christian right, have been constant antagonists.

Right-wing fund-raisers have discovered that antihomosexual propaganda is the surest way to get money from supporters (now that Communists have been largely defanged), and the media inevitably figure prominently in this struggle. In his memoirs Marvin Liebman, a longtime conservative fund-raiser and closeted gay man, acknowledged that "now times are changing.

There is no longer the anti-Communist cement to hold the edifice together. The great enterprise, in which so much time has been invested, is in danger of sinking back to an aggregation of bigotries." He then scolded conservative compatriots "who have recently used homophobia to sell their newsletter, or to raise money for their causes and themselves" (1992:259).

The mass media have a double impact on gay people: not only do they still frequently depict us as wretched or villainous but they simultaneously ignore the existence of lesbians and gay men who are *unexceptional*—just plain "gay folks." Hardly ever shown are gay characters cast in roles or written into plot lines that do *not* emphasize their sexuality, the reaction of heterosexual friends and family. Hardly ever does our sexuality appear as part of the background, introduced in ways that take sexual diversity for granted. For example, there are almost never TV cops who just *happen* to be gay or TV lawyers who *happen* to be lesbians, even when the plot has nothing in particular to do with their sexuality (although characters on *Roseanne*, *Murder One*, and *NYPD Blue* were a start in that direction). Similarly, Matt, the gay man who lived at *Melrose Place* for five years, seemed to be the *only* inhabitant of the entire apartment complex who couldn't get laid. For the most part, like Chekhov's dramaturgical rule of thumb—if a gun is introduced in the first act, it must go off by the play's end—the presence of a lesbian or gay character virtually ensures that his or her sexuality will become the focus of the plot by the program's end.

## THE THREAT MADE FLESH

Stereotypes are one of several general patterns that characterize media coverage of minorities: invisibility, stereotypes, and marginality.

Historically, lesbian and gay people have simply been invisible in the media. Between 1930 and 1961 the Motion Picture Production Code (which went by several names over the decades) formally ensured that lesbian and gay characters did not appear in mainstream Hollywood films or appeared only in subtle, coded forms (Russo 1986). Fearing network censors, television producers followed suit. Likewise, gay and straight reporters and editors alike were comfortable writing about "homosexuals" only when they were involved in a scandal of some sort—e.g., brought up on morals charges, arrested for having sex in public parks or restrooms, or entrapped by the police—and thus rendered "newsworthy" according to the formulae of journalism (Alwood 1996). As a result, generations of Americans came to know gay and lesbian people strictly through the occasional headline ("Pervert Inquiry Ordered," *New York Times*, June 15, 1950), or the steady stream of "sissy" characters supplied by Hollywood (Russo 1986).

With the revision of the code in 1961 explicitly lesbian and gay characters began to appear in Hollywood films—invariably as victims, villains, or clowns of one sort or another. Rarely did media portrayals question or counter these prevailing stereotypes; on the contrary, they took advantage of them. To name but a few examples, by 1963 audiences had already been treated to a self-loathing and suicidal lesbian (*The Children's Hour*), an effete and promiscuous gay libertine (*Suddenly, Last Summer*), a closeted suicidal politician (*Advise and Consent*), a murderous lesbian (*From Russia with Love*), and a psychologically tortured man whose career is threatened because he is gay (*Victim*). Only one of these characters lived to tell about it (Dirk Bogarde in *Victim*). Even today media characterizations invoke popular stereotypes—such as Harvey Fierstein's hysterical character in *Independence Day*, who is never identified as gay but could not be mistaken for anything else—as a sort of code they know will be understood by audiences. Given the limits of time and space faced by screenwriters and directors, these symbolic shortcuts are a convenient way to telegraph character traits without having to spell them out (Turow 1978). Explicitly gay characters are often even more blatantly caricatured. The Fox program *In Living Color* featured a pair of outrageous queens as film critics in a running series of "Men on Men" segments; similarly, it seems that *Saturday Night Live* has never encountered a fag joke it didn't like.

Likewise, storylines involving lesbian or gay characters tended to fall into one of several patterns. As Russo noted in 1986: "It is not insignificant that out of 32 films with major homosexual characters from 1961 through 1976, 13 feature gays who commit suicide and 18 have the homosexual murdered by another character" (32). While our media mortality rate seems to have improved somewhat in the years since (AIDS notwithstanding), films and TV programs continue to feature lesbian and gay characters in comic, secondary, and essentially harmless roles—but, again, with the exception of "Ellen Morgan," not as leading men and women. Witness the background sissies used for comic effect or as sidekicks to the protagonist (a casting strategy also employed with ethnic minorities) in such hit films as *Father of the Bride, Beverly Hills Cop, Mrs. Doubtfire, Prince of Tides,* and *Single White Female.* The 1993 hit *Philadelphia* featured an Oscar-winning performance by Tom Hanks as a gay man, but the dramatic spotlight was shared by Denzel Washington's straight lawyer character.

Television seems more comfortable, however, placing us at the center of "problem dramas" (even on sitcoms) in which the lesbian or gay character's sexuality becomes the dramatic "problem": How will the other characters *deal* with her? What should be *done* about him? This pattern has proven remarkably robust over more than two decades. The August 1997 premiere episode of the TV sitcom *Good News* featured the challenges of a young black gay man coming out and introducing his white boyfriend to his mother and their pastor. As William A. Henry III noted ten years earlier:

> When TV does deal with gays it typically takes the point of view of straights struggling to understand. The central action is the progress of acceptance—not self-acceptance by the homosexual, but grief-stricken resignation to fate by his straight loved ones, who serve as surrogates for the audience. Homosexuality has thus become not a fact of life, but a moral issue on which everyone within earshot is expected to voice some vehement opinion. Just as black characters were long expected to talk almost exclusively about being black, and handicapped characters (when seen at all) were expected to talk chiefly about their disabilities, so homosexual characters have been defined almost entirely by their "problem." (1987:43)

Being defined by their problem, serious lesbian and gay roles are generally confined to TV's problem-of-the-week genre (with occasional exceptions, usually marginal roles such as Matt on *Melrose Place* or Ross's lesbian ex-wife and her lover on *Friends*). But in both television and film central lesbian and gay characters remain exceedingly rare. They typically play comic or supportive dramatic roles and have a nasty of habit of getting killed, going straight, or otherwise vanishing from the plotline. On *One Life to Live*, for example, the gay teenager, Billy, disappeared from the program when he "went to Yale."

In her study of the making of a TV program that included a lesbian character, Montgomery

(1981) observed several unwritten rules regarding lesbian and gay characters or themes:

> Throughout the process all the decisions affecting the portrayal of gay life were influenced by the constraints which commercial television as a mass medium imposes upon the creation of its content. The fundamental goal of garnering the largest possible audience necessitated that (a) the program be placed in a familiar and successful television genre . . . (b) the story focus upon the heterosexual male lead character and his reactions to the gay characters rather than upon the homosexual characters themselves; and (c) the film avoid any overt display of affection which might be offensive to certain segments of the audience. These requirements served as a filter through which the issue of homosexuality was processed, resulting in a televised picture of gay life designed to be acceptable to the gay community and still palatable to a mass audience. (56)

Acceptability to the gay community, in this case, meant only that the movie or program was not an outright attack on our basic humanity—even if it could never be mistaken for an expression of our values or perspectives. But, of course, the networks weren't seeking lesbian and gay viewers in the first place; they simply wanted to avoid a fight later on. As Russo remarked: "Mainstream films about homosexuals are not for homosexuals. They address themselves exclusively to the majority." Inevitably, however, we will be in the audience (1986:32).

Yet even this minimal and peripheral presence seems sufficiently threatening to the "industry" that gay characterizations and plot elements are routinely accompanied by pressbook qualifications and backpedaling (Russo 1986). "*The Children's Hour* is not about lesbianism, it's about the power of lies to destroy people's lives," according to its director William Wyler (1962). Likewise, director John Schlesinger (1972) assures us that "*Sunday, Bloody Sunday* is not about the sexuality of these people, it's about human loneliness." Similarly, "*Windows* is not about homosexuality, it's about insanity," according to director Gordon Willis (1979). When *Making Love* was released in 1982 there were two publicity posters, only one of which—the one intended for the gay press—made it clear that the two men were lovers. More recently, Jonathan Demme defended his 1993 film *Philadelphia* by insisting that it was not about gays, but about civil rights, bigotry, and the power of human tragedy to bring families together.

But it isn't only audiences who seem to require protective distancing from gay characters and themes. We are frequently treated to show-biz gossip intended to convey the heterosexual bona fides of any actor cast in a gay role. When the Broadway play *The Boys in the Band* opened in 1968, Cliff Gorman, the actor playing Emory, "the definitive screaming queen," made sure the public knew he was *only acting*. As Judy Klemesrud (1968) explains in a *New York Times* interview entitled "You Don't Have to Be One to Play One," it's "not exactly the kind of part you'd imagine for a nice (married) Jewish boy from Jamaica." But Cliff "really needed the money" and was so broke he had even taken to "hocking his wife's silver candelabra." Elsewhere in Klemesrud's portrait we are shown Cliff popping open a cold Schlitz ("his second"), listening to country and western music (the only music "that really moves him"), and generally swaggering about the living room. In the accompanying photograph he clutches his "incredibly beautiful" wife, Gayle.

Apparently, the rules haven't changed much since 1968. Despite nearly three decades of lesbian and gay activism since Stonewall, there is not a single major, openly gay Hollywood star, though many could seize this honor simply by coming out (Ellen DeGeneres came out as a television star, and her girlfriend, Anne Heche, who came out with her, was just joining Hollywood's second rank). Media publicity surrounding the 1994 film *Interview with a Vampire*, in which the homoerotic overtones are unmistakable, insisted on the heterosexuality of Tom Cruise and Brad Pitt. In response to persistent rumors that they are homosexual, actor Richard Gere and supermodel Cindy Crawford ran a full-page ad in a British newspaper claiming that, while there is nothing *wrong* with being gay, they simply aren't (a few months later they filed for divorce).

The three patterns we have described—the invisibility of lesbians and gay men, the use of demeaning and limiting stereotypes, and the suppression of positive or even unexceptional portrayals—all serve to support the boundaries of the prevailing moral order. By rendering lesbians and gay men virtually invisible, our very existence is thrown into question. And when we do appear our limited depictions further bolster mainstream values and perspectives. Our opponents are thus quite correct when they assert that the presence of a healthy, nonstereotypic, or even boring lesbian or gay man would threaten the mainstream, if only by throwing into question the "normalcy" of the status quo, introducing choices to people who never realized that such choices could be made.

## RESPONSE STRATEGIES

As we've noted, we are all colonized to some degree by the majority culture. Those of us who belong to one minority group or another may nonetheless have absorbed mainstream values, even when they serve only to demean us. Similarly, although it might seem contrary to their interests, millions of nonwhites across the globe tune in to the U.S. media, with its distinctly "white-angled" view of the world. Recognizing these patterns is a first step toward demanding more even-handed media representation of all cultural groups. Yet this does not, in itself, guarantee a solution. In fact, there are several possible responses to the media's hostile treatment of sexual minorities, including internalization, disengagement, subversion, and self-definition.

### *Internalization*

As we've seen, sexual minorities are particularly vulnerable to the internalization of mainstream values, given that the process of self-identification generally occurs in isolation and relatively late in life. As Hodges and Hutter (this volume) put it: "We learn to loathe homosexuality before it becomes necessary to acknowledge our own. . . . Never having been offered *positive* attitudes to homosexuality, we inevitably adopt *negative* ones, and it is from these that all our values flow." Without realizing it, even lesbians and gay men may be profoundly heterosexist in their thinking and outward behavior.

For these lesbians and gay men, accepting mainstream values often entails the adoption of an assimilationist strategy—an attempt to "pass" as heterosexual, even if it means severing ties to the lesbian and gay community (Woods 1993). Lesbians and gay men are often quite skillful at effecting such a facade; most have been doing it all their lives. But the security such a gambit promises is illusory. Their Faustian bargain does not ultimately shield them from the derogatory values of the straight culture they are attempting to join. Even when they seem to have successfully assimilated they cannot help feeling, in private, the sting of a derogatory comment, a heterosexist joke, a media caricature. As one young gay man wrote to actor Ryan Phillipe, "I act as a straight, normal twenty-one year old . . . Until recently, I would laugh at jokes about gays or would pretend to dislike the way they were. I cannot and will not do that anymore" (Gross 1996:369).

To maintain the facade, lesbian and gay individuals often consider it necessary to protect their closets—even if that means attacking members of their own minority group in order to bolster their (false) credentials as members of the majority. As one journalist put it, describing the media industries:

> For all the organizing that women have done, for instance, in their attempts to break down the barriers, well-placed women executives say they've received very little mutual support from their equally well-placed peers. The old-boy network rules, and the individual women, gays, blacks, or hispanics who attain some degree of success usually have to camouflage themselves in the trappings of their masters." (Kilday 1986:40).

Similarly, gay writer Merle Miller revealed that, "as editor of a city newspaper, he indulged in 'queer-baiting' to conceal his own homosexuality" (Adam 1978:89). Openly gay actor Michael Kearns recalled a gay agent who made it his habit to tell "fag jokes" at the close of interviews with potential clients. If the actor laughed, he was signed up; if he didn't, he wasn't (Hachem 1987:48).

These patterns are not limited to show business or journalism. During the 1996 election campaigns connoisseurs of hypocrisy were treated to the exposure of Republican right-wing guru Arthur Finkelstein as a gay man living quietly with his lover and their adopted children while his clients in the U.S. Senate—Jesse Helms, Lauch Faircloth, Don Nickles, and Robert Smith—led the attack on same-sex marriages (Rich 1996; Rodrick 1996).

Individuals who internalize or fail to challenge mainstream beliefs often fail to realize, however, that by defending antigay and antilesbian values they are essentially doing the work of their oppressors. Political theorists use the term *hegemony* to describe this sort of collusion between master and slave, in which the oppressed are somehow persuaded that their oppression is just, inevitable, or natural. Once a hegemonic

system is in place, those at the top of the hierarchy need only defend the ideologies and structures that convince those below that they belong there. Once homosexuals believe that they are in fact perverted, trivial, or unworthy of public recognition—and therefore lack the grounds to protest their mistreatment—their oppressors' work has been done for them. The Zionist polemicist Ahad Ha-Am drew on a Biblical analogy to describe this phenomenon, in an essay on Moses: "Pharoah is gone, but his work remains; the master has ceased to be master, but the slaves have not ceased to be slaves" (1904/1970:320).

## Disengagement

Once someone sees through the heterosexist fabric of our social order, and renounces the value system that oppresses them, it becomes possible to resist the hegemonic power of the media. The most obvious form of resistance, but possibly the most difficult, is simply to ignore the mass media and refuse to be insulted by their portraits of us. One can simply refuse to watch TV, select films and publications carefully, and turn a deaf ear to antigay and antilesbian slurs.

As we shall see, the religious right has already developed alternative programming to provide its followers with value-congruent media fare. There is a relative absence, however, of equivalent programming on the left end of the spectrum. Leftists are faced with fewer alternatives and consequently may be ambivalent about abandoning the mainstream altogether. In a study of American leftists' relationship to the mass media, Michaud (1994) encountered numerous signs of ambivalence, *despite* which they continued to watch TV:

> We watch network news sometimes, but I feel like it's junkfood news. I find it very frustrating. They never analyze anything. . . . It's also so easy to turn on TV, and there's all this visual stuff. It's so effortless (female, 32).
> I do watch *Nightline*, but it pisses me off to no end . . . the way they manipulate things to put forth a certain point-of-view. It's a total set-up (male, 32).

Although some of us can personally secede from the mass mediated-mainstream or sample it only with great care, not all are willing. The alternatives are simply too few.

Nor can we entirely escape its effects through secession. Indeed, whether we consume or ignore mainstream fare, we are all colonized to some extent by its values. We can always turn off the TV or throw out the newspaper, but cannot always evade the media-inspired conversations and social rituals through which mainstream values become embedded in our ideas about, say, gender roles, materialism, or family structure. Nor can we prevent fellow minority group members from attending to messages that we feel are hostile to their interests (a dilemma familiar to any parent who believes that commercial TV is not in the best interests of children). Given the generally high levels of TV and film viewing on the lower rungs of the socioeconomic ladder, for example, large segments of the population consume media fare that actually serves to maintain their - subordination. For example, black households in the United States are disproportionately poor and uneducated but are also heavy consumers of television despite the racist tone of many programs (Gross 1984). In one report blacks represented only 9 percent of the sample yet accounted for 14 percent of all viewing (Morgan 1986).

Of course, a message's impact can never be judged in a vacuum. Just as *any* mention of lesbians or gay men will seem excessive to some people, the same mention may encourage group solidarity among isolated gays or lesbians. As Freer notes:

> The notion of a "negative" representation is difficult precisely because the meanings are not fixed within the text but generated between text and audience. Hence my memories of certain films (e.g., *A Taste of Honey*) that I saw when young, in which the very existence of a gay character was a positive experience—I recognized myself. The same film, seen today, fills me with horror. Now I know I'm not alone; then I didn't. (1987:62)

Minority audiences facing their living room "window on the world" have had to make do with sparse fare. As African American scholar Patricia Turner put it,

> In 1992 I appeared as a commentator in *Color Adjustment*, a documentary about the images of African Americans in prime-time television. Reflecting back on my childhood in the 1950s and 1960s, I said semifacetiously that while my mother loathed making long distance calls, even when there was a death in the family, she would call long distance to share news that a "Negro" was scheduled to

appear on a television program. African Americans who have seen *Color Adjustment* are forever saying to me that my comments corroborate their personal recollections of the first decade of television. Our images were few and far between, and we hungered for more of them. (1994:xiii–xiv)

In a similar vein, Chinese American actor B. D. Wong, commenting on his role (as a Korean American) on the TV sitcom *All American Girl*, starring Korean American comedienne Margaret Cho, recalled, "When we were growing up, when an Asian person came on TV, somebody would say: 'Come quick! Come into the living room. There's an Asian person on TV.' And everybody would run and go, with this bizarre fascination: 'Oh wow, look at that. That's amazing' " (Southgate 1994:53–54).

We would venture to suggest, however, that neither B. D. Wong nor Margaret Cho would have been called into the living room to witness one of the even more rare appearances of a lesbian or gay character on television. Despite the fact that both Wong and Cho would have had particular reason to be interested in such appearances (to engage in a bit of outing), it is highly unlikely that their families would have been aware of this interest or that they would have indulged it had they suspected. Lesbian and gay people do not share the sort of fond recollections recounted by Turner or Wong.

Likewise, the standards of acceptable media treatment continue to rise. A media representation that was "progressive" for its time may today seem loaded with negative assertions and stereotypes.

Even when a lesbian or gay characterization is meant to be sympathetic (as in the wildly successful *La Cage aux Folles* or its American version, *The Birdcage*), lesbian and gay members of the audience may find themselves laughing at different times than the straight audience, wincing at the falsity of the image. Many gay people watched *Philadelphia* as part of (presumably) straight audiences, only to hear them snicker and laugh at moments not intended to be funny, such as the scene in which Tom Hanks slow dances with Antonio Banderas. To have one's status as "fair game" emphasized in so graphic a fashion—while sitting in a movie theater—is a familiar experience for lesbians and gay men, just as it is for women and racial minorities. Paul Rudnik's 1995 film version of his stage hit, *Jeffrey*, tackled this head-on:

> Early on . . . two men are flirting with each other at the gym. After some suggestive back and forth among the barbells and Nautilus machines, the men kiss. Then the camera cuts away to two young couples sitting in the theater, watching the movie. The girls swoon, sigh and go "Awwww." The guys hurl their popcorn and leap out of their seats, horrified. (Rodriguez 1995).

It can be argued that the best stance for gay people to adopt vis-à-vis the mass media is to repay them with the same indifference and contempt they have shown us. Unfortunately, while this might be a gratifying individual solution it is not realistic as a strategy for the community at large. Even when an individual viewer minimizes his or her irritation by ignoring the media, their reverberations will be felt through others. As we've noted, the media are the primary channel, like it or not, through which society expresses its values and debates the issues affecting our lives; to renounce them entirely is to forego any chance of improving the level of that conversation.

## Subversion

As Raymond Williams has pointed out, hegemony "is never either total or exclusive. At any time, alternative or directly oppositional politics and culture exist as significant elements in the society" (1977:111). One such oppositional strategy is the appropriation and subversion of mainstream media.

For gay males the classic strategy of subversion is camp—an ironic stance toward the straight world rooted in a gay sensibility. As Babuscio defines it, camp reflects "a consciousness that is different from the mainstream; a heightened awareness of certain human complications of feeling that spring from the fact of social oppression; in short, a perception of the world which is coloured, shaped, directed and defined by the fact of one's gayness" (1977:40). This characterization would, of course, fit the comic or aesthetic styles of other oppressed groups—e.g., the fatalism of Jewish humor, the sense of loss in African American folk songs that gave rise to the blues—but the gay sensibility differs in that we encounter and develop it at a later stage in life; it is nobody's native tongue.

Moreover, while sharing much with other minority perspectives, camp is suffused with a theatrical view on the world that is rooted in the particular realities of lesbian and gay life. Forced to "pass for straight" in order to avoid social stigma or physical danger, one develops "a heightened awareness and appreciation for disguise, impersonation, the projection of personality, and the distinctions to be made between instinctive and theatrical behaviour" (Babuscio 1977:45). In short, the gay sensibility incorporates a self-conscious role playing and theatricality—and the knowledge that social and gender roles are ultimately no more than performances, arbitrary guises into which skilled players can step at will. Passing for straight involves play-acting, pretending to be something one is not, either by projecting untruths or withholding truths about ourselves that would lead others to the (correct) conclusion about our sexuality.

Rooted in this sensibility, camp serves several purposes. It supplies an opportunity to express distance from and disdain for mainstream culture. Exchanged in private settings, camp helps forge in-group solidarity, repairing some of the damage inflicted by the majority and preparing us for further onslaughts. Used as a secret code in public settings, it can also be a way to identify and communicate with other "club members" under the unknowing eyes of the straight world—itself an act of subversive solidarity. Politically, it can also be a form of public defiance, a flamboyant expression of sexual variation that dares to show its face. Finally, camp is the quintessential gay strategy for undermining the hegemony of mainstream media images (Babuscio 1977; Dyer 1986). The sting can be taken out of oppressive characterizations and the hot air balloons of official morality can be burst with the weapon of irony. As Sontag put it: "Camp is the solvent of conventional morality. It neutralizes moral indignation" (1967:290).

Camp can also be seen in the appropriation of mainstream personae and products that are adopted as "cult" figures by marginal groups. For gay men, camp cult figures are often female film stars who can be seen as standing up to the pressures of a male-dominated movie industry and, despite all travails, remaining in command of their careers (Bette Davis, Joan Crawford, Mae West), or at least struggling back from defeat (Judy Garland; see Dyer 1986). For lesbians cult figures often include women who are openly, or at least allegedly, lesbians (e.g., Martina Navratilova, k. d. lang, Melissa Etheridge, Amanda Bearse, Jodie

Foster, Lily Tomlin) who have "made it" by beating the boys at their own game.

Most important, by encouraging viewers or readers to evaluate mainstream culture as outsiders, as spectators living beyond its perimeter, a camp sensibility creates a sense of detachment from the dominant ideology:

> The sense of being different . . . made me feel myself as "outside" the mainstream in fundamental ways—and this does give you a kind of knowledge of the mainstream you cannot have if you are immersed in it. I do not necessarily mean a truer perspective, so much as an awareness of the mainstream as a mainstream, and not just the way everything and everybody inevitably are; in other words, it denaturalizes normality. This knowledge is the foundation of camp (Cohen and Dyer 1980:177).

Quite often there is even a perverse pleasure in viewing the mainstream as "unnatural" from a vantage point outside it. Ellsworth describes lesbian feminist reviewers of *Personal Best* (a 1982 film, written and directed by a straight man, that featured a lesbian relationship) who, "expressed pleasure in watching the dominant media 'get it wrong,' and in watching [them] attempt, but fail, to colonize 'real' lesbian space" (1986:54). Nor is it only lesbians and gays who partake of camp sensibilities. For example, in *Making Things Perfectly Queer* (1993), Alexander Doty argues that movies and TV programs elicit a wide range of what he calls "queer" readings—and not exclusively from lesbian and gay audiences.

## Self-Definition

Ultimately, the most effective form of resistance to the hegemony of the mainstream is to speak for oneself, to disseminate narratives and images that counter the accepted, oppressive, or inaccurate ones. The cultural mainstream—defined above as a shared ideology cultivated through the repetition of narrative patterns across illusory differences in medium and genre, and absorbed by otherwise diverse segments of the population—inevitably excludes one group or another. There are exceptions, in short, to the process of cultural mainstreaming. Furthermore, these "deviants" are integral to society's process of self-definition, illustrating acceptable social behavior by serving as counterexamples of it. In the mainstream

media their concerns, values, and even existence may be belittled—an obvious incentive for them to create and consume their own cultural products. But what options do these groups really have to speak for themselves?

The answer to this question depends largely upon who we are talking about. While many groups and interests are ignored or distorted in the media, not all have the same options for resistance. Indeed, the opportunities for opposition are greatest when there is a visible and organized group that can provide solidarity and institutional support for the creation and dissemination of alternative messages. For example, numerous alternatives have sprung up, as it were, along the right bank of the mainstream, the most extensive and visible of which are the Christian cable television networks. These programs provide their viewers with an array of media fare, from news to talk shows to soap operas to sermons, all reflecting perspectives and values that they quite correctly feel are not represented in mainstream, prime-time television, or in the movies. As a conservative religious man explained to researcher Stewart Hoover, he simply doesn't enjoy most mainstream television: "I think a good deal of [television] is written by very liberal, immoral people. . . . Some of the comedies, the things that go on every week, they make extramarital affairs and sex before marriage an everyday thing, like everybody should accept it . . . and they present it in a comic situation, a situation that looks like it could be fun" (1985:382). Fortunately for such viewers, there are options such as Pat Robertson's *700 Club* and the other programs on the *Family Channel*.

The religious sponsoring and producing organizations are not merely engaged in satisfying their audiences' desire for a media environment in which they feel at home. They are also attempting to translate the (usually exaggerated) numbers of their audiences and their (constantly solicited) financial contributions into a power base from which to pull the mainstream closer to where they now reside, up on the right bank. For example, callers to Focus on the Family's toll-free 800 number can sign up for the group's monthly magazines, through which they will be informed about radio and cable-TV programs, offered videocassettes and books for sale, and provided with detailed voters' guides to encourage their support of candidates who favor the agenda of the Christian right.

The United States has no comparable settlement on the left bank of the mainstream, and there are several reasons why the left has been unable to match the right's success in harnessing media technology. Right-wing minority perspectives are ultimately supportive of the dominant ideology and power relationships, however much these groups may be offended by what they see on mainstream television and in the press. Truly oppositional values, by contrast, are fundamentally incompatible with existing power structures because they challenge the gender, class, or sexual hierarchies that undergird the status quo. Or they espouse values (nonmaterialism, alternative sexual norms, fringe politics) that undermine the foundation of our male-dominated, conglomerate-owned, and advertiser-supported media industries.

Consequently, not only will perspectives that present radical challenges to the established order be ignored, they will also be discredited. Those who benefit from the status quo inevitably view their positions as the moderate center, balanced between opposing "extremes." The American news media's fetishized "objectivity" is achieved through an illusory "balance" that, in fact, reflects invisible, taken-for-granted assumptions and ideologies. The fatal flaw in this credo of centrism is that how one defines the "extremes" determines where the center appears to be. In this country the mass media grant legitimacy to positions much further to the right than to the left, which puts the "objectively balanced" mainstream clearly to the right of center. Consequently, Jesse Helms and Strom Thurmond can be elected and reelected to the Senate and Patrick Buchanan and Steve Forbes can run for the Republican presidential nomination, while their opposite numbers on the left could not possibly receive the same degree of visibility and legitimacy (political trivia quiz: who is Larry Agran and what did he run for?).

The success of particular minority groups in educating and exerting pressure on the mainstream media is reflected in the care with which those groups are represented. In fact, the television networks sometimes lament the difficulties they face in avoiding ethnic slurs and stereotypes. "In their desire to avoid stereotyping, I think broadcast standards and practices sometimes goes to an absurd extreme," said Bruce J. Sallan, then ABC's vice president in charge of motion pictures on television. For example, "There are almost no ethnic villains on television. We can't do a Mafia picture at ABC, because broadcast standards won't let us deal with Italians involved in organized crime" (Farber 1985). Similarly, the 1985 ABC-TV film *The Children of Times Square* was allowed to have a black villain *only* if he was balanced by sympathetic black characters: "We had instructions from the network that if a black is shown in a bad light, we must also show a black in a good light" (Farber 1985).

More recently, the networks have moved into what communications researcher Robert Thompson calls the "post-politically correct" period (Seplow 1994:G:11), in which they are once again comfortable showing black criminals. This may reflect a decision on the part of network executives to attend more to the concerns of mainstream audiences on matters of race. According to Bishetta Merritt of Howard University's radio, television, and film department, "Television is asking the questions that white people today in America are asking. It's reflective of the questions that white people have about black people, not the questions black Americans have" (Seplow:G:11). In fact, television programs and audiences present a relatively segregated picture of American media. According to the Nielsen ratings in 1994, there was no overlap between the five most popular shows in white households (*Home Improvement, Grace Under Fire, Seinfeld, Roseanne, NFL Monday Night Football*) and in African-American households (*Living Single, New York Undercover, Martin, Fresh Prince, Me and the Boys*). But however wary the networks remain of presenting African-American villains, they are apparently unafraid of portraying Latin Americans as villainous drug dealers and Arabs as terrorists. Only when Latin and Arab-American groups successfully organize to protest these stereotypes will we see fewer such characters.

Gay people are only now gaining the power and legitimacy needed to demand self-censorship on the part of the media. Consequently, audiences continue to see gay villains, victims, and psychopaths—e.g., the stereotypically gay serial killer in *Silence of the Lambs*, the lesbian psycho-killers in *Basic Instinct*—unbalanced by gay heroes, romantic leads, or just plain gay folks. As Montgomery's research has shown, however, our pressure tactics may at best yield a sort of limited success: screenplays such as *Philadelphia* or *The Birdcage* that offend neither minority nor mainstream sensibilities too much. Should we expect more? Probably not, since we have no way of quantifying the lesbian and gay audience (or any other "invisible" population for that matter) and thus lack the ultimate ammunition in the battle for representation: audience data. For many producers and directors, because we cannot be counted, we simply do not count. Given the commercial success of a mainstream film such as *Philadelphia*, we can surely expect more films with lesbian and gay themes. But we should not assume that these films will tell our stories for us, from our points of view, featuring us as central characters.

The ultimate expression of minority independence from the mainstream is a group's creation and consumption of its own media images. The Christian right, with its syndicated programs and networks, has already moved in this direction. In recent years lesbian women and gay men have also begun, often with difficulty, to gather the resources to do likewise. Typically, the first alternative channels to appear are those with low entry barriers, minimal technological needs, and relatively low operating costs. Thus, newspapers and magazines are the principal media created and consumed by minority groups (Streitmatter 1995). Radio programs, with their low production costs, are often the next to appear. Likewise, videos can be inexpensive to produce, making it possible for anyone with a camera and editing deck (or at least access to them) to produce a crude cable program; in some markets video technology is behind a handful of cable programs, produced during off-hours in local studios, such as *Dyke TV* and *Party Talk*. Video technology also makes possible syndicated cable programs such as *Network Q* and *In the Life* (Closs, this volume). Films, while far more expensive to make, can often recoup their investment through "narrowcasting," by identifying and appealing to a relatively specific niche. Finally, in quite a different way, the internet now utilizes a relatively cheap technology, personal computers, to provide gay chat lines, bulletin boards, and mail networks. By contrast, it is network television—with its numerous regulatory hurdles, high production costs, and demand for broad audiences—that remains the most insular and undemocratic of the media, largely unavailable to most minority groups.

There have always been minority media in the United States. Immigrant groups have long supported newspapers, books, theater, and even movies in their native languages (Goban-Klas 1989). But these voices were gradually stilled as succeeding generations assimilated into main-

stream culture, losing touch with the culture of their immigrant parents or grandparents. Likewise, the African American press initially flourished alongside the mainstream media, and black culture (music and dance in particular) has been the source of countless "crossover" hits and a profound (if rarely acknowledged) influence on white middle-class culture.

Since the 1970s lesbian and gay culture has included a similar range of media output—newspapers and magazines, music, theater, pornography—that are unmistakably the product of a gay sensibility. Here, too, there is the occasional crossover, as when Harvey Fierstein's three one-act plays were snatched up by Broadway producers and retitled *Torch Song Trilogy*, ultimately earning their author/star a Tony award for Best Play. More recently, Tony Kushner's two-part epic *Angels in America* wound its way from regional workshops to Broadway, garnering two successive Tony awards for Best Play, followed shortly by Terrence McNally's *Love! Valour! Compassion!*

But crossing over is no guarantee of protection from the dominant culture. With astounding frequency the critical response to openly lesbian or gay artists is to censure them for not "rising above" their parochial concerns, that is, for addressing themselves specifically to the concerns of fellow lesbians and gay men. Perhaps good literature *has* always transformed a particular subject into something universal. But there is a double standard in the application of the "universality criterion." In an essay entitled "Colonialist Criticism," Nigerian writer Chinua Achebe decried Western critics who evaluate African literature on the basis of whether it overcomes "parochialism" and "achieves universality." As he noted, "It would never occur to them to doubt the universality of their own literature. In the nature of things, the work of a Western writer is automatically informed by universality. It is only others who must strive to achieve it" (1976:11). Similarly, lesbian writer Sarah Schulman described her experience of being marginalized despite having published several novels with major publishers:

> By 1992 I discovered that I was in a ghetto as a lesbian novelist. My fifth novel *Empathy* was published. I got reviewed in *Entertainment Weekly*, but still could not get one straight bookstore in New York City to let me read there except during Gay Pride Month. The best-selling books by lesbians writers had

no lesbian content. When that content was introduced, the books plummeted in the esteem of critics, book buyers, and the general public. My books were translated into eight languages. Straight people never heard of me. I went to my high school reunion. I could tell who was straight and who was gay because the gay people said, "Oh Sarah, you've been doing so much." And the straight people said, "Oh Sarah, what have you been doing?" (1994:xviii–xix).

In recent years lesbian and gay filmmakers have been able, albeit with difficulty, to produce independent documentaries and fictional films that provide a real alternative to mainstream fare. The pioneering documentary *Word Is Out* (1977), and a score of others, including the Oscar-winning *The Times of Harvey Milk, Before Stonewall, Forbidden Love, Last Night at Maud's,* and *The Celluloid Closet,* represent authentic examples of lesbians and gay men speaking for (and to) themselves. True, there were inevitably compromises along the way in order to meet budgets, schedules, and the priggish demands of the Public Broadcasting System, the major outlet for independent documentaries in the United States (see Waugh 1988).

PBS has not proven an especially trustworthy ally, especially when their budget is threatened by pressure from corporate sponsors or politicians. When PBS scheduled a BBC production of gay author David Leavitt's *The Lost Language of Cranes* as part of the Great Performances series in June 1992, the gay themes set off a predictable outcry from the right, and the Texaco Oil Company withdrew its corporate sponsorship from the PBS series (Ehrenstein 1992). Two years later, in January 1994, PBS's American Playhouse series scored one of its biggest ratings successes with the six-hour miniseries *Tales of the City,* coproduced by Channel 4. The story, based on gay author Armistead Maupin's popular novel about San Francisco, impressed most viewers by faithfully capturing the flavor of the original. Rev. Wildmon was also attracted to the series, and in March he sent every member of Congress a "12-minutes bootleg videotape darkly highlighting the series' four-letter words, fleeting nudity, pot-smoking and one prolonged gay kiss" (Rich 1994). The American Family Association's March "Action! Page" mailing was headlined "Your Tax Dollars Used to Air Pornographic, profane, Homosexual TV Series." While listing several programs that "presented homosexuality in a very favorable light," it mostly focused on *Tales of the City*: "Those are your tax dollars PBS used to air this pro-homosexual propaganda. And it's our Judeo-Christian values PBS continues to attack and defame. . . . PBS can rightly be called the Homosexual Pride Taxpayer-Funded TV Network." Within a few weeks PBS announced that it was abandoning plans to coproduce a sequel for which the scripts had already been completed, and the budget for American Playhouse was cut by two-thirds (Carman 1994).

Meanwhile, there is a growing lesbian and gay presence in mainstream (art) theaters, making more of these independently produced films accessible to a national audience. What distinguishes the new breed of lesbian and gay cinema is not merely its content but the frankness and matter-of-factness with which it depicts lesbian and gay lives. As Russo noted: "These films take gayness for granted, and don't shy away from directly addressing the lesbians and gays in the audience." On the contrary, the new lesbian and gay cinema

> neither concerns itself overtly with issues of gay politics nor does it present gay sexuality as society's perennially dirty secret. The key to gay films, whether they are made by heterosexuals or homosexuals, is that they do not view the existence of gay people as controversial. . . . These films may reflect the fear, agitation, and bigotry of a society confronted with such truths, but it is not their view that such emotions are rational or even important to explore. (Russo 1986:34)

The nascent lesbian and gay film movement has found an uncommonly loyal and grateful primary audience. In fact, many of these films have become cult films of a different sort than Hollywood's midnight orphans. *Desert Hearts* was among the first. Made in 1986 on a small budget that was gathered through two-and-a-half years of arduous grassroots fund-raising, *Desert Hearts* achieved both crossover box office success and a cult following among lesbians. As Pat, a forty-seven-year-old secretary in San Francisco, put it,

> I've waited 25 years for this movie. I'm sick of seeing only heterosexual love stories. *Desert Hearts* is a movie I can finally identify with. It's like when I was little, we only had "white dolls" to play with, as if all babies were white. Movie makers have done the same thing:

they've generally ignored gays until the last few years. This movie is a positive step.... I've seen it 22 times and am still not tired of it. (Husten 1987:8)

"I think that lesbians are drawn to [*Desert Hearts*] in the same way that black people were drawn to *Superfly*," says screenwriter Natalie Cooper. "It isn't so much the content. It's a matter of the identification with the content and the way it's been presented." Like Pat, Natalie feels that *Desert Hearts* helped "make people feel okay, instead of feeling peripheral or put down. . . . They can say, 'This is our movie, this is our thing.' It makes them feel—dare I say—not proud, but *viable*" (Husten 1987:8).

In the years since *Desert Hearts* the ranks of independent film have swelled to the point that lesbian and gay film festivals flourish in cities around the country, and lesbian- and gay-themed films have won awards and rave reviews at Sundance and other important festivals. Filmmakers such as Greg Araki (*The Living End*, 1992), Cheryl Dunye (*Watermelon Woman*, 1996), John Greyson (*Zero Patience*, 1993; *Lillies*, 1996), Todd Haynes (*Poison*, 1991), Maria Maggenti (*The Incredibly True Adventures of Two Girls in Love*, 1995), and Rose Troche (*Go Fish*, 1994), and documentarians Arthur Dong (*Coming Out Under Fire*, 1994), Jennie Livingston (*Paris Is Burning*, 1990), Teodoro Maniaci and Francine Rzeznick (*One Nation Under God*, 1993), and Marlon Riggs (*Tongues Untied*, 1989), among others, are telling *our* stories, on *our* terms. Yet, for many lesbian and gay Americans, especially young people exploring their sexuality, these independent films and videos are remote and inaccessible outside of big-city movie theaters and video stores. Their cultural environment is defined by the corporate mass media.

The battlefield of American popular culture is likely to remain active for the foreseeable future, as the forces of conservatism continue their attempts to push the country back to the mythical past of "traditional family values" and the mainstream media, in their search for large and demographically lucrative audiences, inch cautiously toward a more accurate reflection of contemporary realities. In this seesawing progress the lesbian and gay community finds itself simultaneously sought out by adventuresome and opportunistic marketers and scapegoated by equally opportunistic preachers. And we increasingly insist on speaking for ourselves, both behind the

scenes and even on the media stages. Gay advocates and our adversaries agree on one thing: the media are more than "mere" entertainment. The mass media that tell most of the stories to most of the people more of the time are slowly shifting the terms of our public conversation toward a greater inclusiveness and acceptance of diversity.

## References

Achebe, Chinua. 1976. "Colonialist Criticism." In Chinua Achebe, *Morning Yet On Creation Day*. New York: Anchor.

Adam, Barry. 1978. *The Survival of Domination: Inferiorization and Everyday Life*. New York: Elsevier.

Alwood, Edward. 1996. *Straight News: Gays, Lesbians, and the News Media*. New York: Columbia University Press.

Babuscio, Jack. 1977. "Camp and the Gay Sensibility." In R. Dyer, ed., *Gays And Film*, pp. 40–57. London: British Film Institute.

Carman, John. 1994. "PBS Backs Out of Sequel to *Tales of the City*." *San Francisco Chronicle*, April 8.

Cohen, Derek and Richard Dyer. 1980. "The Politics of Gay Culture." In Gay Left Collective, eds., *Homosexuality: Power And Politics*, pp. 172–186. London: Allison and Busby.

Doty, Alexander. 1993. *Making Things Perfectly Queer*. Minneapolis: University of Minnesota Press.

Dyer, Richard. 1986. *Heavenly Bodies: Film Stars and Society*. New York: St. Martin's Press.

Dyer, Richard, ed. 1977. *Gays And Film*. London: British Film Institute.

Ellsworth, Elizabeth. 1986. "Illicit Pleasures: Feminist Spectators and *Personal Best*." *Wide Angle*, 8(2):46–56.

Ehrenstein, David. 1992. "Texaco and the PBS Mess," *Advocate*, June 16, pp. 97–98.

Epstein, Edward. 1974. *News From Nowhere: Television and the News*. New York: Vintage.

Erikson, Kai. 1966. *Wayward Puritans: A Study in the Sociology of Deviance*. New York: Wiley.

Farber, Stephen. 1986. "Minority Villains Are Touchy Network Topic." *New York Times*, March 1, p. 50.

Freer, Pete. 1987. "AIDS and . . . " In Gillian Hanscombe and Martin Humphries, eds., *Heterosexuality*, pp. 52–70. London: GMP.

Gans, Herbert. 1980. *Deciding What's News: A Study of CBS Evening News, NBC Nightly News, Newsweek and Time*. New York: Vintage.

Gerbner, George and Larry Gross. 1976. "Living with Television." *Journal of Communication,* 26(2):172–199.

Gerbner, George and Larry Gross, Michael Morgan, and Nancy Signorielli. 1980. "The 'Mainstreaming' of America." *Journal of Communication,* 30(3):10–29.

— 1982. "Charting the Mainstream: Television's Contributions to Political Orientations." *Journal of Communication,* 32(2):100–127.

— 1986. "Living with Television: The Dynamics of the Cultivation Process." In Jennings Bryant and Dolf Zillmann, eds., *Perspectives On Media Effects.* Hillsdale, N.J.: Lawrence Erlbaum.

— 1994. "Growing Up with Television: The Cultivation Perspective." In Jennings Bryant and Dolf Zillmann, eds., *Media Effects: Advances in Theory and Research,* pp. 17–41. Hillsdale, N.J.: Lawrence Erlbaum.

Goban-Klas, Tomasz. 1989. "Minority Media," In E. Barnouw, ed., *International Encyclopedia of Communications,* 3:30–32. New York: Oxford University Press.

Gross, Larry. 1984. "The Cultivation of Intolerance." In Gabriele Melischek, Karl Erik Rosengreen, and James Stappers, eds., *Cultural Indicators: An International Symposium,* pp. 345–364. Vienna: Austrian Academy of Sciences.

— 1996. "You're The First Person I've Ever Told: Letters to a Fictional Gay Teen." In Michael Bronski, ed., *Taking Liberties: Gay Men's Essays on Politics, Culture, and Sex,* pp. 369–386. New York: Richard Kasak.

Ha-'Am, Ahad (Asher Ginzberg). 1970. "Moses." In Ahad Ha-'Am, *Selected Essays of Ahad Ha-Am.* Ed. Leon Simon. New York: Atheneum.

Hachem, Samir. 1987. "Inside the Tinseled Closet." *Advocate,* March 17, pp. 42–48.

Henry, William. 1987. "That Certain Subject." *Channels,* April, pp. 43–45.

Hodges, Andrew and David Hutter. 1977. *With Downcast Gays: Aspects of Homosexual Self-Oppression.* Toronto: Pink Triangle Press.

Hoover, Stewart. 1985. "The 700 Club as Religion and as Television." Ph.D. diss., University of Pennsylvania.

Horton, Donald and Richard Wohl. 1956. "Mass Communication and Para-Social Interaction: Observation on Intimacy at a Distance." *Psychiatry,* 19(3):188–211.

Huston, Jan. 1987. "Fans Make *Desert Hearts* a Cult Classic." *Gay Community News,* January 25, pp. 8–9.

Kilday, Gregg. 1986. "Hollywood's Homosexuals." *Film Comment,* April pp. 40–43.

Klemesrud, Judy. 1968. "You Don't Have to Be One to Play One." *New York Times,* September 29, II:1.

Kozloff, Sarah Ruth. 1987. "Narrative Theory and Television." In Robert Allen, ed., *Channels of Discourse,* pp. 42–73. Chapel Hill: University of North Carolina Press.

Liebman, Marvin. 1992. *Coming Out Conservative.* San Francisco: Chronicle.

Michaud, Eugene. "The Whole Left Is Watching." Ph.D. diss., University of Pennsylvania, 1994.

Montgomery, Kathleen. 1981. "Gay Activists and the Networks." *Journal of Communication,* 31(3):49–57.

Morgan, Thomas. 1986. "The Black Viewers' New Allure for the Networks." *New York Times,* December 1, pp. III:20.

Rich, Frank. 1994. "The Plot Thickens at PBS." *New York Times,* April 4, p. 17.

— 1996. "The Gay GOP." *New York Times,* September 28, p. 23.

Rodrick, Stephen. 1996. "The Secret Life of Arthur Finkelstein." *Boston Magazine,* October.

Rodriguez, Rene. 1995. "Movie Ads Edging Out of the Closet—Films Such as *Jeffrey* Are Up Front About Gay Love." *San Jose Mercury News,* August 11.

Russo, Vito. 1986. "A State of Being." *Film Comment,* April, pp. 32–34.

— 1987. *The Celluloid Closet: Homosexuality in the Movies.* New York: Harper and Row.

Schulman, Sarah. *My American History.* New York: Routledge, 1994.

Seplow, Stephen. 1994. "The Changing Face of Race on TV." *Philadelphia Inquirer,* October 30, pp. G:1, 11.

Sontag, Susan. 1967. "Notes on Camp." In Susan Sontag, *Against Interpretation, and Other Essays,* pp. 275–292. New York: Delta.

Southgate, Martha. 1994. "A Funny Thing Happened on the Way to Prime Time." *Philadelphia Inquirer,* October 30, pp. 53–54.

Streitmatter, Rodger. 1995. *Unspeakable: The Rise of the Gay and Lesbian Press in America.* Boston: Faber and Faber.

Turow, Joseph. 1978. "Casting for TV Parts: The Anatomy of Social Typing." *Journal of Communication,* 28(4):18–24.

Waugh, Thomas. 1988. "Minority Self-Imaging in Oppositional Film Practice: Lesbian and Gay Documentary." In Larry Gross, John Katz, and Jay Ruby, eds., *Image Ethics,* pp. 248–272. New

York: Oxford University Press.

Weiss, Andrea. 1986. "From the Margins: New Images of Gays in the Cinema." *Cineaste,* 15(1):4–8.

Williams, Raymond. 1977. *Marxism And Literature.*

Oxford: Oxford University Press.

Woods, James D. 1993. *The Corporate Closet: The Professional Lives of Gay Men in America.* New York: Free Press.

# One

# IDENTITY

## THE MODERN HOMOSEXUAL

# I. A

# OTHER TIMES, OTHER CUSTOMS

Based on an outpouring of recent historical and anthropological research, it seems certain that same-sex attractions, relations, and behaviors have been around for a very long time. They can be found in virtually every society, past or present, for which we have adequate data on sexual behavior. To understand the modern "homosexual role," then, it is useful to place it in a broader anthropological and historical context.

In 1951 Ford and Beach published *Patterns of Sexual Behavior*, the first major survey of the cross-cultural data on sexual behavior. Drawing on ethnographic data from 190 human cultures, from the Arctic Circle to the southernmost tip of Australia, as well as numerous mammalian species, the authors endeavored to catalogue cross-cultural variation in courtship, masturbation, intercourse, bestiality, and other sexual behaviors. Their findings were significant in part because they showed that while heterosexual intercourse was the most prevalent form of sexual behavior among adults, never was it the *only* activity practiced in a particular culture. Nor was there consensus on which particular activities were forbidden. Of the 76 human groups for which data on homosexuality were available, the majority (64 percent) considered same-gender sexual relations to be normal and socially acceptable, at least for certain members of the community. In the remaining third of the societies (37 percent), homosexual behavior was reported to be rare, absent, or carried on only in secrecy.

While there is less evidence of same-sex contact between women (given the tendency of male scholars to use male informants and focus on male behavior), it has nonetheless been documented in numerous human societies. Of the seventy-six cultures in which homosexual behavior was noted in Ford and Beach's survey, in seventeen it was reported between women. A more recent survey identified ninety-five cultures in which erotic behavior between females was observed (Blackwood 1985).

Whereas homosexual behavior seems to be a nearly universal feature of human societies (Whitam 1983), sexual contact between same-sex persons may be institutionalized and interpreted in radically different ways, few of which resemble the roles available to lesbians and gay men in our own society. Several of these alternative arrangements are described below:

*Age-structured homosexuality* Many societies prescribe same-sex contact between individuals of different ages, typically older males and boys between late childhood and early adulthood. Quite often these activities are considered a normal and expected part of sexual development. For example, in highly militarized societies (such as ancient Greece, the Azande of Africa, and numerous New Guinea societies) male-male contact is associated with the transmission of courage, prowess, and masculine valor. In some places it is part of formal rituals, such as initiation ceremonies (Herdt 1990:221; Adam 1986).

In various parts of Melanesia, for example, boys between the ages of about seven and thirteen are taken from their mother's household and placed in a boys' house a short distance from the village. For several months to several years, depending on the particular culture, they are denied all contact with females as they are prepared in elaborate initiations for manhood. Central to these rituals is the transmission of semen, which is believed to be the essence of manhood, a scarce resource to be conserved by males (and not squandered unnecessarily on females, who would also be strengthened by it). People in these societies believe that in order to become a ferocious and courageous warrior a boy must repeatedly ingest the semen of mature men. It is crucial during these contacts that the younger boy be the recipient of the semen; reversing roles would be damaging to his growth. At the same time, the boy is expected to sleep with his mentors, who educate him and see that he develops proper male values such as courage, proficiency in hunting, and the ability to dominate women. Homosexual behavior is thus a duty of all adolescent boys, who as adults will reverse roles and supply semen to younger boys; over the course of a life cycle each male serves in both capacities. They do not form lifelong pairings with same-sex partners, nor do they think of themselves as "bisexual" in our sense of the term. Upon achieving adulthood and completing a series of elaborate initiations, they are expected to marry women and produce children, which most apparently do (Williams 1986; Herdt 1981, 1984).

While few societies institutionalize man-boy sex to the same degree as in New Guinea, many have had similar traditions (Williams 1986:264). In ancient Greece, similarly, adolescent boys regularly entered erotic apprenticeships with older males. As in New Guinea societies, the relationship was viewed as a temporary transitional bond; it would have been improper to continue it after the youth matured. While the men might remain friends for life, each ultimately turned to new adolescents as erotic partners (Williams 1986:267).

Examples of age-structured homosexuality between women are less abundant, although there are comparable instances of sexual contact during all-female initiation rituals and training (Blackwood 1985). Among the Dahomeyans of Africa, for example, adolescent girls prepared for marriage by attending initiation schools in which they performed sexual exercises in each other's presence to enlarge their genitalia. Women who continued these activities into adulthood did so in secret (Herskovits 1967). Since at least the 1950s, while their migrant husbands sought work in neighboring South Africa, Lesotho women have formed "mummy-baby" relationships with young girls that include the giving of gifts, the writing of love letters, and the enjoyment of sexual intimacy (Gay 1985).

In these cultures age-structured homosexuality typically involves the assumption that the participating individuals will also marry and have children. Young men and women are expected to outgrow the relationship, after which they may take younger lovers of their own. In this sense same-sex eroticism is viewed as a transitional or phasic activity. Anthropologists do not report finding "homosexuals" in the modern Western sense of a person who is habitually and exclusively sexually bonded to a same-sex partner.

*Cross-gender homosexuality* In cross-gender homosexuality one of the partners relinquishes the role ordinarily associated with his or her anatomical sex and lays claim to that of the other. Males dress and act as females, and females dress and behave as males. Thereafter, homosexual relationships are modeled on the heterosexual pattern. Contact between same-sex partners, one of whom has switched gender roles, is thus consistent with the dictates of the traditional binary gender order (Blackwood 1985:13; Herdt 1990:222).

Williams uses the term *amazon* to designate Native American women who pass for men, dress like men, and marry women (1986:234). Among the Kutenai Indians, for example, there is the legend of "Manlike Woman," a prophet and shaman who claimed that her sex had been surgically altered by a group of white fur traders. After the change she began to dress in men's clothing, carry a gun, participate as a warrior on raids, and court young women, eventually marrying and divorcing several wives. Encountering the couple in the early 1800s, a fur trader wrote of "two strange Indians, in the character of man and wife" (236). Among the Kutenai, who have passed the legend down for over a century, there is great respect for Manlike Woman's reputed supernatural powers.

Elsewhere, males may pass as women. For example, in Polynesian societies males may assume the role of *mahu*. Mahus do women's work, dress in women's clothing, and act as the receptive partner in sexual acts with men. An English captain in Tahiti in 1789 described one of his sailors being "very much smitten" with a dancing girl, only later to discover that she was an anatomical male. The mahu role is much prized among

Tahitians, as only one person at a time in each village is allowed to claim the status. More than other males, mahus are known for forming close ties to both parents and for tending them in old age. When asked, Tahitians explain that the mahu is simply born that way, that "God creates the mahu and that is the way it is" (Williams 1986:257).

## Role-specialized homosexuality

In other societies certain individuals may assume a highly specialized role that incorporates homosexual activity. Rather than switch from one gender to another, they cross over into a sort of third category that differs from both conventional male and female roles, a role recognized and valued by the group.

The most famous example of such a role is the berdache tradition in many Native American cultures. A berdache is an anatomical male whose dress and manner are androgynous, combining aspects of the social roles of both men and women. Berdaches have traditionally fulfilled special ceremonial roles in many Native American religions and are believed to be able to communicate with the spirit world. They are also renowned for their contributions as healers, prophets, matchmakers, and mediators. In their erotic behavior berdaches typically (but not always) assume a nonmasculine role, either becoming asexual or serving as the receptive partner in sex with men. In many cultures a berdache might also become wife to a man (Williams 1986).

Far from threatening the traditional two-gender system, the androgynous berdache is set apart from it (Endleman 1986; Herdt 1990; Greenberg 1988). According to Williams, "They serve a mediating function between women and men, precisely because their character is seen as distinct from either sex. They are not seen as men, yet they are not seen as women either. They occupy an alternative gender role that is a mixture of diverse elements" (1986:2). Because they mediate between the two sexes as well as between the spiritual and physical worlds, berdaches are believed to possess the vision of both. It is often said that they have "double vision," the ability to see more clearly than someone of a single gender, and are often referred to as "seers."

While there is evidence that females sometimes assume special roles comparable to that of the berdache, such transformations are apparently far more common among males (Williams 1986).

## Egalitarian homosexuality

Whereas the three forms of homosexuality described above involve contact between same-sex persons of unequal status, a fourth form involves partners of the same approximate social status. In egalitarian relationships partners are likely to have the same gender and be about the same age. A partner who is insertive on one occasion may be receptive the next, and within the relationship they regard one another as social equals (Greenberg 1986:66).

Cross-culturally, the most common form of egalitarian sexual relationship seems to be the adolescent sex play documented in many cultures (Greenberg 1986). In the East Bay community of a Melanesian island young single men who are good friends or even brothers may take turns in accommodating each other sexually. Young boys of the Kwoma, a New Guinea tribe, play at copulation with one another. Among the Tiwi of Australia, boys inhabit a "bachelor's camp" from age eleven to fourteen, where they form same-sex relationships while living in the bush, isolated from women. And among the !Kung, girls engage in sexual play with one another before doing so with boys (Shostak 1981). In none of these cases does participation necessitate a homosexual orientation in adulthood.

Adults, too, may enter same-sex relationships characterized by intimacy and sexual contact. In the early eighteenth century Joseph François Lafitau, a French Jesuit missionary, described the "special friendships" he witnessed among the "Savages of North America." "They become Companions in hunting, in war, and in fortune," he wrote in his memoirs. "They have a right to food and lodging in each other's cabin. The most affectionate compliment that the friend can make to his friend is to give him the name of Friend." While it is not certain that these intense relationships were sexual, European missionaries attempted to suppress them, believing they would inevitably lead to such "abuses" (Katz 1992:288). Likewise, among women in harems, sisterhoods, and polygynous households, egalitarian sexual relationships are apparently common. Among the Azande, wealthy men married several wives, and built a dwelling in the compound for each wife. Despite the demands of the marriage, co-wives were free to establish sexual partnerships amongst themselves, which may also have facilitated their cooperation in the tasks of the household economy (Blackwood 1985:10).

It should be obvious even from this brief survey that there is tremendous variation in human sexual practices, both in the kinds of activities permitted and the concepts used to make sense of them. The activities we consider pleasurable today might have seemed abhorrent, boring, or sinful to our great grandparents. (Probably our great grandchildren will feel the same way.) Likewise, the sexual customs taken for granted in ancient Greece would be entirely unfamiliar to the Keraki of the New Guinea highlands, the Native American berdache, or the modern-day Houston teenager.

When we turn our gaze back to European ancestors who lived more than a century ago we find no direct parallel to present-day social types. There are no men and women who fit our contemporary conception of the lesbian or gay man, yet there are continuities as well as differences in the labels and images that can be found. Over the centuries numerous terms have been used to designate these erotic preferences. Aristotle believed, as did Thomas Aquinas, that some men were innately attracted to other men. The Greek historian Timaeus wrote of Etruscan men who were "very fond of women, but find more pleasure with boys and young men" (Blumenfeld and Raymond 1988:103). A ninth-century Arabic psychology text noted that "some are disposed towards women," some toward men, and some toward both. And much medieval poetry celebrates or satirizes bisexual inclinations among the rich and powerful. Whereas the term *sexual orientation* would have been unknown to these writers, this does not mean that there was no awareness of specifically homosexual or heterosexual "orientation" in earlier societies. Much evidence indicates that these were common and familiar concepts (Boswell, this volume).

In many ways the paths leading most directly to our current cultural configuration began with the dissolution of the Roman Empire and the rise of Christianity in the third and fourth centuries. Romans made few legal or moral distinctions based on the gender of an individual's erotic partners. In the Greco-Roman world homosexual relationships were widely celebrated in romantic poetry, art, and literature. It was widely known, for example, that virtually all of the Roman emperors took male lovers, exclusively or otherwise. Indeed, Hadrian (who ruled from A.D. 117 to 138) and the Greek youth Antinous were seen as models of erotic fidelity and romantic love (Boswell 1980:85).

With the rise of Christianity new beliefs about homosexuality would gradually displace the Greco-Roman attitude of indifference; the reasons for this shift have not been fully explained. In the third and fourth centuries Christian theologians increasingly held that procreation was the only moral function of sexual intercourse and argued, variously, that homosexual contacts were animalistic, unnatural, and degrading (especially for those males who took the receptive role during intercourse). Greco-Roman ideas about spiritual love and eroticism gave way to the ascetic notion that sexual pleasure, even for married couples, was morally suspect. As historians have pointed out, the reasons for these restrictive sexual values had as much to do with attempts to consolidate power and ensure moral conformity (by using Jews, heretics, foreigners, and homosexuals as scapegoats for other social tensions) as with purely theological objections to homosexuality.

In fact, there is compelling evidence that intolerance toward homosexuality during the late Middle Ages was primarily a function of changing political fortunes. For more than a millennium the Christian church had largely accommodated or ignored homosexual activities; theologians who *did* condemn homosexuality typically saw it in the same category of sins as adultery, usury, or gluttony (Boswell 1980). Only in the late Middle Ages, as the church consolidated its power, did antihomosexual rhetoric gradually become a centerpiece of Christian morality. Homosexual behavior was increasingly viewed as a dangerous, antisocial, and sinful aberration associated with heresy and witchcraft. Between 1250 and 1300 homosexual activity passed from being completely legal in most of Europe to incurring the death penalty in all but a few areas. Many of today's most deeply held beliefs about sexuality—in particular the equation of sexual pleasure with sin and procreative sex with "nature"—had taken shape by the end of the fourteenth century (Boswell 1980). The centuries that followed saw the reworking of these same themes and moral ideologies. By the seventeenth century prohibitions on homosexuality—and other forms of sodomy—formed the bedrock of Puritan morality in this country (D'Emilio and Freedman 1988).

In an era of secularization, in which "science" increasingly challenged religion as the source of fundamental "truth," the nineteenth century saw an important shift in the prevailing view of homosexuality. Emerging theories advanced a view of homosexuality as the attribute of individuals for whom this was the *natural* inclination, rather than an unnatural deviation from "normal" sexuality.

Variously labeled "Urnings," the "intermediate sex," the "third sex," or "homosexuals," these attempts rapidly fell victim to the "pathological" view of homosexuality that recast the longstanding "sin" as a "sickness." As a result, homosexuality was gradually "medicalized," reconceived as the proper concern of physicians who could diagnose and treat it (Weeks 1981).

While ancient civil and ecclesiastic codes had viewed sodomy as a category of forbidden acts, a transgression anyone might commit in a moment of weakness, medicine increasingly viewed it as the behavior of a distinct *class* of persons. Indeed, by the turn of the century there was a near consensus among proponents of the medical model that homosexuality was hereditary in origin. The new medical discourse insisted "that only a subspecies of human beings, now called 'homosexuals' for the first time, felt such same-gender impulses, and that such impulses, wherever present, *always* constituted a personality disorder" (Duberman 1986:445). Previously, one might have engaged in homosexual *behavior*, but now one simply *was* a homosexual; isolated "sins" became symptoms of an underlying personality type. As Michel Foucault (1978:43) wrote, in a famous passage: "The nineteenth-century homosexual became a personage, a past, a case history, and a childhood.... The sodomite had been a temporary aberration; the homosexual was now a species."

Nor was there always a homosexual "community" as we today know it. Indeed, it wasn't until the late 1800s that a discernible gay subculture began to emerge in American cities. Urbanization and industrialization created a context in which individuals could escape the confines of traditional family life and an intimate community for the impersonality of the city. Ironically, the social stigmatization and legal oppression they experienced were among the key factors encouraging the rise of a distinct gay subculture (D'Emilio, Chauncey, this volume).

With the rise of the homophile movement in the late 1950s and the 1960s a visible community with its own rules, beliefs, literature, and language began to emerge, most notably in New York and San Francisco. For individuals who experienced same-sex attractions there were now bars, neighborhoods, restaurants, modes of dress, publications, and symbols such as the pink triangle, used by the Nazis to designate homosexual prisoners but now appropriated as a symbol of gay pride.

It should be emphasized in this context that heterosexuality, too, has a history. While we imagine that "heterosexuality is as old as procreation, ancient as the lust of Eve and Adam" (Katz 1995:13), we must keep in mind that while people have always had heterosexual sex, they have not always thought of themselves as *heterosexuals*. It wasn't until the late 1800s that medical researchers began to define sexuality in terms of two polarized erotic states, heterosexual and homosexual. In America the word *heterosexual* first appears in an 1892 medical journal article, and it is absent from the 1901 edition of the comprehensive *Oxford English Dictionary*. It does not appear in the *New York Times* until 1930. Before that time there had been Victorian notions of "true love" and lust, of virtue and sin, but these were quite different from our present-day concept of heterosexuality, defined in terms of normalcy, naturalness, and health. As the historian Jonathan Ned Katz has pointed out, past Americans and other peoples named, perceived, and socially organized the bodies, lusts, and intercourse of the sexes in ways radically different from the way we do (Katz 1995).

The sexual identities that seem natural and possible depend largely on the society into which one has been socialized. No sexual practice is *inherently* sinful, moral, deviant, or desirable except insofar as it is defined as such (Becker 1963). In the fourth century a man who enjoyed sex with other men might have used no particular label for these activities. A thousand years later, in the Christian world, he might have viewed these same activities as sins or transgressions against God. By the start of the present century he might have thought of himself as an "invert" or "homosexual," while today he would most likely consider himself gay. Thus an individual's self concept takes shape as erotic yearnings are organized and directed through social contact with others, as he or she learns about and experiments with the sexual identities made available by the culture.

## REFERENCES

Adam, Barry D. 1986. "Age, Structure, and Sexuality: Reflections on the Anthropological Evidence on Homosexual Relations." *Journal of Homosexuality*, 11(3/4):19–33.

Becker, Howard S. 1963. *Outsiders: Studies in the Sociology of Deviance.* New York: Free Press.

Blackwood, Evelyn. 1985. "Breaking the Mirror: The Construction of Lesbianism and the Anthropological Discourse on Homosexuality." *Journal of Homosexuality*, 11(3/4):1–17.

Blumenfeld, Warren J., and Diane Raymond. 1988. *Looking at Gay and Lesbian Life*. Boston: Beacon.

Boswell, John. 1980. *Christianity, Social Tolerance, and Homosexuality*. Chicago: University of Chicago.

Boswell, John. 1990. "Sexual and Ethical Categories in Premodern Europe." In David McWhirter, Stephanie Sanders, and June Machover Reinisch, eds., *Homosexuality/Heterosexuality: Concepts of Sexual Orientation*, pp. 15–31. New York: Oxford University Press.

Boswell, John. 1994. *Same-Sex Unions in Premodern Europe*. New York: Villard.

D'Emilio, John and Estelle Freedman. 1988. *Intimate Matters: A History of Sexuality in America*. New York: Harper and Row.

Duberman, Martin B. 1986. *About Time: Exploring the Gay Past*. New York: Meridian.

Endleman, Robert. 1986. "Homosexuality in Tribal Societies." *Transcultural Psychiatric Research Review*, 23:187–218.

Ford, Clellan S. and Frank A. Beach. 1951. *Patterns of Sexual Behavior*. New York: Harper.

Foucault, Michel. 1978. *The History of Sexuality*. Vol. 1. New York: Random House.

Gay, Judith. 1985. " 'Mummies and Babies' and Friends and Lovers in Lesotho." *Journal of Homosexuality*, 11(3/4):97–116.

Greenberg, David F. 1988. *The Construction of Homosexuality*. Chicago: University of Chicago Press.

Herdt, Gilbert H. 1981. *Guardians of the Flutes: Idioms of Masculinity*. New York: Columbia University Press.

— 1990. "Developmental Discontinuities and Sexual Orientation Across Cultures." In David McWhirter, Stephanie Sanders, and June Machover Reinisch, eds., *Homosexuality/Heterosexuality: Concepts of Sexual Orientation*, pp. 208–236. New York: Oxford University Press.

Herdt, Gilbert H., ed. 1984. *Ritualized Homosexuality in Melanesia*. Berkeley: University of California Press.

Herskovits, M. J. 1967. *Dahomey: An Ancient West African Kingdom*. 2 vols. Evanston: Northwestern University Press.

Katz, Jonathan Ned. 1992. *Gay American History*. Rev. ed. New York: Meridian.

— 1995. *The Invention of Heterosexuality*. New York: Dutton.

Shostak, Marjorie. 1981. *Nisa, The Life and Words of a !Kung Woman*. Cambridge: Harvard University Press.

Weeks, Jeffrey. 1981. *Sex, Politics and Society: The Regulation of Sexuality Since 1800*. New York: Longman.

Whitam, Frederick L. 1983. "Culturally Invariable Properties of Male Homosexuality: Tentative Conclusions from Cross-Cultural Research." *Archives of Sexual Behavior*, 12(3):207–226.

Williams, Walter. 1986. *The Spirit and the Flesh: Sexual Diversity in American Indian Culture*. Boston: Beacon.

# | 1 |

# A Matter of Difference

## Martin Duberman

Virginia Woolf slept with Vita Sackville-West. Does that make her "lesbian"? Cary Grant had a long-standing affair with Randolph Scott. Does that make him "gay"? And what do we do with Colette, the lover of young men, once we learn of her involvement with the film star Marguerite Moreno? And is there a category for Lord Byron, notorious for his many affairs with women *and* at one point madly in love with the choirboy John Edleston?

Queer theory has taught us to distrust categories as needless calcifications of what is purportedly our fluid, meandering erotic natures. We are told to move beyond Freud's notions of inherent bisexuality to posit a malleable sexuality that, if allowed to run free, would create all sorts of trisexual permutations. Most of us, alas, however attracted to the theory of infinite malleability, have been trained in a culture that regards sexual appetite as consisting of two, and only two, contrasting variations—gay or straight. And most of us have internalized that perhaps false dichotomy to such a degree that it has become as deeply imprinted in us—as immutable—as any genetically mandated trait.

Historians, often deeply conservative by temperament—who else would devote a lifetime to conserving the past?—tend to have little patience with the implicit injunction of queer theorists to reinvent ourselves constantly, and dismiss such a view as utopian. Yet even historians cannot blink away, much as they might wish, the ambiguities about human sexual nature that have arisen in the wake of the burgeoning scholarship on the gay and lesbian past.

A mere twenty years ago, the notion of a formal, scholarly, institutionalized inquiry into gay history would have been unthinkable, literally not nameable, yet there are now enough serious-minded scholars devoting their full-time efforts to its reclamation to fill conference rooms. Some are engaged in documenting the history of genital sex between members of the same gender. Others pursue evidence of passionate, romantic, *nongenital* friendships. Yet another group of scholars is at work detailing the history of gender nonconformity and of cross-gender identifications in dress, speech, mannerisms and attitudes—studies that center on the phenomena of transvestism and transsexualism or, cross-culturally, on "third gender" figures like the Native American *berdache*, the Indian *hijra*, and the Polynesian *mahu*. Finally, there are scholars whose primary inquiry is describing how and why cultural definitions of sexual and gender unorthodoxy have shifted over time; their interest is not in the nonconforming behavior itself but in understanding the shifting ways it has been regarded.

Although all these enterprises, and more, have swiftly accelerated in the past few years, their interconnections are not always clear, and the complex nature of the evidence being unearthed has often been difficult to interpret. To take just one example—the history of passionate friendship—scholars continue to debate earnestly, yet inconclusively, the connection of that phenomenon to the history of erotic arousal. Are they one and the same? Is passionate friendship best seen as an instance of erotic sublimation? Is overt sexuality a natural extension of emotional closeness and should we therefore view its absence as an instance of cultural repression? And some would argue that the pursuit of evidence of genital sex

*Nation*, July 5, 1993, pp. 22–24.

between two people of the same gender is itself a misguided enterprise, the "true" history of "gays" and "lesbians" residing not in the record of same-gender erotic arousal but in the story of gender nonconformity.

There is no question—to stay with the example of passionate friendship—but that many pairs of women in the United States and England lived together during the latter part of the nineteenth and the early part of the twentieth century in devoted partnerships, sharing all aspects of their lives. Well, nearly all. Emotional intimacy—yes. Frequent hand-holding, touching, even kissing—yes. But genital sexuality—apparently no. Should we therefore refrain from calling them lesbians?

Perhaps the answer lies not in these women's (apparently) celibate behavior but in their fantasy lives; perhaps these women secretly admitted to themselves what they were loath to act upon. Perhaps—but it is unlikely we will ever know. We almost never have enough information about the inner lives of people in the past to talk confidently about the content of their subjective desires. Maps to the psychological interior (in the form, say, of elaborate, unbridled diaries and letters) are almost always lacking for historical figures. In their absence, we form judgments from *behavioral* evidence alone—itself not easy to gauge and interpret.

And what of the additionally complicating factor of *self*-definition? Should we reserve the label "lesbian" (or "gay") for those who are subjectively conscious of having a different sexuality, which they in turn reify into a different "identity"? In regard to those pair-bonded women involved in "Boston marriages" (as they were sometimes called in this country), the historian Leila Rupp has concluded that they would most probably have rejected the label "lesbian" for themselves.

Indeed, some of those women lived on into a more self-conscious era when the terminology and categories "gay" and "lesbian," not earlier available, had come into common usage, and they often reacted with angry disgust to the suggestion that *their* relationships could be so characterized. True, their very vehemence can be taken as a classic instance of denial. But if we insist on that interpretation, we have placed ourselves in the position of claiming to know the "truth" of a relationship better than the participants in it—to say nothing of placing ourselves in danger (one to which historians commonly succumb) of projecting *our* descriptive categories backward in time onto those who might have nei-

ther understood nor approved of them.

The problem of interpreting "Boston marriages" is but one example of the conundrums facing those engaged in trying to unearth a usable past for today's lesbian and gay community, trying somehow to lay claim to an extended history that can provide needed nourishment and legitimacy. The large majority of gay men and lesbians share the mainstream American view, common to most cultures, that legitimacy is predicated on the ability to lay claim to "roots"—to antecedents; to hoist the counter banner of being "something new under the sun" is tantamount to declaring impotence. Again like other mainstream Americans, most gay men and lesbians hanker after and rhetorically hallow the past even as they insist on its irrelevance.

In the case of gay people, the hankering takes on particular poignancy. Having been excluded from the textbooks, having been denied the kind of alternate, family-centered oral tradition available to other minorities, gay people long for some proof—some legitimizing evidence—that we have always existed, and in pretty much the same form as we currently do, and that we are therefore automatically entitled to the same status and rights other "official" minorities lay claim to.

Alas, we can never find *exact* precursors in the past, and any search for them is doomed to disappointment. This is not less true for heterosexuals than for homosexuals (as we have quaintly learned to call ourselves). Heterosexuality, too, has a history, a record of shifting definitions of what has been considered "healthy" or "authentic"—and thereforez allowable—behavior. Women in this country and in England in the mid-nineteenth century, for example, were commonly viewed as passionless. Any woman who exhibited "undue" interest in sex was likely to be labeled disturbed—"neurasthenic"; she would be sent away for a rest cure and, should that fail, would become a candidate for a clitoridectomy. Yet a mere hundred years later a common feminist view is that women are "naturally" *more* sexual than men, capable of that indefinite number of orgasms and ever-heightened pleasure that the low-performing male can only fantasize about (and envy so furiously in the female that he invents the domestic lockup to curtail her).

Neither gays nor straights, in short, can hope to lay claim to any kind of history other than an endlessly changing one. We can never confirm our present images by citing lengthy lineages in the past. What the past *can* be said to confirm is that "human nature," far from being a constant, has taken on, under varying cultural imperatives, a wide range of shapes—the very starting point of queer theory.

Reclaiming the history of gender nonconformity—which some argue is conterminous if not wholly synonymous with the history of "gays" and "lesbians"—is also a way of confirming another truth of value to *all* human beings, regardless of their sexual orientation. And that is the demonstrable ability of people who are "different" to develop, in the face of denunciation and oppression, creative strategies for survival that then open up new possibilities for everyone. We are all far more different (though not necessarily in sexual ways) than most of us would care to admit in our conformist culture. The emerging history of lesbians and gay men has begun to provide empowering evidence for anyone insistent on allowing their differentness to emerge—and on it being respected.

# | 2 |

## *"Intimate Friendships"*

### Erica E. Goode, with Betsy Wagner

History shows that the lines between "straight" and "gay" sexuality are much more fluid than today's debate suggests.

"Ah, how I love you," wrote President Grover Cleveland's sister Rose to her friend Evangeline Whipple in 1890. "It makes me heavy with emotion. . . . All my whole being leans out to you. . . . I dare not think of your arms." The letter was one of many the two women exchanged, their tone as impassioned and yearning as any billet-doux, their language, at least to modern ears, tinged with eroticism. Evangeline, a young widow, eventually remarried, taking as her husband an aging Episcopalian bishop. But when he died, she resumed her correspondence with Rose, and in 1910 the two women went off to Italy, living together until Cleveland's death eight years later.

Today, such fervor between women—or men—would have a ready name, draw champions and detractors, perhaps spark a spirited defense on the op-ed page. The 1990s focus a stark light on matters of affection and desire, the corners scrutinized, the edges hard and precise. But Rose Cleveland and Evangeline Whipple loved in the waning years of another time, when the lines were drawn differently, the urge to categorize and dissect not so overpowering. Belonging to the 19th century, they were not yet initiated into the idea of "sexual identity," knew nothing of gay bars or marches on Washington and considered even the display of a bare ankle risqué. If, at a garden party or high tea, they encountered the terms "homosexual," "sexual invert" or "lesbian"—labels slowly filtering down in the 1890s from medical circles into common use—they probably would have found them curious, would have shaken their heads and said, "Oh, but surely such things have nothing to do with us!"

Every era clings to the belief that the way it views the world reflects not the influence of culture and location but the way the world is. In the most intimate area of life, in questions of what behind bedroom doors is acceptable or frowned upon, of what sexuality means and how it is expressed, such convictions gain particular force. Yet historians, who only in recent years have begun to reconstruct how other epochs regarded amorous relations between members of the same sex, do not see a fixed scene but a moving landscape, a shifting of boundaries and definitions that defies contemporary labeling. Says Univer-

*U.S. News and World Report*, July 5, 1993, pp. 49–52.

sity of North Caroline historian John D'Emilio, "What we've learned . . . is that sexuality is much more fluid than any of us wants to admit."

## A GAY "MOVEMENT"

Asked to pinpoint the birth of the gay liberation movement, many gay and lesbian activists point to a June night in 1969, when a police raid on a Greenwich Village gay bar, the Stonewall Inn, triggered a riot that mobilized the gay community. Others cite earlier milestones: the founding of the Mattachine Society and the Daughters of Bilitis in the 1950s; the 1948 publication of the Kinsey report, with its controversial estimate that 1 in 10 men is homosexual, or perhaps the creation of the first lesbian newsletter, *Vice Versa*, distributed informally in 1947 by a Los Angeles secretary, Lisa Ben. Yet for any of these events to have taken place, something more fundamental was needed: a realization, among those attracted toward members of their own gender, that there were others like them, facing the same difficulties and concerns. And before that, something even more basic: the idea that sexual orientation was an important characteristic, that it set a group of people apart, defining them as different in some essential way from a "heterosexual" majority, a development scholar Jonathan Katz has called "the invention of the homosexual."

Love between men was celebrated as "Eros" in ancient Greece and flourished in other societies like Japan, where it formed a respected subculture as late as the mid-1800s. In Europe, legal and religious sanctions against homosexual behavior at first became common in the Middle Ages, a turbulent period during which the state grew increasingly hostile toward nonconformity of many types. Yet early laws, even the death penalties meted out for sodomy in colonial America, spoke not to a certain type of person, but to any sexual act that departed from the true purpose of sexual intercourse: procreation. Homosexual sex was just one of many ways a person could run afoul of God. In a blistering 1674 sermon, the Rev. Samuel Danforth holds forth equally against the man who "lyeth with mankind, as he lyeth with a woman" and against those who committed other sodomitical acts, such as "self-pollution" (masturbation), adultery and bestiality.

The roots of prescriptions against sodomy and other forms of sexual waywardness were biblical. But the underlying danger of nonprocreative sex lay in its threat to marriage and family, insitutions vital to a young society struggling to survive against difficult odds. Yet no one in early America considered homosexuality a trait of particular people; through weakness or "inclination," anyone could fall prey to sodomitical sins. Nor, it appears, did those who today would readily embrace the term "gay" see themselves as a distinct group. Embedded in families, they had no hope for a life apart; nor could they have one, until the coming of cities and railroad tracks, of urban meeting places and jobs that allowed men (and much later women) to strike out on their own, gradually turning what had been a series of sexual "sins" into an identity, a way of being. Even then, the transformation was not complete. To create a person called a homosexual required a new way of thinking about sexuality, less tightly bound to fertility, and the work of a newly bold circle of scientists determined to make explicit what had hitherto been unspoken.

## DAWN OF SEXOLOGY

"The majority of homosexuals," wrote Dr. Richard von Krafft-Ebing in 1886, "are happy in their perverse sexual feeling and impulse, and unhappy only in so far as social and legal barriers stand in the way of the satisfaction of their instinct toward their own sex." Krafft-Ebing and other turn-of-the-century "sexologists" set out to cleanse homosexuality of its moral taint, removing it from the realm of the criminal into what they saw as the kindlier province of medicine. They were radicals, brazenly describing sexual passion as a healthy part of life and exposing sexual details long shrouded in Victorian modesty. Among their friends, they counted gay intellectuals, like those in London's Bloomsbury group, and early champions of homosexual emancipation, like British writer Edward Carpenter.

Yet, however well-intentioned, the sexologists' contribution in the end proved double-edged. By identifying homosexuality as an inborn abnormality, a "sexual inversion," they hoped to engender pity and legal leniency. But they also, for the first time, focused attention—and disapproval—on a group of individuals rather than on specific behaviors. As historian Michel Foucault put it: "The sodomite had been a temporary aberration; the homosexual was now a species."

The vivid images conjured by the medical doctors, misleading caricatures of mannish women and effeminate men based on extreme cases, seeped into society. In the United States, where the new books on sexuality were widely read, they created an uneasy self-awareness and sensitivity to sexual overtones new and foreign to men and women still immersed in 19th-century notions of romanticism and sentimental friendship.

In this earlier, expansive climate, effusive exchanges between same-sex friends—homosexual or not—had been commonplace. Walt Whitman, now celebrated as America's most famous homoerotic poet, extolled the virtues of "manly love" and "fervent comradeship." But even nonsexual relationships between men found expression in purple prose. In the late 1700s, for example, Alexander Hamilton wrote unself-consciously to his military comrade John Laurens, "I wish, my dear Laurens . . . it might be in my power, by action rather than words, [to] convince you that I love you." And Henry David Thoreau wrote of men's friendship as "Two sturdy oaks . . . which side by side / Withstand the winter's storm . . . Their roots are intertwined / Inseparably." As for Rose Cleveland and Evangeline Whipple, in nineteenth-century eyes theirs was a "romantic friendship," an attachment both high-minded and encouraged in an era when extramarital or premarital liaisons with men were unacceptable.

Were such friendships sexual? We ask the question easily, but the women themselves likely did not—being not yet baptized into a sexually explicit age. Historians are equivocal: "Many were not. Some probably were," they say. Sex, for most of Victorian society, required a male organ, and what women could do together was not deemed of great importance. "If sex entered into it," writes California State University English Prof. Lillian Faderman, "they may have considered it somewhat irregular, but they did not feel compelled to spend too many daytime hours analyzing its implications."

## END OF INNOCENCE

The arrival of sexology and its sequel, Freudianism, gradually put an end to such innocence. The boundaries of friendship narrowed. Affectionate links once seen as harmless—schoolgirl crushes, for example, or overt affection between men—began to arouse suspicion. Thus, in the 1800s, writers happily described "smashes" and "spoons" between college women, infatuations involving elaborate courtship rituals. By 1928, a novel about Vassar asserted that "intimacy between girls was watched with keen distrustful eyes. Among

one's classmates, one looked for . . . the masculine girl searching for a feminine counterpart, and one ridiculed their devotions."

Homosexuality as a sickness, a perverse condition, could not just be ignored. Transferred into the arena of medicine, it demanded a cure, and doctors began an all-out campaign. Trying to locate same-sex desire in the body, they pointed to the structure of the pelvis, the size of the penis, to body hair. They warned of the deep-voiced female or the contralto male. They associated homosexuality with degeneracy, then genius and then misguided parenting. And with speculations about cause came attempts at treatment: castration, hypnosis, electric shock, hysterectomies, and later, in a slightly less brutal era, psychoanalysis.

To a young person, confused about sexual feelings and in search of information, the picture of same-sex love gleaned from books and articles in the early 1900s was uniformly depressing and at times perplexing. One early medical test, for example, stated confidently that male homosexuals could not whistle and favored the color green. Popular culture was not much more optimistic. The publication of Blair Niles' *Strange Brother* in 1931 and Radclyffe Hall's *The Well of Loneliness*, three years earlier, offered sympathetic portraits of homosexuality. But Tom, a gay character in Niles' novel, renounces his lover, explaining, "There's no happiness for such as us, Mark, except in overcoming. Put into your work all that you feel—all that you suffer. . . . Don't let our handicap destroy you.

Such portrayals did not provide promising soil for the growth of a "gay pride" movement. Yet the appropriation of homosexuality by the medical profession—and its increased visibility in popular writing—had unexpected consequences. Love between members of the same sex might be deplored and vilified, but it was publicly discussed, and through the accounts of "patients" and the tribulations of "twisted" characters in pulp novels, gay men and lesbians across the country discovered that there were others like them. They traveled to urban areas, where a burgeoning gay subculture awaited them. And eventually, they began to shift the terms of the dialogue, shedding the language of perversion and self-hate for a new vocabulary of self-respect, staking out a birthing ground for political awareness. It was a movement that would grow and solidify and finally come of age, its strength forged in the cries of young men dying of AIDS.

## BLURRING BOUNDARIES

"Same person, no difference at all. Just a different sex," says Orlando, the protagonist of director Sally Potter's newly released film, upon awaking one morning, looking in the mirror, and discovering that "he" has become a "she." Virginia Woolf, in her tongue-in-cheek 1928 novel upon which the movie is based, concedes that Orlando's transformation may strain credibility: "Many people . . . holding that such a change of sex is against nature, have been at great pains to prove (1) that Orlando had always been a woman, (2) that Orlando is at this moment a man," she writes. "But let other pens treat of sex and sexuality; we quit such odious subjects as soon as we can." Woolf's literary exercise grew out of her affair with writer Vita Sackville-West, but her message is a contemporary one: gender and sexuality are inextricably entangled, and a discussion of either one can quickly lead into perilous and uncertain territory.

Scientists who first studied homosexuality often confused the social niche that men and women occupied with their choice of whom to take to bed. In women, a desire for higher education or an interest in a professional career was seen as a mark of lesbian tendencies; in men, passivity was a sure sign that they were "Urnings"—the term coined in 1864 by German lawyer Karl Heinrich Ulrichs for a female soul trapped in a male body. Today, derisive names for homosexu-

als still reflect this confounding, focusing less on sexual orientation than on departures from accepted gender roles: male homosexuals are "pansies" or "fairies," lesbians are "butches" or "bull dykes."

Slowly, as openly gay men and women become more familiar, appearing on television sitcoms, on late-night talk shows, in newspapers and magazines, the rigidity of such conceptions is giving way. But the resistance to change is not surprising. It is never easy to admit that things were not always the way they are now, or that they might be different in the future. Once the crucial line divided procreative and nonprocreative sex; today, many forms of pleasure-driven sexuality have lost their stigma; premarital sex, masturbation and a variety of erotic practices raise scarcely an eyebrow.

Yet the boundaries that persist are held tightly. They serve, it seems, other purposes, shoring up political arguments and providing reassurance that a kiss or fond embrace will not lead to polymorphous chaos. In part, suggests Brown University historian Lisa Duggan, homophobia may reflect the fear that if that taboo, too, disappears, the distinctions between the genders will simply dissolve. For a culture where love between men and women is the norm, homosexuality traces a line of definition, an "Other" that demarcates what heterosexuality is and is not. As lesbian activist and poet Judy Grahn puts it: "We are essential to them knowing who they are."

# I 3 I

# *Categories, Experience, and Sexuality*

## JOHN BOSWELL

For nearly a decade the historiography of homosexuality has been both enriched and complicated by a controversy over the epistemology of human sexuality, often referred to as the "constructionist/essentialist" debate. It is not actually a debate: one of many ironies about the controversy is that no one deliberately involved in it identifies himself as an "essentialist," although

constructionists (of whom, in contrast, there are many) sometimes so label other writers. Even when applied by its opponents the label seems to fit extremely few contemporary scholars. This

In Ed Stein, ed., *Forms of Desire*, pp. 133–174. Excerpt. New York: Routledge, 1992.

fact is revealing, and provides a basis for understanding the controversy more accurately not as a dialogue between two schools of thought, but as a critique by revisionists of assumptions believed to underlie traditional historiography.

Most fields of historical enquiry go through phases of self-questioning about basic assumptions, and after an early period of rather simplistic "who-was-and-who-wasn't?" history by and about gay people it was to be expected that there would be a period of reconsideration and an effort to formulate a more sophisticated analytical base. Although welcome and fruitful, this evolution in gay historiography has not been uniformly successful. In some areas it has greatly heightened critical sensibilities on issues of sexuality and sexual identity; in others, the range of opinions and approaches it has produced has blurred rather than refined the focus of discussion.

Like most radical critiques facing the presumed superior numbers and longevity deployed by established, older notions, constructionism wages a kind of guerrilla warfare: its partisans tend to devote more energy to exposing the weaknesses of the "essentialist" position than to articulating and refining their own. This tactic is a bit misleading, since there are few if any works intended to express an "essentialist" position, but it affords constructionism a great defensive strength, since it is very difficult to react to an unidentifiable or deftly moving opponent (opposing one of its manifestations may have no effect on others). It is beneficial to scholarship in the long run, because it does reveal fallacies in earlier writing, but it also makes difficult the task of understanding or defining what newer truth emerges: by the time the reporters have located the "constructionist" camp to interview its leaders, they have usually moved on to a new position.

There are probably as many ways to define "constructionism" as there are "constructionists." Very broadly speaking, they have in common the view that "sexuality" is an artifact or "construct" of human society and therefore specific to any given social situation. Some would argue that there are no underlying diachronic constants of human sexuality involved in this social construction, others that whatever underlying phenomena there may be are of much less importance than social overlay, or cannot be identified and should not be assumed. Part of the reason it is so difficult to identify "essentialists" is that no reasonable person would disagree with the proposition implicit in the constructionist critique that the experience, including the sexual experience, of every human being in every time and place is distinct from that of every other human being, and that the social matrix in which she or he lives will determine that experience in a largely irresistible way, including creating (or not creating) opportunities for sexual expression and possibly even awareness of sexual feelings and desires.

Agreeing on this, however, hardly begins to address the problematic underlying questions, such as whether society is itself responding to sexual phenomena that are generic to humans and *not created* by social structures. In this context one can see that the controversy is not simply a variant of the ongoing interdisciplinary nature/nurture debate about biological determinism versus social development, because no one who believes that there are biological aspects to human sexuality would claim that there are not also individual psychological, familial and social factors operating alongside and in conjunction with these. Indeed, in any careful epistemology these would have to be considered "biological" as well, since they are a ubiquitous part of the life of human organisms. Constructionists, moreover, can hardly argue that there are not "natural" (i.e., physiological) components to human sexuality in terms of the functioning of body parts, response to stimulus, etc.

It is at the secondary level—where constructionists also disagree among themselves—that the epistemological differences between "constructionists" and the writings they criticize seem most pronounced, although here, too, there is confusion and overlap, and some constructionists seem as far from other constructionists as all do from the so-called "essentialists." Some constructionists argue that a "homosexual identity" did not exist before a certain date (often the second half of the nineteenth century); others that "homosexuality" was not found before such a date; others that although "homosexuality" was known throughout history, "gay people" did not exist until relatively recently. Some writers argue generally that "sexuality" is not a constant; others posit more specifically that social constructs of sexuality are not constant. A more sweeping and profound version of these is that there is no aspect of sexuality that is not socially constructed.

These are all very different propositions, based on distinct premises, presupposing varying definitions of similar terms, and requiring individual analysis. It would be impossible to do justice to this range of views in a brief essay; they are presented here in summary form to help the reader appreciate their relationship to the idea postulated as the fundamental assumption of "essentialists": that humans are differentiated at an individual level in terms of erotic attraction, so that some are more attracted sexually to their own gender, some to the opposite gender, and some to both, in all cultures.

This is, for example, the assumption usually alleged to make *Christianity, Social Tolerance and Homosexuality* (Boswell, 1980, hereafter *CSTH*) an "essentialist" work: the supposition that there have been in all Western societies "gay people" and "non-gay people."[1] This is not false attribution: it was, in fact, the working hypothesis of the book. Logically this view is not necessarily opposed to all constructionist positions: even if societies create or formulate "sexualities," it might happen that different societies would construct similar ones, as they often construct similar political or class structures (of course, if a constructionist position holds that "gay person" refers only to a particular, modern identity, it is then, tautologically, not applicable to the past).

Most constructionist critiques, however, assume that the essentialist position necessarily entails a further supposition: that society does not *create* these attractions, but only acts on them. Some other force—genes, psychological influences, etc.—creates "sexuality," which is essentially independent of culture. This was certainly not a working hypothesis of *CSTH*; I can state with reasonable certainty that its author was (and is) agnostic about the *origins* of human sexuality.

The etiology of human sexual interest could be a crucial facet of the controversy. If a predilection for sexual activity with one gender could be shown to be innate in all humans or fixed in childhood in all (or even many) known cultures, then it would be rather pointless to argue that all "sexuality" is socially constructed. If it could be demonstrated conclusively, on the other hand, that people learn all sexual behavior socially and would be completely non-sexual or undifferentiated in desire if brought up alone on a desert island, then some strains of "constructionism" would be statements of empirical fact rather than critical theory.

For the present, however, data concerning the provenances of human sexuality are so unsatisfactory as to be almost perfectly moot, and if, as seems likely, they turn out ultimately to be a complex interaction of physiological, psychological and cultural factors, it will still be crucial to assess

and discuss the extent to which social factors create, shape and determine human sexuality. To do so intelligently requires an appreciation of both the strengths and limitations of the "constructionist" controversy and alternative approaches to the history of human sexuality. It may be helpful to divide them into four different areas: 1) philosophical; 2) semantic; 3) political; and 4) empirical.

## Philosophical

Two major philosophical issues underlie much of the constructionist critique of conventional historiography. The first is a general reaction against post-enlightenment positivism and its tendency to treat abstractions as concrete signifiers rather than abbreviations for loose generalizations. The reification, for example, of terms like "capitalism," "feudalism," or "sexuality"—defensible only as short-hand rubrics for congeries of ideas—can obscure through oversimplification more than is gained through organizational efficiency. This problem is exacerbated, the constructionist critique rightly notes, by anachronistic assumptions that any abstract categories of one culture (e.g., "gender," "class") can be projected onto others.

These problems are both general and specific. They derive from the most basic puzzle of human epistemology: to what extent do the abstractions of human thought and speech correspond to an objective reality? But they also arise from more specific questions about the reality or accuracy of particular concepts and abstractions such as "gender" and "sexuality." Both sorts of questions are useful, but they have played a somewhat confusing role in the constructionist controversy, because they are often adduced in a haphazard and ad hoc way as a criticism of the concept of homosexuality (or sexuality, or "gay person," etc.) alone, without any coherent acknowledgement or exploration of the much broader and more complicated issues they pose for historical writing (and human thought). If constructionists arguing against the transhistorical reality of "sexuality" or "homosexuality" would make clear that they also do not believe there is any such thing as a historical "heterosexuality," "family," "kinship," "state," "government," or other such familiar abstractions, their audience would have a more realistic perception of their position. As it is, readers are usually left with the impression that other diachronic abstractions are accurate as commonly applied, while this one alone is singularly inaccurate.

Almost any thoughtful person would agree with the first point—that all categories are inadequate and abstractions can be misleading; it is the second—namely, this one abstraction is much more removed from reality than any others—that is difficult to accept. If it is not a distortion of their position and constructionists actually believe it, they have yet to demonstrate why this one abstraction is so much less accurate than all others. There is a further subtlety: whatever inadequacies abstract categorizations of sexual experience have transhistorically they may also have in the present. An additional layer of misconception is introduced by implicitly suggesting to readers that it is only across time that conceptual inaccuracy arises, as if "homosexuality" were a perfectly clear and concrete concept in the present.

While it is certainly a valuable intellectual strategy to deflate and refine positivist assumptions, it must be undertaken consistently and with perspective. It is unwise, for example, to ignore the fact that abstractions and their application constitute a useful intellectual strategy in themselves, and are in the long run perhaps the most indispensable element of human thought (all words and terms being, in the most basic sense, abstractions). It is pointless and naive to portray them as inherently false or inimical to accuracy rather than as tools that may be employed well or ill.

A second philosophical problem inherent in the controversy is the issue of "free will." Although it is rarely directly addressed, much discussion about "sexual identity," "sexual orientation," "sexual preference," "homosexuality," "heterosexuality," "sexuality," "gay identity" and related concepts in fact implicitly centers on the extent to which humans determine their own character, preferences, interests, desires, etc., as opposed to passively experiencing or inheriting them. This is one of the oldest riddles of the mind, and has baffled the investigations of philosophers for millennia and psychologists for decades. Introducing it as a casual premise or factor in discussions of human sexuality is jejune and almost guarantees misunderstanding and non-productive argument. Where it is in fact relevant, it needs to be articulated clearly and coherently as a major philosophical difficulty, so that all parties can at least face the real puzzle and not attempt to resolve it obliquely by defining the nature of "sexuality" first and hoping that the question of the will will somehow fall into line.

## Semantic

Semantic difficulties are not neatly distinguishable from philosophical problems, but it may be useful to view them from a slightly different perspective. All human disagreements are "semantic" problems in the sense that words are the implements of verbal dispute. A great many different lexical issues make up the constructionist controversy, but some of the most important ones can be subsumed under a single question: is it legitimate to ask questions of the past using the categories of the present, regardless of whether they would have had meaning for the persons being studied, or should the investigator adopt the categories with which denizens of the past would have described their own lives and culture? More simply, should we look at the past through the alembic of our terms or through the alembic of theirs?

Obviously we can not escape our filters entirely, but we could strive to get beyond them. If "sexual orientation" or "gay person" or "homosexual identity" are modern constructs (conceptually or socially, or both) it is grossly misleading, the argument goes, to apply them to premodern people, somewhat like applying the term "feminist" to Joan of Arc or "democrat" to Cicero.

Constructionist answers to this question generally presuppose that we should suppress modern categories as irrelevant and focus instead on the categories the ancients would have used themselves, as more reflective of the reality of their structures and experience. This assumes, politely but oddly, that humans are inevitably the best analysts of their own lives and environments. One would have thought that, in fact, the aim of good historical writing was to get beyond the mere descriptions of contemporaries and to organize information in its most revealing way.

To be more concrete: there are few, possibly no words in any ancient or medieval language corresponding precisely to "gay" or "homosexual." Some nouns and verbs categorize homosexual activities or persons involved in them, but the abstractions "homosexual" or "homosexuality" are uncommon or unknown in most premodern languages. Constructionists reasonably argue that this is one of a number of indications that these categories did not exist in the past (either conceptually or "really"), and that forcing the modern terms onto data from the past is a distortion. Moreover, the extant indications of sexuality from ancient Greece and Rome suggest categories of organization—e.g., along lines of age or status—quite different from modern patterns. This constitutes, for constructionists, evidence that "sexuality" in such societies was fundamentally different from "sexuality" in the modern West, and should be assessed in its own distinctive terms and categories.

Three problems reduce the value of this line of thought: 1) there may be reasons for the structure of a language other than its reflection of "objective reality"; 2) modern terms for sexuality are not necessarily any more comprehensive or accurate about the present than ancient ones are for the past; 3) application of modern categories to the past, even if they do not match precisely, may be a useful strategy for determining the relationship between the two.

In regard to the first, the absence of a concept can hardly be taken to demonstrate the absence of what it applies to. All languages respond to structural and developmental pressures beyond accurate description. There is no word in French for "shallow" and no word in Latin for "religion." These facts have very different significances. The first is simply a semantic accident: it is hardly the case that there is nothing "shallow" in France or that the French do not recognize "shallowness." They simply happen not to have developed a single word for this concept, and instead use the negation "not deep."

The lack of a word for "religion" in Rome (and well into the Middle Ages) may be to some extent a semantic accident as well, but it is also related to social reality: there was no "religion" at Rome comparable to "religion" as known in the modern West—i.e., a comprehensive, exclusive system of theology and ethics. Even the word "cult," which in the nineteenth century could be used of Roman religion, now connotes a kind of total commitment which was not an essential component of Roman religion (though not necessarily lacking in it).

Does this mean that there was no "religion" in Rome, and that historians are distorting reality by talking and writing about "Roman religion"? Should some new word, free of the contaminants of modern concepts, be coined to characterize the veneration of Roman deities and the cult of Cybele? No. There was obviously "religion" in Rome, including Christianity itself—which gave us our sense of "religion." . . .

Is it revealing that Romans and Greeks had many words for age-related sexual categories and no word to describe persons, regardless of gender, involved in what we call "homosexual activity"? Probably not. The relationship of concrete nouns to abstract concepts is not regular or predictable. For example, there is no abstraction in English for both "aunts" and "uncles" in the way that "sibling" applies to brothers and sisters. Does that mean that we conceive a greater gender difference between aunts and uncles than between brothers and sisters? It is conceivable, but it seems unlikely when one considers the capricious and independent forms of gender pairing in English. There is, for example, no word to distinguish gender for cousins, although all other relatives are so differentiated—brother/sister, father/mother, daughter/son, aunt/uncle, niece/nephew. Should we infer that English speakers do not distinguish between male and female cousins? Of course not; the necessary and relevant information is simply conveyed otherwise—in a name or phrase. "My cousin Jane" conveys the same amount of information as "My sister Jane"; the reasons for the difference are linguistically interesting, but not socially significant. Several hundred miles north of New Haven, my contemporaries can make the distinction by saying "cousin" or "cousine": is theirs a fundamentally different attitude to gender? No; and since one can not generalize about North America in 1988, we should pause before making inferences from language about "the ancient world."

There is an enormous vocabulary in all ancient languages referring to aspects of homosexuality, and no reason to suppose that the lack of a perfect match with English in terms of its organization proves a fundamental discontinuity either of experience or conceptualizations. It may reveal no more than a linguistic boundary.

Nor should the prevalence of age-related terminology in such languages, in and of itself, be considered evidence of a wholly different sexual structure. Why are "boyfriend" and "girlfriend" common English words, while "manfriend" and "womanfriend" are not in the language at all? Because friendship is limited to the young? Or because older people usually have younger "friends"? Or because love makes us feel "young" again? In fact, these terms, like many words in all languages, are only very obliquely related to their obvious meaning, and apply less often to "friendship" than to romantic love. Sexual and romantic terminology tends to be deformed by reticence, decorum and taboo, and must be addressed with enormous caution by scholars. "Boyfriend" and "girlfriend" are certainly not indications of a general propensity for older persons to date "boys" or "girls" as those terms are understood in English cultures. They are simply conventions, perfectly unambiguous to native speakers even to degrees of great subtlety: the point of "boyfriend" is in fact to distinguish the person so designated from a "friend," so the "friend" is wholly misleading, and the term is doubly or trebly removed from reality; by contrast, "girlfriend" could be used of a "friend" by a female or a romantic interest by a male. Scholars of the future would be completely wrong to infer from these terms a preoccupation with younger sexual partners on the part of most English speakers, or to suspect lesbianism in a case where a teenage girl has a "girlfriend," but would be correct to infer homosexuality if a teenage boy had a "boyfriend." These are, moreover, not odd or little used terms; they are the most basic and familiar words for such relationships in our language.

How will we determine, then, whether premodern sexuality was fundamentally different from our experience? Partly by defining our terms, beginning with "fundamentally different." Being a Catholic in Rome in the fourth century, when choosing to join the minority religion incurred the threat of death, was obviously "fundamentally different" from being a Catholic in the fifteenth century, when failing to observe the official Catholic religion meant death, and from being a Catholic in present-day Italy, where it is an ethnic heritage of little moment to many Italians. Is it wrong or misleading to use "Catholic" to describe all of these categories? On the contrary, it is necessary, since they are all fundamentally related as well as fundamentally different. The task of the historian is to convey both aspects to readers.

To apply this to constructionism would require separate and lengthy analysis of the use of each of the possible terms relating to sexual identity, orientation, etc. "Gay" is probably the most problematic and revealing. If by a "gay person" one means someone having a specific social identity beyond predominant erotic interest in one's own gender, it will be difficult to apply the term to the past, but no more difficult than it is to apply it to the present outside one or two narrow circles. Leaving aside the problem of "latent" or "closeted" homosexual desires, which might be predominant but unacknowledged or unrecognized, there are still a great many types of conscious "gay identities": single gay men vacationing in Key West or living on Castro Street may have very little in common with a lesbian couple on a farm in New Hampshire, with self-consciously lesbian nuns in Cameroun, with members of a gay fathers group in Des Moines, with a Mexican who prides himself on being "macho" because he takes only the active role and only with younger boys, with the *xanitha* of the Middle East who play only a passive role with older or richer men. Because all these people have erotic interactions primarily with their own gender, which is statistically less frequent in most human cultures, they have something interesting and important in common. It may not be a fundamental basis of identity in all cases (even on Castro Street), but it must play some role, as any noticeable and important divergence from the norm will. On the other hand, there is as much difference in "sexual identity" among them as there is between them and the characters in the Satyricon whose eroticism is focussed on their own gender. One might well argue that other issues are more important for some of these persons in defining their "sexuality" than the sex of their partner—gender roles, monogamy, politics, celibacy, preferred activity—but that does not efface what they have in common; it simply privileges another category for purposes of discussion.

Some constructionists would, in fact, argue that only the first group (unmarried homosexual men or women in a subculture of such persons) meets their definition of "gay," and that some other term should be used for other categories of same-sex eroticism. It is obviously legitimate and potentially helpful for some scholars to employ terms like "homosexual" or "gay" with definitions different from or more specialized than others, and to criticize writing in which such categories are used imprecisely or inconsistently, although not writings in which they are used differently, as if such terms had a "natural" meaning. Equally obviously, such specialized use of language must be articulated and defended: a universal or self-evident meaning of words cannot be assumed, and if a default meaning of "gay" can be claimed, it should probably be that of common parlance, where it is juxtaposed by the population at large with "straight" to refer to (also using common parlance) "sexual preference." ("Homosexuality," even more simply, has a nearly ubiquitous meaning in English of sexuality between persons of the same gender.) Gay people themselves will often remark of someone that he does not yet "realize" he is gay—a clear indication that the category is not necessarily a self-conscious one in their view.

Specialists and scholars, of course, need not be confined to ordinary speech in technical writing, but can hardly afford to ignore it in communicating with the public.

## Political

This raises the third and most explosive underlying issue of constructionism. The controversy evokes, subtly, a wide range of political and emotional connotations without consciously addressing them. These create an emotional undertone to the arguments, and invest them with a force out of proportion to the ostensible intellectual differences. Although there may be no practicing essentialists, "essentialism" as a mode of thought is associated with generally conservative assumptions about positivist historiography, less than up-to-date views of sexuality, biological determinism, and a general failure to think critically about underlying assumptions. By contrast, constructionism seems a more empowering concept, affirming in some ways the interactive strength and control of the individual, and locating the essence of sexuality in mutable social structures rather than inexorable evolutionary processes. Constructionism also fits well with anthropology and contemporary literary theory and their intellectual forebears, structural linguistics and structuralism, which all emphasize the ultimate relativity and subjectivity of language and observation.

If there are essentialists who say they know that homosexuality and heterosexuality are constants in history, they are certainly proceeding on faith rather than empirical evidence, but the same must be said of constructionists who claim to know the opposite. Since it is perfectly unclear what factors—social, psychological, genetic, etc.—produce varieties of sexual interest, no one can claim to "know" that there were or were not such interests in the past. He could say that he has not or has seen evidence for their existence, but to start from a position of certainty about sexuality in the past is a stance of faith, not really appropriate for historical enquiry. This is different from raising questions about whether there are social "constructions" of sexuality which affect personal identity. Doubtless there are and they do, but the relationship of these to the existence of "gay people" in the past is extremely subtle and has barely been broached to date in the literature on this subject, which tends to imply that a positive answer to the first question necessarily implies a negative to the second.

An additional political fillip is contributed by the claim of some constructionists that essentialists are solipsistically seeking themselves in the past while the constructionists are more open-mindedly looking for differences. This unprovable (and probably fanciful) charge raises an interesting point: since every human being (is the category "human being" a social construct? no doubt) is both like others and different from them, there seems little reason a priori to assume that one strategy is better than another, unless there is a political reason to emphasize differences over similarities. A conscientious quest for either one will necessarily disclose the other as well.

There is also a more cogent political dimension to the controversy, ultimately related to the issue of "fundamental difference" addressed above. At one level it is simply a matter of convention to refer to the residents of the Italian peninsula in the fifth century—1,400 years before the creation of the modern state of Italy—as "fifth-century Italians." But it could become a highly political issue if, for example, Mussolini wished to argue that something which happened in fifth-century Italy justified an act of aggression in the twentieth century by the "heirs" or "descendants" of those "Italians." . . . We all use such terms, or do not use them, for political reasons, and if constructionists or essentialists wish to make political arguments for certain ways of conceptualizing or writing about the mysteries of sexuality they have as much right as anyone else to introduce political considerations into semantic, philosophical, or historical discussions. It is more helpful, obviously, if such issues are carefully and honestly identified as such.

## Empirical

In the last analysis the theoretical revisions of constructionism will be of little value if there is no empirical basis for them. Does the historical record in fact suggest that premodern patterns of sexuality were fundamentally different from modern ones? Yes and no. Public discourse about sexuality in ancient and medieval Europe was markedly different from its modern descendants and rarely directed attention to the issues subsumed under or implied by the rubrics "orientation," "preference," or "identity."[2]

For example, in the Mediterranean city-states of the ancient world (ca. 400 B.C.–400 A.D.) both public and private "norms" for human conduct were largely social and behavioral (as opposed, e.g., to intentional, psychological, or spiritual), and based on codes of public conduct and behavior anyone could follow, regardless of (what modern writers would call) "sexual orientation." Ideals of human action focused on the fulfillment of social roles and expectations: being a good citizen by serving in the army or civil service or donating resources or labor to the state, or being a responsible family member by treating one's spouse properly and caring well for children. "Sexual identity" had little to do with any of these—including the roles of spouse and parent, since marriage and parenthood were not thought to depend on erotic attachment.

Opportunities for sexual expression also tended to obviate questions of orientation. Marriage was a duty for all Roman citizens, in the eyes of the family and the state, but was not generally supposed to fulfill erotic needs. Every male was expected to marry, as were most females, regardless of whether conjugal relations afforded an opportunity for erotic satisfaction or not. In the case of males, extramarital sexuality was normal and accepted; in the case of married females, it was not, but for the latter, erotic fulfillment was not a public issue—fair treatment, affection and respect were the expected rewards of being a good wife and mother.

Ethical ideals (as opposed to ordinary behavior)[3] were slightly more complicated, and can be distinguished according to three general approaches, depending on whether they emphasized (1) the responsibilities, (2) dangers or (3) religious significance of human sexuality. (1) The moral views on human sexuality of the "average Greco-Roman" were rarely articulated and are difficult to reconstruct with precision. They seem to have presupposed that sexuality is good or neutral so long as it is responsible—i.e., does not interfere with duties to the state or family, and does not involve the abuse of freeborn children or married women (a reminder that class and citizenship were real for Greco-Romans in a way we can no longer appreciate). This loose code is implicit in much of Greek and Roman literature, art, mythology and law, and it is against it that (2) a second, more ascetic approach began in the centuries before the beginning of the Christian Era to urge that sexuality was an inherently dangerous force and should be avoided as much as possible. Some adherents of this view would call their followers to celibacy, some would limit sexual expression to marriage, others to procreative

acts within marriage. Although the latter two prescriptions would apply to homosexual and heterosexual acts differentially (since the former would be categorically precluded, while the latter would only be circumscribed), they were not aimed at homosexuality or predicated on any invidious distinction between homosexual or heterosexual: their objective was primarily to curtail promiscuous or pleasure-centered heterosexual activity. They excluded homosexual acts incidentally or along with activities—such as masturbation—which were not special to any group. (3) A few specific religions attached theological or ceremonial significance to particular aspects of sexuality: traditional Romans idealized the sacrifice of sexual pleasure made by Vestal Virgins, while others embraced mystery cults which incorporated sexual acts in religious observance. Jews had very detailed rules about licit sexuality. Such practices and proscriptions had little impact on popular views: both Jews and Vestal Virgins were considered distinctive precisely because the standards they followed were exceptional. Apart from Judaism, no religion of the ancient world categorically prohibited homosexual relations, although some preached celibacy.

There was thus relatively little reason for Romans to confront or pose questions of sexual orientation. Opportunities for erotic expression were organized around issues of class and age or marital status rather than gender; personal worth was measured in terms of public contributions and family responsibility, neither essentially related to personal erotic interest; private sexual behavior was not an arena of judgement or concern; and even ethical systems did not make the gender of sexual object choice a criterion of moral action.

This does not mean that everyone was at liberty to perform any sort of sexual act with anyone of either gender. Gender, age, class, social standing, and in some cases citizenship set limitations on the range of acceptable forms of sexual expression for each individual. With a few exceptions, the higher one's social status the more restrictions would apply to sexual acts, and the fewer to sexual partners. A wealthy and powerful adult male citizen, for example, at the top of the status hierarchy, could penetrate any other person without loss of social status (although a dispute might arise if the other party were the wife or child of another citizen). "What does it matter," Antony wrote to Augustus, "where or in whom you stick it?" But for the same male to be penetrated—by anyone—would incur disrespect if it were known, and might even subject him to loss of civil privilege. By contrast, although a slave (or even a freedman) would lose no status for being penetrated by someone more powerful, he might suffer greatly (a slave could forfeit his life) if he penetrated a citizen.

The restrictions on the sexual behavior of adult male citizens were not the result of prejudice against homosexuality: the same man could penetrate as many other men as he wished without incurring any stigma. The code of propriety was related to gender—penetration and power were associated with the prerogatives of the ruling male elite; surrendering to penetration was a symbolic abrogation of power and authority—but in a way which posed a polarity of domination-subjection rather than of homosexual-heterosexual. It was generally acceptable for a member of a less powerful group to submit to penetration by a member of a more powerful one: this was not thought to characterize any defect of personality or to indicate any special psychological constitution or status.

The urgent personal question for males in Augustan Rome was not the gender with which one did it but what one did. Martial titillated his audience by speculating on the possibility of "passive" sexual behavior on the part of well-known Roman citizens, and a number of prominent Athenians and Romans were the butt of humor because they had performed an activity inappropriate to their status; conversely, Juvenal composed a long satire on the several inversions of the prevailing ethic involved in someone of low status (a male prostitute) taking the active role with male citizen clients. The issue in all such cases was behavior, not gender preference: no citizen was ridiculed for having recourse to passive partners of either sex, nor were prostitutes or slaves—male or female—pilloried for receptivity.

Beginning around 400 A.D., Christianity began to introduce a new sexual code, focussed on religious concepts of "holiness" and "purity." The origins and sources of its norms—the New Testament, Alexandrian Judaism, popular taboos, neo-Platonic philosophy, Roman legal principles—are imperfectly understood and too complex to penetrate here. For the most part its regulations, like their Greco-Roman predecessors, were conceptually unrelated to sexual "identity" or "orientation." But because Christianity, unlike ancient ethical systems, used obedience to sexual ethics as a primary symbol and test of human conduct, its code was both more detailed and more prominent, and in practice it laid the groundwork for distinctions based on "orientation."

Two general approaches to Christian sexuality can be discerned in the early church, distinct in their relation to "orientation." The earliest, evident in the New Testament, is similar to the "sex is dangerous" approach of pagan ethics: eroticism is a troublesome aspect of a fallen world; Christians should attempt to control it through responsible use. This approach would not, in itself, create distinctions based on gender object choice, because it focuses on the permanence and fidelity of erotic relationships, qualities that could be and were present in both heterosexual and homosexual relationships in the ancient world. Longlasting homosexual unions and even official marriages were known in Greece and Rome, and Christian ceremonies of union for males closely resembling, if not actually constituting, marriage were also common in parts of the Christian world throughout the Early Middle Ages; they invoked well known pairs of saints as models for permanent, erotic same-sex relationships (cf. Boswell, 1994). Even in areas where such relationships were not recognized, there was through the end of the twelfth century a strong tradition in Christian thought which regarded homosexuality and heterosexuality as two sides of the same coin— either could be put to good or bad use, depending on the extent to which it was directed toward godly or ungodly ends. Any faithful and selfless passion subordinated to God's love, in this tradition, might be holy and sanctifying, just as any selfish lust was sinful.

An opposing school of thought held that to be sinless a sexual act must be procreative. Even non-procreative sexual activity between husband and wife was sinful, since procreative purpose was the sole justification for any sexual act. This idea was almost certainly borrowed from strands of late antique pagan ethics, and was at first limited to ascetic Christian writers deeply imbued with Hellenistic philosophy, especially in Alexandria. (Other Christians opposed sexuality *especially* when it was procreative, because birth trapped good souls in evil matter.) But the procreative-purpose stance gradually spread throughout the Christian world and became the favored position of ascetics in the West, since it both limited sexuality to the smallest possible arena and appealed to an easily articulated and understood principle. Ultimately it became the standard of Catholic orthodoxy.

By the end of the Middle Ages, although in parts of the Catholic world the "separate but equal" tradition survived, the majority of Catholic churchmen and states had accepted the principle of procreative justification, and as a result non-procreative sexual behavior was considered a serious sin everywhere in Western Europe. Most civil law codes included penalties for "unnatural acts," which were, theologically, the discharge of semen in any non-procreative context: non-procreative heterosexual activity (i.e., oral or anal), masturbation, homosexual acts, bestiality. At least from the time of Augustine influential theologians had argued that non-procreative acts within marriage were even more sinful than those outside, but public legal systems found them difficult to detect and punish, and civil codes and popular attitudes often reduced the distinction to extra-marital versus marital sexuality, or heterosexual versus homosexual acts.

This created a kind of dichotomy loosely related to sexual object choice: although many forms of heterosexual activity (even within marriage) and masturbation suffered the same moral sanctions as homosexual acts, only the latter two were *categorically* prohibited, while forms of the first could be entirely moral. It is essential to note, nonetheless, that whereas this late medieval system placed homosexual activity generically in an inferior category, it did not create a concept of sexual dimorphism in which a homosexual "orientation" or erotic preference was stigmatized as characterizing a special category of person. Those who engaged in forbidden sexual activity — homosexual or heterosexual — were sinners, but everyone in Catholic Europe was a sinner. All humans in all times (except Adam and Eve before the fall and the Virgin Mary after) were sinners. The rationale which made homosexual acts morally reprehensible also condemned contraception, masturbation, sexual expression between husband and wife undertaken for reasons of affection or pleasure, divorce, lending at interest, and a host of other common, everyday activities, familiar to (if not practiced by) most Europeans. "Sinner" was a universal, not a special, category, and if the particular vice which placed someone in this category was unusual, the category itself was thoroughly familiar to his neighbors.

Moreover, being "sinful" was a temporary state, no matter how often or for how long one found oneself in it. Anyone could cease being "sinful" at any moment, through repentance and contrition, ideally but not necessarily solemnized in the sacrament of penance. In this regard the public discourse of Catholic Europe regarding sexual ethics was much like the public ethos of ancient city-states, despite the change from secular to religious justification. Both were predicated on norms of external, modifiable behavior, rather than on internal disposition or inclination; and the ethical codes of both either treated homosexuality and heterosexuality as morally indistinguishable or focused on elements of sexual behavior which usually affected all varieties of sexual expression.

The splintering of the Christian tradition during the Reformation rendered it increasingly difficult in Early Modern Europe to sustain public codes of conduct based on a particular set of transcendental values, and religious concepts of holy versus sinful behavior gradually ceased to be the defining terms of public discourse about sexual conduct, even in officially Catholic countries. By the early twentieth century scientific — especially medical — values had replaced the consensus once based on theological principles, and as public attention focused less and less on the salvation of the soul and more and more on the body and its well-being the paramount standard in both public and private codes came to be the norm of health, both physical and psychological. The desirability of persons, actions and things is generally assessed in modern industrial nations against the "norm" of "health": what is physically or mentally "normal" is what would be found in a "healthy" person. That this is tautological is not particularly unusual or striking; what is more interesting is that "normality" and "health" are characteristics rather than modes of behavior, and one generally has less control over them than over actions or conduct. Paradoxically, many individuals in modern liberal states have less control over their status than they would have had in ancient or medieval societies.

The medieval notion of the unholiness of homosexual acts was transformed by this change into the abnormality of the homosexual "condition." The "condition" has been variously conceptualized as a genetic "trait," a psychological "state," an "inclination," or a "preference"; though these terms vary in their implications of permanence and mutability, all suggest an essential, internal characteristic of a person rather than an external, voluntary activity.

The importance of the difference between the modern view and preceding systems of conceptualizing sexuality can scarcely be exaggerated.

Contemporary concepts have drastically altered social views of sexual behavior and its significance by focusing on sexual object choice and correlating it with an inherent, defining personal characteristic. The majority supposes itself to have the trait, condition, or preference of heterosexuality, which is "healthy" and "normal," and believes that a minority of persons have the "opposite" trait, condition or preference, which is "unhealthy" and "not normal." The difference is rendered more profound and alienating by the fact that the "normal" or "healthy" state is generally considered, like all forms of sexuality in the past, to be primarily behavioral. Because "heterosexual" is conceived to be the norm, it is unmarked and unnoticed. "Heterosexual person" is unnecessary: "person" implies heterosexual without indication to the contrary. And yet the normal person is not "heterosexual" in any defining sense; he engages in heterosexual activity from time to time, but hardly any information about his or her character, behavior, lifestyle or interest is inferable from this fact. "Homosexual," on the other hand, is understood as a primary and permanent category, a constant and defining characteristic which implies a great deal beyond occasional sexual behavior about the person to whom the term is applied. Not only, it is imagined, does his or her sexuality define all other aspects of personality and lifestyle—which are implicitly subordinate to sex in the case of homosexuals but not heterosexuals—but the connotations of the term and its place in the modern construction of sexuality suggest that homosexuals are much more sexual than heterosexuals. The majority chooses sexual "orientation" or object-choice-based-identity as the key polarity in sexual discourse, marks certain people on the basis of this, and then imagines that its categorization corresponds to the actual importance in their lives of the characteristic so marked.

The conceptual distance between "homosexual" and "heterosexual" is vastly greater in modern understandings of sexuality than its nearest correlates in ancient or medieval systems. "Homosexual/heterosexual" is the major dialectical foundation of all modern discourse about sexuality—scientific, social and ethical—and it seems urgent, intuitive and profoundly important to most Americans. This greatly complicates analysis of either the discourse about or the reality of sexuality in premodern Europe, since these primary modern rubrics were of little import or interest to ancient and medieval writers, and the categories the latter employed (e.g., active/passive; sinful/holy) often filter or obscure information necessary to answer questions of interest to modern researchers about sexual "orientation."

While, as the constructionists rightly note, premodern societies did not employ categories fully comparable to the modern "homosexual/heterosexual" dichotomy, this does not demonstrate that the polarity is not *applicable* to those societies as a way of understanding the lives and experiences of their members. A common thread of constructionist argument at the empirical level is that no one in antiquity or the Middle Ages experienced homosexuality (or heterosexuality, in some versions) as an exclusive, permanent or defining mode of sexuality. This argument can be shown to be factually incorrect (or at least a misleading oversimplification) fairly easily once philosophical, semantic and political difficulties have been identified as separate issues.

▼ ▼ ▼

In addition to comments about preference or orientation, discussions of particular sexual practices sometimes disclose evidence relatable to sexual preference. As noted, the issue of males being penetrated was problematic in some social contexts, and discussions of men who prefer to be penetrated provide indirect evidence that their preferred sexual activity necessarily involved other males. Although slaves and boys may have accepted rather than sought a passive role, there is no reason to assume that some of them did not enjoy it, and adult males who preferred to be penetrated were common enough not only to have special names (not derogatory for anyone other than an adult male citizen), but also to provoke scientific speculation on the origin of their unusual "orientation." Satirists depict passive adult citizens as hiring bisexual males to satisfy their needs and impregnate their wives.

Both Greek and Latin, moreover, use verbs which primarily or exclusively denote a male's penetrating another male, as opposed to a female, suggesting that in addition to the most prominent distinctions between active and passive there were common and familiar distinctions about preferred object choice.

Suppose, for the sake of discussion, that the rough proportions of Kinsey 0s, 1s, 5s, 6s, etc. were the same in most populations. How would one then explain the casual ubiquity of homosexual activity at Athens or Rome? Do the data from these cultures in and of themselves suggest a sexual topography profoundly different from that of twentieth-century democracies? Actually, no. Kinsey and other researchers have found an incidence of homosexual behavior among males even in the most highly repressive societies which shocked and outraged contemporaries who had never suspected such a thing was possible. If 30%–50% of American males, in the face of overwhelming social condemnation, have homosexual experiences, it is hardly surprising that a large percentage of males should do so in cultures where it is a morally neutral activity, or that this should then cause the muniments of that civilization to appear rather different from the records available in highly repressive societies. If all of the American males who indulged in homosexual behavior felt free to acknowledge it, American erotic literature might well resemble that of Athens or Rome. This same percentage of men might not, however, consider themselves predominantly interested in their own gender, any more than the majority of Athenians or Romans did.

Cognizance of the social significance of sexual behavior in given times and places is fundamental to understanding both the reality and the perception of sexuality. These have varied so widely in the Western tradition that the most basic taxonomic distinctions of one age may seem almost entirely irrelevant to those of another. Primary ancient and medieval sexual constructs were unrelated to the modern differentiation between homosexual and heterosexual "orientation," "identity," or "preference." This does not mean that there was no awareness of specifically homosexual or heterosexual "orientation" in earlier societies. Much evidence indicates that these were common and familiar concepts, which received little attention in the records of these cultures not because few people recognized them, but because they had little social or ethical impact.

Challenges to the received wisdom are a major fuel for the advance of scholarship, and all scholars on any side of a controversy benefit from the energy it generates. Just as revolutionary ideals, however, once in power, often shift from being an innovative solution to being part of the problem, radical critiques of established positions rapidly become established themselves, and then require the same sort of critical scrutiny they once

offered to older approaches. Constructionism may have much to offer the history and analysis of human sexuality, but it will be more effective if it diverts some of the critical energy presently aimed at the scarce "essentialists" to refining and questioning more of its own assumptions and conclusions.

## NOTES

1. Definitions are at the heart of the controversy, and most constructionists would disagree with my use of "gay." I defined "gay persons" in *CSTH* (44) as those "who are conscious of erotic inclination toward their own gender as a distinguishing characteristic"; I would now simplify this and designate as a gay person anyone whose erotic interest is predominantly directed toward his or her own gender (i.e., regardless of consciousness of this as a distinguishing characteristic). This seems to me the normal meaning of the term among American speakers of English.

2. The terminology of sexual preference, identity and orientation is not uniform, and there are no standard definitions or distinctions to cite. "Preference" and "orientation" clearly could mean different things and either could be the basis of an "identity," but all three are often used interchangeably, even in scientific literature. Precise use of such words depends on premises about the will which have yet to be established and agreed upon.

3. I.e., standards proposed as to how people *should* behave, as opposed to an empirical description of how they did. In some societies—e.g., among Orthodox Jews—rules for proper conduct (such as laws of kashrut) may shape daily life, but among Greeks and Romans the ideals of patrician philosophers probably had little impact on the lives even of other members of their own class until Christian emperors began legislating morality in the fourth century.

## REFERENCES

Boswell, John. 1980. *Christianity, Social Tolerance and Homosexuality*. Chicago: University of Chicago Press.

Boswell, John. 1994. *Same-Sex Unions in Pre-Modern Europe*. New York: Villard.

# | 4 |

# Capitalism and Gay Identity

## John D'Emilio

*This essay is a revised version of a talk I gave before several gay audiences during 1979 and 1980. I was searching for a large historical framework in which to set the history of the pre-Stonewall movement. Why, I wanted to know, did a movement begin only in 1950, when many of the elements of gay and lesbian oppression stretched much farther back in time? Michel Foucault in The History of Sexuality and Jeffrey Weeks in Coming Out had each argued that "the homosexual" was a creation of the nineteenth century, but without convincingly specifying why or how this came to be. I wanted to be able to ground social construction theory, which posited that gay identity was historically specific rather than universal, in concrete social processes. Using Marxist analyses of capitalism, I argued that two aspects of capitalism—wage labor and commodity production—created the social conditions that made possible the emergence of a distinctive gay and lesbian identity. I was not trying to claim that capitalism causes homosexuality nor that it determines the form that homosexual desire takes.*

*The essay had political motivation as well. Early gay liberationists had argued that sexuality was malleable and fluid ("polymorphously perverse") and that homosexuality and heterosexuality were both oppressive social categories designed to contain the erotic potential of human beings. By the late 1970s this belief was fading. In its place, gay activists laid claim to the concept of "sexual orientation," a fixed condition established in life, if not at birth. This perspective was immediately useful in a political environment that sought "rights" for "minorities," but it also fudged some troubling issues, which the conclusion to this essay addresses.*

▼ ▼ ▼

For gay men and lesbians, the 1970s were years of significant achievement. Gay liberation and women's liberation changed the sexual landscape of the nation. Hundreds of thousands of gay women and men came out and openly affirmed same-sex eroticism. We won repeal of sodomy laws in half the states, a partial lifting of the exclusion of lesbians and gay men from federal employment, civil rights protection in a few dozen cities, the inclusion of gay rights in the platform of the Democratic Party, and the elimination of homosexuality from the psychiatric profession's list of mental illnesses. The gay male subculture expanded and became increasingly visible in large cities, and lesbian feminists pioneered in building alternative institutions and an alternative culture that attempted to embody a liberating vision of the future.

In the 1980s, however, with the resurgence of an active right wing, gay men and lesbians face the future warily. Our victories appear tenuous and fragile; the relative freedom of the past few years seems too recent to be permanent. In some parts of the lesbian and gay male community, a feeling of doom is growing: analogies with McCarthy's America, when "sexual perverts" were a special target of the right, and with Nazi Germany, where gays were shipped to concentration camps, surface with increasing frequency. Everywhere there is a sense that new strategies are in order if we want to preserve our gains and move ahead.

I believe that a new, more accurate theory of gay history must be part of this political enter-

In Ann Snitow, ed., *Powers of Desire: The Politics of Sexuality*, pp. 100–113. New York: Monthly Review Press, 1983.

prise. When the gay liberation movement began at the end of the 1960s, gay men and lesbians had no history that we could use to fashion our goals and strategy. In the ensuing years, in building a movement without a knowledge of our history, we instead invented a mythology. This mythical history drew on personal experience, which we read backward in time. For instance, most lesbians and gay men in the 1960s first discovered their homosexual desires in isolation, unaware of others, and without resources for naming and understanding what they felt. From this experience, we constructed a myth of silence, invisibility, and isolation as the essential characteristics of gay life in the past as well as the present. Moreover, because we faced so many oppressive laws, public policies, and cultural beliefs, we projected this into an image of the abysmal past: until gay liberation, lesbians and gay men were always the victims of systematic, undifferentiated, terrible oppression.

These myths have limited our political perspective. They have contributed, for instance, to an overreliance on a strategy of coming out—if every gay man and lesbian in America came out, gay oppression would end—and have allowed us to ignore the institutionalized ways in which homophobia and heterosexism are reproduced. They have encouraged, at times, an incapacitating despair, especially at moments like the present: how can we unravel a gay oppression so pervasive and unchanging?

There is another historical myth that enjoys nearly universal acceptance in the gay movement, the myth of the "eternal homosexual." The argument runs something like this: Gay men and lesbians always were and always will be. We are everywhere; not just now, but throughout history, in all societies and all periods. This myth served a positive political function in the first years of gay liberation. In the early 1970s, when we battled an ideology that either denied our existence or defined us as psychopathic individuals or freaks of nature, it was empowering to assert that "we are everywhere." But in recent years it has confined us as surely as the most homophobic medical theories, and locked our movement in place.

Here I wish to challenge this myth. I want to argue that gay men and lesbians have not always existed. Instead, they are a product of history and have come into existence in a specific historical era. Their emergence is associated with the relations of capitalism; it has been the historical development of capitalism—more specifically, its free-labor system—that has allowed large num-

bers of men and women in the late twentieth century to call themselves gay, to see themselves as part of a community of similar men and women, and to organize politically on the basis of that identity.[1] Finally, I want to suggest some political lessons we can draw from this view of history.

▼  ▼  ▼

What, then, are the relationships between the free-labor system of capitalism and homosexuality? First, let me review some features of capitalism. Under capitalism workers are "free" laborers in two ways. We have the freedom to look for a job. We own our ability to work and have the freedom to sell our labor power for wages to anyone willing to buy it. We are also freed from the ownership of anything except our labor power. Most of us do not own the land or the tools that produce what we need, but rather have to work for a living in order to survive. So, if we are free to sell our labor power in the positive sense, we are also freed, in the negative sense, from any other alternative. This dialectic—the constant interplay between exploitation and some measure of autonomy—informs all of the history of those who have lived under capitalism.

As capital—money used to make more money—expands so does this system of free labor. Capital expands in several ways. Usually it expands in the same place, transforming small firms into larger ones, but it also expands by taking over new areas of production: the weaving of cloth, for instance, or the baking of bread. Finally, capital expands geographically. In the United States, capitalism initially took root in the Northeast, at a time when slavery was the dominant system in the South and when noncapitalist Native American societies occupied the western half of the continent. During the nineteenth century, capital spread from the Atlantic to the Pacific, and in the twentieth, U.S. capital has penetrated almost every part of the world.

The expansion of capital and the spread of wage labor have affected a profound transformation in the structure and functions of the nuclear family, the ideology of family life, and the meaning of heterosexual relations. It is these changes in the family that are most directly linked to the appearance of a collective gay life.

The white colonists in seventeenth-century New England established villages structured around a household economy, composed of family units that were basically self-sufficient, independent, and patriarchal. Men, women, and children farmed land owned by the male head of the household. Although there was a division of labor between men and women, the family was truly an interdependent unit of production: the survival of each member depended on the cooperation of all. The home was a workplace where women processed raw farm products into food for daily consumption, where they made clothing, soap, and candies, and where husbands, wives, and children worked together to produce the goods they consumed.

By the nineteenth century, this system of household production was in decline. In the Northeast, as merchant capitalists invested the money accumulated through trade in the production of goods, wage labor became more common. Men and women were drawn out of the largely self-sufficient household economy of the colonial era into a capitalist system of free labor. For women in the nineteenth century, working for wages rarely lasted beyond marriage; for men, it became a permanent condition.

The family was thus no longer an independent unit of production. But although no longer independent, the family was still interdependent. Because capitalism had not expanded very far, because it had not yet taken over—or socialized—the production of consumer goods, women still performed necessary productive labor in the home. Many families no longer produced grain, but wives still baked into bread the flour they bought with their husbands' wages; or, when they purchased yarn or cloth, they still made clothing for their families. By the mid-nineteenth century, capitalism had destroyed the economic self-sufficiency of many families, but not the mutual dependence of the members.

This transition away from the household family-based economy to a fully developed capitalist free-labor economy occurred very slowly, over almost two centuries. As late as 1920, fifty percent of the U.S. population lived in communities of fewer than 2,500 people. The vast majority of blacks in the early twentieth century lived outside the free-labor economy, in a system of sharecropping and tenancy that rested on the family. Not only did independent farming as a way of life still exist for millions of Americans, but even in towns and small cities women continued to grow and process food, make clothing, and engage in other kinds of domestic production.

But for those people who felt the brunt of these changes, the family took on new significance as an affective unit, an institution that provided not goods but emotional satisfaction and happiness. By the 1920s among the white middle class, the ideology surrounding the family described it as the means through which men and women formed satisfying, mutually enhancing relationships and created an environment that nurtured children. The family became the setting for a "personal life," sharply distinguished and disconnected from the public world of work and production.[2]

The meaning of heterosexual relations also changed. In colonial New England the birth rate averaged over seven children per woman of childbearing age. Men and women needed the labor of children. Producing offspring was as necessary for survival as producing grain. Sex was harnessed to procreation. The Puritans did not celebrate heterosexuality but rather marriage; they condemned all sexual expression outside the marriage bond and did not differentiate sharply between sodomy and heterosexual fornication.

By the 1970s, however, the birth rate had dropped to under two. With the exception of the post-World War II baby boom, the decline has been continuous for two centuries, paralleling the spread of capitalist relations of production. It occurred even when access to contraceptive devices and abortion was systematically curtailed. The decline has included every segment of the population—urban and rural families, blacks and whites, ethnics and WASPS, the middle class and the working class.

As wage labor spread and production became socialized, then, it became possible to release sexuality from the "imperative" to procreate. Ideologically, heterosexual expression came to be a means of establishing intimacy, promoting happiness, and experiencing pleasure. In divesting the household of its economic independence and fostering the separation of sexuality from procreation, capitalism has created conditions that allow some men and women to organize a personal life around their erotic/emotional attraction to their own sex. It has made possible the formation of urban communities of lesbians and gay men and, more recently, of a politics based on sexual identity.

Evidence from colonial New England court records and church sermons indicates that male and female homosexual behavior existed in the seventeenth century. Homosexual behavior, however, is different from homosexual identity. There was, quite simply, no "social space" in the colonial system of production that allowed men and women to be gay. Survival was structured around participation in a nuclear family. There were certain homosexual acts—sodomy among men, "lewdness" among women—in which individuals engaged, but family was so pervasive that colonial society lacked even the category of homosexual or lesbian to describe a person. It is quite possible that some men and women experienced a stronger attraction to their own sex than to the opposite sex—in fact, some colonial court cases refer to men who persisted in their "unnatural" attractions—but one could not fashion out of that preference a way of life. Colonial Massachusetts even had laws prohibiting unmarried adults from living outside family units.[3]

By the second half of the nineteenth century, this situation was noticeably changing as the capitalist system of free labor took hold. Only when individuals began to make their living through wage labor, instead of as parts of an interdependent family unit, was it possible for homosexual desire to coalesce into a personal identity—an identity based on the ability to remain outside the heterosexual family and to construct a personal life based on attraction to one's own sex. By the end of the century, a class of men and women existed who recognized their erotic interest in their own sex, saw it as a trait that set them apart from the majority, and sought others like themselves. These early gay lives came from a wide social spectrum: civil servants and business executives, department store clerks and college professors, factory operatives, ministers, lawyers, cooks, domestics, hoboes, and the idle rich; men and women, black and white, immigrant and native-born.

In this period, gay men and lesbians began to invent ways of meeting each other and sustaining a group life. Already, in the early twentieth century, large cities contained male homosexual bars. Gay men staked out cruising areas, such as Riverside Drive in New York City and Lafayette Park in Washington. In St. Louis and the nation's capital, annual drag balls brought together large numbers of black gay men. Public bathhouses and YMCAs became gathering spots for male homosexuals. Lesbians formed literary societies and private social clubs. Some working-class women "passed" as men to obtain better-paying jobs and lived with other women—forming lesbian couples who appeared to the world as husband and wife. Among the faculties of women's colleges, in the settlement houses, and in the professional associations and clubs that women

formed, one could find lifelong intimate relationships supported by a web of lesbian friends. By the 1920S and 1930s, large cities such as New York and Chicago contained lesbian bars. These patterns of living could evolve because capitalism allowed individuals to survive beyond the confines of the family.[4]

Simultaneously, ideological definitions of homosexual behavior changed. Doctors developed theories about homosexuality, describing it as a condition, something that was inherent in a person, a part of his or her "nature." These theories did not represent scientific breakthroughs, elucidations of previously undiscovered areas of knowledge; rather, they were an ideological response to a new way of organizing one's personal life. The popularization of the medical model, in turn, affected the consciousness of the women and men who experienced homosexual desire, so that they came to define themselves through their erotic life.[5]

These new forms of gay identity and patterns of group life also reflected the differentiation of people according to gender, race, and class that is so pervasive in capitalist societies. Among whites, for instance, gay men have traditionally been more visible than lesbians. This partly stems from the division between the public male sphere and the private female sphere. Streets, parks, and bars, especially at night, were "male space." Yet the greater visibility of white men also reflected their larger numbers. The Kinsey studies of the 1940s and 1950s found significantly more men than women with predominantly homosexual histories, a situation caused, I would argue, by the fact that capitalism had drawn far more men than women into the labor force, and at higher wages. Men could more easily construct a personal life independent of attachments to the opposite sex, whereas women were more likely to remain economically dependent on men. Kinsey also found a strong positive correlation between years of schooling and lesbian activity. College educated white women, far more able than their working-class sisters to support themselves, could survive more easily without intimate relationships with men.[6]

Among working-class immigrants in the early twentieth century, closely knit kin networks and an ethic of family solidarity placed constraints on individual autonomy that made gayness a difficult option to pursue. In contrast, for reasons not altogether clear, urban black communities appeared relatively tolerant of homosexuality. The popularity in the 1920s and 1930s of songs with lesbian and gay male themes—"B. D. Woman," "Prove It on Me," "Sissy Man," "Fairey Blues"—suggests an openness about homosexual expression at odds with the mores of whites. Among men in the rural West in the 1940s, Kinsey found extensive incidence of homosexual behavior, but, in contrast with the men in large cities, little consciousness of gay identity. Thus even as capitalism exerted a homogenizing influence by gradually transforming more individuals into wage laborers and separating them from traditional communities, different groups of people were affected in different ways.[7]

The decisions of particular men and women to act on their erotic/emotional preference for the same sex, along with the new consciousness that this preference made them different, led to the formation of an urban subculture of gay men and lesbians. Yet at least through the 1930s this subculture remained rudimentary, unstable, and difficult to find. How, then, did the complex, well-developed gay community emerge that existed by the time the gay liberation movement exploded? The answer is to be found in the dislocations of World War II, a time when the cumulative changes of several decades coalesced into a qualitatively new shape.

The war severely disrupted traditional patterns of gender relations and sexuality, and temporarily created a new erotic situation conducive to homosexual expression. It plucked millions of young men and women, whose sexual identities were just forming, out of their homes, out of towns and small cities, out of the heterosexual environment of the family, and dropped them into sex-segregated situations—as GIs, as WACs and WAVEs, in same-sex rooming houses for women workers who relocated to seek employment. The war freed millions of men and women from the settings where heterosexuality was normally imposed. For men and women already gay, it provided an opportunity to meet people like themselves. Others could become gay because of the temporary freedom to explore sexuality that the war provided.[8]

The gay men and women of the 1940s were pioneers. Their decisions to act on their desires formed the underpinnings of an urban subculture of gay men and lesbians. Throughout the 1950s and 1960s the gay subculture grew and stabilized, so that people coming out then could more easily find other gay women and men than in the past. Newspapers and magazines published

articles describing gay male life. Literally hundreds of novels with lesbian themes were published.[9] Psychoanalysts complained about the new ease with which their gay male patients found sexual partners. And the gay subculture was not to be found just in the largest cities. Lesbian and gay male bars existed in places like Worcester, Massachusetts, and Buffalo, New York; in Columbia, South Carolina, and Des Moines, Iowa. Gay life in the 1950s and 1960s became a nationwide phenomenon. By the time of the Stonewall Riot in New York City in 1969—the event that ignited the gay liberation movement—our situation was hardly one of silence, invisibility, and isolation. A massive, grass-roots liberation movement could form almost overnight precisely because communities of lesbians and gay men existed.

Although gay community was a precondition for a mass movement, the oppression of lesbians and gay men was the force that propelled the movement into existence. As the subculture expanded and grew more visible in the post-World War II era, oppression by the state intensified, becoming more systematic and inclusive. The Right scapegoated "sexual perverts" during the McCarthy era. Eisenhower imposed a total ban on the employment of gay women and men by the federal government and government contractors. Purges of lesbians and homosexuals from the military rose sharply. The FBI instituted widespread surveillance of gay meeting places and of lesbian and gay organizations, such as the Daughters of Bilitis and the Mattachine Society. The Post Office placed tracers on the correspondence of gay men and passed evidence of homosexual activity on to employers. Urban vice squads invaded private homes, made sweeps of lesbian and gay male bars, entrapped gay men in public places, and fomented local witchhunts. The danger involved in being gay rose even as the possibilities of being gay were enhanced. Gay liberation was a response to this contradiction.

▼ ▼ ▼

Although lesbians and gay men won significant victories in the 1970s and opened up some safe social space in which to exist, we can hardly claim to have dealt a fatal blow to heterosexism and homophobia. One could even argue that the enforcement of gay oppression has merely changed locales, shifting somewhat from the state to the arena of extralegal violence in the form of increasingly open physical attacks on lesbians and gay men. And, as our movements have grown, they have generated a backlash that threatens to wipe out our gains. Significantly, this New Right opposition has taken shape as a "pro-family" movement. How is it that capitalism, whose structure made possible the emergence of a gay identity and the creation of urban gay communities, appears unable to accept gay men and lesbians in its midst? Why do heterosexism and homophobia appear so resistant to assault?

The answers, I think, can be found in the contradictory relationship of capitalism to the family. On the one hand, as I argued earlier, capitalism has gradually undermined the material basis of the nuclear family by taking away the economic functions that cemented the ties between family members. As more adults have been drawn into the free-labor system, and as capital has expanded its sphere until it produces as commodities most goods and services we need for our survival, the forces that propelled men and women into families and kept them there have weakened. On the other hand, the ideology of capitalist society has enshrined the family as the source of love, affection, and emotional security, the place where our need for stable, intimate human relationships is satisfied.

This elevation of the nuclear family to preeminence in the sphere of personal life is not accidental. Every society needs structures for reproduction and childrearing, but the possibilities are not limited to the nuclear family. Yet the privatized family fits well with capitalist relations of production. Capitalism has socialized production while maintaining that the products of socialized labor belong to the owners of private property. In many ways, childrearing has also been progressively socialized over the last two centuries, with schools, the media, peer groups, and employers taking over functions that once belonged to parents. Nevertheless, capitalist society maintains that reproduction and childrearing are private tasks, that children "belong" to parents, who exercise the rights of ownership. Ideologically, capitalism drives people into heterosexual families: each generation comes of age having internalized a heterosexist model of intimacy and personal relationships. Materially, capitalism weakens the bonds that once kept families together so that their members experience a growing instability in the place they have come to expect happiness and emotional security. Thus, while capitalism has knocked the material foundation away from family life, lesbians, gay men, and heterosexual feminists have become the scapegoats for the social instability of the system.

This analysis, if persuasive, has implications for us today. It can affect our perception of our identity, our formulation of political goals, and our decisions about strategy.

I have argued that lesbian and gay identity and communities are historically created, the result of a process of capitalist development that has spanned many generations. A corollary of this argument is that we are not a fixed social minority composed for all time of a certain percentage of the population. There are more of us than one hundred years ago, more of us than forty years ago. And there may very well be more gay men and lesbians in the future. Claims made by gays and nongays that sexual orientation is fixed at an early age, that large numbers of visible gay men and lesbians in society, the media, and the schools will have no influence on the sexual identities of the young, are wrong. Capitalism has created the material conditions for homosexual desire to express itself as a central component of some individuals' lives; now, our political movements are changing consciousness, creating the ideological conditions that make it easier for people to make that choice.

To be sure, this argument confirms the worst fears and most rabid rhetoric of our political opponents. But our response must be to challenge the underlying belief that homosexual relations are bad, a poor second choice. We must not slip into the opportunistic defense that society need not worry about tolerating us, since only homosexuals become homosexuals. At best, a minority group analysis and a civil rights strategy pertain to those of us who already are gay. It leaves today's youth—tomorrow's lesbians and gay men—to internalize heterosexist models that it can take a lifetime to expunge.

I have also argued that capitalism has led to the separation of sexuality from procreation. Human sexual desire need no longer be harnessed to reproductive imperatives, to procreation; its expression has increasingly entered the realm of choice. Lesbians and homosexuals most clearly embody the potential of this spirit, since our gay relationships stand entirely outside a procreative framework. The acceptance of our erotic choices ultimately depends on the degree to which society is willing to affirm sexual expression as a form of play, positive and life-enhancing. Our movement may have begun as the struggle of a "minority," but what we should now be trying to "liberate" is an aspect of the personal lives of all people's sexual expression.[10]

Finally, I have suggested that the relationship between capitalism and the family is fundamentally contradictory. On the one hand, capitalism continually weakens the material foundation of family life, making it possible for individuals to live outside the family, and for a lesbian and gay male identity to develop. On the other, it needs to push men and women into families, at least long enough to reproduce the next generation of workers. The elevation of the family to ideological pre-eminence guarantees that a capitalist society will reproduce not just children, but heterosexism and homophobia. In the most profound sense, capitalism is the problem.[11]

How do we avoid remaining the scapegoats, the political victims of the social instability that capitalism generates? How can we take this contradictory relationship and use it to move toward liberation?

Gay men and lesbians exist on social terrain beyond the boundaries of the heterosexual nuclear family. Our communities have formed in that social space. Our survival and liberation depend on our ability to defend and expand that terrain, not just for ourselves but for everyone. That means, in part, support for issues that broaden the opportunities for living outside traditional heterosexual family units: issues like the availability of abortion and the ratification of the Equal Rights Amendment, affirmative action for people of color and for women, publicly funded day care and other essential social services, decent welfare payments, full employment, the rights of young people—in other words, programs and issues that provide a material basis for personal autonomy.

The rights of young people are especially critical. The acceptance of children as dependents, as belonging to parents, is so deeply ingrained that we can scarcely imagine what it would mean to treat them as autonomous human beings, particularly in the realm of sexual expression and choice. Yet until that happens, gay liberation will remain out of our reach.

But personal autonomy is only half the story. The instability of families and the sense of impermanence and insecurity that people are now experiencing in their personal relationships are real social problems that need to be addressed. We need political solutions for these difficulties of personal life. These solutions should not come in the form of a radical version of the pro-family position, of some left-wing proposals to strengthen the family. Socialists do not generally respond to the exploitation and economic inequality of industrial capitalism by calling for a return to the family farm and handicraft production. We recognize that the vastly increased productivity that capitalism has made possible by socializing production is one of its progressive features. Similarly, we should not be trying to turn back the clock to some mythic age of the happy family.

We do need, however, structures and programs that will help to dissolve the boundaries that isolate the family, particularly those that privatize childrearing. We need community- or worker-controlled day care, housing where privacy and community coexist, neighborhood institutions—from medical clinics to performance centers—that enlarge the social unit where each of us has a secure place. As we create structures beyond the nuclear family that provide a sense of belonging, the family will wane in significance. Less and less will it seem to make or break our emotional security.

In this respect gay men and lesbians are well situated to play a special role. Already excluded from families as most of us are, we have had to create, for our survival, networks of support that do not depend on the bonds of blood or the license of the state, but that are freely chosen and nurtured. The building of an "affectional community" must be as much a part of our political movement as are campaigns for civil rights. In this way we may prefigure the shape of personal relationships in a society grounded in equality and justice rather than exploitation and oppression, a society where autonomy and security do not preclude each other but coexist.

## NOTES

1. I do not mean to suggest that no one has ever proposed that gay identity is a product of historical change. See, for instance, Mary McIntosh, "The Homosexual Role," *Social Problems* 16 (1968): 182–92; Jeffrey Weeks, *Coming Out: Homosexual Politics in Britain* (New York: Quartet, 1977). It is also implied in Michel Foucault, *The History of Sexuality*, vol. 1: *An Introduction*, trans. Robert Hurley (New York: Pantheon, 1978). However, this does represent a minority viewpoint and the works cited above have not specified how it is that capitalism as a system of production has allowed for the emergence of a gay male and lesbian identity. As an ex-

ample of the "eternal homosexual" thesis, see John Boswell, *Christianity, Social Tolerance, and Homosexuality* (Chicago: University of Chicago Press, 1980), where "gay people" remains an unchanged social category through fifteen centuries of Mediterranean and Western Europe history.

2. See Eli Zaretsky, *Capitalism, the Family, and Personal Life* (New York: Harper and Row, 1976); and Paula Fass, *The Damned and the Beautiful: American Youth in the 1920s* (New York: Oxford University Press, 1977).

3. Robert F. Oaks, " 'Things Fearful to Name': Sodomy and Buggery in Seventeenth-Century New England," *Journal of Social History* 12 (1978): 268–81; J. R. Roberts, "The Case of Sarah Norman and Mary Hammond," *Sinister Wisdom* 24 (1980): 57–62; and Jonathan Katz, *Gay American History* (New York: Crowell, 1976), 16–24, 568–71.

4. For the period from 1870 to 1940 see the documents in Katz, *Gay American History*, and idem, *Gay/Lesbian Almanac* (New York: Crowell, 1983). Other sources include Allan Bérubé, "Lesbians and Gay Men in Early San Francisco: Notes Toward a Social History of Lesbians and Gay Men in America," unpublished paper, 1979; Vern Bullough and Bonnie Bullough, "Lesbianism in the 1920s and 1930s: A Newfound Study," *Signs* 2 (Summer 1977): 895–904.

5. On the medical model see Weeks, *Coming Out*, 23–32. The impact of the medical model on the consciousness of men and women can be seen in Louis Hyde, ed., *Rat and the Devil: The Journal Letters of F. 0. Matthiessen and Russell Cheney* (Hamden, Conn.: Archon, 1978), 47, and in the story of Lucille Hart in Katz, *Gay American History*, 258–79. Radclyffe Hall's classic novel about lesbianism, *The Well of Loneliness*, published in 1928, was perhaps one of the most important vehicles for the popularization of the medical model.

6. See Alfred Kinsey et al., *Sexual Behavior in the Human Male* (Philadelphia: W. B. Saunders, 1948), and *Sexual Behavior in the Human Female* (Philadelphia: W. B. Saunders, 1953).

7. On black music, see "AC/DC Blues: Gay Jazz Reissues," Stash Records, ST-106 (1977), and Chris Albertson, *Bessie* (New York: Stein and Day, 1974); on the persistence of kin networks in white ethnic communities see Judith Smith, "Our Own Kind: Family and Community Networks in Providence," in *A Heritage of Her Own*, eds. Nancy F. Cott and Elizabeth H. Pleck (New York: Simon and Schuster, 1979), 393–411; on differences between rural and urban male homoeroticism see Kinsey et al., *Sexual Behavior in the Human Male*, 455–57, 630–31.

8. The argument and the information in this and the following paragraphs come from my book, *Sexual Politics, Sexual Communities: The Making of Homosexual Minority in the United States, 1940–1970* (Chicago: University of Chicago Press, 1983). I have also developed it with reference to San Francisco in "Gay Politics, Gay Community: San Francisco's Experience," *Socialist Review* 55 (January-February 1981): 77–104.

9. On lesbian novels see the *Ladder*, March 1958, 18; February 1960, 14–15; April 1961, 12–13; February 1962, 6–11; January 1963, 6–13; February 1964, 12–19; February 1965, 19–23; March 1966, 22–26; and April 1967, 8–13. The *Ladder* was the magazine published by the Daughters of Bilitis.

10. This especially needs to be emphasized today. The 1980 annual conference of the National Organization for Women, for instance, passed a lesbian rights resolution that defined the issue as one of "discrimination based on affectional/sexual preference/ orientation," and explicitly disassociated the issue from other questions of sexuality such as pornography, sadomasochism, public sex, and pederasty.

11. I do not mean to suggest that homophobia is "caused" by capitalism, or is to be found only in capitalist societies. Severe sanctions against homoeroticism can be found in European feudal society and in contemporary socialist countries. But my focus in this essay has been the emergence of a gay identity under capitalism, and the mechanisms specific to capitalism that made this possible and that reproduce homophobia as well.

# | 5 |

# A Worm in the Bud: The Early Sexologists and Love Between Women

## LILLIAN FADERMAN

Avoid girls who are too affectionate and demonstrative in their manner of talking and acting with you. . . . When sleeping in the same bed with another girl, old or young, avoid
"snuggling up" close together. . . . And, after going to bed, if you are sleeping alone or with
others, just bear in mind that beds are sleeping places. When you go to bed, go to sleep just
as quickly as you can.

—IRVING D. STEINHARDT, *TEN SEX TALKS TO GIRLS*, 1914

Because nineteenth-century women of the working class were largely illiterate and thus have left
little in the way of letters, journals, or autobiographies, it is difficult to know to what extent some
form of romantic friendship may have been
prevalent among them. Historians such as Mar-
ion Goldman have suggested a picture of relationships between nineteenth-century American
prostitutes that appears to have commonalties
with nineteenth-century middle-class romantic
friends. They spent all their free time together,
traveled together, protected each other, loved
each other. Goldman talks about two who were so
devoted that they even tried to die together. The
deviance of prostitutes' roles, which set them
apart and circumscribed their activities, encouraged them in a "female solidarity and bonding"
that were not unlike romantic friendship. However, because their sexuality was so much more
available to them than to the typical nineteenth-
century middle-class woman, love between
women who were prostitutes was much more
likely to have manifested itself in genital relations.

Women in penal institutions during the late
nineteenth and early twentieth century seem also
to have engaged in some form of romantic friendships. The early twentieth-century psychologist

Margaret Otis described such passionate but
apparently largely nonsexual relationships
between black and white women in reform
schools. Otis claimed that those relationships
occurred only along cross-racial lines, "the difference in color . . . tak[ing] the place of difference
in sex" and the black woman generally playing
the "man's role." But since the black and white
women were physically segregated in the institutions Otis observed, the relationships usually
could have no consummation outside of romantic notes passed surreptitiously between the
women and quick utterances of endearment and
high sentiments—which would have rendered
those affections as emotionally intense and
ungenital as most romantic friendships probably
were. Had the women not been segregated, however, the nature of the relationships might have
been quite different.

But in the era when romantic friendships
between middle-class women in America were an
important social institution, during the eighteenth and much of the nineteenth century, they

In Lillian Faderman, *Odd Girls and Twilight Lovers*, pp.
37–61. Excerpt. New York: Columbia University Press,
1991.

appear not to have been common for working-class women, perhaps because the intimacy necessary for the development of such relationships required leisure and some degree of social privacy. Working-class women, who were generally employed in a domestic setting, had little of either. At the end of the nineteenth century, however, their situation began to change. American working-class women made a move into the public sphere parallel with their middle-class counterparts, taking the new jobs that were opening up with the rapid growth of American corporations and industry. There was now employment for them outside of homes, not only in factories but also in service occupations such as sales and clerical work, and the number of women in unskilled and semi-skilled occupations grew rapidly. The low-paid female wage worker figured heavily in the tripling of the female labor force between 1870 and 1900 (from 1.8 million to 5.3 million, twice the increase in the number of women in the general population).

Many young working-class women left parents' or domestic employers' homes and moved to big cities where they were on their own—away from perpetual supervision and scrutiny for the first time. Such a move accounts for their changing heterosexual practices—which seem to have constituted a (hetero)sexual revolution that preceded the revolution of the 1920s by at least a couple of decades. But such a move also drew young working-class women together in ways that would have been impractical or impossible earlier. Because they lived and worked away from a domestic setting and often made less than subsistence wages, they frequently shared rooms, sometimes on a long-term basis. One historian gives several examples of women who not only lived together but moved together from city to city to find work, and she suggests that such long-term partnerships indicated "close personal bonds that existed among some lower-paid working women similar to the bonds of love and friendship [among] nineteenth century American middle-class women."

But that many of those relationships were really similar to romantic friendship as middle-class women experienced it is perhaps dubious. Working-class women may have realistically felt that they did not have the luxury to engage in a connection that neither promoted survival as its chief aim nor promised starker sensual pleasures that could help them forget the bleakness of their labors. The most convincing depictions of these relationships suggest that they were far more concretely oriented—either sexually or practically—than those between romantic friends usually appear to have been. Kathy Peiss, for example, in *Cheap Amusements: Working Women and Leisure in Turn-of-the-Century New York*, observes that working-class women's same-sex friendships generally occurred in a context that permitted them to negotiate the world of heterosexual commercial amusements in order to make appropriate heterosexual contacts without being accosted by unwelcomed advances as lone women would be. Peiss contrasts this arrangement to the romantic friendships of middle-class women whose purpose was often to help them maintain their privatized same-sex world.

▼ ▼ ▼

Regardless of the extent or nature of romantic friendship and love between working-class women, when the sexologists (primarily medical men with middle-class backgrounds) who began writing about sexuality in the latter half of the nineteenth century turned their attention to homosexuality, they were more easily able to acknowledge that intimate relations between women in the classes "beneath" them could go beyond the platonic than they could with reference to women of their own class. Their early definitions of the female "sexual invert" (their term for the lesbian) were based on women of the working class. However, although they made their first observations about these women, it was not many decades before relationships between middle-class women (who were becoming entirely too independent) came to be seen by sexologists as similar to what they had observed in the "lower" classes. They were oblivious to the social and economic factors that created important differences between the women's relationships in each class.

The "scientific" classification of the lesbian in the latter half of the nineteenth century may be seen as consistent with the passion for taxonomy (the minute classification of almost everything) that had overtaken scientific circles at that time. But while they were convinced of the objectivity of their classifications, the scientists—and particularly the medical men who turned their attention to sexology—were often motivated by the moral vision of their day. Influenced by the theories of evolution, they formulated the notion that those who did not contribute to what was considered the human race's move forward—criminals and deviants and, by virtue of their socioeconomic position, the "lower classes"—owed their backwardness to bad heredity. They were "degenerate" because, as the term itself suggests, their genes were defective. Their deviant or backward behavior was thought to have a physiological basis. Through this explanation of the misfit, science came to replace religion as the definer and upholder of mores. White middle-class European values and behaviors that reflected the background of the scientists came to be seen as scientifically normal and healthy. Those who did not conform were "abnormal." The sexologists thus developed a medical model to study various problems that were earlier considered social or ethical. While in previous eras a person who had a sexual relationship with an individual of the same sex would have been considered a sinner, by the late nineteenth century that person became a "congenital invert," a victim of inborn "contrary sexual feeling," a "homosexual"—all ways of looking at same-sex love that had not existed in the first part of the nineteenth century or earlier.

Much of the nineteenth-century classification was done in the name of the eugenics movement, which often attacked the poor and also marked the beginning of a long history of attempted "genocide" of those who loved the same sex. It was now claimed that sexual anomalies were congenital and would not occur without tainted heredity; thus eugenicists were determined to educate the rest of the medical community about the need to make those who were not—as an American doctor, William Lee Howard, said—in "the prime of physiological life" refrain from procreation. Masculine females and feminine males, Howard stated, were only born to parents of the degenerate class who themselves lacked the appropriate "strong sex characteristics."

## SEXUAL INVERSION AND "MASCULINE" OR TRANSVESTITE WOMEN

These medical men first observed that inappropriate sex role behavior was sometimes characteristic of women of the working class. The females that the earliest sexologists such as Karl Westphal, Richard von Krafft-Ebing and Cesare Lombroso defined as sexual inverts were often a captive population in prisons and insane asylums, daughters of the poor. Westphal, a German psychiatrist writing in 1869, was the first to describe extensively love between women in medical terms. His subject was a thirty-five-year old servant who was admitted to the Berlin Charite Hospital because of hysteria and bizarre behavior. She claimed to be profoundly disturbed by her love for a young girl. Westphal suggested that she was really a man trapped in a woman's body. As a child she had been fond of boy's games, she liked to dress in a masculine way, she had dreams in which she appeared to herself to be a man—and she apparently had sexual desires for women. To Westphal and the sexologists who came after him, the romantic interests of women like this one were inextricably linked to what the sexologists saw as their masculine behavior and their conception of themselves as male. Some historians have suggested a shift in the early sexologists' views from a concern with inappropriate gender behavior, that is, inversion of personality traits so that a female looks and behaves like a male—to a concern with inappropriate sexual object choice, or homosexuality. But such a distinction is not to be found in Westphal's work, which clearly connected the two. Nor is it to be found in the work of many sexologists well into the twentieth century or in the popular imagination, which often assumes, even today, that lesbians are necessarily masculine and that female "masculinity" is a sure sign of lesbianism.

Westphal must have often witnessed passionate expression of love between women of his class since it was so prevalent in Germany during his day, but he would have regarded it as romantic friendship. In the poor servant woman he observed, who was also hysterical and not "feminine" as were refined women of his class, he could dare to see a deviant sexuality. What he could not understand about her life, however, was the reality of the perception that more feminine-looking and -acting females might have more difficulty surviving in her rough environment. He connected her "masculinity" with her "inappropriate" sexual drive, assuming a tie between the two. Despite his limited perceptions, Westphal's writing alerted other medical men to a supposed correlation between "masculinity" and female same-sex love.

There were many masculine-looking women of the working class, not only in Europe but in America as well, during Westphal's day. While women of the middle class in the latter part of the nineteenth century were enjoying a tremendous expansion of opportunities in terms of education and the slow but sure opening of various professions to them, the situation of working-class women was not to change much until the end of the century. The jobs that were open to them—usually of a domestic nature or in a factory—offered little beyond bare subsistence and no vistas of opportunity such as women from wealthier families were beginning to enjoy. It appeared to a good number of them that had they at least been men, life would have been more fair. Wages would have been higher for work that was not more difficult, and they would have been socially freer to engage in activities such as travel. There were good reasons for them to envy the privileges that males even of their class enjoyed and that were far above what was available to any female.

Most of them suffered in silence. But a few were more active in their resentment, and the most adventurous or the most desperate of them even formulated an ingenious solution to their plight. They figured out that if they moved to an area where they were not known, cut their hair, and wore men's clothes, their potential in terms of meaningful adventure and finances would increase tremendously. They often saw themselves not as men trapped in women's bodies, as the sexologists suggested they were, but rather as women in masquerade, trying to get more freedom and decent wages. Their aims were not unlike those that any feminist would applaud today.

They had few problems with detection. It was relatively easy for women to pass as men in earlier times because, unlike in the latter half of the twentieth century, women never wore pants. A person in pants would have been assumed to be male, and only the most suspicious would have scrutinized facial features or body movements to discern a woman beneath the external appearance.

Obviously there were more working-class women who were disgruntled with their limitations as females but simply eschewed feminine behavior in mild protest than who actually chose to become transvestites and try to pass as men, but the number of the latter was sizable. One researcher has estimated through Union Army doctors' accounts that at least four hundred women transvestites fought in the Civil War. Many continued as transvestites even into the twentieth century, such as "Harry Gorman," who, around the turn of the century, did heavy work as an employee of the New York Central Railway and frequented saloons and dance houses every night. Gorman was discovered to be a woman when she was hospitalized for a broken limb. She admitted that she had been passing as a man for twenty years. She also declared that she knew of "at least ten other women," also employed by the New York Central, who passed as men, appeared wholly manlike, and "were never suspected of being otherwise." Since there were at least eleven such women working for the New York Central alone and there are records of myriad other such cases, one can safely guess that transvestism and attempts to pass were not so rare and that there must have been thousands of women wandering around America in the latter part of the nineteenth century and the early twentieth century who were passing as men.

Most of these working-class women appear to have begun their "masculine" careers not because they had an overwhelming passion for another woman and wanted to be a man to her, but rather because of economic necessity or a desire for adventure beyond the narrow limits that they could enjoy as women. But once the sexologists became aware of them, they often took such women or those who showed any discontent whatsoever with their sex roles for their newly conceptualized model of the invert, since they had little difficulty believing in the sexuality of women of that class, and they assumed that a masculine-looking creature must also have a masculine sex instinct.

Autobiographical accounts of transvestite women or those who assumed a masculine demeanor suggest, if they can be believed at all, that the women's primary motives were seldom sexual. Many of them were simply dramatizing vividly the frustrations that so many more women of their class felt. They sought private solutions to those frustrations, since there was no social movement of equality for them such as had emerged for middle-class women. Lucy Ann Lobdell, for example, who passed as a man for more than ten years in the mid-nineteenth century, declared in her autobiography: "I feel that I cannot submit to all the bondage with which woman is oppressed," and explained that she made up her mind to leave her home and dress as a man to seek labor because she would "work harder at housework, and only get a dollar per week, and I was capable of doing men's work and getting men's wages." "Charles Warner," an upstate New York woman who passed as a man for most of her life, explained that in the 1860s:

> When I was about twenty I decided that I was almost at the end of my rope. I had no money

and a woman's wages were not enough to keep me alive. I looked around and saw men getting more money and more work, and more money for the same kind of work. I decided to become a man. It was simple. I just put on men's clothing and applied for a man's job. I got it and got good money for those times, so I stuck to it.

A transvestite woman who could actually pass as a man had male privileges and could do all manner of things other women could not: open a bank account, write checks, own property, go anywhere unaccompanied, vote in elections. The appeal was obvious. Even those passing women who denied they were "women's-righters," as did Babe Bean, had to admit, "As a man I can travel freely though unprotected and find work."

Transvestism may have had a particular appeal to some minority women, who suffered doubly from the handicaps visited on women because of gender and on minorities because of racial prejudice. If they could pass as a man they obliterated at least one set of handicaps. Thus a black woman, Mary Fields, who had been born a slave in Tennessee, found remunerative and honorable employment as a stagecoach driver, even accompanying and protecting a group of nuns on a trek out West. As late as 1914 gender passing obviously provided more opportunities for a minority female than she would have had living as a woman. Ralph Kerwinieo (nee Cora Anderson), an American Indian woman who found employment for years as a man and claimed that she "legally" married another woman in order to "protect" her from the sexist world, also expressed feminist awareness for her decision to pass as a man:

This world is made by man—for man alone. . . . In the future centuries it is probable that woman will be the owner of her own body and the custodian of her own soul. But until that time you can expect that the statutes [concerning] women will be all wrong. The well-cared for woman is a parasite, and the woman who must work is a slave. . . . Do you blame me for wanting to be a man—free to live as a man in a man-made world? Do you blame me for hating to again resume a woman's clothes?

There must have been many women, with or without a sexual interest in other women, who would have answered her two questions with a resounding "no!"

It appears that an interest in sexual relations with other females came only later in the careers of many of these transvestite women (and in some cases was never of interest to them). But it is plausible that often transvestites did not become lovers with other women until they took on the persona of men and had available to them only those sexual opportunities typically open to men. As subtle as such developments may have been, the sexologists saw only the obvious when they formulated their early definitions of the lesbian. They could not recognize a woman's wish to be masculine and even to pass as a man as a desire for more economic and social freedom. In their own narrow views she acted masculine because she was a man trapped in a woman's body and all her instincts were inverted, including her sexual instinct. The sexologists conflated sex role behavior (in this case, acting in ways that have been termed masculine), gender identity (seeing oneself as male), and sexual object choice (preferring a love relationship with another woman). They believed in an inevitable coherence among the three. It was thus that transvestite women and women who behaved as men traditionally behaved, generally women of the working class whose masculinity was most apparent, came to be seen by the early sexologists as the prime example of the lesbian, whether or not those women had sexual relations with other females. And conversely, women who were passionately in love with other females but did not appear to be masculine were considered for some years more as merely romantic friends or devoted companions.

## FEMINISTS AS SEXUAL FREAKS

Masculine appearance, especially among working-class women, figured heavily in the early definitions of the female invert. A typical description was one by Krafft-Ebing in 1888: "She had coarse male features, a rough and rather deep voice, and with the exception of the bosom and female contour of the pelvis, looked more like a man in women's clothing than like a woman." But as the late nineteenth-century feminist movement grew in strength and in its potential to overthrow the old sex roles, it was not too long before feminism itself was also equated with sexual inversion and many women of the middle class came to be suspected of that anomaly, since as feminists they acted in ways inappropriate to their gender, desiring to get an education, for example, or to work in a challenging, lucrative profession.

It was the European sexologists who were the first to connect sexual inversion and feminism. Havelock Ellis stated in his chapter "Sexual Inversion Among Women" in *Studies in the Psychology of Sex* that female homosexuality was increasing because of feminism, which taught women to be independent and to disdain marriage. Ellis, as a congenitalist who believed that homosexuality was hereditary, hastened to add that the women's movement could not directly cause sexual inversion unless one had the potential for it to begin with, but the movement definitely "developed the germs of it" in those who were that way inclined; and in other women it caused a "spurious imitation" of homosexuality.

Like the leading English and German sexologists, the French sexologist Julien Chevalier, in his 1893 work *Inversion sexuelle*, suggested that homosexuality was congenital and that the lesbian was born with "organic elements" of the male; but despite that conviction he also observed that the number of lesbians had grown over the last decades because women were getting educations, demanding careers, emancipating themselves from male tutelage, "making men of themselves" by cultivating masculine sports, and becoming politically active. All of this "male emulation," according to him, resulted in female sexual inversion.

American sexologists followed the lead of the Europeans. Frequently their goal also seemed to be to discredit both the women's movement and love between women by equating them with masculine drives and thus freakishness. They were ready to wage war on any form of women's bonding, which now, in the context of feminism, seemed threatening to the preservation of old-fashioned femininity. . . .

In his article "Effeminate Men and Masculine Women," the psychiatrist William Lee Howard, a staunch congenitalist, explains that these feminist-viragent-lesbians—all "unsightly and abnormal beings"—are victims of poor mating. They must have had feminist mothers who neglected their maternal instincts and dainty feminine characteristics, preferred the laboratory to the nursery, and engaged in political campaigns. Thus they reproduced these mental and physical monstrosities. Howard is, however, optimistic about the future. Soon "disgusted Nature, no longer tolerant of the woman who would be a man," will allow all such types to "shrink unto death," he affirms.

Howard had the assurance of the Darwinists behind him in his conviction that society and nature had evolved for the better in doing away with matriarchy and establishing patriarchy. Whatever was, at that point in time, had to be superior to what had preceded it. Nature would thus see to it that feminists and lesbians, Amazonian throwbacks in Howard's view, would go the way of the dinosaur and the dodo bird.

The early sexologists, who have been considered so brave for daring to write about sex at all in the sexually inhibited nineteenth century, were, in important ways, not much more imaginative or flexible regarding sex and sex roles than the conservative masses around them. Despite the occasional lip service to feminism such as Ellis paid, they clearly believed that there were men's roles and women's roles, and if any woman wanted to diverge from what was appropriate it could only be because she had a congenital anomaly (a degeneracy, most sexologists believed) that made her an invert. A top item on their hidden agenda, whether they were conscious of it or not, finally came to be to discourage feminism and maintain traditional sex roles by connecting the women's movement to sexual abnormality.

## THE ATTACK ON "ROMANTIC FRIENDSHIP"

It was still possible in the early twentieth century for some women to vow great love for each other, sleep together, see themselves as life mates, perhaps even make love, and yet have no idea that their relationship was what the sexologists were now considering "inverted" and "abnormal." Such naïveté was possible for women who came out of the nineteenth-century tradition of romantic friendship and were steeped in its literature. Even had they been exposed to the writings of the sexologists, which were by now being slowly disseminated in America, they might have been unable to recognize themselves and their relationships in those medical descriptions. Their innocence became increasingly difficult to maintain, however, as the twentieth century progressed.

Perhaps the sexual possibilities of romantic friendship among middle-class women were overlooked by outside observers throughout much of nineteenth-century America because "illicit" sexuality in general was uncommon then (compared to earlier and later eras), judging at least from the birthrate of children born prior to the ninth month of marriage. During the Revolutionary era, for example, 33 percent of all first children were born before the ninth month of marriage. In Victorian America, between 1841 and 1880, only 12.6 percent of all first births were before the ninth month of marriage. If unmarried women, especially those of the "better classes," appeared to be by and large inactive in terms of heterosexual relations, it was probably difficult to conceive of them being homosexually active. Popular wisdom had it that decent women were uninterested in genital sexuality and merely tolerated their marriage duties. As an 1869 book, *The Physiology of Women*, observed with conviction:

> There can be no doubt that sexual feeling in the female is, in the majority of cases, in abeyance, and that it requires positive and considerable excitement to be roused at all; and, even if roused (which in many instances it never can be), is very moderate compared with that of the male.

It could easily be believed that romantic friendship between two women was a "mental passion," spiritual, uplifting, and nothing more.

Lesbianism became a popular topic of exotic and erotic French novels by the mid nineteenth century and a subject of great interest to later nineteenth-century European sexologists, but in America it was quite ignored almost to the end of the century. The *Index Catalogue of the Library of the Surgeon General's Office* lists only one article on lesbians between 1740 and 1895. However, soon after that point sexological writings began to fascinate American medical men tremendously. The second series of the same catalogue lists almost 100 books and 566 articles between 1896 and 1916 on women's sexual "perversions," "inversions," and "disorders."

Turn-of-the-century American writers on lesbianism generally acknowledged the influence of the European sexologists while extending their observations to the American scene. For example, a 1902 article titled "Dr. Havelock Ellis on Sexual Inversion" observed that it was women's colleges that were "the great breeding ground" of lesbianism. These discussions were often very explicit about the dangers of female friendships that had hitherto seemed perfectly innocent. A medical work that appeared at the beginning of the century alerted doctors that when young girls are thrown together they manifest

an increasing affection by the usual tokens. They kiss each other fondly on every occasion. They embrace each other with mutual satisfaction. It is most natural, in the interchange of visits, for them to sleep together. They learn the pleasure of direct contact, and in the course of their fondling they resort to cunni-linguistic practices. . . . After this the normal sex act fails to satisfy [them].

But even romantic friendship that clearly had no sexual manifestations was now coming to be classified as homosexual. Medical writers began to comment on "numerous phases of *inversion* where men are passionately attached to men, and women to women, *without the slightest desire for sexual intercourse.* [Italics are mine.]"

American doctors were now genuinely disturbed that the public was still naive about what had recently become so apparent to the medical men. Bernard Talmey, for example, in his 1904 treatise *Woman*, insisted that homosexuality in females had never been made a legal offense only because of "the ignorance of the law-making power of the existence of this anomaly. The layman generally does not even surmise its existence." Because of such ignorance, he concluded, women's intimate attachments with each other are considered often erroneously as "mere friendship." They are fostered by parents and guardians and are "praised and commended" rather than suspected of being "of a homosexual origin," as they often are. Some doctors believed they were doing a public service in attempting to close the gap in knowledge as quickly as possible. However, since their writings were for the most part "scientific" it was only very gradually that they began to filter through to popular awareness. Early twentieth-century popular magazine fiction in America continued to treat intense love between women as innocent and often ennobling romantic friendships.

Thus lacking the concept, two women in the late nineteenth or early twentieth century might still live in a relationship that would certainly be defined as lesbian today and yet have no awareness of themselves as lesbians. If their relationship was genital they could have felt the same guilt over it that their contemporaries might have experienced over masturbation—it was sexual pleasure without the excuse of inescapable marital duties—but they would not necessarily have felt themselves abnormal. In 1914 psychoanalysts were still noting that "homosexual women are often not acquainted with their condition."

Yet there were a few indications of a change in public consciousness as early as the late nineteenth century in America. In contrast to William Alger's 1868 view of romantic friendships bringing to women "freshness, stimulant charm, noble truths and aspirations," an 1895 work, *Side Talks with Girls*, warns the young female that it is dangerous for her to have "a girl-sweetheart" because if she wastes her love on another female she will not have any to give "Prince Charming when he comes to claim his bride." A couple of decades later, advice books of that nature were somewhat more explicit about the possibilities of sex between females, although the word "lesbian" or "invert" was never used. In fact, a 1914 book, *Ten Sex Talks to Girls*, which like its 1895 predecessor was aimed at adolescents and post-adolescents, specifically classified sexual relations between females with masturbation, which, the author admonished, "when practiced by one girl is harmful enough, but when practised between girls . . . is a most pernicious habit which should be vigorously fought against." This author was quite explicit in his warning to girls to avoid just those manifestations of romantic friendship that were accepted and even encouraged a few decades earlier, such as hugging and exchanging intimacies. Parents were especially alerted to be suspicious of their daughters' attachments. Articles such as a 1913 piece in *Harper's Bazaar* titled "Your Daughter: What Are Her Friendships?" and signed "by a College Graduate" informed parents that most college friendships were innocent, but a tenth of them (how that figure is arrived at is never made clear) were morally degenerate and caused guilt and unhappiness because they were "not legitimate."

The medical journals sometimes went much further in their imputation of wild sexual practices between females, though again their focus was generally on women of the working class. Dr. Irving Rosse, for example, discussed sex between women in sensationalistic, excessive, and bizarre terms that appear to have come right out of French novels rather than reality. In an 1892 article for the *Journal of Nervous and Mental Disease* he described one case of a prostitute who had "out of curiosity" visited various women who made a "speciality of the lesbian vice" and on submitting herself "by way of experiment to [their] lingual and oral maneuvers . . . had a violent hystero-cataleptic attack from which she was a long time in recovering." Another case he described was of a young unmarried woman who became pregnant through her married sister, "who committed the simulacrum of the male act on her just after copulating with her husband." To divine the means she used to transfer her husband's semen from her vagina to her unmarried sister's challenges the average imagination, but Dr. Rosse seemed to find nothing dubious in such a feat. In a 1906 work, August Forel, a Swiss psychiatrist and director of the Zurich Insane Asylum, wrote about lesbian sexual orgies "seasoned with alcohol" and nymphomaniacal lesbians. "The [sexual] excess of femal inverts exceed those of the male," he stated. "This is their one thought, night and day, almost without interruption." The literature disseminated to the lay public was considerably tamer.

Nevertheless, the new perspective undoubtedly created great confusion in women who were brought up in the previous century to believe in the virtues, beauty, and idealism of romantic friendship. Suddenly they learned that what was socially condoned so recently was considered unsalutary and dangerous. One woman remembered the shock of the new "knowledge" that came to her when she was eighteen, in 1905. She had been raised with the idea of the preciousness of intimate attachments between females, but almost overnight all changed, she suggested: "Public opinion, formed by cheap medical reprints and tabloid gossip, dubbed such contacts perverted, called such women lesbians, such affection and understanding destructive." She was, however, a tall, broad-shouldered woman with a deep voice who sold books door-to-door. Females of more "refinement," who were more feminine-looking and had a more protected social status, were apparently able to continue relationships such as earlier eras viewed as romantic friendship much longer into the twentieth century than unsheltered women who looked as though they had stepped out of the pages of Krafft-Ebing.

Class may have accounted for profound differences here. The luxury of naïveté regarding lesbianism that many socially sheltered middle-class American college women were able to enjoy even into the sophisticated 1920s is illustrated in their yearbooks. The Oberlin College yearbook of 1920, for example, contains a page of thirty-two photographs of women who are identified by name under the heading "Lesbians." They were members of the Oberlin Lesbian Society, a woman's group devoted to writing poetry.

▼ ▼ ▼

However, not all females of their social class remained as innocent. Although some early twentieth-century women apparently saw no need to hide their same-sex relationships, many apparently did. Willa Cather was perhaps representative in this regard. At the beginning of her college career at the University of Nebraska in the late nineteenth century she called herself Dr. William and dressed virtually in male drag. By the end of her college years her presentation was considerably more feminine, but she continued her amorous relationships with other women—Louise Pound, Isabelle McClung, with whom she was involved for about twelve years, and later Edith Lewis, with whom she lived for forty years. Yet she cultivated the image of celibacy and pretended to reject all human ties for the sake of art. She claimed that she could not become "entangled" with anyone because to be free to work at her writing table was "all in all" to her. She seems to have felt that it was necessary to conceal the ways in which the women she loved and lived with, and was very "entangled" with, contributed to her ability to create, although the latest Cather biographers have not seen the need for such reticence (see O'Brien, this volume).

Cather became very secretive about her private life around the turn of the century because she was cognizant of the fall from grace that love between women was beginning to suffer. Other women who had same-sex relationships at about that time, when society's view of such love started to turn, adopted a much more aggressive and sadder ploy to conceal what was coming to be considered their transgressions: they bitterly denounced love between women in public. Jeannette Marks, professor at Mount Holyoke, lived for fifty-five years in a devoted relationship with Mary Woolley, president of Mount Holyoke, and yet wrote and attempted to publish an essay in 1908 on "unwise college friendships." She called such relationships "unpleasant or worse," an "abnormal condition," and a sickness requiring a "moral antiseptic." Marks appears not even to be talking about full-fledged lesbianism, since she describes those loves only as "sentimental" friendships. But against all her own experiences and those of her closest friends, she baldly states in this essay that the only relationship that can "fulfill itself and be complete is that between a man and a woman." Later Marks even began work on a book dealing with homosexuality in literature in which she intended to show that insanity and suicide were the result of same-sex love. Were those

works a pathetic attempt to deny to the world that her domestic arrangement, which all Mount Holyoke knew about, was not what it seemed?

Perhaps it would be more charitable to try to understand her ostensible dishonesty through a revelation that her contemporary Mary Casal makes in her autobiography, *The Stone Wall*. Casal, writing about the turn of the century a number of years later (1930), talks frankly about her own earlier lesbian sexual relationship with Juno, which she describes as being "the very highest type of human love," but she insists on a distinction between their homosexuality and that of "the other" lesbians:

> Our lives were on a much higher plane than those of *the real inverts*. While we did indulge in *our sexual intercourse*, that was never the thought uppermost in our minds. . . . But we had seen evidences of overindulgence on the part of some of those with whom we came in contact, in loss of vitality and weakened health, ending in consumption. [Italics are mine.]

*True* lesbianism for her had nothing to do with whether or not one has sexual relations with a person of the same sex. Rather it is a matter of balance: Those who do it a lot are the real ones. She and Juno are "something else."

It is likely that many early twentieth-century women, having discovered the judgments of the sexologists, formulated similar rationalizations to make a distinction between their love and what they read about in medical books. That perception may have permitted many of them to live their lives as publicly as they did—in the presidents' houses on college campuses, the directors' apartments in settlement houses, the chiefs' offices in betterment organizations. They knew they were not men trapped in women's bodies, the inverts and perverts the sexologists were bringing to public attention. If they had to call themselves anything, they were romantic friends, devoted companions, unusual only in that they were anachronisms left over from purer times.

▼ ▼ ▼

## WHY SOME LESBIANS ACCEPTED THE CONGENITAL INVERT THEORY

Most sexologists were not very flattering in their views of inversion. August Forel was representative in his assumption that homosexual love is pathological in nature and "nearly all inverts are in a more or less marked degree psychopaths or neurotics." The new explanations for love between women made it degenerative and abnormal where earlier it was socially sanctioned. Those "explanations" eventually blew the cover of women whose sexual relationships with other women may have been hidden under the guise of romantic friendship. It would be logical to assume that women who loved other women would in a mass, categorically, reject the sexologists' theories, tainted as they were with traditionalism and stereotypes. And many women, finding the sexologists' theories disabling, did reject them. But a surprising number of women found them extremely enabling. They perceived real benefits in presenting themselves as congenital inverts.

It meant to some of them that romantic friendship would not have to give way to heterosexuality and marriage with the advent of a creditable male suitor. If they were born into the "intermediate sex," no family pressure or social pressure could change them. Their love for women was mysteriously determined by God or Nature. If their attraction to women was genital and they failed to keep that a secret, they could not in any case be seen as moral lepers. They were simply biological sports, as Natalie Barney, an American lesbian, wrote in her autobiography, reflecting the sexologists' influence on her conception of her own homosexuality: "I considered myself without shame: albinos aren't reproached for having pink eyes and whitish hair; why should they hold it against me for being a lesbian? It's a question of Nature. My queerness isn't a vice, isn't deliberate, and harms no one." The sexologists had provided that ready-made defense for homosexuality.

For the woman who was caught up with notions of gender-apppropriate behavior, the sexologists' views of the lesbian as a "man trapped in a woman's body" could be turned in her favor sexually if she wished: she could give herself permission to be sexual as no "normal" woman could. In her essay "The Mythic Mannish Lesbian," Esther Newton suggests that the congenital inversion theory must have appealed to some women because it was one of the few ways a woman could "lay claim to her full sexuality." The "normal" female's sexuality was supposed to be available for procreation and her husband's conjugal pleasure only. But if a female were not a female at all but a man trapped in a woman's body, it should not be condemnable nor surprising that her sexuality would assert itself as would a man's. Newton suggests that for decades the female invert was alone among women in her privilege of being avowedly sexual. Frances Wilder is an example of a woman who took that privilege. In a letter she wrote in 1915 to Edward Carpenter, a leading promoter of the congenital theory, she confessed that she harbored a "strong desire to caress and fondle" another female. Hoping to justify her sex drive, she explained that she experienced such a desire because she had within her not just "a dash of the masculine" but also a "masculine mind."

Such defenses, which attributed sexual difference to nature, also meant that those who identified themselves as homosexual could, for the first time, speak out against legal and social persecution. Lesbians (as women) were generally seen as being beneath the law and therefore ignored, with a few rare exceptions. But homosexual men and the lesbians who identified with their struggle through such groups as the German Scientific Humanitarian Committee used the congenital inversion theory to challenge legal sanctions against sodomy: the law and society had no business persecuting homosexuals, since their behavior was normal for them. And there was no reason for social concern about homosexual seduction, since someone who was not a congenital invert could not be seduced by a person of the same sex.

It was, in fact, much better to be a congenital invert than one who had the option of being heterosexual and chose homosexuality out of free will. Such a conscious choice in those unexistential times was an offense to society. As one American medical doctor, Joseph Parke, observed in 1906, "If the abnormality is congenital, clearly it cannot be a crime. If it be acquired it may be both vicious and criminal." For many, to claim a birth defect was preferable to admitting to willful perversity.

The spread of the congenital theory also informed many who loved the same sex that there were others like them. That information carried with it potential political and personal benefits that would have been impossible earlier. First in Europe and later in America, it encouraged those who wished to define themselves as homosexuals to organize publicly. The sexologists virtually gave them not only an identity and vocabulary to describe themselves, but also an armor of moral innocence. Once they knew there was a sizable minority like them, they could start looking for each other.

Already by 1890 some female "inverts" had joined the sexual underworld of big cities such as New York, where, along with male "inverts" in evening gowns, they attended balls at places such as Valhalla Hall in the Bowery, wearing tuxedos and waltzing with other more feminine-looking women. The women who attended such functions were perhaps the first conscious "butches" and "femmes." There could be no such social equivalents for women who loved women before the sexologists turned their attention to them, since earlier they had had no awareness of themselves as a group. In effect, the sexologists gave many of them a concept and a descriptive vocabulary for themselves, which was as necessary in forming a lesbian subculture as the modicum of economic independence they were able to attain at about the same time in history. Historian George Chauncey points out with regard to male homosexuals that the sexologists were merely "investigating an [existing] subculture rather than creating one" through their formulations of sexual inversion. And, indeed, there is good evidence to suggest that homosexual male subcultures have been in existence at least since the beginning of the eighteenth century. But for women who loved women the situation was somewhat different, since economic dependency on marriage had made it impossible for them to form such a subculture as early as male homosexuals did. The sexologists, emerging just as women's economic position was beginning to change, provided the crucial concept of sexual *type*—the female invert—for women who in earlier times could have seen themselves only as romantic friends or isolated women who passed as men. If the sexologist did not *create* a lesbian subculture, they certainly were the midwives to it.

The usefulness of the writings of the early sexologists has been felt even in more recent times by lesbians. Barbara Gittings recalls that in 1950 when she first realized she was homosexual she went to the library looking for more understanding of what that meant. Although she had to search under "Abnormal," "Perversion," and "Deviation," she remembers: "I did find my way to some good material. Though I couldn't identify with the women Ellis described, at least I knew that other female homosexuals existed. They were real-life people. That helped." The sexologists crystallized possiblities for young women that they would have had difficulty in conceptualizing on their own.

Thus some women who loved women were

happy about the sexologists' explanations of the etiology of their "problem." Perhaps those theories even seemed accurate to women who desired to be active, strong, ambitious, and aggressive and to enjoy physical relationships with other women: since their society adamantly defined all those attributes as male, they internalized that definition and did indeed think of themselves as having been born men trapped in women's bodies. For many of them, the image of their masculinity was an integral part of their sexual relationships and they became "butches" in the working-class and young lesbian subcultures, especially during the 1950s. If the only cultural models they saw of lovers of women were male, it is not unlikely that they might have pictured themselves as male when making love to a woman, just as the sexologists suggested.

The congenital theory even enjoyed some revival in the 1980s. While Freud's explanation of lesbianism as determined in childhood was the dominant view from the 1920s through the 1960s and the feminist explanation of lesbianism as a political choice held sway in the 1970s, more recently, perhaps in response to a perceived climate of conservatism, the congenital theory has reappeared in the guise of essentialism. Ignoring the evidence of the 1970s, when many women came to be lesbians through their feminist awareness, essentialists say that biology alone explains lesbianism, which is a permanent, fixed characteristic. One is a lesbian if one is born a lesbian, and nothing can make a lesbian a heterosexual. Heterosexuality is "natural" only to one who is born heterosexual, just as homosexuality is "natural" to the born lesbian. As an Austin, Texas, woman observed, "I'm a lesbian because of genetics, I'm sure my great-grandmother and grandmother were lesbians, even though they never came out." Her proof of their lesbianism, like many of the sexologists' "proofs," is only their feminism and their "masculinity": "They rebelled against playing traditional roles. They smoked, hunted, did carpentry at home. And they let me know it was okay for a young girl to do things." An adherence to the congenital theory is perhaps the safest position homosexuals can take during homophobic times when they fear they might be forced to undergo "treatment" to change their sexual orientation. And it serves to get parents or detractors off one's back. Essentialism is also a political strategy. Even in conservative periods, it encourages homosexuals to build their own culture and institutions with the conviction that since they are born different from heterosexuals they must find ways to rely on only themselves and others like them.

However, historically no less than today, there were other females who did not see themselves as having been born men trapped in women's bodies, despite the fact that they made their lives with other females and even had sexual relations with them. For these women, much of what the sexologists wrote was frightening or meaningless. Those who were scared by the sexologists' pronouncements perhaps ran into heterosexual marriages that would mask their feelings or lived as homosexuals but practiced furious homophobic

denial to the world. But many others must have been outraged at the imputation of degeneracy and rejected the theories out of hand, believing perhaps that there were some freaks somewhere such as those the medical men wrote about, but it had nothing to do with them. They simply loved a particular female, or they preferred to make their life with another woman because it was a more viable arrangement if one were going to pursue a career, or they did not think about it at all—they lived as they pleased and saw themselves as uncategorizable individuals.

# 1 6 1

# The Bowery as Haven and Spectacle

## GEORGE CHAUNCEY

At the end of the 1890s, Columbia Hall (better known as Paresis Hall), on the Bowery at Fifth Street, was, by all accounts, the principal resort in New York for degenerates and well known as such to the public. An investigator who visited the place several times in 1899 noted that he had heard of it constantly and that it made no attempt to disguise its well-known character as a resort for male prostitutes. Like other men, he found it easy to gain admittance to the Hall, despite the spectacle to be found within:

> These men . . . act effeminately; most of them are painted and powdered; they are called Princess this and Lady So and So and the Duchess of Marlboro, and get up and sing as women, and dance; ape the female character; call each other sisters and take people out for immoral purposes. I have had these propositions made to me, and made repeatedly.

An officer of the Reverend Charles Parkhurst's City Vigilance League, who had visited the place fully half a dozen times in April and May, added

that the "male degenerates" there worked the tables in the same manner female prostitutes did: "[They] solicit men at the tables, and I believe they get a commission on all drinks that are purchased there."

But if Paresis Hall was the principal such establishment in the red-light district centered in the working-class neighborhoods south of the Rialto (Fourteenth Street) at the turn of the century, it was hardly the only one. One well-informed investigator claimed in 1899 that there were at least six such "resorts" (saloons or dance halls) on the Bowery alone, including one called Little Bucks located across the street from Paresis. New York's chief of police added Manilla Hall, the Palm Club of Chrystie Street, and the Black Rabbit at 183 Bleecker Street to the list. North of the Rialto, on West Thirteenth Street between Fifth and Sixth Avenues, stood Samuel Bickard's Artistic Club, whose patrons were summarily arrested and fined for disorderly conduct on sev-

*Gay New York*, pp. 33–45. New York: Basic, 1994.

eral occasions. Five years later, just before a crackdown closed most of the resorts, the Jumbo and several other halls on the Bowery still functioned as "notorious degenerate resorts," according to the men who organized the crackdown, while the "chief attraction" of several places on Bleecker and Cornelia Streets was said to be "perversion."

This chapter sets the stage for our investigation of male (homo)sexual practices, cultures, and identities in the early twentieth century by offering a brief tour of the Bowery fairy resorts, an introduction to the neighborhood in which they developed, and an overview of the different places occupied by queer life in working- and middle-class culture. As the anti-vice crusaders who sought to reform the moral order of turn-of-the-century American cities discovered, gay male society was a highly visible part of the urban and sexual underworld and was much more fully and publicly integrated into working-class than middle-class culture. The subculture of the flamboyantly effeminate "fairies" (or "male degenerates") who gathered at Paresis Hall and other Bowery resorts was not the only gay subculture in the city, but it established the dominant public images of male sexual abnormality. Other men from different social milieus crafted different kinds of homosexual identities, as we shall see. But the prominence of the Bowery fairies and their consistency with the gender ideology of the turn of the century meant their image influenced the manner in which all homosexually active men understood their behavior.

It is not surprising that the Bowery was the center of the city's best-known sites of homosexual rendezvous at the turn of the century, for it was a center of other "commercialized vice" as well. Since early in the nineteenth century the Bowery, a wide boulevard cutting diagonally through the center of Manhattan's Lower East Side, had been the epicenter of a distinct working-class public culture, with its own codes of behavior, dress, and public sociability. When Italians, Jews, and other new immigrant groups replaced the Irish, Germans, and native-born white "Americans" as the largest working-class communities in that area of New York near the end of the century, the Bowery continued to play that role. The boulevard and surrounding streets were alive with theaters, dime museums, saloons, and dance halls, where men and women found relief from their jobs and crowded tenement homes.

To the horror of respectable but politically powerless Jews and Italians living nearby, the Bowery (along with an area known as the Tenderloin, which stretched up Broadway and Sixth Avenue from Twenty-third Street to Fortieth) was also a center of the city's institutions of "commercialized" sex. Next to the theaters and amusement halls stood the tenement brothels and assignation hotels that served the sexual interests of the large numbers of unmarried workingmen and married immigrants, unaccompanied by their wives, who lived in the neighborhood during their sojourn in this country. Along Broadway, Allen Street, Second Avenue, Fourteenth Street, and the Bowery itself, female prostitutes congregated to ply their trade. They made no effort to disguise their purpose, and the children who grew up on the Lower East Side quickly learned to identify them. The left-wing Jewish writer Mike Gold recalled of his street that "on sunshiny days the whores sat on chairs along the sidewalks. . . . [They] winked and leered, made lascivious gestures at passing males . . . call[ing] their wares like pushcart peddlers. At five years I knew what it was they sold."

He and his contemporaries also learned to recognize the fairies (as they were called) who congregated on many of the same streets. As one man complained in 1899, not only were there "male degenerates upon the Bowery in sufficient number to be noticeable," but "boys and girls get into these dance halls on the East Side [referring to Paresis and Manilla Halls], . . . [and] watch these horrible things." In 1908, when he was fifteen, Jimmy Durante got a job as a pianist at a Coney Island dive, where the customers included "the usual number of girls," by which he meant prostitutes, and the "entertainers were all boys who danced together and lisped." He insisted that none of this bothered him. On "the Bowery, where I was brought up," he boasted, "I had seen enough to get acclimated to almost anything."

But if the Bowery, like the Tenderloin, was an area where working-class men and women could engage in sexually charged encounters in public, it also took on particular significance in bourgeois ideology and life in the late nineteenth century as a so-called red-light district. Sociability was, in most respects, more privatized and ritualized in the city's middle-class neighborhoods. Higher incomes bought apartments or townhouses that provided greater privacy than was imaginable in the tenements, and socializing tended to take place at home, in restaurants, or in private clubs rather than on the stoop or in saloons open to the street. Indeed, men and women of the urban middle class increasingly defined themselves as a class by the boundaries they established between the "private life" of the home and the rough-and-tumble of the city streets, between the quiet order of their neighborhoods and the noisy overcrowded character of the working-class districts. The privacy and order of their sexual lives also became a way of defining their difference from the lower classes. Sexual reticence and devotion to family became hallmarks of the middle-class gentleman in bourgeois ideology, which presumed that middle-class men conserved their sexual energy along with their other resources. The poor and working classes, by contrast, were characterized in that ideology by their lack of such control; the apparent licentiousness of the poor, as well as their poverty, was taken as a sign of the degeneracy of the class as a whole. Middle-class ideology frequently interpreted actual differences in sexual values and in the social organization of middle-class versus working-class family life that grew out of their quite different material circumstances and cultural traditions as evidence of working-class depravity. It also tended to interpret even those working-class strategies adopted to sustain the integrity of the family as evidence of flagrant disregard for family values. Working-class families often took in boarders as a way to help preserve the family household by allowing women to stay at home with their children while also contributing to the family income, for instance. But middle-class observers condemned the practice as invasive of the privacy of the home and as a threat to the mother's sexual purity.

In this ideological context, the red-light district provided the middle class with a graphic representation of the difference between bourgeois reticence and working-class degeneracy. The spatial segregation of openly displayed "vice" in the slums had both practical and ideological consequences: it kept the most obvious streetwalkers out of middle-class neighborhoods, and it reinforced the association of such immorality with the poor. If the Bowery resorts served the interests of some working-class men and women and also appalled others of the same class who felt powerless to eliminate them, the red-light district also came to represent the sexual immorality of the working class as a whole in bourgeois ideology. This representation could take quite tangible form. Going slumming in the resorts of the Bowery and the Tenderloin was a popular activity among middle-class men (and even among some

women), in part as a way to witness working-class "depravity" and to confirm their sense of superiority. Mary Casal, a woman who took the tour, recalled years later that "it was considered very smart to go slumming in New York" in the 1890s, and many of her friends "were anxious to go again and again." But she went only once, she said, for she was stunned by "the ugliness of the displays we saw as we hurried from one horrid but famous resort to another in and about the Bowery," many of them full of male "inverts."

But if most slummers were suitably scandalized by what they saw, many were also titillated. Slumming gave men, in particular, a chance to cultivate and explore sexual fantasies by opening up to them a subordinate social world in which they felt fewer constraints on their behavior. It allowed them to escape the norms of middle-class propriety and, in particular, to shed the constraints they felt imposed on their conduct by the presence of respectable women of their own families or class. Resorts competed to offer them the most scandalous shows as well as music, drink, dancing, and, for a price, access to women and fairies of the lower classes with whom they could engage in ribald behavior inconceivable in their own social worlds.

At a time when New York was famous for being a "wide-open town," some clubs went so far as to stage live sexual performances, some of them designed to startle and engage their audiences by their transgression of normal racial and gender boundaries. In 1904, for instance, three hundred men, most of them apparently middle class, paid $2.50 (a fee high enough to exclude most laborers) to crowd into the back room of a saloon on Thirty-third Street between First and Second Avenues known as Tecumseh Hall & Hotel, which unions hired for their meetings on other nights. The lure was a live sex show that included sex between a black man and a white woman, between two women, and between a woman and a man in women's clothes. The employees arrested in 1900 in a raid on another club, the Black Rabbit on Bleecker Street, included the French floorman, known as the "Jarbean Fairy"; a twenty-year-old woman called a "sodomite for pay" by the anti-vice crusader Anthony Comstock (she had apparently engaged in sodomy with two men as part of the floor show); and a third person Comstock called a hermaphrodite, who had displayed her/his genitalia as part of the show.

A number of resorts made "male degenerates"

pivotal figures in their portrayal of working-class "depravity." Billy McGlory had realized as early as the late 1870s that he could further the infamy of Armory Hall, his enormous dance hall on Hester Street at the corner of Elizabeth, by hiring fairies—powdered, rouged, and sometimes even dressed in women's clothes—as entertainers. Circulating through the crowd, they sang, danced, and sometimes joined the best-paying customers in their curtained booths to thrill or disgust them with the sort of private sexual exhibitions (or "circuses") normally offered only by female prostitutes. By 1890, several more halls had added fairies as attractions, and the Slide, Frank Stevenson's resort at 157 Bleecker Street, had taken Armory Hall's place as New York's "worst dive" because of the fairies he gathered there.

The fairies' presence made such clubs a mandatory stop for New Yorkers out slumming and for the urban entrepreneurs who had made a business out of whetting and then satisfying the urge of men visiting the city to see the spectacle of the Sodom and Gomorrah that New York seemed to have become. As a *New York Herald* reporter observed in 1892:

> It is a fact that the Slide and the unspeakable nature of the orgies practised there are a matter of common talk among men who are bent on taking in the town, making a night of it. . . . Let a detective be opportuned by people from a distance to show them something *outre* in the way of fast life, the first ptace he thinks of is the Slide, if he believes the out-of-towner can stand it.

A retrospective account of slumming agreed. In 1915 a lawyer recalled the "Famous Old Time Dives [whose] Nation-Wide Evil Reputation Nightly Drew Throngs of 'Spenders' ": "No visitor ever left New York feeling satisfied unless he had inspected the mysteries of [Chinatown]," the heart of any city's red-light district, he claimed, but on his way back uptown the visitor almost always stopped on Bleecker Street to visit the Slide,

> one of the most vile, vulgar resorts in the city, where no man of decent inclinations would remain for five minutes without being nauseated. Here men of degenerate type were the waiters, some of them going to the extent of rouging their necks. In falsetto voices they sang filthy ditties, and when not otherwise

busy would drop into a chair at the table of any visitor who would brook their awful presence.

As the *Herald* story suggests, New Yorkers did not need to leave their armchairs to go slumming in the Bowery, for a new kind of metropolitan press had emerged in the city in the 1880s and 1890s that constructed a mass audience by focusing the public's attention on precisely such manifestations of urban culture. Joseph Pulitzer's *World* and William Randolph Hearst's *Journal* pioneered in those years a new style of journalism that portrayed itself as the nonpartisan defender (and definer) of the "public interest," waged campaigns on behalf of moral and municipal reform, and paid extravagant attention to local crimes, high-society scandals, and the most "sensational" aspects of the urban underworld. Their low prices and nonpartisan character allowed these newspapers to build a mass market to which advertisers could sell products; their journalistic voyeurism turned urban life itself into a commodity to be hawked at a penny a copy and helped mark the boundaries of acceptable public sociability. Fairies were not a staple of the new journalism's press campaigns, but they appeared regularly enough in the pages of New York's newspapers to alert any reader to their existence. The 1892 *Herald* story about the Slide, to take one example, included an extensive description of the resort, which must be regarded as an effort to titillate readers by supplying them with fulsome detail even as the paper asserted its own respectability by adopting a tone of reproach. "Here, Mr. Nicoll, Is a Place to Prosecute," the paper announced to the district attorney and the public in the headline it placed over the story.

But what the *Herald* reporter identified as evidence of depravity also points to the importance of the Bowery resorts to men who were fairies, for he made it clear that the Slide was a place where they felt free to socialize with their friends and to entertain not only the tourists but also the saloon's regulars and one another with their campy banter and antics. The night the reporter visited, he saw a group of men "bandying unspeakable jests with other fashionably dressed young fellows, whose cheeks were rouged and whose manner," he noted, using an expression normally reserved for describing female prostitutes, "suggested the infamy to which they had fallen." He later saw "half a score of the rouged and powdered men" sitting at a table on a raised dais in the center of the barroom, where they normally ensconced themselves to "amuse the company with their songs and simpering requests for drinks." One of them, either suspicious of the reporter's motives or interested in including him in the merriment, actually approached him (or "minced up to me and lisped," as the reporter put it) and asked for a drink.

While the reporter at least feigned outrage at the request, the other men present, as his account suggests, did not. Moreover, the record of another man's conversation with a "degenerate type" at the Slide also indicates that the men who were made part of the spectacle at such resorts nonetheless managed to turn them into something of a haven, where they could gather and find support. Charles Nesbitt, a medical student from North Carolina who visited the city around 1890, took the slummer's tour with a friend. As he later recalled, he visited several beer gardens on the Bowery where "male perverts, dressed in elaborate feminine evening costumes, 'sat for company' and received a commission on all the drinks served by the house to them and their customers." Such men dressed in male attire at the Slide, he discovered, but still sat for company as their transvestite counterparts did elsewhere. Intrigued, Nesbitt asked one of the men, known as "Princess Toto," to join his table; to his surprise, he found the fellow "unusually intelligent" and sophisticated. Princess Toto, he quickly decided, was "the social queen of this group" and "had pretty clear cut ideas about his own mental state and that of his fellows." Nature had made him this way, Toto assured the young medical student, and there were many men such as he. He indicated his pride in the openness of "my kind" at places like the Slide, calling them "superior" to the "perverts in artistic, professional and other circles who practice perversion surreptitiously." "Believe me," the student remembered him commenting, "there are plenty of them and they are good customers of ours."

Sensing the medical student's interest, Toto invited him to attend a ball at Walhalla Hall, one of the most prominent of the many Lower East Side halls that neighborhood social clubs rented to hold their affairs. Nesbitt went and discovered some five hundred same-sex male and female couples in attendance, "waltzing sedately to the music of a good band." Along with the male couples there were "quite a few . . . masculine looking women in male evening dress" dancing with other women, many of whom seem to have impressed the student as being of "good" background. "One could quite easily imagine oneself," he recalled with amused incredulity, "in a formal evening ball room among respectable people."

As the medical student discovered, the Bowery resorts were only the most famous element of an extensive, organized, and highly visible gay world. The men who sat for company at the Slide were part of a subculture that planned its own social events, such as the Walhalla ball, and had its own regular meeting places, institutions, argot, norms and traditions, and neighborhood enclaves. To worried anti-vice investigators and newspaper reporters, the Slide was an egregious manifestation of urban disorder and degeneracy. But to the men who gathered there, it served as a crucial institution in which to forge an alternative social order. Although middle-class gay men participated in the gay world, its public sites were restricted at the turn of the century to the working-class neighborhoods of the Bowery and waterfront, their very existence contingent on the ambivalent tolerance afforded them by working-class men.

The institutions and social forms of the gay subculture were patterned in many respects on those of the working-class culture in which it took shape: the saloons, small social clubs, and large fancy-dress balls around which fairy life revolved were all typical elements of working-class life. The core institutions of the gay subculture were a number of Lower East Side saloons, a few of them famous among slummers as "resorts" but most of them not on the slummers' map.

The role of the saloons is hardly surprising, since they were central to the social life of most working-class men, although their precise character varied among immigrant and other cultural groups. Located on every block in some tenement districts, saloons served as informal labor exchanges, where men could learn of jobs and union activities. Saloons cashed paychecks and made loans to men who had little access to banks, and they provided such basic amenities as drinking water and toilet facilities to men who lived in tenements without plumbing. Above all, they became virtual "workingmen's clubs," where poor men could escape crowded tenements, get a cheap meal, discuss politics and other affairs of the day, and in a variety of ways sustain their native cultural traditions of male sociability. Saloons were often attached to large public halls, which saloonkeepers made available for meetings of unions or social clubs, whose members returned the favor by patron-izing the bar. Most saloons also had smaller, more private back rooms, behind the public front barroom, where unmarried women and prostitutes sometimes were allowed to meet men and where patrons could engage in more intimate behavior than would be possible in the front.

Although saloons of varying degrees of affluence could be found throughout the city, they played a particularly critical role in those neighborhoods where social life was likely to be conducted on a sex-segregated basis and where housing was so crowded and inadequate that men had no alternative but to seek out such public spaces in which to socialize. In such neighborhoods these most public of establishments also afforded a degree of privacy unattainable in the patrons' own flophouses and tenements; many of the saloons even rented private rooms on an hourly basis to prostitutes and their customers and to other couples.

"Normal" men and "fairies" intermingled casually at many saloons, some of which were well known as "fairy places" in their neighborhoods. At some of them, fairies and their partners used the back rooms for sexual encounters, just as mixed-sex couples did. The Sharon Hotel, on Third Avenue just above Fourteenth Street, for instance, was known in the neighborhood as "Cock Suckers Hall," and investigators found a room behind the first-floor saloon where a dozen or more youths waited on male customers. "The boys have powder on their faces like girls and talk to you like disorderly girls talk to men," one investigator reported in the summer of 1901. He even observed several men having sex in the back room. On one occasion two of the fairies sat at a stout man's table, had him buy them drinks, and then unbuttoned his trousers and masturbated him "in front of everybody who was in the place." Five blocks north on Third Avenue at Twentieth Street stood Billy's Hotel, which investigators called "without a doubt . . . one of the worst houses of perverts in NYC." Seventy-five "Fairies" were found in the back room one evening in the spring of 1901, "dressed as women, [with] low neck dresses, short skirts, [and] blond wigs." Fairies who met men in the saloon could take them to rooms upstairs or to the basement, where they had keys to a row of bathhouse-like closets in which they could "carry on their business."

Although anti-vice investigators focused on the saloons' role as a site for sexual assignations, the saloons also functioned as important social centers for gay men, just as they did for other working-class men. They provided a place for gay men to meet, socialize, and enjoy one another's company. At Paresis Hall, for instance, Ralph Werther, a student living in New York in the 1890s and 1900s who later wrote an account of his experiences, discovered a whole society of "men of my type," for whom the hall was not the degenerate resort seen by slummers but a center of community and source of support. The fairies' appropriation of the resources available at Paresis Hall was emblematic of the way gay men appropriated and transformed the practices and institutions of their natal cultures as they forged their own. Many youths in the tenement districts, for instance, organized informal social clubs that rented rooms, often connected to saloons, as places for unsupervised gatherings, and that periodically sponsored larger parties or dances serving both to entertain the club's members and to raise funds for other outings. The Cercle Hermaphroditis, which Werther learned some of the men at Paresis Hall had organized, was such a club. It permanently rented a room above the bar, where members could gather by themselves and store their personal effects, since the laws against transvestism and the hostility of some men made it dangerous for them to be seen on the Bowery in women's attire. A "small colony of pederasts" said to exist on the Lower East Side in 1902 may have been another such social club, whose members organized social events and entertained other men at a saloon. "The members of this band," a surgeon reported having been told, "have a *théâtre comique*, where they perform and have their exclusive dances; they also 'pair off,' living together as husband and wife."

Such loosely constituted clubs and other gay social networks fostered and sustained a distinctive gay culture in a variety of ways. In addition to organizing dances and other social activities, the men who gathered at saloons and dance halls shared topical information about developments affecting them, ranging from police activity to upcoming cultural events. They assimilated into the gay world men just beginning to identify themselves as fairies, teaching them subcultural styles of dress, speech, and behavior. The clubs also strengthened the sense of kinship such men felt toward one another, which they expressed by calling themselves "sisters." Perhaps most important, they provided support to men ostracized by much of society, helping their members reject some of the harsh judgments rendered against them by many of their contemporaries. According to Ralph Werther, many of the fairies at Paresis Hall disparaged the implications of the slang name the slummers had given their meeting place, officially named Columbia Hall; paresis was a medical term for insanity, which outsiders thought men might acquire at the hall from syphilis or simply from asssociating with the fairies. Werther and his associates, by contrast, defended the hall as "the headquarters for avocational female-impersonators of the upper and middle classes." "Culturally and ethically," he emphasized in his account of the place, "its distinctive clientele ranked high." Werther also recorded numerous conversations among club members about the humiliations and harassment they had suffered at the hands of slummers, the police, and young toughs, but his reports also suggested that the conversations helped the men resist internalizing such hostility.

While the Bowery resorts and other saloons served as meeting places primarily for working-class men, gay and "normal" alike, they were also visited by middle-class men, and not only by uptown "sporting men" keen to spend an uninhibited night out on the town. Many uptown gay men visited them as well in order to escape the restrictions imposed on their conduct in their own social circles. Werther lived such a "double life," as he called it. At least once a week he left his respectable routine as a student at an uptown university (probably Columbia) in order to visit the streets and resorts of the Lower East Side, exchanging his normal gentleman's garb for more feminine attire. He took extravagant precautions to avoid being seen by his everyday acquaintances on the train or on the Bowery, for fear that "even my best friend would be likely to get me thrown out of my economic and social position" if he learned of Werther's life as a fairy. Werther and the other middle-class men he met on the Bowery went there because they found working-class men to be more tolerant of their kind than their middle-class colleagues and acquaintances were. Since "the 'classy,' hypocritical, and bigoted Overworld considers a bisexual [by which he meant an "intermediate type" or fairy] as monster and outcast," Werther claimed, "I was driven to a career in the democratic, frank, and liberal-minded Underworld." Drawing on the same imagery of heights and depths and light and shadow that many middle-class writers used to characterize the different class worlds and moral orders coexisting in the city, he added: "While my male soul was a leader in scholarship at the university uptown, my female soul, one evening a week, flaunted itself as a French doll-baby in the shadowy haunts of night life downtown." He quoted another middle-class man who claimed that he revealed his character only on the Bowery, and not in his own social circles, because "the world [by which he meant his own, middle-class world] thinks female impersonation disgraceful, [and] I had to spare my family all risk."

▼ ▼ ▼

As even this brief tour suggests, the gay world had become part of the spectacle of the Bowery by the 1890s. At a time when New York was a notoriously "wide-open" city, "degenerate resorts" and "fairy back room saloons" were a highly visible feature of the city's sexual underworld, spotlighted by the press and frequented by out-of-town businessmen and uptown slummers alike. The gay world was, moreover, remarkably integrated into the life of the working-class neighborhoods in which it took shape. Gay men not only modeled their own social clubs and events on those of other working-class men, but socialized extensively and overtly with "normal" working-men as well. Most of the saloons they frequented were patronized by a mixed crowd of gay and straight men. This was not because there were too few gay men to support a separate gay saloon culture. One investigator reported seeing some seventy-five fairies at a single saloon in 1901, after all, and a decade earlier a medical student had seen hundreds of same-sex couples dancing at a masquerade hall. The number of "mixed" saloons reveals instead the degree to which gay culture was tolerated by—and integrated into—working-class culture and the degree to which social and sexual interactions between "queer" and "normal" men were central to gay life. Gay men, as we shall see, sometimes had to fight to claim their place in working-class neighborhoods, but there was room for them in working-class culture to claim such a place.

Indeed, the saloons and other resorts where gay and straight men interacted were a highly revealing part of male sexual culture at the turn of the century, complex institutions playing varying roles for different constituencies and capable of multiple cultural meanings. In keeping with their working-class origins, they were the most commercialized and visible sites of gay sociability in the city; middle-class gay culture, as we shall see, tended to be more circumspect, as was middle-class culture generally at the turn of the century. A source of scandal and titillation for uptown slummers, the resorts were also a source of support and communal ties for middle- and working-class fairies alike. And to the horror of middle-class reformers—and the great curiosity of latter-day historians—they were a central site of a distinctly working-class male culture in which "fairies" and "normal" men publicly— and sexually—interacted with remarkable ease.

# I. B
# WHO'S A QUEER? IDENTITIES IN QUESTION

People are not born with the awareness that they are homosexual, bisexual, or heterosexual. Before they can identify themselves in terms of these categories they must learn that such categories exist, discover that other people occupy them, and perceive that their own needs or attractions qualify them for membership. To "become" a lesbian or gay man, then, one must first learn the system of social meanings associated with such a role and interpret one's own desires accordingly (Troiden 1988).

In a society that expects all children to become heterosexuals, however, lesbians and gay men follow a different developmental pathway than their heterosexual peers. As adolescents, most yield to parental and peer pressure and participate in the heterosexual "rating, dating, and mating" scene (Troiden 1988:13). They experiment sexually and romantically with members of the other sex. Meanwhile, they may be aware of same-sex attractions that prevent them from integrating these experiences psychologically. Perhaps they have sensed since childhood that they are "different" from others, even when they lacked words or concepts with which to articulate this difference. As a result, gays and lesbians often identify themselves relatively late in life, and to do so must "unlearn" certain assumptions acquired during childhood. As Troiden has noted, "becoming homosexual is a form of adult resocialization" (1988:2).

Several researchers have described the stages through which individuals typically pass as they consolidate a lesbian or gay identity. These so-called stage models are based on the averaged

experiences of many people and may not describe the trajectory of any particular individual. Not all lesbians or gay men pass through the stages in exactly the same way; nor do the stages always follow the same order. As Troiden has remarked: "Progress through the stages occurs in a back-and-forth, up-and-down fashion," like a spring lying on its side (42). Even so, stage models are useful generalizations, and several have been proposed (Ponse 1978; Cass 1979; McDonald 1982; Plummer 1975). The four-stage model below was described by Troiden (1988).

1. The first stage, *sensitization*, typically begins before puberty. During this stage, youngsters may not think that homosexuality has anything to do with them—if they think about sexual identities at all. Indeed, they may have little or no awareness that homosexuality even exists. Since childhood they have been pressured by parents and peers to assume that they are heterosexual and may already have experimented with friends of the other sex. At the same time, however, they experience "generalized feelings of marginality, perceptions of being different from same-sex peers" (Troiden 1988:43).

While these childhood feelings are not yet sexual in nature, they sensitize an individual to subsequent self-definition as homosexual. For example, when asked if they felt "very much or somewhat different" from the other boys and girls in grade school, gay men were twice as likely as heterosexual men (72 percent versus 39 percent of heterosexual controls) to report that they had experienced such feelings. Likewise, 72 percent of lesbians (versus 54 percent) reported having felt different and set apart during childhood. While as children few of the men and women (20 percent) interpreted these feelings in sexual terms, they now look back on them as signs of an emerging lesbian or gay identity (Bell, Weinberg and Hammersmith 1981).

2. The second stage is *identity confusion*. By adolescence lesbians and gay men typically have begun to personalize homosexuality, as same-sex feelings or experiences lead them to question their own sexual identities. They no longer take heterosexuality for granted, but have not yet affirmed a lesbian or gay identity; the result is a period of turmoil and uncertainty. Cass (1984) describes the onset of identity confusion in this way: "You are not sure who you are. You are confused about what sort of person you are and where your life is going. You ask yourself the questions 'Who am I?,' 'Am I a homosexual?,' 'Am I really a heterosexual?' " (156).

As the confusion is resolved, childhood anxieties about being different begin to crystallize in the perception that one is *sexually* different. It is during this phase that individuals first seek out information about homosexuals and homosexuality. Before they can see themselves as lesbian or gay, they must realize that such categories exist, learn what they entail, and perceive themselves as being similar to those who are so labeled. As a seventeen year old, Christopher, recalls: "It is impossible to say just when I realized I was gay. Looking back, I can see that I have always liked other boys, but it wasn't until I was thirteen that I learned the name for my passion was 'homosexuality' " (Heron 1983:19).

In areas where accurate information about homosexuality is unavailable, individuals may find it difficult to acknowledge and label their own homosexual feelings; in other settings, in which information is widely disseminated, adolescents may be well-informed and may pass through this phase more quickly.

3. In the stage of *identity assumption* individuals learn more about homosexuality and begin to define themselves as homosexuals. They may seek out other homosexuals, experiment sexually, and explore the lesbian and gay subculture by frequenting places where other homosexuals are thought to congregate: lesbian or gay bars, parties, parks, gyms, or neighborhoods (Lynch 1987). As Troiden (1988) explains, these early contacts are of tremendous significance. Positive experiences facilitate lesbian or gay identity formation, providing opportunities for an individual to obtain information about the community, to reexamine

his or her own ideas about homosexuality, and to see similarities between him or herself and those labeled "homosexual." Conversely, unfavorable contacts may prompt an individual to reject a lesbian or gay identity ("I'm not really a homosexual"), abandon homosexual behavior ("I can get along without it"), or reject both identity and behavior ("I can become heterosexual and learn to desire the opposite sex") (Troiden 1988:53).

By the end of the identity assumption stage people have begun to accept themselves as lesbians or gay men, perhaps even to reveal this identity to others. While ages vary, retrospective studies of adult homosexuals suggest that gay males arrive at these self-definitions between the ages of nineteen and twenty-one (Harry and Devall 1978; McDonald 1982; Troiden 1988), while lesbians recall achieving self-definition slightly later, between the ages of twenty-one and twenty-three (Califia 1979; Riddle and Morin 1977).

4. The final phase, *commitment*, involves increased comfort with a lesbian or gay identity and affirmation of the accompanying lifestyle. There are both internal and external signs of this final stage. Externally, individuals may enter their first long-term love relationships, participate in community activities, subscribe to gay publications, or become politically active. Internally, individuals' same-sex attractions are reconceptualized as being "natural" or "normal," an essential part of their personality rather than a passing phase (Ponse 1978). They begin to distinguish "true" homosexuals from those who are merely experimenting or confused (Warren 1974). They may also begin to view homosexuality more positively, questioning the negative associations they acquired in childhood. Not every individual achieves the commitment stage of self-identification as lesbian or gay. Indeed, one limitation of all stage models is their tendency to imply a linear "gay trajectory": initial awareness of same-sex feelings that progresses to homosexual behavior, self-labelling, self-disclosure, and the eventual stabilization of a positive gay identity. Not all men or women follow this path or reach the same milestones. One study (McDonald 1982) found that *on the average* it took eleven years from the time respondents became aware of same-sex feelings to the point at which they viewed themselves as positively gay-identified. Typically, they became aware of same-sex attractions at age thirteen, first learning the word *homosexual* two years later, about the time they had their first sexual experiences. Self-labeling occurred four years later, at an average age of nineteen, and self-disclosure to

a significant nongay person (such as a parent, friend, or employer) took place at age twenty-three.

But there were numerous deviations from the path. One in five men (18 percent) skipped a stage, labeling themselves homosexual in the absence of any overt same-sex experiences. Others (15 percent) had not yet reached the fourth stage and were still plagued by identity confusion. In his 1977 study of the Toronto gay community, for example, Lee estimated that between twenty and thirty thousand men were engaging in sex with other men. Yet less than half this number frequented gay institutions (such as bars, bookstores, or political meetings) in which they could socialize with other gay men, learn about gay life, and see themselves as members of a gay community.

The models outlined by these researchers often implicity accept the notion of a "lesbian and gay community" as the (desirable) endpoint of the coming out trajectory. But we should be wary of an unquestioning belief in either the form or the function of that community. As Stein ( "Becoming Lesbian," this volume) illustrates with the example of an Asian American lesbian arriving in the Castro in the mid-1970s, the image and behavior patterns that comprise lesbian and gay identities are generally defined by the experiences and expectations of white, middle-class women and men. This is entirely consistent with the overall influence of race and class bias in American society and is further amplified by the selectivity with which the mass media choose and craft the images they will disseminate. Finally, the relative privilege of the white and well-off is reflected in the burgeoning lesbian and gay media that market increasingly upscale products in their expanding glossy pages. For many lesbian women and gay men of color the pull of competing identities complicates their relationships to an overarching lesbian and gay community, however much they may resonate to its claim of an underlying basis for membership. And these alternative identity categories themselves are not without their own complexities and internal divisions (Beam,"Making Ourselves from Scratch"; Takagi, "Maiden Voyage," this volume).

The proliferation of ethnic and national identities has a parallel within the sexual minority community. The possibility of a unified lesbian and gay identity has been further challenged in recent years by the emergence of groups claiming a distinct identity and equal billing under the larger umbrella of sexual nonconformity. Leading the way in this latest labeling campaign are bisexuals (Queen, "Strangers at Home"; Wilson, "Just Add

Water," this volume). No longer willing to be seen as occupying a halfway house in the coming out process, or as being a hybrid category occupying positions 2 through 5 on Kinsey's zero-to-six scale of sexual behaviors, women and men who insist that they are attracted to members of both sex have claimed an independently valid identity. "When asked why their struggle is emerging now, some bis draw comparisons to the late '60s, when lesbians and gays who had apprenticed in the civil rights and peace movements grew radicalized enough to make their own demands. Today, bis who apprenticed in the gay movement claim a similar awakening" (Rotello 1992). It is easy to see why many have been attracted to the simple inclusiveness of the label *queer* to gather all nonconformist sexualities under one big tent. But a big tent does not guarantee peaceable coexistence.

In the early years of lesbian and gay liberation there was a widely shared sense that gay people were suddenly free to discover and reveal the "true" self that had been denied and erased by heterosexist society. In this way lesbians and gay men would be freed from the straitjacket of gender conformity. As Stein (this volume) notes, the result often was the substitution of a new conformity for the old. An early devotion to the concept of fluidity in sexuality—"overcoming the enormous amount of repression of bisexuality that is part of our whole social fabric" (Altman 1972:18)—quickly turned into an (often politicized) expectation of exclusive homosexuality. However, the waters did not remain neatly parted, with lesbians, gay men, and heterosexuals neatly confined to their distinct riverbeds. As Gayle Rubin put it,

> In the 1960s, the important stratifications were pretty much understood to be caste, class, and race. One of the great contributions of feminism was to add gender to that list. By the early 1980s, it had become clear to me that adding gender did not take care of the issues of sexual persecution, and that sexuality needed to be included as well. (1994:91).

Adding a focus on sexuality meant acknowledging the variability of sexual orientation and sexual behavior both over a lifetime and, even more controversially, at more or less the same time. Sex radical Pat Califia, noting that "gay people have responded to persecution and homophobia by creating our own mythologies about homosexuality," set off a steady barrage of ideological depth charges by writing candidly about her sexual experiences and identities (this volume). But even without going as "far out" as Califia—a lesbian sadomasochist who has sex with faggots—it was not difficult to encounter queers who resist being confined within the neat categories of lesbian and gay. And it was also not difficult to witness firestorms of emotion and hostile attacks in response to such manifestations of nonconformity. In the 1980s the "sex wars" featured denunciations and excommunications of women considered unworthy of the title lesbian or feminist (see "The Good Parts: Pornography," this volume). In 1990 longtime lesbian activist Jan Clausen wrote about her involvement with a man—"my interesting condition"—and provoked numerous letters denouncing her as "a danger to the lesbian community far greater than any threat by homophobes" (Conforti 1990).

On campus after campus across the country in the late 1980s student groups were challenged to reflect the diversity of alternative sexual identities. At the University of Pennsylvania the group that began life in the mid-seventies as Gays at Penn and changed its name in the early eighties to Lesbians and Gays at Penn was, by 1989, called the Lesbian, Gay and Bisexual Alliance. Similarly, at the Fifth Lesbian and Gay Studies Conference, held at Rutgers in 1991, a motion was adopted that henceforth there would be Lesbian, Gay and Bisexual Studies Conferences. But it didn't stop there; it wasn't long before demands were heard for further expansion to include transsexuals and transgendered people, the latest group demanding to be accepted on its own terms (Feinberg, "To Be or Not to Be," this volume). The term *trans* is coming into use to cover everyone who challenges the boundaries of sex and gender. It is also used to draw a distinction between those who reassign the sex they were labeled at birth and those of us whose gender expression is considered inappropriate for our sex (Feinberg 1996:x).

As we approach a new century we know that the definitions and demands associated with sexual and gender identities will not remain fixed. We are far from the apparent certainty of the 1950s, but it is not yet clear where our journey will end.

## REFERENCES

Altman, Dennis. 1981 [1972]. "Forum on Sexual Liberation." In Dennis Altman, *Coming Out in the Seventies*, pp. 16–20. Boston: Alyson.

Bell, Alan P., Martin S. Weinberg, and Sue Kiefer Hammersmith. 1981. *Sexual Preference: Its Development in Men and Women*. Bloomington: Indiana University Press.

Califia, Pat. 1979. "Lesbian Sexuality." *Journal of Homosexuality*, 4(3):255–266.

Cass, Vivienne C. 1979. "Homosexual Identity Formation: A Theoretical Model." *Journal of Homosexuality*, 4(3):219–235.

Cass, Vivienne C. 1984. "Homosexual Identity: A Concept in Need of Definition." *Journal of Homosexuality*, 9(2–3):105–126.

Clausen, Jan. 1990. "My Interesting Condition." *Out/Look* (winter), pp. 10–21.

Conforti, Lucia. 1990. "Letter to the Editor." *Out/Look* (summer), pp. 7, 78.

Feinberg, Leslie. 1996. *Transgender Warriors*. Boston: Beacon.

Harry, Joseph and William B. DeVall. 1978. *The Social Organization of Gay Males*. New York: Praeger.

Heron, Ann, ed. 1983. *One Teenager in Ten: Writings by Gay and Lesbian Youth*. Boston: Alyson.

Lee, John Alan. 1977. "Going Public: A Study in the Sociology of Homosexual Liberation," *Journal of Homosexuality*, 3(1):49–78.

Lynch, Frederick R. 1987. "Non-Ghetto Gays: A Sociological Study of Suburban Homosexuals." *Journal of Homosexuality*, 13(4):13–42.

McDonald, Gary J. 1982. "Individual Differences in the Coming Out Process for Gay Men." *Journal of Homosexuality*, 8(1):47–60.

Plummer, Kenneth. 1975. *Sexual Stigma: An Interactionist Account*. London: Routledge and Kegan Paul.

Ponse, Barbara. 1978. *Identities in the Lesbian World: The Social Construction of Self*. Westport, Conn.: Greenwood.

Riddle, Dorothy I. and Stephen F. Morin. 1977. "Removing the Stigma: Data from Individuals." *APA Monitor*, November, pp. 16, 28.

Rotello, Gabriel. 1992. "Bi Any Means Necessary." *Village Voice*, June 30, pp. 37–38.

Rubin, Gayle. 1994. "Sexual Traffic: Interview with Judith Butler" *Differences*, 6(2–3):62–99.

Troiden, Richard R. 1988. *Gay and Lesbian Identity: A Sociological Analysis*. New York: General Hall.

Warren, Carol A. B. 1974. *Identity and Community in the Gay World*. New York: Wiley.

# | 7 |

## *Making Ourselves from Scratch*

### Joseph Beam

Each morning as I wipe the sleep from my eyes, don the costume that alleges my safety, and propel myself onto the stoop, I know with the surety of the laws of gravity that my footsteps fall in a world not created in my image. It is not in the newspapers, in store windows, nor is it on the television screen. Too often, it is not in the eyes of my sisters who fear my crack, nor is it present in the countenance of my brothers who fear the face that mirrors our anger. At day's end, having done their bidding, I rush home to do my own: creating myself from scratch as a black gay man.

My desk and typing table anchor the northeast corner of my one-room apartment. There are days that I cling to both objects as if for sanity. On the walls surrounding me are pictures of powerful people, mentors if you will. Among them are: Audre Lorde, James Baldwin, John Edgar Wideman, Essex Hemphill, Lamont Steptoe, Judy Grahn, Tommi Avicolli, Charles Fuller, Toni Morrison, and Barbara Smith. These writers, of local and international fame, are connected by their desire to create images by which they could survive as gays and lesbians, as blacks, and as poor people. Their presence in my writing space bespeaks what another writer, Samuel Delany, calls "the possibility of possibilities."

But it has not always been this way. I have not always known of the possibilities. In the winter of '79, in grad school, in the hinterlands of Iowa, I thought I was the first black gay man to have ever lived. I knew not how to live my life as a man who desired emotional, physical, and spiritual fulfillment from other men. I lived a guarded existence: I watched how I crossed my legs, held my cigarettes, the brightness of the colors I wore. I was sure that some effeminate action would alert the world to my homosexuality. I spent so much

energy in self-observation that little was left for classwork and still less to challenge the institutionalized racism I found there. I needed heroes, men and women I could emulate. I left without a degree; the closet door tightly shut.

Several years passed before I realized that my burden of shame could be a source of strength. It was imperative for my survival that I did not attend to or believe the images that were presented of black people or gay people. Perhaps that was the beginning of my passage from passivism to activism, that I needed to create my reality, that I needed to create images by which I, and other black gay men to follow, could live this life.

The gay life is about affectation, but style is not image making. Style, at best, is an attitude, a reaction to oppression, a way of being perceived as less oppressed, a way of feeling attractive when we are deemed unattractive. The most beleaguered groups—women, people of color, gays, and the poor—attend most intently to style and fashion. But is it important to know who tailored the suit Malcolm X wore when he was killed? For a people who fashioned beautiful gowns and topcoats from gunnysack, it's nothing, nothing at all, that we can work some leather, fur, or gold. The lives we lead are richer than Gucci or Waterford; our bodies more fit than Fila or Adidas; our survival more real than Coca-Cola.

As African Americans, we do not bequeath dazzling financial portfolios. We pass from generation to generation our tenacity. So I ask you: What is it that we are passing along to our cousin

In Essex Hemphill, ed., *Brother to Brother: New Writings by Black Gay Men*, pp. 261–262. Boston: Alyson, 1991.

from North Carolina, the boy down the block, our nephew who is a year old, or our sons who may follow us in this life? What is it that we leave them beyond this shadow-play: the search for a candlelit romance in a poorly lit bar, the rhythm and the beat, the furtive sex in the back street? What is it that we pass along to them or do they, too, need to start from scratch?

# | 8 |

# Becoming Lesbian: Identity Work and the Performance of Sexuality

## ARLENE STEIN

When Margaret Berg first slept with a woman, her lover declared herself to be a lesbian immediately afterward. She had what she calls a "coming home" experience. For Margaret, however, the experience was far less significant.

> After the first time we made love, for her it was like, Well, now we were lovers. And to me, it was much more, OK, I tried this, but it was much more along the lines of sexual experimentation. . . . Maybe I'll do it again, maybe I won't.

Margaret's lover had "much more self-consciously identified homoerotic feelings" than she did. "I hadn't thought about the whole thing very much. It was much more consciously on her agenda," she recalled. "She was the one to make the first moves." At times, this sense of dissonance was echoed by others. Margaret recalls her lover saying to her early in their relationship: "Sometimes I think I'm a lesbian and you're not."

Laura Stone recalls her first lesbian experience as a nineteen year old in 1969, "We slept together and kind of fumbled through it." While her friend declared herself to be a lesbian immediately after this experience, she resisted. "I knew that I didn't feel like *aha*, I was coming home. I didn't feel like, What a relief to shed this charade. I didn't feel like where have I been all my life. But I wasn't repulsed either." After recognizing that her initial sexual response to women was muted in comparison to other women she knew, Laura quickly became known to others as "the straight woman who was messing around with gay women." These feelings were seen as a source of inadequacy and were therefore kept private, con-

fined to a sort of personal inner dialogue.

Within the culture of a social movement in which identity provided an entry into political participation, and was often seen as a end in itself, some women's worst fear was that they would be unable to develop *any* identity at all. Mary Lipton recalled:

> For the longest time, I was afraid that I wasn't anything. I wasn't gay or straight. That I was the only person in the entire world who wasn't anything. I was turned off to men but hadn't fallen in love with a woman. I actually slept with a woman, but it was not a good experience. . . . I really wasn't sure what I was. I thought maybe I was nothing.

Unlike those who experienced themselves as more *internally* driven toward homosexuality, some women initially experienced a lack of congruence between their "deep" sense of self (or personal identity) and the social category lesbian; they "tried on" a lesbian identity and decided it didn't quite "fit." Sometimes this incongruence was manifested as a lack of emotional and physical response in initial sexual encounters; homosexual *behavior* did not itself guarantee the development of a lesbian *identity*. A sexual involvement alone was not enough to authenticate their lesbianism; it did not necessarily move them through the path of lesbian development.[1] Some left the lesbian fold, driven out by their perception that they were not "real" lesbians.

But the recognition that there were different

Arlene Stein, *Sex and Sensibility: Stories of a Lesbian Generation*, pp. 65–90. Berkeley: University of California Press, 1997. Excerpt.

types of lesbians, and that some women initially had an easier time claiming an identity than others, strengthened their resolve to undertake "identity work" to claim lesbian selfhood. As Laura Stone put it,

> I knew that some part of me felt like I couldn't move further towards women, and that I was being scared off from that, being scared off from going my own route. Part of me thought that it's because it's not supposed to be. . . . So it was almost like I saw myself desensitized to the socialization of the society, but I was straight identified. At no point in that process did I think of myself as a lesbian. But I thought I could *become* a lesbian.

## IDENTITY WORK

Accounts of "coming out" among lesbian feminists imagined the process as a journey that began with a discovery of the lesbian within one's sense of self and proceeded through time, as the individual moves from an oppressive environment to one that permits a freer and bolder state of self and public expression (Zimmerman, 1990:34–75). Coming out signified the claiming, or reclaiming, of that which is essential, true, unchanging. But coming out is as much a practical creation of the self, a "be-coming out," as a matter of revealing or discovering one's sexuality.

"Coming out is partially a process of revealing something kept hidden, but it is also more than that," writes political philosopher Shane Phelan. "It is a process of fashioning a self—a lesbian or gay self—that did not exist before coming out began" (1993:774).[2] Identities do not spring forth effortlessly from individuals: individuals reflexively effect change in the meanings of particular identities. Becoming a lesbian always entails participating in particular communities and discourses, and conforming to historical and localized norms for "being" a lesbian. A lesbian identity is learned and performed in a myriad of different ways. Particularly for women who "originally" experienced themselves as heterosexual or bisexual, and who became lesbians in a very self-conscious way, through the influence of feminism, coming out as a lesbian often entailed a great deal of work.

Sociologist Barbara Ponse describes identity work as the "processes and procedures engaged in by groups designed to effect change in the meanings of particular identities" (Ponse, 1978). I use the term similarly, to signify the process by which

many individuals sought to achieve congruence between their emergent social identity as lesbian and their subjective sense of self, and to narrow the experiential gap separating them from other, more experienced lesbians. For women of the baby boom cohort the identity work required to "become lesbian" took different forms, forms that often derived from feminist reinterpretations and reversals of dominant gender and sexual norms.

Erving Goffman has shown that on the level of surfaces, of self-presentation, individuals use gestures and symbols, "signs that convey social information," as a means of self-presentation. This type of identity work signals membership in the group to others.[3] A second dimension of emotion work offers instructions about how to do "deep acting," by trying to alter one's inner thoughts so as to feel differently and so look as though one feels differently too.[4] Arlie Hochschild proposes that people are more likely to seek interactional rules for both of these levels of management in "times of great social transition," when they often find themselves in previously unknown situations with no social rules at hand. An emergent culture would need to codify rules for management of both symbols and emotions in order to successfully organize members' interactions (Kraus, 1992:4–8).

Indeed, my interviewees described a period, the 1970s, when gender and norms were highly contested and often very fluid. Acts of identity work conveyed membership and position within the lesbian subculture to other members while at the same time managing the communication of this stigmatic information to members of the larger society. They also effected change in personal identities, altering the ways in which individuals thought about themselves. In terms of "surface" identity work, individuals changed their dress and mannerisms to more closely conform to what a real lesbian "looked like." They also engaged in the public telling of coming out stories. But, on a deeper level, individuals consciously alter not only surface characteristics, such as symbols or gestures, but also inner characteristics such as emotions and desires. By looking at these performances we can more fully grasp the complexity of sexual identity formation.

## TELLING STORIES

In modern life there are numerous incitements for individuals to "confess" the "truth" of our lives. The Catholic confessional, in which an individual speaks of deep dark secrets in order to expunge one's sins is joined by the psychoanalytic couch, in which the analysand is encouraged to probe the depths of her unconscious. Among lesbians and gay men the coming out narrative has become a kind of collective confessional that seeks to free the individual from his/her sexual repression, and, at the same time, to build a culture and community around a "reverse affirmation" of shared stigma.[5]

Many of my interviewees who came of age during the 1970s were introduced to the idea of coming out through their participation in feminist "consciousness-raising." In c-r groups women talked about their personal problems as women — their unsatisfying relationships with men, their feelings of inferiority and powerlessness. Within the context of a consciousness-raising group, "small group," or "rap group," as they were sometimes called, many women came to recognize that the "personal is political" and to think of themselves as members of a collectivity of women. They also came to recognize their deep feelings for other women. One woman recalled:

As women turned to each other for affection and support that we had previously sought in men, many sensual feelings were liberated. At meetings we gave each other hugs and backrubs; in the streets we began to walk arm in arm. We felt a new freedom to explore our feelings for each other. Some of us made love with women we loved; some of us "came out." For some women lesbianism was an extension of the desire to be completely self-sufficient. Or, many times, the women's movement provided a safe enough place to open up new sexual feelings.

As gender and sexual boundaries were being blurred, and the meanings of sexuality were being redefined, consciousness-raising groups often became coming out groups in which individuals were socialized into the lesbian world. In the language of the day, discovering one's lesbianism was a matter of unearthing that which was repressed and hidden, that which was negated by the compulsory heterosexuality of the dominant culture.

As Laura Stone recalled: "People didn't feel so freaked out about the idea of women loving women. It was the idea of women not loving men that was so offensive." Hence, it took a great deal of courage, and a new set of values, to go against the social grain. As a 1972 lesbian feminist tract suggested, this passage entailed the fashioning of

a new self, but a self that, in contrast to the formerly "feigned" heterosexual self, was actually "truer" to the individual (Abbott and Love, 1972:223).

Coming out was conceptualized as a difficult "task," which one had to be "ready" to undertake and for which homosexual desire was not necessarily a prerequisite. The core sense of self was imagined to be fluid and malleable, a rough piece of clay that needed to be shaped. Coming out was a matter of "coming to consciousness" and socializing the individual into a new existence as a lesbian. Consciousness-raising was "a reconditioning experience designed to shed layer after layer of trained negative thinking and free the vital self which oppression has so effectively buried" (Esther Newton, in Abbott and Love, 218).

The coming out story, the account of the passage into the lesbian/gay world, was the gay community's "development myth." It was an account of heroism in the face of tremendous odds and societal pressure that was based on the ideal of being "true to oneself," expressing one's "authentic" self, a central theme in American culture in the twentieth century.[6] When forty-four-year-old Sarah Marcus became involved with a woman for the first time, she did not think of herself as a "lesbian." A lesbian, she thought, was a woman for whom lesbian desires had always been "primary," a woman who had never desired men. She did not fit this description. But it was through her involvement in feminism that Sarah joined a consciousness-raising group. In that group she began to self-identify as lesbian. The coming out group helped to bridge the gap between herself and more "experienced" lesbians. Sarah took great joy in telling her coming out story every opportunity she got.

The telling of coming out stories was a public act that served as a type of "identity announcement," which directed an individual's conduct and influenced that of others. Telling one's coming out story had the effect of announcing one's membership in the group to others. But it also had the effect of defining and sharpening the teller's interest in a situation and thus more sharply focusing attention on those situated events found relevant to that identity (Hewitt, 1989:167). In telling these stories, individuals ordered their subjective reality, isolating and recalling the defining events, contexts, or ideas gave symbolic order to their lesbian trajectory. This telling served to reinforce the teller's commitment to a lesbian identity. As Judith Butler suggests, "It is through the repeated play of this sexuality that the 'I' is insistently reconstituted as a lesbian 'I.' In other words, the repetition of a culturally constructed characteristic reproduces the identity of lesbianism, of homosexuality (Butler, 1991:311).

In the context of the lesbian/gay community, coming out is a status passage that tends to be highly ritualized. It is a collective narrative, an "identity story" that possessed certain conventions and rules. Describing the coming out narrative as it operated in a Southern city in the mid-1970s, Barbara Ponse isolated five atemporal component elements that she called the "gay trajectory." The first element is that the individual has a "subjective sense of being different" from heterosexual persons and "identifies this difference as feelings of sexual-emotional attachment to her own sex." Second, she develops an understanding of the "homosexual or lesbian significance of these feelings." Third, the individual "accepts these feelings and their implications for identity"—the individual comes out or accepts the identity as lesbian. Fourth, the individual "seeks a community of like persons. "Given one of these elements," says Ponse, "irrespective of their order in time, it is commonly assumed in the lesbian world that the others will logically come to pass" (Ponse, 1978:125).

When coming out stories were told publicly, there was a tendency to present a relatively homogeneous, seamless narrative. Some individuals reported experiencing a strain toward rewriting their personal biographies in order to emphasize their sense of authenticity. Though they recognized that early on they did not "feel" like lesbians, upon coming out they conceived of their new status as a personal essence, some inner quality of being, which came to feel "natural." Laura Stone acknowledged that, unlike many of her lesbian friends, her coming out was not a matter of "coming home." She did not experience her lesbianism as "primary" or highly driven. Yet through the process of consciousness-raising she came to see herself as a lesbian, albeit one who was "going through a different path of coming out."

Symbolic interactionist literature on identity construction speaks of the ways people experiencing "conversions" of identity are prone to "recasting the past" to bring the past into line with the present (Berger and Luckmann, 1967; Ponse, 1978). Coming out stories, like all narratives of the self, are incomplete selective renderings of personal history, shaped by the needs of the present as much as the past. In interviewing people about their lives, particularly about the past, it is impossible to know the "truth." What we know is what individuals want us to know, how they represent themselves to those around them.

Many women who came out "through the women's movement," such as Laura or Sarah, who had never thought of themselves as lesbians—or even bisexuals—before their exposure to feminism, self-consciously constructed their stories to resemble those of women for whom lesbianism was more internally motivated. Individuals were often quite self-conscious about having done this. Speaking of the pressures to rewrite her coming out narrative along such lines, one woman complained:

> I've gotten the feeling from fringe feminists and older lesbians that if you didn't grow up as a tomboy and fall in love with your high school classmates, you ain't no fer-real dyke. . . . When asked how I came out I have gotten into adding a fictitious struggle with lesbianism from way back in talking with some women. It helps to show your scars, even fake ones.[7]

Psychoanalytic developmental theory tends to correlate the degree of pathology in a trait with the earliness of its origins, enabling a pathologization of sexualities determined to have early origins, such as homosexuality (Epstein, 1991). While imagining a highly constructionist conception of lesbianism that viewed sexual identities as malleable, in practice lesbian feminists often turned the standard psychoanalytic account on its head, attributing "most favored" status to those individuals who were commonly believed to be most pathological. For a woman trying to authenticate her lesbianism to herself and to others, early homosocial or homosexual events, relationships, and personal feelings that may not have seemed particularly sexual or even significant at the time of their occurrence were recast to reveal a continuous lesbian history (Ponse, 1978). But often, despite these conscious commitments, heterosexual desires intruded. "Deeper" forms of identity work, such as resocializing desires, were therefore in order.

## DEFINING DESIRES

Lesbian feminism normalized relationships between women by deprecating heterosexual relationships and by generating a culture and vocabulary that valued and even *idealized* lesbianism. Feminists privileged lesbianism as the most effective challenge to compulsory heterosexuality. They attributed a woman's heterosexual past to some "pre-enlightened phase" and created a new cultural repertoire of desire, a new set of "sexual scripts" that would guide sexual desire and behavior and provide an alternative to the dominant heterosexual ones.[8]

For many women, exclusive commitment to homosexuality was never in question. But for others, including some of those who came out "through feminism," heterosexual desires persisted beneath the surface, despite their best efforts. Even as they identified as lesbians, some women reported experiencing a sense of "role distance." They felt that the term *lesbian* did not fully express "who they were." Nearly half the women I interviewed acknowledged various levels of continuing heterosexual desire, even after having come out and declared their lesbianism.

In *Lesbian Connection*, a Michigan-based national newsletter, a pained letter writer from Madison, Wisconsin, described herself as having been married for six years and having enjoyed "good relations with her husband and with other men long after her marriage." But eventually, she wrote, "It started growing in me that I was interested in women, and then I was very interested, and eventually, after my first Michigan [Women's Music] Festival, I wanted a woman so badly I cried." She described the process of identifying as a lesbian, despite the fact that she continued to enjoy sexual relations with men. "I think of myself as a lesbian who is attracted to men," she wrote, "or a bisexual who has no desire to get involved with men but feels a sexual attraction for them."

Unconscious fantasies tend to pose intractable problems for "politically correct" voluntarism (see Segal, 1983). Among lesbians heterosexual desires were seen as evidence of "internalized oppression." Once recognized and brought to consciousness, some imagined that internalized heterosexuality, much like internalized homophobia, could be erased.

Some suggested that heterosexual desires are compatible with a lesbian identity. But having heterosexual desires was one thing, and acting on them quite another. While conducting fieldwork in a lesbian community in the mid-1970s, Barbara Ponse reported encountering strong norms prohibiting heterosexual contacts among lesbians

and mandating a high degree of consistency between identity, behavior, and practices. "The importance placed on lesbian identity," she concluded, "would tend to limit experimentation with heterosexual relationships once a woman had made the identification. . . . A lesbian who engages in relationships with men could expect censure from other lesbians" (Ponse, 1978:184).

In the context of a movement that was attempting to imagine an alternative sexual order, it is understandable that heterosexuality and bisexuality would be prohibited. As Margaret Berg said, "There was such a great premium placed on being a lesbian that there was no place to be if you didn't fit into the categories." She drew a strict separation between personal and social identity and, like many members of her age cohort, privileged the social over the personal. The "social categories" that were available were heterosexuality and homosexuality. One could think of oneself as bisexual but, said Margaret, there was no "social context" for that in her world.

The gay liberation movement had initially supported bisexuality as the ideal form of sexuality, suggesting that it transcended binary identity categories, questioned the homosexual/heterosexual opposition, and affirmed polymorphously perverse pleasures. But by the early 1970s, in many lesbian circles, bisexuality was anathema; bisexuals were at best inferior lesbians and at worst collaborators with the enemy. Although lesbian feminism had attracted many women who had previously imagined themselves as heterosexual or bisexual, once having self-identified as lesbian, persistent sexual fantasies about men were not readily discussed. One woman told me that she had long thought of herself as being bisexual, but started calling herself a lesbian at some point because she wasn't having sex with men. "It wasn't that I wasn't still attracted to men," she said. "It was simply that they were out of the picture."

Bisexuality was not considered legitimate or authentic within the lesbian world. In terms of the "gay trajectory" women who harbored continued heterosexual desires were imagined as "having trouble dealing with their gayness" (Ponse, 1978). In view of these negative sanctions, some believed that even if they were originally attracted to men, and their initial lesbian experiences were not universally positive, they could resocialize themselves to be sexually interested in women. They believed that they were originally bisexual but had been socialized to be straight. Coming out therefore entailed identity work designed to "get in touch with one's lesbianism" and resocialize oneself to be gay.[9]

Sharon Lieberman said that after several unsuccessful relationships with men she decided that she was not going to find a man to suit her needs, that "all men were impossible." At the time, she was working with a women's newspaper in Eugene, Oregon, where everyone told her that she was "really" a lesbian. She recalls,

> I decided to change my masturbation fantasies. I made myself. It was like an internal decision on my part: I'm not going to find the partner I want among men. So one night I was lying in bed, ready to go to sleep and I masturbated about a woman.

Eventually, Sharon says, she came to have little desire for men and her sexual relationships with women became stronger and more pleasurable. Several other women told me about having consciously sought to redirect their sexual fantasies toward women. When interests and desires for men intruded, some reinterpreted them as the residues of compulsory heterosexuality and "false consciousness."

## DOING GENDER

When one becomes a lesbian, gendered bodily significations of hairstyle, clothing, and even comportment are problematized. Lesbians tend to be members of, or at least travelers through, both heterosexual and the homosexual worlds. Unless they pass as men (historically the case for a very small minority of women) in order to live, work, and love, they must satisfy the requirements of both worlds. In the straight world they must "pass" as straight, or at least develop a self-presentation that marks them as female. In the lesbian world they must conform to different norms of membership.

The codification and eroticization of gendered differences have long been a central part of lesbian subcultures. The most visible manifestation of lesbian "gender" is tied to appearance. But lesbian gender is much more than this. Speaking of the linkages between gender, self-presentation, and eroticism in the context of the working-class bar scene of the 1950s, Joan Nestle has written:

> Lesbian life in America . . . was organized around a highly developed sense of sexual ceremony and dialogue. Indeed, because of

the surrounding oppression, ritual and code were often all we had to make public erotic connections. Dress, stance, gestures, even jewelry and hairstyles had to carry the weight of sexual communications. The pinky ring flashing in the subway car, the DA haircut combed more severely in front of a mirror always made me catch my breath, symbolizing as they did a butch woman announcing her erotic competence. (Nestle, 1992:14–15)

Members of working-class bar subcultures eroticized gender differences. Butch-femme roles, which adapted conventional gender roles to the lesbian context, were, in Joan Nestle's words, "a conspicuous flag of rebellion" in a highly stigmatized, secretive world, a means of survival in an age when gender rules were heavy as lead weights (Kennedy and Davis, 1993). Being a butch, or "mannish woman," was an assertion of strength against very narrow conceptions of what it meant to be a woman. Wearing a leather jacket and slicking back short hair wasn't simply an experiment with style—it was an embrace of one's "true nature" in the face of dominant culture's notions of what it meant to be a woman: feminine and coy (Nestle, 1981; see also Califia, 1983).

Nearly twenty years later, in the context of the women's liberation movement, a very different politics of gender and the body emerged. Seventies feminists attempted to free women's bodies from their possession by men, which they viewed as being synonymous with their sexualization. As Deborah Gerson has written of this period:

> Women looked at their vulvas and cervix, examined their breasts and took up sports and recreational activities. . . . How we lived in our bodies, not only how we thought about our bodies was transformed. A growing awareness of alienation from and oppression to our bodies was met not only by a new consciousness in our minds, that is new ideology and new information, but by a new set of practices that enabled women to both learn about their bodies and live differently in them. (Gerson, 1995)

As part of a movement devoted to empowering women by reconstituting gendered bodies lesbian feminists attempted to erase gender differences, recodify gender and sexuality, and position themselves outside of the dominant culture. Early lesbian feminists saw lesbians as the embodiment of the androgynous ideal of a world without gender.

Minimizing the differences between women and men, they embraced an antinatalist, housewifery politics that placed lesbians in a cross-gender position. As Sidney Abbott and Barbara Love wrote:

> Lesbians have been critically examining sex roles. Instead of accepting the old explanation that was handed out to them that gay women were trying to be more male and gay men more female, they have identified cross-behavior as an important breakthrough, going beyond the confines of sex-role-categorized behavior. For the lesbian this means that she is not trying to be like a man, but she is trying to be more of a human being. (Abbott and Love, 1972:173).

For feminists, who were committed to minimizing gender differences, the exaggerated gender roles of butch-femme were little more than a self-hating reflection of the dominant heterosexual culture.

Butches, some charged, were "male-identified" in the truest sense: they looked and acted like men. Femmes were little better. Feminists, in response, wished to free themselves from norms that associated women with their bodies and made a fetish of personal appearance. The practice of femininity, they believed, constrained women and encouraged them to display sociability rather than technical competence, to accept marriage and childcare in response to labor market discrimination against women, and to organize their lives around themes of "sexual receptivity" and "motherhood."

It is not surprising that clothing, an important bodily marker of gender, would figure prominently in the effort to remake "lesbian gender." The struggle over identity and strategies for countering dominant constructions of identity, through the reconstitution of cultural codes, are central to marginalized groups and related to the forms of expression they produce. Like punk subcultures of the 1970s and early eighties in Britain and the United States, lesbian subcultures construct resistance partly through style and self-presentation.[10]

Not only did feminist lesbians wish to free themselves from gender roles, they wished to free themselves from fashion and style altogether, which they saw as synonymous with women's oppression. Toward this end they embraced androgynous styles of self-presentation. They wore jeans and T-shirts, flannel shirts and work boots. They wore their hair relatively short. They forged a style that embodied ideals of authenticity and naturalness against what was seen as the artificial, feigned styles of butch-femme and "normal femininity."

"We went to great pains to look as bad as we could," Jackie Henry recalled. "That outfit—the flannel and jeans, and so on—came out of some conscious planning out of the feminist movement about restrictive clothing. There was a lot of talk about clothing as chains." Feminists burned their bras and donned flannel shirts, denim vests, and blue jeans.[11] The look that became de riguer among young lesbians and many feminists in the 1970s was an attempt to replace the artifice of fashion with a supposed naturalness, freed of gender roles and commercialized pretense. It was derived, as Jackie put it, "from the wish on the part of a bunch of upper-middle-class lesbians to identify with working-class groups." The lesbian look was styled after simple, functional working-class clothing, symbolizing the wish on the part of many middle-class lesbians to be downwardly mobile, or at least to identify with the least fortunate members of society.

Clothing was an emblem of refusal, an attempt to strike a blow against the twin evils of capitalism and patriarchy, the fashion industry and the female objectification that fueled it (Stein, 1992).

Several women who had thought of themselves as tomboys from an early age spoke about the "lesbian look" in much the same terms as they described their own coming out: as a coming home. This sense of coming home was not universal, however. Though intending to minimize the differences between lesbians, differences of style persisted and sometimes posed problems. Thirty-two-year-old Dale Hoshiko arrived in San Francisco in the mid-1970s from Hawaii, eager to become a part of the lesbian/gay "scene." A friend from Hawaii, a lesbian, showed her around when she arrived, but, Dale recalled, "she didn't like hanging out with me because it pointed to the fact that we were all Asian. People would ask if I was her sister. She liked to view herself as white." Because Dale was Asian American, she was viewed as an oddity on Castro Street, in the heart of the gay ghetto.

> The men looked at me strangely. They couldn't figure out what I was doing there. I didn't have the lesbian look. I carried a handbag. I wasn't seen as a lesbian. I was seen as an Asian woman.

The women's community of San Francisco, which was at that point fairly distinct from the gay male ghetto, was much more receptive and welcoming toward Dale. But despite the efforts of some feminists to welcome women of color into their circles Dale's comments suggest that dominant visual codes in lesbian/gay communities often assumed whiteness and marked women of color as heterosexual. The identity work required of women of color was therefore doubly demanding, requiring the skillful manipulation of white-defined visual codes.

Many women I interviewed also spoke about the persistent differences between lesbians who could pass as straight and those who couldn't. Jackie Henry differentiated between her own experience as someone who appears "less threatening to the straight world" and those who "from an early age fit the stereotype of the butch lesbian and were brutally punished for it." She believed that it was important to remove herself from the heterosexual world and from the attentions of men and to make herself look less feminine. But some feminine-appearing women found themselves in a quandary trying to figure out how to present their "gendered" selves.

Sarah Marcus said: "I tried to look more butch. I drabbed it up a bit. But I always had a lot of trouble, and that was a source of great discomfort to me." Women who felt that they were "originally" more feminine in comportment, hairstyle, or dress sometimes felt they had to be "pretend butches" in order to be lesbians. And, despite their efforts to move toward androgyny, lesbian feminists were often more sympathetic toward "butchy" women. They affirmed that which the dominant culture had historically stigmatized as lesbian—the masculine woman. But being *too* masculine was also scorned on the grounds that it imitated men and carried the taint of butch-femme roles.

Styles that emphasized dichotomous masculine and feminine codes were seen as vestiges of the prefeminist days and reflections of an oppressive hegemonic culture. Sunny Connelly described herself as a "baby butch, through and through." During the hippie era there was a lot of "fluid sexuality and gender play." At that time, she said, "it was easy to blend in the crowd. It was a time of 'anything goes.'" In the late 1960s she used to wear tuxedo jackets and slick her hair back, in the "old gay" style. But with time, she said, feminists "got on her case" for that. So she grew her hair longer and tried to blend in. But the knotty problem of gender refused to go away.

Despite their efforts to neutralize gender (and race), many women experienced a continuing disjuncture between the person they were and the person they wished to be. Some changed their gendered self-presentation, or "surface identity," but still felt that "deep down" they could never entirely free themselves from gender roles. One needed to be butch to subvert femininity, but being too butch was tantamount to wandering into the field of butch-femme roles, which were generally anathema to women of the baby boom cohort. As Gayle Rubin has suggested: "In spite of their prevalence, issues of gender variance are strangely out of focus in lesbian thought, analysis and terminology. The intricacies of gender are infrequently addressed" (Rubin, 1992:468). Despite their ostensible attempt to erase gender differences, recodify gender and sexuality, and position themselves outside of the dominant culture, lesbian feminists were ultimately utterly dependent on the dominant gender codes they tried to subvert.

## FINDING AN "OTHER" LOVER

Recasting the past, resocializing one's sexual attractions, and changing one's appearance were important steps toward developing a lesbian identity for women of the baby boom cohort. But perhaps the most important step was the establishment of a same-sex relationship, which was often synonymous with involvement with an identifiable lesbian community. Many women described the erotic flavor of many community interactions, the fusion of the personal and the political that made lesbianism a plausible and even exciting alternative.

If the community was in some sense a "significant other" that fused personal and political relationships and provided a source of potential lovers and friends, the building block of the community was the couple. For sexually inexperienced women entry into a romantic relationship with another woman was one way of gaining membership into the lesbian subculture. Many women spoke of the importance of their first relationship as distinct from a first sexual experience that may or may not have been considered to be significant.

Women who experienced their sexuality as relatively fluid and their lesbianism as largely "elective" described themselves as forming an emotional attachment with a more experienced lesbian. The more experienced lesbian helped to construct the new lesbian's coming out experience and participate in the formation of her new sexual identity. No one said that they consciously became involved with a woman for this reason alone; nonetheless, many were highly conscious of the role that this dynamic played in their attractions and relationships. In 1971, soon after she declared herself a lesbian, Sally Kirk became involved with a woman who was older, who had come out before the women's movement. "I got to have the sense that I was really a lesbian because Jane was really a lesbian," she recalls. It is common for an "experienced" lesbian to introduce a "novice" lesbian to a new social world, whereby the novice shapes her sexual identity based on her position as a woman in love.

Sally told me that in order to be attracted to women she "always had to be attracted to people who were really different. Otherwise it was too much of the same thing." Sally was Jewish and middle class; her lovers tended to be non-Jewish and working class. "Everything was different. There was always this excitement, this dynamism." If class and ethnicity were two important ways in which her lovers differed from herself, sexual identity was an additional difference, though she did not become conscious of that dynamic until much later. Sally experienced her lesbianism as elective. Her lovers all experienced their lesbianism as more primary and driven. She was a "daughter of the movement." Her lovers thought of themselves as lifelong lesbians, who would have been lesbians regardless of history, contingency, or chance.

More than half the women who described their lesbianism as "elective" identified similar relationship dynamics. They found themselves consistently attracted to, and involved with "more experienced" lesbians. Many "new" lesbians described their involvement with "old gay" women who had then come into the women's movement. Others chose as lovers women of their own age, "new gay" women for whom lesbianism was, as some women described it, a coming home experience. Several women reported that more experienced, more internally driven lesbians courted them and were attracted to what they saw as their femininity. They, in turn, were attracted to what they perceived as the more "androgynous" or masculine sense of self of "lifelong lesbians."

Though few women identified with butch-femme roles per se, many described eroticizing certain traits that signify gender in our culture:

sexual aggressiveness, shyness, a willingness to take the initiative, and a range of others. For Toby Miller, who says she consistently became involved with "the most shut-down male-identified women"—this wasn't a particularly positive dynamic. When two women come together in a lesbian relationship they often bring to that relationship two very different conceptions of self. The eroticization of difference flew in the face of the ideology of lesbian feminism, which imagined lesbian relationships, in contrast to heterosexual or even lesbian butch-femme couples, as a partnering of equals, united in their similarity.

But over time some reported that these differences diminished. Some feminine women, for example, described becoming more like their "butchier" girlfriends. One might see this as an example of the tendency, described in psychoanalytic literature on lesbian relationships, for women lovers to merge. The very fact that there are two women in a relationship is likely to produce greater possibilities for fusion, or loss of self, it is suggested, because of the possibility that lesbian relationships offer for bodily and psychic oneness. Lesbians in relationship enjoy an "intimacy of familiarity, comfort and reciprocity," writes Joyce Lindenbaum. "There is a sense of shared identification, of knowing what the other feels." But as merging progresses the differences between partners often give way to sameness. Differences come to be experienced as a threat and are thus submerged (Lindenbaum, 1985:85–103; also Burch, 1987). In terms of gender roles, masculine women may become "femmier," and femmier women "butchier." The qualities that once attracted two individuals to each other—their differences—give way to similarity and sameness.

## THE ACTORS BEHIND THE ACTS

The dominant social-psychological conception of lesbian development, embodied by stage models of sexual identity formation, claims that lesbian identity formation is an objective unilinear process that ends at the moment at which one comes out, or consciously identifies as lesbian. As the preceding suggests, such models may offer little insight into the production of gendered and sexed subjectivity, with all of its inconsistencies. Identity is not a "truth" that is discovered, it is a performance enacted.

Identities often do not spring forth effortlessly from individuals: individuals reflexively effect change in the meanings of particular identities.

One is not born a lesbian; one becomes a lesbian through acts of reflexive self-fashioning. The formation of a lesbian identity is at least partly a matter of donning codes and symbols. It involves conforming to historically specific and localized codes for what it means to be a lesbian.

Women of the baby boom performed their lesbianism by rewriting their autobiography or consciously trying to resocialize themselves to be sexually attracted to women and to repress their feelings for men. Sometimes they changed their self-presentation to bring it more in line with what they considered to be authentically lesbian. At other times they pursued relationships with someone whom they identified as a real lesbian.

In the 1970s, when feminism and gay liberation were highly influential, such performances took place within a system that highly valued authenticity—being true to oneself. Lesbian feminism was founded on the belief that women could retrieve a self that had been denied to them by the dominant culture. Authenticity was an important criteria for building trust between individuals within lesbian communities, particularly in view of the persistence of stigma. In the "dominant culture" lesbians often feel like inauthentic, deviant, "failed" women, but within the lesbian subculture they imagined that it was possible to "be themselves."

The effect of this identity work was often, paradoxically, to impose a rather rigid normative conception of what it means to be a lesbian. To become a lesbian in the context of the gender/sexual politics of the 1970s was to be implicated in that which one opposed: binary sexual and gender categories.[12]

While identity may consist of a string of performances made consistent only through their repetition, individuals, I have suggested, varied in terms of their "skills" as performers and the success of their performances. For many women performing lesbianism came relatively easy and effortlessly; becoming a lesbian meant coming home, reengaging with what they believed to be their authentic self, and embracing the desires they had long embraced in secret. It permitted them to adopt a *surface* identity as a lesbian to match the *deep* sense of difference they already possessed.

To others coming out meant "discovering" their lesbianism. They had experienced themselves as originally heterosexual or bisexual. For these women desire was often not the primary determinant of a lesbian identification; their deep identification as lesbian was preceded by an identification with lesbianism as a sociosexual category. Even after having come out, some in this group felt that their sense of lesbian self was inauthentic; they felt that they were just "going through the motions,"compelled to undertake rigorous identity work to consolidate a sense of lesbian self.

By engaging in identity work some individuals in this latter group were able to narrow the experiential gap separating them from other more experienced lesbians. They "became lesbians." But others continued to experience a dissonance between the person they felt that they "were" and the person they wished to "become." Identity work did not close the gap between their subjective sense of self and the social sexual typology *lesbian*. For some of these women lesbian identity often felt "put on" or "not part of them" (Hochschild, 1983:36). They changed their self-presentation, which operated as a surface identity,, but still felt that deep down they could never entirely free themselves from gender roles. For them, gender and sexuality inhered in traits "possessed" rather than presentations enacted (Weston, 1991:13).

## NOTES

1. Recent literature has argued that emotional experience, including physiological, is essential to the authenticating process as a clue to self-knowledge/self-identity. See Carolyn Ellis (1991). This emotional experience was often linked to physiological sexual response, a relationship that is difficult to ascertain from my interviews but worth probing in a future study.

2. For Judith Butler (1991) the performance of sexuality, like the performance of gender, is an act of resistance waged by actors who are situated to see through the illusion of gender and sexuality as coherent core identities. See also Diana Fuss (1991). For a cogent, grounded critique of performative theory, see Kath Weston (1993). For an earlier, seminal treatment of identity work undertaken by an "intersexed" person, see Harold Garfinkel (1967).

3. Goffman (1959) distinguishes between use of symbols to denote prestige or stigma. A prestige symbol serves to "establish a special claim to prestige, honor, or desirable class position," while a stigma symbol "draw[s] attention to a debasing identity discrepancy" (43–44). But a symbol that denotes stigma to society at large may well serve as a prestige symbol within a subculture. Such a symbol "adds

another layer of complexity to the act of managing information in self-presentation."

4. Here, writes Arlie Hochschild, "the actor does not try to seem happy or sad but rather expresses spontaneously" (1983:35).

5. Ken Plummer (1995) situates the confessional mode of sexual storytelling in late modernity. The coming out story is one of many types of sexual stories that have come to be told in the late modern world, and exists alongside them.

6. For examples of this "development myth," see Julia Penelope Stanley and Susan J. Wolfe (1980). For a critical review of this literature, see Bonnie Zimmerman (1990). On the importance of authenticity and expressive individualism in American culture, see Bellah et al. (1985).

7. *Lesbian Connection*, 1(8), no. 75.

8. John Gagnon and William Simon (1973) conceptualized the "sexual script" as a counterpoint to "drive theory," suggesting that sexual behavior is, for the most part, a simple, everyday occurrence constructed from social motives and settings that are variable. Also see Ken Plummer (1982).

9. Barbara Risman and Pepper Schwartz (1988) suggest that lesbians' "transformation of sexual orientation to suit political beliefs deserves more analytical attention" (138).

10. On subcultural style as resistance, and punk subcultures in particular, see Dick Hebdige (1988).

11. As Deborah Gerson (1995) notes, what was burned "was not the literal bra but the social bra, the political bra; the brassiere and symbol and practice of the exploited breast, the controlled breast, the subordinated, domesticated, playboy breast, the imperfect if not perfect breast, the man's breast" (18–19).

12. On the "paradox of performativity," see Judith Butler (1993), p. 241.

## SOURCES CITED

Abbott, Sidney and Barbara Love. 1972. *Sappho Was a Right-On Woman*. New York: Stein and Day.

Bellah, Robert, et al. 1985. *Habits of the Heart*. Berkeley: University of California.

Berger, Peter and T. Luckmann. 1966. *The Social Construction of Reality*. New York: Anchor.

Burch, Beverly. 1987. "Barriers to Intimacy: Conflicts Over Power, Dependency, and Nurturing in Lesbian Relationships." In Boston Lesbian Psychologies Collective, ed. *Lesbian Psychologies: Explorations and Challenges*. Urbana: University of Illinois Press.

Butler, Judith. 1991. "Imitation and Gender Insubordination." In Diana Fuss, ed., *Inside/Out: Lesbian Theories, Gay Theories*. New York: Routledge.

Butler, Judith. 1993. *Bodies That Matter*. New York: Routledge.

Califia, Pat. 1983. "Gender Bending." *Advocate*, September 15.

Ellis, Carolyn. 1991. "Sociological Introspection and Emotional Experience." *Symbolic Interaction* (Spring), 14(1).

Epstein, Steven. 1991. Sexuality and Identity: The Contribution of Object Relations Theory to a Constructionist Sociology." *Theory and Society*, 20:825–873.

Fuss, Diana, ed. 1991. *Inside/Out: Lesbian Theories/Gay Theories*. New York: Routledge.

Gagnon, J. H. and William Simon. 1973. *Sexual Conduct: The Social Sources of Human Sexuality*. Chicago: Aldine.

Garfinkel, Harold. 1967. *Studies in Ethnomethodology*. Englewood Cliffs: Prentice Hall.

Gerson, Deborah. 1995. "Speculums and Small Groups: New Visions of Women's Bodies." Unpublished ms.

Goffman, Erving. 1959. *The Presentation of Self in Everyday Life*. Garden City: Doubleday.

Hebdige, Dick. 1988. *Subculture: The Meaning of Style*. New York/London: Routledge.

Hewitt, John P. 1989. *Dilemmas of the American Self*. Philadelphia: Temple University Press.

Hochschild, Arlie. 1983. *The Managed Heart: Commercialization of Human Feeling*. Berkeley: University of California Press.

Kennedy, Elizabeth and Madeline Davis. 1993. *Boots of Leather, Slippers of Gold: The History of a Lesbian Community*. New York: Routledge.

Kraus, Natasha Kirsten. 1990. "Butch/Fem Relations of the 1940s and 50s: Desire Work and the Structuring of a Community." Unpublished paper, Department of Sociology, University of California, Berkeley.

Lindenbaum, Joyce. 1987. "The Shattering of an Illusion: The Problem of Competition in Lesbian Relationships." In V. Miner and H. Longino, eds., *Competition: A Feminist Taboo?* New York: Feminist Press.

Nestle, Joan. 1981. "Butch-Fem Relationships: Sexual Courage in the 1950s." *Heresies*, 3(4):21–24.

— 1992. *The Persistent Desire: A Fem-Butch Reader*. Boston: Alyson.

Phelan, Shane. 1994. *Getting Specific. Postmodern Lesbian Politics*. Minneapolis: Minnesota.

Plummer, Kenneth. 1983. *Documents of Life*. London: Allen and Unwin.

— 1995. *Telling Sexual Stories: Power, Change, and Social Worlds*. New York: Routledge.

Ponse, Barbara. 1978. *Identities in the Lesbian World: The Social Construction of Self*. Westport: Greenwood.

Risman, Barbara and Pepper Schwartz. 1988. "Sociological Research on Male and Female Homosexuality." *Annual Review of Sociology*, 14:125–147.

Rubin, Gayle. 1992. "Of Catamites and Kings: Reflections on Butch, Gender, and Boundaries." In Joan Nestle, ed., *The Persistent Desire*. Boston: Alyson.

Segal, Lynne. 1983. "Sensual Uncertainty; or, Why the Clitoris Is Not Enough." In S. Cartledge and J. Ryan, eds., *Sex and Love*. London: Women's Press.

Stanley, Julia Penelope and Susan Wolfe. 1980. *The Coming Out Stories*. Watertown, Mass.: Persephone.

Stein, Arlene. 1992. "All Dressed Up But No Place to Go: Style Wars and the New Lesbianism." In Joan Nestle, ed., *The Persistent Desire: A Fem-Butch Reader*. Boston: Alyson.

Weston, Kath. 1991. *Families We Choose: Lesbians, Gay Men, Kinship*. New York: Columbia University.

Weston, Kath. 1993. "Do Clothes Make the Woman? Gender, Performance Theory, and Lesbian Eroticism," *GENDERS* (Fall), no. 17, pp. 1–21.

Zimmerman, Bonnie. 1990. *The Safe Sea of Women: Lesbian Fiction 1969–1989*. Boston: Beacon.

# | 9 |

# Gay Men, Lesbians, and Sex: Doing It Together

## PAT CALIFIA

I have sex with faggots. And I'm a lesbian. You think *you're* confused? How did this happen to a woman who maintained a spotless record as a militant lesbian separatist for eight years, a woman who had sex with only three men (once apiece) before coming out, a woman who gets called a dyke on the street at least once a week, a woman who has slept (and not stayed to sleep) with hundreds of other women?

To explain, I need to go back to 1977. Those of you who aren't ready for this have my permission to leave the room. But don't slam the door on your way out. Who knows who will be sitting on *your* face in 1984?

In 1977 when I bought my first dog collar, there was no such thing as a lesbian S/M community. There probably were a few isolated dykes who owned rope they never intended to string up for clothesline—but I couldn't find them. So

when I heard about a women's S/M support group, I joined it even though most of the members were straight or bisexual. I was surprised to discover that most of them were honest, intelligent perverts—and feminists! One of them, a professional dominatrix, became my lover.

My lover found the straight S/M scene pretty joyless, so she hung out with a small group of gay men who were into fisting and S/M. She was especially attached to Steve McEachern, who ran private hand-balling parties in his extremely well-equipped basement. This club was called The Catacombs. The Christmas after we became lovers, she took me to a party at his house. About fifteen men were present. She and I were the only women. After a huge dinner, everybody just

*Advocate*, July 7, 1983, pp. 24–27.

started taking off his clothes. I found myself sitting alone in a corner, wondering if I was going to spend the entire orgy feeling sorry for myself (my girlfriend had wandered off with Steve). A tall, handsome man (albeit a little skinny) sat down beside me and said, "Hi, my name's Joe. How would you like to fist me?"

I took a deep breath and said, "I'd like that, but you'll have to show me what to do." That was fine with him. He got me an emery board and some nail clippers and showed me how to perform the very severe manicure handballing requires. He took for granted that a novice had to receive detailed instructions, and he didn't expect me to dazzle him with a magic show of sexual expertise. This attitude was very reassuring and completely different from the way anybody else I'd met had approached sex. When Joe approved my hands, we went downstairs, located some towels and Crisco, and climbed onto the waterbed.

Joe lay on his back. He wrapped his arms around his thighs and held them apart. My first handful of grease melted right into his ass. It was like feeding a hungry animal—an animal that talked back. He gave me such careful instructions about when to push and when to pull back that I got into him easily, I can't remember how deep. It seemed like miles. I came to at one point and realized just how vulnerable he was, this big man clutching his thighs and groaning uncontrollably because I was so far into him. The walls of his gut hugged my hand and forearm, smoother and softer and more fragile than anything I'd ever touched before. I think I cried. I know I got wet.

Well, that's how it started. I've lost track of exactly how many men I've put my hand(s) into, and it still puts me in a trance. It's awesome to be that close to another human being. In between cans of Crisco. I've thought a lot about why it's possible to cross the "gender line" in the context of this kind of sex. First of all, in fisting the emphasis is not on the genitals. Men at handballing parties don't usually cruise each other's dicks. They cruise each other's hands and forearms. It is not unusual for fisters to go all night without a hard-on. Tops with small hands are in demand, and my glove size is a popular one. Gay men who are into handballing usually think of themselves as sexually different from other gay men. They get a lot of attitude about being sick, kinky, and excessive. Hence some of them are willing to break a gay taboo and do it with a woman.

As I acquired more experience in the S/M community, I realized this, too, was a sexuality that allowed people to step outside the usually rigid boundaries of sexual orientation. I met lesbians who topped straight men for money (and did that myself for a while). I met straight men who would go down on other men or be fucked by them if their mistresses ordered them to do it. Since the acts took place under the authority of women, they thought of them as heterosexual behavior. (I also met a lot of bisexuals who didn't need any excuses.)

These combined experiences have resulted in a lifestyle that doesn't fit the homosexual stereotype. I live with my woman lover of five years. I have lots of casual sex with women. Once in a while, I have casual sex with gay men. I have a three-year relationship with a homosexual man who doesn't use the term *gay*. And I call myself a lesbian.

Of course. I've modified my sexual pattern in the face of the AIDS crisis. I've become much more conscious of the need to maintain good general health by getting enough sleep, eating a nutritious diet, and reducing stress and recreational drug use. I've also quit having sex with strangers. I have the same amount of sex but with fewer people—and none of them are taking excessive risks with their health, either. I have not dropped fisting from my repertoire. I am simply more selective about whom I do it with. I have yet to be convinced that fisting exposes me or my partners to more danger than other kinds of sexual contact.

Why not identify as bi? That's a complicated question. For a while, I thought I was simply being biphobic. There's a lot of that going around in the gay community. Most of us had to struggle so hard to be exclusively homosexual that we resent people who don't make a similar commitment. A self-identified bisexual is saying, "Men and women are of equal importance to me." That's simply not true of me. I'm a Kinsey Five, and when I turn on to a man it's because he shares some aspect of my sexuality (like S/M or fisting) that turns me on *despite* his biological sex.

There's yet another twist, I have eroticized queerness, gayness, homosexuality—in men and women. The leatherman and the drag queen are sexy to me, along with the diesel dyke with greased-back hair, and the femme stalking across the bar in her miniskirt and high-heeled shoes. I'm a fag hag.

The gay community's attitude toward fag hags and dyke daddies has been pretty nasty and unkind. Fag hags are supposed to be frustrated, traditionally feminine, heterosexual women who never have sex with their handsome, slightly effeminate escorts—but desperately want to. Consequently, their nails tend to be long and sharp, and their lipstick runs to the bloodier shades of carmine. And They Drink. Dyke daddies are supposed to be beer-bellied rednecks who hang out at lesbian bars to sexually harass the female patrons. The nicer ones are suckers who get taken for drinks or loans that will never be repaid.

These stereotypes don't do justice to the complete range of modern faghaggotry and dyke daddydom. Today fag hags and dyke daddies are as likely to be gay themselves as the objects of their admiration.

I call myself a fag hag because sex with men outside the context of the gay community doesn't interest me at all. In a funny way, when two gay people of opposite sexes make it, it's still gay sex. No heterosexual couple brings the same experiences and attitudes to bed that we do. These generalizations aren't perfectly true, but more often than straight sex, gay sex assumes that the use of hands or the mouth is as important as genital-to-genital contact. Penetration is not assumed to be the only goal of a sexual encounter. When penetration does happen, dildos and fingers are as acceptable as (maybe even preferable to) cocks. During gay sex, more often than during straight sex, people think about things like lubrication and "fit." There's no such thing as "foreplay." There's good sex, which includes lots of touching, and there's bad sex, which is nonsensual. Sex roles are more flexible, so nobody is automatically on the top or the bottom. There's no stigma attached to masturbation, and gay people are much more accepting of porn, fantasies, and fetishes.

And, most importantly, there is no intention to "cure" anybody. I know that a gay man who has sex with me is making an exception and that he's still gay after we come and clean up. In return I can make an exception for him because I know he isn't trying to convert me to heterosexuality.

I have no way of knowing how many lesbians and gay men are less than exclusively homosexual. But I do know I'm not the only one. Our actual behavior (as opposed to the ideology that says homosexuality means being sexual only with members of the same sex) leads me to ask questions about the nature of sexual orientation, how people (especially gay people) define it, and how

they choose to let those definitions control and limit their lives.

During one of our interminable discussions in Samois[*] about whether or not to keep the group open to bi women, Gayle Rubin pointed out that a new, movement-oriented definition of lesbianism was in conflict with an older, bar-oriented definition. Membership in the old gay culture consisted of managing to locate a gay bar and making a place for yourself in bar society. Even today, nobody in a bar asks you how long you've been celibate with half the human race before they will check your coat and take your order for a drink. But in the movement, people insist on a kind of purity that has little to do with affection, lust, or even political commitment. Gayness becomes a state of sexual grace, like virginity. A fanatical insistence on one hundred percent exclusive, same-sex behavior often sounds to me like superstitious fear of contamination or pollution. Gayness that has more to do with abhorrence for the other sex than with an appreciation of your own sex degenerates into a rabid and destructive separatism.

It is very odd that sexual orientation is defined solely in terms of the sex of one's partners. I don't think I can assume anything about another person simply because I've been told she or he is bisexual, heterosexual, or homosexual. A person's politics may be conservative, liberal, radical, or nonexistent, regardless of sexual orientation. In fact, a sexual orientation label tells you nothing about her or his sex life, for God's sake. There are lots of "heterosexual" men who have plenty of anonymous sex with other men. There are celibate faggots and dykes. There are lesbians who've been married for thirty years and have six children. There are heterosexual women who frequently have sex with other women at swing parties. For many people, if a partner or a sexual situation has other desirable qualities it is possible to overlook the partner's sex. Some examples: a preference for group sex, for a particular socioeconomic background, for paid sex, for S/M, for a specific age group, for a physical type or race, for anal or oral sex.

I no longer believe that there is some ahistorical entity called homosexuality. Sexuality is socially constructed within the limits imposed by physiology, and it changes over time with the sur-

---

[*] Samois, founded in San Francisco in 1978, was a group of feminist lesbians who shared an interest in sadomasochism.

rounding culture. There was no such thing as a Castro clone, a lesbian-feminist, or a Kinsey Six a century ago, and one hundred years from now these types will be as extinct as *Urnings*.

This is not to say that in a sexual utopia we would all be bisexual. There is nothing wrong with having sex exclusively with members of your own sex (or the opposite sex). I simply question some of the assumptions or attitudes that have grown around the fact that some people have an erotic preference for same-sex behavior. Gay people have responded to persecution and homophobia by creating our own mythology about homosexuality. Whenever desire and behavior conflict with rhetoric, it's time to reexamine the rhetoric. Some lesbians and gay men are having opposite-sex experiences. Why? What are they learning?

Gay male friends and lovers have taught me things that I would never have learned in the lesbian community. I can't exaggerate my admiration for the well-developed technology, etiquette, attitudes, and institutions that gay men have developed to express their sexuality. (Remember, this is from the perspective of a woman who can't go to the baths every night or answer fifty sex ads in the "Pink Pages.") There's a basic attitude that sex is good in and of itself and that people ought to get what they want and treat each other well while they pursue it. That includes taking responsibility for preventing and treating sexually transmitted diseases. There's certainly room for improvement, but gay men are better educated about STDs and deal with them more promptly than typical heterosexual swingers or nonmonogamous lesbians.

Having good sex with men also allowed me to confront some of my fears about what it might "mean" to be a lesbian. You know, all that stuff about dykes being too unattractive to get a man and all the psychobabble about penis envy. I now feel that having sex with women really is a choice for me. I know that sexually active women are in demand in any straight sex environment, and I could walk into most of those joints and take my pick. I just don't want what they have to offer. I no longer feel threatened by sexual come-ons from men. Once you've had vice presidents of large corporations on your leash, straight men lose a lot of their power to intimidate you.

As for penis envy, I often think it would be nice to have a cock. I love fucking people, and because there's all this cultural meaning assigned to getting fucked with a cock (as opposed to fingers or a dildo), I'd like to have that sexual power. But I'm better with a strap-on dildo than most straight boys are at using their own cocks, and besides, I can change sizes. Once you've gotten two hands up somebody's ass, you aren't likely to feel jealous of a penis. Nobody's cock is *that* big. So, while I wouldn't mind having one, I think after I was done using it, I'd want to be able to take it off and leave it on a shelf. I don't want to have to be adjusting it in my pants all the time. And I *like* sitting down to pee. It makes it easier to read, and if you're outdoors, the grass tickles your heinie.

It's been very nice to lose my phobia about cocks. Our culture's phallic mythology has given the male sex organ so much highly charged symbolic significance that anything powerful is a phallic symbol. A lot of feminist antiporn ideology puts out the idea that cocks are ugly weapons that do nothing but defile or murder women. This symbolic system is very harmful. If cocks really have an inherent power to pollute and damage women, the only solution is to forcibly excise them from the male body. Instead I'd like to see women become more phallic (i.e., more powerful). Cocks seem more fragile than thermonuclear to me. There's a vulnerability about getting an erection that I'm really grateful I don't have to experience before I can give someone a night to remember.

The last and most painful thing I've learned from my contacts with gay men is how the war between the sexes looks from the other side. As embarrassing as it is, I finally had to concede that women engage in a lot of behavior that is homophobic or sexist, and that it is women who enforce much of the sexual repression of the children they raise. This doesn't mean that I think women are equally responsible for their own oppression. Men get most of the goodies from the system and have the highest investment in keeping it running. But I no longer feel that all women are innocent victims, and all men are misogynist monsters.

The information flows both ways. I don't remember how many times I've explained to a gay man what rape is and why women, being physically smaller, feel less safety and mobility on the streets than men do. Then there's economics. Many gay men really don't understand what kinds of jobs women can readily obtain and what these jobs pay.

And of course they get to learn a lot about things like menstrual cycles and multiple orgasms. I can still hear the quaver in the voice of the first gay man who ever went down on me. "Let's see," he said bravely, as he gently spread my labia apart, "where's that famous clitoris I've heard so much about?"

In the midst of the craziness, hostility, ignorance, and angst that plague human relations and sexuality, I feel entitled to whatever comfort or gratification I can find. I'll be looking for some more tonight, in the company of a girlfriend of mine. We have a date to tie up a furry little number and show him a good time. If it bothers you to envision the details, consider it in the abstract. Think of it as a fine example of lesbian/gay solidarity . . . just queers doing queer things together!

# | 10 |

# *Maiden Voyage: Excursion Into Sexuality and Identity Politics in Asian America*

## DANA Y. TAKAGI

Like black men and women who refused to be the exceptional "pet" Negro for whites, and who instead said they were "niggers" too (the original "crime" of "niggers" and lesbians is that they prefer themselves), perhaps black women writers and non-writers should say, simply, whenever black lesbians are being put down, held up, messed over, and generally told their lives should not be encouraged, *We are all lesbians.* For surely it is better to be thought a lesbian, and to say and write your life exactly as you experience it, than to be a token "pet" black woman for those whose contempt for our autonomous existence makes them a menace to human life.[1]

—ALICE WALKER

The topic of sexualities—in particular, lesbian, gay, and bisexual identities—is an important and timely issue in that place we imagine as Asian America. *All of us* in Asian American Studies ought to be thinking about sexuality and Asian American history for at least two compelling reasons.

One, while there has been a good deal of talk about the "diversity" of Asian American communities, we are relatively uninformed about Asian American subcultures organized specifically around sexuality. There are Asian American gay and lesbian social organizations, gay bars that are known for Asian clientele, conferences that have focused on Asian American lesbian and gay experiences, and as Tsang notes in this issue,* electronic bulletin boards catering primarily to gay

Asians, their friends, and their lovers. I use the term "subcultures" here rather loosely and not in the classic sociological sense, mindful that the term is somewhat inaccurate since gay Asian organizations are not likely to view themselves as a gay subculture within Asian America any more than they are likely to think of themselves as an Asian American subculture within gay America. If anything, I expect that many of us view ourselves as on the margins of both communities. That state of marginalization in both communities is what prompts this essay and makes the issues raised in it all the more urgent for all of us—gay, straight, somewhere-in-between. For as

*Amerasia Journal*, 20(1):1–17, 1994.

* Chapter 83 of this volume.—EDS.

Haraway has suggested, the view is often clearest from the margins where, "The split and contradictory self is the one who can interrogate positionings and be accountable, the one who can construct and join rational conversations and fantastic imaginings that change history."[2]

To be honest, it is not clear to me exactly *how* we ought to be thinking about these organizations, places, and activities. On the one hand, I would argue that an organization like the Association of Lesbians and Gay Asians (ALGA) ought to be catalogued in the annals of Asian American history. But on the other hand, having noted that ALGA is as Asian American as Sansei Live! or the National Coalition for Redress and Reparation, the very act of including lesbian and gay experiences in Asian American history, which seems important in a symbolic sense, produces in me a moment of hesitation. Not because I do not think that lesbian and gay sexualities are not deserving of a place in Asian American history, but rather, because the inscription of non-straight sexualities in Asian American history immediately casts theoretical doubt about how to do it. As I will suggest, the recognition of different sexual practices and identities that also claim the label *Asian American* presents a useful opportunity for re-thinking and re-evaluating notions of identity that have been used, for the most part, unproblematically and uncritically in Asian American Studies.

The second reason, then, that we ought to be thinking about gay and lesbian sexuality and Asian American Studies is for the theoretical trouble we encounter in our attempts to situate and think about sexual identity *and* racial identity. Our attempts to locate gay Asian experiences in Asian American history render us "uninformed" in an ironic double sense. On the one hand, the field of Asian American Studies is mostly ignorant about the multiple ways that gay identities are often hidden or invisible within Asian American communities. But the irony is that the more we know, the less we know about the ways of knowing. On the other hand, just at the moment that we attempt to rectify our ignorance by adding say, the lesbian, to Asian American history, we arrive at a stumbling block, an ignorance of how to add her. Surely the quickest and simplest way to add her is to think of lesbianism as a kind of ad hoc subject-position, a minority within a minority. But efforts to think of sexuality in the same terms that we think of race, yet simultaneously different from race in certain ways, and therefore, the

inevitable "revelation" that gays/lesbians/bisexuals are like minorities but also different too, is often inconclusive, frequently ending in "counting" practice. While many minority women speak of "triple jeopardy" oppression—as if class, race, and gender could be disentangled into discrete additive parts—some Asian American lesbians could rightfully claim quadruple jeopardy oppression—class, race, gender, and sexuality. Enough counting. Marginalization is not as much about the *quantities* of experiences as it is about *qualities* of experience. And, as many writers, most notably feminists, have argued, identities whether sourced from sexual desire, racial origins, languages of gender, or class roots, are simply not additive.[3]

## I. NOT COUNTING

A discussion of sexualities is fraught with all sorts of definition conundrums. What exactly does it mean, sexualities? The plurality of the term may be unsettling to some who recognize three (or two, or one) forms of sexual identity: gay, straight, bisexual. But there are those who identify as straight, but regularly indulge in homoeroticism, and, of course, there are those who claim the identity gay/lesbian, but engage in heterosexual sex. In addition, some people identify themselves sexually but do not actually have sex, and, there are those who claim celibacy as a sexual practice. For those who profess a form of sexual identity that is, at some point, at odds with their sexual practice or sexual desire, the idea of a single, permanent, or even stable sexual identity is confining and inaccurate. Therefore, in an effort to capture the widest possible range of human sexual practices, I use the term sexualities to refer to the variety of practices and identities that range from homoerotic to heterosexual desire. In this essay, I am concerned mainly with homosexual desire and the question of what happens when we try to locate homosexual identities in Asian American history.

Writing, speaking, acting queer. Against a backdrop of lotus leaves, sliding *shoji* panels, and the mountains of Guilin. Amid the bustling enclaves of Little Saigon, Koreatown, Chinatown, and Little Tokyo. Sexual identity, like racial identity, is one of many types of recognized "difference." If marginalization is a qualitative state of being and not simply a quantitative one, then what is it about being "gay" that is different from "Asian American?"

The terms "lesbian" and "gay," like "Third

World," "woman," and "Asian American," are political categories that serve as rallying calls and personal affirmations. In concatenating these identities we create and locate ourselves in phrases that seem a familiar fit: black gay man, third world woman, working class Chicana lesbian, Asian American bisexual, etc. But is it possible to write these identities—like Asian American gay—without writing oneself into the corners that are either gay and only gay, or, Asian American and only Asian American? Or, as Trinh T. Minh-ha put it, "How do you inscribe difference without bursting into a series of euphoric narcissistic accounts of yourself and your own kind?"[4]

It is vogue these days to celebrate difference. But underlying much contemporary talk about difference is the assumption that differences are comparable things. For example, many new social movements activists, including those in the gay and lesbian movement, think of themselves as patterned on the "ethnic model."[5] And for many ethnic minorities, the belief that "gays are oppressed too" is a reminder of a sameness, a common political project in moving margin to center, that unites race-based movements with gays, feminists, and greens. The notion that our differences are "separate but equal" can be used to call attention to the specificity of experiences or to rally the troops under a collective banner. Thus, the concept of difference espoused in identity politics may be articulated in moments of what Spivak refers to as "strategic essentialism" or in what Hall coins "positionalities." But in the heat of local political struggles and coalition building, it turns out that not all differences are created equally. For example, Ellsworth recounts how differences of race, nationality, and gender, unfolded in the context of a relatively safe environment, the university classroom:

> Women found it difficult to prioritize expressions of racial privilege and oppression when such prioritizing threatened to perpetuate their gender oppression. Among international students, both those who were of color and those who were White found it difficult to join their voices with those of U.S. students of color when it meant a subordination of their oppressions as people living under U.S. imperialist policies and as students for whom English was a second language. Asian American women found it difficult to join their voices with other students of color when it meant subordinating their specific oppressions as Asian Americans. I found it difficult to speak as a White woman about gender oppression

when I occupied positions of institutional power relative to all students in the class, men and women, but positions of gender oppression relative to students who were White men, and in different terms, relative to students who were men of color.[6]

The above example demonstrates the tensions between sameness and difference that haunt identity politics. Referring to race and sexuality, Cohen suggests that the "sameness" that underlies difference may be more fiction than fact:

> The implied isomorphism between the "arbitrariness of racial categorizations" and the "sexual order" elides the complex processes of social differentiation that assign, legitimate, and enforce qualitative distinctions between different types of individuals. Here the explicit parallel drawn between "race" and "sexuality," familiar to so many polemical affirmations of (non-racial) identity politics, is meant to evoke an underlying and apparently indisputable common sense that naturalizes this particular choice of political strategy almost as if the "naturalness" of racial "identity" could confer a corollary stability on the less "visible" dynamics of sexuality.[7]

There are numerous ways that being "gay" is not like being "Asian." Two broad distinctions are worth noting. The first, mentioned by Cohen above, is the relative invisibility of sexual identity compared with racial identity. While both can be said to be socially constructed, the former are performed, acted out, and produced, often in individual routines, whereas the latter tends to be more obviously "written" on the body and negotiated by political groups.[8] Put another way, there is a quality of voluntarism in being gay/lesbian that is usually not possible as an Asian American. One has the option to present oneself as "gay" or "lesbian," or alternatively, to attempt to "pass," or, to stay in "the closet," that is, to hide one's sexual preference.[9] However, these same options are not available to most racial minorities in face-to-face interactions with others.

As Asian Americans, we do not think in advance about whether or not to present ourselves as "Asian American," rather, that is an identification that is worn by us, whether we like it or not, and which is easily read off of us by others.

A second major reason that the category "gay" ought to be distinguished from the category "Asian American" is for the very different histories of each group. Studying the politics of being "gay" entails on the one hand, an analysis of discursive fields, ideologies, and rhetoric about sexual identity, and on the other hand, knowledge of the history of gays/lesbians as subordinated minorities relative to heterosexuals. . . . Similarly, studying "Asian America" requires analysis of semantic and rhetorical discourse in its variegated forms, racist, apologist, and paternalist, and requires in addition, an understanding of the specific histories of the peoples who recognize themselves as Asian or Asian American. But the specific discourses and histories in each case are quite different. Even though we make the same intellectual moves to approach each form of identity, that is, a two-tracked study of ideology on the one hand, and history on the other, the particular ideologies and histories of each are very different.[10]

In other words, many of us experience the worlds of Asian America and gay America as separate places—emotionally, physically, intellectually. We sustain the separation of these worlds with our folk knowledge about the family-centeredness and supra-homophobic beliefs of ethnic communities. Moreover, it is not just that these communities know so little of one another, but, we frequently take great care to keep those worlds distant from each other. What could be more different than the scene at gay bars like "The End Up" in San Francisco, or "Faces" in Hollywood, and, on the other hand, the annual Buddhist church bazaars in the Japanese American community or Filipino revivalist meetings?[11] These disparate worlds occasionally collide through individuals who manage to move, for the most part, stealthily, between these spaces. But it is the act of deliberately bringing these worlds closer together that seems unthinkable. Imagining your parents, clutching bento box lunches, thrust into the smoky haze of a South of Market leather bar in San Francisco is no less strange a vision than the idea of Lowie taking Ishi, the last of his tribe, for a cruise on Lucas' Star Tours at Disneyland. "Cultural strain," the anthropologists would say. Or, as Wynn Young, laughing at the prospect of mixing his family with his boyfriend, said, "Somehow I just can't picture this conversation at the dinner table, over my mother's homemade barbecued pork: 'Hey, Ma. I'm sleeping with a sixty-year-old white guy who's got three kids, and would you please pass the soy sauce?'"[12]

Thus, "not counting" is a warning about the ways to think about the relationship of lesbian/gay identities to Asian American history. While it may seem politically efficacious to toss the lesbian onto the diversity pile, adding one more form of subordination to the heap of inequalities, such a strategy glosses over the particular or distinctive ways sexuality is troped in Asian America. Before examining the possibilities for theorizing "gay" and "Asian American" as non-mutually exclusive identities, I turn first to a fuller description of the chasm of silence that separates them.

## II. SILENCES

The concept of silence is a doggedly familiar one in Asian American history. For example, Hosokawa characterized the Nisei as "Quiet Americans" and popular media discussions of the "model minority" typically describe Asian American students as "quiet" along with "hard working" and "successful." In the popular dressing of Asian American identity, silence has functioned as a metaphor for the assimilative and positive imagery of the "good" minorities. More recently, analysis of popular imagery of the "model minority" suggest that silence ought to be understood as an adaptive mechanism to a racially discriminatory society rather than as an intrinsic part of Asian American culture.[13]

If silence has been a powerful metaphor in Asian American history, it is also a crucial element of discussions of gay/lesbian identity, albeit in a *somewhat* different way. In both cases, silence may be viewed as the oppressive cost of a racially biased or heterosexist society. For gays and lesbians, the act of coming out takes on symbolic importance, not just as a personal affirmation of "this is who I am," but additionally as a critique of expected norms in society, "we are everywhere." While "breaking the silence" about Asian Americans refers to crashing popular stereotypes about them, and shares with the gay act of "coming out" the desire to define oneself rather than be defined by others, there remains an important difference between the two.

The relative invisibility of homosexuality compared with Asian American identity means that silence and its corollary space, the closet, are more ephemeral, appear less fixed as boundaries of social identities, less likely to be taken-for-granted than markers of race, and consequently, more likely to be problematized and theorized in discussions that have as yet barely begun on racial identity. Put another way, homosexuality is more clearly seen as *constructed* than racial identity.[14] Theoretically speaking, homosexual identity does not enjoy the same privileged stability as racial identity. The borders that separate gay from straight, and, "in" from "out," are so fluid that in the final moment we can only be sure that sexual identities are as Diana Fuss notes, "in Foucaldian terms, less a matter of final discovery than a matter of perpetual invention."[15]

Thus, while silence is a central piece of theoretical discussions of homosexuality, it is viewed primarily as a negative stereotype in the case of Asian Americans. What seems at first a simple question in gay identity of being "in" or "out" is actually laced in epistemological knots.

For example, a common question asked of gays and lesbians by one another, or by straights, is, "Are you out?" The answer to that question (yes and no) is typically followed by a list of who knows and who does not (e.g., my coworkers know, but my family doesn't . . . ). But the question of who knows or how many people know about one's gayness raises yet another question, "how many, or which, people need to know one is gay before one qualifies as "out?" Or as Fuss says, "To be out, in common gay parlance, is precisely to be no longer out; to be out is to be finally outside of exteriority and all the exclusions and deprivations such outsider-hood imposes. Or, put another way, to be out is really to be in — inside the realm of the visible, the speakable, the culturally intelligible."[16]

Returning to the issue of silence and homosexuality in Asian America, it seems that topics of sex, sexuality, and gender, are *already* diffused through discussions of Asian America.[17] For example, numerous writers have disclosed, and challenged, the panoply of contradictory sexually-charged images of Asian American women as docile and subservient on the one hand, and as ruthless matahari, dragon-lady aggressors on the other. And of course, Frank Chin's tirades against the feminization of Asian American men has been one reaction to the particular way in which Asian Americans have been historically (de)sexualized as racial subjects. Moving from popular imagery of Asian Americans, *the people*, to Asia, *the nation*, Chow uses Bertolucci's blockbuster film, *The Last Emperor*, to illustrate what she calls, "the metaphysics of feminizing the other (culture)" wherein China is predictably cast as a "feminized, eroticized, space."[18]

That the topic of *homo*-sexuality in Asian American studies is often treated in whispers, if mentioned at all, should be some indication of trouble. It is noteworthy, I think, that in the last major anthology on Asian American women, *Making Waves*, the author of the essay on Asian

American lesbians was the only contributor who did not wish her last name to be published.[19] Of course, as we all know, a chorus of sympathetic bystanders is chanting about homophobia, saying, "she was worried about her job, her family, her community." Therefore, perhaps a good starting point to consider lesbian and gay identities in Asian American studies is by problematizing the silences surrounding homosexuality in Asian America.

It would be easy enough for me to say that I often feel a part of me is "silenced" in Asian American Studies. But I can hardly place all of the blame on my colleagues. Sometimes I silence myself as much as I feel silenced by them. And my silencing act is a blaring welter of false starts, uncertainties, and anxieties. For example, on the one hand, an omnipresent little voice tells me that visibility is better than invisibility, and therefore, coming out is an affirming social act. On the other hand, I fear the awkward silences and struggle for conversation that sometimes follow the business of coming out. One has to think about when and where to time the act since virtually no one has ever asked me, "Are you a lesbian?" Another voice reminds me that the act of coming out, once accomplished, almost always leaves me wondering whether I did it for myself or them. Not only that, but at the moment that I have come out, relief that is born of honesty and integrity quickly turns to new uncertainty. This time, my worry is that someone will think that in my coming out, they will now have a ready-made label for me, lesbian. The prospect that someone may think that they know *me* because they comprehend the category *lesbian* fills me with stubborn resistance. The category lesbian calls up so many different images of women who love other women that I do not think that any one — gay or straight — could possibly know or find me through that category alone. No wonder that I mostly find it easier to completely avoid the whole issue of sexual identity in discussions with colleagues.

There are so many different and subtle ways to come out. I am not much of a queer nation type, an "in your face" queer — I catalogue my own brand of lesbian identity as a kind of Asian American "take" on gay identity. I do not wear pink triangles, have photos of girls kissing in my living room, or, make a point of bringing up my girlfriend in conversation. In effect, my sexual identity is often backgrounded or stored somewhere in between domains of public and private. I used to think that my style of being gay was dignified and polite—sophisticated, civilized, and genteel. Work was work and home was home. The separation of work and home has been an easy gulf to maintain, less simple to bridge. However, recently, I have come to think otherwise.

But all this talk about me is getting away from my point which is that while it would be easy enough for me to say many of us feel "silenced," which alone might argue for inclusion of gay sexualities in discourse about the Asian American experience, that is not enough. Technically speaking then, the terms "addition" and "inclusion" are misleading. I'm afraid that in using such terms, the reader will assume that by adding gay/lesbian experiences to the last week's topics in a course on Asian American contemporary issues, or, by including lesbians in a discussion of Asian women, the deed is done. Instead, I want to suggest that the task is better thought of as just begun, that the topic of sexualities ought to be envisioned as a means, not an end, to theorizing about the Asian American experience.

For example, one way that homosexuality may be seen as a vehicle for theorizing identity in Asian America is for the missteps, questions, and silences that are often clearest in collisions at the margins (identities as opposed to people). In the following discussion, I describe two such confrontations—the coming out of a white student in an Asian American Studies class and the problem of authenticity in gay/lesbian Asian American writing. Each tells in its own way the awkward limits of ethnic-based models of identity.

### a. the coming out incident

Once, when I was a teaching assistant in Asian American Studies at Berkeley during the early 1980s, a lesbian, one of only two white students in my section, decided to come out during the first section meeting. I had asked each student to explain their interest, personal and intellectual, in Asian American Studies. Many students mentioned wanting to know "more about their heritage," and "knowing the past in order to understand the present." The lesbian was nearly last to speak. After explaining that she wanted to understand the heritage of a friend who was Asian American, her final words came out tentatively, as if she had been deliberating about whether or not to say them, "And, I guess I also want you all to know that I am a lesbian." In the silence that followed I quickly surveyed the room. A dozen or

so Asian American students whom I had forced into a semi-circular seating arrangement stared glumly at their shoes. The two white students, both of whom were lesbians, as I recall, sat together, at one end of the semi-circle. They glanced expectantly around the circle, and then, they too, looked at the ground. I felt as though my own world had split apart, and the two pieces were in front of me, drifting, surrounding, and at that moment, both silent.

I knew both parts well. On the one side, I imagined that the Asian American students in the class, recoiled in private horror at the lesbian, not so much because she was a lesbian or white, but because she insisted on publicly baring her soul in front of them. I empathized with the Asian American students because they reminded me of myself as an undergraduate. I rarely spoke in class or section, unless of course, I was asked a direct question. While my fellow white students, most often the males, chatted effortlessly in section about readings or lectures, I was almost always mute. I marveled at the ease with which questions, thoughts, answers, and even half-baked ideas rolled off their tongues and floated discussion. For them, it all seemed so easy. As for me, I struggled with the act of talking in class. Occasionally, I managed to add a question to the discussion, but more often, I found that after silently practicing my entry into a fast-moving exchange, the discussion had moved on. In my silence, I chastised myself for moving too slowly, for hesitating where others did not, and alternately, chastised the other students for their bull-dozing, loose lips. I valorized and resented the verbal abilities of my fellow classmates. And I imagined how the Asian American students who sat in my class the day the lesbian decided to come out, like me, named the ability to bare one's soul through words, "white." On the other side, I empathized as well with the lesbian. I identified with what I imagined as her compelling need to claim her identity, to be like the others in the class, indeed to be an "other" at all in a class where a majority of the students were in search of their "roots." I figured that being a lesbian, while not quite like being Asian American, must have seemed to the intrepid student as close to the ethnic model as she could get. Finally, I thought she represented a side of me that always wanted, but never could quite manage, to drop the coming out bomb in groups that did not expect it. Part of the pleasure in being an "outsider" can be in the affirmation of the identity abhorred by "insiders." I imagined that she and her friend had signed up for my section because they *knew* I too was a lesbian, and I worried that they assumed that I might be able to protect them from the silence of the closet.

In the silence that followed the act of coming out, and indeed, in the ten weeks of class in which no one spoke of it again, I felt an awkwardness settle over our discussions in section. I was never sure exactly how the Asian American students perceived the lesbian—as a wannabe "minority," as a comrade in marginality, as any White Other, or perhaps, they did not think of it at all. Nor did I ever know if the lesbian found what she was looking for, a better understanding of the Asian American experience, in the silence that greeted her coming out.

The silences I have described here dramatize how dialogue between identities is hampered by the assumption of what Wittig calls the "discourses of heterosexuality." She says:

> These discourses of heterosexuality oppress us in the sense that they prevent us from speaking unless we speak in their terms. Everything which puts them into question is at once disregarded as elementary. Our refusal of the totalizing interpretation of psychoanalysis makes the theoreticians say that we neglect the symbolic dimension. These discourses deny us every possibility of creating our own categories. But their most ferocious action is the unrelenting tyranny that they exert upon our physical and mental selves.[20]

More important, the coming out incident suggests that marginalization is no guarantee for dialogue. If there is to be an interconnectedness between different vantage points, we will need to establish an art of political conversation that allows for affirmation of difference without choking secularization. The construction of such a politics is based implicitly on our vision of what happens, or, what ought to happen, when difference meets itself—queer meets Asian, black meets Korean, feminist meets Greens, etc., at times, all in one person.[21] What exactly must we know about these other identities in order to engage in dialogue?

### b. the question of authenticity

What we do know about Asian American gays and lesbians must be gleaned from personal narratives, literature, poetry, short stories, and essays. But first, what falls under the mantle, *Asian American*

*gay and lesbian* writings? Clearly, lesbians and gays whose writings are self-conscious reflections on Asian American identity and sexual identity ought to be categorized as Asian American gay/lesbian writers. For example, Kitty Tsui, Barbara Noda, and Merle Woo are individuals who have identified themselves, and are identified by others, as *Asian American lesbian voices*. Similarly, in a recent collection of essays from a special issue of *Amerasia, Burning Cane,* Alice Hom ruminates on how an assortment of Others—white dykes, Asian dykes, family, and communities—react to her as butchy/androgynous, as Asian American, as a lesbian. These writers are lesbians and they write about themselves as lesbians which grants them authorial voice *as a lesbian*. But they also identify as *Asian American*, and are concerned with the ways in which these different sources of community—lesbian and Asian American—function in their everyday lives.

But what then about those who do not write explicitly or self-consciously about their sexuality or racial identity? For example, an essay on AIDS and mourning by Jeff Nunokawa, while written by a Japanese-American English professor, does not focus on issues of racial and sexual *identity*, and as such, is neither self-consciously gay nor Asian American.[22] What are we to make of such work? On the one hand, we might wish to categorize the author as a gay Asian American writer, whether he wishes to take this sign or not, presuming of course, that he is gay since his essay appears in an anthology subtitled, "gay theories," and, in addition presuming that he is Asian American, or at least identifies as such given his last name. On the other hand, we might instead argue that it is the author's work, his subject matter, and not the status of the author, that marks the work as gay, Asian American, or both. . . . In this case, we might infer that since the topic of the essay is AIDS and men, the work is best categorized as "gay," but not Asian American.

This may seem a mundane example, but it illustrates well how authorial voice and subject matter enter into our deliberations of what counts and what does not as Asian American gay/lesbian writings. . . . The university is filled with those of us, who while we live under signs like gay, Asian, feminist, ecologist, middle-class, etc., do not make such signs the central subject of our research. And what about those individuals who write about gays/lesbians, but who identify themselves as heterosexual? In the same way that colonizers write about the colonized, and more recently, the colonized write back, blacks write about whites and vice versa, "we" write about "them" and so on.

I want to be clear, here. I am not suggesting that we try to locate Asian American gay/lesbian sensibilities as if they exist in some pure form and are waiting to be discovered. Rather, I think we ought to take seriously Trinh T. Minh-ha's warning that, "Trying to find the other by defining otherness or by explaining the other through laws and generalities is, as Zen says, like beating the moon with a pole or scratching an itching foot from the outside of a shoe."[23] My concern here is to turn the question from one about a particular identity to the more general question of the way in which the concept of identity is deployed in Asian American history.

Thus, not only is marginalization no guarantee for dialogue, but the state of being marginalized itself may not be capturable as a fixed, coherent, and holistic identity. Our attempts to define categories like "Asian American" or "gay" are necessarily incomplete. For example, as Judith Butler has noted:

> To write or speak *as a lesbian* appears a paradoxical appearance of this "I," one which feels neither true nor false. For it is a production, usually in response to a request, to come out or write in the name of an identity which, once produced, sometimes functions as a politically efficacious phantasm.
> . . . This is not to say that I will not appear at political occasions under the sign of the lesbian, but that I would like to have it permanently unclear what precisely that sign signifies.[24]

A politics of identity and whatever kind of politics ensues from that project—multiculturalism, feminism, and gay movements—is first of all a politics *about* identity. That is, about the lack of a wholistic and "coherent narrative" derived from race, class, gender, and sexuality. . . . Because no sooner do we define, for example, "Japanese American" as a person of Japanese ancestry when we are forced back to the drawing board by the biracial child of Japanese American and an African American who thinks of herself as "black" or "feminist."

## III. RETHINKING IDENTITY POLITICS

Lisa Lowe in her discussion of identity politics affirms the articulation of "Asian American" identity while simultaneously warning us of its overarching, consuming, and essentializing dangers. She (Lowe) closes her discussion saying:

> I want simply to remark that in the 1990s, we can afford to rethink the notion of ethnic identity in terms of cultural, class, and gender differences, rather than presuming similarities and making the erasure of particularity the basis of unity. In the 1990s, we can diversify our political practices to include a more heterogeneous group and to enable crucial alliances with other groups—ethnicity-based, class-based, and sexuality-based—in the ongoing work of transforming hegemony.[25]

I have intended this essay, in part, as an answer to Lowe's call to broaden the scope of Asian American discourse about identity. But there is a caveat. The gist of this essay has been to insist that our valuation of heterogeneity not be ad-hoc and that we seize the opportunity to recognize non-ethnic based differences—like homosexuality—as an occasion to critique the tendency toward essentialist currents in ethnic-based narratives and disciplines. In short, the practice of including gayness in Asian America rebounds into a reconsideration of the theoretical status of the concept of "Asian American" identity. The interior of the category "Asian American" ought not be viewed as a hierarchy of identities led by ethnic-based narratives, but rather, the complicated interplay and collision of different identities.

At the heart of Lowe's argument for recognizing diversity within Asian American, generational, national, gender, and class, as well as my insistence in this essay on a qualitative, not quantitative view of difference, is a particular notion of subjectivity. That notion of the subject as non-unitary stands in sharp contrast to the wholistic and coherent identities that find expression in much contemporary talk and writing about Asian Americans. At times, our need to "reclaim history" has been bluntly translated into a possessiveness about *the* Asian American experience (politics, history, literature) or perspectives as if such experiences or perspectives were not diffuse, shifting, and often contradictory. Feminists and gay writers, animated by post-structuralism's decentering practices offer an alternative, to theorize the subject rather than assume its truth, or worse yet, assign to it a truth.

Concretely, to theorize the subject means to uncover in magnificent detail the "situatedness"[26] of perspectives or identities as knowledge which even as it pleas for an elusive common language or claims to establish truth, cannot guarantee a genuine politics of diversity, that is, political conversation *and* argument, between the margins.[27] Such a politics will be marked by moments of frustration and tension because the participants will be pulling and pushing one another with statements such as, "I am like you," and "I am not like you." But the rewards for an identity politics that is not primarily ethnic-based or essentialist along some other axis will be that conversations like the one which never took place in my Asian American studies section many years ago will finally begin. Moreover, our search for authenticity of voice—whether in gay/lesbian Asian American writing or in some other identity string—will be tempered by the realization that in spite of our impulse to clearly (de)limit them, there is perpetual uncertainty and flux governing the construction and expression of identities.

## NOTES

My special thanks to Russell Leong for his encouragement and commentary on this essay.

1. Alice Walker, *Conditions: Five, the Black Women's Issue* (1984), 288–89.

2. See Donna Haraway, "Situated Knowledges: The Science Question in Feminism and the Privilege of Partial Perspective," *Feminist Studies* 14:3 (1988), 575–99.

3. See Teresa de Lauretis, "Feminist Studies/Critical Studies: Issues, Terms, and Contexts," in *Feminist Studies/Critical Studies*, edited by Teresa de Lauretis (Bloomington: Indiana University Press, 1986), 1–19; bell hooks, *Yearning: Race, Gender and Cultural Politics* (Boston: South End Press, 1990); Trinh T. Minh-ha, *Woman, Native, Other* (Bloomington: Indiana University Press, 1989); Chandra Talpade Mohanty, "Under Western Eyes: Feminist Scholarship and Colonialist Discourses," *Third World Women and the Politics of Feminism*, Chandra Talpade Mohanty, Ann Russo and Lourdes Torres, eds. (Bloomington: Indiana University Press, 1991), 52–80; Linda Alcoff, "Cultural Feminism Versus Post-Structuralism: The Identity Crisis in Feminist Theory," *Signs*, 13:3 (1988), 405–37.

4. Trinh T. Minh-ha, 28.

5. Epstein (1987). Jeffrey Escoffier, editor of *Outlook* magazine made this point in a speech at the American Educational Research Association meetings in San Francisco, April 24, 1992.

6. See Elizabeth Ellsworth, "Why Doesn't This Feel Empowering? Working through the Repressive Myths of Critical Pedagogy," 59:3 (1989), 297–324.

7. Ed Cohen, "Who Are We?" Gay "Identity" as Political (E)motion," *inside/out*, Diana Fuss, ed. (New York and London: Routledge, 1991), 71–92.

8. Of course there are exceptions, for example, blacks that "pass" and perhaps this is where homosexuality and racial identity come closest to one another, amongst those minorities who "pass" and gays who can also "pass."

9. I do not mean to suggest that there is only one presentation of self as lesbian. For example, one development recently featured in the *Los Angeles Times* is the evolution of "lipstick lesbians" (Van Gelder, 1991). The fashion issue has also been discussed in gay/lesbian publications. For example, Stein (1988) writing for *Outlook* has commented on the lack of correspondence between fashion and sexual identity, "For many, you can dress as femme one day and as butch the next."

10. Compare for example the histories: Takaki's *Strangers from a Different Shore*, Sucheng Chan's *Asian Americans*, and Roger Daniels' *Chinese and Japanese in America* with Jonathan Katz' *Gay American History*, Jeffrey Week's *The History of Sexuality*, Michel Foucault's *The History of Sexuality*, and David Greenberg, *The Construction of Homosexuality*.

11. See Steffi San Buenaventura, "The Master and the Federation: A Filipino-American Social Movement in California and Hawaii," *Social Process in Hawaii* 33 (1991), 169–193.

12. Wynn Young, "Poor Butterfly" *Amerasia Journal* 17:2 (1991), 118.

13. See Keith Osajima, "Asian Americans as the Model Minority: An Analysis of the Popular Press Image in the 1960s and 1980s," *Reflections on Shattered Windows: Promises and Prospects for Asian American Studies*, Gary Y. Okihiro, Shirley Hune, Arthur A. Hansen and John M. Liu, eds. (Pullman: Washington State University Press, 1988), 165–174.

14. See Judith Butler, *Gender Trouble* (New York: Routledge 1990); Michel Foucault, *The History of Sexuality, Volume 1: An Introduction*, trans. Robert Hurley (New York: Vintage, 1980); Monique Wittig, *The Straight Mind and Other Essays* (Boston: Beacon Press 1992); David Greenberg, *The Construction of Homosexuality*.

15. Diana Fuss, "Inside/Out," *inside/out*, Diana Fuss, ed. (New York: Routledge, 1991), 1–10.

16. *Ibid.*

17. Consider for example debates in recent times over intermarriage patterns, the controversy over Asian Americans dating white men, the Asian Men's calendar, and the continuation of discussions started

over a decade ago about gender, assimilation and nativism in Asian American literature.

18. See Rey Chow, *Woman and Chinese Modernity* (Minneapolis: University of Minnesota Press, 1991).

19. See Asian Women United, *Making Waves* (Boston: Beacon Press, 1989).

20. Monique Wittig, "The Straight Mind," *The Straight Mind and Other Essays* (Boston: Beacon Press, 1992), 25.

21. All too often we conceptualize different identities as separate, discrete, and given (as opposed to continually constructed and shifting). For an example of how "identity" might be conceptualized as contradictory and shifting moments rather than discrete and warring "homes" see Minnie Bruce Pratt,

"Identity: Skin Blood Heart" and commentary by Biddy Martin and Chandra Talpade Mohanty, "Feminist Politics: What's Home Got to Do with It?"

22. See Jeff Nunokawa, " 'All the Sad Young Men': Aids and the Work of Mourning," *inside/out*, Diana Fuss, ed., 311–323.

23. Trinh T. Minh-ha, 76.

24. Judith Butler, "Imitation and Gender Subordination," *inside/out*, Diana Fuss, ed., 13–31.

25. Lisa Lowe, "Heterogeneity, Hybridity and Multiplicity: Marking Asian American Differences," *Diaspora* (Spring 1991), 24–44.

26. Haraway, "Situated Knowledges."

27. I am indebted to Wendy Brown for this point. See Wendy Brown "Feminist Hesitations, Postmodern Exposures," *Differences* 2:1 (1991).

# | 11 |

# *Strangers at Home: Bisexuals in the Queer Movement*

## CAROL QUEEN

As a bisexually-identified adolescent, I was alone with my difference. My lot was no different from that of all the lesbian, gay, bisexual, gender-bent, and otherwise queer youths whose hearts and hormones send different messages than those heard by our straight "peers."

I went off to college vowing to find others, and did, at the Gay People's Alliance. They were warm and welcoming until I said I was bi. Then their eyes rolled, and I know in retrospect what they were thinking: "Another poor closet case influenced by Elton John." Patiently it was explained to me that almost every young gay person eases into her or his rightful homosexual identity by leaning on a "safer" and "more socially acceptable" bisexual identification, which provided the person just coming out a cushion of "heterosexual privilege" until s/he had acquired enough gay pride to drop the charade.

In short, I'd grow out of it.

Not much had been written about bisexual-

ity—it was 1974. I found only a couple of bi-positive pieces written from what I now might call a "queer Utopian" perspective: "In a nonsexist and nonhomophobic world, we might all be bisexual." There was a queer movement twenty years ago too, embracing a wider rainbow of non-hetero alternative sexualities than the already-becoming-staid gay movement found acceptable; but before long the radical discourse about queerdom fell out of favor as the gay movement worked its way towards the political mainstream.

I was barely seventeen. I had just kissed my first woman. Maybe my new friends in the gay community were right about, as they termed it, this "phase."

I saw that the polite distance between my new gay friends and me would be an obstacle to establishing relationships with women. My few forays

*Out/Look*, 16:23, 29–33, 1992.

into erotic desire for straight women bore the same fruit they usually do for "gold-star" lesbians—frustration and emotional pain. There was no community of bisexual women with whom to explore my attractions. I did what many other bisexual people have done—I stopped insisting I be acknowledged and accepted as bisexual. I lived and loved, passing, in the gay community, and for many years only a few people realized that I still harbored erotic desires for men and that, occasionally, I acted on them.

Please understand that identifying as heterosexual—relying on that elusive "privilege"—never once occurred to me. I was not and am not heterosexual. Discourse was binary, with only two possible sexual orientations from which to choose, and identifying as heterosexual was not an option. Closeting myself about my bisexuality gave me access to a community where I desperately wanted to belong, and for the next ten years *did* belong, as an activist, an advocate, and a lover of women—a lesbian.

Perhaps only a queer who has had the narrowness of the closet work at her/his sense of self will understand how this felt to me, and to the many other lesbian and gay community members who hide the truths of their sexual lives. I was an out lesbian with a dirty secret, at odds with the expressed ethics of a queer community which said "out" was good—but hadn't accepted me warmly when, naively, I had taken them at their word.

The bones of this story are not just mine. Many other bisexuals have carved out lives (hidden or not) among lesbians and gays. The lesbian and gay movement must come to terms with the position of bisexual people within it because we're already here. It won't help to vote whether or not bisexuals should be let in: we *are* in. Nor can there be a vote to exclude us; bisexual people whose longtime and cherished home is the lesbian and gay community will do what we've always done to stay affiliated with it—we will fight, or lie and deny that our opposite sex relationships have any meaning. Many of us come out of our closet only when we get so sick of it that staying in threatens our sanity or our sense of authenticity. Some of us come out when sexual behavior with an other-sex partner leads to love and we can't bring ourselves to deny it. And, increasingly these days, bisexuals are coming out because they realize they can—that a growing bisexual community exists to welcome them.

## WHY ARE WE ARGUING?

Why are we, even for a minute, searching for the experiences and attitudes that divide bisexuals from lesbians and gay men? Why aren't we searching for what we hold in common? As bisexual theorist Amanda Udis Kessler notes, we "share the same issues, and not just 'half the time.' We don't get half-gaybashed when we walk down the street with our same-sex lovers. . . . We don't get half-fired from our jobs, or lose only half of our children in court battles. . . . Lesbian/gay issues are our issues, and we want to work on them with lesbians and gay men."

Working in concert with lesbians and gay men, though, can be emotionally difficult; we're forced to contend with the feeling that many of our queer sisters and brothers see us as strangers in the house. These and other factors have led bisexual women and men to look to each other for community.

The question of bisexual participation in the lesbian and gay movement is not new, in spite of the attention the recent resurgence of the bisexual movement has received. Bisexuals have generated debate at least as far back as Stonewall. The lesbian and gay movement grapples with issues of sexual diversity—bi and otherwise—because it's fully diverse itself, a microcosm of the larger society in which homosexuality is only the biggest of many secrets that refuse to stay silenced.

I assume that what is healthy for us in our workplaces and families of origin—to own our experience and insist it be honored—is equally right in our queer families of choice and our political organizations. When I finally came out again as bisexual, ten years after my first attempt, I was struck by how many people in my small-city gay community found excuses to chat with me privately so they could confide their feelings of concern about their own opposite-sex desires or to confess that they'd even gone so far as to secretly act on them. These whispered confidences show me that Kinsey, who did so much to help us all out of the closet earlier in this century, was right to sketch us on a continuum, not in fixed categories. But Kinsey had nothing to say about our community affiliations, and it is clear to me that one reason these secrets are not usually aired is because they threaten our sense of who we are and where we are at home.

Many lesbians and gay men seem to have bought the line that bisexuals, "confused" about their sexual identities, make unstable mates and community members. Absent from the discourse has been the revelation that many bisexuals are in fact not confused—that the confusion lies, if anywhere, in the reactions of monosexuals to us. Nothing in either our homophobic culture or our homosexual counterculture helps us with the shock that our desires and affections are not always labeled "either/or." Sometimes a bisexual "phase" may be an indicator of confusion generated by a person's internalized homophobia, but I think a more common confusion comes from a monosexual's realization that the walls of her/his box are beginning to crumble.

Many bisexuals do not seek refuge in a homophobic closet that contains both pleasure and privilege. Those who do are the people many lesbians and gays think of as representative of biness. That "honor" has gone to those who mirror the gay community's own antipathy. Heterosexuals are not the only people who fall prey to stereotyped thinking: thus the bisexual role models my gay community of the seventies recognized were mostly rock stars who were said to be closeted about their homosexuality. This is a gay cultural version of our parents' assumptions that homosexual Boy Scouts would grow up to be Liberace—other models of being gay aren't envisioned because they're not seen. When our role models are circumscribed or removed, how are we to be guided in our development?

The lesbian and gay community knows the effects of this silencing, but has ironically adopted as forebears some historical figures who were probably bisexual. Some bisexuals want to take back the Virginia Woolfs and Oscar Wildes, but I think we ought to share them—the sexually divergent, and often gender-bent, people of yesterday can be heroes to all of us. Besides, it can be argued that none of us has any business labeling people who are no longer around to speak for themselves; it displays a distressingly ahistorical perspective to use late-twentieth-century constructs to describe the lives lived in a social context we can never fully understand. Lesbians and gay men might argue that in the presence of the kind of supportive community we now rely on, people having same- as well as other-sex relationships in other times might have elected to be what we now define as gay. We'll never know. Many people in other eras have exhibited exclusively same-sex erotic behavior. Denying that both homo- and heterosexual activity might naturally occur in one person's lifetime (either then or now) is just an academic version of some monosexuals' favorite game: Make Them Choose.

Some gays and lesbians wonder at many bisexuals' angry emphasis on biphobia in the gay community: Don't we know who our real enemies are? The answer is yes, and the dismal truth is that we *expect* homophobia—who in this culture hasn't been subtly or overtly warned against crossing that line? Bisexual anger has a simple genesis: We expected more of others who have faced homophobia.

## SEEDS OF ANGER

Representatives of lesbian-feminist separatism may feel singled out as special targets of our anger and distress. To the extent that this is true, the seeds of anger lie in lesbian separatism as a politic: In this reading of feminism, specific sex acts take on politicized meaning. These are said to have consequences for the consciousness of the person performing them. Lesbian feminism is arguably the most proscriptive gay or lesbian politic, generating in its adherents the greatest tendency to judge others' (especially sexual) behavior. Gay men, for example, seem more likely to cite personal antipathy or simple stereotypes about bisexuals as a source of their chagrin. A great many bisexual women, particularly those who are feminist and lesbian-identified, have felt both personally and politically rejected and judged by the separatist sisters. Even those with no such experience may feel wary having heard other bisexual women's stories. No one likes to feel attacked, even politically.

In today's climate of attack against sexual minorities, we have little to gain from separatism. Much as we need to honor our differences, we must understand that the strategic risks we run as fractionalized peoples are greater than any risks to individuals' identities. Struggling toward a more inclusive community does not mean we have to put an end to difference—it means we have to deal with it.

I understand the antipathy some gays and lesbians feel about bisexuals; I felt it myself when I was trying to live within a normative lesbian community. I sometimes feel it today in the presence of bisexual people who are not queer identified: Once a faggot-bi boyfriend and I were at a bi Thanksgiving celebration at which all the men were visibly nervous about Boyfriend's fey mannerisms. The two of us left shaking our heads, having felt not home, but homophobia. The dif-

ference between a gay-identified and a heterosexually-identified bisexuality challenges us when
we come together to build bisexual identity. But I
have to ask: how will any of those (mostly newly-
out) bisexuals ever come to be queer identified if
they have no access to the queer community?
How will they learn the folkways of the
lesbian/gay world if that world does not welcome
them as bisexuals?

Ironically, there is a strongly feminist bent to
the organized bisexual movement today. Activists
push to include political issues that have seen
more play in the lesbian feminist community
than elsewhere in the lesbian and gay world.
Issues of access and inclusion around race, economic status, and dis/abilities have been high priorities at nationally and regionally-organized conferences. Bisexual women are no more comfortable with sexism than lesbians, in spite of the fact
that some lesbians code some bi women's sexual

practices as inherently sexist.

With the rise of the queer movement we still
define ourselves in relation — nay, opposition — to
a culturally conservative heterosexual norm, but
we are increasingly aware that gold-star lesbians
and gay men are not the only people who lead dissident lives and that, in fact, heterosexual behavior does not always equal "straight." When I strap
on a dildo and fuck my male partner, we are
engaging in "heterosexual" behavior, but I can
tell you that it feels altogether *queer*, and I'm sure
my grandmother and Jesse Helms would say the
same. Reifying other-sex behavior and making its
absence the basis of gay politics doesn't strike me
as very careful analysis. Sexual variation brought
out of the closet is seen as dangerous and dissident by the status quo — please remember that
homosexuality is not the only sexual behavior for
which people have been arrested, institutionalized, or persecuted.

# | 12 |

# *Just Add Water: Searching for the Bisexual Politic*

## ARA WILSON

Imagine a world in which our genders had nothing to do with whom we fell into bed with. To be
sure, for some lesbian and gay readers, that image
is a nightmare. But for many anti-authoritarian
and progressive groups, from the Bloomsbury circle of Woolf and Keynes to socialist sects, the
relaxed freedom, radical plurality, and sheer poly-
morphic humanity of a bisexual world is a recurring utopian ideal. From the sounds of it, the new
"bisexual movement" may be the latest incarnation of the longing for an existence free from constricting gender and sex classifications.

Ignoring, for a moment, that one movement's
utopia may be another movement's hell, I'll allow
the possibility that a radical, humanistic ideal
underpins this fledgling bisexual "movement."
First I have to ask, though: what kind of "movement" is this? It doesn't seem to be about civil

rights (especially since gay and lesbian reforms
have fought discrimination that is based on "sexual preference"); nor is it revolutionary in the
classic sense of that term.

One explanation of what the "movement" is
about can be found in the premiere issue of a new
bisexual magazine. On the inside cover, a six-part
dictionary definition of "move" accompanies the
publication's clever name, *Anything That Moves*.
The final instance of the last meaning, "to set in
motion," is emphasized: "STIR OR SHAKE."
Not advance, progress, change, or take action,
but movement pure and simple. And, from the
perspective of an embattled lesbian, this emphasis indeed seems to be appropriate for the bisexual

*Out/Look*, 16:22, 24–28, 1992.

movement's political practices and endeavors thus far: movement and shaking, not direction and vision. Underpinning this understanding of a movement as disruption, noise, motion—a quite prevalent notion these days—is, I think, an ideal of sexual freedom that is probably not so different from the vision held by many gays, queers, and even lesbians. So why are so many of us reluctant to unquestioningly acquiesce to the bisexual political agenda?

Turn from inspiration to movement: If bisexuals need to move—whether toward an ideal, or just shake shake shake—what are they moving *against*? What is it that prevents the world from realizing plural erogeneity? To have movement where there had been none or little, the activists organizing around their complex sexuality must have some picture of what blocks their progress.

## WHAT'S THE THEORY?

The most visible model for organizing around sexuality is the kind of gay and lesbian—or "queer"—politics in the foreground today. Gay men and lesbians have taken a sexual identity and organized a political community around that. And who could ignore the appeal of QUEER NATION, queer politics, and in-your-face strategies of recent or young—post 1985, say—gay and lesbian activism?

Like one big gay pride march, gay and lesbian politics of recent years have heralded our sheer existence: "We're here, we're queer, and we're not going shopping." This brash tack diagnoses homophobia as the problem, and loud and proud public identity as the cure. It is often described as the perfect instance of "identity politics," a double-edged label.

The lesson of this queer politics for people who consider their bisexual practices and desires to be of vital importance is this: naming bisexuality in the face of silence or misrepresentation is the key. In this queer-style politics, individual sexual practices and desires, especially those criticized, condemned or scorned, are political precisely because of that scorn. This pervasive idea is yet another interpretation of "the personal is political." Declaring one's deviant, transgressive erotic biography is a political act brimming with the potential to subvert repression and to facilitate the exploration of sexual practices and beings.

So, according to the logic of this queer moment in political time, one reason that a poly-

sexual world does not exist, or exists only precariously, is that bisexuals and bisexuality are invisible and misrepresented. The neglect, denial, and coercion surrounding a person's erotic engagements with both men and women is oppressive; it misrepresents the truth, and recreates a socio-cultural regime that falls far short of a polyerotic utopia. This is so even, or especially, if the repression comes from within the embattled gay and lesbian world itself. Therefore, the chief political strategy of bisexual politics is the enunciation of the existence of men and women who have sex with both men and women. And so we see a florescence of declarations of bisexuality—and even, in some corners, a reclaiming of famous but hidden-from-history bisexuals. Bisexual activists and anthologists Lani Kaahumanu and Loraine Hutchins argue in *Anything That Moves* for reclaiming Langston Hughes, Ma Rainey, and Bessie Smith, "who wrote and sang wonderfully heterosexual lyrics," as bisexual. The truth is important, and the truth is that many of us have had sex with, or desires for, both men and women (a point widely recognized in gay, lesbian, and queer circles). The bisexual spokespeople understand the expression of this truth about the existence of bisexuality as a political mission. But applying a literal or clinical definition of bisexual—as anyone whose erotic life engages both males and females—is unsettling to many gays and lesbians because it disregards the involuntary, dare we say compulsory, status of heterosexuality. It is also a political problem because of its focus on the identities of individuals.

## WHAT ARE THEY AGAINST?

In this schema, the self-definition of bisexual individuals is of paramount importance. But is declaring a literal bisexual identity politically or otherwise satisfying enough? Following the model of Queer Nation and other movements, individual bisexual identity suggests the possibility of some kind of group identity, or even "community." Unhappily, the move from individual to community has so far been a tricky one for the bisexual movement. The historians of bisexuality cited above address this question:

Why have we "accepted" invisibility, and why haven't we, up until this point, projected a more visible presence, creating a prominent community that even the most virulent biphobe would have to recognize? The answer, of course, is that this is the way oppression operates, in this case bisexual oppression.

This logic suggests that the formation of community is inhibited by oppression and not the complexities of bisexual identity.

The opening editorial of *Anything That Moves* declares: "It is time for the bisexual voice to be heard." It asserts:

> We are tired of being analyzed, defined and represented by people other than ourselves—or worse yet, not considered at all. We are frustrated by the imposed isolation and invisibility that comes from being told or expected to "choose" either a homosexual or a heterosexual identity. . . . We are angered by those who refuse to accept our existence; our issues; our contributions . . . our voice.

I am intrigued by the incensed demand for recognition. Of course there are the dominant objectionable representations of bisexuals and bisexuality, notably the stereotypes of promiscuity and indecisive immaturity (although, like many guardians, the stepmother of a college friend definitely preferred indecisiveness to the finality of homosexuality, lamenting, "Couldn't you at least be bisexual?"). My library search for recent academic and media references demonstrated that the most striking image of the bisexual in the popular mind is of the AIDS-carrying bisexual man (there were also many references to the problem of a bisexual husband). And even if I'm not bi-identified, I am offended by the depiction of bisexuals in mainstream pornography—after all what are all those soft-focus depictions of sapphic love but the suggestion of a bisexual woman on a female swing?

I just don't think, though, that the preponderance of annoying (and in the case of bisexual AIDS carriers, dangerous) representations in dominant culture is what the bisexual movement's concern with silence and oppression is all about. What is really preventing the enunciation of bisexual voices? Who expects the choice between het or homo? Who refuses bisexuals?

Enter the generic 1970s-vintage lesbian feminist, who wishes to goddess these women giving energy to men would just quit, and who is committed to condemning, or better yet, policing the bisexual behaviors that underpin the movement. Or so some bisexual spokespeople imagine. It's easy to predict, and in fact to construct, the les-

bian-feminist separatist stance on bisexuality, since the figure of the dour lesbian on patrol for incorrect practices and attitudes has become a staple in contemporary gay and lesbian discourse.

"Biphobia!" as hostility toward bisexuals has been dubbed, was chanted against a lesbian feminist's speech in Northampton's Pride celebrations. It is lesbians who most often display, or are said to display, "biphobia." Now why is that? Undoubtably, there are whole covens of women cursing the drain of bisexual womens' energy (and when there aren't, we'll have to hire them). But the treatment of lesbian-feminist resistance to the bisexual movement highlights the flaws in the bisexual political picture.

## RETHINKING THE ENEMY

Bisexual activists seem not only uninterested in the actual lesbian-feminist stance, but dismissive of underlying worries that a rush of bisexuals will clamor into the queer world, possibly with heterosexual lovers—like straight men—in tow. The lack of curiosity about lesbian-feminist anxiety is in part a result of the dismissal of lesbians as stereotypically humorless, PC terrors, with no sense of style. It also shows a complete amnesia about feminist critiques of male dominance and of the increasingly documented but long-argued understanding that men get more money, attention, love, sex, power, and energy than similarly situated women do.

The easy dismissal of lesbian feminists is a symptom of the displacement of feminism to the background of contemporary sexual identity politics. Only through persistent effort (which is also called "being difficult" or "having no sense of humor") have lesbians won visibility, money, publications, and teeny bits of power in the predominantly male gay world. Still, in the current "queer" landscape, it is lesbians who are hardest to see. If bisexuals are "successful" in claiming a greater share of gay, lesbian, and queer space and resources, it is lesbians who have the most to lose.

In May of 1991, bisexual agitators staged a theatrical critique of "bi-phobia" in response to a flap (from lesbians) because the *San Francisco Bay Times* added the word "bisexual" to its masthead. The guerrilla troupe chose the Castro for this staging, a site decidedly famous for its unambiguous male queerness and, as an afterthought, for the presence of unarguably junior lesbian colleagues. In order to show that excluding bisexuals from gay and lesbian organizations weakens the fight against heterosexism and homophobia, the actors drew on right-wing motifs. The group called itself HUAC, "Homosexual Unity And Conformity." Just to remind you, the acronym parodies Joseph McCarthy's (absolutely non-parodic) House UnAmerican Activities Committee of the 1950s. A caption under a photograph printed in *Anything That Moves* identifies an actress: "A 'Real' Dyke in Steel Boots & Earth Mother for Pure Womynspace coaxing bisexual Cianna Stewart to 'Forswear dick forever.' " The guerrilla enterprise went to some pains to skewer gay men as well ("a nerdy faggot in trendy glasses" is the other photo's caption—ouch!), but the real focus of critique is against PC dykes.

This image of the righteous, irritable lesbian-feminist sourpuss is not new: what is new is the notion that these small pockets of women hold real power, power enough to oppress, police, and censor the behaviors of young people who have barely encountered this subculture in person. To be sure, some groups do hold sway over arenas of women's culture—publishing and festivals—and were in evidence at the much maligned national lesbian conference in Atlanta. But the notion of an all-powerful politically correct sex police leads to some curious political statements and priorities. A bisexual activist said that "queer het sex" takes place between young, sex-radical gay men and women as a revolt against PC sex. Radical, dude.

The bisexual identity movement frames itself with a self-comforting sense of equivalence: oppression by downwardly mobile lesbian feminists is equivalent to the anti-sex morality of the right and the church. Bi-phobic lesbians are interchangeable with HUAC, a government group which destroyed lives, careers, and a powerful radical spirit. Fellating a man is equivalent to going down on a woman. "Biphobia" becomes equivalent to homophobia because it restricts the freedom of these energetic individuals.

This equation is a delusion: a woman's fellatio and cunnilingus are not political equivalents. Not if you take a good look at the way sexual practices and identities are located, defined, and controlled in the social world, and see that men and women are not equivalent as sexual objects (even if we want them to be). Fellatio and cunnilingus may very well be comparable sexual practices in the life of a specific woman. But, as bisexual women must know all too well, compulsory heterosexuality and male domination mean that heterosex (except some interracial forms) brings privileges denied to lesbian sex.

## OPPRESSORS ARE NOT ALIKE

One of the reasons why the bisexual movement is so vexing to me, aside from my insidious biphobia, is this fuzziness of perspective on oppression. The bisexual movement *sounds* like other progressive political projects. The political identities and moves of lesbians and gays, feminists, lefties, and anti-racists are motivated by a critique of powerful social systems that oppress them. For instance, if patriarchy is the social system at fault, positioning women as lower-status adjuncts to male life, then some lesbian feminists advocate escape to an allwomyn self-sufficient farm and create a womon's culture. It's easy to mock but it has its own sophisticated mechanism. Who or what has the power in the bisexual vision? Can activists really think that lesbian feminists *oppress* them? Perhaps in San Francisco or Northampton—locations of strong gay and lesbian enclaves and, therefore, of bisexual activism—the queer world can *seem* powerful and secure, but of course this is a place-specific illusion.

Given our vulnerability, the priorities of bisexual declarations are baffling: do oppression and phobia from the gay world warrant more attention than, say, Jesse Helms or global capitalist patriarchy? Is it vitally important to declare that an African Amercan male poet, whose sex with men during an aggressively virile phase of US history has been an "open secret," is bisexual rather than gay? Locating a compelling or comprehensible project in the bisexual movement is hard.

The confident understanding of identity as a political site makes sense for gays and lesbians because of the nature of our histories. The homosexual identity was forged in the laboratories of power and imposed on a diverse group. Identity—identifying, exposing, naming, defining—has been a critical component of hunting and watching and threatening gays and lesbians. Our ghettoized identity has been a central component of our struggles, and dangerous borders have defined a real or imagined gay and lesbian community. Over the hundred years of shouldering stigmas, homosexuals learned to wield them, reform them, redefine them, transforming the sickness into strength, the label into an emblem. The new bisexual movement yearns for recognition and community, but thankfully it has not emerged out of such an involuntary/voluntary process of painful identity formation.

If the bisexual movement isn't a similar kind of political "movement" or community in its own right, it nonetheless aspires to achieve political, liberatory aims through broadening the scope of the gay and lesbian world. In the chilly political climate in which we find ourselves, perhaps any motion to disrupt boundaries is politically useful. Some people think it would be ideal—utopian even—to get rid of most or all identity boundaries. But what a good look at the current, decidedly non-utopian world of ours should tell us is

that expanding the human potential of some individuals—through positive visualization or boundary transgression—can quite happily co-exist with diminished life chances for many, many others. While the movement for bisexual recognition undoubtedly offers a liberating framework for some men and women, some lesbians and gay men remain unmoved by heterosexual transgressions into our entrenched, yet fun, little world.

# | 13 |

## *To Be or Not to Be*

### LESLIE FEINBERG

"You were born female, right?" The reporter asked me for the third time. I nodded patiently. "So do you identify as female now, or male?"

She rolled her eyes as I repeated my answer. "I am transgendered. I was born female, but my masculine gender expression is seen as male. It's not my sex that defines me, and it's not my gender expression. It's the fact that my gender expression appears to be at odds with my sex. Do you understand? It's the social contradiction between the two that defines me."

The reporter's eyes glazed over as I spoke. When I finished she said, "So you're a *third* sex?" Clearly, I realized, we had very little language with which to understand each other.

When I try to discuss sex and gender, people can only imagine woman or man, feminine or masculine. We've been taught that nothing else exists in nature. Yet, as I've shown, this has not been true in all cultures or in all historical periods. In fact, Western law took centuries to neatly partition the sexes into only two categories and mandate two corresponding gender expressions.

"The paradigm that there are two genders founded on two biological sexes began to predominate in western culture only in the early eighteenth century," historian Randolph Trumbach notes in his essay, "London's Sapphists: From Three Sexes to Four Genders in the Making of

Modern Culture."[1] Trumbach explains that as late as the eighteenth century, in northwestern Europe, feminine men and masculine women— known as mollies and tommies respectively— were thought of as third and fourth genders.

But how many sexes and genders *do* exist? All too frequently, this question is presented as an abstract one, like how many angels can dance on the head of a pin. But the search for the answer to this question has to be understood within the context of oppression.

Those of us who cross the "man-made" boundaries of sex and gender run afoul of the law, are subject to extreme harassment and brutality, and are denied employment, housing, and medical care. We have grown up mostly unable to find ourselves represented in the dominant culture.

So how can we have a discussion of how much sex and gender diversity actually exists in society, when all the mechanisms of legal and extralegal repression render our lives invisible? Gender theorists can't just function as census takers who count how much sex and gender diversity exists; they must be part of the struggle to defend our

In Leslie Feinberg, *Transgender Warriors*, pp. 101–107. Boston: Beacon, 1996.

right to exist, or most of us will be forced to remain underground.

The more inclusive the trans liberation movement becomes, and the more visible our movement is in society, the more clearly sex and gender variation will be seen. However, as the trans movement grows and develops, part of its impact has been to pose questions: What is the relationship between birth sex, gender expression, and desire? Does the body you are born with determine your sex for life? How many variations of sex and gender exist today?

The gradations of sex and gender self-definition are limitless. When I first opened an America Online account, I tried to establish the *nom de net* "stone butch" or "drag king." I discovered these names were already taken. As I later prowled through AOL and UNIX bulletin boards, I found a world of infinite sex and gender identities, which cyberspace has given people the freedom to explore with a degree of anonymity.

But although this fluidity and variation exists, there still aren't many more words to express sex and gender than there were when I was growing up. All of the complexity of my gender expression is reduced to looking "like a man." Since I'm not a man, what does it mean when people tell me I look like one? When I was growing up, other kids told me I pitched baseballs and shot marbles "like a boy." As a young adult, I suffered a torrent of criticism from adults who admonished me for standing, walking, and sitting "like a boy." Strangers felt free to stop me on the street to confront me with this observation. Something about me was inappropriate, but what?

The "gender theory" I learned in school, at home, in books, and at the movies was very simple. There are men and women. Men are masculine and women are feminine. End of subject. But clearly the subject didn't end there for me.

I had no words to discuss this with anyone. The way I expressed myself was wrong. There was no language to dispute this because the right way was assumed to be natural. Thank goodness, by the time I was sixteen years old the women's liberation movement was beginning to vocally denounce the outrageously separate and unequal indoctrination of girls and boys. For the first time, I was able to separate my birth sex from the gender education I received as a girl. Since sex and gender had always been seen as synonymous when I was growing up, disconnecting the two was a very important advance in my own thinking.

In addition, one of the gifts the women's movement gave me was a closer look at the values that have been attached to masculinity and femininity. In my social education, masculinity had been inaccurately contrasted as stronger, more analytical, more stable, and more rational than femininity.

But it was not until the rise of the movement for transgender liberation that I began to see the important distinction between the negative gender *values* attached to being masculine or feminine and my right to my own gender *expression*. I am subjugated by the values attached to gender expression. But I am not oppressing other people by the way I express my gender when I wear a tie. Nor are other people's clothing or makeup crushing my freedom.

Both women's and trans liberation have presented me with two important tasks. One is to join the fight to strip away the discriminatory and oppressive values attached to masculinity and femininity. The other is to defend gender freedom—the right of each individual to express their gender in any way they choose, whether feminine, androgynous, masculine, or any point on the spectrum between. And that includes the right to gender ambiguity and gender contradiction.

It's equally important that each person have the right to define, determine, or change their sex in any way they choose—whether female, male, or any point on the spectrum between. And that includes the right to physical ambiguity and contradiction.

This struggle affects millions of people, because, as it turns out, sex and gender are a lot more complicated than woman and man, pink and blue. As the brochure of the Intersex Society of North America explains: "Our culture conceives sex anatomy as a dichotomy: humans come in two sexes, conceived of as so different as to be nearly different species. However, developmental embryology, as well as the existence of intersexuals, proves this to be a cultural construction. Anatomic sex differentiation occurs on a male/female continuum, and there are several dimensions."[2]

In an article entitled, "The Five Sexes: Why Male and Female Are Not Enough," geneticist Dr. Anne Fausto-Sterling stresses that "Western culture is deeply committed to the idea that there are only two sexes." But, she adds, "If the state and the legal system have an interest in maintaining a two-party sexual system, they are in defiance of nature. For biologically speaking, there are many gradations running from female to male; and depending on how one calls the shots, one can argue that along that spectrum lie at least five sexes—and perhaps even more."[3]

The right to physical ambiguity and contradiction are surgically and hormonally denied to newborn intersexual infants who fall between the "poles" of female and male. If doctors refrained from immediately "fixing" infants who don't fit the clear-cut categories of male and female, we would be spared the most commonly asked question: "What a beautiful baby! Is it a boy or a girl?"

And imagine what a difference it would make if parents replied, "We don't know, our child hasn't told us yet."

Why are infants being shoehorned into male or female? As Fausto-Sterling points out, "For questions of inheritance, legitimacy, paternity, succession to title, and eligibility for certain professions to be determined, modern Anglo-Saxon legal systems require that newborns be registered as either male or female." As a result, infants are surgically and hormonally manipulated into one sex or the other after birth, sometimes without even the parents' knowledge. Fausto-Sterling concludes that society, therefore, "mandates the control of intersexed bodies because they blur and bridge the great divide."[4]

Intersexuality is not news; it's been recorded since antiquity. Creation legends on every continent incorporate a sacred view of intersexuality. But with the rise of patriarchal, sex-segregated societies in Greece and Rome, for example, intersexual babies were burned alive, or otherwise murdered. In recent centuries, intersexuals were ordered to pick one sex in which to live, and were killed if they changed their minds.[5]

What's news is hearing courageous intersexual people voice their own demands. Day-old infants can't give informed consent to genital surgery. Intersexed babies have a right to grow up and make their own decisions about the body they will live in for the rest of their lives. Parents need counseling; intersexual youth need intersexual advisors. These are basic human rights, yet they are being violated every day. Cheryl Chase, founder of the Intersex Society of North America, describes this nightmare:

When an intersexual infant is born, the parents are confronted with a shocking fact that violates their understanding of the world. Physicians treat the birth of such an infant as a medical emergency. A medical team, generally including a surgeon and an endocrinologist, is roused from bed, if need be, and assembled to manage the situation. Intersexual bodies are rarely sick ones; the emergency here is culturally constructed. The team analyzes the genetic makeup, anatomy, and endocrine status of the infant, "assigns" it male or female, and informs the parents of their child's "true" sex. They then proceed to enforce this sex with surgical and hormonal intervention.

The parents are so traumatized and shamed that they will not reveal their ordeal to anyone, including the child as he/she comes of age. The child is left genitally and emotionally mutilated, isolated, and without access to information about what has happened to them. The burden of pain and shame is so great that virtually all intersexuals stay deep in the closet throughout their adult lives.[6]

Even reactionaries might agree with the struggle against the surgical alteration of infants, but with a twist: Let no man put asunder what God has brought together. However, this argument must not be used as a weapon against the rights of transsexual adults who choose sex-reassignment surgery. Not all transsexuals want or can afford that elective. But for those who do, there's no contradiction between the rights of transsexuals and those of intersexuals. The heart of the struggle of both communities is the right of each individual to control their own body.

I can remember standing in front of an abortion clinic in Buffalo, my arms linked with others in the dim glint of dawn, with cold rain dripping off my face. We were defending the women's health clinic against a right-wing assault on the right of women to choose abortion. I certainly knew politically what I was supporting. But that morning, perhaps because I was so miserably cold and wet, I felt the intersection of the demands of the trans movement and the women's movement in my own body. The heart of both is the right of each individual to make decisions about our own bodies and to define ourselves.

That is a right of each woman, each intersexed person, each transsexual man or woman—each human being. I believe that people who don't identify as transsexual also have a right to hormones and surgery. There are many of us who have wanted to shape our bodies without changing our sex. Since sex-reassignment programs won't prescribe hormones or arrange surgery for a person who does not identify as a transsexual, we have to lie, buy hormones on the street, or go to quacks who sell prescriptions for a hefty fee.

Legions of people in this society do all sorts of things to make themselves more comfortable in their own bodies: myriad types of cosmetic surgery, nose jobs, piercing, tattooing, augmentation, liposuction, dieting, bodybuilding, circumcision, bleaching, coloring, and electrolysis. But many of the people who add, subtract, reshape, or adorn their bodies criticize those transsexuals who elect surgery for *their* life decisions. I believe that the centuries-old fears and taboos about genitals, buried deep in the dominant Western culture, make the subject of surgical sex-change highly sensational. Today some opponents of sex-reassignment argue that sex-change is merely a high-tech phenomenon, a consequence of people being squeezed into narrow cultural definitions of what it means to be a woman or a man because surgical and hormonal options are now available. It's true that the development of anesthesia, and the commercial synthesis of hormones, opened up new opportunities for sex-reassignment. However, the argument that transsexuals are merely escaping rigid sex roles doesn't take into account ancient surgical techniques of sex-change developed in communal societies that offered more flexible gender choices.

It all comes down to this. Each person has the right to control their own body. If each individual doesn't have that right, then who gets to judge and make decision? Should we hand over that power to the church or the state? Should we make these rights subject to a poll?

And equally important to me is the right of each person to express their gender in any way they choose. But currently, strangers don't have to ask a parent if their infant is a boy or a girl if the child is dressed in pink or blue. Even gender color-coded diapers are now marketed in the United States.

As I researched this book, I was surprised to discover that this pink-for-girls, blue-for-boys gender assignment is a relatively recent development in the United States.[7] In the last century in this country, babies of all sexes wore little white dresses, which didn't seem to skew the gender expressions of these generations of children. Furthermore, the pink-blue gender values used to be just the opposite.

"Gender-based color schemes were adopted only at the onset of the twentieth century, as plumbing, cloth diapers, and color-fast fabrics became more available," wrote historians Vern and Bonnie Bullough. "However, different countries adopted different color schemes. In fact, there were heated arguments in the American popular press that pink was a more masculine color than light blue."[8]

How did the current pink and blue finally get assigned? Pink became a "girl's" color and blue a "boy's" in the United States in the early twentieth century after a media circus surrounding the acquisition of Thomas Gainsborough's painting *Blue Boy* and Sir Thomas Lawrence's *Pinkie* by wealthy art aficionado Henry Edwards Huntington.[9]

But the problem with the binary categories of pink and blue is that I'm not so easily color-coded, and neither are a lot of people I know. I've been taught that feminine and masculine are two polar opposites, but when I ride the subways or walk the streets of New York City, I see women who range from feminine to androgynous to masculine and men who range from masculine to androgynous to feminine. That forms a circle—a much more liberating concept than two poles with a raging void in between. A circle has room on it for each person to explore, and it offers the freedom for people to move on that circle throughout their lives if they choose.

Even today, when sex and gender choices have been so narrowed, when there are such degrading and murderous social penalties for crossing the boundaries of sex and gender, many of us can't—and don't want to—fit. We have to fight for the right of each person to express their gender in any way they choose. Who says our self-expression has to match our genitals? Who has the right to tell anyone else how to define their identities? And who has the right to decide what happens to each of our bodies? We cannot let these fundamental freedoms be taken away from us.

But those rights can't be won and protected without a fight. Strong bonds between the women's and trans liberation movements would put even more muscle into that struggle.

## NOTES

1. Randolph Trumbach, "London's Sapphists: From Three Sexes to Four Genders in the Making of Modern Culture," *Bodyguards: The Cultural Politics of Gender Ambiguity*, eds. Julia Epstein and Kristina Straub (New York: Routledge, 1991) 112–13.

2. *What Is Intersexuality?* (San Francisco: Intersex Society of North America, n.d.).

3. Anne Fausto-Sterling, "The Five Sexes: Why Male and Female Are Not Enough," *Sciences* March/April 1993: 20–21.

4. Ibid., 23–24.

5. The prevalence of intersexual myths is reflected in documentation as diverse as "Androgyne," *The Woman's Encyclopedia of Myths and Secrets,* ed. Barbara G. Walker (San Francisco: Harper and Row, 1983) 32–34; the Greek *androgyne* of Plato, *The Symposium,* trans. Walter Hamilton (London: Penguin Books, 1951) 58–65; the Japanese *Izanagi/Izanami* unity described in Mircea Eliade, *Myths, Dreams, and Mysteries: The Encounter between Contemporary Faiths and Archaic Realities,* trans. Philip Mairet (1957; New York: Harper and Row, 1975) 179–83; the Yoruban and Dahomean *Mawulisa* and *Seboulisa* of Audre Lorde, *The Black Unicorn* (New York: W. W. Norton, 1978), William Bascom, *The Yoruba of Southwestern Nigeria* (New York: Holt, Rinehart and Winston, 1969), and Melville Herskovits, *Dahomey,* 2 vols. (New York: J. J. Augustin, 1934); the "twofold gods" of Crete, Cyprus, Rome, Greece in Marie Delcourt, *Hermaphrodite: Myths and Rites of the Bisexual Figure in Classical Antiquity,* trans. Jennifer Nicholson (1956; London: Studio Books, 1961) 17–43; and the *Warharmi* of the Kamia of southwestern North America in Walter Williams, *The Spirit and the Flesh: Sexual Diversity in American Indian Culture* (Boston: Beacon Press, 1986) 18. For some information on persecution of hermaphrodites, see the original classical sources referenced in P. M. C. Forbes Irving, *Metamorphosis in Greek Myths* (Oxford: Clarendon Press, 1990) 149–50, and the French sources in Eugene de Savitsch, *Homosexuality, Transvestism and Change of Sex* (Springfield, IL: Charles C. Thomas, 1958) 30.

6. Cheryl Chase, e-mail communication, 2 February 1995.

7. Sandra Salmans, "Objects and Gender: When an It Evolves Into a He or a She," *New York Times* 16 November 1989: B1.

8. Vern L. Bullough and Bonnie Bullough, *Cross Dressing, Sex, and Gender* (Philadelphia: University of Pennsylvania Press, 1993) viii.

9. Ibid.

# Two

# INSTITUTIONS

## AND OPINION MAKERS

# II.A

# INVENTING SIN: RELIGION AND THE CHURCH

Every culture offers answers to fundamental questions concerning the origin and meaning of things: how the world came to exist and what lies beyond it, what is important and how things relate to each other, and what moral principles can be derived from these answers in order to define appropriate behavior. In nearly all societies throughout human history the answers to these questions have been formulated as religious beliefs: explanatory and moral systems that focus on the actions, intentions, and preferences of supernatural powers. Religious systems of explanation offer accounts of the creation of the world and its inhabitants, especially humans, as well as specifying the rules for proper behavior—and the consequences for infractions—that have been imposed by the creator. In *Civilization and Its Discontents* Freud summarized in similar fashion what "the common man understands by his religion—the system of doctrines and promises which on the one hand explains to him the riddle of life with enviable completeness, and, on the other, assures him that a careful Providence will watch over his life and will compensate him in a future life for any frustrations he suffers here" (1962 [1930]:21).

In Western culture the dominant religious traditions for the past two millennia have been Christian, built upon but significantly differing from Judaism. In contrast to most other major world religions—Hinduism, Buddhism, Confucianism, and Islam—Christianity has been marked by what sex historian Vernon Bullough terms a general hostility toward sexual expression, and hence can be labeled sex-negative (1979:ix). However, homosexuality has been singled out in Judaism and Christianity for condemnation that exceeds the minimum requirements of sex negativity.

Early Judaic views on sexuality were shaped by

principles that resulted in antipathy to homosexual acts. The first was a focus on procreation as a necessary goal and duty, embodied in the commandment to "be fruitful and multiply." This fundamental injunction led to the expectation that everyone would marry as early as possible and engage in marital sexual intercourse on a regular basis (Bullough 1979:77). In this context any sexual act that could not promote appropriate procreation was sinful. Thus, because conception was viewed as the product of male semen planted in the female womb, lesbianism did not evoke the same sort of condemnation: "In lesbianism there is no spilling of seed. Thus life is not symbolically lost, and therefore lesbianism is not prohibited in the Bible" (Milgrom 1993:11).

The second consideration pervading early Judaic views of sexuality was the fear of assimilation into neighboring cultures, which prompted the prohibition of many sexual practices associated with outsiders (this is a common explanation as well for many of the biblical dietary requirements known as kashrut). At earlier stages in Jewish history the hostility to foreign religions focused on the temple prostitutes, both male and female, common in many Middle Eastern societies, and this has been seen as a source of the famous prohibition in Leviticus against a man "lying with a man as one lies with a woman." (It might be worth noting that this biblical prohibition, part of the Holiness Code, is addressed only to Jews and did not apply to gentiles). At the same time, other forms of emotional, and possibly physical, attachment between men and between women might be celebrated. The love of David and Jonathan, that "surpassed the love of women," and the devotion of Ruth to Naomi, can certainly sustain a homosexual interpretation. In the later period of the Second Temple widespread fear of assimilation into Greek culture led to a greater antipathy toward homosexuality that was carried into exile in Talmudic Judaism. These condemnations of homosexuality were also absorbed into and amplified by early Christianity.

The Gospels are quite silent on the topic of homosexuality, but St. Paul provided sufficient ammunition for those seeking New Testament support for condemnation of homosexuality, as well as any other sexual acts outside of marriage. The early Church adopted a suspicion toward sexuality based on Jesus's possible endorsement of celibacy and on Paul's expressed preference for sexual continence. Ultimately, as in the influential formulation of St. Augustine, core Christian belief defines sexuality as sinful, and only exculpated by the sacrament of marriage. But even matrimony did not remove the sinfulness of sexuality: "Though [marital] coitus must be regarded as a good, because it came from God, every concrete act of intercourse was evil, with the result that every child could literally be said to have been conceived in the sin of its parents" (Bullough 1979:193). Ultimately, Augustine concluded that although celibacy was the highest good marital intercourse was justified by the need—and the commandment—to procreate. All other forms of intercourse were evil.

Despite the hostility of the Church fathers to sexuality outside of marriage, and the specific condemnation of homosexuality as a diversion of the sexual organs from the procreative purpose, historian John Boswell has argued that the early Middle Ages were *relatively* tolerant of homosexuality (1980, 1994). For various reasons, not completely understood, during the twelfth and thirteenth centuries homosexuality came to be viewed as "a dangerous, antisocial, and severely sinful aberration. . . . By 1300 . . . a single homosexual act was enough . . . in many places, to merit the death penalty" (Boswell 1980:295).

The most influential formulation of the emerging view of sexuality was that of St. Thomas Aquinas (1225–1274), "whose *Summa theologiae* became the standard of orthodox opinion on every point of Catholic dogma for nearly a millennium and permanently and irrevocably established the 'natural' as the touchstone of Roman Catholic sexual ethics" (Boswell 1980:318). For Aquinas sins against nature were those forms of lust that were directed solely toward the pursuit of pleasure and entirely precluded procreation. These included, in ascending order of sinfulness: masturbation

(spilling seed), deviation from the natural manner of coitus (which, according to Aquinas, was limited to face-to-face with the woman on her back, the "missionary position"), homosexuality, and bestiality.

In the sixteenth century Christianity was in turmoil, as the Protestant movement begun by Luther set loose a torrent of schism and strife that transformed the Western world. However, while the leading Protestant theologians differed from the Catholic Church on many issues of sexuality, such as divorce and clerical celibacy, Luther and Calvin both followed Aquinas in condemning homosexuality as contrary to nature. At the same time, the Catholic Church responded to the Protestant challenge by convening the Council of Trent (1545–1564), which reasserted traditional views and enshrined Aquinas as the "doctor of the church." Because "Catholic moralists were not eager to appear to abandon a moral doctrine of the Fathers if the Protestants still held it" (Noonan 1966:353), both sides emphasized their intolerance of nonprocreative sexuality. These restrictive views were carried to the New World by both Catholic and Protestant colonizers, where they were imposed upon both Native American cultures and the emerging European American societies.

The past five centuries have seen a decline in the role of religion as the institution that explained the world and defined morality, and this process of secularization has extended to the realm of sexuality. Although the replacement of church authority by civil law did not result in any immediate liberalization, as the condemnation of "sins against nature" was translated into "crimes against nature," now punished by the state, the ultimate trajectory has been toward greater sexual freedom. The emergence of science as the dominant source of explanation for human behavior, including sexuality, further weakened the hold of traditional religious perspectives, although it would be a mistake to discount the power of institutional religion even to this day.

The views of human nature and actions introduced by science and medicine in the nineteenth century led to significant changes in Western attitudes toward sexuality. By the mid-twentieth century progressive forces within many religious denominations had joined the effort to liberate lesbian, gay, and bisexual people. In the early 1950s reform efforts in Great Britain spearheaded by progressive Anglican clergy led to the Wolfenden Report of 1957 and the sodomy law reform of 1967. In the United States progressive clerics and denominations, such as the Quakers, Unitarian Universalists, and some Episcopal dioceses, lent support to homophile groups and lesbian/gay liberation. In 1965 the Council on Religion and the Homosexual, an alliance of liberal church leaders in San Francisco, joined with lesbian and gay groups to protest police harassment. In 1969 the United Church of Christ called for the decriminalization of homosexual activities between consenting adults, a position soon joined by the Unitarian Universalist Association. Similar stands were taken by significant factions within the Presbyterian and Methodist Churches (Melton 1991). Within Judaism the Reconstructionist movement has long ordained lesbian and gay rabbis, and they were joined in this by the Reform wing of American Judaism in 1990.

In 1968 the Reverend Troy Perry (ordained in a Southern Pentecostal denomination) started the first gay church in his Los Angeles home. Within a short period Perry's Metropolitan Community Church had grown to several hundred members, drawn from numerous Christian denominations, and it began to spread beyond Southern California. By the mid-1980s the Universal Fellowship of Metropolitan Community Churches included nearly two hundred congregations in ten countries. The example of the UFMCC led to the founding of lesbian/gay congregations within other religious persuasions. In 1972 the first lesbian and gay synagogue, Beth Chayim Chadashim ("House of New Life") was founded in Los Angeles, followed shortly by synagogues in New York, San Francisco, and, ultimately, over thirty other locations in the United States and other countries.

In some instances lesbian and gay organizations have attempted to obtain official recognition, sometimes holding services within established churches. Dignity, founded by gay Catholics in San Diego in 1969, was emulated by organizations of lesbian and gay Episcopalians (Integrity), United Methodists (Affirmation), Mormons (Affinity), and other Protestant denominations.

After an initial period of quasi toleration of Dignity, which had grown to be among the largest lesbian and gay organizations in the country, the Catholic Church began to reassert its traditional hostility toward homosexuality. In 1975 the Sacred Congregation for the Doctrine of the Faith published a "Declaration on Certain Questions Concerning Sexual Ethics" in which the Catholic Church tried to come to terms with the changing sexual attitudes of the times. In that document the church acknowledged the existence of individuals

who are homosexual "because of some kind of innate instinct or a pathological constitution judged to be incurable." This was taken by many as a sign of progress, despite the document's insistence that "homosexual acts are intrinsically disordered and can in no case be approved," and it might have encouraged liberal factions within the Church. But since the election of Pope John Paul II in 1978 conservative voices have dominated the choir. Father John McNeill, a Jesuit priest who wrote *The Church and the Homosexual* in 1979, was first silenced and then expelled from his order, and other liberal theologians were disciplined for espousing pro-gay positions.

These measures did not suffice to reverse the liberal trends found throughout American Catholicism and, in 1986, Cardinal Ratzinger, head of the Congregation for the Doctrine of the Faith, issued a letter on "the Pastoral Care of Homosexual Persons" (reprinted in this volume). This new document repeated and strengthened the message of the 1975 declaration that homosexual acts are "intrinsically disordered," and then specifically condemned efforts to enact civil legislation "to protect behavior to which no one has any conceivable right." If such efforts provoke "irrational and violent reactions," Cardinal Ratzinger suggested, it was only to be expected. The letter went on to state that "all support should be withdrawn from any organizations which seek to undermine the teachings of the Church, which are ambiguous about it, or which neglect it entirely." This official pronouncement effectively ended the access to churches previously enjoyed by Dignity chapters in dioceses across the United States and Canada.

In the period since the Ratzinger letter the Catholic Church has not relented in its hostility to lesbian and gay people, and prominent clerics such as Cardinals O'Connor of New York and Bevilacqua of Philadelphia have been in the forefront of efforts to defeat lesbian and gay causes. Conservative Catholic laypersons such as Paul Weyrich, Phyllis Schlafly, William F. Buckley, and Patrick Buchanan have also played leading roles in the rise of the New Right that has made attacks on gay people a centerpiece of its political rhetoric.

Despite the evident enmity of the Catholic Church some lesbian and gay Catholics have sought a silver lining in the dark cloud of religious bigotry. Conservative journalist Andrew Sullivan tried to reconcile his homosexuality and his religion, arguing that the Church made a monumental concession by using the term "homosexual persons" because "the term 'person' constitutes in Catholic moral teaching a profound statement about the individual's humanity, dignity and worth; it invokes a whole range of rights and needs" (1994:52). But not, of course, the right to sexual expression; that, we're told by Ratzinger, is "behavior to which no one has any conceivable right." Sullivan seems less concerned with whether his church grants him the right to express his sexuality than he is grateful that they have found a place for him in the natural order. And what is this place? "As albinos remind us of the brilliance of color . . . as the disabled person reveals to us in negative form the beauty of the fully functioning human body; so the homosexual person might be seen as a natural foil to the heterosexual norm, a variation that does not eclipse the theme, but resonates with it" (Sullivan 1994:55).

The view that homosexuality can be seen only as the distorted reflection of a heterosexual norm is not limited, of course, to tortured gay apologists. The religious right has placed what they call "family values" as the centerpiece of their crusade against minorities (single mothers on welfare), feminism (women daring to seek employment and careers outside the home), and gay people (who "recruit because they can't reproduce"). In this ecumenical enterprise the vulnerability of the "traditional nuclear family" and of heterosexuality itself is constantly emphasized. In the words of the Ramsey Colloquium, a group of conservative theologians [excerpted in this volume], heterosexual marriage, despite its divine origins, is a fragile institution in need of careful and continuing support. And, as Jewish theologian Samuel Dressner worries, acceptance of homosexuality is the first step down a familiar slippery slope: once "heterosexuality within the marital bond is dismissed, then how can adultery, pedophilia, incest or bestiality be rejected?" (1991:320).

Among mainline Protestant denominations only the United Church of Christ permits the ordination of open lesbians and gay men. In 1992 the Presbyterian Church initiated a three-year study of homosexuality that failed to resolve the issue of ordination of gay people. In 1993 a draft statement on homosexuality by a committee of the Evangelical Lutheran Church in America set off what a church official called "the most volatile explosion in the life of this church." And, although in 1996 conservative Episcopal bishops failed in their attempt to force a heresy trial for a bishop who ordained a noncelibate gay man, the issue contin-

ues to roil most mainline Protestant denominations.

Beyond the fringe of mainline denominations lies the rapidly growing domain of the Protestant fundamentalists who erupted onto the public stage in the late 1970s, amassing enormous financial and political power through broadcast and cable programming, direct mail, and video cassette distribution. Organizations such as Rev. Jerry Falwell's the Moral Majority, Beverly LaHaye's Concerned Women for America, Rev. Donald Wildmon's American Family Association, Dr. James Dobson's Focus on the Family, Rev. Lou Sheldon's Traditional Values Coalition, and, most notably, the Christian Coalition, founded by 1988 Republican presidential hopeful and televangelist Pat Robertson, have made attacks on lesbian and gay people a centerpiece of their crusades and their fund-raising.

As the century and the millennium draw to an end religious leaders and institutions play important roles on both sides of the cultural wars raging in the United States. Progressive clergy, often openly lesbian and gay, are reshaping rituals and beliefs and challenging their colleagues to evolve and adapt. On the other side the religious right has been the engine of social and political reaction for the past two decades, and homosexuality has been among their most consistent targets. Catholic, Protestant, Jewish, and Moslem fundamentalists have made common cause in their unrelenting hostility to lesbian and gay people's demands for civil and religious equality. In Iran the revolutionary government of Ayatollah Khomeini demonstrated its fundamentalism by executing gay men. In Colorado Pastor Peter Peters published a pamphlet entitled *Intolerance of, Discrimination Against, and the Death Penalty for Homosexuals Is Prescribed in the Bible* (1992) — only somewhat less subtle than many of his allies on the right.

## REFERENCES

Boswell, John. 1980. *Christianity, Social Tolerance, and Homosexuality*. Chicago: University of Chicago Press.

Boswell, John. 1994. *Same-Sex Unions in Premodern Europe*. New York: Villard.

Bullough, Vernon. 1979. *Sexual Variance in Society and History*. Chicago: University of Chicago Press.

Dressner, Samuel. 1991. "Homosexuality and the Order of Creation," *Judaism*, 40(3):309–321.

Freud, Sigmund. 1962 [1930]. *Civilization and Its Discontents*. Trans. James Strachey. New York: Norton.

Melton, J. Gordon. 1991. *The Churches Speak on Homosexuality: Official Statements from Religious Bodies and Ecumenical Organizations*. Detroit: Gale Research.

Milgrom, Jacob. 1993. "Does the Bible Prohibit Homosexuality?" *Bible Review*, 9(6):11.

Noonan, John. 1966. *Contraception: A History of Its Treatment by the Catholic Theologians and Canonists*. Cambridge: Harvard University Press.

Peters, Peter J. 1992. *Intolerance of, Discrimination Against, and the Death Penalty for Homosexuals Is Prescribed in the Bible*. LaPorte, Col.: Scriptures for America.

Sullivan, Andrew. 1994. "Alone Again, Naturally: The Catholic Church and the Homosexual." *New Republic*, November 28, pp. 47–55.

# | 14 |

## The Abominable Sin: The Spanish Campaign Against "Sodomy," and Its Results in Modern Latin America

### WALTER WILLIAMS

Soon after Christopher Columbus recognized that his voyage across the Atlantic Ocean had not taken him to Asia, Europeans realized that he had discovered a previously unknown continent. To them it was, in a very real sense, a "New World." The peoples they found there were as unfamiliar as beings from another planet, and their history had not prepared them for such extensive dealings with peoples of other cultures. In contrast to Middle Eastern civilizations, which had been at the center of commercial and intellectual interaction from three continents, Europeans after the fall of the Roman Empire had been relatively isolated from outside contact. Accordingly, Europeans held their own cultural values, and were little used to accepting differing viewpoints.

Such intolerance of cultural variation extended to sexuality, and at least since the thirteenth century European thought condemned same-sex relations as a major sin. Despite a tradition of homoeroticism going back to the ancient Greeks, when the Roman Empire adopted Christianity as its state religion it also adopted the antisexual heritage of the Hebrews. Weakened as it was by the otherworldly concerns of Christianity, and divided by sectarian divisions and persecutions within this new state religion, the late Roman Empire began condemning sexual practices that had previously been well accepted.

During the early medieval era a new culture formed, arising from the Greco-Roman-Christian tradition combined with folk cultures from Europe. Some historians have suggested that this medieval culture was not as concerned about condemning homosexual relations, and tolerated emotional expressions of love between people of the same sex. But by the fourteenth and fifteenth centuries, Europe was in the midst of an extremely homophobic outburst. Part of this antihomosexualism was due to Church dogma, and to political opportunism. Jealous political leaders used outlandish rumors to associate homosexual behavior with heresy and treason. By emphasizing the evilness of homosexuality, these factions could justify confiscating the wealth of those accused. The frenzy that resulted also had much to do with simple scapegoating. Europe convulsed itself with mass executions of anyone perceived as different: Jews, Christian nonconformists, woman-centered folk spiritualists known as witches, and "sodomites." The term *sodomy* was taken from the biblical story of God's destruction of the ancient city of Sodom. The original moral of this story is that Sodom was destroyed because of its inhospitality to strangers, but later writers emphasized a sexual interpretation. Especially during the Inquisition the Christian establishment killed and tortured Jews, heretics, witches, and sodomites alike, and not so incidentally confiscated condemned persons' property, thus increasing its own wealth. With this combination of economic, political, and psychological factors, same-sex relations had become a dogmatic issue.

In Walter Williams, *The Spirit and the Flesh: Sexual Diversity in American Indian Culture*, pp. 131–140. Excerpt. Boston: Beacon, 1986.

## SPANISH HOMOPHOBIA

By the time European explorers landed in America, Europe was more firmly committed than any other culture in the world to persecuting sodomy. While homophobia was typical of Christian Europe generally, the Spanish seemed to be at the forefront of this persecution. In Spain the Inquisition reached sadistic extremes in its suppression of sexual diversity. Sodomy was defined loosely as any nonreproductive sexual act (usually a same-sex act but sometimes anal sex between a male and a female). Sodomy was a serious crime in Spain, being considered second only to crimes against the person of the king and to heresy. It was treated as a much more serious offense than murder. Circumstantial evidence or uncollaborated testimony was easily accepted as proof of the crime. Without any concept of religious freedom, or separation of church and state, sodomy was also considered a mortal sin. Those convicted by the inquisitorial courts were burned at the stake.

Why were the Spanish so morbidly incensed over a sexual act? In what way did it threaten their society so severely as to be classified as more serious than murder? In many ways the Spanish were not much different from other Europeans in their homophobic reactions. Yet they had additional reasons to be upset over sodomy, quite likely growing out of their struggle against the Moors. These North African Muslims had occupied the Iberian peninsula for over seven hundred years, and for just that long the European natives had been resisting. Since warfare depleted the population, Spanish culture encouraged propagation. As in some other societies that emphasized population growth, the Spanish tried to suppress birth control, abortion, and nonreproductive forms of sexuality. In an attempt to regain their homeland—similar to the struggles of the ancient Hebrews—the Spanish emphasized the same pro-population values that they had absorbed from the Jews via Christianity. Moreover, since all Europe had been devastated in the fourteenth century by the bubonic plague, with an estimated loss of half its population, even more pressures were added for maximizing reproduction.

The Spanish had an additional reason for opposing homosexuality. In technology and intellectual thought, the Islamic civilization of the Moors was clearly more advanced than that of the Castilians. If the Spanish were going to challenge their culturally superior Muslim enemy, they were going to have to overcome their sense of inferiority by overcompensating—they had to see themselves as superior. They obviously could not do this in regard to technological or intellectual matters, so they had to turn to ideological values. In short, the Spanish had to create a culture that emphasized its difference from the Moors. Christianity, with its intolerance for other religions, served that function, supplying a unifying theme around which the non-Muslim Spanish could rally and proclaim their superiority. Their religious fanaticism sustained them in their struggles to drive out the Moors, and it left a heritage of intolerance and persecution of nonconformists.

One aspect of Moorish society that clearly stood out as different from the Christians was its relaxed attitude toward same-sex relations. After centuries of continuous warfare, Spanish men displayed contempt for behavior that they associated with their Islamic enemy. When the Spanish regained control of the peninsula by the late fifteenth century, this offered the Church an unprecedented opportunity to impose its rules on the newly conquered lands. By confiscating the property of condemned individuals, the Church could gain a vast base of wealth in Spain as well as eliminate possible competitors for control of the population. This, along with the need for maximizing population growth and differentiation from the Moors, makes it clear why the Spanish treated sodomy as such a serious breach of civil and religious standards. Behind their fanatical condemnation was a striving for economic and political power, and uncertainty about being able to keep their Christian culture free from any taint of Moorish influence. They might not be able to challenge the Moors on technological or intellectual grounds, but they could do so by emphasizing "morals"—social taboos that the Muslims did not share.

## THE SPANISH IN THE AMERICAS

Before 1492 the Spanish had so little contact with other cultures, except for their enemy the Moors, that they could not know that homosexual behavior was commonly accepted among many of the world's cultures. But no sooner had they finished the colossal effort to expel the Moors than the discovery of the New World brought them face to face with another cross-cultural struggle. To their horror, the Spanish soon discovered that the Native Americans accepted homosexual behavior even more readily than the Moors. Since this was an inflammatory subject on which the Spanish had strong feelings, the battle lines were soon drawn. Sodomy became a major justification for Spanish conquest of the peoples called Indians.

The Spanish recognized, as would the other Europeans who followed them into the Americas, that the peoples of the New World represented a vast diversity of cultures. Nevertheless, most of the commentators did not often bother to make such distinctions in their rush to condemn Indian eroticism. In one of the least condemnatory accounts of Indian sexuality, for example, Pedro Cieza de Leon wrote in his "Chronicles of Peru" that the two worst sins of the Indians were cannibalism and sodomy. But he cautioned against condemning all Indians on these grounds:

> Certain persons speak great ill of the Indians, comparing them with beasts, saying that their customs and living habits belong more properly to brutes than to men, that they are so evil that not only do they make use of the abominable sin but also that they eat one another. . . . It is not my intention to say that these things apply to all of them. . . . If in one province they practice the abominable sin against nature, in many others it is regarded as unseemly and is not practiced or indeed may be abhorred. . . . So that it would be an unjust thing to voice a general condemnation of them all.

In his rush to defend Indians, Cieza de León does not question the Spanish antihomosexual consensus, but only points out that not all Indians practiced sodomy. For those who did, he equated them with cannibals, worthy of no defense.

The Spanish did find, however, that same-sex acts were quite common. In many cases this was first observed through native art. Particularly in Mexico and Peru, there was a rich artistic tradition of erotic art. Sexual customs were depicted in detail, including homosexual behavior. For example, Bernal Diaz, on an exploration of the coast of Yucatán in 1517, reported discovering many clay "idols" in which "the Indians seemed to be engaged in sodomy one with the other." Fernandez de Oviedo, the chronicler for the king, wrote about another expedition to a Yucatán coastal island on which Diego Velazquez reported entering a Maya temple and being shocked to see a large wooden statue of two males engaged in intercourse. In Panama in 1515, Oviedo himself saw some of this intricate artwork: "In some part of these Indies, they carry as a jewel a man mounted upon another in that diabolic

and nefarious act of Sodom, made in gold relief. I saw one of these jewels of the devil twenty pesos gold in weight. . . . I broke it down with a hammer and smashed it under my own hand." The Spanish melted down untold quantities of Indian artwork in precious metals, but they took a special delight in destroying these "jewels of the devil."

As a result of this systematic destruction, we cannot know the extent to which pre-Columbian art expressed homosexual themes. Unfortunately, this obliteration did not end with the colonial era. Even as late as 1915, a Peruvian art collector knew of many Moche and Vicus ceramic pieces depicting "sodomy or pederasty . . . [which] a misunderstood modesty has led many collectors to destroy." The director of the Peru National Museum of Anthropology and Archaeology points out that such censorship over the centuries continues at the hands of modern "iconoclasts."

The Spanish destruction of art is typical of their refusal to see things in a different light. They did not use this knowledge to gain a wider understanding of sexual diversity, or to question their strange notion that the only function of sexual desire is procreative. Upon no authority other than the Bible, they declared that any other sexual act than that designed to reproduce was "against nature." Accordingly, they could only report in amazement the high incidence of same-sexuality among the Indians. Bernal Díaz del Castillo, accompanying Hernán Cortés during his conquest of Mexico in 1519, commented frequently on the widespread practice of same-sex relations as a well-established custom. The chronicler López de Gomara reported that the Indians "are sodomitic like no other generation of men."

The Spanish were also amazed that homosexuality was often associated with cross-dressing, and that the practice had religious connotations. Cieza de León reported in 1553 that he punished the Indians of Puerto Viejo in Peru because of temple prostitution. He wrote in disgust: "The devil held such sway in this land that, not satisfied with making them fall into so great sin, he made them believe that this vice was a kind of holiness and religion."

Instead of learning lessons about human variability in erotic attraction and gender role, the Spanish used the existence of homosexuality as evidence of Indian inferiority. In his first report to Emperor Charles V, conquistador Hernán Cortés wrote on July 10, 1519, that the Indians of Mexico "are all sodomites and have recourse to that abominable sin." Bernal Díaz del Castillo said Cortés paused in the fighting along the coast near Xocotlan long enough to order his Indian allies: "You must not commit sodomy or do the other ugly things you are accustomed to do."

These matters were emphasized by the Spanish conquistadors and writers for more than just human interest. The Indians' acceptance of homosexuality provided a major justification for the conquest and subjugation of the New World. With their belief that same-sex behavior was one of God's major crimes, the Spanish could easily persuade themselves that their plunder, murder, and rape of the Americas was righteous. They could fight their way to heaven by stamping out the sodomites, rather than by crusading to the Holy Land.

The condemnation of Indian homosexual behavior was a major factor in proving the virtue of the Spanish conquest, and the conquistadors acted resolutely to suppress it by any means necessary. The priests of course tried to convince the Indians to change voluntarily, but sometimes the military leaders did not even give the natives an opportunity to change. For example, the conquistador Nuño de Guzmán recalled that in 1530 the last person taken in battle, who had "fought most courageously, was a man in the habit of a woman, which confessed that from a child he had gotten his living by that filthiness, for which I caused him to be burned." Likewise, Antonio de la Calancha, a Spanish official in Lima, sang the praises of Vasco Núñez de Balboa, who on his expedition across Panama "saw men dressed like women; Balboa learnt that they were sodomites and threw the king and forty others to be eaten by his dogs, a fine action of an honorable and Catholic Spaniard."

Even Francisco de Vitoria, the leading Spanish liberal theologian who argued that the pope and the emperor had no dominion over American Indians, made a few exceptions. The natives, he avowed, could not be legally dispossessed of their lands except for three reasons: cannibalism, incest, and sodomy. The Spanish did not, however, merely take the lands of the Indians. The Europeans' mere presence led to native decimation in numbers unprecedented in human history. A major reason the Spanish were able to prevail over the Indians was that the Europeans brought with them many deadly germs to which the Indians had no immunity. Europeans at this time had very high levels of pathogens left over from the plague. Diseases that only sickened the hardened white survivors caused the American natives to die

in huge numbers. Old World diseases were without a doubt the deadliest weapon of the conquistadors, killing probably ninety percent of precontact populations.

The Spanish did not realize why the Indians were wasting away from disease, but took it as an indication that it was part of God's plan to wipe out the infidels. Oviedo concluded, "It is not without cause that God permits them to be destroyed. And I have no doubts that for their sins God is going to do away with them very soon." He further reasoned, in a letter to the king condemning the Mayas for accepting homosexual behavior: "I wish to mention it in order to declare more strongly the guilt for which God punishes the Indians and the reasons why they have not been granted his mercy."

The Spanish did not understand that the diseases had more to do with the will of microbes than the will of God. With such misunderstandings, the theologian Juan Gines de Sepulveda stated: "How can we doubt that these people so uncivilized, so barbaric, so contaminated with so many sins and obscenities . . . have been justly conquered by such a humane nation which is excellent in every kind of virtue?"

Almost as soon as they were able to establish control, representatives of the Church and the state began imposing their notions of proper behavior on the Indians. As early as 1613 in Florida, Spanish priests were trying to get Timucua Indian men and boys in confessional to admit being "sodomites." A Spanish missionary who saw some *"maricas"* among the Yuma Indians during a 1775 expedition in California condemned them as "sodomites, dedicated to nefarious practices. From all the foregoing I conclude that in this matter of incontinence there will be much to do when the Holy Faith and the Christian religion are established among them."

What happened when the Spanish had a chance to intervene is seen in an incident that occurred at the mission near Santa Barbara, California, in the 1780s. When a Chumash *joya* and his husband visited another Indian who was a laborer at the mission, the suspicious priest burst into their quarters and caught them "in the act of committing the nefarious sin." The priest reported in indignation that he punished them, but not "with the severity it properly deserved. When they were rebuked for such an enormous crime, the layman [Indian man] answered that the *Joya* was his wife!" What the Indian man stated as a justification for his relationship, the missionary took as an outrage.

After this incident, the priest reported, no more of "these disreputable people" came to any of the southern California missions, "although many *Joyas* can be seen in the area. . . . Almost every village has two or three." Obviously the berdaches and their husbands had quickly learned to avoid the Spanish, but the priests were not satisfied with this. The writer concluded: "We place our trust in God and expect that these accursed people will disappear with the growth of the missions. The abominable vice will be eliminated to the extent that the Catholic faith and all the other virtues are firmly implanted there, for the glory of God."

The Spanish began a concerted effort to wipe out berdachism in California, and by the 1820s a missionary at San Juan Capistrano was able to report that while berdaches were once very numerous among the Mission Indians, "At the present time this horrible custom is entirely unknown among them." Evidently the Spanish were successful in this suppression, because I was able to locate no trace of even a memory of a berdache tradition among Mission Indians today.

With the harsh impact of disease, military conquest, and cultural imposition that the Indians experienced from the Spanish, it is difficult to learn native reactions to the suppression of homosexuality. Yet the Spanish documents do tell us a few things. After stating that most of the Peruvian Indians of Puerto Viejo "publically and openly [practiced] the nefarious sin of sodomy, on which they greatly prided themselves," Cieza de León complimented the local Spanish authorities for having "given punishment to those who committed the above mentioned sin, warning them how our all powerful God is displeased. And they put fear into them in such a way that now this sin is used little or not at all." By 1552 the historian López de Gomora reported that Native American sodomy was being successfully wiped out by the Spanish.

## NATIVE RESPONSE

How did the Indians react to the intense suppression of berdachism that the Spanish enforced? It is hard enough to get the Indian viewpoint from the documentary record on any subject, and especially difficult on something like taboo sexual behavior. The Spanish claimed that they had wiped out homosexual practices. Certainly the Spanish got the impression that "sodomy" no longer existed, and without a doubt it was not openly engaged in as it had been before the arrival of the Europeans. But that does not mean that a recognized and respected status for berdaches no longer existed, or that private same-sex behavior vanished.

To find evidence of such continuity is extremely difficult. The researcher must be a detective, searching for a shred of information that might tell how native cultures adapted to these enforced changes on their ways of life. Traditionalist Indians tend not to record their thoughts in written form, and certainly not their thoughts about anything that would only bring them trouble from whites. As a result, there is a large documentary gap beginning with the establishment of colonial control, and it seems unlikely that documents will be found that verify the continuity of accepted and common homosexual behavior among Indians. The lack of documentation requires present-day ethnographers to investigate the position of contemporary Indians, to see if a respected berdache role survives. Such research cannot be done by just any fieldworker, since Indian people long ago learned not to open up to whites on this topic. It requires a person with sensitivity and a feeling of trust developed with informants.

One such ethnographer is Clark Taylor, who had the advantage of being openly gay during his fieldwork among the Zoque Indians. As a result of his open identity, Taylor's informants confided in him. They reported that among the Zoque, as well as with the Huichol and the Cora Indians, berdaches still play a part in modern-day Indian rituals in springtime. They do not share the *mestizo* values of machismo, and do not think of gender variance and male-male sexual behavior as deviant.

Ethnographic reports on the Indians of present-day central Chile offer a clue to one type of reaction to Spanish suppression. Among the precontact Araucanians, the Mapuchem and probably other peoples, shaman religious leaders were all berdaches. When the Spanish suppressed this religious institution because of its association with male-male sex, the Indians switched to a totally new pattern. Women became the shamans. So strong was the association of femininity with spiritual power that if the androgynous males could not fill the role, then the Indians would use the next most spiritually powerful persons. In striving for effective spirituality, they responded in a creative way to Spanish genocidal pressures.

One possible conclusion that might be drawn from this change would be that the Indians merely turned against the berdache priests. But such a sudden and unified move would seem unlikely when considering the previously high status of the shamans. More likely the Indians may have employed a clever strategy to remove the berdaches from a public institutionalized role, to protect them from the Spanish wrath. Once the berdaches were no longer in public leadership positions they would not be obvious to the homophobic Spanish officials. Gender variation and same-sex behavior could continue in private, unnoticed by the Spanish overlords.

Such examples may lead us to speculate that once Indians realized how much the Europeans hated sodomy, indigenous groups in various areas of the Americas quickly adapted to colonial control by keeping such things secret. This meant that berdachism would no longer be associated with ceremonialism. We have seen that the religious aspect is an important element in berdachism, but does this mean that without it berdache status would disappear? Evidently it does not. In fact, there are ethnographic reports of certain tribes in which berdache status from the beginning did not involve religious office, and though such cultures were probably rare, they do demonstrate that berdachism is not restricted to a society in which it serves an active religious leadership function.

More recent examples reveal that berdachism can survive without religious connotations. If the religious element of a group's berdache tradition has not survived, what elements do continue? The evidence suggests that the three features most notable in modern Indian groups are an androgynous personality, a woman's or mixed-gender work role, and the passive role in sexual behavior with men. The continuity of a respected social position for such nonmasculine males indicates that these three features are at the core of berdache identity. All three are equally important elements, and are considered to be personality traits that are intertwined. These traits are today more important even than cross-dressing or spirituality.

It was not until after she had been doing fieldwork among the Isthmus Zapotecs of Oaxaca, Mexico, for several years that Beverly Chiñas developed the kind of trust that would allow informants to talk openly with her about this topic. The Zapotec word for berdaches, *ira' muxe*, which means "males who manifest some degree of effeminate behavior," can also be applied to known homosexual or bisexual males, even if they do not display feminine behavior. Chiñas found that Zapotecs do not agree on a precise meaning beyond this, nor on exactly to which individuals it should be applied. But the definition does show a strong connection between nonmasculine personality and homosexual behavior. "*Ira' muxe* are respected by Zapotecs, who emphasize their differences from the general heterosexual population." *Ira' muxe* have no special religious role, but Zapotecs "defend them and their rights to their sexual and gender identity because 'God made them that way.' " Zapotecs reject the idea that *ira' muxe* could choose to be or could be forced into being different from the way they are. Berdachism is seen as a reflection of a person's basic character.

## SURVIVAL AMONG MAYAS TODAY

Knowing of the sporadic reports of continued berdache behavior in Latin America, I resolved to investigate a culture about which there was abundant evidence of aboriginal homosexuality: the Mayas. After my fieldwork among berdaches of the northern Plains tribes, I next made a trip to Yucatán to see if I could collect any information on modern Maya berdaches. Since the early Spanish documents contained many references to sodomy among these people, I decided to test my assumptions that such traditions have not disappeared. By luck, I met a man in Key West, Florida, who had previously lived in Yucatán and who had brought back with him a young Mayan as his lover. He had no knowledge of Mayan history, but what he said fit with precontact patterns. He stated, "Maya Indians have a very accepting attitude toward sex; 'If it feels good, do it.' Homosexuality is very open and common, with boys between the early teens to the mid twenties. But after then, men have much social pressure exerted on them to get married to a woman, and to stop dressing effeminately." What he said reflected a remarkable continuity from precolonial Mayan culture, with its institutionalized male marriages of boys and young men.

In trying to understand modern Yucatán folk traditions deriving from the Maya heritage, it is necessary to recognize the unbroken aboriginal influence. Though technological society has made inroads into the daily life of the traditional people, especially in the last decade, when improved transportation made outside access easier, Yucatán retains its separation even from the rest of Mexico. Yucatán is most famous for its surviving archeological ruins, with their large pyramids and intricately carved temples. At several of the ruins, most notably Uxmal, it is difficult to ignore the fascination that the Mayas had with the male penis. Huge stone phallic symbols occupy central positions in the ceremonial grounds.

The situation of homosexually inclined males in Yucatán is much different from that of members of the urban gay subculture of the United States. Because homoeroticism is much more diffuse in the society, there are not separate subcultural institutions for homosexuals. There are, however, known meeting places for males who want to have sexual relations. In small villages, this will usually be a certain area near the central plaza. In the cities, it may be on certain streets. "Cruising" for partners is much easier than in the United States, where the population is polarized between "gay" and "straight" men. In Yucatán, with its more fluid approach to sexuality, there is much more of a chance of meeting someone of the same sex for erotic interests. There is also not a strict separation by age as in the United States, so that even males below the age of eighteen may enter a steam bath. What they do in the privacy of their room is considered no one else's business. Puberty, rather than the arbitrary age of eighteen or twenty-one, is seen as a more proper dividing point concerning sexual matters.

After my arrival in Yucatán, I soon learned that the society provides a de facto acceptance of same-sex relations for males. It did not take long to establish contacts, and my informants suggested that a large majority of the male population is at certain times sexually active with other males. This usually occurs in the years between thirteen and thirty, when sexual desire is strongest, but it also involves men older then that. Marriage to a woman does not seem to have much effect on the occurrence and amount of homosexual behavior.

The limitation that the culture imposes is not to prohibit male-male sexual behavior entirely, but instead to regulate it by placing males in active masculine (hombre or mayate) or passive feminine (homosexual or loca) roles. Homosexuales are de ambiente, having an androgynous ambience. They take the passive role in either anal or oral sex, and are considered the true homosexual. They often share a sense of community with other androgynous males, revolving around drag names, "campy" language, and gender-referenced humor. While they are not seen as

"real men," they occupy an accepted position in society and are not subject to homophobic violence as in Anglo-America.

Their masculine sexual partners, the hombres (literally "men"), have no sense of identity as homosexuals. As long as they effect a macho demeanor and at least express some interest in getting married to a female at some time in the future, they are free to follow their sexual desires with males. They have no burden of being labeled "abnormal," because in fact their behavior is normal for that society. The surprising configuration of their society is that a particular person might take either role in sex, depending on the particular relationship established with the other partner. Some persons, referred to as inernacionales, take both roles sexually, but most males identify with one role more than the other and assume either an active or passive role. It is generally assumed that the more masculine of the two will take the active role in sex, but this may vary sometimes. Passive homosexuals have told me of instances when their hombre boyfriends played the passive role in sex, but this was done only after a level of trust had been established so that such a role reversal would be kept secret. Sex with a male is not something to be embarrassed about, but role reversal is.

Perhaps the best way to explain the social role of homosexual Mayas is to examine the words of particular people. In a small Maya village, it is easy to be introduced to those who are known as homosexual. As the man who introduced me said of such persons, "Everyone knows they're homosexual, and accepts them. There are people like that everywhere in the world. There are some homosexuals in every Maya village." With such a matter-of-fact attitude he introduced me to a young man in his mid-twenties who did not seem very feminine but not macho either. He was a typical de ambiente, with a pleasant, friendly personality. He was popular with the men in his village, being nicknamed El Sexy. When I met him, I noticed a macho man making a noticeably sexual come-on to him, publicly and without any sense of subterfuge. Later, when he was riding with me in my car, a boy smiled and yelled to him, "I see you have found your husband," referring to me. It was not a negative or derogatory joke, just a relaxed kidding that reflected the general knowledge of the villagers that my informant preferred men. He enjoyed the joke immensely.

The men had no reluctance to be seen with him, and had none of the stiffness so apparent in "straight" males in the United States. When he goes to the village tavern, or *cantina*, the men may dance with him. During carnival time, he dresses as a woman and is especially popular as a dance partner. Everyone accepts him. He says of his respected position:

> The other people appreciate me very much. Because I behave properly. *Hombres* will have sex with each other when they get drunk, but I consider that to be bad. It should only be done with an *homosexual*, then it's alright. I would not have sex with another *homosexual*; I don't consider them to be completely men. They're like a third group, different from men or women.

He never takes the initiative in sex, since the men always come to him. He has had relations with most of the men in his village, from teenagers to the elderly. "They know I'm good," he remarks. The men take him to a place, usually behind the church or in the sports field. Since he lives with his mother, he never brings a man home for sex, although he does do social entertaining there. His mother seems quite comfortable with his male visitors, and had no objection to me staying in their home. Since everyone sleeps in a separate hammock, sex is not usually associated with the bedroom. Sexual acts, male-female as well as male-male, are more likely done outside in the bush. Despite his character and behavior, which in the United States would be defined as gay, "El Sexy" plans to get married to a woman after he is thirty, "so that I won't be alone." He might decide to have children, but otherwise he feels that marriage will not inhibit his sexual activities with men.

A few days later, a young man who was visiting let it be known that he enjoyed sex with males. He does not identify himself as homosexual, but rather as *hombre*. He explained that his *hombre* social role required that he take only the "active" role. To do otherwise (at least where others would know about it) would require a changed social role that he was not prepared to make.

For those who follow the cultural dictates of taking on a clearly defined homosexual role, there is an easy acceptance by society. This can apply even for those who follow the role for their entire lives. In another Maya town in southern Yucatán, I visited a forty-year-old man who dresses in a mixture of men's and women's clothing. He owns a popular beauty shop, and is one of the most prosperous persons in the town. When I and a friend visited him, he was calmly doing a manicure for a middle-aged, proper-looking woman. While I talked with him, the woman's husband continually exchanged erotic glances with the young man who accompanied me. As the beautician sat with his thinning hair in pink rollers, he talked freely about his sex life while continuing the woman's manicure. One cannot even imagine such a situation in the typical Anglo-American beauty parlor. He told me:

> Everyone knows I'm *homosexual*, and I am well respected. There are hundreds of *homosexuales* in town, most openly so, but I am the only one who dresses as a woman. The people treat me as a woman, and there are never any problems. I attend mass devotedly; the priest often visits my house for meals because I'm one of the best cooks in town. People respect my good citizenship. The men come to visit me for sex; I have to turn them away. I had a lover for several years, and we walked around town holding hands being completely open. No one objected. I feel no discrimination for being different.

Next I visited a fifty-five-year-old Maya in the same town. He dresses as a man, and is not recognizably feminine. But he has identified as *homosexual* for his entire life, and everyone in his village knows this. He rents out hammock spaces in his house to local high school students, whose parents want them living near the school in a trustworthy environment. He allows men to visit him for sex only during the weekends, when the students are gone.

He had recognized himself as homosexual when he was still a young boy, and had had an open and active sex life with men since his early teens. His family and everyone in town knew, and he had never had any problems. He never felt in danger, and my statements about the attacks against gay people in the United States seemed almost unbelievable to him. He could not even conceive of why someone would want to hurt others merely because they were homosexual. He had not noticed any changes in people's attitudes toward homosexuality since his youth, and stated that attitudes had always been accepting. For those who accept their society's mores and the available roles open to them, there is a recognized and respected position that continues aspects of the aboriginal tradition of the berdache.

## MESTIZO MALES

While the Spanish writers were not correct in their belief that they had wiped out the berdache traditions among the Indians, their antisodomy campaign did have a significant impact on the emerging *mestizo* society. Since relatively few Spanish women came to America, most of the early colonists were men. They had sex with Indian women, and produced biracial progeny that were also bicultural. As a result, the *mestizo* culture absorbed opposing notions of sexuality from the aboriginal and Spanish heritages. With Spanish influence being so strong, it is not surprising that homophobia is an element of *mestizo* social attitudes.

In Mexico at least, an antihomosexual feeling may also be a reflection of condemnation of same-sex behavior by the Aztecs. Unlike most of their neighbors, the Aztec conquerers who invaded central Mexico from the north a century before the Spanish seem to have had taboos against homosexuality. Like the Spanish, the Aztecs were a militarized conquering people, and both societies pursued an ideal of absolute machismo that condemned effeminacy. The modern Mexican *mestizo* identifies with the Spanish or the Aztecs, rather than with the more traditional civilizations of classical Meso-America. Those other cultures, with their easy acceptance of homosexuality, are seen as weak.

Many people do not publicly admit to being Indian, and claim not to understand a Native American language when in fact they do. This acculturative pressure, which is just beginning to be felt in more remote areas, has existed in central Mexico for centuries. The process of acculturation has caused tremendous problems in personal identity that have an impact on sexual behavior. With such conflicting cultural values in *mestizo* society, there are contradictory messages for homosexually inclined individuals.

The major impact that the Spanish campaign has had on modern *mestizo* culture is a decline in status for androgynous males. These individuals have lost the respected status they had in many traditional cultures, and instead are often criticized as being traitors to the macho ideal. Yet, even in *mestizo* culture, the Spanish were not able to wipe out the behavior they so detested. Ironically, what emerged was a kind of de facto cultural approval for masculine males who wish to have sex with these *homosexuales*. Establishing who is *homosexual*, however, leads to a confusion of roles. Erskine Lane, a gay man from the United States who has lived in Latin America for several years, expresses this confusing situation: "The gay gringo who lingers for awhile in Spanish America soon comes to understand how Alice felt when she fell down the rabbit hole. Disorientation in a topsy-turvy wonderland where many old familiar standards of sexual behavior no longer apply at all and most of the others have been reversed. Who is gay? What is gay? For a while you're not sure any more."

Lane characterizes *mestizo* males as almost completely bisexual in their behavior. Yet, they manage to avoid defining themselves as such. By their view, manhood is defined as one who takes the active role in sex. The sex of the person he sleeps with is less important than the position he takes in the sex act. "The macho can actively court and pursue other males; he can even, in some circumstances, admit to a preference for males, all without compromising his heterosexuality." He can do this, however, only as long as he plays the inserter, or "man's," role.

This feeling is illustrated by one *hombre* who would take only the active role in sex, saying, "If I let him fuck me I'd probably like it and then I'd do it again. And then I'd be queer." This fear of the enjoyment of anal sex partly explains the strict separation of active and passive roles in *mestizo* society. Lane asked some of his macho male sexual partners which sex they really preferred. This kind of question was puzzling to them, and they had to think about it before giving an answer. One responded: "It really wouldn't matter to me . . . I guess I really have no preference, but sometimes I think it feels better with a man." The North American writer concluded: "The pansexuality of some guys here amazes me. Male, female, fat, skinny, tall, short, young, old, whatever. No apparent preference. Or, if they have a preference, it is overridden by the supreme macho mandate, which simply says Fuck!"

A similar pattern has been observed by Paul Kutsche, an anthropologist who did fieldwork in Costa Rica. He speaks of the relaxed attitude about sex that is common among mestizo males, and explains it as due to their general approach to life: "Latins are less prone to pigeonhole other individuals or themselves, and more prone to approach each event existentially without [having categories determined by] the foregoing events." Though it is easy to see the continuities of aboriginal culture in these sexual patterns, among modern *mestizos* the androgynous male has lost the high status and religious association that was formerly held by Indians. The pejorative term *maricón* means effeminate, swish, but not homosexual per se. So while a masculine man who has sex with other males is not an object of concern, the androgynous male is the brunt of jokes.

Just as the status of women has declined with the imposition of a misogynist Spanish culture, so too has the status of non-masculine males. There are many similarities between these two groups, in that the social position of both is contradictory. There is the *madre*, who is saintly and sexless, but there is a contrasting species of female, the *bicha*. These social constructs are models of femininity, and an androgynous male fits into this pattern. Lane concludes, "He may be treated with something resembling tenderness or with something bordering on contempt. Or, more probably, with a strange mixture of the two. Just as the woman is treated."

In such a cultural context, specifically "gay" establishments—like bars where homosexuals congregate—are rare. Until recently at least, attempts to organize a separate subculture were met with repression. Police may arrest customers if an openly gay bar opens, and an attempt to start a gay newspaper would most assuredly meet with police opposition. But the focus of such repression, would not be against the sexuality itself, as it would be in the United States. It would be against

the political implications of the rise of a separate gay subculture. Since same-sex contacts can occur in just about any location, there is little need for separate subcultural institutions. As a consequence, people are not polarized into opposite identities based on sexual behavior. So the irony is that while the androgynous male may be derided, as women are derided, there is still a place in society for him. Lane contrasts the situation in Anglo-America, "where a flamboyant painted queen wandering into a straight bar by accident may get thrown out, beat up, or abused. Here he will more likely be invited to dance by some admiring macho."

Since Latin American *mestizo* cultures are the product of two cultures with such opposing attitudes toward gender variation and same-sex behavior, it is understandable that they should have contradictory and confusing tendencies. The fieldwork in Latin America reported in this chapter indicates that in areas where a precolonial berdache tradition existed, and where the Indian traditions are still followed, berdaches continue to be respected. Such is also the case in North America. But for *mestizos*, the contradictory position of homosexually inclined males, whether feminine or masculine, is a product of the historic changes forced on Native Americans by the Spanish. It is part of the heritage of cultural genocide.

# | 15 |

# Letter to the Bishops of the Catholic Church on the Pastoral Care of Homosexual Persons

JOSEPH CARDINAL RATZINGER, CONGREGATION FOR THE DOCTRINE OF THE FAITH

1. The issue of homosexuality and the moral evaluation of homosexual acts have increasingly become a matter of public debate, even in Catholic circles. Since this debate often advances arguments and makes assertions inconsistent with the teaching of the Catholic Church, it is quite rightly a cause for concern to all engaged in the pastoral ministry, and this Congregation has judged it to be of sufficiently grave and widespread importance to address to the Bishops of the Catholic Church this Letter on the Pastoral Care of Homosexual Persons.

2. . . .

3. Explicit treatment of the problem was given in this Congregation's "Declaration on Certain Questions Concerning Sexual Ethics" of December 29, 1975. That document stressed the duty of trying to understand the homosexual condition and noted that culpability for homosexual acts should only be judged with prudence. At the same time the Congregation took note of the distinction commonly drawn between the homosexual condition or tendency and individual homosexual actions. These were described as deprived of their essential and indispensable finality, as being "intrinsically disordered," and able in no case to be approved of.

In the discussion which followed the publication of the Declaration, however, an overly benign interpretation was given to the homosexual condition itself, some going so far as to call it neutral, or even good. Although the particular inclination of the homosexual person is not a sin, it is a more or less strong tendency ordered toward an intrinsic moral evil; and thus the inclination itself must be seen as an objective disorder.

Therefore special concern and pastoral attention should be directed toward those who have this condition, lest they be led to believe that the living out of this orientation in homosexual activity is a morally acceptable option. It is not.

4. An essential dimension of authentic pastoral care is the identification of causes of confusion regarding the Church's teaching. One is a new exegesis of Sacred Scripture which claims variously that Scripture has nothing to say on the subject of homosexuality, or that it somehow tacitly approves of it, or that all of its moral injunctions are so culture-bound that they are no longer applicable to contemporary life. These views are gravely erroneous and call for particular attention here.

5. . . .

6. Providing a basic plan for understanding this entire discussion of homosexuality is the theology of creation we find in Genesis. God, in his infinite wisdom and love, brings into existence all of reality as a reflection of his goodness. He fashions mankind, male and female, in his own image and likeness. Human beings, therefore, are nothing less than the work of God himself; and in the complementarity of the sexes, they are called to reflect the inner unity of the Creator. They do this in a striking way in their cooperation with him in the transmission of life by a mutual donation of the self to the other.

In Genesis 3, we find that this truth about persons being an image of God has been obscured by original sin. There inevitably follows a loss of awareness of the covenantal character of the union these persons had with God and with each other. The human body retains its "spousal significance" but this is now clouded by sin. Thus, in Genesis 19:1–11, the deterioration due to sin continues in the story of the men of Sodom. There can be no doubt of the moral judgement made there against homosexual relations. In Leviticus 18:22 and 20:13, in the course of describing the conditions necessary for belonging to the Chosen People, the author excludes from the People of God those who behave in a homosexual fashion.

Against the background of this exposition of theocratic law, an eschatological perspective is developed by St. Paul when, in I Cor. 6:9, he proposes the same doctrine and lists those who behave in a homosexual fashion among those who shall not enter the Kingdom of God.

In Romans 1:18–32, still building on the moral traditions of his forebears, but in the new context of the confrontation between Christianity and the pagan society of his day, Paul uses homosexual behaviour as an example of the blindness which has overcome humankind. Instead of the original harmony between Creator and creatures, the acute distortion of idolatry has led to all kinds of moral excess. Paul is at a loss to find a clearer example of this disharmony than homosexual relations. Finally, 1 Tim. 1, in full continuity with the Biblical position, singles out those who spread wrong doctrine and in v. 10 explicitly names as sinners those who engage in homosexual acts.

7. The Church, obedient to the Lord who founded her and gave to her the sacramental life, celebrates the divine plan of the loving and life-giving union of men and women in the sacrament of marriage. It is only in the marital relationship that the use of the sexual faculty can be morally good. A person engaging in homosexual behaviour therefore acts immorally.

To choose someone of the same sex for one's sexual activity is to annul the rich symbolism and meaning, not to mention the goals, of the Creator's sexual design. Homosexual activity is not a complementary union, able to transmit life; and so it thwarts the call to a life of that form of self-giving which the Gospel says is the essence of Christian living. This does not mean that homosexual persons are not often generous and giving of themselves; but when they engage in homosexual activity they confirm within themselves a disordered sexual inclination which is essentially self-indulgent. As in every moral disorder, homosexual activity prevents one's own fulfillment and

happiness by acting contrary to the creative wisdom of God. The Church, in rejecting erroneous opinions regarding homosexuality, does not limit but rather defends personal freedom and dignity realistically and authentically understood.

8. Thus, the Church's teaching today is in organic continuity with the Scriptural perspective and with her own constant Tradition. Though today's world is in many ways quite new, the Christian community senses the profound and lasting bonds which join us to those generations who have gone before us, "marked with the sign of faith."

Nevertheless, increasing numbers of people today, even within the Church, are bringing enormous pressure to bear on the Church to accept the homosexual condition as though it were not disordered and to condone homosexual activity. Those within the Church who argue in this fashion often have close ties with those with similar views outside it. These latter groups are guided by a vision opposed to the truth about the human person, which is fully disclosed in the mystery of Christ. They reflect, even if not entirely consciously, a materialistic ideology which denies the transcendent nature of the human person as well as the supernatural vocation of every individual.

The Church's ministers must ensure that homosexual persons in their care will not be misled by this point of view, so profoundly opposed to the teaching of the Church. But the risk is great and there are many who seek to create confusion regarding the Church's position, and then to use that confusion to their own advantage.

9. . . .

10. It is deplorable that homosexual persons have been and are the object of violent malice in speech or in action. Such treatment deserves condemnation from the Church's pastors wherever it occurs. It reveals a kind of disregard for others which endangers the most fundamental principles of a healthy society. The intrinsic dignity of each person must always be respected in word, in action and in law.

But the proper reaction to crimes committed against homosexual persons should not be to claim that the homosexual condition is not disordered. When such a claim is made and when homosexual activity is consequently condoned, or when civil legislation is introduced to protect behavior to which no one has any conceivable right, neither the Church nor society at large should be surprised when other distorted notions and practices gain ground, and irrational and violent reactions increase.

11. It has been argued that the homosexual orientation in certain cases is not the result of deliberate choice; and so the homosexual person would then have no choice but to behave in a homosexual fashion. Lacking freedom, such a person, even if engaged in homosexual activity, would not be culpable.

Here, the Church's wise moral tradition is necessary since it warns against generalizations in judging individual cases. In fact, circumstances may exist, or may have existed in the past, which would reduce or remove the culpability of the individual in a given instance; or other circumstances may increase it. What is at all costs to be avoided is the unfounded and demeaning assumption that the sexual behaviour of homosexual persons is always and totally compulsive and therefore inculpable. What is essential is that the fundamental liberty which characterizes the human person and gives him his dignity be recognized as belonging to the homosexual person as well. As in every conversion from evil, the abandonment of homosexual activity will require a profound collaboration of the individual with God's liberating grace.

12. What, then, are homosexual persons to do who seek to follow the Lord? Fundamentally, they are called to enact the will of God in their life by joining whatever sufferings and difficulties they experience in virtue of their condition to the sacrifice of the Lord's Cross. That Cross, for the believer, is a fruitful sacrifice since from that death come life and redemption. While any call to carry the cross or to understand a Christian's suffering in this way will predictably be met with bitter ridicule by some, it should be remembered that this is the way to eternal life for all who follow Christ.

▼ ▼ ▼

Christians who are homosexual are called, as all of us are, to a chaste life. As they dedicate their lives to understanding the nature of God's personal call to them, they will be able to celebrate the Sacrament of Penance more faithfully and receive the Lord's grace so freely offered there in order to convert their lives more fully to his Way.

13. . . . .

14. . . . .

15. We encourage the Bishops, then, to provide pastoral care in full accord with the teaching of the Church for homosexual persons of their dioceses. No authentic pastoral programme will include organizations in which homosexual persons associate with each other without clearly stating that homosexual activity is immoral. A truly pastoral approach will appreciate the need for homosexual persons to avoid the near occasions of sin.

We would heartily encourage programmes where these dangers are avoided. But we wish to make it clear that departure from the Church's teaching, or silence about it, in an effort to provide pastoral care is neither caring nor pastoral. Only what is true can ultimately be pastoral. The neglect of the Church's position prevents homosexual men and women from receiving the care they need and deserve.

An authentic pastoral programme will assist homosexual persons at all levels of the spiritual life: through the sacraments, and in particular through the frequent and sincere use of the sacrament of Reconciliation, through prayer, witness, counsel and individual care. In such a way, the entire Christian community can come to recognize its own call to assist its brothers and sisters, without deluding them or isolating them.

16. . . . .

17. In bringing this entire matter to the Bishops' attention, this Congregation wishes to support their efforts to assure that the teaching of the Lord and his Church on this important question be communicated fully to all the faithful.

▼ ▼ ▼

In a particular way, we would ask the Bishops to support, with the means at their disposal, the development of appropriate forms of pastoral care for homosexual persons. These would include the assistance of the psychological, sociological and medical sciences, in full accord with the teaching of the Church.

. . .

All support should be withdrawn from any organizations which seek to undermine the teaching of the Church, which are ambiguous about it, or which neglect it entirely. Such support, or even the semblance of such support, can be gravely misinterpreted. Special attention should be given to the practice of scheduling religious services and to the use of Church buildings by these groups, including the facilities of Catholic schools and colleges. To some, such permission to use Church property may seem only just and charitable; but in reality it is contradictory to the purpose for which these institutions were founded, it is misleading and often scandalous.

In assessing proposed legislation, the Bishops should keep as their uppermost concern the responsibility to defend and promote family life.

18. . . .

(During an audience granted to the under-signed Prefect, His Holiness, Pope John Paul II, approved this Letter, adopted in an ordinary session of the Congregation for the Doctrine of the Faith, and ordered it to be published.)

—*Given at Rome, 1 October 1986.*
JOSEPH CARDINAL RATZINGER
PREFECT

# | 16 |

# *Homophobic? Re-Read Your Bible*

## PETER J. GOMES

Opposition to gays' civil rights has become one of the most visible symbols of American civic conflict this year, and religion has become the weapon of choice. The army of the discontented, eager for clear villains and simple solutions and ready for a crusade in which political self-interest and social anxiety can be cloaked in morality, has found hatred of homosexuality to be the last respectable prejudice of the century.

Ballot initiatives in Oregon and Maine would deny homosexuals the protection of civil rights laws. The Pentagon has steadfastly refused to allow gays into the armed forces. Vice President Dan Quayle is crusading for "traditional family values." And Pat Buchanan, who is scheduled to speak at the Republican National Convention this evening, regards homosexuality as a litmus test of moral purity.

Nothing has illuminated this crusade more effectively than a work of fiction, *The Drowning of Stephan Jones*, by Bette Greene. Preparing for her novel, Ms. Greene interviewed more than 400 young men incarcerated for gay-bashing, and scrutinized their case studies. In an interview published in *The Boston Globe* this spring, she said she found that the gay-bashers generally saw nothing wrong in what they did, and, more often than not, said their religious leaders and traditions sanctioned their behavior. One convicted teenage gay-basher told her that the pastor of his church had said, "Homosexuals represent the

devil, Satan," and that the Rev. Jerry Falwell had echoed that charge.

Christians opposed to political and social equality for homosexuals nearly always appeal to the moral injunctions of the Bible, claiming that Scripture is very clear on the matter and citing verses that support their opinion. They accuse others of perverting and distorting texts contrary to their "clear" meaning. They do not, however, necessarily see quite as clear a meaning in biblical passages on economic conduct, the burdens of wealth and the sin of greed.

Nine biblical citations are customarily invoked as relating to homosexuality. Four (Deuteronomy 23:17, I Kings 14:24, I Kings 22:46 and II Kings 23:7) simply forbid prostitution, by men and women.

Two others (Leviticus 18:19–23 and Leviticus 20:10–16) are part of what biblical scholars call the Holiness Code. The code explicitly bans homosexual acts. But it also prohibits eating raw meat, planting two different kinds of seed in the same field and wearing garments with two different kinds of yarn. Tattoos, adultery and sexual intercourse during a woman's menstrual period are similarly outlawed.

There is no mention of homosexuality in the four Gospels of the New Testament. The moral

*New York Times*, August 17, 1992. p. A:19.

teachings of Jesus are not concerned with the subject.

Three references from St. Paul are frequently cited (Romans 1:26–2:1, I Corinthians 6:9–11 and I Timothy 1:10). But St. Paul was concerned with homosexuality only because in Greco-Roman culture it represented a secular sensuality that was contrary to his Jewish-Christian spiritual idealism. He was against lust and sensuality in anyone, including heterosexuals. To say that homosexuality is bad because homosexuals are tempted to do morally doubtful things is to say that heterosexuality is bad because heterosexuals are likewise tempted. For St. Paul, anyone who puts his or her interest ahead of God's is condemned, a verdict that falls equally upon everyone.

And lest we forget Sodom and Gomorrah, recall that the story is not about sexual perversion and homosexual practice. It is about inhospitality, according to Luke 10:10–13, and failure to care for the poor, according to Ezekiel 16:49–50: "Behold, this was the iniquity of thy sister Sodom, pride, fullness of bread, and abundance of idleness was in her and in her daughters, neither did she strengthen the hand of the poor and needy." To suggest that Sodom and Gomorrah is about homosexual sex is an analysis of about as much worth as suggesting that the story of Jonah and the whale is a treatise on fishing.

Part of the problem is a question of interpretation. Fundamentalists and literalists, the storm troopers of the religious right, are terrified that Scripture, "wrongly interpreted," may separate them from their values. That fear stems from their own recognition that their "values" are not derived from Scripture, as they publicly claim. Indeed, it is through the lens of their own prejudices and personal values that they "read" Scripture and cloak their own views in its authority. We all interpret Scripture: Make no mistake. And no one truly is a literalist, despite the pious temptation. The questions are, By what principle of interpretation do we proceed, and by what means do we reconcile "what it meant then" to "what it means now?"

These matters are far too important to be left to scholars and seminarians alone. Our ability to judge ourselves and others rests on our ability to interpret Scripture intelligently. The right use of the Bible, an exercise as old as the church itself, means that we confront our prejudices rather than merely confirm them.

For Christians, the principle by which Scripture is read is nothing less than an appreciation of the work and will of God as revealed in that of Jesus. To recover a liberating and inclusive Christ is to be freed from the semantic bondage that makes us curators of a dead culture rather than creatures of a new creation.

Religious fundamentalism is dangerous because it cannot accept ambiguity and diversity and is therefore inherently intolerant. Such intolerance, in the name of virtue, is ruthless and uses political power to destroy what it cannot convert.

It is dangerous, especially in America, because it is anti-democratic and is suspicious of "the other," in whatever form that "other" might appear. To maintain itself, fundamentalism must always define "the other" as deviant.

But the chief reason that fundamentalism is dangerous is that, at the hands of the Rev. Pat Robertson, the Rev. Jerry Falwell and hundreds of lesser-known but equally worrisome clerics, preachers and pundits, it uses Scripture and the Christian practice to encourage ordinarily good people to act upon their fears rather than their virtues.

Fortunately, those who speak for the religious right do not speak for all American Christians, and the Bible is not theirs alone to interpret. The same Bible that the advocates of slavery used to protect their wicked self-interests is the Bible that inspired slaves to revolt and their liberators to action.

The same Bible that the predecessors of Mr. Falwell and Mr. Robertson used to keep white churches white is the source of the inspiration of the Rev. Martin Luther King Jr. and the social reformation of the 1960's. The same Bible that anti-feminists use to keep women silent in the churches is the Bible that preaches liberation to captives and says that in Christ there is neither male nor female, slave nor free.

And the same Bible that on the basis of an archaic social code of ancient Israel and a tortured reading of Paul is used to condemn all homosexuals and homosexual behavior includes metaphors of redemption, renewal, inclusion and love—principles that invite homosexuals to accept their freedom and responsibility in Christ and demands that their fellow Christians accept them as well.

The political piety of the fundamentalist religious right must not be exercised at the expense of our precious freedoms. And in this summer of our discontent, one of the most precious freedoms for which we must all fight is freedom from this last prejudice.

# | 17 |

## Biblical Verse: Is It a Reason or an Excuse?

### DEB PRICE

An Engineering professor is treating her husband, a loan officer, to dinner for finally giving in to her pleas to shave off the scraggly beard he grew on vacation.

His favorite restaurant is a casual place where they both feel comfortable in slacks and cotton-polyester blend golf shirts. But, as always, she wears the gold and pearl pendant he gave her the day her divorce to her first husband was final.

They're laughing over their menus because they know he always ends up diving into a giant plate of ribs, but she won't be talked into anything more fattening than shrimp.

Quiz: How many Biblical prohibitions are they violating? Well, wives must be "submissive" to their husbands (I Peter 3:1). And all women are forbidden to teach men (I Timothy 2:12), wear gold or pearls (I Timothy 2:9) or dress in clothing that "pertains to a man" (Deuteronomy 22:5).

Shellfish and pork are definitely out (Leviticus 11:7,10), as are usury (Deuteronomy 23:19), shaving (Leviticus 19:27) and clothes of more than one fabric (Leviticus 19:19). And since the Bible rarely recognizes divorce, they're committing adultery, which carries the rather harsh penalty of death by stoning (Deuteronomy 22:22).

So why are they having such a good time? Probably because they wouldn't think of worrying about rules that seem absurd, anachronistic or—at best—unrealistic.

Yet this same modern-day couple easily could be among the millions of people who never hesitate to lean on the Bible to justify their own anti-gay attitudes.

Bible verses have long been used selectively to support many kinds of discrimination. Some-where along the way, Jesus' second-greatest commandment gets lost: "You shall love your neighbor as yourself."

Once a given form of prejudice falls out of favor with society, so do the verses that had seemed to condone it. It's unimaginable today, for example, that anyone would use the Bible to try to justify slavery.

Yet when the abolitionist movement began to gain momentum in the early 19th century, many Southern ministers defended the owning of human beings as a divinely approved system: "Slaves, obey in everything those who are your earthly masters . . . " (Colossians 3:22).

In an influential anti-abolitionist essay, South Carolina Baptist leader Richard Furman declared in 1822 that "the right of holding slaves is clearly established in the Holy Scriptures."

Meanwhile, anti-slavery crusaders were taking an interpretative approach to the Bible since a literal reading "gave little or no support to an abolitionist position," author Carl Degler says in *Place Over Time: The Continuity of Southern Distinctiveness.*

Nearly 100 years after the Emancipation Proclamation, a Virginia court defended racial segregation by saying, "The Almighty God created the races white, black, yellow, Malay and red, and He placed them on separate continents. . . . He did not intend for the races to mix." The U.S. Supreme Court rejected that reasoning in 1967 when it struck down laws in 16 states forbidding interracial marriage.

Like advocates of racial equality, suffragists

*Detroit News*, August 24, 1993.

found the literal reading of the Bible was their biggest stumbling block. Many ministers even condemned using anesthesia during labor because pain in childbirth was punishment for Eve's bite of forbidden fruit (Genesis 3:16).

Susan B. Anthony eventually declared in frustration: "I distrust those people who know so well what God wants them to do, because I notice it always coincides with their own desires."

Studying the Bible is often akin to looking at Rohrschach ink blots, says Biblical scholar Joe Barnhart, author of *The Southern Baptist Holy War.*

"What we get out of it is sometimes what we put in," he explains.

The punishment the Bible metes out to all men for Adam's downfall is toiling "in the sweat of your face" (Genesis 3:19).

Yet, Barnhart notes with a laugh, there's one bit of progress never denounced by preachers hot under the clerical collar: air-conditioning.

# | 18 |

# *The Homosexual Movement: A Response by the Ramsey Colloquium*

## RAMSEY COLLOQUIUM

## I. THE NEW THING

Homosexual behavior is a phenomenon with a long history, to which there have been various cultural and moral responses. But today in our public life there is something new, a *novum*, which demands our attention and deserves a careful moral response.

The new thing is a movement that variously presents itself as an appeal for compassion, as an extension of civil rights to minorities, and as a cultural revolution. The last of these seems to us the best description of the phenomenon; indeed, that is what its most assertive and passionate defenders say it is. *The Nation*, for example, asserts (May 3, 1993): "All the crosscurrents of present-day liberation struggles are subsumed in the gay struggle. The gay movement is in some way similar to the movement that other communities have experienced in the nation's past, but it is also something more, because sexual identity is in crisis throughout the population, and gay people—at once the most conspicuous subjects and objects of the crisis—have been forced to invent a complete cosmology to grasp it. No one says the changes will come easily. But it's just possible that a small and despised sexual minority will change America forever."

Although some date "the movement" from the "Stonewall Riot" of June 1969, we have more recently witnessed a concerted and intense campaign, in the media and in leading cultural institutions, to advance the gay and lesbian cause. Despite the fact that the Jewish and Christian traditions have, in a clear and sustained manner, judged homosexual behavior to be morally wrong, this campaign has not left our religious communities unaffected. The great majority of Americans have been surprised, puzzled, shocked, and sometimes outraged by this movement for radical change. At the same time, the movement has attracted considerable support from heterosexual Americans who accept its claim to be the course of social justice and tolerance.

*First Things*, March 1994, pp. 15–20.

We share a measure of ambivalence and confusion regarding this remarkable insurgency in our common life. We do not present ourselves as experts on the subject of homosexuality. We are committed Christians and Jews and we try to be thoughtful citizens. In this statement, we do our best to respond to the claims made by the gay and lesbian movement and to form a moral judgment regarding this new thing in our public life.

We are not a "representative group" of Americans, nor are we sure what such a group would look like. No group can encompass the maddening and heartening diversity of sex, race, class, cultural background, and ideological disposition that is to be found among the American people. We are who we are. As such, we offer this product of our study, reflection, and conversation in the hope that others may find it helpful.

Our aim is to present arguments that are public in character and accessible to all reasonable persons. In doing so, we draw readily on the religious and moral traditions that have shaped our civilization and our own lives. We are confident that arguments based, inter alia, on religious conviction and insight cannot legitimately be excluded from public discourse in a democratic society.

In discussing homosexuality, homosexuals, and the gay and lesbian movement, it is necessary to make certain distinctions. Homosexuality is sometimes considered a matter of sexual "orientation," referring to those whose erotic desires are predominantly or exclusively directed to members of the same sex. Many such persons live lives of discipline and chastity. Others act upon their homosexual orientation through homogenital acts. Many in this second group are "in the closet," although under the pressure of the current movement, they may be uneasy about that distinction between public and private. Still another sector of the homosexual population is public about its orientation and behavior and insists that a gay "lifestyle" be not simply tolerated but affirmed. These differences account for some of the tensions within the "movement." Some aim at "mainstreaming" homosexuality, while others declare their aim to be cultural, moral, and political revolution.

We confront, therefore, a movement of considerable complexity, and we must respect the diversity to be found among our homosexual fellow citizens and fellow believers. Some want no more than help and understanding in coping with what they view as their problem; others ask no more than that they be left alone.

The new thing, the *novum*, is a gay and lesbian movement that aggressively proposes radical changes in social behavior, religion, morality, and law. It is important to distinguish public policy considerations from the judgment of particular individuals. Our statement is directed chiefly to debates over public policy and what should be socially normative. We share the uneasiness of most Americans with the proposals advanced by the gay and lesbian movement, and we seek to articulate reasons for the largely intuitive and pre-articulate anxiety of most Americans regarding homosexuality and its increasing impact on our public life.

## II. NEW THING/OLD THING: THE SEXUAL REVOLUTION

While the gay and lesbian movement is indeed a new thing, its way was prepared by, and it is in large part a logical extension of, what has been called the "sexual revolution." The understanding of marriage and family once considered normative is very commonly dishonored in our society and, too frequently, in our communities of faith. Religious communities and leaderships have been, and in too many cases remain, deeply complicit in the demeaning of social norms essential to human flourishing.

Thus moral criticism of the homosexual world and movement is unbalanced, unfair, and implausible if it is not, at the same time, criticism of attitudes and behaviors that have debased heterosexual relations. The gay and lesbian insurgency has raised a sharp moral challenge to the hypocrisy and decadence of our culture. In the light of widespread changes in sexual mores, some homosexuals understandably protest that the sexual license extended to "straights" cannot be denied to them.

We believe that any understanding of sexuality, including heterosexuality, that makes it chiefly an arena for the satisfaction of personal desire is harmful to individuals and society. Any way of life that accepts or encourages sexual relations for pleasure or personal satisfaction alone turns away from the disciplined community that marriage is intended to engender and foster. Religious communities that have in recent decades winked at promiscuity (even among the clergy), that have solemnly repeated marriage vows that their own congregation do not take seriously, and that have failed to concern themselves with the devastating effects of divorce upon children cannot with integrity condemn homosexual behavior unless they are also willing to reassert the heterosexual norm more believably and effectively in their pastoral care. In other words, those determined to resist the gay and lesbian movement must be equally concerned for the renewal of integrity, in teaching and practice, regarding "traditional sexual ethics."

It is testimony to the perduring role of religion in American life that many within the gay and lesbian movement seek the blessing of religious institutions. The movement correctly perceives that attaining such formal approbation—through, for example, the content and style of seminary education and the ordination of practicing homosexuals—will give it an effective hold upon the primary institutions of moral legitimation in our popular culture. The movement also correctly perceives that our churches and synagogues have typically been inarticulate and unpersuasive in offering reasons for withholding the blessing that is sought.

One reason for the discomfort of religious leaders in the face of this new movement is the past and continuing failure to offer supportive and knowledgeable pastoral care to persons coping with the problems of their homosexuality. Without condoning homogenital acts, it is necessary to recognize that many such persons are, with fear and trembling, seeking as best they can to live lives pleasing to God and in service to others. Confronted by the vearing ambiguities of eros in human life, religious communities should be better equipped to support people in their struggle, recognizing that we all fall short of the vocation to holiness of life.

The sexual revolution is motored by presuppositions that can and ought to be effectively challenged. Perhaps the key presupposition of the revolution is that human health and flourishing require that sexual desire, understood as a "need," be acted upon and satisfied. Any discipline of denial or restraint has been popularly depicted as unhealthy and dehumanizing. We insist, however, that it is dehumanizing to define ourselves, or our personhood as male and female, by our desires alone. Nor does it seem plausible to suggest that what millennia of human experience have taught us to regard as self-command should now be dismissed as mere repression.

At the same time that the place of sex has been grotesquely exaggerated by the sexual revolution, it has also been trivialized. The mysteries of human sexuality are commonly reduced to matters of recreation or taste, not unlike one's preferences in diet, dress, or sport. This peculiar mix of the exaggerated and the trivialized makes it possible for the gay and lesbian movement to demand, simultaneously, a respect for what is claimed to be most importantly and constitutively true of homosexuals, and tolerance for what is, after all, simply a difference in "lifestyle."

It is important to recognize the linkages among the component parts of the sexual revolution. Permissive abortion, widespread adultery, easy divorce, radical feminism, and the gay and lesbian movement have not by accident appeared at the same historical moment. They have in common a declared desire for liberation from constraint—especially constraint associated with an allegedly oppressive culture and religious tradition. They also have in common the presuppositions that the body is little more than an instrument for the fulfillment of desire, and that the fulfillment of desire is the essence of the self. On biblical and philosophical grounds, we reject this radical dualism between the self and the body. Our bodies have their own dignity, bear their own truths, and are participant in our personhood in a fundamental way.

This constellation of movements, of which the gay movement is part, rests upon an anthropological doctrine of the autonomous self. With respect to abortion and the socialization of sexuality, this anthropology has gone a long way toward entrenching itself in the jurisprudence of our society as well as in popular habits of mind and behavior. We believe it is a false doctrine that leads neither to individual flourishing nor to social well-being.

## III. THE HETEROSEXUAL NORM

Marriage and the family—husband, wife and children, joined by public recognition and legal bond—are the most effective institutions for the rearing of children, the directing of sexual passion, and human flourishing in community. Not all marriages and families "work," but it is unwise to let pathology and failure, rather than a vision of what is normative and ideal, guide us in the development of social policy.

Of course many today doubt that we can speak of what is normatively human. The claim that all social institutions and patterns of behavior are social constructions that we may, if we wish, alter without harm to ourselves is a proposal even more radical in origin and implication that the sexual revolution. That the institutions of marriage and family are culturally conditioned and subject to change and development no one should doubt, but such recognition should not undermine our ability to discern patterns of community that best serve human well-being. Judaism and Christianity did not invent the heterosexual norm, but these faith traditions affirm that norm and can open our eyes to see in it important truths about human life.

Fundamental to human life in society is the creation of humankind as male and female, which is typically and paradigmatically expressed in the marriage of a man and a woman who form a union of persons in which two become one flesh—a union which, in the biblical tradition, is the foundation of all human community. In faithful marriage, three important elements of human life are made manifest and given support.

(1) Human society extends over time; it has a history. It does so because, through the mysterious participation of our procreative powers in God's own creative work, we transmit life to those who will succeed us. We become a people with a shared history over time and with a common stake in that history. Only the heterosexual norm gives full expression to the commitment to time and history evident in having and caring for children.

(2) Human society requires that we learn to value difference within community. In the complementarity of male and female we find the paradigmatic instance of this truth. Of course, persons may complement each other in many different ways, but the complementarity of male and female is grounded in, and fully embraces, our bodies and their structure. It does not sever the meaning of the person from bodily life, as if human beings were simply desire, reason, or will. The complementarity of male and female invites us to learn to accept and affirm the natural world from which we are too often alienated.

Moreover, in the creative complementarity of male and female we are directed toward community with those unlike us. In the community between male and famale, we do not and cannot see in each other mere reflections of ourselves. In learning to appreciate this most basic difference, and in forming a marital bond, we take both difference and community seriously. (And ultimately, we begin to be prepared for communion with God, in Whom we never find simply a reflection of ourselves.)

(3) Human society requires the direction and

restraint of many impulses. Few of those impulses are more powerful or unpredictable than sexual desire. Throughout history societies have taken particular care to socialize sexuality toward marriage and the family. Marriage is a place where, in a singular manner, our waywardness begins to be healed and our fear of commitment overcome, where we may learn to place another person's needs rather than our own desires at the center of life.

Thus, reflection on the heterosexual norm directs our attention to certain social necessities: the continuation of human life, the place of difference within community, the redirection of our tendency to place our own desires first. These necessities cannot be supported by rational calculations of self-interest alone; they require commitments that go well beyond the demands of personal satisfaction. Having and rearing children is among the most difficult of human projects. Men and women need all the support they can get to maintain stable marriages in which the next generation can flourish. Even marriages that do not give rise to children exist in accord with, rather than in opposition to, the heterosexual norm. To depict marriage as simply one of several alternative "lifestyles" is seriously to undermine the normative vision required for social well-being.

There are legitimate and honorable forms of love other than marriage. Indeed, one of the goods at stake in today's disputes is a long-honored tradition of friendship between men and men, women and women, women and men. In the current climate of sexualizing and politicizing all intense interpersonal relationships, the place of sexually chaste friendship and of religiously motivated celibacy is gravely jeopardized. In our cultural moment of narrow-eyed prurience, the single life of chastity has come under the shadow of suspicion and is no longer credible to many people. Indeed, the non-satisfaction of sexual "needs" is widely viewed as a form of deviance.

In this context it becomes imperative to affirm the reality and beauty of sexually chaste relationships of deep affectional intensity. We do not accept the notion that self-command is an unhealthy form of repression on the part of single people, whether their inclination be heterosexual or homosexual. Put differently, the choice is not limited to heterosexual marriage on the one hand, or relationships involving homogenital sex on the other.

## IV. THE CLAIMS OF THE MOVEMENT

We turn our attention now to a few of the important public claims made by gay and lesbian advocates (even as we recognize that the movement is not monolithic). As we noted earlier, there is an important distinction between those who wish to "mainstream" homosexual life and those who aim at restructuring culture. This is roughly the distinction between those who seek integration and those who seek revolution. Although these different streams of the movement need to be distinguished, a few claims are so frequently encountered that they require attention.

Many gays argue that they have no choice, that they could not be otherwise than they are. Such an assertion can take a variety of forms—for example, that "being gay is natural for me" or even that "God made me this way."

We cannot settle the dispute about the roots—genetic or environmental—of homosexual orientation. Although some scientific evidence suggests a genetic predisposition for homosexual orientation, the case is not significantly different from evidence of predispositions toward other traits—for example, alcoholism or violence. In each instance we must still ask whether such a predisposition should be acted upon or whether it should be resisted. Whether or not a homosexual orientation can be changed—and it is important to recognize that there are responsible authorities on both sides of this question—we affirm the obligation of pastors and therapists to assist those who recognize the value of chaste living to resist the impulse to act on their desire for homogenital gratification.

The Kinsey data, which suggested that 10 percent of males are homosexual, have now been convincingly discredited. Current research suggests that the percentage of males whose sexual desires and behavior are exclusively homosexual is as low as 1 percent or 2 percent in developed societies. In any case, the statistical frequency of an act or desire does not determine its moral status. Racial discrimination and child abuse occur frequently in society, but that does not make them "natural" in the moral sense. What is in accord with human nature is behavior appropriate to what we are meant to be—appropriate to what God created and calls us to be.

In a fallen creation, many quite common attitudes and behaviors must be straightforwardly designated as sin. Although we are equal before God, we are not born equal in terms of our strengths and weaknesses, our tendencies and dispositions, our nature and nurture. We cannot utterly change the hand we have been dealt by inheritance and family circumstances, but we are responsible for how we play that hand. Inclination and temptation are not sinful, although they surely result from humanity's fallen condition. Sin occurs in the joining of the will, freely and knowingly, to an act or way of life that is contrary to God's purpose. Religious communities in particular must lovingly support all the faithful in their struggle against temptation, while at the same time insisting that precisely for their sake we must describe as sinful the homogenital and extramarital heterosexual behavior to which some are drawn.

Many in our society—both straight and gay—also contend that what people do sexually is entirely a private matter and no one's business but their own. The form this claim takes is often puzzling to many people—and rightly so. For what were once considered private acts are now highly publicized, while, for the same acts, public privilege is claimed because they are private. What is confusedly at work here is an extreme individualism, a claim for autonomy so extreme that it must undercut the common good.

To be sure, there should in our society be a wide zone for private behavior, including behavior that most Americans would deem wrong. Some of us oppose anti-sodomy statutes. In a society premised upon limited government there are realms of behavior that ought to be beyond the supervision of the state. In addition to the way sexual wrongdoing harms character, however, there are often other harms involved. We have in mind the alarming rates of sexual promiscuity, depression, and suicide and the ominous presence of AIDS within the homosexual subculture. No one can doubt that these are reasons for public concern. Another legitimate reason for public concern is the harm done to the social order when policies are advanced that would increase the incidence of gay lifestyle and undermine the normative character of marriage and family life.

Since there are good reasons to support the heterosexual norm, since it has been developed with great difficulty, and since it can be maintained only if it is cared for and supported, we cannot be indifferent to attacks upon it. The social norms by which sexual behavior is inculcated and controlled are of urgent importance for families and for the society as a whole. Advocates of the gay and lesbian movement have the responsibility to set forth publicly their alternative proposals. This must mean more than calling for liberation from established standards. They must clarify for all of us how sexual mores are to be inculcated in the young, who are particularly vulnerable to seduction and solicitation. Public anxiety about homosexuality is preeminently a concern about the vulnerabilities of the young. This, we are persuaded, is a matter of legitimate and urgent public concern.

Gay and lesbian advocates sometimes claim that they are asking for no more than an end to discrimination, drawing an analogy with the earlier civil rights movement that sought justice for black Americans. The analogy is unconvincing and misleading. Differences of race are in accord with — not contrary to — our nature, and such differences do not provide justification for behavior otherwise unacceptable. It is sometimes claimed that homosexuals want only a recognition of their status, not necessarily of their behavior. But in this case the distinction between status and behavior does not hold. The public declaration of status ("coming out of the closet") is a declaration of intended behavior.

Certain discriminations are in fact necessary within society; it is not too much to say that civilization itself depends on the making of such distinctions (between, finally, right and wrong). In our public life, some discrimination is in order — when, for example, in education and programs involving young people the intent is to prevent predatory behavior that can take place under the guise of supporting young people in their anxieties about their "sexual identity." It is necessary to discriminate between relationships. Gay and lesbian "domestic partnerships," for example, should not be socially recognized as the moral equivalent of marriage. Marriage and the family are institutions necessary for our continued social well-being and, in an individualistic society that tends to liberation from all constraint, they are fragile institutions in need of careful and continuing support.

## V. Conclusion

We do not doubt that many gays and lesbians — perhaps especially those who seek the blessing of our religious communities — believe that theirs is the only form of love, understood as affection and erotic satisfaction, of which they are capable. Nor do we doubt that they have found in such relationships something of great personal significance, since even a distorted love retains traces of

love's grandeur. Where there is love in morally disordered relationships we do not censure the love. We censure the form in which that love seeks expression. To those who say that this disordered behavior is so much at the core of their being that the person cannot be (and should not be) distinguished from the behavior, we can only respond that we earnestly hope they are wrong.

We are well aware that this declaration will be dismissed by some as a display of "homophobia," but such dismissals have become unpersuasive and have ceased to intimidate. Indeed, we do not think it a bad thing that people should experience a reflexive recoil from what is wrong. To achieve such a recoil is precisely the point of moral education of the young. What we have tried to do here is to bring this reflexive and often pre-articulate recoil to reasonable expression.

Our society is, we fear, progressing precisely in the manner given poetic expression by Alexander Pope:

> Vice is a monster of so frightful mien,
> As to be hated needs but to be seen;
> Yet seen too oft, familiar with her face,
> We first endure, then pity, then embrace.

To endure (tolerance), to pity (compassion), to embrace (affirmation): that is the sequence of change in attitude and judgment that has been advanced by the gay and lesbian movement with notable success. We expect that this success will encounter certain limits and that what is truly natural will reassert itself, but this may not happen before more damage is done to innumerable individuals and to our common life.

Perhaps some of this damage can be prevented. For most people marriage and family is the most important project in their lives. For it they have made sacrifices beyond numbering; they want to be succeeded in an ongoing, shared history by children and grandchildren; they want to transmit to their children the beliefs that have claimed their hearts and minds. They should be supported in that attempt. To that end, we have tried to set forth our view and the reasons that inform it. Whatever the inadequacies of this declaration, we hope it will be useful to others. The gay and lesbian movement, and the dramatic changes in sexual attitudes and behavior of which that movement is part, have unloosed a great moral agitation in our culture. Our hope is that this statement will contribute to turning that agitation into civil conversation about the kind of people we are and hope to be.

# | 19 |

# *In God's Image: Coming to Terms with Leviticus*

## REBECCA T. ALPERT

Joan and Leslie have been lovers for the past five years. This year, they decided to go home for the Jewish holidays to Joan's family in upstate New York. It was an important milestone. Joan's parents had become more comfortable with their daughter's lesbian life-style and lover; this would be a way of acknowledging the growth in the relationships among Leslie, Joan, her parents, and her younger brother.

Joan's family is deeply involved in their local Conservative synagogue, and it was truly an act of courage for all of them to go to Kol Nidre services together. Joan was excited—proud of her family and eager to reenter the Jewish life she had left behind. Leslie was scared, but interested in learning more about involvement in the Jewish community. Although Leslie's parents are Jewish, she was raised without religious training.

Yom Kippur evening turned out to be a good experience. The congregants were friendly and welcoming to Joan and her "friend." Religiously, too, the women were moved by the powerful experience of communal prayer. They decided that night to spend the entire next day in shul, continuing their fasting and waiting for the stirring blast of the *shofar* to bring an end to the day.

All went well until the afternoon service. The rabbi explained that for the Torah portion, they would be reading from the book of Leviticus, chapter 18, a description of forbidden sexual practices. Why read that on the holiest day of the year? No explanation was offered. As the Torah

In Christie Balka and Andy Rose, eds., *Twice Blessed: On Being Gay and Jewish*, pp. 61–70. Excerpt. Boston: Beacon, 1989.

was read, Joan and Leslie followed along in the translation until they read the words: "Do not lie with a male as one lies with a woman; it is an abomination."

Joan and Leslie froze, recognizing the meaning for them as lesbians, even though the language refers only to men. They looked at one another, disappointment spreading across Joan's face while a tear formed in the corner of Leslie's eye, as if to say, "This place is really not for us, after all."

Three times a year, on Yom Kippur afternoon and then twice during the annual cycle of Torah readings, every year for the past 2,500 years, Jews around the world have listened to the public reading of the words of Leviticus declaring a sexual act between two men "an abomination." When the prohibition is read from Leviticus 20, during the third yearly reading, it is declared not only an abomination, but also a capital crime.

What could be more profoundly alienating than to know that the most sacred text of your people, read aloud on the holiest day of the year, calls that which is central to your life an abomination? What could be more terrifying than to know that what for you is a sacred loving act was considered by your ancestors to be punishable by death?

Coming to terms with Leviticus may be the greatest single struggle facing gay men and lesbians seeking to find a religious home within the Jewish community. Before we examine strategies for all of us to cope with this dilemma, we must understand the power and authority of this text: What is Leviticus, and why is it so important?

Leviticus is the third book of the Pentateuch, the five books of Moses. These books comprise the story of the birth of our people and the beginnings of the Jewish legal system. Traditionally, they are understood as revelation—God's words, written down by Moses, God's prophet, on Mt. Sinai. Thus, these words are considered not only a record of our past, but God's explanation of God's will for the people of Israel as well. Laws codified in these books are the ultimate source of authority and are the starting point for the later development of Jewish civilization. According to strict interpretation of Jewish law, no law stated in the Torah can ever be nullified or abrogated.

Beyond its implications for the Jewish legal system, the Torah has deep symbolic power. It is preserved on a handwritten parchment scroll. It is kept in the ark, a sacred space at the front or center of every synagogue, under a flame that burns perpetually. It is adorned with a special cover and ornaments. It is removed from the ark with great pageantry to be chanted aloud three times weekly. The public reading of Torah is the central event of the Sabbath morning service. To be called to the Torah to recite the blessing for reading from the scroll is a great honor. Blessing and reading from the Torah forms the central experience of the bar/bat mitzvah ceremony. (Imagine, if you will, the adolescent who thinks he or she might be gay having to read from Leviticus 18 or 20 at the rite of passage!)

Clearly, the words of the Torah cannot be dismissed lightly, nor would we wish them to be. The Torah contains concepts that are vital to us: that we should love our neighbors as ourselves and deal respectfully with the stranger, the poor, and the lonely in society. The Torah instructs us to all see ourselves as having been created in God's image, and therefore as the bearers of holiness in the world. It also contains wonderful and challenging stories of the world's beginnings and our people's journey from slavery to freedom.

Those of us who choose to remain identified with the Jewish tradition do so in part because of the foundation laid by Torah. We cannot simply excise what we do not like; it is our heritage and the primary text of our people. Yet a piercing question arises and reverberates through our lives: How do we live as Jews when the same text that tells us we were created in God's image also tells us that our sacred loving acts are punishable by death by decree of that same God?

This question may impel us to deny the power of Leviticus, but in truth we cannot. For all of us involved in any way in Jewish life, this text has authority. It has authority in that it is used by others to support the belief that homosexuality is wrong. (Of course, this is true not only for Jews. Leviticus is quoted by right-wing Christian religious groups to the same end.) And whether we ourselves consciously accept the authority of the text or not, we would be foolish to think that it does not affect us deeply, sometimes in subtle or insidious ways. For those of us who are lesbian or gay, it can undermine our pride in ourselves, feeding our own homophobia as well as that of others.

Let me suggest, then, three methods of coming to terms with Leviticus. We can, as did our ancestors, interpret the text to enable us to function with it on its own terms. We can, like biblical scholars, treat the text as a historical record and draw conclusions based on the way it functions in a given context. Or we can encounter the text directly with our emotions and our self-knowledge, allowing it to move us to anger, and then beyond anger, to action.

Each method comes to terms with the text's authority in a different way. Through interpreting the text we stay within the system and redirect it. Through historical reasoning we place limits on the text's authority by examining it with the lens of another system. Through encountering the text emotionally, we confront it and therefore use it as an instrument of transformation.

## THE INTERPRETIVE METHOD

*Midrash*—the process of making commentary to interpret the text—is a vital aspect of attempts throughout Jewish history to make the Bible come alive. Throughout the generations, interpreters have sought to make the text accessible to their contemporaries who may not understand its original meaning. The text may be ambiguous, unclear, or redundant. A word or custom may be unfamiliar and need explanation. One part of the text may contradict another part, and a resolution of the conflict is necessary. The same word or phrase may be repeated, seemingly without purpose, and commentators have sought to explain these repetitions by assigning different meanings to them. Finally, there are cases in which the grammar or syntax is unusual and lends itself to providing a new interpretation.

While interpretive methods are legitimate and widely practiced, it should be noted that many would claim that the text is not really in need of interpretation. It stands on its own as God's word.

With this understanding as our background, let us look at how Leviticus 18:22 and 20:13 have been interpreted by traditional Jewish commentators. We find that this prohibition is mentioned less often than others in the Torah. Some have assumed that this lack of discussion is due to the fact that homosexuality was not common among Jews. Suffice to say that we can only speculate about the extent of homosexual practice, but we can say with certainty that the subject was not considered problematic enough to require extensive public discussion. For whatever reason, to be sure, homosexuality was not a visible issue in the Jewish world until contemporary times.

Most of the interpretations of Leviticus 18:22 hinge on an unclear word—*to'evah*—which is generally translated as "abomination." In fact, the meaning of this word is obscure. Therefore, interpreters have taken the opportunity to translate it

in ways that explain the prohibition. After all, the text never tells us why lying with a man is *to'evah*, but only that it is.

What might *to'evah* mean? According to the second-century commentator Bar Kapparah, it means "*to'eh ata ba*—you go astray because of it" (see Babylonian Talmud, Nedarim 51b). This play on words has been taken to mean that it is not intrinsically an evil to engage in homosexual acts, but rather that they have negative consequences. Bar Kapparah did not spell out those negative consequences—rather, it was left to later commentators to interpret his interpretation.

Certain medieval texts suggest that one is being led astray from the main function of sexual behavior, namely procreation. Some Rabbinic commentators assume that to go astray means to abandon your wife and to disrupt family life. This interpretation is reinforced by medieval commentator Saadiah Gaon's general pronouncement that the Bible's moral legislation is directed at preserving the structure of the family (*Emunot ve-Deot* 3:1). Finally, modern commentator R. Baruch haLevi Epstein, author of the commentary *Torah Temimah*, suggests that going astray means not following the anatomically appropriate manner of sexual union.

The most well-known biblical commentator, Rashi, who lived in eleventh-century France, had but one comment on the subject. Wanting to make the text clearer to his readers, he explained rather graphically the meaning of the phrase, "as with a woman": "He enters as the painting stick is inserted in the tube."

In the contemporary era, traditional Jews have had to come to terms with the fact that gay men and lesbians have made ourselves a presence in the Jewish community. The most serious and thorough traditional response on the subject has been made by Norman Lamm. Lamm affirms the text as it is simply understood—a strong prohibition against homosexuality. While he claims interpretation to be unnecessary to explain the text, in fact, he makes an interpretation of his own of the meaning of *to'evah*: "The very variety of interpretations of *to'evah* points to a far more fundamental meaning, namely, that an act characterized as an abomination is prima facie disgusting and cannot be further defined or explained." While the term *to'evah* is not a problem for Lamm, the fact that this is considered a capital crime is at least distressing. But since capital punishment was one of the things the rabbis interpreted out of existence making it impossible to convict someone of a capital crime, Lamm does oppose penalizing homosexual behavior.

It is not only Orthodox Jews who assert interpretations to substantiate their antihomosexual points of view. Note the following responsum by the well-known Reform rabbi, Solomon Freehof: "In Scripture (Leviticus 18:22) homosexuality is considered to be an 'abomination.' So too in Leviticus 20:13. If Scripture calls it an abomination, it means that it is more than a violation of a mere legal enactment, it reveals a deep-rooted ethical attitude."

So far, we have examined traditional interpretations of the text. These interpretations either support the plain meaning of the text, explain difficult or unclear words in the verse, or use the text to create legal pronouncements on unrelated subjects.

Yet the interpretive method is also used to alter the meaning of other biblical verses, sometimes even contravening the original meaning. This fact creates an opportunity among contemporary commentators to alter or expand the meaning of our verse.

Contemporary commentators in the first instance see a contradiction between Leviticus 18:22 and the idea as stated in Genesis that we were all created in God's image. This contradiction must be resolved. We must assume that those of us who were created lesbian and gay are also in God's image, and that acts central to our identity cannot therefore be an abomination.

In another interpretation, it is pointed out that the text refers only to certain sexual acts, not to same-sex love relationships. Therefore, the text is not relevant to a style of life and love and family of which it was ignorant.

It has often been pointed out that lesbians are not included in the Leviticus prohibition. This fact has led to a variety of interpretations: that women's sexual activities don't matter, that lesbian activity is acceptable, or that the absence of this rule makes the ruling against gay men invalid.

Perhaps the text is addressing the issue of sexual experimentation. According to this interpretation, straight men who are considering a "fling" and in the process hurting their current partner should refrain from doing so.

Other commentators, including Arthur Waskow, have suggested that the text is only trying to tell us not to make love to a male as if he were a female—that is to say, gay love and straight love are indeed different. One should not be confused with the other. (The acts do not evoke the same feelings or fulfill the same commandments.)

To some readers, this whole process of textual interpretation may seem irrational and unnecessary, and even amusing. Why go to the trouble to validate this text? Why play by these rules? There are many gay and lesbian Jews who feel compelled by the absolute authority and immutability of the Torah text. For them this is the only solution that will enable them to affirm both their gay and Jewish selves, and help them to feel whole. And for all of us, as noted earlier, the traditional interpretations affect us in subtle and destructive ways. It is for these reasons that more creative work needs to take place in the area of interpreting the text.

## BIBLICAL CRITICISM

A little more than one hundred years ago, Jewish and Christian thinkers began to study the Bible as a document created by human hands. The early biblical critics' questioning of divine authorship is viewed as commonplace today, but in their times their views were heretical.

Biblical scholars sought to place the Bible in its context in the Ancient Near East. They explained much of what was unclear in the biblical text by reference to practices in other cultures. They explained redundancies as the result of compilation of documents by multiple authors. They introduced the concept of evolution and attempted to date biblical materials. Biblical critics developed sensitivity to the nuances of the text, developing concerns about linguistic and literary patterns.

The viewpoint of biblical criticism enables us to look at our verse in its historical, linguistic, and cultural context and understand it in a new, more objective light. Of course, we must bear in mind that complete objectivity is unattainable. Even looking at the text from outside, we are bound by our own cultural norms and expectations. In truth, we are looking at our verse through another kind of lens. While we think the approach of biblical criticism is a valid way to look at the text, we do not think that we have found in this method a way of obtaining "the truth."

From this perspective we certainly see the simple meaning of the text—that in biblical times, homosexual acts were forbidden. Yet this method does not require that we affirm the truth of that reality for today. We can, as biblical critics, acknowledge the need for a reexamination of biblical norms. (After all, the Bible also countenanced other things we no longer accept as moral—slavery and a second-class status for women and people with disabilities, for example.)

Furthermore, we can explain why homosexual acts were considered *to'evah* from a different perspective, by examining parallel linguistic uses of the word. We discover that *to'evah* is actually a technical term used to refer to a forbidden idolatrous act. From this information, we may conclude that the references in Leviticus are specific to cultic practices of homosexuality, and not sexual relationships as we know them today. This explanation is supported by reference to the other legal condemnation of homosexuality in Deuteronomy, which directly interdicts homosexual practices related to cultic worship.

Second, we understand that much of the Bible is an effort to make the separations between acts considered holy and those considered profane, to create an ordered perception of the universe. Accordingly, the sexual prohibitions described fit into the larger category of laws about kosher foods, the separation of the sexes and their clothing, and the prohibitions against plowing with two types of animals and of mixing certain types of fabric. We can reexamine, today, which of these separations are still meaningful.

Looking at the text from the outside also enables us to explain the repetition of the law as being derived from two different sources, written at different times. So the death penalty may have been applied at one period in biblical history, but not at another time.

Through this approach, we are able to step back from the text and ask questions about how the text functioned. We can see from some of the suggestions above that the text functioned to keep order and define it and to separate the Israelite people from the practices of their neighbors. This gives us the opportunity to conclude that values may be disengaged from specific laws, and that there may be other means of perpetuating values if we indeed still share them today. Further, if we are not bound by the assumptions of divine authorship, we can assert that while the prohibition against homosexual acts functioned in its time, it is no longer appropriate to our ethical sensibilities today.

## ENCOUNTERING THE TEXT

There is one last approach for coping with Leviti-cus. In this method, we confront the text directly. We do not look to the midrashist or the scholar to interpret the text for us. Rather we face the text in its immediacy—seeking its meaning in our lives, coming to terms with all that implies, and then going beyond it.

To face the simple meaning of Leviticus is to acknowledge the source of much of lesbian and gay oppression. The Bible does tell us that sexual acts between people of the same sex are *to'evah*—an abomination—and that they are punishable by death. And we know very well that this text has given generations the permission to find those of us who are lesbian or gay disgusting, to use Norman Lamm's word; to hate us; and even to do violence against us.

In our encounter with Leviticus, we experience the pain and terror and anger that this statement arouses in us. We imagine the untold damage done to generations of men, women, and children who experienced same-sex feelings and were forced to cloak or repress them. We reflect on those who acted on those feelings and were forced to feel shame and guilt and to fear for their lives. We remember how we felt when we first heard those words and knew their holy source. And we get angry—at the power these words have had over our lives, at the pain we have experienced in no small part because of these words.

Then, if we can, we grow beyond the rage. We begin to see these words as tools with which to educate people about the deep-rooted history of lesbian and gay oppression. We begin to use these very words to begin to break down the silence that surrounds us.

We proclaim the two consecutive weeks in the spring during which these words are read (*Parshat Ahare Mot* and *Parshat Kedoshim*) as Jewish Lesbian and Gay Awareness Weeks. During this time we urge that Torah study sessions be held in every synagogue to open the discussion of the role of gay and lesbian Jews in the community. Those of us who can take the risks of visibility must make ourselves available to tell our stories—of our alienation from the community, and of our desire to return. Each of us can tell the story of what this prohibition has meant in our lives—how we have struggled with it, and where we are on the road to resolution. And we expect to be listened to, with full attention and respect, as we do so.

In this way, we can transform Torah from a stumbling block to an entry path. We become more honest with ourselves and with our community about the barriers to our involvement, about our need for separate places to worship, and about our demand to be accepted as an integral part of Jewish life.

Whether we try interpreting, criticizing, or confronting, there are no easy answers for coming to terms with Leviticus. But we cannot desist from the challenge of finding creative solutions to deal with this dimension of our oppression. To be whole as Jewish lesbians and gay men we must acknowledge with what great difficulty those pieces of our lives fit together. But we must also demand—of ourselves and of our community—that those pieces be made to fit.

We marvel at the fact that words written thousands of years ago still have so much power to affect our lives. Words are powerful. Now it is up to us to make the words that will transform our lives and give new meaning to our existence as gay and lesbian Jews.

# II. B

# MAKING US SICK: THE MEDICAL AND PSYCHIATRIC ESTABLISHMENT

The belief that homosexuality is a disease, psychiatric syndrome, or consequence of scrambled genes is of relatively recent origin. Until the late nineteenth century Western medicine did not consider sexuality a proper medical concern. Criminal courts had consulted specialists in forensic medicine since the 1600s, usually to determine whether a defendant had engaged in anal intercourse. But the involvement of physicians in public discourse regarding homosexuality was limited. Homosexual acts were viewed as sins, moral lapses to which anyone might succumb. They were isolated transgressions, not manifestations of a persistent, stable condition or personality type. They belonged under the jurisdiction of moral authorities, not doctors.

In the late 1800s physicians began to play an expanding role in public discourse on sexuality, and homosexuality in particular. No longer were they speaking only when called upon. Now physicians were inventing medical terms for what had long been seen as moral defects. They were writing books and articles expounding their views, leading social purity organizations, and calling on legislators to consult them as experts on sexuality. Sexologists, especially those in Germany and Austria, began to treat sexual dysfunctions in their clinical practices. Sexual variation was increasingly viewed in terms of normalcy and pathology, and new diagnostic categories were invented to allow treatment of the latter. Writing in a medical journal in 1884, Dr. George Shrady argued, with respect to men and women with "abnormal instincts," that "conditions once considered criminal are really pathological and have come within the province of the physician" (Greenberg 1988:403). Increasingly, physicians won the "explanation rights" that had long been monopolized by the clergy.

Several developments encouraged the new activism among physicians. Most physicians were members of the middle class and were trying to upgrade their profession. Expanded jurisdiction for physicians meant not only greater prestige but new sources of income. To this end long-standing social problems such as drunkenness were recast as diseases: The term *alcoholism* was coined in 1852 by a Swedish physician, who declared it a new disease that should henceforth be treated by physicians (Greenberg 1988:403). Moreover, scientific modes of thought were gaining ground in related fields, creating a constituency for writings that were free of metaphysics and religious superstition. Inspired by Darwin and his followers, it was now fashionable to advance biological and evolutionary explanations for such problems as crime, violence, class conflict, and sexual deviance (Bullough 1994:45).

At the same time, the conversion to scientific modes of thought inspired a profusion of medical theories about homosexuality. Significantly, the writers who first voiced these ideas included many homosexuals, including Karl Heinrich Ulrichs and Magnus Hirschfeld in Germany and J. A. Symonds and Edward Carpenter in England. Not surprisingly, they were motivated by a liberatory impulse. In science and medicine they saw a benevolent and compassionate alternative to the moral condemnations of religion. Sinners were thus reconceptualized as victims of a medical condition or members of a "third gender" (Weeks 1977).

The German attorney and sexologist Karl Heinrich Ulrichs was among the first to write extensively about homosexuality, contending that homosexuals (or "Urnings," as he called them) comprised a third sex, the result of a prenatal inversion that placed female minds in male bodies, and vice versa. Between 1862 and his death in 1895 he published numerous books and pamphlets promoting his theory and arguing in favor of legal reform.

Richard von Krafft-Ebing, a Viennese professor of psychiatry, repeatedly revised his encyclopedic *Psychopathia Sexualis* between 1886 and his death in 1902, expounding the notion that any nonprocreative sexuality was perverse. Even more influential were the teachings of Sigmund Freud. While Freud resisted the view that homosexuality was a sickness, he held the view that homosexuals were "stuck" at an early, immature stage of psychosexual development. Inside every homosexual, he reasoned, was a thwarted heterosexual. Other sexologists attributed a supposed increase in homosexuality to feminism. American physician William Lee Howard warned that women who prefer "the laboratory to the nursery" will produce children who are "perverts, moral or psychical"—effeminate sons and masculine daughters (Chauncey 1982:141).

With the new medical theories came attempts at cure. In *Gay American History* Jonathan Ned Katz (1976) documents a horrifying range of measures intended to relieve homosexuals of their unnatural impulses. Surgical treatments have included castration, hysterectomy, and vasectomy. In the 1800s, the removal of the ovaries and clitoris was prescribed to "cure" various forms of female "erotomania," including lesbianism. Lobotomies were performed as recently as the 1950s. Drug therapies have included the administration of hormones, LSD, stimulants, and depressants. Other documented "cures" have included electric shock, sensitization therapy designed to arouse heterosexual impulses through the display of pornography, and aversion therapy designed to suppress homosexual impulses by pairing erotic images with powerful nausea-producing drugs. As historian Jeffrey Weeks notes, these treatments had little to do with real medicine or proper science, and none did more than temporarily thwart same-sex attractions. Rather, they represent "medicine acting as the moral policeman of the mind and body" (1977:31).

As doctors busied themselves seeking a cure, medical terms and concepts about homosexuality filtered into the popular consciousness. Words like *sodomite* were gradually replaced by their medical counterparts: *homosexual* or *sex deviate*. Sodomy laws were rewritten to incorporate psychiatric terms such as *sexual psychopath*. Ironically, it was the U.S. military that made the greatest contribution toward the medical redefinition of homosexuality. Gearing up for World War II, the military established an elaborate screening system focused on detecting and excluding homosexuals. Over 6,400 local draft boards and 108 induction stations were established to perform the screening ("Homosexuals in Uniform," this volume). Observing that the government had spent over $1 billion on psychiatric casualties from World War I, the psychiatric establishment claimed it could save the government money by prescreening those individuals who were prone to mental illness. As historian Allan Bérubé (1990) notes:

> These psychiatrists also promoted screening to enhance the prestige, influence, and legitimacy of their profession, which other physicians had for decades dismissed as the "Cinderella" of the medical specialties. Military screening offered psychiatrists the opportunity to introduce tens of thousands of physicians and draft board members to the value and basic principles of psychiatry. (10)

Among potential soldiers, then, it became common knowledge that homosexuality was a "psychopathic personality disorder" that could disqualify them from service. For many it was their first contact with a psychiatrist.

After the war the psychiatric establishment largely retained the view that homosexuality was pathological. The Kinsey reports of 1948 and 1953 found that same-sex eroticism was far more common than anyone had expected, yet these findings had little impact on mainstream medical thought. Therapists continued to subject their homosexual patients to hypnosis, electroshock, and aversion therapy (Katz 1976). In 1962 psychoanalyst Irving Bieber and his colleagues published a study of 106 homosexuals who were undergoing psychoanalytic treatment. By examining their backgrounds, Bieber claimed to find a particular "family configuration" that produced homosexuals. Today he is best remembered for the theory that "overclose mothers" and "distant fathers" produced homosexual children. Countless mothers, having heard some version of this theory, still blame themselves for "causing" their children to become lesbian or gay ("I Was Raising a Homosexual Child," this volume). Charles Socarides, another psychiatrist who wrote on homosexuality, contributed the notion that homosexuality resulted when a child failed to pass unscathed through the Oedipal complex, leaving him "fixated" on his mother.

By the late 1960s, however, medical consensus on homosexuality was fragmenting. Bieber and Socarides claimed that homosexuals are inherently unhappy and maladjusted, yet both had studied only psychiatric patients, thus committing a glaring methodological tautology: clinical samples are by definition unhappy or maladjusted and reveal little about individuals who do not seek therapy. Bieber claimed a cure rate of 27 percent but could provide no details of treatment. Socarides could identify only five accounts of successful cure (Lewes 1988).

As the discrepancy between theory and clinical practice expanded, other researchers began to question the basic assumption that homosexuality was a sign of pathology. In the 1950s Evelyn Hooker initiated a landmark series of studies of gay men that would ultimately refute these assumptions ("The Psychologist—Evelyn Hooker," this volume). Evidence mounted that homosexuality was neither disease nor dysfunction, and the American Psychiatric Association and the American Psychological Association were forced to reconsider their views on the subject. Increasingly, gay activists—who had never been permitted to address either group—demanded that they be heard. In 1970 protesters disrupted an American Psychiatric Association session on behavioral therapy, demanding that psychiatrists must "stop talking *about* us, and start talking *with* us." In 1972, after much haggling, the annual meeting convened a panel discussion entitled, "Psychiatry, Friend or Foe to Homosexuals?" The one gay psychiatrist who agreed to participate was listed in the program as "Dr. Henry Anonymous." He wore a mask and spoke into a special microphone that distorted his voice. To this day he has not publicly identified himself to the APA.

A year later the convention followed with a panel of "experts" on homosexuality, including Bieber and Socarides as well as psychiatrists and a gay activist who challenged their beliefs ("Should Homosexuality Be in the APA nomenclature?" excerpted in this volume). One of the central debates revolved around the appropriate locus of therapy: was it homosexuals or those who reviled them who suffered a pathological condition? George Weinberg's 1972 book, *Society and the Health Homosexual,* had introduced the term *homophobia* to characterize irrational fear and prejudice toward homosexuals. It was homophobia, Weinberg argued, that the mental health establishment must combat. Increasingly, the physicians began to agree, although there was and remains resistance to this view (see, for example, "If Freud Had Been a Neurotic Colored Woman: Reading Dr. Frances Cress Welsing," this volume). With a dozen publications on homosexuality over a twenty-five-year period, Socarides became the leading expert and spokesman for psychoanalytic reactionaries. His 1995 book, *A Freedom Too Far*, replays the psychoanalytic dogma that childhood trauma produces adult homosexuality. As the back cover explains, Dr. Socarides has concluded that "the seeds of his patients' homosexual orientation were planted in the earliest years, usually before the age of three, and their appropriate gender-defined self identity impaired as the result of abuse and neglect." Socarides' views took on an ironic twist when his own son emerged as a gay activist in the 1990s.

After a lively debate the American Psychiatric Association in 1973 voted to declassify homosexuality. In its official Diagnostic and Statistical Manual (DSM) homosexuality would not be listed as a disease. Doctors could no longer use it as a diagnostic category—a change denounced by Bieber and Socarides. The less stigmatizing diagnosis "ego-dystonic homosexuality" (homosexuality that is "unwanted and a source of distress") would remain in the DSM until 1987 to mollify psychiatrists who wished to treat unhappy homosexuals. But by acknowledging that homosexuality per se was not a pathology the APA set the stage for sweeping changes in public opinion and in the psychiatric profession. By the 1980s there emerged a body of psychiatric and psychoanalytic thought that did not approach homosexuality with the familiar question, "What went wrong?" or its colloraries, "How can we prevent, or change it?" Notable in this regard is the work of gay and lesbian therapists (e.g., Isay 1989; O'Connor and Ryan 1993) whose perspectives are not "biased by the notion that all homosexuals are latent heterosexuals who are deviant or perverted in their sexuality because of emotional trauma" (Isay 1989:10).

## REFERENCES

Bérubé, Allan. 1990. *Coming Out Under Fire: Lesbian and Gay Americans and the Military During World War Two*. New York: Free Press.

Chauncey, George. 1982. "From Sexual Inversion to Homosexuality: Medicine and the Changing Conceptualization of Female Deviance." *Salmagundi*, 58/59:114–146.

Greenberg, David. 1988. *The Construction of Homosexuality*. Chicago: University of Chicago Press.

Isay, Richard. 1989. *Being Homosexual: Gay Men and Their Development*. New York: Avon.

Katz, Jonathan Ned. 1976. *Gay American History*. New York: Crowell.

Lewes, Kenneth. 1988. *The Psychoanalytic Theory of Male Homosexuality*. New York: Simon and Schuster.

O'Connor, Noreen and Joanna Ryan. 1993. *Wild Desires and Mistaken Identities: Lesbianism and Psychoanalysis*. New York: Columbia University Press.

Socarides, Charles. 1995. *A Freedom Too Far*. Phoenix: Margrave.

Weeks, Jeffrey. 1977. *Coming Out: Homosexual Politics in Britain, from the Nineteenth Century to the Present*. London: Quartet.

Weinberg, George. 1972. *Society and the Healthy Homosexual*. New York: St. Martin's.

# | 20 |

## The Product Conversion—From Heresy to Illness

### Thomas Szasz

> The most prejudiced must admit that this religion without theology [positivism] is not chargeable with relaxation of moral restraints. On the contrary, it prodigiously exaggerates them.
>
> —John Stuart Mill

In the work of Benjamin Rush, we have traced the manifestations of the great ideological conversion from theology to science. We saw how Rush had redefined sin as sickness, and moral sanction as medical treatment. In this chapter I shall analyze this process in broader terms and shall show that as the dominant social ethic changed from a religious to a secular one, the problem of heresy disappeared, and the problem of madness arose and became of great social significance. In the next chapter I shall examine the creation of social deviants, and shall show that as formerly priests had manufactured heretics, so physicians, as the new guardians of social conduct and morality, began to manufacture madmen.

The change from a religious and moral to a social and medical conceptualization and control of personal conduct affects the entire discipline of psychiatry and allied fields. Perhaps nowhere is this transformation more evident than in the modern perspective on so-called sexual deviation, and especially on homosexuality. We shall therefore compare the concept of homosexuality as heresy, prevalent in the days of the witch-hunts, with the concept of homosexuality as mental illness, prevalent today.

Homosexual behavior—like heterosexual and autoerotic behavior—occurs among higher apes and among human beings living in a wide variety of cultural conditions. Judging by artistic, historical, and literary records, it also occurred in past ages and societies. Today it is part of the dogma of American psychiatrically enlightened opinion that homosexuality is an illness—a form of mental illness. This is a relatively recent view. In the past, men held quite different views on homosexuality, from accepting it as a perfectly natural activity to prohibiting it as the most heinous of crimes. We shall not explore the cultural and historical aspects of homosexuality; instead, we shall confine ourselves to a comparison of the attitude toward homosexuality during the witch-hunts and at the present time. Since late medieval and Renaissance societies were deeply imbued with the teachings of Christianity, we shall first survey the principal Biblical references to this subject.

The Bible prohibits almost every form of sexual activity other than heterosexual, genital intercourse. Homosexuality is prohibited first in Genesis, in the story of Lot. . . .

Homosexuality is again prohibited in Leviticus. "You shall not lie with a male as with a woman: it is an abomination." Adultery, incest, and bestiality are also forbidden. The punishment for transgression is death: "If a man lies with a male as with a woman, both of them have committed an abomination; they shall be put to death, their blood is upon them."

It is important to note that only male homosexuality is forbidden: "You shall not lie with a

In Thomas Szasz, *The Manufacture of Madness*, pp. 160–179. Excerpt. New York: Harper and Row, 1970.

| 157 |

male as with a woman . . . " God addresses males only. He does not command woman not to lie with a female as with a man. Here by omission and implication, and elsewhere by more explicit phrasing, woman is treated as a kind of human animal, not as a full human being. The most up-to-date legal statutes of Western nations dealing with homosexuality continue to maintain this posture toward women: Though homosexual intercourse between consenting adults continues to be prohibited in many countries, nowhere does this apply to women. The inference about the less than human status of women is inevitable. No wonder that in his morning prayer, the Orthodox Jew says, "Blessed be God . . . that He did not make me a woman," while the woman says, "Blessed be the Lord, who created me according to His will."

Biblical prohibitions against homosexuality had of course a profound influence on the medieval equation of this practice with heresy; on our contemporary criminal laws and social attitudes, which regard homosexuality as a hybrid of crime and disease; and on the language we still use to describe many so-called sexually deviant acts. Sodomy is an example.

Webster's *Unabridged Dictionary* (Third Edition) defines sodomy as "The homosexual proclivities of the men of the city as narrated in Gen. 19:1–11; carnal copulation with a member of the same sex or with an animal or unnatural carnal copulation with a member of the opposite sex; specif.: the penetration of the male organ into the mouth or anus of another." This definition is pragmatically correct. In both psychiatric and literary works, the term "sodomy" is used to describe sexual activity involving contact between penis and mouth or anus, regardless of whether the "passive" partner is male or female. Fellatio is thus a type of sodomy. Because human beings frequently engage in these and other nongenital sexual acts, Kinsey correctly emphasized that there are few Americans who, in their everyday sexual lives, do not violate both the religious prohibitions of their faith and the criminal laws of their country.

In short, the Church opposed homosexuality not only, or even primarily, because it was "abnormal" or "unnatural," but rather because it satisfied carnal lust and yielded bodily pleasure. This condemnation of homosexuality, says Rattray Taylor, "was merely an aspect of the general condemnation of sexual pleasure and indeed of sexual activity not directly necessary to ensure the continuation of the race. Even within marriage, sexual activity was severely restricted, and virginity was declared a more blessed state than matrimony." It is no accident, then, that carnal lust, leading to nonprocreative sexual practices and pleasure of all kinds, was a characteristic passion of witches. They were supposed to satisfy their cravings by copulating with the Devil, a male figure of superhuman masculinity, equipped with a "forked penis," enabling him to penetrate the woman at once vaginally and anally.

As we turn to a consideration of the Church's attitudes toward sex during the witch-hunts, we discover a concrete connection between notions of religious deviance and sexual offense: Heresy and homosexuality become one and the same thing. For centuries, no penological distinction is made between religious unorthodoxy and sexual misbehavior, especially homosexuality. "During the Middle Ages," says Westermarck, "heretics were accused of unnatural vice [homosexuality] as a matter of course. . . . In medieval laws sodomy was also repeatedly mentioned together with heresy, and the punishment was the same for both."

In thirteenth-century Spain, the penalty for homosexuality was castration and "lapidation" [execution by stoning]. Ferdinand and Isabella changed this, in 1479, to "burning alive and confiscation. irrespective of the station of the culprit." In other words, then the crime was subject to punishment by both secular and ecclesiastic courts—just as now it is subject to punishment by both penal and psychiatric sanctions. In 1451, Nicholas V empowered the Inquisition to deal with it. "When the institution [Inquisition] was founded in Spain," Lea writes, " . . . the Seville tribunal made it [homosexuality] the subject of a special inquest; there were many arrests and many fugitives, and twelve convicts were duly burnt."

In English-speaking countries, the connection between heresy and homosexuality is expressed through the use of a single word to denote both concepts: buggery. The double meaning of this word persists to this day. Webster's *Unabridged Dictionary* (Third Edition) defines "buggery" as "heresy, sodomy": and "bugger" as "heretic, sodomite." The word is derived from the medieval Latin *Bugarus* and *Bulgarus*, literally Bulgarian, "from the adherence of the Bulgarians to the Eastern Church considered heretical."

This connection, at once semantic and conceptual, between unorthodoxy and sodomy, was firmly established during the late Middle Ages, and has never been severed. It is as strong today as it was six hundred years ago. To be stigmatized as a heretic or bugger in the fourteenth century was to be cast out of society. Since the dominant ideology was theological, religious deviance was considered so grave an offense as to render the individual a nonperson. Whatever redeeming qualities he might have had counted for nought. The sin of heresy eclipsed all contradictory, personal characteristics, just as the teachings of God and the Church eclipsed all contradictory, empirical observations. The disease called "mental illness"—and its subspecies "homosexuality"—plays the same role today. The late Senator Joseph McCarthy thus equated the social sin of Communism with the sexual sin of homosexuality and used the two labels as if they were synonymous. He could not have done this had there been no general belief that, like medieval heretics, men labeled "homosexual" are somehow totally bad. They can have no compensating or redeeming features: They cannot be talented writers or patriotic Americans. Given this premise—which McCarthy did not invent, but only appropriated for his use—it follows that homosexuals must also be politically deviant, that is, Communists. The same logic applies in reverse. If Communists are the modern, secular incarnations of the Devil—political incubi and succubi, as it were—then it follows that they, too, can have no redeeming features. They must be completely bad. They must be homosexuals. . . .

We are ready now to consider the problem of homosexuality in its contemporary form: that is, is homosexuality a disease? In a recent authoritative volume on "sexual inversion," Judd Marmor, the editor, raises this question, and answers that "Most of the psycho-analysts in this volume, except Szasz, are of the opinion that homosexuality is definitely an illness to be treated and *corrected*." (Italics added.) The correctional zeal of the modern psychiatric therapist shows itself here in a way that cannot be mistaken. Disease as a biological condition and as a social role are confused. Cancer of the bladder is a disease; but whether it is treated or not depends on the person who has the disease, not on the physician who makes the diagnosis! Marmor, like so many contemporary psychiatrists, forgets or ignores this distinction. There is, to be sure, good reason why he, and other "mental health workers," do so: By pretending that convention is Nature, that disobeying a personal prohibition is a medical illness,

they establish themselves as agents of social control and at the same time disguise their punitive interventions in the semantic and social trappings of medical practice.

René Guyon, a French student of sexual customs, has recognized this characteristic tendency of modern psychiatry to brand as sick that which is merely unconventional. "The trouble to which the psychiatrists have gone," he observes, "to explain . . . nature in terms of convention, health in terms of mental disease, is scarcely to be believed. . . . The distinctive method of its system is that every time it comes across a natural act that is contrary to the prevailing conventions, it brands this act as a symptom of mental derangement or abnormality."

The question of whether or not homosexuality is an illness is therefore a pseudo problem. If by disease we mean deviation from an anatomical or physiological norm—as in the case of a fractured leg or diabetes—then homosexuality is clearly not an illness. Still, it may be asked if there is a genetic predisposition to homosexuality, as there is to a stocky body build; or is it entirely a learned pattern of behavior? This question cannot be answered with assurance. At present, the evidence for such predisposition is slim, if any. The biologically oriented person may argue, however, that more evidence for it might be discovered in the future. Perhaps so. But even if homosexuals were proven to have certain sexual preferences because of their nature, rather than nurture, what would that prove? People who are prematurely bald are sick, in a stricter sense of this word, than homosexuals could possibly be. What of it? Clearly, the question that is really being posed for us is not whether a given person manifests deviations from an anatomical and physiological norm, but what moral and social significance society attaches to his behavior—whether it be due to infectious illness (as was the case with leprosy in the past), or to learned preference (as is the case with homosexuality today).

Psychiatric preoccupation with the disease concept of homosexuality—as with the disease concept of all so-called mental illnesses, such as alcoholism, drug addiction, or suicide—conceals the fact that homosexuals are a group of medically stigmatized and socially persecuted individuals. The noise generated by their persecution and their anguished cries of protest are drowned out by the rhetoric of therapy—just as the rhetoric of salvation drowned out the noise generated by the persecution of heretics and their anguished cries of protest. It is a heartless hypocrisy to pretend that physicians, psychiatrists, or "normal" laymen for that matter, really care about the welfare of the mentally ill in general, or the homosexual in particular. If they did, they would stop torturing him while claiming to help him. But this is just what reformers—whether theological or medical—refuse to do.

The idea that the homosexual is "sick" only in the sense that he is so categorized by others, and himself accepts this categorization, goes back at least to André Gide's autobiographical work, *Corydon*, and perhaps earlier. . . .

The "diagnosis" of homosexuality is in actuality a stigmatizing label which, to protect his authentic identity, the subject must reject. To escape from medical control, the homosexual must repudiate the diagnosis ascribed to him by the physician. In other words, homosexuality is an illness in the same sense as we have seen Negritude described as an illness. Benjamin Rush claimed that Negroes had black skin because they were ill; and he proposed to use their illness as a justification for their social control. Rush's modern follower asserts that men whose sexual conduct he disapproves of are ill; and he uses their illness as a justification for their social control.

Only in our day have Negroes been able to escape from the semantic and social trap in which white men have held them fast after their legal shackles had been cast off a century ago. So-called mental patients, whose fetters—forged of commitment papers, asylum walls, and fiendish tortures passed off as "medical treatments"—have a strangle hold on their bodies and souls are only now learning how to properly abase themselves before their psychiatric masters. It seems probable that many more people will have to be injured by means of psychiatric labeling and its social consequences than have been so far, before men will recognize, and protect themselves from, the dangers of Institutional Psychiatry. This, at least, is the lesson which the history of witchcraft suggests.

So long as men could denounce others as witches—so that the witch could always be considered the Other, never the Self—witchcraft remained an easily exploitable concept and the Inquisition a flourishing institution. Only loss of faith in the authority of the inquisitors and their religious mission brought an end to this practice of symbolic cannibalism. Similarly, so long as men can denounce each other as mentally sick (homosexual, addicted, insane, and so forth)—so

that the madman can always be considered the Other, never the Self—mental illness will remain an easily exploitable concept, and Coercive Psychiatry a flourishing institution. If this is so, only loss of faith in the authority of institutional psychiatrists and their medical mission will bring an end to the Psychiatric Inquisition. This day is not imminent.

My contention that the psychiatric perspective on homosexuality is but a thinly disguised replica of the religious perspective which it displaced, and that efforts to "treat" this kind of conduct medically are but thinly disguised methods for suppressing it, may be verified by examining any contemporary psychiatric account of homosexuality. . . .

Contemporary psychiatrists will not admit to the possibility that they might be wrong in categorizing sexual inversion as an illness. "In a discussion of homosexuality, psychiatrists would probably agree unanimously on at least one point: the belief that the homosexual is a sick person." This statement appears in the introduction to a pamphlet on homosexuality, distributed free to the profession by Roche Laboratories, one of the principal manufacturers of so-called psychopharmacologic drugs. Like the inquisitor, the psychiatrist defines, and thereby authenticates, his own existential position by what he opposes—as heresy or illness. In stubbornly insisting that the homosexual is sick, the psychiatrist is merely pleading to be accepted as a physician.

As befits the ministrations of a modern inquisitor, the persecutory practices of the institutional psychiatrist are couched in the vocabulary of medicine. Pretending to be diagnosing a measles-like illness during its incubation period in order the better to treat it, the psychiatrist actually imposes pseudomedical labels on society's scapegoats in order the better to handicap, reject, and destroy them. Not satisfied with diagnosing overt homosexuals as "sick," psychiatrists claim to be able to discover the presence of this supposed disease (in its "latent" form, of course), in persons who show no outward sign of it. They also claim to be able to diagnose homosexuality during childhood, while it is incubating, as it were. "We have noted," write Holemon and Winokur, "that this [effeminate behavior] often antedated homosexual orientation and homosexual relations. In these patients effeminacy seems to be the primary problem and the sexual behavior is secondary. From this one should be able to predict which children will develop effeminate homosexuality by selecting those with objective signs of effemi-nacy." In a similar vein, Shearer declares that "excessive clinging to the parent of the opposite sex, especially between father and daughter, should also alert the physician to the possibility of homosexuality." What constitutes "excessive clinging"? How much affection between child and parent of the opposite sex is permitted with-out it signifying the presence of the dread disease, homosexuality?

From the foregoing we may safely conclude that psychiatric opinion about homosexuals is not a scientific proposition but a medical prejudice. It is pertinent to recall here that the more attention the inquisitors paid to witchcraft, the more the witches multiplied. The same principle applies to mental illness in general, and to homosexuality in particular. Zealous efforts to eradicate and pre-vent such "disorders" actually create the condi-tions in which the assumption and ascription of such roles flourish. . . .

It is clear that psychiatrists have a vested inter-est in diagnosing as mentally ill as many people as possible, just as inquisitors had in branding them as heretics. The "conscientious" psychiatrist authenticates himself as a competent medical man by holding that sexual deviants (and all kinds of other people, perhaps all of mankind, as Karl Menninger would have it) are mentally ill, just as the "conscientious" inquisitor authenticated him-self as a faithful Christian by holding that homo-sexuals (and all kinds of other people) were heretics. We must realize that in situations of this kind we are confronted, not with scientific prob-lems to be solved, but with social roles to be con-firmed. Inquisitor and witch, psychiatrist and mental patient, create each other and authenti-cate each other's roles. For an inquisitor to have maintained that witches were not heretics and that their souls required no special effort at salva-tion would have amounted to asserting that there was no need for witch-hunters. Similarly, for a psychopathologist to maintain that homosexuals are not patients and that neither their bodies nor their minds require special efforts at cure would amount to asserting that there is no need for coer-cive psychiatrists.

It is necessary to keep in mind here that most people diagnosed as physically ill *feel* sick and *consider themselves* sick; whereas most people diagnosed as mentally ill *do not feel* sick and *do not consider themselves* sick. Consider again the homosexual. As a rule, he neither feels ill, nor considers himself ill. Hence, he usually does not seek the help of a physician or psychiatrist. All this, as we have seen, parallels the situation of the witch. As a rule, she, too, neither felt sinful, nor considered herself a witch. Hence, she did not seek the help of the inquisitor. If, then, a psychia-trist is to have a patient of this kind, or a priest such a parishioner, each must have the power to impose his "care" on an unwilling subject. The State gives this power to the psychiatrist, just as the Church gave it to the inquisitor.

But these are not the only possible, or indeed actually existing, relationships between psychia-trists and patients, or priests and parishioners. Some of their relationships are, and were, wholly voluntary and mutually consensual. The discus-sion about the disease concept of homosexuality (and mental illness generally) narrows down to two questions, and our answers to them. First, should psychiatrists have the right to consider homosexuality a disease (however defined)? I say: Of course they should. If that concept helps them, they will be wealthier; if it helps their patients, the patients will be happier. Second, should psychiatrists have the power, through alliance with the State, to impose their definition of homosexuality as a disease on unwilling clients? I say: Of course they should not.

Psychiatrists and others who like, and plead for the adoption of, the disease concept of homosex-uality (and of other types of human behavior) often seem to be talking about the first question — that is, what kind of disease the alleged "patient" has. But, as a rule, consciously or unwittingly, they are concerned with the second question — that is, how to control or "correct" (to use Mar-mor's term) the patient's alleged "sickness." The president of the Mattachine Society, the nation's largest organization of homosexuals, rightly warns that "when doctors rush into print with wild claims of 'cures' for homosexuality they are not serving the homosexual. Indeed, they are doing just the opposite; they are increasing social pres-sure on him. . . . A 'cure' would be a sort of 'final solution' to the homosexual problem."

Our position on the disease concept of homo-sexuality and its social control through medicine could be vastly clarified were we to apply to it our experience with the heresy concept of homosexuality and its social control through religion. Indeed, the parallels between these two sets of theoretical concepts and social sanctions need to be extended only to include one addi-tional consideration — the legitimacy or illegiti-macy of combining religious and medical *ideas* and *practices* with political *power*.

If it is true that God rewards faithful Christians with eternal bliss in a life hereafter, is this not inducement enough to insure true belief? Why should the State use its police power to impose religious faith on nonbelievers, when, if left alone, such heretics are sure to suffer eternal damnation? In the past, the zealous Christian countered this challenge by affirming his boundless love for his "misguided" brother whom it was his duty to "save" from his horrible fate. Since the heathen could usually not be saved by persuasion alone, the use of force—justified by the lofty theological goal—was in order.

Witnessing the tragic consequences of this logic translated into everyday life, the Founders of the American Republic reasserted the classic distinction between truth and power, and sought to embody this distinction in appropriate political institutions. The Founding Fathers thus reasoned that if the Christian religions were "true" (as many of them believed they were), then their value (or the value of other religions) ought to become manifest to rational men (and they treated men generally as rational). Entertaining the possibility of religious falsehood, they refused to endorse any particular faith as the only true one. In short, they held that should there be error in religion, men should be left unhampered to discover it for themselves and to act freely on their discoveries. The upshot was the uniquely American concept of religious freedom and pluralism, based on a separation of Church and State. This concept, which depends wholly on the blocking of the official guardians of religious dogma from access to the police power of the State, is embodied in the First Amendment to the Constitution, which states that "Congress shall make no law respecting an establishment of religion, or prohibiting the free exercise thereof . . ."

Inasmuch as the ideology that now threatens individual liberties is not religious but medical, the individual needs protection not from priests but from physicians. Logic thus dictates—however much expediency and "common sense" make this seem absurd—that the traditional constitutional protections from oppression by a State-recognized and supported Church be extended to protections from oppression by a State-recognized and supported Medicine. The justification now for a separation of Medicine and State is similar to that which obtained formerly for a separation of Church and State.

As the Christian concept of sin carries with it its own deterrent of suffering in hell, so the scientific concept of disease carries with it its own deterrent of suffering on earth. Moreover, if it is true that nature rewards faithful believers in medicine (and especially those who seek prompt and properly authorized medical care for their illnesses) with a long and healthy life, is this not inducement enough to insure true belief? Why should the State use its police power to impose medical dogma on nonbelievers, when, if left alone, such heretics are sure to suffer the ravages of bodily and mental deterioration? Today, the zealous psychiatrist counters this challenge by affirming his limitless medical obligation to his "sick" brother whom it is his duty to "treat" for his dread disease. Since the madman cannot usually be cured by persuasion alone, the use of force—justified by the lofty therapeutic goal—is in order.

Witnessing the tragic consequences of this logic translated into everyday life, we ought to emulate the wisdom and the courage of our forebears and trust men to know what is in their own best medical interests. If we truly value medical healing and refuse to confuse it with therapeutic oppression—as they truly valued religious faith and refused to confuse it with theological oppression—then we ought to let each man seek his own medical salvation and erect an invisible but impenetrable wall separating Medicine and the State.

# | 21 |

## *Homosexuals in Uniform*

### NEWSWEEK

Although Army regulations strictly forbade the drafting of homosexuals, scores of these inverts managed to slip through induction centers during the second world war. Between 3,000 and 4,000 were discharged for this abnormality; others were released as neuropsychiatric cases. Last week, with most of the records on homosexuals tabulated, Army medical officers, for the first time, summed up their strange story.

To screen out this undesirable soldier-material, psychiatrists in induction-station interviews tried to detect them (1) by their effeminate looks or behavior and (2) by repeating certain words from the homosexual vocabulary and watching for signs of recognition. In some instances, the urinary hormone secretion test showed a higher degree of estrogens (female hormones) than androgens (male hormones), just the opposite of a normal man. But this test was too uncertain and too expensive to try on every inductee.

Frequently, a latent homosexual, who had no knowledge of his predilection, was inducted into the service, only to develop alarming symptoms in camp and on the battlefield. Many of these men refused to admit homosexuality, even to themselves, and went to elaborate lengths to prove their masculinity. One of these ruses was regular and conspicuous absence without leave, always with female companions. Often the soldier's primary trouble was not discovered until he was haled before Army psychiatrists on an AWOL charge.

From case histories in Army files, these facts about homosexuals were gleaned:

▼ They topped the average soldier in intelligence, education, and rating. At least 10 per cent were college graduates: more than 50 per cent had finished high school. Only a handful were illiterate.

▼ Including all ages, there were more whites than Negroes in this group. They came mostly from the cities rather than the country.

▼ Although the majority had no family history of nervous or mental disease, many were from homes broken by divorce or separation. In many instances the man had been brought up by his mother as a girl, or had been an only son in a large family of girls. About half assumed a "feminine" role, the other half "masculine." Most were either unmarried or had made a failure of marriage.

▼ As a whole, these men were law-abiding and hard-working. In spite of nervous, unstable, and often hysterical temperaments, they performed admirably as workers. Many tried to be good soldiers.

Once this abnormality was detected, the man was usually evacuated by the unit doctors to a general hospital where he received psychiatric treatment while a military board decided whether or not he was reclaimable. A good number begged to be cured, but doctors usually doubted their sincerity, and recommended discharge. At least half of the confirmed homosexuals, one psychiatrist estimated, were well-adjusted to their condition, and neither needed nor would respond to treatment. The majority, therefore, were released.

*Newsweek*, June 9, 1947, p. 54.

**The Blue Discharge:** Early in the war, the homosexuals were sent up for court-martial, but in 1943–1944, the Army decided to separate most of them quietly with a "blue" discharge (neither honorable nor dishonorable) unless some other breach of military law had been committed. Last week, however, the Army announced a stiff new policy, effective July 1.

Instead of leaving the service with the vague and protective "blue" discharge, the homosexuals who had not been guilty of a definite offense would receive an "undesirable" discharge. A few of this group with outstanding combat records might receive an honorable discharge. Those found guilty of homosexual violence or of impairing the morals of minors would receive a "yellow" or dishonorable discharge.

# | 22 |

# *I Was Raising a Homosexual Child*

## FLORA RHETA SCHREIBER

There are so many things I know now, that I was foolishly, almost criminally ignorant of that night. It is why I am telling this story. I also know now that millions of other mothers can make, and perhaps are making, the same mistakes I made, mistakes born not out of an evil will, but out of misguided love.

My education began on that catastrophic night four years ago. There was the sudden ringing of the telephone: it was the police, and they were calling to say that my son Don* had been picked up—in Central Park—in the embrace of another man. They wanted my husband to come down to the station. He rushed out immediately, barely pausing long enough to tell me what had happened. And then, while I was alone, the full import of the news began to sink in. I scurried frantically through my memories, trying to find evidence of the mistake I could not believe I had made. Don always had been what mothers call a good boy. Even in his early teens, he had perfect manners. He never got into fights or any other kind of trouble. His school grades were excellent. He always took pride in his personal appearance. Even at five, nothing delighted him more than new clothes. He had grown into a handsome teenager, tall for his age, with a proud, almost cocky, way of walking.

## ALWAYS MY FAVORITE

Don had always been my favorite son. Our younger boy, Peter, had a personality exactly like Arthur's, my chemist husband. He was quiet, almost withdrawn, and fanatically interested in mathematics and science. Don had my outgoing, cheerful temperament, and he had my artistic interests. This meant he also had much of my sensitivity. Whereas Peter went to bed and slept like a stone, Don was always waking up in the middle of the night, frightened by some street noise or the wind or rain. Often it was difficult to calm him, and I would oust my husband from his bed and let Don sleep in the same room with me.

Don and I were close, from his babyhood. I realize now that my husband and I made an unspoken agreement to divide our children. As a result, Don went everywhere with me. On Saturdays he would help me do the shopping, and then

*Cosmopolitan*, January 1963, no. 154, pp. 61–64.

* The names of this family have been changed.

in the afternoon we'd usually go to one of the art museums. We went to the movies together. He even came along when I went shopping for clothes, and always had fascinating comments on what I bought. I could have worn a potato sack around the house as far as my husband and Peter were concerned, but Don was always telling me that my new hat was lovely, or the new dress made me look really beautiful. Even at ten, he was more considerate than most adults. When his father invited him to go to football or baseball games with him and Peter, he would look at me, and I would say: "Go ahead. I don't mind being alone." But he would always refuse. "No thanks, I'll go to the movies with Mom," he would say.

I never had to order Don to do anything. All I had to do was suggest. When he asked for a bicycle, and I told him how worried I would be about him riding in the city streets, that was the last I heard of it. Peter, on the other hand, complained and moaned until his father bought him a bicycle over my objections. Peter was always coming home with a broken tooth or a black eye from a sandlot football game, but Don seemed instinctively to dislike such roughneck fun, and I was glad of it. "I prefer gentlemen myself," I would tell him, and give him a warm hug and kiss.

## Set Apart From Other Boys

He developed his own interests, which set him apart from the boys in the neighborhood. He built up a marvelous stamp collection, and after that he collected miniature furniture with which he would decorate tiny rooms. Except for swimming, which he enjoyed all year round, he had no interest in athletics. He was different, but I saw nothing wrong with that. I was proud of it.

I was also frankly glad that my marriage had given me at least one person with whom I could share my real feelings. Over the years, a gulf had opened between Arthur and me. Our quarrels, which were all too frequent in the early years of our marriage, were replaced by vast deserts of silence. I often talked about it to Don, especially when I was feeling blue. I would tell him how hard it was to find yourself married to a man who had no love to give, a man who was somehow self-contained, within a strange stubborn armor. "Don't ever marry someone like that," I would say. Don always listened sorrowfully to me in those depressed hours. Often he would touch me deeply by saying: "Don't worry, Mom, I'm going to marry someone like you."

How could he say things like that, and then become involved in this awful mess? How did it creep up on me without the least hint of warning? Don seemed to be a perfectly normal sixteen year old, once we make allowances for his rather special personality. He did not shun girls. He took Joan, the pert teen-ager who lived on the floor above us, to the movies occasionally. Lately, he had been staying out rather late on Friday and Saturday nights, and I had spoken to him about it—rather halfheartedly, I must admit. After all, he was big for his age, and he was a sophomore in high school now. It was natural for him to be making new friends.

No, I told myself, no. The call had to be an insane mistake, a twisted misunderstanding. I lived on this emotion for over an hour . . . . until Don and his father came home.

One look at my husband's ashen face, at Don's trembling mouth, and I knew it was true. "Oh darling, tell me what happened," I cried, rushing to throw my arms around him, to hold him the way I held him when he was a frightened little boy in the dark bedroom. But this was not a boy. It was a man, hurt, sullen, who stepped back, avoiding my arms.

## Couldn't You See It Coming?

"Leave me alone. Mother," he said. I stood aside, stunned, while he brushed past me and went slowly up the stairs to his room. "I only want to help . . . to understand. . . . " I called after him. But he did not look back.

I stumbled into the living room to face my husband. He told me, in his maddening, monosyllabic fashion, that the call was completely correct. Don *had* been caught on a bench in Central Park, being embraced by another man. Suddenly Arthur lashed out at me: "Couldn't you see it? I knew something was wrong for over a year. Always in the bathroom rubbing cream on his face, slicking his hair. The way he walked. Pete told me that all the boys in his class call him Miss Gibbons. . . . "

"I didn't see it," I said dazedly. "I didn't see anything. I'm only his mother."

Arthur's anger suddenly faded. For the first time in years I heard genuine emotion in his voice. "And I'm only his father." He put his face in his hands in a gesture of supreme weariness. "Maybe some of it—a lot of it—is my fault, too, Eve. I realize that, too. I'm not blaming you for everything."

"Why should we be blamed for anything—you or I? What have we done?"

"I don't know," Arthur said. "But I think we had better find out. I talked to a lawyer down in the police station. He told me that the judge would probably dismiss Don with a warning. But I'm afraid if he gets caught this way again, he could be sent away."

Sent away. The vision of my son in some vast, impersonal institution, wearing the stigma of a record for the rest of his life, was almost too much to bear. "I'll do whatever you say," I told Arthur. Never had I felt so helpless.

## "Maybe I'm Just . . . Different"

The next morning Don stayed in his room, ignoring my calls for breakfast. Finally I could stand his silence no longer, and knocked on his door. "Can I come in?" I said.

"If you want to."

I found him sitting by the window, staring morosely out at the spring sunshine. "Don," I said. "Can't you tell me anything about what happened last night?"

"I got trapped," he said.

"What do you mean?"

"The police had a trap all set up. The minute this other fellow sat down on the bench and put his arm around me, they jumped out of the bushes and arrested us both."

"Then you didn't . . . do anything?"

"No," he said, still looking away.

"But . . . why were you there?"

"I had to go. I wanted to see what would happen."

"*Why*, Don?"

He shook his head hopelessly. "You just don't understand, Mom. I don't think you ever will. I have these . . . feelings. I don't want to have them, but I have them. And I can't help it. Maybe Wally is right. Maybe I am just . . . different."

"Wally? Who's Wally?"

"Someone I met at the pool. He's a freshman in college. He writes me letters—like this one." He pulled open his desk drawer and handed me a piece of pale blue stationery. On it, in tiny handwriting, were the words: "*I've thought it all over seriously. I can't picture any happiness without you.*" The note was signed "*Wally.*"

"Why he's responsible. He's the one—"

"No, Mother," Don said abruptly. "No he's not. He's one of the finest persons I've ever met. But if he's right . . . about the feelings . . . " He put his face in his hands, in a gesture remarkably similar to the one his father had made the previous night. "I went to the park to find out. I wanted to see what would happen, what I felt."

That night, Arthur brought home our family doctor. We had both known him for years. In fact, he had treated my parents when I was a child. He and Arthur were good friends. They often went on fishing trips together. Now he sat beside my husband while I told him what I had heard from Don that morning. "The boy needs psychiatric help," he said in his quiet, matter-of-fact way.

"Psychiatric?" I gasped. "Does that mean he's crazy?"

"It means he's disturbed," the doctor said. "We don't know why. Would you like me to recommend a psychiatrist?"

I nodded. My talk with Don had convinced me of my own helplessness. The doctor named a woman psychiatrist, Dr. Cornelia B. Wilbur. "She's had a lot of experience in treating problems such as Don's—and considerable success. Let me know how things go."

As my husband predicted, the court dismissed the charge against Don, but suggested our son seek psychiatric guidance. This made it all the more important for him to get help, and early the following week we made an appointment with Dr. Wilbur. I went with him to the office, and sat in the waiting room while the doctor talked with Don. He was with her for almost an hour. On the way home he was silent and remote. Finally he turned to me and said: "She sure asks some funny questions. I'm going to see her three times a week."

## From Son to Stranger

Those first few months of treatment did not seem to do Don much good. I kept looking for the reappearance of the gentle, friendly, talkative boy I'd known. Instead he was moody and distant, spending most of his time in his room and going out of his way, I felt, to avoid me. One Sunday, while Arthur and Peter were off to a football game, I was especially lonely, and knocked on Don's door. "Would you like some lunch?" I asked.

He came storming out of the room as if I had made some hideous proposal. "Can't you let me alone?" he shouted.

"Don," I pleaded, "I only want what's best for you."

"No you don't," he snarled.

"Don, don't talk to me that way," I gasped.

"I'll talk to you any way I please," he roared. "When I think of what you've done to me—"

He snatched his overcoat and dashed into the street. I felt worse, in that moment, than the night of his arrest. He seemed lost to me now, in a far more terrible way. Was this what psychiatry did? Half in anguish, half in rage, I decided to see Dr. Wilbur and find out for myself.

## FIRST HOPE OF A CURE

"You're not helping my son," I told her. "You're destroying him. You're turning him against me—the one person who loves him for his own sake."

Dr. Wilbur shook her head. "I haven't turned your son against you or anyone else, Mrs. Gibbons," she said. "Analysis doesn't work that way. Don is making certain discoveries about the part you've played in his life which are disturbing to him. But eventually, if all goes well, he will work out these negative feelings."

"You mean that he'll be cured? I can't believe it. He doesn't show one sign of progress."

"He does to me," Dr. Wilbur said. "Don has a good chance to be completely cured. He's very young. He doesn't flaunt his homosexuality. Above all, he wants to change."

"It is possible then?" I asked, revealing for the first time the fear that had been haunting me.

"Even among older men," Dr. Wilbur said, "change is possible. As we have shown in the book* on which I collaborated, twenty-seven per cent of the men we studied abandoned their homosexuality completely. That isn't a large percentage, I know. But these were older men and some did not stay in treatment. Don is continuing his treatment with great seriousness and his chances are greater."

"Can I do anything to help him?" I asked.

Dr. Wilbur hesitated, then said: "You can perhaps help Don most by undergoing analysis yourself—with another psychiatrist, of course."

The mere suggestion of treatment made me furious. "My boy may need treatment, but I don't," I cried, and stamped out of the office.

But in the next few weeks, I began to change my mind. Don's persistent coldness had a really alarming effect on me. I began having terrible depressions, in which I would find myself sitting in the kitchen, weeping over nothing. I felt totally exhausted all the time, so listless that the tiniest bit of housework was an enormous effort. My husband became genuinely alarmed about my condition and tried to draw me out of the grey swamp into which I seemed to be sinking. I was very touched by this first hint of tenderness after more than a decade of indifference, but it was too little too late. I felt that I was the victim of a cruel joke.

Finally it became evident even to me that I, too, needed psychiatric help. My husband was anxious to see me get it even though the expense of paying for both Don and me simultaneously would be murderous. "We just won't take any vacations for a while," he said. "And Pete and I will watch our football games on television. I'll even give up my fishing trips. You and Don get well; that's the only thing that matters."

I was not at all impressed with my early sessions with the psychiatrist Dr. Wilbur recommended. They only seemed to result in further disturbing me. We talked about my attitude toward sex, for instance. I was perfectly honest with him. I told him that I never enjoyed it. I told him how I had pitied my poor fragile mother for having to submit to my unkempt father with his tavern breath and bawdy jokes. With Arthur—well, very little happened between us. Perhaps I needed an especially strong, vital man to arouse me. My husband was not that man. After a year or two, we both realized and admitted it—in that awful, silent way such decisions are made in a marriage.

It was not easy, thinking about all these painful memories. I finally asked the doctor what it had to do with my depressions, or, more important, Don's trouble. "I'm here to help him, you know." I was not prepared for what followed.

## IS HOMOSEXUALITY INHERITED?

"Mrs. Gibbons," he said, "why do you think Don has this trouble, as you prefer to call it?"

"The more I think of it," I said, "the more I am convinced that he was seduced by that older boy, Wally. He took advantage of Don's innocence . . ."

"But you told me yourself what Don has said—about having these feelings about being forced to go into Central Park that night . . ."

"Maybe it's something he was born with," I said wildly. "Something he inherited—from his father."

I can still hear my psychiatrist's deep soothing

* Irving Bieber et al., *Homosexuality: A Psychoanalytic Study of Male Homosexuals*, New York: Basic, 1962.

voice, carefully but firmly disagreeing. "No, Mrs. Gibbons. We now assume that most homosexuals are born with the capacity to become normal men and women. When a boy turns to homosexuality, it is because he is *afraid* of developing his feelings for girls. Whenever it occurs, in adolescence or late in life, homosexuality is a symptom of fear and is the inhibition of normal sexual expression."

"Why would Don be afraid?" I asked.

"Because you dominated his life so totally, Mrs. Gibbons. When your marriage failed, you turned for consolation to your son. You totally absorbed his attention, his love. By prolonging this close attachment into his adolescence, you forced him, unintentionally, to choose you as the object of his first sexual feelings. He resisted these feelings. of course; he was probably frightened by them. But the experience caused a block in his sexual life. Unconsciously, to escape the guilt of desiring his mother, Don turned toward homosexuality."

When I first heard these words, they seemed gibberish. It took many weeks of thinking and talking with my doctor, before I realized they were true. It took more time before I stopped blaming myself. I came to realize that I did not deliberately try to ruin my son's life. I was only groping for what every human being must have: another person's love.

Another mistake also became obvious in these dramatic months. By monopolizing my son, I had pushed his father out of sight. This, my psychiatrist told me, also probably played a part in Don's turning toward homosexuality. He was searching for friendship and affection from an older man, a substitute, however pale, for the father he never really possessed. Arthur and I talked this over. We discussed many of my "couch thoughts," as we began calling them. We talked more in those first six months of my analysis than we had in the previous five years.

## WEAK MOMENTS IN THE STRUGGLE

The dark brown shades in which I had been seeing the world began to change. I no longer felt the terrible draining sense of loss which Don's coldness had inflicted on me. But Don's struggle was by no means over. There were nights when he would go into Manhattan, and come home long after midnight. For the next few days, he would be more withdrawn than ever. I knew that meant he had seen Wally again. But I also knew that no words from me were going to help him win his battle. The only help I could give was indirect. "Why don't you take Don with you to the ball game next Sunday?" I asked my husband one night.

At first he glowed at the idea. Then he was uneasy. "I've asked him before. He told me it was for morons."

"Ask him again," I said. "He still might think it's for morons, but maybe he'd enjoy going out with you and Pete afterward. Have dinner some place."

Minutes later, my husband came into the kitchen, wide-eyed. "He said yes."

That was the beginning of a cautious friendship between Don and his father. There were many things that separated them: they still exist. Don's interest in art and music is genuine; to my husband these always would be a bore. But they found things to talk about; Don announced he was considering a career in architecture. This turned out to be something Arthur had once planned to do. "Until I found out I couldn't draw," he said. He dug out some books on the subject which he'd buried in a cellar trunk.

Don's relationship with his brother Peter improved, too. Where before Peter had tended to ignore him, even to treat him with callous contempt, he now began to ask Don's advice on books and art, areas where he admitted his big brother's superiority. Gone were the sneering remarks about "sissy stuff." But all these hopeful signs were only improvements. After eighteen months, Don was still going to see Dr. Wilbur twice a week. He was still struggling with feelings that disturbed him, still prone to sudden depressions and fierce irritability. Then, one day, a letter came for him—on delicate blue stationery.

It was a test for me. I handed it to him without a word. Standing right there, he ripped it open and read it. With his face expressionless, he handed it back to me. "*I shall miss you, but you are right. We can't see each other any more.*" It was signed: "*Wally.*" I looked up, my eyes blurred with tears. I heard a husky man's voice, my son's voice, saying: "I think it's going to be all right now."

I wanted to hug him and kiss him. But I just nodded. I had learned something from my analysis, too. I understood now that I had to let him go, to let him move away from my side, into the world. I heard Peter yelling to him from the front porch: "Hey Don. Bunch of guys're going to the movies tonight. Wanna go?"

"Sure," Don said. "You bringing dates?"

"Some are, some aren't."

"Okay. I might bring a date."

## A MAJOR MILESTONE

I learned then that Don had been going out with several girls in his high school class for the past six months. But only after the letter from Wally did he begin bringing them home to meet me and Arthur. They were charming girls, and they seemed to enjoy Don's company. He was perfectly at ease with them. One night, after several couples had come over for dancing and Cokes, Don was helping me clean up in the kitchen, and as he poked a glass under the hot water faucet, he said: "Being with girls is a lot more comfortable than that other thing. I never really wanted to be that way."

My psychiatrist told me that this was a major milestone. "If he can talk about it that objectively, he's pretty much freed himself from fear of his feelings." Both our psychiatrists have assured us that Don has in all probability been permanently cured.

Looking back, I now thank God that Don was arrested. If that crisis had not exploded in our faces, our ignorance would have let him drift into deep-rooted, habitual homosexuality. The crisis changed all that. It changed not only Don's life, but the life of our whole family. It gave Peter a brother, it gave my husband another son, and it gave me a husband. Perhaps for the first time in our marriage, there is some real affection between my husband and me. Don's anguish awoke in all of us the realization that our family had accepted a sickly substitute for genuine love. When that happens, no family is safe.

# | 23 |

# *The Psychologist—Dr. Evelyn Hooker*

## ERIC MARCUS

*Psychiatrists and psychologists in the postwar period, with few exceptions, believed that all homosexuals were mentally ill and that their illness was treatable: You could make a homosexual into a healthy heterosexual. Despite the near absence of dissenting opinion, some homosexuals refused to accept the prevailing dogma, but they were almost powerless to challenge it. Who would do the research and write the papers that questioned the opinions of the American Psychiatric and Psychological Associations?*

*In 1945, a young gay man and his friends found an ally, Dr. Evelyn Hooker, a professor of psychology at UCLA. Through their encouragement, Dr. Hooker pursued pioneering research that led to her controversial and widely publicized conclusion that there was no inherent connection between homosexuality and psychopathology. Remarkably,*

*until Dr. Hooker began her work, no one had scientifically tested the stated belief of the mental health profession that homosexuals were mentally ill.*

*When Dr. Hooker speaks, it is easy to imagine her commanding the attention of any audience, regardless of what she has to say. Now in her early eighties, she still has a powerful voice, which resonates through the double-height living room of her Santa Monica apartment. Hobbled by spinal arthritis, Dr. Hooker no longer moves with the same determination she once did. But as she took her seat in a comfortable high-backed easy chair in*

Excerpt. In Eric Marcus, ed., *Making History: The Struggle for Lesbian and Gay Equal Rights*, pp. 18–25. New York: HarperCollins, 1992.

*the living room of her book-filled apartment, cigarette in hand, speaking and gesturing emphatically, her independence of thought and strength of character were apparent.*

▼ ▼ ▼

It was during World War II, and I was teaching for the University Extension Division at UCLA and doing some research. Sammy was in one of my small introductory night classes. It became clear almost immediately that he was the most outstanding student in the class. He talked with me at intermission. He asked questions. There was just no doubt that he was the bright and shining star. You know, when a teacher finds a person like that, you fall for it hook, line, and sinker. Sammy would walk me downstairs after class. When he discovered that I was taking the streetcar home, to save gasoline, instead of driving, he began driving me home. Sammy had all the gasoline he wanted because he was writing million-dollar contracts between the air force and the aircraft industry in this area. He had a high school education. His father was a junk dealer.

Our friendship developed gradually, but I had an idiotic policy then. I thought instructors should not fraternize with their students. It wasn't until he had finished my course that Sammy called me and asked if he could come over. We spent the evening talking. When he left, Don, my first husband, turned to me and said, "Well, you told me everything else about him, why didn't you tell me he was queer?" I assume that's the word he used. It was the 1940s, after all. I said, "How could you possibly tell? You're crazy!" To which Don replied, "He did everything but fly out the window." Sam had a fragile build, but it wouldn't occur to you that he was gay. A thought might enter your head if you knew enough. But usually not, because he could put on a macho sort of manner. Not too exaggerated.

Sammy was very eager to get to know us. He and his lover, George, who was introduced as his cousin, invited us to dinner, and we went. George was a much older man. They wanted my approval so much that they were afraid to let me know they were gay. It was a delicious dinner.

Gradually, the fog came down and they became very good friends of ours. I liked them. They were very interesting people. I don't remember a time when Sammy or George said, "We're gay." They just gradually let down their hair. They adored Don. Don was very handsome, a marvelous talker. He was a sort of free-lance

writer in Hollywood and also worked on radio and did some painting. He liked them very much. He wasn't bothered by the fact that they were gay. It wouldn't have occurred to him to be bothered by things like that because he had lived in Hollywood for a long time.

I've tried hard to remember what I knew about homosexuality before I met Sammy, George, and their friends. I didn't know much. As a matter of fact, when I was in college at the University of Colorado, *The Well of Loneliness* was circulating quietly. I remember reading it and thinking, *Oh, gee. I wouldn't like to have to live my life with all that secrecy.* It makes a lot of sense to me and has always made a lot of sense to me when gay people say, "I had to have been born this way because almost from the very beginning of my sexual consciousness I was interested in men" or "I was interested in women." I was interested in men from the time I was an adolescent, and there was never any question about that. I think that understanding, together with the rather extraordinary cross section of society into which I was introduced by Sammy, made the difference.

▼ ▼ ▼

In 1945, after I had known them for about a year, Sam and George invited us to join them on a Thanksgiving holiday in San Francisco. We had an absolutely marvelous time. Sammy was one of these people I described as an "If" personality. If all restraints were off, if he didn't have to behave like a businessman or a manager, then he was funny, funny, funny! He was dramatic, campy. On the first night we were there, Sammy insisted that we go to Finocchio's—to see female impersonators. My eyes were wide. I had never seen anything like that.

It was a tourist place, not a gay bar, where they did dance routines. And it was a place for transvestites and would-be transvestites. Besides the dance routines, there were two old bags from Oakland who did a lot of female patter; it was funny, funny, funny! You absolutely believed that these female impersonators were the real thing. Then all of a sudden, they took out their breasts and bounced them up and down on the stage! The whole house just came down. The part that was most impressive and most astonishing as you watched these—you can only say—beautiful women in their beautiful evening clothes was their feminine curves. Whether they were on hormones, I don't know.

After the show, we came back to the Fairmont

Hotel on Nob Hill for a snack. I was unprepared for what came next. Sammy turned to me and said, "We have let you see us as we are, and now it is your scientific duty to make a study of people like us." Imagine that! This bright young man, somewhere in his early thirties, had obviously been thinking about this for a long time. And by "people like us" he meant, "We're homosexual, but we don't need psychiatrists. We don't need psychologists. We're not insane. We're not any of those things they say we are."

But I demurred. I was already teaching about eighteen hours a week and doing some animal research and God knows what else. I said, "I can't study you because you're my friends. I couldn't be objective about you." He replied that they could get me a hundred men, any number of men I wanted.

I couldn't see how I could do it. The thought of it was not in any way disturbing. It was not that. But I couldn't see how I could add anything more to what I was already doing. Sammy would not let me go. He said, "You're the person to do it. You know us. You have the training."

The purpose of the study Sammy wanted me to do was to show the world what they were really like. What he wanted countered was the kind of thing that I was teaching at the time. I taught everything in the psychology domain, including abnormal psychology and social psychology. You name it, I did it. And I probably taught the usual junk that homosexuality is psychopathological, that it's a criminal offense, and that it's a sin. I had no reason to think that these three things weren't true.

Sammy was pressing me hard, so I said I would talk to a colleague about it. I had a colleague with whom I shared an office. He was half-time, and I was part-time research. His name was Bruno Klopfer. Bruno was one of the world's greatest experts on the Rorschach test. So I went to Bruno and I told him about this suggestion. He jumped out of his chair and said, "You must do it, Eee-vah-leeeen! You must do it! Your friend is absolutely right. We don't know anything about people like him. The only ones we know about are the people who come to us as patients. And, of course, many of those who come to us are very disturbed, pathological. You must do it!" So I told Bruno I would do it. Bruno later served in my research as a judge. Unfortunately, Sammy was killed in a tragic automobile accident and never learned the outcome of what he urged me to do.

Despite my decision to proceed with the study, I was so pressed in my work and my personal life that it was difficult to do the research. I started to do a sort of hand-to-mouth study. My gay friends—and their friends—all longed to be in the study, of course. And I would say, "Now, don't talk to anybody else about what you saw in the Rorschach. Don't tell them how many responses you had or what you saw." With the Rorschach, you show an individual ten different ink blots and ask him to describe what he sees. The normal number of responses might be something like fifty. Well, the first thing you know, I was getting three hundred to four hundred responses to the Rorschach test. If they are really creative, and many of these men were, then you're going to have a lot of unique responses and that, of course, is fine. But not three hundred or four hundred. They certainly were talking to their friends.

In the middle of all this, my own house of cards blew up. I had known for some time that Don, my husband, was an alcoholic. He finally decided to be divorced. He said, "It's enough that I destroy myself; I can't bear to destroy you." I wrote to my friends in the East and said, "If you hear of a job there, let me know." I'm a Hopkins Ph.D., and a lot of my psychological friends were in the East. I didn't think that I could stand staying in California. It was awful. Dreadful. And just like that, I was hired at Bryn Mawr, outside Philadelphia. It was crazy. So I just dropped the project. By then I had done maybe fifty or seventy-five interviews.

I stayed one year at Bryn Mawr. If I had stayed there, you never would have heard from me. I wouldn't have done the study without the guys in California. But after one year, I came back to my old job at UCLA. It was 1948. The housing situation was dreadful. It so happened that I met Helena, the wife of a man named Edward Hooker who. . . . Shall I make it dramatic? It was dramatic, I can tell you. They had this beautiful home in Brentwood. When I met Helena, she said, "I am leaving my husband and I'm not coming back." They lived on an acre of ground, with a big orchard in front. There was a main house and then there was a little house that Helena had been living in separately from her husband. She invited me for dinner and asked me, "Would you like me to talk my husband into renting you the house once I'm gone?" I said yes because it was perfect, only fifteen minutes from UCLA.

The fateful day arrived, and I went over for dinner, and after a bit Edward Hooker came out

▼ ▼ ▼

from the bedroom. He was deaf and wore a hearing aid. He walked over to me and said, "I'm Edward Hooker, and I think it's time we met." He knew we had something in common, that we took our Ph.D.s on the same commencement platform at Johns Hopkins University, in 1932, though we had never met until that day.

He was delighted to rent the little house to me. So Helena moved out, and I moved in. I had been told by Helena that Edward was very asocial and that I must not have any parties. One night I was coming home and I said to myself, "I don't care if he's asocial. He's always there working, working, working. And I'm going to stop and buy some food and I'm going to invite him to dinner."

I invited him to dinner. A few months later, we were having dinner again, and we were sitting in my living room, eating at the card table. I was giving him a lecture about how he had a lot to give to some woman and he ought to do something about it. He looked up at me, with his eyes twinkling, and said, "Do I have to go out and look?" I looked at him seriously and said, "Well, of course, how else do you think you're going to find someone?"

One thing led to another, of course. Edward was a distinguished professor at UCLA. He had a Guggenheim Fellowship at Cambridge, England, in 1950 to 1951. I had an appointment at the Tavistock Clinic in London, just by chance, you know. So at the end of that year, we were married in the Kensington Registry on High Street, and then returned home to California.

For the first time in my life I was really free. I was in love. I didn't have to teach eighteen hours a week. I had just heard that the National Institute of Mental Health [NIMH] had been founded, which started me thinking. I began looking through the interviews that I had done with the original group of gay men and knew I couldn't use them. First of all, they were not planned enough. And second, I didn't have anything to compare them with.

What I had learned, of course, with every step I took, was that these men represented a cross section of personality, talent, background, adjustment, and mental health. The whole kit and caboodle was there. But I had to prove it.

As I was sitting there in my study, I said to myself, "What I think I'll do is apply to NIMH. If the study section thinks this project is worth doing, I'll do it." So I wrote out an application for a grant. I said that I could get any number of gay men.

The chief of the grants division, John Eberhart, flew out and spent the day with me. He wanted to see what kind of a kook this was. "Is she crazy or can she do this?" At the end of the day he said, "We're prepared to make you this grant, but you may not get it." By this time it was 1953, the height of the McCarthy era. The concern was that if somebody were to come across my name in connection with homosexuality and come across the fact that my first husband was in the Bureau of Medical Aid to Spain in the Spanish Civil War, they would have killed the research. And here I was proposing to study normal male homosexuals in 1953? As John had said to me, "If you get the grant, you won't know why, and we won't know why." And to this day, I have no idea why I got it because several years later, I learned that McCarthy's henchmen had indeed been keeping an eye on me.

Later, once the results were known, I was often asked by gay women, "Why didn't you do for us what you did for the gay men?" First I said, "You didn't ask me, and the men did." But there's more to it than that. Suppose I had gone to NIMH in 1953 and said, "I want to do a study of lesbians." The first thing that would have happened, I am convinced, is that they would have said, "We think this bears investigation." They would have been thinking, "Perhaps she herself is a lesbian." I think that may have been one question in John Eberhart's mind when he came and spent the day with me. He knew that if I was going to go into this field, I had to be above reproach. I would have to be as pure as the driven snow.

▼ ▼ ▼

The real excitement began when NIMH gave me the grant. There was excitement about doing something you felt was going to be ground breaking, whatever it led to. It was exciting because it would have been the first time anybody ever looked at this behavior and said, "We'll use scientific tests to determine whether or not homosexu-

---

\* Alfred Kinsey's *Sexual Behavior in the Human Male*, published in 1948, challenged widely held beliefs concerning male sexuality. Among Kinsey's conclusions: 37 percent of American men had at least one postadolescent homosexual experience leading to orgasm, and 4 percent were exclusively homosexual throughout adulthood. Homosexuality, as evidenced by the Kinsey reports, was far more widespread than anyone had imagined. Kinsey's human sexuality scale ranges from zero to six: Zero is exclusively heterosexual; six is exclusively homosexual.

ality is pathological."

When I set out to find the thirty gay men I needed for the study, I had a few rules. I wanted to be certain that they were all what Kinsey called a "five" or "six" — exclusively homosexual.* I didn't want anyone who had extended therapy or arrest records.

I found the gay men primarily through friendship networks, the Mattachine Society* — I had been invited to some of the original public meetings of the organization — and ONE, Incorporated. I interviewed them in the apartment in back of our garage. I could not have carried on my study at UCLA. No one would have participated because they would have been afraid of the stigma. Everyone knew that I was doing this research, so these men would have been identified immediately as homosexuals.

▼ ▼ ▼

I had no difficulty getting these men to talk. And I had no difficulty finding many more gay men than the thirty I needed, although I only used thirty. The problem was getting the straight men. Remember, this was the early 1950s. I thought that if I went to a labor union and asked for the personnel director and told him what I was doing, he would be willing to speak individually to men he thought were thoroughgoing heterosexual men. Not a bit of it. The personnel director I went to wouldn't do it. He said, "Are you doing a Kinsey study?" I said, "No, I'm not." "Any study that involves sexuality," he said, "might boomerang, and I would lose my job."

I was just at my wit's end to find heterosexuals who were of the general educational, economic, et cetera level of my gay group. So I got heterosexuals in the most unusual ways. One day, for example, I was sitting in the study and I heard some steps coming down the driveway. I looked out, and there were blue trouser legs, four of them. I said, "Oh boy!" It turned out that they were firemen who had come by to look at our fire precautions. I went out to meet them, and as we walked toward my office, one of them said, "Oh, you're a writer?" I said, "No, not exactly. I'm a psychologist." "Oh," he said, "I have two boys, and they're in a psychology experiment at UCLA." I asked him if he would be willing to be in a psychology experiment. He said he couldn't because

of work. When I asked him about participating on his days off, he said he had to take care of his boys. So I offered to pay for a baby-sitter. Finally, he agreed to participate. That's when my husband said, "No man is safe on Saltair Avenue."

The fireman introduced me to a cop. The cop wanted to come to me because he was having marital troubles and was willing to exchange a little information for some advice. I learned all about the ins and outs of the police department downtown. In my search I also went to the maintenance department at UCLA, but instead of getting a maintenance man, I found a man who was working on his master's degree in sociology. After two years, I got my thirty and thirty.

Each of the sixty subjects was given three projective personality tests widely used at the time: the Rorschach test, the Thematic Apperception test, and the Make A Picture Story test. The assumption underlying their use was that the person being tested would reveal his anxieties, fears, and fundamental personality predispositions without being fully aware that he was doing so.

The test results were then submitted to three judges, all nationally and internationally known psychological experts who did not know whether a subject was homosexual or heterosexual. The judges evaluated each test and assigned a rating of overall psychological adjustment on a scale of one — superior — to five — maladjusted. On all three tests, two-thirds of the heterosexuals *and* homosexuals were assigned a rating of three, which was average, or *better!* There was *no* inherent association between maladjustment or psychopathology and homosexuality. This finding was validated later by my own use of objective psychological tests and the reports of other psychologists.

Bruno Klopfer was one of the original judges who evaluated the responses. He was living in Carmel. When I went up there, people said, "You'll never get away with this. Your face will reveal who is and who isn't. He'll know." I said, "Oh, nonsense. He's the great Rorschach expert." I think we spent ten days just going over the materials, one after the other. It was terribly exciting to see Bruno make his decisions. It was simply that he was sure he could pick out the homosexuals from the heterosexuals, but he couldn't.

At that time, the 1950s, every clinical psychologist worth his soul would tell you that if he gave those projective tests he could tell whether a person was gay or not. I showed that they couldn't do it. I was very pleased with that. Bruno could

---

* The Mattachine Society was an organization for homosexuals founded by a small group of men in Los Angeles in 1950.

hardly believe his eyes. He was absolutely positive that the dynamics would be such that he would know immediately who was gay and who wasn't. But he didn't know.

One of the most exciting days of my life was the day I presented that paper—my study—at a meeting of the American Psychological Association in Chicago in 1956. The title of the paper was "The Adjustment of the Male Overt Homosexual." In my paper I presented the evidence that gay men can be as well adjusted as straight men and that some are even better adjusted than some straight men. In other words, so far as the evidence was concerned, there was no difference between the two groups of men in the study. There was just as much pathology in one group as in the other.

My presentation was held in one of the big ballrooms in one of the big hotels. The air was electric. We were still going strong at the end of the hour, so they moved us to another ballroom. Of course, there were some people, not too many, who were saying, "That can't be right." And they set off to prove that I was crazy. At the time, the hard-liners among the psychoanalysts, like Irving Bieber, would as soon shoot me as look at me.

I think for everybody—unless they were severely prejudiced, as lots of people were and are—what I had to say was a very exciting concept. And, of course, I made it electric. I used to have a fairly good speaking voice. A woman came up to me after I finished reading the paper and said, "If I had your voice, I'd patent it."

When I came back from Chicago, I remember a meeting at a restaurant in Hollywood. I had promised the gay men that I would let them know what the results were. Oh, they were uproarious with laughter. "This is great. We knew it all the time!" I didn't meet with the straight men. They didn't have the motivation to follow an old lady around.

In his book, *Homosexuality and American Psy-*chiatry: The Politics of Diagnosis, Ronald Bayer wrote about me and his reaction to my study. He described the study quite accurately and then said—I'm paraphrasing—"But in spite of the fact that she drew tentative conclusions"—which, of course, any scientific study does—"she nevertheless accepted the honors of the gay community. She was an advocate for them. . . . " There's a slight no-no in that, I think. But I don't care. As far as he's concerned, I was tainted by my association. I ought to be that perfectly impartial, objective researcher. That's why I had to use judges, so I couldn't be accused of anything.

▼ ▼ ▼

I think that the net impact of my study was felt in a number of ways. My friend Ed Shneidman described it when the Clinical Division of the American Psychological Association gave me the Distinguished Contribution Award: Among the things he wrote was that I had made homosexuality a respectable field of study. That cannot be discounted. It paved the way for a lot of people who had the courage—gay and straight psychologists alike—to do research.

But what means the most to me, I think, is. . . . Excuse me while I cry. . . . If I went to a gay gathering of some kind, I was sure to have at least one person come up to me and say, "I wanted to meet you because I wanted to tell you what you saved me from." I'm thinking of a young woman who came up to me and said that when her parents discovered she was a lesbian, they put her in a psychiatric hospital. The standard procedure for treating homosexuals in that hospital was electroshock therapy. Her psychiatrist was familiar with my work, and he was able to keep them from giving it to her. She had tears streaming down her face as she told me this. I know that wherever I go, there are men and women for whom my little bit of work and my caring enough to do it has made an enormous difference in their lives.

# | 24 |

# A Symposium: Should Homosexuality Be in the APA Nomenclature?

JUDD MARMOR, IRVING BIEBER, RONALD GOLD

## HOMOSEXUALITY AND CULTURAL VALUE SYSTEMS

### Judd Marmor, M.D.

Proponents of the mental illness label for homosexuality base their arguments on three major themes: 1) that homosexuality is the consequence of "disordered sexual development," 2) that it is a deviation from the biological norm, and 3) that psychodynamic studies of homosexuals always reveal them to be deeply disturbed individuals.

The disordered sexual development theme is based on the finding that a certain type of disturbed parent-child relationship is a background factor in most cases. There seems to be an assumption in this theme that if there is a disturbed parent-child relationship in the background of someone with variant sexual behavior this proves that the individual with such variant behavior must be mentally ill.

There are a number of fallacies in this argument. First, we know that although most homosexuals show the "typical" family constellation, by no means do all of them. Secondly, not all people who do have such family constellations in their background become homosexual. Third (and most importantly) to call homosexuality the result of disturbed sexual development really says nothing other than that you disapprove of the outcome of that development. *All* personality idiosyncrasies are the result of background developmental differences, and *all* have specific historical antecedents. The concept of illness cannot be extrapolated on the basis of background but must rest on its own merits.

## DEVIANT BEHAVIOR NOT NECESSARILY PSYCHOPATHOLOGY

It is my conviction that we do not have the right to label behavior that is deviant from that currently favored by the majority as evidence per se of psychopathology. And, as a matter of fact, we do not do so except where we are reflecting our culture's bias toward a particular kind of deviance. In a democratic society we recognize the rights of individuals to hold widely divergent religious or ideational preferences, as long as their holders do not attempt to force their beliefs on others who do not share them. Our attitudes toward divergent sexual preferences, however, are quite different, obviously because moral values, couched in "medical" and "scientific" rationalizations, are involved.

There are some psychiatrists who would argue that individuals who adhere to unusual life-styles are indeed neurotic and that they suffer from various developmental fixations or arrests that account for their inability to adhere to the behavioral or ideational standards of the majority. Such labeling tends to define normality in terms of behavioral adjustment to cultural conventions rather than in terms of ego strengths and ego-adaptive capacities, and it puts psychiatry clearly in the role of an agent of cultural control rather than of a branch of the healing arts.

Moreover, the relativity of our contemporary sexual mores should not be ignored in any scientific approach to sexual behavior. In a cross-cul-

*American Journal of Psychiatry*, 130(11):1207–1216, 1973. Excerpt.

tural study of 76 societies other than our own, Ford and Beach (3) found that in nearly two-thirds of them homosexual activities were considered normal and socially acceptable, at least for certain members of the community. Nor were all these societies necessarily "primitive" ones. In ancient Greece—a society that we admire and feel indebted to culturally, philosophically, and scientifically—overt homosexual relations between older men and youths was not only considered acceptable but was an institutionalized practice cultivated by heterosexual, healthy, honorable, normal men.

## BI-SEXUALITY—OUR MAMMALIAN INHERITANCE

The second major argument for the illness viewpoint is that homosexuality, in contrast to other forms of behavior deviance, is biologically unnatural. Dr. Frank Beach, the eminent biologist, has summarized the evidence on this by pointing out that bisexual behavior has been observed in more than a dozen mammalian species and "undoubtedly occurs in many others not yet studied." He concluded: "Human homosexuality reflects the essential bisexual character of our mammalian inheritance. The extreme modifiability of man's sex life makes possible the conversion of this essential bisexuality into a form of unisexuality with the result that a member of the same sex eventually becomes the only acceptable stimulus to arousal" (4).

Thus, from an objective biological viewpoint there is nothing "unnatural" about homosexual object choice. To illustrate how serious the argument if concerning the supposed biological unnaturalness of homosexuality let us consider some other conditions that are also outside of the presumable customary biological patterns. What about vegetarians? After all, most human beings are "naturally" meat-eaters, but we don't automatically label vegetarians as mentally ill. Or what about celibacy? Do we automatically assume that all people who choose a life of sexual abstinence are mentally ill simply because they do not follow the "natural" biological mating patterns? Obviously, we do not.

The third argument is that is often advanced is that any careful study of the personality of homosexuals will show that they are really disturbed individuals. In contrast to Socarides, who holds the view that all homosexuals are practically bor-

derline psychotics, Bieber concedes that many homosexuals can be well-adjusted individuals, but he argues that they still suffer from "pathology."

## HAPPY, CONSTRUCTIVE, AND REALISTIC HOMOSEXUALS

What *does* constitute the intrinsic "pathology" of a socially well adjusted homosexual? I submit that in the view of Bieber, Socarides, and others who share their viewpoint, it is primarily that his sexual preference differs from that of the majority of society. I do not deny that there are homosexuals who, just like heterosexuals, suffer from a wide variety of personality disorders and serious mental illnesses, although much of the dis-ease that they suffer from is not intrinsic to their homosexuality but is a consequence of the prejudice and discrimination that they encounter in society.

But I believe there is now an incontrovertible body of evidence that there are homosexual individuals who, except for their variant objective sex choice, are happy with their lives and have made a constructive and realistic adaptation to being a member of a minority group in our society. I consider the kind of evidence that Socarides marshals from his clinical practice as essentially meaningless in this regard. As I have often pointed out, if our judgment about the mental health of heterosexuals were based only on those whom we see in our clinical practices we would have to conclude that all heterosexuals are also mentally ill.

The final absurdity of this is the impossibility of trying to define at what point a person becomes a homosexual who is labeled as having a mental disorder. Some defendants of the illness theory try to justify it by saying that it applies only to obligatory homosexuality. Does this mean that only type 6 homosexuals are mentally ill and all the others are not? Or that types 4, 5, and 6 are ill but no 1, 2, and 3? The whole process of such labeling is unpleasantly reminiscent of the Hitlerian process of trying to determine what fraction of black or Jewish ancestry a person might be permitted to have and still be considered an acceptable member of society with full legal rights.

Surely the time has come for psychiatry to give up the archaic practice of classifying the millions of men and women who accept or prefer homosexual object choices as being, by virtue of that fact alone, mentally ill. The fact that their alternative life-style happens to be out of favor with current cultural conventions must not be a basis in itself for a diagnosis of psychopathology. It is our task as psychiatrists to be healers of the distressed, not watchdogs of our social mores.

# HOMOSEXUALITY—AN ADAPTIVE CONSEQUENCE OF DISORDER IN PSYCHOSEXUAL DEVELOPMENT

## Irving Bieber

Three questions seem most relevant to the question of removing the term "homosexuality" from the *Diagnostic and Statistical Manual of Mental Disorders* or changing the current designation:

1. Is homosexuality a normal variant of sexual development and sexual functioning? The long-term study that my colleagues and I reported in 1962 (1), further investigations of colleagues, and the extensive clinical experience of myself and others since then leave no doubt that homosexuality is not merely a variation of normal adult sexuality. Observations on olfaction offer supporting evidence that humans born with normal gonads and genitals are biologically programmed for heterosexual development. From early life, olfaction plays a central role in sexual organization and functioning; it steers the infant toward heterosexual objects and works as an important triggering mechanism in sexual arousal (5,6). Homosexuality does not occur without antecedent heterosexual development; it appears only *after* sexual responsivity to heterosexual objects has been established. Psychoanalytic evidence of heterosexual responses in homosexuals can almost always be demonstrated.

I have repeatedly emphasized that the dislocations in heterosexual organization of biologically normal children occur as a consequence of pathological family contexts—more specifically, pathologic relationships between parents and child. Typically, mothers of homosexuals are inappropriately close, binding, often seductive, and tend to inhibit boyish aggressiveness. The fathers are overtly or covertly hostile; thi  is expressed in detachment, streaks of cruelty, or frank brutality. The relationship between the parents is generally poor; often the husband is held in contempt by a wife who prefers her son. The pre-homosexual child may be exposed to rejection and hostility from other significant males,

such as brothers and peer mates. Defective masculine relationships deprive such a boy of needed masculine figures for identification and modeling that are ultimately sought, in part, in homosexuality. It then becomes a substitute adaptation, replacing the heterosexuality that is made inadequate or unavailable by a network of induced fears about heterosexual behavior. Within a substitutive adaptation, attempts are made to acquire missing sexual and romantic gratification. Through various homosexual maneuvers and activities, reparative attempts are made to strengthen masculine self-esteem and to alleviate profound feelings of rejection from men. Through homosexuality, reassurance and acceptance are sought from other men. Contrary to p      o      p      -ular notions, homosexuality is not an adaptation of choice; it is brought about by fears that inhibit satisfactory heterosexual functioning.

## INHERENT PSYCHOLOGICAL PAIN

The gay activists and their proponents among some psychiatrists claim that many men are neurotic about their homosexuality only because society is prejudiced. Extinct cultures, such as the ancient Greek, are held up as prejudice free examples, while cultures and present-day societies where there is no homosexuality are disregarded. The animal evidence has rested heavily on statements by Frank Beach. His position on animal homosexuality has changed, however, and in 1971 he wrote, "I don't know any authenticated instances of males or females in the animal world preferring a homosexual partner, if by homosexuality you mean complete sexual relationships, including climax. . . . It's questionable that mounting in itself can be properly called sexual" (7).

Opponents of my views have accused me and other colleagues with similar ideas of being prejudiced, reactionary, and homophobic. The trouble with such ad hominem attacks is that they do not get to the heart of the matter but serve merely as a diversionary method to discredit without risking an objective engagement with the evidence. As I see it, society at large does not produce a homosexual condition nor can it mitigate the inherent psychological pain. If all discrimination against homosexuals ceased immediately, as indeed it should, I do not think their anxieties, conflicts, loneliness, and frequent depressions would be short-circuited.

2. If homosexuality is not normal, how should it be categorized? In the past century, psychiatry and that allied behavioral sciences have amassed an enormous body of data, although psychiatric diagnostic classification is the weakest part of this extraordinary development. Our present nosology is based on very different categories of criteria. The diagnoses of mania and depression are based in the salient symptom; of schizophrenia, on a constellation or cluster of signs and symptoms; of personality disorders, on pschodynamic formulations; and on sociopathy, on sociologic criteria. Classification of homosexuality has reflected this medley of psychiatric criteria. It is often referred to as "sexual deviation." Literally, deviation is a statistical term denoting movement away from a median or statistical norm. Deviation and pathology are not necessarily related; genius is as deviant as is mental deficiency. In my opinion, the term "sexual deviation" is ambiguous, vague, and not useful as a diagnosis or as a nosologic category.

## HOMOSEXUALITY: SEXUAL INADEQUACY

Masters and Johnson (8) used criteria that qualified as functional and dysfunctional to classify sexual disorders, and they introduced the term "sexual inadequacy." Under this rubric, they included frigidity and sexual impotence. The psychodynamic common denominator of frigidity, impotence, premature ejaculation, and homosexuality consists of a network of fears about being effective in heterosexual activity. I suggest that homosexuality be characterized as a type of sexual inadequacy since most homosexuals (especially those who are exclusively homosexual) cannot function heterosexually.

I think, too, that adaptational concepts are very useful in formulating broader diagnostic contexts. Homosexuality could be classified as an adaptation to inhibited, dislocated, heterosexual functioning; this would leave room for an expanded description of the patient's heterosexual difficulties.

3. Does the inclusion of homosexuality in the diagnostic manual make homosexuals "sick," as they claim? Discrimination against homosexuals existed long before modern psychiatric and diagnostic manuals. Psychiatry, particularly psychoanalysis, has contributed significantly toward altering archaic, moralistic, and pseudoscientific

concepts. Freud (9) was the first to discard the notion that homosexuality was a degenerative disease. He classified it as a disorder of psychosexual development rather than as sinful and antisocial.

There is no reason to believe that if homosexuality were removed from the diagnostic manual there would be a significant alteration in existing social attitudes. Even if it could be shown that improved social attitudes would eventuate, this would not be reason enough to exclude the term if we agree that homosexuality is not normal and is a treatable condition.

Removal of the term from the manual would be tantamount to an official declaration by APA that homosexuality is normal. Undoubtedly, it would be interpreted that way. More importantly, dropping the term would be a serious scientific error. Such an action would also interfere with effective prophylaxis. Prehomosexual boys are easily identifiable and should be treated. Further, young men in conflict about their sexual direction may be discouraged from seeking treatment by those who would assure them that their homosexual proclivities are normal and that it is only "society," with its outmoded value system, that makes them reject a homosexual preference.

## STOP IT, YOU'RE MAKING ME SICK!

### Ronald Gold

I have come to an unshakable conclusion: The illness theory of homosexuality is a pack of lies, concocted out of the myths of a patriarchal society for a political purpose. Psychiatry—dedicated to making sick people well—has been the cornerstone of a system of oppression that makes gay people sick.

To be viewed as psychologically disturbed in our society is to be thought of and treated as a second-class citizen: being a second-class citizen is not good for mental health. But that isn't the worst thing about a psychiatric diagnosis. The worst thing is that gay people believe it.

Nothing is more likely to create neurotic anxiety as "a lack of feeling of wholeness," and nothing is more likely to alienate you from a major aspect of yourself than to be told incessantly that it's sick.

At 14 years of age I discovered what the "experts" said about the way I love: "infantile sex," "inevitable emotional bankruptcy," "a masquer-

So I went to my older sister and she sent me to a psychiatrist. He shot me full of sodium pentothal and scared me out of my wits. It is amazing how I could have kept on believing this nonsense about homosexuality when so little of it had anything to do with my life. But I went on willingly to other psychiatrists and learned from them that a part of me I didn't want to give up needed to be excised. I was ready for "psychic annihilation"; I became a heroin addict. This time I was sent to the Menninger Clinic, and there I was convinced that my "cure" must include a change in sexual orientation. So when it was agreed that I was through with treatment, it seemed to me I'd done only half a job. But I soon found that all I needed for another person to love me was to like myself better, I met a young man, and we had a good, happy life for 12 years. When we broke up our conflicts weren't out of the psychiatric literature. They were just like the tales of heterosexual divorce you read about in *Redbook*.

The man I live with now is a warm, loving, open person. For the past two years we've been going through the joyful process of discovering the full repertory of mutuality—easier for two members of the same sex.

## Psychological Growth Through Resisting Oppression

There are advantages to being gay. I learned that in the gay movement. And I learned something else: that I was oppressed and must make the choice to do everything I can to cease being an accomplice in my own oppression. I've had an immense sense of psychological growth through this decision. I've fought through to a sense of myself as a whole person—a good, concerned, loving, fighting-mad homosexual. I'm fighting the psychiatric profession now, but I know that a false adversary situation has been drawn between psychiatry and Gay Liberation. We can save you the trouble of treating some people, and we can be a helpful adjunct for many of your patients by pointing them along the road to self-esteem.

After our meeting with your Committee on Nomenclature and Statistics, its chairman said that "whether a person prefers to have sexual rela-tions with a member of the same or of the oppo-site sex is in itself not an indicator of mental dis-order." But, he added, "What are we to do about the homosexual who comes to us and says he's miserable, that he wants to change?" Such people do need help. But is it their homosexuality that's doing them in? Or is it something that psychiatry has helped to create: irrational fear and hatred of homosexuality? Instead of acceding to requests for brainwashing, what you can help these people realize is that there are many successful, well-adjusted people in various professions (including psychiatry) who are homosexual. You can help them to see that successful sexual adjustment of any kind cannot be achieved in a climate of guilt and fear.

When these patients see themselves as people, not sets of stereotypical patterns, I suspect that most of them (about as many as you can get with your current techniques) will go on being gay. Only they'll be happy about it. Perhaps the same percentage you have now will wind up predominantly heterosexual. And many of those who had been exclusively homosexual—many more than you now count as treatment "successes"—will discover a heterosexual component in themselves. We have found that such things happen frequently in the Gay Liberation movement.

I feel better since I've joined Gay Liberation. I work better, I'm happier in love. Would you rather have me the way I am? Or would you suggest another round of therapy? I think you really know that I'm not sick now, that my homosexuality is simply a part of me that in the past I wasn't allowed to accept. And I think you're prepared to agree that my previous illness was at least in part a direct result of the crimes perpetrated on me by a hostile society. You have been willing accomplices in such crimes. It is now time for you to prevent them. Take the damning label of sickness away from us. Take us out of your nomenclature. Work for repeal of sodomy laws, for civil-rights protections for gay people.

Most important of all, speak out. You've allowed a handful of homophobes to tell the public what you think. It's up to you now to get on the talk shows and write for the weeklies, as they do. You've got to tell the world what you believe—that Gay is Good.

# | 25 |

# *If Freud Had Been a Neurotic Colored Woman: Reading Dr. Frances Cress Welsing*

Any force which estranges and alienates us from one another serves the interests of racist domination.

—BELL HOOKS

That there is homophobia among Black people in America is largely reflective of the homophobic culture in which we live. . . . Yet, we cannot rationalize the disease of homophobia among Black people as the white man's fault, for to do so is to absolve ourselves of our responsibility to transform ourselves.

—CHERYL CLARKE

In 1974, the year that Dr. Frances Cress Welsing wrote "The Politics Behind Black Male Passivity, Effeminization, Bisexuality, and Homosexuality," I entered my final year of senior high school.

By that time, I had arrived at a very clear understanding of how dangerous it was to be a homosexual in my Black neighborhood and in society. I had no particular inclinations to slip on a dress like skin, wear loud lipstick, and wiggle my hips through the four A.M. shadows and street lights of the tenderloin or the boulevards where erotic desire was claimed by the highest bidder or the loneliest man. Facing this then-limited perception of homosexual life, I could only wonder, where did I fit in? I had no particular inclination to chase down men while wearing platform pumps and a miniskirt. None of this behavior was the least bit appealing to me.

Conversely, I was perfecting my heterosexual disguise; I was practicing the necessary use of masks for survival; I was calculating the distance between the first day of class and graduation, the distance between graduation from high school and departure for college—and ultimately, the arrival of my freedom from home, community, and my immediate peers. I believed my immi-

nent independence would allow me to explore what my hetero-disguise and my masks allowed me to conceal.

It is fortunate that the essay by Dr. Welsing I am citing here had not come to my attention during my adolescence. I can only imagine how little resistance the assault of her ideas would have been met with by me at that time. At seventeen, I wasn't coming out of anything I couldn't get back into immediately, and that included closets. But in 1974, the concept of "closets" had not come to my attention. I knew not to reveal my homosexual desires to my peers or discuss them with my family or any school counselor.

During the course of the next sixteen years I would articulate and politicize my sexuality. I would discover that homo sex did not constitute a whole life nor did it negate my racial identity or constitute a substantive reason to be estranged from my family and Black culture. I discovered, too, that the work ahead for me included, most importantly, being able to integrate all of my identities into a functioning self, instead of

In Essex Hemphill, *Ceremonies: Prose and Poetry*, pp. 52–64. New York: Plume, 1992.

accepting a dysfunctional existence as the consequence of my homosexual desires.

▼ ▼ ▼

Dr. Frances Cress Welsing, a controversial Washington, D.C.-based general and child psychiatrist, emerged on the Black cultural scene in the early 1970s. Her claim to fame is her controversial essay "The Cress Theory of Color Confrontation and Racism (White Supremacy): A Psychogenetic Theory and World Outlook" (1970). This widely disseminated essay appears with her article "Black Male Passivity" in her recently released book, *The Isis Papers: The Keys to the Colors* (Chicago: Third World Press, 1990). She is a sought-after public speaker, and in recent years, her ideas have been embraced in the reemergence of Black cultural nationalism, particularly by rap groups such as Public Enemy.

Welsing's "Theory of Color Confrontation" forms the intellectual and political basis for her examination of various issues confronting Black Americans, including issues of sexuality and homosexuality. Her arguments about race and sexuality, based on her theories, are her *sincerely* held beliefs. She contextualizes her positions on sexuality in a myopic analysis of Black masculinity, an analysis constructed from a still very limited, very patriarchal, and culturally conservative view of what Black liberation should be.

For Black gays and lesbians, Dr. Welsing is not as easily dismissed as Shahrazad Ali, author of the notorious book of internal strife, *The Blackman's Guide to Understanding the Blackwoman* (Philadelphia: Civilized Publications, 1989). While Ali, like Welsing, attacks Black homosexuality, she reserves her harshest commentary for Black lesbians. She writes, "The lesbian Blackwoman has arrived at her final limit and literally blows a fuse in her brain which blocks out her real gender and replaces it with a masculine role. Of course, just as male homosexuals, she overdoes it and makes herself a spectacle that is not welcome among civilized people. She is rough and tough and ready to battle. . . . She needs a special exorcism" (pp. 151–152). This is what Ali advised Black males. By dismissing the lives of Black lesbians and gay men, Ali is clearly not advocating the necessary healing Black communities presently require; she is advocating further factionalization. Her virulently homophobic ideas lack credibility and are easily dismissed as incendiary.

Dr. Welsing is much more dangerous because she attempts to justify *her* homophobia and heterosexism precisely by grounding it in an acute understanding of African-American history and an analysis of the psychological effects of centuries of racist oppression and violence. Rather than dismissing Black homosexuality, Welsing explains it as evidence of Black males *adapting* to oppression. While we may disagree with Welsing's views, we must acknowledge her own obviously fertile intellect and the power that her ideas have in many parts of the Black community. Welsing's seductive fusion of her own ideology with widely held Black nationalist concepts only shows how potentially misdirected the effort to counterattack racism can be, even for those intelligent enough to see the connections between racism, homophobia, heterosexism, classism, and all other oppressions spawned by patriarchal and white-supremacist domination.

In "Black Male Passivity," Welsing refutes any logical understanding of sexuality. By espousing Black homophobia and heterosexism — imitations of the very oppressive forces of hegemonic white male heterosexuality she attempts to challenge — she places herself in direct collusion with the forces that continually move against Blacks, gays, lesbians, and all people of color. Thus, every time a gay man or a lesbian woman is violently attacked, blood is figuratively on Dr. Welsing's hands as surely as blood is on the hands of the attackers. Her ideas reinforce the belief that gay and lesbian lives are expendable, and her views also provide a clue as to why the Black community has failed to intelligently and coherently address critical, life-threatening issues such as AIDS.

Arguing against an acceptance of homosexuality within the Black community, Dr. Welsing cautions:

> Black psychiatrists must understand that whites may condone homosexuality for themselves, but we as Blacks must see it as a strategy for destroying Black people that must be countered. Homosexuals or bisexuals should neither be condemned nor degraded, as they did not decide that they would be so programmed in childhood. The racist system should be held responsible. Our task is to treat and prevent its continuing and increasing occurrence (p. 91).

In other words, Dr. Welsing is suggesting that Black homosexuals are engaged in sexual genocide, in treason against the race, and are programmed by white racism to commit acts of *sup-*

*posed* self-destruction such as choosing to love and be loved by members of the same gender. If we dare follow her ideas to their illogical conclusions, then we could easily argue that every Black action that fails to conform to Black societal codes of morality and ethics is caused by racism. Such reasoning allows for the shirking of responsibility for our actions and choices. It is simply too easy to say, "The devil made me do it."

Welsing's widely disseminated color-confrontation theory is the justification for her homophobic and heterosexist assault. Her theory is very seductive, particularly for Black people oppressed for so long. It is very much like cocaine; a dose of her ideas momentarily provides one with a rush of empowerment, but after the high is gone the harsh realities of racism still remain, just as sexual diversity, as created by nature, still remains irrevocable, uncontrollable.

Yet, what gives her ideas power is her capacity to *account for* Black male homosexuality and bisexuality by presenting them as predictable behaviors within her color confrontation model.

The basis of her theory, which forms the framework for her puritanical assertions about sexuality and gender in general, is as follows:

> Racism (white supremacy) is the dominant social system in today's world. Its fundamental dynamic is predicated upon the genetic recessive deficiency state of albinism, which is responsible for skin whiteness and thus the so-called "white race." This genetic recessive trait is dominated by the genetic capacity to produce any of the various degrees of skin melanination—whether black, brown, red or yellow. In other words, it can be annihilated as a phenotypic condition. . . . Therefore, white survival and white power are dependent upon the various methodologies, tactics, and strategies developed to control all "non-white" men, as well as to bring them into cooperative submission. This is especially important in the case of Black men because they have the greatest capacity to produce melanin and, in turn, the greatest genetic potential for the annihilation of skin albinism or skin whiteness (p. 83).

This theory grounds Welsing's perspective on Black male homosexuality and bisexuality, allowing her to define them as dysfunctional behavioral responses to oppression. Asserting that "Black male homosexuality and bisexuality are only the long-run by-products of males submit-

ting in fear to other males" (p. 91), she claims that Black male homosexuality and bisexuality have "been used by the white collective in its effort to survive genetically in a world dominated by colored people, and Black acceptance of this imposition does not solve the major problem of our oppression but only further retards its ultimate solution" (p. 92).

In attempting to account for homosexuality among whites, Welsing writes:

> White male and female homosexuality can be viewed as the final expression of their dislike of their genetic albinism in a world numerically dominated by colored people. This dislike of their appearance, though deeply repressed, causes a negation of the act of self-reproduction (sex) in various forms. This is the eventual origin of homosexuality. . . .
>
> Unlike the white male, the Black male does not arrive at the effeminate, bisexual or homosexual stance from any deeply repressed sense of genetic weakness, inadequacy, or disgust, which I refer to as primary effeminancy (effeminancy that is self-derived and not imposed forcibly by others). Instead, the Black male arrives at this position secondarily, as the result of the imposed power and cruelty of the white male and the totality of the white supremacy social and political apparatus that has forced 20 generations of Black males into submission (p. 86).

It is less than sophisticated reasoning to reduce the social complexities of sexuality and its expression to the governing control and influence of white supremacy. To the extent that the history of racism has undeniably affected all facets of the lives of people of color (and whites as well), it is a legitimate concern to bring to any examination of sexuality. But to the extent that sexual identity and sexual practices represent conscious, personal choices, the most we can do is examine how sexuality is impacted upon and influenced by racism, in the same way that we can examine the impact of capitalism, religion, or patriarchy on sexuality.

To argue, as Welsing does, that racism causes homosexuality is to suggest that Black liberation will somehow eradicate Black homosexuality. If such eradication is to occur in the process of dismantling and destroying white supremacy, then what method(s) will be employed to achieve this? Does Black liberation ultimately require the confinement or extermination of Black homosexuals? Will Black liberation cancel out homosexual desire? The answer is surely a resounding no! Will Black liberation fail without the unqualified support and participation of Black gays and lesbians? The answer is an equally resounding *yes!*

In the glaring absence of a progressive feminist analysis, Welsing expediently ignores all efforts to achieve a cogendered liberation. By arguing that Black men are alienated from their manhood by Black women (their mothers in single-parent contexts) and society (white mates), Dr. Weising embarks upon the classic, homobashing tirade of Black nationalist patriarchs who have consistently attacked homosexuals as weak, irrelevant cocksuckers. She also buys into the patriarchal concept that the only legitimate family is one headed by a man with a submissive woman by his side. She blames Black women who have been hurt by Black men and left with raising children alone for fostering the existence of Black homosexuality, because "the alienation, hate, and disgust felt towards adult males are visited upon their sons subtly" (p. 88).

This transference of "hate and disgust" supposedly alienates Black male children from themselves and their manhood. "Black males soon learn that it is easier to be a female child than a male child, and more promising to be an adult Black female than an adult Black male" (p. 88). She additionally argues that this attitude is reinforced in Black male children by the Black female teachers they come into contact with who may also be "hurt and disgusted" with Black men and, again, transfer this to Black male children.

Arguing that the alienation between Black men and women and the absence of male role models in the home and in the community promote the occurrence of homosexuality, bisexuality, effeminization, and passivity, Welsing writes:

> There is only one solution—that Black males collectively face the horrendous presence of white males and conquer the accompanying fear engendered by this act. After the white man is faced, he must be resisted steadfastly and fought if he continues to wage war on Black people—as he has demonstrated historically that he intends to do. And it is Black males and not females who must do the fighting (p. 90).

Finally, Dr. Weltsing tmts out the standard beliefs regarding prisons and the confinement of Black men—that they, too, *breed* homosexuality. Writing of an ex-prisoner patient whom she identifies

as an example of twenty generations of racist abuse, Welsing confides in us that he said:

> "It is easier to endure the life on the inside than to try to put up with the pressures of being a man, a husband, and a father in the street." The intent of racist programming had been achieved: "Give up trying to be a Black man. Why not be a woman?" Many Black males have answered unconsciously, "Why not!" The braided and curled hair, the earrings and bracelets, the midriff tops, the cinch waisted pants, the flowered underwear, the high-heeled shoes with platforms and the pocketbooks are all behavioral answers to the above. They say in loud and clear language, "White man, I will never come after you. I cannot run in my high-heels—you know that. And I may mess up my hair."

Welsing's reasoning is so flawed, outdated, and totally hereto-reactionary that I am curiously reminded of the child who found himself faced with having to tell the emperor he's wearing none of the beautiful clothes that his court is leading him to believe he's wearing—or, as in a more recent example, of the discovery that Milli Vanilli didn't really sing a note of their hit song "Girl You Know It's True."

I suspect, however, that if Freud had been a neurotic, Black nationalist colored woman living in the noxious racism of America, out of desperation he might very well have formulated homophobic and heterosexist theories such as Dr. Welsing's. Even among the oppressed there is a disturbing need for a convenient "other" to vent anger against, to blame, to disparage, to denigrate. Such behavior is surely as detrimental as any an oppressor can exercise against the oppressed. There is no excuse for such behavior just as there is no credibility for Dr. Welsing's theories regarding sexuality. At best, her views reinforce the rampant homophobia and heterosexism that have paralyzed the Black liberation struggle. She widens the existing breach between Black gays and lesbians and their heterosexual counterparts, offering no bridges for joining our differences. And throughout it all, she does not foster an understanding of our differences as she would lead us to believe, but instead offers justification for homophobia and heterosexism to continue disabling Black communities.

Despite the popularity of Dr. Welsing's views among many Black nationalists and some who claim Afrocentricity, Black gays and lesbians and advocates of diversity can take sustenance and inspiration from the words of Cheryl Clarke, who in her 1983 essay from *Home Girls: A Black Feminist Anthology* (New York: Kitchen Table Press, 1983), "The Failure to Transform: Homophobia in the Black Community," firmly urges us:

> Open and proud Black gay men and lesbians must take an assertive stand against the blatant homophobia expressed by members of the Black intellectual and political community who consider themselves custodians of the revolution. For if we will not tolerate the homophobia of the culture in general, we cannot tolerate it from Black people, no matter what their positions in the Black liberation movement. Homophobia is a measure of how far removed we are from the psychological transformations we so desperately need to engender. The expression of homophobic sentiments, the threatening political postures assumed by Black radicals and Progressives of the nationalist/communist ilk, and the seeming lack of any willingness to understand the politics of gay and lesbian liberation collude with the dominant white male culture to repress not only gay men and lesbians, but also to repress a natural part of all human beings, namely the bisexual potential in us all. Homophobia divides Black people as political allies, it cuts off political growth, stifles revolution, and perpetuates patriarchal domination (p. 207).

So, Dr. Welsing, you say you want to have a revolution, or are you just talking like you do?

# II. C
# CAUSES AND CURES: THE ETIOLOGY DEBATE

Few topics have filled more headlines or inspired more public speculation about homosexuality than the question of etiology, What *causes* homosexuality? If our answers remain laughably crude, it isn't because no one applied themselves to the task. On the contrary, the question may be unanswered (or unaswerable) because it is itself based on a fundamental misunderstanding of the phenomenon.

The wording of the question reveals much about the motives of those asking it—and the kind of answer they expect. First, by making *homosexuality* a singular noun, we assert that it is a unitary construct, a largely undifferentiated phenomenon that has essentially the same cause wherever it turns up.

At the same time, the wording of the question reveals a therapeutic impulse. We typically ask about causes when we wish to devise remedies. By asking what causes homosexuality, we define it as a Problem to Be Solved. Heterosexuality is taken for granted; it is an unmarked category and needs no particular explanation. But homosexuality represents a departure from conventional expectations, one that must be explained, contained, and cured. For this reason it seems odd to ask the converse: "What causes heterosexuality?" or simply, "What causes sexuality?" (Sedgwick, "How to Bring Your Kids Up Gay," this volume).

Having framed the question in this way, many researchers have adopted the tools and vocabulary of the biological sciences. Indeed, some strand of biologism can be found in the earliest theories about homosexuality. In the 1860s Karl

Heinrich Ulrichs theorized that sexual preferences were as innate as the sexual organs themselves. Homosexual men and women were members of a "third sex," to which he gave the names "Uranians" and "Dionings." At the century's end the third-sex theory attracted Magnus Hirschfeld, leader of the early German Scientific Humanitarian Committee, which held that because homosexuality was congenital it should be decriminalized. Meanwhile, in Great Britain, Havelock Ellis wrote in *Sexual Inversion* that homosexuality was almost certainly an anomaly in gender formation. Inversion, he speculated, was the result of recessive genes (Irvine, "Sexology and Homosexuality," this volume).

Common to all these theories is some variant of biological determinism, the assumption that sexual orientation is entirely, or at least substantially, the product of biological causes. Theories differ on the specifics. Some propose that orientation is hardwired into some crevice of the brain, while others stress the possible role of genes or hormones. But whatever homosexuality's specific cause(s), the argument goes, it is relatively impervious to cultural or developmental influences. One does not acquire it by consorting with a particular kind of people, having certain formative sexual experiences, or making "choices." It isn't something your parents can control, and it is fixed long before the Oedipal drama envisioned by Freud. It is rooted in the body itself.

As scientific technologies and methods achieve greater precision, it has become possible to seek the causal mechanism in ever more minuscule bodily structures. With their new armamen-tarium of electronic microscopes and scanners, contemporary scientists have revived the hope that sexuality will someday be pinned to a partic-ular chromosome, structure, or bundle of nerves — a sort of "sex center" in the brain. The familiar speculations of psychiatrists, who had for decades shaped public discourse on homosexual-ity with talk of overclose mothers and distant fathers, gave way to authoritative-sounding reports from the biological sciences. Now it was biologists, geneticists, and neuroanatomists who seized the microphone, promising "scientific" answers to age-old questions about sexuality. The public's fascination with this new wave of research demonstrates how deeply we crave such answers — and how credulous we can be when they arrive in the form of "science." When asked in a 1993 survey what caused homosexuality, Ameri-can adults were evenly split between those who thought it is chosen and those who believe it isn't (*New York Times*/CBS News Poll 3/5/93).

The latest wave of biological research began with the 1991 publication of Simon LeVay's three-page report in *Science*, which claimed a link between sexual orientation and a microscopic structure in the hypothalamus. LeVay's findings quickly entered the media echo chamber, pushed along by the publicists at *Science* (Diaz, "Are Gay Men Born That Way?" this volume). His story was repeated in the *New York Times*, the *L.A. Times, Newsweek, Time*, the *Wall Street Journal* . . . the list goes on. LeVay himself appeared on countless news and entertainment programs, patiently explaining his research to the likes of Phil Don-ahue. His personal odyssey was then replayed in his 1993 book, *The Sexual Brain*.

Less than five months after his findings were published, the research team of Michael Bailey and Richard Pillard (1991) inspired another round of headlines. Bailey and Pillard had studied the incidence of homosexuality among 167 men whose brothers were gay. The findings again sug-gested that biological mechanisms were at work. When a subject was an identical twin (thus sharing 100 percent of his genes with a gay sibling), he stood a 52 percent chance of being gay himself. Among nonidentical twins (whose genetic overlap was not as great), 22 percent were gay. And among men who were genetically unrelated to their gay siblings (such as those who had been adopted), only 11 percent were gay. In other words, the closer the genetic relation, the more likely the brothers were to share the same sexual orientation. Again,

the media took notice. A few months after the ini-tial report, *Newsweek* ran a cover photo of a plas-tic-looking white infant under the headline "Is This Child Gay?"

Next came a study published by Dean Hamer and his colleagues at the National Cancer Insti-tute, which found an unexpectedly high probabil-ity that gay men would also have gay brothers, maternal uncles, and maternal cousins. Paternal relatives, by contrast, were less likely to be gay. This pattern of inheritance is typical of traits car-ried on the X chromosome, such as hemophilia, which boys inherit from their mothers. Analyzing the X chromosomes of forty pairs of gay brothers, Hamer found that thirty-three of them shared strips of DNA of identical length. While emphasiz-ing that they had not yet located a "gay gene," the research team continues to map the X chromo-some in the search for further clues; Hamer's col-league Angela Pattatuci is pursuing similar stud-ies with lesbians (Burr 1996).

The appeal of such theories is not difficult to fathom. First, biological determinism seems to refute moral arguments against homosexu-ality. To those who condemn homosexuality as immoral, biology answers that it is beyond an indi-vidual's control, something that cannot be changed. Because an act must be voluntaristic to have moral consequences, homosexuality and other immutable traits such as eye color and height cannot be judged in moral terms. In this way biologism appeals to many lesbians and gay men because it confirms a deeply felt conviction: "I had no choice in the matter," or, "I was born this way." It also figures in public support for, or hos-tility toward, gay people: polls show that a respon-dent's belief about the "cause" of homosexuality is the best predictor of that person's attitudes on issues related to gay rights.

Biological theories are also appealing because they seem to align homosexuality with accepted notions of "natural behavior." Nature, in this sense of the term, is contrasted with that which is "unnatural" and thus dangerous, perverse, or pathological. Naturalism asserts that there is a single normative way of conducting human events, ordained by God or tradition or evolution. To violate it is to risk retribution of one kind or another. Homosexuality is thus condemned because heterosexuality is considered nature's "intended" form of sexual behavior. The response from biology is that homosexuality does indeed have a place in the natural order because it *does* occur in nature. Its passage from one generation to another—whether through genes or hormones or some other mechanism—is part of nature's plan. The conclusion follows: If homosexuality has biological origins, it must be natural.

Naturalism is problematic for those on all sides of the argument, however. While they can be used to illustrate homosexuality's place in the natural order, the same arguments seem to rationalize a status quo that is hostile toward it. As sociologist Barry Adam observes, arguments based on assumptions about nature tend to obscure the social origins of oppression. Indeed, the "biologization of social phenomena shrouds them in a casing of immutability and permanence" (1978:35). The status quo is thus exonerated. Social problems—bigotry and oppression among them—are cast as inescapable, if undesirable, aspects of life. In this way naturalism forestalls creative thinking and debate about alternative visions of society. It "innoculates against reason or critical inquiry" (Adam 1978:34).

A third appeal of biological arguments is the parallels they draw between heterosexism and other isms based on immutable traits. By arguing that sexual orientation is fixed and natural, we liken it to race, gender, age, and other forms of human variation on the basis of which it is socially (and often legally) unacceptable to discriminate. This argument, too, has its limitations. In the first place, there is little historical evidence that the immutability of a trait ensures its social acceptance. Biological determinism does not save African Americans from racism, or women from sexism, or the elderly from ageism. Further, if one argues that one's rights are rooted in biology one risks the reversal of future scientific research. Suppose that the final conclusion is that sexual orientation is not biologically determined—does one then concede that lesbian and gay people do not deserve full civic equality? Better to base one's claims on consitutional guarantees such as those that protect freedom of religion, an attribute no one links to biological immutability (Diaz, "Are Gay Men Born That Way?"; Jefferson, "Studying the Biology of Sexual Orientation Has Political Fallout," this volume).

If many lesbian and gay people welcome suggestions of biological determinism, the political and religious right are determined to deny that homosexuality is the result of anything but perverse choice (Jefferson, "Studying the Biology of Sexual Orientation Has Political Fallout," this volume). Most press accounts reported that LeVay and Pilliard are openly gay, but right-wing colum-nist Cal Thomas went further, outing Dean Hamer and citing the media's failure to report Hamer's homosexuality (which Hamer himself has not publicly acknowledged, though his colleague Angela Pattatuci is openly lesbian) as evidence of journalistic complicity in furthering gay interests (1995). Certainly Thomas is correct that the mainstream media have by and large adopted the biological origins position, and it can regularly be encountered from such opinion leaders as Oprah and Ann Landers, who informed her readers that "there is now a growing body of evidence that human sexual orientation is determined at birth. I hope that when these scientific findings become better known, gay bashing will become totally unacceptable" (Landers 1993).

The media are more divided, however, on the matter of early childhood signs of future orientation. Anxiety about their children's sexuality seems to perturb many parents, and the psychiatric profession is all too ready to treat Gender Identity Disorder (Sedgwick, "How to Bring Your Kids Up Gay," this volume). But what's a parent to do when faced with conflicting advice? *Chicago Tribune* readers worried because their young sons like to dress up as women might have been reassured to read that "in children under 5, such play is neither a symptom of gender confusion nor an early sign of homosexuality" (Brotman 1994). But, a few months later, a wire service report, "Very Feminine Boys Likely to Become Homosexual Adults" (1/19/95), warned that "playing with dolls does not cause homosexuality, but it's a possible early sign." In an NBC News special in 1995 psychologist Richard Green delivered this soundbite: "Barbie dolls at five, sex with men at twenty-five."

If there is any question that fascinates the media, and much of the public, as much as the cause of homosexuality, it's estimating the size of the homosexual population. Deflation fever hit the media after a 1991 survey purported that gay men may be less than 2 percent of the population. The report brought rejoicing to the political right, including those in congress who, in the 1980s, killed the funding of the first major survey of adult sexual behavior proposed in the United States since the 1950s, because they were afraid that the numbers of gays might be higher than the famous 10 percent figure derived from the Kinsey studies.

Numbers like this are always political—the very term *statistics* reflects the origin of demographic counting techniques as eighteenth-century political tools for state control—as the framers of the U.S. Constitution knew when they mandated a census every ten years. But their importance has dramatically increased with the explosion of opinion polling and sophisticated demographic marketing. The public arena is now cluttered with the competing claims of partisan polls, self-serving audience surveys, one-sided letter-writing campaigns and biased phone-in talleys. Gays, too, became caught up in the numbers game and often came dangerously close to arguing that our right to social and legal equality rests on our supposedly substantial numbers. At the same time, we must insist that human rights not be granted—or denied—on the basis of constituency size.

In fact, the time was long overdue to retire the 10 percent Kinsey pseudo-statistic and admit that the only truly honest reply to the question how many gay people are there is that *there is no scientifically valid answer*. For one thing, the impressively accurate methods of modern probability sampling fail unless the population to be sampled can be specified, and this of course is precisely what cannot be done with a largely invisible and closeted group. But the difficulties facing those who wish to count the queers only start with pervasive invisibility, because it isn't at all clear what or who it is who should be counted.

The Kinsey studies that gave birth to the 10 percent figure were focused on sex acts, not sexual identity. In the 1948 report on sexual behavior in the human (read white American) male, Kinsey categorized his informants along a scale from 0 (100 percent heterosexual) to 6 (100 percent homosexual) and astounded his fellow citizens by the revelation that so many of them failed to achieve the expected purity of heterosexuality. Within the space of two pages Kinsey reported thirteen different percentages relating to homosexual activity, the most notorious of which at the time was that 37 percent have at least some overt homosexual experience to the point of orgasm between adolescence and old age. The lowest of these was the finding that 4 percent of the white males are exclusively homosexual throughout their lives and, in the middle, 10 percent of the males are more or less exclusively homosexual for at least three years between the ages of sixteen and fifty-five. In fact, the 4 percent category seems the most appropriate one to chose if you want to pick out the "true gays," and it's easy to see that the popularity and longevity of the 10 percent figure owes more to politics and folklore than to science.

Recall that Kinsey wasn't counting kinds of people; he didn't believe there "were two discrete populations. . . . The world is not to be divided into sheep and goats." But we are a society that likes people neatly pigeonholed—and not only for the purpose of constructing or claiming political constituencies. We artificially divide people into racial groups and then, in white supremacist societies, define anyone with *any* African heritage as Black (just as the Nazis perfected a pseudoscientific system for detecting Jews).

The likelihood is that more extensive and careful surveys would produce figures closer to Kinsey's 4 percent of adults who "are more or less exclusively homosexual." In fact, a 1993 study of American sexuality reported 2.8 percent of men and 1.4 percent of women identifying as homosexual or bisexual (Laumann et al. 1994). A 1994 study found 4.1 percent of men and 2.3 percent of women reporting having only homosexual sex, while 10 percent of men and 6.4 percent of women have had sex with someone of their own gender at least once (Usdansky 1994). In other words, queers might be comparable numerically to Jews—another semiinvisible minority familiar with the "don't ask, don't tell" closet. That shouldn't give our enemies too much comfort.

But the right's real nightmare isn't limited to our numbers—it's our potential to recruit that should disturb their slumber. Because whatever numbers emerge from better studies will miss the point that many more men and women are potentially queer if—and when—circumstances permit them to explore their feelings and act on their desires. Heterosexism keeps us all in closets of restricted choices. Open and visible queers proclaiming their right to slide up and down the Kinsey continuum challenge the assumption that the world is divided into sheep and goats. If we do not allow numbers to define us but demand our place in the sun, loudly and queerly showing and telling, then our numbers will also increase.

## REFERENCES

Adam, Barry. 1978. *The Survival of Domination: Inferiorization and Everyday Life.* New York: Elsevier.

Bailey, J. Michael and Richard Pillard. 1991. "A Genetic Study of Male Sexual Orientation." *Archives of General Psychiatry*, 48:1089–1096.

Burr, Chandler. 1996. *A Separate Creation: The Search for the Biological Origins of Sexual Orientation.* New York: Hyperion.

Hamer, Dean, Stella Hu, Victoria Magnuson, Nan

Hu, and Angela Pattatucci. 1993. "A Linkage Between DNA Markers on X Chromosome and Male Sexual Orientation," *Science*, 261:321–327.

Kinsey, Alfred, Wardell Pomeroy, and Clide Martin. 1948. *Sexual Behavior in the Human Male*. New York: Saunders.

Kinsey, Alfred, Wardell Pomeroy, Clide Martin, and Paul Gebhard. 1953. *Sexual Behavior in the Human Female*. New York: Saunders.

Landers, Ann. 1993. "Fighting Ignorance About Gays." *Philadelphia Inquirer*, April 25.

Laumann, Edward, John Gagnon, Robert Michael, and Stuart Michaels. 1994. *The Social Organization of Sexuality: Sexual Practices in the United States*. Chicago: University of Chicago Press.

LeVay, Simon. 1991. "A Difference in Hypothalamic Structure Between Heterosexual and Homosexual Men." *Science*, 253:1034–1037.

LeVay, Simon. 1993. *The Sexual Brain*. Cambridge: MIT Press.

Thomas, Cal. 1995. "Syndicated Column." *Los Angeles Times Syndicate*, November 2.

Usdansky, Margaret. 1994. "Study Fuels Homosexuality Debate." *USA Today*, August 17, p. 8A.

# | 26 |

# Boys Will Be Girls: Sexology and Homosexuality

## JANICE IRVINE

Perhaps the most significant impact of sexology on homosexuality was its role in the invention of the category itself. Michel Foucault, Jeffrey Weeks, and others have detailed the shift in the late eighteenth and early nineteenth centuries from a focus on specific sexual behaviors to one on sexual identities or individual "conditions."[1] Whereas, earlier, religion and the law took note of *acts* of sodomy, the new medical discourse recognized a distinct kind of *person*—the homosexual. Historians have differed on the significance of medical labeling: did it create a subculture that organized around the new concept of homosexual identity, or was medicalization a response to, and an attempt to define and control, preexisting sexual communities?[2] Although evidence indicates that the determinative role of medical literature in shaping homosexual activity and identity was limited, medicalization shifted the locus of moral authority to the medicopsychiatric profession, and much early research focused on descriptive and etiological studies of this new individual. This newly medicalized condition was variously conceptualized as a disease or, as in the case of Havelock Ellis, an anomaly akin to color blindness.[3] Whatever the specific diagnosis, homosexuality was seen as an individual condition, and interventions were subject to the current theories and treatment modalities of medicine and psychiatry.

The new category of "the homosexual" brought new complexities. The advantage for society was the safety implied by the existence of a distinct type of person who was homosexual. Since deviance was allegedly marked and separate, an "us-them" philosophy was possible. A related advantage for sexologists was the creation of a new population of research subjects and, later, clients. But practical and theoretical dilemmas were introduced with the new conceptual category. Primary questions centered on definitional boundaries: who were the individuals who were homosexuals, and how did they get that way? The texts of the early sexologists offered an array of complicated, sometimes contrived, theories, which form the backdrop for modern sex research on homosexuality.[4]

Although it is a hallmark of modern sexology that gender identity, gender role, and sexual preference are at least nominally distinct, early sexological theories of homosexuality amalgamated sex and gender. Physiological characteristics and cross-gender mannerisms were targeted by sexologists as essential features of "inverts," "the intermediate sex," or "the third sex." Carroll Smith-Rosenberg describes the role of the early sexologists in the struggle over "the social and sexual legitimacy of the New Woman" in the late nineteenth and early twentieth centuries.[5] Bourgeois women who were educated, independent, unmarried, and desirous of male privilege became symbols of female rebellion and a crisis of gender. It was precisely for their aspirations to male power and privilege that these women were targeted by the Viennese neurologist and sexologist Krafft-Ebing as "Mannish Lesbians."[6] In an analysis that is remarkably predictive of some late twentieth-century research, Krafft-Ebing argued that homosexuality was characterized by cross-gender behavior in early childhood. In one of his case studies he reported: "Even in her earliest childhood she preferred playing at soldiers and

In Janice Irvine, *Disorders of Desire*, pp. 242–257. Philadelphia: Temple University Press, 1990.

other boys' games; she was bold and tom-boyish and tried even to excel her little companions of the other sex. She never had a liking for dolls, needlework or domestic duties."[7] This conflation of sexual variation, gender role, and social status was common in the sexological gender discourse throughout the century. It is, as Smith-Rosenberg notes, a metaphoric system in which "disease again bespoke social disorder."[8]

Gender rebellion thus became a primary signifier of the homosexual condition. There remained questions about the origins of this condition, for it was vital to the social order to understand how it might be "caught" and whether it might be prevented or cured. Krafft-Ebing promulgated the notions of congenital and acquired inversion. Masturbation, the *bête noire* of the nineteenth century, was seen as a major cause of acquired inversion.[9] For Havelock Ellis, inversion was rooted in biology, and the male or female invert suffered from some genetic or chromosomal abnormality.[10] Yet Ellis distinguished between inversion, which was biologically inevitable, and homosexuality, which was an acquired characteristic. The homosexual woman, for example, was viewed as simply having a weakness or a predisposition to seduction by female inverts, who were considered to be congenitally deviant.

The ramifications of etiological theories are clearly political and remain controversial among gay activists as well as sexologists. Biological determinism, as in Ellis' notion of the invert, can be the basis for an appeal to social tolerance: an individual who is powerless to change should not be subjected to legal or moral censure, or to therapeutic attempts at change. And if homosexuality is congenital, then there is no social threat of seduction or conversion. This is the social agenda behind some sexological theories based on biology,[11] and, significantly, their essentialism resonates with the personal experience of many gay people, for whom sexual desire and attraction are so powerfully compelling and consistent that they feel as if they were "born this way." Yet the essentialist sword can cut both ways. Biological theories of homosexuality can also connote a sense of "wrongness" or disease. Since heterosexuality is normative, homosexuality can be considered unnatural and abnormal, whether it is biological or not. Thus, essentialism within a culture dominated by a medical discourse can raise the specter of disease and thus prevention, a theme evident in the work of Krafft-Ebing and hinted at by contemporary scientists such as Gunter Doerner.[12]

A theory based on "acquired" or socially mediated factors can also engender responses aimed toward prevention or cure. If homosexuality is not innately programmed, some believe, it should be possible to determine the developmental factors involved and eliminate them. This, in fact, is the impetus behind some modern sex research that seeks to identify, and modify factors thought to be related to homosexuality, such as cross-gender behavior. If we can derail a boy from "sissy" behaviors, some hope, we can avert future homosexuality. Social learning theory is also interpreted by some as highlighting the threat of homosexual seduction, and thus may increase efforts at social control. If one is not born homosexual, in this view, vulnerable and impressionable children should be protected from deviants who might want to convert them. Over the decades, psychoanalytic therapy, hypnotherapy, and aversion treatment have been directed toward eliminating homosexual behavior, reshaping desire, or liberating "blocked" heterosexual expression. Such theories about homosexual etiology, which appear to be less biologically determined and which introduce the role of culture, still reflect essentialist thinking, in that there is the presumption of an immutable sexual force that, at birth, begins to be shaped by the exigencies of individual and social learning. Such thinking still typically views homosexuality as a perversion of normal development and as an identity whose meaning is stable through time.[13]

Sex research is always shaped by the cultural context, and the social relations of gender and homosexuality are characterized by inequality. Political considerations are present in any discourse on homosexuality, since gay people, as a persecuted minority, are vulnerable to the ideological ramifications of research hypotheses. Unfortunately, modern research on homosexuality is often conducted by scientists committed to the pretense of "neutrality," who either ignore the political implications of their work or fail to act in behalf of those whom they study. Research on homosexuality has flourished in the last several decades, but given the myriad conflicting social and professional pressures surrounding it, it is indeed a mixed bag.

## HOMOSEXUALITY IN THE LABORATORY

The two institutional pillars of scientific sex research both embarked on major research projects into homosexuality beginning in the 1960s.

The Kinsey Institute for Research in Sex, Gender, and Reproduction and the Masters and Johnson Institute, although dissimilar in methodology and research focus, have viewed the study of homosexuality as a logical step in their scientific investigations into human sexuality. Both institutes have published massive texts presenting their findings. In 1979 Masters and Johnson released *Homosexuality in Perspective*. The Kinsey Institute has been more prolific over the years. It has published *Homosexuality: An Annotated Bibliography* (1972), *Male Homosexuals: Their Problems and Adaptations* (1974), *Homosexualities: A Style of Diversity Among Men and Women* (1978), and *Sexual Preference: Its Development in Men and Women* (1981).

Research into homosexuality has been the major research endeavor of the Kinsey Institute since the late 1960s. Kinsey himself had planned, after the release of his works on male and female sexuality, a publication on homosexuality, but he died before realizing this goal. The Institute went in a different research direction after his death, but returned to the subject in 1967, aided by funding from the National Institute of Mental Health.[14] Like Kinsey himself, the Institute researchers have found many friends in the gay community because of their liberal acceptance of homosexuality.

The theoretical orientation of the Institute's work on homosexuality has been predominantly sociological. Their data come from ethnographic studies and survey research in major gay communities in the United States, the Netherlands, and Denmark, as well as extensive fieldwork with lesbians and gay men. The Kinsey Institute research is framed by the societal reaction (or "labeling") theory of deviance. This perspective criticizes the notion that certain behaviors are deviant per se and instead focuses on the processes by which such acts come to be labeled as deviant by society.[15] Martin Weinberg has noted that his research on homosexuality is more related to his training as a sociologist than to sexology.[16] A focus on the social context and how people deal with stigmatization clearly distinguishes the work of Weinberg and Colin Williams from that of psychoanalysts, who view homosexuality as an illness. In *Male Homosexuals*, the authors state, "The paramount problems faced by homosexuals are a function of the social and cultural contexts within which they pursue their sexual expression."[17] By deriving its approach from labeling theory, the Kinsey Institute shifted the research emphasis at least somewhat from lesbians and gays and addressed the sociopolitical context. This has led to a fairly consistent liberalism in its publications, which frequently call for "tolerance" and "the day when homosexuality is no longer regarded as a 'sin' or a 'sickness' but rather as another important form of human diversity."[18] The books pragmatically advise homosexuals to find homosexual roommates and not live with their parents, and admonish therapists not to attempt to convert homosexuals to heterosexuality.[19]

In its ethnographic inquiries into the gay "lifestyle" and its developmental research on the origins of homosexuality, the Kinsey program mirrors the research goals of the early sexologists who sought to explain who was homosexual and why. Both assume the uniqueness of a homosexual person, despite Kinsey's admonition that "the world is not to be divided into sheep and goats."[20] Significantly, the Institute's research is unable to delineate developmental differences between gay people and non-gays. Traditional etiological theories simply did not hold up under their longitudinal studies. Yet the research did uphold the connection between homosexuality and cross-gender behavior posited by the early sexologists.

The major tenets about homosexuality advanced by the research of the Kinsey Institute are as follows:

1. Homosexuality is not deviant per se, but must be viewed within the broader social context in which it is perceived with hostility.

2. There is no such entity as "the" homosexual, but rather a range of homosexual lifestyles. The Institute has chosen to refer to "homosexualities," and has developed a typology of expressions of gay behavior.

3. Contrary to traditional developmental theories of psychiatry, there are no significant differences in the families of heterosexuals and homosexuals. Specifically, there has been no support for the "dominant mother, absent father" syndrome advanced by psychiatry as the etiology of male homosexuality.

4. Among both lesbians and gay men, there is a significant link between nonconformity to stereotypic gender roles and the development of homosexuality.

This was the major finding of the Institute's most recent book, *Sexual Preference:*

> While gender nonconformity appears to have been an aspect of the development of homosexuality in many of our respondents, it was by no means universal, and conversely, gender nonconformity does not inevitably signal future homosexuality. Nonetheless, according to our findings, a child's display of gender nonconformity greatly increases the likelihood of that child's becoming homosexual regardless of his or her family background and regardless of how much the child identifies with either parent.[21]

For lesbians and gay men, assessing the Kinsey Institute research is problematic. It is tempting, in a virulently homophobic culture, to praise any scientific treatise that is as progay as the Institute studies. In the finest tradition of Havelock Ellis, *Homosexualities* proclaims that "few homosexual men and women conform to the hideous stereotype most people have of them."[22] The studies methodically document that, cultural stereotypes to the contrary, there are no psychological differences between homosexuals and heterosexuals. In retrospective analysis, Weinberg notes that, given the detrimental social consequences of the myriad developmental theories about homosexuality, the very inconclusiveness of the Kinsey studies serves an important function.[23]

Yet gay activists have not been blind to the shortcomings of the Kinsey Institute research. Major criticisms include the inevitable focus on white males; sampling difficulties, such as the pitfalls of generalizing from respondents concentrated in San Francisco to gay people living in more homophobic areas; the unwieldy nature of the five-hour interview; and insufficient attention to demographic data in their final analysis.[24] A review in *Gay Community News* went to the heart of the issue, describing the flaws listed above as "secondary considerations":

> There is no need to worry about diction when we should be worrying about asking the wrong question. The question is not, "*Why* are there homosexuals?" but rather "*What* is a homosexual?" That is a question science cannot answer, because there is no such thing as a homosexual. (Emphasis in original.)[25]

Sexological research, however enlightened, unquestioningly supports the idea of homosexuals and heterosexuals as two distinct and mutually exclusive brands of human beings, rather than understanding sexual orientation as a fluid concept.

The latest release from the Institute shows a tendency toward biologism. Although the authors carefully state that their study contained no data that would allow them to determine any possible biological etiology of homosexuality, they nevertheless make numerous speculations and state: "Our findings are not inconsistent with what we would expect to find if, indeed, there were a biological basis for sexual preference."[26] In addition, they review the research of the late 1970s that attempted to isolate a biological cause of homosexuality. They conclude that there is mounting evidence for a physiological, and specifically hormonal, determinant of homosexuality and report a growing momentum of support for this theory within scholarly circles. This drift toward biological determinism is congruent with the new biomedical and physiological emphasis at the Kinsey Institute under the directorship of June Reinisch.[27]

The Kinsey Institute authors hypothesize that the scientific determination of a physiological basis for homosexuality would loosen societal oppression. Like Masters and Johnson and Kinsey himself, they equate the biological with the "natural" and think that proving that a behavior has physiological origins will undermine the basis for social, political, and moral condemnation. Alan Bell and his colleagues write:

> Those who argue that homosexuality is "unnatural" will be forced to reconsider their belief, because something that is biologically innate must certainly be natural for a particular person, regardless of how unusual it may be. People might ultimately come to the conclusion that everyone is unique, biologically and socially, and that natural physiological factors will make it inevitable that a certain percentage of people in any society will be fundamentally homosexual regardless of whether they are momentarily (or even continuously) engaged in heterosexual behaviors.[28]

The latest theoretical tendency of the Kinsey Institute researchers is a disappointing shift away from their earlier commitment to research on homosexuality from a societal reaction perspective. Although they still criticize discrimination against lesbians and gays, they have shifted their lens back to the individual rather than the social environment. Their current references to biology, physiology, and "natural" sexual behavior reflect less their sociological roots and more the medical ideology of Masters and Johnson.

Masters and Johnson's research on homosexuality reflects their belief in the biomedical model and the primacy of physiology in understanding human sexuality. Sociological and psychological research is helpful, they believe, but "unless these two areas are supported by basic science and preclinical work, it's going to fall right back into the old traps of speculative hypothesis."[29] In 1964 they began their physiological research on homosexuality, and they published *Homosexuality in Perspective* in 1979. The research for *HIP* took longer than that for either *Human Sexual Response* or *Human Sexual Inadequacy* because, essentially, it is a "homosexual composite" of both. It contains data on the physiological sexual response of homosexuals as well as information on the treatment of sexual dysfunction and dissatisfaction.

Masters and Johnson's initial goal had simply been to study and report on the physiological sexual response of homosexuals. They added the second component when, after years in the laboratory, they concluded, "No real differences exist between homosexual men and women and heterosexual men and women in their physiological capacity to respond to sexual stimuli."[30] This finding, by itself, produced yawns within sexology. Helen Singer Kaplan responded that any medical person would have known that there would be no physiological differences, and added, "Nobody would have thought penises would react any differently—the penis doesn't know what brand of sex it's having."[31] Anticipating criticism, Masters and Johnson had expanded their work, and also expanded their potential market to include clinical interventions with homosexuals and research into the sexual fantasies of both heterosexuals and homosexuals.

Perhaps the most controversial aspect of the book was its report on clinical programs to convert homosexuals into heterosexuals. In a two-week intensive therapy program that emphasized reeducation and sensate focus techniques, Masters and Johnson treated sixty-seven lesbians and gay men who had expressed a desire to function heterosexually, and claimed success in changing all but 35 percent of them. In addition, although they essentially maintain that homosexuality is learned behavior, they, like the Kinsey researchers, opened the door to possible physiological determinants, concluding that in some instances "hormonal predispositions may interact with social and environmental factors to lead toward a homosexual orientation."[32].

The research biases in *HIP* reflect the ideology of all of Masters and Johnson's work: a belief that physiological data will reveal essential "truths" about human sexuality; an ethos that stresses the superiority of marriage and commitment; and a liberal tendency that emphasizes individualism and free choice while minimizing the importance of the sociopolitical context. The research sample reveals the same inadequacies as their earlier investigations. The majority of subjects were white and of high socioeconomic and educational levels. In addition, they chose subjects whom they defined as "committed"—that is, homosexuals who had lived together for at least one year. This was clearly an ideological decision, since in *HSR* they had demonstrated that physiological response was not affected by marriage.

Masters and Johnson are unclear about the purpose of their research on homosexuality. On the one hand, they insist that increased scientific evidence will alter cultural conceptualizations of homosexuality: "Now that it has been established that homosexual men and women are not physiologically different, it is also reasonable to speculate that in the near future, a significant measure of the current onus of public opprobrium will be eased from the men and women with homosexual preference."[33] Yet they quickly retreat from confronting homophobia and take refuge in their alleged professional and scientific neutrality. In the preface they caution that *HIP* "must not be construed as a statement of social, legal, or religious position," and in the conclusion they emphasize: "It is not our intention to assume a role in interpreting or implementing moral judgment. These privileges and their accompanying awesome responsibilities are not within the purview of a research group devoted to psychophysiologic aspects of human sexuality."[34]

The sex research institutes of both Kinsey and Masters and Johnson acknowledge the environment of social and political oppression of lesbians and gay men, yet they fail to deal with the implication that this is also the context in which their work will be received. Masters and Johnson were particularly naive in believing that their data showing that homosexuals and heterosexuals had the same physiological responses during sex would decrease homophobia. In fact, a *Newsweek* poll revealed that in July 1983, 58 percent of respondents said that homosexuality should *not* be considered an accepted alternative lifestyle, up from 51 percent in June 1982. Like their insistence on the similarities between women and men, it reflected their belief that people can understand and accept each other only when they are proven to be the same. Differences are unacceptable, alienating, and intolerable.

Although Masters and Johnson are theoretically consistent in their emphasis on the "sameness" of gay and straight individuals, sexology faces a theoretical tension in research and clinical work on homosexuality. It is both economically and politically practical to focus on the differentness of gay people. This widens the potential market for sexologists in terms of research on the establishment of sexual identity, the development of preventive measures, and clinical treatment programs. Ideologically, it aligns sexology with an antigay dominant culture—a move that could effect broader acceptance and credibility for the aspiring profession. Conversely, an overemphasis on difference is untenable in a field that largely professes a liberal stance toward homosexuality. Further, many sexologists are themselves gay, and subgroups of the profession, such as humanistic sexology, have a legacy of gay advocacy. Indeed, one market strategy encourages sexologists to deemphasize difference, since practitioners cannot afford to alienate their constituency. Sexologists must walk a fine line that casts homosexuality as a disease or even a benign abnormality while simultaneously offering the hope and compassion that will attract clients. Given the widespread but erroneous conflation of sameness and equality, sexologists like Masters and Johnson are in the tricky position of espousing ideological liberalism by positing the similarity of gay and straight people while also offering a cure. They bridge the inconsistency by deferring to the "choice" of clients who seek out a conversion program because of their own desire to change sexual orientation.

*HIP* had two major effects within popular culture: it validated notions of a cure for homosexuality and, by comparing the lovemaking techniques of homosexuals and heterosexuals, functioned as a sex manual for heterosexuals. Some of its findings were extrapolated by the media into the conclusion that gay people had better sex than heterosexuals. This emerged from the finding that heterosexuals tended to be more goal-oriented in sex, moving rapidly and predictably into

intercourse, whereas the homosexual sample tended to "move more slowly through excitement and to linger at plateau stages of stimulative response"[35] According to Masters and Johnson, same-sex couples have the advantage of better communication, the "it takes one to know one" principle that is reflected in their own dual-sex teams. In addition, they have suggested that poor sexual communication between the sexes is built on the assumption of male sexual expertise. Thus, they advocate in *HIP*, as in their other publications, that in the interest of better heterosexual sex, men should give up the position of sex expert and women should take more sexual responsibility.

The homosexual conversion programs have been more controversial within sexology and the gay community. Shortly after the publication of *HIP*, the *New York Times* ran a front-page story announcing "New Treatment for Homosexuals."[36] Despite Masters and Johnson's claims that homosexuality was an acceptable lifestyle, their implementation of a treatment program to convert gay people conveyed legitimacy to homophobic attacks. The inherent superiority of heterosexuality was implicit in that they developed no programs facilitating the "free choice" of heterosexuals to convert to homosexuality.

The search for a cure for homosexuality has deep roots in the history of American psychiatry. Homosexuality had been listed as an official category of mental illness in the first *Diagnostic and Statistical Manual* (1952) of the American Psychiatric Association, lending official credence to the profoundly antihomosexual sentiment of Western culture. In the 1940s, analysts began voicing optimism about the potential to "cure" gay people.[37] Irving Bieber and Charles Socarides rose to prominence in the 1960s with their oedipal and preoedipal theories of the pathological development of homosexuality. Socarides claimed that psychoanalysis could cure up to 50 percent of "strongly motivated obligatory homosexuals."[38]

By the early 1970s, however, gay activists had begun to challenge the very definition of homosexuality as a pathological condition. After several years of bitter political dispute, the board of trustees of the American Psychiatric Association removed homosexuality from the *DSM-III*. As a compromise gesture, ego-dystonic homosexuality was included in its place. This measure has remained controversial into the 1990s, and gay activists, gay psychiatrists, and their supporters have lobbied to remove the classification. Most members of the APA's Advisory Committee on Sexual Dysfunction remain supportive of the new diagnosis, however. Several of these members are prominent sexologists, such as Helen Singer Kaplan, Harold Lief, and Joseph LoPiccolo. The links between psychiatry and sexology ensure the perpetuation of the ideology of disease and cure within sexual science, and the conversion programs are merely an extension of a historical struggle.

Yet Masters and Johnson are virtually oblivious to this history of sexual and gender politics. They write that there are "any number of good reasons" for gays to convert to heterosexuality, including concern for job security and increased social respectability.[39] In the 1990s, AIDS would presumably be one of those "good reasons." For women, "the lesbian role was described as preferable because women reported that it was not only more sexually stimulating, but it was psychosocially more enhancing to the individual. Women in this study consistently reported that they experienced far more freedom of self-expression during their commitment to a lesbian orientation." Therapy focused on convincing a woman that a man could be retrained to provide her "with some opportunity for the self-expression she had grown to appreciate in her experience with lesbian society." Treatment included communication training of the male partner, to attempt to raise him up to the level of "receptivity of communicative exchange"[40] to which the woman had been accustomed in her lesbian relationships.

Masters and Johnson's medical strategy is to change the individual, not society. Their conversion program could serve as legitimation for their research focus on homosexuality, since it yielded clinical tools for returning social and sexual "deviates" to the mainstream. It would also buffer their more culturally challenging enterprise, which was to offer homosexuals treatment for sexual dysfunctions within homosexual relationships. Both treatment programs could significantly expand the market for professional sex therapists, but it was their "cure" for homosexuality that received the most attention.

In the early 1980s, the homosexual "cure" brought sexologists and the gay community head-to-head. The two modalities of intervention and treatment were conversion of adult homosexuals to heterosexuality, and retraining potentially gay children, most notably "sissy boys," in more "gender-normal" behavior. Conceptually, the cures reflect a mix of biological determinism and cultural acquisition theories. The premise that homosexuality is developmentally acquired, combined with research that correlates adult homosexuality with childhood gender anomaly, fosters a sense that being gay is a composite of environmentally induced characteristics such as effeminate mannerisms. Conversion to heterosexuality, then, is merely a function of changing mannerisms and behavior patterns. Hypnotherapy, aversion therapy, and other behavioral techniques are employed to that end. On the other hand, the programs operate on the notion that the core nature that will ultimately be released is heterosexual. Helen Singer Kaplan, a maven of homosexual conversion programs, stated that, with effective therapy, "very often a man's latent heterosexuality will blossom."[41]

Kaplan's work is a striking example of the role of sexologists in pathologizing behavior that is not culturally normative. Having integrated her theory on homosexual conversion with her work on inhibited sexual desire, she considers homosexuality a pathological deviation of the desire phase because it entails "desire for an object or situation which does not interest the majority of persons."[42] She crafted the diagnosis "situationally inhibited sexual desire," which is described as appropriate for people who experience "little or no desire in situations which most persons would find erotic, i.e., an intimate sexual relationship with an attractive partner of the opposite gender."[43] In this view, homosexual desire is considered sick simply because of its minority status.

Gay psychiatrists have challenged conversion programs on the grounds of both their homophobia and the questionable effectiveness of their techniques. As with sex therapy, critics have argued that sexologists provide little or no outcome data to support their extravagant claims of success. Emery Hetrick, president of the Institute for the Protection of Lesbian and Gay Youth, said: "Neither Kaplan nor any of the other cure people have ever demonstrated that their achievement is anything more than the most transient and circumstantial kind of performance."[44] Kaplan, however, incensed many members of the gay psychiatric community by implying that their criticisms were motivated by self-interest:

The gay psychiatric community insists that there is no such thing as successful treatment when success is measured by capacity of heterosexual pleasure markedly increased over homosexual pleasure. They deny it, yet everyone who has focused on that issue in therapy has seen it. The gay psychiatric community feels threatened by this concept. They would have to look upon themselves as possibly having a pathological condition if they don't deny it.[45]

Since the conversion programs are premised on contempt for a sexual minority, any effective professional opposition must affirm gay sexuality as a viable option. Currently this strategy is most effectively pursued by openly gay sexologists such as David McWhirter and Andrew Mattison. Trained in psychiatry and psychology respectively, McWhirter and Mattison nevertheless moved beyond the paradigms of homosexual pathology to conduct a sophisticated research study on the everyday lives of male couples. In a model predicated on stage theory, McWhirter and Mattison discuss issues relevant to gay men such as intimacy, sexuality, trust, and risk taking in relationships. Thus, they have abandoned the traditional sexological emphases on determining what causes homosexuality, and how to prevent it, instead sketching a lively and compassionate view of how men structure their relationships together. In *The Male Couple: How Relationships Develop*, the authors discuss their own initial internalized homophobia and then proceed to locate their work in a context deeply hostile to gay male relationships. They recommend not only that support systems for gay couples be strengthened, but that gay couples be recognized as legitimate family units, and that this recognition be widely visible, particularly to young gay persons.[46]

*The Male Couple* is a pivotal text in sexological research. Its acceptance of gay sexuality is reminiscent of some of the earlier work on homosexuality produced by the Kinsey Institute. But the courage of the authors in coming out is unprecedented since the era of Magnus Hirschfeld, who once faced the charge that his own research on homosexuality was self-serving.[47] McWhirter and Mattison comment on this fact:

Not many years ago, the very fact that we are a male couple ourselves would have been an issue used by some to discredit our study. Fortunately, as the times and attitudes have changed, most people recognize that our status as a male couple actually gives the research a more firm footing in truth. . . . It

would have been more difficult for nongay researchers to obtain the same degree of accuracy we achieved.[48]

The emergence of openly gay sexologists is a promising step toward more helpful and sophisticated research on homosexuality.

As a whole, the research on homosexuality, conducted by the scientific sexologists is characterized by a superficially liberal tolerance that frequently masks a deeper strain of fear and prejudice. Care is taken to emphasize that homosexuality is an acceptable alternative lifestyle and to criticize societal discrimination against gay people. As noted, both the Kinsey Institute and Masters and Johnson publications wistfully hypothesize that their contributions to the scientific study of homosexuality will result in a loosening of social strictures. Yet most gender sexologists hide behind their scientific status and refuse to utilize their research to alleviate the oppression of the very population they have been studying. Shortly after *HIP* was published, for example, Masters and Johnson refused to comment on the antigay Briggs Initiative in California. "We just don't feel qualified to answer," they told the audience.[49]

Moreover, the research creates frightening possibilities for lesbians and gay men. Despite the Kinsey researchers' hopes that societal oppression might erode with evidence of a biological basis for homosexuality, they concede that, in fact, the opposite is just as likely. More often than not, biological determinants trigger a momentum toward eradication, not acceptance, of a minority position. The Kinsey writers acknowledge:

Already we have heard the suggestion that pregnant women be closely monitored—that those carrying boys be regularly checked for fetal androgen levels and that where hormone levels are low, there be medical intervention to supplement them artificially. And some homosexual adults have allegedly been "cured" by brain surgery to destroy "inappropriate" sexual response centers.[50]

Similarly, the clinical work of Masters and Johnson, Kaplan, and others implies that it is both possible and appropriate to cure homosexuality through therapeutic intervention.

Research on homosexuality is merely one enterprise by which scientific sexologists attempt to understand sex and gender. The connection is perhaps made most explicitly in *Sexual Prefer-*

*ence*, which reports a link between homosexuality and early gender nonconformity. The authors conclude in the epilogue, "A principal issue raised by homosexuality in both males and females has to do with what it means to be a man or a woman."[51] Although sexologists generally urge a loosening of cultural stereotypes of masculinity and femininity, their work stands on a continuum alongside that of more open gender engineers—sexologists who have developed and implemented programs for the surgical reassignment of sex.

## NOTES

1. See Michel Foucault, *The History of Sexuality*, vol. I: *An Introduction* (New York: Pantheon, 1978); Jeffrey Weeks, *Sex, Politics, and Society* (London: Longman, 1981); Diane Richardson, "The Dilemma of Essentiality in Homosexual Theory," *Journal of Homosexuality* 9, no. 2–3 (Winter 1983/Spring 1984): 79–90.

2. See, for example, Esther Newton, "The Mythic Mannish Lesbian: Radclyffe Hall and the New Woman," *Signs* 9 (1984): 557–575; George Chauncey, Jr., "From Sexual Inversion to Homosexuality: Medicine and the Changing Conceptualization of Female Deviance," *Salmagundi* 58–59 (Fall 1982–Winter 1983): 114–146; John D'Emilio and Estelle Freedman, *Intimate Matters: A History of Sexuality in America* (New York: Harper and Row, 1988); Lillian Faderman, *Surpassing the Love of Men* (New York: William Morrow, 1981); Carroll Smith-Rosenberg, *Disorderly Conduct: Visions of Gender in Victorian America* (New York: Alfred Knopf, 1985).

3. Phyllis Grosskurth, *John Addington Symonds* (London: Longman, 1964), p. 273.

4. For a more detailed exegesis of early sex research on homosexuality, see Jeffrey Weeks, *Coming Out: Homosexual Politics in Britain, from the Nineteenth Century to the Present* (London: Quartet Books, 1977); Carroll Smith-Rosenberg, "The New Woman as Androgyne: Social Disorder and Gender Crisis, 1870–1936," in *Disorderly Conduct*, pp. 245–296.

5. Smith-Rosenberg, "The New Woman."

6. Esther Newton argues convincingly that "mannish lesbians" or "butches" were not simply victims of sexological medical discourse; in fact, the identity was useful to them as a signifier of explicit sexuality. See Newton, "The Mythic Mannish Lesbian."

7. Quoted in Smith-Rosenberg, "The New Woman," p. 271.

8. Ibid., p. 272.

9. Richard von Krafft-Ebing, *Psychopathia Sexualis*, 12th (revised and enlarged) ed. (1902.), trans. Franklin Klaf (New York, 1965), pp. 222–368.

10. Havelock Ellis, "Sexual Inversion with an Analysis of Thirty-three New Cases," *Medico-Legal Journal* 13 (1895–96).

11. See, for example, Richard Green, "Navigating the Straits of Oedipus," *New York Times*, December 11, 1988.

12. See Jeffrey Weeks, *Sexuality and Its Discontents: Meanings, Myths and Modern Sexualities* (London: Routledge and Kegan Paul, 1985); Weeks, *Sex, Politics and Society*; and Linda Murray, "Sexual Destinies," *Omni*, April 1987.

13. Notions of acquired etiology, because they introduce the role of culture, are sometimes confused with social construction theory. Yet there are important differences. Although social factors are stressed in theories of acquired etiology, these influences are seen as molding a stable sexual drive or energy that, under developmentally "normal" circumstances, is heterosexual. There is, therefore, a tendency within such theories to pathologize homosexuality, although some social learning theorists espouse a liberal tolerance for diversity. Unlike social learning theories, social construction theory avoids the medicalized nomenclature of disease and cure. Constructionism does not see gay people as hapless members of a fixed and deviant sexual category, but examines how the meaning of same-gender sexual behavior has emerged and changed in different eras and cultures. It acknowledges social, political, historical, and economic factors as essential to the development of homosexual identity and community. The gay individual is positioned as an empowered social actor. Because of this, social construction theory is sometimes misconstrued as implying that sexuality is flexible and easily changed. This implication may be upsetting to a gay person who does not experience sexuality as a "choice" or mere "preference." But the critique of stable categories of meaning that social constructionism offers does not suggest that sexuality is quixotic or that different configurations of desire and expression can be easily interchanged. Rather, by refusing to accept traditional ideas of sexuality as a transcendent force, the theory allows for imaginative questions that probe for more sophisticated analyses of the development of sexual desire and behavior.

I am grateful to Lisa Duggan and Carole Vance for discussions on this topic.

14. Alan Bell and Martin Weinberg, *Homosexu-

*alities: A Study of Diversity Among Men and Women* (New York: Simon and Schuster, 1978), p. 14.

15. See, for example, John Kitsuse. "Societal Reaction to Deviant Behavior," in *Deviance: The Interactionist Perspective*, ed. Earl Rubington and Martin Weinberg (New York: Macmillan, 1968), pp. 19–29.

16. Telephone interview with Martin Weinberg, October 7, 1988.

17. Martin Weinberg and Colin Williams, *Male Homosexuals: Their Problems and Adaptations* (New York: Oxford University Press, 1974), p. 8.

18. Alan Bell, Martin Weinberg, and Sue Hammersmith, *Sexual Preference* (New York: Simon and Schuster, 1980), p. xii.

19. Ibid.; Weinberg and Williams, *Male Homosexuals*.

20. Alfred C. Kinsey, Wardell B. Pomeroy, Clyde E. Martin, and Paul H. Gebhard, *Sexual Behavior in the Human Male* (Philadelphia: W. B. Saunders, 1948), p. 639.

21. Bell, Weinberg, and Hammersmith, *Sexual Preference*, p. 189.

22. Bell and Weinberg, *Homosexualities*, p. 230.

23. Weinberg interview.

24. See, for example, Robert Etherington, "A Monumental Study: Less Than Monumental Results," *Gay Community News*, September 30, 1978, pp. 10–11; Nancy Walker, "Nothing New About Lesbians," *Gay Community News*, September 30, 1978, p. 13.

25. Larry Goldsmith, "Science vs. Real Life," *Gay Community News*, February 6, 1982, p. 6.

26. Bell, Weinberg, and Hammersmith, *Sexual Preference*, p. 216.

27. Hall, "New Directions for the Kinsey Institute."

28. Bell, Weinberg, and Hammersmith, *Sexual Preference*, p. 218.

29. "Playboy Interview: Masters and Johnson," *Playboy*, November 1979, pp. 87–121.

30. Ibid., p. 104; William Masters and Virginia Johnson, *Homosexuality in Perspective* (New York: Bantam, 1979); hereafter cited as *HIP*.

31. Quoted in "Sex and the Homosexual," *Newsweek*, April 30, 1979.

32. *HIP*, p. 411.

33. Ibid., p. 227

34. Ibid., pp. ix, 403.

35. Ibid.

36. Noted in "Playboy Interview," p. 87.

37. Richard Bayer, *Homosexuality and American Psychiatry: The Politics of Diagnosis* (New York: Basic Books, 1981).

38. Ibid., p. 37.

39. *HIP*, p. 357.

40. Ibid., p. 377.

41. Diane Klein, "Interview with Helen Singer Kaplan," *Omni*, August 1981, p. 92.

42. Helen Singer Kaplan, *Disorders of Sexual Desire, and Other New Concepts and Techniques in Sex Therapy* (New York: Brunner/Mazel, 1979), p. 64.

43. Ibid.

44. Quoted in Lawrence Mass, "Shrinking Homophobia: AMA Report Echoes the Same Old Prejudices," *New York Native*, April 12–25, 1982.

45. *Sexuality Today*, March 8, 1982.

46. David P. McWhirter and Andrew Mattison, *The Male Couple: How Relationships Develop* (Englewood Cliffs, N.J.: Prentice Hall, 1984), p. 292.

47. Edwin Haeberle, "Swastika, Pink Triangle and Yellow Star—The Destruction of Sexology and the Persecution of Homosexuals in Nazi Germany," *Journal of Sex Research* 17 (1981): 270–287.

48. McWhirter and Mattison, *Male Couple*, p. xii.

49. Quoted in Thomas Szasz, *Sex by Prescription* (New York: Anchor Press/Doubleday, 1980), p. 44.

50. Bell, Weinberg, and Hammersmith, *Sexual Preference*, p. 219.

51. Ibid., p. 221.

# | 27 |

# How to Bring Your Kids Up Gay: The War on Effeminate Boys

## Eve Kosofsky Sedgwick

In the summer of 1989 the U.S. Department of Health and Human Services released a study entitled *Report of the Secretary's Task Force on Youth Suicide*. Written in response to the apparently burgeoning epidemic of suicides and suicide attempts by children and adolescents in the United States, the 110-page report contained a section analyzing the situation of gay and lesbian youth. It concluded that, because "gay youth face a hostile and condemning environment, verbal and physical abuse, and rejection and isolation from families and peers," young gays and lesbians are two to three times more likely than other young people to attempt and to commit suicide. The report recommends, modestly enough, an "end [to] discrimination against youths on the basis of such characteristics as . . . sexual orientation."

On 13 October 1989, Dr. Louis W. Sullivan, secretary of the Department of Health and Human Services, repudiated this section of the report—impugning not its accuracy, but, it seems, its very existence. In a written statement Sullivan said, "the views expressed in the paper entitled 'Gay Male and Lesbian Youth Suicide' do not in any way represent my personal beliefs or the policy of this Department. I am strongly committed to advancing traditional family values. . . . In my opinion, the views expressed in the paper run contrary to that aim."[1]

It's always open season on gay kids. But where, in all this, are psychoanalysis and psychiatry? Where are the "helping professions"? In this discussion of institutions, I mean to ask, not about Freud and the possibly spacious affordances of the mother-texts, but about psychoanalysis and psychiatry as they are functioning in the United States today.[2]

I am especially interested in revisionist psychoanalysis, including ego psychology, and in developments following on the American Psychiatric Association's much-publicized 1973 decision to drop the pathologizing diagnosis of homosexuality from its next Diagnostic and Statistical Manual (DSM-III). What is likely to be the fate of children brought under the influence of psychoanalysis and psychiatry today, post-DSM-III, on account of parents' or teachers' anxieties about their sexuality?

The monographic literature on the subject is, to begin with, as far as I can tell exclusively about boys. A representative example of this revisionist, ego-based psychoanalytic theory would be Richard C. Friedman's *Male Homosexuality: A Contemporary Psychoanalytic Perspective*, published by Yale University Press in 1988.[3] (A sort of companion volume, though by a nonpsychoanalyst psychiatrist, is Richard Green's The *"Sissy Boy Syndrome" and the Development of Homosexuality* [1987], also from Yale.)[4] Friedman's book, which lavishly acknowledges his wife and children, is strongly marked by his sympathetic involvement with the 1973 depathologizing movement. It contains several visibly admiring histories of gay men, many of them encountered in nontherapeutic contexts. These include "Luke, a forty-five-year-old career army officer and a life-long exclusively homosexual man" (1988, p. 152); and Tim, who was "burly, strong, and could work side by side with anyone at the

In Michael Warner, ed., *Fear of a Queer Planet*, pp. 69–81. Minneapolis: University of Minnesota, 1993.

most strenuous jobs"; "gregarious and likable," "an excellent athlete," Tim was "captain of [his high school] wrestling team and editor of the school newspaper" (pp. 206–7). Bob, another "well-integrated individual," "had regular sexual activity with a few different partners but never cruised or visited gay bars or baths. He did not belong to a gay organization. As an adult, Bob had had a stable, productive work history. He had loyal, caring, durable friendships with both men and women" (pp. 92–93). Friedman also, by way of comparison, gives an example of a *hetero*sexual man with what he considers a highly integrated personality who happens to be a combat jet pilot: "Fit and trim, in his late twenties, he had the quietly commanding style of an effective decision maker" (p. 86).[5]

Is a pattern emerging? Revisionist analysts seem prepared to like some gay men, but the healthy homosexual is one who (a) is already grown up, and (b) acts masculine. In fact, Friedman correlates, in so many words, adult gay male effeminacy with "global character pathology" and what he calls "the lower part of the psychostructural spectrum" (p. 93). In the obligatory paragraphs of his book concerning "the question of when behavioral deviation from a defined norm should be considered psychopathology," Friedman makes explicit that, while clinical concepts are often somewhat imprecise and admittedly fail to do justice to the rich variability of human behavior," a certain baseline concept of pathology will be maintained in his study, and that that baseline will be drawn in a very particular place. "The distinction between nonconformists and people with psychopathology is usually clear enough during childhood. Extremely and chronically effeminate boys, for example, should be understood as falling into the latter category" (pp. 32–33).

"For example," "extremely and chronically effeminate boys"—this is the abject that haunts revisionist psychoanalysis. The same DSM-III that, published in 1980, was the first that did not contain an entry for "homosexuality," was also the first that *did* contain a new diagnosis, numbered (for insurance purposes) 302.60: "Gender Identity Disorder of Childhood." Nominally gender-neutral, this diagnosis is actually highly differential between boys and girls: a girl gets this pathologizing label only in the rare case of asserting that she actually is anatomically male (e.g., "that she has, or will grow, a penis"); while a boy can be

treated for Gender Identity Disorder of Childhood if he merely asserts "that it would be better not to have a penis"—*or* alternatively if he displays a "preoccupation with female stereotypical activities as manifested by a preference for either cross-dressing or simulating female attire, or by a compelling desire to participate in the games and pastimes of girls."[6] While the decision to remove "homosexuality" from DSM-III was a highly polemicized and public one, accomplished only under intense pressure from gay activists outside the profession, the addition to DSM-III of "Gender Identity Disorder of Childhood" appears to have attracted no outside attention at all—nor even to have been perceived as part of the same conceptual shift.[7]

Indeed, the gay movement has never been quick to attend to issues concerning effeminate boys. There is a discreditable reason for this in the marginal or stigmatized position to which even adult men who are effeminate have often been relegated in the movement.[8] A more understandable reason than effeminophobia, however, is the conceptual need of the gay movement to interrupt a long tradition of viewing gender and sexuality as continuous and collapsible categories—a tradition of assuming that anyone, male or female, who desires a man must by definition be feminine; and that anyone, male or female, who desires a woman must by the same token be masculine. That one woman, *as a woman*, might desire another; that one man, *as a man*, might desire another: the indispensable need to make these powerful, subversive assertions has seemed, perhaps, to require a relative deemphasis of the links between gay adults and gender-nonconforming children. To begin to theorize gender and sexuality as distinct though intimately entangled axes of analysis has been, indeed, a great advance of recent lesbian and gay thought.

There is a danger, however, that that advance may leave the effeminate boy once more in the position of the haunting abject—this time the haunting abject of gay thought itself. This is an especially horrifying possibility if—as many studies launched from many different theoretical and political positions have suggested—for any given adult gay man, wherever he may be at present on a scale of self-perceived or socially ascribed masculinity (ranging from extremely masculine to extremely feminine), the likelihood is disproportionately high that he will have a childhood history of self-perceived effeminacy, femininity, or nonmasculinity.[9] In this case the eclipse of the effeminate boy from adult gay discourse would represent more than a damaging theoretical gap; it would represent a node of annihilating homophobic, gynephobic, and pedophobic hatred internalized and made central to gay-affirmative analysis. The effeminate boy would come to function as the discrediting open secret of many politicized adult gay men.

One of the most interesting aspects—and by interesting I mean cautionary—of the new psychoanalytic developments is that they are based on *precisely* the theoretical move of distinguishing gender from sexuality. This is how it happens that the *depathologization* of an atypical sexual object-choice can be yoked to the *new* pathologization of an atypical gender identification. Integrating the gender-constructivist research of, for example, John Money and Robert Stoller, research that many have taken (though perhaps wrongly) as having potential for feminist uses, this work posits the very early consolidation of something called Core Gender Identity—one's basal sense of being male or female—as a separate stage prior to, even conceivably independent of, any crystallization of sexual fantasy or sexual object choice. Gender Identity Disorder of Childhood is seen as a pathology involving the Core Gender Identity (failure to develop a CGI consistent with one's biological sex); sexual object-choice, on the other hand, is unbundled from this Core Gender Identity through a reasonably space-making series of two-phase narrative moves. Under the pressure, ironically, of having to show how gay adults whom he considers well-integrated personalities do sometimes evolve from children seen as the very definition of psychopathology, Friedman unpacks several developmental steps that have often otherwise been seen as rigidly unitary.[10]

One serious problem with this way of distinguishing between gender and sexuality is that, while denaturalizing sexual object-choice, it radically *renaturalizes* gender. All ego psychology is prone, in the first place, to structuring developmental narrative around a none-too-dialectical trope of progressive *consolidation* of self. To place a very early core-gender determinant (however little biologized it may be) at the center of that process of consolidation seems to mean, essentially, that for a nontranssexual person with a penis, nothing can ever be assimilated to the self through this process of consolidation unless it can be assimilated *as masculinity*. For even the most

feminine-self-identified boys, Friedman uses the phrases "sense of masculine self-regard" (RF, p. 245), "masculine competency" (p. 20), and "self-evaluation as appropriately masculine" (p. 244) as synonyms for any self-esteem and, ultimately, for any *self*. As he describes the interactive process that leads to any ego consolidation in a boy:

> Boys measure themselves in relation to others whom they estimate to be similar. [For Friedman, this means only men and other boys.] Similarity of self-assessment depends on consensual validation. The others must agree that the boy is and will remain similar to them. The boy must also view both groups of males (peers and older men) as appropriate for idealization. Not only must he be like them in some ways, he must want to be like them in others. They in turn must want him to be like them. Unconsciously, they must have the capacity to identify with him. This naturally occurring [!] fit between the male social world and the boy's inner object world is the juvenile phase-specific counterpoint to the preoedipal child's relationship with the mother. (p. 237)

The reason effeminate boys turn out gay, according to this account, is that other men don't validate them as masculine. There is a persistent, wistful fantasy in this book: "One cannot help but wonder how these [prehomosexual boys] would have developed if the males they idealized had had a more flexible and abstract sense of masculine competency" (p. 20). For Friedman, the increasing flexibility in what kinds of attributes or activities *can* be processed as masculine, with increasing maturity, seems fully to account for the fact that so many "gender-disturbed" (effeminate) little boys manage to grow up into "healthy" (masculine) men, albeit after the phase where their sexuality has differentiated as gay.

Or rather, it *almost* fully accounts for it. There is a residue of mystery, resurfacing at several points in the book, about why most gay men turn out so resilient—about how they even survive—given the profound initial deficit of "masculine self-regard" characteristic of many proto-gay childhoods, and the late and relatively superficial remediation of it that comes with increasing maturity. Given that "the virulence and chronicity of [social] stress [against it] puts homosexuality in a unique position in the human behavioral repertoire," how to account for "the fact that severe, persistent morbidity does not occur more frequently" among gay adolescents (RF, p. 205)? Friedman essentially throws up his hands at these moments. "A number of possible explanations arise, but one seems particularly likely to me: namely, that homosexuality is associated with some psychological mechanism, not understood or even studied to date, that protects the individual from diverse psychiatric disorders" (p. 236). It "might include mechanisms influencing ego resiliency, growth potential, and the capacity to form intimate relationships" (p. 205). And "it is possible that, for reasons that have not yet been well described, [gender-disturbed boys'] mechanisms for coping with anguish and adversity are unusually effective" (p. 201).

These are huge blank spaces to be left in what purports to be a developmental account of proto-gay children. But given that ego-syntonic consolidation for a boy can come only in the form of masculinity, given that masculinity can be conferred only by men (p. 20), and given that femininity, in a person with a penis, can represent nothing but deficit and disorder, the one explanation that could never be broached is that these mysterious skills of survival, filiation, and resistance could derive from a secure identification with the resource richness of a mother. Mothers, indeed, have nothing to contribute to this process of masculine validation, and women are reduced in the light of its urgency to a null set: any involvement in it by a woman is overinvolvement, any protectiveness is overprotectiveness, and, for instance, mothers "proud of their sons' nonviolent qualities" are manifesting unmistakable "family pathology" (p. 193).

For both Friedman and Green, then, the first, imperative developmental task of a male child or his parents and caretakers is to get a properly male Core Gender Identity in place as a basis for further and perhaps more flexible explorations of what it may be to be masculine—i.e., for a male person, to be *human*. Friedman is rather equivocal about whether this masculine CGI necessarily entails any particular content, or whether it is an almost purely formal, preconditional differentiation that, once firmly in place, can cover an almost infinite range of behaviors and attitudes. He certainly does not see a necessary connection between masculinity and any scapegoating of male homosexuality; since ego psychology treats the development of male heterosexuality as non-problematical after adolescence, as not involving the suppression of any homosexual or bisexual possibility (pp. 263–67), and therefore as com-

pletely unimplicated with homosexual panic (p. 178), it seems merely an unfortunate, perhaps rectifiable misunderstanding that for a proto-gay child to identify "masculinely" might involve his identification with his own erasure.

The renaturalization and enforcement of gender assignment is not the worst news about the new psychiatry of gay acceptance, however. The worst is that it not only fails to offer, but seems conceptually incapable of offering, even the slightest resistance to the wish endemic in the culture surrounding and supporting it: the wish that gay people *not exist*. There are many people in the worlds we inhabit, and these psychiatrists are unmistakably among them, who have a strong interest in the dignified treatment of any gay people who may happen already to exist. But the number of persons or institutions by whom the existence of gay people is treated as a precious desideratum, a needed condition of life, is small. The presiding asymmetry of value assignment between hetero and homo goes unchallenged everywhere: advice on how to help your kids turn out gay, not to mention your students, your parishioners, your therapy clients, or your military subordinates, is less ubiquitous than you might think. On the other hand, the scope of institutions whose programmatic undertaking is to prevent the development of gay people is unimaginably large. There is no major institutionalized discourse that offers a firm resistance to that undertaking: in the United States, at any rate, most sites of the state, the military, education, law, penal institutions, the church, medicine, and mass culture enforce it all but unquestioningly, and with little hesitation at even the recourse to invasive violence.

These books, and the associated therapeutic strategies and institutions, are not about invasive violence. What they are about is a train of squalid lies. The overarching lie is the lie that they are predicated on anything but the therapists' disavowed desire for a nongay outcome. Friedman, for instance, speculates wistfully that—with proper therapeutic intervention—the sexual orientation of one gay man whom he describes as quite healthy might conceivably (not have *been changed* but) "have shifted *on its own*" (Friedman's italics) : a speculation, he artlessly remarks, "not value-laden with regard to sexual orientation" (p. 212). Green's book, composed largely of interview transcripts, is a tissue of his lies to children about their parents' motives for bringing them in. (It was "not to prevent you from becoming homosexual," he tells one young man who had been subjected to behavior modification, "it was because you were unhappy" (RG, p. 318); but later on the very same page, he unself-consciously confirms to his trusted reader that "parents of sons who entered therapy were . . . worried that the cross-gender behavior portended problems with later sexuality.") He encourages predominantly gay young men to "reassure" their parents that they are "bisexual" ("Tell him just enough so he feels better" [RG, p. 207]) and to consider favorably the option of marrying and keeping their wives in the dark about their sexual activities (p. 205). He lies to himself and to us in encouraging patients to lie to him. In a series of interviews with Kyle, for instance, the boy subjected to behavioral therapy, Green reports him as saying that he is unusually withdrawn—" 'I suppose I've been overly sensitive when guys look at me or something ever since I can remember, you know, after my mom told me why I have to go to UCLA because they were afraid I'd turn into a homosexual' " (p. 307); as saying that homosexuality "is pretty bad, and I don't think they should be around to influence children. . . . I don't think they should be hurt by society or anything like that—especially in New York. You have them who are into leather and stuff like that. I mean, I think that is really sick, and I think that maybe they should be put away" (p. 307); as saying that he wants to commit violence on men who look at him (p. 307); and as saying that if he had a child like himself, he "would take him where he would be helped" (p. 317). The very image of serene self-acceptance?

Green's summary:

> Opponents of therapy have argued that intervention underscores the child's "deviance," renders him ashamed of who he is, and makes him suppress his "true self." Data on psychological tests do not support this contention; nor does the content of clinical interviews. The boys look back favorably on treatment. They would endorse such intervention if they were the father of a "feminine" boy. Their reason is to reduce childhood conflict and social stigma. Therapy with these boys appeared to accomplish this. (p. 319)

Consistent with this, Green is obscenely eager to convince parents that their hatred and rage at their effeminate sons is really only a desire to protect them from peer-group cruelty—even when the parents name *their* own feelings as hatred and

rage (pp. 391–92). Even when fully one-quarter of parents of gay sons are so interested in protecting them from social cruelty that, when the boys fail to change, their parents kick them out on the street! Green is withering about mothers who display any tolerance of their sons' cross-gender behavior (pp. 373–75). In fact, his bottom-line identifications as a clinician actually seem to lie with the enforcing peer group: he refers approvingly at one point to "therapy, be it formal (delivered by paid professionals) or informal (delivered by the peer group and the larger society via teasing and sex-role standards)" (p. 388).

Referring blandly on one page to "psychological intervention directed at increasing [effeminate boys'] comfort with being male" (p. 259), Green says much more candidly on the next page, "the rights of parents to oversee the development of children is a long-established principle. Who is to dictate that parents may not try to raise their children in a manner that maximizes the possibility of a heterosexual outcome?" (p. 260). Who indeed—if the members of this profession can't stop seeing the prevention of gay people as an ethical use of their skills?

Even outside the mental health professions and within more authentically gay-affirmative discourses, the theoretical space for supporting gay development is, as I've pointed out in the introduction to *Epistemology of the Closet*, narrow. Constructivist arguments have tended to keep hands off the experience of gay and proto-gay kids. For gay and gay-loving people, even though the space of cultural malleability is the only conceivable theater for our effective politics, every step of this constructivist nature/culture argument holds danger: the danger of the difficulty of intervening in the seemingly natural trajectory from identifying a place of cultural malleability, to inventing an ethical or therapeutic mandate for cultural manipulation, to the overarching, hygienic Western fantasy of a world without any more homosexuals in it.

That's one set of dangers, and it is as against them, as I've argued, that essentialist and biologizing understandings of sexual identity accrue a certain gravity. The resistance that seems to be offered by conceptualizing an unalterably *homosexual body*, to the social-engineering momentum apparently built into every one of the human sciences of the West, can reassure profoundly. At the same time, however, in the postmodern era it is becoming increasingly problematical to assume that grounding an identity in biology or "essential nature" is a stable way of insulating it from societal interference. If anything, the gestalt of assumptions that undergirds nature/nurture debates may be in process of direct reversal. Increasingly it is the conjecture that a particular trait is genetically or biologically based, *not* that it is "only cultural," that seems to trigger an estrus of manipulative fantasy in the technological institutions of the culture. A relative depressiveness about the efficacy of social-engineering techniques, a high mania about biological control: the Cartesian bipolar psychosis that always underlay the nature/nurture debates has switched its polar assignments without surrendering a bit of its hold over the collective life. And in this unstable context, the dependence on a specified *homosexual body* to offer resistance to any gay-eradicating momentum is tremblingly vulnerable. AIDS, though it is used to proffer every single day to the news-consuming public the crystallized vision of a world after the homosexual, could never by itself bring about such a world. What whets these fantasies more dangerously, because more blandly, is the presentation, often in ostensibly or authentically gay-affirmative contexts, of biologically based "explanations" for deviant behavior that are absolutely invariably couched in terms of "excess," "deficiency," or "imbalance"—whether in the hormones, in the genetic material, or, as is currently fashionable, in the fetal endocrine environment. If I had ever, in any medium, seen any researcher or popularizer refer even once to any supposed gay-producing circumstance as the *proper* hormone balance, or the *conducive* endocrine environment, for gay generation, I would be less chilled by the breezes of all this technological confidence. As things are, a medicalized dream of the prevention of gay bodies seems to be the less visible, far more respectable underside of the AIDS-fueled public dream of their extirpation.

In this unstable balance of assumptions between nature and culture, at any rate, under the overarching, relatively unchallenged aegis of a culture's desire that gay people *not be*, there is no unthreatened, unthreatening theoretical home for a concept of gay and lesbian origins. What the books I have been discussing, and the institutions to which they are attached, demonstrate is that the wish for the dignified treatment of already-gay people is necessarily destined to turn into either trivializing apologetics or, much worse, a silkily camouflaged complicity in oppression—in the absence of a strong, explicit,

*erotically invested* affirmation of some people's felt desire or need that there be gay people in the immediate world.

## NOTES

"How to Bring Your Kids Up Gay" was written in 1989 for a Modern Language Association panel. Jack Cameron pointed me in the direction of the texts discussed here, and Cindy Patton fortified my resistance to them.

1. This information comes from reports in the *New York Native*, 23 September 1989, pp. 9–10; 13 November 1989, p. 14; 27 November 1989, p. 7.

2. A particularly illuminating overview of psychoanalytic approaches to male homosexuality is available in Kenneth Lewes, *The Psychoanalytic Theory of Male Homosexuality* (New York: Penguin/NAL/Meridian, 1989).

3. Richard C. Friedman, *Male Homosexuality: A Contemporary Psychoanalytic Perspective* (New Haven, Conn.: Yale University Press, 1988). All citations will appear in parentheses in the text with RF.

4. Richard Green, *The "Sissy Boy Syndrome" and the Development of Homosexuality* (New Haven, Conn.: Yale University Press, 1987). Citations will appear in the text with RG.

5. It is worth noting that the gay men Friedman admires always have completely discretionary control over everyone else's knowledge of their sexuality; no sense that others may have their own intuitions that they are gay; no sense of physical effeminacy; no visible participation in gay (physical, cultural, sartorial) semiotics or community. For many contemporary gay people, such an existence would be impossible; for a great many, it would seem starvingly impoverished in terms of culture, community, and meaning.

6. *Diagnostic and Statistical Manual of Mental Disorders* 3d ed. (Washington, D.C.: American Psychiatric Association, 1980), pp. 265–66.

7. The exception to this generalization is Lawrence Mass, whose *Dialogues of the Sexual Revolution*, vol. I, *Homosexuality and Sexuality* (New York: Harrington Park Press, 1990) collects a decade's worth of interviews with psychiatrists and sex researchers, originally conducted for and published in the gay press. In these often illuminating interviews, a number of Mass's questions are asked under the premise that "American psychiatry is simply engaged in a long, subtle process of reconceptualizing homosexuality as a mental illness with another name—the 'gender identity disorder of childhood' " (p. 214).

8. That relegation may be diminishing as, in many places, "queer" politics come to overlap and/or compete with "gay" politics. Part of what I understand to be the exciting charge of the very word "queer" is that it embraces, instead of repudiating, what have for many of us been formative childhood experiences of difference and stigmatization.

9. For descriptions of this literature, see Friedman, *Male Homosexuality*, pp. 33–48, and Green, *The "Sissy Boy, Syndrome"*, pp 70–390. The most credible of these studies from a gay-affirmative standpoint would be A. P. Bell, M. S. Weinberg, and S. K. Hammersmith, *Sexual Preference: Its Development in Men and Women* (Bloomington: Indiana University Press, 1981), which concludes: "Childhood Gender Nonconformity turned out to be more strongly connected to adult homosexuality than was any other variable in the study" (p. 80).

10. Priding himself on his interdisciplinarity, moreover, he is much taken with recent neuroendocrinological work suggesting that prenatal stress on the mother may affect structuration of the fetal brain in such a way that hormonal cues to the child as late as adolescence may be processed differen-

tially. His treatment of these data as data is neither very responsible (e.g., problematical results that point only to "hypothetical differences" in one chapter [p. 24] have been silently upgraded to positive "knowledge" two chapters later [p. 51]) nor very impartial (for instance, the conditions hypothesized as conducing to gay development are invariably referred to as inadequate androgenization [p. 14], a *deficit* [p. 15], etc.). But his infatuation with this model does have two useful effects. First, it seems to generate by direct analogy this further series of two-phase narratives about psychic development, narratives that discriminate between the circumstances under which a particular psychic structure is organized and those under which it is *activated*, that may turn out to enable some new sinuosities for other, more gay-embracing and pluralist projects of developmental narration. (This analogical process is made explicit on pp. 241–45.) And second, it goes a long way toward detotalizing, demystifying, and narrativizing in a recognizable way any reader's sense of the threat (the promise?) presented by a supposed neurobiological vision of the already-gay male body.

# | 28 |

# *Studying the Biology of Sexual Orientation Has Political Fallout*

Neurobiologist Simon LeVay didn't anticipate political fallout when he published his 1991 study indicating that a tiny segment of the hypothalamus believed to regulate sexual activity is smaller in homosexual men than in heterosexuals.

Then the Salk Institute researcher began fielding questions from reporters asking what impact his work would have on gay rights.

"I hadn't really thought about how it would be interpreted or the social consequences it would

have," says Dr. LeVay, who has since left the institute in La Jolla, Calif., to actively espouse gay rights. He formed a gay-studies school in West Hollywood, works the lecture circuit and rides in gay-pride parades.

Science doesn't operate in a vacuum—particularly when it comes to explaining homosexuality. Far from "rescuing homosexuality from the

*Wall Street Journal*, August 12, 1993, pp. 1+.

claws of a religious or political environment to a medically-safe environment"—as neurobiologist Heino Meyer-Bahlburg suggested at a recent seminar on the subject—the search for a cause of homosexuality has simply shifted an increasingly nasty debate to the nation's research laboratories.

## POLITICAL FODDER

Though they are far from conclusive, recent biological studies have become crucial political fodder for both gay-rights activists and their opponents. For example, last month's announcement of a National Cancer Institute study showing that some men may have inherited one or more genes that predispose them to homosexuality has interpretations for both sides. "Some people may say to me, 'Your research is really pro-gay,'" says Dean Hamer, a molecular biologist who led the genetics study. "But others may say that it proves homosexuality is a genetic disease like alcoholism."

It is hardly the first time science has had to deal with political and social ramifications, from the fury over creationism vs. evolution in the Scopes monkey trial of 1925, to the bitter debate over the French "morning-after" abortion pill, RU-486.

But most scientists studying sexual orientation say they are uneasy with this commingling of politics and research. "I've come to the realization that it's very difficult to predict what will be the political impact of anything that happens in the world, much less any particular scientific finding," says Dr. Hamer.

## PROCESS AT RISK

The politics can get overwhelming at times, threatening to impinge on the scientific process. Scientists who pour cold water on the biological-cause theories have found themselves scolded by gay-rights activists. "I'm told my criticism is not politically correct," says William Byne, a New York psychiatrist and former neurobiologist who questions the latest scientific findings, primarily because they haven't been replicated. "What they're saying, therefore, is that I should subjugate scientific rigor to political expediency."

The discovery of a definitive biological cause of homosexuality could go a long way toward advancing the gay-rights cause. If homosexuality were found to be an immutable trait, like skin color, then laws criminalizing homosexual sex

might be overturned. A Hawaii supreme-court judge recently noted that a biological basis for homosexuality could tip the scales toward legalization of same-sex marriages. Job protection for homosexuals—the law in eight states—might be extended throughout the country.

Moreover, a biological link could do much to dispel the belief that people choose to be homosexual. Recent polls indicate Americans who think homosexuality isn't chosen are far more likely to favor gay rights than those who believe otherwise.

It is such shifts in public opinion that antihomosexual groups fear most. "If I were a gay-rights manager, I'd say, 'Guys, whatever we do, we have to make them believe we were born that way,'" says Paul Cameron, chairman of Family Research Institute Inc., a lobbying group whose slogan is "Scientists Defending Traditional Family Values." "If they can get a majority of Americans believing it, they're home free."

## DEARTH OF FUNDING

Until recently, fear of getting embroiled in the political battle put a lid on research. In 1982, Laura Allen was studying sex-linked brain differences in rats as a graduate student at UCLA, and she wanted to see if similar differences could be found in the brains of gay men. Her superior, Dr. Roger Gorski, told her to stick with rats. "I was not allowed to do that study because of the fear of controversy it would cause. Dr. Gorski told me, 'This could end your career,'" she says.

Despite the initial trepidation, Dr. Allen persisted. Last year, she and Dr. Gorski published a study showing that a structure connecting the left and right sides of the brain, called the anterior commissure, was 34 percent larger in the 30 gay men studied than in 30 heterosexual men. Ironically, "what hurt my career was not publishing my results right away," Dr. Allen says.

Sexual-orientation research, along with sex research in general, also has suffered from lack of funding. "Most of what's being done is by people paid to do other things, on smuggled time," says Richard Pillard, a professor of psychiatry at Boston University. His studies on gay twins, with research partner J. Michael Bailey of Northwestern University's department of psychology, were largely funded "on a shoestring" by a combination of money from Northwestern and an $8,000 loan.

"It's clear that sex research is regarded with great suspicion by at least some branches of the government," Dr. Pillard says.

"When you're dealing with something as socially significant as homosexuality, you have the increased responsibility to consider the public reaction to what you're announcing," says Thomas Murray, director of the Center for Biomedical Ethics at Case Western Reserve University in Cleveland, and an ethics adviser on the Human Genome Project.

## ACCUSATIONS OF BIAS

Despite Dr. Hamer's efforts, though, conservative groups opposed to homosexuality have blasted him. They point to possible holes in the study and accuse the researchers of bias in their statements that male homosexuality is "a normal variation in human behavior."

"Their literature review is entirely pro-homosexual," says the Family Research Institute's Dr. Cameron, who faults the researchers for "not including any major discussion of the hypothesis of recruitment"—the belief that gays and lesbians "recruit" heterosexuals into a life of homosexuality. He also complains that the researchers ignored "the traditional psychological model of disturbed families producing more homosexuals." (The American Psychiatric Association removed homosexuality from its list of disorders in 1973.)

Dr. LeVay readily acknowledges that as a gay man, "I was very interested in the question of what makes people gay," although he says his study wasn't done to advance gay rights.

Boston University's Dr. Pillard, who also is homosexual, thinks the criticism about biases is bunk. "What does a bias mean? Do they think we're altering the data?" he asks regarding his studies that found a 52 percent correlation for homosexuality between sets of identical male twins and a 48 percent correlation between female identical twins.

Dr. Hamer's work is the first of the recent sexual-orientation studies to receive federal funding, but that is mainly because it is part of a larger study of certain types of cancer in gay men who test positive for HIV, the virus that causes acquired immune deficiency syndrome. And the go-ahead for the study went all the way to the Department of Health and Human Services because officials at the National Institutes of Health were concerned it would be "potentially controversial," Dr. Hamer says.

"It's common for one of the institutes of the NIH, if they have something unusual or contro-versial, to pass that information up the line," acknowledges Bill Grigg, spokesman for HHS's U.S. Public Health Service arm. "And if a big story may come up out of it, it might even be mentioned to the White House."

Such skittishness is understandable, given the controversy that erupted when Dr. LeVay published his research about the hypothalamus two years ago. Gay-rights leaders were quick to tout the study as proof that homosexuality isn't a choice, while cautioning against the possible use of the findings to somehow "cure" homosexuals.

Critics zeroed in on the fact that Dr. LeVay is homosexual, suggesting that he may have been biased. Questions also were raised whether the differences in brain structure might have been due to the ravages of AIDS, since the 19 gay men whose brains were studied all had died from the disease. (Dr. LeVay says that is unlikely.) Some religious fundamentalists even suggested that homosexual activity somehow could have caused the structural differences.

To mitigate a similar frenzy over his genetic study, Dr. Hamer says he sought the advice of an advisory committee of two bioethicists, a Presbyterian minister, a lawyer, a member of the Federation of Parents and Friends of Lesbians and Gays and a representative of the NIH director's office. He asked them "how to present the results to the general press in a way that wouldn't be sensationalist or misleading or cause people undue fears."

## WRANGLING OVER WORDS

Even the very words used in scientific language come up for political interpretation these days when discussing homosexuality. Take, for example, the flare-up at the American Psychiatric Association's annual convention in May, where biologists in one panel discussion were explaining how certain hormonal deficiencies and prenatal stresses could be linked to homosexuality.

"I'd like not to hear the words 'deficiency' or 'distress' used in discussing hormones," complained audience member James Krajeski, a San Francisco psychiatrist. "We need to move away from pathological models where the assumption is that homosexuality is a negative outcome."

The biologists insisted that the terms are strictly scientific. "I see nothing pejorative," said Walter Miller, a pediatrician lecturing about congenital adrenal hyperplasia, a disorder where genetic females develop male genitals, and which may provide some hints about hormones and homosexuality. "This is science. The interpretation and assignment of value judgments is something society can do."

With genetic and biological research now fueling gay-rights debates, antihomosexual groups have realized the importance of a scientific component to their arguments. "We spent $30,000 doing focus groups, and found that our public wasn't able to articulate what was wrong with homosexuality, other than to say it was 'evil,' " says the Rev. Lou Sheldon of the Traditional Values Coalition. "They couldn't speak about it from the public-health risks standpoint. All they could say was, 'The Bible says . . . ' "

Opponents of homosexuality therefore have been quick to cite such writings as those by Dr. Byne, the New York psychiatrist, to bolster their claims that homosexuality is a sinful, chosen behavior. Dr. Byne contends that while studies showing a biological link to homosexuality have gotten lots of attention, those that show no link get buried on the back pages if they are reported at all. "The problem is that negative replication studies tend to go unheeded," he says. "For example, there are 25 studies looking at testosterone levels in gay men. Three found lower levels, two found higher levels, 20 found no difference. But for decades, the predominant belief was that homosexuality was caused by low testosterone levels."

Dr. Cameron of the Family Research Institute is one who makes extensive use of Dr. Byne's work to support his own views of homosexuality. Dr. Cameron is the author of such writings as a pamphlet called "Medical Consequences of What Homosexuals Do," which purports to give information about gay men's sexual practices, calling them "a medical horror story."

Dr. Cameron was dropped from the American Psychological Association in 1983 for allegedly violating the preamble of the APA's code of ethics with his antihomosexual views. He says he resigned, but agrees that the split was related to his views on homosexuality.

As the man in the middle, Dr. Byne says being quoted by antihomosexual groups irks him as much as the criticism he gets from gay-rights groups. "They have picked up on my work arguing against biological causation, and they have interpreted it as arguing for choice," he says. "Rejecting the idea that there's a simple biological cause is not arguing for choice." He says he also has "taken a lot of heat from gay scientists doing biological research in this area. They say I have to take responsibility for the misuse of my work."

Their opponents' interest in science has gay-rights activists nervous that any new biological data will be turned against them. They ask: Couldn't a prenatal test be developed to determine a child's predisposition to homosexuality?

"That certainly is a possibility," says UCLA's Dr. Allen. "If a gay gene is isolated, then maybe amniocentesis could be used to identify the genetic composition of the unborn baby."

That, and the implication that a pregnancy could be terminated based on such information, is something that weighs heavily on the minds of scientists in the field. "We have an obligation to make sure we don't do things that could be used to harm people," Dr. Hamer says.

But he and others say they are hopeful that their research will one day lead to a more level-headed debate over sexual orientation. "I'm perfectly aware there are many people who are not interested in the facts, who have their own deeply-held beliefs, which I respect, that will not be swayed by science," Dr. Hamer says. "But I'm optimistic that the majority of Americans are willing to listen to the facts."

# | 29 |

## Are Gay Men Born That Way?

Gay men can't win. Lesbians can't play. Bisexuals—well, hey, they don't exist. Yet there is a seemingly endless fascination with figuring out the "causes" of homosexuality. It just never ends. (Remember the Sissy Boy Syndrome and hormonal studies of recent years past? Well, there's at least a 100-year history of such studies.) And unlike really important news, the mainstream straight media can't get enough of it. The "news" of what causes homosexuality does become important, however, because of how gay people are portrayed; more than different, they are congenital defects. Never has there been such a quest to locate in the body what causes the condition of heterosexuality.

The latest riptide came in August 1991, in a study of the hypothalami of gay men; in its wake, came a study of gay twins a couple of months later. Both studies were conducted by gay men, which the press used to ward off charges of homophobia in both coverage of the stories and their fundamental underlying inquiries.

First, hard-wired homosexuality. Neuroanatomist Simon LeVay, a scientist with the Salk Institute in La Jolla, California, concerned himself with four particular nuclei (called INAH 1,2,3 and 4) in the hypothalamus, a grape-sized region in the brain. The nuclei under consideration are about the size of a grain of sand. Previous studies allegedly demonstrated that two small groups of the neurons in the nuclei are larger in men than women. LeVay compared the nuclei of 41 persons: 18 homosexuals and one bisexual who had so declared themselves before death, all of whom died of AIDS; 16 "presumed" (the word is his) heterosexuals, 6 who died of AIDS, 10 who died of other causes; and 9 "presumed" heterosexual women, one who died of AIDS. LeVay found no significant differences in three of the nuclei, but he did find differences between the supposed straight men and straight women and the supposed straight men and homosexual men with respect to nucleus INAH 3: in LeVay's words, it exhibited dimorphism, that is different properties in the same species, here, the scattering of cells. The cells in the "straight" INAH 3 nuclei were spread out over a larger area than those in the "gay" and "female" nuclei. INAH 3 was presumed to be the nucleus that correlated to sexual orientation.

LeVay concludes his study by humbly stating: "The discovery that a nucleus differs in size between heterosexual and homosexual men illustrates that sexual orientation in humans is amenable to study at the biological level. Further interpretation of the results must be considered speculative. In particular, the results do not allow one to decide if the size of INAH 3 in an individual is the cause or consequence of sexual orientation . . ." (*Science*, Vol. 253, August 30, 1991).

Which is worse to contemplate, that you were born different or that the punishment for acting on your desires will be a scarlet letter in your brain? And if you chose celibacy because the second prospect is too much to bear, where would that place you in the scheme of things? Does it matter if you are a Kinsey 6 (exclusively homosexual fantasies and practices) or a Kinsey 3? These are but a few questions the study raises.

The media had a field day with the finding, aided by *Science*'s own marketing efforts. In addition to giving LeVay top billing in the issue's news release, editors chose to supplement LeVay's piece with a "News and Comment" on the study and stories on gender differences and the brain.

*Z Magazine*, December 1992, pp. 42–46.

However, the American Association for the Advancement of Science, which publishes *Science*, did not bother to send its release or advance sheets of the article to the gay press for reporting or comment; the straight press received such materials and reported on the study even before subscribers had received it (the publication is not available at newsstands). Thus, throughout the coverage, the gay community was represented as the "other"; it could not represent itself. A perhaps fitting coincidence is that the story was out just days after psychoanalyst Irving Bieber died (an observation I owe to John Mitzel). Bieber was a leading advocate of psychoanalytic treatments to cure homosexuality. About his study, LeVay was quoted in the *Times* saying, "It's not just the province of the psychologists and psychoanalysts anymore."

Emblazoned atop its logotype, the September 9, 1991 issue of *Time* asked, "Are Gay Men Born That Way?" Perhaps editors really wanted to ask, "Are gay men born *that* way?" *Time* typified the mainstream press' sensationalist coverage of Dr. LeVay's study. The media not only discussed whether biology is destiny but also delved into, sometimes unknowingly, the contested terrain of nature/nurture, nature/culture and sex/gender. The same press that a week earlier had decried as fascistic the Soviet Union's brain studies of long-dead geniuses celebrated a brain study of people who died of AIDS.

The representation of gay men through photographs, not words, in the *Time* article is telling. In the table of contents appears a picture of two white men holding hands. Both have blond hair, mustaches, the same muscular build. Both are sporting T-shirts that say "Mr. Right" and both are wearing white shorts. In a picture accompanying the article are two white men, one with his arm around the other. Both are balding with closely cropped beards and both are wearing Keith Haring T-shirts. The message is not that all gay men are "clones," for surely the two pairs do not look alike. Rather, the message is that gay men seek partners that mirror themselves; they are twins of sorts—the biological proof exists. But is their sameness the result of deliberative acts (grooming, clothing) or the result of biology? The result of nature or (gay) culture? Moreover, their state, or perhaps "condition," is depicted as infantile, dressed identically as parents suit up toddler twins. The message is that gay men are the inverse of heterosexuals, for what heterosexual couple could ever look so much alike?

Contrast this depiction of potential subjects of the study with how LeVay himself was portrayed in the popular media. Although he works with tiny slices of brain tissue, photographs typically showed LeVay holding an entire unmutilated human brain, probing it with an instrument, a scientist-god divining the mysteries of the brain, and therefore humanity itself. Is this because it would be too boring if he was shown as he actually is, peering through a microscope at stained tissue samples? Would readers be incredulous that such methods could unlock the secrets of sexuality?

How about fish? The *New York Times* next featured a story on November 12, 1991 about "macho fish."—a study by neurobiologist Dr. Russell Fernald allegedly proving that in aggressive male fish "brain cells in the hypothalamus that allow the fish to mate are six to eight times larger than are equivalent cells in mild-mannered males with no social clout." Then came the twin study (adding the "reality" of science to *Time's* conception of gay couples) conducted by Dr. J. Michael Bailey of Northwestern University and Dr. Richard Pillard of Boston University School of General Medicine and published in the December 1991 issue of the *Archives of General Psychiatry*. Pillard and Bailey studied the rates of homosexuality in 167 identical and nonidentical twin brothers of gay men, as well as adoptive brothers of gay men. They found that 52 percent of the identical twin brothers were gay, as against 22 percent of the nonidentical twins and 1 percent of the adoptive, genetically unrelated brothers.

The obvious question here is whether a more persuasive study, fully discounting any social factors, would demonstrate that a majority of twins separated at birth are both gay. (Dr. Pillard has publicly stated that since there is no family environment that specifically supports being gay, the argument that they were only measuring familiality can be discounted.)

This too, was picked up by the national media, with banner headlines proclaiming such enlightening facts as "Gay Men in Twin Study" or "Genes Linked to Being Gay," but it didn't receive quite the same play as the brain study. Most often, it was used to buttress LeVay's findings. Moreover, the notion that the human animal has essential tendencies, independent of prevailing social factors and located in the body, has been frequently recycled by the media and politicians to keep women at bay. With feminist anger mounting anew by events this year, *Time* saw fit in its January 20, 1992 cover story to effectively blame women for their problems, or at least dampen their spirit to organize politically. Who can fight biology to try and control one's destiny? Asked and answered by *Time*: "Why Are Men and Women Different? It Isn't Just Upbringing. New Studies Show They are Born That Way." On the cover is a photograph of a little girl in a dress watching a little boy make a muscle.

Amonth later came *Newsweek*, again with the gay question, although one would have thought the news was old by then. The February 24, 1992 cover featured a plastic-looking blond and blue-eyed Aryan infant. "Is This Child Gay? Born or Bred: The Origins of Homosexuality." The article of course doesn't answer the question because it can't be answered. But it leaves little doubt for the reader that gay people are *queer*. One of two lesbians pictured is lying on her bed, cuddling a live pig! Given reports that some health clinics have been inundated with calls from straight parents-to-be wanting to know if, in light of LeVay's study, their fetus could be "tested" for gayness and possibly aborted, the depiction of the baby was manipulative at best.

The suggestion of genetic engineering wasn't just made by paranoid parents. The Moonie-owned *Washington Times*, under the headline "Scientist links brain anomaly, homosexuality" (if women and gay men have similar brains, maybe it's straight men, a relative minority, that are the anomaly) quoted none other than Kevin Klivington, assistant to the president of the Salk Institute as saying, "It's far out. . . . But since the cluster of cells is smaller in homosexuals, you could envision a transplant of additional cells into the area [to turn a homosexual into a heterosexual]." Klivington appears to misread the study, since LeVay specifically states "no attempt was made to measure cell number or density." LeVay only showed that the *spacing* of the cells is over a different size area. But accuracy doesn't much matter, either to the press or to LeVay, for that matter.

I asked LeVay whether he thought results of his study were misconstrued or blown out of proportion by commentators who interpreted them as tending to prove an innate biological correlate to homosexuality. His response was equivocal, even contradictory at times, but ultimately approving of such an interpretation. While he was forthright about the shortcomings of his study, even stating, "I was embarrassed about having to simplify things down to 19 of this and 16 of that as if that's how men come," he added, "The question that people are really interested in is

what causes people to be gay or straight which is not anything one could surmise from the article. It only opened up a new avenue [of research]. But still, I have to say that what we know from work on minds is that we would expect homosexuality to have arisen early in life and that it is tied to events in fetal or early life and not later. The work tends to support the idea that it is not a matter of socialization."

Others would disagree. Notes Anne Fausto-Sterling, Professor of Medical Science at Brown University and author *of Myths of Gender: Biological Theories About Women and Men*, "I am bothered by a number of technical aspects of the article. These include (1) the fact that nothing is known about the actual sexual behavior of the supposedly straight men used in the study, (2) that there were only six straight and no gay women in the study, (3) that the range of sizes found for the special "sexuality" area of the brain almost completely overlapped in the gay and straight samples and (4) that all of the gay men in the study died of AIDS, a disease known to cause brain degeneration."

LeVay placed the one bisexual man in the study in the "gay group." LeVay's assumption that his preference must be men may have a sexist element to it or it may not. There are millions of men, married to women, who regularly seek out sex with other men. Lots have sex with their wives too. Are they gay? Isn't their assumed heterosexuality socially constructed? What of the high percentage of "otherwise straight" men in prison who engage in sex with other men during the period of their incarceration, but not after? What about cross-cultural differences, such as initiation rites involving same-sex sexual practices?

The point is that such studies failed to account for the fluidity and complexity of sexuality. And science, which prides itself on dispassionate research in the search for "objective truths" gets sloppy, using anecdotal evidence when dealing with issues of sexuality. Notes historian of sexuality Jennifer Terry, co-editor (with Jacqueline Urla) of the forthcoming *Deviant Bodies: Scientific Constructions of Pathologized Subjects*, "LeVay's very rough and ready classifications seem shocking when they come from the scientific world where precision is the name of the game, and yet this way of dealing with social variables of sexuality is all too common among natural scientists even when they are gay and should know better. LeVay, like many other scientists working on matters related to sexuality, went to considerable lengths to measure an area of the brain where 'significant' differences between presumably heterosexual and homosexual men are no larger than a grain of sand. But he used no precision in his measurement of social variables—things as analytically complex as sexual orientation, sexual desire and gender identification. Typically, these social variables are never measured by biological scientists; instead, like LeVay, they substitute simple folk understandings for complex analytical constructs and systems. And these folk understandings tend to be crystallizations of dominant ideology regarding sex and sexuality."

Adds Fausto-Sterling, "The study's rationale confuses sexuality with gender roles, placing both on a single continuum. Would, for example, a stereotypically masculine homosexual (i.e., a football player) be expected to have a feminine brain? In fact, this formulation ignores current work in animal behavior which suggests that masculinity and femininity are not mutually exclusive."

LeVay fails to acknowledge a host of studies and experiments performed on homosexuals that have proven fatally flawed. Even *Science* has published studies with complicity that could not be duplicated relating to purported anatomical differences between men and women and homosexuals and heterosexuals. Writes Dr. William M. Byne (Letters, *New York Times*, September 19, 1991), "[I]n recent years *Science* has published provocative, sexually and politically charged studies that enjoyed widespread news media coverage and acceptance by the scientific community before being discredited . . . (1) A study claiming to demonstrate a sex difference in the splenium, a portion of the brain connecting its two halves (*Science*, No. 216, pages 1431–32, 1982). Owing to premature acceptance of this "finding"— popularly interpreted as the biological explanation for gender differences in social roles, aptitudes and achievements—it is entrenched in the scientific literature, where it is unlikely to be dislodged for years. Studies published by at least six independent research groups subsequently failed to detect the reported sex difference. (2) A claim that a hormonal test could distinguish between homosexual and heterosexual men (*Science*, No. 225, pages 1496–99, 1984) . . . also failed duplication . . ."

The harmful and anti-intellectual yen for constructing difference (from the dominant culture, from the elites) at the biological level is an old one. There is a long and baneful history of brain studies on politically marginalized groups, women and Blacks in particular. But even those, such as Stephen Jay Gould, who highlighted the ignominious history of scientific racism and biological determinism in his 1981 book *The Mismeasure of Man*, cautiously responded to the issue of biological destiny for homosexuality. When I asked him to comment on LeVay's study, he replied, "No comment. I am not a brain scientist," but added, "The notion itself is not implausible, although there is a problem with all biological argumentation [because it has so often proven wrong], but there can be overuse of social explanations which swing the pendulum too far the other way." Gould emphasizes in his work that science is a creative, socially embedded process and that scientists, often unintentionally, were prejudicially motivated in their decisions about what to study, their methodology, and interpretations of results. What motivated Richard Pillard and Simon LeVay? Foremost that they are gay.

Pillard asked himself, "Does being gay run in families? It runs in my family. I have a lesbian daughter, a lesbian sister, a gay brother, a father who I have reason to think was more than accidentally gay, and so on." To Pillard's credit, he asks a question inclusive of straight people. "The big question is, 'How does sexual orientation unfold in human beings?' We sort of don't notice it because most of society just takes being straight for granted: men and women sort of grow up being attracted to each other. How does it happen? Well, they just learn; like the way we learn the multiplication tables, it just comes about. Society invests in that being how it happens. But really, we don't know how it happens."

LeVay told me, "I've always been intensely curious about my sexuality and I always intended to work on this issue but I couldn't until other researchers studied it too. To me, it seemed the most natural thing to do. Just because some see it as stereotyping, pigeon holing or saying there's some deficiency, I don't think it is being taken that way. Historically, there were studies of male-female differences [by] researchers who were thought to be prejudicial [against women] who said there were intrinsic differences [between the sexes], but now, there is no question anymore that there are differences between males and females at [the level of the brain], but you must preface that by saying there is an overlap both ways with both sexes. Society as a whole is smart enough to assimilate these ideas and while there are intrinsic differences, not to pigeon hole . . . I don't think gays and lesbians have any reason to be threatened by findings or differences or causes."

LeVay's historical reference is significant, for some reasons already mentioned. He also naively fails to acknowledge, to cite but one example, the fate of Magnus Hirschfeld and the Scientific Humanitarian Committee in Germany who, in 1908, compiled data on homosexuals in the hopes of influencing efforts to decriminalize sodomy. Hirschfeld, too, believed that homosexuality was a function of biology. When the Nazi's came to power, they ransacked and burned his institute. But they remembered what he said about locating difference in the body. The rest is history.

Can science ever be immune from experiments conceived out of prejudices and stereotypes, conscious or not? (Which is not to suggest that it cannot in discrete areas identify and locate verifiable phenomena in nature.) I await the study that says lesbians have a region of the hypothalamus that resembles straight men and I would not be surprised if, at this very moment, some scientist somewhere is studying brains of deceased Asians to see if they have an enlarged "math region" of the brain.

The studies themselves may be irrelevant, compared to their social implications; compared to why the straight cultural imagination is so enamored with making homosexuality a matter of genetics and why some gay people think it will kill the social ill of homophobia. The reactions are connected. As long as straight people feel they have won a "genetic lottery," discrimination against gay people will persist. Consider the exchange on the Oprah Winfrey show of April 25, 1992 (the show was on gay and straight twins):

Oprah: "Do you think society will change if it were proven beyond a shadow of a doubt that you're born that way?"

Straight white male twin: "It would be easier . . . the acceptance, but you understand that people still don't accept Blacks and Hispanics and handicapped . . . Gays are right in there with them . . . people don't accept obese people."

(Chagrined) Oprah: "I forgot about that. Let's take a break."

(Another bright spot on the show was a straight mother asking Oprah, "I sometimes would like you Oprah to put on your panel nongay people and ask them how they got to be that way.")

LeVay's study spoke to his experience and those of many gay men, in his opinion. "Basically

I tend to sympathize with people who say this proves what I have always thought—that I was born that way. That it wasn't thought processes or interpersonal relationships later in life." He admitted that he is mostly in contact with "white, educated gay men" for such opinions and that it doesn't speak to the experiences of many gay men, lesbians, and bisexuals. But let's face it, his is regarded as the emblematic experience.

But challenging the essentialist construct of homosexuality is not to say that sexuality is necessarily volitional. When that light bulb goes off, it certainly seems hardwired. Explains Jennifer Terry, "I don't believe in any simple way that we 'choose' our sexual orientation . . . it has to do with how one negotiates consciously and unconsciously their surrounding cultural and historical condition. . . . We narrate our experiences of profound difference from heterosexuals through these amazing moments of awakened but prohibited bodily lust. In modern Western culture, which is obsessed with rationality, the body is contrasted with the mind as a place where 'involuntary' responses happen that may be irrational, mysterious, powerful and inexplicable. . . . I'm sympathetic to the strategic use of things like the LeVay study in order to say, 'Don't fuck with me. I'm not going to change and I feel good about this.' But that position does not have to rely on the body for its articulation."

Discussions of whether homosexuality is biologically determined are chock full of tension and emotion. It is the subject of fractious debate in gay social, political, academic, and legal circles. If nothing else, the controversy proves that disparate experiences—even conscious experiences separate and apart from Terry's more nuanced approach to the matter—of millions of gay people cannot be conflated into scattered cells in one region of the hypothalamus; for one thing, the "community" is hardly monolithic.

Most obviously ignored is the experience of bisexuals, often regarded as an enigma by both gays and straights. Bisexuals are rightfully angry at existing sexual politics and they are organizing. At OutWrite 1992, the third annual lesbian and gay writers conference, activists passed out flyers stating "WE'RE FED UP WITH BEING SET UP" referring to a recent cover story in Outlook magazine with the provocative title, "What do Bisexuals Want?"—"What do you think we want?" asked the flyer, "Anything different from what you want? We doubt it." They were also angered by a decision by 1993 March on Washington organizers to use the title "For Lesbian, Gay and Bi Equal Rights and Liberation" because "bisexual" sounds too—yes—sexual.

Many gay men and lesbians knew from early childhood that they were different, "queer." Others did not have an inkling of preference for the same sex until adulthood. The former group may find solace in studies such as LeVay's, because they may believe it will relieve them of the pressure to become heterosexual. The latter may be troubled by it, caught between their very different experience and perhaps some internalized homophobia that they do not wish to be viewed as a "defect" and yet not knowing how to connect their experience with the former group. The bridge is bigotry towards all gay people who "act" on it.

Many liberal straight people, like Oprah, and many gay people cited for comment in the mainstream press applauded these studies. The reactions are replete with happy expectancy of enhanced legal protections and greater tolerance. If sexuality is an immutable characteristic, then perhaps gay people won't be discriminated against, the reasoning goes. Cases of discrimination will be afforded heightened scrutiny like other "suspect" classes under a 14th Amendment equal protection analysis. The argument has been tried, and it's been largely unsuccessful. It also gets forced into a dichotomy of status versus conduct that once again reduces the complexity of sexual experience. If discrimination is not rational and rarely needs justification, why willingly give so much authority to science to define the debate?

Because attorneys on behalf of gay men and lesbians must craft legal arguments in an effort to win cases. And judges are often as intellectually lazy as journalists, whom they are no doubt influenced by (the most egregious example being the Second Circuit's decision two years ago banning begging on New York City subways in which the esteemed Court cited a Harris Poll on how commuters feel about beggars—since when are First Amendment rights decided by public opinion polls?). The challenge is how to fashion anti-discrimination arguments plausible in the eyes of the courts that embrace an identity politics not based on rigid identities.

There are gay people who think the study is totally irrelevant to their experience or to gay rights—and believe that nondiscrimination should be on moral grounds, not biological grounds (the wording is actually Gould's, however), or that they should be able to choose the object of their sexual desire in any consensual way they please, as others are free to choose the vehicle of their spirituality via religion, whichever one they choose. But Jerry Falwell also deems the study irrelevant; to Falwell, the mind, not the brain, has to do with homosexuality. Of course, his agenda is different. The irony of an unintended alliance is twofold—between gay people who believe they either choose their sexuality or those who believe they should be left alone to sleep with whomever they want, together with some scientists and scholars, who believe sexuality is a complex interactive social process—and the Falwells of the world.

Like feminism continuously having to reinvent itself because of the collective amnesia that afflicts politics in the U.S., so too, must gay liberation. Nowhere is this more clear than in the present debate. The gay community may never reach true consensus, but its take on biological determinism has often reflected either the movement's political demands at the time or the resultant backlash. Prior to the late 1960s-early 1970s gay liberation movement, the homophile movement of the 1950s deployed an assimilationist strategy, that homosexuals are "normal" productive members of society whose sexual orientation should be tolerated (despite the fact that Kinsey's 1948 study demonstrated the high incidence of "homosexual" experience among presumed heterosexuals). Then, the gay liberation movement, influenced by its activists' New Left politics, tested boundaries, arguing that everyone is potentially gay, but defining a very separate gay culture. The New Right, epitomized by Anita Bryant's Save Our Children campaign literally crusaded against gay rights with evangelical zeal. (And the last time there were major riots in California was in the spring of 1979, after an all-straight jury convicted Harvey Milk's assassin Dan White of the lesser charge of manslaughter). Faced with the Reagan reaction and the ascendancy of the Religious Right and the crisis of AIDS, the movement's sexual politics retreated a bit; its back was against the wall, friends were getting sick and dying and mainstream straight society said gay men got what they deserved. Despite ACT-UP's street-smart politics, much of the push for change was to be advanced largely in traditional political corridors: lobbying legislatures, trying cases and challenging bureaucratic intransigence, with one important caveat relevant here: gay white men who previously considered themselves relatively privileged began to question the medical and scientific establishment, realizing as Blacks and women have long known, that science is not always friendly. Nevertheless, political exigencies required a definition of identity based once again on somewhat fixed notions of sexual orientation. But now, a new generation of young activists, such as those in the organization Queer Nation, are proclaiming, "We're here, we're queer. Get used to it." They ascribe to a liberation politics of choice, pushing sexual boundaries with "gay sensibility" as identity politics, embracing bisexuality and even a gay and lesbian identity where gay sex includes cross gender sex.

At a time when gay rights activists have probably reached a point when they could agree to dis-agree on what determines sexuality, and to map out political and legal strategies most inclusive of the whole range of self-identification, fantasy, desires and actions; at a time when different experiences are beside the point, given that so many gay men are fighting for their lives, and recent experience, like the Thomas confirmation hearings, renewed gay-baiting of feminists such as NOW president Patricia Ireland, the Willie Smith and Rodney King verdicts, and the LA riots, have reminded both lesbians and gay men of color as well as white lesbians of their multiple vulnerabilities, galvanizing efforts at coalition politics, it's no accident the powers that be find solace in hearing that gay biology is destiny. They want a cure.

# II. D

# CREATING CRIMINALS: GOVERNMENT AND THE LEGAL SYSTEM

Sexuality is probably the most highly charged domain of human activity, its regulation one of the central mechanisms of social control. The modern state, like earlier ruling authorities, both secular and religious, takes a particular interest in sexual behavior. Just as the state reserves to itself and its agents the sole legal right to commit acts of violence, it also asserts the right to determine which sexual acts are permissible and who may commit them. The state's interest need not always be defined in the same fashion. Sometimes states adopt policies intended to increase the birthrate and thus promote heterosexual marriage and occasionally even extramarital childbirth, as in Nazi Germany; in other instances, such as contemporary China and India, states intervene to limit the number of children by promoting sterilization and abortion.

Whatever form the state's interest takes, sexuality seems fated never to be regarded with benign neglect. In Western societies, such as the United States, that derive their codes of sexual behavior from the jurisprudence of medieval Christianity, sexual behavior is always presumed guilty until proven innocent.

In Gayle Rubin's words, "The only adult sexual behavior that is legal in every state is the placement of the penis in the vagina in wedlock" (1984:291). The complete prescription for acceptable sex according to the "traditional family values" of this country would be marital intercourse (for Catholics, with procreative intent or, at least, the absence of contraception), at night, in bed, with lights out, in missionary position. In the wake

of the "sexual revolution" of the 1960s and 1970s most of these prescriptions have been weakened if not overturned: couples are now encouraged by counselors, therapists, and even ministers, to "vary" their sexual diet by experimenting with the time, place, position, and even content of their sexual diet. Nonmarital sex was once a crime in most states. In 1950 movie star Ingrid Bergman was drummed out of Hollywood, denounced on the floor of the Senate as a "powerful influence for evil," and forced to leave the country because she had a child out of wedlock (Friedrich 1986:410). Today celebrities and just plain folk on talk shows discuss their unmarried romances and parenthood.

In contrast to most non-Western cultures, the regulation of sexual behavior in the West has long been especially punitive in the case of male homosexual activity. Historically, "sodomy" laws were drawn to proscribe sexual activity that did not have the possibility of procreation, thus forbidding oral and anal sexual contact between opposite- as well as same-sex couples as well as sex with animals. In England the 1533 Act of Henry VIII, which superseded ecclesiastical law, adopted the criteria used by the Church, and thus such acts were defined, following medieval Christian "natural law," as crimes against nature. Thus, in British law, the penalty for "the abominable vice of buggery" was death, and the law was enforced. In 1806 there were more executions for sodomy than for murder, and the "law appears to have been particularly severe on members of the armed forces" (Weeks 1981:100). British law was reformed in the late nineteenth century, replacing death with harsh prison sentences, such as that given to Oscar Wilde in 1895.

The British punishments for sodomy and buggery were carried over to the American colonies, then incorporated into the legal statutes of the United States, which meant that the punishment often was execution, although in 1777 Thomas Jefferson urged Virginia to substitute castration. Over the course of nearly two hundred years there were other reforms in the severity of the punishment, but in 1961 every state in the United States had a sodomy law on its books. In that year Illinois became the first state to enact a "Model Penal Code" that was drafted by a group of legal scholars in an effort to modernize state penal codes. Among the many provisions of that code was the decriminalization of homosexual conduct between consenting adults in private. It was likely that many of the Illinois legislators who voted for the reforms were unaware of this provision. In several states that followed Illinois in adopting the Model Penal Code, legislators later realized they had legalized homosexual acts and added new sodomy laws barring lesbian and gay sex acts. Since 1961 twenty-seven other states have removed their sodomy laws (in a few cases this was done by state courts ruling the laws unconstitutional), but twenty-three states still treat sexual activity between consenting adults of the same sex as a crime. In many of these "sodomy" between opposite-sex partners is also a crime, although even in states that prohibit heterosexual sodomy actual prosecutions are overwhelmingly aimed at lesbian and gay people. Whether the sodomy laws are actually enforced or generally ignored, their very existence places a burden of criminality on gay people that is often invoked to justify discrimination in other domains.

The realm of legally protected sexual behavior in the United States began to expand in the 1960s on the basis of legal arguments using the concept of a "right to privacy" that was interpreted as keeping the state out of adults' bedrooms. In 1965 the Supreme Court's *Griswold vs. Connecticut* decision ruled that married couples had the right to purchase contraceptives because of this right to sexual privacy. The same principle prevailed in subsequent decisions permitting the possession of contraceptives by unmarried couples and, most controversially, affirming a woman's right to choose abortion in the first two trimesters of a pregnancy. But the right to privacy was not sufficient to overcome the institutionalized heterosexism of the U.S. legal system.

In 1986, in the infamous *Bowers v. Hardwick* decision, the Supreme Court stripped the right to privacy argument of its credibility as a defense of gay sexuality. Diverging from the logic of sexual liberty implicit in *Griswold* and many subsequent decisions, and showing what Justice Blackmun termed an "almost obsessive focus on homosexual activity," the Court asserted that the right to privacy does not extend to homosexual acts, even when committed by consenting adults in private. Simply put, "The Constitution does not confer a fundamental right upon homosexuals to engage in sodomy. . . . Any claim that . . . any kind of private sexual conduct between consenting adults is constitutionally insulated from state proscription is unsupportable." The rationale for the decision was most clearly evident in Chief Justice Burger's concurring opinion, in which, with flagrant disregard for the First Amendment, he proclaimed that "condemnation of those practices is firmly rooted in Judeo-Christian moral and ethical standards."

The *Hardwick* decision underscored the legal barriers to full equality that lesbian and gay Americans face. In addition to being defined as criminals in 23 states, we are also subject to discrimination against which we have little protection. In 1971 there were no legal protections against discrimination for lesbians and gay men anywhere in the United States. In 1997 Maine and New Hampshire became the latest states to enact civil rights legislation prohibiting discrimination on the basis of sexual orientation, joining (in chronological order) Wisconsin, Massachusetts, Connecticut, Hawaii, New Jersey, Vermont, California (partial protection), Minnesota, and Rhode Island. More than 140 municipalities have enacted similar protective measures. Despite these hard-won and limited advances, in 39 states, and most municipalities, there are literally no protections against discrimination in housing, employment, or public accommodation, and those who engage in such discrimination can point to sodomy laws as well as religious strictures to justify their bigotry. When the Cracker Barrel restaurant chain fired many lesbian and gay employees in 1991 to demonstrate their devotion to family values, they had no fear of legal action in any of the many Southern and Midwestern states where they operate.

The attacks on the civil rights of lesbian and gay people are not limited to small-minded restaurant chains wishing to ingratiate themselves with intolerant diners. The government at the highest levels, and in all three branches, has shown itself to be similarly bigoted and opportunistic. Constitutional protections have rarely been extended to lesbian and gay men, not only in the privacy of their bedrooms but also in the workplace. Governmental agencies, from the Federal government down to local school boards and police departments, have denied employment to openly lesbian and gay citizens, and the courts have generally refused to intervene. In the most widely publicized instance President Clinton's half-hearted attempt to end discrimination against gay people in the military concluded in his shameful pretense that the "don't ask, don't tell, don't pursue" formula was anything other than surrender.

During the cold war government witch-hunts targeted homosexuals along with suspected Communists as prime sources of subversion. Lesbian and gay employees were routinely fired as "security risks"—a Senate committee reported 4,954 cases between 1947 and 1950 (Van Dyne 1980:99)—before a federal court ruled in 1965 that the government could not fire a gay person simply because of homosexuality. Yet the government still considers homosexuality—if visible—"incompatible with military service," and before President Clinton's executive order of August 1995 homosexuality was grounds for denying a security clearance.

Modeled as it was on the civil rights struggles of the 1960s, the fight for equality for gay people began in the arena of civil rights protection and decriminalization. Yet in recent years issues of domestic and personal rights have moved to the forefront. Beginning in the late 1970s there has been a concerted effort by the right in the United States to reverse the gains of racial minorities, women, and lesbian and gay people. These efforts have often taken the form of attacking what Senator Jesse Helms referred to as "the wayward, warped sexual revolution which has ravaged this Nation for the past quarter of a century" (Congressional Record, 10/14/87, S14203). The tactics of the sexual counterrevolutionaries included a deliberate move to extend the scope of the "family" as political symbol from the private domestic sphere, using it as a vehicle to recapture the *public* world they feared was being usurped by minorities, feminists, and queers.

One of the clearest manifestations of institutionalized heterosexism has long been the denial of custody and even visitation rights to lesbian mothers and gay fathers engaged in legal battles with their former spouses. Despite many advances in the area of family law, such as the possibility of adoption by gay people and even "second parent" adoption within lesbian and gay couples, there have also been terrible setbacks. In a much publicized 1993 case a Virginia mother, Sharon Bottoms, lost custody of her young son to her mother, who challenged her daughter's fitness as a parent because she was living in a lesbian relationship and thus could be considered a criminal under Virginia's sodomy law. The lower court ruling was upheld by the Virginia Supreme Court in 1995 (Reske 1995).

When Sharon Kowalski was injured in an automobile accident in 1983, her parents prevented her lover, Karen Thompson, from being with her and caring for her. It took eight years of legal battles before a Minnesota court responded to Kowalski's own wishes and awarded Thompson custody of her injured lover (Hunter 1995). This experience has unfortunately been a familiar one to many gay men who have been kept away by family members from lovers dying of AIDS or evicted from the home a couple shared together. Although many municipalities and hundreds of private employers now recognize and provide benefits to "domestic partners," those benefits are still far from the equivalent of those available to married partners.

Marriage provides immediate and substantial benefits in many domains, including Social Security and tax benefits, parenting and property rights, health insurance, veteran's discounts, medical decision making, bereavement or sick leave, immigration protection, and automatic inheritance. As Hawaii began moving toward the legalization of same-sex marriages in that state, the issue of lesbian and gay marriage served as a lightning rod for political attacks. By mid-1996 bills had been introduced in thirty-four states, and passed in twelve, that would preclude recognition of same-sex marriages. In May 1996 thrice-married Republican congressman Robert Barr introduced a federal Defense of Marriage Act, defining marriage as "the legal union between one man and one woman," permitting states to disregard the Full Faith and Credit clause of the U.S. Constitution by not recognizing same-sex marriages granted by another state and denying same-sex partners marital tax or survivor benefits. Twice-married Republican presidential candidate Bob Dole was a cosponsor of the bill, and President Clinton was quick to announce that he would sign the bill once it passed Congress (Purdom 1996).

The climate of political hostility and public debates over the rights of gay people to legal equality fuel an environment in which antilesbian and antigay violence is common. In a survey of 3,086 lesbian and gay Pennsylvanians the Philadelphia Lesbian and Gay Task Force found that their rates of victimization were at least three times higher than the criminal violence victimization rates compiled by the U.S. Department of Justice for the adult population (Gross and Aurand 1996). Similar patterns have been reported elsewhere. In 1995 the Klan Watch of the Southern Poverty Law Center reported that hate crimes were up 25 percent over 1994 and that homophobia was the motive for one-quarter of the assaults and nearly two-thirds of the homicides (Moran 1995).

In 1977 the passage of a "gay rights" ordinance in Dade County, Florida, brought on a counterattack spearheaded by singer Anita Bryant under the guise of "saving our children." The campaign was successful. Subsequently repeated referenda have been placed on state and local election ballots, and in many of these gay people have been defeated.

In 1992 an antigay initiative, Amendment 2, was passed in Colorado, prohibiting the state or any local government from enacting civil rights protection for gay people. The amendment was ruled unconstitutional by the state courts, and when the case was appealed to the U.S. Supreme Court in 1995 the Clinton administration refused to file a brief in support of the Colorado court decision, saying there was "no federal issue at stake" in a case that would determine whether a state could deprive its citizens of equal protection under the law! The Supreme Court's six to three ruling in *Romer v. Evans* in May 1996 was the most significant legal victory yet for lesbians and gay people. In his decision Justice Anthony Kennedy wrote that "Amendment 2 classifies homosexuals not to fur-

ther a proper legislative end but to make them unequal to everyone else. This Colorado cannot do."

## REFERENCES

Friedrich, Otto. 1986. *City of Nets: Hollywood in the 1940s.* London: Headline.

Gross, Larry and Steven Aurand. 1996. *Discrimination and Violence Against Lesbian Women and Gay Men in Philadelphia and the Commonwealth of Pennsylvania.* Philadelphia: Philadelphia Lesbian and Gay Task Force.

Hunter, Nan. 1995. "Sexual Dissent and the Family: The Sharon Kowalski Case." In Lisa Duggan and Nan Hunter, eds., *Sex Wars: Sexual Dissent and Political Culture*, pp. 101–106. New York: Routledge.

Moran, Robert. 1995. "House Panel Urged to Adopt Expanded Hate Crime Legislation—Supporters Want a Law to Address Attacks Against Homosexuals. Lawmakers Show Little Interest." *Philadelphia Inquirer*, August 29.

Purdom, Todd. 1996. "White House Is Avoiding Gay Marriage as an Issue." *New York Times*, May 16.

Reske, Henry. 1995. "Lesbianism at Center of Custody Dispute." *ABA Journal*, July, p. 28.

Rubin, Gayle. 1984. "Thinking Sex." In Carole Vance, ed., *Pleasure and Danger*, pp. 267–319. Boston: Routledge and Kegan Paul.

Van Dyne, Larry. 1980. "Is DC Becoming the Gay Capital of America?" *Washingtonian*, September, pp. 96–101.

Weeks, Jeffrey. 1981. *Sex, Politics and Society: The Regulation of Sexuality Since 1800.* London: Longman.

# | 30 |

## *Crime Story*

STEN RUSSELL

Regular viewers of *Crime Story*, a panel discussion type television show presented in the Los Angeles area late Sunday nights at 11:00 by station KTLA, channel 5, may have been gratified, if surprised, by the unexpectedly friendly attitudes toward homosexuality expressed on the program July 20th. The show focuses attention upon such questions as narcotics, law enforcement, prisons and prison reform, international crime, and sex crime, and perversion under which latter headings they classify homosexuality.

Past programs have been decidedly anti-homosexual whenever that has been the subject of discussion, but always, fortunately, rather ineffective productions due, perhaps, to an amateur high school debate quality about them, and to the fact that the panel of "experts," as they are known, is often desperately recruited from among members of the program's own staff.

But the July 20th program in the absence of its regular moderator Sandy Howard, presented a most reasonable picture of the homosexual. The members of the qualified panel made effective, intelligent observations, and many positive and constructive points. The whole show was guided carefully by the guest moderator. Credit for the success of the program must go to Herbert Selwyn, attorney for the Los Angeles Chapter of the Mattachine Society who was a member of the panel.

### "PART III—SEX CRIMES: ONE OF THE NATION'S PROBLEMS"

The Panel: Dr. Isidore Ziferstein, Psychiatrist and Psychoanalyst—worked at Iowa State Penitentiary for four years. Attorney, Herbert Selwyn, Los Angeles, California. Dr. Wm. Graves, Psychiatrist—an assistant at San Quentin; member of Friends' Subcommittee for legislation (on the California Penal Code). Mr. Fred Otash, Private Detective—former Los Angeles Policeman, one-time investigator for "Confidential Magazine," and "An authority on all types of crime," according to Bill Bradley the moderator.

Bill Bradley began by asking the panel to define "sex crime."

Dr. Ziferstein said that a sex crime is a sexual act that does harm to another individual. He did not consider a sex act between consenting adults that causes no harm a sex crime.

Mr. Otash began by explaining Sec. 288A of California's Penal Code. This, he said, involved "sex perversion" and more precisely, copulation by mouth. It was Mr. Otash's "opinion" that this particular sex crime was the most prevalent in the nation. In most cases the police have to deal with, where the charge could be a violation of Sec. 288A, the charge is often reduced to a simple "vag-lewd." Husbands and wives can commit this crime, but the police would not likely be peeking into bedroom windows according to Mr. Otash.

Mr. Selwyn divided sex crimes into direct, where the sexual organs are involved, and indirect, where burglary or arson, etc., are the crimes but frequently motivated by sexual conflicts.

Dr. Ziferstein reacting to Mr. Otash's definition of a "sex criminal"—namely anyone who broke the penal code in this regard—said "yes, the penal code regarding sexual acts would make nearly every American citizen a sex criminal." However, he felt that a great error was involved and that the term sex criminal should only apply to those who used sex as a means of perpetrating

ONE, September 1958, pp. 26–28.

harmful acts upon other persons.

Dr. Graves concurred with Dr. Ziferstein.

Mr. Bradley asked—are all homosexuals sex criminals and why do they receive special consideration?

Mr. Otash explained—all homosexuals are sex criminals by the letter of the law. Further, in his opinion, this was rightly so. He felt that homosexuals went about breeding more homosexuals, simply by contact. According to Mr. Otash they could not keep to their own kind but "preyed on normal men" and converted them to their way of life. He added, "You may call them homosexuals; I call them 'fags.'"

Mr. Selwyn said that he would leave the question to the psychiatrists as to whether a homosexual could convert a "normal man" to a homosexual simply with one or two casual sex experiences. However, he was most interested in the manner in which the police got their evidence and their "homosexual sex criminals." He denounced the peep-hole techniques in latrines and the quasi-entrapment methods widely used by the vice-squad. In the former, he felt that while the men involved were indiscreet to have sexual acts in a public place, that nevertheless it could hardly be assumed that they were other than consenting adults and that this should not be penalized with as much as 15 years in jail. In the latter, the technique consisted of playing up to a homosexual's weakness, getting him to make "a pass," and then flashing a badge. Mr. Selwyn took a very dim view, indeed, of this latter practice.

Mr. Otash appeared to be stung at this bald statement of police tactics and said that while he was one of those who had been staked out at peep-hole sights in public "commodes" at Venice, Calif., that the police did not do this without complaints—that complaints had come in that homosexuals were seducing children and propositioning normal men in the latrines—further that the police investigated, found this to be true and took to jail the offending homosexuals.

Mr. Selwyn felt all sex crimes should be divided into three parts: those perpetrated by force, those involving children, and those involving consenting adults. The latter group he felt should be removed from the category, altogether. He did not believe that the percentage of homosexuals that molested children to be nearly as high as the percentage of heterosexuals that molested children—from the simple fact of there being not more than 5-10 homosexuals per 100 of population.

Dr. Ziferstein felt that all this "peeping and prying" only gave evidence and a continuing climate to the undercurrent of feeling that there is a special dirtiness about sex in general.

Dr. Graves was queried as to the incidence of homosexuality in prison. He guessed that at times it could go as high as 50 percent of the male population—but that it was looked on differently in prison than in the outside society. By the psychiatrists it was called "situational sex behavior"—that is, something most of the men involved would not do if they had normal outlets for the sex drives and that therefore, it was not judged as harshly by prison officials—although they tried to keep homosexual practices to a minimum.

Dr. Graves did not feel that homosexual criminals should be given any more special treatment than any other criminal. All criminals were special unto themselves, he felt, and should be treated for their own individual problems.

Mr. Selwyn queried Dr. Graves as to the feasibility of allowing prisoners the right to have sexual intercourse with their wives or sweethearts as is permitted in Mexican jails. Would not this practice cut down on the "situational homosexuality?" he asked.

Dr. Graves agreed that it probably would if there were some way to bring about our society's acceptance of this practice.

Dr. Ziferstein pointed out that our society was basically an anti-sex society, not just an anti-homosexual society. He implied that it was because of this that there were so many sex deviates, homosexuals included. Homosexuals, per se, he did not feel were dangerous to the common good. The "homosexual neurosis" is no worse than any other neurosis, he said.

Dr. Graves did not seem to necessarily agree with Dr. Ziferstein as to homosexuality being a neurosis to start with. In this society where homosexuality is connected with great moral repugnance, he felt that naturally most homosexuals were going to get neurotic over the state of affairs.

The other panelists seemd to ignore Mr. Otash except when the Moderator asked him a direct question, at which point the other panelists would take off from his answer and kick it around among themselves.

The next question was directed to Mr. Otash. Why is there such a big difference in the viewpoints of Law, Law Enforcement and Medical Opinion? asked Mr. Bradley.

Mr. Otash's answer was, "If you think these people [Homosexuals] are all right you should change the laws."

Mr. Selwyn and the rest of the panel agreed wholeheartedly. After all, it was explained, the police don't draft the laws, but are duty bound to enforce them. The laws should be changed, so that the police are not faced with this problem.

Dr. Ziferstein felt that the difference lay in the occupational hazard of each job. The policeman becomes involved in the "cops and robbers" chase at the expense of human values and the psychiatrists and social workers become involved in the human values to the exclusion of all else. He

felt, however, that the latter bias was a better one.

Mr. Selwyn felt that there needed to be a balance between social protection and the rights of the individual. He mentioned the work of the Church of England's Moral Welfare Counsel and their recommendation that sex between consenting adults should not be considered a legal question at all. He concluded by adding that it may be a moral question between the private individual and his conscience, but there were no legal values involved.

# | 31 |

# Public Policy and Private Prejudice: Psychology and Law on Gay Rights

### GARY B. MELTON

By a razor-thin majority, the Supreme Court held in *Bowers v. Hardwick* (1986; hereafter cited as *Bowers*) that the constitutional right to privacy does not extend to "homosexual sodomy." The majority was convinced that the "ancient roots" of criminal sanctions for homosexual conduct demonstrated that such behavior is outside the realm of privacy fundamental to Western law. In the opinion for the Court, Justice White seemed not only to recognize sodomy laws as constitutional, but also to approve of such laws as consistent with proscription of "adultery, incest, and other sexual crimes" (p. 196). In a concurring opinion, Chief Justice Burger put the matter most bluntly:

Decisions of individuals relating to homosexual conduct have been subject to state intervention throughout the history of Western Civilization. Condemnation of those practices is firmly rooted in Judeao-Christian moral and ethical standards. . . . To hold that the act of homosexual sodomy is somehow

protected as a fundamental right would be to cast aside millennia of moral teaching. (pp. 196–197, citations omitted)

Relying heavily on an amicus brief submitted by the American Psychological Association (APA) and the American Public Health Association, Justice Blackmun wrote an impassioned dissent, joined by Justices Brennan, Marshall, and Stevens, in which he recognized that the key issue was respect for personhood: the protection of rights that "form so central a part of an individual's life" (p. 204), just as "homosexual orientation may well form part of the very fiber of an individual's personality" (p. 203, footnote 2). Noting the particular centrality of sexual intimacy in personal life, Justice Blackmun argued that the fact that individuals define themselves in a significant way through their intimate sexual relationships with others suggests, in a Nation as diverse

*American Psychologist,* 44(6):933–940, 1989.

as ours, that there may be many "right" ways of conducting those relationships, and that much of the richness of a relationship will come from the freedom an individual has to *choose* the form and nature of these intensely personal bonds (p. 205).

With obvious exasperation, Justice Blackmun concluded,

> I can only hope that here, too, the Court soon will reconsider its analysis and conclude that depriving individuals of the right to choose for themselves how to conduct their intimate relationships poses a far greater threat to the values most deeply rooted in our Nation's history than tolerance of nonconformity could ever do. (p. 214)

In a separate dissent, Justice Stevens, joined by Justices Brennan and Marshall, agreed with Justice Blackmun that consensual homosexual behavior is well within the bounds of intimate expression protected by the right to privacy. Justice Stevens also suggested that prosecution only of *homosexual* sodomy raised serious questions of equal protection:

> From the standpoint of the individual, the homosexual and the heterosexual have the same interest in deciding how he will live his own life, and, more narrowly, how he will conduct himself in his personal and voluntary associations with his companions. State intrusion into the private conduct of either is equally burdensome. (pp. 218–219)

Moreover, Justice Stevens noted, differential intrusions into the private lives of homosexuals "must be supported by a neutral and legitimate interest—something more substantial than a habitual dislike for, or ignorance about, the disfavored group" (p. 219), but Georgia had failed to provide an adequate justification for its criminal sanctions for homosexual conduct.

*Bowers* was a serious defeat for lesbians and gay men. However, as Justice Stevens's opinion implied, the holding that homosexual conduct is not protected by the right to privacy does not foreclose all constitutional arguments to protect lesbians and gay men from discrimination. First, the *Bowers* holding may not preempt a claim that homosexual *orientation*, apart from homosexual *conduct*, lies within a constitutionally protected zone of privacy. Second, even if homosexual orientation lies outside such boundaries, special

restrictions on lesbians and gay men must comport with the equal protection clause. The state cannot enforce discriminatory policies unless those provisions pass at least a rational basis test. Indeed, given the continuing history of discrimination against lesbians and gay men in matters unrelated to homosexual behavior, a strong case can be made for treating homosexuality as a quasi-suspect or suspect classification and, therefore, requiring heightened judicial scrutiny of the constitutionality of discrimination against lesbians and gay men. At a minimum, state-sanctioned discrimination against homosexuals should invite the sort of searching rational-basis inquiry that the Supreme Court has applied in cases involving discrimination on the basis of mental disability, even though it has failed to recognize people with mental disabilities as a class needing special judicial protection against discrimination.

Several subsequent courts have noted that *Bowers* dealt only with homosexual sodomy and not with other homosexual conduct (e.g., kissing) or affectional preferences. In two of these cases the courts went further and held that homosexuals are a suspect class and that discriminatory policies thus must be subjected to strict scrutiny. Applying such an analysis, the courts struck down discrimination against homosexuals in the defense industry and the military.

The Ninth Circuit Court of Appeals has agreed to rehear *Watkins v. United States Army* (before the full court rather than a three-judge panel). The determination of suspect classification involves a series of empirical questions that psychology may help to answer. Courts considering such issues must decide whether the class at issue has suffered a history of purposeful invidious discrimination. Suspect classes are defined by traits (*e.g.*, skin color) that are irrelevant to legitimate state purposes; they are subjected to discrimination because of prejudice and inaccurate stereotypes; and their membership is based on an immutable characteristic. Psychology can contribute to courts' understanding of the depth of antigay prejudice that persists in the United States, the lack of relationship between homosexuality and ability to respond to job requirements and other social demands, the near-impossibility of changing homosexual orientation, and the deleterious effects of continuing discrimination on mental health and social relations.

The nature of the inquiry is illustrated by the conclusions about social reality that a federal district court in California reached in *High Tech Gays:*

> Wholly unfounded, degrading stereotypes about lesbians and gay men abound in American society. Examples of such stereotypes include that gay people desire and attempt to molest young children, that gay people attempt to recruit and convert other people, and that gay people inevitably engage in promiscuous sexual activity. Many people erroneously believe that the sexual experience of lesbians and gay men represents the gratification of purely prurient interests, not the expression of mutual affection and love. They fail to recognize that gay people seek and engage in stable, monogamous relationships. Instead, to many, the very existence of lesbians and gay men is inimical to the family. For years, many people have branded gay people as abominations to nature and considered lesbians and gay men mentally ill and psychologically unstable.
>
> As with attitudes about racial groups . . . , these attitudes about gay people reflect "prejudice and antipathy" against gay people, because they do not conform to the mainstream. The stereotypes have no basis in reality and represent outmoded notions about homosexuality, analogous to the "outmoded notions" of the relative capabilities of the sexes that require heightened scrutiny of classifications based on gender. The fact that a person is lesbian or gay bears on relation to the person's ability to contribute to society. Rather than somehow being enemies of American culture and values, lesbians and gay men occupy positions in all walks of American life, participate in diverse aspects of family life, and contribute enormously to many elements of American culture. (*High Tech Gays*, pp. 1369–1370, citations omitted)

The prejudices embedded in the "millennia of moral teaching" that the Supreme Court used as its foundation in *Bowers* stand in contrast to the recognition in post-*Bowers* decisions that "lesbians and gay men have been the object of some of the deepest prejudice and hatred in American society . . . hatred so deep that many gay people face the threat of physical violence on American streets today" (*High Tech Gays*, p. 1369). With the openness of some courts to consideration of such issues, the potential social consequences of their decisions, and the availability of relevant body of psychological research, the social responsibility of psychology to bring its knowledge to the legal system is clear (see Melton, 1987).

This duty is heightened by the fact that psychology and the other mental health disciplines historically have contributed to societal prejudice against lesbians and gay men. Just as organized psychology has acted in both judicial and legislative forums to redress wrongs against mentally disabled people in which it once participated (Melton and Greenberg, 1987), so too should it seek to right the wrongs that were supported historically by branding lesbians and gay men as "mentally ill and psychologically unstable." In that regard, the court in *High Tech Gays*, the three-judge panel in *Watkins*, and the dissenting justices in *Bowers* all noted the change in psychology's understanding of homosexuality.

At the same time, the majority view in *Bowers*, the continuing prejudice of many courts against lesbians and gay men in contexts other than employment law, and the animosity often experienced by gay people in everyday life illustrate the need for continuous vigilance to correct the misconceptions about homosexuality by legal and political decision makers. Whatever else the case may stand for, *Bowers* was an unmistakable anti-gay decision incompatible with the law's reverence for human dignity. In the age of the acquired immunodeficiency syndrome (AIDS), such mean-spirited responses to homosexuality may be particularly difficult to overcome (Blendon and Donelan, 1988; Herek and Glunt, 1988), but the challenge is compelling for both psychology and law to redress the wrongs of past and present and to reject unequivocally tacit support for private biases.

## REFERENCES

Blendon, R. J., and Donelan, K. (1988). Discrimination against people with AIDS: The public's perspective. *New England Journal of Medicine, 318,* 1022–1026.

Bowers v. Hardwick, 478 U. S. 186 (1986).

City of Cleburne v. Cleburne Living Center, 473 U. S. 432 (1985).

Doe v. Casey, 796 F.2d 1508 (D. C. Cir. 1986), *aff'd in part, rev'd in part subnom.* Doe v. Webster, 107 S. Ct. 3182 (1987), *cert. denied,* 108 S. Ct. 2883 (1988).

Falk, P. J. (1989). Lesbian Mothers: Psychological assumptions in family law. *American Psychologist, 44,* 941–947.

Herek, G. M. (1989). Hate crimes against lesbians and gay men: Issues for research and policy. *American Psychologist, 44,* 948–955.

Herek, G. M., and Glunt, E. K. (1988). An epidemic of stigma: public reactions to AIDS. *American Psychologist, 43,* 886–891.

High Tech Gays v. Defense Industrial Security Clearance Office, 668 F. Supp. 1361 (N. D. Cal. 1987).

Melton, G. B. (1987). Bringing psychology to the legal system: Opportunities, obstacles, and efficacy. *American Psychologist, 42,* 488–495.

Melton, G. B., and Greenberg, E. G. (1987). Fear, prejudice, and neglect: Discrimination against mentally disabled people. *American Psychologist, 42,* 1007–1026.

New York v. Uplinger, *cert. granted,* 464 U. S. 812 (1983), *cert. dismissed,* 467 U. S. 246 (1984).

Padula v. Webster, 822 F.2d 97 (D. C. Cir. 1987).

Palmore v. Sidoti, 466 U. S. 429 (1984).

Watkins v. United States Army, 837 F.2d 1428, *re-h'g en banc granted,* 847 F.2d 1362 (9th Cir. 1988).

# | 32 |

## *Crimes of Lesbian Sex*

### Ruthann Robson

About half the jurisdictions in the United States have statutes that criminalize lesbian sexual expressions, and virtually every state has had a statute as recently as 1968 that would imprison someone for lesbian sexual expression. Many of us tend to dismiss such statutes as not really applicable to us: the statutes are anachronisms; the statutes are law in states that are conservative; the statutes are meant to apply to acts other than what we do; the statutes are directed at other sorts of lesbians. Rarely do we know what these statutes actually say. Yet these statutes are the legal text of lesbian sexuality. Enacted and codified, interpreted and applied, these statutes are the legislative pronouncements and judicial interpretations.

The statutes are generally referred to as sodomy statutes and usually discussed in terms of gay male sexuality. Centering lesbian concerns, I instead refer to the statutes as the lesbian sex statutes. This does not mean, however, that I concede the statutes always or only apply to lesbian sexuality. The statutes, individually, and collectively, are idiosyncratic in their application to various expressions of lesbian sexuality.

The existing lesbian sex statutes employ what I consider to be three different strategies to describe that which they criminalize: oral/anal, natural, and gender specificity. These strategies may overlap within a given statute, or a state may have a statutory scheme that utilizes more than one.

What I am calling the oral/anal strategy usually prohibits any sexual contact between the sex organs (described also as genitals) of one person, and the mouth or anus of another. These statutes are anatomically specific to a certain extent, but they also target what is generally considered sodomy—sexual contact between a man's penis and an anus, or sexual contact between a man's penis and a mouth, also called fellatio. A few states broaden this strategy by also including objects, fingers, and body parts as prohibited penetrators of sexual organs.

The second strategy relies on so-called natural understanding for its meaning. Statutes criminalize the "the crime against nature," or the "abominable and detestable crime against nature," or reversing the adjectives, "the detestable and abominable crime against nature" or the "infamous crime against nature." This strategy, stand-

In Ruthann Robson, *Lesbian (Out)law*. Ithaca, N.Y.: Firebrand, 1992; repr. in William Rubenstein, ed., *Lesbians, Gay Men, and the Law,* pp. 80–86. New York: New Press.

ing alone, is amazingly insufficient to advise any-one of any acts that are within the prohibition. Nevertheless, many courts—including the United States Supreme Court—have upheld such statutes from constitutional vagueness attacks by reasoning that our common under-standing includes knowledge of what such statutes prohibit, or that even if common knowl-edge is not so definite, judges interpreting the statute can rely on established legal understand-ings. The failure to name what is prohibited, rem-iniscent of the tactics of the sixteenth-century jurist Germain Colladon and the 1920s members of British Parliament, is inherent in statutes that rely on natural understandings. If one wanted to learn specifics about lesbian sexuality, or about any type of sexuality, the natural strategy statutes would definitely not be the place to go.

The third strategy relies on gender specificity for meaning. Often, although not always, gender specificity targets persons of the same sex, and often, although again not always, this strategy is combined with either the oral/anal or the natural strategies. Interestingly, the specificity of gender is also usually coupled with a prohibition against sexual contact with animals. Statutes within this strategy can be some of the broadest in terms of criminalizing lesbian sexual expressions, espe-cially if such statutes criminalize sexual contact between person of the same sex.

There are not many reported cases—cases which have been through an appeal process and are printed in official state reporters—in which any of these statutes have been applied to con-sensual activity, and even fewer of those cases involve adult women. There are a few cases, how-ever, and in one a 1968 Michigan appellate court upheld the conviction and prison sentence of one and one-half to five years in the Detroit House of Corrections based on facts it described as follows:

> Defendant [Julie Livermore] visited Mrs. Carolyn French at the pubic camping grounds at Sunrise Lake in Osceola County. Michigan. Mrs. French had been tent-camp-ing with her 4 children at Sunrise Lake for several days.
>
> About 9 p.m. that same evening, defen-dant and Mrs. French were observed by com-plainant Jerry Branch and others, to be in close bodily contact with each other, which continued for approximately one hour. The defendant and Mrs. French then entered the latter's tent.

Later, on receiving a complaint, Troopers . . . of the Michigan State Police, proceeded to the Sun-rise Lake camping ground. They arrived there about midnight, talked to the complainant and others and then stood within 15 feet of the French tent. Obscene language and conversation indica-tive of sexual conduct occurring between two female persons was overheard by the troopers for about ten minutes. From the information received from complainant, the obscene lan-guage and conversation, and noises overheard, the troopers took action in the belief that a felony had been committed or was being committed at that time. They approached the tent, identified themselves and requested admittance; there was no reply; the troopers unzipped the outer flap, and aided by a flashlight observed a cot located directly in front of the doorway on which defen-dant and Mrs. French were lying, partially cov-ered by a blanket; the two females were advised that they were under arrest and after taking sev-eral flash pictures the troopers permitted them to dress in private.[1]

No matter the wording of any particular statute, each statute has the capacity to be inter-preted to include two women "lying, partially covered by a blanket" who have been overheard engaged in "obscene language and conversation indicative of sexual conduct." This case indicates the horrific potential that all the statutes possess.

The case is also typical in its lack of specificity. A lesbian sex statute may explicitly exempt the state from a requirement that it specify the acts alleged to be criminal.[2] Judicial opinions often decline to relate the actual acts that constitute the crime.[3] When described at all, lesbian sexuality is described in clinical terms or with reference to male sexuality, or simply as unnatural, deviant, or sexual. The few factual descriptions are not pro-vided by lesbians, but by lawyers and judges inter-preting lesbian sexual activity. Similarly, I think it is a fairly safe assumption, given the continuing infrequency of women legislators, that none of the lesbian sex statutes was authored by a lesbian. Lesbians are at the margins of the legal text of our own sexuality. One way to center lesbians is to engage in a specific and contextualized analysis of the legal interpretations of some common les-bian sexual activities as described from a lesbian point of view.

The main character, and sometimes narrator, of Judith McDaniel's recent novel *Just Say Yes* is the twenty-six-year-old lesbian, Lindsey.[4] She is waitressing in Provincetown for the summer, wondering about her life, and experiencing sexual encounters. The following five passages and their legal analyses reveal how our sexual practices violate—and fail to violate—the various laws in various states in idiosyncratic ways.

## 1.

*Ra's hands spread the lips of her cunt wide and her voice invited Lindsey to stroke the clitoris, move slowly up to the shell-pink little button hiding under the flashy hood. . . . Letting her one hand follow Ra's rhythm, Lindsey began to stroke lightly with her other, up the belly first, then to the bottom cup of one breast, then the other. . . . Suddenly Ra's knees jerked, and Lindsey felt the orgasm starting under her fingers. She rubbed Ra's clitoris until she was sure she'd gone over the edge, then let her fingers burrow into Ra's wet center and catch at the waves of orgasm pulsing down her abdomen.*

Whether Lindsey and Ra are guilty of criminal conduct depends, in part, upon which strategy a state uses in its lesbian sex statute(s). However, in all states that might criminalize this encounter—as well as any other lesbian encounter—if one party is guilty, then both are guilty, assuming consent. The state can choose to prosecute only one person, which will assist the state in proving its case if the other person cooperates. Consent will not be a defense.

In states that employ only the oral/anal strategy, the sexual encounter between Lindsey and Ra is not within the statute. Thus in Alabama, Kentucky, Georgia, and Utah, Lindsey has not committed any crime. Whether Lindsey's acts violate statutes dedicated to the natural strategy depends on whether the courts in the particular state have chosen to interpret the statute narrowly (to prohibit only oral/anal sexual activity) or broadly (to "cover the entire field of unnatural acts," as a Nevada court expressed it). In Idaho, committed to a broad interpretation by prior case law, if a court found Lindsey's acts within the statute, the mandatory minimum sentence would be five years; since no maximum sentence is listed, it could legally be imprisonment.

Lindsey's acts are most likely to violate the statutes that target not acts, but actors—persons of the same gender. In Louisiana, for example, the "use of genital organ of one of the offenders" is sufficient to constitute the crime if both parties are of the same sex. And in Missouri, "any sexual act involving the genitals of one person and the

mouth, tongue, hand, or anus of another preson" is a crime if the parties are of the same sex. In Arkansas, the statute combines anatomical specificity with gender specificity to criminalize penetration of the vagina or anus by any body member of a person of the same sex. Lindsey's fingers surely qualify as body members, but how does their "burrowing" translate into the legally required penetration? Arkansas' penetration requirement is not unique, and statutes that resort to any of the three strategies often include a penetration requirement either in the statute itself or in judicial interpretations of the statute. But even if *burrow* means legal penetration, Lindsey might not be a criminal in Texas, where the recently enacted statute criminalizes deviate sexual intercourse defined as activities between persons of the same sex in which "the penetration of the genitals or the anus of another person with an object" occurs. In Texas, then, if Lindsey had burrowed with a dildo, she would violate the statute, but the question remains as to whether her fingers qualify as an object. While our everyday understanding of the word object might be limited to the inanimate, a Texas court could decide to give effect to the intention of the legislature. Confronted with Lindsey and Ra, a court might attempt to decide whether Texas legislators intended to include fingers as objects, or whether criminalizing Lindsey and Ra's activities had been their intention.

## 2.

*Ra knelt, and Lindsey felt her shoulders between her knees, her tongue probing as her fingers parted the lips of Lindsey's vagina. Ra sucked and nibbled, swallowed from Lindsey's smooth wetness, then moved her tongue hard against Lindsey's clitoris, pushing, circling, then pushing again until an orgasm pulsed out of Lindsey's toes, pushing up to her thighs, swelling her cunt, and throbbing finally into her uterus.*

In states that rely upon the oral/anal strategy in their lesbian sex statutes, Ra's tongue on Lindsey's clitoris is a crime. Lindsey and Ra could be jailed for twenty years in Georgia, five years in Virginia, one year in Alabama and Kentucky, and six months in Utah. The absence of anal sex will not help Lindsey and Ra, unless they are in the California prison system, which only criminalizes anal penetration by a penis by inmates, and possibly if they are in South Carolina, which only criminalizes the undefined act of "buggery."[5]

One of the more interesting states in which to consider the placement of Ra's tongue is Kansas. Kansas criminalizes what it calls sodomy between persons of the same sex, but the statute explicitly defines sodomy as "oral-anal copulation, including oral-genital stimulation between the tongue of a male and the genital area of a female." The "including" in the Kansas statute, added by a 1990 amendment, is an excluding of female tongues. At least this is the interpretation of authoritative comments to the statutes, as well as the state's highest court. In Kansas, Ra and Lindsey do not violate the proscription of oral sex.

The Kansas situation is not historically unique. A 1939 Georgia court held that lesbian cunnilingus was not a crime under the statute that prohibited the "carnal knowledge and connection against the order of nature, by man with man, or in the same unnatural manner with woman." The court concluded that "man" was the exclusive actor, and held the unspecified acts between two women were excluded even though they were "just as loathsome." The Georgia legislature subsequently amended the statue to rely on the oral/anal strategy and eliminate any gender references.

Courts in other states, however, have found lesbian cunnilingus clearly illegal. Under Louisiana's prior crime against nature statute (since amended to reflect the oral/anal strategy), the women who participated in "oral copulation by and between both of the accused" had their convictions of thirty months in prison affirmed. In Oklahoma, under a crime against nature statute still in effect, in a case involving interracial lesbian (and heterosexual) acts, the court had no difficulty accepting the proposition that the statute's reference to "mankind" included both male and female and that "copulation *per os* between two females" was criminal. Yet because Oklahoma's statutory scheme also includes a requirement of "penetration, however slight" an appellate court—despite its expressed disagreement with the penetration requirement— reversed the conviction of a woman who admitted performing cunnilingus on another female because the prosecutor "made no effort to introduce any evidence, either direct or circumstantial, proving the essential element of penetration." What penetration means—and what it is that must be penetrated—is unclear. Is Ra's tongue against Lindsey's clitoris penetration?

## 3.

*They didn't undress, and there seemed to be little urgency in their movements at first, just a gentle rocking of bodies entwined, interlocked in the right way. Sindar had slipped her hard, round thigh between Lindsey's legs, brought it right up against the rough seam of her pants crotch, and began to move up and down, up and down. Mesmerized, Lindsey lay quietly at first, one hand holding Sindar's shoulder as she rocked, the other resting on the back of her head, feeling the tightly braided dreads, pressing Sindar's mouth tight into her own. . . . Together they rocked, feeling the tension build, the wetness seep through the cloth. . . . Lindsey felt Sindar's orgasm begin when her rhythm changed, became more urgent, forceful, and her faster thrusts brought Lindsey over the edge too, let her gasp with relief as she felt the orgasm ripple up her thighs and into her belly.*

The clinical term for Lindsey and Sindar's lovemaking is *tribadism,* and as an activity that does not include oral/anal contact with sexual organs, or any penetration, it is criminalized only by the most broadly worded statutes that would also criminalize Lindsey's previously discussed interactions with Ra. Among the broadest of these statutes are ones that clearly target same-sex activities. For example, Montana's criminalization of "deviate sexual intercourse" includes "any touching of the sexual or other intimate parts of another [of the same sex] for the purposes of arousing or gratifying the sexual desire of either party." If the touchings between Lindsey and Sindar are intended to sexually arouse or gratify either of them, they are guilty in Montana and could be sentenced to ten years. Michigan's statute prohibiting gross indecency between women—the statute under which Julie Livermore was convicted because of her activities at the campground with Carolyn French—is also sufficiently broad to allow a conviction of Lindsey and Sindar, as well as many lesbians at the annual Michigan Women's Music Festival.

## 4.

*Carol was leading the way now, walking toward the end of the pier. . . . Suddenly, Carol did what she had been doing all week in the freedom of this new environment—she threw her natural caution into the breeze blowing off the ocean and put her arms around Lindsey. Lindsey's lips were waiting. . . . They kissed slowly at first, lips exploring the contours of a face, tasting the skin, breathing in the scent of a new person. Once again her bare thighs were touching Carol's. She began to explore the velvet-smooth skin under Carol's blouse. . . . Her fingers traced the length of Carol's spine, up from the waist to the back of her neck, beneath the shorts to her tailbone, to her firm ass.*

*"Oh, my." Carol moved away from the kiss and took a deep breath.*

Carol and Lindsey are kissing and touching on a public pier, and although each of the previous three scenes also took place in public in Judith McDaniel's novel, I analyzed them as if they occurred behind the proverbial drapes-drawn, locked-door bedroom. We need to reconsider privacy. In the context of lesbian sex statutes, lesbian sex in public—or in any place with a window or other indication that might be interpreted to be less than absolutely private—is subject to being criminalized as indecent exposure, public lewdness, or open and gross lewdness.

Every state in the United Sates has some sort of statute that prohibits public lesbian sexual expressions. Many of these statutes are aimed at "flashers," and thus target exposure of the genitals in public in a manner likely to be observed. So limited, the statutes would not criminalize Lindsey and Carol's activities on the pier, although Lindsey's prior acts with Ra on that same pier would be criminalized. However, even relatively benign statutes enacted in states that do not have specific lesbian sex statutes contain words that could be interpreted to criminalize Lindsey and Carol. New Jersey prohibits any "flagrantly lewd and offensive act." New York prohibits any "lewd act." New Mexico criminalizes exposure of the breasts. And in Vermont, "open and gross lewdness and lascivious behavior" is a crime that can provoke a five-year prison sentence.

### 5.

*I was learning real quick that arguing with a lawyer can take a lot of time and preparation. I let it drop for then because we were climbing those narrow steps again, Carol ahead, me behind. I put both hands under her ass as she climbed. "I don't know about legal definitions," I told her, "but I'd be glad to show you in person what I think a lesbian is."*

That Lindsey's new lover is an attorney with the public defender's office might be convenient

should Lindsey be arrested for the crime of solicitation to violate a lesbian sex statute. Soliciting a person to commit a crime is an independent offense in many jurisdictions. Solicitation is often used to prosecute what the state considers prostitution, but there need not be a mention of money if the act solicited is lesbian sex. In the District of Columbia, for example, it is illegal "for any person to invite, entice, persuade, or address for the purpose of inviting, enticing, or persuading" any person for an "immoral or lewd purpose." The D.C. courts have expressly limited "immoral and lewd" to acts encompassed by their sodomy statute, which uses the oral/anal strategy to criminalize lesbian sex. The courts have rejected free speech challenges to this criminal solicitation statute and have also held that the solicitation need not occur in a public place. So, depending on whether or not Lindsey thinks oral sex would demonstrate "what a lesbian is," she could be subject to a $300 fine. And for her second offense, perhaps inviting Carol over the next day with a similar promise, Lindsey is subject to another $300 fine and ten days in jail. And for every invitation, enticement, or persuasion thereafter Lindsey is subject to an additional $300 fine and ninety days in jail.

As the crimes of Lindsey, Carol, Sindar, and Ra demonstrate, lesbian sexual expressions and various lesbian sex statutes have a rather idiosyncratic relationship. Cunnilingus between women is not criminal in Kansas, but should the tongue stray toward the anus and any "penetration, however slight" occur, then it is a crime with a sentence of six months in prison. A finger inside a lesbian lover is illegal in Missouri; a dildo is legal. But not in Texas, where dildo use will be a criminal act and fingers, unless they are objects, are legal. Such disparities are partially explained by the commitment to male sexuality embedded in the statutes. While the statutes seek to criminalize lesbian sex—I cannot think of any applicable statute that actually intends to exclude lesbianism from sexual deviancy—the attempted criminalization occurs within a frame of reference that centers male sexuality.

There are several lesbian theorists, most notably Marilyn Frye, arguing that sex is a term not applicable to lesbians. Frye's view is supported by the haphazard manner in which the lesbian sex statutes, considered as a whole, apply to lesbians. When we consider statutes or interpretations that require penetration, for example, it does not mean that lesbians have a uniform disdain or appreciation for penetration—whatever penetration means—but that penetration is not definitional of lesbian sex. Whatever our personal preferences, I think most of us would describe both Lindsey's interactions with Ra and with Sindar as "sex," and most of us would not consider one encounter as "less sex" than any other from Lindsey's point of view. The lesbian sex statutes and their judicial constructions centralize male sexuality, however, not lesbian sexuality.

While I am certainly not advocating that all statutes be broadened to include all lesbian relating, the statutes and their interpretations do constitute the legal text of our sexuality, and we need to think about the absences and rationales in that text. The refusal to explicitly state the acts criminalized is a violence. The absence is violent not only because if one wished to comply with the law (as the law assumes), one would need to avoid a wide spectrum of activities, but also because the only references to our sexuality within the legal text are constructed around profound absences. The rationales in the text are also violent. Although it is a relief in some ways to know that in Kansas my tongue on another lesbian's clitoris is legal, this relief is tempered by its rationale: my tongue is somehow less sexual because it shares a body with a clitoris instead of a penis. There is a random violence inherent in determinations of my criminal culpability based upon how deep my tongue penetrates, whether I use my tongue or my fingers, my fingers or an object, whether I eroticize a lover's clitoris, her anus, or her mouth, whether we are clothed or inside or in what state we happen to find ourselves. There is also a violence in the legal text of our sexuality that would describe any activities within our lovemaking as "deviate," as "perverted," as "unnatural," or even with reference to words like *intercourse* or *copulation.*

The violence of the lesbian sex statutes is the violence of propaganda, the propaganda of non-lesbianism. Because the statutes are rarely enforced—a rarity that insulates them from being challenged or attracting interest—we are tempted to think of the lesbian sex statutes as ineffectual attempts at brainwashing. Yet as propaganda they are effective, not because they prevent us from engaging in lesbian activity, but because they perpetuate violence upon our lesbian survival. They negatively affect our daily survival as support for legal determinations that tolerate discrimination against us, that remove our children from us as threats that regulate our choices about being open with our sexuality.

The rules of the law that are the lesbian sex statutes domesticate us. They are the supporting legal text for any feelings any of us might have that our sexuality is wrong. These laws domesticate us with their paradoxical message: our sexuality is not worthy of inclusion within any legal text; our sexuality is worthy only of being criminalized. It is a violence that may seem intangible, but it is ultimately supported by very tangible people like police, prosecutors, judges, and prison guards. When we appeal to the law as lesbians, we appeal to a legal text that has historically criminalized us and continues to do so.

## NOTES

1. People v. Livermore, 9 Mich. App. 47, 155 N.W. 2d 711, 712 (Mich. Ct. App. 1968).

2. For example, the District of Columbia statute entitled Sodomy provides in part that any indictment for such offenses "it shall not be necessary to set forth the particular unnatural or perverted sexual practice with the commission of which the defendant may be charged, nor to set forth the manner in which said unnatural or perverted sexual practice was committed."

3. As one judge states, "the sordid unnatural acts testified to by this witness are such that little could be gained by setting them forth in this opinion." Warner v. State, 489 P.2d 526 (Cr. Ct. App. Okl. 1971) (case involved "oral sodomy" between two women and between a woman and a man).

4. All italicized passages are excerpted and slightly edited from Judith McDaniel, *Just Say Yes* (Ithaca, New York: Firebrand Books, 1990). The passages appear on pages 15, 36, 124–5, 67–8, and 172.

5. *Buggery* is often interchangeably with *sodomy,* but according to *Black's Law Dictionary,* even when so used it does not necessarily include fellatio.

# II. E

# DENIAL AND ERASURE: EDUCATION AND CULTURE

"Whatever is unnamed, undepicted in images, whatever is omitted from biography, censored in collections of letters, whatever is misnamed as something else, made difficult-to-come-by, whatever is buried in the memory by the collapse of meaning under an inadequate or lying language—this will become, not merely unspoken, but unspeakable."
—Adrienne Rich

In his concurring opinion in *Bowers v. Hardwick* then Chief Justice Burger drew upon sources of hostility to homosexuality ranging from "Judeo-Christian moral and ethical standards" to the "common law of England . . . [that] became the received law of Georgia and the other colonies." Burger seemed particularly impressed with the contribution to this tradition of bigotry by the influential eighteenth-century British jurist William Blackstone, who referred to " 'the infamous *crime against nature*' as . . . a heinous act 'the very mention of which is a disgrace to human nature,' and 'a crime not fit to be named.' " Blackstone and Burger thus join the company of those who have hoped that the reality of sexual variation can be erased through denial.

One result of this conspiracy of silencing was that young lesbian, gay, and bisexual people encountering the schools and the mass media were unable to find images and information to help them understand their sexuality and overcome the hostility of family, peers, teachers, and preachers.

When lesbian and gay people in the United States began to organize in the 1950s and press for social change, they did so in an atmosphere that defined them as sinful, sick, and criminal. The first post-World-War-II homophile organization (as the lesbian and gay movement was then known), the Mattachine Society, was named for medieval court jesters who could speak unpopular truths

from behind masks (D'Emilio 1983). The Mattachine Society took an assimilationist approach that backed away from any open or confrontational strategy, preferring to work behind the scenes by encouraging mainstream professionals to educate the public. This "was an approach founded on an implicit contract with the larger society wherein gay identity, culture, and values would be disavowed (or at least concealed) in return for the *promise* of equal treatment. . . . Tolerance would be earned by making difference unspeakable" (Adam 1978:121).

But another approach began to surface, exemplified by Washington, D.C. activist Frank Kameny. In 1957, as a thirty-two-year-old astronomer recently hired by the Army Map Service, Kameny was confronted by Civil Service investigators with a charge of homosexuality and fired. Unlike most of those dismissed during the witch-hunts of the period, Kameny fought back through the federal courts, taking his case all the way to the U.S. Supreme Court, which refused to hear his appeal. Kameny did not take even this defeat as final, and in 1961 he joined with others to form the Mattachine Society of Washington. Stepping out from behind the masked modesty of the Mattachine's dependence on liberal professional authorities, Kameny modeled his strategies on the civil rights movement, arguing for unapologetic public actions. Articulating a minority civil rights analysis clearly paralleling other groups' struggles,

Kameny noted that we do not see "the NAACP and CORE worrying about which chromosome and gene produced a black skin, or about the possibility of bleaching the Negro" (Adam 1978:153).

The cornerstone of Kameny's political position was the cultivation of gay pride and the conviction that "we must instill in the homosexual community a sense of worth of the individual homosexual." This could only be done by a movement openly led by homosexuals themselves, because "the ONLY people in the world who are doing this are the pitifully small handful of us in the homophile movement" (quoted in Marotta 1981:62–3). Although small in numbers, the newly militant homosexual activists were marking significant new territory, and, while still overshadowed by the much larger civil rights and antiwar movements of the 1960s, they represented a significant change in the rules of the game.

This new generation of gay leaders was faced with the problem of creating a 1960s-style mass movement out of a group that had long learned to hide its identity from public view. One of the first institutions to feel the impact of the newly visible gay liberation was the academy. The presence of lesbian and gay scholars and students in colleges and universities was not new, but the emergence of openly gay academics was revolutionary. In 1967 the first gay student group was started at Columbia University by Robert A. Martin (a.k.a. Stephen Donaldson), a sophomore who had been influenced by Kameny. Later that same year another milestone was passed when Craig Rodwell opened the world's first lesbian and gay bookstore, the Oscar Wilde Memorial Bookstore, in Greenwich Village, with about twenty-five titles on its sparse shelves (Duberman 1993:164).

"In March 1973, seven men and one woman—college faculty, graduate students, a writer and a director, all gay—gathered informally in a Manhattan apartment . . . [and] talked in highly personal terms of the difficulties of being gay in a university setting." By the fourth meeting the participants decided that they "could contribute to the gay movement and to our own liberation by organizing in a formal way," and thus was formed the Gay Academic Union (D'Emilio 1974:13).

The founders of the Gay Academic Union decided to go public by sponsoring a conference on "universities and the gay experience." The two-day event held on Thanksgiving 1973 at the City University of New York, drew three hundred; the third conference two years later drew over a thousand. One of the keynote speakers at the first conference was Barbara Gittings, longtime lesbian activist and former editor of the *Ladder*, who began her talk with a fairy tale—"an untrue story about what life is like for the gay person in academia today:

> Every lesbian growing up finds that the signs of her sexual orientation are welcomed and encouraged by her parents and relatives. In school she gets massive peer support, and plenty of opportunities to develop a homosexual social life. Her sex-education courses teach her that being gay is positive, desirable. And valuable. Her church approves her orientation and encourages her to express it, and in her church she feels both socially comfortable and spiritually attuned.
>
> Again in college everyone and everything is geared to reinforcing her lesbianism and making her feel proud of it. She knows she'll never be called into the dean's office for a stern lecture, or a maudlin lecture, or a patronizing lecture, or for threats to tell her parents or to take away her scholarship. She knows that she can confidently go to the student counseling center and get constructive help for any love and sex problems that she may have. There is even a gay lounge on campus, which she can make her special place for meeting friends and for browsing through duplicate copies of good gay books in the main library.
>
> Later, as a teacher, she has no fear of a witch hunt or malicious accusations, because she knows that the full power of the faculty senate, the administration, and the board of trustees supports her right to be openly gay in the same way and to the same extent that most people are "known" to be straight. And there is a great variety of ways for her to meet other gay women openly in happy, civilized atmospheres.
>
> Throughout her life she can draw upon a rich literature about her kind of life and her kind of love. And the images of gay people in the mass media give her strength and dignity in her orientation and a sense of community with other gay people. The church blesses her love relationship with another woman, the world smiles and approves, and the state rewards the couple with special legal and economic advantages. And they all live happily ever after in academia. (1974:29–30)

In the more than two decades since this fairy tale was told to those who were bravely attending the first public meeting of lesbian and gay academics, much of what Gittings described *has* come to pass—especially those portions dealing with colleges and universities. While parents, public schools, churches, and the state have, for the most part, not yet lived up to Gittings's pretty picture, academia has changed in ways that her 1973 audience would truly have thought inconceivable. And most of the credit goes to those whose energies were unleashed by the advent of the lesbian and gay liberation movement.

Lesbian and gay caucuses began to emerge within many academic disciplines, with particularly strong forces in languages and literature, sociology, psychology, and history. But some of the most important progress in establishing lesbian and gay studies was happening outside the groves of academe. In 1976 independent scholar and playwright Jonathan Ned Katz published *Gay American History*, nearly seven hundred pages of documents and commentary to demonstrate "that the heretofore suppressed, hidden history of homosexual Americans does exist, and to insure that, like Gay Americans today, its existence can no longer be denied" (Katz 1976:2). Following Katz's inspiring model, grassroots lesbian and gay history projects sprang up around the country—in Boston, Buffalo, Chicago, San Francisco—and the results of their research appeared in the pages of the newspapers and journals spawned by the lesbian and gay liberation movement. Toronto's *The Body Politic* played a crucial role, both by publishing the work of the scholars who were pioneering what was then a far from respectable field and by convening international conferences in 1982 and 1985 that were key moments in the coalescing of an "invisible college" of lesbian and gay scholars both inside and outside of the academy (two other conferences in Amsterdam, in 1983 and 1987, also contributed to this process). In addition to sessions organized within academic disciplinary conferences, large-scale lesbian, gay, and bisexual studies conferences were held, first at Yale in the late 1980s, and subsequently at Harvard, Rutgers, and the University of Iowa.

Traditional avenues of academic publishing also opened in response to the flowering of lesbian and gay studies, beginning with the founding of the *Journal of Homosexuality* by John DeCecco in 1976 and continuing as important university and trade presses began to venture into areas previously considered too risky. In 1980 John Boswell's *Christianity, Social Tolerance, and Homosexuality* was both an award-winning scholarly success and a best-seller, and publishers took heed. The Oscar Wilde Memorial Bookstore now keeps company with Giovanni's Room in Philadelphia, the Different Light bookstores in Los Angeles, San Francisco, and New York, Lambda Rising in Washington and Baltimore, Glad Day in Boston and Toronto, and others in many cities across the continent. Equally important, major chains such as Barnes and Noble and Borders regularly include lesbian and gay sections (Mann, "The Gay and Lesbian Publishing Boom," this volume). However, as novelist Sarah Schulman has noted, the most dramatic literary successes have been achieved by gay male writers and by lesbians whose work contains "no primary lesbian content. . . . Books with primary lesbian characters are diminished and demeaned . . . [considered] 'political, not literary'" (Schulman 1996).

Many colleges and universities across the United States and Canada offer courses focused on lesbian and gay issues, and graduate students are no longer routinely warned that lesbian and gay topics are a kiss of death on the job market. Still, it would be an exaggeration to say that such research is invariably viewed with positive or even neutral eyes. In a 1993 survey conducted by the American Political Science Association among their members, 43 percent of the gay respondents said they had experienced or witnessed a situation in which a person's perceived homosexuality had hurt them in a job search. Yet progress is continuing. In 1989 City College of San Francisco inaugurated a department of lesbian and gay studies, and many institutions are exploring and introducing minors in gay studies. In 1991 City University of New York's Graduate School opened the Center for Lesbian and Gay Studies (CLAGS), the brainchild of prominent gay historian Martin Duberman. One of CLAGS's first projects was to assemble and publish a directory of lesbian and gay studies, listing some six hundred scholars from across the United States, Canada, and twelve other countries working in a wide variety of fields and disciplines.

Despite the remarkable success of lesbian and gay studies within the academic world, the important work of those outside academia has neither ended nor been rendered superfluous. One of the true treasures of grassroots scholarship, the Lesbian Herstory Archives founded by Joan Nestle and Deb Edel, succeeded in acquiring a building in Brooklyn as a permanent home and continues to serve as an invaluable resource for scholars. Independent scholars, writers, and editors such as Allan Bérubé, Michael Bronski, Pat Califia, Jewelle Gomez, Jonathan Ned Katz, and Barbara Smith continue to make major contributions.

As is often the case, the success of a social movement can be judged by the opposition it provokes, and lesbian and gay studies are no exception. In recent years the pages of conservative and even mainstream publications have been full of anxiety over the increased visibility of lesbian and gay faculty, students, courses, and topics. Much of this hostility has become entangled with the attacks mounted from the right on what they term the tyranny of political correctness now supposedly dominating American campuses. In one of the most extensive bombing runs of this campaign, Dinesh D'Souza's *Illiberal Education* (1991), lesbians and gay students are listed among the foremost villains in the PC drama.

However much the achievements of lesbian and gay studies, and scholars, within higher education, have fulfilled the dream of Barbara Gittings's 1973 fairy tale, the story is much bleaker in the realm of primary and secondary education. The public schools, in particular, have become a major battleground of the 1990s, as conservatives and fundamentalists have attempted to reverse the successes of minorities, women and gay people. Public education in the United States is uniquely decentralized, and the fight to improve the conditions faced by lesbian, gay, and bisexual youth must be fought district by district, state by state. While Massachusetts enacted a state law in 1993 prohibiting discrimination based on sexual orientation in education, the California state Board of Education was embroiled in controversy over three references to lesbian, gay, and bisexual people that threatened to prevent adoption of a Health Education Framework for the state's schools.

Gay people may be increasingly visible on college campus and in college curricula and textbooks, but "educational information about sexual orientation has long been censored in our nation's public schools. On the other hand . . . anti-gay slurs are the most-common and most-feared form of verbal harassment in U.S. schools" (Kielwasser and Wolf 1994:61). Bookstores and libraries may stock books and academic journals written for and by lesbian and gay academics, but *"The Readers' Guide to Periodical Literature* (a favorite index for high school students, as well as the general public) has refused to index many gay and lesbian publications" (Kielwasser and Wolf 1994:60).

In 1992 progressive New York City Schools Chancellor Joseph Fernandez was forced out of office in a political struggle fought largely over the issue of lesbian and gay content in the multicultural "Rainbow Curriculum" (Irvine 1994). When Minnesota enacted statewide protection for lesbian and gay people in employment, housing, and public accommodations in 1993, the bill also included a provision prohibiting teaching about homosexuality in the public schools. In August 1995 a coalition led by the Catholic Defense League and the Christian Coalition demanded that St. Paul, Minnesota, end a school district program that provides information, referrals, and support groups for gay, lesbian, and bisexual students (Burson 1995). In February 1996 the Salt Lake City Board of Education voted to eliminate all extracurricular clubs in order to block a lesbian-gay-straight alliance recently formed at a local high school. Ironically, under the federal Equal Access Act sponsored by Utah Senator Orin Hatch to ensure that Christian Bible clubs could use school facilities, they were not able to simply forbid one category of club (Sahagun 1996). In response, three teachers announced the formation of a gay and straight teachers alliance and a veteran public high school teacher came out publicly (Cortez 1996).

On the other side of this continuing struggle are organizations, from Virginia Uribe's pioneering Project 10 in the Los Angeles high schools, to the PERSON (Public Education Regarding Sexual Orientation Nationally) Project in San Francisco, to the Gay, Lesbian, and Straight Education Network (GLSEN), a national federation founded in Boston in 1990 that by 1997 had over 40 chapters across the United States, to the efforts of individuals and groups in states and local districts around the country. The fight to end the silence is far from over.

## REFERENCES

Adam, Barry. 1978. *The Survival of Domination.* New York: Elsevier/Greenwood.

Burson, Pat. 1995. "Groups Protest School District's Gay Program." *St. Paul Pioneer Press,* August 15.

Cortez, Marjorie. 1996. "Gay Teacher Says Silence Would Be Hypocritical." *Deseret News,* February 28.

D'Emilio, John. 1974. "Introduction." In *The Universities and the Gay Experience: A Conference Sponsored by the Women and Men of the Gay Academic Union,* pp. 9–18. New York: Gay Academic Union.

— 1983. *Sexual Politics, Sexual Communities.* Chicago: University of Chicago Press.

— 1992. "Gay and Lesbian Studies: New Kid on the

Block?" In John D'Emilio, *Making Trouble: Essays on Gay History, Politics, and the University*, pp. 166–175. New York: Routledge.

D'Souza, Dinesh. 1991. *Illiberal Education: The Politics of Race and Sex on Campus*. New York: Free Press.

Duberman, Martin. 1993. *Stonewall*. New York: Dutton.

Gittings, Barbara. 1974. "Keynote." In *The Universities and the Gay Experience: A Conference Sponsored by the Women and Men of the Gay Academic Union*, pp. 29–32. New York: Gay Academic Union.

Irvine, Janice. 1994. "A Place in the Rainbow: Theorizing Lesbian and Gay Culture." *Sociological Theory*, 12(2):232–248.

Katz, Jonathan Ned. 1976. *Gay American History: Lesbians and Gay Men in the USA*. New York: Crowell.

Kielwasser, Alfred and Michelle Wolf. 1994. "Silence, Difference, and Annihilation: Understanding the Impact of Mediated Heterosexism on High School Students." *High School Journal*, 77(1/2):58–79.

Marotta, Toby. 1981. *The Politics of Homosexuality*. Boston: Houghton Mifflin.

Rich, Adrienne. 1976/1979. "It Is the Lesbian in Us." In Adrienne Rich, *On Lies, Secrets, and Silence*, pp. 199–202. New York: Norton.

Sahagun, Lois. 1996. "Utah Takes Sweeping Approach to Ban Gay Teens Club." *Los Angeles Times*, February 22.

Schulman, Sarah. 1996. "Lesbian Content: The Kiss of Death." OutWrite 96, the Sixth National Lesbian, Gay, Bisexual and Transgendered Writers Conference, Boston, February 23–25.

Shea, Lois. 1995. "Teaching on Gays Banned by Board." *Boston Globe*, August 16.

# | 33 |

## Who Hid Lesbian History?

### LILLIAN FADERMAN

Before the rise of the lesbian-feminist movement in the early 1970s, twentieth-century women writers with great ambition were generally intimidated into silence about the lesbian experiences in their lives. In their literature, they gave male personae the voice of their most autobiographical characters, and they were thus permitted to love other women; or they disguised their homoerotic subject matter in code which is sometimes all but unreadable; or when they wrote of love most feelingly and even laid down rules for loving well as Margaret Anderson did, they left out gender altogether. We cannot blame them for not providing us with a clear picture of what it was like for a woman to love other women in their day. If they had they would have borne the brunt of anti-lesbian prejudice which followed society's enlightenment by late-nineteenth-century and early-twentieth-century sexologists about love between women,[1] and they knew that if they wished to be taken seriously they had to hide their arrested development and neuropathic natures. But we might expect that before the twentieth century, before love between women was counted among the diseases, women would have had little reason to disguise their emotional attachments; therefore, they should have left a record of their love of other women. And they did. However, it is impossible to discover that record by reading what most of their twentieth-century biographers have had to say about their lives.

While pre-twentieth century women would not have thought that their intensest feelings toward other women needed to be hidden, their twentieth-century biographers, who were brought up in a post-Krafft-Ebing, Havelock Ellis, Sigmund Freud world, did think that, and they often altered their subjects' papers. Other twentieth-century biographers have refused to accept that their subjeccts "suffered from homosexuality," and have discounted the most intense expressions of love between their subjects and other women. And where it was impossible to ignore the fact that their subjects were despondent over some love relationship, many twentieth-century biographers frantically searched for some hidden man who must have been the object of their subject's affection, even though a beloved woman was in plain view. These techniques of bowdlerization, avoidance of the obvious, and *cherchez l'homme* appear in countless pre-1970s biographies about women of whom there is reason to suspect lesbian attachments.

In our heterocentric society, the latter technique is the most frequent. What can it mean when a woman expresses great affection for another woman? It means that she is trying to get a man through that woman. What can it mean when a woman grieves for years over the marriage or death of a woman friend? It means that she is really unhappy because she had hoped to procure her friend's husband for herself, or she is unhappy because there must have been another man somewhere in the background who coincidentally jilted her at the same time—only all concrete evidence has been lost to posterity. So why did Lady Mary Montagu write to Anne Wortley in 1709 letters which reveal a romantic passion? e.g.,

> My dear, dear, adieu! I am entirely yours, and wish nothing more than it may be some time or other in my power to convince you that there is nobody dearer (to me) than yourself . . . [2]

In Margaret Cruikshank, ed., *Lesbian Studies*, pp. 115–122. Old Westbury, N.Y.: Feminist Press, 1982.

I cannot bear to be accused of coldness by one whom I shall love all my life. . . . You will think I forget you, who are never out of my thoughts. . . . I esteem you as I ought in esteeming you above the world.[3]

. . . your friendship is the only happiness of my life; and whenever I lose it, I have nothing to do but to take one of my garters and search for a convenient beam.[4]

Nobody ever was so entirely, so faithfully yours. . . . I put in your lovers, for I don't allow it possible for a man to be so sincere as I am.[5]

Lady Mary's 1920s biographer admits that Mary's letters to Anne carry "heartburnings and reproaches and apologies" which might make us, the readers, "fancy ourselves in Lesbos,"[6] but, she assures us, Lady Mary knew that Anne's brother, Edward, would read what she wrote to Anne, "and she tried to shine in these letters for him."[7] Thus, Mary was not writing of her love for Anne; she was only showing Edward how smart, noble, and sensitive she was, so that he might be interested in her.

Why did Anna Seward, the eighteenth-century poet, grieve for thirty years over the marriage of Honora Sneyd? Why in a sonnet of 1773 does she accuse Honora of killing "more than life, —e'en all that makes life dear"?[8] Why in another does she beg for merciful sleep which would "charm to rest the thoughts of whence, or how / Vanish'd that priz'd Affection"?[9] Why in still another poem does she weep because the "plighted love" of the woman she called "my life's adorner"[10] has now "changed to cold disdain"?[11] Well, speculates her 1930s biographer, it was probably because Anna Seward wished to marry the recently widowed Robert Edgeworth (whom Honora ensnared) herself. After all, "She was thirty years old—better suited to him in age and experience than Honora. Was she jealous of the easy success of [Honora]? Would she have snatched away, if she could have done so, the mature yet youthful bridegroom, so providentially released from his years of bondage?"[12]

But surely such distortions could not be made by a biographer of Mary Wollstonecraft. Even her husband, William Godwin, admitted in his memoirs of her that Mary's love for Fanny Blood had been "so fervent, as for years to have constituted the ruling passion of her mind."[13] But what was regarded as a fact of life by an eighteenth-century husband, boggles the mind of a twentieth-century scholar. For example, how was one biographer of the early 1950s to deal with the

information that in 1785 Mary underwent a terrible depression and that she complained in a letter to Fanny Blood's brother, George, "My harassed mind will in time wear out my body. . . . I have lost all relish for life—and my almost broken heart is only cheered by the prospect of death. . . . I almost hate the Green [her last home with Fanny] for it seems that grave of all my comforts"?[14] The biographer states himself that at the Green Fanny's health worsened and she could no longer teach, and for that reason Mary urged her to marry a man who would take her to a warm climate where she might recover. Then he asks, quoting the above letter to George Blood, "What had happened [to cause her great depression]? Surely her father's difficulties could not have suddenly plunged her into such a despondent state; nor could loneliness for Fanny or George."[15] His explanation is that Mary must have been madly in love with the Reverend Joshua Waterhouse and had been spurned by him. The biographer admits that there is no evidence he can offer to prove his hypothesis, and even that "On the surface Waterhouse seems like the last man in the world who would have attracted Mary Wollstonecraft." But he was the only man around at the time so "apparently he did."[16] "Something drastic," the biographer points out, must have happened "to provoke such despair," and the loss of a much-loved woman friend cannot be seen as "drastic" by a heterocentric scholar.

When there is no proof that a subject was involved in a heterosexual relationship, such biographers have been happy enough to accept circumstantial evidence rather than acknowledge the power of a same sex attachment. Characteristically, the same Wollstonecraft scholar quotes a letter to George Blood which Mary wrote six months after Fanny's death ("My poor heart still throbs with selfish anguish. It is formed for friendship and confidence—yet how often it is wounded") and then points out that the next sixteen lines have been obliterated by a later hand and suggests that they must have referred to her affair with Waterhouse. "Surely the censor did not go to such pains to conceal Mary's lamentations on the death of her friends," he asserts. It must have been Mary's love of a man the censor was trying to hide.[17] However, considering Godwin's complete honesty regarding Mary's affairs with Fuseli, Imlay, and himself, it is doubtful that a considerate censor would wish to spare her the embarrassment of one more youthful affair. What is more likely is that the letter was censored by someone from our century, aware of the twentieth-century stigma regarding "lesbianism," who wished to spare Mary that more serious accusation.

Despite that biographer's flimsy proof of the Waterhouse affair, subsequent Wollstonecraft biographers, uncomfortable with the evidence of her attachment to Fanny, have been happy to accept Waterhouse as fact. The myth is even propagated in a 1970s biography of Wollstonecraft by a woman. After discussing Mary's attachment to Fanny and pointedly distinguishing it from "lesbianism," she introduces Mary's "affair" with Waterhouse with the statement, "In spite of these emotions and professions [to Fanny], a certain secret disloyalty to Fanny did take place. It is rather a relief to discover it" [sic].[18]

The *cherchez l'homme* technique has been used most frequently by biographers of Emily Dickinson who have filled up tomes looking for the poet's elusive lover and have come up with no fewer than ten candidates, generally with the vaguest bits of "evidence." Concrete evidence that the ruling passion of Dickinson's life may well have been Sue Gilbert was eradicated from Dickinson's published letters and has become available only within the last couple of decades through Thomas Johnson's complete edition of her correspondence.[19] The earlier publications of a sizable number of Dickinson's letters was the work of her niece, Martha Dickinson Bianchi, the author of *The Life and Letters of Emily Dickinson* (1924) and *Emily Dickinson Face to Face* (1932). Bianchi, a post-Freudian, felt compelled to hide what her aunt expressed without self-consciousness. Therefore, Bianchi reproduced a February 16, 1852 (Johnson date) letter to Sue thus:

> Sometimes I shut my eyes and shut my heart towards you and try hard to forget you, but you'll never go away. Susie, forgive me, forget all that I say.[20]

What she did not produce of that letter tells a much more potent story:

> . . . Sometimes I shut my eyes, and shut my heart towards you, and try hard to forget you because you grieve me so, but you'll never go away, Oh, you never will—say, Susie, promise me again, and I will smile faintly—and take

up my little cross of sad—*sad* separation. How vain it seems to *write*, when one knows how to feel—how much more near and dear to sit beside you, talk with you, hear the tones of your voice; so hard to "deny thyself, and take up thy cross, and follow me"!—give me strength, Susie, write me of hope and love, and of hearts that *endured*, and great was their reward of "Our Father who art in Heaven." I don't know how I shall bear it, when the gentle spring comes; if she should come and see me and talk to me of you, Oh it would surely kill me! While the frost clings to the windows, and the World is stern and drear; this absence is easier; the Earth mourns too, for all her little birds; but when they all come back again, and she sings and is so merry—pray, what will become of me? Susie, forgive me, forget all that I say. . . .

Similarly, in the letter of June 11, 1852 (Johnson date) Bianchi tells us that Emily wrote to Sue:

> Susie, forgive me Darling, for every word I say, my heart is full of you, yet when I seek to say to you something not for the world, words fail me. I try to bring you nearer, I chase the weeks away till they are quite departed—three weeks—they can't last always, for surely they must go with their little brothers and sisters to their long home in the West![21]

But by checking the complete letter in the Johnson edition we find that what Emily wrote to Sue in that letter of June 11, when Sue was about to return to Amherst from her semester-long stint as a schoolteacher, was much more in the nature of a love letter than we could have guessed from the Bianchi version:

> Susie, forgive me Darling, for every word I say—my heart is full of you, none other than you in my thoughts, yet when I seek to say to you something not for the world, words fail me. If you were here—and Oh that you were, my Susie, we need not talk at all, our eyes would whisper for us, and your hand fast in mine, we would not ask for language—I try to bring you nearer, I chase the weeks away till they are quite departed, and fancy you have come, and I am on my way through the green lane to meet you, and my heart goes scampering so, that I have much ado to bring it back again, and learn it to be patient, till that dear Susie comes. Three weeks—they can't last always, for surely they must go with their

little brothers and sisters to their long home in the West!

Sue Gilbert was later to marry Austin Dickinson, Emily's brother, and Martha Dickinson Bianchi was the daughter of Sue and Austin. As anxious as she was to prove that Sue played a great part in making Emily a poet and to show that they were the closest of friends, she was even more anxious to prove that Emily and Sue were *only* friends. Thus, she includes in *Face to Face* an affectionate note that Emily sent Sue on June 27, 1852 (Johnson date):

Susie, will you indeed come home next Saturday? Shall I indeed behold you, not "darkly, but face to face" or am I *fancying* so and dreaming blessed dreams from which the day will wake me? I hope for you so much and feel so eager for you—feel I cannot wait. Sometimes I must have Saturday before tomorrow comes.[22]

But what Emily really said in that note, as Johnson shows, places their relationship in quite a different light:

Susie, will you indeed come home next Saturday, and be my own again, and kiss me as you used to? Shall I indeed behold you, not "darkly, but face to face" or am I *fancying* so, and dreaming blessed dreams from which the day will wake me? I hope for you so much, and feel so eager for you, feel I cannot wait, feel that *now*, I must have you—that the expectation once more to see your face again, makes me feel hot and feverish, and my heart beats so fast—I go to sleep at night, and the first thing I know, I am sitting there wide awake, and clasping my hands tightly, and thinking of next Saturday, and "never a bit" of you.

Sometimes I must have Saturday before tomorrow comes.

Where biographers have been too scrupulous to bowdlerize they have nevertheless managed to distort lesbian history by avoiding the obvious. Sometimes this has been done to "save" the reputations of their subjects (e.g., Emma Stebbins, Alice B. Toklas, and Edith Lewis were the "companions," respectively, of Charlotte Cushman, Gertrude Stein, and Willa Cather), although illicit heterosexual affairs are seldom treated with such discretion by even the most sensitive biographers. Sometimes this has been done out of willful ignorance. For example, while Amy Lowell so obviously made her "companion," Ada Russell, the subject of her most erotic love poetry that even a casual acquaintance could observe it, and Lowell herself admitted, "How could so exact a portrait remain unrecognized?"[23] it did remain unrecognized by those who saw Lowell only as an overweight unmarried woman whose "sources of inspiration are literary and secondary rather than primarily the expression of emotional experience,"[24] and whose characters thus never breathe, except for those "few frustrated persons such as the childless old women in 'The Doll,' " who share Lowell's "limited personal experiences."[25]

Although many biographers of the 1970s have been much more perceptive and honest with regard to their subjects' lesbian loves (e.g., Jean Gould's *Amy: The World of Amy Lowell and the Imagist Movement*, New York: Dodd, Mead, 1975; and Virginia Spencer Carr's *The Lonely Hunter: A Biography of Carson McCullers*, Garden City, New York: Doubleday, 1975) we cannot assume that lesbian history will never again be hidden by scholars who live in this heterocentric world. One otherwise careful, contemporary feminist critic totally ignores Margaret Anderson's successive passionate relationships with Jane Heap, Georgette LeBlanc, and Dorothy Caruso, and explains that ambitious women of Anderson's day were forced into loveless existences. But even where lesbian relationships are admitted in biographies of the 1970s, their importance is often discounted. A recent author of an Edna St. Vincent Millay biography squeezes Millay's lesbian relationships into a chapter entitled "Millay's Childhood and Youth" and organizes each of the subsequent chapters around a male with whom Millay had some contact, all of them ostensibly her lovers. Six who had relatively short contact with her are treated together in a chapter entitled "Millay's Other Men," although the author admits in that chapter that three of "Millay's other men" were homosexual.

This essay no doubt reads like a long complaint. It is. But it is also a warning and a hope. It is as difficult for heterocentric biographers to deal with love between women in their subjects' lives as it is for ethnocentric white scholars to deal with Third World subject matter, and their products are generally not to be trusted. If we wish to know about the lives of women it is vital to get back to their diaries, letters (praying that they have not already been expurgated by some well-meaning heterosexist hand), and any original source material that is available. It is also vital to produce biographies divested of the heterocentric perspective. Women's lives need to be reinterpreted, and we need to do it ourselves.

## NOTES

1. See my article, "The Morbidification of Love Between Women by Nineteenth-Century Sexologists," *Journal of Homosexuality* 4 (Fall 1978):73–90.

2. *The Complete Letters of Lady Mary Wortley Montague*, ed. Robert Halsband (Oxford: Clarendon Press, 1965), I:4.

3. Ibid., I:5.

4. Ibid., I:12.

5. Ibid.

6. Iris Barry, *Portrait of Lady Mary Wortley Montague* (Indianapolis: Bobbs-Merrill, 1928), p. 61.

7. Ibid., p. 54.

8. Walter Scott, ed., *The Poetical Works of Anna Seward with Extracts from her Literary Correspondence* (Edinburgh: John Ballantyne and Co., 1810) III:135.

9. Ibid., III:134.

10. Ibid., I:76–77.

11. Ibid., III:133.

12. Margaret Ashmun, *The Singing Swan: An Account of Anna Seward and her Acquaintance with Dr. Johnson, Boswell, and Others of their Time* (New Haven: Yale University Press, 1931), pp. 28–29.

13. William Godwin, *Memoirs of Mary Wollstonecraft*, ed. W. Clark Durant (1798; reprinted London: Constable and Co., 1927), p. 18.

14. Quoted in Ralph M. Wardle, *Mary Wollstonecraft: A Critical Biography* (Lawrence: University of Kansas Press, 1951), pp. 40–41.

15. Ibid., p. 41.

16. Ibid., p. 37.

17. Ibid., pp. 41–42.

18. Claire Tomalin, *The Life and Death of Mary Wollstonecraft* (London: Harcourt Brace Jovanovich, 1974), p. 18.

19. Thomas Johnson and Theodora Ward, eds., *The Letters of Emily Dickinson* (Cambridge: Harvard University Press, 1958).

20. Martha Dickinson Bianchi, *Emily Dickinson Face to Face* (Boston: Houghton Mifflin, 1932), p. 184.

21. Ibid., p. 216.

22. Ibid., p. 218. I discuss these letters at greater length in "Emily Dickinson's Letters to Sue Gilbert," *Massachusetts Review* 18 (Summer 1977).

23. Letter John Livingston Lowes, February 13, 1918 in S. Foster Damon, *Amy Lowell: A Chronicle, With Extracts from Her Correspondence* (Boston: Houghton Mifflin Co., 1935), p. 441.

24. Hervey Allen, "Amy Lowell as a Poet," *Saturday Review of Literature* 3 (February 5, 1927): 558. See also Horace Gregory, *Amy Lowell: Portrait of the Poet in Her Time* (New York: Thomas Nelson and Sons, 1958), p. 212; and Walter Lippmann, "Miss Lowell and Things," *New Republic* 6 (March 18, 1916):178–179.

25. Allen, "Amy Lowell as a Poet," p. 568.

# I 34 I

# *Stolen Goods*

## MICHAEL BRONSKI

*Close to a year and a half ago I was asked by Warren Blumenfeld to write an essay for an anthology he was editing entitled* Backfire: How Homophobia Harms Heterosexuals. *In the letter that accompanied my contract Blumenfeld wrote, "As we discussed a few months ago, I would be very much honored to include an essay written by you on the cultural contributions of gays and lesbians, which, for various reasons (especially those dealing with*

*Gay Community News*, July 21, 1991, pp. 8–9.

homophobia) have not been accepted or acknowl-edged within mainstream culture." This sentence pleased me because I had had some problems with the title and possible thrust of the book. Theoreti-cally, I suppose, heterosexuals are harmed—or at any rate diminished—by their homophobia, just as white people are by their racism and men by their misogyny. It is simply that in this time of AIDS hysteria and queer bashing, of organized, methodical attacks by the Republican party on both civil and abortion rights, of a Supreme Court that seems determined to chip away every inch of personal freedom we have gained in the past forty years, the theoretics of how homophobia hurts het-erosexuals lay low on my list of worries. But I was more than willing to write about how the contribu-tions of gay men went unaccepted and unacknowl-edged because of homophobia. I thought that the book's title—How Homophobia Harms Hetero-sexuals—might be viewed as a question, one that I would be willing to pursue and answer. When I did, my answer was that, certainly in terms of pop-ular culture, homophobia did not hurt heterosexu-als, but rather worked to their advantage.

I wrote my essay for Blumenfeld to edit and was told that it was excellent, but needed a few changes. Much of the editing was sensitive and useful, and informs this version of the piece, but there were several sentences—crucial, I felt to my argument—that were removed wholesale or changed to mean something entirely different.

In discussing the dynamic of how gay culture is assimilated I stated, "The bottom line is that straight culture is willing to take what they want and need from the gay sensibility and never admit or acknowledge its existence." In summing up I stated that "in cultural matters straight people's homophobia never hurts them in the same deadly and destructive way that it hurts queers; it merely allows them to steal without guilt and to cover the tracks of their hate with their own enjoyment." These sentiments, I was told, were unacceptable because they would alienate straight readers. The crux of the problem seemed to be clarified when a phrase in which heterosexuals are described as manifesting a "hateful and destructive homopho-bia" was changed to refer to their "destructive homophobic conditioning." And while it is impor-tant to remember that homophobia (like racism and misogyny) is a learned, not innate, behavior, it is equally important to hold people responsible for their actions and thoughts and not pretend that homophobia "just happens."

After three contentious phone calls—in which I was told that several straight people had also found my fictional introduction to the piece offensive because it conveyed a "gay elitism" and painted all heterosexuals as bores—I agreed to think about some changes that would bring my essay more politically in line with others in the book. But Blu-menfeld's editor at Beacon Press conveyed, in what I felt to be a homophobic letter, her feeling that even more drastic—including removing the fic-tional preface, which she felt was highly insulting to heterosexuals—changes were necessary.

It was clear, then, that neither was my essay suited for Backfire: How Homophobia Harms Heterosexuals nor did I want it published there, and I withdrew it.

## Part I: A Fairyless Tale

The evening began most curiously. Leah Hatch left her office at New York University after teach-ing her seminar on the Shakespearian sonnet and noticed that while the West Village streets seemed rather empty she could not find a cab to go uptown to meet her husband Gerald for dinner and the opera. Grabbing an uptown bus she observed that the other passengers, and there were only a few, seemed particularly noisy and rambunctious. Gerald was waiting for her outside of Morgan la Fay, their favorite new restaurant, and on entering were surprised that Alfredo, the maitre d', was not there. They found their own table and settled in: he complained about the lack of attention his new line of non-sexist chil-dren's books was getting in the industry and that most of his authors were not at home when he called today, she about the newest demands by fringe student political groups on campus. "After all," she muttered over her dry Beefeaters martini, "it's not as though the school doesn't already have more liberal policies than most other universi-ties."

Their waiter, a new man who seemed to have just been hired that afternoon, informed them that several entrées were not available and unfor-tunately there were no fresh deserts to be had. Gerald and Leah ate their steak and baked pota-toes—there apparently was no *gratin de pommes de terre provençal* (strange, since it was Chef Bertholle's specialty)—quietly engaging only in that elliptical small talk that couples married for more than two decades use to communicate the business of their day. Finishing up, they walked the few blocks to the Metropolitan Opera only to discover that Tchaikovsky's *Pique-Dame* had been cancelled. There were not many people in the Lincoln Center Plaza, but those who were there were buzzing about some rumor that most of the orchestra and many of the singers never showed up for the performance. Deciding to have a drink and some music, they took a cab to the Carlyle only to be told, by the assistant manager filling in for the missing doorman, that not only hadn't most of the waiters and bartenders shown up for work, but Bobby Short was also nowhere to be found and every other cabaret performer they called to fill in was also missing.

Giving up on their evening out, Leah and Gerald picked up a copy of the *New York Times* and started home noticing on their way downtown that most of the Broadway theaters seemed to have darkened their lights. Settling down with a drink, Gerald—who had taken the first two sections—noticed the paper's thinness. Not only was there less news, the only advertisements seemed to be for Club Med cruises (and those seemed to be missing some of the male models) and nothing for Calvin Kline underwear, or Bloomingdales, or men's sweaters. Leah was shocked that the Arts pages were almost completely bare—no reviews or features, only an announcement for a Tom Jones concert graced the page. Even the book review was missing. What at first seemed curious was now becoming downright bizarre. What was going on? Where was everybody? Well, not everybody, just the chefs, the musicians, the entertainers, the models, the waiters, photographers, the writers, the designers, the artists, actors, and well, lots of people out on the streets.

At the same moment Gerald and Leah looked at one another and began to understand. As affluent, moderately sophisticated middle-class, liberal, New Yorkers, they of course knew that gay men were behind some of what was usually called "culture." They just never knew—or admitted—how many. Could it be that all of the gay men in New York disappeared, vanished, became tired of having their endless efforts presumed to be the work of straight people or ignored or blatantly scorned *precisely* because they were by gay men? The ultimate ramifications of this were horrifying—no classical music, no experimental theater, no new fashions, no Broadway musicals, no alternative films, no opera, no avant garde art scene. In the midst of constructing this cultural nightmare, Gerald and Leah both had the same thought and raced down the long hallway to their fifteen-year-old son Chris's room, past the framed photographs that had won him first prize in his

school competition, and stood there. Afraid to open the door, they wondered if they would be met by only emptiness and silence.

## PART II: STOLEN GOODS

Homosexual behavior has always existed throughout history. Occasionally it has been sanctioned in specific instances in specific cultures—the ancient Greeks, for instance, allowed relationships between older men and younger freeborn boys—but for the most part it has been persecuted. Most Western cultures categorized it as a sin—a transgression against the moral order. As the power of religion began to be replaced by materialism, homosexuality grew to be defined as a transgression against the social order—a crime against the state. After the Freudian revolution homoeroticism and behavior—under the auspices of medicine and psychology—was understood as a sickness which might have been either psychological or physical depending on which theory was in current vogue.

Since the development of an open, and oppositional, homosexual identity in the late Victorian era—thanks to the writings of such men as John Addington Symonds, Havelock Ellis, and Edward Carpenter—homosexual people have viewed themselves as a distinct group brought together as much by their shared "sensibility" as their common sexuality. This did not eliminate their status as social outcasts; if anything, it increased visibility, which many times facilitated persecution. But what it did do was create a distinct cultural identity that in turn created distinct cultural products. Over the years a very complex, quite unequal, and very uneasy relationship has existed between gay male culture and mainstream culture. As religious, social, and legal prohibitions against homosexual acts remained intact, homosexual identity retained its stigma. However, although identified and defined as outcast, homosexual countercultures developed a positive gay identity, and, from the late nineteenth century on, homosexual writers and artists created a distinct political, artistic, and social identity. There were, of course, homosexuals pioneering in other fields as well—Alan Turing invented the modern computer, Wittgenstein broke important new ground in philosophy, and Maynard Keynes essentially invented contemporary economics—but because Western European society only allows gay male visibility in the "feminine" realm of culture the sexuality of these men, as well as many others, is twice hidden.

From Oscar Wilde's comedy of public and private personas in *The Importance of Being Ernest*, to Tennessee Williams's examination of the power of eroticism in *A Streetcar Named Desire*, to the ecstatic disco music of the seventies, to the highly sexualized photographs of Robert Mapplethorpe, gay artists have developed a way of looking at the world that has always presented not only a critique of the prevailing, dominant culture—what Christopher Isherwood has called the "heterosexual dictatorship"—but an alternative.

When the social order demanded that sexual activity result in procreation, gay artists promoted the idea of purely recreational sexuality. When mainstream culture—particularly industrialized British Victorian culture—insisted that art be utilitarian, gay artists promoted the idea of "art for art's sake"; a radical notion of beauty existing for the pleasure it gave the viewer. When, under the strictures of religion, moralism, and production, the patriarchal and hierarchical culture insisted on day-by-day literalism, gay artists proved that the imagination could bring not only emotional solace but psychological freedom.

From the very beginning the straight world enjoyed many aspects of gay culture. Oscar Wilde was lauded until his sexuality became too public to ignore. Writers like Edward Lear (who hid his sexuality in cryptic limericks) and Gerard Manley Hopkins (who converted his homoeroticism into subversive religious poetry) learned to write in code to avoid persecution. You can see a gay sensibility in the films of such Hollywood directors as George Cukor and James Whale and in the Broadway plays of John van Druten and lyrics of Cole Porter and Lorenze Hart. During the fifties and sixties Tennessee Williams and Edward Albee managed to have Broadway hits despite the accusations that they were attempting a homosexual subversion of American theater. Andy Warhol and David Hockney changed the face of the art world with their inventiveness and daring use of their gay sensibility.

For over one hundred years gay men have been creating culture that in turn has been assimilated into the mainstream. This culture and sensibility, in addition to being one of the most important forces shaping Western culture, has also been one of the most progressive, liberating, and visionary. The association of homosexuality with the sexual and the cry of "sex obsession" have been used to attack homosexuals, but it is precisely this quality, this "obsession with sex"

that is at the basis of the liberation offered by the gay sensibility. Gay artists have constantly argued in favor of an open imagination, sought to present images of beauty to a culture that has demanded only the most utilitarian necessities, and portrayed alternative worlds as a release from an oppressive reality. Freeing sexuality and eroticism is an impulse everyone feels on some level, no matter how much they consciously support the existing system. And this has always been the potent threat of the gay sensibility—a threat mainstream culture constantly attempts to co-opt and defuse by assimilation.

It is interesting to note that when gay men of color such as Bruce Nugent, Langston Hughes, Alain Locke, James Baldwin, among many others, produce culture their work is viewed almost always in relationship to their racial, not sexual, identities. This is due, in part, to the racism of the mostly white historical development of the gay sensibility but also to the incredibly stifling pressures that the dominant culture places on both gay and Black artists; pressures that make it extraordinarily risky to publicly claim more than one outsider identity. A look at the outstanding cultural production of the Harlem Renaissance—a movement that provided outlets for a great many gay men and lesbians—gives us a perfect example of how the urban American Black sensibility and a gay sensibility might work hand in hand. But all this work is labeled, by mainstream white, heterosexual culture, as only Black, never *gay*. The development of a U.S. gay culture runs, to a large degree, on a parallel track with that of a Black culture and there are few overlaps.

A good example of how trends—culture in the broadest sense—that originate in the white gay community move over to the straight world is men's fashions. In rebellion against the button-down-grey-flannel-suit image that was de rigueur for the fifties man—a look that minimalized sexuality, reinforced conformism, and promoted social authority—gay style sported tennis shoes, loafers, Levis, and chinos. In the early fifties, particularly in a gay community like New York's Greenwich Village, such clothing was identifiably "gay." These fashion choices—especially in opposition to the accepted standard—were understood in two ways. The first was that gay men could recognize one another because of the style (thus giving cohesion to a somewhat covert, hidden community), and its reverse was that the straight world could identify "what a homosexual looked like."

This dynamic was not particularly secret. In Ruth McKinney's 1947 humorous autobiography, *My Sister Eileen*, she notes, after the sisters move to a basement apartment on Christopher Street, how many of the neighborhood men wear tennis shoes. The phrase "light in the loafers"— implying that someone was gay, possibly because like a fairy they floated a bit when they walked— was so common that it even appears as late as 1987 in the Robin Williams's film *Good Morning, Viet Nam*. And it wasn't just that these clothes were less traditional, a bit rebellious— they were also sexy.

The Rev. Robert Wood, in his groundbreaking 1960 book *Christ and the Homosexual* traces the origins of blue jeans as a gay style in the context of an emerging postwar gay culture. Discovering dungarees while on basic training in the West, many gay GIs began to wear them back East after the war. "But it wasn't just the wearability of the jeans which commended them; they were also sexy. Tight cut, low on the hips, rugged in appearance, different in style, able to be shrunk to a form-fit, the more worn and faded the better, they quickly became the costume of the homosexual who wanted to look trim, to be a bit revealing in the crotch and rump, and to feel 'butch.' " If you read through the gay novels of the time— James Barr's *Quatrefoil*, Fritz Peters's *Finistere*, Michael Forrest's *The Gay Year*—it is clear from the description how these clothes functioned to define, socially and emotionally, what it meant to be gay in a contemporary urban setting.

Of course, what eventually happened was that the straight world was drawn to the erotic and psychological freedom that these gay clothes represented and they, in time, became an accepted staple of U.S. apparel. The same pattern is seen in man's styles throughout the next decades. The sixties brought flowered shirts and tight pants, wide ties and bellbottoms, men's jewelry, long hair, and sexy underwear. The seventies brought on a clone look with short hair and trim mustaches, flannel shirts, tight jeans, and work boots. The eighties provided an older, more butch leather/Levi look and even sexier underwear ads. Each of these looks started in urban gay male communities and were quickly taken up by the fashion industry and marketed as the "new look" for the heterosexual male. Each "look" is progressively more sexual and more open—the "tough" Levi outside covers suggestively sexual undergarments. These looks became commonplace to U.S. culture: the Marlboro Man and the Calvin

Klein underwear man—to choose the two most obvious and mythical types—peered out of almost every magazine and newspaper, down from billboards, out of televisions. American men were discovering that they were sexual and they were learning it from queers.

This dynamic can be seen widespread through U.S. culture: Andy Warhol and Robert Mapplethorpe, disco and acid house music all started in the gay culture. Drag shows lead the way not only to *La Cage aux Folles* but to *Tootsie* and *Victor/Victoria*. Off-Broadway theater started in Greenwich Village's Cafe Cino; American experimental film grew from the Kucher Brothers and Jack Smith. The various nostalgia crazes over the past thirty years began as gay male phenomenon. Bette Midler, Barbra Streisand, Jane Olivor all started in gay culture. The comebacks of Blossom Dearie, Eartha Kitt, Barbara Cook, and Yma Sumac were all due to a gay following. Quiche, brunch, and Perrier (none of which real men ate—or drank) gained popularity through gay culture. The idea of Camp altered the very notions of how we looked at popular culture. There is no doubt that the gay male sensibility—after it had been assimilated—has been one of the most dynamic transformers of U.S. culture. But, one must ask, at what cost?

Assimilation is the word used by mainstream culture to describe what is *supposedly* an equal cultural exchange—the dominant culture appropriates an enjoyable aspect of the counterculture, which receives, in return, some form of acceptance. But the reality is that most of these artifacts, interests, ideas, styles, and visions are stolen, appropriated without credit, and their origins lied about. The prohibition against speaking honestly about the lives of gay people is almost universally enforced by the media, and gay culture *meisters* are forced to remain silent about the sexuality or suffer homophobic attacks. Those who are willing (and able) to remain closeted are rewarded and those who choose to be open are ignored or attacked.If audiences knew that the four men responsible for *West Side Story*—Leonard Bernstein, Arthur Laurents, Stephen Sondheim, and Jerome Robbins—were gay, it is unlikely the show would have been greeted with the praise it received. On the other hand, once Tennessee Williams, in the sixties, became more open about his sexuality—declaring it rather than just letting it be presumed—he was attacked as a cultural subversive. Even Edward Albee, who never played the game of *pretending* to be straight, was regaled with homophobic attacks. Playwrights like Robert Patrick—surely one of the best stage writers of the last thirty years—have never received the praise or fame he deserves simply because he refuses to be quiet about his sexuality. (This situation has its exceptions—Harvey Fierstein managed to be both out and critically acclaimed, and some critics are willing to allow a genius like Charles Ludlam some small praise as an oddity act.) But the bottom line is that straight culture is willing to take what they want and need from the gay sensibility and never admit or acknowledge its existence.

The situation is not without ironies: some bitter, some simply ironic. Many times the products of preassimilated gay sensibility—especially when they might be used to publicly identify a homosexual—could be mortally dangerous: think of all of the men who were queer-bashed because they were wearing loafers and jeans (or leather and boots) only to have their attackers wearing the same styles two years later. This same dynamic happens, on a less deadly level, with cultural queer-bashing. The work of openly gay artists has always been dismissed as "insignificant," "immature," "frivolous," "self-indulgent," "contentless," and "supercilious" (all words that have been used to describe nonreproductive sexuality or fall into homophobic categorizations in the standard psychological attacks on gay people). Once these artists, or works, are assimilated the traits that were once vilified are praised with words like "inventive," "imaginative," "triumph of form over content," "androgynous," and "daringly erotic." On the lighter side, a good case might be made for the fact that gay sensibility and taste—in fashion, film, music, or theater—exists precisely to create, and manifest, an open gay identity. Once these are assimilated—that is, stolen—by straight culture, gay people have to begin inventing something new to distinguish themselves from the more mundane herd. The fact remains that the tremendous impact of gay culture upon the straight world is never acknowledged.

Every now and then the question is posed (as it was fancifully in the opening to this piece): Would heterosexuals suffer if there were no gay sensibility input into mainstream culture? And the answer would have be to a resounding *yes*. But that is not really the question to be asked. For while it is true that many heterosexuals have, because of their own hateful and destructive homophobia, cut themselves off from who and what they identify as gay—women, men, and culture: look at Leah and Gerald's relationship with their son Chris—they *never* deny themselves the benefits of assimilated gay culture and sensibility because they never have to admit or deal with the fact that it *is* gay culture. The lie of assimilation is that while the straight world can revel in the pleasure of the gay imagination they don't have to give anything in return. In cultural matters straight people's homophobia never hurts them in the same deadly and destructive way that it hurts queers; it merely allows them to steal without guilt and to cover the tracks of their hate with their own enjoyment.

## PART III: HAPPY ENDING?

There is no way to stop the dominant culture from stealing and co-opting gay culture. Nor should there be. The evolution of a pluralistic society—as ours is blithely called; a phase obscuring the inequities that hurt and damage those of us who are at some disadvantage—is dependent on the contributions of all. The assimilation of gay culture is merely one in a series of thefts; African American, Latino, Asian, Native American Indian cultures, and those of every cultural and ethnic group face the same threat. The difference is that almost all of these other cultures receive some acknowledgment: the Motown sound is accepted as "Black music," Frank Sinatra is proud of his Italian heritage, Philip Roth recognizes the effect that American Judaism has had upon his life and work, Linda Ronstadt works with the Mexican music of her childhood. This is not to say that any of these groups do not face cultural oppressions—they do, it is just that while the process of assimilation will dilute and defuse their original intention and power, it generally does not totally ignore and lie about their place of origin.

In the past twenty years the lesbian and gay liberation movement has been battling not only for basic civil rights and equal protection under the law—a seemingly endless fight with the Supreme Court deciding in 1987 that homosexual acts are not even legal in the privacy of the bedroom—but for the right to be visible, to be open, to be ourselves. This basic right is denied us not only because of the lies, distortions, and disinformation perpetrated by the media but because of the consistent assimilation of gay culture without acknowledgment. The message of the Stonewall riots was to be out, open, and demand what you want: a message repeated today by Queer Nation's "We're Here, We're Queer, We're Fabulous, Get Used to It." The relationship between gay culture, homophobia, and the dominant culture is complex. The first step in resolving it is for lesbians and gay men to insist not only on visibility but on the open acknowledgment of their sexuality, life, and culture. The second step is for heterosexuals to acknowledge the many ways they benefit from gay culture and the many ways they contribute to gay invisibility. The fact that homophobia, like racism, is socially conditioned—learned—behavior cannot obscure the reality of who is hurt by it and who is responsible. To simply pose the question of how straight people are culturally harmed by their homophobia is to resolve nothing.

## NOTE

This essay deals with gay male contributions to culture. Historically, because of the existing cultural male bias, gay men have always had more visibility than lesbians. This has rendered lesbians doubly invisible and their cultural contributions twice lost. Lesbian cultural contributions have been brought to light, explored, and explicated more through the lens of the second wave of feminism than through the focus of gay liberation.

Thanks to both cartoonist Gary Ostrom of the now defunct *Body Politic* and Carl Morse in his poem "Dream of the Artfairy," who both explored the idea of what the world would be like without the contributions of gay men.

# | 35 |

# *Remembering Lenny: Parting Notes on a Friend Who Never Quite Came Out*

## PAUL MOOR

On Oct. 15, 1990, the *New York Times* carried a three-column headline across the top of its front page: LEONARD BERNSTEIN, 72, MUSIC'S MONARCH, DIES. Not often does the good gray *Times* use language like that—"music's monarch"—particularly in a headline.

Neither I nor *The Advocate* had any interest in outing Bernstein, whom I knew for the last 40-odd years of his life. I also knew Felicia Montealegre, the lovely Chilean-American actress, for years before she married him. A logistical coincidence abetted our triplex friendship: Lenny lived at 32 W. Tenth St., I at 184 W. Tenth St., and Felicia at 69 Washington Pl., a few blocks farther downtown. A group that gathered at Felicia's for Sunday brunch included me and frequently Lenny, whose really big career had begun shortly before.

More than once, while waiting for the food, Lenny and I played Mozart four-hand sonatas on Felicia's upright; more than once, on less happy occasions, Felicia sobbed on my shoulder when Lenny would change his mind and say he didn't think he wanted to get married after all. Aaron Copland, discussing that troubled relationship with me on one occasion, expressed moral misgivings that Lenny was attracted to Felicia as "window dressing"—as camouflage.

In those days, as for the rest of his life, except when sleeping or on the podium or at synagogue, Lenny had a cigarette always in his hand, and he

*Advocate*, November 22, 1990, pp. 66–67.

sucked on it like a breast-feeding infant—even after lung cancer killed Felicia in 1978.

Being in the field of contemporary music in the 1940s in New York, Lenny and I—not to mention Samuel Barber, Marc Blitzstein, Paul Bowles, John Cage, Copland, Henry Cowell, David Diamond, Gian Carlo Menotti, and Virgil Thomson, to name only the gay composers—ran into one another frequently at concerts and over supper afterward. Virtually everybody in the entire international music world "knew about" Lenny.

When I recently reviewed the second volume of Copland's memoirs for *Musical America*, I wrote:

> With the publication of a bumptious, unauthorized book some years back, the homosexuality of a number of 20-century American composers . . . became a matter of public record. I have conducted a little experiment by drawing up a generously fair list of their straight contemporaries: Carter, Foss, Hanson, Harris, Ives, Moore, Piston, Riegger, Ruggles, Schuman, and Sessions. Those two lists provide an astonishing ratio of (*at least*) ten homosexual to 11 heterosexual composers; about half have been gay—a truly astonishing, possibly unique statistic in all musical history.

## LIVING A LIE

I find it fair to say that Lenny, in his youth, permitted social pressures to force him into a trap. He found his first principal mentor in Copland and his second in Boston Symphony conductor Serge Koussevitzky, who called him Lenyusha (pronounced LENyusha). Koussie (as his adoring Tanglewood students referred to him) heard rumors about Lenny and raised the subject one day himself: "My old friend Tchaikovsky—pederastical. My Aaron—pederastical. Lenyusha, even I have heard *you* are pederastical."

Lenny knew that Koussie, whom he worshiped, wanted it not to be true—so he dissembled. He also did this for his immigrant parents (his father sold beauty supplies, and his mother had worked in a textile mill).

The New York Philharmonic did manage to survive a gay conductor, Dimitri Mitropoulos, thanks to the fact that he apparently lived a personal life of almost monastic austerity; had the board of directors known, they would never have engaged him. (Have things in the music field changed since then?) Lenny stood on the threshold of a great career, and he knew what his society considered his duty.

One memory seems ironic in view of the flourishing conducting career that Copland himself enjoyed in later life. Copland, who grew up 18 years before Lenny did, told me he'd once asked Lenny, "How in the world can you stand up there on the podium and try to conduct 100 or so men when you know all the time that they *know* about you?" In that regard, certainly, Lenny had no problems.

Lenny's behavior, on many other occasions, manifested that contorted sort of guilt that derives from self-hating homophobia. During the Holland Festival around 1950, we lunched together at the Kurhaus in Scheveningen. He talked about a waiter on the *Nieuw Amsterdam* who had fallen hard for him during the voyage over and declared his readiness to follow Lenny anywhere, under any circumstances.

In a manner I found chilling, Lenny told how he had sketched what that poor devil would have had to submit to: servant's quarters and so on. Lenny made it clear he couldn't even think of him—lover or not—as anything but a menial.

During the early years of our friendship, Lenny had already concluded a serious, live-in relationship with another musician (who, like Lenny, went on to marriage and prominence in another area of music). After that, he seemed uninterested in anything more than casual contacts. During a debate between us about stable as opposed to overnight relationships, Lenny summed up his own outlook in five memorable words: "Homosexuality without promiscuity is impossible!"

Tom Waddell, the physician and Olympic athlete, told me (shortly before he died of AIDS) about a San Francisco party Lenny had attended along with the upper crust of the city's gay society. When the host introduced Waddell as the founder of the Gay Olympics, Lenny (by that time quite drunk, according to Waddell) launched a gratuitous attack: "Who the hell needs Gay Olympics?" As Waddell walked away, seething, Lenny's infuriated voice followed him: "Who the hell's *that* fucking queen!" ("I still wish I'd punched him," Waddell said.)

## FAMILY HONOR

In pursuing Lenny, Felicia showed pathetic, almost desperate persistence. When all seemed lost, she began a relationship with actor Richard Basehart. Felicia and Lenny, back together, finally not only married but had three children. Lenny wholeheartedly adored his children—and, in what he thought was their best interest, he continued to maintain the charade, the facade.

As Lenny's children grew up, he gradually became more open. After 25 years of turbulent marriage, he and Felicia began a trial separation. (Lenny returned to her only after her cancer diagnosis.) Incidents got into the news; one involved an ex-Marine who had left with Lenny's car—which Lenny neglected to report to the police.

As the AIDS epidemic became ever more hideous, Lenny became ever more eager to help. Last year, to protest what he considered censorship of an AIDS exhibit by the National Endowment for the Arts, he refused a Bush administration medal. He conducted AIDS benefit concerts, lining up as soloists some of the greatest names in the world. Archival tape I saw the night

he died included a clip of him paying tribute to "those I love who have died of AIDS." Over and over, he gave every appearance of a profoundly troubled man desperately trying to come out.

Years earlier he had audaciously composed his *Serenade for Violin, Strings, and Percussion* after Plato's *Symposium,* one of all literature's greatest paeans to homosexual love. In *Songfest,* the poems he set included a late discovery by Walt Whitman, "To What You Said," in which the poet went perhaps farther than ever in writing of men's love for men. When Lenny conducted *Songfest* in Munich for a television film, he turned and recited that entire poem to an enormous, spellbound audience.

If Lenny never came out in the customary sense, he did everything just short of it. Those of us with nobody to hide from any longer know, for certain, that if he had, it would have made him a far less unhappy man.

# | 36 |

## *Willa Cather*

### SHARON O'BRIEN

Willa Cather did not make it easy for her biographers. In the last years of her life, she destroyed the letters in her possession and wrote a will in which she forebade quotation from her correspondence. Like many writers, Cather wanted to protect her privacy, and she did not trust future biographers and critics to address her life or her work sympathetically.

But Willa Cather had another reason for wanting to guard her private life. Judging from her letters, she was willing to be viewed as a woman, but not as a lesbian. Her love for women was a source of great strength and imaginative power to her, but she feared misunderstanding and repudiation

if this love were to be publicly named—quite a legitimate fear in her time. But since I am writing in a more enlightened era than hers, I can assume that I am addressing the sympathetic readers that Cather, given her historical moment, could not have imagined.

I am still aware that Willa Cather would not have approved of my writing a biography that mentions her lesbianism. When I was working on my full-length biography of her, *Willa Cather:*

In Sharon O'Brien, *Willa Cather*, pp. 15–19.
Philadelphia: Chelsea House, 1994.

*The Emerging Voice,* I knew that scholarly integrity required me to explore the connections between sexuality and creativity; but I still felt some guilt about venturing into personal territory that she wanted to guard. One night, I dreamed that Cather invited me to tea in her Greenwich Village apartment. Pouring me a cup from her silver teapot, she turned to me and said, "I just want you to know that I'm not gay." Ever the biographer, I stood my ground and asked, "What about the letters to Louise Pound [Cather's first lover]?" She did not reply, and the dream ended. Later, my anxiety surfaced again: I dreamed that Edith Lewis, Cather's longtime companion, called me up and said, "I just want you to keep the word 'lesbian' out of the biography." Of course, I could not promise I would, and she hung up.

Finally, though, Willa Cather and I came to a reconciliation, at least in my unconscious. As I was finishing up the manuscript, I dreamed I was a guest in her house. She came downstairs with my bags packed—not a gesture of rejection but a sign of a considerate hostess. It was time for me to go.

As these dreams suggest, writing a biography is not just an intellectual experience. The biographer forms a close emotional and imaginative relationship with the subject, and at times that relationship may seem more real, more intense, than bonds with people in one's daily life. All in all, I spent 15 years on my full-length biography of Willa Cather, and when it was finished I thought I would never want to write about her again.

I changed my mind when I was asked to write a biography for readers in a series to be called *Lives of Notable Gay Men and Lesbians.* I thought that the series was needed, and the publisher was brave and imaginative to create it. I also thought that Cather's life—itself filled with bravery and imagination—had much to offer readers in their teens and early twenties, a period of difficult transition when we all need hopeful stories to help us grow up.

Although novels such as *My Ántonia* and stories such as "Paul's Case" are now frequently taught in high schools, paradoxically Willa Cather did not want her fiction to be read in high school. She did everything she could during her lifetime to limit the dissemination of her fiction. She controlled the excerpts from her fiction that could appear in anthologies and refused permission to anthologies intended for use in high schools. She successfully kept all her novels out of paperback and prevailed upon Houghton Mif-

flin, her publisher, not to sell *My Ántonia* to the movies. As the publisher Alfred Knopf recalls, Cather did not want her books to be read in the classroom because she feared that if readers were exposed to her in a coercive, authoritarian environment, they might "grow up hating her." In other words, she did not want to be on reading lists, syllabi, or tests.

Cather resisted being "taught" to students because her view of the ideal relationship between writer and reader was based on the model of friendship. She wanted readers to respond voluntarily and imaginatively to her work because her writing struck some chord of affection in them. "When we find ourselves on shipboard, among hundreds of strangers," she wrote, "we very soon recognize those who are sympathetic to us. We like a writer much as we like individuals, for what he is, simply, underneath his accomplishments." But if her novels were assigned, then the relationship between the reader and the text would be enforced, not freely chosen. To follow out the implications of her metaphor, reading a writer in the classroom would be like a hostage forming a bond with a captor, not like a traveler striking up a shipboard friendship.

So strongly did Cather wish readers to discover her fiction independently that throughout the 1920s she refused to allow her novels to be adopted by book clubs. She relented only with *Shadows on the Rock,* in part responding to the private claims of friendship: Dorothy Canfield Fisher, then one of the judges of the Book-of-the-Month Club, prevailed upon her.

After Cather's death, Edna Lewis, who became executor of her estate, agreed finally to paperback editions, and Cather's fiction has long been taught in high schools. So it is certainly possible that some of you reading this biography have encountered Willa Cather because her work has been assigned to you. You may have been required to write a paper on her work or take an examination in which questions were asked about *My Ántonia.* So you may not have yet approached Willa Cather freely, as a literary friend.

But friendship can often develop after assigned meetings. Such was the case for me. I read *My Ántonia* in high school because I had to, and then I forgot all about Willa Cather. I associated her with conservatism and Catholicism because my Irish Catholic father kept telling me I should read *Death Comes for the Archbishop* and *Shadows on the Rock*—a sure way to keep Cather off my reading list. When I was in graduate school, during the early years of the women's movement, I complained to a friend that American fiction was terribly hard on strong women. "I'm tired of reading books where women end up dead or punished," I said. "Try Willa Cather," he said.

So I read *O Pioneers!* and found a new literary world opening to me: here was a writer who could imagine a female character as creative and strong, and who didn't end the novel by making her heroine walk into the ocean. I also fell in love with Cather's lucid, evocative, pure style. Having spent too much time wandering in the convoluted prose of Henry James's late novels—brilliant writing, of course, but not my cup of tea—I found entering Cather's verbal landscape the equivalent of leaving a labyrinth for the thrilling openness of the Nebraska plains.

I wrote my dissertation on Cather and then spent 10 years writing a biography. In my work, I could write about issues that concerned me deeply—gender, sexuality, the creative process—and still be in the company of a writer whose prose made me happy. For the first time, I felt that my private and public worlds might come together, that I might be able to teach and write what I cared about. So my literary friendship with Cather allowed me to stay in graduate school (I'd been on the verge of leaving) and become a teacher and a writer.

I hope, then, that if you have encountered Willa Cather in the classroom, you can hold open the possibility of developing a literary friendship with her—if not now, perhaps sometime in the future. I still turn back to her fiction for inspiration and guidance; sometimes she is a friend, sometimes a mentor, sometimes the voice of my best self. One passage from *My Ántonia* I read and reread, and quote to anyone who will listen. It's the beautiful section in which Jim is lying drowsily in the garden, surrounded by yellowing pumpkins and ladybugs, and it leads to the quotation that Cather wanted on her gravestone:

The earth was warm under me, and warm as I crumbled it through my fingers. Queer little red bugs came out and moved in slow squadrons around me. Their backs were polished vermilion, with black spots. I kept as still as I could. Nothing happened. I did not expect anything to happen. I was something that lay under the sun and felt it, like the pumpkins, and I did not want to be anything more. I was entirely happy. Perhaps we feel like that when we die and become a part of something entire, whether it is sun and air, or goodness and knowledge. At any rate, that is happiness; to be dissolved into something complete and great. When it comes to one, it comes as naturally as sleep.

Whenever I become enmeshed in that curse of American life, a narcissistic preoccupation with myself and my accomplishments (or lack thereof), I like to say to myself "that is happiness; to be dissolved into something complete and great." Cather's voice helps remind me of the pleasure that can come from leaving the self behind, "dissolving" as I place my attention outward on my students, or my friends, or the words that flow from my fountain pen. (Like Cather, I do first drafts by hand.)

I am grateful to Cather for those words, for the literary friendship we have had, and for the novels she has left us. I am also glad that her work is available in paperback and taught in high schools. According to Cather, a fine writer leaves in the mind of the receptive reader a "cadence, a quality of voice that is exclusively the writer's own, individual, unique." Perhaps some of you have heard Cather's distinctive voice speaking to you even from within the structure of a classroom or a syllabus, and you will some day begin an enriching friendship with her. If so, as a reader you will receive the emotional and spiritual connection with a writer that Willa Cather, speaking of her own literary friendship with Sarah Orne Jewett, called "a gift from heart to heart."

# I 37 I

# Closets in the Museum: Homophobia and Art History

## JAMES SASLOW

*This essay was written nearly two decades ago, when I was a beginning graduate student—the only one, so far as I knew, who was openly gay and wanted to pursue my own "roots" in the field of art. Its analysis accurately reflects the situation in academia and the art world at that time, but much has since changed, and largely for the better. I had a bit of fun in this piece at the expense of some obviously fuddy-duddy professors, but Columbia University deserves gratitude for later encouraging me to write one of the first doctoral dissertations on a gay theme (the myth of Ganymede, mentioned below). Acceptance, even appreciation of gay artists and history is now quite widespread in the discipline, including the formation of a Gay and Lesbian Caucus of the College Art Association in 1989 and an explosive growth of research, theory, panels, and publications.*

*Precisely because of that progress, the following essay now needs to be placed in a longer historical perspective. Its analysis and agenda grew out of the political passion and emerging identity politics that animated the first wave of contemporary gay activism, which was closely associated with the broader cultural values of the now mythical sixties. In this early phase of gay art studies, from Stonewall into the mid-1980s, a handful of scholars concentrated on rescuing a putative "canon" of artists and works from historical neglect. As in many other disciplines, the subsequent, more methodologically sophisticated second stage, inspired by Foucault's theories of the social construction of culture, has aggressively modified the traditional notions of homosexual identity upon which such a sought after canon was founded. This article, predating such developments, tacitly accepts a constant form of "homosexuality" throughout history, and largely defines "gay subject matter" as erotic images—both assumptions that I, like many others, later reexamined.*

*In retrospect, I remain deeply fond of this essay, intended in the fire of youth as a manifesto for changes that did, in large part, come to pass. Both mainstream and community-based galleries, periodicals, and collectors have made possible a flowering of gay and lesbian visual artists, and an expansion of their art beyond erotica to portraits, genre scenes, and conceptual works. All is not rosy: museums have been less welcoming than academia, obscenity remains a rallying point for the religious right, and our definition of gay art has unfortunately also had to make room for the AIDS Quilt and political graphics from ACT-UP. All the same, the realization that, twenty years on, the article has turned into something of a period piece inspires both nostalgia and gratification.*

▼   ▼   ▼

Perched on a rocky bluff at the edge of downtown, the stately colonnades of the Philadelphia Museum are surrounded by high stone walls, elaborate fountains, and cascading staircases. This overpowering monumentality could be looked upon as symbolizing either of two ideas: the dignity of art's function, or the power of the institution itself.

One glance at the surrounding landscape makes clear which connection is intended. The vista down the imposing boulevard from the museum's front plaza leads the visitor's eye directly to the great tower of City Hall. The rear

In Karla Jay and Allen Young, eds., *Lavender Culture*, pp. 215–227. New York: Harcourt Brace, 1978.

façade overlooks the historic palaces of the 1876 Centennial Exhibition. Art lies on axis with temporal power and national glory.

A coincidence of urban planning, perhaps—but a revealing one. Over the last several years, as a student, writer, and lecturer on art, I have been investigating our gay heritage in the visual arts, and find that it is richer than many of us are yet aware of. I have also found that the powerful complex of institutions that are the custodians of our artistic heritage—museums, galleries, universities—tends to overlook or suppress the historical evidence of gay artists and gay themes. Based on my own experience, I will attempt here to provide a brief overview of the art world's present attitudes toward homosexuality and homoerotic art, and of some progress that has been made toward breaking the hold of tradition on our past.

The art world has declared gay people and their emotions "obscene"—which derives from the Latin *obscaenus*, literally "offstage." As one element of society's existing structure, the art world has good reason to curtail the subversive power of gay images. To allow visual expression of gay themes would have two effects: it would show that the existing order is incomplete, and thus illegitimate; and it might lead to a threatening sense of solidarity among those who share a sense of beauty in the same "forbidden" images.

Tennessee Williams eloquently evoked this power of images in his poem "The Dangerous Painters":

I told him about the galleries upstairs, the gilt and velour insulation of dangerous painters. I said, if they let these plunging creations remain where they sprung from easels, in rooms accessible to the subjects of them . . .

they would be stored fuel for a massive indignation. The fingers of misshapen bodies would point them out, and there would be always the goat-like cry of "Brother!"

The cry of "Brother!" is worse than the shouting of "Fire!," contains more danger. For centuries now it has been struck out of our language.

Museums are our culture's most visible art institution—often the only setting in which most people come into contact with "fine art," especially art of the past. A surprising number of our "dangerous" gay brothers—and sisters—are represented on museum walls. Often, however, their art "sneaks through" because it is barely recognized as such, even by the curators. And if *they*

don't recognize it, you probably won't either; the average viewer lacks the specialized knowledge needed to catch the gay references. On the other hand, trust your eyes: the gay viewer is usually far more open to suggestions of gay emotion than the art "experts." This is one field where the old taunt is meaningful: it takes one to know one.

"Gay art" really includes several different aspects. First, gay artists and gay subject matter are separate, though related, issues. Second, within gay subject matter it is necessary to consider separately the twin categories of male eroticism and female eroticism.

When confronted with the first issue—secrecy regarding artists who were themselves gay—museum staffs could well argue that it is not the museum's role to explicate the private lives of the artists whose work it displays. This argument might hold true, unless that private life has some relevance to the meaning or intention of the individual's work. Unfortunately, it is precisely that relevance which the art world is unwilling or unable to perceive.

If a heterosexual male artist paints a portrait of his wife, or even his mistress, for example, that relationship is usually evident from the title or conveniently noted on the frame or nearby wall plaque. This information calls our attention to a potential layer of meaning in the work. Yet in 1975 Francis Bacon, a highly respected painter from Britain, exhibited several dramatic canvases depicting the death of his lover of many years, George Dyer; New York's Metropolitan Museum coyly identified Dyer as a "close friend and model."

Such sins of omission are especially unfortunate in the modern period, where the subject matter of a work is often intimately bound up with the artist's personal concerns. Knowing that the great Baroque painter Caravaggio was suspected of sodomy may have only tangential bearing on his seventeenth-century depictions of Madonnas. But it is essential to our understanding of Marsden Hartley's 1915 "Painting #47, Berlin" that we be informed the initials "KvF" on an army helmet stands for Kurt von Freibourg, and that Hartley lost his young German lover in the Great War.

Sometimes even admitted facts are misleadingly interpreted to fit established values. I once heard a Metropolitan tour guide's commentary on "The Horse Fair," the major work by the French artist Rosa Bonheur (1822–1899). Bonheur lived with another woman for forty years, and had a government permit to wear men's clothes—a preference the guide excused as somehow necessitated by outdoor sketching, even though Bonheur also wore trousers to sit in her garden, and wore her hair so short she at times passed as a man. While we can't know precisely what she and fellow artist Nathalie Micas "did in bed," it comes as a shock to anyone familiar with available nineteenth-century options for gay expression to hear the guide airily assume that "Rosa had some problems in that she never married." The guide simply could not see Bonheur's unorthodox life as anything but the one thing it was not—unfulfilled.

Naturally, we want to learn about past gay artists and take pride in their achievements. More important than these "guessing games," however, is exposing the gay content of works of art. In this sphere the uncomfortable curator has a distinct advantage: interpretation of the past often requires information that was commonplace to original viewers but is now unfamiliar.

Neo-classic subjects of the late eighteenth and early nineteenth centuries, for example, are particularly rich in gay imagery—at least partly because the artists sought inspiration in ancient Greece, the last Western culture to depict homosexuality freely and positively in literature and on vases and other paintings. But Benjamin West's "Death of Hyacinthus" (on extended loan to the Philadelphia Museum), which portrays the stricken boy expiring in the arms of Apollo, would probably strike an unknowing observer as a sort of 1770s colonial Red Cross poster. To appreciate the real pathos of the scene, you have to know that the two men were lovers—a bit of mythology not likely to have come out in grade school. Thomas Sully's "Orestes and Pylades" (1809; Brooklyn Museum) illustrates one of the most famous loving male couples of antiquity—but come prepared with a copy of Bulfinch's *Mythology*.

Similarly, the suggestiveness of Pierre Mignard's delicately boyish "Ganymede" (seventeenth century), in San Francisco's Palace of the Legion of Honor, will elude the visitor who doesn't know that Ganymede was "cupbearer" to Zeus, who swooped to earth as an eagle to carry him off. It might be possible to infer the full interpretation from the details within the picture itself—if you know that the pitcher in his hand used to symbolize, for young girls, virginity about to be broken. However, that interpretation is hardly, as straight people are fond of requesting, "pushed in our faces": given the total lack of explanatory material about the painting, the museum staff could be accused of shirking its educational duty.

One small but noteworthy exception to this "benign neglect" was the treatment accorded the French painters known as Les Barbus (the bearded ones) in the mammoth exhibit, "Age of Revolution: French Painting 1774–1830" (Louvre and Detroit Institute of Arts, 1975). The wall plaques for two paintings by Barbu artists, including another "Apollo and Hyacinthus" by Jean Broc (1801), noted matter-of-factly that "homoerotic" themes were frequent in their work.

Intimacy between women has been permitted in Western art more frequently than male eroticism for several reasons. As in much contemporary pornography, the close physical contact between women in Ingres' Turkish bath scenes, Degas' prints of brothels, or Courbet's "Sleep" titillates straight men. The deeper implications of such scenes are overlooked, thanks to the traditional notion that women cannot really be sexual by themselves. This conception of women as passive, "decorative" objects may effectively prevent even the historian from imagining any emotional interaction between them. Hence the Hellenistic Greek statuettes of women seated together in intimate poses are usually assumed to represent trivial scenes entitled something like "Women Gossiping."

In the enthusiasm of revisionism, we must be careful not to impute to every depiction of women a conscious intent on the artist's part to portray lesbianism. Nevertheless, we today are more sensitized to the broad range of possible meanings inherent in a portrayal of women alone together. One of the most complex examples of lesbian portrayal-*cum*-avoidance is the frequently painted myth of Diana and Callisto. François Boucher's eighteenth-century French version (now in San Francisco) shows us two women lying together in the woods, one slyly tickling the other's face with a straw. Viewers are supposed to disallow this obvious lesbian eroticism because (*if* you know the plot) the tickler isn't "really" a woman. It's actually Zeus again, this time disguised as a woman to gain the affection of Callisto, a chaste devotee of the virgin goddess Diana. That explanation used to both titillate and pacify more innocent observers; today, we would probably make a case for how such inversions actually heighten the picture's eroticism. (There is more than a hint of "women-identified women," by the way, in pictures of Diana's Amazon cortège, who destroy men who intrude on their rituals.)

(Although I am concentrating here on Western art, it should be pointed out that most of the major non-Western cultures have long, valued traditions of erotic art, more extensive and more explicit than our own — and usually including gay subjects on a more equal footing. From mass-produced woodblock prints in Japan to illustrations of Chinese lesbian novels, or the manuscript illuminations of India, depiction of gay love — more frequently female than male — is widespread and accepted.)

Despite a general rise in the social consciousness of museums over the last decade and a half, increased visibility for gay artists and subjects will probably come first through the exhibits of individual contemporary artists who happen to be gay and feel comfortable about letting that be known. We must, therefore, touch briefly on the role of the commercial art gallery; fortunately, the news in this sphere is somewhat encouraging.

The gallery world, like the museum world, is notoriously gay, at least by reputation; for familiar reasons, it too used to be discreetly closeted. A few gay artists, like Paul Cadmus in New York and David Hockney in England, have been able to show somewhat erotic works for as long as the last thirty years, but these artists are a tiny minority.

However, the first stimulus a commercial venture responds to is money. As gay people, primarily men, begin to constitute a visible market, with its own channels of publicity, galleries have begun to react favorably. New York artist John Button recalls how his gallery panicked when he proposed a show of his male nudes; the management was won over when every work on display sold out on opening day.

Gallery owners now tend to be glad to see me coming to review a show for *The Advocate*. Some owners even seek out the gay clientele: last year New York's Fabian Gallery invited the gay press to an opening of works (some with gay content) by Brazilian constructionist Hely Lima, and calmly pinned up favorable reviews from other gay magazines — including semi-beefcake photos of the artist. On the other hand, a group of lesbian artists met with so much hostility from established New York outlets that in 1976 they formed their own collective to provide exhibit space. The majority of the galleries the women approached expressed the opinion that it was commercially acceptable to be feminist, but not *lesbian* feminist. This attitude, too, has some economic stimulus: lesbians

are perceived to be a small market, and, like women as a class, to have less expendable income.

For truly significant signals of a "push" for new information and interpretations in art, we must look to the academic community. The history of art is primarily preserved, researched, and disseminated in the university. Art history is, therefore, subject to the same conservative tendencies as most academic disciplines — plus a few added problems of its own.

In the very recent past, a few cracks have appeared in the formerly monolithic silence of the academic world on gay matters; there are hopeful, even exciting, signs. It is at least possible to indicate on a graduate school application that you are gay — as I did — and not be summarily rejected. But in assessing present gay awareness in the academic world, I am still reminded of the Red Queen's remark to Alice in Wonderland, "I've seen gardens, compared to which this would be a wilderness."

It is oversimplified to suspect conscious prejudice and deliberate suppression behind every professor's door. Academia is a gerontocracy: a student who entered college the year of Stonewall is finishing the Ph.D. just this year — with luck. Most of today's academics, lacking exposure to a coherent philosophy of sexual politics, are (with significant exceptions) unprepared to grasp the importance of gay art or its broader ramifications. When I informed an adviser, now nearing retirement age, that I wanted to write a psychological study of images of women in the work of Sandro Botticelli (the Renaissance master whose life contains more than a hint of homosexuality), he looked bemusedly startled, then shrugged that he couldn't see "any reason why you *can't* do it."

Of course, such topics have been all too easy to avoid until recently. Homosexuality is only now entering art history as an issue to be openly confronted, because the first generation of modern Western artists that could be openly gay — around World War I — has only recently receded far enough into the past to become the province of historians.

Among the juicier anecdotes art historians now have to cope with, my personal favorites involve the artists who served Serge Diaghilev's Ballets Russes. Léon Bakst created the scenery and costumes for *Jeux* and *Afternoon of a Faun* (1912), including a famous watercolor of Nijinsky as the Faun. Nijinsky's autobiography frankly recounts his five-year affair with Diaghilev, commenting significantly, "The Faun is me, and *Jeux* is the life of which Diaghilev dreamed." Nijinsky's revelations also shed light on the paintings by Picasso for the 1917 production of *La Parade*; Picasso's backdrop contains portraits alluding to the relationships among some of the same personalities.

Such inside information is, unfortunately, rare. Especially in researching earlier periods, art historians (those who are trying) share with other disciplines the enormous obstacles to uncovering gay people's private lives. Until very recently, artists would seldom commit such revelations to paper. Even in contemporary times, surviving friends and relatives are notoriously the worst source: they often think they are helping the artist's memory by covering up "embarrassing" information.

What little we know of the private life of painter Florine Stettheimer (1871–1944), for example (designer of the innovative cellophane sets for Gertrude Stein and Virgil Thomson's opera, *Four Saints in Three Acts*), strongly suggests at least a woman-identified woman: she never married, living all her life with two also unmarried sisters and their mother. But this information may remain a permanent riddle. After her death, Stettheimer's sisters physically cut from her diaries all entries they said "pertained only to family matters."

Despite the difficulties of "de-closeting" artists of the past, once homoeroticism can be proved scholars do accept the new information. Whether such discoveries will be absorbed in a professor's total outlook is another matter: they are still considered at best irrelevant, at worst shameful.

While the scholarly literature has long acknowledged the unavoidable documentation of gay leanings in such figures as Michelangelo and Leonardo da Vinci, the tendency persists to try to explain away prima facie evidence of homosexuality. Botticelli's arrest for sodomy in 1502 has always been considered insufficient reason to pursue possible gay content, on the grounds that "in those days, *everyone* was accused of it." The obvious suspicion is never seriously entertained: that perhaps everyone was accused of it because everyone was *doing* it (Raymond deBecker alleges precisely this interpretation in his full-length study of homosexuality in art and society, *The Other Face of Love*).

Even where an artist's sexuality was clearly known to his or her contemporaries, and relevant to the work, this information is usually discreetly ignored in lectures and publications. The most infamous example is the Italian Renaissance artist Giovanni Bazzi, whose sexual proclivities earned him the nickname *Il Sodoma*, "because he always mixed and lived with beardless boys, and answered willingly enough to that name," as the chronicler Giorgio Vasari recounts. Bazzi is listed in encyclopedias under "Sodoma," but mention is seldom made of the origin of his sobriquet, or of what connection this knowledge might have to his work. His portrayal of the baby Jesus fingering an arrow proffered by an androgynous nude Saint Sebastian, for example, takes on new suggested overtones if we recall Vasari's report that "most of the young men of Siena followed Sodoma."

This silence is self-perpetuating. Art historians trained in such a milieu can enjoy the false luxury of treating Michelangelo and Leonardo as great exceptions, "excused" by genius. Thence the pathetic, and infuriating, ignorance of a professor to whom I once revealed my desire to investigate gay art history. After inching his chair back two strides from mine, he replied blandly, "That's fine, but don't you think you'll run out of material pretty quickly?"

This professor's pointed withdrawal brings up a second, more personal reason for avoiding gay topics—a reason which remains virtually unspoken among art historians, yet subtly influences their behavior even today. Few male professors in that past have been willing to broach homoeroticism in the classroom for fear of bringing suspicion on their own heads. As much victims as perpetrators of current stereotypes, they still suffer from the ancient specter of effeminacy that haunts men engaged in any way with "the arts."

In part because of homophobic stereotypes, the field of art history is, in fact, dominated by women students (though women are still not proportionally represented on many faculties; sex discrimination suits have been filed at such colleges as Tufts University). The predominance of women has helped art history become a pioneering field in feminist scholarship; the impact of the women's movement has provided at least the beginnings of a similar openness to gay scholarship for two reasons.

At the most basic level, any serious research into creative women was bound to turn up a percentage of them who loved other women. The clearest case in point is the legendary "Paris in the Twenties," where the literary and artistic community included, besides Stein and Toklas, the American painter Romaine Brooks, who painted portraits of her lover, author Natalie Clifford Barney, as well as pictures of the dancer Ida Rubinstein (with whom Brooks was infatuated) and of Una, Lady Troubridge.

On a more philosophical level, the issues raised by feminist art historians have begun to "clear the ground" for a more sympathetic understanding of concepts important to developing a theoretical justification for gay art. Prominent critics like Linda Nochlin of Vassar and Lucy Lippard bring to their analyses a concern for gender roles and androgyny as well as a psychological and sociological understanding of oppression, both of which clearly overlap with gay concerns.

The greatly increased attention given to women's issues in recent scholarship is heartening evidence of the flexibility of academia. There are some snags, however, to extrapolating a parallel future for gay studies. While oppression of the two groups shares a clear relation, resistance to admitting the reality of homosexuality is even more deeply ingrained than resistance to the value of women. More practically, women are a much bigger presence in art than gay people, particularly since, unlike women, gays can choose to remain closeted.

The obstacles to gay acceptance make the events of the 1977 College Art Association Conference all the more striking and encouraging. The venerable professional association for artists and teachers issued a call for its first panel session ever on "Homosexuality and Art: Classical to Modern Times" and, according to the committee chairperson, was deluged with forty-two requests to submit papers. Nine studies were eventually presented at the Los Angeles colloquium, on topics ranging from male/male courtship scenes on Greek vases to the lesbian vision of Romaine Brooks, who died in 1970. The panel was well attended, and caused little overt outcry from conferees.

Two of the topics discussed at the session illustrate the kinds of essential work just now beginning to "rehabilitate" neglected aspects of art history. Both deal with bisexual figures whose gay sides have often been bowdlerized. Wayne Dynes, well known in New York as an openly gay art scholar, recounted the adventures of Orpheus after he lost his beloved Eurydice. Greek art often depicted his subsequent activity, the introduction of pederasty to Thrace (for which the city's angry maidens decapitated him). Similarly, Judith Stein of the Tyler School of Art discussed depictions of Sappho, who most often appealed to later painters not in her documented role as the great-

est creative lesbian of antiquity, but for the supposed drama of her suicide after rejection by a legendary male lover.

Such openness is to be lauded, but it is still a novelty in "official" circles. Within the gay community itself, however, the Gay Academic Union has consistently provided a forum for gay-related research at its annual conferences, each of which has included some discussion of the visual arts. Topics have ranged from Michael Lynch's research on Hartley, to silent films by Eisenstein and Genet, and the visual imagery in contemporary gay publications.

Art historians rely on a number of scholarly and general publications to disseminate new findings such as these. Here again, while an occasional article surfaces dealing with topics like homoerotic imagery in Caravaggio, the number of such studies to see print does not yet seem commensurate with the potential material for study. Fortunately magazines, unlike museums, are already within the gay community's own capabilities. A number of respected publications such as *Gay Sunshine* and *Body Politic* already devote space to scholarship and criticism in art. Also, the newly formed Gay Academic Union Journal *Gai Saber* will cover art among many gay-related scholarly topics.

In summation, we have seen that museums are storehouses—and, like most storehouses, they are full of closets.

But what is shut up in the basements of great classical temples across the land is more than musty canvas and crackled varnish: it is the visible record of human consciousness.

Part of that consciousness, in virtually all times and all places, has been gay. And, contrary to what most of us have been led to believe, that gay consciousness has found innumerable, sometimes truly beautiful ways to break through to artistic expression. But for the most part, access to these expressions is still effectively denied to us—indeed, to the entire culture.

The history of America—if you will, of Western civilization since the decline of feudalism—has been a struggle for gradual extension of pride and power to an increasing number of individuals. In this struggle, art has been utilized by ruling elites as well as by the insurgents.

For their part, the powers that control society are well aware of the usefulness of structured uniformity. The Soviet Union sponsors "Socialist Realism," an official state vision of industrialized optimism; dissident artists made headlines a few years ago when their impromptu outdoor show of abstract works was obliterated by government bulldozers. In America intervention is less obvious; nevertheless, one need only look at the crazy-quilt of restrictions imposed on "obscenity" to see that our society, too, acknowledges and fears the power of art to encourage nonconforming thoughts and behavior.

For art is also the first and ideal weapon of those groups who seek to establish *new* cosmologies that will legitimize that group's particular values. From Eugène Delacroix's 1830 "Liberty Leading the People" to the explicit illustrations for *Fag Rag's* "Cocksucking as an Act of Revolution," as well as in myriad less polemical ways, art has served as midwife to new social values. Once visualized, ideas and images which were formerly only the property of a few scattered minds can be shared, can serve as the basis for a more complete imagining of shared consciousness.

In *Counterrevolution and Revolt*, Herbert Marcuse clearly defines the role of art in social change:

> *Cultural revolution:* the phrase, in the West, first suggests that ideological developments are ahead of development at the *base* of soci-

ety: cultural but *not* [yet] political and economic revolution. . . . The strong emphasis on the political potential of the arts . . . is the effort to find forms of communication that may break the oppressive rule of the established language and images over the mind and body of man—language and images which have long since become a means of domination, indoctrination, and deception.

Art is a major battleground in the struggle for self-determination—for gay people even more than for others, because, unique among subgroups, we are not born into our own culture. We discover its relevance only later in life, and it is then we desperately need models and images that are too seldom available.

By continuing to ferret out these images, hitherto ignored or suppressed, that prove gay people are a continuous presence in human culture, art historians will be adding to the "stored fuel" needed to establish gay people as an intrinsic and beautiful part of the larger universe. Marcuse envisioned this role of art in sociological terms. Tennessee Williams, later in "The Dangerous Painters," phrased the same thought more poetically: "Revolutions only need good dreamers."

# | 38 |

# *Imagine a Lesbian, a Black Lesbian*

## JEWELLE GOMEZ

Black women are still in the position of having to "imagine," discover and verify Black lesbian literature because so little has been written from an avowedly lesbian perspective. The near nonexistence of Black lesbian literature [which other Black lesbians and I do deeply feel] has everything to do with the politics of our lives, the total suppression of identity that all Black women, lesbian or not, must face.

—BARBARA SMITH[1]

In the more than fifteen years since that statement appeared in Barbara Smith's article, "Toward a Black Feminist Criticism," much has changed in the literary arena for Black women writers, but too much has remained the same for Black lesbian

writers and critics. While some attention has been given to the numbers of books published by Black

In Jewelle Gomez, *Forty-Three Septembers*, pp. 129–149. Ithaca, N.Y.: Firebrand, 1993.

women, little of the critical discussion has directly addressed the politics of publishing for Black women in general and Black lesbians specifically. Nor has it placed that work which does get published in a strong critical, literary context.

Sexuality has been raised as an issue in much of the recent analysis of such important writers as Toni Morrison and Alice Walker, yet it has consistently remained peripheral. Critics rarely address it as a substantial issue. Even the free-wheeling explicitness of Terry McMillan, or the sensual epics of Gloria Naylor, more often spark debates about male/female conflict rather than female sexuality or desire. Gender and sexuality have a profound effect on the quantity and quality of writing done by Black women (and concomitantly on that of other women of color in this country), and on the critical response to that work, as well as on the possibilities of publication.

It is specifically in the work of Black lesbian writers and critics that these two issues are unremittingly linked to themes and style. Yet many Black critical writers—feminist or not—still resist utilizing the expanded vision that Smith called for in discussing the work of Black women writers. I keep not finding myself within their analyses.

## I.

The quality of light by which we scrutinize our lives has direct bearing upon the product which we live, and upon the changes which we hope to bring about through those lives.

—AUDRE LORDE[2]

Barbara Smith's demand for an alteration in the quality of the light by which our lives and our work are examined is the central focus of her initiation of the discussion of Black feminist thought and its relationship to developing the art of critical writing by and about Black women. For me, it was a trumpet, startling and welcome. It was a call to take my own work seriously, to take the work of other women and women of color seriously. No longer were my poems and stories of consequence solely within the context of a lesbian or a Black social circle. And my work's value in one arena no longer meant inconsequence in the other, or in the world at large. The basic principles of Black feminist criticism as outlined by Smith are relatively elementary: a commitment

to explore gender as well as racial politics; the assertion of a need to work from the assumption that Black women's writing is part of an identifiable literary tradition; and acceptance of the importance of a search for a commonality of language and culture in the work of Black women.

These principles offer an expanded area of concentration in which we can examine the work of African-American women; and using one or all of the aspects Smith mentioned, we can be naturally inclusive of the work of lesbians. What I would add to Smith's groundbreaking essay is a more detailed discussion of work by Black lesbian writers, something not possible earlier because of the (even greater) scarcity of material in print. The primary work Smith examined was Toni Morrison's *Sula*. It is interesting to look at the lesbian bonds reflected in ostensibly heterosexual works if only because it reveals just how much of a lesbian subtext exists within the Black community despite attempts to conceal or deny it. But it is now crucial to examine the work of out Black lesbian writers and discuss the many ways in which we approach the issues that affect us both as Black women and as lesbians. Such consideration assists me in assessing my own work and contributes to the development of other Black lesbian writers and of Black literature overall.

Smith's thesis set off a reactionary response from Black critics quite out of proportion to the modest suggestions she made. For many feminist critics years later—both heterosexual and lesbian, Black and white—race, not sex or gender, remains the predominant feature in any discussion of work by women of color. It is, as Alice Walker said, "that perhaps white women feminists, no less that white women generally, cannot imagine black women have vaginas. Or if they can, where imagination leads them is too far to go."[3]

This observation was prompted by Patricia Meyer Spacks' introduction to her book. *The Female Imagination.* In it Spacks excuses the omission of African-American women with this statement: ". . . the books I talk about describe familiar experience, belong to a familiar cultural setting; their particular immediacy depends partly on these facts."[4] In one brief sentence she dismisses the value of the ability to live outside of ourselves when, in fact, that ability is at the core of imagination and any true liberation struggle. In that introduction the author admits to the failure of her imagination when it comes to Black women. As Alice Walker says, "Spacks never lived in nineteenth-century Yorkshire, so why theorize about the Brontés?"[5]

Expanding historical discussion to include Black women seems to stall some white feminist critics. In a parallel way, linking sexuality to race seems to make the interpretation of the work of Black lesbians intimidating for Black critics. The lives of "the other" are too remote, perhaps too explicit even for those of us who think of ourselves as being in the vanguard of change.

The question always hanging in the air around Black critics is: *Why do we have to talk about being lesbians in our work? Can't we just concentrate on the Black struggle?* It is disturbing to hear our work being dismissed by other Black feminist critics using terms such as *reductionist.* Hazel Carby, in her otherwise very useful book, *Reconstructing Womanhood,* poorly reconstructs Smith's call for an expansion of our critical perspective. She makes it sound as if Black lesbians are demanding that we each cordon off our specific areas of interest and not venture outside of them. Smith's message is not that looking at literature with a Black feminist eye reduces "the experience of all black women to a common denominator and [limits] black feminist critics to an exposition of an equivalent black female imagination,"[6] as Carby presumes. The idea is rather that such a perspective adds a layer of information and experience from which all critics, lesbian or not, would benefit.

It is the explicitly lesbian nature of Smith's discussion which sends many Black feminist critics scuttling backward. Asking feminist critics (Black or white) to express solidarity with a lesbian vision is asking them to also question their accommodation to the status quo (or the patriarchy, to use an unfashionable term) in order to succeed. Because a great many of the Black women critics being published today have academia rather than community activism as their base of legitimacy, lesbianism may be an aspect of our culture they can't afford to identify with professionally.

One example of such distancing occurred in 1987 when Rutgers University held a conference called "Changing Our Own Words." The two-day event featured presentations by almost every major critic of Black women's work in print— Hazel Carby, Hortense J. Spillers, Mary Helen Washington, Claudia Tate, Deborah McDowell, Houston Baker among them. Although Barbara Smith's article was a reference for several of the speakers, no lesbian critics spoke on the program. (There were several of us in the audience.) The

two critics—Carby and Baker—who addressed work with explicit lesbian content (the film of Alice Walker's *The Color Purple,* and *Sassafras, Cypress and Indigo,* a novel by Ntozake Shange) never mentioned the word *lesbian* nor the importance of the lesbian perspective. When questioned at the end of the sessions neither speaker could rationally explain why. Each essentially said that the lesbian content was not significant or germane to their discussion. In works with interpersonal relationships at their core, the relevance of the form of those relationships seems obvious.

Some critical essayists such as Calvin Hernton, Alice Walker, and Barbara Christian[7] have not fallen into this sin of omission, but for many feminist critics (white as well as Black), the work of lesbian writers remains foreign territory they see little advantage in exploring. For all African-Americans, female and male, who were forbidden by law the right to read, politics can never be separated from our literary tradition. For women who have been so callously forbidden the right to control our own bodies, the issues of sexuality and gender are equally intrinsic to the discussion of our work. For Black lesbians, and all women of color who are lesbians and whose frame of reference is colonialism, the inclusion of both perspectives is even more critical given the historical position of nonwhite women in this country. I cannot afford to overlook the full spectrum of work created by writers—the writing of Hazel Carby or Patricia Meyer Spacks has the potential to inform what all of us write. But I do not rely on critics to offer me legitimacy, especially when they insist on my invisibility. I must continue to move toward a Black feminist criticism. The three points of reference that Smith defines in her article serve as an important jumping off point for me.

## II.

Within the celebration of the erotic in all our endeavors, my work becomes a conscious decision, a longed-for bed which I enter gratefully and from which I rise up empowered.

AUDRE LORDE[8]

We must continue to insist that being a lesbian is larger than simply what we do in bed, that it has pervasive social and political implications. But it *is* what we do in bed, or that our identity depends on what we do in bed, that presents a sticking point for critics. This is more than simply homophobia. It is, as Amber Hollibaugh termed it, "erotophobia"[9]—fear of anything pertaining to the erotic or desire, especially connected with women. The fear is a part of the deeply puritanical roots of this country, as well as the response of oppressed people of color, and women, whose identities have often been reduced simply to sexual functions. This erotophobia seems to be at the heart of Black feminist critics' inability to address the work of lesbians and Black lesbians within the Black literary context. Even where sexuality is not a predominant or central element, the work of Black lesbian writers may be presumed to be explicit. And in work where sexuality is explicit or directly implied (as in *The Color Purple*), it is ignored.

"Miss Esther's Land," a story by Barbara Banks published in *Home Girls*, captures an essence of Black lesbian life and writing. It is full of the cultural references of Black life, and strongly articulates the perceptions of Black women through the eyes of Black lesbians in rural circumstances. It is a fine example of a wholistic view of Black women's lives, a view that cannot dismiss the questions of either race or sexuality. And because it is particularly well written, this story provides the opportunity to discuss the fullness of writing by Black women.

"Miss Esther's Land" tells of an enduring lesbian relationship as recounted by one of the partners as she nears her last days. On her seventy-fifth birthday, Esther must decide between leaving her land to her lover of forty years, Molly, or doing as Molly would prefer and deeding it to the Black townspeople who want to design a new community. Within a few pages Banks raises a wide range of interlocking concerns. Esther must confront what her obsessive love of her land has meant to her relationship with both Molly and the townspeople, Black and white. Shown from her perspective, Esther's sense of preservation is natural—the land is a powerful symbol of freedom. She is a farm woman who remembers her grandfather, an ex-slave, and his toil to work the land. But to the townspeople and to Molly, who has been their school teacher and champion, the acreage is more than a pastoral monument to their history: it is a seed for the future, one only Esther can secure.

Within this layered context, Banks reveals the subtle issues Molly and Esther face. Leaving the land to Molly in her will is not safe. Molly is not blood relation, her status as lover/partner is unde-

fined within the Black community. Their union is accepted but unacknowledged publicly. The Black community has a desperate interest in the land: whites will not let them develop their section of town to provide services and suitable homes. This land offers them the chance to take control of their own lives for the first time since slavery. And Esther's son, who does not take the long view, would have little difficulty retrieving the bequeathed land from Molly in court and delivering it into the hands of white land developers for the highest price. Esther, living at the edge of the intruding Route 60 and searching herself for the meaning of the sudden death of her ancient apple tree, can only feel sorrow that everyone else does not love her farm as she does—for its memories.

The crucial subtext of her dilemma is that she and Molly are lovers. Their physical relationship is made clear by Esther's recollection of their first days together:

> Esther kissed her. She pressed her mouth softly upon Molly's and was struck still by the newness of the thing, by her own naiveté. She did not know how to touch her, was not sure if she should, was afraid she'd spoil this wonderful thing by making it carnal.
>
> Frustrated she stammered, "Now what do I do?" By morning, the issue had been resolved.[10]

Molly and Esther relate physically in an easy way. Their sexuality is not a source of guilt for them, but rather one of joy. Yet they are aware of the social dangers such a relationship presents. On the day of Esther's seventy-fifth birthday, Molly removes her things from their bedroom to a guest room, a task obviously repeated many times during their four decades together. Presumably this allays the suspicions of the family visiting for the celebration; it at least provides a way for those who are suspicious to dismiss their misgivings. Yet, even as she packs her things, Molly says to Esther, "What makes you think they don't know anyway? If anyone of them has ever thought about it, they know. But people are wonderful at ignoring things when it's to their advantage. . . ."[11]

In these few pages Barbara Banks tells us much about what it might really be like to have a relationship with another woman in a Black rural community. It is also emblematic of the position in which Black lesbians find ourselves within the Black and the feminist literary communities: our sexual lives remain unacknowledged (as were Celie and Shug's at the Rutgers conference), yet those same sexual lives are a solid wall blocking out full consideration of our work and existence.

Banks' story begins exploring the strength of family by portraying one of the classic attitudes to lesbianism in the Black community without forgetting the historical perspective. It is the analysis of lesbian works like this that opens up the meaning of race and sex in our society.

*Her,* written by Cherry Muhanji, is a novel to similarly consider. It is a lyrical narrative about life on a block in Detroit in the 1950s and '60s. While the main action of the novel is not explicitly lesbian, the underpinnings certainly are. A young girl, Sunshine, is brought home by her boyfriend to live in his mother's house, where an assortment of sisters and aunts and uncles up from the South also live. Accustomed to bearing the scorn of other Black women because of her exceptionally fair skin, the girl is sullen and uncommunicative. She mistrusts the friendship offered by her mother-in-law, Charlotte, since she's unused to the gruff interchange that is common in a house full of working-class Black women. She cannot find her voice, or even her own name.

Sunshine flees this family and moves in with Mrs. Ricky Wintergreen, a notorious and mysterious owner of a local night club. Sunshine takes the name Kali and remakes herself in the image of Mrs. Wintergreen. But in finding a new persona she also finds herself under the dangerous influence of a psychotic pimp. The neighborhood and its characters represent a full cross section of a very dynamic world, much like the one I grew up in: pimps, prostitutes, white hustlers living in close proximity to people working as maids, Pullman porters, hairdressers—with the gay characters easily distributed on either side of the law. It is an interdependent neighborhood that has yet to devolve into the urban isolation characteristic of the '70s and '80s.

Wintergreen, as she is called reverently by the patrons of her club where she sings, is an enigma. We learn that the subtle tension that resonates on the block between her and Charlotte exists because they had been lovers during the war years. The tragedy comes not from their desire but from their failure to have fulfilled themselves. But Kali's potential tragedy draws them back to each other, shaking the foundation of the lives they've built separately. Meeting Wintergreen up close for the first time in years Charlotte sees the dramatic damage that has been done to her feet during the war. With little hesitation, "Charlotte planted tiny kisses along the high and low places of the broken feet, washing them with great tears."[12]

The expression of their love is so powerful it draws Charlotte's husband to the door of the room. "For the first time he saw that his wife was capable of deep feeling. And that discovery moved him in ways that he couldn't articulate then. . . . The only thing he heard was the name Ricky repeated over and over again. He removed his head from the parlor door and shut it quietly."[13] Ricky Wintergreen bridges the years and lives between them: "Gently she brought Charlotte's head close and kissed her mouth. After the first lingering taste, Ricky pushed her tongue inside Charlotte's mouth and stayed."[14] When their desire can be met fully, a circle is completed and action can be taken. Their reunion is at the heart of the community of women who rescue Kali.

Muhanji is able to draw the picture of lesbian love within the context of a Black community without sacrificing the integrity of either reality. The mingled working class/underclass roots of her story represent a world I feel a kinship with. Use of that historic period allows Muhanji to capture a moment in our history before Black innocence is completely lost, when the mythology surrounding one character, Wintergreen, can carry a community forward to action. Economic survival, community integrity, and desire are at the heart of Muhanji's characters just as they are for Banks.'

The strongest writing by Black lesbians reflects these multiple concerns. It examines how Black lesbians survived within the context of the legacy of slavery and racism and utilizes the complex nature of social and sexual interactions to reflect society at large. The development of methods of absorbing or ignoring differences within the African-American community; the contrast between the response to homosexuality by the traditional Black working poor and that of the striving, Black middle class; the flowering of gay life in the Black community that lived outside of the law; the difference between Black urban and Black rural lesbian life—all are areas of study that aid in expanding the Black feminist vision.

## III.

At the same time that I emphasize the recognition of the specifics of racial and sexual politics I also suggest, as Smith does, that no work be considered without placing it within some additional literary context. In her book, *How to Suppress Women's Writing*,[15] Joanna Russ catalogues a number of insidious practices for dismissing women's literature. Isolation, Russ points out, has been a chief method in the critical establishment and it is manifested in many different ways. Many feminist critics and historians have been guilty of using isolation against the work of Black women and Black lesbians.

As a writer of fantasy fiction, I am always pushing doubly hard to have my work seen within the context of other fantasy writing. Because I am Black and a lesbian, critics of the genre don't quite know where to place a Black lesbian vampire novel. And many feminist critics don't have the background in genre fiction that would allow them to place the work in a context (Susanne Sturgis, who reviewed my novel in *Feminist Bookstore News*, and Patricia Roth Schwartz in *Sojourner* were two exceptions). Reviewers for African-American publications ignored the book completely, as if mystified by a complexity of vision.

A narrowness, similar to that which plagues science fiction critics, has also afflicted me at times. When looking at comic fiction I have found it difficult to appreciate, or even recognize, humor on the printed page. Several times in past articles I've discussed Ann Allen Shockley's novel, *Say Jesus and Come to Me*.[16] Shockley (the author of *Loving Her*, the first explicit and sympathetic novel about a Black lesbian, published in 1974), drew on a short story she'd written earlier to describe the life of a Black preacher, Reverend Myrtle Black. Lust and ambition seem to drive her from one pastorate to the next seeking new converts, new conquests, and power. That is until she meets Travis Lee, a soul singer who's recently repented her sins and been born again. As it stands, this work presents problems for me. Its transitions feel too abrupt. It ignores the patently homophobic stance of most Fundamentalist Christian dogma. The core of Rev. Black's political campaign is feminism at its most self-absorbed—a difficult point to overcome if we're to sympathize with the reverend.

Yet as someone pointed out to me sometime after I had read and reviewed the book, *Say Jesus and Come to Me* may work for many people as that rare form: comic fiction. Perhaps because I, like others who feel they are in an embattled community, have needed each piece of literature to

represent the best of all that I feel and believe, I had been unable to see its comic possibilities and the value of that genre. I had not looked at it in relationship to the comic sketches of Alice Childress or the bawdy humor of comedian Jackie Moms Mabley. In light of those traditions it makes sense that Rev. Black's licentious spirit and Travis' miraculous conversion take on such melodramatic proportions rather than the more mundane framework I anticipated. I realized that I had not considered Shockley's work fully to assess the value within the comic genre, much as other critics have neglected placing my novel within the context of vampire fiction or African-American historical fiction. Ignoring the cultural or literary context is another way of isolating our work and denying it the critical attention it deserves.

Another form of isolation, even within the appropriate cultural or literary context, grows out of the fear some feminist critics seem to have of raising questions about the quality of the writing of Black women. Linda Powell pointed out in *Conditions* magazine that ". . . if a black woman speaks the language and is nice around white folks . . . she can speak at conferences. She can write reviews. And even if she's mediocre it's not bad for a negro?"[17] It falls to Black feminist and lesbian critics to explore the crucial issues of literary quality even if others will not. And by literary quality I do not mean adherence to traditional forms or content, but rather how well a writer uses her own language to achieve her goals within the piece being examined.

My work may be isolated by not being addressed within the genre where it might rightfully belong but more importantly, it is isolated, and the development of my craft is impeded, by not being discussed professionally as well as politically. This lack of serious consideration on the part of magazine and anthology editors may come simply from a shortage of time and money, or even skills. But often it is attributable to the low expectations editors have for the work of women, and women of color in particular. As a response I've come to rely on a circle of writers/editors whom I trust to be tough, to question what I don't know and what they don't know, so that my writing, even where flawed, represents a sincere effort to communicate, not simply time spent at a typewriter.

Another method of isolation is that of offering up one Black lesbian writer as the spokeswoman and the authority and ignoring the work of others. Black feminist critics seem to have fallen into this error as easily as others. At any African-American literary gathering, if the question of Black lesbians is raised, Audre Lorde's name is offered as the token. Certainly Lorde is the most well-known out Black lesbian writer, but what of Cheryl Clarke, Alexis DeVeaux, Terri Jewell, Michelle Cliff, Sapphire, Kate Rushin, Angela Bowen, Lindajean Brown, and the many more who have been publishing for the past fifteen years?

It was Audre, herself, who made me most aware of this issue when I called to ask if I could interview her for the film, *Before Stonewall.* Her response was to ask if she were the only Black lesbian in the film. She did not want white audiences to use her to feel satisfied, as if having seen her they'd seen all Black lesbians. To avoid this Audre suggested the inclusion of another of her contemporaries, Muaua Flowers. The result is a lively discussion between friends who are relating their experiences rather than a singular Black spokesperson.

Unfortunately, the same tokenizing tactic is used by Black feminist critics as well. For them to rely on knowing the work of one Black lesbian, or two, effectively stunts the growth of other Black lesbian writers and renders them invisible. In preparing this work it was possible to locate full-length works by a larger number of Black lesbians than was possible when "Toward a Black Feminist Criticism" was originally published. Some of these writers, such as Audre Lorde, are already quite well-known to us, and my goal is to expand our critical field of reference. Discussing the work of little-known writers, such as Cherry Muhanji and Barbara Banks, along with the standard-bearers, helps enrich the field. This is in opposition to the prevailing concept behind commercial presses: *We have one already.* A philosophy like this leaves individual Black lesbian writers with too much responsibility and not enough room to create. Imagine a publisher saying: We have enough white male writers from the East Coast this year. Let's not bother with those submissions. And why don't we just skip that new Norman Mailer book.

## IV.

Language—however we adapt it or adapt to it—is eternally political, because language reveals to what degree the writer accepts or rejects the prevailing culture.

CHERYL CLARKE[18]

My attempt to break through these forms of isolation and place my work within the appropriate tradition is an acknowledgment of the value of Black women's use of our own language and cultural experience. Some feminists emphasize the idea that *We can do anything men can do.* Women can hold nontraditional jobs, maintain a corporate image, sound and act as aggressively as a man. This is much the same type of message delivered to Blacks by civil rights leaders—show white people we were just like them. But another equally important aspect of feminism is the exploration of things that are not the same as men, that are more particular to women: crafts, music, religions, ways of processing information.

For Black women writers whose language and inflection, as well as interpretation of cultural experiences, are a complex amalgam of European-American and African or Caribbean influences, the acknowledgment of difference is central to liberation and to writing. Questions about narrative voice, dialects, occupations and preoccupations certainly yield revealing information when raised about the work of Black lesbian writers. In 1992 the American Family Association excerpted the work of Black lesbian poet, Sapphire, in an attempt to stir up controversy about the funding of *The Portable Lower East Side,* a New York magazine.[19] Taking her work out of context AFA attempted to show that she was supporting "wilding" or gang rape, when in fact her poem was an attempt to step inside the minds and hearts of the boys who perpetrated the Central Park jogger rape. While I expect the Religious Right to deliberately misread our language and perspective, I always hope that Black feminist critics will not make that error. I wondered where they were as this Black writer was vilified in the national press.

Critics must be able to admit when our experience or sensibilities are limited and do not allow us the openness to analyze material that is outside our definitions. We then have to do the work to be open and to learn. To demand academic language, or classical European-American references or structure, is to deny the voice of Black women. For many, my entire discussion may be discounted if my choice of references is drawn from short story writers and novelists and poets equally; or if they are drawn from lesbian literary presses and placed right alongside university or commercial presses unapologetically. To be prejudiced against that mix ignores the political considerations that influence who has access to publication and who does not. In examining the voice of Black lesbians it is the element of difference which often alienates Black feminist critics. It is more valuable to embrace that difference, whether comfortable or not, and learn from it.

## V.

I am trying to point out that lesbian-feminism has the potential of reversing and transforming a major component in the system of women's oppression. . . . If radical lesbian-feminism purports an anti-racist, anti-classist, anti-woman-hating vision of bonding . . . then all people struggling to transform the character of relationships in this culture have something to learn from lesbians.

CHERYL CLARKE[20]

The articulation of guiding principles and the practice of them is not "from my mouth to God," as my Aunt Irene says. A major stumbling block for me is that 90 percent of the time when I'm asked to write about the work of another Black woman, the review or article is being requested for a white and often straight publication. My reticence to write something which will be perceived as negative about a Black woman or Black lesbian in a mainstream journal (no matter how "constructively critical" it might be) is as hard as a plaster cast. The discussion among several Black women critics (myself included) that I mentioned earlier was published in *Conditions: Nine*. Some readers who felt our remarks were too critical of established Black lesbian writers cancelled subscriptions or harangued us personally for publishing such work and in a "white" publication (although the magazine's editorial collective had a substantial representation of women of color). Some protesters, Black and white, appeared to feel that the work of Black lesbians is too delicate to withstand close examination. If one is able to see our work within the context of years of tradition, both written and oral, that assumption is absurd.

I do believe that we have much to learn from each other's work but still, like those who criticized our contribution to *Conditions: Nine*, I can't dismiss the racism and homophobia that has operated within progressive journals of all kinds. This means that my choice of words has a softer edge when discussing a Black woman whose work does not satisfy me, or that I avoid discussion of another Black lesbian writer altogether. Still it is important for me to speak so that I do not succumb to the same alienation I find inexcusable in others. It's crucial that all writers interested in serious critical work acknowledge our limitations and, rather than resigning ourselves to alienation or ignorance, begin to bridge the gaps that separate us from new experiences.

I find the principles of Black feminist criticism offer me the broadest perspective so that this loss or exclusion does not occur. I'm not at all interested in assessing, dismissing, or promoting one particular genre, school, or writer. Nor do I advocate censoring out what might be considered "incorrect" for the Black image or the Black lesbian image and supporting only idealized, sanitized images. I'm more interested in the personal and literary chances that Black women take and how we can surprise and sometimes delight each other.

For me, feminist criticism must encompass that place where philosophy and activism intersect. The quality of life and work must be defined by principles that may seem academic on paper but are vital points of reference in our lives, and starting places for action. While some critics may be able to avoid examination of the discomforting space between thought and action, there are also many who will not want to. Black lesbian feminist writers have little choice.

I began this discussion by exploring what has not been done. But I continue to believe that there is a lot that can be done, and that the effort benefits all writers. Now, as was always true, recognizing these possibilities does require a great deal of realignment of how we think, feel, and react. The first step is, as always, imagination.

## NOTES

1. Barbara Smith, "Toward a Black Feminist Criticism," *Conditions: Two* (1977), 39.

2. Audre Lorde, "Poetry Is Not a Luxury," in *Sister Outsider* (Trumansburg, NY: Crossing Press, 1984), 36.

3. Alice Walker, "One Child of One's Own," in *In Search of Our Mothers' Gardens* (New York: Harcourt Brace Jovanovich, 1983), 373.

4. Ibid., 372.

5. Ibid., 373.

6. Hazel U. Carby, *Reconstructing Womanhood* (New York: Oxford University Press, 1987), 10.

7. Calvin Hernton, *The Sexual Mountain and*

*Black Women Writers* (New York Doubleday, 1989); Alice Walker, *In Search of Our Mothers' Gardens*; Barbara Christian, *Black Feminist Criticism* (New York: Pergamon Press, 1985).

8. Audre Lorde, "Uses of the Erotic," in *Sister Outsider*, 55.

9. Amber Hollibaugh, "The Erotophobic Voice of Women," *New York Native*, No. 7, September 25, 1983, 33.

10. Barbara Banks, "Miss Esther's Land," in *Home Girls: A Black Feminist Anthology*, edited by Barbara Smith (New York: Kitchen Table: Women of Color Press, 1983), 185.

11. Ibid., 194.

12. Cherry Muhanji, *Her* (San Francisco: Aunt Lute Foundation, 1990), 156.

13. Ibid., 157.

14. Ibid., 158.

15. Joanna Russ, *How to Suppress Women's Writing* (Austin: University of Texas Press, 1983).

16. Ann Allen Shockley, *Say Jesus and Come to Me* (New York Avon Books, 1982).

17. Cheryl Clarke, Jewelle Gomez, Evelynn Hammonds, Bonnie Johnson, Linda Powell. "Black Women on Black Women Writers," *Conditions: Nine* (1983), 101.

18. Cheryl Clarke, review of *Nappy Edges* by Ntozake Shange, *Conditions: Five* (1979), 160.

19. Sapphire "Wild Thing," *The Portable Lower East Side: Queer City*, Vol. 8, No. 2 (1991), 41.

20. Cheryl Clarke, "Lesbianism: An Act of Resistance," in *This Bridge Called My Back*, edited by Cherríe Moraga and Gloria Anzaldúa (New York: Kitchen Table: Women of Color Press, 1983), 134.

# | 39 |

# Too Queer for College: Notes on Homophobia

## ESTHER NEWTON

My wrist was broken in three places when I collided with the hardwood floor of a roller skating rink on a summer night six years ago. After six weeks in a cast and three months of physical therapy, my hand worked again, but not the way it had before. My right wrist—I am right-handed—is askew, thickened and chronically painful.

That was the price for holding hands with another woman in public. As a lesbian who looks it, I hardly ever express affection where straight people might see. But this skating rink was in Greenwich Village, gay capital of the East Coast. I remember a young man shouting something angry at us. The words were blurred but the meaning was clear from his tone, his glower, and the girlfriend clinging to him. The next lap around the rink, something—I never saw what or who—felled me from behind.

The physical therapists were wonderful, but they dealt with physical trauma, and the mental shock proved even more intractable. I had to eat this man's anonymous hatred, accept the fact that, in a spiteful spasm, he could ruin my beautiful, capable hand. I could neither vomit the hatred back on him nor forgive, since I had not seen the attack. I couldn't even be certain it wasn't an accident. That would have been the more comforting explanation. Who wants to believe herself despised by total strangers? But if my assailant's hostility was impersonal, it was *my* wrist, not his, that was broken. The worst effect of homophobia, in the academic world or anywhere, is the damage done to lesbians and gay men. To a lesser degree, straight people are harmed by the lies they force us to tell.

*Gay Studies Association Newsletter*, March 1987, pp. 1–3.

For Kenneth W. Payne, fieldworker, scholar, brilliant teacher, and cherished gay colleague at Purchase in the early 1980s, who never got a tenure track job. Ken Payne died of AIDS in 1988.

Homophobia in the academic world is not the violent shove in the back. It occurs in a privileged context where hostility is rarely so "crudely" expressed. But it does break spirits, damage careers, ruin lives. Like my attacker at the skating rink, homophobia among academics is usually a sneak. It strikes in closed-door meetings of tenure-review and promotion committees and in secret letters of recommendation. Rejection and denial are almost always attributed to the victim's alleged personal and intellectual shortcomings. In twenty-eight years in higher education, the fact that I am a lesbian was never given as the reason for attacking me.

What little systematic data there are confirms that there's nothing exceptional or personal about discrimination against lesbians and gay men in higher education. The American Sociological Association's Task Group on Homosexuality surveyed 2,000 sociology department heads about their attitudes toward gays and lesbians in academia. Based on the 640 responses, the ASA Task Group concluded that:

> sociologists and students who are known as homosexuals or, even more so, as activists, run considerable risk, according to the perceptions of department heads and chairs, of experiencing discrimination in being hired or promoted in a sociology department. Hence the vast majority remain closeted within their colleagues. This, in turn, inhibits them from displaying interest in, and engaging in, research, advising, or teaching courses on, the topic of homosexuality.

Academic homophobia first struck me in college, when the dean of women threatened me with expulsion because I had been seen in a phone booth with another woman. We were not lovers; we had simply been talking to a mutual friend. But the dean was rumored to be a lesbian herself; I knew she *knew*. She didn't say, "I'm going to expel you because you're a lesbian." She said something about inappropriate behavior and not tolerating a bad attitude. Unlike the heroine of *Rubyfruit Jungle*, I cowered before the dean, and thanked my lucky stars when she decided to accept my story. I was left in that permanent state of fearfulness and vulnerability which is the fate of those with a dirty secret.

In 1965, when I was a graduate student in anthropology, I decided to write, or rather felt impelled to write my thesis on female impersonators as symbolic leaders of the gay community. I

was lucky to be at an elite graduate school—one that could afford to take chances on some students.

Even so, my topic was widely viewed as an inappropriate dirty joke. Without the support of several powerful straight white male faculty members, my project would have been squashed. I dared not mention in my dissertation that my being a lesbian had anything to do with my choice of topic, my perspective, or the relative ease with which I had gained my informants' confidence.

In 1968, after I got my first job, I became a passionately committed feminist. People had always looked at me askance because I didn't smile enough, because my body language was all wrong, in short because I wasn't feminine. But now they could label me feminist as well as, or instead of, lesbian. The movement also attracted many straight women. Some have been staunch allies; others have capitulated under straight male pressure to get rid of the queer perspective my person and my work have represented.

I was denied tenure on my first job. The rejection felled me like a dumb ox. The process was secret, but privately and as a favor, the woman department head told me some people had trouble with my "personality." There was also a question about my "commitment to anthropology." It was like the menacing encounter I'd had with the college Dean: "You're doing something wrong and I won't say what, but we *know* about it."

In 1973, when I came up for tenure at my second job, I was more sophisticated. I had found my feet as a feminist teacher, and had a network of supporters. Also, my dissertation had been published (*Mother Camp: Female Impersonators in America*. University of Chicago Press, 1972, 1979). My review committee split. The negative majority accused me of having a "feminist bias" and asserted, contrary to glowing student evaluations, that I was unfair to male students. My detractors were so confident that they committed these observations to paper. After a protracted campus struggle, the college president granted me tenure, with a one-year delay to make sure I didn't get overconfident. Neither my opponents nor my supporters ever said publicly that I was a lesbian. Most of my colleagues got tenure easily.

Now that I had tenure, I "came out" on my job. I began to refer to my home life honestly among my colleagues and mentioned my homosexuality in class when *I* thought it appropriate. I also started to write about it. For instance, I added a section dealing with my graduate school experience in the closet to a paper I had written about life as an academic woman. A feminist philosophy professor who was editing a book on women and work solicited my piece, commenting, "I'm surprised how much the inclusion of 'lesbianism' changes the tone of the essay—making it more serious, more moving, and in an odd way more seriously political." But the publisher saw it differently, and the professor was persuaded to drop my piece. It "assumed a feminist audience," she wrote in a subsequent letter, and was too focused on the academic world. Also, she said, her collection was now more about the relation of work to "mothering," not "personal relations"; so the topic of lesbianism was inappropriate. She advised me that in revising the piece for publication elsewhere I should be more upbeat, lest people think that lesbians are bitter.

That article has never been published. The professor's book, which sold widely to feminists, included a bitter meditation on graduate school by a "straight" woman with whom I had had a clandestine affair. Not one author in that book on women and work, including several who are gay, mentions lesbianism.

Another paper of mine concerned the anthropological and feminist controversy over the existence of "primitive matriarchies." This work too was solicited and accepted by straight feminist editors, but in due course the publisher's reader expressed

> disbelief that the paper was actually submitted for publication. It is bad. It is poorly written, poorly organized, poorly thought out and bereft of ideas of its own. . . . I could see a good visionary article that would revolve around some real things [such as] . . . total control of women over the reproductive process through chemical contraception and legal abortion; the shrinking of the family.

These comments were sent on to me and my co-author by the editors to justify their decision to "agree to drop [your paper] from the collection." Like female impersonation, the vision of a female-dominated society was just not a legitimate topic, but phony "standards" were cited to strengthen the case. This kind of thing can drive you crazy. You end by distrusting everyone and shying away from the editorial help all writers need.

It took me a long time to get over a string of such rejections, but eventually a community of lesbian and gay scholars, primarily historians, provided the support and intellectual stimulation that enabled me to resume academic research. With fifteen years of outstanding teaching, one edited book and two authored ones, and a number of articles on gay and feminist topics I had the nerve to propose myself for a promotion to full professor. Whether I had a "strong" enough publication record to make full professor at a major research university, I do not know. Obviously previous rejections of my work didn't help. I do claim to be the equal of the full professors at my state college.

But my colleagues split again. The majority wrote that I hadn't published enough to merit promotion, and that eight lengthy favorable outside letters (many from full professors at major universities, some of whom called my first book a "classic" in urban anthropology) were outweighed by two cursory negative ones. One male member of the review committee reportedly dropped some of my work on the table with disdain, saying, "Have you *read* this?" In that atmosphere several more neutral colleagues, including a full professor who is a heterosexual feminist, found it more comfortable to vote against my promotion. Later, the feminist professor admitted disliking the irrational hostility of certain committee members toward me, but, she explained, she agreed with them about my lack of publications. "But I've written two books," I objected, "you were just promoted for editing one!" The insufficient publication note was also publicly sounded by a male administrator involved in my case. A colleague later reported this man's off-the-record remark: "Can you imagine promoting someone who writes this shit?"

How have these experiences affected my career? On the face of it, I have been held back, paid less, disrespected by many of the people I work with. More profoundly, homophobia has forced me to frame my life by its imperatives. Without it, I would not identify so strongly with other gay people. My work might have been on Paleolithic arrowheads instead of on people who are marginal and different. I have found my intellectual voice in the silence society tried to impose on me. Although the kind of writing and teaching I do best—interdisciplinary, controversial—has been scorned by many of my colleagues, it has gained me the respect of others and the admiration of students, who continue to flock to my classes.

Now that I have job security, what I fear most is the bitterness that can trap you in a perpetual dance with the limits straight society sets. That is the inner wasteland from which Malcolm X emerged when, toward the end of his life, he saw that "white man" was a set of attitudes which might possibly, through hard political and spiritual action, be transformed. He was pushed to the floor of the skating rink a hundred times over, and turned that rage and that pain into his own growth, his own project. That is the kind of victory over homophobia I seek.

# | 40 |

# The Gay and Lesbian Publishing Boom

## WILLIAM J. MANN

By the end of last year, the gay and lesbian publishing industry had undergone a revolution that left many giddy with excitement and others cautious with apprehension. The gay book publishing world had suddenly produced a "boom"—remarkable, unprecedented activity, and what had been a niche market was abruptly steered into the big bucks game. The phenomenal success of *Straight from the Heart*, penned by gay hunk role models Rod and Bob Jackson-Paris, paved the way for other queer celeb titles: Victoria Starr's k.d. lang bio, Martina's mystery, Joe Steffan's *Honor Bound*, the Herb Ritts photo fest of Rod and Bob (back again). Then there were the advances: Led by Dorothy Allison's deal with Penguin, it was no longer unthinkable for a queer writer to receive a six-figure advance. Or seven-figure attention: Allison's *Skin*, published by the lesbian-feminist press Firebrand, was excerpted in *The New York Times*.

Suddenly, by 1994, every Barnes and Noble—from the cities to the suburbs and into the blue-collar malls—had hung "Gay and Lesbian" category signs over bookshelves. Nearly every major publishing house began pumping out its own line of gay and lesbian titles. And there is little sense in the industry that the boom has reached its peak. Indeed, the activity is still there: more celebrity autobiographies (Margarethe Cammermeyer's *Serving in Silence*, Greg Louganis' *Breaking the Surface*), another photo book of Rod and Bob, and continued brisk sales at the nation's gay bookstores.

Quantifying this "boom," however, is difficult. Exact figures are hard to come by, if only because of the fluid nature of what constitutes a "gay book." Does a gay or lesbian writer automatically write a gay or lesbian book? What about a gay-themed story or biography of a gay person written by a non-gay author? The Lambda Literary Awards considered Jeannette Winterson's *Written On the Body* enough of a lesbian book to give it the award for Best Lesbian Novel, even though the very gender of its protagonist was left unclear.

A very rough estimate used by *Publishers Weekly* is that about three percent of the roughly 58,000 titles published in this country in 1993 were gay or lesbian books (these are the most recent figures available, and 1994 is generally considered to have expanded upon 1993). That translates into just under 2,000 titles—not an "explosion," perhaps, but certainly a marked improvement over years past.

## ORIGINS

Those "years past" could hardly have predicted the current interest. Even as the first political advancements were made in the immediate post-Stonewall era of the early '70's, gay literature was

*Harvard Gay and Lesbian Review*, Spring 1995, pp. 24–27.

slow to emerge. Of course, there had always been books with gay themes. James Baldwin, Tennessee Williams, Gore Vidal, Radclyffe Hall, and Christopher Isherwood had all produced what critic Reed Woodhouse has called (in his article, "The Five Houses of Gay Fiction") "closet" or "proto-ghetto" literature by the 60's. But the earliest unabashedly *gay books* came from the Berkeley-based Gay Sunshine Press, a flower-child collective founded by Winston Leyland that spawned the *Manroot* poetry series and other radical gay male titles. This was followed fairly quickly by two lesbian-feminist presses: Daughters, Inc., founded by June Arnold, Parke Bowman, Charlotte Bunch, and Bertha Harris in 1973, and Naiad Press, founded by Barbara Grier and Donna McBride. While Daughters, Inc. folded in 1978, Naiad remains in business today and is an important player in the independent press.

Outlets for gay titles, however, remained few and far between. Although Craig Rodwell's groundbreaking Oscar Wilde Memorial Bookstore opened its doors in New York's Greenwich Village in 1967, the real advent of the independent gay bookstore didn't occur until the late 1970's or early 80's, with the emergence of A Different Light in New York, Los Angeles and San Francisco, Lambda Rising in Washington, D.C., Giovanni's Room in Philadelphia, Glad Day in Boston and Toronto, People Like Us in Chicago, among others. Gay titles were often given little more than half a shelf in the alternative independent and feminist bookstores that had been proliferating since the 50's. I can recall venturing into a bookstore my parents called "that hippie place" outside Hartford, Connecticut as a newly awakened gay teenager in the late 70's and asking whether they carried any homosexual titles. "We don't sell pornography," I was told. When I explained I wasn't interested in porn (at least, not at that particular moment), I was told they didn't carry anything "perverted." This from a proprietor who stocked shelves with titles on the oppression of women, of workers, of minorities, and of animals!

Michael Denneny, the unofficial dean of gay publishing, says that things weren't much different in the major publishing houses at the time. A great deal of convincing was needed to get publishers to agree to try a book with any kind of queer content. As a gay man (and one of the founders of the pioneering gay literary journal, *Christopher Street*), Denneny had been instru-

mental in getting his bosses at Macmillan to publish the non-fiction book, *The Homosexuals: Who and What We Are*, in 1975—but not without a lot of struggle. When he arrived at St. Martin's Press a few years later, he was determined to launch a regular series of gay books, and he told upper management of his intent.

"I saw this as a new market, and I saw it as potentially profitable," Denneny recalls. "I didn't want to go through the type of struggle on every single book I had gone through with one book at Macmillan. It would be too exhausting. I wanted them to work with me for the first couple of years because I knew it would be priming the pump."

The priming paid off, for the pump proved bountiful. Within a few years, starting with Edmund White's *Nocturnes for the King of Naples* in 1978, St. Martin's gay books had become classics—and moneymakers. They were joined by a new surge in independent gay publishing. White's Violet Quill comrade Felice Picano had founded SeaHorse Press in 1977, which published groundbreaking gay male books by Doric Wilson and Martin Duberman. Picano then joined forces with several other small presses to create Gay Presses of New York, which published, among other titles, Harvey Fierstein's *Torch Song Trilogy* in 1981.

Also in 1977, Sasha Alyson founded the long-running Alyson Publications in Boston. For more than a decade, Alyson has been the leader in gay genre fiction (mysteries, science fiction) as well as in important non-fiction studies of gay life and culture (youth issues, AIDS, coming out stories.)

By the mid-1980's a new crop of lesbian-feminist independent presses had sprung up, many still operating today: among them, Firebrand Books, founded by Nancy Bereano; Kitchen Table/Women of Color Press, the first press to specifically target lesbians of color, founded by Audre Lorde, Barbara Smith and Cherrie Moraga; and New Victoria Books, founded by Beth Dingham. By this time, too, other mainstream houses had followed St. Martin's lead in developing their own lesbian and gay titles, particularly Crown, Dutton and HarperCollins. Such openly gay editors as Denneny, Carole DeSanti, Bill Whitehead, and David Groff encouraged queer writers and helped navigate their books into print. By the late 1980's, the Publishing Triangle, an organization of gay and lesbian publishing professionals in New York, had formed with a membership of more than 600.

Among the more interesting developments of

late is Richard Kasak's Masquerade, BadBoy and Hard Candy books. Starting out with slickly produced pornographic novels and collections, Kasak has recently begun publishing notable work by such authors as Samuel Delany and Stan Leventhal, expanding into what was a void for gay male writers among independent presses, as most of the independent, smaller houses (Alyson being a notable exception) are devoted exclusively to women.

So there's no question that a torrent of queer book publishing, selling, and buying has washed over the publishing industry for the past couple of years. But is the tide getting ready to crest? Only so much money can keep going out to lure gay authors into the fold before publishers start looking at the bottom line. Every publisher I spoke with made that point: as soon as the money stops, so will the titles. And, inevitably, not every book for which publishers have offered big advances will turn into a blockbuster. St. Martin's was very disappointed with sales for *Honor Bound,* midshipman Joe Steffan's account of being expelled from West Point after admitting he was gay. Even Randy Shilts' acclaimed *Conduct Unbecoming* was not the financial success of his earlier *And the Band Played On.* The message is clear: individual gay titles will no doubt continue to be published, but gay books as a *category* that excites publishers' interest could be threatened by disappointing performances of highly touted (and expensive) projects.

## SMALL VERSUS BIG

If money remains a problem at the big houses — where five- and six-figure advances to the likes of Dorothy Allison and Urvashi Vaid made news last year — it is even more of an issue for the smaller gay and lesbian presses. Barbara Smith of Kitchen Table/Women of Color Press points out: "The irony is we [the independent small presses] built up the markets and then they [the mainstream publishers] move in and make the profits."

A further irony is that while smaller houses cannot afford to pay the big advances, they *can* afford to take risks the bigger houses cannot. Sales in the tens of thousands are not needed for a small press to consider a book successful. More modest print runs and less ambitious expectations allow them to publish without fearing the passing of a fad. Something that's not economically viable for a big house might be just the ticket for a small press. It's their long-term economic viability that

many small presses must ultimately consider. Directors at several of the small presses have told me that they simply refuse to be intimidated by the big advance wars. They may end up missing out on some projects or losing some authors to the major houses, but at least they won't be closing their doors. The growth of a small press like Alyson has been slow but steady. While they still operate out of an office that's an alcove of their own warehouse on a nearly deserted block in Boston, most observers predict that Alyson will be around for the long haul.

That's comforting for those who think the mainstream houses will eventually tire of gay and lesbian titles in their "flavor-of-the-month" search for new ideas. But queer books seem to be settling in with an unexpected determination. Crown's acquisition of Denneny signals a long-term investment. Crown, a division of Random House, now hopes to achieve a similar reputation as St. Martin's had in the 1980's as a publisher of important gay titles. Already in the works under Denneny's stewardship are a full-fledged biography of Edmund White, an examination of the religious right's war against gays by *Advocate* reporters Chris Bull and John Gallagher, and several "very exciting" fiction projects. "Over the next year, we're going to be taking a major stand on gay and lesbian books," Denneny promises. "Crown will hopefully become the leading mainstream publisher of gay and lesbian titles."

Such activity does not seem to portend a downturn in interest, as many feared in the heady first days of the gay and lesbian publishing boom last year. With Douglas Sadownick's *Sacred Lips of the Bronx* and other queer titles now regularly chosen as selections by the Book of the Month Club, gay books have definitely become an established category, much as women's and African-American titles have. Whether or not the boom peaks, that much at least is not going to change. What *is* going to change, however, is the dynamic between the big and small presses: who will do what, and what will get done?

The cornerstone for the smaller houses is a commitment to a wide range of titles and writers. Alyson, for example, has focused on publishing books that reflect the queer experience outside the urban centers of New York or San Francisco, long the chief settings for most gay fiction and much nonfiction. As far back as *Shadows of Love,* Alyson's 1988 fiction anthology, the stated aim was to "represent the geographic and ethnic diversity of gay America and the multifariousness of its inhabitants." The company's lead title from last fall, *Small Favors*, by James Russell Mayes, follows that philosophy, presenting a collection of stories set in the rural Midwest.

The smaller houses tend to be on the cutting edge in general. Firebrand was the first to publish Dorothy Allison. A book such as *A Lotus of Another Color*, an anthology of South Asian gay and lesbian writers, can be more feasibly published by the independents than by the majors. And the many manifestations of queer sexuality can be more fully explored in a series of small volumes from Alyson (*Doing it for Daddy* by Pat Califia) or BadBoy (*The Kiss of the Whip* by Jim Prezwalski) than they can in a bigger book from a bigger house, where Crown's *Culture of Desire* by Frank Browning barely scratched the latex of current gay sexual trends.

But such freedom rarely translates into big dollars (although Richard Kasak's titles, even his more "literary" excursions, have been particularly big money-makers). For a writer, it is still the dream of a big advance from a major house that motivates. One writer I know, who has had considerable success publishing with the independent presses, still awaits "the big break" with a mainstream house, as if success with the smaller houses was just a stepping stone.

And, predictably, as mainstream publishers have increasingly turned to lesbian and gay writers, turf-war tensions between big and small houses have intensified. Small presses have often felt abandoned by a writer they have nurtured, and they resent the publicity and money generated by big publishers like Crown or Dutton, when they have often been publishing quality queer writers for more than a decade. They fear losing some of their top talent to the undeniable temptation of a big house. "There's just no way to compete with a big advance," Beth Dingham of New Victoria Press told me plainly.

"For a lot of books, the smaller gay or lesbian press can do as good a job as a mainstream publisher," admits Michael Denneny. "But there will be a point where a certain writer, like a Dorothy Allison, will become successful enough and will move to the bigger houses, simply because there are more resources there. There's a lot of conflict about that today and I don't think there should be."

Surprisingly, Nancy Bereano of Firebrand—who published Allison's first book, *Trash*, only to watch as she moved on to Viking Penguin with *Bastard Out of Carolina* and became a finalist for the National Book Award, agrees. "The net result of Dorothy Allison's success is very good for the smaller houses," she says. "The effect on Firebrand has been an incredibly positive one." In fact, while Penguin will publish Allison's next novel, she insisted that Firebrand publish her collection of personal essays, *Skin*, which brought Firebrand considerable notoriety last year, and was excerpted in *The New York Times*. "I think this could be a model for other writers who start in the smaller houses and move into the mainstream," Bereano says.

## MARKET FORCES AT WORK

Yet success at the mainstream houses has generally been reserved for gay white male writers: Edmund White, David Leavitt, Michelangelo Signorile, Dennis Cooper, Rod and Bob. (Dorothy Allison is a notable exception.) Even an author as respected as Sarah Schulman has had difficulty being consistently published by the mainstream houses, and she has made no secret of her anger about this, publicly confronting former Crown editor David Groff at an OutWrite gathering a few years ago and asking why he hadn't published more lesbians.

If anything can be generalized about the smaller houses, it's that they have produced a high quality lesbian output, a telling contrast to the dearth of lesbian books from the big houses. Perhaps this is because the fundamental thinking at lesbian presses is often quite different from the bottom-line thinking of the big publishing houses. "Virtually no one involved in the women's presses comes out of a trade publishing background," Nancy Bereano explained to me. "We've come out of a grassroots political background. We make a choice to support less commercially viable books, like poetry and books by women of color, and that's a political choice."

That the world of gay and lesbian publishing—like the industry itself—is relentlessly white as well as male was made clear as, one after another, few of the key players I interviewed were persons of color. There are just three gay-lesbian small presses in this country that target an African-American audience: Vega Press; Kitchen Table/Women of Color Press; and Woman in the Moon Press. (A fourth, Galiens Press, dissolved when founder Assoto Saint died of AIDS last year.)

The current attention to gay and lesbian titles "hasn't had much impact on us as lesbians of color," Barbara Smith of Kitchen Table told me. "I think that's because women of color tend to be quite political, quite critical of the status quo, in their writing. And that makes institutions like mainstream publishers uncomfortable."

Meanwhile, other small presses continue to struggle with issues of diversity in their titles, some with more success than others. Alyson Publications has had an increasing number of books by writers of color, and has been the moving force behind the career growth of African-American writer Larry Duplechan. James Earl Hardy's *B-Boy Blues* is attracting considerable notice and selling very well. At Firebrand, a third of their list is by women of color.

There are encouraging signs at the bigger houses as well. According to Denneny, the most promising books to cross his new desk at Crown are by young lesbian writers. What may have been lip service by mainstream publishers to issues of diversity in the past now seems to be more authentic, especially given such successes as Allison, Schulman's *My American History* and Randall Kenan's *Let the Dead Bury Their Dead*, which was a finalist for the 1992 Los Angeles Times Book Prize. In addition, Dutton broke new ground last month by signing poet and essayist Kenny Fries to write a memoir about his life as a disabled gay man.

If there remain concerns about the future of gay books — and there should be — chief among them is the "Hollywoodization" that seems to be creeping in. Gay books, like their straight counterparts, are increasingly expected to be blockbusters. Even at the smaller presses, as some editors confided to me, book proposals that would have been given more of a chance in the past are in for heavier scrutiny. More and more, big and small publishers alike are looking for titles that will sell a record number of copies, encouraged by the phenomenal success of last year's *Straight From the Heart*, the biggest-selling gay book of all time. "It's as if every movie had to be *Jurassic Park*, and none of them could be *Paris Is Burning*," Matthew Sartwell of the Publishing Triangle lamented to me.

What we're also seeing is what agent Malaga Baldi calls "gay lite": celebrity memoirs, mysteries, humor books and lifestyle companions like the recent *Unofficial Gay Manual*. While lightweight and easy to dismiss as trivia, such books are an important bridge to readers who might not pick up a more "literary" tome. And that's important: for if the bottom line on the future of gay

publishing is how much money queer books make — which in turn will prompt publishers to put out more queer books — then the key is to get more people to buy them. There are two markets for such a sales strategy. One is the "crossover" market, a dim and dangerous proposition. Books like *And the Band Played On* are rare: most publishers I spoke with said straight people are only in the most unusual circumstances going to buy a clearly gay-identified book. The success of a gay book must therefore depend almost exclusively on the gay consumer.

And that market has yet to be fully tapped. As the gay press has grown in both quality and quantity over the last five years, so has the potential for a literary gay market. A straight book, even a good straight book, might get reviewed in a half dozen newspapers. But a gay book, even a mediocre one, is often reviewed in upwards of twenty or thirty publications, from the national glossies to the free weeklies published in nearly every American city of at least moderate size. In addition, the handful of gay bookstores that existed around the country by the early 80's has grown to between 60 and 70 today, and counting feminist and gay-friendly bookstores, that figure skyrockets to 250. Such outlets host book readings and signings that give queer authors more of a head start than many of their straight counterparts, at least among the target population.

The aim for publishers, then, should be an expanded queer market, which ultimately may prove more promising than any hope of crossover appeal. There remain hordes of gay and lesbian consumers who still do not regularly buy queer books, who take Stephen King or Danielle Steel to the beach, and who *could* provide the dollars to keep the big gay titles rolling off the presses. Michael Denneny calls these "the boys in the bars"; they're also the dykes in the poolrooms and the emerging queer youth market, all of whom would potentially buy gay books if they were offered the same variety straight readers have at any drugstore paperback rack. The gay Stephen King or lesbian Danielle Steel has yet to be found, but "the gay illiteracy," as David Groff calls it, could be bridged by finding them.

Yet there remain real concerns. If anything jeopardizes the continued growth of queer books, it's AIDS. The publishing world has already lost such giants as Paul Monette, Robert Ferro, George Stambolian, John Preston, and David Feinberg, to name a few. Nearly the entire first generation of gay African-American writers has died (Melvin Dixon and Assoto Saint, among others). What might they have written ten years from now, or after a lifetime of writing? How many of the younger crop of writers will also have their careers short-circuited?

While book publishing in general has become much more dependent on the bottom line, gay and lesbian writers are no worse off than straight writers. Consider how new writing by different minorities has come into the mainstream since World War II. In the 1950's and early 1960's, the majority of significant writing came from urban male Jewish writers: Mailer, Bellow, Roth. In the 70's and early 80's, there was a wave of important books by African-American women. Gay and lesbian writers are the newest group to have titles brought into mainstream publishing.

Booksellers agree, but cautiously. The current conservative trend in Washington could eventually make publishing or distributing queer-themed literature difficult. But the cultural war is being won even as individual political battles are lost. Queer titles are being institutionalized at the mainstream publishing houses, becoming book categories and often full-scale imprints. The independent presses have never been healthier, with a renewed commitment to a diversity of titles, especially as the majors increasingly go for the blockbusters.

Barbara Grier put things in perspective for me when she told me that Naiad was reprinting a series of lesbian titles from the 30's. "We mustn't pretend we invented the wheel," she said. "There is a tradition, and that tradition will continue."

# | 41 |

# *A Lesson in Tolerance*

## DAVID RUENZEL

On Tuesday, March 22, Rodney Wilson returned to his teaching job at Mehlville (Mo.) High School from a two-day trip to Washington, D.C., where he had visited the Holocaust Museum. There he had purchased a poster depicting the various ID patches concentration camp inmates were compelled to wear, and he brought it with him that day to his junior history class. Pulling a chair to the front of the classroom, the 28-year-old teacher sat down and told his students he was gay. Wilson pointed to the pink triangle on the poster and said, "If I had been in Europe during World War II, I would have been forced to wear this pink triangle, and I would have been gassed to death."

To Wilson, it seemed an auspicious time to reveal his homosexuality, although he admits he was not certain he would do it until the very last moment. Pedagogically, it made good sense: his students were studying the events of World War II and had just finished watching the movie *Escape*

*from Sobibor,* an account of the only successful mass escape from a Nazi death camp. His mention of his homosexuality and the extermination of homosexuals were made in the context of the larger genocide.

There had been rumors around school that Wilson was gay—rumors that began to proliferate in January, when the *St. Louis Post-Dispatch* published a letter from Wilson supporting a column that advocated same-sex marriage. He cited Biblical passages to argue his case. "Many among the faculty were very, very upset," Wilson recalls. He was told that one teacher who always thought highly of him cried because of the letter. The person was outraged, Wilson says, "that I could be so arrogant as to use the Bible to support gay-lesbian marriage." He also heard that a male faculty

*Teacher Magazine,* September 1994, pp. 24–29.

member got down on his knees in the school office to propose to another, making fun of what Wilson had written.

But addressing the rumors was the least of Wilson's reasons for coming out. Much more important was his conviction that students needed to see, as he puts it, "a human face behind the 'evil' word 'homosexual.' " This conviction had been intensifying since the fall of 1991, his second year of teaching in Mehlville, a St. Louis suburb, when his students debated whether a lesbian couple should be allowed to adopt children. The answer was a belligerent "no." In fact, some of the students said they would burn down the house of any lesbian couple that moved near them.

Wilson is a compulsive writer, fastidiously documenting events and offering provocative analyses of them. In a single-spaced, five-page account of the events of March 22, Wilson makes an analogy that had been gestating since the discussion of the lesbian couple. "If I were black in 1956 Montgomery, Ala.," he writes, "teaching blind students who were white, and I discovered that the students hated blacks (not knowing I was black), as a teacher I would have to reveal my blackness in an attempt to help them overcome their bigotry. Similarly, I needed to reveal my gayness to my students."

Both Wilson and his students agree that his disclosure met with an overwhelmingly sympathetic response. One student, and then another, praised his courage. And as they began to clap, the others joined in. Wilson told the class that what he had done was risky, that he could suffer "on-the-job discrimination as a result." His students asked questions: "Do your parents know?" "How did you know you were gay?" "How did your being gay affect your growing up?" Wilson replied that he knew he was gay from the age of 7 and that his parents, whom he informed three years ago, were accepting. Three girls, overcome by the emotion in the room, began to cry.

Encouraged by this response, Wilson decided to make the same disclosure to his next class. Here the reaction was much more prosaic. After one or two cursory questions, students asked: "Are we getting our tests back?" By the end of the day, the news had traveled through much of the 2,000-student school. Wilson's students supported him unreservedly; they said they would file petitions, organize marches, or do whatever was necessary to protect him should he face any harassment. Most students had little reaction at all, although the ensuing gossip, which exhausted itself within

a week or two, was a temporary diversion from the everyday routine. Occasionally, students dropped by to offer encouragement; others strode into his classroom and peered at him, apparently wanting to see what a gay person actually looked like.

Wilson concludes his document on the events of March 22 this way: "I could write a thousand pages and speak a million words in support of what I have done. If necessary, I will do just that. In the meantime, may God bless my beloved students for their righteousness and bring into existence a world in which their opinions dominate."

In making his disclosure, Wilson was taking some serious professional risks. He is eligible for tenure at the end of the 1994–1995 school year, his fifth year of teaching, and many of his colleagues believe his actions have jeopardized his chances. "This won't blow over," says on teacher, who asks to remain anonymous. "Of course, they won't fire him because he acknowledged to his students that he was gay. That would cause them all kinds of legal and political problems. But next year, he'd better watch his step because they may be looking to nab him on some pretense."

At the time, Wilson was relatively unconcerned. His teaching record was impeccable. The evaluations he had received from assistant principal John Brandenberg and social studies department chairman Don Dulin praised him for everything form "staying on lesson objectives" to establishing "a 'safe zone' for differing viewpoints." Several of his students say they have learned more from him than anyone else. And many of his fellow teachers—even those who are wary of gays and gay rights—applaud his work and integrity. Veteran math teacher Bill Henchel, who had been Wilson's mentor during his first year at Mehlville High, claims that "Wilson is one of the finest young teachers I've ever seen. Intelligent, caring, committed. I've learned a lot from him and have tried to emulate some of the things he does in the classroom."

But there are, according to Henchel, "a lot of CYA"—cover your ass—"people in our administration. If anything comes up out of the ordinary, they take some action so they can say, 'We took action, so you can't do anything to us,' They were anticipating a lot of problems and were shocked when there were none."

Wilson is the antitheses of the kind of wild-eyed iconoclast who strikes fear into the hearts of administrators. He grew up in a conservative Missouri town and is a former member of the fundamentalist Assembly of God Church. He remembers his father once saying, "I don't want a queer within a mile of this house." Wilson disparages moral relativism—what he calls the "you-do-your-thing-and-I'll-do-mine philosophy"—and is pro-life, though he doesn't share this information with his students. "I don't want to stifle debate," he says. A tee-totaler and nonsmoker who has hung perhaps 50 "Proud to be Drug-Free" ribbons from the light fixtures of his classroom, he headed a "Students Against Drinking and Driving" group at the school for three years. Still a Christian (if no longer a fundamentalist), he says he is saddened by the fact that so much of the antagonism toward gays and lesbians is rooted in the church. He greatly resents that some Christians are taught to associate homosexuality and immorality. Hate, he says, is the ultimate evil.

Wilson, then, was not fearful on March 24, when, in the midst of a lesson, he was summoned from his classroom to principal Ron Jones' office. Jones and assistant principal Brandenburg were waiting for him there.

"Is this about the gay issue?" Wilson asked.

"Yes," Brandenburg said.

Wilson agreed to give them an account of what happened on March 22, but first he asked that Gail Egleston, a Mehlville High English teacher and the school's union representative, be permitted to sit in. It was, Egleston says, one of the gentlest meetings she has ever attended. Wilson talked and the administrators took notes. During the meeting, Brandenburg praised Wilson's "articulateness and intellect," acknowledging that he was an outstanding teacher. He did regret, though, that Wilson had not immediately informed him of what had occurred in class; he and other administrators had felt "blindsided." They had heard, for instance, that Wilson had cried in class (which had not happened) and were concerned about his emotional state. They had also heard a rumor that Wilson had told his class he would be fired. Finally, Brandenburg expressed concern about the impact of such personal information and viewpoints—here he referred to the *Post-Dispatch* letter-to-the-editor—could have on the school community. Did Wilson think individual rights were more important than institutional rights?

Two weeks later, Jones called Wilson back into his office and told him that he would soon be receiving a memorandum, written by assistant superintendent Maureen Spence and a district lawyer, asking that homosexuality not be a topic of discussion unless the issue has "relevance to the curriculum." According to Wilson, Jones tried to disassociate himself from the memorandum—even though the principal's name would appear on it—by saying, "I have no problem with you" and "you have broken no policy."

The two-paragraph memorandum, which Wilson received on April 14, is a sort of masterwork of bureaucratic evasiveness. In essence, it is a reprimand that wants to be something other than a reprimand, a spanking that doesn't want to be perceived as a threat. The memo begins, "Mehlville School District considers it inappropriate conduct for a teacher to discuss facts and beliefs of a personal nature, regardless of the nature of those beliefs, in the classroom." After emphasizing that the memorandum is not an attempt to "suppress your personal viewpoint," it stipulates that district policy "requires a teacher to employ appropriate instructional methods and to accept suggestions from principals and supervisors to improve the educational practice. Your primary responsibility is to teach the curriculum as outlined by the Mehlville School District." This last point—namely that the teacher has an obligation to adhere to the curriculum—is apparently crucial to the administration, for it is reiterated in the last paragraph, along with the reminder that "viewpoints on facts of a personal nature [should be left] outside the classroom." Not once in the memorandum do the words "gay" or "homosexual" appear.

Wilson immediately construed the memo as a gag order. "The more I read it, the more disturbed I became," he says. "What they were saying to me, in effect, was that I can't bear witness to the Holocaust. They say it's inappropriate to discuss facts of a personal nature. But how can it be wrong to say that I, as a homosexual, would have died had I then been living in Europe? To accuse me of inappropriate behavior is blatantly discriminatory. Thirty years from now people will look back on such a memo with disbelief."

While Wilson believes teachers must not proselytize and insists that he does not advocate gay rights to his students, he just as adamantly insists that he be permitted to exercise the same rights a heterosexual teachers. "You see," he says, "gay people are not talked about. Therefore, when you talk about a gay person, even one time, they say, 'Here he goes, ramming it down our throats.' My third period class wondered about me because I would occasionally make reference to gay and lesbian people. But heterosexual people announce their heterosexuality on many occasions. I'll talk to someone barely five minutes when he tells me he's heterosexual in a billion different ways. We must be given the same freedom. If a heterosexual teacher is allowed to put a picture of his wife and child on his desk, than a homosexual teacher can't be told not to do that. Of course, they don't allow us to marry in this state. But if I am in my heart married to someone, I'll put his picture on my desk. If heterosexuals do it, I'll do it, too."

From the day Wilson received the memorandum, he has indefatigably worked to have the administration remove it from his file. "They can redeem themselves by rescinding the memo," he says. "It belongs in the dustbin of history. We young people just aren't going to hide anymore. We must live above ground, not in parks and dark places."

Wilson responded to the district memorandum with a 29-page document of his own. It is a document that ostensibly asks Jones for clarification but which is, in effect, a polemic, remarkable for its thoroughness breadth and tone of barely contained rage. Largely, it consists of questions with a vituperative edge. He begins by asking if heterosexual teachers are also subject to the memorandum and are, therefore, being advised, among other things, not to wear wedding rings or to talk about their children, as these things constitute a disclosure of personal views. He asks if the following classroom statements, which parallel his own about the Holocaust, would be violations of school policy: "As a Jew, I would have been gassed to death." "As a Jehovah's Witness, I would have been forced to renounce my religion or face execution." If these statements would have been acceptable, he asks, then why not his own?

Clearly prodding the district administrators to acknowledge that they don't truly object to espousal of personal views, as long as they're conventional views, Wilson continues with his questioning: Is it a violation to tell students that drug use is a vice? May teachers voice their support of civil rights? Finally, after asking the administration to define a "personal fact," Wilson asks: "Is the fact that one is a vegetarian a 'fact of a personal nature'? Is the fact that one has been to Rome a 'fact of a personal nature'?"

One particular question seems to contain the others, addressing just how far teachers must go to separate their personal lives from their professional lives. "If a teacher is unable to speak from personal experience, I must ask, are we teachers simply robots whose life is activated at 7:35 a.m. and deactivated at 2:10 p.m.?"

Even before Wilson received the memorandum and composed his response, he was planning to step up coverage in his classes of gay and lesbian history, which he considers woefully inadequate. Wilson points out his history text book and shakes his head with disdain. "Eight hundred pages," he says, "and not a word about gays and lesbians. You wouldn't even know we existed—that's how buried our history is. I don't want to be pushy, but I do want to be true to history. History is sacred."

Wanting to know if the memorandum would affect his plans to explore gay and lesbian history with his students, Wilson asked that it be rescinded or clarified within two weeks. Receiving no response, he informed Jones on May 9 of a number of topics he hoped to cover that would entail mention or discussion of gays and lesbians. The administration continued to acquiesce, and Wilson continued to press. He sent yet another written request and then followed it up with phone calls to the assistant superintendent's office.

Finally, on June 8, Wilson received a response in the form of a certified letter from the district's law firm, Kohn, Shands, Elbert and Giljum. The April 8 district memorandum, it stated, would not be retracted. The Mehlville School District remain fully convinced that Wilson's behavior was inappropriate. Because the outcome of his case is far from certain (it may end up in court), Wilson does not want the specific contents of the letter made public. But it is essentially a restatement of the original district memorandum. As a teacher, it says Wilson's job is to present the curriculum and refrain from interjecting personal viewpoints. While it is appropriate for him to present a variety of viewpoints on different issues, and indeed he is encouraged to do so, he must not personally espouse any given position.

In what was becoming a cat-and-mouse game, Wilson responded with a nine-page letter of his own. In it, he agrees that the classroom must not become a forum for one's personal views, yet he strenuously argues that such a position carried to an extreme is both ludicrous and a violation of a teacher's right to free speech. Could a teacher, for example, not advocate for the equal rights of African Americans and women? Must he, in discussing the status of African Americans, present as reasonable the viewpoint of skinheads as well as the NAACP's?

Having outlined the details of his position, the concluding paragraphs of Wilson's letter are both resolute and sorrowful: "It is self-evident to me that I am experiencing woes with the Mehlville School District. . . . I have no doubt that the Mehlville School District does not want me to be granted tenure; therefore, they are at this time attempting to create the rope with which to hang me. . . . I am of the opinion that this case involves a violation of my right to free speech and that of the 700 other teachers in the Mehlville School District. I am of the opinion, therefore, that the Mehlville School District must be stopped in its tracks."

Wilson says he has to "walk on eggshells" until he is granted or denied tenure, but he is determined to address in the classroom aspects of the gay and lesbian history he believes are important. Most notable, he is organizing a national movement to designate October 1994 as the first gay history/awareness month across the United States. He plans to celebrate the month in his classroom, just as he now celebrates black history month and women's history month. "From now on," he says, "I'm going to exercise all the rights straight people have. I know some parents will probably go berserk. I don't mean to provoke. But if exercising my rights means provoking people, then I'm sorry. It's like Martin Luther King. He was a rabble-rouser, but he was only doing what was right. The country hadn't caught up with him yet because he was way ahead of the curve."

Wilson's actions raise difficult questions: How familiar with students should a teacher be? Does good teaching inevitably and necessarily involve an expression of self? Or should a teacher's single task be to impart only the skills and information contained in the curriculum? Does the teacher who express his or her viewpoint or makes a personal revelation guide students toward an opinion they have not yet formed on their own? This last point was a principal concern of social studies chairman Dulin, who in the past had given Wilson outstanding evaluations. "When it comes to contemporary issues," he says, "I think it's best to take a neutral position. Lead the discussion off with free inquiry then get the students to explore different sides of the issue. The discussion should be free and open because the kids are more comfortable if they feel they can say anything."

While Dulin praises Wilson's teaching, he declines to offer an opinion on his particular case. (Neither Mehlville superintendent of schools Robert Rogers nor assistant superintendent Spence returned phone calls regarding the Wilson matter.) But principal Ron Jones is forthright.

"Personally, yes, I feel he made a mistake," he says. "The potential for using that information in a negative sense is enormous." The principal notes that if Wilson were to give a male student an F, the student could blackmail the teacher by saying that he tried to fondle him.

"Rodney had a Kodak moment with the kids," Jones says, "one of those times when everything just seems to flow. But he should have kept it hidden."

Did that mean that Wilson should lie about his homosexuality?

"He shouldn't deny it," Jones says. "But he shouldn't admit it either."

Jones looks and sounds world-weary. He speaks sadly of the changes he has witnessed during his four decades in education—changes that have required teachers to be more and more impersonal. "I myself am a hugger, but I don't even do that anymore," he says. "We've got to be careful about touching for legal reasons. It scares the death out of me. It used to be that when I came across a boy I knew, I'd give him a friendly little pop in the shoulder, but I don't even do that anymore. At one time, we used to take a kid home if he or she got sick, but those days are past."

Jones admires Wilson, saying he is a natural teacher who has a tremendous rapport with his students. He also acknowledges that teachers can't avoid talking about their personal lives but then asserts—seemingly reiterating the district memo—that "the teacher is there to present the facts the best he can." While he agrees that the memo could have been better phrased, he says its intent was "to make sure Wilson understood the parameters as far as the curriculum was concerned. If Rodney wants to teach facts as facts, as they pertain to the subject matter, people will accept it." While his remarks sound almost as fuzzy as those in the memo, Jones clearly believes Wilson's duty is to present the curriculum and *only* the curriculum.

It's easy to appreciate Jones' lament about the increasing distance between teachers and students, made necessary by a sensitivity—some would say hypersensitivity—to harassment and abuse issues. And there may be sound reasons why Wilson shouldn't have discussed his homosexuality. But the reasons enumerated by Jones and the administration in the memorandum and certified letter present problems.

For one thing, the implication that a teacher must not depart from the prescribed curriculum is troubling, if not ludicrous. No one visits a favorite former high school teacher and says, "What I like best about you was the way you always stuck to the curriculum." In fact, a teacher who slavishly follows a curriculum is most likely to be remembered as a pedant.

Good teachers digress from the curriculum all the time, understanding that it's but a broad outline, not a decree. They know that the curriculum is the most ephemeral of documents, constantly changing to meet social and political pressures. Schools sometimes like to pretend, especially when they want to keep teachers "on track," that the curriculum is a document of immutable wisdom, when it is all too often the product of compromises made in the face of intrepid lobbying.

Even if a magical curriculum could be developed that would somehow please everyone, it is unlikely that teachers would want to follow it to the letter. "If you covered the curriculum just as it was given to you," Wilson says, "you'd go insane, and your students would go insane, too. They'd hate learning history, and that would be a crime. I don't care if they leave not knowing a particular fact, but I do care that they leave liking history a bit more than they did coming in."

This gets at another odd assumption the district memoranda make: namely that education largely consists of facts. Indeed, Jones' statement about "teaching facts as facts" brings to mind Thomas Gradgrind, the dictatorial schoolmaster in Charles Dickens' novel *Hard Times*, who, in an attempt to bridle the dangerous imagination, tells a teacher, "Now, what I want is, Facts. Teach these boys and girls nothing but Facts. . . . Plant nothing else, and root out everything else. . . . Stick to Facts, sir!"

Complicating the issue is the insistence that teachers avoid "personal facts," as if these sorts of facts could be pitted against facts of a purely objective nature. Of course, there is information about a teacher's personal life that he or she is best off not divulging; but to suggest, on the other hand, that there is a universe of unbiased facts is fallacious. The very facts a teacher chooses to present, as Wilson points out in his last response to the district, invariably indicate some degree of subjectivity. The certified letter from the district's law firm takes a slightly different tack, in that it encourages Wilson to present a variety of viewpoints as long as he doesn't avow any single viewpoint as his own. In essence, though, viewpoints presented this way merely become facts of a more expansive nature, as in "feminists believe $x$

because of $y$, while conservatives are opposed to $x$ because of $z$."

What kind of teacher would be content simply to dispense facts? Probably not a very good one. A teacher who is merely a purveyor of information could easily be replaces by a faster, more comprehensive machine the computer, for instance. Furthermore, the teacher who believes that it is his or her job to disseminate a plethora of viewpoints with absolute neutrality is prone to the charge of moral relativism, which some people believe has led to the decline of American public education.

According to Kevin Jennings, a history teacher at Concord Academy in Massachusetts and author of *One Teacher in 10: Gay and Lesbian Educators Tell Their Stories*, teachers are always better off coming out. "Even people who experience some harassment still feel better after acknowledging their homosexuality universally," he says. "Fear of violence goes away, along with fear of job loss. When you're gay, you don't know where your support may be, and gay teachers inevitably find they have many straight allies. Having to be silent when confronted with homophobia is enormously degrading to teachers.

"More often than not, the fears don't come true—students, for instance, don't engage in name-calling. This generation grew up during a time when gay people became visible, and they're not as freaked about homosexuality. Besides, young people are by nature idealistic, reacting with indignation to manifest unfairness. They're the biggest allies of gay teachers. When there is harassment, it's almost always from administrators."

In Wilson's case, there wasn't so much as a single complaint lodged by parents regarding Wilson's disclosure, as principal Jones acknowledges. Why then did the administration take any action at all? Karen Harbeck, a Massachusetts lawyer specializing in the legal needs of lesbian and gay clients and editor of a book titled *Coming Out of the Classroom Closet*, says a prudent employer wouldn't harass gay or lesbian educators since recent legal judgments have consistently gone against those who have.

Harbeck, who has corresponded with Wilson and followed his situation, surmises that the administration was anticipating trouble that never came. "We've found that administrations are typically swayed by the first phone calls that come in, which are typically hostile calls," she explains. Yet, experience demonstrates that they're watching the wrong phone calls. The rights belong with the accused."

Harbeck is impatient with the notion that Wilson made a mistake in disclosing his homosexuality. "Teachers talk about their personal lives all the time," she says. "It's astounding how much goes on. I recently came across a situation in which a 4th grade math teacher was talking in class about a leather watch that turns him on. The amount of heterosexism"—discrimination against homosexuals by heterosexuals—"in classrooms is amazing, right down to the wedding ring. So in the case of gay and lesbian teachers, it's 'Oh, Lord, I don't want these hostile phone calls.' But if a phone call scares them, if they run because one person calls about Rodney Wilson, then why are they in education?"

While defending Wilson and the right of teachers "to come out," Harbeck emphasizes that teachers have no license, morally or legally, to expatiate upon their personal lives. Any mention of one's homosexuality had at best be done within the context of a lesson, and even then it has to be approached with extreme caution. "I would bring in speakers—gays and lesbians from the community—rather than talk extensively about my personal life," Harbeck says. "I told that to Rodney in person. If he's invited to give a presentation to the faculty or to students, that's one thing. But to sit in class and talk about his struggles at age 12 is inappropriate for any educator. You're supposed to stay on course with the curriculum. Rodney can talk about Stonewall [the 1969 gay uprising in New York City] without going into his personal life. He can put it into a historical context without exposing himself directly.

"If I were Rodney Wilson, I would form a club. A gay-straight alliance of which I would offer to be a faculty advisor. It could meet after school like the ski club or anything else. Here's where I would talk to students one on one—not in the midst of course work."

Harbeck believes that Wilson spent too much time generating documents when he should have been establishing an open dialogue with district administrators. Citing a 1989 U.S. Department of Health and Human Services report estimating that almost one-third of teen suicides are committed by homosexuals, she believes that Wilson should have emphasized the importance of being a positive role model for gay and lesbian students.

"Unfortunately, Rodney lost contact, and now he has a stalemate in which no one is really talking," she says. "He needs to create a larger educa-

tional context so that people know what it's all about. People say, 'Why does he have to talk about it?' There's an answer to that. We've been invisible for 300 years. The world is so heterosexist that we need to overbalance it until it comes out level. So what Rodney has done is incredibly important. But now he must work on the interpersonal level. You must be expansive instead of pedantic."

The Rodney Wilson case can perhaps be distilled into a single question: Just how much of themselves—their passions, their ideas, their personal histories—should teachers be expected to leave at the school door? To dwell too much upon themselves, especially if the conversation does not converge with the subject they teach, can be a futile exercise in narcissism. The teacher, prey to his or her own egotism, wants to be admired rather than to instruct. But to go to the opposite extreme—to draw a line of demarcation between oneself as a teacher and oneself as a person—can be schizophrenic for the teacher and deadening for the students. By constructing a facade of emotional neutrality, the teacher creates an arid climate in which nothing can flourish but facts.

Most of the teachers interviewed for this story—both gay and straight—say they generally strive to maintain a "middle ground." While they reserve the right to make personal statements, they do so cautiously, not wanting to make themselves the center of attention. Interestingly enough, a number of gay teachers who have not disclosed their homosexuality to their students say they remain silent in the classroom for this very reason. As far as their teaching is concerned, they believe that their homosexuality is irrelevant, and public disclosure would place them in the limelight, where the students belong.

Gail Egelston, the Mehlville High English teacher and union representative, elaborated upon the difference between giving an opinion and proselytizing. "If a student has a right to interpret an event," she says, "we have a right to interpret it, too. We do both ourselves and our students a disservice if we continually feign neutrality. If a student says, 'Want a steak?' I'll say, 'No, I'm a vegetarian' and explain why I think not eating meat is a good thing. But we don't present our views a gospel. We present them as opinions."

Wilson agrees with Egelston. Gesturing to the walls of his classroom, which are covered with pictures of everyone from movie stars to Reagan and Bush to Martin Luther King Jr. and Malcolm X, he says he is primarily interested in celebrating diversity. Eclecticism is his modus operandi: "When it comes to expressing your opinions, there are two lines of thought," he says. "One is that teachers should express their biases so that students can respond accordingly. The other is that teachers should not express bias. I generally lean toward not expressing my bias. For instance, if you ask my students if I'm pro-life or pro-choice, it would probably be a 50–50 vote. While I'm pro-life, they're not going to know that. My students are going to know, just by looking around the room, that I support African-American rights and that I believe African Americans have been violated, abused. But I want to be careful with interjecting my opinions because you want your students to think on their own. You don't want to crush their ability to create ideas. I would be crossing the line at the point where I begin to impose my ideas in an inappropriate way upon my students."

It is perhaps too easy to think of Wilson's situation solely in terms of a teacher's right to free expression. Wilson insists that he has a right to say who he is, just as heterosexual teachers every day say who they are "in a billion different ways." But he also wants people to consider the impact his revelation could have upon gay and lesbian students who, as part of a group disparaged by society, often endure a self-loathing that can be scar-

ring and even fatal. His coming out of the closet, he says, has enabled him to work openly and honestly with gay and lesbian students who are sometimes perched on the edge of the abyss.

Sitting in Wilson's classroom after school are four such students—one girl and three boys. One of the boys says that from the time he was in elementary school he has always felt different, an oddity in what he has come to identify as a heterosexual world. He, like the other three students seated with him, endured taunting and the accompanying sense of shame throughout his childhood. Wilson's coming out for him and his friends, was an event of enormous significance, he says, helping gay students move toward self-acceptance.

One of the other boys offers what is surely the most important perspective on Rodney Wilson's disclosure that March day. Wilson, the boy says, saw him through a tumultuous period during which he was battling with his parents, who insisted that he was just "going through a phase." He decided he could no longer live at home. "I dropped out of school, but Mr. Wilson stayed in contact with me," he says. "He said I had to stay in school, so I finally went back. In my mind, he's a true teacher. Only when you can bring something of life from outside the building into the school can you call yourself a real teacher."

# 42

# *Gay Teachers Make Their Lives Whole Again*

### DEB PRICE

Is she in the closet? The question makes being gay sound like a high-stakes game of Sardines—either you're crammed into an overcrowded hiding place or visible to the whole world. But for most of us, the coming-out process is more like playing Mother May I: a lot of hesitant baby steps, a few giant steps and a couple of playmates equally unsure of their footing.

For gay teachers, the scariest step often bridges

the chasm they've dug to separate their professional and personal lives. Most fear losing their credibility or careers. "People wouldn't be able to see beyond my lesbian identity to see me as a good teacher," a closeted teacher told researcher Pat Griffin.

*Detroit News*, March 11, 1993.

Special-education teacher Mary Lorenz of Northampton, Mass., recalls years of clamming up whenever conversation in the faculty lounge turned to life beyond the schoolhouse walls. "I was always very, very careful," she says. "I never made up stories or changed pronouns, but I was reticent. I definitely felt isolated."

Lorenz and a dozen other Massachusetts educators found the courage to integrate the two halves of their lives during a 15-month research project designed by Griffin, a University of Massachusetts education professor.

When Griffin first met them, many of the 13 were trying to be Super Teacher. "They just knocked themselves out to create a reputation that was above reproach," Griffin said. Yet their hard work failed to banish the terror "that they'll be accused either of molestation or recruitment just by being gay or lesbian," she found.

Such fears had long kept them quiet about anti-gay remarks and AIDS, even though they instinctively felt a duty to educate their students and fellow teachers.

"The conflict between concealing and revealing their lesbian and gay identities was as much a part of every school day as were lesson plans and faculty meetings," Griffin writes in "Coming Out of the Classroom Closet," a collection of essays edited by Karen M. Harbeck.

The 13 educators in her project included a principal, a librarian and a guidance counselor, as well as classroom teachers. In the beginning, none was publicly out at school or completely closeted elsewhere. By the end, through positive reinforcement, all of them had taken steps—whether giant or baby-sized—toward openness at school, all felt more effective professionally and none had suffered job repercussions.

At first, nine of the 13 said being gay had nothing to do with being an educator. "I don't think of myself as a gay teacher," one said. "I'm just a teacher who happens to be gay."

But as they met together month after month, they realized how much energy they devoted to compartmentalizing their lives. And they began to see ways that being gay was an asset to them as educators.

Gradually, "I'm out at school" stopped seeming like a true-false question. Instead, they saw multiple choices, which they expressed at a gay-pride parade.

Nancy Hoff, a high-school shop teacher, recalls that the group's bravery helped her "to go to the next steps—little steps of being bolder at school and hiding less, starting to use my partner's name and talking about my life."

Thanks to the strides she made while in Griffin's group, Hoff felt free to take her partner to the prom that she chaperoned as senior adviser. Then, taking one more step in a round of Truth or Consequences, they danced.

In the game of life, example can be the best teacher: Homosexuality is nothing to hide.

# | 43 |

# *Pop Tune Can Comfort Teens Unsure of Their Sexuality*

## Victoria Brownworth

It was a crisp spring night and I was driving past my old school—a Catholic girls academy. A lovely clear night with a sky full of stars, in a quiet, tree-shrouded neighborhood. The big white stone convent of my Catholic girlhood loomed near.

On my favorite alternative rock station, a lyri-

*Philadelphia Daily News*, July 25, 1995.

cal but upbeat song started to play. The words did-n't catch me right away. Then I heard the female singer bouncing out the first stanza of the chorus:

Her lips were soft,
Her lips were sweet.
She was just like me;
I kissed a girl.

I pulled over in the shadow of the school where I first kissed a girl. I turned the radio up. I was listening to the hit song "I Kissed a Girl" by singer-songwriter Jill Sobule; no negative tale of adolescent angst and suicidal woe, but an uplift-ing tune about romantic experimentation in which lesbianism is more attractive than hetero-sexuality.

They'll have their diamonds,
But we'll have our pearls.
I kissed a girl—
I might do it again—
I'm so glad I kissed a girl.

Three minutes of a good danceable beat, a clear pretty voice and lyrics unmistakenly direct—all in all a catchy tune. And with a delightful pro-queer message.

This song, on my favorite radio station, the one every Philadelphia teenager listens to. I was shocked—and thrilled. Positive songs about queer romance—especially as sweetly innocent as this—simply don't exist. Or at least don't get played on radio during prime time.

"I Kissed a Girl" was the song I'd been waiting to hear for more than 20 years. It would have made the first time I kissed a girl very different. It no doubt will change the lives of thousands of young lesbian and bisexual girls. Because "I Kissed a Girl" is a song that makes girls kissing other girls sound the way young love is supposed to sound—simple and tender—like it's OK. Jill Souble's message is succinct: girls kissing girls is good; don't feel bad about it.

That positive, affirming message would have helped me and my queer friends when we were teens. The nice normal images of women loving other women invoked by the song would have made me feel less different and less isolated because I would have known other girls felt just like I did.

I was 13 when another girl first kissed me, a girl a few grades ahead of me. She was very smart, very pretty, very popular. Everybody liked her. Nobody knew—except the girls she kissed—she was a lesbian. It was secret.

That's because sexuality was never discussed in Catholic school—except in the schoolyard. The nuns told us: If a boy asks you, say no. Some of us weren't even sure what it was we were sup-posed to say no to. We were told a good girl saves herself for marriage; boys only want one thing. These covert messages the nuns taught were very specific: Boys are bad, girls are good and girls who stay away from boys are best of all (but they didn't mean lesbians). The sin of homosexuality was never discussed, merely implied; all sex was sin-ful.

These messages reduce sex to victim (girl) and victimizer (boy), and imply sex is always wrong. Teens are made to feel normal adolescent sexual urges are bad. But not all boys force themselves on girls and not all girls are attracted to boys. So a song like Souble's isn't just for young lesbians, it's for any teen feeling her or his way sexually. This song doesn't promote sex—it's about a kiss, hand on a knee, talking to someone who understands you. It's a song about feelings. Tune to the latest hip-hop song from TLC about oral, anal and other sex, and Souble's song seems incredibly tame.

Sex is a complicated thing, especially in these days of killer diseases. But examining sexual feel-ings doesn't have to be so complicated, as Sou-ble's song explains. No sexual choice is irrevoca-ble, except the one made carelessly. One kiss doesn't necessarily make a girl a lesbian. But one positive song can certainly make her feel better about being queer.

# *Three*
# MAINSTREAM
## MEDIA

# III. A
# UP FROM INVISIBILITY: FILM AND TELEVISION

In 1895 Thomas Edison and his colleagues were perfecting an invention that would transform the world: motion pictures. One of the first films made at the Edison Studio in New Jersey was a five-minute experimental film, directed by William Dickson, that showed two men dancing together to the music of a waltz played on an Edison gramophone. It was called *The Gay Brothers*. While we don't know what Dickson intended this light-hearted scene to suggest, we do know that this brief curtain raiser did not prove typical of the thousands of movies that have followed.

Like other minorities, gay people have mostly been invisible on the screen. When members of a minority do begin to appear on movie and television screens, the roles they are permitted to play are generally limited to two categories: villains and victims (of violence and of ridicule). In the case of African Americans these two types can be seen, on the one hand, in Griffith's *Birth of a Nation*, in which black men are vicious rapists whose attacks on white women are foiled by the white male heroes of the KKK, and, on the other hand, in the caricatured lazy and foolish servants portrayed by Stepin Fetchit and Butterfly McQueen. By representing a threat to be defeated or a fun house mirror that highlights the hero's normal image, both villains and victims uphold the importance of staying on the straight and narrow path.

In the case of racial and ethnic minorities— African Americans, Native Americans, Asian Americans, and, through the 1950s, even "white ethnics" such as Italian, Polish, and Jewish Ameri-

cans—these characters may have represented a threat to the values but not the identity, of "mainstream" Americans. Hollywood felt compelled to protect "real" Americans from the threat of aliens who might move into their neighborhood and even marry their daughters. But sexual minorities presented a different, and more insidious, danger. Lesbian, gay, and bisexual people are not easily identifiable by skin color, facial features, or accents, and they are not segregated in ethnic neighborhoods. As with the "red menace" of the 1940s and 1950s, when Americans were warned that Communists hid, metaphorically, under our beds, in the case of lesbians and gays Americans were afraid of who might literally be *in* their beds.

American movies have been preoccupied with lesbian and gay people, but for decades this took the form of hidden and coded representations (Russo 1987). In the case of women the disguise was often just that: cross-dressing that allowed the audience to enjoy the discomfort of the other characters because they were "in on the joke." Women dressed as men were allowed to evoke ambiguous responses from their male co-stars, as long as the roles were "straightened out" by the final clinch. But while the mystery lasted it could send mixed messages to audiences, and we can assume that lesbians and gay men sitting in darkened theaters in 1936 paid close attention when Cary Grant told Katherine Hepburn, whose character in *Sylvia Scarlett* is disguised as a young man, "There's something that gives me a queer feeling every time I look at you" (Weiss 1992).

The early history of the movies, and especially

the period after the introduction of the Motion Picture Production Code in the 1930s, was full of what Vito Russo described as "frivolous, asexual sissies" (1987:31) who provided comic relief playing sidekicks, servants, and scapegoats. What was almost completely forbidden was any character who was explicitly lesbian or gay (Custen, "Where Is the Life That Late He Led?" this volume).

There is a Hollywood legend that producer Sam Goldwyn was told that Radclyffe Hall's *The Well of Loneliness* wouldn't work as a movie because it was the story of a lesbian, to which Goldwyn was supposed to have replied, "So what? We'll make her an American." That exchange may never have occurred, but in 1936 Goldwyn produced a film version of Lillian Hellman's Broadway play, *The Children's Hour,* in which lesbianism was erased completely. In the film *These Three* Hellman's play about two women schoolteachers whose lives are destroyed when a vicious child falsely accuses them of being lovers was transformed by Goldwyn and director William Wyler into a more suitably American tale in which the liar accuses one teacher of an affair with the other teacher's fiancé.

Throughout the period of the code lesbian and gay characters were often implied in movies, but always as threatening or pathetic or ridiculous figures. Female characters with sinister lesbian overtones appeared in prison and mental hospital plots (*Caged, Snake Pit*) and as predatory and unscrupulous (*Young Man with a Horn, All About Eve*). Male roles with gay overtones depicted sad young men (*Tea and Sympathy, Rebel Without a Cause*) and vicious degenerates (*Suddenly Last Summer*).

By the end of the 1950s the Motion Picture Production Code was weakening. In 1961 Otto Preminger filmed the best-selling novel *Advise and Consent*, a story of political intrigue in Washington, D.C., in which a senator commits suicide when an early homosexual episode is brought to light. The Motion Picture Association of America was forced to accept that times had changed, and issued a policy on October 3, 1961, stating, "In keeping with the culture, the mores and the values of our time, homosexuality and other sexual aberrations may now be treated with care, discretion and restraint." Discretion and restraint meant, as the MPAA cautioned, that "sexual aberration could be suggested but not actually spelled out." It also still meant that lesbian and gay people would be depicted, in Vito Russo's words, as "pathological, predatory and dangerous; villains and fools, but never heroes" (1987:122).

Director William Wyler took advantage of the new rules to make a second film version of Lillian Hellman's *The Children's Hour* (1962), and this time he retained the original version of the lie told by a little girl. Wyler was quoted as saying that "the lie has to have such a devastating effect that to be credible it must be appalling." Apparently he also meant it had to be unspeakable: although it is clear that the child is alleging that the teachers are carrying on a lesbian relationship, the word *lesbian* is never uttered. What is more, no one in the film suggests in any way that were it true it would not be a tragedy. In fact, the climax of the film occurs when one of the teachers realizes that she is, in fact, attracted to the other woman. "I'm guilty!" she cries, "I've ruined your life, and I've ruined my own. I feel so damn sick and dirty I just can't stand it anymore." The consequence of this realization of her lesbianism is that she promptly commits suicide, only one of many lesbian and gay characters of the period who take their lives when faced with the "awful truth" about their sexuality.

The 1960s were a period of cultural change and growing openness to aspects of sexuality previously denied and repressed in American society, but in Hollywood the climate remained chilly for lesbian and gay characters. Hollywood studios avoided the risk of being denied a code seal by steering clear of depictions of sympathetic or happy homosexuals (the code was superseded in 1968 by the MPAA "alphabet soup" ratings system still in effect today). The story line pioneered by *The Children's Hour* was repeated with variations by other writers and directors, except that the exposure of a character's homosexuality did not depend on the perceptiveness of a vicious child. In *The Sergeant* (1968) Rod Steiger plays a sexually repressed homosexual who doesn't seem to understand why he is obsessed with a handsome young soldier. When his secret eventually explodes in his face—Steiger kisses the enlisted man and is rebuffed—he runs off into the woods and shoots himself. In *Reflections in a Golden Eye* (1967) Marlon Brando is another sexually repressed military man, this time a colonel who follows a young private around, spying on him at night. When he realizes that the private is attracted to his wife and not to him, the colonel shoots the young man.

As the decade of the sixties moved toward the explosion of the Stonewall riots, two movies presented unusually explicit portraits of lesbian and gay life. *The Killing of Sister George* (1968) and *The Boys in the Band* (1970) were presented by the producers and accepted by the critics as unflinching glimpses of gay life: "tacky, tawdry, repellent and true," in the words of *Life* critic Richard Shickel (see discussions by Sheldon, "Lesbians and Film: Some Thoughts," and Dyer, "Stereotyping," in this volume). *Sister George* is the name of a character in a British television soap opera, and she is "killed off" in the program because the real-life actress who plays her is too blatantly lesbian for the producers. George's aggressively butch personality—and her heavy drinking—lead to her complete ruin. Although the film was condemned by lesbian and gay critics as yet another story of a doomed homosexual, *Sister George* has also been seen in a more positive light as an unapologetic feisty lesbian who is undone as much by her own honesty as by her abrasiveness. The real message of the film was that being out of the closet was dangerous to your health. This message was repeated eight-fold in *The Boys in the Band*.

The story of *Boys* focuses on a collection of assorted gay stereotypes who gather at a birthday party and proceed to savage each other in a drunken orgy of self-hate. Critics hailed it as "a landslide of truths," accepting both the stereotypical gay characters and their acute self-hatred. For gay people the film prompted a more complex set of responses. While stereotypical, the characters rang true as well, and they weren't all unhappy or dysfunctional. The film also allowed its gay characters to display a biting wit and a determination to survive despite the odds.

When the central character surveys the wreckage of his apartment at the end of the party and says, "You show me a happy homosexual and I'll show you a gay corpse," he was summarizing an entire genre of movies: out of thirty-two films with major lesbian or gay characters between 1961 and 1976, thirteen feature gays who commit suicide and eighteen have the homosexual character murdered. To gay protests about the film of *Boys in the Band* director William Friedkin responded, "This film is not about homosexuality, it's about human problems. I hope there are happy homosexuals. They just don't happen to be in my film." Nor have they been in many other major American films since.

In February 1971, just a few years after Stonewall, network television's first sympathetic portrait of a gay man appeared, when the controversial sitcom *All in the Family* aired an episode, "Judging Books by Covers," in which Archie Bunker discovers that a football player pal is gay. Possibly because *All in the Family* wasn't yet the ratings giant it soon became the gay-theme show received comparatively little attention.

The following year there was the more significant breakthrough of the ABC made-for-TV movie *That Certain Summer*, in which two gay men actually were shown touching (on the shoulder), and none of the gay characters had to die at the end of the story. Still, the main character, a gay father who comes out to his son, says that if he were given a choice he would choose not to be homosexual. This "breakthrough" was something of a false spring, however, as it did not herald the blooming of a hundred (or even a dozen) gay and lesbian characters. Yet gay and lesbian characters did begin to appear from time to time for one-shot appearances on network series, and in 1978 two TV movies were based on real-life experiences of lesbian and gay people: *Sergeant Matlovich vs. the U.S. Air Force* told the story of the Vietnam vet who said, "They gave me a medal for killing two men and a discharge for loving one," and *A Question of Love* recounted a lesbian mother's child custody case (the women never kiss, but one is shown tenderly drying her lover's hair).

The slight increase in gay (and less often lesbian) visibility in the mid-seventies was quickly seized upon by the right wing as a sign of media capitulation to what in the 1980s came to be called "special interests." The nastiness of the attacks on gay visibility on television is well represented in a nationally syndicated column by Nicholas Von Hoffman, who noted that the "old-style Chinese have the Year of the Tiger and the Year of the Pig," but the "new-style Americans are having the Year of the Fag" (11/4/76). Von Hoffman plaintively asks, "Is a new stereotype being born? Is network television about to kill off the bitchy, old-time outrageous fruit and replace him with a new type homo?" But, although the right wing consistently attacked the networks for what they considered to be overly favorable attention to gay people, in fact, gay people are mostly portrayed and used in news and dramatic media in ways that serve to reinforce rather than challenge the prevailing images. As critic William Henry noted in an overview of TV's treatment of gays through the late 1980s, "When TV does deal with gays it typically takes the point of view of straights struggling to understand. The central action is the progress of acceptance—not self-acceptance by the homosexual, but grief-stricken resignation to fate by his straight loved ones, who serve as surrogates for the audience" (1987:43).

Being defined dramatically as a "problem," it is

no surprise that gay characters were generally confined to television's favorite problem-of-the-week-genre, the made-for-TV movie, with a very occasional one-shot appearance of a lesbian or gay character on a dramatic series. Continuing gay male characters began to appear in the 1980s, but they tended to be so subtle as to be readily misunderstood by the innocent or confused about their sexuality and never seen in an ongoing romantic gay relationship.

Although the lesbian character Dr. Lynne Carlson appeared for a few months in 1983 on the daytime serial *All My Children*, a regular lesbian character did not appear on prime-time television until the short-lived medical series *Heartbeat* in 1989. The role of the lesbian nurse practitioner Marilyn McGrath played by Gail Strickland on *Heartbeat* demonstrated that behind the superficial feminism of the program beat a familiar patriarchal heart (see Moritz, "Old Strategies for New Texts," this volume). Apparently, for program executives progress means constructing images of lesbians and gays that are nonthreatening to heterosexuals by erasing any sign of lesbian and gay sexuality. The desexualization of Marilyn McGrath did not, however, deflect the wrath of the Rev. Donald Wildmon's American Family Association, whose massive campaign against the program may have contributed to the cancellation of *Heartbeat* after one season.

Also in 1989 ABC broadcast a four-hour miniseries based on Gloria Naylor's novel, *The Women of Brewster Place*. The story traces the tales of a group of African American women over several decades living in tenements on a walled-off, dead-end block. A major portion of the plot concerns a lesbian couple who live on the block. In the words of the *New York Times*'s John O'Connor, the women "are portrayed with relative candor and sympathy in a plot development that turns into a condemnation of homophobia" (1989). The two women become the targets of the neighborhood busybody, who is horrified when she spies on them and, as she repeats to everyone in the vicinity, "I thought they was gonna kiss each other smack on the face." But, despite the sympathetic representation of the couple, they do no such thing (see Bruni, "Culture Stays Screen Shy of Showing the Gay Kiss," this volume).

In 1990 an episode of the popular series *thirtysomething* included a scene showing two gay men in bed—but not touching. The subsequent furor, and alleged loss of $1 million in ad revenues, led ABC to withdraw the episode from the rerun schedule. In this context no one should have been surprised at the furor aroused in February 1991 when two female attorneys on NBC's *LA Law* engaged in the first lesbian kiss on network television. Predictably, Rev. Wildmon geared up his fundamentalist letter-writing battalions to browbeat the networks and advertisers into censoring such acts by threatening them with product boycotts. Equally predictably, NBC began hedging its bets: "We were not attempting to create a lesbian character in that episode," said NBC spokeswoman Sue Binford. "It was much more of an attempt to add texture to C.J.'s character. It was a minor part of the overall story line" (Enrico 1991).

In the early 1990s three successful TV series made history, of a sort, by introducing lesbian or gay characters with continuing if secondary roles. Ratings queen Roseanne brought into the circle of her eponymous heroine the character of her gay boss (and later partner), Leon Carp (played by Martin Mull), followed by her bisexual friend Nancy (Sandra Bernhard). The story of the founding of the fictional town of Cicely, Alaska (the setting of *Northern Exposure*), by lesbian lovers Roslyn and Cicely was told in the final episode of the 1992 season. The series earlier introduced the secondary characters of Ron and Erick, a gay couple who owned a bed-and-breakfast inn in Cicely. The twenty-something ensemble show *Melrose Place* featured a gay man, Matt Fielding (Doug Savant), among the residents of a West Hollywood apartment complex. The 1994 season introduced an enormously successful sitcom about a group of twenty-something *Friends*, and the secondary characters included the lesbian former wife of one central figure, her lover, and the baby she gives birth to during one episode. The success of these programs, despite the rising temperature of homophobic rhetoric on the political right, led television producers to include lesbian or gay weddings on *Roseanne* and *Friends* (neither wedding, however, featured a visible kiss between the partners). The question remains, however, whether any lesbian and gay characters will be permitted to have lives as full as their heterosexual counterparts or will they remain relegated to the margins as sympathetic if witty celibates?

The fall 1996 television season opened with a leaked story that Ellen Morgan, the lead character played by Ellen DeGeneres on the sitcom *Ellen*, would come out as a lesbian later in the season. A predictable wave of articles, columns, and editorials followed, some urging ABC/Disney to permit the unprecedented coming out of a TV series lead and others decrying this latest nail in the coffin of family values. The media frenzy escalated when DeGeneres herself came out—on the cover of *Time,* in a two-part interview with Diane Sawyer and, along with her new girlfriend, actress Anne Heche, on *Oprah.* The one-hour "coming out" episode pulled the highest ratings of the season, along with critical acclaim, but ABC officials cautioned that Ellen Morgan's future would not be filled with lesbian romantic liaisons. Network executives were not the only ones experiencing ambivalence. Lesbian cartoonist Alison Bechdel spoke for many when she commented, "It's kind of sad to me, even though in one way it's progress. It's sad because I like being on the margins. I think you have a richer kind of life that way. I don't want to see queer life turned into a commodity on network TV."

One television format that has proved hospitable to lesbian and gay people is the daytime talk show pioneered by Phil Donahue in the late 1970s. By the early 1990s there were numerous variations running every day on broadcast and cable channels. One thing these shows have in common is that they all schedule lesbian, gay, and bisexual guests and themes with great frequency, especially during the crucial sweeps months. The hosts and, increasingly, the studio audiences, can be counted on to take a liberal view toward sexual minorities—they are especially fascinated with transgendered people of any sort—and to endorse a "live and let live" attitude toward homosexuality (Gamson, "Do Ask, Do Tell," this volume). By the 1990s it is safe to say that most Americans were more likely to encounter an openly lesbian or gay person on daytime TV talk shows than anywhere else in our public culture. The talk shows have reduced their reliance on "experts" brought on to "explain" lesbian and gay guests to the audience (or to themselves), and they are also less likely than in the past to feel the need to include a homophobe for "balance" whenever scheduling lesbian or gay guests.

There is another arena in which lesbian and gay people have been able to speak for themselves. For decades lesbian and gay artists, including many people of color, have been prominent in the ranks of avant-garde and independent filmmakers. These range from the widely known, such as Andy Warhol, to those whose fame is limited to festival, campus, and art house circles, such as Barbara Hammer and Isaac Julien. Some have "broken through" and reached wider audiences, as the late Marlon Riggs did with his widely

admired *Tongues Untied,* an exploration of black gay life that was broadcast on Public Television and singled out for attack by Patrick Buchanan in ads run during his campaign for the Republican presidential nomination in 1992. Independently financed lesbian and gay films that reached wider theatrical audiences include Donna Deitch's 1985 *Desert Hearts,* Bill Sherwood's 1986 *Parting Glances,* Jennie Livingston's 1991 *Paris Is Burning,* Gregg Araki's 1992 *The Living End,* Ang Lee's 1993 *The Wedding Banquet,* Rose Troche's 1994 *Go Fish,* and Maria Maggenti's *The Incredibly True Adventure of Two Girls in Love* in 1995. By the summer of 1996 Hollywood studio scouts were flocking to lesbian and gay film festivals in San Francisco and Los Angeles, noting, in the words of one marketing executive, that "any time a niche is under-represented on the screen, there's a certain amount of money to be made. The gay audience is certainly one that is under-represented" (Irvine 1996).

The industry's interest in independent lesbian and gay films is also spurred by the continuing success of mainstream films that utilize that oldest of movie clichés, the drag queen with a heart of gold. Beginning with the Australian *Priscilla, Queen of the Desert,* followed by the moderately successful *To Wong Foo, With Love, Julie Newmar,* starring certifiably straight Patrick Swayze, Wesley Snipes, and John Leguizamo, and culminating in the smash hit *The Birdcage,* starring Robin Williams, Hollywood has been seeing gay characters—admittedly in their most outdated manifestation—earning respect the old fashioned way: at the box office. Gay filmmaker Jeffrey Friedman, co-director of *Celluloid Closet,* based on Vito Russo's pioneering book, noted that

> the *Birdcage* characters are direct descendants of the sissy characters from the '50s. I still don't think we're at a point of having gay characters without them being a plot point or fitting into one of these Hollywood templates. Still, the fact it's made so much money points to the fact audiences are willing to shell out money to see a movie about gay people, and that's got to have an effect. (Fleming 1996)

## REFERENCES

Enrico, Dottie. 1991. "The Media Fallout from 'Lesbian Kiss': Advertisers on LA Law Caught in the Middle." San Francisco Chronicle, March 5, p. E1.

Fleming, Michael. 1996. "Is Gay OK at Box Office?" *Variety*, April 8.

Henry, William. 1987. "That Certain Subject." *Channels*, April, pp. 43–45.

Irvine, Martha. 1996. "Hollywood Scouts Flock to Gay and Lesbian Film Festivals." *Associated Press*, July 5.

O'Connor, John. 1989. "In 'Brewster Place,' Women Lead the Way." *New York Times*, March 19.

Russo, Vito. 1987. *The Celluloid Closet: Homosexuality in the Movies*. Rev. ed. New York: Harper and Row.

Weiss, Andrea. 1992. *Vampires and Violets: Lesbians in Film*. New York: Penguin.

# | 44 |

## *Stereotyping*

### RICHARD DYER

Gay people, whether activists or not, have resented and attacked the images of homosexuality in films (and the other arts and media) for as long as we have managed to achieve any self-respect. (Before that, we simply accepted them as true and inevitable). The principle line of attack has been on stereotyping.

The target is a correct one. There is plenty of evidence to suggest that stereotypes are not just put out in books and films, but are widely agreed upon and believed to be right. Particularly damaging is the fact that many gay people believe them, leading on the one hand to the self-oppression so characteristic of gay people's lives,[1] and on the other to behaviour in conformity with the stereotypes which of course only serves to confirm their truth. Equally, there can be no doubt that most stereotypes of gays in films are demeaning and offensive. Just think of the line-up—the butch dyke and the camp queen, the lesbian vampire and the sadistic queer, the predatory schoolmistress and the neurotic faggot, and all the rest. The amount of hatred, fear, ridicule and disgust packed into those images is unmistakable.

But we cannot leave the question of stereotyping at that. Just as recent work on images of blacks and women has done, thinking about images of gayness needs to go beyond simply dismissing stereotypes as wrong and distorted. Righteous dismissal does not make the stereotypes go away, and tends to prevent us from understanding just what stereotypes are, how they function, ideologically and aesthetically, and why they are so resilient in the face of our rejection of them. In addition, there is a real problem as to just what we would put in their place. It is often assumed that the aim of character construction should be the creation of "realistic individuals," but, as I will argue, this may have as many drawbacks as its apparent oppo-

site, "unreal" stereotypes, and some form of typing may actually be preferable to it. These then are the issues that I want to look at in this article—the definition and function of stereotyping and what the alternatives to it are.

## IDEOLOGY AND TYPES

How do we come to our "understanding" of the people we encounter, in fiction as in life? We get our information about them partly from what other people tell us—although we may not necessarily trust this—and, in fiction, from narrators and from the "thoughts" of the characters, but most of our knowledge about them is based on the evidence in front of us: what they do and how they do it, what they say and how they say it, dress, mannerisms, where they live and so on. That is where the information comes from—but how do we make sense of it? Sociological theory suggests four different, though inter-related, ways of organising this information: *role, individual, type* and *member*. When we regard a person in their *role*, we are thinking of them purely in terms of the particular set of actions (which I take to include dress, speech and gesture) that they are performing at the moment we encounter them. Thus I may walk down the street and see a road-sweeper, a housewife, a child, a milkman. I know from what they are doing what their social role is, and I know, because I live in this society, that that role is defined by what sociologists call "variables" of occupation, gender, age and kinship. Although this notion of role has developed within a tradition of sociology that views social

In Richard Dyer, ed., *Gays and Film*, pp. 27–39.
Excerpt. New York: Zoetrope, 1977.

structure as neutral (not founded upon power and inequality), it is nonetheless valuable because it allows us to distinguish, theoretically at least, between what people do and what they are. However we seldom in practice stop at that, and role usually forms the basis for other inferences we make about people we encounter. We can see a person in the totality of her/his roles — their sum total, specific combination and interaction — a totality that we call an *individual*, complex, specific, unique. Or we can see a person according to a logic that assumes a certain kind-of-person performs a given role, hence is a *type*. Both individual and type relate the information that has been coded into roles to a notion of "personality" — they are psychological, or social psychological, inferences. The last inference we can make, however, is based on the realisation that roles are related not just to abstract, neutral structures but to divisions in society, to groups that are in struggle with each other, primarily along class and gender lines but also along racial and sexual lines. In this perspective, we can see the person — or character, if we're dealing with a novel or film — as a *member* of a given class or social group.

One of the implications of this break-down is that there is no way of making sense of people, or of constructing characters, that is somehow given, natural or correct. Role, individual, type and member relate to different, wider, and politically significant ways of understanding the world — the first to a reified view of social structures as things that exist independently of human praxis, the second and third to explanations of the world in terms of personal dispositions and individual psychologies, and the fourth to an understanding of history in terms of class struggle (though I extend the traditional concept of class here to include race, gender and sex caste). Since the main focus of this article is stereotyping, I shall deal first and at greatest length with the question of type, but I also want to go on to deal with the two chief alternatives to it, individuals and members.

When discussing modes of character construction, it is I think better to use the broad term type and then to make distinctions within it. A type is any simple, vivid, memorable, easily-grasped and widely recognised characterisation in which a few traits are foregrounded and change or "development" is kept to a minimum. Within this, however, we may make distinctions between social types, stereotypes and member types. (I leave out of account here typing from essentially earlier forms of fiction — *e.g.* archetypes and allegorical types — where the type is linked to metaphysical or moral principles rather than social or personal ones.) I shall deal with the first two now, and member types in the last section, since they are in important ways different from social and stereotypes.

The distinction between social type and stereotype I take from Orrin E. Klapp's book *Heroes, Villains and Fools*. The general aim of this book is to describe the social types prevalent in American society at the time at which Klapp was writing (pre-1962), that is to say, the range of kinds-of-people that, Klapp claims, Americans would expect to encounter in day-to-day life. Like much mainstream sociology Klapp's book is valuable not so much for what it asserts as for what it betrays about that which is "taken for granted" in an established intellectual discourse. Klapp's distinction between a social type and a stereotype is very revealing in its implications:

> . . . stereotypes refer to things outside one's social world, whereas social types refer to things with which one is familiar; stereotypes tend to be conceived as functionless or dysfunctional (or, if functional, serving prejudice and conflict mainly), whereas social types serve the structure of society at many points.[2]

The point is not that Klapp is wrong — on the contrary, this is a very useful distinction — but that he is so unaware of the political implications of it that he does not even try to cover himself. For we have to ask — who is the "one" referred to? and whom does the social structure itself serve? As Klapp proceeds to describe the American social types (*i.e.* those within "one's social world"), the answer becomes clear — for nearly all his social types turn out to be white, middle-class, heterosexual and male. One might expect this to be true of the heroes, but it is also largely true of the villains and fools as well. That is to say that there are accepted, even recognised, ways of being bad or ridiculous, ways that "belong" to "one's social world." And there are also ways of being bad, ridiculous and even heroic that do not "belong."

In other words, a system of social- and stereotypes refers to what is, as it were, within and beyond the pale of normalcy. Types are instances which indicate those who live by the rules of society (social types) and those whom the rules are designed to exclude (stereotypes). For this reason, stereotypes are also more rigid than social types. The latter are open-ended, more provisional, more flexible, to create the sense of freedom, choice, self-definition for those within the boundaries of normalcy. These boundaries themselves, however, must be clearly delineated, and so stereotypes, one of the mechanisms of boundary maintenance, are characteristically fixed, clear-cut, unalterable. You appear to choose your social type in some measure, whereas you are condemned to a stereotype. Moreover, the dramatic, ridiculous or horrific quality of stereotypes, as Paul Rock argues, serves to show how important it is to live by the rules:

> It is plausible that much of the expensive drama and ritual which surround the apprehension and denunciation of the deviant are directed at maintaining the daemonic and isolated character of deviancy. Without these demonstrations, typifications would be weakened and social control would suffer correspondingly.

It is not surprising then that the *genres* in which gays most often appear are horror films and comedy.

The establishment of normalcy through social- and stereotypes is one aspect of the habit of ruling groups—a habit of such enormous political consequences that we tend to think of it as far more premeditated than it actually is—to attempt to fashion the whole of society according to their own world-view, value-system, sensibility and ideology. So right is this world-view for the ruling groups, that they make it appear (as it does to them) as "natural" and "inevitable"—and for everyone—and, in so far as they succeed, they establish their hegemony. However, and this cannot be stressed too emphatically, hegemony is an *active* concept—it is something that must be ceaselessly built and rebuilt in the face of both implicit and explicit challenges to it. The subcultures of subordinated groups are implicit challenges to it, recuperable certainly but a nuisance, a thorn in the flesh; and the political struggles that are built within these sub-cultures are directly and explicitly about who shall have the power to fashion the world.

The establishment of hegemony through stereotyping has then two principle features which Roger Brown has termed ethnocentrism, which he defines as thinking "of the norms of one's group as right for men [*sic*] everywhere," and the assumption that given social groups "have inborn and unalterable psychological characteristics."[3] Although Brown is writing in the context of cross-cultural and inter-racial stereotyping, what he says seems to me eminently transferable to the stereotyping of gays. Let me illustrate this from *The Killing of Sister George*.

By ethnocentrism, Brown means the application of the norms appropriate to one's own culture to that of others. Recasting this politically (within a culture rather than between cultures), we can say that in stereotyping the dominant groups apply their norms to subordinated groups, find the latter wanting, hence inadequate, inferior, sick or grotesque and hence reinforcing the dominant groups' own sense of the legitimacy of their domination. One of the modes of doing this for gays is casting gay relationships and characters in terms of heterosexual sex roles. Thus in *The Killing of Sister George*, George and Childie are very much presented as the man and woman respectively of the relationship, with George's masculinity expressed in her name, gruff voice, male clothes and by association with such icons of virility as horse brasses, pipes, beer and tweeds. However, George is not a man, and is "therefore" inadequate to the role. Her "masculinity" has to be asserted in set pieces of domination (shot to full dramatic hilt, with low angles, chiaroscuro lighting and menacing music), and her straining after male postures is a source of humour. *Sister George* emphasises the absence of men in the lesbian milieu, by structuring Childie and George's quarrels around the latter's fears of any man with whom Childie has dealings and by the imagery of dolls as surrogate children which are used in a cumulatively horrific way to suggest the grotesque sterility of a woman loving another woman (and so denying herself the chance of truly being a woman, *i.e.* a heterosexual mother).

The idea that this image of lesbianism indicates an inborn trait (hence reinforcing the idea that the way the dominant culture defines gays is the way we must always be) is enforced in *Sister George* partly through dialogue to that effect and partly through a chain of imagery linking lesbianism with the natural, bestial or low.

The link between lesbians and animals is a strong feature of the iconography of gay women in films—they often wear furs, suede or leather, are interested in horses or dogs, or are connected, through composition, montage or allusion, with animals.

What is wrong with these stereotypes is not that they are inaccurate. The implications of attacking them on that ground (one of the most common forms of attack) raise enormous problems for gay politics—first of all, it flies in the face of the actual efficacy of the hegemonic definitions enshrined in stereotypes, that is to say, gay people often believe (I did) that the stereotypes are accurate and act accordingly in line with them; and second, one of the things the stereotypes are onto is the fact that gay people do cross the gender barriers, so that many gay women do refuse to be typically "feminine" just as many gay men refuse to be typically "masculine" and we must beware of getting ourselves into a situation where we cannot defend, still less applaud, such sex-caste transgressions. What we should be attacking in stereotypes is the attempt of heterosexual society to define us for ourselves, in terms that inevitably fall short of the "ideal" of heterosexuality (that is, taken to be the norm of being human), and to pass this definition off as necessary and natural. Both these simply bolster heterosexual hegemony, and the task is to develop our own alternative and challenging definitions of ourselves.

## STEREOTYPING THROUGH ICONOGRAPHY

In a film, one of the methods of stereotyping is through iconography. That is, films use a certain set of visual and aural signs which immediately bespeak homosexuality and connote the qualities associated, stereotypically, with it.

The opening of *The Boys in the Band* shows this very clearly. In a series of brief shots or scenelets, each of the major characters in the subsequent film is introduced and their gay identity established. This can be quite subtle. For instance, while there is the "obvious" imagery of Emory—mincing walk, accompanied by a poodle, shutting up an over-chic, over-gilded furniture store—there is also, cross cut with it, and with shots of the other "boys," Michael going shopping. He wears a blue blazer and slacks, we do not see what he buys. It is a plain image. Except that the blazer, a sports garment, is too smart, the slacks too well pressed—the casualness of the garment type is belied by the fastidiousness of the grooming style. When he signs a cheque, at chic store Gucci's, we get a close-up of his hand, with a large, elaborate ring on it. Thus the same

stereotypical connotations are present, whether obviously or mutedly, in the iconography of both Emory and Michael—over-concern with appearance, association with a "good taste" that is just shading into decadence. The other "boys" are similarly signalled, and although there is a range of stereotypes, nearly all of them carry this connotation of fastidiousness and concern with appearance. This observation can be extended to most gay male iconography—whether it be the emphasis on the grotesque artifices of make-up and obvious wigs, body-building or sickliness of features, connoting not only depravity and mental illness but also the primped, unexposed face of the indoors (non-active, non-sporting) man.

Iconography is a kind of short-hand—it places a character quickly and economically. This is particularly useful for gay characters, for, short of showing physical gayness or having elaborate dialogue to establish it in the first few minutes, some means of communicating immediately that a character is gay has to be used. This of course is not a problem facing other stereotyped groups such as women or blacks (but it may include the working class), since the basis of their difference (gender, colour) shows whereas ours does not. However, while this is true, and, as I want to argue later, some kind of typing has positive value, it does seem that there may be a further ideological function to the gay iconography. Why, after all, is it felt so necessary to establish from the word go that a character is gay? The answer lies in one of the prime mechanisms of gay stereotyping, synechdoche—that is, taking the part for the whole. It is felt necessary to establish the character's gayness, because that one aspect of her or his personality is held to give you, and explain, the rest of the personality. By signalling gayness from the character's first appearance, all the character's subsequent actions and words can be understood, explained, and explained away, as those of a gay person. Moreover, it seems probable that gayness is, as a material category, far more fluid than class, gender or race—that is, most people are not either gay or non-gay, but have, to varying degrees, the capacity for both. However, this fluidity is unsettling both to the rigidity of social categorisation and to the maintenance of heterosexual hegemony. What's more, the invisibility of gayness may come creeping up on heterosexuality unawares and, fluid-like, seep into the citadel. It is therefore reassuring to have gayness firmly categorised and kept separate from the start through a widely known iconography.

## NOTES

1. The concept of self-oppression is crucial to an understanding of the politics of homosexuality. It is excellently examined in Andrew Hodges and David Hutter, *With Downcast Gays*, Pomegranate Press, London, 1974.

2. Orrin E. Klapp, *Heroes, Villains and Fools*, Prentice-Hall, Englewood Cliffs, 1962, p. 16.

3. Roger Brown, *Social Psychology*. Macmillan. New York and London, 1965, p. 183.

# | 45 |

# *Lesbians and Film: Some Thoughts*

## CAROLINE SHELDON

The average gay woman goes to the cinema as much as everyone else, and like the bulk of the cinema public is hardly catered for in terms of her own reality. Films in general distribution tend to emphasise either middle-class life styles (lesbians are not necessarily middle-class) or escapist male heroics of a kind unavailable to the public. Unfortunately when lesbians do appear the effect is far more negative than their simple absence. Lesbianism is usually shown as an aberration, an individual psycho-social problem, which may not be the condition of every lesbian in the audience but may help to precipitate a few into believing that it is. This analysis in itself could become a psycho-social one—which could be useful for those still doubting that dominant ideologies have any effect in the make-up of a particular class, caste or group's expectations.

As commodities (determined by the profit motive in production and distribution) and as ideological products (determined by a multitude of historical, social and cultural factors), films are often tools to maintain depoliticisation. At the same time, they may give clues as to the mode of operation of capitalist/patriarchal power. Given the political perspective of lesbianfeminism, a term which I shall clarify, I shall be discussing quite a large number of films, made by men and women, which reflect on the position of lesbians in society. Out of this political stance, a number of distinct areas appear as needing analysis and I shall be indicating some possibilities of approach to a) pornographic and *avant-garde* cinema and

homosexuality; b) stereotyping of lesbians in contemporary film; c) films of interest to lesbians; d) women's films and lesbians' films.

▼ ▼ ▼

## STEREOTYPES AND MYTHS: MEN'S FILMS ABOUT LESBIANS

The myths on which the cinema is based relate to the complex and often contradictory mythology of women, which operates in society as a whole.
—CLAIRE JOHNSTON,
*NOTES ON WOMEN'S CINEMA*

The struggle to change the social and economic conditions of women has all along the line been a struggle with women's own consciousness of their condition, basic to which is a constantly reconditioned sense of powerlessness (either as an individual or collectively). Studies have been made on a wide variety of topics: literature, fashion, psychology, job-conditions, advertising, language, history, etc. that repeatedly show how sexism operates to keep women oppressed. The cinema is included in this brief as it has reflected, and continues to reflect, the expectations and role models available to women.[1]

In Richard Dyer, ed., *Gays and Film*, pp. 5–26. Excerpt. New York: Zoetrope, 1977.

The contradictory stereotypes that women are expected to fulfil (little girl, sex object, mother, career-girl, goddess, etc. *ad nauseam*) are probably at the root of the possibility for a new women's consciousness: the tensions between these expectations can no longer be glossed over in a rapidly changing society, in which class or social status varies from one generation to the next.[2] None of these options describes a whole person, and the fulfilment of any one of these by one woman has been a task demanding considerable strength and resourcefulness, not to mention a great deal of self-mutilation.

Like other women, lesbians are victims to the twin processes of stereotyping and mythologising. Myths, such as those exploited and perpetrated by porn films ("Lesbians are fantastic in bed" and "all a lesbian needs is a good screw") although quite contradictory (why should a woman need a screw if her sex life is that good independent of men?) can either be subscribed to independently of each other . . . or they can be found together without obvious disjunction *because of their mythical status.* Myths about lesbians have the added value of reflecting on other women: the first of these myths finds straight (heterosexual) women wanting, the second puts all women, gay or straight, onto the same level as sex-objects for men.

The other side of the coin of men's fantasies about lesbians (and women) is quite a deep fund of fear, which finds its expression in representing lesbians as castrating bitches or sadists. These fears serve to maintain divisions between women on the basis of sexual orientation. Looking at the media not one but three lesbian stereotypes emerge:

the butch/mannish lesbian (bar dyke/foot-stomper, often working-class and dominant in her relationships with other women)

the sophisticated lesbian (often an older woman, who is rich and successful in a man's world)

the neurotic lesbian (often *femme* or closet)

Often these stereotypes and fears are combined to form one lesbian character. In *Rome, Open City* the lesbian is at the same time a sophisticated older woman, who is mannish in appearance, and a sadistic castrating bitch (literally, in the scene where the priest is tortured). Like Rosa Klebb, the sadistic dyke in *From Russia with Love* (whose castrating behaviour takes the form of aiming her knife-pointed shoe at Bond's crotch at the end of the film!), the character is at the service of an ideological statement, with the rejection of "normal" sexuality allied with unacceptable political doctrine: in *Rome, Open City* the lesbian is a Nazi; in *From Russia with Love* she is a Communist.

*The Killing of Sister George* (as a stage-play written by a man, and as a film directed by a man—as are all of the films in this section) is one of the best-known and apparently respected films about lesbians in England. The reason is not simply the apparent social realism of its approach: the film displays all three of the major stereotypes of lesbians as separate characters, the better to show the repulsiveness of each. Sister George (Beryl Reid) is the essence of revolting butch in her outrageous (often sadistic) dominating behaviour (paralleled by the cloying sentimentality of her television role as a district nurse), while Childie (Susanna York) is the ultimate of the neurotic (regressed) lesbian with her dolls and shyness. In fact both women display psychological imbalance, since George is also a heavy drinker, and is equally capable of childlike behaviour. . . . Coral Brown's role, as Mrs. Mercy Croft, is that of the successful and sophisticated career woman, who will take Childie away. Her behaviour also shows her to be the castrating bitch of the film. This trait is particularly apparent in her destruction of George, despite the fact that she is another woman—or is this a contradiction based on George's ambiguous sex role?

There is certainly little or no solidarity between any of the women, consistent with male assumptions about women not getting on together (rooted in their fears about women allying). Lesbianism here is not woman-identification in any way. The voyeuristically necessary seduction scene is as nasty as the women: though it is hard to work out what is happening, the dark setting and strange musical score indicate that it is certainly perverted. The events and the portraits of the three women, drawn as quite emotionally repellent, make no attraction to the idea of lesbianism possible. Little threat is implicit in these women's presence in the world since they are destructive of themselves and each other. This is true even of Mrs. Croft, despite her real power in her job and her ability to pass as a straight (heterosexual) woman, since there is an implication in the final dialogue, that she too will be destroyed by her lesbianism in relating to Childie, even if she discards her newly acquired lover rapidly. . . .

*Les Bitches* picks up where *Sister George* leaves off with the rich sophisticated predatory older woman picking up an innocent young girl from the streets; the theme is stereotypically overdetermined from the start. With superb film artistry the director shows the playing out of the destruction of innocence, pulling heavily both on voyeuristic interest in lesbian love-making, and the myth that "all a lesbian needs is a good screw." Ultimately Frédérique abandons Why for a young man, and Why, maddened by her rejection by both lovers (Paul was originally interested in her) knifes (note the Freudian overtones) her "protector" and assumes the woman's identity. . . .

Apparently more sympathetic views of lesbians in the cinema are present in the works of three other male film makers: *The Conformist*, and *Thérèse and Isabelle*. The lesbians in *The Children's Hour* and *The Conformist* are both portrayed with a certain stereotyping: Shirley MacLaine's character, Martha, is a neurotic (closet) lesbian; Dominique Sanda as Anna Quadri is sophisticated and bourgeois. Thérèse and Isabelle are both safely unstereotyped, being schoolgirls.

Despite her stereotyping, Martha in *The Children's Hour* is portrayed because the concept that she is dangerous and predatory (a child molester) is attacked by the film's exposure of society's paranoia. The film is important in that there is solidarity between the two woman, and a certain ambivalence is found in Karen's behaviour since she is not anxious to leave her life with Martha in order to get married—she even brings her along on dates with her fiancé. (In the end she decides not to marry him, so the film does not use lesbianism to service heterosexuality.) It is the self-disgust of the realisation that she really is a lesbian that causes Martha to commit suicide. In doing this she remains a victim of her society to the end, having internalised its rejection of homosexuality. It is useful to note that this film is based on a play by a woman, Lillian Hellman, which goes a long way in explaining its positive aspects. As a film, however, it was made just after the McCarthy era and one feels it is as much a statement against the regime of false rumour spreading and intolerance of deviance as it is about lesbianism, which never appears as a valid option.

The interests of *The Conformist* are definitely elsewhere: in the psychological and social pressures that make Marcello Clerici a fascist capable of being responsible for the deaths of people he admires and loves. Anna Quadri's sympathetic portrayal is in part due to her attractiveness, and in part due to the fact that she is anti-fascist and victim. However, her initial overstated "butchness" and her predatory behaviour towards the stereotypically silly Giulia (who plays the feminine role to the hilt) show her in a less positive light: as a bored bourgeoise, she is a long way from the street vendor who sings the Internationale or the ordinary working people at the dance. The key to the film is in Bertolucci's attitude to the bourgeoisie and its impotence. There is even a certain ambiguity in Anna's relationship with Clerici, which seems made up of a stated revulsion and an unstated fascination (the myth that "every woman loves a facist" covering "all a lesbian needs . . . "?) The film is better at shedding light on the male characters than on the female ones, and their attitude to Anna's lesbianism is instructive: Professor Quadri's attitude is purely voyeuristic ("They are so beautiful"); Clerici's is the desire to conquer, wishing to see Anna as a sex-object, like his wife, and her role in the film is partly to emphasise his repressed homosexuality, already hinted at in his guilt about the childhood incident with the chauffeur. Her final shooting indicates the sorry end to which decadent bourgeois lesbians must come.

*Thérèse and Isabelle* is quite a different kettle of fish, apparently, being based on Violet Leduc's autobiographical novel of the same name, and is exclusively about the relationship between two girls at boarding school (those notorious hotbeds of adolescent lesbianism!!), a relationship where no patterns of dominance emerge, and where both emotions and sexuality are on a give-and-take basis. Unfortunately three factors betray the film as unliberated in its attitude to the girls: the fact that they are played by two actresses clearly out of their teens; the graphic and beautiful portrayal of their sexual encounters (which clearly puts the film in the soft porn *genre*); and the fact that the events are in the memory of one of the women about to marry and settle into her correct role in life. It was "just a phase they were going through" like Emmanuelle, March, and countless others in hard porn flicks.

In general it appears that despite the emergence of a new consciousness about gayness and womanity, the cinema is entrenched in viewing both as negative and potentially destructive (either of self or others) unless a safe domesticity prevails in marriage to a 'strong' man.

## LESBIANS AT THE MOVIES

> I myself never go to the cinema or
> hardly ever practically and the cin-
> ema has never read my work or
> hardly ever.
>
> GERTRUDE STEIN

As an ever greater number of lesbians come out
(live out their gayness openly), film makers are
cashing in on this market as well by producing
explicitly lesbian films for mass audiences. But
how do we lesbians respond, react, feel and think
about these films and others?

I remember being depressed for days after seeing *Sister George*, feeling: "Sure, such a relationship may exist, but what a miserable one, and what's
it doing on film to pervert young minds about lesbians? . . . " I talked with a friend, who said she
thought it was a good film, well acted and all, but
she was furious at the stereotyping. Others enjoyed
some of George's outrageous anti-establishment
behavior (particularly the incident with the nuns)
and others yet spoke of the character played by
Coral Brown as a turn-on (the myth of the sophisticated older woman rules OK apparently); but the
general impression was a certain unease, despite
the desire to have a film that was lesbian.

The only other widely seen film of this group
(apart from *The Fox*, which in no way is claimed
as a lesbian film), *Emmanuelle*, seems to have
had a similar response. Despite the pleasure felt
at the ease of the relationship between
Emmanuelle and Bee and the rarity of seeing lesbian sex so positively depicted, there is a general
feeling that the film is a rip-off, basically geared to
a straight audience both in its *Vogue* glossy sophisticated innocence and its "moral" ending. This
becomes particularly apparent in trying to explain
the way in which Bee leaves Emmanuelle to her
fate with little or no concern over her future. This
heterosexual model of playboy behaviour ("The
adventure is over, bye-bye.") simply does not ring
true in women's relationships to each other; the
small details that we are given to characterise Bee
(a sensitive woman, who has achieved a certain
independence of men in her work) are not consistent with such a lack of concern. One simply
feels the need of the director to wind up the affair
in order to get back to the nitty-gritty.

On the whole, lesbians' interest in the cinema
seems to be oriented towards those exceptional
films made in Hollywood during the late 1930s
and 40s, when the needs of the patriarchy/capi-
talism to make war and money demanded that
women be oriented away from home-making and
into industry to replace men sent away as cannon-
fodder. These films often had as central characters strong and resilient women, played by such
actresses as Lauren Bacall, Joan Crawford, Bette
Davis, Marlene Dietrich, Greta Garbo,
Katharine Hepburn and Barbara Stanwyck. More
recently, the cowgirl films (*Annie Get Your Gun*
[1950], *Calamity Jane* [1953], etc.) and films with
Jeanne Moreau and Glenda Jackson enjoy some
such popularity.

The popularity of these films is consistent with
my having defined lesbianism primarily as
woman-identification. There is a real need for lesbians to see and know about women who define
themselves in their own terms. In the strength of
actresses often playing parts in which they are
comparatively independent of domestic expectations and of men is found a far greater affirmation
than in the kind of "lesbian films" that have been
produced. Most lesbians have been through a
heterosexual phase, so the plot demand that the
heroine be attracted to a man is not particularly
disturbing (irritating maybe), and the explanation
for the plot development could lie in the fact that
there is no woman around of equal strength to
attract the heroine. . . .

In the few Hollywood films of the 1930s and
40s where any kind of overt lesbianism is apparent
it is treated in an episodic, almost irrelevant fashion (except that it has the function of making the
heroine even more attractive to the men in the
film, giving rise to both repressed homosexuality
and the conqueror instinct discussed previously).
Marlene Dietrich is famous for her appearance in
drag in her film-stage numbers, but significantly
less remembered for her flirtations with the
women in her audiences in *Blonde Venus* (1932)
and *Morocco* (1930). Both Katharine Hepburn
and Garbo have also appeared on film in men's
clothing. In *Sylvia Scarlett* (1935) Katharine
Hepburn, dressed as a boy, is approached by a
young woman who playfully draws a moustache
on Sylvia's lip and kisses her; Sylvia jumps up and
runs away. In *Queen Christina* (1933), a rewrite of
the life of the famous Swedish lesbian queen who
gave up her throne rather than marry, Garbo is
initially involved in an affair with her chamber-
maid and the two even kiss quite passionately on
the screen, the lovers argue and separate, leaving
the bulk of the film to be taken up with a heterosexual affair (but how lesbians cheer when Garbo
says "I want to be alone"!).

Janet Meyers, discussing this phenomenon, says of these three stars:

> Most lesbians I know feel a strong response to these women on screen. The qualities they projected, of being inscrutable to the men in the films and aloof, passionate, direct, could not be missed. They are all strong, tough and yet genuinely tender. In short, though rarely permitted to hint it, they are lesbians. Because of the old star system in the Hollywood studios, where movie projects were "created" to suit particular stars, that lesbian reality surfaced in memorable ways.[4]

Positive and self-reliant women in modern Hollywood cinema are more rare—and, as pointed out earlier, usually punished for unsocial behaviour. . . .

## CONCLUDING NOTES

In describing lesbianism as woman-identification, I have given myself a wider brief in my discussion than simply to analyse films from the point of view of women sexually orientated towards women. The power structure that restricts all women's roles in the cinema is one that delimits the roles of lesbians, making it hard to see lesbianism in any other terms than sexual. Conversely, because of the political nature of an anti-social choice of sexuality by women, the way films do represent lesbians is highly relevant to all women: the kinds of myths, stereotypes and plots of "lesbian films" reflect the need of patriarchal capitalist society to divide in order to rule. A way to do this is to make both hetero-sexism (in the representation of homosexuality) and sexism (in the representation of women) appear natural. Film is an excellent vehicle for this strategy in its pretension to reality, dependent on our conditioned acceptance of the meaning of film language, hiding behind the notion of simple entertainment. "Lesbian films" are clearly made for the general public and serve to reinforce negative images of lesbianism—as such, few lesbians find anything to identify with in these films, whose purpose is to continue to support the *status quo*. These films fulfil voyeuristic desires whilst warning women to stay in safe heterosexual domesticity, despite the implied inadequacy of their own sexual competence.

As I have pointed out, on the whole, lesbians (and indeed feminists) are attracted by films containing independent and sensitive strong women, but a frustration for lesbians in watching such films is the potential lesbianism of the heroine(s) which never surfaces. It would be pleasant to see a film in general distribution using a traditional Hollywood plot of the type in which a self-sufficient heroine *does something* (saves the firm from bankruptcy, organises a successful strike, or whatever) with a male peer who, come the inevitable romantic ending, suggests they "get hitched"; she replies, "Sorry, I'm not interested. I have no intention of involving myself in such oppressive relationships. I'm a lesbian," and walks off into the sunset either alone or with another woman! This little fantasy on a well-worn plot (variations are endless, as Hollywood discovered) serves to emphasise a point made by Joan Mellen that lesbians are rarely represented in films as having anything more important to do than deal with their relationships—their work, when they have any (such as Mrs. Croft's job in television administration), is of minimal interest except inasmuch as it highlights their perversity (*e.g.* George's sugary television role). Indeed, unless a woman's lesbianism is a closely-guarded secret it becomes a major known fact about her life: Vita Sackville-West is better known nowadays as a lesbian than as either a gardener or a novelist. The taboo nature of homosexuality made it for a long time an unknown fact (how many people realised that Gertrude Stein was a lesbian?), but now there is scurrilous interest (was Virginia Woolfe really a lesbian?), although this is perhaps an improvement on invisibility it remains negative and is paralleled by the type of greater visibility of lesbians in modern cinema.

▼ ▼ ▼

However, as Claire Johnston so correctly points out, the work of feminist film makers should not limit itself to replacing heroes of the patriarchy with feminist heroines, although this is an important and necessary part of a feminist film struggle. If we are concerned about the way that film promotes its illusions, then there is a need to reflect in our film making practice on these devices and strategies (as Jan Oxenberg has begun to do in *Home Movie* and, with the help of the lesbian community, in *Comedy in Six Unnatural Acts*). This work of analysis and negation of the way patriarchal culture operates in film to buttress the unthinkingness of male fears and fantasies (in women as well as men) is a first step in developing and affirming a new consciousness which may eventually produce a radically different women's film language. Inasmuch as women are beginning to establish the ways in which the language is male in its assumptions they are also discovering that this is true of film language. This essay has been an early discussion of a certain filmic vocabulary related to lesbianism. The search for a woman's language in all domains (science, poetry etc.) is one that is also taking place in film. It is one that will only take place in the public eye if a wider variety of films are in general distribution and the techniques of film criticism and film making are in the hands of that very public.

## NOTES

1. E.g., the journal *Women and Film* (Berkeley, California, 4 issues, 1973–75, no longer in publication); Claire Johnston (ed.), *Notes on Women's Cinema*, SEFT; Molly Haskell, *From Reverence to Rape*, Penguin, 1974; Joan Mellen, *Women and their Sex-*

*uality in the New Film*, Horizon Press, New York, 1973; Marjorie Rosen, *Popcorn Venus*, Avon Books, New York, 1974; Musidora, *Paroles . . . elles tournent*, Librairie des Femmes, Paris, 1976; as well as a number of articles in feminist journals all over the world, including *Spare Rib* (London).

2. "Wherever there is a general attempt on the part of the women of a society to readjust their position in it, a close analysis will always show the changed or changing conditions of the society have made women's acquiescence no longer necessary or desirable," quoted from Olive Scheiner, Introduction to *Women and Labour*, 1911, in *Dyke*, Spring 1976 (New York).

3. Recently two very interesting feminist films were made by California film makers, Roberta Friedman and Graham Wembren of the Oasis group: *The Making Of Americans*, based on a section of the book of the same name by Gertrude Stein, and *Bertha's Children*.

4. Janet Meyers, "Dyke Goes to the Movies," *Dyke* (New York), Spring 1976, p. 38.

# | 46 |

# *Where Is the Life That Late He Led?*
# *Hollywood's Construction of Sexuality in the Life of Cole Porter*

## GEORGE F. CUSTEN

Cole Porter, the American composer and lyricist, valorized the bright, brittle world of sophisticated heterosexual romantic entanglements. In songs like "Night and Day" and "Every Time We Say Goodbye" Porter created a world of romantic desire that addressed the emotions of yearning and sexual passion more directly than the work of his contemporaries Irving Berlin, Rogers and Hart, Jerome Kern (with his various lyricists), or the brothers Gershwin. In his own life this balladeer of male/female passion worked assiduously to maintain the public image of a sophisticated,

happily married cosmopolite. Yet the truth of Porter's life was far different from the public facade; he was, in fact, a homosexual (married to a lesbian). According to every available biographical source, Porter's sexual life was limited to a series of brief, often paid, male encounters (see Schwartz 1977, Bergreen 1990). Bergreen, despite overwhelming data available in many popular sources confirming that Porter was exclu-

Original manuscript, 1994.

sively gay, states the case for Porter's sexuality like this: "He was married to a woman of means, who was older than he, and who *probably* excused him from conjugal relations. She tolerated his homosexual affairs as he tolerated her lesbian encounters" (417).

In the life of Cole Porter, and in its celluloid fabrication *Night and Day*, we have the case of a celebrity who created a facade of heterosexuality in an age when to openly proclaim one's homosexuality was to trade celebrity for notoriety. Allied with the Hollywood film, other popular media all constructed fame and success as the province of heterosexuals. These diverse sources of information—popular biographical sketches in mass circulation magazines, advertisements for films, celebrity endorsements, and the myriad publicity discourses spun out by the Hollywood studios—erected about the lives of those nominated for public veneration a wall that limited the taxonomy of greatness and banished homosexuality from the territories of movies and life. The Porter biopic *Night and Day*, slyly dubbed by writer Ethan Mordden "one of the outstanding science-fiction films of the age," is thus connected to other fields of popular culture in its suppression of the homosexual's story and his connection to fame. All of these texts denied that homosexuality and greatness could ever share the same sentence, let alone the same movie marquee (Mordden 1991). Film was supported by other forums of culture in ignoring this aspect of a life. As late as 1991, when I called the Yale library, where some of the Porter papers repose, the librarian scoffed at the idea that Porter was gay, defying me to produce a single letter or document that could prove this.

Here I will examine how one genre of a mass medium, the film biopic, created specific strategies to deal with problematic categories like homosexuality. Through an analysis of the production practices that shaped *Night and Day*, we can see how Hollywood's treatment of sexuality and sexual relations came to form part of a larger agenda, the production and reproduction of conventional wisdom about famous, accomplished, and noteworthy lives. Hollywood, ever mindful of its role as the keeper of the flame of public history, sought to control elements of life it deemed problematic. It did so by maintaining strict control over the content of any film released during the studio era, and no subject was more fraught with peril than the depiction of sexuality, sexual preference, and sexual difference.

## MASS MEDIATED FAME

In the films overseen by the censorship arm of the industry, the Motion Picture Producers and Distributors of America (MPPDA), and its office of enforcement, the Production Code Administration (PCA), Hollywood associated itself with a notion of accomplishment acceptable for the American family.[1] Nowhere is this process seen more clearly than in the biographical films produced during the studio era. In the studio era, as today, Hollywood went to great lengths to suggest to the public that these films *were* true versions of a life. A Warner Brothers publicity brochure circulated for *Night and Day* told the reader that "*Night and Day* posed many technical and artistic problems. The time covered, from 1914 to the present, demanded great stress on authenticity of costumes, scenes, backgrounds and manners. . . . Cole Porter's personal scrap books also proved valuable in the research that proceeded the shooting of *Night and Day*." In addition to publicity materials sent to film exhibitors, commodity tie-ins, like the educational magazine *Photoplay Studies*, were sent to educational associations and schools nationwide, and the circulation of these materials, often with the approval of educational organizations like the powerful National Council of Teachers of English, made certain that literature and history were rendered understandable courtesy of MGM, Fox, and the other film corporations (Maltby 1993:60). Such tie-ins also validate moviegoing as an educational, uplifting enterprise, so that its texts came to be perceived, suggests Vivian Sobchack (1990), as "constructions of general historical eventfulness," that is, as factual history.

In addition to studio publicity materials, the texts of the films themselves were framed as accurate, valuable historical narratives. Ninety percent of the film biographies produced during the studio era opened with a written or spoken assertion of the veracity of the film that would follow.

Films such as *Night and Day*, rather than merely altering some Emersonian essentialist concept of "the great life," were patterned ideological constructions that, while framed as true and natural, made sure that unique greatness conformed to limited and constricting narrative templates. Any viewer of 1946 who responded to *Night and Day*'s peculiar ideas about the kind of person Cole Porter was also responded to previous film biographies, movie musicals, magazine articles, and radio programs in which Porter, biography, and popular music might figure. As Lawrence Grossberg notes, "Culture 'communicates' only in particular contexts in which a range of texts, practices and languages are brought together." In a pre-TV world film biography was the most popular source of relaying the possibilities of the great life to the American public, but it interacted with other symbolic forms to perform this task (Grossberg 1992).

## SEXUALITY AND GREATNESS

The issue of how accurate a life on film is—whether it presents key incidents in the life of the figure, whether its psychological portrayal is recognizable to those who knew the historical personage—dodges the more interesting question of how popular representation of history are constructed in film, and how they helped shape a sense of history and a sense of the self. Because the representation of sexuality as it impinges upon social relations is such a jealously guarded trope, filmic representation in these areas has always come under close scrutiny, and particular control has adhered to public sexual representations. Gay men and lesbians, because of our official invisibility during the studio era, were particularly vulnerable to mass media power simply because of our elimination from the scripts of history. Our inability to speak for ourselves within the discursive spaces of official popular culture rendered us a social group defined by the very people to whom gays find ourselves in opposition. Homosexuality was one of the most censored bits of behavior in the public narratives of the biopic.

In the studio era—roughly 1927–1960—outing was virtually impossible, a nonoption in journalistic or historical discourses. As a result, Hollywood filled the vacuum of lesbianism and homosexuality with what Freud might have called "family romances," idealized versions of life in which homosexuality was marginalized by extinction and the dominant sexual ideology was produced and reproduced through narratives that limited options and rewrote the scripts of history. The biopic created a highly codified sense of public history that limited cinematic fame as the province of happily married heterosexuals. Under the Hollywood studio system it was impossible to produce a clearly articulated biography of a gay person. This obvious lacuna is but one fold of a conscious operation that, for lack of a better word, heterosexualized well-known gay and lesbian figures. The absence of sexual minorities, and our subsequent reconstruction as heterosexual, is significant for what it suggests about public history made in Hollywood. Rather than being the disinterested chronicle of a set of "naturally" selected heroes and heroines, public history cum biography is instead always written (or filmed) with a particular set of priorities and values in mind. The elimination of a gay and lesbian history from these scripts presumes heterosexuality as the precondition for—and eventually a confirmation of—accomplishment and renown. Poignantly, this false front of heterosexuality was abetted by some of the subjects themselves, who used the media to construct a public fiction out of the facts of their lives. By buying into the front of heterosexuality, men like Cole Porter protected their career image ("happily married sophisticate Cole Porter") at the expense of their actual self.

In a sense, the "whitewashed" version of history created by Hollywood may have been a way of voiding criticism of the movies (and movie people) as a source of influence for viewers, valorizing the world of entertainment itself as pure, worthy, and admirable. Seen in this light, it is no coincidence that the largest proportion of film biographies made by Hollywood were about performing artists (36 percent), subtly legitimizing the movies' own system of representation and buttressing the superstructure of popular entertainment that may have been threatened by revelations in other noncinematic sources. It is almost as if certain media in the studio era—fan and gossip magazines, tabloid journals—were allocated a culture's fair share of criticism, so that the popular tales of society came to be narrated on the screen only as stories of veneration (cf. Custen 1992).

Like all films, the Porter biopic was shaped by at least six factors: the Motion Picture Producers and Distributors of America (MPPDA) with its formal system of censorship overseen by the Production Code Administration (PCA), the legal difficulties one engaged when picturing the life of a living (or even a deceased) figure, the image of the star persona impersonating the famous figure, and the intertextual influence of other biographical discourses upon the movies make up four elements; interacting with all these factors was the figure of the producer. The producer's own ideas on how one pictured a life, formed by cultural notions of sexuality and its representation, were perhaps the most powerful determinants of what figures would have their histories recorded and what a famous life should contain. Last, as Thomas Schatz (1989) has noted, Hollywood relied on star/genre formulations as a device to stabilize the variability of the many kinds of narratives and stars present in the world of film and film biography. *Night and Day*, and the narrative it constructed, was affected by the evolving demands of the musical film, Hollywood's sense of self-interest when narrating a film about its own community, the interests of the living Cole Porter, the star image of Cary Grant, the interstudio conventions, and Warner's own internal understanding of how the great life should be told, in this case complete with song, dance, and romance.[2]

*Night and Day* is fairly representative of the Hollywood biopic. To Hollywood the famous person was likely to be that all too common figure: the straight, white American male whose doings were situated somewhere after his twentieth year. Given this already limited taxonomy of fame, it is no surprise that the Hollywood producer and the workers at the MPPDA would cooperate in constructing a congruent ideology of fame that eliminated nonmainstream areas of behavior from these tales of valorization. Specifically, section 2, subsection 4 of the Production Code constructed sex in unambiguous, missionary terms. "The sanctity of the institution of marriage and the home shall be upheld. Pictures shall not infer that low forms of sex relationship are the accepted or common thing." The code specifically precluded the picturing of "sex perversion or any inference" thereof without labeling what these horrible practices might entail. The love that dared not speak its name was, in fact, not named. Homosexuality was thus relegated to a linguistic netherworld Foucault refers to as a "silence," albeit an absence with a plurality of forms.

Despite the absence of a specific prohibition against homosexuality, the specter of nonmainstream behavior had to be controlled, and there appeared frequent and highly coded discursive utterances about these unnamable practices that were mutually understood by film personnel and strictly enforced within the industry. This prohibition, which precluded gay or lesbian narratives from being part of the biographical text, did not preclude the use of gay characters for ridicule in fiction films. Readers at the PCA warned Hal Wallis, Warner production head during the making of *Night and Day*, to eliminate dangerous "pansy action" from a minor gay character (a

choreographer), but gay characters were allowed as background in many fictive films, most often as the butt of jokes establishing the dominance and superiority of heterosexuality. Rather than being the obvious subjects of a film, gay characters and gay sexuality were pervasively present in forms of negation, "textually submerged, but ubiquitous," to use Ella Shohat's apt term for the representation of minorities in film. Although they never had starring roles, Grady Sutton, Franklin Pangborn, and Richard Hayden played countless victims of heterosexual humor. In biopics, however, films with the patina of history behind them, it was particularly important to eliminate references to homosexuality, even negative ones. Time and again censorship memoranda from the readers at the MPPDA warned producers to eliminate "pansy action," MPPDA and studioese code for effeminate male behavior.

So anxious was Hollywood to banish gays and lesbians from their scripts of history that even figures known as heterosexual had their lives recast to eliminate the producer's anxieties concerning even the possibility of misconstruction. One of the more distasteful examples of Hollywood homophobia surfaced in the production of a film about a heterosexual who was well-known, Alexander Graham Bell. *The Story of Alexander Graham Bell*, produced by Twentieth Century-Fox (nominally under the guidance of Kenneth MacGowan, but, as ever, under the watchful eyes of Darryl Zanuck) contained, in one version of the screenplay, the accurate depiction of the famed inventor as an elocution instructor. This seemingly harmless bow to historical accuracy elicited from Zanuck the fearful injunction that anything less than a "normal" version of the life of a great person was a betrayal of the public trust the studios saw themselves as upholding in these historical outings. Fearing the impact this "unmasculine" profession might have on the star image of the (then) proposed impersonator of Bell, Tyrone Power (the part eventually went to Don Ameche), Zanuck forbade the accurate picturing of the life. "Despite the fact that elocution was the rage at the time," Zanuck wrote to one screenwriter, "casting a leading man of today as an out-and-out elocution enthusiast is like asking Tyrone Power to wear lace on his under-drawers."[3] If a profession construed as nontraditional for males could earn such stigma, the possibility of depicting a homosexual character (Cole Porter) or a well-known lesbian (Queen Christina) with any accuracy was never a remote possibility under the studio system, particularly since neither figure was "out" in their respective era.

In nonhistorical films the avoidance of homosexuality was, if possible, greater, so that even in films whose original sources were *about* homosexuality Hollywood strove to eliminate this subject. *Tea and Sympathy* was a controversial hit play of 1953–1954 in which a young boy is cured of his homosexuality by a sympathetic headmaster's wife; when it was filmed, noted liberal MGM producer Dory Schary had to reassure the MPPDA:

> as for the character of the boy himself, Mr. Schary protested that he did not wish to bring up the question of homosexuality. He wished rather to center the boy's problem on the fact that he was an "off-horse," who liked long haired music, who did not date girls like other boys did. . . . He kept saying that what he wanted to emphasize in the boy's character was that he was a non-conformist. (Harvey 1989:249)

Hollywood strove to eliminate homosexuality from all its scripts, both historically constituted ones and those that were not. Of course, all the editing in the world could not prevent oppositional readings by members of gay and lesbian communities who attempted to recuperate content from films like *Queen Christina* or from gay and lesbian performers acting out straight parts, and in these films there may have occurred those bursts of Ernst Bloch's anticipatory consciousness and the inevitable utopian moments Frederic Jameson assures us are part of all popular culture (Jameson 1990:9–34).[4] Nevertheless, preferred constructions that eliminated homosexuality continued to be the dominant ways of making film history.

Yet, Hollywood, via the route of absence, went beyond the annihilation of homosexuality. It created a false front of heterosexuality that served to ensure the ideological that the figures audiences were supposed to emulate were emphatically heterosexual, and, moreover, to teach that the handiwork of their genius was *specifically motivated by* the glow of heterosexual love. We thus have a more powerful case of film being used to obfuscate and create a false history, not merely to cover up a version of the truth but to invent a normative formula to which all must adhere.

Even in a cinema that, through renaming, typecasting, stereotyping, and other strategies, thrived on reducing the "other" status of a per-

former to mainstream acceptability, the treatment of homosexuality was unique. Other minority groups denied screen presence, or burdened with harmful film stereotypes, could nevertheless resort to circulating positive images in print and other media. Those intertexts available, in varying degrees, to other minority groups — the publicity, the news and information shared by social groups — had the potential to be used as fuel for oppositional readings of Hollywood. Such material was denied the gay and lesbian spectator, reader, or auditor, for we were an absence in almost any forum. Because such potentially liberating sources of information were as heavily censored as gay and lesbian screen roles, we were figures to be inscribed and animated by others, creatures to be rewritten and reconfigured at will. Other minority groups did not suffer this same fate. Eddie Cantor, who was told by producer Sam Goldwyn to suppress his "Jewishness" on screen so he might be more acceptable to nonurban audiences, could nevertheless let this aspect of his identity surface in publicity material extolling his connection to Jewish charities. This option was closed to gays and lesbians, and because of such cloture the talented and famous homosexual was a null set, a category without membership, a logical contradiction in the studio era. Here film biography naturalized one mode of sexual orientation and linked it to desired states of status, profession, and achievement. Heterosexuality was not so much a correlate of genius or fame as an explanation of and a motivation for that exalted state. Heterosexual romance, one of the standard plot lines that buttress almost all Hollywood narratives, runs throughout *Night and Day*, not just in the relationship of Cole and Linda Porter but in a ludicrous depiction of Monty Woolley (playing himself) as a relentless "skirt chaser" despite the fact that the real life Woolley, himself gay, chased pants (particularly if they encased a sailor) and not skirts. Further, the film makes a conventional fictive explanation for marital discord; Cole is always surrounded by young chorus girls, providing a constant backdrop suggesting that Porter's sexual interest was aroused by these women and that his wife was jealous of their competition.

Porter himself was as successful a businessman as he was a composer. Through protracted negotiations with Jack Warner he had raised the asking price for rights to use thirty-eight of his songs in a film based on his life to $300,000. Well aware of the conventions of show business biographies, and experienced in business negotiations concerning artistic properties, Porter was willing to sign away certain of his biographical rights as part of the business of putting on a show. To this end, he and his wife and mother signed release forms allowing six-foot-two-inch Cary Grant and youthful Alexis Smith to impersonate the diminutive (five-foot-six-inch) balding Porter and his older wife in a film that bore only the most superficial resemblance to their actual lives. Porter's contract stipulated that

> it is understood that Producer in the development of the story . . . upon which the photoplay shall be based shall be free to dramatize, fictionalize, or emphasize any or all incidents in the life of Seller, or interpolate such incidents as Producers may deem necessary in order to obtain a treatment or continuity of commercial value.[5]

Porter thus realized that the events of his life were not necessarily the same as a story of his life. Born into a wealthy family in Peru, Indiana, he was a pampered only child. Educated privately, he enrolled in Yale, graduating in 1913. It was there that he apparently had his first gay experiences, and it was at Yale that he seriously developed a love of the theater and things theatrical (he was voted the "most entertaining" by his classmates). He also formed a lifelong friendship with another gay man, classmate Monty Woolley (depicted in the film as his law professor). After graduating from Yale, Porter enrolled in Harvard Law School to please his wealthy grandfather but left after a short time. He volunteered for the Duryea Relief Party, an organization formed by wealthy Americans to distribute food to war-beleaguered France and, while "over there," met his future wife, the wealthy, older divorcee, Linda Lee. Cole Porter and Linda Lee married in Paris in 1919. After living and studying composition (briefly, with Vincent d'Indy at the Schola Cantorum) in France and Italy, supported by his trust fund and his wife's ample alimony settlement, Porter returned to the United States. In 1929 he scored a huge success with *Fifty Million Frenchman*, which contained the hit, "You Do Something to Me," as well as the coded gay paean, "Find Me a Primitive Man." *The Gay Divorcé* (1932) and *Anything Goes* (1934) cemented his fame. From the 1930s on, he commuted between New York and California (with frequent side trips all over the world), where, like his equally successful contemporaries Kern, Gershwin, and Berlin, he alternately created shows for Broadway and wrote for films. His unconventional marriage was ruptured in 1936 by Cole's increasingly "out" behavior. While aware of his gay life, Porter's wife Linda had reached a mutual accommodation with her husband. Simply stated, Porter could act on his gay desires as long as he publicly played straight. Charles Schwartz, an early biographer of Porter, notes that Linda Porter's main concern about Cole's gay life was "that if word got out to the media of how he was carrying on, it would be terribly damaging to his reputation and career" (1977:176). Despite a serious separation in the mid-1930s, Cole's crippling riding accident in 1937 reunited the couple. Until he virtually ceased composition in 1958 (the year he had his accident-damaged leg amputated at the hip), and his death in 1964, Porter was a major celebrity, whose very image—the slicked-back hair, full-toothed, dazzling smile, and debonair dress—embodied sophistication for the American public.

## FRAMING "COLE PORTER"

How, then, did one deal with a life in which the public narrative was at odds with its private behavior? While this has always been a problem of the popular biography—printing the legend or the fact—the substantial cash investment of Warner Brothers in a film of Porter's life meant that all strategic possibilities would be invoked to assure that a profitable and therefore conventional tale be created. A film of his life *had to* reaffirm to the public both Cole's genius as well as his heterosexual life. For Porter the remuneration and untold free publicity such a film would generate were worth the distortions of the strange concoction that was eventually made. Further, while Porter profited in a public sense from the tale of his life, *Night and Day* cemented, through the physique of Cary Grant, the image of Porter as the dashing heterosexual and thus helped construct a self that the private Porter could use and, presumably, be pleased with.

Like Porter's, every life presented scenarists and producers with problems in narratization. These problems could concern condensation of events, censorship, the elimination of morally objectionable materials, legal entanglements with surviving relatives, and, absorbing all these considerations, Hollywood's shifting conventions for what constituted a life worth depicting. In the Porter case there were more than the usual number of obstacles to overcome. Warner's solutions to these problems illustrate the machinery of studio production at its most characteristic.

Porter himself seemed as adept as any Warner's writer at constructing the narrative of his own life. The gay man or lesbian—unlike many other minorities—can, if he or she so desires, adopt the various public postures associated with heterosexuality. Invoking this strategy of enclosure, Porter carried on a very active gay life in private, while his public life as a glamorously married cosmopolite was much chronicled in gossip columns and other journalistic reports. Occasionally, Porter was able to refer to homosexuality in his lyrics, but this had to be done in a highly coded manner. As Michael Bronski notes, this subterfuge was deemed necessary in the public image of figures of the studio era even while the Broadway theater, from the time of Tennessee Williams on, was able to add homosexuality to the menu of permissible plots. "Although gay men may have been everywhere working and writing and directing and producing theater, there was no social permission for them to openly express their sexuality either in their lives or in their work. They resorted to hidden references" (Bronski 1984:113).

Having constructed a front of heterosexuality in his real life, the task of aiding Warner's in depicting this artifice was arguably in Cole's best interest. Although he was absorbing the values of the culture that repressed him and other gays and lesbians by energetically buying into the front of heterosexuality and marriage, Porter wanted to continue to profit by the rules of this culture. Films like *Night and Day*, and men like Cole Porter, reinforced a kind of sexual and class hegemony through their willful banishing of gay elements from their scripts. Thus, a history the movies would not make (that of the gay Cole Porter whose witty songs of "Love for Sale" could have referred to his frequent taste for male hustlers) becomes a nonhistory. For Hollywood, as a sustainer of the social status quo, the first problem of picturing a life, then, might be to eliminate those areas that the culture tells us should not exist.[6]

The second problem of a life is dealing "properly" with the elements that are deemed worthy of existence. Porter's marriage to the older, wealthy Linda Lee was hardly the stuff of other Warner's biopics of this period. Full of periods of estrange-

ment due to his extramarital affairs, his marriage would be unfilmable were the facts ever brought to the attention of the Breen Office. Of course, since homosexuality (section 2, subsection 4 of the 1934 Production Code) was so far beyond the pale of discussible topics in the 1940s, the nature of the marriage never surfaced as a debatable issue. Nevertheless, while the fact of his marriage was real, its cinematic depiction was pure Hollywood. Beyond that, in his social attitudes Porter was not the lofty, benevolent individual a great man, in the mold of other biopics, was supposed to be. As Charles Schwartz has suggested, Porter was more than a bit of a snob and at times even quite bigoted. Although born in Peru, Indiana, his identity was not with Middle America but centered about the New York-Paris-Beverly Hills axis, with all the wit contained therein. He was not Will Rogers. On the surface, Porter's life was hardly the stuff of inspiration for movie audiences (Schwartz 1977).

Yet the Porter life had much that could be inspiring. In addition to the words and music that were strong selling points with various sheet music and record tie-ins, there was Porter's very real courage in overcoming a crippling riding accident that left him, at age forty-five, nearly paralyzed and in excruciating pain. Here, in Porter's fight to resume his life and career in the aftermath of his accident, was that necessary component of the lowest common denominator, what Darryl Zanuck, of the rival Fox studio, referred to as a rooting interest. If this particular angle was not enough of a lure for audiences, Warners could—and did—invent other attractions.

The case of sanitizing the Porter life story is noted in a memo of July 7, 1943, from Jack Moffitt, the writer assigned to the screenplay, to production supervisor Hal Wallis.

> The life of Cole Porter can be a "wholesome" story. It is the triumph of the hick. It will be doubly amusing because he triumphs as a sophisticate. . . . Mr. Porter's life, though rich in incident, follows a simple, straight story line. My talk with Mr. Porter convinces me he will show a very cooperative attitude. He recognizes the plot needs of movie entertainment and agrees to interpretations that will assist the picture's box office.[7]

The memo further indicated guidelines that would help the film's box office, suggesting that the focus had to be on the music Porter composed and not the life that he led. The dangers of accuracy were hinted at by Jack Moffitt, one of the screenwriters employed by Warner's for the film and film critic for the magazine *Esquire*. "Instead of dramatizing Cole Porter songs, which all Americans know and love, Mr. Schwartz [the producer] has dramatized the man Cole Porter, whom few people know and most people would dislike."[8] In order to sell Warner's Cole Porter to the American public, other facts of his life would have to be rewritten. Porter had inherited a sizable fortune from his grandfather, and before his success as a composer he had, floated by his grandfather's and wife's money, led a life in Europe filled with sex, booze, and the distinct absence of a specific career. The average viewer, it was reasoned, would hardly find these circumstances congruent with his or her own life. However, by foregrounding Porter's struggles and physical tragedy rather than his rather freewheeling lifestyle, and by redefining his relationship with his wife to conform to existing contours of glamorous heterosexual romance, the film could be reframed. As a studio employee and a film critic, scriptwriter Moffitt knew the rules of the biopic game, and, in a desperate attempt to have his—and not some other writer's—version of a Porter life appear beneath the Warner's logo (after all, writers were the least powerful figures in the calculus of studio-era Hollywood), warned Jack Warner to manufacture a life congruent with his audiences' values, not one filled with "Oscar Wilde dialogue" and "Noel Coward characterizations"; "There are 124,224,128 Americans living outside of New York City," Moffitt cautioned, "and Mr. Schwartz has made no effort to please any of them. Despite the box-office value of such films as *Meet Me in St. Louis*, the opportunity to show Cole Porter and his songs springing from the heart of a normal American home life has been ignored."[9]

But the disaffected writer (who was removed from the film) need not have counseled Warner on this matter. *Night and Day* became the wholesome story Warner's production supervisor Wallis foresaw, the tale of a fellow who, given the gift of music (which he generously shared on the Warner's soundtrack), nevertheless created (with the aid of his adoring, loving wife) his greatest work in his triumph over pain. Like other great public figures whose tales Hollywood had told (Madame Curie, Emile Zola, Dr. Ehrlich), Porter was abetted by his spouse and buttressed by the institution of marriage. The absence of marriage or, even more pointedly, the denial of heterosexual love is the punishment for and an explanation of failure. Thus, in *Night and Day*, we see Porter at the front in World War I, pining for his wife-to-be, Linda. Injured in a bombardment (in the midst of composing "Begin the Beguine"!), he lapses into melancholy. Linda, instantly (and fictitiously) transformed into a nurse's aide, miraculously materializes by his side. Keenly aware of the special needs of the genius Porter, and well socialized into her subordinate role as keeper of genius, she purchases a piano so Cole can "snap out" of his misery through the therapy of work and love. Inspired by her gift, and spurred on by her presence, Cole conjures up one of his greatest creations, "Night and Day," composed amid pointedly displayed falling bombs, ticking clocks, and the drip, drip, drip of rainy France.

In *Night and Day* the title song appears some fifteen years ahead of its actual composition. But this chronological gaffe was an intentional strategic gamble; Warners traded off the few people who might spot this slip for the role the song played in motivating Porter's love for his wife and her role as supporter of the career and donor of the source of inspiration.[10] His heterosexual romantic desire motivates the specific composition, nicely normalizing the composer, enabling audiences to view the song as a valentine to marriage, love, and the support of the male career. Charm and surface had been transformed into character and depth, and marginalized sexual behavior, or even longing, was eliminated.

## TELEVISION AND BIOGRAPHY

By the time television came to narrate the lives of the famous, the rules for the construction of a life had altered. Whereas in *Night and Day* Porter's homosexuality was something to be hidden and transformed, Rock Hudson's homosexuality is, in his TV biopic, revealed but equally transformed. Like all biographies on TV and film, *Rock Hudson* (1990) is teleological; but here, in the age of TV, the career trajectory has a new mortal lesson and a chilling deadly payoff. A denizen of the studio era, the cinematic Cole Porter can only attain success with his devoted wife; monogamy is rewarded with success, veneration, and triumph. The poststudio biography of Hudson, himself one of the last "products" of the studio system, who opted to deny monogamy with men or women in life and on film, ultimately suffers for this "code" lapse. Without the restrictive Production Code to annihilate Hudson's sexuality, the producers are "free" to tell his tale; but *freedom* is a word that transmutes into merely another, different set of limitations, and the gay man or lesbian on TV is more likely than not, as Vito Russo (1987), Larry Gross (1989), and others have noted, to have his or her tale imbricated with tragedy, violence, or victimhood. Having joined the cast of world history, the gay man or lesbian is limited in the scripts he or she can play. Thus, Hudson's life is a teleology of tragedy, not triumph. This "flaw" in his narrative is activated by the time bomb of AIDS, which "finally" goes off in the last act of the script and the life. Where Porter's cinematic marriage helps him to sustain a triumph over adversity, Rock Hudson is denied this critical crucible so necessary to the Hollywood formula of genius and happiness; Hudson's divorced state and his "failed" marriage (like Porter, to a lesbian) is correlated with tragedy, and his career is framed as mere luck—and not with the gilt of pure genius. In *Rock Hudson*, the actor's analysis of his own sexuality suggests he had internalized mainstream notions of the self, that he had taken to heart Hollywood's biopic lessons on the marriage of career, self, and sexuality. It is his outing—and not his self-suppression—that he takes as the cause of his death, and in some ways the outing "killed" the image while letting the real man emerge. In a deathbed valediction, a feature of many biopics that allows one final message to be telegraphed to the viewer, he sums up his self-suppression:

> I spent my whole life keeping everything inside, denying everything. And now, everybody knows anyway. You know what's so damn funny? All the time I kept pretending I wasn't gay, I kept on thinking I was the perfect man, the perfect star. If it ever came out that I was gay, oh it would kill me. And look; it has.

It is as if the whole life was a public service announcement approved by the MPPDA; that Hudson's end is the wages of sin, the price paid for nonconformity to the TV code of happiness selectively culled from the prescribed social code of life. Hudson, as a *gay* victim of the punitive code of biography, must pay with something far more valuable than a tarnished image. The price of fame is not equal for all, and minorities pay a higher price than others for entering the exclusive club of renown.

As the legal definition of what constitutes a "public figure" has, since *New York Times v. Sullivan* (1964), become more broadly inclusive, journalistic conventions for celebrity exposés have increasingly become more prying than in Porter's day. Yet the two scripts of the lives of Porter and Hudson are instructive. In both homosexuality is only presentable as fiction—in one case, of heterosexuality, in the other, of a laundered version of a sexless homosexuality—created by heterosexuals to advance their mainstream arguments for marriage and fidelity and the payoffs that come with these gestures. Hudson's death is even told from the point of view of his litigious surviving lover. The film opens at the posthumous trial, at which Hudson, in the person of his estate, has been sued by his lover for knowingly having sexual relations with him while infected with the HIV virus. The film that is wedged between the opening charge and the ultimate judgment relentlessly proves the justice of the verdict. This perspective—Hudson as a violator of the law—privileges a condemnation of the actor's life seen from the vantage point of the "state," a site often opposed to gay culture. Moreover, by selecting a trial to frame the issues of both life and film, *Rock Hudson* utilized one of the most standard devices of the classical Hollywood cinema to reproduce the culture of domination in the guise of openly representing and fairly evaluating an alternative lifestyle. *Rock Hudson* naturalizes the verdict on the life by encasing it within the official power of the law, telegraphing to viewers what the film is *really* about, laying bare the judgment of a life for all to see. The judgment against the character of Hudson and his manager—that they conspired to hide Hudson's illness from his lover—has the force of the community behind it. In death the famous homosexual is still an outlaw.

The differences between these two lives on film, separated as they are by over forty years, are remarkably small. Both *Rock Hudson* and *Night and Day* were not naive outputs of Hollywood that relied on a randomly selected notion of the public self; they were products of institutional systems that controlled definitions of culture through the manipulation and censorship of content. The lives were shaped by similar pressures: constrained by legal anxieties, controlled by a production system that eliminated any behavior deemed "offensive" to the mainstream audience, altered to fit the star persona of an actor, and constructed with the conservative producer's intertextual notion of how a life should be lived. The differences between the night of the screen and the days of their lives is poignant and constant, a testimonial to the conservative power of media in regard to sexual minorities.

## Notes

Many of the numeric data cited here are drawn from an earlier version of this essay that appeared in my book, *Bio/Pics: How Hollywood Constructed Public History* (New Brunswick, 1992), pp. 110–147. Percentages quoted throughout the text are based on my purposive sample of one hundred biopics.

1. The PCA was founded in 1930, and enforcement of its strictures was a serious affair from 1934–1966. It attained its power through an agreement, signed by all the major studios, not to distribute a film that did not bear the PCA seal of approval. By 1968, with the world a very different place than it had been when the PCA was formed, the less powerful "ratings system" had replaced this once powerful agency as an arbiter of content.

2. There was a general feeling that Warner Brothers may have strayed too far into biofantasyland with the Porter film. An August 1946 article in *Life* magazine, " 'Night and Day' vs. Cole Porter," presents a catalogue of inaccuracies in the film, noting, "It may be a matter of no great consequence that moviegoers are misled concerning the life of a popular composer. But . . . such disregard for facts destroys the validity of the movie formula. *Night and Day* . . . marks a sad decline from the great Warner Brothers biographies of Zola and Pasteur" (1946, 101). For an overview of how star/genre formulations shaped studio era Hollywood, see Schatz 1989.

3. Zanuck to Harris, Memorandum of May 21, 1938, MacGowan Collection, Research Library, University of California at Los Angeles, box 887, folder 1.

4. See Noriega 1990 for the inevitable "leakage" of gay and lesbian content into film reviews despite Hollywood's protests that films were, following the Production Code, not supposed to have this as a subject matter.

5. Warner's Collection, University of Southern California, Doheny Library, Contract, p. 6, *Night and Day* file.

6. Porter's homosexuality illustrates the difficulty of doing institutional histories of film based on written material alone. Simply stated, that which can't be discussed, or written about, ceases to exist as a bit of archival data. These "holes" in the language—the refusal to commit to writing about certain prac-

tices—parallel similar gaps in the subject matter of the film life. The author is forced to use secondary material and, interestingly, material often not deemed officially appropriate for serious academic study, like Kenneth Anger's hugely entertaining *Hollywood Babylon*. It is often only in such nonmainstream media sources that banished or taboo behavior can be chronicled at all.

7. Warner Brothers Collection, University of Southern California, Doheny Library, Memo of July 7, 1943, from Jack Moffitt to Hal Wallis, *Night and Day* file.

8. Warner Brothers Collection, University of Southern California, Doheny Library, Memo from Jack Moffitt to Hal Wallis, April 14, 1944.

9. Ibid.

10. Cole did not meet his future wife until 1918. In the film this occurs at his family home when he is in his early twenties. Linda's age (she was eight years older than Cole), her previous marriage and divorce, and of course her lesbianism were also elided from the script. *Life* magazine poked fun at the inaccuracies in the film yet inadvertently supplied free publicity by giving it a six-page spread in their August 5, 1946, issue.

## Works Cited

Bergreen, Lawrence. 1990. *As Thousands Cheer: The Life of Irving Berlin*. New York: Viking.

Bronski, Michael. 1984. *Culture Clash: The Making of Gay Sensibility*. Boston: South End.

Custen, George F. 1992. *Bio/Pics: How Hollywood Constructed Public History*. New Brunswick: Rutgers University Press.

Gross, Larry. 1989. "Out of the Mainstream: Sexual Minorities and the Mass Media." In Ellen Seiter, Hans Borchers, Gabriele Kreutzner, Eva-Maria Warth, eds., *Remote Control: Television, Audiences, and Cultural Power*, pp. 130–149. London: Routledge.

Grossberg, Larry. 1992. "The Affective Sensibility of Fandom." In Lisa Lewis, ed., *Adoring Audience: Fan Culture and Popular Media*, pp. 50–65. New York: Routledge.

Harvey, Stephen. 1989. *Directed by Vincente Minelli*. New York: Harper and Row.

Lucasfilm, Intl. 1992. *The Young Indiana Jones Chronicles: Study Guide* San Rafael: Lucas Films.

Maltby, Richard. 1993. "The Production Code and the Hays Office." In Tino Balio, ed., *Grand Design: Hollywood as a Modern Business Enterprise, 1930–1939*, pp. 37–72. New York: Scribner's.

Mordden, Ethan. 1991. "Rock and Cole," *New Yorker*, October 28, 1991, pp. 91–113.

" 'Night and Day' vs. Cole Porter." 1946. *Life*, August 5, 1946, pp. 101–107.

Noriega, Chon. 1990. "Something's Missing Here: Homosexuality and Film Reviews During the Production Code Era, 1934–1962." *Cinema Journal*, 30(1):20–41.

Production Code Administration. 1953. Minutes of a Meeting on *Tea and Sympathy*, 11/2/53. *Tea and Sympathy* file. Los Angeles: PCA Collection, Library of the Academy of Motion Picture Arts and Sciences.

Russo, Vito. 1987. *The Celluloid Closet: Homosexuality in the Movies*. Rev. ed. New York: Harper and Row.

Schatz, Thomas. 1989. *The Genius of the System*. New York: Pantheon.

Schwartz, Charles. 1977. *Cole Porter: A Biography*. New York: Dial.

Shohat, Ella. 1990. "Ethnicities-in-Relation: Towards a Multi-Cultural Reading of American Cinema." In Lester Friedman, ed., *Ethnicity and American Cinema*. Urbana: University of Illinois Press.

Sobchack, Vivian. 1990. " 'Surge and Splendor': A Phenomenology of the Hollywood Historical Epic." *Representations* (Winter), no. 29.

Warner Brothers Pictures. 1946. Publicity Brochure for *Night and Day*.

# | 47 |

# Old Strategies for New Texts: How American Television Is Creating and Treating Lesbian Characters

## MARGUERITE J. MORITZ

In response to the Women's Liberation Movement, Hollywood in the 1970s began producing what came to be called New Women's films. *Alice Doesn't Live Here Anymore* (1975), *Julia* (1977), *An Unmarried Woman* (1977), and *Starting Over* (1979) are among the most popular of that genre, which is generally characterized by its focus on women seeking new definitions of themselves and their personal relationships. Those movies and many more like them have been the center of several important discussions among feminist critics who have demonstrated the many ways in which the visual and narrative codes of cinema have often worked to restore female characters to their "proper place," often within the traditional family structure.

These film strategies have direct application to the portrayal of women on American television. Prime-time television programming, like Holly-wood cinema, can be considered "the limiting case, the ideal-type," so pervasive that it serves as a "model for modes of production and modes of representation" all over the world (Kuhn 1982, 21). Just as dominant cinema relies on fictional characters playing out their roles in a narrative context, so too does American television find its entertainment value in storytelling. The similarities and connections between film and television are also clear from an institutional standpoint: indeed, many Hollywood studios now routinely produce television programming while aspiring Hollywood filmmakers often begin their careers in television. And most significantly, these indus-

In R. Jeffrey Ringer, ed., *Queer Words, Queer Images: Communication and the Construction of Homosexuality*, pp. 122–142. New York: New York University Press, 1994.

tries share a long and well-documented history of being white, male, heterosexual, and capitalistic both in terms of what they produce and how they produce it (Kuhn 1982, 25).

Just as feminist film critics have demonstrated that the post-Liberation women created by Hollywood are often not so liberated after all, this essay will show that lesbian characters created for prime-time American television may offer viewers little more than new texts created with old strategies in mind.

## RECUPERATION AND AMBIGUITY IN HOLLYWOOD CINEMA

Early Hollywood cinema in its classic era of big studio and big star films provided several stories in which strong women characters defy convention, only to be brought to the brink of ruin by their bold behavior. Before the closing credits, however, they are rescued from their shaky precipice and repositioned in a more socially acceptable space. *Mildred Pierce* (1945), a melodramatic murder mystery starring Joan Crawford, offers perhaps the most analyzed example of how this kind of recuperation plays out.

The main character, in the person of Crawford, is possessed of traits not typically associated with her wife-mother-homemaker status. She is ambitious, aggressive, determined, and decisive. When her unemployed husband fails to provide sufficiently for her and her daughters, she asserts herself, proceeding to banish him from their home and to accomplish what he apparently cannot. Within a short time the uneducated but savvy Mildred builds up a booming restaurant business. But then success begins to take its toll. Mildred's personal life starts to unravel. Her youngest daughter succumbs to a tragic illness. Her oldest daughter is defiant and deceitful. And when it looks as though Mildred herself will be revealed as a murderer, the real culprit is uncovered and a devastated Mildred is taken back by her husband, presumably ready to retreat from her role in the outside world.

> Mildred's take-over of the place of the father has brought about the collapse of all social and moral order in her world. . . . In the face of impending chaos and confusion the patriarchal order is called upon to reassert itself and take the Law back into its own hands, divesting women completely of any power they may have gained while the patriarchal

order was temporarily impaired. This involves establishing the truth without a doubt, restoring "normal" sexual relationships and reconstituting the family unit, in spite of the pain and suffering which such repressive action must cause. (Cook 1978, 75)

The outcome presented in *Mildred Pierce* is seen by many feminist critics as prototypical of classical Hollywood films portraying strong female characters. "Often narrative closure itself seems to necessitate the resolution of problems and ambiguities brought up by the desire of women characters to go to work, to be sexual beings, or both. The end of the story becomes the solution of that story when the woman is returned to her 'proper' place, i.e., with her husband, at home" (Walker 1982, 167). While other narrative closures for these kinds of stories do exist, they run a narrow range. Kuhn suggests that recuperation is inevitable and is accomplished "thematically in a limited number of ways: a woman character may be restored to the family by falling in love, by 'getting her man,' by getting married, or otherwise accepting a 'normative' female role. If not, she may be directly punished for her narrative and social transgression by exclusion, outlawing or even death" (Kuhn 1982, 34).

Given that they were prompted by the women's rights movement and directed toward a more liberated female audience, it might be expected that the New Women's films of the 1970s would deal differently with narrative closure. But like history, Hollywood has a way of repeating itself. *Klute* (1971), starring Jane Fonda as prostitute Bree Daniels, is one of the first of this genre and, like *Mildred Pierce*, one of the most analyzed. At the time of its release, some feminists hailed the film for its gripping portrayal of a strong woman by a politically active star. "*Klute* became a focus of critical attention because of the questions it raised about audience pleasure. It immediately attracted feminist approval for the powerful image of Jane Fonda's Bree Daniels. She seemed to be, at last, a positive Hollywood heroine, an 'independent' woman for other women to identify with" (Lovell and Frith 1981, 15). But many other feminist writers developed a far different reading of the film. Gledhill argues that precisely because of its contemporariness, this film text is more able to mask its real message. For her, the Bree Daniels role is simply an updated version of the evil woman created in 1940s film noir.

The film is trying to articulate, within the ambiance of the thriller, a modern version of the independent woman, conceived of as the sexually liberated, unattached, hip woman and without mentioning feminism or women's liberation arguably trying to cash in on these concerns to enhance the modernity of the type.

I would argue that *Klute's* production of the stereotype is no different in its ultimate effect, and that the film operates in a profoundly anti-feminist way, perhaps even more so than the '40s thrillers from which it derives. (Gledhill 1978, 114)

▼ ▼ ▼

Not all of Hollywood's efforts to woo the New Women's audience relied on the restoration of male dominance. In fact, one of the marks of these films is their use of textual ambiguity. *Julia* is a case in point. The film is an account of writer Lillian Hellman (played by Jane Fonda) and her revolutionary friend Julia (Vanessa Redgrave). The film clearly raises a question as to whether the two women had a romantic sexual relationship, yet deliberately avoids answering it. "While most reviewers agree that the relationship portrayed between the women is central to the film . . . there are almost as many opinions as there are reviews concerning the precise nature of that relationship" (Kuhn 1982, 38). In *An Unmarried Woman* and *Alice Doesn't Live Here Anymore*, ambiguity itself becomes a form of resolution. By making the future of the female protagonist unclear, these texts provide a way in which the narrative can simultaneously appeal to audiences that want to see patriarchy challenged and those that expect to see it restored.

It would be problematic for a cinematic institution whose products are directed at a politically heterogeneous audience overtly to take up positions which might alienate certain sections of that audience. Films whose address sustains a degree of polysemy—which open up rather than restrict potential readings, in other words—may appeal to a relatively broad-based audience. Openness permits readings to be made which accord more or less with spectators' prior stances on feminist issues. *Julia* illustrates the point quite well: while lesbians may be free to read the film as an affirmation of lesbianism, such a reading—just as it is not ruled out—is by no

means privileged by the text. (Kuhn 1982, 139)

If strong female characters have typically been dealt with through recuperation or ambiguity by cinema in earlier decades, are the same strategies finding their way into American television portrayals today? The question is of particular interest when it is raised about stories with lesbian characters because these scripts might be seen as network television's most progressive efforts.

## HOMOSEXUALITY AND AMERICAN TELEVISION

During most of its history, American television effectively banned the portrayal of homosexuals. The three major networks were never legally bound to do so, but claimed instead that they were governed by what they termed matters of public taste. "In the '50s, they couldn't use the word pregnant when Lucy was expecting a baby [on *I Love Lucy*]," explains Dianna Borri, NBC's manager of standards and practices in Chicago (quoted in Moritz 1989, 13). The networks contend that they reflect societal trends rather than set them. Therefore, as homosexuality has become more socially acceptable, so have gay characters.

It was only in 1973 that American television offered its first fictional portrayal of homosexuality with the made-for-TV movie *That Certain Summer*, starring Hal Holbrook as a gay father coming out to his son (Henry 1987, 43). A few other shows with homosexual themes followed, but that abruptly changed in 1980 when a more conservative national mood gave rise to the Moral Majority's campaign against television shows with too much sex and violence. ABC and CBS canceled their plans for four separate productions with gay themes and NBC revamped its *Love, Sidney* sitcom to virtually eliminate any reference to the main character's homosexuality (Moritz 1989, 14).

By the second half of the 1980s, network attitudes appeared to be shifting once again, this time toward a more liberal approach to both language and story themes. The emergence of AIDS, the relatively marginalized position of broadcast television brought on by increasing cable penetration and home video ownership, the demonstrated commercial viability of gay-themed material in other mass media, and the appeal of emerging social issues in general as a backdrop for broadcast productions all contributed to the creation of a climate in which homosexuality was once again permitted to emerge on American television. Lesbian characters, always a rarity in the past, were no longer invisible.

Starting in the mid-1980s, lesbian characters and story lines began their fictional coming out, the result at least in part of a changing institutional context in which what was once taboo had become potentially viable and sellable. *Golden Girls, Kate and Allie, L.A. Law, Hill Street Blues, Moonlighting, Hunter,* and *Hotel*—some of the most popular shows on TV—all have had episodes (since 1985) with lesbian parts. *My Two Loves,* an ABC Monday Night Movie, explored in uncommonly explicit visual detail two women involved in a love affair. In addition, ABC introduced a series in the spring of 1988 that featured prime time's first regular cast member with a lesbian identity: *Heartbeat,* an hour long drama about a women's medical clinic, presented actress Gail Strickland as Marilyn McGrath. Her role as an older woman, a nurse-practitioner, a mother, and a lesbian no doubt gave her considerable demographic appeal. After its initial six-episode spring run, ABC renewed the show and put it on its fall 1988 schedule. It was canceled later that season because of consistently weak ratings.

Of course the fact that lesbians are now being portrayed may simply reflect the industry's current attempt to give a contemporary look to its standard fare of sitcoms, cop shows, and nighttime soaps. In fact, if these portrayals do nothing more than extend negative stereotypes about women in general and about lesbians in particular, then they are neither indicators of pro-social programming nor of progressive politics at the networks. It is with that in mind that we look at how five recent prime-time American television shows construct and frame lesbian characters. They are *Heartbeat* (two episodes), *Hunter, Hotel,* and *Golden Girls.* These episodes were selected because the lesbian characters in them are central rather than peripheral to the structure of the narrative.

## RECUPERATION AND NARRATIVE CLOSURE

The most striking case of recuperation to bring about narrative closure is seen in "From San Francisco with Love," an episode of the detective show *Hunter* in which the macho Los Angeles cop for whom the show is named tries to unravel the murders of a millionaire and his son. As the story unfolds, Hunter goes to the scene of the first murder in San Francisco and meets Sgt. Valerie Foster, who originally investigated the case. She is more than cooperative, sharing not only her police files with him, but her bed as well. She claims to be eager to help break the case and introduces Hunter to the millionaire's cool, cunning, very young widow. But Sgt. Foster is really trying to throw Hunter off the track. She is also plotting to murder the millionaire's son and in fact, we see her calmly shoot him in the head, her way of eliminating his claim to his father's fortune.

Why is Sgt. Foster doing all this? Because she is the lesbian lover of the millionaire's widow and together they plan on getting away with murder and an $80 million fortune. Eventually Hunter uncovers the fact that the cop and the widow are actually lovers, but he still can't prove that they are murderers. Hunter now prepares a plan in which he plays on the women's basic distrust of each other. The plan works, and the widow turns the cop in. But the cop has herself covered. She produces a tape recording she secretly made the night the women planned the killings. Both women are therefore implicated, both are caught, and both are guilty. The recuperation in this denouement is both unambiguous and complete. The women lovers prove to be their own undoing. They have, in fact, been cunning enough to get away with murder, but their deceitfulness and lack of trust is so total that they are doomed to fail in any venture that requires mutual reliance. Thus they have transgressed by being lesbians, murderers, and disloyal lovers. They obviously are beyond restoration to a "normative" female role. For these actions, they must and will be removed from society and properly punished.

This episode of *Hunter* was considered to portray lesbians so negatively that it drew a protest from the Alliance of Gay and Lesbian Artists (AGLA), an activist group based in Los Angeles that has been working to improve the image of homosexuals on television. "The network realized why [we protested] and afterwards came to us and asked us to submit scripts [that would be acceptable]," AGLA member Jill Blacher says (Moritz 1989, 11).

The episode of *Hotel,* an hour-long drama about the people who work in a luxury San Francisco hostelry, takes a far different approach to its narrative closure, but the recuperation of its lesbian subjects is no less complete. Here the sexual involvement of hotel coworkers Carol Bowman and Joanne Lambert comes out only after Joanne tragically dies in a car crash. Carol is left not only to grieve her lost mate but also to deal with Joanne's father, who comes from the East Coast to take home his daughter's body and her personal effects. The father has no idea that his daughter has been living with a female lover, but he finds out when a hotel attendant brings him a package from his daughter's employee locker that is addressed to him. The package contains a videotape that he watches from his suite.

*Joanne (on videotape):* Happy birthday, Dad. My gift to you this year is a heart-to-heart talk, at least my half of it.
I know it's never been easy between us. . . .
I know you never meant to be so stern, so unapproachable. . . . [Carol and I have] been together for six years now, Dad. Like they say, I guess it must be love.

Enraged, the father now storms into the office of the hotel's top executive, Mr. McDermott, and accuses Carol Bowman of corrupting his daughter.

*Lambert:* My daughter was always a good girl. Unfortunately, she and I were not very close. At home, she was rather shy, quiet. I always felt she was too easily led, influenced by others. One of her friends, a member of your staff, took advantage of Joanne, corrupted her. . . . Whatever our problems might have been at home, my daughter was not abnormal. She dated a great deal. She was not interested in other women.

*McDermott:* Why are you telling me this?

*Lambert:* Good Lord, man, isn't it obvious? This Bowman woman works with the public every single day representing you and your hotel.

*McDermott:* What do you want me to do? Fire her?

*Lambert:* You certainly aren't going to leave her in a position of being able to prey on other unsuspecting young women.

Given Mr. Lambert's distinct disapproval, Carol Bowman decides that he can have everything; she will be satisfied with her memories. In the final scene, we see Carol and Mr. Lambert packing up Joanne's things. The opening shot has the camera positioned high above them, shooting down, which both diminishes their presence and suggests that the deceased lover, Joanne, may be looking on from above. When Mr. Lambert finds a doll that he gave his daughter at age five, he begins to cry and Carol comes to his side to comfort him.

*Lambert:* Maybe you're right. Maybe memories are the most important things. I was always a better talker than a listener. . . . Maybe it's time I started listening a little.

*Carol:* What do you mean?

*Lambert:* You're the only one who can help me fill in all the blanks. Keep what's important to you. . . . Just do me a favor. Just take me through them, tell me what they meant . . . and maybe I can understand who Joanne grew up to be while I wasn't looking.

They embrace and the camera begins a long, slow pullout, again from the perspective of Joanne, looking on from above.

This narrative closure is ambiguous in that it does offer a degree of hope and acceptance for the lesbian lover. The irate father does after all admit that he wants and needs to know about his daughter's life, and that he will rely on her lover to give him that very personal information. Even though the daughter and her lover both are granted a measure of acceptance, that happens only after their relationship has been irrevocably terminated. The daughter is recuperated by virtue of her ultimate exclusion, and her lover is restored only now that she no longer is in the illicit relationship. In other words, the terms of their acceptance are based on their separation by death.

In two episodes of *Heartbeat* with lesbian themes, recuperation is achieved not through punishment or death but through the reaffirmation of patriarchy as it plays out in the lives of the other characters in the show. The fifth and sixth episodes, the final two programs of the show's first season, were aired on two consecutive nights during the critical May ratings sweeps. The narrative involves four separate story lines, each one tracking a problematic relationship in which medical staff members are embroiled. One follows an impotent doctor and his impatient fiancée, a second involves the resident psychiatrist's efforts to deal with his life after his marriage falls apart, and the third deals with a jealous romance between two doctors on the staff. The lesbian story centers on nurse-practitioner Marilyn McGrath and her unresolved relationship with her daughter Allison. Allison is coming back to California to be married in the home of her father, which her mother had left a decade earlier after revealing her lesbian identity. She makes it clear that she does not want her mother's lover, Patti, to attend the wedding, that she does not accept her mother's lifestyle, and that she is embarrassed by it.

> *Allison:* Dad and Elaine [his new wife] would be more comfortable if you sat in the front row but didn't walk down the aisle.
>
> *Marilyn:* I see. Is that what you want?
>
> *Allison:* I want things to go smoothly.
>
> *Marilyn:* So do I. Patti and I will do anything we can to help.
>
> *Allison:* I don't want there to be any tension. I don't think it would be a good idea for you to bring her. I'm sure she's a lovely person but a lot of my friends don't know about you.

Marilyn agrees to her daughter's request, but later feels guilty and upset. ("She doesn't want you to come to her wedding and I agreed," she confesses to lover Patti. "I don't want to go without you. I want to be with my partner.") Her lover, however, assures her that she has done the right thing.

It is Patti who urges Marilyn to make amends with her daughter ("It's your daughter and it's the biggest piece of unfinished business in your life. You've got to try to get through to her. Go and see her.") Marilyn indeed does go back to the family home she once left and has a painful exchange with Allison.

> *Allison:* It's not that you're a lesbian. That's not what bothers me. It's, why did you marry Dad? Why did you have me?

> *Marilyn:* I thought I could make a life with your father. I wasn't in love, but I liked him and I wanted children. And I decided I could keep those different feelings buried deep within me.
>
> *Allison:* But you left me.
>
> *Marilyn:* I didn't have a choice. It was the hardest thing I ever did, but believe me it would have been more devastating for you if I had stayed.

After Marilyn assures Allison that she will not turn out to be a lesbian too, the mother and daughter cry, embrace, and apparently patch up their differences. Patti is allowed to go to the wedding, and it is here that all four story lines are resolved.

The scene opens with a shot of Marilyn and Patti seated next to each other in the front row, as the organist plays "Here Comes the Bride." After the ceremony, the story turns to the still-impotent doctor and his increasingly uninterested fiancée as they line up at the buffet table. When she strikes up a conversation with another man, the impotent doctor asserts his proprietary rights and tells the man to "take a hike." At this, the fiancée stalks out, but the doctor catches up with her in the bedroom where she has left her coat. They quarrel. She slaps him. He grabs her, kisses her, throws her down on the bed and begins making passionate love to her, his potency obviously restored. Thus ends one story line.

Next, we see the two doctors who have been having a difficult time with their newly established relationship. She has accused him of being secretly involved with Eve, the sexy blond breast-implant surgeon at the clinic. Only now, as they dance cheek to cheek at the reception, does she accept his pledge of love and loyalty. He kisses her fingers, she strokes his hair, they smile lovingly and embrace. Thus ends the second story line.

The third narrative concludes with the psychiatrist waiting for his car to be brought around by the attendant so he can leave the reception. The seductive Eve appears, makes sarcastic note of his depression, and strikes a very responsive chord.

> *Eve:* What's the matter Stan? No one to dance with?
>
> *Stan (the psychiatrist):* I don't feel much like dancing.
>
> *Eve:* Wedding's a little painful, huh?

*Stan:* You really like to kick 'em when their down, don't you?

*Eve:* You call this down? No, you've got a lot more room to drop.

*Stan (looking angry):* This must be your way of showing affection, right?

The camera cuts to a close up of Eve looking at Stan alluringly. Then we see him grab her, wrap his arms around her, and kiss her. At that moment, the attendant drives up with Stan's car. Stan opens the door and pushes Eve inside.

*Stan:* Get in.

*Eve:* So doctor, where are we going?

*Stan:* You'll know when we get there.

Show credits start to roll as he screeches out of the driveway, apparently off to a place where they can continue what they've started.

The narrative closure in *Heartbeat* is accomplished through the restoration of the patriarchal system not just once, but four separate times, beginning with the ceremony most symbolic of patriarchy: the wedding. In direct succession we see the three heterosexual couples who have shared the narrative's focus with the homosexual couple. In each case, the resolution of their problems revolves around an overtly sexual exchange in which the men exert their virility and dominance over the women in their lives. The impotent doctor rekindles his manhood by confronting another suitor, calling his girlfriend a "slut," and having a sexual response to getting slapped in the face. The ever-collected and rational psychiatrist finally lets loose, getting physical and assertive with a colleague whom he treats like a young thing he's picked up at a party. Even Leo, the gentle pediatrician, makes it clear he is in charge as he tells his jealous mate on the dance floor, "If you're looking for a fight, baby, you ain't gonna find it here."

While the heterosexual couples find resolution in romance, passion, and drama, the lesbian couple is depicted as utterly prim and proper, completely self-contained and unobtrusive. The narrative closure of *Heartbeat* clearly shows that what does not happen to the lesbian couple is more important than what does.

The script is open-ended or ambiguous to the extent that the lesbian couple, after a considerable struggle, has achieved a victory. But even though

they have obtained permission to come to the wedding, this narrative closure does not permit them to participate in the event. Marilyn has one line of dialogue ("I think I'm going to cry"). She and Patti are seen in one shot as the processional starts and in a second shot as the ceremony opens; then they become invisible. While the heterosexual couples exhibit an outpouring of desire as the wedding reception plays out, the lesbians are politely kept from our view, never intruding on the show's vision of what it is to be a couple or to be in a romantic relationship. They agree to accept a limited place, not walking down the aisle, apparently not dancing, eating, or mingling with anyone but nicely tucked back in the closet, out of view from the rest of the guests and from the audience as well. The overall effect is to reaffirm the patriarchal order and to tell the audience that what really counts goes on in the heterosexual world, the arena of passion, desire, and drama.

It is interesting and perhaps not simply coincidental that the one situation comedy in the group of television shows under discussion is the one show in which the narrative closure does not rely on punishment, death, or exclusion to bring about narrative closure. *Golden Girls* is a half-hour sitcom that regularly features four women characters, three friends in late middle age and one of their mothers who is in her eighties. All four women live together in an upscale Miami home. This particular episode opens with Dorothy telling her elderly mother that she's expecting a visit from her college friend Jean. The crusty old mother, one of the more knowledgeable of this group, immediately recalls Jean as a lesbian, astonishing Dorothy.

*Dorothy:* How did you know?

*Mother:* A mother knows.

Now Dorothy and her mother have to decide whether to tell Rose and Blanche, the other women in the house, about Jean's sexual identity. When Jean arrives Dorothy and her mother take up the topic with her.

*Dorothy:* I wanted to make sure it was okay with you before I told them.

*Jean:* . . . If you think they can handle it, I prefer to tell them.

At this moment, Rose walks in with a tray of her special "clown sundaes," which she makes with raisin eyes and chocolate chip noses. The gesture epitomizes Rose's lack of sophistication and general inability to grasp what is going on around her and prompts Jean to deliver this aside to Dorothy.

> *Jean:* It'll just be our little secret.

As the show unfolds, Jean finds herself increasingly drawn to the kindhearted Rose. They both grew up on farms, and both like sad movies and staying up late playing card games. Eventually, Jean tells Dorothy that she thinks she has fallen in love with Rose. Dorothy passes on the information to her mother and together they reveal the story to Blanche. Now only Rose is unaware that Jean is a lesbian and that Jean is in love with her. When Jean tries to tell her how she is feeling ("I'm quite fond of you"), Rose finally begins to suspect something.

In the final scene, Jean asks to speak with Rose alone and she explains some of what she has been going through. Since her longtime lover died last year, Jean says, she has been in mourning.

> *Jean:* I thought I could never care for anyone again, until I met you.
>
> *Rose:* Well I have to admit I don't understand these kinds of feelings. But if I did understand, if I were—you know—like you, I think I'd be very flattered and proud that you thought of me that way.

As the two women put their arms around each other, the crotchety old mother enters and they hasten to explain lest she get the wrong impression. But she is still one step ahead of them.

> *Jean:* This isn't what it looks like.
>
> *Mother:* I know, I was listening at the door.
>
> *Rose:* Why were you listening at the door?
>
> *Mother:* Because I'm not tall enough to see through the window.

The camera cuts to Dorothy and Blanche, who have obviously been listening in at an open window all along. They give a sheepish wave, in effect admitting their intense curiosity over the Jean and Rose affair, and bring the show to its conclusion.

This narrative closure exhibits little need for recuperating the lesbian character. Jean will go back home and go on with her life and her lifestyle and will be better off knowing that she is once again willing to take risks and to engage with people. Thanks to Rose, she now realizes she can have feelings for women other than her deceased lover. Rose will also carry on with her life but will be enriched and enlightened by her experience with Jean. This is a story ending where differences are allowed to exist. The message to the audience is that a lesbian and a straight woman can have a friendship and can accept each other without finding fault or choosing sides.

Throughout the show, however, the subject matter is never treated seriously. Instead, lesbianism is represented as outside the experience of these women, something they don't even know about. One of them confuses lesbians with Lebanese people, saying they can't be so bad because Danny Thomas is one. Another says she may not know what a lesbian is but she could look it up in a dictionary. Only the tough old mother, who often speaks of connections with the Cosa Nostra in her native Sicily, knows about women like that. Since the topic is never treated seriously, it cannot pose a serious threat and therefore does not require any serious redress. Like the rest of the show, the ending is permitted to be basically lighthearted and humorous.

## RECUPERATION AND CINEMATIC STRUCTURES

One of the chief contributions of feminist film scholars to cinema studies is their work on textual analysis. This approach attempts to uncover the ways in which cinema specifically creates meanings through its visual as well as its spoken story. The analysis therefore looks not just at character and plot but also at lighting, camera framing and movement, editing, and other aspects of the visual to see how it operates in conjunction with character and plot to create specific cinematic meaning. Textual analysis is pertinent in television studies because television has adopted many of its codes directly from Hollywood cinema. It is pertinent here since in both film and television texts, at least some aspects of recuperation and ambiguity are carried out visually, not simply in accomplishing closure, but in structuring and positioning the lesbian characters throughout the narrative. Feminist film theory asks how women are *not* represented in a script; it also asks how women are represented visually, what fixed images of women are appealed to, and how those images operate interactively in the story line and in the visual structuring (Kuhn 1988, 81). We now look at these same five television programs with these questions in mind, examining specifically how television treats lesbian characters with respect to three significant areas of depiction: sexuality, personal rights, and publicity or public disclosure.

## Sexuality

With the exception of the conspiring murderers in *Hunter*, none of these lesbian characters is permitted to be sexual or even romantic. The contrast between the lesbian lovers and their straight counterparts in *Heartbeat* is stark. The lesbian couple never even approaches getting physical, but the male-female couples are frequently shown in close-up passionately embracing, kissing, and alluding to their love-making plans. In one instance a couple is shown undressed in the bed where the guests have left their coats at an afternoon wedding reception. At the same time, in the entire two-hour course of the show, the lesbian lovers are limited to one medium shot in which they share a limp, passionless embrace. That comes at a moment when they are reassuring each other that their problems will work out. Thus when they embrace, rather than being sexual with each other, they really are consoling each other. In the final scene there is a close-up of their hands touching, one woman's hand resting on top of the other's. Again, the context of the story makes it clear that this also is not a sexual moment. It is a tender moment and a reassuring gesture, but sexual it is not.

In *Hotel*, to cite another example, the lesbians are never shown together. The script uses a videotape as a device through which to bring the dead lover on camera. It could have used that same device to show the women together. Similarly, it could have used flashback to accomplish the same purpose. But it did not. The only shot of the lesbians together is in the still photos that remain in the apartment they shared and even here there is not a hint of sexuality or romance. We see close ups of very innocent "vacation" pictures; the two women might just as easily be companions and friends as lovers and partners for the previous six years. One photo shows the two women bicycling with two men, as heterosexual a depiction as possible given the story line.

In *Golden Girls*, recuperation is carried out in the looks, dress, and demeanor of the lesbian character. First, the lesbian part is played by Lois Nettleton, a well-known and respected actress. She is feminine, quiet, soft, and soft-spoken. She wears pretty dresses and high heels. Like the Carol Bowman character in *Hotel*, like Marilyn and Patti in *Heartbeat*, she is depicted visually as distinctly feminine. This kind of visual rendering combines with narrative story lines that produce characters who basically are desexualized.

The exception are the lesbian killers in *Hunter*. These characters are clearly not drawn in the timid fashion used with the other lesbians. They are at the opposite end of both the visual and the emotional spectrum. These women are obviously sexual. They dress in sophisticated, revealing clothes. ("The way she's dressed," says Hunter's partner of Sgt. Foster, "she's got herself a date.") Of all the lesbian characters under discussion, these two are the only ones who are shown expressing their sexual passion for each other. The following exchange, for example, takes place as we see a close-up of the two women, facing each other, their bodies touching as Casey runs her hand slowly down Valerie's cheek, throat, and low-cut blouse.

*Casey:* It's cold out, Val.

*Valerie:* When do I get my mink?

*Casey:* As soon as the dust clears. But you will look better in sable.

They have been given narrative permission to be sexual because they are evil and willing to use their sexuality to achieve evil ends. The young widow, after all, ensnared the millionaire into marriage, not for his love, but for his money. Her lover, Sgt. Foster, slept with Hunter to see what he would reveal about his investigation ("She thought I was going to be one of those after-sex talkers," Hunter tells his partner.) The connection seems clear: if they are sexual then they also must be vicious, greedy, deceitful, cunning, and deadly—direct inheritors of the film noir genre.

## Personal Rights

In both *Heartbeat* and *Hotel* the lesbian characters discover that they have limited personal rights and go on to accept that limitation without challenge. Marilyn, for example, agrees to her daughter's demand that lover Patti stay away from the wedding. When she confesses that to her lover,

Patti not only shows no anger or resentment but tells Marilyn that she should agree to whatever her daughter wants so as to seize this "golden moment."

At another point in the show, Marilyn recounts what happened when she revealed her sexual identity to her husband several years earlier. He effectively banished her from their home and demanded that she give up any claim on custody of their daughter. She agreed because she felt she had little choice.

And now, years later, Marilyn is still agreeing and feeling as though she has little choice. Not once does she insist on having the same rights as her ex-husband, who is bringing his new mate to the wedding without hesitation. Indeed, Marilyn's demeanor throughout conveys her sense of responsibility for having caused heartache in the life of her daughter. While she is continually agonizing over what she did in the past and what she should do to make things better in the present, it is the daughter who is given the right to be angry and enraged. If the daughter is mature enough to marry, one might argue that she is mature enough to accept her mother's choices. Yet her mother never makes that demand. Even though Marilyn admits that she is "terrified" to do it, we see her returning to her ex-husband's home to find her daughter and once again apologize for being who she is. Marilyn is positioned as the person who is at fault, a position she never takes issue with. Her daughter is positioned as the person who was injured or wronged and that gives her every right to vent her considerable anger both publicly and privately.

A similar kind of inequity of rights plays out in *Hotel*, only now it is the parent who is given the right to be angry and enraged and the lesbian daughter and her lover who must seek forgiveness for their transgression.

First we see, via videotape, the deceased daughter trying to explain to her father who she is and how she lives her life. It is an explanation she could never bring herself to make in person. As in *Heartbeat*, it is the lesbian whose appearance conveys nervousness and guilt, positions that carry over to the main character in the show, her lover, Carol Bowman.

This character emerges as a person without power or knowledge. We see her proceed through a series of steps, all attempts at discovering the real limitations of her world, her situation, herself. Her first step is to seek advice and emotional support from a friend and co-worker. The "tell me what to do, Julie" scene sets the stage for her encounters with the three individuals who really can determine her future and describe her personal rights. Carol goes to three men in succession to find out her fate. First, she meets with her boss, Mr. McDermott, to ask if her job is in jeopardy now that he knows about her sexual relationship with Joanne.

> *Carol:* Will this affect my job? I know people can be, well, oversensitive about . . . [pause] . . . things.

> *McDermott:* You should know by now: the only thing Miss Frances and I are sensitive about is the way our guests are treated.

Next Carol goes to her dead lover's father and briefly puts up her one fight. She tells Mr. Lambert that his daughter never got up the courage to actually mail him that videotape because she was afraid of his rejection. She accuses him of rarely phoning, never visiting, and now wanting to stake his claim on a daughter he barely knew.

> *Carol:* You think you can just sail in here and pick up the pieces. Well some of those pieces belong to me and you can't have them. . . . I'm going to fight you on this.

> *Lambert:* Don't do it, Miss Bowman. I will use the courts. I will use publicity, whatever it takes, and you will regret it. I swear you will.

Finally, she consults with a lawyer, but his advice in not encouraging.

> *Lawyer:* It's not what you or Mr. Lambert wants, but what state law dictates. In the absence of a will, Joanne's family becomes her sole heir. . . . Realistically, the most you could hope for is some sort of nuisance settlement, you know, to make you go away.

> *Carol:* But it's not fair.

> *Lawyer:* But it is the law. You know my advice to you is to ask yourself whether a court fight would be worth it. The time, the money, and [he gives her a knowing look] the public exposure.

It is only after these three men have spoken that Carol knows what she can and cannot do, what her rights are. Her lack of power and control over her own fate is reiterated three times over. Even though she is a lesbian she is a character very much living in and dominated by a man's world. And this she is neither willing to challenge nor to fight. Rather than expressing anger at her lack of legal standing, she acquiesces. She not only agrees to give up any claim to her small, personal treasures, she helps the man who is determined to take them away from her. And when he experiences the grief that she has been dealing with all along, it is she who unhesitatingly comforts him, her subservience to him emphasized all the more by her kneeling at his feet.

### *Public Disclosure*

The idea of public disclosure appears in the scripts of all five shows. In *Hunter*, the killer cop assures her lover that the worst that can happen to them is a little bad publicity. In *Hotel*, the father threatens to use publicity to win his case and the lawyer cautions that a court fight might not be worth the "public exposure." In *Heartbeat*, the daughter won't allow her mother's lesbian lover at her wedding because she wants things to go smoothly and because some of her friends don't know about her mother's sexual identity. The idea of keeping the lesbian character's sexual identity secret comes up in *Golden Girls* as well. And indeed, the decision is made to keep that identity private, even though the character says she prefers to be open about who she is.

Implicit in each of these constructions is the idea that public disclosure is likely to result in public scorn. This has interesting parallels in *I Passed for White*, a Hollywood film in which a light-skinned black woman tries to keep her identity hidden in an effort to win social approval or at least to avoid social rejection. Why, if being homosexual is acceptable, is it necessary for any of these characters to keep their identities secret? Obviously, the implied message in all these scripts suggests that it is not socially acceptable to be a lesbian, that caution is always advised in revealing these matters. Just as the lesbian characters show little heart for fighting for their personal rights, they show little inclination to reveal their personal identities. That message is revealed as much in how they look as in what they actually do. In *Hotel*, when her lawyer suggests she consider the public exposure, the camera cuts to a close-up of Carol to show her horrified countenance.

### CONCLUSION

We began this examination by asking whether the same strategies that have been used in constructing strong women characters in both early and later Hollywood films are being used today by American television in its recent introduction of lesbian characters to prime-time television. Our examination makes it clear that the answer is yes. Except for *Hunter*, in which recuperation is total, these scripts employ a certain amount of ambiguity in that lesbian characters are permitted some degree of victory in their own personal battles. But in almost every instance, that victory is balanced by other messages, both in the text and in the visual content of the shows, that suggest these characters have a long way to go before achieving equal status with their heterosexual counterparts.

When we ask a question that has become central to feminist film criticism—how are these characters not depicted?—several interesting answers emerge. They are not depicted as sexual or passionate, even when they are labeled as lovers in the script. They are not depicted as angry, even though their circumstances suggest they have many reasons to be so. They are not shown as independent or assertive, particularly when it comes to securing their own personal rights. They are not shown making demands but rather are seen continually agreeing to the demands of others.

When we ask how are they depicted visually, the other part of the equation falls into place. In dress and manner both, they are shown to be feminine but not sexy, never daring. Any kind of physical exchange with a female partner is either omitted altogether or drawn in the most timid way (a hand resting atop another hand, a sweet but sexless hug). Close-ups of their faces often reveal an agonizing look, a repeated suggestion that their sexuality has caused others problems and for this they must take the blame and suffer the consequences.

These are not scripts that argue for the rights, legal or otherwise, of homosexuals. They are, instead, productions designed to attract mass audiences who will have varying degrees of willingness to accept any lesbian depictions in the first place. Just as Hollywood producers have been careful to incorporate a degree of polysemy into their cinematic texts, so too are American television producers careful to avoid alienating audience members by producing scripts that might be construed as too strident. While it may be argued that these scripts are by design relatively unconcerned with gay rights and more concerned with ratings, it is also true that once-taboo subjects in both cinema and television have gained acceptance only gradually. This may not be the first choice of feminists and lesbians, but it is a first step in working toward at least a small measure of social change.

## WORKS CITED

Cook, Pam. 1978. "Duplicity in *Mildred Pierce*." In E. Ann Kaplan, ed., *Women and Film Noir*, pp. 68–82. London: British Film Institute.

Gledhill, Christine. 1978. "*Klute*: Part 2: Feminism and *Klute*." In E. Ann Kaplan, ed., *Women and Film Noir*, pp. 112–128. London: British Film Institute.

Henry, William. 1987. "That Certain Subject." *Channels* (April), pp. 43–45.

Kaplan, E. Ann. 1982. *Women and Film*. New York and London: Methuen.

Kuhn, Annette. 1982. *Women's Pictures: Feminism and Cinema*. London: Routledge and Kegan Paul.

Lovell, Terry, and Simon Frith. 1981. "How Do You Get Pleasure? Another Look at *Klute*." *Screen Education*, 39:15–24.

Moritz, Marguerite J. 1989. "Coming Out Stories: The Creation of Lesbian Images on Prime Time TV." *Journal of Communication Inquiry*, vol. 13, no. 2.

Walker, Janet. 1982. "Feminist Critical Practice: Female Discourse in *Mildred Pierce*." In *Film Readers: Feminist Film Criticism*, pp. 164–172. Evanston, Ill.: Northwestern University Press.

# | 48 |

# *Culture Stays Screen-Shy of Showing the Gay Kiss*

FRANK BRUNI

As popular television shows and movies slouch toward greater inclusion of sympathetic gay characters, the step they seem most reluctant to take is the candid portrayal of same-sex desire or intimacy.

They recoil from kisses.

*Philadelphia* does not have one, an omission that has triggered widespread debate and disappointment among gay audiences.

*Six Degrees of Separation* does—sort of. It suggests two men kissing, but the smooch is obscured from view because star Will Smith refused to pucker up.

And the TV show *Roseanne* may or may not have one, depending on the outcome of Roseanne Arnold's battle with network executives. She says they have refused to air an episode in which her character ventures into a gay bar and brushes lips with Mariel Hemingway.

*Detroit Free Press*, February 11, 1994, p. 1.

Whether or not Arnold wins, this much is already clear: On the big and little screens, a kiss is not just a kiss when the lips engaged belong to two women or two men.

"I think it really is the flashpoint," said gay playwright and screenwriter Paul Rudnick, who scripted *Addams Family Values* and writes a monthly column on the film industry for *Premiere* magazine.

Rudnick and others note that this taboo reflects the feelings of many Americans who believe it's OK for gays to do what they want behind closed doors, but not to "flaunt" their sexual orientation in public. Asked to define flaunting, many of these people mention kissing.

Seeing a same-sex couple kiss makes it impossible for an observer to think about homosexuality only as an abstraction or to interpret warm interaction between two men or two women as something else—something less disturbing.

"It's indisputably real," said Martin Duberman, founder and director of the Center for Lesbian and Gay Studies at the City University of New York.

"If you hear two people talking affectionately, you can still fit that into your brain in one of a variety of categories—these people just have a friendship, or just care about each other," Duberman said. "But if you see two people romantically kissing, you can't avoid thinking about where that may lead—genital sex."

Such kisses have indeed been shared in the past, both in movies and on TV.

In the 1971 British film *Sunday, Bloody Sunday*, for example, Peter Finch kissed Murray Head; he said in interviews at the time that he got through the scene by closing his eyes and thinking of England.

There have been gay kisses or clear intimations of gay sex in a host of other films as well, from *Personal Best*, with Mariel Hemingway, to *My Own Private Idaho*, with the late River Phoenix; and from *Cruising*, which plumbed sadomasochism, to *Midnight Express*, which journeyed into a Turkish prison.

But nearly all these films either served up their gay and lesbian characters as eccentrics, put them in exotic milieus or were marketed, at least initially, to a limited audience, usually the sophisticated art-house crowd.

One of the few exceptions, 1982's mass-marketed *Making Love*, couldn't recruit a big-name star—Michael Douglas and Harrison Ford turned down the lead role ultimately played by

Michael Ontkean—and did a belly flop at the box office.

Mainstream TV shows that have dared to broach gay physical affection have beat quick retreats.

One episode of *thirtysomething* opened with two men in bed together sharing post-coital thoughts; protests from viewers and sponsors made ABC pull the episode from syndication, never to be broadcast again.

A bisexual attorney on *L.A. Law* planted a kiss on a confused but excited female colleague's lips; after, the storyline abruptly stopped.

Although last month's TV miniseries *Tales of the City* went further than these programs, showing a prolonged deep kiss between two gay men, it was broadcast not by one of the four big networks but by PBS—and some local affiliates declined to air it.

The reluctance of those producing mainstream commercial entertainments to show lesbians or gay men kissing has plenty of precedents and parallels.

Even to this day, it's rare to see an interracial couple kiss on-screen. It's not all that common, either, to see an elderly or ugly couple kiss.

Hollywood traffics in idealized fantasies, and the ideal that contemporary American culture has developed for romance and passion is "youth, beauty, Caucasian skin and heterosexuality," noted Rudnick.

Images of gay and lesbian affection, though, carry the extra baggage of homophobia, which the entertainment industry is confronting and battling at a slow pace, careful not to get too far ahead of its public.

"It's certainly getting better," said Scott Robbe, founder of a Los Angeles group of openly gay writers, producers, directors and actors called Out in Film. Robbe notes that *Philadelphia*, as a big-budget, big-star vehicle focusing on a gay character, marks an impressive milestone with or without a kiss.

Robbe said the next test was to see what happens with *Interview With the Vampire*, an adaptation of Anne Rice's book now filming in New Orleans. According to published reports, star Tom Cruise has demanded that the story's homoerotic content be toned down; Cruise has denied this.

One of the heads of production happens to be Hollywood titan David Geffen, who is openly gay.

"Geffen has been fabulous in the past few

years," said Robbe. "*Interview with the Vampire* will be a good indicator of how mature Hollywood has become in regard to gay and lesbian themes."

Gay cultural critics and activists say putting same-sex kisses on-screen—and giving those kisses to respectable, appealing characters in unremarkable settings—is a vital step toward full acceptance of gays in society at large.

Unlike bizarre scenes of gays in strange underground bars, which movies have seldom hesitated to show, a simple kiss affirms not how different gays and lesbians are to everyone else, but how similar.

"It's proof," Rudnick said. "It's proof of our humanity."

▼ ▼ ▼

NEW YORK (AP) — There may not be a kiss-off for *Roseanne* after all.

ABC said Thursday it will air an episode of the popular comedy March 1 that features Roseanne Arnold exchanging a kiss with Mariel Hemingway in a gay bar.

Exactly how that encounter will play remains to be seen, according to ABC spokesman Steve Battaglio, who said the segment had been shot but postproduction was not complete.

"There have been discussions concerning how the kiss will be depicted," Battaglio said. "Those talks are continuing."

He said the episode will also carry a parental discretion advisory.

In the episode, titled "Don't Ask, Don't Tell," Arnold's character, Roseanne Conner, goes to a bar with bisexual friend Nancy, played by Sandra Bernhard. After dancing with Hemingway, Roseanne makes a wisecrack that is misinterpreted. The kiss results.

Earlier this month, Tom Arnold, husband of the star and the series' co-executive producer, charged that ABC was refusing to air the episode because of the kiss. He called the network's decision misguided and "homophobic," adding, "Roseanne is shocked."

"We've always been supportive of the episode," Battaglio said. "The network is working with the Arnolds to bring this to a conclusion that both parties will be satisfied with."

# | 49 |

## *Do Ask, Do Tell: Freak Talk on TV*

### JOSHUA GAMSON

At the end of his 22 years, when Pedro Zamora lost his capacity to speak, all sorts of people stepped into the vacuum created by multifocal leukoencephalopathy, the AIDS-related brain disease that shut him up. MTV began running a marathon of The Real World, its seven-kids-in-an-apartment-with-the-cameras-running show on which Pedro Zamora starred as Pedro Zamora, a version of himself: openly gay, Miami Cuban, HIV-positive, youth activist. MTV offered the marathon as a tribute to Zamora, which it was, and as a way to raise funds, especially crucial since Zamora, like so many people with HIV, did not have private insurance. Yet, of course, MTV was also paying tribute to itself, capitalizing on Pedro's death without quite seeming as monstrous as all that.

President Clinton and Florida Governor Lawton Chiles made public statements and publicized phone calls to the hospital room, praising Zamora as a heroic point of light rather than as the routinely outspoken critic of their own HIV and AIDS policies. The Clinton administration,

*American Prospect*, Fall 1995, no. 23, pp. 44–50.

in the midst of its clampdown on Cuban immigration, even granted immigration visas to Zamora's three brothers and a sister in Cuba—a kindly if cynical act, given the realities of people with AIDS awaiting visas and health care in Guantanamo Bay.

Thus, according to People magazine, did Zamora reach a bittersweet ending. He was unable to see, hear, or speak, yet with his family reunited, "his dream had come true." Behind the scenes, one who was there for Zamora's last weeks told me, the family actually separated Zamora from his boyfriend, quite out of keeping with the "dreams" of Pedro's life. When Pedro had his own voice, he had spoken powerfully of how antigay ideology and policy, typically framed as "pro-family," contributed to teen suicides and the spread of HIV; in death, those speaking for him emphasized individual heroism and the triumph of the heterosexual family.

That others appropriated Zamora on his deathbed hardly tarnishes his accomplishment. As an MTV star, Pedro had probably reduced suffering by more lesbian and gay teenagers, and generally affected the thinking of more teenagers, than a zillion social service programs. He spoke publicly to millions in his own words and with the backing of a reputable media institution, and he did not just tell them to wear condoms, or that AIDS is an equal-opportunity destroyer, and he did not just explicitly fill in the sexual blanks left by prudish government prevention campaigns. He also told them and showed them: Here is me loving my boyfriend; here is what a self-possessed gay man looks like, hanging out with his roommates; here is what my Cuban family might have to say about my bringing home a black man; here is me at an AIDS demonstration, getting medical news, exchanging love vows.

To speak for and about yourself as a gay man or a lesbian on television, to break silences that are systematically and ubiquitously enforced in public life, is profoundly political. "Don't tell" is more than a U.S. military policy; it remains U.S. public policy, formally and informally, on sex and gender nonconformity. Sex and gender outsiders-gay men, transsexuals, lesbians, bisexuals-are constantly invited to lose their voices, or suffer the consequences (job losses, baseball bats) of using them. Outside of the occasional opening on MTV or sporadic coverage of a demonstration or a parade, if one is not Melissa Etheridge or David Geffen, opportunities to speak for oneself as a nonheterosexual, or to listen to one, are few and

far between. Even if the cameras soon turn elsewhere, these moments are big breakthroughs, and they are irresistible, giddy moments for the shut-up.

Yet, in a media culture, holding the microphone and the spotlight is a complicated sort of power, not just because people grab them back from you but because they are never really yours. If you speak, you must prepare to be used. The voice that comes out is not quite yours: It is like listening to yourself on tape (a bit deeper, or more clipped) or to a version dubbed by your twin. It is you and it is not you. Zamora's trick, until his voice was taken, was to walk the line between talking and being dubbed. The troubling question, for the silenced and the heard alike, is whether the line is indeed walkable. Perhaps the best place to turn for answers is the main public space in which the edict to shut up is reversed: daytime television talk shows.

## DAYTIME EXPOSURE

For lesbians, gay men, bisexuals, drag queens, or transsexuals, or some combination thereof, watching daytime television has got to be spooky. Suddenly, there are renditions of you, chattering away in a system that otherwise ignores or steals your voice at every turn. Sally Jessy Raphael wants to know what it's like to pass as a different sex, Phil Donahue wants to support you in your battle against gay bashing, Ricki Lake wants to get you a date, Oprah Winfrey wants you to love without lying. Most of all, they all want you to talk about it publicly, just at a time when everyone else wants you not to. They are interested, if not precisely in "reality," at least not (with possible exceptions) in fictional accounts. For people whose desires and identities go against the norm, this is the only spot in mainstream media culture to speak on our own terms or to hear others speaking for themselves. The fact that it is so much maligned, and for so many good reasons, does not close the case.

I happened to turn on the Ricki Lake Show yesterday, for example, which, as the fastest rising talk show ever, has quickly reached first place among its target audience of 18-to-34-year-old women. The topic: "I don't want gays around my kids." I caught the last twenty minutes of what amounted to a pro-gay screamfest. Ricki and her audience explicitly attacked a large woman who was denying visitation rights to her gay ex-husband ("I had to explain to a nine-year-old what 'gay' means," and "My child started having night-mares after he visited his father"). And they went at a young couple who believed in keeping children away from gay people on the grounds that the Bible says "homosexuals should die." The gay guests and their supporters had the last word, brought on to argue, to much audience whooping, that loving gays are a positive influence and hateful heterosexuals should stay away from children. The antigay guests were denounced on any number of grounds, by host, other guests, and numerous audience members: They are denying children loving influences, they are bigots, they are misinformed, they read the Bible incorrectly, they sound like Mormons, they are resentful that they have put on more weight than their exes. One suburban-looking audience member angrily addressed each "child protector" in turn, along the way coming up with my new favorite apostrophe, and possible new pageant theme, as she lit into a blue-dressed woman: "And as for you, Miss Homophobia . . ."

The show was a typical mess, with guests yelling and audiences hooting at the best one-liners about bigotry or body weight, but the virulence with which homophobia was attacked is both typical of these shows and stunning. When Ms. Lake cut off a long-sideburned man's argument that "it's a fact that the easiest way to get AIDS is by homosexual sex" ("That is not a fact, sir, that is not correct"), I found myself ready to start the chant of "Go, Ricki! Go, Ricki!" that apparently wraps each taping. Even such elementary corrections, and even such a weird form of visibility and support, stand out sharply. Here, the homophobe is the deviant, the freak.

Lake's show is among the new breed of rowdy youth-oriented programs, celebrated as "rock and roll television" by veteran Geraldo Rivera and denigrated as "exploitalk" by cultural critic Neal Gabler. Their sibling shows, the older, tamer "service" programs such as Oprah and Donahue, support "alternative" sexualities and genders in quieter, but not weaker, ways. Peruse last year's Donahue: two teenage lesbian lovers ("Young, courageous people like yourself are blazing the way for other people," says Phil), a gay construction worker suing his gay boss for harassment ("There's only eight states that protect sexual persuasion," his attorney informs), a bisexual minister, a black lesbian activist and two members of the African American theater group Pomo Afro Homos ("We're about trying to build a black gay community," says one), the stars of the gender-crossing Priscilla, Queen of the Desert ("I have a lot of friends that are transsexuals," declares an audience member, "and they're the neatest people"), heterosexuals whose best friends are gay, lesbians starting families, gay teens, gay cops, gay men reuniting with their high school sweethearts, a gay talk show. This is a more diverse, self-possessed, and politically outspoken group of non-heterosexuals than I might find, say, at the gay bar around the corner; I can only imagine what this means for people experiencing sexual difference where none is locally visible.

Certainly Donahue makes moves to counter its "liberal" reputation, inviting right-wing black preachers and widely discredited and relatively loony "psychologist" Paul Cameron, who argues that cross-dressing preceded the fall of Rome, that people with AIDS should be quarantined, and that sexuality "is going to get us." But more often than not, Phil himself is making statements about how "homophobia is global" and "respects no nation," how "we're beating up homosexual people, calling them names, throwing them out of apartments, jobs." The "we" being asserted is an "intolerant" population that needs to get over itself. We are, he says at times, "medieval." In fact, Donahue regularly asserts that "for an advanced, so-called, 'industrialized' nation, I think we're the worst." Questioning an officer about the treatment of gay police, for example, he cannot stop the almost desperate how're-we-doing flow: "But what would you say, regarding law enforcement today? How are we? Are we getting there? Are you pleased? Is it better than in the military? Is it worse? What?"

Oprah Winfrey, the industry leader, is less concerned with the political treatment of difference; she is overwhelmingly oriented towards "honesty" and "openness," especially in interpersonal relationships. As on Lake's show, lesbians and gays are routinely included without incident in more general themes (meeting people through personal ads, fools for love, sons and daughters you never knew), and bigotry is routinely attacked. But Winfrey's distinctive mark is an attack on lies, and thus the closet comes under attack—especially the gay male closet—not just for the damage it does to those in it, but for the betrayals of women it engenders.

On a recent program in which a man revealed his "orientation" after 19 years of marriage, for example, the biggest concern of both Winfrey and her audience was not that Steve is gay, but that he was not up-front with his wife. As Winfrey put it on that program, "For me, always the issue is how you can be more truthful in your life." One of Steve's two supportive sons echoes Winfrey ("I want people to be able to be who they are"), as does his ex-wife, whose anger is widely supported by the audience ("It makes me feel like my life has been a sham"), and the requisite psychologist ("The main thing underneath all of this is the importance of loving ourselves and being honest and authentic and real in our lives"). Being truthful, revealing secrets, learning to love oneself: These are the staples of Winfrey-style talk shows. Because of them, not only do gay and bisexual guests find a place to speak as gays and bisexuals, but the pathology becomes not sexual "deviance" but the socially imposed closet.

All of this, however, should not be mistaken for dedicated friendship. Even when ideological commitments to truth and freedom are at work, the primary commitment of talk shows is, of course, to money. What makes these such inviting spots for nonconforming sex and gender identities has mostly to do with the niche talk shows have carved out for ratings. The shows are about talk; the more silence there has been on a subject, the more not-telling, the better talk topic it is. On talk shows, as media scholar Wayne Munson points out in his book All Talk, "differences are no longer repressed" but "become the talk show's emphasis," as the shows confront "boredom and channel clutter with constant, intensified novelty and 'reality.' " Indeed, according to Munson, Richard Mincer, Donahue's executive producer, encourages prospective guests "to be especially unique or different, to take advantage of rather than repress difference."

## THIS SIDE OF A FISTFIGHT

While they highlight different sex and gender identities, expressions, and practices, the talk shows can be a dangerous place to speak and a difficult place to get heard. With around 20 syndicated talk shows competing for audiences, shows that trade in confrontation and surprise (Ricki Lake, Jenny Jones, Jerry Springer) are edging out the milder, topical programs (Oprah, Donahue). Although Winfrey is still number one, with an estimated 9.4 million viewers, her ratings have declined significantly. Unquestionably, "exploitalk" is winning out, and the prize is big: A successful talk show, relatively cheap to produce, can reportedly make more than $50 million a year in profits.

One way to the prize, the "ambush" of guests with surprises, is fast becoming a talk show staple. As Ricki Lake, whose show reaches an estimated audience of 5.8 million, told a reporter, the ambush "does so much for the energy of the show." Even without an ambush, a former Jane Whitney Show producer told TV Guide, "When you're booking guests, you're thinking, 'How much confrontation can this person provide me?' The more confrontation, the better. You want people just this side of a fistfight."

For members of groups already subject to violence, the visibility of television can prompt more than just a fistfight, as this year's Jenny Jones murder underlined. In March, when Scott Amedure appeared on a "secret admirer" episode of the Jenny Jones Show (currently number three in the national syndicated talk show ratings), the admired Jonathan Schmitz was apparently expecting a female admirer. Schmitz, not warming to Amedure's fantasy of tying him up in a hammock and spraying whipped cream and champagne on his body, declared himself "100 percent heterosexual." Later, back in Michigan, he punctuated this claim by shooting Amedure with a 12-gauge shotgun, telling police that the embarrassment from the program had "eaten away" at him. Or, as he reportedly put it in his 911 call, Amedure "fucked me on national TV."

Critics were quick to point out that programming that creates conflict tends to exacerbate it. "The producers made professions of regret," Gabler wrote in the Los Angeles Times after the Amedure murder, "but one suspects what they really regretted was the killer's indecency of not having pulled out his rifle and committed the crime before their cameras." In the wake of the murder, talk show producers were likened over and over to drug dealers:

Publicist Ken Maley told the San Francisco Chronicle that "they've got people strung out on an adrenaline rush," and "they keep raising the dosage"; sociologist Vicki Abt told People that "TV allows us to mainline deviance"; Michelangelo Signorile argued in Out that some talk show producers "are like crack dealers scouring trailer park America." True enough. Entering the unruly talk show world one tends to become, at best, a source of adrenaline rush, and at worst a target of violence.

What most reporting tended to gloss, however, was that most antigay violence does not require a talk show "ambush" to trigger it. Like the Oakland County, Michigan, prosecutor, who argued that "Jenny Jones's producers' cynical pursuit of ratings and total insensitivity to what could occur here left one person dead and Mr. Schmitz now facing life in prison," many critics focused on the "humiliating" surprise attack on Schmitz with the news that he was desired by another man. As in the image of the "straight" soldier being ogled in the shower, in this logic the revelation of same-sex desire is treated as the danger, and the desired as a victim. The talk show critics thus played to the same "don't tell" logic that makes talk shows such a necessary, if uncomfortable, refuge for some of us.

Although producers' pursuit of ratings is indeed, unsurprisingly, cynical and insensitive, the talk show environment is one of the very few in which the declaration of same-sex desire (and, to a lesser degree, atypical gender identity) is common, heartily defended, and often even incidental. Although they overlook this in their haste to hate trash, the critics of exploitative talk shows help illuminate the odd sort of opportunity these cacophonous settings provide. Same-sex desires become "normalized" on these programs not so much because different sorts of lives become clearly visible, but because they get sucked into the spectacular whirlpool of relationship conflicts. They offer a particular kind of visibility and voice. On yesterday's Ricki Lake, it was the voice of an aggressive, screechy gay man who continually reminded viewers, between laughing at his own nasty comments, that he was a regular guy. On other days, it's the take-your-hands-off-my-woman lesbian, or the I'm-more-of-a-woman-than-you'll-ever-be transsexual. Here is the first voice talk shows promote, one price of entry into mainstream public visibility: the vicious one, shouting that we gay people can be as mean, or petty, or just plain loud, as anybody else.

## SPECTACLE AND CONVERSATION

The guests on the talk shows seem to march in what psychologist Jeanne Heaton, coauthor of the forthcoming Tuning in Trouble, calls a "parade of pathology." Many talk shows have more than a passing resemblance to freak shows. Neal Gabler, for example, argues that guests are invited to exhibit "their deformities for attention" in a "ritual of debasement" aimed primarily at reassuring the audience of its superiority. Indeed, the evidence for dehumanization is all over the place, especially when it comes to gender crossing, as in the titles of various recent Geraldo programs, in which the calls of sideshow barkers echo: "Star-crossed cross-dressers: bizarre stories of transvestites and their lovers," and "Outrageous impersonators and flamboyant drag queens," and "When your husband wears the dress in the family," and "Girly to burly: women who became men." As long as talk shows make their bids by being, in Gabler's words, "a psychological freak show," sex and gender outsiders entering them arguably reinforce their inhuman, outsider status, by entering a discourse in which they are bizarre, outrageous, flamboyant curiosities. (Often when they do this, for example, they must relinquish their right to define themselves to the ubiquitous talk show "experts.")

Talk shows do indeed trade on voyeurism, and it is no secret that those who break with sex and gender norms and fight with each other on camera help the shows win higher ratings. But there is more to the picture. This is the place where "freaks" talk back. It is a place where Conrad, born and living in a female body, can assert against Sally Jessy Raphael's claims that he "used and betrayed" women in order to have sex with them, that women fall in love with him as a man because he considers himself a man; where months later, in a program on "our most outrageous former guests" (all gender crossers), Conrad can reappear, declare himself to have started hormone treatment, and report that the woman he allegedly "used and betrayed" has stood by him. This is a narrow opening, but an opening nonetheless, for the second voice promoted by the talk show: the proud voice of the "freak," even if the freak refuses that term. The fact that talk shows are exploitative spectacles does not negate the fact that they are also opportunities; as Munson points out, they are both spectacle and conversation. They give voice to those systematically silenced, albeit under conditions out of the speaker's control, and in voices that come out tinny, scratched, distant.

These voices, even when they are discounted, which is often enough, in fact sometimes do more than just assert themselves. The people from whom they emerge, whatever their motivations, can sometimes wind up doing more then just pulling up a chair at a noisy, crowded table. Every so often, they wind up messing with sexual categories in a way that goes beyond a simple expansion of them. Talk shows attract viewers not only through public airings of personal problems, but also through public airings of problematic persons. In addition to reaffirming heterosexuality as normal and natural, or affirming both heterosexuality and homosexuality as normal and natural, talk show producers often make entertainment by mining the in-between: finding guests who are interesting exactly because they don't fit existing notions of "gay" and "straight" and "man" and "woman," raising the provocative suggestion that the categories are not quite working.

The last time I visited the Maury Povich Show, for instance, I found myself distracted by Jason and Tiffanie. Jason, a large 18-year-old from a small town in Ohio, was in love with Calvin. Calvin was having an affair with Jamie (Jason's twin sister, also the mother of a three-month-old), who was interested in Scott, who had sex with, as I recall, both Calvin and Tiffanie. Tiffanie, who walked on stage holding Jamie's hand, had pretty much had sex with everyone except Jamie. During group sex, Tiffanie explained, she and Jamie did not touch each other. "We're not lesbians," she loudly asserted, against the noisy protestations of some audience members.

The studio audience, in fact, was quick to condemn the kids, who were living together in a one-bedroom apartment with Jamie's baby. Their response was predictably accusatory: You are freaks, some people said; immoral, said others; pathetically bored and in need of a hobby, others asserted. Still other aspects of the "discussion" assumed the validity and normality of homosexuality. Jason, who had recently attempted suicide, was told he needed therapy to help him come to terms with his sexuality, and the other boys were told they too needed to "figure themselves out." Yet much talk also struggled to attach sexual labels to an array of partnerships anarchic enough to throw all labels into disarray. "If you are not lesbians, why were you holding hands?" one woman asked Tiffanie. "If you are not gay," another audience member asked Calvin, "how is it you came to have oral sex with two young men?"

This mix was typically contradictory: condemnation of "immoral sex" but not so much of homosexuality per se, openly gay and bisexual teenagers speaking for themselves while their partners in homosexual activities declare heterosexual identities, a situation in which sexual categories are both assumed and up for grabs. I expect the young guests were mainly in it for the free trip to New York, and the studio audience was mainly in it for the brush with television. Yet the discussion they created, the unsettling of categoric assumptions about genders and desires, if only for a few moments in the midst of judgment and laughter, is found almost nowhere else this side of fiction.

The importance of these conversations, both for those who for safety must shut up about their sexual and gender identities, and for those who never think about them, is certainly underestimated. The level of exploitation is certainly not. Like Pedro Zamora, one can keep one's voice for a little while, one finger on the commercial megaphone, until others inevitably step in to claim it for their own purposes. Or one can talk for show, as freak, or expert, or rowdy—limits set by the production strategies within the talk show genre.

Those limits, not the talk shows themselves, are really the point. The story here is not about commercial exploitation, but about just how effective the prohibition on asking and telling is in the United States, how stiff the penalties are, how unsafe this place is for people of atypical sexual and gender identities. You know you're in trouble when Sally Jessy Raphael (strained smile and forced tear behind red glasses) seems your best bet for being heard, understood, respected, and protected.

That for some of us the loopy, hollow light of talk shows seems a safe, shielding haven should give us all pause.

# | 50 |

## More Than Friends

### DAVID EHRENSTEIN

Thursday morning at Paramount studios. On the set of the NBC series Frasier, Daphne is enjoying a rare intimate moment with Frasier's brother, Niles. The cast is rehearsing an episode that is still five days from filming, so no cameras are present and the audience seats overlooking the stage are empty. Jane Leeves, who plays Daphne, is ballroom dancing with David Hyde Pierce, who plays Niles.

Suddenly, she extends one leg high into the air, then lowers it gently onto his shoulder. He can't resist pulling her sensuously toward him. Nearby, standing halfway between the familiar living-room set and the radio-station set, watching the actors intently, is Kelsey Grammer, the show's star and—for this episode, at least—its director. On a movie set, the director is all-powerful, but here in television, the real power lies with the eleven writers standing off to the side, pens in hand. When questions arise about a line or a piece of business, all eyes inevitably turn to them. In response to Grammer's suggestion that a punch line may not be working, one writer assures him, "We're already working on it." When Pierce wants to trim a speech, he seeks a nod of approval from the scribes. Sitcoms are a writer's medium.

The cast prepares to run through the show's opening scene. Grammer sits behind the console of the radio-station set and starts right in from the top. "I think we have time for one call," he says, pushing a button on the telephone console, perfectly in character as radio therapist Frasier Crane. "Hello, Marianne, I'm listening."

"Okay, here it is, Dr. Crane," says a script assistant over a studio speaker. (When the show airs, the caller's voice will be performed by special guest Jodie Foster.) "If my husband and I don't have sex in the next two days I'm going to a department store to pick up a stranger."

Grammer's eyebrows rise a fraction of an inch, but before he can respond, the caller gasps. "Oh, Timmy, look who's here—Nana and Pop-Pop. I'll call you back, Dr. Crane," she says, hanging up.

"To all you Mariannes out there," Grammer says after a long, slow take, "sex with a stranger is never the answer. Better pack the kids off with Nana and Pop-Pop, lead your husband to a sturdy kitchen table, and let the postman ring twice."

It's one of the best lines in the script, and nobody has any doubt who thought of it: staff writer Joe Keenan. "Joe is our Preston Sturges," says fellow writer Anne Fiett-Giordano. "He always seems to come up with the best lines."

Before coming to California to write for Frasier, Keenan was a successful novelist in New York. If he had any dramatic aspirations, they were to write for the Broadway musical stage, not TV.

But two summers ago, Frasier executive producer David Lloyd found himself at a beach on Martha's Vineyard, laughing helplessly while reading Keenan's novel Blue Heaven. "I'd seen a blurb in the New York Times," recalls Lloyd, whose credits include The Mary Tyler Moore Show, Taxi and Cheers. "They said it was as if P. G. Wodehouse had written a gay mafia novel—so I just had to read it." An admitted heterosexual, Lloyd sensed that the openly gay Keenan had the right style for a show like Frasier.

Keenan was hired, and this year he won a Writers Guild Award for an episode in which Grammer is mistaken for gay by a romantically

*Los Angeles Magazine*, May 1996.

inclined male coworker. "Joe Keenan is terrifically talented, a marvel of good taste," says Grammer. "In the gay community, it's acceptable to be very entertaining and charming and witty and urbane. I think everybody should be doing it more often. There are so many dull straight men. They don't seem to want to state an opinion." (Grammer recently optioned the film rights to The Only Thing Worse You Could Have Told Me, a play about gay life by Frasier regular Dan Butler, who, ironically, plays the show's aggressively heterosexual jock, Bulldog.)

There is nothing out of the ordinary about hiring a gay writer to write a straight sitcom. Besides Keenan, the Frasier staff boasts David Lee, a Cheers veteran and co-creator of Wings; and former Kate & Allie writer Chuck Ranberg, who was discovered by Lloyd after he saw a staged reading of Ranberg's successful gay comedy End Of The World Party. There are openly gay and lesbian writers on almost every major prime-time situation comedy you can think of, including Friends, Seinfeld, Murphy Brown, Roseanne, Mad About You, The Nanny, Wings, The Single Guy Caroline in the City, Coach, Dave's World, Home Court, High Society, The Crew and the new Boston Common. Screenwriter Douglas Carter Beane (To Wong Foo, Thanks For Everything—Julie Newmar) is developing a series for the Carsey-Werner company about a straight woman and her gay roommate. The "out" gay writing team of James Berg and Stan Zimmerman (The Brady Bunch Movie) has created a new Fox series called Mommy & Me for Pauly Shore. (Yes, Pauly Shore.) And Kelsey Grammer has a sitcom in development. "Part of it takes place in a drag bar,' he says, and I would imagine that some of the drag queens might be gay." In short, when it comes to sitcoms, gays rule.

Of course, the whole world hasn't gone "gay all of a sudden," as Cary Grant put it in Bringing Up Baby. Sodomy laws remain on the books in more than 20 states, gay-bashing incidents continue to occur with alarming frequency and we still hear antigay diatribes from major presidential candidates. In Hollywood, closeted performers still feel obliged to hide their sexuality behind arranged marriages and publicists who prevent their clients from discussing their "personal lives." In spite of all this, a growing number of talents, unperturbed by their sexual status, have risen through the ranks to dominate sitcoms as never before.

"Gays were always a fact in this industry—a rampant, wonderful, joyous fact," says Mel Brooks, who began his career in television. "In the past, it was never out there, never mainstream. Now it's becoming mainstream." This season, The Crew, High Society, Roseanne, The Larry Sanders Show and the fleeting Pursuit of Happiness had recurring gay characters. There were also the much publicized gay-wedding episodes of Roseanne and Friends. And one week last fall, NBCs entire "Must See TV" lineup—Friends, Frasier, The Single Guy and Seinfeld—featured episodes in which straights were mistaken for gays.

But gay-themed episodes and individual gay characters are really beside the point. In a way, all the episodes of these shows are gay. Like the Jewish moguls who ran Hollywood in the studio era, gay and lesbian sitcom writers are keen observers of the majority culture that surrounds them. MGM's Andy Hardy is a perfect example of how the Jews understood the Gentile sensibility better than the Gentiles did themselves. But where the studio-era Jews were loathe to acknowledge—much less promote—themselves, the gay and lesbian TV writers of today have been pushing the envelope every chance they get. In fact, they're encouraged to do so. Since current comedies are positively obsessed with the intimate sex lives of straight young singles, who better to write them than members of a minority famed for its sexual candor? Keenan's postman joke is exhibit A.

"So much of television has to do with the politics of sexual relationships," says Phil Hartman, star of the sex-obsessed NewsRadio and a veteran of the equally libidinous Saturday Night Live. "The gay community has always had a delightful sense of sarcasm about sexual mores. Unfortunately, to a large segment of our society, gay people are viewed as sexual outlaws . . . God forbid a straight person should acknowledge that there are pleasures associated with their anus. That's a big, big door that people don't want to open."

As a result of the influx of gay writers, even the most heterosexual of sitcoms often possess that most elusive of undertones—the "gay sensibility"—Frasier being a case in point.

Frasier's David Lee is sitting with writing partner Keenan in a plush, wood-paneled office at Paramount, speaking proudly of their series of episodes in which Mercedes Ruehl guest-starred as a domineering station manager who clashes with Frasier professionally, only to find herself attracted to him sexually. The icy Kate and the reserved Frasier throw caution out the window and engage in some precipitous quasi-public sex before coming to their senses. "It was one of the truest arcs of a relationship I've ever seen," Lee says. The affair "began with the passion born out of naughtiness, continued with the passion born out of the fear of discovery, then ended with the two finally getting to know one another on their first—and last—date, and finding they had absolutely nothing in common!"

The story arc seems like a perfect dramatization of a relationship more associated with gays than straights—particularly those who view first-date sex as a matter of course. But Lee shies away from the inference. "I really can't isolate anything about approaches to comedy that is common to the gay writers on the show and not the straight ones," he says. "I can't either," Keenan adds.

"The only thing you will notice," continues Lee, starting to laugh, "is when the subject turns to basketball, Joe, Chuck [Ranberg] and I tend to get up and walk out. Likewise, when it turns to Broadway shows, there's a different exodus."

"Except for David Lloyd, of course," says Keenan of his discoverer. "He's the only straight Broadway show queen I know."

Keenan and Lee banter with the sort of easy camaraderie that many gay men—even if they've known each other briefly—fall into almost automatically. They finish each other's sentences and top off each other's jokes. As they sit back in the office's comfortable chairs, they look less like a pair of TV writers on a high-pressure deadline than a couple of gay supersophisticates having an afternoon coffee. In truth, they're both.

They agree that most gay writers favor playfully malicious dialogue and larger-than-life characters. And they're in sympathy with New York culture critic Jeff Weinstein, who famously remarked: "No, there's no such thing as a gay sensibility, and yes, it has an immense impact on the arts." But, they see it working a bit differently in sitcoms.

"I can understand camp as something that's a little nailed down as specifically gay," says Keenan, "but none of the shows on right now really traffic in camp. All sitcom characters have to be taken seriously on some level, and camp isn't serious."

"When you talk about a gay sensibility," suggests Lee, "you're starting to describe a very urban, very educated—"

"—ironic, detached, iconoclastic attitude," adds Keenan.

"But look," says Lee, "All I have to do is walk down the street into a number of bars and I can show you gay people who don't have a single qualification for a gay sensibility."

Other gays in the industry feel the sensibility question isn't quite so obscure, especially when it comes to Frasier, whose decidedly unmacho leads—Grammer and Pierce—frequently recall comic legends Edward Everett Horton and Franklin Pangborn in their 1930s heyday.

"Frasier has lucked out in terms of gay sensibility by having two characters who—regardless of what their sexuality may actually be—could be seen as gay," says New World Pictures' openly gay vice president of casting, Joel Thurm, who recently turned film producer with the gay drama It's My Party.

"Frasier could easily be an elegant queen," he continues, a playful grin broadening across his features as he peers over the scripts piled on the deck in his Westside office. "So could Niles. It's a lot like it was with The Golden Girls. As far as I'm concerned, Blanche was gay. And I know for a fact I'm not the only gay man who feels this way. Blanche spoke frankly and openly about sex the way many gay men do. In fact, I identify with Blanche, especially now that I'm getting older . . . and hornier."

"The Golden Girls had always been our favorite show," Wooten recalls. "When we got the job, we thought, Oh how fun, we're going to meet so many gay people! We were stunned. We were the only gay writers at the table."

Things are considerably different at the production offices of The Crew. "We have eleven writers on our staff this year—eight of them are gay," says Wooten. "This wasn't out of any plan on our part; we didn't know they were gay when we hired them. In fact, two of them 'came out' for the first time because they felt so comfortable working with us."

Wooten and Cherry agree that this high ratio is still unusual for sitcom staffs. But they don't think the openly gay character they created for The Crew is in any way offbeat. "It's a show about flight attendants, for goodness sake!" says Wooten, laughing behind his desk in a toy-strewn office at KTLA studios in Hollywood. "To write a show about flight attendants, and not have one of them be gay would be a sin!"

"Our theory about gay characters on TV," says Cherry, "is that, to the average housewife, talk shows have gotten so sleazy that a gay man on a sitcom is at least 10 freaks removed from the norm."

The Crew is currently "on hiatus" (industry-ese for being kept alive on life support). But even if the show doesn't make it, the writers' track record ensures their continued employment. TV is in their blood. "Sitcom writing isn't something just any child in America is brought up to want to do," says Wooten. "I'm from poor, white North Carolina trash. There is absolutely no excuse for my being here. Mark is from California, right out of Behind the Orange Curtain Republican land. We're from opposite sides of the country, but we've led parallel lives. We were the children who didn't play outside, didn't play games, but were glued to the TV. So when we made our plans to break into show business—"

"—we just had to do sitcoms!" Cherry chimes in from the couch. "We were made for this sort of thing—"

"—because of our painful childhoods."

"Yeah, don't you love it?" Cherry asks, totally deadpan. "My painful childhood has paid for my new Lexus."

Robert Horn and Daniel Margolis, who wrote for Designing Women and Living Single before creating High Society for CBS, have found a comfort level similar to Wooten and Cherry's. Their show, about a pair of fast-lane New York women (Jean Smart, Mary McDonnell), is right up there with Frasier and The Golden Girls on the gay-sensibility meter.

"There are times when we have done things on our show and been told, 'Only West Hollywood is going to get that,' " Horn says in the show's art deco-trimmed offices at Gower Studios. "My feeling is a lot of that attitude will stay that way. But look at a show like Home Improvement. There's a dynamic there that caters to a certain group I'm not part of. I'm not out there doing carpentry work. But is it written broad enough and funny enough for everybody to enjoy? Yes. So why can't that be true for characters written from a gay point of view, whatever that point may be?"

"—It's not like we get up in the morning, look at ourselves in the mirror and say, 'We're gay men, and that's how we're going to approach everything we do,' " adds Margolis. He bounces gleefully in his chair as he thinks up his next line: "It's not like we're pushing a gay agenda—though we would if it got us more dates!"

Still, Horn and Margolis, like Wooten and Cherry, are well aware of how far they can—and can't—go. "The network is always scared stiff that if you do a lot of gay stuff," says Wooten, "people not into that will turn away, which is probably a

fair assessment—you can't force-feed America."

"You know, it's funny," he adds, "we were watching the promo for the Friends lesbian wedding episode the other night, and my boyfriend said to me, 'You're in big trouble.' I asked why and he said, 'There's going to be a backlash. It's too much.' I said, 'You're kidding.' I thought the show was fine, but we talked about it all weekend. He said, 'They're shoving it down people's throats.' "

Friends cocreators David Crane and Marta Kauffman don't agree. Before unleashing their sitcom supernova, they had worked together for years—from off-Broadway musicals cowritten with Kauffman's composer husband Michael Skloff to unsuccessful sitcoms like The Powers That Be and Family Album. They've become a close-knit team, and they feel their show is right on track.

"Friends is a nine o'clock show that's on at eight," says Kauffman, curled up in a chair alongside Crane in the show's Warner Bros. offices. "I can understand those people who don't want to let their kids watch it. That's part of being a parent—deciding what's appropriate for your kids to see. So when people say, 'These shows should not be on at eight,' fine. Change the channel."

"It's really NBC's call," Crane declares. "They know what this show is."

Kauffman seems almost protective of her writing partner, glancing in his direction whenever he speaks, ready to lend support. "It's not a family show, but I think our characters are in many ways a family," she says. "Friends is very much like it was for David and I when we were in our 20's and living in New York. We took care of each other, kept each other in line. It's a nonfamily family."

Gays and lesbians, more than anyone, know about "nonfamily" families, which is why so many of them have been burning up the Internet about Friends' presumably straight Joey and Chandler (Matt LeBlanc and Matthew Perry), whose emotional interplay is indistinguishable from that of a gay couple. When Joey moved out of Chandler's apartment this winter, it took the form of a full-blown romantic breakup more appropriate to The Way We Were.

Crane and Kauffman, however, don't see it that way. "I don't think there's a specifically gay dimension to this show," says Crane. "So much of writing is just a matter of empathy. Certainly, a gay writer is going to bring certain life experiences to the table. But I don't think friends-as-family is in any way the exclusive domain of gays. I've read scripts by gay writers that don't reflect any knowledge of gay life. On this show, I'm not sure how my being gay fits into the picture."

There are millions of gays and lesbians watching his show every week who could tell Crane in exhaustive detail how same-sexuality "fits into" Friends. But Crane sticks to his guns—although not without an air of ambivalence.

"Inasmuch as I am the sum of my parts," he says, "I don't think there's a . . . I don't know. I hate to define myself. I've been reading a lot of things where I've been called David-Crane-openly-gay-producer. It's virtually become one word!"

"I have to assume," says Kauffman, breaking in on her slightly exasperated partner, "that there are, in the life experience of a gay person, certain things brought to the table, but I don't know that I could tell you what they are or generalize it in any way."

"I certainly can't," says Crane firmly. "I mean, I'm the only gay person in our room."

"That we know of," says Kauffman evenly.

"Yes, that we know of," concedes Crane, starting to smile.

"When you sit down and think about it, it's really remarkable what's happened over the past few years," says industry veteran Joel Thurm, who has done everything from casting the original Broadway production of Hello, Dolly! to playing a casting director in the film I'll Do Anything.

"When I was with The Bob Newhart Show, I never met a gay writer or any other gay person, except maybe in makeup or wardrobe. Same with The Mary Tyler Moore Show. I think there were a couple of gay people backstage, but none of the writers were gay. It was very much a boys' club. Not homophobic, mind you, but a real football-watching crowd.

"Still," he adds, "they did do one thing somewhere in the middle years of Mary, with a wonderful actor-director named Bob Moore, who's dead now. He directed the original production of The Boys In The Band. He played Phyllis' brother. Remember that episode where he kept dating Rhoda and driving Phyllis crazy because she hated Rhoda so much? Then Rhoda told her that the brother was gay, and Phyllis said, 'Thank God!' That was one of the first gay-themed episodes on television. After that show, Bob directed regularly for MTM. But he was the only gay person around in those days. You might say he was the Rosa Parks of The Mary Tyler Moore Show."

But Moore was a blip on the radar screen compared with the man who really leveled the playing field, Tim Flack.

"God, Tim Flack!" says Thurm, gasping at the very name of the former casting director who became one of the most powerful executives in television. "Talk about queens of England! Tim was that category of gay person who, well, let's put it this way: Tim was basically a drag queen. He never wore women's clothes, but he was so wild. And straight men in the network's old boys' clubs aren't afraid of drag queens. Tim was the person who really made a difference for gays in television. He passed away from AIDS about a year ago, but no one will ever forget him. He was my assistant at one time at NBC. Then he went to CBS and became a vice president. So did his assistant, Joe Voci.

"When people in meetings find themselves at an impasse," he adds, "things can get very tense. Tim had this way of breaking that tension with humor—more often than not at his own expense. His favorite expression was, 'I'd rather set my hair on fire!' That's why he rose so quickly from working in casting to working as an executive. He became one of the three people in TV who had the say-sos that puts a show on the air—or keeps it off. And when you're that important, everybody—even the biggest homophobe in town—has to love you."

"When Tim was working with me in casting," Thurm recalls, "we had a TV movie called Mafia Princess. Remember that one? The producers wanted us to go after Glenn Close. Tim and I just sort of looked at each other, because the script was not, shall we say, Oscar caliber. Tim suddenly asked, 'Have you ever thought about Susan Lucci?' And then he got up and did Susan Lucci—hand gestures and everything." (She got the part.)

Former CBS programming chief Jeff Sagansky (now executive vice president of the Sony Corporation) was one of the many straights who truly enjoyed Flack's wild style. "The joke about Tim was that he was as funny as any of the shows he put on the air," Sagansky says. "He was instrumental in getting Designing Women and The Nanny on CBS. He believed in Fran Drescher long before she became a hit. He loved larger-than-life women."

There is a long pause before he adds, "I miss him."

"There's definitely a generational thing going on," Thurm says. "The younger gays aren't as closeted. Their mentality is: if your writing is good, it doesn't matter. Still, it's not okay for any-body to be gay unless they're good at what they do. In fact, you have to be better than anybody else. If you are, then everything's fine."

"There's a pattern within the industry of self-identified liberals who love you when you're a funny queen," says veteran writer Richard Gol-lance, whose credits include Falcoln Crest, Lifestories and Beverly Hills 90210, who isn't shy about admitting he sometimes fits that bill. "But when you have a serious point to make or are upset about something—which happens with AIDS—they have a lot of trouble shifting gears because they're not used to taking gay people seri-ously."

"About two years ago, there was a show I worked on where we did the Gay Episode," Gol-lance continues, his usually genial features sud-denly taking on a deadly serious air. "And there was this enormous conflict on their part about what to do with me. I was the only openly gay man on the set. When I was first interviewed for the job, a show like this was presented as some-thing they wanted to do. It was what I call the Cry Freedom School of Drama—how straight white people are going to deal with this 'other.' I didn't think it'd get done, but I thought it was a very gra-cious thing for them to mention it to me. When the episode actually came to be made, they sud-denly didn't want me to write it. At the same time, they still wanted me to look at the script and tell them what the gay character would or wouldn't do! I have never had that explained to me in any credible way."

He emphasizes that this was some time ago. But Roseanne's William Lucas Walker recalls a more recent incident that occurred while he was writing for a show he would rather not name.

"I had always heard about how liberal Holly-wood was, and I guess I believed it. I was surprised how conservative a town it is in practice, even though they'll say the right things in public. This comedy I worked on was a real straight-boys' club. It reminded me of the high school locker room, only the guys weren't as cute. I wasn't closeted, but I didn't really talk to anyone about it unless they asked. I thought the jungle drumbeats would get out, and everyone would know. They didn't."

The last straw came when a comedian working on another show—whom Walker had considered a friend—dropped by to discuss his recent appear-ance on The Tonight Show with singer-pianist Michael Feinstein. "He was talking about what a 'fag' Feinstein was, and all the writers were join-ing in. I felt my whole insides imploding in slow motion. It was like walking in on a Ku Klux Klan rally."

Walker's experience is by and large an excep-tion to the rule these days. Gays have planted themselves firmly in the comedy business—with the Jews who came before them setting the pace.

So what of Brooks' notion of a gay sitcom being the next step? "I think you can have a gay character leading a show," says Mehlman, "but for it to be truly accepted, the sensibility of its leading character—whether they're gay or Jewish or whatever—has to be that of . . . " It takes him a moment to come up with the words he's looking for. " . . . of a citizen of the world. You got that? I think that's the best thing I've said this entire interview."

# | 51 |

# Anything But Idyllic: Lesbian Filmmaking in the 1980s and 1990s

LIZ KOTZ

Someone must always be more powerful, someone is always more or less powerful. It can be me or you, one woman or another, but power is always there, it is never, ever, absent. Right now, I have it, you're listening to my words and you recognize my strength. . . . It's because we've lost power that we need each other like this.

These words are uttered toward the end of *Let's Play Prisoners* (1988), Julie Zando's provocative and haunting video about love, control, and submission between women—as lovers and friends, as mother and child, or even as artist and viewer. In this video made fifteen years after the beginning of independently produced lesbian media in this country, Zando starts from an assumption of the complete interrelation of power and sexuality—an assumption that couldn't be further from the representations of utopian lesbian worlds found in many of the films, novels, and narratives of the mid-1970s.

Despite fears of censorship, and antifeminist and antigay backlashes during the past decade, more lesbian artists are "out" in public, and more and more often they are taking on controversial issues and experiences. At the same time that the idea of a unified, distinct "lesbian community" has been thrown into question, lesbian filmmakers and videomakers are exploring worlds that are complex, conflicted, and anything but idyllic. An idealized and often painfully sentimentalized "up with lesbians" film aesthetic has, in the past few years, given way to a number of works that probe darker and, at times, distinctly dystopic aspects of women's relationships and communities.

Lesbian film and video provide a corrective to the attitudes, stereotypes, and models of Hollywood films, television, and the popular press, but they also respond to the representations which have been produced within the lesbian community. Films, videos, and art about aspects of lesbian identity are more numerous now than ever, yet the nature of these media—the kinds of audiences they were made for, and the kinds of roles they play—has clearly changed.

Once strongly based in, and accountable to, self-defined "women's communities," lesbian film today is often made by individuals who may feel deeply ambivalent about their relation to these communities—particularly younger women, women of color, or others whose lives are distant from the lesbian feminist utopias envisioned and made visible during the mid-1970s. Often, these filmmakers seek out mixed or lesbian/gay audiences in the context of gay film festivals, the independent film community, or the art world. In the fields of independent and experimental film and video especially, many of the most visible and most successful artists are gay women who create work that sometimes does, and sometimes doesn't, explicitly address lesbian subjects or issues.

Early lesbian experimental cinema of the

In Arlene Stein, ed., *Sisters, Sexperts, Queers*, pp. 67–80. New York: Penguin, 1993.

1970s sprang up at the intersection of several historical forces: a tradition of American experimental cinema committed, against the narrative conventions of the larger culture, to self-made "personal" film-making; an emerging feminist documentary practice, made possible by the development of lightweight, portable equipment that allowed "direct" recordings of events and personal testimonies; and an increasingly separatist lesbian feminist community which, although predominately white and middle class, tried to distance itself not only from the dominant culture, but also from other "deviant" communities, such as gay men and prostitutes.

If any shared trait marked lesbian culture and experimental film culture of the 1970s, it was something like a "tyranny of the radical," in which anything believed to be inherited from the dominant culture was energetically purged. Reacting to the depiction of women in heterosexual pornography, mainstream movies, and advertising, feminists criticized or even proscribed erotic or objectified images of women. These restrictions on content and form made it difficult, for instance, to explore lesbian subjectivity in relation to popular culture, to the cultural and political contradictions of present-day American society, or to diverse ethnic and racial histories. Emerging in response to the modern feminist movement, lesbian experimental film tried to free itself from the repressive, "patriarchal" culture and create a "new language" of lesbian desire and identity. Yet, in its own way, it was unavoidably situated within and shaped by this culture.

The most visible and most prolific producer of early lesbian cinema was Barbara Hammer. Starting in the San Francisco Bay Area in the early 1970s, she has produced almost fifty short experimental films, many of which have been screened internationally. Like that of many feminist artists of the period, Hammer's work initially revolved around the development of a specifically female aesthetic focused on questions of gender and female community. Formally her films are lyrical and imagistic, working with metaphor and superimposition. Thematically, they investigate autobiography, the body, and sexuality, and are often situated in a mythic, pastoral landscape.

Hammer's *Dyketactics* (1974) presents a group of women in nature enacting a communal ritual that celebrates sensuality and lesbian collectivity. By representing the sexual completely divorced from any of the genre conventions of pornography, the film elaborates a tactile, sensual aesthetic. It juxtaposes shots of hands and bodies, water, grass, and women having sex, all situated in an almost mythically pure rural setting, compressing many of the elements that are now seen as stereotypical of this period. In *Double Strength* (1978), Hammer adopts a more explicitly autobiographical form to represent her relationship and breakup with trapeze artist Terry Sendgraft. The camera records an interplay between the two women that is lyrical, harmonious, and egalitarian. The "breakup" occurs offscreen, evoked through metaphor but not recorded directly.

Hammer's 1978 film *Women I Love* is a classic compendium of 1970s-style cunt imagery, represented directly and through various floral and natural symbols. While the intent may be to glorify women's sexuality, the cumulative effect of the images, at least at this historical distance, is deeply romanticizing—a strategy perhaps necessitated by the politicized suspicion of sexual imagery among many feminists. Ironically, much like porn, this idealized iconography of women's bodies and sexuality has the effect of isolating sex from everyday life, from relationships and all their inevitable emotional and political complications. The tendency to locate sexual expression within this pastoral, mythical realm may say a lot about how distant any public expression of sexuality has been from most women's lives, particularly within the kinds of urban spaces that gay men have long had access to. Other films by Hammer, *Menses* (1974), *Superdyke* (1974), and *The Great Goddess* (1977), documented and celebrated various elements of this mythically oriented 1970s lesbian culture.

While many of these once-exploratory tropes became quite conventionalized in 1970s lesbian feminist culture, Hammer helped originate this aesthetic, and her works often have a lyrical power and rhythmic intensity. *Dyketactics*, in particular, was a groundbreaking film, one which helped set the agendas, for better or worse, to which much later lesbian cinema would respond. Energetically embracing sexual expression at a time when many feminists, including lesbians, were unwilling to accept lesbian visual imagery, Hammer's films of the 1970s responded to a complex historical moment full of contradictory possibilities and restrictions. The films are unabashedly gay liberationist, exhibiting all the separatist, experimental, utopian tendencies of the movement in Northern California in the

1970s. These tendencies were rooted in, and contributed to, a model of women's culture which strove to be almost completely outside the structures of "patriarchal," capitalist American society—distinct from the consumerist, urban-based gay male culture of the late 1970s.

Clearly, imagining another world served a purpose. But this retreat from history and from cultural specificity became increasingly problematic. The narrative of "coming out," which dominated much lesbian and gay filmmaking of the 1970's and 1980's, reflected this belief in sexuality as the basis for personal identity, prior to any other cultural or social affiliation. Such a focus on the personal and autobiographical often fit neatly with American individualism and voluntarist strategies of political change. As gay historian and theorist John D'Emilio argues, there has often been "an overreliance on a strategy of coming out" in gay culture, one which has "allowed us to ignore the institutionalized ways in which homophobia and heterosexism are reproduced."

By the 1980's, lesbian artists in many disciplines came to question the predominance of autobiographical genres and the reliance on the coming-out story as the defining narrative of lesbian wok. It is easy to see how such devices had become deeply clichéd, with all the romanticized tales of women breaking with repressive families and the falseness of straight society to find harmony, happiness, and their "real selves" within the lesbian community. Feminist documentaries, in particular, had tended to rely on "talking heads"–style presentations of women telling the "truth" of their won experiences. These strategies, which were believed to create a truer, more immediate, and more self-defined representation of women, tended to deny the mediation and manipulation inherent in any filmed and edited representation.

Yet such naive assumptions, however common, are not inherent in autobiographical work or coming-out stories. A good case in point is *Susana* (1980), by the Argentinian-born San Francisco filmmaker Susana Blaustein Munoz, who went on to make the highly acclaimed documentaries *Las Madres: The Mothers of the Plaza De Mayo* (1986) and *La Ofrenda: The Days of the Dead* (1989) with Lourdes Portillo. A self-reflexive and probing look at family and coming out, *Susana* shows how issues of sexual identity and self-determination can be situated within larger cultural and social histories. Even viewed more than ten years after its making, little except the

clothing and hairstyles seems dated. A bittersweet work about Munoz's tentative reconciliation with her family, the short film implicitly questions the documentary techniques it uses. As Munoz records the reminiscences of her family and close friends, the process of film-making produces a tense encounter between the subjects and the filmmaker, one which often verges on emotional violence.

The film works through disjuncture, probing conflicting points of view rather than creating a seamless narrative flow. Susana's mother recounts her combined love for and rejection of her daughter. She recalls Susana's upbringing in Mendoza, a small town in Argentina, and tries to figure out what went wrong with her smart, headstrong daughter: "Her only problem was to be stubborn. . . . I'm trying to be honest and just, but when I look back on my child's life, I can't find any problem with her." Confronted with her daughter's lesbianism and her departure from the strictures of small-town life, Susana's mother puts it into terms she can understand: "Mendoza was too small for her."

What is at stake, from the outset, is who gets to represent Susana, and how: what genres, narratives, and histories her life will be shaped and understood by. Visually, the film combines Munoz's photographs of herself with home movies and baby pictures, presumably taken by her parents. Even though this is her film, it is clearly not her story only. The film counterposes the perspective of the filmmaker, who sees her parents as having rejected her, with that of her parents, who see their daughter as having rejected them and their way of life. Switching back and forth between speakers, *Susana* probes not only these conflicting opinions but also their irreconcilable ways of making sense of the world. "Yes, Mother," Susana responds with some irony, "I guess Mendoza was too small for me."

The film's most poignant moments focus on Susana's younger sister Graciela, to whom the film is dedicated. Sequences of Graciela reading her written statements are intercut with scenes of two of Susana's lovers. As Graciela describes her fear of Susana, who, her parents have told her, is a "sexual deprivate" and dangerous, Susana's ex-girlfriend recalls how Graciela's visits, as an emissary of her parents and their expectations, would set back Susana's growing self-acceptance. Yet Susana's emerging lesbian identity is not romanticized or idealized. Karen, Susana's first lover, recounts that Susana gave photographs of Karen as presents when they first got involved; one day, after a fight, Karen came home to find her face had been "torn into pieces." Though the violent emotional conflicts between the two lovers are not downplayed, they are shown to be very different from Susana's ruptures with her sister and mother. Munoz, as she presents herself within the film, is tough and angry, but also resilient.

At the end of the film, Susana enters the frame and the two sisters confront each other onscreen. Graciela asks Susana what she thinks, whether they can be friends. "Well, you know, 'friends' is a funny word," Susana replies. "If I do this it's because I think people can communicate. But do you think I really have to change?" When Graciela answers yes, she still thinks Susana must change, that there is no future for her without a man, it is clear that the conflict is as much Graciela's as Susana's. Although she knows she is bolstered by social convention, Graciela paradoxically still looks for her older sister's approval. The relation of power between the two remains ambiguous, and in the end Susana appears to triumph.

Juxtaposing stories and perspectives, the film represents different parts of Susana—her cultural identity as an Argentinian and as a Jew, her family's heritage, her sexual identity, her life as an artist—as conflicting and yet completely interrelated. With its model of personal identity as a composite of disparate, intersecting social forces and narratives, *Susana* foreshadowed much of the lesbian filmmaking that followed in the 1980's.

Like Munoz's *Susana*, the work of New York experimental filmmaker Su Friedrich offers a set of subjective reflections on family and cultural history. Friedrich's works have ranged from the silent, nonnarrative *Cool Hearts, Warm Heart* (1979) and *Gently Down the Stream* (1981) to later works incorporating dramatization, narrative, and documentary techniques, such as *The Ties That Bind* (1984), *Damned If You Don't* (1987), and *Sink or Swim* (1990). Often loosely autobiographical, her films locate the individual in a web of intersecting histories and narratives, chance events, and fantasies, in which forces of empowerment and entrapment cannot fully be separated.

*Gently Down the Stream* uses text and rephotographed imagery to interweave themes of sexual conflicts, troubled relationships, and Catholic guilt. Based on dreams Friedrich recorded in her journal over a number of years, the film meditates on moments of anxiety, doubt, and everyday trauma. The text is scratched word by word into the emulsion, leaving the spectator in a state of waiting and uncertainty: "I / wake / her/ She / is / angry / Smears / spermicidal / jelly / on / my / lips / NO!" "I / draw / a / man / Take / his / skin / Get / Excited / Mount / it / IT'S / LIKE / BEING / IN / LOVE / WITH / A / STRAIGHT / WOMAN." As the film progresses, the anxieties take shape, offering different glimpses of Friedrich's psyche and probing these traumas and tensions. The lesbian experiences evoked by the film are anything but idyllic.

The film's form is itself fractured and disturbed; bits of white leader and punched-out holes insist on the vulnerability and incompleteness of the medium. Series of images—feet walking, water viewed from a boat, a woman rowing, religious artifacts—shift from full-frame to reframed presentations in irregular patterns and rhythms. Their relation to the text is not illustrative but suggestive and oblique, intersecting erratically to create new sets of associations and subjective impressions. The structure of *Gently Down the Stream* is highly permeable, conveying a sense of random and unpredictable encounters that approximate dream logic, as the film proceeds in a stream-of-consciousness flow with constant interruptions and eruptions of unprocessed, sometimes obscure material.

In one of Friedrich's more recent films, *Damned If You Don't* (1987), she returns to the subject of Catholicism, telling a story of a nun's seduction by another woman. Somewhat more conventionally narrative in structure, the film incorporates historical materials into its story: footage from *Black Narcissus*, a 1946 film about nuns; a friend's taped reminiscences of a Catholic-school girlhood; and testimonials from Judith Brown's book, *Immodest Acts: The Life of a Lesbian Nun in Renaissance Italy* (Oxford, 1986). Yet this time, the relationship of lesbian desire to the traditions of Catholicism is more ambiguous. Rather than simply condemning the repressive nature of such religious traditions, the film performs a loosely historical investigation of nuns as embodiments of suppressed and displaced female desires.

Turning the tables on the symbols and structures of institutionalized repression, in its final seduction scene the film gently eroticizes the religious vestments, portraying them as covers hiding potential pleasure and abandon. Sensuality and physical pleasure appear at every turn, as the nun is unable to escape her desires. She flees her pursuer to visit an aquarium, only to be confronted by a pair of beautiful white whales twisting through the water. Throughout the film, the implicit sensuality and perversity of the baroque Catholic iconography is used to create an erotic fascination with concealment and repression. The other woman finally accomplishes her seduction through a gift, a small needlepoint image of Christ with only the mouth embroidered, which she leaves in the nun's room, an eroticized *détournement* of the religious icon.

The underlying strategy of the film revolves around recovering—for pleasure, for suspense, and for fantasy—the mechanisms, anxieties, and twisted representations of the oppressive culture. Rather than questioning the "truth" of its assembled documents, Friedrich probes their pathologized narratives as sources of both history and fascination, documents whose aesthetic excesses and ambiguous powers can be undermined and resituated in a modern tale of "girl gets girl." The structure of the film works to appropriate filmic clichés of voyeuristic pleasure, female sexuality, and happy endings into its highly personal and even humorous meditation on lesbian erotic pursuit and guilt-drenched lust. Rather than using its fragments to create a new fiction of lesbian identity free from repression, the film plays itself out on the level of suggestion and allegory. Perhaps more than anything, it is about fantasy and the processes by which repressive experiences and traumas, when reworked, become turn-ons. Like *Gently Down the Stream, Damned If You Don't* explores the subjective processes of memory, anxiety, and fantasy.

In this alternation between critical and almost nostalgic stances, Friedrich's film explores how a modern lesbian subject is positioned in relation to these representations. *Damned If You Don't* seems to revolve around the possibilities for creating pleasure in the discards of a repressive and constrained past, and of moving beyond feminist critique to selectively reinvest these images and memories with private and erotic meanings. With its sensual and suggestive intercutting, the film probes the complex interplays of voyeurism and identification, guilt, pleasure, and shame, at work in their cautious reappropriation. As Scott MacDonald notes in his discussion of Friedrich's films:

> *Damned If You Don't* . . . energizes feminist deconstruction by locating it within a context of at least two forms of (redirected) film pleasure: the excitement of the melodramatic narrative and the sensuous enjoyment of cinematic texture, rhythm and structure. Friedrich's decision not only to include a representation of female sexuality but to use it as the triumphant conclusion of the film is central to her new direction. Friedrich has cinematically appropriated the pleasure of women for women.[5]

Another artist who in recent years has probed the dense interplay of repression and desire in female relationships is videomaker Julie Zando. Zando's videos raise interesting questions about what constitutes a lesbian work, especially since they don't explicitly focus on sexual relationships between women. Yet the questions she addresses, about female masochism, erotic obsession, and victimization, are clearly located in contemporary lesbian discussions of sexuality and power. Artful and complex, her videos probe the shifting relations of dominance and submission, which are not reducible to the dualistic male-female axis of power on which most earlier feminist analyses were based. Definitely not feminist fairy tales, Zando's works look frankly at desire, submission, and cruelty between women.

Conceptually blurring some of the boundaries between lesbian and straight subjectivity, Zando's films explore how lesbian identity itself is constructed in relation to larger sets of family and social relationships, but without retreating into the closet in the process. *Let's Play Prisoners* (1988) explores power between women through a story about two girls whose childhood rituals and dares take on a distinctly sadomasochistic tone. The story, read by an adult woman (the story's author, Jo Anstey) sitting on a couch, tells of childhood games of imprisonment, physical restraint, humiliation, and pain from the victim's point of view, probing how the girl's masochism and desire for approval compel her to comply with her friend's increasingly cruel requests.

The play of control in the story is echoed in the control exercised by the director in relation to the woman reading the story. Rereadings of lines, interruptions, and instructions from the director are exaggerated, and Zando's hand frequently enters the frame to prompt or adjust Anstey. Combined with the aggressively intrusive and manipulated camera work, this interplay forces the viewer to witness the tension between the two women and to comprehend the making of the video as itself an act of power and seduction. The story is repeated in fragments by a young girl, who is prompted, more gently, by her mother.

As the girls' games become increasingly sadistic, the tension between the storytellers and director also intensifies. At first, the two girls play a simple game of prisoner and guard; then they make an excursion into the forbidden territory of the boys' playground, where they must pull up their skirts so that the boys can see their underpants. Eventually, the friend tells the narrator that they must refrain from going to the bathroom all day and then both wet their pants. Torn between humiliation and an intense fear of rejection, the girl becomes distressed, refuses to comply, and provokes her friend's anger and abandonment.

Exploring this dense relationship between power and love, the video probes the edges of acceptable or comfortable experiences of submission, approval-seeking, and control. It sets up a series of reverberations between the need of the girl reading the story for approval from her mother, the need of the girl in the story for approval from her friend, and the author's need for approval from the director. The video's visually poetic and emotionally gripping play on the inescapably complex and contradictory relations of power forces the viewer to confront her own involvement and complicity in the games of voyeurism and control enacted in the tape.

While many earlier experimental works made by women, such as Hammer's, portray an unproblematic trust and intimacy between filmmaker and subject, and a faith in a direct, unmediated form of representation, Zando's video probes the highly charged undersides of such relations between women, insisting that *all* representations involve some level of control and manipulation. Zando's work implies that this space between women is seductive, but it is not "safe."

Unlike Zando's more psychoanalytically-oriented explorations of power, Indian-British film- and videomaker Pratibha Parmar has investigated levels of racist and colonialist violence in many of her works. Parmar's early video art tape *Sari Red* (1988) poetically examines how the ever-present threat of violence intrudes on the lives of Asian women. Interweaving the account of a racist-motivated murder of a young Indian woman with sensuous images of Asian women in private rituals, *Sari Red* probes the interrelation of public and private spheres and the inseparability of private lives from global forces of colonialism and racist violence.

The tape develops an experimental language, based on South Asian iconography, to explore the intimate spaces between women. Parmar reframes the image of the sari, an icon of Asian female submissiveness in white racist discourse, in order to reclaim it as a symbol of Asian female power, visual pleasure, and cultural identity. While never explicitly sexual or lesbian, the video implicitly politicizes the fragility of this space between women, this possibility for intimacy and subjectivity. The sensuality and lyricism of the images, which suggest an almost erotic embrace of beauty, make the horror of the murder all the more violent and disturbing.

Parmar's more recent work, *Khush* (1991), is an experimental documentary about the lives of South Asian lesbians and gay men. Shifting from Britain to North America, to India and back, the film explores the interplay of cultural identity, racist repression, and sexual desire, and relates the difficulty and danger of coming out for many Asian gays, for whom the family and community are a vital protection from racist societies. The men and women in the film describe the tension of feeling torn between white-dominated gay communities and ethnic communities which, because of racism, are often conservative and inward-looking.

Revolving around the appropriation of the term *khush* (an Urdu word meaning ecstatic pleasure) by the emerging international community of gay South Asians, the film documents their political and cultural self-articulation in the face of legacies of colonialism and diaspora. The film incorporates archival footage of traditional dances, contemporary performance sequences, and images from sculptures and religious icons, to visually evoke culturally specific experiences of sexual pleasure and identity. Like a growing number of other films and videos by women of color, *Khush* affirms a multiplicity of gay identities rooted in diverse historical and cultural traditions, and probes the contradictory intersections of ethnicity, sexual identity, and community.

As different as they are from one another, these works nonetheless reflect some of the shifting agendas of lesbian media. Departing from a conception of lesbian identity and community as unitary, defined by opposition to or exclusion from the larger culture, lesbian artists have over the past fifteen years established a position from which to investigate and redefine elements of both gay and straight cultures. No longer bound to the production of so-called "positive images" or idealized representations, these filmmakers and videomakers are challenging and extending contemporary awareness of the relations between power and sexuality, cultural identity and community.

## NOTES

1. For recent writing on lesbian media, see Teresa de Lauretis, *Technologies of Gender* (Indiana, 1987); Judith Mayne, *The Woman at the Keyhole* (Indiana, 1990); Martha Gever, "The Names We Give Ourselves," in Russell Ferguson et al., eds., *Out There: Marginalization and Contemporary Cultures* (New Museum/MIT, 1990); and Bad Object Choices, eds., *How Do I Look? Queer Film and Theory* (Bay Press, 1992).

2. John D'Emilio, "Capitalism and Gay Identity," in Ann Snitow et al., eds., *Powers of Desire* (Monthly Review Press, 1983), p. 111.

3. Scott Macdonald, "Su Friedrich: Reappropriations," *Film Quarterly* (Winter 1987–88), pp. 41–42.

# III. B
# FIT TO PRINT? JOURNALISM

By the early 1950s newspapers and magazines were being challenged by a new medium that was threatening to become the most powerful source of images and information in the history of the world. In the beginnings of the television era it did not take long before the host of a sensationalistic program in Los Angeles, "Confidential File," decided to broadcast a program on homosexuality. The program, which aired in April of 1954, included an interview with a young gay man who used the pseudonym Curtis White—but only after the host interviewed a psychiatrist and a police department vice officer, who were presented as the representatives of official authority. "Curtis White," who said that he did not consider himself to be abnormal, was asked if his family knew that he was homosexual. In what may have been the first of what is by now a familiar response, White said, "Well, they didn't up until tonight. . . . I think it's almost certain that they will. . . . I think I may very possibly lose my job too." Asked why he had agreed to appear on the program, given these concerns, White said he hoped to be "a little useful to someone besides myself." Unfortunately, despite Curtis White's effective presentation, which was well received by the Los Angeles press, his boss also watched the program and saw through the fake name and the blurring of his face. Curtis White was promptly fired (Alwood 1996:32).

Despite the risks, lesbians and gay men continued to take whatever opportunities presented themselves to appear on television talk shows and to tell their story. In July 1962 a public radio station in New York City, WBAI-FM, broadcast a program in which a panel of heterosexual psychiatrists spent ninety minutes talking about homosexuals and mental illness. This familiar pattern of talking about gay people rather than allowing them to speak for themselves felt like one time too many for a young gay activist named Randy Wicker. Wicker marched into the station the next day and demanded equal time. The station program manager agreed to the demand and scheduled a second program, this time featuring Wicker and seven other gay men.

The following autumn, Randy Wicker received a call from Robert Doty, a reporter at the *New York Times* who had been given an unusual assignment, to investigate the increasingly visible gay male community. Doty was taken on a tour of the gay world by Randy Wicker and introduced to "normal" gay men. Yet, when it came to writing his story, Doty reverted to the familiar journalistic practices of "objectivity" and "balance." What this meant was that direct contact with healthy homosexuals was overruled by the opinions of those defined as "legitimate" authorities—political, legal, medical, and religious—and the only comments that came from gay people were buried at the end of the story. The message was both familiar and clear: gay people were the least important sources of information and opinion about their own lives.

Thus when the *New York Times* first put gay people on the front page, in December 1963, they were motivated by the realization that gay people were beginning to live their lives more openly. That this was an unwelcome development could be seen in the headline and lead paragraph: "*Growth of Overt Homosexuality In City Provokes Wide Concern.* . . . The City's most sensitive open secret—the presence of what is probably the greatest homosexual population in the world and its increasing openness—has become the subject of growing concern of psychiatrists, religious leaders and the police" (Doty 1963).

As hostile as it was, the *Times* article signaled an end to the silence about lesbians and gay men in the press. As the 1960s progressed, more and more articles focusing on gay people began appearing in newspapers and magazines, many of them echoing the *Times*'s concerns over the growing visibility of gay people. Even more alarming to the press was the insistence of many gay people that they were neither morally degenerate nor mentally ill. In March 1964 the *New York Times* ran its second front-page story about homosexuals. Spurred by a report from the New York Academy of Medicine, the article was headlined, "Homosexuals Proud of Deviancy, Medical Academy Study Finds."

The most influential national magazines of the period, *Life*, *Time*, and *Newsweek*, also noticed the presence of the emerging lesbian and gay community and its growing demand for an end to the stigmas imposed by law, medicine, and religion. In June of 1964 *Life* magazine published an extensive article on "Homosexuality in America"—although like most stories of the period it focused exclusively on gay men and ignored lesbians. The introduction to the story captures the stance of the media confronting the specter of homosexuality:

Homosexuality in America: A secret world grows open and bolder. Society is forced to look at it—and try to understand it.
. . . Homosexuality shears across the spectrum of American life—the professions, the arts, business and labor. It always has. But today, especially in big cities, homosexuals are discarding their furtive ways and openly admitting, even flaunting, their deviation. Homosexuals have their own drinking places, their special assignation streets, even their own organizations. And for every obvious homosexual, there are probably nine nearly impossible to detect. This social disorder, which society tries to suppress, has forced itself into the public eye because it does present a problem—and parents especially are concerned. The myth and misconception with which homosexuality has so long been clothed must be cleared away, not to condone it but to cope with it. (6/26/64, p. 66)

This article clearly reflects the familiar concern with "understanding" homosexuals in order to contain the social problem they represent. Still, it was relatively progressive, and *Life* later called on New York State to follow the lead of Illinois, which, in 1961, was the first state to make homosexual behavior between consenting adults legal. But these signs of progress were short-lived, and these national magazines soon reverted to the hostile patterns of earlier years (*Time* magazine's 1966 article, and Kay Tobin's response in the lesbian journal the *Ladder*, this volume).

Although local radio and television stations found homosexuality suitably titillating for talk show audiences, it wasn't until 1967 that any of the television networks were willing to approach the topic. A one-hour documentary on "The Homosexual," narrated by Mike Wallace, was aired in March 1967. Several gay men are shown strategically placed behind potted palms, or otherwise hidden from view, as their tormented psyches are bared. The only gay people identified by name are white, middle-class, and visibly respectable men; the program completely excluded lesbians.

As befits an objective reporter facing an aberration in the natural order, Mike Wallace was anxious to know what causes homosexuality (thus, presumably, helping society to prevent it). For authoritative answers Wallace turned to psychiatrists Irving Bieber and Charles Socarides, two leading proponents of the view—now officially discredited—that gays are mentally ill. In addition to the psychiatrists, Wallace spoke to members of the clergy, who admit that homosexuals, while certainly sinners, are to be pitied and, if possible, saved. Viewers are shown a nineteen-year-old serviceman, arrested in a park for "soliciting" an undercover policeman, being told that his commanding officer and his parents would be informed of his arrest. After an hour-long program in which gay men were defined and framed almost entirely from the outside, Wallace concluded:

The dilemma of the homosexual: told by the medical profession he is sick, by the law that he's a criminal. Shunned by employers. Rejected by heterosexual society. Incapable of a fulfilling relationship with a woman or, for that matter, with a man. At the center of his life, he remains anonymous . . . a displaced person . . . an outsider. (Morgan 1967)

The 1960s are well known as a decade of politics in the streets in which it seemed that one social conflict after another was being taken outside. Among the many landmarks of that turbulent decade, few have achieved the fame and symbolic resonance of the events that began as a fairly routine example of police harassment on a hot night in June of 1969. When the police raided the

Stonewall Bar in Greenwich Village on June 28 they did not expect to set off a riot, but that is what happened when many bar patrons, soon joined by allies outside on the streets, fought back in what turned into several nights of street fighting.

The Stonewall riots set off a flurry of organizing that soon turned into a firestorm of activism across the country. The night of the riots, however, the media were quite unaware of the significance of the events occurring in the Village. The *New York Times*'s brief account of the historic event was buried on page 33 and was told from the perspective of the police. As the riots continued, the *Times* ran a second story the next day, also on page 33, that focused on the official point of view as well: "Police Again Rout 'Village' Youths." Other New York media were less subtle than the *Times*, but no more sympathetic. The *New York Daily News* waited until July 6 to cover the story, but its reporter was at least aware that something significant had occurred. This did not prevent him from treating the riots as an occasion for heavy-handed humor (Lisker, "Homo Nest Raided!" this volume).

On the first anniversary of Stonewall the first gay pride march was held in New York City—it is now an annual event in cities across the country and even beyond—and the *New York Times* took notice. The "quote of the day" was a statement by one of the organizers that summarized the core belief of gay liberation: "We're probably the most harassed, persecuted minority group in history, but we'll never have the freedom and civil rights we deserve as human beings unless we stop hiding in closets and in the shelter of anonymity" (Fosburgh 1970).

The *New York Times* is not just another newspaper. The *Times* sees itself as the leader that other news media follow, and there is a lot of truth in that. The immense power of the *Times* generally has made the paper fairly slow to notice or respond to changes in society, as the paper seems to feel it has a responsibility to serve as a brake rather than a locomotive. The *Times*'s well-known motto is "All the news that's fit to print," and for a long time it was clear that gay people's stories were unfit (Pierson, "Uptight on Gay News"; Signorile, "Out at the New York Times," this volume). In the five years between 1986 and 1992 a series of changes took place that transformed the Gray Lady of 43d Street, as the *New York Times* has long been called in the trade. The first of these changes may have been the most dramatic: homophobic editor Abe Rosenthal retired and was replaced by Max Frankel, who lost little time in letting people

know that times had indeed changed and that included the paper's attitudes toward gay people and stories affecting them.

The transformations at the *New York Times* were accelerated by the revelation in December 1990 that editor Jeffrey Schmalz was gay, and a person with AIDS (Signorile, "Out at the New York Times," this volume). Schmalz's coming out provided the *Times* with an openly gay, trusted insider, and he became, de facto, their first "gay beat" reporter. In the two years that remained before Schmalz died in November 1993, he wrote many articles for the *Times* about AIDS and politics. In 1994 the *Times* appointed veteran David Dunlop to what they now explicitly defined as the gay beat.

Nineteen ninety's second dramatic journalistic coming out happened at the April meetings of the American Society of Newspaper Editors (ASNE). Leroy Aarons, executive editor of the *Oakland Tribune,* had spearheaded a survey of newspapers across the country to gauge tolerance of gays in the newsrooms as well as coverage of lesbian and gay issues. The findings were discouraging. While most papers tolerated gay employees in non-news departments such as the arts, they reported rampant homophobia and few efforts to change by editors or management. Most of the lesbian and gay journalists responding felt isolated and vulnerable. When Aarons spoke at the ASNE meeting to report the results of the survey, he went farther than anyone expected: he came out as gay man.

When Aarons came out of the newsroom closet he inspired hundreds of journalists to follow him, and his speech sowed the seeds of what soon became the National Lesbian and Gay Journalists Association (NLGJA). Aarons retired from the *Oakland Tribune* to devote himself to building NLGJA and spent the following year as a kind of Johnny Appleseed of gay journalism, traveling around the country speaking to lesbian and gay journalists and media activists. By the time the first NLGJA Newsletter was published in September 1991 there were chapters functioning around the country. Issues of the NLGJA Newsletter provided dramatic and emotional reading, printing stories of coming out experiences by lesbian and gay journalists around the country.

▼ *Houston Post* columnist Juan Palomo was told by his editors he could not come out in a column discussing the murder of a gay man. When the story was picked up by an alternative paper, Palomo was fired, only to be rehired the next week following protests from activists.

▼ Gordon Smith, assistant executive editor of the *Providence Journal-Bulletin*, felt he was putting thirty-one years of experience on the line when he told his boss that he is gay, but in fact the reaction was overwhelmingly positive.

▼ Linda Villarosa, senior editor at *Essence* magazine, was out to her colleagues, but she took a giant step farther out when she coauthored with her mother a first-person conversation about their relationship as mother and lesbian daughter.

▼ In May 1992 *Detroit News* Washington bureau news editor Deb Price suddenly became the most widely read openly gay journalist in the world, with an audience upward of 2 million, when the *Detroit News* gave her a regular weekly column devoted to lesbian and gay issues. Deb Price's column is syndicated via the Gannett newspaper chain and appears in papers around the country as well as in *USA Today*.

At its first conference, in San Francisco in June 1992, over three hundred NLGJA members watched *New York Times* publisher Arthur Sulzberger in a videotaped speech.

We can no longer offer our readers a predominately white, straight, male version of events and say that we are doing our job. As a white, straight male, let me quickly add that I don't think that particular vision is any better or worse than a gay or lesbian vision, a black or Hispanic vision, or any other. But in a world as diverse as ours it is simply not complete and therefore not sufficient.

The second NLGJA conference was held in New York, and the six hundred journalists who attended listened to an opening panel comprising television news stars Tom Brokaw, Robert Mac-Neil, Dan Rather, and Judy Woodruff. The panel was not only a dramatic demonstration of the legitimacy the media were granting to NLGJA and its issues, it also put the spotlight on the difference between print and broadcast journalism.

In 1993 NLGJA, together with the Radio and Television News Directors Foundation, conducted a survey of broadcast news directors and of lesbian and gay broadcast journalists. The survey, similar to the 1990 ASNE study, revealed that there is much work to be done before newsrooms are comfortable environments for lesbian and gay journalists and before the news media live up to their responsibilities in covering issues of concern to lesbian and gay people.

Among the signposts of lesbian and gay media visibility in the early 1990s were the coverage of the 1993 March on Washington and the Stonewall Twenty-five celebrations in New York in June 1994. The debate over the military's discriminatory policies figured heavily in the media coverage of the April 1993 march, with photogenic uniform-wearing marchers much favored by television and print photographers. However, despite the prominence of the military issue, or perhaps because of it, the march garnered unprecedented attention from the mass media. Media attention to the march began before the event itself, as reports were published and broadcast on the hundreds of thousands of lesbian and gay people pouring into Washington on the last weekend of April. The march itself was prominently featured on news programs, and the program of speakers was carried live on C-SPAN for over six hours, bringing into homes across the country many words and images never before seen or heard.

In marked contrast to the coverage of previous marches, newspapers across the country carried the story the following day. New York activist William Dobbs analyzed 156 newspapers in the United States, including the 107 largest papers (with 100,000-plus daily circulation), which cumulatively represent more than 50 percent of daily circulation for all newspapers in the country. The results were impressive: 86 percent gave the march front-page coverage and 6 percent had headlines or photos on the front page referring to stories inside. Only two papers did not cover the march in Monday editions, the *Christian Science Monitor* and the Bisbee, Arizona *Daily Review*. Among the largest circulation newspapers, such as the *Wall Street Journal*, *USA Today*, the *Los Angeles Times*, the *Washington Post*, and the *New York Times*, all except the *Wall Street Journal* had substantial front-page coverage including photographs. The *New York Times*'s main article was written by Jeffrey Schmalz.

Similarly extensive coverage occurred the following year during the June 1994 celebrations of the twenty-fifth anniversary of the Stonewall riots and the Gay Games held in New York City. Major essays on the history of the lesbian and gay liberation movement were published in newspapers around the country. *Time* magazine and *Newsweek* published extensive essays on the events. The *New York Times* ran numerous articles about the lesbian and gay community and its achievements as well as several editorials, including one published the day after the march that defended marchers whose unconventional dress had been criticized by gay conservatives: "A just society must offer the same protections to men in leather and chains as to those who wear Brooks Brothers business suits."

An entire subgenre of journalistic attention focused on the sudden discovery of lesbians. As *Newsweek* put it in their lesbian cover story of June 21, 1993, "Lesbians have always been the invisible homosexuals. But suddenly gay women are out of the closet and demonstrating their clout. On sitcoms and in Senate hearing rooms, Americans are finally getting a glimpse behind the old stereotypes and seeing the new diversity of lesbian culture" (3).

Not surprisingly, that new diversity, as represented on *Newsweek*'s cover, was very white and middle-class, as were a spate of articles in *Mademoiselle* (Harris 1993), *Vogue* (Jetter 1993), *Cosmopolitan* (Eaton 1993), and *Glamour* (Sloan 1994). But these articles were also unapologetic, often political, and likely to be written by openly lesbian journalists. The most notorious of the "lesbian chic" covers, however, featured newly out singer k. d. lang dressed as man, sitting in a barber chair while being shaved by (officially straight but oft-rumored to be lesbian) supermodel Cindy Crawford (Bennetts 1993).

By the 1990s lesbian, gay, and bisexual invisibility is truly a thing of the past. Our gains have never been secure, however, as we remain firmly in the gunsights of the right wing. By 1995, with a Republican congressional leadership proclaiming a Contract with America that often read like a contract *on* women and minorities, the NLGJA Newsletter was asking, "Is gay coverage suffering from right-wing backlash?" (Sloan 1995:1). The answer seemed to be that some editors and publishers were, indeed, responding to pressures from the Christian right, and many, of course, had never joined in the movement toward inclusive coverage. Reporter Loraine Anderson of the Traverse City (Mich.) *Record Eagle* studied the stories coming across state and national wires and concluded that "there didn't seem too many stories about minorities, period. . . . [And] most gay stories were about AIDS, most stories about blacks and Hispanics were about crime" (Sloan 1995:12). The article concluded by reiterating a point that has been central to the lesbian and gay movement since the 1960s, quoting openly gay San Francisco TV anchor Hank Plante's belief that improving coverage comes down to gay journalists coming out at work: "If we're out, every time they walk by us [in the newsroom], there the issue is."

## REFERENCES

Alwood, Ed. 1996. *Straight News: Gays, Lesbians, and the News Media*. New York: Columbia University Press.

Bennetts, Leslie. 1993. "k. d. lang Cuts It Close." *Vanity Fair*, August, pp. 94+.

Doty, Robert. 1963. "Growth of Overt Homosexuality in City Provokes Wide Concern." *New York Times*, December 17, p. 1.

Eaton, Catherine. 1993. "A Matter of Pride: Being a Gay Woman in the Nineties." *Cosmopolitan*, November, pp. 226–229.

Fosburgh, Lacey. 1970. "The 'Gay' People Demand Their Rights." *New York Times*, July 5, p. E12.

Harris, Elise. 1993. "Women in Love." *Mademoiselle*, March, pp. 180–183, 208.

Jetter, Alexis. 1993. "Goodbye to the Last Taboo." *Vogue*, July, pp. 86–92.

Morgan, Harry. 1967. "The Homosexuals." *CBS Reports*, March 7.

Sloan, Louise. 1994. "Do Ask, Do Tell: Lesbians Come Out." *Glamour*, May, pp. 242–243, 291–295.

Sloan, Louise. 1995. "Is Gay Coverage Suffering from Right-Wing Backlash?" *Alternatives* (National Lesbian and Gay Journalists Association Newsletter), Summer, p. 1, 11–12.

# | 52 |

## Perverts Called Government Peril

NEW YORK TIMES

Washington, April 18—Guy George Gabrielson, Republican National Chairman, asserted today that "sexual perverts who have infiltrated our Government in recent years" were "perhaps as dangerous as the actual Communists."

He elevated what he called the "homosexual angle" to the national political level in his first news letter of 1950, addressed to about 7,000 party workers, under the heading: "This Is the News from Washington."

Giving National Committee support to the campaign of Senator Joseph R. McCarthy, Republican of Wisconsin, against the State Department, but without mentioning him by name, Mr. Gabrielson said:

"As Americans, it is difficult for us to believe that a National Administration would go to such length to cover up and protect subversives, traitors, working against their country in high Governmental places. But it is happening. If there is but one more (Alger) Hiss or (Judith) Coplon still in a key spot, he should be ferreted out. It's no red herring.

"Perhaps as dangerous as the actual Communists are the sexual perverts who have infiltrated our Government in recent years. The State Department has confessed that it has had to fire ninety-one of these. It is the talk of Washington and of the Washington correspondents' corps.

"The country would be more aroused over this tragic angle of the situation if it were not for the difficulties of the newspapers and radio commentators in adequately presenting the facts, while respecting the decency of their American audiences."

Mr. Gabrielson's letter, appearing over his signature and made available to reporters, did not expand on his assertion that "sexual perverts" were "perhaps" as dangerous as Communists in Government. He was out of the city today and could not be reached for elaboration.

The chairman's letter also attacked President Truman for labeling his trip to the West Coast next month as "non-political," saying that this was "simply a device to carry on politics at the expense of the taxpayers" and "is 'Pendergastism' at its worst."

"We must insure in every way at our command that the people understand the nature of this trip; that the President, in these critical times, spent one month in Florida preparing for another junket away from his White House duties while Congress wallows leaderless," he asserted.

*New York Times*, April 19, 1950, p. 25.

# | 53 |

## The Homosexual in America

*TIME*

It used to be "the abominable crime not to be mentioned." Today it is not only mentioned: it is freely discussed and widely analyzed. Yet the general attitude toward homosexuality is, if anything, more uncertain than before. Beset by inner conflicts, the homosexual is unsure of his position in society, ambivalent about his attitudes and identity—but he gains a certain amount of security through the fact that society is equally ambivalent about him. A vast majority of people retain a deep loathing toward him, but there is a growing mixture of tolerance, empathy or apathy. Society is torn between condemnation and compassion, fear and curiosity, between attempts to turn the problem into a joke and the knowledge that it is anything but funny, between the deviate's plea to be treated just like everybody else and the knowledge that he simply is not like everybody else.

Homosexuality is more in evidence in the U.S. than ever before—as an almost inevitable subject matter in fiction, a considerable influence in the arts, a highly visible presence in the cities, from nighttime sidewalks to the most "in" parties. The latest Rock Hudson movie explicitly jokes about it; Doubleday Book Shops run smirking ads for *The Gay Cookbook*, and newsstands make room for "beefcake" magazines of male nudes. Whether the number of homosexuals has actually increased is hard to say. In 1948, Sexologist Alfred Kinsey published figures that homosexuals found cheering. He estimated that 4% of American white males are exclusively homosexual and that about two in five had "at least some" homosexual experience after puberty. Given Kinsey's naive sampling methods, the figures were almost certainly wrong. But chances are that growing permissiveness about homosexuality and a hedonistic attitude toward all sex have helped "convert" many people who might have repressed their inclinations in another time or place.

Homosexuals are present in every walk of life, on any social level, often anxiously camouflaged; the camouflage will sometimes even include a wife and children, and psychoanalysts are busy treating wives who have suddenly discovered a husband's homosexuality. But increasingly, deviates are out in the open, particularly in fashion and the arts. Women and homosexual men work together designing, marketing, retailing, and wrapping it all up in the fashion magazines. The interior decorator and the stockbroker's wife conspire over curtains. And the symbiosis is not limited to working hours. For many a woman with a busy or absent husband, the presentable homosexual is in demand as an escort—witty, pretty, catty, and no problem to keep at arm's length. Rich dowagers often have a permanent traveling court of charming international types who exert influence over what pictures and houses their patronesses buy, what decorators they use, and where they spend which season.

### THE HOMINTERN

On Broadway, it would be difficult to find a production without homosexuals playing important parts, either onstage or off. And in Hollywood, says Broadway Producer David Merrick, "you have to scrape them off the ceiling." The notion that the arts are dominated by a kind of homosexual mafia—or "Homintern," as it has been called—is sometimes exaggerated, particularly by spiteful failures looking for scapegoats. But in the

*Time*, January 21, 1966, pp. 40–41.

theater, dance and music world, deviates are so widespread that they sometimes seem to be running a kind of closed shop. Art Critic Harold Rosenberg reports a "banding together of homosexual painters and their nonpainting auxiliaries."

There is no denying the considerable talent of a great many homosexuals, and ideally, talent alone is what should count. But the great artists so often cited as evidence of the homosexual's creativity—the Leonardos and Michelangelos—are probably the exceptions of genius. For the most part, thinks Los Angeles Psychiatrist Edward Stainbrook, homosexuals are failed artists, and their special creative gift a myth. No less an authority than Somerset Maugham felt that the homosexual, "however subtly he sees life, cannot see it whole," and lacks "the deep seriousness over certain things that normal men take seriously. . . . He has small power of invention, but a wonderful gift for delightful embroidery. He has vitality, brilliance, but seldom strength."

Homosexual ethics and esthetics are staging a vengeful derisive counterattack on what deviates call the "straight" world. This is evident in "pop," which insists on reducing art to the trivial, and in the "camp" movement, which pretends that the ugly and banal are fun. It is evident among writers, who used to disguise homosexual stories in heterosexual dress but now delight in explicit descriptions of male intercourse and orgiastic nightmares. It is evident in the theater, with many a play dedicated to the degradation of women and the derision of normal sex. The most sophisticated theatrical joke is now built around a homosexual situation; shock comes not from sex but from perversion. Attacks on women or society in general are neither new in U.S. writing nor necessarily homosexual, but they do offer a special opportunity for a consciously or unconsciously homosexual outlook. They represent a kind of inverted romance, since homosexual situations as such can never be made romantic for normal audiences.

## THE GAY SUBCULTURE

Even in ordinary conversation, most homosexuals will sooner or later attack the "things that normal men take seriously." This does not mean that homosexuals do not and cannot talk seriously; but there is often a subtle sea change in the conversation: sex (unspoken) pervades the atmosphere. Among other matters, this raises the question of whether there is such a thing as a discernible homosexual type. Some authorities, notably Research Psychologist Evelyn Hooker of U.C.L.A., deny it—against what seems to be the opinion of most psychiatrists. The late Dr. Edmund Bergler found certain traits present in all homosexuals, including inner depression and guilt, irrational jealousy and a megalomaniac conviction that homosexual trends are universal. Though Bergler conceded that homosexuals are not responsible for their inner conflicts, he found that these conflicts "sap so much of their inner energy that the shell is a mixture of superciliousness, fake aggression and whimpering. Like all psychic masochists, they are subservient when confronted by a stronger person, merciless when in power, unscrupulous about trampling on a weaker person."

Another homosexual trait noted by Bergler and others is chronic dissatisfaction, a constant tendency to prowl or "cruise" in search of new partners. This is one reason why the "gay" bars flourishing all over the U.S. attract even the more respectable deviates. Sociologists regard the gay bar as the center of a kind of minor subculture with its own social scale and class warfare.

As André Gide pointed out long ago from personal experience, there are several varieties of homosexuals that the heterosexual world lumps together but that "feel an irrepressible loathing for one another." Today in the U.S., there are "mixed" bars where all homosexuals, male and female, are *persona grata*; "cuff-linky" bars that cater to the college and junior-executive type; "swish" bars for the effeminates and "hair fairies" with their careful coiffures; "TV" bars, which cater not to television fans but to transvestites; "leather" bars for the tough-guy types with their fondness for chains and belts; San Francisco's new "Topless Boys" discotheques, featuring barechested entertainers. San Francisco and Los Angeles are rivals for the distinction of being the capital of the gay world; the nod probably goes to San Francisco.

Virtually all societies in history have known homosexuality and, with few exceptions, have strongly condemned it—and yet often tolerated it. In 18th century London, for example, Novelist Tobias Smollett sarcastically found that "homosexuality gains ground apace and in all probability will become in a short time a more fashionable device than fornication." But the only society, apart from some primitive ones, that distinctly approved homosexual love was 5th century Greece. "We must blush for Greece," said the enlightened Voltaire. Even this much publicized example has often been over-interpreted. The homosexuality that Socrates and Plato knew rose only with the development of a slave culture and the downgrading of women to the level of uneducated domestics. This resulted in a romantic cult of the beautiful young boy—but not to the exclusion of heterosexual relations—much as the restriction of women to purdah led to a high incidence of pederasty in the Middle East, which is now abating with the growing emancipation of Moslem women.

The once widespread view that homosexuality is caused by heredity, or by some derangement of hormones, has been generally discarded. The consensus is that it is caused psychically, through a disabling fear of the opposite sex. The origins of this fear lie in the homosexual's parents. The mother—either domineering and contemptuous of the father, or feeling rejected by him—makes her son a substitute for her husband, with a close-binding, overprotective relationship. Thus, she unconsciously demasculinizes him. If at the same time the father is weakly submissive to his wife or aloof and unconsciously competitive with his son, he reinforces the process. To attain normal sexual development, according to current psychoanalytic theory, a boy should be able to identify with his father's masculine role.

Fear of the opposite sex is also believed to be the cause of Lesbianism, which is far less visible but, according to many experts, no less widespread than male homosexuality—and far more readily tolerated. Both forms are essentially a case of arrested development, a failure of learning, a refusal to accept the full responsibilities of life. This is nowhere more apparent than in the pathetic pseudo marriages in which many homosexuals act out conventional roles—wearing wedding rings, calling themselves "he" and "she."

Is homosexuality curable? Freud thought not. In the main, he felt that analysis could only bring the deviant patient relief from his neurotic conflicts by giving him "harmony, peace of mind, full efficiency, whether he remains a homosexual or gets changed." Many of Freud's successors are more optimistic. Philadelphia's Dr. Samuel Hadden reported last year that he had achieved twelve conversions out of 32 male homosexuals in group therapy. Paris Psychiatrist Sacha Nacht reports that about a third of his patients turn heterosexual, a third adjust to what they are, and a third get no help at all. But he feels that only about one in ten is moved to seek help in the first place.

## THE WOLFENDEN PROBLEM

That is the crux: most homosexuals apparently do not desire a cure. A generation ago, the view that homosexuality should be treated not as a vice but as a disease was considered progressive. Today in many quarters it is considered reactionary. Homophile opinion rejects the notion that homosexuals are sick, and argues that they simply have different tastes. Kinsey had a lot to do with this, for to him all sexual pleasure was equally valid. "The only unnatural sex act," he said, "is that which you cannot perform." His co-author, Wardell Pomeroy, also argues that homosexuality should be accepted as a fact of human existence, and claims to have known many happy, well-adjusted homosexual couples.

Such views are enthusiastically taken up by several so-called homophile groups, a relatively new phenomenon. Best known of these deviate lobbies is the Mattachine Society, which takes its name from the court jesters of the Middle Ages, who uttered social criticism from behind masks. In recent years, the Mattachines have been increasingly discarding their masks; the Washington branch has even put picket lines outside the White House to protest exclusion of known homosexuals from the civil service and the armed forces, has lately protested exclusion from the Poverty Program. Borrowing a device from the civil rights movement, homophiles have even issued lapel buttons bearing a small equality sign (=) on a lavender background.

Quite apart from the homophile organizations, there is widespread agitation by various groups, including the Civil Liberties Union, for the repeal of laws that in 48 states make various homosexual acts punishable by prison terms ranging from six months to life. The model invariably cited is Britain's 1957 Wolfenden Report—not yet accepted by Parliament—which proposes that homosexual relations between consenting adults should not be illegal. In the U.S. only Illinois has so far adopted this principle. Police, however, claim that many people, including judges, already act as if the Wolfenden rule were the law across the U.S.

## THE MORAL ISSUE

The most telling argument for the Wolfenden rule is that the present statutes are unenforceable anyway as long as the homosexual acts are performed in private (many of the laws also prohibit the same acts between man and wife). In effect, the arrests that are now made are for public or semipublic acts, including "soliciting," with homosexuals often trapped by plainclothesmen posing as deviates. There is also a constant opportunity for blackmail and for shakedowns by real or phony cops, a practice known as "gayola." Advocates of the Wolfenden position argue further that persecution by society only renders the neurotic homosexual more neurotic. A Church of England committee declared that the function of the law is to "protect young people from seduction or assault, and to protect society from nuisances," but not to be the guardian of private morality.

Opponents of this view point out that it is extremely difficult to determine what constitutes "seduction" or even genuine "consent" between adults. Sir Patrick Devlin, formerly a judge on Britain's highest court, argues that the distinction between private and public morality is obscure and indefensible. Many U.S. jurists agree, among them New York State Supreme Court Justice Samuel Hofstadter, who believes that "discretion and privacy" cannot make the difference "between a wrongful and a lawful act"—as, for instance, in the case of incest. He supports a compassionate attitude but feels that "to legalize homosexual conduct is an injustice to society's future and an evasion of the problem."

Beyond the pros and cons of legal reform, there is a separate moral issue. The clear-cut condemnations of the Bible or of traditional moral philosophy have come to be considerably toned down. An influential 1963 statement by British Quakers held that "homosexual affection can be as selfless as heterosexual affection" and therefore is not necessarily a sin. A surprising number of Protestant churchmen accept this idea. Most will still assert that homosexuality is an offense against God and man, but usually with qualifications. Says Los Angeles Methodist Bishop Gerald Kennedy: "The Lord made man and woman, and this implies a sexual relationship and sexual harmony which is in the center of nature." He is echoed by Harvard Divinity School's Harvey Cox, who, from a theological viewpoint, sees "the man-woman relationship as a model of the God-man relationship."

Lack of procreation or of marriage vows is not the issue; even Roman Catholic authorities hold that an illicit heterosexual affair has a degree of "authentication," while a homosexual relationship involves only "negation." Roman Catholic thought generally agrees that homosexuality is of and in itself wrong because, as New York's Msgr. Thomas McGovern says, it is "inordinate, having no direction toward a proper aim." Even in purely nonreligious terms, homosexuality represents a misuse of the sexual faculty and, in the words of one Catholic educator, of "human construction." It is a pathetic little second-rate substitute for reality, a pitiable flight from life. As such it deserves fairness, compassion, understanding and, when possible, treatment. But it deserves no encouragement, no glamorization, no rationalization, no fake status as minority martyrdom, no sophistry about simple differences in taste—and, above all, no pretense that it is anything but a pernicious sickness. •

# | 54 |

# A Rebuke for TIME's Pernicious Prejudice

## KAY TOBIN

An answer to TIME Magazine's essay "The Homosexual in America" (January 21) was delivered in the form of a lecture by Isadore Rubin, Ph.D., editor of SEXOLOGY Magazine and a member of the Sex Information and Education Council of the U.S. (SIECUS). Dr. Rubin's talk, sponsored by the Janus Society, was given in Philadelphia on February 25 and drew an audi-

*Ladder*, February 1966, pp. 20–22.

ence of over 200.

Dr. Rubin said he was appalled when he read this essay in a supposedly responsible publication. He noted that TIME prides itself on being knowledgeable and aware of all the latest things in the fields it discusses. "But if this is so, then I am forced to conclude that if they are not ignorant, the editors of this essay are intellectually dishonest, motivated by prejudice, and guilty of deliberate omission and distortion."

He pointed out that TIME's essay manages to have virtually no mention whatever of any discrimination against homosexuals and indeed it insists they should not be viewed as a martyred minority. Dr. Rubin said that only a prejudiced person could believe homosexuals are *not* the victims of severe injustices.

"Is it discrimination when a person found guilty of a homosexual act in private in a Southern state is condemned to twenty years at hard labor? When college students (in Tallahassee, Florida) are given $10 each by the police for every person they manage to incite or entrap into a homosexual act? When a person in the armed services found to be homosexual is given an other than honorable discharge for no other reason than that he is homosexual? When all homosexuals are excluded from the State Department, regardless of their training and competence, and classed as security risks? When public places are subject to police harassment solely because they serve homosexuals? Perhaps this does not create martyrs," said Dr. Rubin, "but it does create a discriminated-against minority."

While TIME calls for "fairness, compassion, understanding" for homosexuality, Dr. Rubin said he could not find in the essay any example of fairness, compassion, or understanding. It is no plea for understanding, he noted, when TIME claims the arts are dominated by a kind of homosexual Mafia, a "Hominterm," based on the Cominterm, which is supposed to arouse readers' anti-Communist prejudices. Dr. Rubin said he doubted that TIME would be similarly willing to accuse the State Department, which is dominated by heterosexuals, of being a conspiracy of a *heterosexual* Mafia because of its exclusion of homosexuals.

Dr. Rubin gave examples of how the TIME essay tries to discredit opinions favorable to homosexuality. For instance, TIME dismisses the Kinsey research—the best research done on sex so far in this country, Dr. Rubin noted—by calling Kinsey's sampling methods "naive" and saying his fig-

ures "were almost certainly wrong." TIME, suggested Dr. Rubin, may be longing for the old days of hush-and-pretend when people were deceiving themselves that certain sexual activities like homosexuality were merely rare deviations from normal behavior.

When quoting former Kinsey associate Dr. Wardell Pomeroy, the essay says that Dr. Pomeroy "claims to have known many happy, well-adjusted homosexual couples." The word "claims" suggests to the reader that Dr. Pomeroy might be mistaken. On the other hand, when describing the out-of-date and never-proven theories of psychoanalyst Edmund Bergler, TIME blithely states that Bergler *found* certain traits present in *all* homosexuals—with no indication in the essay's wording that Bergler was merely hypothesizing on the basis of those homosexuals who considered themselves sick enough to go to him for treatment, Dr. Rubin charged that Bergler's statements about *all* homosexuals are "arrant and complete nonsense" and that TIME, in reaching back to 1956 to quote Bergler, in the face of all the research done since then, is guilty of intellectual dishonesty.

Dr. Rubin then reviewed recent research to see whether or not the keystone of TIME's essay, the insistence that homosexuality is a sickness, would stand. "No honest scientist can any longer deny that this is an extremely controversial question, and that the burden of proof today rests upon those who claim that homosexuality is necessarily, of itself, an illness."

Dr. Evelyn Hooker, after her comparative study of homosexual and heterosexual men, concluded that severe emotional maladjustments are not more common among homosexuals than among heterosexuals. She has pointed out that the homosexual minority includes many of our most able and useful citizens in all walks of life, including the clergy.

Dr. Virginia Armon repeated Hooker's experiment, using female homosexuals and heterosexuals. She came out with the same findings as Hooker and said that one should not make any generalizations about female homosexuals as a group.

Dr. Joseph DeLuca studied a group of Army inductees being discharged, none having a history of psychiatric hospitalization. His results suggested that homosexuality does not exist as a distinct clinical entity. The homosexuals in his study varied from each other as much as they did from the heterosexuals in regard to personality structure. Dr. DeLuca commented: "The issue of whether homosexuals are more pathologic than normals, in the light of the present findings, seems to have been an unwarranted assumption, based more upon armchair theorizing than experimental evidence."

In South Africa, Renee Liddicoat studied 50 male and 50 female homosexuals, comparing them with a comparable group of heterosexuals, and she concluded: "These people constitute a group of citizens often highly respected, who live useful lives and whose behavior in every way except that of sexual expression conforms to our socially accepted standard of normality."

Dr. Rubin pointed out that these and other studies comprise a body of work, done under scientific rules, which questions the concept of homosexuality as an illness. Yet TIME not only ignored all such research but ended its essay with "the dictatorial editorial statement that homosexuality is 'a pernicious sickness.'" And because this essay is "a tissue of such prejudicial terms (and) is based on deliberate omission and distortion," we have a right to object to it, Dr. Rubin concluded.

# | 55 |

# A Minority's Plea: U.S. Homosexuals Gain in Trying to Persuade Society to Accept Them

## CHARLES ALVERSON

In Washington, they have picketed the White House, Pentagon, State Department and Civil Service Commission. Last fall in San Francisco, candidates for city office actively sought their vote as a bloc. They have recently protested successfully against job discrimination and police harassment in New York. More than 40 regional and national organizations including a newly formed National Legal Defense Fund, fight for their cause.

This sounds like a militant minority, and so it is. But the members of this movement cut across traditional areas of prejudice like race, nationality or religion. What sets them apart is their sexual preferences. They are a tiny but vocal minority of this nation's estimated 10 million homosexuals.

Long the target of whispered comments or off-color jokes, homosexuality is fast coming out in the open. Homosexuals in many instances are boldly challenging the right of others to make them second-class citizens. With growing support from heterosexuals, they are fighting discrimination on legal, economic and social fronts.

## "AGAINST THE MORALS OF THE PUBLIC"

It's a formidable task. Under present laws, homosexual acts—even between consenting adults in private—are illegal in every state except Illinois. A number of occupations—notably teaching—are closed to homosexuals. A military man discovered to be homosexual is abruptly discharged—often with few legal formalities—and is likely to lose his veteran's benefits. Known homosexuals are barred from any post requiring a security clearance and from almost all Federal jobs.

Says Leo M. Pellerzi, general counsel for the Civil Service Commission: "Homosexual conduct is against the morals of the public."

There is a school of psychiatric thought that believes homosexuality is a sickness capable of being cured and thus that efforts to help homosexuals live with their condition are misguided. But the great majority of sex researchers holds

*Wall Street Journal*, July 17, 1968.

that homosexuality is not a disease but is a deep-rooted sexual orientation. Because more and more people are now accepting this latter view, homosexuals are winning ground in their efforts to improve their lives.

Until quite recently, for example, known homosexuals in New York had considerable difficulty getting and keeping city jobs. The Mattachine Society of New York, a homosexual group of 1,000 members, complained to the city's Human Rights Commission and provided case histories of hiring discrimination. Apparently as a result, in January 1967 the city said it had stopped asking job applicants if they were homosexuals.

## "IF YOU'RE GAY, STAY AWAY"

Protests from Mattachine Society members also prompted the New York State Liquor Authority last year to rule that state law doesn't forbid a bar to serve homosexuals. The group had staged a well-publicized "sip in" at a Greenwich Village bar that—to avoid police pressure—had posted a sign reading "If You're Gay, Stay Away."

In several other big cities, police are taking a softer line toward homosexuals. Three years ago San Francisco police regularly raided the social functions of the Society for Individual Rights, a 1,000-member homosexual group. Today, the raids have ceased. Instead, police officers address the group on such topics as the legal rights of homosexuals.

Particularly heartening to homosexuals are signs of changing attitudes on laws relating to homosexual conduct. In 1961, Illinois adopted a penal code that took sexual acts in private between consenting adults out of the province of the law. Nearly a dozen states are studying similar proposals. Abroad, Great Britain last summer passed the Sexual Offenses Act, which removes from criminal statutes private homosexual acts between consenting adults.

That lawmakers are even considering such changes is a major spur to the militancy of homosexuals. Federal agencies are among the biggest targets; homosexuals whose Government jobs or security clearances are threatened are increasingly choosing to stand and fight, either through administrative channels or in the courts.

## THE CASE OF MR. WENTWORTH

"Until recently, the only court cases we got involved in were the ones we couldn't avoid," says

Clark P. Polak, executive secretary of the Homosexual Law Reform Society, a Philadelphia group that offers legal and financial aid to homosexuals in court. "Now we are very much concerned with initiating litigation."

A case in point: Benning Wentworth is a 33-year-old electronics technician at a large private research laboratory in New Jersey. He holds a "secret" security clearance from the Defense Department. In the spring of 1966, Air Force investigators accused Mr. Wentworth of having had homosexual relations with a former Air Force enlisted man. Shortly thereafter, the Defense Department began action to revoke his security clearance, which he has held for seven years.

But instead of quietly quitting his job, as is usually the case with discovered homosexuals, Mr. Wentworth denied the charge—though he admitted he is a practicing homosexual. With the support of the Mattachine Society of Washington, he is fighting revocation of his clearance; he lost a round before the Defense Department's Industrial Security Clearance Review Office in New York and now is appealing. "My sex life is my own private business," says Mr. Wentworth. "It has no bearing on my job or my loyalty."

While not questioning Mr. Wentworth's loyalty, the Government maintains that as a homosexual he is subject to "coercion, influence or pressure that may be likely to cause action contrary to the national interest." In short, say Government officials, his vulnerability to blackmail makes him a poor security risk.

Mr. Wentworth's attorneys argue that, as an admitted homosexual, he can't be blackmailed. "The only one exerting coercion, influence or pressure is the Defense Department," says Franklin E. Kameny, a physicist who is president of the Washington Mattachine Society and who is serving as attorney for Mr. Wentworth in the current administrative hearings.

Except for the controversy, Mr. Wentworth would seem to be the model of a junior technician. An Air Force veteran, he has been with the same employer for seven years and has never been arrested. Soft spoken and shy, he seems anything but a crusader, and nothing in his manner evokes the stereotyped homosexual.

But sitting in the plainly furnished living room of his split-level home in suburban New Jersey, he becomes less reserved and speaks with indignation of the Government action, which could cost him his job as well as his security clearance. "Like anyone else," he says, "I want to be judged by my public acts, not my sexual preferences when they harm no one."

Mr. Wentworth says he was gratified by the reaction of his employer and his fellow workers when it became known that he is a homosexual. "I was worried that there'd be some bad reaction," he says, "but the company never said a thing, and people at work went out of their way to be nice to me." Mr. Wentworth admits that for a time he had considered quitting under pressure from the Defense Department, "but it seemed like a cowardly thing to do, so I decided to fight it."

Mr. Wentworth says he stands ready to take his case to Federal court if the Defense Department turns down his appeal. If so, he will join a growing list of court cases currently in litigation to test laws and rules against homosexuals. Philadelphia's Homosexual Law Reform Society, one of the more active legal aid groups, spent $5,000 for court actions last year, and has set aside another $25,000 for future litigation. (The funds come from membership contributions and profits from the group's monthly magazine, Drum, which has a circulation of 15,000.)

There's no shortage of lawyers to argue cases for homosexuals. Says Mr. Polak of the Philadelphia group, "Volunteer heterosexual lawyers are the backbone of our movement. It's very similar to the early days of the civil rights movement when the strongest supporters were the whites."

One such attorney is Gilbert M. Cantor of Philadelphia, who is currently handling the case of a woman fighting dismissal from a Federal civil service post on the ground that she is a homosexual. Mr. Cantor has been representing homosexual groups and individuals for four years as part of his practice, sometimes at no charge. "Good representation ought to be available to anyone," he says, "and I admire their willingness to assert their rights as citizens rather than acting as members of an underground society."

Among the homosexuals' other allies in the heterosexual world are growing numbers of Protestant clergymen. Churchmen in some of the bigger cities are working not only to help create better public understanding of homosexuals but also to help homosexuals improve their lives.

Rev. Walter D. Dennis, canon of the Episcopal Cathedral Church of St. John the Divine in New York, says Christians must "rethink the usual position that has turned homosexuals into modern-day lepers." The Rev. Robert W. Cromey, an Episcopal clergyman in San Francisco, says, "I believe the sex act is morally neutral."

Of course, only a small minority of churches and clergy accept Mr. Cromey's view. The official position of his own church is that homosexuality is a "mysterious sickness" and a "demon to be cast out, not an incurable condition that can only be endured." The Roman Catholic church holds that "homosexual acts are objectively sinful," although "the condition itself is not sinful."

At least some politicians also are changing their attitudes about homosexuals. In San Francisco last fall, several candidates for mayor, supervisor and sheriff appeared at a candidates' night at the headquarters of a homosexual organization and advertised in the organization's magazine.

Homosexual groups also are starting to form on some college campuses. Last spring a Student Homophile League became an officially recognized student group at Columbia University. (Homophile is a coined word that indicates the group consists of both homosexuals and heterosexuals who support the homosexuals' aims.)

The organization at Columbia has only 16 members, half of them heterosexuals. Nonetheless, they have sponsored lectures and panels on homosexuality and they plan a monthly publication. Similar groups are forming at Stanford University, the University of Miami, the University of Pittsburgh and a handful of other schools.

# | 56 |

## Homo Nest Raided! Queen Bees Are Stinging Mad

### Jerry Lisker

She sat there with her legs crossed, the lashes of her mascara-coated eyes beating like the wings of a hummingbird. She was angry. She was so upset she hadn't bothered to shave. A day old stubble was beginning to push through the pancake makeup. She was a he. A queen of Christopher Street.

Last weekend the queens had turned commandos and stood bra strap to bra strap against an invasion of the helmeted Tactical Patrol Force. The elite police squad had shut down one of their private gay clubs, the Stonewall Inn at 57 Christopher St., in the heart of a three-block homosexual community in Greenwich Village. Queen Power reared its bleached blonde head in revolt. New York City experienced its first homosexual riot. "We may have lost the battle, sweets, but the war is far from over," lisped an unofficial lady-in-waiting from the court of the Queens.

"We've had all we can take from the Gestapo," the spokesman, or spokeswoman, continued. "We're putting our foot down once and for all. "The foot wore a spiked heel. According to reports, the Stonewall Inn, a two-story structure with a sand painted brick and opaque glass facade, was a mecca for the homosexual element in the village who wanted nothing but a private little place where they could congregate, drink, dance and do whatever little girls do when they get together.

The thick glass shut out the outside world of the street. Inside, the Stonewall bathed in wild, bright psychedelic lights, while the patrons writhed to the sounds of a juke box on a square dance floor surrounded by booths and table. The bar did a good business and the waiters, or waitresses, were always kept busy, as they snaked their way around the dancing customers to the booths and tables. For nearly two years, peace and tranquility reigned supreme for the Alice in Wonderland clientele.

### THE RAID LAST FRIDAY

Last Friday the privacy of the Stonewall was invaded by police from the First Division. It was a raid. They had a warrant. After two years, police said they had been informed that liquor was being served on the premises. Since the Stonewall was without a license, the place was being closed. It was the law.

All hell broke loose when the police entered the Stonewall. The girls instinctively reached for each other. Others stood frozen, locked in an embrace of fear.

Only a handful of police were on hand for the initial landing in the homosexual beachhead. They ushered the patrons out onto Christopher Street, just off Sheridan Square. A crowd had formed in front of the Stonewall and the customers were greeted with cheers of encouragement from the gallery.

The whole proceeding took on the aura of a homosexual Academy Awards Night. The Queens pranced out to the street blowing kisses and waving to the crowd. A beauty of a specimen named Stella wailed uncontrollably while being led to the sidewalk in front of the Stonewall by a cop. She later confessed that she didn't protest

*New York Daily News*, July 6, 1969.

the manhandling by the officer, it was just that her hair was in curlers and she was afraid her new beau might be in the crowd and spot her. She didn't want him to see her this way, she wept.

## QUEEN POWER

The crowd began to get out of hand, eye witnesses said. Then, without warning, Queen Power exploded with all the fury of a gay atomic bomb. Queens, princesses and ladies-in-waiting began hurling anything they could get their polished, manicured fingernails on. Bobby pins, compacts, curlers, lipstick tubes and other femme fatale missiles were flying in the direction of the cops. The war was on. The lilies of the valley had become carnivorous jungle plants.

Urged on by cries of "C'mon girls, lets go get'em," the defenders of Stonewall launched an attack. The cops called for assistance. To the rescue came the Tactical Patrol Force.

Flushed with the excitement of battle, a fellow called Gloria pranced around like Wonder Woman, while several Florence Nightingales administered first aid to the fallen warriors. There were some assorted scratches and bruises, but nothing serious was suffered by the honeys turned Madwoman of Chaillot.

Official reports listed four injured policemen with 13 arrests. The War of the Roses lasted about 2 hours from about midnight to 2 a.m. There was a return bout Wednesday night.

Two veterans recently recalled the battle and issued a warning to the cops. "If they close up all the gay joints in this area, there is going to be all out war."

## BRUCE AND NAN

Both said they were refugees from Indiana and had come to New York where they could live together happily ever after. They were in their early 20's. They preferred to be called by their married names, Bruce and Nan.

"I don't like your paper," Nan lisped matter-of-factly. "It's anti-fag and pro-cop."

"I'll bet you didn't see what they did to the Stonewall. Did the pigs tell you that they smashed everything in sight? Did you ask them why they stole money out of the cash register and then smashed it with a sledge hammer? Did you ask them why it took them two years to discover that the Stonewall didn't have a liquor license."

Bruce nodded in agreement and reached over

for Nan's trembling hands.

"Calm down, doll," he said. "Your face is getting all flushed."

Nan wiped her face with a tissue.

"This would have to happen right before the wedding. The reception was going to be held at the Stonewall, too," Nan said, tossing her ashen-tinted hair over her shoulder.

"What wedding?" the bystander asked.

Nan frowned with a how-could-anybody-be-so-stupid look. "Eric and Jack's wedding, of course. They're finally tieing the knot. I thought they'd never get together."

## MEET SHIRLEY

"We'll have to find another place, that's all there is to it," Bruce sighed. "But every time we start a place, the cops break it up sooner or later."

"They let us operate just as long as the payoff is regular," Nan said bitterly. "I believe they closed up the Stonewall because there was some trouble with the payoff to the cops. I think that's the real reason. It's a shame. It was such a lovely place. We never bothered anybody. Why couldn't they leave us alone?"

Shirley Evans, a neighbor with two children, agrees that the Stonewall was not a rowdy place and the persons who frequented the club were never troublesome. She lives at 45 Christopher St.

"Up until the night of the police raid there was never any trouble there," she said. "The homosexuals minded their own business and never bothered a soul. There were never any fights or hollering, or anything like that. They just wanted to be left alone. I don't know what they did inside, but that's their business. I was never in there myself. It was just awful when the police came. It was like a swarm of hornets attacking a bunch of butterflies."

A reporter visited the now closed Stonewall and it indeed looked like a cyclone had struck the premises.

Police said there were over 200 people in the Stonewall when they entered with a warrant. The crowd outside was estimated at 500 to 1,000. According to police, the Stonewall had been under observation for some time. Being a private club plain clothesmen were refused entrance to the inside when they periodically tried to check the place. "They had the tightest security in the Village," a First Division officer said, "We could never get near the place without a warrant."

## POLICE TALK

The men of the First Division were unable to find any humor in the situation, despite the comical overtones of the raid.

"They were throwing more than lace hankies," one inspector said. "I was almost decapitated by a slab of thick glass. It was thrown like a discus and just missed my throat by inches. The beer can didn't miss, though, "it hit me right above the temple."

Police also believe the club was operated by Mafia connected owners. The police did confiscate the Stonewall's cash register as proceeds from an illegal operation. The receipts were counted and are on file at the division headquarters. The warrant was served and the establishment closed on the grounds it was an illegal membership club with no license, and no license to serve liquor.

The police are sure of one thing. They haven't heard the last from the Girls of Christopher Street.

# | 57 |

# *The "Gay" People Demand Their Rights*

## LACEY FOSBURGH

André Gide once wrote that he was "obsessed and haunted . . . expending [himself] crazily to the point of utter exhaustion." Other homosexuals have described the terrible shame and loneliness that shadowed their existence. No such complexes interfered with the march in New York last Sunday of thousands of men and women who hoisted their silk banners high and chanted, "Say it loud, Gay is proud."

Singing their songs as they marched up Sixth Avenue to Central Park, they proclaimed to anyone who would listen the "new strength and pride of the Gay People."

Not long ago the scene would have been unthinkable, but the spirit of militancy and determination is growing so rapidly among the legions of young homosexuals that last weekend thousands of them came from all over the Northeast—eager to participate in the demonstration and to serve notice on the straight world that the passive climate of guilt and inferiority that has long subdued the homosexual world is changing.

## OUT OF THE CLOSETS

"We're probably the most harassed, persecuted minority group in history, but we'll never have the freedom and civil rights we deserve as human beings unless we stop hiding in the closets and in the shelter of anonymity," said 29-year-old Michael Brown, a founder of the Gay Liberation Front, one of the many activist organizations which have sprung up during the last year in response to this new aggressive mood.

The focus of the protest, which brought together almost two dozen divergent groups, was both the laws which make homosexual acts between consenting adults illegal and the social conditions which make it difficult for homosexuals to behave romantically in public, get jobs in government, corporations, banks, airlines, schools or utility companies, or even in some cases rent apartments together.

Such widespread discrimination and inequality, the new homosexual contends, is patently unfair. Now, at a time when blacks, Puerto Ricans, Indians and young people are all refusing to acquiesce in the social values that relegate them to nether worlds, many homosexuals are standing up and saying "I'm proud, too. I'm equal" and the groups who marched last weekend from the "Queens"—men who wore lipstick and dresses—to the Lavender Menace, 30 lesbian members of the Women's Liberation Movement.

*New York Times*, July 5, 1970, p. E-12.

They included politically oriented groups such as the Homosexual Law Reform Society and the socially oriented, like the Institute of Social Ethics and Human Enlightenment, the more collegiate, such as Gay People at Columbia and Tale, and even the revolutionary socialist, such as the Red Butterfly.

Their program, according to Michael Kotis, 28, president of the 15-year-old, 700-member Mattachine Society, is defiance. We're going out in the streets. We're going to protest against every form of bias and discrimination that holds us back."

## MOOD IS EXPLAINED

Bob Kohler, a leading member of the Gay Liberation Front, explained the new mood of militancy this way: "This generation of homosexuals knows that the only way to loosen up society and eliminate the fear and disgust we arouse in people is through an open confrontation. We're going to get loud and angry and then more loud and angry until we get our rights."

Although leaders of the movement firmly believe that such aggressive tactics are the only way to win their legal and social rights, they admit the task is difficult.

"Many people can truly identify with the black civil rights movement or other oppressed minorities, but they still can't accept us," said Mr. Kotis. "The issue of homosexuality hits close to home because it involves the touchy matter of sex. For many people it's too personal and controversial because in their hearts they have secret doubts about their own sexual desires." He pointed out that according to the Kinsey Report 50 per cent of the male population and somewhat less among females are capable of homosexual response.

"We don't belong in the closets any more and people shouldn't be afraid of what we represent," said Becky Irons, a past president of the Daughters of Bilitis, the oldest lesbian organization, with 300 members in New York. "There's just nothing wrong with us, nothing queer or freaky, and as soon as everybody in the Gay World and the straight world recognizes this everything will be alright."

# | 58 |

# The Lesbian Issue and Women's Lib

### JUDY KLEMESRUD

The Lesbian issue, which has been hidden away like a demented child ever since the women's liberation movement came into being in 1966, was brought out of the closet yesterday.

Nine leaders of the movement held a press conference at the Washington Square Methodist Church, 133 West Fourth Street, to express their "solidarity with the struggle of homosexuals to attain their liberation in a sexist society."

The conference was prompted by an article in the Behavior section of the December 14 issue of Time magazine which said that Kate Millett, author of "Sexual Politics" and one of the chief

theoreticians of the movement, had probably "discredited herself as a spokeswoman for her cause" because she disclosed at a recent meeting that she was bisexual.

## PREPARED STATEMENT IS READ

The 36-year-old Miss Millett, sitting in the center of the leaders at a table in the front of the church, read a statement that she said had been prepared last Monday night at a meeting of about 30

*New York Times*, December 18, 1970.

women representing such groups as the National Organization for Women (NOW), Radical Lesbians, Columbia Women's Liberation and Daughters of Bilitis.

The statement said, in part:

"Women's liberation and homosexual liberation are both struggling towards a common goal: A society free from defining and categorizing people by virtue of gender and/or sexual preference. 'Lesbian' is a label used as a psychic weapon to keep women locked into their male-defined 'feminine role.' The essence of that role is that a woman is defined in terms of her relationship to men. A woman is called a Lesbian when she functions autonomously. Women's autonomy is what women's liberation is all about."

Standing behind Miss Millett as she spoke were abut 50 women supporters, who frequently interrupted her statement with cheers. Other leaders in the group were Gloria Steinem, the journalist; Ruth Simpson, president of the New York chapter of Daughters of Bilitis; Florynce Kennedy, a lawyer; Sally Klempton and Susan Brownmiller, journalists and members of the New York Radical Feminists; and Ivy Bottini, Dolores Alexander and Ti-Grace Atkinson of NOW.

"It's not quite my position," Miss Atkinson, a tall, slender blonde in blue sunglasses said afterwards. "It's not radical enough. If men succeed in associating Lesbianism with the women's movement, then they destroy the movement."

The Lesbian issue had been festering for several months, especially since the Women's Strike for Equality last August 26.

At a rally at Bryant Park following the August 26 march down Fifth Avenue, a member of the Radical Lesbians made a plaintive plea for support from her "straight" sisters in the movement. The speaker charged that the police were harassing Lesbians, and that other women in the movement were ignoring their plight.

"We're your sisters, and we need help!" the speaker cried.

The church had been decorated for the press conference with posters that read, "Kate is Great," "We Stand Together as Women, Regardless of Sexual Preference," and "Is the Statue of Liberty a Lesbian, Too?"

During the question period, Miss Alexander said she thought the movement had taken an overly long time to deal with the Lesbian issue because many women in the movement were afraid to confront it.

## "Such an explosive issue"

"It's such an explosive issue," she said. "It can intimidate women. Many women would be reduced to tears if you called them Lesbians."

She added that the movement represented women who were "heterosexuals, homosexuals, tall, short, fat, skinny, black, yellow and white."

"People must speak up a Lesbians," said Barbara Love, of the Gay Liberation Front. "I am a Lesbian. We've got to come out and fight, because we're not going to get anywhere if we don't."

Miss Kennedy, the only black woman among the leaders, called for a total "girlcot" of the products of the major advertisers in Time magazine.

Although they weren't present, supporting statements were distributed from Bella Abzug, Democratic Representative-elect of the 19th Congressional District, Caroline Bird, author of "Born Female," and Aileen C. Hernandez, national president of NOW, who called the attempts to use Lesbianism as a weapon against the women's liberation movement, "sexual McCarthyism."

Betty Friedan, high priestess of the women's liberation movement and a conservative on the Lesbian issue, did not attend the press conference. Leaders said they had tried to contact her, but that she was "out of town."

# | 59 |

## Uptight on Gay News: Can the Straight Press Get the Gay Story Straight? Is Anyone Even Trying?

### RANSDELL PIERSON

Since the 1960s, blacks, women, and other so-called minority groups (women outnumber men in the U.S.) have been hired on in increasing numbers in newsrooms. In many cases their representation is little more than token, but their presence has clearly had a beneficial effect on the way newspapers cover minorities and minority concerns. The gay-rights movement gained momentum in the late 1960s; its aims and tactics are remarkably similar to those of other minority-rights groups; but, gay activists complain, there has been no comparable change in the news media's attitudes toward gays. As they see it, the prevailing attitude is a compound of hostility and ignorance that prevents gay journalists from openly acknowledging their sexual preference and thus virtually guarantees that coverage of the gay-rights movement, of issues arising from the shifting attitudes toward homosexuality, and of the lives led by the majority of gay men and women, will be inadequate and uninformed.

Nearly two hundred interviews at news organizations in ten cities indicate that, with rare exceptions, gay reporters and editors believe they must stay in the closet to keep their jobs, and that their fear of being perceived as gay inhibits them from making suggestions about covering stories about gays.

Last June, this reporter interviewed seven closeted gays at the New Orleans *Times-Picayune/States-Item*; none was willing to be identified. All said they would like to be able to suggest stories relating to gay life and issues but, as one put it: "I am uncomfortable volunteering for covering gay news for fear of being identified as gay. If you're not openly gay—and nobody here

is—questions could be raised about your interest in a gay topic."

This conviction that secrecy is the best policy may be rooted in the fact that, until recently, homosexual acts were illegal in most states and are still nominally so in twenty-five states and the District of Columbia. Social disapproval of homosexuality—much of it, conceivably, based on ignorance—remains a strong deterrent to candor in all states, and not only in the field of journalism. As one reporter said:—It would do no one's career any good at my paper to have [his or her] homosexuality known as a fact. It's the same in law firms where young associates understand the unstated code of their environment: there are certain things which, if done, simply aren't talked about." In New York City, so far as is known, only one reporter for a daily newspaper—Joe Nicholson of the Post—has openly acknowledged that he is gay.

A few news organizations—notably Time Inc., CBS, NBC, and Knight-Ridder Newspapers—have written policies prohibiting discrimination on the basis of sexual preference. Frank Perich, the *Life* magazine typesetter who in February 1981 proposed the nondiscrimination clause adopted that month by Time Inc., says, "Psychologically, the clause is a wonderful benefit. Now I don't have to worry if I suggest we should do something on a gay topic."

Jonathan Z. Larsen, senior editor of *Life*, says that he welcomes the presence of openly gay staff members because "they bring things to our attention." But, Larsen adds, "while I certainly think it is helpful to have open gays on your staff, I'd hate

*Columbia Journalism Review*, March/April 1982, pp. 25–33.

to see a quota saying you have to have x number of politically militant gays around."

## COME OUT—IF YOU DARE

The fact that a news organization has adopted a nondiscrimination policy does not necessarily mean that gays feel free to come out to their colleagues. There are gay journalists on the staff of Knight-Ridder's flagship paper, the *Miami Herald*, for example, but its adoption of the nondiscrimination clause in 1973 did little to change an oppressive atmosphere. Two *Herald* newspeople who are gay said that they did not want to be identified as such because this might impair their working relationships with editors. Brian Jones, a former cub reporter at the *Herald* who is openly gay, says closeted gays "got the message" when in 1977 John McMullan, the *Herald's* executive editor, in a signed column dismissed gay supporters of a proposed Dade County ordinance prohibiting discrimination in housing and employment as "more interested in flaunting their new deviate-freedom than in preventing discrimination," and followed this up with an editorial opposing the ordinance.

An executive in NBC's television news department who describes himself as "openly gay but not for publication" says that, despite the network's official policy on gays, it would be perilous for a newsperson to be too unguarded about revealing his or her homosexuality. "I have to stay personally in touch with Jerry Falwell and Jesse Helms," he says, "so it is distinctly nonuseful to have my homosexuality bandied about. I don't want Falwell to call me up and say, 'You fucking faggot, I'm not going to give you an interview.' "

The nondiscrimination clause, as this executive sees it, is commendable—among other things, it put a stop to the routine exchange of faggot jokes at news conferences—but it provides only a limited sense of security. The clause, he says, "conflicts with a statement news division people at NBC sign, promising they won't get involved in a public way in controversial subjects. If a correspondent came out publicly as gay, NBC would have to pay him off and ask him to leave"—a measure that the executive views as mild compared to what he believes would have happened in the past. "Ten years ago," he says, "the correspondent would not only have been summarily fired, but he'd have been blackballed from all the networks."

The absence of acknowledged gays on news staffs means, of course, that editors are deprived of a ready means of checking on the quality of coverage of stories relating to gays. It also means that editors are not compelled to confront gaps and inconsistencies in their perceptions of homosexuality.

*The New York Times*, in many other respects a trendsetter, is perceived by gay activists and a score of former and present *Times* men and women as being considerably behind the times in its attitude toward, and news treatment of, gays. Interestingly, a decade ago the paper at least compelled its readers to re-examine *their* attitudes toward homosexuality by publishing Merle Miller's Sunday *Magazine* article entitled "What It Means To Be a Homosexual." Miller, a respected television writer, was also the author of *Only You, Dick Daring!*, a classic satire about how networks work; the appearance of his article on January 17, 1971, marked the first time that an American with Miller's kind of credentials had come out in public.

Miller's recollections of how the piece came to be assigned are a useful reminder of an era when gays were just beginning to coalesce for political action in the wake of the so-called Stonewall riots. (Gay Pride Week commemorates the three days of confrontation between police and gays that began on June 28, 1969, when the police raided a Greenwich Village gay bar called the Stonewall Inn.) "In 1970," says Miller, "I was having lunch with two editors from *The New York Times* who were discussing a vicious piece in *Harper's* magazine by Joseph Epstein (now editor of *The American Scholar*). Epstein said that if he had his way he'd wish homosexuals off the face of the earth.[1] And the *Times* editors, both liberals, expressed approval of the piece. It was just a year after Stonewall and I, for the first time, spoke up and said, 'Damn it, I'm a homosexual!' " Miller was promptly invited to write the *Magazine* piece, which drew more than 2,000 letters, mostly favorable.

## DOES THE *TIMES* KNOW ITS OWN MIND?

But if in the past the *Times* boldly tackled a subject most mainstream publications wouldn't touch, in recent years the paper's coverage of gay-related subjects has often seemed timorous, shallow, and hypocritical.

Former *Times* columnist Roger Wilkins—he left the paper in 1979 and is now a commentator on CBS Radio's "Spectrum" program—recalls: "I had a clear sense that [homosexuality] was not a subject which was welcomed at the paper. It was generally known." The first black to be appointed to the Times's editorial board, Wilkins says that during his two years as the paper's urban affairs writer only three of his columns were killed—and two of them were on gay topics. The spiking of a 1978 piece he wrote on the gay-rights bill then coming up before the city council particularly rankled him. "I understood that six hundred thousand to one million gay people live in New York City," says Wilkins, "and their impact on the city is just enormous. I was able to talk to people in the closet who told me how the bill would affect their lives."

Wilkins says he was told by then-assistant metro editor Jonathan Friendly that deputy managing editor Arthur Gelb spiked the column "because it wasn't urban affairs." Friendly, now media reporter for the Times, says he does not recall the incident, adding that his understanding was that the urban affairs column, then as now, was restricted to reporting on two constituencies, "the poor and minorities—ethnic minorities." Wilkins disputes this, saying, "The urban affairs column dealt with everything urban."

Grace Lichtenstein, a general assignment reporter at the Times from 1970 to 1978, comments in a vein somewhat similar to Wilkins's: "I wanted to do more stories on the topic than they wanted. They usually thought one general story [on gays] would do for a year or so. I asked if I could develop gay affairs and women's affairs as a beat on the metropolitan desk, and the request was turned down."

The Times can also be fairly charged with failing to practice what it preaches. Its editorial stance on a bill prohibiting discrimination against gays that has repeatedly failed to pass in the city council has been eloquent: ". . . the city itself is diminished by the manner of the measure's rejection. The bill's intent was merely to guarantee the right not to be discriminated against" (May 25, 1974); ". . . We hope that this time around the bill passes and New Yorkers affirm their belief in equitable treatment for a long-abused minority" (May 3, 1978). But time and again—in 1975, 1978, and 1981—in contract negotiations with The Newspaper Guild, the Times has rejected demands that the paper should accept a nondiscrimination clause protecting gays.

While, at least on its editorial page, the Times regards gays as a minority, editors at other papers hold conflicting views on this basic issue. Peter Weitzel, deputy managing editor at The Miami Herald, says, for example: "My paper doesn't make any effort to cover gays as a specific community that should be regularly covered. I don't think they're a specific minority." Ben Bagdikian, the former Washington Post ombudsman who now teaches journalism at the University of California at Berkeley, disagrees. "Homosexuals have been treated as an inferior group in society," he says, "and therefore deserve regular coverage along with other minorities such as women and blacks."

▼ ▼ ▼

Nor is there any consensus on what to call homosexuals. In New York City, the Daily News and the Post permit the use of the word "gay," as do Newsweek and Time; The New York Times bans its use except when the word appears in quotations or forms part of a group's name. Times news editor Allan M. Siegal, who makes sure reporters conform to the stylebook, explains: "At the Times we are slow to accept change in usage of words, and we feel uncomfortable depriving 'gay' of its traditional meaning."

Strict adherence to this rule can result in bizarre editorial hairsplitting. Sidney Zion, a former Times reporter who now free-lances, wrote an article on the resurgence of bigband jazz that appeared in the June 21, 1981, Times Magazine under the title "Outlasting Rock." Zion's editor spotted a problem in the breezy lead, which ran as follows: "Between the rock and the hard disco, the melody began to slip back in. A piano bar here, a big band there, a touch of Gershwin, a spot of Kern. In gay places and out of the way places." Zion says he was told that he would have to change "gay" to "homosexual" to conform with the paper's style rule. "I said, 'That's crazy,' " Zion recalls. "They said they would leave it 'gay places' only if I meant to say 'happy places.' They knew very well what I meant, but I said, 'Okay, if that makes you feel better.' " And so "gay" was smuggled into print at the Times.

It is curious that a paper like the Times, which editorially grants gays the status of "a long-abused minority," should decline to use the term the activist leaders of that minority use to define themselves. The word "gay" is, of course, as fraught with political significance as, in the past, was "black," which has long since supplanted "Negro" and "colored" in most of the U.S. press. Like "black," "gay" is a term that connotes pride. Moreover, as James Saslow, New York editor of

*The Advocate*, a nationally distributed gay news magazine published in San Mateo, California, explains: "The gay community uses the word 'gay' to get away from the sexual connotations implicit in the word 'homosexual.' I see the resistance by the traditional press to the use of the word 'gay' [as stemming from the fact that] it would force reporters to confront the nonsexual aspects of coverage of gay rights and how our community has organized itself."

## GAPS, LAPSES—BLACKOUTS

Papers that, in one way or another, close themselves off from contact with on-staff gays and from their local gay communities repeatedly incur the risk of missing out on stories and of producing distorted coverage of stories they do report. For example:

The 1980 presidential election marked the emergence of gays as a political force on the national level. Some papers took note of what syndicated columnists Jack W. Germond and Jules Witcover described in a November 29, 1979, piece as "the gay-rights movement's most ambitious project yet . . . to elect homosexual delegates to the Democratic and Republican national conventions next summer to hammer through gay-rights platform planks." on June 25, 1980, for instance, *The Minneapolis Tribune* ran a story headlined DEMOCRATIC PARTY ADOPTS GAY-RIGHTS PLANK; on August 13 of that year *The Washington Star* and *The Washington Post* ran articles on gay caucus activities at the Democratic National Convention and followed up with pieces on the nomination of gay activist Melvin Boozer as a vice-presidential candidate. *The New York Times*, on the other hand, did not mention the gay caucus or the nomination of an openly gay vice-presidential candidate until *after* the convention—and then only in three paragraphs in an August 16 "Reporter's Notebook" piece by Howell Raines and in the last paragraph of a wire-service piece that appeared the same day. (The *Times's* only mention of the adoption by the Democratic Party of a gay-rights plank which had the backing of then-President Carter, and which marked the first time any major American political party had adopted such a plank, was a single sentence in a long June 25, 1980, piece on the platform.)

On June 18, 1981, the U.S. House of Representatives debated the so-called McDonald Amendment, which would specifically deny federal legal services to homosexuals in discrimination cases and other cases in which their sexual preference becomes an issue, and which was attached to a bill authorizing federal funds for the Legal Services Corporation. The following day, *The Washington Post* ran a front-page story, headlined LEGAL SERVICES REPRIEVE VOTED, half of which was devoted to the "bitter, two-hour" debate over the McDonald Amendment.

In New York, by contrast, the emotional debate over the amendment—"the first ever [in Congress] on a gay issue," according to Larry Bush, a writer whose coverage of the McDonald Amendment appeared in several gay papers—was almost completely ignored by the city's dailies. (*The Daily News* carried no mention; the *Post* and the *Times* each devoted only a single sentence to the amendment.) Commenting on this near blackout, Lindsy Van Gelder, a former New York *Daily News* reporter who is a lesbian, says, "I think that if legislation was being passed against any other group, newspapers would know how to cover it, but it's not being done with gays." (The McDonald Amendment passed the House by a vote of 281 to 124, but was ignored by the Senate in the November rush to pass a temporary funding bill.)

On September 9, 1981, Moral Majority leader Jerry Falwell held a press conference in which he called upon Congress to overturn a District of Columbia bill, passed by the district's City Council in July, that removed most criminal penalties for homosexual acts and sodomy between consenting adults. (The bill also reduced the maximum sentence for forcible rape from life imprisonment to twenty years—a change advocated by some women's groups because it could make convictions easier to obtain—and repealed a provision that made it a crime for any male teacher over twenty-one to have consensual sex with any female student under twenty-one.) *The Washington Post* covered the press conference in a September 10 piece. In it, Falwell described the city's sex bill as "a perverted act about perverted acts" and was quoted as saying, "It would be very terrible if Washington D.C. became the gay capital of the world." The article pointed out that Falwell's attempt to overturn the district bill marked "the first major thrust into D.C. politics by the Moral Majority."

There was a flaw in the *Post's* coverage of Falwell's assault on the bill—and it was not rectified during the three weeks between the fundamentalist's press conference and Congress's October 1 vote to overturn the district bill. The paper carried no comment from the segment of the city's population singled out for attack by Falwell: its gays. The *Post* finally got around to providing a comment—in one paragraph—on October 2.

*Washington Post* city editor Milton Coleman concedes that "there should have been an effort to get views of people in the gay community" following Falwell's attack. But, says Coleman, "We did not want to make it look like a gay issue" because heterosexuals were affected by the legislation as well and because the main issue was home rule. Gay writer Larry Bush, who has written op-ed pieces for *The Washington Star* and *The New York Times*, finds this explanation disingenuous. "I think there's no question that Falwell thought he could win by exciting people's feelings about homosexuality," says Bush, "and I think *The Washington Post* let him get away with it," in part by not giving Washington's powerful gay community . . . a chance to respond."

Last spring, two Florida state legislators introduced the so-called Trask-Bush amendment—a rider attached to the state's general appropriations bill that was designed to deny funding to state universities that provide a meeting place for any group that "recommends or advocates sexual relations between persons not married to each other." The amendment was "directed directly at homosexuals," declared Representative Tom Bush, one of its sponsors. (Senator Alan Trask was the other sponsor.) The amendment was attached to the Senate's appropriations bill on April 24, to the House's bill on May 11. The bill was passed by the House on June 16, by the Senate on June 17.

*The Miami Herald* ran dozens of appropriations stories during those months but, according to the paper's morgue, it did not once mention the Trask-Bush amendment. *The Miami News* carried a single piece on the amendment—an April 25 AP story—and on May 12 briefly mentioned its passage in the House. The *News*, according to its morgue, then dropped the subject until August 28, when Florida's commissioner of education announced that he would challenge the amendment in the courts on the ground that it violated First Amendment guarantees of free speech and free assembly. The *Herald* got onto the story on September 15. (The state's Supreme Court struck down the amendment in February 1982.)

During the spring and summer of 1981, when public discussion could have affected legislation, the only Miami paper to explain the significance of the Trask-Bush amendment, and to keep reading

ers posted on its progress through the Senate and House, was South Florida's gay paper, *The Weekly News*.

Over a period of three days on the weekend of April 24, 1981, New Orleans police rounded up and jailed more than 100 gay men and women in a series of raids in the French Quarter. (Those arrested were charged with "obstructing sidewalks" in front of gay bars.) The arrests prompted a vigorous political response from the local gay community, which charged that the police were trying to drive gays out of the French Quarter. A protest meeting attended by 700 gays helped to persuade Mayor Ernest Morial and Police Chief Henry Morris to promise to investigate charges of police harassment. (All charges against the arrested gays were subsequently dropped.)

Two of the city's three network television stations—WDSU (NBC) and WVUE (ABC)—followed the breaking story and sent film crews to the protest meeting held on the Tuesday following the weekend arrests. The *Times-Picayune/States-Item* got around to the story on Wednesday, April 29—five days after the first arrests. The account, buried in section 5, said nothing about the protest meeting, which would seem to have been the logical peg, and failed to include in its tally of arrests a group of thirty-nine gay men picked up the previous Sunday. Reporter Allan Katz, who wrote the story, says: "They wanted somebody to do something in a hurry. You would think that because the story was four days old before they assigned it to a reporter they didn't consider it a major story. About the only time in my experience we really try to relate to gay news," Katz explains, "is when something really controversial comes up." Apparently, the arrest of more than 100 men and women in a city not under martial law was not considered "really controversial."

(Last October, to its credit, the *Times-Picayune/States-Item* published two pieces of enterprise reporting on issues related to gay rights. As a rule, however, the paper relies on wire stories. "It's easier for them to pick up a wire story," says Iris Kelso, a political writer for the paper, "because it doesn't involve a lot of decision about doing it and who to assign it to." The paper's index for 1981 lists twenty-eight references to, and stories about, homosexual topics; all but five were wire stories.)

Anti-gay violence is a phenomenon common to many cities, including, notoriously, New York. A grim example occurred on November 19, 1980, when a man who later told police that he hated homosexuals fired several rounds of ammunition into a gay bar in Greenwich Village, killing two men and wounding six others. A month later, a group of teenagers went on a "gay-bashing spree" in the Village, attacking a dozen men, most of whom were gay. Beatings by gangs are almost a routine occurrence. According to Jay Watkins, a spokesperson for the 1,000-member Chelsea Gay Association, which monitors attacks against the city's gays, its Violent Crime Victim's Hotline receives an average of twelve calls each week. (One of the hotline's purposes is to bring the cases to the attention of the police.) This would mean that, at the very least, roughly 600 such assaults take place yearly in New York City.

The *Times* covered the November shooting rampage, as did the *Daily News* and the *Post*. But, unlike its tabloid competitors, the *Times* never sought any personal reaction from the city's shaken gay community and, indeed, it seems unwilling to acknowledge the day-to-day existence of antigay violence in its own backyard, even while admitting its existence elsewhere. (An example is a November 27, 1981, piece, bearing a San Francisco dateline, headed COAST CITY TO CURB ASSAULTS BY GANGS.) The *Times*, says Watkins, treats such attacks as "random violence, not targeted at gays," adding, "When *The New York Times* presents them as just another street assault, you wonder why they even bother to cover them." (Peter Millones, the *Times*'s metropolitan editor, declined to be interviewed for this article.) Among the city's papers that do cover such assaults, and define them as anti-gay, are the *Daily News*, the *Post*, *The Village Voice*, the *Soho News*, the *Chelsea-Clinton News*, a neighborhood weekly, and *The New York Native*, a gay biweekly.

The *San Francisco Chronicle* is one mainstream daily that has begun to pursue news relating to the lives gays lead and the issues that concern them as it would any other story. The *Chronicle*'s recent coverage of anti-gay violence is a clear case in point. Between September 15 and December 10, 1981, the paper ran at least six articles on the subject. Some were brief, such as GAY ACTIVIST NEARLY KILLED BY S.F. KNIFERs and, two months later, GAYS OUTRAGED OVER STABBINGS; a few were long, such as VIOLENCE AND GAYS—A TURN OF THE TIDE, a fifty-paragraph piece accompanied by five photos. This last article, pegged to the sentencing of a confessed killer of four gay men, con-

cluded with with a cogent quote that has implications for editors. Tht, murders, said Gwenn Craig, president of the Harvey Milk Gay Democratic Club, prove "the fundamental point we've been trying to make for years. We've been saying that hatred of gay people is an issue that our society has to deal with. It's real and it brings tragedies like this."

▼ ▼ ▼

The author of these six pieces was Randy Shilts, who joined the *Chronicle*'s staff last summer after the paper made it known that it was looking for an openly gay reporter. Shilts says his instructions are to do general reporting (most of his pieces are in this category) while keeping an eye on gay topics. Among other stories, he has written features on "the first acknowledged lesbian judge in the country" and "the city's first openly gay cop."

Shilts believes that his presence on the staff has had beneficial effects both on the way the paper is perceived by the city's gay community and on the quality of the paper's coverage of it. "The gay community doesn't feel as alienated" as it did previously, he says. "They know they have somebody they can call up who won't make queer jokes when they hang up the phone. And within the paper I think a lot of dumb things that are written because of ignorance, not malice, don't appear because [his colleagues] can come to me and feel like they're getting things in clearer perspective."

Asked if a gay reporter could objectively cover the city's gay community, city editor Jerry Burns replied that the question was comparable to asking "whether a black reporter can cover black stories or a Jewish person a Jewish story. You want to build a staff composed of people of a variety of backgrounds."

## CONSCIOUSNESS-RAISING IN THE NEWSROOM

Hiring an openly gay reporter, as the *Chronicle* did, or keeping on and making the best use of a reporter who comes out to his editor and colleagues, as the *New York Post* has done, are obvious means of upgrading a paper's coverage of gays. But the prerequisite for improving coverage is an awareness that something is lacking in the existing news product. Gay activists have tried for years to raise the press's consciousness on this score, and here and there they can point to change. In Boston, for example, the *Globe* altered its style rule to allow the use of "gay" as a noun and ran a profile of a lesbian grandmother following meetings with a local group called Lesbian and Gay Media Advocates. In Minneapolis, *Tribune* assistant city editor John Addington says that meetings with "vocal gay leaders in the community," together with the presence of two openly gay reporters who have since moved on to other jobs, resulted in increased coverage of gay news.

Ron Gold, a former *TV Guide* editor and *Variety* reporter who served as media liaison for the National Gay Task Force until 1979, believes that activists must not only "consult with" editors but also "confront" them to end what he regards as "a literal conspiracy in the major media to suppress gay news." What Gold and others find particularly wrongheaded about present coverage of gays is its focus on the wilder fringes of gay life at the expense of the domesticity of the lives led by the majority of gay men and women and of the development of professional caucuses and gay communities. James Saslow, New York editor of *The Advocate*, says in this connection: "Always what captures the public's mind are the sexual or sensational aspects, rather than the full picture of the lives we lead. Nothing else gets through. It's as if there's a filter on the city editor's brain."

Conceivably, the establishment this spring of a national gay wire service could alert attentive mainstream editors to a range of stories they would otherwise not pick up on. The wire service, which is being set up by the Gay Press Association, will be based in New York City. In the meantime, the paucity of nonsensational and nonpolitical pieces on gays suggests that the "filter on the city editor's brain" may, over the years, have become virtually impermeable. This reporter's survey of coverage indicated that, while papers frequently present gays in a crime or drag-queen context and sporadically report on their political activities, they almost never treat the wider issues of how gays live, or the problems a gay child faces, or the psychological and social aspects of being gay. The *Globe*'s February 2, 1981, profile of a lesbian grandmother; a June 21, 1981, *Washington Post* piece headlined GAY COUPLE LIVING TOGETHER FINDS OLD RULES DO NOT FIT; and Randy Shilts's *San Francisco Chronicle* pieces demonstrate that papers can present gays as, quite simply, people—but such pieces are rare.

In the January 21, 1982, *Advocate*, media columnist Randy Alfred observed: "If the gay angle is essentially irrelevant to the story's news value, it will be mentioned only if the story is negative. An alleged arsonist who claims to be gay is a 'gay arsonist,' but a humanitarian doctor who's partly closeted is a 'bachelor.' "

The observation is apt, but it begs the question of how journalists can extricate themselves from this bind until more gays whom the public respects step out of the closet, thus making it possible for them to be defined as gay. To do so, of course, requires guts. Not to do so, meanwhile, helps to perpetuate the present stasis, in which the press transmits to an intolerant and ill-informed society the kind of coverage that, being only marginally better informed, does little to educate that society out of its intolerance.

"The biggest enemies [faced by gay activists trying to effect change] are the totally closeted people who have real power," says the NBC news executive who describes himself as "openly gay but not for publication." His comment is echoed by many gays in the news media, who perceive promotion to power as a means by which institutions unwittingly force closeted gays to become, or appear, homophobic: the more they have to protect, the more careful they are to disguise themselves—some, by marrying and raising a family; some, by expressing their contempt for "faggots" in a variety of ways at the office.

▼ ▼ ▼

Joan Cook, a metro desk reporter at *The New York Times* and chairperson of The Newspaper Guild's unit at the paper, says: "I know it's a problem felt by homosexuals—the uncertainty of knowing what will happen if they become open. I don't know that there are any guarantees for anyone advancing the body social. Everybody takes risks. You decide whether you're going to be a risk-taker or not."

It would be unfair, however, to place the burden of change on the shoulders of gays. Surely, at the very least, editors have a responsibility to provide a newsroom climate in which reporters, straight or gay, can suggest that stories about gays be pursued without fearing that their motives will be questioned or their future at the paper imperiled. Surely, too, one might expect conscientious editors and reporters to review their past coverage of stories relating to gays and then to ask themselves one question: Have their attitudes toward homosexuality affected their ability to perceive and report reality?

1. What Epstein wrote in "Homo/Hetero, The Struggle For Sexual Identity," the cover article of the September 1970 Harper's, was: "If I had the power to do so, I would wish homosexuality off the face of this earth. I would do so because I think that it brings infinitely more pain than pleasure to those who are forced to live with it; because I think there is no resolution for this pain in our lifetimes . . . ; and because . . . I find myself completely incapable of coming to terms with it."

# | 60 |

# Out at the New York Times

## MICHELANGELO SIGNORILE

### A "LAVENDER ENLIGHTENMENT" IS UNDER WAY AT AMERICA'S NEWSPAPER OF RECORD

It was an afternoon during the Persian Gulf war. The editors of the *New York Times* were gathered in the conference room adjacent to executive editor Max Frankel's office for a daily event: the page 1 meeting. As usual, some people sat on chairs lining the room's walls. An inner circle of people sat around a long, narrow table, while Frankel and managing editor Joseph Lelyveld sat at the head of the table.

With the paper's Washington, D.C., bureau staff participating in the meeting with the help of speakers and a microphone hidden somewhere in the room, editors from each of the paper's departments described the articles they had in the works for the next day's paper and suggested what should be on page 1. On that particular day, there were at least five gay people in the room.

When it came time for foreign news editor Bernard Gwertzman to deliver his report, he decided to relay a story. One of his reporters had written about the elaborate display of multicolored tents stretched across the Saudi Arabian desert where U.S. troops were stationed. Something about the way the description was worded had irked Gwertzman. "I told the reporter to change it," Gwertzman explained to the group, laughing, "because he made the soldiers look like a bunch of faggots."

A cold silence came over the room for several seconds. Then the meeting continued, although in a tense manner. Later, a couple of the gay individuals who had been present privately told Gwertzman what they thought of his comment. But more significant, in what some say was a first, Frankel and Lelyveld took Gwertzman to task, letting him know that from then on gay slurs would not be tolerated at the *New York Times*. "They came down on him hard—tore him out a new asshole," quips *Times* deputy news editor Russell King, who is gay.

Several months later, Philip Gefter, who'd just been hired as a *Times* picture editor, was sitting at the picture desk when he overheard a straight male editor retelling an event to a group of people. In his account, the male editor used the word "fruits" to describe gay men. A straight female editor who was present became incensed. She told the male editor that his words were hurtful. Gefter, empowered by the woman, reeled around, looked the male editor in the face, and said, "Yeah. You never know when there might be a gay person around." The male editor mumbled an apology and loped off.

In January, two weeks after becoming the new *Times* publisher, Arthur Ochs Sulzberger Jr. held a meeting with the editorial staff in the newsroom. It was a new year and a new *Times*. He told the staff that from then on "diversity" would be a

*Advocate*, May 5 and 19, 1992, pp. 34–42 and 38–42.

priority at the paper, and eventually he blurted out the phrase "sexual orientation."

"We almost fell off our chairs," recalls photographer Sara Krulwich, a lesbian who's been with the *Times* for 13 years. "It was the first time any top executive at the *Times* had ever used those words."

And just a few weeks ago, in an unprecedented appearance, Lelyveld spoke to the newly formed National Lesbian and Gay Journalists Association at New York's Lesbian and Gay Community Services Center. He gave several reasons for appearing before the crowd of 250, including his desire "to show solidarity with my gay colleagues at the *Times*."

While what some have dubbed the Lavender Enlightenment was occurring behind the scenes at the *Times* in the last year or so, it seemed like all manner of gay and lesbian news was suddenly fit to print on the paper's pages as well. There were stories about suburban gays, Jewish gays in search of a rabbi, powerful lesbians in the gay and lesbian civil rights movement, the paucity of gay and lesbian characters on television, and even a travel piece — with recommendations from a New York hotel concierge — on things for gay male couples from Los Angeles to do while visiting the Big Apple. One *Times* headline asked, WAS ST. PAUL GAY?, while another queried, WAS SCHUBERT GAY? But the eyebrow raiser of 1991 had to be MILITANTS BACK "QUEER." SHOVING "GAY" THE WAY OF "NEGRO."

Throughout 1991 and into 1992, page 1 of the *Times* addressed such subjects as a battle between Irish-American gays and the organizers of New York City's St. Patrick's Day parade, the outcome of a gay-bashing murder trial in Queens, children growing up in gay households, a controversy over banning military recruiters from college campuses in New York State because of the Pentagon's ban on enlistment of gays and lesbians, the mainstreaming of the gay press, and a Bronx hospital giving spousal benefits to gay employees.

The editorial page was lit up. President George Bush received a severe lashing on more than one occasion for his fumbling of the AIDS crisis — with the *Times* actually nominating Earvin "Magic" Johnson for president the day after he revealed he tested positive for antibodies to HIV, the suspected AIDS virus. Defense secretary Dick Cheney was urged to end the Pentagon's ban on enlisting gays and lesbians in the military in a lengthy editorial complete with a chart showing that the public was in favor of ending the ban. The *Times* went after the New York

State legislature on several issues, not only demanding passage of a hate-crimes bill stalled by antigay Republicans in the state senate but also calling for something far more radical: complete civil rights for lesbians and gay men. The behavior of the Ancient Order of Hibernians, the organizers of the St. Patrick's Day parade, was "deplorable" according to the *Times*. And Marvel Comics was given a pat on the back for breaking ground in having one of its superheroes, Northstar, come out of the closet. Said the *Times*: "Mainstream culture will one day make its peace with gay Americans. When that time comes, Northstar's revelation will be seen for what it is: a welcome indicator of social change."

Op-ed page columnist Anna Quindlen, who's always been out-front on gay and AIDS issues, seemed more personally moved by the AIDS crisis, writing, "This is what AIDS looks like — good people, lovable people, people you want to hug."

Even op-ed columnist and former *Times* executive editor A.M. "Abe" Rosenthal, long reviled by many gays and lesbians as the most homophobic force at the *Times*, went through a surprising transformation. As executive editor during the early and mid '80s, Rosenthal had the *Times* virtually ignore the AIDS crisis. "The lack of coverage in the early years of the epidemic was just criminal," notes Stephen Miller, a spokesman for the New York chapter of the Gay and Lesbian Alliance Against Defamation (GLAAD). But in 1991, Rosenthal wrote a column assailing Bush for remaining "silent" on the epidemic. In yet another column last year, the man who some say tyrannized gays and lesbians at the *Times* for many years and who wouldn't even allow the word *gay* to be used in the paper, declared that "harassment and assault of gay men and lesbians is an illness in our society."

To the astute lesbian and gay reader, it was all very clear: Something had happened at the *New York Times*.

▼  ▼  ▼

Jeff Schmalz has spent more than half of his life at the *Times*. He began there 20 years ago, at the age of 18, as a copyboy and worked his way up to the position of deputy national editor. His path from there would be easy to predict: He'd probably become national editor in a short time, after current national editor Soma Golden retired or moved on. "I'd have gone to work abroad for a year or two first before taking over the national editor spot," he says. And that would most likely have occurred after the 1990 elections; Schmalz was slated to oversee all the election coverage.

But on Dec. 21, 1990, it became evident that his life would change dramatically. Schmalz came back from lunch that day, sat down at his computer terminal, and began editing a news story on the computer screen. For weeks he'd had vision problems, and his left eye had been twitching. Assuming that he was overworked he had taken off ten days and gone to St. Thomas in the Virgin Islands to relax. But the twitching didn't stop. And now the words on the screen were getting blurry as he tried to edit. Suddenly, he got very dizzy. He stood up and took a few steps. Then he blacked out.

Schmalz was having a grand mal seizure in the middle of the newsroom at the *New York Times*. He fell to the floor and immediately went into violent convulsions. "It was absolutely frightening," recalls one observer. "Everyone was horrified. It's one of those situations where you just don't know what to do. You're helpless."

Dr. Lawrence Altman, from the science desk, was summoned downstairs, and soon a team of paramedics arrived. The entire newsroom was shaken, and reporters, editors, and photographers stood dumbstruck and watched Schmalz come to. "As I was waking up, a crowd was gathered around me, and Max [Frankel] was holding my hand," Schmalz remembers. "He was quite wonderful. He was just right there."

It wasn't until a month later that Schmalz found out what was happening to his body. But the newsroom grapevine had already surmised the truth. "I'd wondered about it," says Frankel. "Previously, I didn't know he was gay. But there was speculation that it was AIDS and that he was gay."

Schmalz tested HIV-positive. His T-helper cell count—a key measure of immune-system health—was zero. There was a fear that his vision problems and the convulsions stemmed from toxoplasmosis, a deadly opportunistic infection in the brain. But when a spinal tap indicated no presence of toxoplasmosis, Schmalz's doctors decided they wanted to do exploratory brain surgery to find out what was going on.

"I had to tell the paper at that point—I'd spent my whole life exploring the truth and reporting the truth," he says. "I just went in and told them I had AIDS."

"It was a sad moment," recounts Frankel with a rasp in his voice. Frankel has been at the paper for 42 years. He watched Schmalz grow up there. And since Frankel took over as executive editor in 1986, their relationship has become closer. Schmalz also has a warm friendship with Lelyveld, who's been at the *Times* since 1962 and who also began there as a copyboy.

"Max [Frankel] cried," Schmalz recalls. "Lelyveld cried. They were just deeply and genuinely moved. They told me that the *Times* would do anything it could. Historically, the *Times* has always rallied around employees who are sick and has always treated people exceptionally well, including people with AIDS."

Throughout the '80s there were several people at the paper, mostly on the business side and therefore with no day-to-day contact with the editors, who'd quietly died of complications from AIDS. In 1988, 33-year-old Robert Barrios, a copy editor, became the first person in the editorial department who was known to have died of complications from AIDS. Barrios was close with a few newsroom staffers, and his death certainly had an impact. But he'd been at the paper for only a little over a year. He hadn't become an intimate friend of the top editors and executives of the *Times*.

Larry Josephs, a former *Times* staffer who became well-known for two harrowing articles he wrote for the *New York Times Magazine* chronicling his battle with AIDS, also died of the disease, in 1991. In the mid '80s he'd worked as a news assistant on the editorial page. "I hired him, and I thought probably he was gay, but I didn't care," says editorial page editor Jack Rosenthal. "But I later realized that I should have cared, in an affirmative way. I realized afterward that he was able to correct people who were being thoughtless because he had the experience of being gay and thus was more sensitive to the AIDS epidemic."

Josephs's death was a big blow to many at the paper, but Josephs, like Barrios, was not a major force in the newsroom; he'd been with the paper on and off throughout the early and mid '80s and hadn't worked in the *Times* offices since 1987.

Schmalz, on the other hand, had a violent seizure right under everyone's nose. And though he's now stepped down as deputy national editor, he's working at the *Times* every day in the position of assistant national editor in charge of projects, providing the top brass with front-row seats to the most horrific epidemic in America. He's someone they know well, who's been in the newsroom of the *Times* for 20 years—a wonder boy, admired by many of the executives. "He's a tremendously talented journalist and a very good friend," says current publisher Sulzberger. For several years Schmalz has socialized with Sulzberger and his wife—regularly taking a gay date along for evenings out with the couple or spending much time at their home.

Quindlen, another close friend of Schmalz's, noticed the impact his getting sick had at the paper. "People were really affected by it," she says. "This is probably the most vivid case of someone at the *Times* having AIDS. A lot of us knew Larry Josephs, but with Jeff actually being here, well, he's just so much a part of the place."

"I think things were already changing, but my illness couldn't do anything but make them more aware of AIDS," Schmalz says. He now also sees his homosexuality from a different perspective. "I regret that I wasn't more out all along," he adds. "I regret that I didn't do more talking about being gay, overall. It's important for people to know that the deputy national editor of the *New York Times* can be gay—people both on the outside and at the paper."

Frankel shrugs off the notion that the awareness of Schmalz's illness might have influenced coverage, "I can't say that I've noticed a change," he says. "It's hard to measure change. It's evolutionary."

But one *Times* staffer, who wishes to remain anonymous, is adamant about the significance of Schmalz's experience: "There have always been gay people here at the *Times*, and I'm sure that Frankel and Lelyveld have always known gay people, but there's never been anyone that high up, that close to them in the newsroom, who is so well-liked. His coming out has had a profound effect."

▼ ▼ ▼

Of course, one man's profound is another's incremental.

"I've noticed an improvement," says Robert Bray, communications director of the National Gay and Lesbian Task Force, a political group. "But it's episodic. I don't want more articles about gays specifically. I'd rather see our visibility permeate the paper at all levels. I want to see the gay rodeo on the sports pages. I want to see gays included in the stories about Valentine's Day."

If the Lavender Enlightenment is under way in the Manhattan newsroom, it has yet to reach the foreign bureaus or even the Washington and Los Angeles bureaus. GLAAD's Miller, who has met with *Times* management on several occasions, says that the organization "praises the *Times* for the progress" but still has problems with much of the coverage.

"Their political and Washington reporters don't ask the presidential candidates—or even the President—about gay civil rights, about gays in the military, or even about AIDS" he says. "The international coverage of gays is woeful. Their foreign correspondents are ignorant and not educated on gay issues. The pieces on China's repression, for example, never talk about the rounding up of homosexuals. The articles on skinhead violence in Germany never recount the horrible antigay attacks."

If you read only the *Times* for coverage of California's protests and rioting over Gov. Pete Wilson's veto of a measure that would have banned antigay employment discrimination, you didn't find out until six weeks after the demonstrations began that the daily protests by lesbians and gays marked a turning point in the gay civil rights movement. Actually, you didn't even know they occurred until a week after they began, when the *Times* finally decided to run an Associated Press photo and a blurb. The *Times's* Los Angeles correspondent, Robert Reinhold, after writing one piece at the outset about the politics behind the veto (which landed on page A16), seemed to fall asleep at the wheel. And no one in New York was trying to wake him up.

"I don't really cover demonstrations," Reinhold explains. "As I recall I did tell them to pick it up on the wires. The [broad story that was written six weeks later] would have been done earlier had I not gotten involved in other things. We're spread pretty thin here. But I think there was some advantage to the delay, to see whether the anger that had been stirred by the veto was more enduring and more substantial than just a few protests." By contrast, starting the day after the protests began, *USA Today* had the story on page 1A, 2A, or 3A every day for a full week as well as on editorial and op-ed pages.

When it comes to physical contact between homosexuals, the *Times* is still squeamish. Last year, assistant managing editor Allan M. Siegal removed from an article a photo of two women kissing on the television series *L.A. Law*. (Ironically, it was to accompany an article by television critic John J. O'Connor about how television makes gays invisible.) Siegal, the *Times's* resident monitor of taste, also caused an uproar among gays at the paper last year when he pulled a photo of a Connecticut lawmaker kissing his male lover (as a public act of coming out) during a session of the legislature The implication seems to be that kissing between men and women, certainly something the *Times* has shown before, is OK, while same-sex kissing is in some way distasteful or even prurient.

And coverage of the AIDS crisis, while it has improved substantially, has never caught up to its potential.

"The *Times* is slow on AIDS," observes Peter Millones, a former metropolitan editor and a former assistant managing editor at the paper, now an assistant professor at Columbia University School of Journalism. "Back then [in the beginning of the epidemic], it didn't click, it didn't register."

Some even say that the coverage of the AIDS crisis, while it has improved somewhat from six years ago, may have actually declined again in the last two years, particularly around the issues of drug development and treatment. Two years ago the AIDS Coalition to Unleash Power (ACT UP), a direct-action group, waged a campaign against the *Times* and later against one person specifically: science reporter Gina Kolata. She was charged with having "an unquestioning acceptance of the Establishment point of view of how to do research," according to Mark Harrington of the New York chapter of ACT UP.

After a blistering article attacking Kolata's reporting appeared in the *Village Voice* (Kolata calls it "the nastiest article I have ever seen in my life"), some activists noticed that she was taken off the beat for a while. Not true, says Kolata. "I had letters and memos from top management telling me not to stop what I was doing."

But there certainly are fewer stories now regarding drug research. Harrington thinks the *Times* pulled Kolata back a bit because of the controversy. "In a way, our attacks on her weren't a success," he says, "because it didn't result in their improving the coverage but rather in their taking her off the beat without replacing her and then throwing the drug-development stories onto the business pages."

The reason that the *Times* has been so carefully scrutinized is simply because it is the most influential, most important news organization in America—not because it's worse than any other newspaper. In actuality, the *New York Times* is better on gay and AIDS issues than most other metropolitan dailies, including the country's other largest papers: the *Los Angeles Times*, the *Washington Post*, and the *Chicago Tribune*.

A comparison of major dailies during the period from 1990 to 1992 using Nexis, a computer information service that catalogs numerous newspapers, showed that the *L.A. Times*, because it is a substantially larger paper than most, had

significantly more stories about gays than any of the other three papers and almost double that of the *New York Times*.

The *Los Angels Times*'s Victor F. Zonana, who is gay, has done some of the most incisive AIDS reporting in the country and has written noteworthy pieces about the gay community. "As a member of an embattled community and a survivor of the AIDS epidemic, I feel a profound responsibility to bear witness," he says. "But I use the same professional standards and ethics when I write about AIDS as when I write about the stock exchange. I'm critical of the community's organizations because I believe they are a public trust, and I hold them to very high standards." The paper's media and television critic, Howard Rosenberg, has also done some exceptional work on gay issues.

But a closer look at the *Los Angeles Times* shows that the stories about lesbians and gays turn up predominantly in the View, Calendar, and Metro sections of the paper and rarely in the national news section. While the *Los Angeles Times* had twice as many stories as the *New York Times*, the *New York Times* was twice as likely to put stories about gays and lesbians on the front page.

Compared to the *New York Times*, the *Washington Post* and the *Chicago Tribune* both had pitifully litle coverage on gay issues for the two-year period, each with half the number of stories the *New York Times* had and with very few on page A1. On AIDS issues alone, the *New York Times* beat out all three other papers, with 20% more stories than the *Los Angeles Times*, 50% more than the *Washington Post*, and 75% more than the *Chicago Tribune*.

But perhaps the most telling figures are the percentage increase of stories about the gay community from 1990 to 1991. The *Los Angeles Times* had 40% more stories in 1991 than in the previous year (but this includes last fall's protests, which occurred in the paper's own backyard). The *Washington Post* and *Chicago Tribune* each had an increase of less than 10%. But the *New York Times* showed a whopping increase of 65%.

▼ ▼ ▼

"We have a long way to go, but I think the *Times* is moving in that direction," says Sulzberger regarding his ambitious master plan to make the paper more representative of different cultures. "I believe fundamentally that diversity is the single most important issue that this newspaper faces—

coming to terms with the diversity of its work force. I want to create a workplace where all people—black, female, gay, disabled—are comfortable and can succeed. Diversity of the workplace is also important because we reach a diverse audience. I'm more interested in how the coverage is viewed, and it has to be influenced by my people who are gay."

In mid January of this year, 40-year-old Sulzberger became the fifth publisher of the *New York Times* since his great-grandfather, Adolph S. Ochs, bought the newspaper in 1896. Sulzberger succeeded his father, Arthur Ochs "Punch' Sulzberger, when the elder Sulzberger retired at age 65 after running the paper since 1963.

The younger Sulzberger has been described in the media as "brash" and even as an activist. Currently, he serves on a committee of the Newspaper Publishers Association aimed at combating racism and sexism in the workplace. He made sure that sexual orientation was part of the program of a recent conference on diversity that he held at the *Times* for newspaper publishers from around the country.

It was under Sulzberger's supervision that Gerald Boyd, an African-American, was brought in as metropolitan editor. "Boyd has a genuine interest in the disenfranchised," observes a *Times* staffer. "When Boyd was told about the importance to the gay community of the Julio Rivera murder trial [in which the victim, a Queens man, was gay-bashed], he made sure that it was given the same prominence that the Howard Beach racial murder trial was given."

And it was under Sulzberger's supervision that openly gay and outspoken Adam Moss, the former editor of the now-defunct New York weekly *7 Days*, was brought in under contract as a consultant to the *Times*. While it is unclear what future the *Times* and Moss have together, some say that Moss, who has Lelyveld's ear, has been very vocal and has had an effect in the newsroom regarding gay issues.

Sulzberger has worked in various departments of the paper since 1978 and has gotten to know much of the staff. About seven years ago, he separately approached a number of staff members whom he knew to be gay. Anticipating his eventual role as publisher, he wanted to discuss the problems they faced as gay people at the *Times*. "Actually, he took me to lunch and asked, 'So when are you going to tell me that you're gay?' " laughs Schmalz. "He was genuinely interested in what I had to say."

Of course, first and foremost, Sulzberger is a businessman. He is said to scrupulously study market research. Having worked much of the time on the business side of the paper, he knows that diversity does more than serve humanity: It's also the only commercially viable way to go now. He's taking over the *Times* during the biggest slump in the newspaper industry in history. Nationally, *USA Today* has taken center stage, becoming the largest-circulation newspaper in the country; much of its success can be attributed to the fact that it's the most culturally diverse news organization in America. Locally, the bulk of the *Times*'s straight, white, upper-middle-class readership is increasingly fleeing the city and turning to the *Times* less and less.

"*New York Newsday* has made no secret of the fact that it is intensely covering gay and lesbian issues," notes Stuart Elliott, the *Times*'s popular advertising columnist, regarding the tabloid competition whose circulation is steadily increasing. "It's clear that *Newsday* is prominently placing these stories so that gays will turn to it."

Elliott, a gay man, spent three years at *USA Today*, which he describes as "the gorgeous mosaic. They're in the forefront on gay issues. It's about wanting to be inclusive of gays, but it's also a dollars-and-cents issue. We're a target audience that they would like to reach."

Sulzberger has made his mark on the paper in recent years, and now, as full-fledged publisher, he will no doubt make a much stronger impression. However, it's myopic if not unfair to suggest that the changes at the *Times* are occurring only because of the new publisher or even solely because of the impact of Schmalz's illness.

In actuality, the *Times* has been subtly changing for the past six years, battling institutionalized homophobia that was embedded in the very fiber of the paper by an editor who ran his empire not unlike recent Eastern European despots. And, like them, he would live to see his monuments toppled.

## "LAVENDER ENLIGHTENMENT" CONTINUES AT AMERICA'S NEWSPAPER OF RECORD

*In part 1 of "Out at the New York Times," which ran in the last issue of* The ADVOCATE, *Jeff Schmalz, a 20-year veteran of the paper who had risen to the position of deputy national editor,* came out as gay and as a person with AIDS and described a violent seizure he'd suffered in the Times *newsroom last year. Though the* Times *still has a long way to go with regard to lesbian and gay issues, coverage has improved dramatically over the past year. Some say it is the effect that Schmalz's illness has had on the newsroom and the top brass. Others say the changes—which have been dubbed the Lavender Enlightenment—are also due to the new publisher, 40-year-old Arthur Ochs Sulzberger Jr., who took over from his father, Arthur Ochs "Punch" Sulzberger, who retired in January. The new publisher has been described as an "activist" who speaks often of his commitment to "diversity" at the paper. In actuality, the changes at the* Times *have been subtly occurring over the past six years, as editors and staffers recovered from the reign of a despotic editor, A. M. "Abe" Rosenthal.*

▼ ▼ ▼

In 1963 Abe Rosenthal arrived back in New York. The Pulitzer prize-winning reporter who began his career at the *Times* in 1946 had been away for nine years. He'd spent those years as a correspondent in India, Poland, Switzerland, and Japan and wrote from many other countries in Eastern Europe, Africa, and Asia. He was now the paper's metropolitan editor. His focus would be on New York City.

Shortly after settling in, Rosenthal noticed something while walking down Riverside Drive. New York had dramatically changed while he was gone: There was a thriving male homosexual subculture emerging. Men were meeting on the streets and touching on the streets. To Rosenthal, this was alarming.

The next day he raced into the office and assigned reporter Robert Doty a story that would forever take a place in the paper's history. On Dec. 16, 1963, a headline blared from the front page: GROWTH OF OVERT HOMOSEXUALITY IN CITY PROVOKES WIDE CONCERN. "The overt homosexual—and those who are identifiable probably represent no more than half of the total—has become such an obtrusive part of the New York scene that the phenomenon needs public discussion," the story read.

At the time of the article's appearance, many other media organizations were also beginning to break the silence on homosexuality. Noted historian John D'Emilio observed in his book *Sexual Politics, Sexual Communities: The Making of a Homosexual Minority in the United States* that in

their articles, "the *Washington Post* and *Life* acknowledged a range of opinions, including those of homophile leaders and mental health professionals who took issue with the sickness theory [of homosexuality]." But the *Times* story, he pointed out, "emphasized the stance of vice squad officers and the segment of the medical profession that categorized homosexuals as 'crippled psychically.'"

In 1969 author Gay Talese, a close friend of Rosenthal's and a former *Times* reporter, wrote in *The Kingdom and the Power*, his book about the *Times*, that "it seemed to Rosenthal that homosexuals were more obvious on city streets . . . and this led to a superb article that was by old-time standards, quite revolutionary."

▼ ▼ ▼

Shortly after he arrived at the *Times* in 1972, Jeff Schmalz, who began working as a copyboy, remembers hearing "much screaming and yelling over various articles" about gays. The modern gay rights movement had come into being with the Stonewall riots, a series of demonstrations in New York City in 1969, the same year Rosenthal was named the paper's managing editor. Many writers and editors at the *Times* were eager to cover the burgeoning movement and report on the gay and lesbian community. "We'd done a piece about a gay cruise on the cover of the travel section," Schmalz recalls. "There was a lot of shouting about it. Abe thought that it was a total mistake and that we never should have done it. And we'd used the word *gay*. He said we could never use that word again."

Throughout the '70s and into the '80s most gay men and lesbians who worked at the *Times* were deeply closeted. "There was some sleeping around among people in the newsroom," Schmalz says, "but we didn't even nod or wink at each other while in the office." Gay people at the *Times* say that they were immensely frightened and frustrated under Rosenthal, who moved into the top position of executive editor in 1977. They couldn't complain bemuse to do so they'd have to come out. But they felt they couldn't come out because it would definitely jeopardize their jobs.

*Times* assistant news editor Russell King remembers writing a first-person piece in the early '80s about AIDS that he was going to submit to the *New York Times Magazine*. "I showed it to a friend at the *Times*, who said, 'You can't [submit] this. Everyone will know you're gay,'" King recalls. "I then showed it to my editor. He was a good person, knew I was gay, and accepted it but agreed that it would be trouble for me if it was printed, that it would hurt me."

Charles Kaiser is the author of *1968 in America* and is a former staffer at both the *Times* and the *Wall Street Journal*. In 1982, having worked as a news clerk for Rosenthal at the *Times*, he was the media critic at *Newsweek*. He wrote a column criticizing the *Times* and Rosenthal specifically, saying that Rosenthal had used the paper to reward his friends and punish his enemies. Rosenthal, never able to stomach criticism, flew into a frenzy.

Though years later, in 1991, he would opine that "the outing of gays who want to keep their sex lives private" is a form of "sexual harassment," Rosenthal revealed Kaiser's homosexuality to people throughout the media industry, Kaiser asserts. "Within days Rosenthal was telling everyone he knew that I'd written this article about him because I'm gay," Kaiser says. "I assume that what he meant was that because he had a reputation for being homophobic, I was doing this to retaliate against him, which was a complete non sequitur. I was a media critic, and I was doing my job." At the time, Kaiser was completely closeted and hadn't ever discussed his homosexuality with Rosenthal. "He outed me," Kaiser asserts. "I kept hearing it from people in Washington [D.C.], people in New York. It was very uncomfortable."

Rosenthal denies the entire scenario, claiming to only vaguely remember the attack in *Newsweek*. "He's a fantasizer," he says of Kaiser. "He obviously fantasized about the *New York Times*, and he fantasized about my attitude toward him. He has a grievance against this paper. It comes from his inability to be successful."

In the mid '80s, *Times* reporter Richard Meislin, who had a plum spot as the bureau chief in Mexico City, got sick while abroad. There was speculation that it was AIDS (it wasn't). When news of his illness got back to Rosenthal—who was then informed that Meislin was gay—he blew his stack. Staffers say he chastised two editors for not telling him previously that Meislin was a homosexual. Rosenthal apparently decided that Meislin, as a homosexual, shouldn't represent the *Times* in Mexico and eventually pulled him back, though Meislin was doing what some editors considered to be exemplary work.

Meislin was not assigned another foreign post or sent to Washington, D.C., which would be a usual next step. Instead, he was brought back to the New York newsroom to do a job he hated.

"What kept me from leaving the paper," says Meislin, "was that one of the [other] editors took me in his office and said, 'We know you've been screwed, but don't do anything rash. You have a long career ahead of you, and Rosenthal will be leaving soon.'"

Peter Millones, an assistant professor at the Columbia University School of Journalism, was at that time an assistant managing editor at the *Times*. He recalls hiring Meislin. "It didn't occur to me to tell Rosenthal or anyone else that [Meislin] was gay," he says "I don't recall why the decision was made to make him come back, but it would make sense [that it was because he was gay]. Abe was a tyrannical executive."

Rosenthal says the entire incident "never happened," claiming that "this is the first time I've ever heard of that." He also comments that "people who are used to being discriminated against will sometimes take certain acts as being discriminatory when they're not."

▼ ▼ ▼

No matter how much activists protested, Rosenthal refused to let the word *gay* be used in the paper—even after 15 years of pressure—except in names of organizations or in quotes.

Dudley Clendinen, who recently stepped down from a position as a managing editor at the *Baltimore Sun*, was a reporter at the *Times* in the early '80s. "Abe had a dinner party at his home on Central Park West for me and [theater critic] Frank Rich when we joined the *Times* in 1980," he recalls. "Part of the conversation that night was about the *Times* policy with regard to the use of the word *homosexual* instead of *gay*. I argued that *homosexual* was a clinical word that robbed people of their humanity. Abe didn't agree. His attitude was that the general culture only saw the subject scientifically. The conversation went nowhere."

Rosenthal now says that he banned the word *gay* in the early '70s because he "felt at that time that the *Times* should not use a word for political purposes until that word has become accepted as part of the language," as if the *Times* is merely a barometer of public opinion and not also a powerful catalyst for change. How could the word be "accepted as part of the language" if the *Times* refused to acknowledge it? And wasn't it equally "political" to not use the word? By not using *gay*, the *Times* held back a social movement, refusing to give it legitimacy. Rosenthal admits, "It may be quite possible that I should have approved of the word *gay* earlier."

But perhaps the most devastating of Rosenthal's misdeeds was his callous indifference to the AIDS crisis early in the epidemic, a catastrophic ignorance on his part, the outcome of which can never be reversed. In 1976, when a mysterious illness struck several American Legion convention attendees in Philadelphia, the *Times* immediately ran the story on the front page (where it stayed for months), ensuring that the government, the medical establishment, and the rest of the media switch into emergency mode. Within days, the nation's resources and attention were focused on what came to be called Legionnaires' disease, an illness that killed 29 people.

But as the number of AIDS-related deaths of gay men rose steadily into the hundreds and later the thousands, the *Times* coverage of the disease amounted mostly to minuscule reports buried in the B and C sections Ironically. Rosenthal, who attacks anti-Semitism in the media, never realized that the way he was treating the AIDS epidemic wasn't much different from the way that news organizations treated the Holocaust early on.

When asked about this failure, Rosenthal becomes defensive. "I'm not going to talk about all that," he says. "I'm not going back to then. Look, it's quite true that we should have or could have had more stories about AIDS, but then again, there wasn't much known about it."

But isn't it the *Times*'s job to explore that? "Well, yes," he responds. "It is the *Times*'s job to explore that, but, well, I guess we all should have done more."

"The way the *Times* worked under Rosenthal," explains Kaiser, "was that everyone below him spent all of their time trying to figure out what to do to cater to his prejudices. One of those widely perceived prejudices was Abe's homophobia. So editors throughout the paper would keep stories concerning gays out of the paper."

As soon as Rosenthal retired in 1986 to become a twice-weekly op-ed columnist at the paper and Max Frankel took over as executive editor, the walls of repression came tumbling down, staffers say. "I knew they'd had a hard time," recalls Frankel, "and I knew they weren't comfortable identifying themselves as gay." Almost immediately Frankel let it be known that things were going to be different. One way was in quickly allowing the use of the word *gay* in the paper. A former staffer recalls seeing a memo that Frankel sent to then publisher Punch Sulzberger soon

after taking over: "Punch, you're going to have to swallow hard on this one: We're going to start using the word *gay*."

Photographer Sara Krulwich, a lesbian, says Frankel was immediately "a positive force" that helped her and others to relax. Agrees Schmalz: "Things changed completely with Max."

"Previously, everyone was terrified," notes deputy photo editor Nancy Lee, a lesbian. "I was away when Max took over. When I came back the entire newsroom had changed. There was a general loosening up. The next year I organized a bunch of people for the [gay pride] parade, and we marched holding hands. We haven't marched since, but every year now we have a party. Last year we had about 60 people. I now have pictures of my partner under the glass on my desk. Everyone on my staff knows and I take Marie to any *Times* function that she cares to go to. I didn't do that under Abe."

Lee, who has been with the paper for 11 years, feels that her being out of the closet has changed attitudes at the paper. "On my staff, which is photographers, editors, and lab personnel, I was the first person that many of them ever knew was a lesbian," she says "I'm sure they were grossed out at first. You got the sense that they disapproved. But because they know me, they like me, and so it helps them to accept not just me but other gay people and homosexuality in general."

The combination of the departure of Rosenthal, the efforts by Frankel to dismantle the ingrained homophobia, the attempts by the new publisher, Arthur Ochs Sulzberger Jr., to achieve diversity, and, perhaps most important, the coming out of people like Lee, Schmalz, and many others has created a general feeling in recent months among gay staffers at the *Times* that they can speak up about their experiences.

"People are now very vocal when they need to be," says Lee. In January, *Times* business reporter Kim Foltz wrote a piece in the *New York Times Magazine* in which he revealed his HIV-positive status, discussed his gay relationship, and even complained that the paper's health plan would not be adequate for him when and if he is unable to work.

While the editors may not always follow the advice of gays and lesbians in the newsroom, gay staffers say they are now asked their opinions about sensitive issues. Regarding the decision on whether to out Assistant Secretary of Defense Pete Williams last August, Schmalz says, "I argued that we should have outed him. He was publicly defending the Pentagon's policy of excluding homosexuals. I argued that it was a case that fit into the guidelines, that it was a case of hypocrisy." The *Times*, still smarting from the controversy around having named the woman who accused William Kennedy Smith of raping her, decided against naming Williams in a story that referred to his outing. But Schmalz thought it was significant that he was brought into the discussion.

"The changes regarding gays at the *Times* are a little bit commensurate with the situation with women here," says *Times* op-ed columnist Anna Quindlen. "There was a period when women had to pass. When you're passing, you can't really come into the office with your particular life concerns. You don't want to draw attention to the fact that you're female. But when you don't have to pass any longer, you can come in with your life stories and say, 'At least half of our readers are interested in this story, and I know about it because it's part of my experience.' " Quindlen has noticed that gay people at the *Times* are now much more at ease socially. "My gay friends now talk openly with me, out loud in the newsroom, about their dates" she says.

Philip Gefter, who is training to become a picture editor, says that even longtime gay staffers are amazed at how many gays and lesbians there are at the paper whom they previously didn't know about. "Every time I want a 'proclivity check' on a man I find attractive," he says. "I'll ask a gay man who's been here a long time and that person will say. 'No, he's not gay,' but then I'll find out later that the person in question is, in fact, gay."

One observer who's worked at several New York papers is astonished: "The closet doors are just flying off their hinges up there—and everyone has been talking about it."

The Lavender Enlightenment's effect on Rosenthal, who wrote gay-positive columns last year, is probably the most interesting of all. "All this time people have assumed I had certain attitudes, but they weren't really true," he claims. "They say that I'm suddenly interested in gays and AIDS and that I'm now writing about these issues. But I'm interested in it because I've always had an interest in it; I just never had occasion to write about it."

"It's like the guy who yells 'nigger, nigger, nigger' and then goes into work one day and sees that everyone is black," says one staffer. "What happened was that Abe realized that some of his own clerks and some of the people he's worked with

for years are gay because they are suddenly more open. These were like his spiritual sons. And it just blew him away."

Meislin, who was pulled back from Mexico City's foreign desk by Rosenthal, is now back on track and content in his position as graphics editor at the *Times*. "You can't live in the past when the present is much improved," he says.

But others don't forget so easily. Shortly after Schmalz had his seizure in the newsroom and subsequently revealed that he had AIDS, Rosenthal began asking about him. "He told somebody that he wanted to hear from me, that he wanted me to call him," Schmalz says. "I never called. It was just too late. You can't wait until somebody's dying and then decide to be there. Where was he all those years?"

▼ ▼ ▼

On a Friday evening two weeks before Christmas 1991, several hundred lesbians and gay men were crammed in an upper East Side townhouse for a joint Christmas party of the Publishing Triangle, an organization of gays and lesbians in the book publishing field, and the newly formed New York chapter of the National Lesbian and Gay Journalists Association.

Everyone was there—a who's who of queer writers, editors, photographers, reporters, publicists, and literary agents. They came from *Time* and *Newsweek*, Reuters and the Associated Press, Random House and Simon and Schuster, *People* and *Entertainment Weekly*, *New York Newsday* and the *New York Post*, ABC and CBS, and many more media outlets. The party went on far longer than expected, as people commented about the unstoppable energy in the room. This was all very new, and power was what they were getting off on—the extraordinary collective power that they all realized could be harnessed if they worked together.

The first meeting of the New York chapter of the National Lesbian and Gay Journalists Association had occurred just six weeks before. At that meeting, attended by 60 people, there were at least 15 people from the *Times*, some of whom didn't even know each other or know about each other's sexuality. "That was important," says Gefter. "I think that as gay people at the *Times* become more and more visible to each other, there are more informal avenues of dialogue that create a kind of advocacy block."

That advocacy block is only just beginning to form at the *Times*. "There is now a loose, informal social network of gay men and women here at the *Times*," says real-estate reporter David Dunlap. "We have talked about the possibility of sitting down with some editors and managers. There is no specific agenda of which I'm aware, though there certainly are issues we want to raise in time, such as spousal benefits."

Other staffers talk about asking for a full-time reporter to cover gay issues and the gay movement, arguing that during the black civil rights movement there were reporters whose beat was solely that movement as it was crystallizing. Still other staffers have agendas ranging from adding commitment ceremony announcements to changing obituaries (currently the *Times* will not use the word *lover* and will not say the deceased is "survived by" his or her companion). In almost all cases, gay *Times* editors, reporters, and photographers are guarded, in that *New York Times* way, about sounding too much like what they call advocates, because they are, after all, "journal-ists." But at least one, propelled by forces beyond his control, has comfortably crossed that line.

"Sometimes greatness is thrust upon you," says Schmalz, grinning. "Having AIDS has changed my politics. The paper trains you to be apolitical. I grew up at the paper and have been apolitical throughout. Now I'm having a political awakening."

Schmalz has been in and out of the hospital six times in the last year and a half, has had brain surgery, survived viral pneumonia, and outlasted a rare and often immediately fatal brain infection, progressive multifocal leukoencephalopathy. He's lived far longer than his doctors had hoped for, looks great, and has tremendous energy. He's now pondering what direction he'd like to go in, what kind of meaningful writing about his experience he'd like to do for the paper.

"I have a voice that needs to get out now," he says, beaming with the glow of the activist. "AIDS is not just a disease. It is a revolution in your life."

# III. C

# CRIES AND WHISPERS: AIDS AND THE MEDIA

At the end of the 1970s America was confronted with the specter of a seemingly incurable disease contracted through sexual contact: genital herpes. The media were quick to point out that the causes of the epidemic were to be found in the so-called sexual revolution. Accounts were rife with thinly disguised moral judgments, mixing opinion with facts as they told us that "herpes could be an unpleasant fact of life for virtually an entire generation. The price, [health experts] say, of the sexual revolution" (CBS AM, 5/7/82). The sexual revolution, it was frequently emphasized, was characterized by permissiveness and promiscuity, and now the bills were coming due.

Despite all the attention it received, the panic was short-lived and the fear of herpes did not ring down the curtain on the sexual revolution. Perhaps the extent of the "epidemic" was exaggerated, or perhaps herpes, while incurable, was not a sufficient deterrent as the chief weapon of the emerging sexual counterrevolution of the 1980s. But the stage was set for the arrival of a much more potent and deadly threat: AIDS.

The AIDS epidemic was a challenge to the institutions and the values that typify the achievements of modern Western society: science and medicine, respect for the rights and concern for the welfare of all citizens. So far, the record of our societal and institutional response has been mixed at best, possibly because AIDS came upon us in ways that put our motives and our institutions to a particularly rigorous test. By emerging among groups that are largely despised and rejected, AIDS proved once again the truism that the importance of an event may be determined less by what happened than by whom it happened to. In the early days of the AIDS epidemic (at a point when widespread educational efforts might

have saved tens of thousands of lives since lost), Congressman Henry Waxman of California contrasted public response to AIDS and to Legionnaire's Disease: "What society judged was not the severity of the disease but the social acceptability of the individuals affected with it" (quoted in Shilts 1987:143–144).

In the June 5, 1981, issue of the Centers for Disease Control's *Morbidity and Mortality Weekly Report* there was an article about five gay men in Los Angeles diagnosed with a rare disease called Pneumocystis carinii. The article noted that "the occurrence of pneumocystis in these five previously healthy individuals . . . is unusual. The fact that these patients were all homosexuals suggests an association between some aspect of a homosexual lifestyle or disease acquired through sexual contact." The first notice of AIDS in the *New York Times* came in a brief article that appeared on July 3, 1981, on page 20: "Rare Cancer Seen in 41 Homosexuals." At this point the newly emerging disease was being called GRID—Gay Related Immune Deficiency—and the name embodied the association between gay men and AIDS that has lasted ever since. The first story on AIDS aired by NBC news appeared in June 1982, and it began with Tom Brokaw framing the issue in a fashion that remained constant in much subsequent coverage: "Scientists at the National Centers for Disease Control in Atlanta today released the results of a study that shows that the lifestyle of some male homosexuals has triggered an epidemic of a rare form of cancer."

The media alternated depictions that distanced AIDS as the fate befalling those gay men in the "fast lane" whose lifestyles have put them far outside the mainstream ("Investigators also believe that AIDS is principally a phenomenon of the raunchy subculture in large cities, where bars and bathhouses are literal hotbeds of sexual promiscuity," *Rolling Stone*, 2/3/83) with stories that intimated that AIDS might also threaten the "general population."

The media's mainstream orientation was clearly reflected in the oft-expressed concern over the fate of the "general population" if and when AIDS spread beyond the deviant "risk groups" in which it mostly appeared (Albert, "Illness and Deviance," this volume). For example, although the *Philadelphia Inquirer* was an exception to the rule among newspapers because its medical reporter, Donald Drake, gave the epidemic serious attention in the early period, AIDS did not make the paper's front page until he wrote an article stating that heterosexuals might be at risk. In a CBS news special ("AIDS Hits Home," October 22, 1986) correspondent Bernard Goldberg commented, "A scary reality is starting to hit home, that the AIDS virus is out there and it's not just gays who are catching it."

The initial flicker of attention in the mass media was not only late, it was also short-lived. There were a total of five network television stories on AIDS in 1982 (three of which focused on persons considered by the media to be "innocent victims"—hemophiliacs, children, recipients of blood transfusions). In 1983 that number rose to thirty-nine, but the following year it dropped to twenty-five even as the death rate continued to climb.

Between January and June of 1985 the *New York Times* published 52 articles about AIDS; from July to December of 1985 the *New York Times* ran 323 articles about AIDS. What reversed the trend? On July 25, 1985, Rock Hudson announced that he had AIDS; he died three months later. The *Times* was not unusual. The week after the announcement, Rock Hudson appeared on the covers of *Newsweek*, *People*, and *McLean's*, the largest Canadian newsweekly. From July to December 1985, NBC broadcast over 200 stories on AIDS—three times as many as during the entire 1980 to 1984 period. The other news media reacted similarly (Milavsky 1988).

There may still be much mystery surrounding the causes and possible cures of AIDS, but there is little that is mysterious about the response of the media and other institutions to the epidemic. As many analysts have described, and many news professionals have admitted, the homophobia of the press, combined with their assumption that their audiences shared their biases, led them to ignore and downplay the story for much too long.

In August 1982 Dan Rather on the "CBS Evening News" was blunt about the fact that the majority of people with AIDS were gay men, but not until May of 1983 could CBS bring itself to report that the major way AIDS is transmitted is through sexual contacts. Broadcast news media even today almost always use phrases like *bodily fluids* rather than use the word *semen* or, heaven forbid, vernacular terms such as *cum*. Television networks are unwilling to accept advertisements for condoms, and public service announcements intended to educate the public about AIDS are tongue-tied by censorship.

Print media have been considerably more forthcoming with accurate information. Harry Nelson could write an article for the *Los Angeles Times* in April 1983 reporting that the risk of AIDS "is associated with passive (receptive) anal intercourse" because of "the presence of the agent in the semen of the active partner." After a long period of sticking to the vague term "sexual contact" the *New York Times* published an article by Jane Brody, in the "Personal Health" column for February 12, 1986, which reported that "infected semen can spread AIDS through intercourse in which the virus comes in contact with broken blood vessels or lesions in the anus or vagina."

The media were not alone in their reluctance to deal with the topic of AIDS. President Ronald Reagan did not give a speech on this unprecedented health crisis until June 1987, by which point over twenty thousand people had died of AIDS in the United States. But the media are not politicians, and they are expected to rise above their own prejudices. In fact, of course, they do not set aside their biases, much of the time, and AIDS was no exception. As James Kinsella ("The Second Wave," excerpted in this volume) and Randy Shilts (1987) documented, homophobia among media personnel discouraged reporters and editors from tackling AIDS in the early years. Before it became an "official major story," any reporter suggesting an AIDS-related story to his or her editor would be provoking the question: Why are you interested? The implication that wouldn't need to be spelled out was, are you interested in something that affects gay men because you are gay yourself? This is a question few reporters wanted to face, whether they were gay (and many were) or straight. Thus it is not surprising that the most extensive AIDS coverage in the mainstream press was written by Randy Shilts for the *San Francisco Chronicle;* for Shilts was one of the few openly gay reporters in the country, and the first ever to be hired as an openly gay person (Greenman, "More to the Shilts Story," this volume).

It was only after Rock Hudson had raised the status of AIDS to that of a front-page story that reporters could safely be associated with the topic. Even then, media attention to AIDS seemed always to erupt whenever there was a dramatic story that involved heterosexuals. A young hemophiliac named Ryan White who was harassed by schoolmates when they discovered he had AIDS became a national figure after massive media exposure; a major AIDS funding bill was eventually named the Ryan White Act. In 1991 Kimberly Bergalis claimed she contracted AIDS through a dental procedure and became a media celebrity. That same year AIDS-related coverage exploded when basketball star "Magic" Johnson announced that he was HIV-positive. Six months later tennis star Arthur Ashe announced that he was suffering from AIDS, contracted through a blood transfusion years before, and yet another heterosexual AIDS story dominated the front pages for weeks. This time the homophobia implicit in the media's over-reaction to heterosexual AIDS stories was barely hidden, as in *Philadelphia Inquirer* columnist Claude Lewis's comment, "Because of (Ashe), AIDS is perhaps a bit more respectable today" (1992).

Despite the unprecedented publicity surrounding Rock Hudson, other famous bachelors preferred to die of other causes, and for a long time the media cooperated in turning celebrity coffins into permanent closets. As sociologist Peter Nardi found, many newspapers chose not to report any male lovers as survivors. When mentioned, they are typically referred to in the concealing language of "long-time companion" (1990). Part of the reason for this posthumous euphemizing lies in the routines of newspaper obituary preparation. Most often it is the families of those who have died of AIDS who try to hide the true cause of death. In writing an obituary, reporters must call the deceased person's family to verify the cause of the death, and they usually take explanations at face value, even if their instincts tell them they are not getting the truth. When Tommy Lasorda, Jr., a thirty-three-year-old gay artist who was the son of Los Angeles Dodgers manager Tommy Lasorda, died of AIDS in 1991, the media reported that he died of pneumonia and severe dehydration. Not only is the stigma removed from the cause of death but so is the stigma of a gay identity.

The 1988 death of Max Robinson, who in 1978 became the first black news anchor on network television, occasioned a flurry of defensive maneuvering. Robinson himself had kept his AIDS-related illness a secret, but he was later reported to have wanted his death to emphasize the need for AIDS awareness among black people. However, as critic Phillip Harper wrote, the palpable desire on the part of Robinson's friends to distance their late friend from any suspicion of homosexuality undermined these efforts (1991).

By May 1992, when television actor Robert Reed died, his family was unable to keep the secret for long that AIDS contributed to the death of the Brady Bunch's dad or to suppress the related fact of his homosexuality. The changes that had begun to take place in media practice over the decade of the AIDS epidemic can best be seen in the response of openly gay *New York Times* editor Jeffrey Schmalz: "It's important that people know that someone like this died of AIDS." Schmalz was angry when he saw that his own newspaper's obituary writer had accepted the family's story apparently without question. "An obituary is a news article; it's not an article written to please the survivors; it's not written for any other reason than to tell the truth."

Media accounts tend to portray AIDS as a disease of white gay men, on the one hand, and injection drug-using people of color, on the other. Some of this can be traced to homophobia in the African American press and other community institutions (Kinsella, "The Second Wave," this volume), but it also accords with the media's unshakeable attraction to simple central-casting stereotypes.

In fictional formats as well as the news AIDS reinvigorated the two primary roles the mass media offer to minority groups: victim and villain. Victims, as in the family-centered television movies *An Early Frost* (NBC, 1985), *Our Sons* (ABC, 1991), and *In the Gloaming* (HBO, 1997), are objects of pity, and when treated well by the authors they end by being tearfully reconciled with their families. Television dramatists have presented the plight of (white middle-class) gay men with AIDS, but their particular concern is the agony of the families/friends who have to face the awful truth: their son (brother, boyfriend, husband, etc.) is, gasp, gay! But, even with AIDS, not too gay, mind you. In the first network made-for-TV movie on AIDS, NBC's *An Early Frost*, a young, rich, white, handsome lawyer is forced out of the closet by AIDS. As lesbian critic Andrea Weiss put it, "We know he is gay because he tells his disbelieving parents so, but his lack of a gay sensibility, politics and sense of community make him one of those homosexuals heterosexuals love" (1986:6).

There are some truly dramatic and important AIDS stories that we never see enacted or even reflected glancingly in TV drama, but they aren't stories of victims who may finally be accepted back into the arms of their families. These are stories of how the gay *community* responded to an unparalleled health crisis with unprecedented grassroots feats of social service and medical organizing. They are stories of sex and public health education, of research-backed militant agitation for reforms in the testing and approval of drugs, of coalition building with other marginalized groups suffering from disproportionate AIDS risk.

The consistent feature of all TV dramatic programming on AIDS (and most news, public affairs, and documentary programming as well) has been to focus on *individual* people suffering from AIDS, and, if the angle of vision is widened at all, it will then include (straight) family members and possibly a lover (as long as they barely touch) and perhaps one or two friends (more likely to be straight than gay). What is wrong with this picture?

What's wrong is that it not only leaves out the important—and dramatic—achievements of the gay community noted above, but that it falsely suggests that gay people with AIDS *are* alone and abandoned, unless and until they are taken back into the bosom of their family.

The pattern of portraying people with AIDS outside the context of the gay community and the service organizations created in response to AIDS was dramatically reinforced in Hollywood's first major film centering on the epidemic, Jonathan Demme's *Philadelphia*. Once again we meet a white gay man who lives an upper-middle-class life as a closeted lawyer—although he has a lover and he is out to his family—until he is stricken with AIDS, whereupon he is promptly fired from the big-time law firm where he had been a rising star. Shortly afterward he shows up in the office of a (black) homophobic ambulance-chasing lawyer and asks him to represent him in suing his old law firm, because he has been turned down by other lawyers. The ambulance chaser refuses but later reconsiders, takes the case, and wins it, at the same time undergoing a conversion to tolerance and acceptance of at least one person (we have no reason to think that the character would not be horrified were he later to learn that his newborn child was gay). The film was presented and largely

received as a landmark of progress in Hollywood's approach to AIDS and gay people, but, in fact, it was mired in the same old, same old.

True, the protagonist is supported by his completely accepting family, but in most ways the film continues the familiar practice of marginalization. The homophobic lawyer is shown repeatedly in intimate scenes with his wife and children, but the gay lawyer and his lover are barely allowed to touch, and their only (brief) kiss is obscured by the back of the lover's head. A scene showing the two of them talking in bed was reportedly shot but not used. The gay couple seems to have gay friends, but those friends have few lines and are mostly confined to a costume party, presumably representing the true image of gay life.

Most dishonest, however, is the erasure of the organized response to AIDS. The biggest lie in the movie is told when the gay lawyer fired because he has AIDS says that he was turned down by ten lawyers before ending up in the office of an ambulance-chasing homophobe. In Philadelphia, as in many other large cities, a person in his position would have been able to avail himself of lesbian and gay legal services or even ones especially created to deal with AIDS-related cases. In other words, the dramatic premise of the film—the victimized person with AIDS ends up at the mercy of a homophobe who can then be converted to tolerance—requires the erasure of the accomplishments of the gay community, just as the fear of heterosexual audiences' sensibilities requires the denial of the realities of gay life.

In 1996 the arrival of a new class of antiviral drugs was greeted as "The End of AIDS?" (on *Newsweek*'s cover, December 2, 1996). In a lengthy *New York Times Magazine* cover story titled "When Plagues End" Andrew Sullivan's perfunctory acknowledgment that "the vast majority of HIV positive people in the world, and a significant minority in America, will not have access to the expensive and effective new drug treatments," was overshadowed—in the article and in the larger media celebration—by his claim that HIV "no longer signifies death. It merely signifies illness."

The much-heralded promise of the new treatments was soon complicated with attacks by gay journalists Gabriel Rotello and Michelangelo Signorile on what they characterized as a culture of promiscuity obsessed with sex, drugs, and muscles. Rotello's and Signorile's writings, described by the *Boston Globe* as "so overwhelmingly conservative that they might turn up on Pat Robertson's *The 700 Club*" (Biddle 1997), fueled a campaign by political and real estate interests in New York that were targeting sex businesses. Ignoring the unprecedented success of AIDS education efforts as compared with virtually all other public health campaigns, they argued that prevention efforts have failed and that stronger measures are needed. Signorile's alarm over lapses from "safe sex" quickly moved from the pages of *Out* to the *New York Times* op ed page (2/26/95). In his New York *Newsday* column Rotello claimed "Sex Clubs Are the Killing Fields of AIDS" (4/28/96), an attack he developed in his book, *Sexual Ecology,* which concludes that salvation for gay men lies in a "two-tiered gay society in which married couples would be viewed as legitimate, while those who were unmarried would be considered social outcasts" (1997a:16). Rotello's prescription, which ignores the legal barriers to same-sex marriage, was paralleled by Signorile's celebration of gay men who abandon the fast lane of the "circuit" parties (a world most of his readers had never approached any closer than in the pages of glossy magazines) for the sober maturity of suburbia.

## REFERENCES

Biddle, Frederic. 1997. "Grim Warning on AIDS in the '90s." *Boston Globe,* July 23.

Harper, Phillip Brian. 1991. "Eloquence and Epitaph: Black Nationalism and the Homophobic Impulse in Responses to the Death of Max Robinson." *Social Text,* 28:68–86.

Kinsella, James. 1989. *Covering the Plague: AIDS and the American Media.* New Brunswick, N.J.: Rutgers University Press.

Lewis, Claude. 1992. "Ashe's Star Quality Extended Far Beyond the Tennis Courts." *Philadelphia Inquirer,* April 15, p. A19.

Milavsky, Ron. 1988. "AIDS and the Media." American Psychological Association, Atlanta, August 15.

Nardi, Peter. 1990. "AIDS and Obituaries: The Perpetuation of Stigma in the Press." In Douglas Feldman, ed., *Culture and AIDS,* pp. 159–168. New York: Praeger.

Rotello, Gabriel. 1997a. "Creating a New Gay Culture: Balancing Fidelity and Freedom." *Nation,* April 21, pp. 11–16.

— 1997b. *Sexual Ecology: AIDS and the Destiny of Gay Men.* New York: Dutton.

Shilts, Randy. 1987. *And the Band Played On: People, Politics, and the AIDS Epidemic.* New York: St. Martin's.

Signorile, Michelangelo. 1997. *Life Outside: The Signorile Report on Gay Men: Drugs, Muscles, and the Passages of Life.* New York: HarperCollins.

Sullivan, Andrew. 1996. "When Plagues End." *New York Times Magazine,* November 10, pp. 52+.

Weiss, Andrea. 1986. "From the Margins: New Images of Gays in the Cinema." *Cineaste,* 15(1):4–8.

# | 61 |

# Illness and Deviance: The Response of the Press to AIDS

### EDWARD ALBERT

AIDS has been the subject of considerable press coverage since 1981. AIDS-related material has filled the columns not only of news outlets directly connected to affected groups (e.g., the homosexual [gay] press), but also of general interest publications. The purpose here is to address the AIDS phenomenon as it has been brought to the public in the general circulation, popular magazine press.

The role of the press in reporting AIDS cannot be seen as simply one of an observer on the scene, chronicler of some finite set of events available for anyone to see. Rather, media coverage reveals a selectivity of perspective. For the population at large, those with no direct contact with AIDS or its sufferers, the awareness of this disease is media related. It is to these portrayals that one must turn to help explicate popular reactions to AIDS. Such portrayals can be understood in terms of the larger context of a general confounding in contemporary society of issues of medicine and morality that often results in the stigmatization of the victims of illness.

## METHODOLOGY

This paper is based on a content analysis of AIDS-related articles that appeared in national circulation magazines between May 1982 and December 1983. The sample, drawn from the Magazine Index of the Information Access Corporation, begins with the first article listed under a separate AIDS heading and is limited to those articles that appeared in general-interest publications. Articles from science-oriented magazines (e.g., *Scientific American* and *Science*) were

excluded. With the exception of several articles appearing in magazines not readily available at the time, the sample represents the population of published magazine treatments on the topic. In total, 57 articles, from forty-four separate issues of 25 different publications were surveyed.[1]

## THE THEORETICAL ISSUE OF MORAL VERSUS MEDICAL DECISION MAKING

The production of distinctions that have as their effect the defining of approved and disapproved behavior and the creation of valued and devalued persons is an inescapable feature of social life. The consequences flowing from such distinctions vary from mild expressions of disapproval or praise to the conferring of high or outcast statuses. The magnitude of social response is relative to the nature and centrality of the distinction to the values upon which the society is based. In all cases, however, social distinctions and their implied social judgments have relevance for individual and group identity and ranking within a community. Our interest here is in documenting the production of negative judgments and in observing the creation of disapproved or outcast persons. This process has been variously called stigmatization (Goffman 1963), status degradation, identity transformation (Sarbin 1967), or labeling (Schur 1971).

In all societies, the production of such distinc-

In Douglas A. Feldman and Thomas M. Johnson, eds., *Social Dimensions of AIDS*, pp. 163–178. Westport, Conn.: Praeger, 1986.

tions is institutionalized; various occupational groups—referred to by Becker (1963) as moral entrepreneurs—function as arbiters of the normal. Parsons (1958) and others have noted the ways by which magicians or priests fulfilled such functions in more undifferentiated societies. As societies become more specialized and differentiated, however, so also do their normative systems. Concomitantly, an increased specialization occurs in the work roles that arbitrate adherence to such complex systems.

The process of social decision making is being transformed from one emphasizing a "moral" accent to one increasingly taking on a technical/secular character. This process, often involving the transformation of perception from a moral cast to one of illness, has been called "medicalization." Conrad and Schneider (1980:28) define medicalization as the finding of "medical solutions for deviant behaviors or conditions." This process can be seen to contain several elements: the focus of decisions is no longer the designation of "crime" or "sin" but "illness"; those designated become "patients" rather than "criminals"; doctors replace police or priests as agents of social control; and societal reaction alters from one of punishment to treatment.

Various categories of behaviors can be transformed to a greater or lesser degree by the tendency toward medicalization. When successful, such transformations involve not only the changes noted above, but alterations in perception: new categorical distinctions operating at the institutional level similar to the new identity transformations occurring on the individual level. Behaviors undergoing such alteration from the "deviant" to the "ill" include many now subsumed under the rubric "mental illness" (Foucault 1965; Sarbin 1968a, 1968b; Szasz 1970; Wooten 1959), alcoholism (Robinson 1972), drug abuse, hyperactivity in children (Conrad 1975), child abuse and, perhaps, obesity.

On the individual level the transference of decision making from moral to medical auspices has been consequential. Although, as Wooten (1959) suggested, the medical model of mental illness deemphasized "punitive" reactions and went hand in hand with increasing humanitarianism, this trend did not necessarily result in destigmatization. Illnesses for which victims can be held "accountable" are still condemned. As the brutish world of bacteria decreasingly accounted for illness, lifestyle (over which individual control is viewed as possible) became increasingly impor-

tant and with it so did the possibility of individual responsibility (Sontag 1977).

In this vein, many taken-for-granted behaviors (e.g., smoking, a sedentary lifestyle, driving without seat belts) have been identified as contributing to morbidity. However, as McKinley (1981) points out, only select behaviors resulting in illness are defined in such a way as to place those who engage in them in the position of risking definition as "deviant" rather than "ill" to the degree that they are made motivationally responsible for their situation. Specifically, behaviors that call into question community moral standards may result in an individual's loss of the illness role and its replacement with the label "deviant."

It has been in this area of the violation of moral standards that, as a society, we have been most reluctant to give up the deviance model for the medical one. Each time a child molester is treated, a John Hinkley hospitalized, or help sought for the drunk driver who commits vehicular homicide, a call goes up for a return to traditional values and a turning away from "permissiveness." Such reactions derive more from the ambiguity attached to such issues in the first place than from a backlash, and such ambiguity is in part explained through the use of Parsons' (1958) typology of deviance. He proposed two variables: the first characterizes the deviant act, which can, in this schema, either be situational or normative; the second characterizes the generality of the deviance, representing a disturbance in the total person or merely in a particular role commitment. Along the first continuum we move from disturbances of role performance (illness) to ones of "character" (sin). On the second, we move from total disturbances over which the individual lacks control to disturbances of particular "volitional" commitments to social expectations. Ambiguity emerges, in the minds of observers, from situations not clearly on one or another pole of these variables. Such ambiguity is consequential, because it carries with it decisiveness in the use of stigmatizing labels with their implications for social identity and life changes.

Sarbin (1967) raises a related issue when he notes that sanctions and their intensity vary on a continuum related to performance of ascribed and achieved role expectations. Toward the achieved role expectation pole, negative labeling is relatively minimal whereas meritorious performance is highly rewarded. On the other hand, no positive reward is attached to ascribed role performance, whereas negative performance is accompanied by strong sanction. With the AIDS/homosexuality connection we have the potential for a confused response to the degree that it becomes unclear whether the sick individual exhibits, on the one hand, deviance (Parsons) and, on the other, role failure (Sarbin). AIDS (as illness) represents situational deviance related to achieved statuses, whereas homosexuality remains normative deviance related to an ascribed status (see Table 1). Taken together, we have a bipolarity that may be at the base of situations of evaluative ambiguity wherein those labeled are faced with a structurally induced inability to discern consistent social identities for themselves or, likewise, others for them.

## HOMOSEXUALITY: THE MORAL/MEDICAL AMBIGUITY

Observations conducted on AIDS as it is represented in popular magazines document the ambiguity with which we, as a society, view both homosexuality and illness. The nature of the reaction to AIDS as expressed in the media is such that it has, from the very outset, been impossible to separate the disease from the varied contexts of its occurrence. Tied to stigmatized groups (including gays), AIDS has emerged in public perceptions as problematic in that it occurs simultaneously on the two very clearly defined poles of the situational/normative continuum used by Parsons.

Furthermore, to the extent that AIDS affects homosexuals, it has raised the issue, at least in the eyes of an already unaccepting public, of sexual orientation as a violation of one's ascribed status rather than as a matter of individual choice. The resulting confusion, as we shall discuss, might be understood as the conflict between the increasing hegemony of medical decision making and the remnants of the more undifferentiated patterns of moral decision making that continue in public opinion.

Conrad and Schneider (1980) observe that processes criminalizing and medicalizing homosexuality were both increasing during the late nineteenth century. Medicalizing occurred, perhaps, in reaction to added punitive action taken against homosexuals. Such ambivalence remains. Public opinion surveys continue to document the confusion of illness versus deviance perspectives as they relate to gays. Recent surveys of attitudes toward homosexual behavior indicate

predominantly negative reaction. Glen and Weaver (1979) find no significant increase in positive attitudes toward homosexuality during the early to mid-1970s. And, in a recent Gallup Report (1982) survey, a national sample rejected

| Table 1 | |
|---|---|
| *Illness versus Moral Evaluations* | |
| AIDS (Illness) | Homosexuality (Deviance) |
| Situational | Normative |
| Impaired role performance | Sin |
| Lack of personal control | Individual choice |
| Achieved role failure | Ascribed role failure |

the assertion of homosexuality as an "alternative lifestyle" by 51 to 34%. This is highlighted in the internal battle that occurred in the American Psychiatric Association (APA) over the retention or elimination of homosexuality from its list of disorders in the 1968 revision of its second *Diagnostic and Statistical Manual (DSM II)*. The forces favoring demedicalization of homosexuality won in 1974, and homosexuality was removed from the list of illnesses. From the official perspective of the APA, homosexuality became, by fiat, an alternative lifestyle. However, as noted in Conrad and Schneider (1980), a 1977 study of 2,500 psychiatrists (Leif 1977) showed that 69% still saw homosexuality as "pathological."

The occurrence of AIDS exacerbates this confusion by overlaying an undisputed illness on a highly disputed behavior that carries with it three judgmental options: alternative lifestyle, illness, or deviance. AIDS presents a situation in which the physiological problem occasions the reaffirmation of one of these already-held conceptions concerning the nature of homosexuality.

The media portrayals of AIDS reflect the confusion and ambiguity experienced by the society at large. Further, the media's confusion over the illness/deviance character of people with AIDS has resulted in the raising of issues of personal responsibility in ways that give rise to questions of the degree to which situational difference becomes normative violation.

It is important to note that the perspective here is one that sees the media as reflecting public attitudes rather than producing them. Although this paper will not deal at length with one aspect of the media's AIDS coverage—self-criticism for the re-creation of the stigma attached to homosexuality—it should be remember that the highly publicized liberalization of attitudes toward alternate sexual lifestyles that AIDS coverage is said to have jeopardized did not, in fact, ever really occur.

## AIDS: THE MAGAZINE VERSION

The actual portrayal of AIDS in the media, and the groups affected by it, can be seen to focus on several interconnected issues. The themes that emerged cannot be understood as merely the result of reporting on a reality that would be, should anyone wish to look, readily available. Rather, those themes must be seen in the context of the exigencies of news production. We follow a social-constructionist perspective on AIDS coverage, viewing it as, at least in part, related to the problems of getting out the news. Thus, for example, AIDS coverage is slotted into the already extant news categories of "science news" or "lifestyle" sections. Further, such categories appear with a predictable regularity and must be filled whether news is breaking or not.[2] Magazine portrayals have tended to reflect themes of an unfolding, rather than a breaking, character. These are themes congruent with the timing of magazine production. In this way, long-term issues of lifestyle, historic perspective, biography, and rising fear are developed, as opposed to the hit-and-run newspaper presentations of new findings or new categories of sufferers.

On one level, magazine coverage of AIDS appears to be a function of its own attention. The distribution of articles over the period studied is not an accurate reflection of actual increases or decreases in morbidity rates but, rather, appears to follow a "bandwagon effect" generated by media attention in the first place (see Table 2). Having uncovered an issue, the media seem to have then set out to fill the need that, at least in part, was its own creation. The upshot, AIDS coverage, is interesting and can be studied not only for the actual issues raised, but for the manner of development.

Particularly curious behavior is usually confined, in the popular press, to the tabloids (e.g., the *Star*, *National Enquirer*, and the *Globe*). Unlike the tabloids, however, other media outlets seem to require a pretext for giving us the non-normative side of life. For example, a crime like the Manson murders was an opportunity to read about the inside scoop on sex, drugs, and communal living in the 1960s. Jim Jones provided a similar journalistic opportunity to read about a cult that rehearsed mass suicides. AIDS has provided an occasion for such an excursion into a world perceived of as "strange" and "disordered" by the nontabloid media. No in-depth exploration of the lifestyles of the members of the American Legion followed reports of Legionnaire's disease or of the U.S. woman in the case of toxic-shock syndrome.

Primarily concerned with homosexual patients, portrayals of AIDS have focused on sociocultural qualities. In this way, gay life has been made to appear to occur in geographic isolation—in bathhouses, on Christopher Street in New York, in San Francisco, at a gay parade, in a prison. This sense of distance is produced in three distinct ways. In the first, gay behavior is made topical in a way that highlights its normative difference. For example:

> Investigators also believe that AIDS is principally a phenomenon of the raunchy subculture in large cities, where bars and bathhouses are literal hotbeds of sexual promiscuity (*Rolling Stone* 1983:19).

> The gays who get AIDS, it turned out, have often had many more sexual contacts (a lifetime average of 1,100 partners) than the controls (500 partners) (*Newsweek* 1983a:76).

> . . . Many of the early cases involved men with vigorous sex lives. Dr. Linda Laubenstein . . . describes the hospital's first patients as having had anywhere from 25 to 500 different sex partners in the course of a year. . . . They were also frequent drug users, partial to inhalents like cocaine and marijuana and especially nitrites—amyl, butyl, and isobutyl, popularly known as "poppers," which they used about as frequently as they had sex (*New York* 1982).

> But clearly, urban gay life-style has put many homosexual males at risk. An infectious agent loose in the hothouse environment of a gay bath, where some men have as many as 10 anonymous sexual contacts in one night . . . (*Newsweek* 1983b:80).

> Some gays are attempting to remain celibate. . . . Others have set up sexual collectives, usually groups of three to twelve men, who promise to have sex only within the group (*Time* 1983:57).

> Over the next year, Callen pursued his sex life in toilet stalls, referred to as tea rooms. . . . Soon Callen was going to the baths every other day. There were no windows, there were no clocks, there was no music. There was only continuous, impersonal sex, often with men whose early lives had been as tortured as his own (*New York* 1983:26).

> The vast majority of sufferers—75 percent—are homosexual males, many of them highly promiscuous, some with sexual histo-

ries involving many hundreds, even thousands of partners (*Macleans* 1983a:34).

Such descriptions began with the early coverage of the illness in the spring of 1982 and seemed to reach a peak in the spring and summer of 1983. Emphasizing non-normative sexual practices, a picture of gay life emerged that was basically and irretrievably at odds with accepted U.S. lifestyles.

*York Times Magazine* 1983:36).

As nightmare rumors become fact, fear of contagion prompts a slowing down of life in the fast lane (*Newsweek* 1983b:80).

Perhaps it is here, better than anywhere else, that the distancing of AIDS sufferers can be seen: the "problem group" is detached from the rest of society. In the failure of AIDS to touch the general population and in the face of such massive

| | | | |
|---|---|---|---|
| | | Table 2 | |
| | *Quarterly Incidence of Surveyed AIDS-Related Articles and New AIDS Cases* | | |
| | *Quarter* | *Number of Articles* | *New AIDS Cases* |
| 1982 | Jan-March | 0 | 100 |
| | April-June | 1 | 155 |
| | July-Sept. | 2 | 225 |
| | Oct.-Dec. | 3 | 275 |
| 1983 | Jan.-March | 6 | 400 |
| | April-June | 12 | 525 |
| | July-Sept. | 27 | 515 |
| | Oct.-Dec. | 6 | 200 |

Secondly, people with AIDS, especially gay men, are portrayed as experiencing a reign of terror justified by an exponentially increasing death toll. We see a group in panic, its institutions crumbling and its lifestyle becoming increasingly tenuous.

Believed to be sexually transmitted, AIDS has thrown homosexual communities into near panic (*People* 1983:42).

According to Gottlieb, homosexuals in the Los Angeles area are aware of AIDS and are frightened by it (*Saturday Evening Post* 1982:26).

. . . an epidemic of fear is sweeping San Francisco where at least one new case is reported each day (*Macleans* 1983b:6).

Panic has set in on Greenwich Village streets and in "the Castro," San Francisco's gay quarter (*Time* 1982:55).

AIDS has struck terror throughout the homosexual population. . . . A frightened gay community is cooperating with public-health officials to track down AIDS victims (*Newsweek* 1982b:63–64).

. . . the specter of AIDS haunts every member of the homosexual community, especially in the cities where it is most prevalent (*New*

damage it becomes like a faraway earthquake, a war involving others, or merely a great famine that sweeps across some other place. In short, it becomes something that, due to its lack of effect on "me" and due to its reported serious nature, must be happening somewhere else. In these two ways, media coverage highlights an already present social distance between affected and nonaffected groups.

Such difference is exacerbated in a third way: through the use of characterizations that help produce the very difference that they are seen to report. Regularly, those who ran a higher risk of AIDS were characterized either as belonging to "at-risk groups" or as "victims." Such unfortunates, from the outset, were specifiable in terms of some particular quality: they were homosexual men, Haitians, IV-drug users, or hemophiliacs. In early reports, gay men were variously described as "tinderboxes waiting for an opportunistic disease" (*New York* 1982), "walking time bombs" (*Newsweek* 1982a:101:), or "living playgrounds for infectious agents" (*Time* 1982:55). On the other hand, those not immediately in danger have been left, in large part, to undifferentiated categories reported as the "population at large" or the "general population."

These differences highlight social categories already firmly established. The strength and persistence of such categories lies in the perception that the associated characteristics and/or behaviors place in question the normative grounds for social order. AIDS, because it occurs to "those people," extends a gap and transforms it from a previously moral one to a physiological one.

In this light, one gay man is quoted as expressing the not completely irrational fear that, due to AIDS, homosexuals would all be "shipped off to some leper colony" (*Newsweek* 1983:20). This is ironic, because gays (and drug users) have always risked isolation. The "Typhoid Marys" associated with these behaviors were teachers, musicians, exposed politicians, and peers.[3] AIDS, as portrayed in the media, has merely helped to transform a metaphorically contagious disease into one concretely so. AIDS concretizes the moral category of homosexuality, and the media—by merging homosexuality with organic disease—very nearly creates a biological distinction between "straights" (heterosexuals) and gays where only normative differences existed before.

The association between lifestyles and disease is such as to become seemingly inseparable.[4] This synthesis has not been made, however, in reports of IV-drug users whose lifestyle also seems linearly related to AIDS. In fact, the lifestyle of the addict seems, for the most part, entirely ignored in the press. We have been willing to see drug addiction as, on the face of it, empirically damaging; however, gay lifestyles have only been assumed to be so. The fact that gays are now dying from disease (as addicts die from overdoses) reaffirms a social difference that lacked twentieth-century evidence (i.e., scientific evidence that one can see, touch, and measure). In the way that psychiatry searches for chemical causes for mental disorders that, if found, prove the appropriateness of the label "illness," so too the finding of physiological consequences of homosexuality—albeit not causal—gives renewed credibility to social distinctions perceived to have been significantly weakened in recent years. Further, although drug addiction has, since the early part of the century, carried a stigma, that stigma is one reflecting violations of conventional norms governing commitment to work and role obligations. The stigma attached to homosexuality reflects a perceived violation of the societal ground for being "human" in the first place: that all individual are clearly of one or another gender, and that

gender is ascribed at birth (see Raymond 1979 for a discussion of this issue).

## AIDS AS THE UNKNOWN: THE "CREEPING" THREAT TO US ALL

That the AIDS epidemic poses no immediate threat to the "population at large" is vouchsafed by a social barrier that, it is taken for granted, preserves a critical separation between populations. However, the barrier *is* permeable. Underlying and fueling the stigmatization of AIDS risk groups is the fear that the social distinctions that protect will be breached, leaving the general population open to the onslaught of fatal infections that AIDS permits. The press in some ways has circled the wagons. Outside are predominantly gay males subject no longer only to opportunistic infections due to disease, but now to an opportunistic morality by which they are held at arm's length. Inside is a population reading about a progressive contagion that moves from homosexual males, IV-drug users, Haitians, and hemophiliacs to health-care workers, children, surgery patients, and heterosexual women (families), with the explicit implication that it will not stop there.

From the perspective of the gay community itself (and from the several media critics who have addressed this issue) the fear of contagion must be seen as a double-edged sword.[5] On the one hand, it is the fear that contributes to the reestablishment of gays as outcasts. On the other, public fear (at least as a reported expression of gay opinion) is perceived to have generated public reaction in the form of research towards a cure.

It cannot be proven that research began in earnest only after the perception that AIDS was—as one article reported—"creeping out of well-defined epidemiological confines." (*Newsweek* 1983a:74). However, a reader of AIDS portrayals would easily become aware of the place and importance of just that fear. Although concern for one's physical well being is at issue, an overriding concern for the spread of disorder and chaos of which gays and other deviant actors can be seen as carriers prevails. Fear of contagion is often, but never clearly, expressed. Beginning as "GRID" (Gay-Related Immune Deficiency), it was given the informal appellation in the press of the "Gay Plague." Although these terms were generally dropped, references to a plague have continued. It is "plague" that conjures up the image of the Dark Ages, of death and disorder against which the modern world lives in fear and must constantly struggle. The hopelessness and disorder of such a world is made available in the descriptions of the people with AIDS.

## THE THEME OF BLAME IN MEDIA PORTRAYALS

Perhaps of singular importance to the issue of stigma, and the maintenance of social distance, is the invidious implication of blame and personal responsibility for one's disability that is contained in media coverage. At its most virulent are the reports of accusations that gays are justifiable objects of the righteous punishment of God for sinful behavior. Such condemnations also occasionally arise from within the gay community as expressions of self-doubt and "recrimination concerning gay lifestyles. A gay physician is quoted as saying that "perhaps we've needed a situation like this to demonstrate what we've known all along: depravity kills!" (*New York* 1982).

However, of more concern is the implicit use of blame as an indicator of social worth. Three categories of people with AIDS can be documented: the innocent, the suspect, and the guilty. The first category includes hemophiliacs, children, and, more recently, surgery patients. They are portrayed as innocent bystanders who cannot be held responsible for their illness; occupying a valued social position, they thus deserve all the benefits that accrue to any unremarkable sick person. Comparative references such as the following are typical:

> Some of the most tragic victims . . . are . . . children. . . . If the cases among children are the most wrenching . . . (*Newsweek* 1963a:77).
> Among the most tragic victims of the disease are the young children. (*Vanity Fair* 1983:31).

The innocence of children is exemplified in pictures of doctors and others, with benevolent and concerned faces, holding babies suspected of having the disease. Remarkable in such photos is the apparent absence of protective gear (see *Time* 1983:57; *Newsweek* 1982b:63). In other AIDS-contact situations wherein the social characteristics of the victims are suspect, such gear is clearly a mandatory barrier. Thus, a *Newsweek* photograph shows three correctional personnel wearing their protective gear for use in dealing with prisoners suspected of AIDS. Two wear heavy

gloves, what appear to be jump suits, and riot helmets with plastic face plates. The third, in a surgical gown, cap, mask, and gloves also carries a walkie-talkie. Other photos show police with special "resuscitation gear" to minimize the chance of contact with a possible at-risk patient (*U.S. News and World Report* 1983:13).

Haitian-Americans who contract AIDS are often seen as closet homosexuals or drug abusers who conceal this fact from medical investigators due to the strong stigma attached to such activities by Haitian society. They are in the second category of the "suspect." Other reports suggest that Haitians prostitute themselves to vacationing gays and so either contract or spread the disease. It might be observed that their reported concealment, even if not actually the case, helps to create a picture of a group who violates a basic assumption associated with illness: the responsibility to cooperate with professional help in one's cure (Parsons 1951).

In this case, they also present pre-existing characteristics of an already non-normative character. They are black, tend to be poor, are recent immigrants, and the association of Haiti with cult-religious practices fuels the current tendency to see deviance in groups at-risk for AIDS.

The third category is, of course, the most invidious: the category of the guilty. Moral spokesmen such as Jerry Falwell aside, the press on its own terms effectively attaches blame to both the homosexual and the drug user. Blame implicitly results in cases in which the attribution of "illness" can be used in situations for which personal responsibility can be seen as both contributory and significant. Such responsibility is an integral part of any illness label that is accompanied by what is seen as a non-normative environment within which the illness was seen to have its origin. Such environments or activities related to at-risk AIDS populations are described in the media as "anonymous sexual contacts," ". . . the paraphernalia of kinky sex . . . ," recreational injection of drugs, "especially with dirty needles . . ," (*Newsweek* 1983a); the use of "inhalants," a "fast-track" lifestyle (*New York* 1982) or frequently visiting "places of random sex" (*New York* 1983).

It is noteworthy that blame and sanction seem contingent on the finding of a causal link with non-normative behavior. For example, the use of tampons in the case of toxic shock did not result in women being blamed for bringing that upon themselves. Nor was any serious attribution of responsibility assigned for the consequences in women who continued to use tampons.

In a more general context, McKinley (1981:10) notes that:

> Indeed one can argue that certain at-risk behaviors have become so inextricably intertwined with our dominant cultural system (perhaps even symbolic of it), that the routine public display of such behaviors almost signifies membership in this society.

Further, he contends, that to then ask persons to give up such behaviors is tantamount to asking them to abandon their culture. With this in mind then, blame is not so much related to at-risk behaviors per se, but to non-normative at-risk behaviors; sex is sanctionable, smoking is not. In fact, industrialized societies have raised the hazardous lifestyle to heroic proportions insofar as such lifestyles affirm valued cultural traits like machismo or the achieving of worldly goals in the face of adversity. Statistically, however, more deaths result from participation in hazardous sports than from participation in hazardous sex.

## CONCLUSION

Although media coverage of AIDS does not appear, for the most part, to have been intentionally stigmatizing, it can, in fact, be seen to have approached the story in ways that have appeared to reaffirm the outcast status of at-risk groups, especially homosexual men. This consequence, however regrettable, is not altogether surprising. The issues surrounding homosexuality, its unclear relationship to illness and medical decision making, and the consequent questions of personal responsibility for deviance all can be seen as problematic in contemporary U.S. society. Media coverage reflects the ambiguity and ambivalence already associated with these issues.

In a larger context, the role of the media in the perception of illness has yet to be addressed in any systematic manner. Its obvious impact in the present context merely serves to point out the necessity for such research if any complete understanding of the experience of illness is to be produced.

## NOTES

1. Several articles referred to in this paper were taken from outside of the population defined by the Magazine Index. These occurrences are noted.
2. For discussions of the methods utilized by the media to produce the news see Gans, 1979; Molotch

and Lester, 1974; Tuchman, 1972, 1973, 1978.
3. It is interesting in this regard to note that the recent Gallup Report (1982) on attitudes toward homosexuality shows a general increase in approval for "equal job opportunities" for homosexuals since the last poll in 1977: 59% in favor in 1982 as compared to 52% in 1977. A full 50% responded favorably to "homosexuals as doctors," 52% to homosexuals in the "armed forces," 70% to homosexuals as "salespersons," but, significantly, only 38% responded favorably to homosexuals in the "clergy" and only 32% to homosexuals as "elementary school teachers." Further, in this context, we might speculate as to the significance of another Gallup finding: that when asked whether homosexuality was innate or acquired, 17% said "born with," 52% said "environment," whereas 13% noted "both." Given the weight placed on environment, the perception of possible "contagion" becomes all the more real not just from AIDS but from homosexuality itself.
4. Not only has AIDS become inextricably tied to homosexuality, but over the course of AIDS coverage, homosexuality's tie to other diseases has been emphasized. References to gays and hepatitis B, syphilis, gonorrhea, herpes, amebiasis, and others are not uncommon.
5. A small number of articles that take a critical stance have appeared in this group. In general, they argue that AIDS has been underfunded due to the stigmatized group that it affects. Further, there is some discussion of the setback that AIDS has given to the movement to normalize alternative sexual lifestyles. (See *Life* 1983; *Ms* 1983; *The Nation* 1983; *National Review* 1983; *The New Leader* 1983; *The New Republic* 1983; *New York* 1983; *Playboy* 1983a, 1983b; *The Progressive* 1983; *Vanity Fair* 1983).

## REFERENCES

Becker, Howard S. 1963. *Outsiders: Studies in the Sociology of Deviance*. New York. Free Press of Glencoe.

Conrad, Peter. 1975. The Discovery of Hyperkinesis: Notes on the Medicalization of Deviant Behavior. *Social Problems* 23 (October): 12–21.

Conrad, Peter and Joseph W. Schneider. 1980. *Deviance and Medicalization: From Badness to Sickness*. St. Louis: C.V. Mosby.

Foucault, Michel. 1965. *Madness and Civilization: A History of Insanity in the Age of Reason*. New York: Random House.

Gallup Report. 1982. American Pro Equal Rights for Gays . . . but Hedge in Some Areas. *Gallup*

*Report Number* 205 (October): 3–19.

Gans, Herbert. 1979. *Deciding What's News.* New York: Pantheon Books.

Glen, Norval and Charles Weaver. 1979. Attitudes Toward Premarital, Extramarital, and Homosexual Relations in the U.S. in the 1970's. *Journal of Sex Research* 15 (May): 108–118.

Goffman, Erving. 1963. *Stigma: Notes on the Management of a Spoiled Identity.* Englewood Cliffs, N.J.: Prentice-Hall.

Leif, M. I. 1977. Sexual Survey: #4 Current Thinking on Homosexuality. *Medical Aspects of Human Sexuality* 11:110–111.

*Life.* 1983. The View from Here. *Life* 6 ( July): 6–7.

*Macleans.* 1983a. The Growing Canadian AIDS Alarm. *Macleans* 96 (July 11): 34–35.

*Macleans.* 1983b. A Crisis of Mounting AIDS Hysteria. *Macleans* 96 (August 1): 6–8.

McKinley, John B. 1981. A Case for Refocusing Upstream: The Political Economy of Illness. In *The Sociology of Health and Illness*, pp. 613–633. Peter Conrad and Rochelle Kern, eds., New York: St. Martin's Press.

Molotch, Harvey and Marilyn Lester. 1974. News as Purposive Behavior: On the Strategic Use of Routine Events, Accidents, and Scandals. *American Sociological Review* 39:101–112.

*Ms.* 1983. The Politics of AIDS. *Ms.* (May):103.

*The Nation.* 1983. AIDS Neglect. *The Nation.* (May 21):627.

*National Review.* 1983. AIDS and Public Policy. *National Review* 35 (July 8): 796.

*The New Leader.* 1983. AIDS and the Moral Majority. *The New Leader* 66 (July 11): 12.

*The New Republic.* 1983. The Politics of a Plague. *New Republic* (August 1): 18–21.

*Newsweek.* 1982a. Homosexual Plague Strikes New Victims. *Newsweek* 100 (August 23): 10.

_____. 1982b. AIDS: A Lethal Mystery Story. *Newsweek* 100 (December 27): 63–64.

_____. 1983a. The AIDS Epidemic: the Search for a Cure. *Newsweek* 101 (April 18): 74–79.

_____. 1983b. The Change in Gay Life-Style. *Newsweek* 101 (April 18): 80.

_____. 1983c. The Panic Over AIDS. *Newsweek* 101 (July 4): 20–21.

*New York.* 1982. The Gay Plague. *New York* 15 (May 31): 52–61.

_____. 1983. AIDS Anxiety. *New York* 16 (June 20): 24–29.

*New York Times Magazine.* 1983. A New Disease's Deadly Odyssey. *New York Times Magazine* (February 6): 28–44.

Parsons, Talcott. 1951. *The Social System.* Glencoe, Ill.: Free Press.

_____. 1958. Definitions of Health and Illness in the Light of American Values and Social Structure. In *Patients, Physicians and Illness*, E. Gartly Jaco, ed. New York: Free Press.

*People.* 1983. AIDS, A Mysterious Disease, Plagues Homosexual Men from New York to California. *People* 19 (February 14): 42–44.

*Playboy.* 1983a. AIDS: Journalism in a Plague Year. *Playboy* 30(October):35–36.

_____. 1983b. The Desexing of America *Playboy* 30 (December): 109.

*Progressive.* 1983. Everybody Out of the Pool. *Progressive* 47 (September): 11–12.

Raymond, Janice G. 1979. *The Transsexual Empire: The Making of the She-Male.* Boston: Beacon Press.

Robinson, D. 1972. The Alcohologist's Addiction — Some Implications of Having Lost Control over the Disease Concept of Alcoholism. *Quarterly Journal of Studies in Alcoholism* 33:1028–1042.

*Rolling Stone.* 1983. Is There Death After Sex? *Rolling Stone* (February 3):17ff.

Sarbin, T. R. 1967. The Dangerous Individual: An Outcome of Social Identity Transformation. *British Journal of Criminology* 7:285–295.

_____. 1968a. Ontology Recapitulates Philogy: The Mythic Nature of Anxiety. *American Psychologist* 23:411–418.

_____. 1968b. The Transformation of Social Identity: A New Metaphor for the Helping Professions. In *Comprehensive Mental Health*, Leigh M. Roberts, Norman S. Greenfield, and Milton H. Miller, eds., pp. 97–115. Madison: University of Wisconsin Press.

*Saturday Evening Post.* 1982. Being Gay Is a Health Hazard. *Saturday Evening Post* 254 (October): 26.

Schur, Edwin M. 1971. *Labeling Deviant Behavior.* New York: Harper and Row.

Sontag, Susan. 1977. *Illness as Metaphor.* New York: Farrar, Straus and Giroux.

Szasz, Thomas. 1970. *The Manufacture of Madness.* New York: Harper and Row.

*Time.* 1982. The Deadly Spread of AIDS. *Time* 120 (September 6): 55.

_____. 1983. The Real Epidemic: Fear and Despair. *Time* 121 (July): 56–58.

Tuchman, Gaye. 1972. Objectivity as Strategic Ritual: An Examination of Newsmen's Notions of Objectivity. *American Journal of Sociology* 77 (January): 660–679.

_____. 1973. Making News by Doing Work: Routinizing the Unexpected. *American Journal of So-*

*ciology* 79 (July): 110–131.

_____. 1978. *Making News: A Study in the Construction of Reality.* New York: Free Press.

U.S. *News and World Report.* 1983. Fear of AIDS Infects the Nation. *U.S. News and World Report* 94

(June 27): 13.

*Vanity Fair.* 1983. A Moral Epidemic. *Vanity Fair* 46 (September): 130–132.

Wooton, Barbara. 1959. *Social Science and Social Pathology.* London: George Allen Unwin.

# I 62 I

# *The Second Wave*

## JAMES KINSELLA

Max Robinson, the first black anchor on network television, was sitting for an interview with the *Washington Post* in the late spring of 1988, when the question of his lengthy illness came up. Was it AIDS? "I'm just not going to get into the subject of what I have," Robinson said. For months the rumors had been circulating throughout the Northeast media establishment, and in Chicago, from where the poised and professional broadcaster had last coanchored ABC's "World News Tonight." Ironically, one of the last stories he broadcast was on AIDS hysteria. He left the network months later, in early 1984.

Robinson's refusal to confirm or deny the whispers did not make them go away. He had an infectious disease and he almost died in December of 1987: that was as much as he would admit. Once the most influential black in American journalism, the forty-nine-year-old now was cloistered in his lakefront apartment.

Seven years since the epidemic first made news, the mainstream media establishment was giving occasional AIDS-related stories big play, though coverage of the epidemic overall was decreasing. The Robinson feature ran on the cover of the *Post*'s well-respected "Style" section. In the minority press, however, Robinson's illness was routinely disregarded, even though he had become a TV personality on the "Essence" shows, the black magazine-format program shown mostly on cable.

In the early 1980s, the mainstream media made AIDS a well-kept secret. Now the minority press was underplaying almost every aspect of the

disease that was increasingly claiming the lives of blacks and Hispanics. And both the mainstream and minority media were ignoring the biggest threat to the larger population: the spread of the disease to heterosexual minorities.

## PROTECTING THEM FROM THE NEWS

"We have a family newspaper here," said William Egyir, managing editor of' the New York *Amsterdam News*, the granddaddy of the black media. It was the spring of 1988 when Egyir made his defense of the newspaper's poor AIDS coverage. The statement echoed the attitude in the mainstream press a half decade earlier. The rationale was still dangerously faulty. Of the nearly 76,000 cases of AIDS diagnosed in the United States by late 1988, one in four were black, three in 20 were Hispanic. That meant blacks and Hispanics were being infected at more than twice the rate of whites in the United States. Increasingly those coming down with the disease were not gay and middle-class. They were junkies from the barrio and the ghetto. In New York, the infection rate for drug addicts was estimated at about 60 percent in 1988. In Newark, New Jersey, authorities pegged it closer to 100 percent.

"These people don't read the paper," said

In James Kinsella, *Covering the Plague: AIDS and the American Media*, pp. 242–253. New Brunswick, N.J.: Rutgers University Press, 1989.

Egyir. For the most part, he was right: addicts do not read any newspapers, as a rule.

In 1988, it already may have been too late to reach the junkies in New York and Newark. But it was not too late to warn their sex partners who did not use drugs. If addicts weren't reading the *Amsterdam News* or other minority-community newspapers, many of their partners were. Unfortunately, the newspapers largely turned their backs on these people, too.

## THE VOICE OF HARLEM

When it was founded in 1909, the weekly *Amsterdam News* targeted itself toward the residents of the nation's most astute black community: Harlem. The paper built a reputation for covering every side of race politics, from the 1940s desegregation of the hometown Dodgers to the civil rights marches of the 1960s. In its most influential days during the mid- and late 1960s, it had a circulation of almost ninety thousand and was considered black America's paper of record.

The *Amsterdam News* necessarily became its own agenda-setter, because the issues it considered most pressing were often overlooked entirely by the mainstream press. The paper is much more likely to feature the latest jousting between Jesse Jackson and Mayor Ed Koch than news about Soviet-American arms negotiations or even a strike by New York Rapid Transit workers. "Few movers use the *Amsterdam News* as their sole news source," according to one black journalist. As its circulation slid, to thirty-five thousand in the 1980s, the *Amsterdam News* became less influential in the black community. The paper also was hit with competition from both within and without its own community. New York papers like the *Caribbean News*, for example, focused on immigrant populations and expanded coverage to cut into the *News*'s territory. And the city's growing black middle class, much of which no longer called Harlem home, reached more and more for what were formerly considered the "white" papers.

The *Amsterdam News* continued to focus on its traditional audience, that community-minded, middle-class, and politically interested black — the kind of reader who was also likely to patronize the restaurant or shop that advertises in the newspaper. Thus coverage at the *News* was determined by the same criterion that the mainstream media used: try to guess what that target audience wants to read.

## AIDS COVERAGE AT THE AMSTERDAM NEWS

For editors like Egyir, it was clear early on in the AIDS epidemic that his readers would not be interested in what the mainstream media defined as a disease mostly affecting gays. "That's not a part of the community that the black media covers," said Gil Gerald, director of the National AIDS Network, a public education project. Not until 1987 would the paper begin to give any attention to the plague that had taken hold in Harlem. Yet its coverage was about the best the minority press in New York City offered. During a twelve-month period ending in mid-1988, the *Amsterdam News* published about twice as many AIDS-related stories as the *Caribbean News*, and nearly as many articles as the two major Spanish-language daily papers, *El Diario-La Prensa* and *Noticias del Mundo*. Still, in that year-long period, the *Amsterdam News* ran only fifty articles on the epidemic.

Many of those articles were no more than three-inch notices of AIDS information meetings, for example. And there were opinion pieces from politicians like Harlem Representative Charles Rangel and public health officials, describing the epidemic and what it meant for the black community. But the most dramatic articles were those written by community members lashing out at "the white media." For instance, on a June 6, 1987, in "Putting the AIDS Blame on 'Black Mames,'" an unidentified writer complained about, and labeled as racist, recent articles in newspapers like the *New York Times* that cited the danger of transmission between black women and men. "Now that the AIDS disease is developing into an international health catastrophe they would put the blame between the sheets of 'Black Mames.' . . . What's most maddening is the deafening silence of our influential community in the face of this calculated media mud onslaught which continues to besmear our image."

As in its heyday, when the faithful read it in part to track the civil rights struggle, the *Amsterdam News*'s strength was its political sensibility. And as in the 1960s, it found itself playing the role of guardian to a community too often under siege. As a result, the tone of its AIDS news was often defensive. The coverage was also weak. When it described how the disease was transmitted, the most important information for its readers, the prose was often so subtle as to be misleading: "While white homosexuals contract AIDS from 'action' between themselves, the majority of Blacks and Hispanics get it as IVDU," the paper reported on April 4, 1987. Neither "action" (presumably anal and possibly oral sex) nor IVDU (intravenous drug use) were explained.

There were also repeated articles attacking basic, common-sense methods of prevention such as condom use. "Don't Give Convicts Condoms" read a headline on May 2, 1987, supporting City Councilman Enoch Williams's attempt to shut down the practice in New York City's jails.

Some of the newspaper's most ambitious reporting on the epidemic was done to track down conspiracy theories about the disease, such as the idea that AIDS is a product of a CIA experiment run afoul in the Congo. Other black media have printed the claims of Steve Cokely, who was an aide to Chicago's acting mayor, Eugene Sawyer. In 1988 Cokely charged that doctors, most of them Jewish, were responsible for the spread of AIDS by injecting the disease into blacks. He no longer works for the city of Chicago.

## WHAT UNCLE SAM DIDN'T DO

Distrust of the federal government obviously underlay much of the coverage of the epidemic at the *Amsterdam News*. The minority media cannot be entirely blamed for taking this tack. The mainstream media also overlooked the fact that the crisis was affecting minorities disproportionately, and to a large extent still does. The image of the AIDS victim that appears on the TV screen, for example, is almost always white and is much more likely to be that of a middle-class person than someone who is poor. The CDC has done little to promote the real picture of this epidemic until very recently.

As early as 1983, the CDC had such a clear understanding of how AIDS was spreading that the agency broke down the victims into racial groups: "57 percent of those [AIDS cases] reported have been white, 26 percent black, 14 percent Hispanic and 3 percent other or unknown," the CDC's *Morbidity and Mortality Weekly Report* declared on September 9 of that year. Even then it was obvious the disease was accelerating among minorities. Blacks, for example, were being hit far harder proportionately than whites. It was obvious that AIDS was not going to be contained exclusively in the gay population.

However, not until three years after that initial racial-group breakdown did the CDC get around to featuring the problem in the MMWR. Finally, in the issue of October 24, 1986, the CDC warned public health officials that "until an effective therapy or vaccine is available, prevention of [HIV] infection depends on education and behavioral modification of persons at increased risk," including minorities.

CDC officials could not explain why they had waited to publish the information. Perhaps it was because Dr. James Curran, Dr. Harold Jaffe, and other CDC officials were much better connected to gays than to the communities of blacks and Hispanics in the inner city, having worked with homosexual organizations on other diseases like hepatitis B. Some familiar with the agency also said that doctors there were afraid of stumbling into the same political mess as when early in the epidemic they labeled Haitians a high-risk group for the disease. The CDC was attacked as racist by black and Haitian groups both in the United States and abroad for that move.

Nonetheless, "the government should have reached out to the black press," said Gerald of the National AIDS Network. In the early years, that vehicle for public health information was almost completely ignored. In the fall of 1987, the Department of Health and Human Services commissioned the National Black Entertainment Network to produce a one-hour documentary. Called "AIDS in the Black Community," it was a straightforward introduction to how the disease was making headway mostly among heterosexual minorities.

Since then, the U.S. Public Health Service has generated ad campaigns directed specifically at blacks and Hispanics.

## AIDS COVERAGE IN THE OTHER BLACK MEDIA

As in all other media, the most important spur to the black media to cover the epidemic was personal involvement in the crisis. Some journalists at the black publications mourned the loss of friends who had died of AIDS, and certain "celebrity" obituaries shook the entire black community. Willi Smith's death was one of those.

The thirty-nine-year-old fashion designer, whose Williwear creations had grown into a multimillion-dollar business during the mid-1980s, was diagnosed with the disease. He died April 17, 1987. His death was covered by much of the black media and helped bring home the fact that the epidemic was touching black lives. As with Rock Hudson, the fact that Smith was gay would be largely overlooked.

However, there was one black medium that did not shy away from the epidemic, in any of its forms. From January 1984, the gossipy *Jet* magazine had been covering the disease as closely as *Newsweek* and *Time*, and far more closely than its counterpart. *People*. By 1985 the glossy weekly was running regular stories, from how the disease was spreading to how to prevent it. Its mainstay, of course, was the inside scoop on the black elite: "Richard Pryor denies having AIDS," one 1986 article began.

With a circulation of some 835,000, *Jet's* influence in the black community is substantial. Unfortunately, its sister publication, *Ebony*, with more than 1.7 million subscribers monthly, largely overlooked the crisis. Both magazines are published by the conservative Johnson family, which has long sought to put the best light on the black community. "The 100 Most Influential Black Americans," an *Ebony* article, is typical of the features run in the magazine.

## ROCK WHO?

In the Hispanic community, there was no equivalent to the Rock Hudson death. Unlike the black media, Spanish-language print journalists and broadcasters tend to use Associated Press or United Press International news services. However, even as these resources began exploding with AIDS information after Rock Hudson's diagnosis in 1985, "Hispanics saw [the epidemic] as a Hollywood story," said Josefina Vidal, health editor of *La Opinion*. "It wasn't news that was affecting us."

The daily newspaper, based in Los Angeles, had run some news items on AIDS, beginning in February of 1985. But the same inhibitions keeping the story untold in the black and mainstream media also kept a lid on coverage in the Hispanic media. The Spanish-speaking community in the United States, though it comes from very different cultures ranging from South and Central America to the Caribbean, is generally considered conservative and very family-oriented. "Sex isn't a topic discussed much in the home," said Emilio Nicolas, Jr., general manager of WXTV, a popular Hispanic station in New York. If homosexuality is ignored by the black media, it is denied by many Hispanic journalists. José Sanz, a producer of a Spanish-language series on the disease, said the multi-part program did not use the word "homosexual" until a gay male being interviewed uttered the term himself.

Not until 1986 did progressive media like *La Opinion* produce original articles on AIDS. By that time, said Vidal, "the statistics were clear about the danger the disease posed for the Hispanic community." In fact, anyone closely covering either the Hispanic or black communities should have recognized much earlier that the epidemic was spreading fast among their ranks.

From late 1986 on, the figures on those coming down with the disease showed that AIDS was claiming two and three times as many victims, proportionately, among those two minority groups than among whites. Not all of the minority victims were junkies and gays. In Los Angeles, intravenous drug users were spreading the disease to their spouses, children, and lovers, though at a much slower rate than in such big cities as New York, Newark, and Chicago. The difference, according to experts, was that in sprawling Los Angeles, the distances that separated pockets of drug addicts kept those users from spreading the disease more rapidly among themselves. In addition, the dangerous habit of passing needles from one user to the next in a shooting gallery was much less common on the West Coast than in the East.

Hispanics on both coasts, however, shared special problems in trying to tackle the disease. For instance, in attempting to get the word out about AIDS, communicating it in simple terms could be extremely confusing when dealing with Hispanic immigrants from five or more countries— Mexico, Cuba, Puerto Rico, El Salvador, Nicaragua, etc.—each familiar only with their very distinctive dialect.

## TELLING SONIA'S STORY

Despite the difficulties, there were some impressive information campaigns kicked off in Hispanic print and broadcast media.

At *La Opinion* Josefina Vidal and other editors pulled together a special supplement, "SIDA: Epidemia sin fronteras" (AIDS: Epidemic without Boundaries), that ran in July 1987. The twenty-page tabloid was included in the eighty-five thousand copies of *La Opinion*. Since most of the paper's readers are conservative Catholics,

Vidal focused on families to gain the attention and sympathy of this group.

There was Sonia, a young immigrant mother of two. She had been infected with the AIDS virus by her drug-using boyfriend. Worse still, she was pregnant, and the doctors told her that she might have infected her child. "I cried and beat my head with my hands. This couldn't be happening to my baby," she said. "[The doctor] recommended that I have an abortion, but I didn't have the heart for that and I told him I wanted to have my baby." Sonia did have her baby, and he was infected with the disease.

Even the gay men *La Opinion* reported on, such as thirty-two-year-old Sergio Rebolledo, were described in a family context. "[He] is a religious man, who goes to church to pray often, as his grandmother taught him. For him, God is a compassionate being, not someone that judges and punishes.'" His parents and sister still live in his native Mexico City, and they all know about his illness. "My mother is very worried, but when she comes to see me she feels much better," he said.

*La Opinion* followed up its first supplement with a second one in October 1988, "Juntos contra el SIDA" (Together against AIDS).

Perhaps because Vidal, who oversaw these special sections, was careful to couch these gripping stories in terms her audience could relate to— family, church, home—there was little negative response from the community. In fact, there were demands from throughout Los Angeles and even in San Francisco for reprints of the special sections. They eventually were distributed in clinics as well as at the San Francisco and L.A. AIDS projects.

Another significant effort was a documentary on AIDS in the Hispanic community, spearheaded by broadcaster Emilio Nicolas while at the Hispanic station in San Francisco. KDTV. And Univision, the Hispanic network with some 450 affiliates, in 1987 featured a series of AIDS shows on its "America," a more entertainment-oriented, Spanish-language version of "60 Minutes." Not surprisingly, these productions looked like their English-language counterparts: Although they avoided many of the foolish errors the networks and print media committed in the early years, the programs often focused on children even though adults make up the majority of those actually getting the disease.

Little Celeste was one such subject. The ten-year-old girl was described as the longest-living survivor of AIDS, and "among the youngest, and most innocent victims," on the "America" show of April 28, 1987. She had been infected in the womb, and her mother, father, and younger brother all had since died of the disease. The story of Celeste's horror was told mostly through her grandmother, Toy Santiago. Reaction to the piece was strong and quick. Thousands of phone calls poured into the network's affiliates across the country, some viewers offering compliments, a few complaints, and many wanting more information.

The event indicated the power of the televised word, perhaps especially in the Hispanic community. Many Latinos, even those who are completely bilingual, prefer to watch TV in their mother tongue. Although well-educated Hispanics traditionally have preferred English-language TV, even some of them are switching over to Univision and its competitor network, Telemundo Group, as their programming becomes more sophisticated. One of the strongest stations, KMEX in Los Angeles, part of the Univision network, often pulls in larger audiences than many of the English-language stations, even though it is stuck on the outback of local TV's channel 31.

## THEIRS VERSUS OURS

U.S. mainstream media have ignored minorities as both a source of and an audience for news. With efforts like Univision's "America" segments on AIDS, it's even easier for editors at daily newspapers and TV producers to dismiss their responsibility to inform *all* Americans about pressing health issues like AIDS. The minority media tend to set their own agenda and, particularly in the black press, to ignore major events other media have deemed important. As a result, some frustrated editors at metropolitan dailies have decided that minority readers concerns are so different from their own that they can't possibly produce a paper that appeals at the same time to white surburbanites, black city dwellers, and Hispanics in the barrio.

That notion is wrong, according to the findings of an exhaustive study undertaken by the American Society of Newspaper Editors in 1986. To produce a paper that blacks will read, editors need no more to "mirror" that community—as the *Amsterdam News* claims to do, but fails resoundingly—than they need to understand Hibernian rituals to get the Irish to subscribe. Whether a person—white, black, Hispanic—regularly reads the newspaper depends on whether he or she has the habit. Helping to shape such practices early on, through schools, for instance, is more important to the future of newspaper readership than targeting minority groups for coverage.

But mainstream newspapers do a miserable job of attracting black and Hispanic readers. Despite feeble attempts by some dailies to capitalize on this untapped market, newspaper management has changed only slightly since the Kerner Commission report of 1968 excoriated the white media establishment for its racist practices. Print journalism is doing little to halt the move, especially by minority audiences, to television as the single source for news.

That has alarming implications for an American population that is increasingly minority-dominated. For the first time in the history of modern California, a majority of the state's public school students are black, Hispanic, or Asian—not white. When those children become adults, they very likely won't have the newspaper reading habit and will rely on TV news.

Does it matter that most Americans get their news exclusively from the television? Coverage of the AIDS epidemic shows just how much. TV news will continue to discount minority communities, even as crises like AIDS affect blacks and Hispanics more, and present fairly complex issues like disease prevention in dangerously simplistic terms, when it airs them at all.

Who will speak for the group now being devastated by AIDS: drug-using, poor, disenfranchised blacks and Hispanics? Who will tell their story? Who will air their concerns?

## "PERSONAL THREAT" RULE

Journalists are still led by the rule that has consistently determined how AIDS would be covered: the closer the threat of the disease seemed to move toward those setting the agenda, the bigger the story became. That was true in the spring of 1983, when data from a study of pediatric AIDS cases were wrongly interpreted to suggest the disease could be spread through routine, household contact. In the summer of 1985, when the diagnosis of virile "Every Man" Rock Hudson was made public, the press once again wrote itself into a frenzy. And in the spring of 1987, when the AIDS agenda turned to discussions of who should be tested, and how can "we" protect ourselves from "them," media interest boomed again. Since then, fears have largely been quelled, and so has the coverage. The media are slow to learn their lessons, but when they do they generally commit them to memory. So it has been with the fact that AIDS is not a threat to the average white, heterosexual, middle-class person. Even a flamboyant study like the March 1988 report by Dr. William Masters and Virginia Johnson, claiming that everyone was at risk of catching the disease, perhaps even from toilet seats, did not draw the firestorm of reaction they had hoped for.

As the media grasped that reality, coverage dropped off precipitously. Public health officials like Surgeon General C. Everett Koop feared that turn of events. Now that the epidemic has moved into its second wave, overwhelming Third World America, widely accessible information should be more important than ever in the fight against AIDS. But except for features done by the *New York Times*, the *Washington Post*, the *Philadelphia Inquirer*, and a handful of other outlets, the media are not responding. In some cities, more has been written about the purported transmission of AIDS by mosquitoes, which was proved impossible, than about the very evident spread of the disease from intravenous drug-using father to wife to child. The disease is shaping communities and cities, and yet the implications of this crisis are being disregarded.

There is also a pattern of missing out on even more obvious news opportunities to educate minorities about the disease. Max Robinson, for example, probably the most recognized black journalist in America, died in late 1988, without ever publicly acknowledging his illness. The following day, a close friend announced that Robinson had died of AIDS, and that the former network anchor had wanted his demise to serve as a means of informing others about the disease. He could and should have used his life more effectively for the same purpose.

# | 63 |

# A Test of Who We Are As a People:
# ACT UP Rally, Albany, New York, May 7, 1988

VITO RUSSO

A friend of mine has a half-fare transit card which he uses on buses and subways. The other day when he showed his card, the token attendant asked what his disability was. He said, "I have AIDS," and the attendant said, "No you don't. If you had AIDS you'd be home—dying."

I'm here to speak out today as a PWA who is not dying *from*—but for the last three years quite successfully living *with*—AIDS. Members of my family who get all their information from reading the newspapers and watching television know two things about me—that I'm going to die and that the government is doing everything in its power to save me. They're wrong on both counts.

If I'm dying from anything it's from homophobia. If I'm dying from anything it's from racism. If I'm dying from anything it's from indifference and red tape. If I'm dying from anything I'm dying from Jesse Helms. If I'm dying from anything I'm dying from Ronald Reagan. If I'm dying from anything I'm dying from the sensationalism of newspapers and magazines and television shows that are interested in me as a human interest story only as long as I'm willing to be a helpless victim but not if I'm fighting for my life. If I'm dying from anything I'm dying from the fact that not enough rich, white, heterosexual men have gotten AIDS for anyone to give a shit.

Living with AIDS in this country is like living in the twilight zone. Living with AIDS is living through a war which is happening only for those people who are in the trenches. Every time a shell explodes you look around to discover that you've lost more of your friends. But nobody else notices—it isn't happening to them. They're walking the streets as though we weren't living through a nightmare; only *you* can hear the screams of the people dying and their cries for help. No one else seems to be noticing.

It's worse than wartime because during a war the people are united in a shared experience. This war has not united us—it's divided us. It's separated those of us with AIDS and those of us who fight for people with AIDS from the rest of the population.

Two-and-a-half years ago I read a *Life* magazine editorial on AIDS that said it's time to pay attention because "this disease is now beginning to strike the rest of us." It was as if I wasn't the one holding the magazine in my hand. Since then nothing has changed to alter the perception that AIDS is not happening to the real people in this country—it's not happening to *us* in the United States—it's happening to *them*—to the disposable populations of fags and junkies who deserve what they get. The media tell people they don't have to care because the citizens who really matter are in no danger. Twice, three times, maybe four, the *New York Times* has published editorials saying "Don't Panic Yet Over AIDS"—it still hasn't entered the general population and until it does we don't have to give a shit.

And the days and the months—and the years pass by, and *they* don't spend those days and nights and months and years trying to figure out how to get ahold of the latest experimental drug and which dose to take it at and in which combination with what other drugs and from what source and for how much money because it isn't happening to them so they don't give a shit. And they don't sit in television studios surrounded by technicians

In Brian Wallis, ed., *Democracy: Discussions in Contemporary Culture*, 5:299–302. Seattle: Bay Press, 1990.

who wear rubber gloves and refuse to put a body mike on them because it isn't happening to them so they don't give a shit. And they don't have their houses burned down by bigots and morons. They only watch it on the news and then they eat their dinner and they go to bed because it isn't happening to them so they don't give a shit.

They don't spend their waking hours going from one hospital to another, watching the people they love die slowly of neglect and bigotry because it isn't happening to them so they don't give a shit. They haven't been to two funerals a week for the last three, four, or five years so they don't give a shit. It's not happening to them.

We read on the front page of the *New York Times* that Dr. Anthony Fauci now says that all sorts of promising drugs for treatment haven't even been tested in the last two years because he can't afford to hire the people to test them. We're supposed to be grateful that this story has appeared. Nobody wonders why some reporter didn't dig up that story and print it eighteen months ago, before Fauci went public with his complaints before a congressional committee. How many people died in the last two years who might be alive today if those drugs had been speedily tested?

Reporters all over the country are busy printing government press releases. They don't give a shit—it isn't happening to them—meaning that it isn't happening to the real people, the world famous general public we all keep hearing about. Legionnaires' disease was happening to them because the people who got it looked like them, sounded like them, were the same color as them—and that fucking story about a couple of dozen people hit the front pages of every newspaper and magazine in the country and stayed there until the mystery was over.

All I read in the newspapers tells me that the mainstream heterosexual population is not at risk for this disease. All the newspapers I read tell me that IV drug users and homosexuals still account for the overwhelming majority of cases and those at risk. Then can somebody please tell me why every single penny allocated for education and prevention gets spent on ad campaigns directed almost exclusively to white, heterosexual teenagers who they keep telling us are *not at risk for this disease?*

Can somebody tell me why the only television movie ever produced by a major network in this country is not about a young man with AIDS but about the impact of the disease on his straight, white nuclear family? Why for eight years every single newspaper and magazine in this country has done cover stories on AIDS only when the threat of heterosexual transmission is raised? Why for eight years every single educational film designed for use in high schools has eliminated any gay positive material before being approved by the board of education? Why in the past eight years every single public information pamphlet and videotape distributed by establishment sources has ignored specific homosexual content? Why every bus and subway ad I read and every advertisement and billboard I see is specifically not directed at gay men?

Don't believe the lie that the gay community has done its job and done it well and has successfully educated its people. The gay community and IV drug users are not all politicized people living in New York and San Francisco. Members of minority populations, including so-called sophisticated gay men, are abysmally ignorant about AIDS. If it is true that gay men and IV drug users are the populations at risk for this disease we have a right to demand that education and prevention be targeted specifically to these people and *it is not happening*. We are being allowed to die while low risk populations are being panicked—not educated—panicked into believing that we deserve to die.

AIDS is not what it appears to be at this moment in history. It is more than just a disease that ignorant people have turned into an excuse to exercise bigotry they already feel. It is more than a horror story to be exploited by the tabloids.

AIDS is a test of who we are as a people. When future generations ask what we did in the war we have to be able to tell them that we were out here fighting. And we have to leave a legacy to the generations of people who will come after us. Remember that someday the AIDS crisis will be over. And when that day has come and gone there will be people alive on this earth—gay people and straight people—black people and white people—men and women—who will hear the story that once there was a terrible disease—and that a brave group of people stood up and fought and in some cases died so that others might live and be free. I'm proud to be out here today with the people I love and to see the faces of those heroes who are fighting this war and to be part of that fight. To steal a phrase from Mike Callen's song, "Love is all we have for now—what we don't have is time."

Like the unsung, anonymous doctors who are

fighting this disease and are so busy putting out fires that they don't have time to strategize, AIDS activists are stretched to the limit of their time and energy, putting out the fires of bigotry and hatred and misinformation when they need to be fighting for drugs and research money. We need luxury time to strategize the next year of this battle and we need our friends to join us so we can buy that time. And after we kick the shit out of this disease I intend to be alive to kick the shit out of this system so that this will never happen again.

# | 64 |

# *More to the Shilts Story*

## Jessea Greenman

It is but a few days after Randy's death. Print and electronic tributes to his opus continue to mount. I have been taking in as many of these commentaries as cross my path, and it appears that several important points remain, at this moment in time, unelucidated. Please note, there is a natural human tendency to lionize the just deceased, and this brief analysis is NOT an attempt to defang or declaw the lion. Rather, it is an effort to describe the environment in which Randy wrote, the "jungle," to continue the metaphor.

Almost universally, commentators on Shilts' legacy note that he was the first openly gay reporter hired for a major mainstream newspaper when taken on by the San Francisco Chronicle in 1981. It is vital to rephrase that when hired by the Chronicle, Shilts became the *only* openly gay reporter writing on lesbian and gay issues for a major mainstream newspaper, and he was to remain the *only* such reporter for some time *after* 1981.

So what's the difference and why is it important? As you read on, perhaps it will become evident to you that this analysis of representation in the media can and does apply to any number of minority groups. Being the first is important, especially because the presumption is that others soon will follow. That was not the case for lesbian and gay reporters in the media. It was to be years before there were any other "out" lesbian and gay mainstream journalists writing about the lesbian and gay community.

Point one: As a consequence, Randy Shilts was regarded by mainstream media and the public as the only voice for lesbian and gay America. There were no other sources known to the media against which to compare Randy's perceptions and perspective. The natural issue of this situation is that everything that Randy wrote in those days was considered authoritative and given tremendous weight. This made his role highly problematic for the lesbian and gay community.

Media have a "take me to your leader" mentality. Randy was taken to be a leader (since he was the only one they knew and trusted) by the media, and so his opinion was sought out on any number of subjects. The question remains: did Randy Shilts represent anyone and, if so whom? Randy was not an officer of any organization in the lesbian/gay community. Randy no doubt talked to people in the lesbian and gay community, but that does not mean he represented them or their views.

The question of representation in media is enormous and complex; it is not my intention to explore it in depth here. The point being made is that oppressed communities have little access to mainstream media. A few "voices" are selected by the media to represent those communities. These media figures may very well not represent their communities at all, particularly since most communities are highly diversified. Thus, media and the public need to be mindful when the same one voice or few voices are cited over and over again on behalf of any given group of people. That one

*MediaFile*, May 1994, pp. 1–4.

or those few voices cannot possibly represent a community.

Point two: everything that anyone says about lesbian and gay people is and always has been automatically problematized. This is because we are, by mainstream definition, controversial. In part this is because the interaction of fear of us and ignorance about us has kept those who are ignorant fearful and those who are fearful ignorant, thereby neatly perpetuating the conception of us as controversial. This is also, in part, because the hatred and violence arrayed against us have led the vast majority of lesbian and gay people to hide, making it impossible to do valid studies of our population and to demystify who we really are. It is hard to refute lies and distortions when there aren't many real facts. All of this was even more true in the early 1980's when Randy Shilts was the only out queer reporter.

This means that there is nothing that anyone can safely say about us without causing or feeding into controversy. If someone claims to have figures showing that lesbian and gay people have high per capita average incomes (and a lesbian/gay marketing research firm has released such figures, flawed though they are for the reason cited above), then the right wing turns that into a rationale for claiming we are over-privileged already and therefore do not deserve protection from employment discrimination. If someone else were to release figures purportedly showing that lesbian and gay people had LOW per capita average incomes, then just as surely that would be corrupted by the right wing into an argument for not providing us with social services since such figures demonstrate that we are a lazy and shiftless lot. Whatever Randy Shilts wrote, and I do mean whether he wrote a spirited defense of bath houses or a spirited condemnation, it was bound to be caught up in the ongoing firestorm of controversy which always flames around our community. The brouhaha over lesbians and gays in the military is just the latest in an unbroken line of issues having to do with lesbian and gay people which our society is apparently incapable of discussing rationally and our media incapable of covering rationally. There is no neutral ground in a free-fire zone.

Just as firestorms suck oxygen out of the atmosphere, so the ever-flaring firestorms of controversy to which our community is subjected suck away the life's breath of free speech. Our community cannot work on its own issues, for we are being watched. I am proud of our community for voluntarily and pro-actively addressing issues such as domestic partner abuse, yet the right wing jumps on such discussions as more fuel for controversy, as in "Those sick perverts are incapable of loving and committed relationships. Look, they beat each other up all the time. Here's a story from one of their own newspapers to prove it." Thus, our efforts to address issue within our community are turned into factoid weapons against us. Our community needs to be discussing, fully and fairly and accurately, whether or not there is a resurgence of unsafe sex in order to figure out whether new education strategies are needed, but we are inhibited from such a life-saving discussion because we know what the media will do with such a debate: inflame it. We know what the right wing would do with the facts presented during such a discussion: turn them into media Molotov cocktails against us. In Randy's time, when so few heterosexual people knew anything at all about us, this chilling effect on free speech and free journalism was even more powerful. Randy did deal with the bath house issue, and others. It was not possible then, and it is still not possible now, to discuss such matters in an atmosphere of calm.

Point three: as with many other minorities, lesbian and gay people are considered to be inherently incapable of being objective about their own community. Whether it is right-wingers asserting that lesbian and gay scientists and doctors cannot be relied upon to do valid studies or mainstream assignment editors asserting that we are ipso facto "interested parties" when it comes to issues having to do with sexual orientation, this is a pervasive and powerful dynamic carrying the seductive glitter of superficial truth. However, it is deeply flawed.

If matters regarding sexual orientation (or race, or gender) automatically make people into "interested parties," then NO ONE is neutral. That is, heterosexuals (or whites, or men), who presumably also have identity and rights at stake in these matters, must be regarded as equally biased if queers (or journalists of color or women commentators) are to be regarded as biased in these matters. Rarely, however, are heterosexuals (or whites, or men) disqualified from commenting on issues for reasons relating solely to their status, yet this commonly happens to minority journalists.

On the contrary, far from being biased, lesbian and gay people are THE EXPERTS on issues having to do with sexual orientation. The censorship of fair and accurate information about lesbian and gay people has been so terribly complete that only by dint of long and diligent study can one become expert in this area. Most heterosexual people do not have the inclination to pursue such studies; most queer people do this work as a matter of course, as part of their own search to make sense of the universe and to survive in it.

What makes Randy Shilts unique is that, for a longish and crucial period in history, he was accepted by the mainstream as an expert, not only on AIDS, but also on the "gay" community. Perhaps the "credit" for this should go to the San Francisco Chronicle, perhaps to the peculiar exigencies of those times—we need not resolve this age-old theoretical debate about what makes people famous. We do need to note that Randy's writing was so powerful because, for that moment, his insider status as a gay man was recognized as a form of expertise. While I would hypothesize that his expertise was limited and partial, in that he very much exhibited the perspective of a gay white man of the 80's rather than an expertise reflecting our entire community, we can leave

this, too, to subsequent study. I would urge Bill German at the Chronicle to collect into one volume and publish ALL of Randy's articles for the paper, so that serious students of such questions can conduct comprehensive analyses. The unassailable point remains: Randy Shilts' milestone is that he was perhaps the first gay journalist accepted as an expert on our community.

This brief essay is an attempt to put Randy's work into context so that people can understand why he was viewed as such a controversial and powerful figure within our community, a historical fact which is being lost in the current plethora of eulogies. It is also an attempt to begin the discussion of how such dynamics shape media coverage of most minorities. What is needed are more voices, more representation, more self-representation, and discussion in an atmosphere of reason, and we could use these right now whether we are covering undocumented workers, the rights of criminals, or lesbian and gay issues into the 21st century.

# 65

# *Big Science: What Ever Happened to Safer Sex?*

Richard Goldstein

Safer sex isn't what it used to be (if it ever was). The old curriculum—with its emphasis on condoms and classification of sex acts into crude categories of risk—has given way to workshops on negotiation and meditations on the L-word, as in l-u-v. Gay guides to "dating and mating" have hit the stands. (One Baedeker breathlessly advises, "Learn from the lesbians: Keep your fingernails short.") Old-fangled ideas about fidelity are being revived under the rubric of what Michelangelo Signorile, in his *Life Outside*, calls "postmodern monogamy."

It's all part of the New Prevention, a still-evolving strategy stemming from the realization that AIDS is a condition rather than a crisis. A robust

debate has broken out over the best way to keep gay men from taking the recent good news as permission to return to the randy days. It's clear that the old safe-sex techniques are inadequate to the task. We need a diet we can stick to. We also need an analysis that empowers us to change what is destructive, and preserve what is distinctive, about gay male sexuality.

No wonder queer theorists have begun to focus on the failings of safer sex. A flurry of books has appeared arguing that the old guidelines were more effective as a response to the AIDS hysteria

*Out*, May 1997, no. 43, pp. 62–66.

of the '80s than they are as a teaching tool for gay men in the '90s. Cindy Patton's *Fatal Advice: How Safe-Sex Education Went Wrong* (Duke University Press) contends that prevention discourse served the purposes of the Right by deadening gay male sexuality and severing it from its radical potential. Walt Odets' *In the Shadow of the Epidemic* (Duke University Press) proposes a new safer-sex ethic in which each individual learns to calibrate a balance between pleasure and risk.

Both these books attempt to recapture "the joy of gay sex," as it once was known, and they take a nurturing, therapeutic tone. But the loudest voices in this debate have always been those that castigate. Ever since Larry Kramer put the ire in fire and brimstone, AIDS activism has thrown up home-grown prophets wielding the threat of death unless the community changes its ways.

Kramer is the gay Jeremiah. As the epidemic surged, he spoke at rallies, funerals, and AIDS conferences combining rage against an indifferent America with a crushing critique of gay liberation. "You're all going to die," Kramer would thunder at his gay listeners, producing mass cringing and rapt attention. His message of mobilization took hold, but so, unfortunately, did the idea that the best way to reach gay men is to terrify and shame them.

By now, the hectoring tone Kramer unleashed has become a new literary genre: the Gay Jeremiad. It begins with contempt for the superficiality of gay life, builds to an attack on sexual excess, and culminates in a heroic enemy-of-the-people stance, in which the prophet stands alone against the denial of his brothers. Straight people relish this spectacle, but gay people love it too. The Gay Jeremiad taps into the guilt we cannot overcome, and turns it into a two-edged sword. On the one hand, it empowers us to change our lives; on the other, it blames us for what we cannot change.

Gabriel Rotello's new book, *Sexual Ecology: AIDS and the Destiny of Gay Men*, published by Dutton in April, is a case in point. It urges gay men to devise alternatives to promiscuity while haranguing them for failing to be restrained. It preaches communal solidarity while demonizing those who dissent. It offers a message of empathy laced with contempt. Yet these contradictions are precisely what it takes to be a gay prophet, not to mention a darling of those who would police gay sexuality. And so, Rotello's book is likely to become a sensation, less because of its message than for its tough-love tone.

For years Rotello has argued, as a *New York Newsday* columnist and an OUT contributor, against the "myths" of safer sex: that fellatio is risk-free, that sex clubs' self-policing is sufficient, and that teaching people to use condoms is more important than urging them to have fewer partners. Rotello holds that none of these have prevented a large group of gay men from having unsafe sex. And he is convinced that this perpetual pool of risk springs from the very values of sexual liberty that theorists like Patton and Odets are determined to preserve.

Rotello goes even further, arguing that if it hadn't been for "gay sexual extremism," HIV would never have become a plague. To bolster this point, he borrows heavily from the work of *Newsday* colleague Laurie Garrett (*The Coming Plague: Newly Emerging Diseases in a World Out of Balance*, Farrar, Straus and Giroux), postulating that HIV has been with us for decades, possibly centuries. What made this virus achieve pandemic proportions, Garrett and Rotello believe, was the rise of social factors favoring its spread. For Rotello, this hypothesis is proof positive that the proliferation of promiscuity and anal sex among gay men during the post-Stonewall years is what made HIV emerge from its dormancy. In other words, "the gains of the gay sexual revolution . . . brought us AIDS."

There are brief passages sprinkled throughout Rotello's book about why gay liberation developed an affinity for promiscuity. But these crumbs of empathy are not as likely to stick to the ribs as words like "toxic," phrases like "a culture of disease," and assertions like the following: "For gay men, Dionysus is the god that failed."

Some of his most bizarre statements are related to this charge: for example, that enormous numbers of homosexuals abruptly discovered anal sex in the 1970S at the urging of a cadre of liberationists. Never mind that such an event could never be documented (except in anecdotal reminiscences of the sort Rotello quotes); never mind the ancient association between homosexuals and the crime against nature known as "buggery." If anal sex did become more commonplace after Stonewall, it had little to do with sex radicals. Our desires are shaped by complex social and natural forces. But to explore the structure of sexuality is not the prophet's mission. He needs an enemy within.

Rotello finds his foe among AIDS prevention workers who created "the condom code." He maintains that they did nothing to reduce the frequency or change the nature of gay male sex; as a result he accuses them of fostering something epidemiologists call the Second Wave—an unexpected rise in HIV infections over the past few years among young gay men.

There is no disputing the danger of the Second Wave. But does the annual rate of new infections (about 2 percent, according to researchers in San Francisco and New York) really demonstrate that AIDS prevention failed? Consider that during the early years of AIDS gay men were getting infected at rates up to 12 percent per year. Consider how difficult it has been to stem sexually transmitted diseases in the general population, and you might conclude that the gay community has been remarkably successful at changing its behavior—though perhaps not successful enough.

Still, Rotello piles on the statistics to show that many gay men getting infected today are well integrated into the community and highly aware of AIDS. But this picture is hardly complete, and Rotello ignores data that contradict it. For example, he neglects to mention a 1995 study by researchers at the Columbia University School of Public Health that found that although integrated gay men are more likely to practice anal sex, they are also more likely to use condoms than those who are closeted or conflicted about their sexuality. Rotello also overlooks the fact that young gay men of color have the highest rate of new infections, suggesting that racism, alienation, and poverty all have an impact on sexual behavior.

Rotello's incomplete use of the social research and his offhand hyperbole ("Gay men are experiencing a form of extinction as devastating as that inflicted upon any dying species") stem from his desire to present a simple explanation for a complex phenomenon. Jeremiah blamed decadence for the defeat of the Israelites; Rotello blames gay promiscuity for the rise of AIDS. He isn't entirely wrong, and neither was the prophet, but in both cases, there was more to it than that.

The gay '70s was a psychic Intifada: a sloughing off of centuries of shame and a venting of pent-up desire. A generation of gay men raced through a second puberty, casting ancient taboos away. But this rush of self-discovery proceeded amid immense social stigma: Gay men left their wives, families cast out their sons, and violence haunted the new community. How could gay sex *not* have been excessive? Revolutions do not incorporate the rules of salubrity.

Still, it's important to ask, What can be done about the ominous rate of new infections? There is a general consensus that AIDS prevention needs to include a number of options, from using condoms in casual encounters to an emerging practice called "negotiated safety," in which both members of a couple set rules for each other's behavior and vow to stick by them. Rotello subscribes to most of this. But engendering safety is not enough, he avers; the community needs to direct its members toward a design for living. "Taking a lesson from environmentalism and population control," he writes, "immediate and tangible social rewards need to be implemented to encourage safety and restraint. And these rewards will have to be built right into the structure of gay society."

We can do this because of the "new gay ideal" from which this book takes its name. Sexual ecology is an ideology whose reverence for the natural world inspires a determination to live in sync with its processes. Naturally (as it were), this includes a decision to embrace moderation, since that's the holistic way to control disease. The new ideal also involves a yearning for marriage and family, and a commitment to community. If this sounds like your standard heterosexual lifestyle with a little more deep throat, guess again: Rotello invokes "deep ecology."

Do gay men need a high concept in order to love, honor, or at least stick to safer sex? Rotello thinks we do. After all, we've been denied the inducements of straight society: marriage, children, the whole moon-June schmear. Rotello credits these institutions, and the fidelity they inspire, with preventing AIDS: In order to stop the epidemic, gay men need to live like that.

In fact, Rotello thinks we can program ourselves to reject promiscuity. This is where the book differs most dramatically from other safer-sex critiques. History teaches us that sexual morality is closely related to social status. As long as heterosexuality is regarded as a natural part of life, and homosexuality is not, it's hard to imagine gay men incorporating the majority's code of conduct.

Yet Rotello would apply the rules of straight society—from stigma to enforcement—to anyone who refuses to practice sex in a responsible way. This is the dark side of sexual ecology, for in the real world, the same laws that penalize prostitutes and their johns can punish homosexuals who cruise in the park. Public lewdness laws are already being used against gay men who neck too avidly on the streets of Rudolph Giuliani's New York.

But enforcement is only part of Rotello's program. He also calls for the disapproval, if not shunning, of gay men who have unsafe sex. That would be a far more radical step than same-sex marriage; it would mean rejecting the sex outlaw within. This is a strategy for behavior modification that an aversion therapist might envy: If we regard those who practice promiscuity with shame, we will look with shame upon this yearning in ourselves.

But shame is even harder to suppress than sex. An undertone of disgust keeps popping up under Rotello's New Age homilies, and this animus intrudes on his worthy goal of fidelity as a prevention strategy, making his book seem more like an exercise in punishment than an agenda for reform. Take Rotello's attack on slutting around. In his eyes, it's not just dangerous, or even pathological, but "immoral," because it does "ecological harm." How different is that notion from Pat Buchanan's assertion that AIDS is nature's revenge on homosexuals?

You'd think Rotello would consider the history of gay male promiscuity. It may not be eternal, but neither was it invented in 1969. Oscar Wilde described it as "feasting with panthers" and Walt Whitman celebrated it as "the need of comrades." Stigma is what ties these passions to ours. Generation after generation, gay men grow up intensely conflicted, not just about our desires but over the way we have sex. As long as we live in this unhealthy environment—and we will for the foreseeable future—we will be dealing with the libidinal consequences.

The task of AIDS prevention is to help us reconcile those risky needs with survival. Achieving that requires a different sort of prophecy than either Rotello or his competitors on the safer-sex beat are able to provide. It takes a delicate balance among scientific reasoning, philosophical acuity, and emotional empathy. In the absence of that kind of leadership, the best we can do is engage in fierce debate. But as the fur flies, it's worth remembering the golden rule of liberation: You can't get to the promised land in a state of shame.

# III. D

# NAMING NAMES: OUTING

When the National Lesbian and Gay Journalists Assocation met for its first convention in 1992, according to the *New York Times* account, "the morality of identifying secretly gay public officials, a practice known as 'outing,' was the question discussed most often." The issue of outing burst onto the journalistic scene in 1990, but the concept, although not the term, arose at the very dawn of modern gay consciousness at the end of the nineteenth century. The idea that homosexuals constitute a "people" set apart from the society they live among, however invisibly, leads inevitably to the question of what obligations they have to this "community" (Gross, *Contested Closets*, this volume). Until recently, lesbian and gay journalists, like gay people in general, abided by a social contract they never actually signed but were informed about when they came out into the gay community: we keep each other's secrets. But after nearly ten years and more than a hundred thousand deaths from AIDS this contract was becoming frayed.

The AIDS Coalition to Unleash Power, or ACT UP, came into being in March 1987 and quickly infused a new burst of militant energy into the AIDS and gay movements. ACT UP combined streetwise activists and newly radicalized middle-class professionals. The journalists who tore up the social contract are members of the ACT UP generation. This is also a generation that has lived its entire life in the age of mass media gossip and infotainment. From *People Magazine* to Liz Smith, from Jay Leno and David Letterman to Oprah and Ricki Lake, from the *National Enquirer* and the *Globe* to the *Philadelphia Inquirer* and the *Boston Globe*, we have become a society drenched in gossip and "news" about celebrities of all sorts. Whether it's the fifteen minutes of fame haphaz-

ardly awarded to random individuals or the perennial allure of Liz Taylor or John F. Kennedy, Jr., on the cover of a magazine, we have come to expect that anyone hit by the media spotlight will share his or her private life with us.

In such a climate it should not surprise us that some gay journalists became increasingly impatient with the code that bound the media in a conspiracy of silence and deception about the real lives of lesbian and gay celebrities. Not only do the media draw the line of discretion much farther from home when writing about gay people than when writing about nongay figures; they actively engage in obfuscation and collude in outright lies—what could be called "inning." Outing was adopted as a tactic in opposition to the tacit agreement by which gay private lives were granted an exemption from the public's "right to know," thus protecting the closets of the rich and famous and leaving unchallenged the distaste of the media—and the public—for facing the reality of lesbian and gay existence.

In June 1989 *OutWeek*, a new lesbian and gay weekly news magazine, signed AIDS activist Michelangelo Signorile as features editor and columnist. His disillusionment with the ethics of gossip journalists, fueled by his militant gay politics and AIDS activism, turned to anger, which he unleashed in his "Gossip Watch" column. This was not the usual gossipy listing of who had been seen where and with whom, but a weekly dissection of New York's and Hollywood's celebrity and gossip elite, who were attacked for failing to pay enough attention to AIDS, for pretending that lesbian and gay celebrities are heterosexual, and for flattering politicians "who are keeping us down at best, murdering us at worst." Signorile's most frequent targets were the gossip writers who reported on the doings of the elite, flattering their egos and, in many cases, reporting on their nonexistent heterosexual romances.

Around the same time gay author Armistead Maupin began to dare the gay press to name names: "If the gay press has any function at all," Maupin believes, "it's to tweak the conscience of famous people who are in the closet; and certainly we shouldn't continue to lionize those among us who are making a success of themselves in the mainstream while remaining so determinedly in the closet. . . . I'm taking the hard line on it and saying homophobia is homophobia" (Warren 1989).

Maupin's disclosures were printed in many gay papers and periodicals, but the mainstream press ignored this novelty, just as they had earlier declined to specify precisely what ACT UP demonstrators were saying about Illinois governor James Thompson. Within a few months, however, the mainstream media had joined the gay press in playing the game while simultaneously debating the rules. *Time* media critic William Henry noted the ethical conflict between the right to privacy and the importance of coming out, and decided that outing "claims an unjustifiable right to sacrifice the lives of others" (1990).

In February 1990 Malcolm Forbes died, and the outing season was soon to be in full swing. The March 18 cover of *OutWeek* showed a photo of Malcolm Forbes on his motorcycle, with the bold headline, "The Secret Gay Life of Malcolm Forbes." Signorile's article begins with Forbes's funeral, noting the presence among the mourners of many prominent homophobes, including Richard Nixon and William F. Buckley, and asks whether they knew "that they were coming to pay homage to someone who embodied what they ultimately detested?" Signorile concluded his article with a defense of outing Forbes. First, he noted, "All too often history is distorted," and the fact that one of the most influential men in America was gay should be recorded. Second, "it sends a clear message to the public at large that we are everywhere" (1990).

Although several papers outside New York picked up the Forbes story, the New York press ignored it until reports from other places made it difficult to avoid (Signorile, "How I Brought Out Malcolm Forbes and the Media Blinked," this volume). Stories began appearing that focused on the conflict between privacy and the tactics of outing. The next round of mainstream newspaper analyses emphasized the dilemma outing posed for the media. The *Sunday Oregonian* accompa-

nied its thoughtful article on outing with a sidebar: "Practice puts press on spot," quoting the editor's determination to make decisions on a case-by-case basis.

The *New York Times* would refer only to "an Illinois politician" and "a famous businessman who had recently died," saying that the paper would not print "hearsay," even if the subject is no longer living. The *New York Times*'s reluctance to name gay names even when the person in question was dead was tellingly contrasted with their printing of the name and many personal details about the woman who accused a Kennedy of rape; this "outing" of a private person caused an intense debate within the *Times* itself.

The alternative and gay press joined the debate over outing, but in these cases the articles were written by openly gay people who presented the issues in a longer historical context and with a more complex awareness of the arguments on both sides (Carr, "Why Outing Must Stop," this volume). In the letters column of the *Village Voice*, lesbian novelist Sarah Schulman, while admitting her ambivalence over the morality of outing, objected to the characterization of the tactic as an invasion of privacy: "Most gay people stay in the closet—i.e., dishonor their relationships—because to do so is a prerequisite for employment. Having to hide the way you live because of fear of punishment isn't a 'right,' nor is it 'privacy.' Being in the closet is not an objective, neutral, or value-free condition. It is maintained by force, not choice" (1990).

In the same issue gay activist and writer Vito Russo noted that to say someone is gay is to talk "about *sexual orientation*, not their sexual activity." But, most critically, he pointed out, "Signorile is saying that if being gay is *not* disgusting, is *not* awful, then why can't we talk about it? After all, it's not an insult to call someone gay. Is it?" (1990).

By the end of 1990 Michelangelo Signorile had long been receiving tips about Assistant Secretary of Defense Pete Williams from people angry over the Department of Defense's discrimination against lesbian and gay people, but with Williams's sudden media visibility during the gulf war he "got a tidal wave of information about the topic once again as well as a lot of pressure from colleagues urging me to expose the truth." Signorile's story about Pete Williams was on the cover of the *Advocate's* August 27, 1991, issue. Aware that mainstream media had ducked the story when Queer Nation outed Williams in Washington that June, the *Advocate* decided to build an irresistible groundswell by distributing advance copies of the article and by linking the outing of Williams to the military's increasingly fierce exclusion of gays and lesbians from the armed forces.

The strategy paid off, because the story broke through the resistance of the media gatekeepers, running in hundreds of papers. The majority of the articles, whether they included Pete Williams's name or declined to print it, clearly framed the issue in terms of hypocrisy and discrimination, as when *New York Newsday* coyly referred to "a prominent, high-ranking civilian official of the Department of Defense, an agency that routinely discharges members of the armed forces for being gay or lesbian."

The exposure of Pete Williams's homosexuality just as the Pentagon was booting out lesbian and gay gulf war veterans put the military on the defensive. The *New York Times* reported that Defense Secretary Dick Cheney "defended the right of homosexuals to hold civilian jobs at the Pentagon, saying that as long as they fulfilled their professional responsibilities their private lives were their own business." But though Cheney stood by the basic military policy of exclusion, repeating the official mantra that "homosexuality is incompatible with military service," the magical powers of this phrase had been seriously weakened by the exposure of the hypocrisy embodied by Pete Williams. Within weeks of the *Advocate* article both the *New York Times* and the *Washington Post* ran editorials attacking the military's antigay policy, and *Time* magazine published a lengthy account that was clearly sympathetic to the gay cause.

The outing of Pete Williams is a prime exhibit for the defense of outing as a political strategy: it placed the issue of military antigay discrimination squarely on the public agenda. Thomas Stoddard, then executive director of the Lambda Legal Defense and Education Fund, who had previously criticized outing, said that the Pete Williams story was "the *only* example in which outing has advanced the interests of gay people." Some writers in mainstream media agreed with this judgment, such as openly gay *Detroit News* media critic Michael McWilliams, who argued that "outing should be used only in extreme cases . . . some cause-and-effect relationship must be established between a gay person doing his or her job and doing damage to other gay people" (McWilliams 1991).

*Washington Post* reporter Marjorie Williams, writing in the *Washington Monthly* (1991), argued for privacy: "It does terrible violence to the ideal of a common interest to carry too far the insistence

that a particular person, by virtue of gender or sexual orientation or color or any other index, has a greater responsibility than others to address a particular issue." But this is precisely the heart of the issue of outing as it is considered by gay people. While the mainstream media are preoccupied with the question of political hypocrisy, calibrating their measuring instruments to determine whether a particular case reaches their threshold of outrage; lesbian and gay activists and journalists are more likely to factor into their calculations the question of communal responsibility. The involuntary exposure of closeted homosexuals was long a favored tactic used by the enemies of gays as a form of social control. Now the adoption of outing as a political tactic challenges their ability to determine the meaning of gay identity and the consequences of its visibility.

The furor over outing shifted the line toward more equal treatment of public figures by the news media and a greater willingness to include someone's homosexuality when it is relevant to a story. Congressman Steve Gunderson (R-Wis.), had never supported any gay causes in his eleven years in office. After activists made his homosexuality public, Gunderson began to be more supportive of gay issues and even to be more open about his sexuality. In October 1994 he was the subject of a profile in the *New York Times Magazine,* with the headline "Congressman (R) Wisconsin. Fiscal Conservative. Social Moderate. Gay." By 1996 Gunderson, who decided not to run for reelection, had published a memoir together with his lover, architect Rob Morse.

In March 1995 the *Wall Street Journal* ran a front-page article reporting that *Rolling Stone* founder Jann Wenner "left the home he shared with his wife and three young children and began a relationship with a young male staffer at Calvin Klein." As former *OutWeek* editor Gabriel Rotello ("The Inning of Outing," this volume) put it, "If *OutWeek's* Forbes article ignited the outing war with a bang, the *Journal's* piece on Wenner—and follow-up articles in *Newsweek,* the *Washington Post,* and elsewhere—symbolically ends it with a whimper."

The war might have ended, but outing remains a tactic in activists' arsenals, as closeted legislators Senator Barbara Mikulski (D-Md.) and Congressman Jim Kolbe (R-Ariz.) discovered after they voted for the Defense of Marriage Act in 1996. Kolbe beat the *Advocate* to the punch, by coming out himself, telling a reporter, " I feel a tremendous burden lifted. It's a relief" (Willey 1996). After confronting Mikulski at a New York book-signing, Signorile and media activist Ann Northrop proposed October 10 as National Outing Day (Keen 1996). "From this day forward, the day before National Coming Out Day will be National Outing Day," Signorile said. "It's a day to out a favorite public figure to everyone you know, through e-mail messages, voice mail messages, notes and letters in the mail, and in casual conversation throughout the day. And if there happens to be an elected official who voted anti-gay and who is making a public appearance, it's a day to go and confront that person."

## REFERENCES

Henry, William III. 1990. "Forcing Gays Out of the Closet." *Time*, January 29, p. 67.

Keen, Lisa. 1996. "Mikulski Swept by Outing Fray." *Washington Blade*, November 1.

McWilliams, Michael. 1991. "Will Magazine's 'Outing' of Gulf War Spokesman Change Pentagon Policy Toward Gays?" *Detroit News*, August 3, C-1, 12.

Russo, Vito. 1990. "Letter to the Editor." *Village Voice*, April 24.

Schulman, Sarah. 1990. "Letter to the Editor." *Village Voice*, April 24.

Signorile, Michelangelo. 1990. "The Other Side of Malcolm." *OutWeek*, March 18, pp. 40–45.

Signorile, Michelangelo. 1991. "The Outing of Assistant Secretary of Defense Pete Williams." *Advocate*, August 27, pp. 34–44.

Warren, Steve. 1989. "Telling 'Tales' About Celebrity Closets." *Au Courant* (Philadelphia), October 23, p. 12.

Willey, Keven. 1996. "Kolbe Steps Forward: Gay Lawmaker Gets Priorities Straight." *Arizona Republic*, August 4.

Williams, Marjorie. 1991. "Is It Any of Your Business?" *Washington Monthly*, September, pp. 39–44.

# | 66 |

# Contested Closets: The Politics and Ethics of Outing

## LARRY GROSS

Outing has a long past, if only a short history. The issue of outing, although not the term, arises at the very dawn of modern gay consciousness. The idea that homosexuals—lesbian women and gay men—constitute a "people" set apart from the society they live among, however invisibly, leads inevitably to the question of what obligations they have to this "community." Indeed, history reveals that the temptation to proclaim publicly the secret of prominent persons' homosexuality has frequently been felt though rarely yielded to. On the contrary, until recently the only exposure gay people feared came through inadvertence, or the prying and publicity of public authorities and media sensationalism.

The issue of outing is part of the story of the emergence and evolution of the lesbian and gay community in this country, and of its usually adversarial relationship with the institutions that define and control the public agenda of issues and images. It is also part of the story of the changing role and norms of journalism and other mass media. The involuntary exposure of closeted homosexuals was long a favored tactic of social control threatened and employed by our enemies. The adoption of outing as a political tactic has challenged their ability to determine the meaning of gay identity and the consequences of its visibility.

## THE PATH OVER CORPSES

The political tactic of exposing closeted homosexuals had been used by homosexuals themselves in at least one instance long before the emergence of the contemporary gay liberation movement. To understand the context of the first outings we have to briefly set the stage for this *fin-de-siecle* drama. . . .

In the early years of the century Imperial Germany was rocked by scandals centering on accusations that many of the Kaiser's closest associates were homosexual (Steakley, 1975; 1989). In 1902 German "munitions king" Alfred Krupp was expelled from Italy by the authorities when his homosexual activities on Capri came to the attention of the police. The story was widely publicized by the Italian socialist press and subsequently picked up by the German press. The anti-government Social Democratic newspaper *Vorwarts* ran the story under the headline "Krupp On Capri" (the German Catholic paper had reported the story without naming Krupp), and suggested that the authorities invoke Paragraph 175 against the powerful ally of the Kaiser. Although Krupp began to bring legal action against the paper, he died of an apparent suicide a week after the article appeared (Manchester, 1968).

The Krupp scandal occurred at the moment when the newly emerging German homosexual emancipation movement was working for the abolition of the laws against homosexual acts. In 1897 Magnus Hirschfeld founded the first homosexual emancipation organization, the Scientific-Humanitarian Committee, and in the preface to its first *Jahrbuch*, in 1899, he hoped that Paragraph 175, "whose existence besmirches the

In Larry Gross, *Contested Closets: The Politics and Ethics of Outing*, pp. 1–12, 35–45, 124–132. Excerpt. Minneapolis: University of Minnesota, 1993.

escutcheon of German justice, will not be carried into the new century." When Krupp was exposed by a socialist press which also called for the repeal of Paragraph 175, the Scientific Humanitarian Committee was caught in a tactical and ethical dilemma. The decision of the Committee was that exposure of prominent homosexuals would not be an effective or moral strategy, and the *Jahrbuch* for 1903 promised that "the frequently suggested 'path over corpses' will not be taken by us under any circumstances" (Steakley, 1975, p. 24, 33). . . . But now another wing of the movement took the initiative.

Adolf Brand was the founder of *Der Eigene*, the first homosexual periodical in the world. Like Hirschfeld, Brand was a crusader for the abolition of Paragraph 175, but unlike Hirschfeld Brand was an anti-Catholic anarchist who favored the exposure of homosexual hypocrites. Brand published a pamphlet which revealed that a leader of the anti-reform Center Party had been the blackmail victim of a male prostitute. Under threat of libel action Brand printed a retraction, yet many viewed the incident as a success for the homosexual movement.

The most serious round of scandals began when a socialist journalist, Maximilian Harden, exposed the homosexuality of Prince Philipp zu Eulenburg, known as the Kaiser's closest friend, in an attempt to undermine his political influence. The result was a series of civil and criminal trials in which figures on both sides were charged—with libel or with violations of the law prohibiting homosexual behavior. In some of these trials two of the pioneers of the early homosexual emancipation movement played major roles. When the mayor of Berlin, General Kuno Count von Moltke sued Harden for implying that he and Eulenburg were lovers, Hirschfeld testified that Moltke's " 'unconscious orientation' could 'objectively' be labelled 'homosexual,' even if he had never committed sodomy" (Steakley, 1989, p. 242).

The next major trial pitted the Imperial Chancellor, Prince von Bülow, against Brand, who was charged with writing a new pamphlet that claimed that Bülow had been blackmailed because of homosexuality, that he had participated in all-male gatherings hosted by Eulenburg at which homosexual activities occurred, and that he was "morally obligated as a homosexual to use his influence for the repeal of Paragraph 175," (op. cit.). Brand's defense of his exposure of Bülow is little different from many present day defenses of outing public figures:

> On the stand, Brand maintained the truth of the leaflet and stated that he had by no means intended to insult Bülow by calling him a homosexual, since he had a positive view of those who shared his own sexual orientation. He had exposed Bülow with the political goal of hastening the repeal of Paragraph 175, for he had come to believe that this could only be achieved by creating martyrs—the strategy of "the path over corpses." (op. cit.)

. . . After the judge prevented him from presenting his evidence, Brand's trial ended in a conviction for libelling Bulow and he served an 18-month prison term. Eventually Brand, too, renounced the tactic of exposing highly placed homosexuals, because "decent society can not stand the truth" (Gray, 1991: 49).

The rise of the Nazis revived the debate about the tactic of outing because of the prominence of Ernst Röhm, the chief of staff of Hitler's SA paramilitary organization and a known homosexual. In the early 1930s, in a political move reminiscent of the Krupp and Eulenberg scandals, "Röhm and other SA leaders were attacked for their homosexuality in the left-wing media. Social Democrats and Communists suggested that nepotism and abuse of power in the SA and the Hitler Youth had contributed to making homosexuality an essential characteristic of the fascist system" (Oosterhuis, 1991: 251).

Writing about "the Röhm case" in *Der Eigene* Adolph Brand once again stated the argument for outing. Declaring that "every sexual contact is a private matter," he went on to note,

> In the moment, however, when someone— as teacher, priest, representative, or statesman . . . would like to set in the most damaging way the intimate love contact of others under degrading control—in that moment has his own love-life also ceased to be a private matter and forfeits every claim to remain protected henceforward from public scrutiny and suspicious oversight.
>
> Rather, from that moment on the public has the undoubted right to be occupied also with his own love-life, to hold up to him the mirror of his strict party morality and—if only the least trace of erotic inclinations and sexual acts are established, which his party morality publicly condemns—to relentlessly accuse him personally, as the representative of that party morality, of political hypocrisy

and to expose him as an insolent swindler of the people! For he is then enjoying the joys of life that he wants to withhold from the people. (Brand, 1991, p. 235–236)

Possibly daunted by the memory of the earlier outing scandals, Brand limited himself to naming Röhm, who had already been exposed by the left press, noting somewhat surprisingly, "I will not name names here, although many deserve nothing else. For the deserters from our ranks really should be mercilessly pilloried in public" (ibid.). . . .

▼ ▼ ▼

In June 1986 the U.S. Supreme Court dealt a devastating blow to lesbian and gay hopes for constitutional redress through the Federal courts. The Supreme Court explained, in *Bowers v. Hardwick*, that gay people simply did not enjoy the right to privacy now taken for granted as a constitutional guarantee by Americans. On October 14, 1987, two days after the National March on Washington for Lesbian and Gay Rights had assembled one of the largest demonstrations in the capitol's history, and one day after 600 civilly disobedient demonstrators had been arrested on the steps of the Supreme Court, Jesse Helms rose on the floor of the U.S. Senate to introduce an amendment to a health funding bill. The amendment states that "none of the funds made available . . . shall be used to provide AIDS education, information, or prevention materials and activities that promote, encourage, or condone homosexual activities." In fact, the amendment forbids funding anything which might "promote, condone or encourage sexual activity outside a sexually monogamous marriage"(S 14204). . . .

The amendment was passed 96 to 4 and turned out to be only the first of what has become a steady stream of similar amendments introduced by Jesse Helms and his friends.

In this atmosphere of relentless attack from the right, with supposed friends caving in to Helms' blackmail, despite the unparalleled size of the October 1987 march, it is easy to understand that the movement began to question its strategies. In February 1988 the National Gay and Lesbian Task Force organized a "war conference" to consider and debate a range of options for the political struggles of the late 1980s. At this conference the option of exposing closeted politicians was once more put on the table and debated. Some advocated "bringing out" those who were proving to be unreliable allies in the fight against anti-gay politicians; several of the senators who voted for the Helms amendment on AIDS funding, and many in both houses who caved in on the NEA restrictions, were potential targets for such action. As one activist put it, "we're going to have to change the rules of the game, . . . to take away the protection of the code, the code of silence" from closeted politicians who do not support gay interests" (Weiser, 1989).

But, despite the new willingness to think the previously unthinkable, the war conferees did not decide to break the uneasy truce that protected Washington's closets of power. Not everyone was willing unconditionally to respect the code of silence, however. Although the executive director of the National Gay and Lesbian Task Force, Urvashi Vaid, maintained that "our movement should [not] be about the business of dragging other people out of the closet," Vic Basile, then head of the Human Rights Campaign Fund, the leading gay PAC, was quoted as saying that "those who participate in the gay community and then vote against it are guilty of hypocrisy—hypocrisy that causes harm to a whole class of people. They are like Jews who put other Jews into the ovens. Their duplicitous, devious, harmful behavior ought to be exposed" (ibid.). It wasn't long before members of ACT UP acted on that belief, organizing a demonstration against Oregon senator Mark Hatfield after he cast a vote they considered anti-gay.

As a tactic, however, outing depended on media cooperation. Like the proverbial tree falling in a forest, outing a politician required an audience to be heard, and this proved to be an obstacle to those who were willing to break the code of silence. When Chicago ACT UP members decided to expose Governor James Thompson after he supported legislation allowing hospitals to test patients for HIV without their consent, they marched outside his home carrying signs naming him as a homosexual, but "the mainstream press ignored their claims, reporting only that a protest had taken place" (Richardson, 1989). New York activist Andy Humm, one of those who favored outing in the war conference discussions, agreed that "As a tactic, it isn't going to work until we start getting some attention from the mainstream press. If it never gets picked up, it doesn't make any difference" (ibid.).

Gay activists did not expect the mainstream press to assist them by reporting their charges, but they may have been more disappointed that the gay press was not willing to join in outing politicians. The *Washington Blade*, the capital's gay newspaper, refused to carry outing stories. According to *Blade* editor Lisa Keen, "The allegation of hypocrisy was not enough. . . . Privacy is supreme" (Weiser, A-5). The code of silence may have been weakened, but as long as the mainstream and the gay media refused to play the game, outing remained a fairly ineffective weapon.

The next threat to the code came from the other side. In June 1989, the Republican National Committee circulated a memo "saying that soon-to-be-elected House Speaker Tom Foley was 'out of the liberal closet' " (Matza, 1990), thus implying that Foley is homosexual. In response, Barney Frank threatened to expose the names of closeted Republican officeholders; the memo was withdrawn, its author was sacrificially fired, and the rumors ceased. "Frank did not carry out his threat, and he was at pains to underscore the limited circumstances in which he would apply it: 'I referred only to those gay people who shamefully use the fact or accusation of homosexuality as a weapon against others.' " (Henry, 1990).

But the genie was out of the bottle again, and this time it wouldn't get back in. The political landscape in 1989 was very different from earlier years, and the "path over corpses" had a very different meaning after 100,000 deaths from AIDS. The Republican smear and Frank's counterthreat had ignited a spark in the gay press.

"That got us thinking," said Gabriel Rotello, editor-in-chief of the New York magazine *Out-Week*, which has led the way with outing. . . . The billionaire Malcolm Forbes was the first target. After his death, *OutWeek* revealed that he was gay in anger at the fiction of his glamorous heterosexual activities. It was a story that worked globally. Show business was next. (Appleyard, 1990)

## GLITTER AND BE DISCREET

In a society increasingly inclined to choose entertainment figures as its cultural heroes, it is hardly surprising that the stars of stage and screen have been as devoted to the sanctity of the closet as any Washington politician. Despite, or perhaps because of, the stereotypical assumption that Broadway and Hollywood are havens for homosexuals, there has never been a major star of stage,

screen or television who has voluntarily come out. This is not exactly a matter of personal choice. The entire industry operates on the principle that the American public is suffused by prejudices that must be catered to. In earlier decades the same logic required Jewish actors to submerge and hide their ethnicity.

New York actor Jules Garfinkle changed his name to Jules Garfield for the Broadway stage, but when he arrived in Hollywood Jack Warner told him that Garfield didn't sound like an American name. Upon being told that Garfield had been the name of an American president Warner relented, but the Jules had to go. As one of Warner's executives put it," . . . we wouldn't want people to get the wrong idea." "But I *am* Jewish," said the future John Garfield. "Of course you are," said the Warners executive. "So are we . . . most of us. But a lot of people who buy tickets think they don't like Jews. . . . And Jules is a Jew's name." (Friedrich, 1986, p. 355)

With only minor changes the same discussion could have occurred in connection with homosexuality. But while there may be less pressure on Jewish actors to change their names or, *pace* Barbra Streisand, their noses, lesbian and gay performers are still expected to stay quietly in the closet.

Rock Hudson (formerly Roy Fitzgerald) was hastily married off to his agent's secretary after *Confidential* magazine threatened to expose him as homosexual. Similar pressures and motives are widely rumored to lie behind many of Hollywood's most prominent and apparently romantic couplings, prompting movie star Nelson Eddy to joke to Noel Coward that "marriage is the tax on stardom" (Hadleigh, 1991: 72). Nowadays, at least, they aren't necessarily required to get married or engage in other charades. What *is* required, of course, is that they steadfastly present themselves as heterosexual. . . .

▼ ▼ ▼

There is an unshakable conviction on the part of most people in positions of power in the entertainment industry that the American public will not accept openly lesbian and gay performers, and isn't too crazy about them in backstage roles, either. The consequence of all this is a continuing devotion to the sanctity of the closet that pervades show business in the United States. Lesbian and gay actors and others who begin to achieve success and celebrity are quickly taught the rules of the game, if they haven't already demonstrated their discretion.

"One of the unwritten laws of gay life," [writer Armistead] Maupin sighs, "is where you reach a certain level of fame, you shut up about your homosexuality. You're not told this by straight people, you're told it by other famous homosexuals who are ushering you into the pantheon of the right." (Warren, 1989)

## NOSTALGIA FOR A PLACE ONE HAS NEVER SEEN

"Rumor and gossip constitute the unrecorded history of the gay subculture" (Weiss, 1991, p. 283). Writing about the emergence of lesbian identities in the 1930s, Andrea Weiss cites Patricia Spacks' analysis of gossip as an alternative discourse through which "those who are otherwise powerless can assign meanings and assume the power of representation . . . reinterpreting . . . materials from the dominant culture into shared private meanings" (ibid.). The gossip that Weiss is concerned with, however, is not the exchange of stories about one's friends and acquaintances, but the circulation of rumor and speculation about the lives of movie stars and other celebrities. Lesbian and gay media scholars have demonstrated the central importance of stars in gay ghetto culture and the special relationship gays have had to film (see Dyer, 1977, 1986). Living in a world which despised and rejected their feelings, gay people found both escape and affirmation in the darkness of the theater and the luminance of the silver screen.

The crystallizing of lesbian and gay identities is somewhat akin to the re-discovery of their "ethnic roots" by third generation Americans whose parents had successfully assimilated into the mainstream. But, for gay people there were no grandparents to visit and the stars and stories of popular culture often took the place of the "old country." As Vito Russo put it, "In *Queen Christina*, Garbo tells Gilbert . . . 'It is possible to feel nostalgia for a place one has never seen.' Similarly, the film *Queen Christina* created in gay people a nostalgia for something they had never seen" (1987: 65). "For a people who were striving toward self-knowledge," Weiss writes of 1930s lesbian women, "Hollywood stars became important models in the formulation of gay identity" (Weiss, 1991, p. 291). . . .

Despite the explosion of lesbian and gay visibility since the late 1960s, the near total absence of openly gay celebrities insures the continuing importance of gossip in the crafting of gay subcultural identity. Insider gay gossip has always focussed heavily on the exchange of names of famous people who are secretly gay, just as Jews (and, I'm told, Canadians, or Hoosiers) have told each other with pride about rich and famous people who are, but are not generally known to be, Jewish (or Canadian, or Hoosier).

The denial and erasure of lesbian women and gay men from the formal curricula of our schools and from the informal but even more influential curriculum of our mass media leads to the understandable desire to discover and celebrate the contributions of lesbian and gay figures. Just as African American activists and educators have brought out the often obscured achievements of people of color, and just as feminist art historians have uncovered the accomplishments of women artists whose work had been misattributed to men (Nochlin and Sutherland, 1976), so too have lesbian and gay scholars assembled lists of famous people who were homosexual. These range from the "Great Queens of History" school of celebratory catalogues (from Sappho and Socrates, to Leonardo and Michelangelo, to Frederick the Great and James Buchanan, to Marcel Proust and Gertrude Stein, and so forth) to the rosters of more contemporary celebrities that are compiled and traded through gossip networks (from Cole Porter and Mary Martin, to Cary Grant and Barbara Stanwyck, to Merv Griffin and Jodie Foster, to Lily Tomlin and John Travolta, to Martina Navratilova and Greg Louganis, to . . . ). Such lists present scholars, journalists and activists with important issues of evidence and ethics: what constitutes proof of someone's sexual identity, especially when evidence is likely to have been suppressed or destroyed, and what considerations should influence the decision to reveal a person's previously hidden homosexuality? Are historians the outers of the past, or are outers the historians of the present?

It is lists like these that are meant when outing proponents talk about role models to help gay people as well as the rest of society counter the stigmatizing images fostered by invisibility and stereotypes. The lack of lesbian and gay role models has been cited as a contributory factor to the alarming statistic that "up to 30 percent of completed adolescent suicides annually" may be accounted for by gay teens (Gibson, 1989, p. 110). *Village Voice* columnist Michael Musto, defending outing in response to a hostile letter, claimed to "get letters from formerly suicidal lesbian teens who now feel empowered" by the knowledge that an outed celebrity is also gay (Musto, 1991).

This is a *celebratory* form of outing, good for building internal morale, and easily translated into a public tactic, as when marchers in annual June gay pride parades carry signs with the pictures and names of famous lesbian and gay "ancestors." The more political form of outing that focuses on exposing hypocrites who actively work against gay interests while hiding their own homosexuality has also been a commonplace of gay gossip, and its move into the public arena is the least controversial aspect of outing. But the most radical aspect of outing is the argument that all homosexuals are members of a community, whether they admit it or not, to which they owe a measure of accountability and allegiance.

> Whether gay public figures have an obligation to the gay commons is at the heart of the outing debate. By proclaiming that they do, we redefine the concept of a gay and lesbian community. Because such an assertion presupposes that the gay community is a genuine, inescapable minority like the Black or Latino community, into which one is born, from which one derives advantages and disadvantages, and to which one owes inherent allegiance. It brands as immoral the attempt by powerful gays to escape the social penalties of homosexuality, and asserts a claim of moral kinship where none existed before. (Rotello, 1990: 52)

But even gay activists who would not subscribe to such a radical statement are caught in the web of rhetoric spun around the concept "that gay men and women were an oppressed minority and that, like other minorities, they possessed a culture of their own" (D'Emilio, 1983: 248). If gay people constitute a *minority* in this sense then the rhetoric of allegiance and accountability is not as far fetched as it sounds to many who respond to outing as an unwarranted invasion of privacy. Criticizing outing, the co-chair of the Iowa Lesbian and Gay Political Caucus refers to an *ethic*, "and that ethic is that we protect each other" (Johnson, 1990); but the concept of an ethic is clearly rooted in the sense of a community. Conventional notions of a community include the expectation that it is expected to protect its members, and may on occasion sacrifice some members to protect or further the interests of the

group. Outing would appear to be an example of such a sacrifice. In traditional political liberalism, the members will, it is assumed, offer themselves voluntarily for possible sacrifice, but there are cases, such as the military draft, where the community compels members to sacrifice themselves. The question, therefore, is whether the present embattled conditions—AIDS, antigay violence, virulent political attacks—override the "longstanding tradition that required sodomites to keep each other's secrets" (Goldstein, 1990).

Those threatened with outing are likely to invoke images from our contemporary rogues gallery of villains, as in writer Fran Lebowitz' characterization of *OutWeek*: "It's damaging, it's immoral, it's McCarthyism, it's terrorism, it's cannibalism, it's beneath contempt. . . . To me this is a bunch of Jews lining up other Jews to go to a concentration camp" (Lewin, 1990). But the analogy to Jews and concentration camps is also used by the proponents of outing, who see powerful closeted gays as analogous to the assimilated Jews who never believed that they would be touched by the crude anti-semitism directed at the ghetto dwellers. To such people gay liberationists might well reply by citing Hannah Arendt's account of her experience as a Jew expelled from Germany:

> For many years I considered the only adequate reply to the question, Who are you? to be: a Jew. That answer alone took into account the reality of persecution. . . . The statement: I am a man—I would have considered as nothing but a grotesque and dangerous evasion of reality. . . . The basically simple principle here is one that is particularly hard to understand in times of defamation and persecution: *the principle that one can resist only in terms of the identity that is under attack*. Those who reject such identifications on the part of a hostile world may feel wonderfully superior to the world, but their superiority is then truly no longer of this world; it is the superiority of more or less well-equipped cloud-cuckoo-land" (1968: 17–18, my emphasis).

However, even without focussing on the present crises of AIDS and right-wing anti-gay campaigns, as the achievements of the lesbian and gay movement steadily expand the possibilities of being openly gay in many places and occupations, there is a corresponding increase in the resentment and hostility towards those who choose to remain closeted, while reaping the benefits of expanded psychological and social breathing space created through others' efforts. This resentment is not directed indiscriminately. Just as no one has outed such nonpublic citizens as our hypothetical lesbian gym teacher, no one is blaming the truly vulnerable for remaining in the closet, even though militants who have themselves taken the risks and suffered the costs of being out might wish everyone would follow their lead. On the other hand, to cite an example used by Richard Goldstein, why should a candid performer confined to gay cabaret look kindly on a closet case who gets to chat with Arsenio Hall? Lesbian writer Victoria Brownworth turned the ethical question around, saying that,

> every gay man and lesbian woman who "passes" (and tries to) oppresses me further and reaps the benefits of my activism while hiding the strength of our numbers from the people to whom those numbers would make a difference. . . . Is it ethical to stay in the closet, pass for straight, assume the mantle of heterosexual privilege and enjoy its benefits while those who are openly gay suffer the oppression of their minority status? (1990)

It might be objected that the closeted celebrities and media "big fish" who have been the targets of outing are not harming anyone, and not obviously taking advantage of other gay people merely because they are living "private" lives. We may be amused by the disingenuousness of the claim of privacy when it's made by show biz celebrities who "share" their lives with millions of television viewers along with Jay Leno, Arsenio Hall, and any other talk show host who'll have them, or invite *People* magazine into their home. But, beyond the shallowness of the argument that celebrities deserve to have their privacy protected—when they're not parading their "private" lives before the media—there is the fact that stars not only take advantage of the presumption of heterosexuality but actually promulgate the assumption of the ubiquity and normality of heterosexuality. In other words, their very public pseudo-real lives, endlessly circulated by the gossip media, are cultivating the images and undergirding the ideology that oppresses gay people. No one is obliged to make a fabulous living as a movie, television, recording, etc., star, and those who do take on this burden can be held accountable for the images they promote.

Quite aside from the question of the ideological consequences of their public personae, closeted celebrities and public officials are disingenuous in another way when they claim that their private lives are unrelated to the larger lesbian and gay community. There are important ways in which they benefit from the accomplishments of the lesbian and gay movement, even if they lack a sense of political engagement or responsibility. This is not exactly the same as the "minority community" claim that parallels the claims made on prominent Jews or Blacks. Any analysis of the changes wrought by the gay liberation movement would note the emergence and flowering of a fully elaborated subculture, and suggest that these people are indeed enjoying the fruits of others' labors.

The successful gay and lesbian figures who live in well-appointed closets are able to enjoy much fuller gay lives than their counterparts in past generations. Although the upper classes have always been able to indulge in private tastes behind the high walls of their preserves, today's rich and famous have the option to partake of private pleasures in the semi-public precincts of the gay world. Until recently they have done so in the security of knowing that we kept each other's secrets (although we certainly gossiped about them among ourselves). Assistant Secretary of Defense Pete Williams and Congressman Steve Gundersen were two of the many closeted gay men who frequent the gay bars in and around Washington, D.C., and elsewhere. Such people can be condemned as tourists who exploit the freedoms provided by others' efforts and risks, while refusing to use the power provided by their positions and visibility for the good of the community, and even occasionally using that power in ways that directly hurt gay people. The response of openly gay people in many instances, understandably, is resentment and, sometimes, outing.

What is certain is that extremists have always pushed beyond the boundaries respected by the moderates, and thus instigated the process of radical change that eventually redraws those boundaries. Just as the young radicals of the gay liberation movement of the early 1970s outraged many of the older "homophile" leaders who stressed education and assimilation, so too today's outers are denounced by the leaders of the established gay movement. But they have nevertheless cracked the code of conduct, and broken some prominent eggs in the process of making their new sort of omelet.

## REFERENCES

Appleyard, Brian. 1990. "Closet gays fear terrorism by a militant tendency," *The Sunday Times* (London), May 6.

Arendt, Hannah. 1968. *Men In Dark Times.* New York: Harcourt Brace and World.

Brand, Adolph. 1991. "Political criminals: A word about the Rohm case" (1931), in Harry Oosterhuis, ed., *Homosexuality and Male Bonding in Pre-Nazi Germany.* New York: Haworth Press, pp. 235–240.

Brownworth, Victoria. 1990. "Campus Queer Query," *OutWeek,* May 16, pp. 48–49.

D'Emilio, John. 1983. *Sexual Politics, Sexual Communities.* Chicago: University of Chicago Press.

Dyer, Richard. 1977. "Stereotyping," in Richard Dyer, ed., *Gays and Film,* London: British Film Institute.

Dyer, Richard. 1986. *Heavenly Bodies: Film Stars and Society.* New York: St. Martin's Press.

Friedrich, Otto. 1986. *City of Nets: A Portrait of Hollywood in the 1940s.* London: Headline.

Gibson, P. 1989. "Gay male and lesbian youth suicide," *Report of the Secretary's Task Force on Youth Suicide, Vol. 1: Overview and Recommendations.* Washington, D.C.: U.S. Department of Health and Human Services, 3: 110–142.

Goldstein, Richard. 1990. "The Art of Outing: When Is It Right to Name Gay Names?" *The Village Voice,* May 1, 33–37.

Gray, Natasha. 1991. "Outing's German Roots," *NYQ,* November 3, 48–49.

Hadleigh, Boze. 1991. *The Vinyl Closet: Gays in the Music World.* San Diego: Los Hombres Press.

Henry, William III. 1990. "Forcing Gays Out of the Closet," *Time,* January 29, p. 67.

Hentoff, Nat. 1991. "Armageddon in Adrian, Michigan," *The Village Voice,* March 5, p. 20.

Herzer, Manfred. 1990. "Kertbeny, Karoly Maria," Wayne Dynes, ed. *Encyclopedia of Homosexuality,* New York: Garland.

Johnson, Dirk. 1990. "Privacy vs. the Pursuit of Gay Rights," *The New York Times,* March 27, p. A:21.

Lewin, Rebecca. 1990. "A Few Minutes With Fractious Fran," *The ADVOCATE,* July 3, p. 63.

Manchester, William. 1968. *The Arms of Krupp,* Boston: Little Brown.

Matza, Michael. 1990. "Out/Rage," *The Philadelphia Inquirer,* June 28, p. E:1.

Musto, Michael. 1991. "Reply" (to several letters), *Village Voice,* April 23, p. 5.

Nochlin, Linda and Harris Sutherland. 1976. *Women Artists: 1550 - 1950.* New York: Knopf.

Oosterhuis, Harry. 1991. "Male bonding and homosexuality in German Nationalism," in Harry Oosterhuis, ed., *Homosexuality and Male Bonding in Pre-Nazi Germany.* New York: Haworth Press, pp. 241–264.

Richardson, Valerie. 1989. "Gay activists drag 'hypocrites' out of the closet," *The Washington Times,* September 20, p. A-5.

Rotello, Gabriel. 1990. "Tactical Considerations," *OutWeek,* May 16, pp. 52–53.

Russo, Vito. 1987. *The Celluloid Closet: Homosexuality in the Movies.* New York: Harper and Row (Revised edition).

Steakley, James. 1975. *The Homosexual Emancipation Movement in Germany.* New York: Arno Press.

Steakley, James. 1989. "Iconography of a Scandal: Political Cartoons and the Eulenburg Affair in Wilhelmin Germany," in M. Duberman, M. Vicinus and G. Chauncey, eds., *Hidden From History: Reclaiming the Gay and Lesbian Past,* NY: NAL Books, pp. 233–263.

Warren, Steve. 1989. "Telling 'Tales' About Celebrity Closets," *Au Courant* (Philadelphia), October 23, p. 12.

Weiss, Andrea. 1991. " 'A Queer Feeling When I Look At You': Hollywood stars and lesbian spectatorship in the 1930s," in Christine Gledhill, ed., *Stardom: Industry of Desire.* London: Routledge, pp. 283–299.

Wieser, Benjamin. 1989. "Gay Activists Divided on Whether to 'Bring Out" Politicians," *The Washington Post,* September 19, p. A4.

# | 67 |

# How I Brought Out Malcolm Forbes—and the Media Flinched

MICHELANGELO SIGNORILE

Malcolm Forbes was gay.

But nobody wants to hear it.

Not the powers-that-be. Not even our scoop-hungry, scandal-mongering, dirt-dishing media. They will go to any length to report the most intimate detail about The Donald's latest extramarital affair. That's heterosexuality: Juicy, tantalizing, steeped in glamour. But sodomy? Too disgusting. Why expose such proclivities, especially on the occasion of an icon's death?

For months, I'd been keeping a file on Malcolm Forbes' secret gay life. In my Gossip Watch column for *OutWeek*, the gay and lesbian weekly, I've referred several times to what was well-known in New York society circles. At one point, I even urged Forbes to "stop living lies while truth is ultimately the most powerful weapon." Obviously I sensed a story, and so did my editor, but there was more to it than that.

Whether you regard Malcolm Forbes as a knight in shining leather or an emblem of capitalism's oppression, the fact is he was one of the most influential men in America—and he was gay. When Forbes died, the world had to be told right away. All the homophobes with whom he trotted about the globe, and all the bigots who praised him, had to have it thrown in their faces. There was a truth to be reported.

So I fleshed out my sources and wrote a story. It hit the stands, and then . . .

NOTHING.

Our publicist had given advance copies of the issue to all major media. *The Daily News* demanded—and got—our permission to break it exclusively. Their story was written, pasted down, and scheduled for the Sunday edition. But at the very last minute it was killed. At the *Post*, where

such news would usually make for screaming front-page headlines, the story "laid there like a *latke*," according to editor Jerry Nachman, while his colleagues were "thrashing" about what to do with it. *Entertainment Tonight* ditched its segment on the topic, which had been scheduled to air that week, while, one producer told me, "a debate raged" over its fate. And *The New York Times* is "still deciding," according to one reporter, whether this news is fit to print.

Meanwhile . . . Malcolm Forbes was gay.

It is a fact I wanted to make known. But I knew it wouldn't be easy. I decided to round up the usual suspects. I called Liz Smith.

She wouldn't take my call, but she sent a fax "I knew Malcolm Forbes only as a family man. . . . The subject you mention never came up at any time. I never saw any evidence of it: In fact, it never occurred to me. . . . If [another side of his life] existed, I guess I was too square to be included." (Poor Liz. That same week, in response to my incessant prodding in print, she'd told *7 Days*: "What do they want me to be—the great lesbian of the Western world?")

Other journalists were more defensive and downright indignant when I contacted them. One editor at an upscale glossy hung up on me. The honcho at a pseudo-downtown monthly called me "scum." Most writers wouldn't even return my calls. And those who did (except for *Newsday*'s James Revson and the *News*'s William Norwich, both of whom said they'd always heard the rumors) simply refused to discuss the issue.

They were all following the Unwritten Rule: If

*Village Voice*, April 3, 1990, pp. 23–24.

you're gay, don't say it, and always cover for everyone who is. This rule was carved in stone a long time ago, and it's been followed scrupulously by closet cases in the press, who've learned that, if they kiss the asses of the rich and keep quiet about what they do with their assess, they'll be rewarded with parties and perks. This rule perpetuates the tyranny of the closet, warping the lives of those who won't come out, endangering the precious few who do, and making homosexuality seem rare.

The Unwritten Rule must be broken—and I had hurled the first stone. But instead of a resounding crash, all I heard was a modest thud. The story ran deep inside *USA Today*. *The Miami Herald* put it in the C section. *The San Francisco Chronicle* and *Los Angeles Times* did pieces focusing on the gay debate about bringing out the rich and famous. A blurb appeared in the Personalities column of *The Washington Post*. But, for the most part, my story became fodder for the supermarket tabs. "MALCOLM FORBES HAD AIDS & KILLED HIMSELF," opined the *Globe*. "LIZ IN SHOCK . . . , "the *National Enquirer* screamed. I took solace in the thought that, in trailer parks all over America, the message—however grossly distorted—had gotten through.

But where were Ted Koppel and Barbara Walters? For that matter, where was Andy Rooney?

*Entertainment Tonight* had promised to cover the reports of Forbes's homosexuality, spreading the word to millions of viewers, who, I can assure you, did not want to know he was gay. The piece was to run on the day *OutWeek*'s story hit the stands. It didn't.

Following up on a previous discussion, I called producer Mary Ann Norbom to find out why the segment hadn't run. A "debate is raging," she said. Two other producers at *E.T.* had serious reservations about the segment. Their reason was not unlike something I'd said on camera: "The media doesn't like to tell people that their icons are gay."

I asked Norbom: "Are we in the business of telling people what they *want* to hear or do we tell them the truth?" She replied that gossip is a "subjective" art, and informed me that "most people in America don't think homosexuality is normal." I was reminded that "this is an entertainment show." (At presstime, *E.T.* is still undecided about running the story.)

I did get to go on one show: *9 Broadcast Plaza*. "How many people didn't want to know that Malcolm Forbes was gay?" host Sara Lee Kessler asked the audience. Everyone except my two

friends in the crowd raised their hands. Aside from the manic musings of Howard Stern, there was a virtual blackout on the air. Not even *CNN*'s mad dog, Patrick Buchanan, would go near this story.

*The Daily News*'s Ann Adams had been calling me for days prior to our publication to get the scoop. Though she won't confirm this, an independent source at the *News* says orders came down from news editor James Willse to get the story. (Willse would not return my calls, and neither would the *News*'s own press office.) After refusing for four days to give Adams an exclusive, I finally agreed. She had to practically break the presses to get the story in. But, shortly before the press run, Willse apparently killed the story. Adams wouldn't say why, but sources at the *News* say he was skeptical of *OutWeek*'s credibility. (This is strange, considering that we'd worked with the *News* on several stories.)

Last Friday—just one day after a *Voice* fact-checker called Willse's office in regard to this piece—the *News* ran an item in its Apple Sauce column addressing Forbes's gay life. In an attempt to cover its ass, the blurb quoted a weekly giveaway paper that had called my *OutWeek* story "sensationalized." That same day's front-page headline in the *Daily News* blared: "MARLA HID IN TRUMP TOWER" (referring to a piece inside by Liz Smith).

While *Newsday* fumbled—reporter Jesse Mangaliman said he was tossed "from editor to editor"—*The New York Times* was fraught with confusion. Media columnist Martin Arnold, who'd been hungry for the story, said he didn't do a piece because, "We don't write about people's sex lives." When I pointed out that the *Times* creatively found a way to tell its readers that Donald Trump was having an extramarital affair with Marla Maples. Arnold said the Trumps "are alive and are filing legal documents." But he thought it was "important" that the gay community write about Forbes being gay, nonetheless. "I don't think you were doing a nasty thing," Arnold offered. "But it's against the culture of this place to write about people's sex lives. Which is not to say you shouldn't do it."

'Science reporter Gina Kolata would like to do a story in the *Times*, but her editors are ". . . still deciding. The *Times* doesn't want to do a story just about Malcolm Forbes and his secret gay life," she says. "That would only be gossiping, if we did that right now, and it would only feed into homophobia. It's better if we wait, and if we decide to do a story, do one that is a more serious piece about why someone such as Forbes, as powerful as he was, didn't want to come out of the closet, and about the feeling among people in the gay community that naming names may be important."

At the *Post*, Page Six's Richard Johnson proclaimed, "I don't believe in dancing on people's graves. It's a respect for the dead." But that hasn't stopped him from running postmortem items about people like Joan Crawford and Bette Davis—and most of the time they weren't the prettiest of stories either. I wasn't revealing anything terrible about Forbes—simply that he was gay. But I guess *bad* is in the eye of the beholder.

After much questioning, Johnson did admit: "Maybe I should have covered it."

*Post* editor Jerry Nachman is also conciliatory, "Was there a political decision behind it? No. We have always found *OutWeek* to be reliable and credible. We've worked with you and have always found you to be a good source. . . . Like everyone else, we're thrashing. Everyone's thought a lot about it. . . . I'm not saying we won't run it."

It may be relevant that Nachman, along with other editors and publishers, was chummy with Forbes. (Nachman even tells of a lunch Forbes threw for him when the *Post* editor arrived in New York.) Perhaps, as some have suggested,

there was an attempt to spare Forbes's heirs; or perhaps the survivors have enough clout to make sure that they are spared. It's also true that many reporters are reluctant to bring anyone out because they don't want to make gays and lesbians visible—especially if they're rich and famous.

There are those in the gay community who feel the same way. Some think the right to privacy should never be abridged, others feel bringing someone out can only be justified when they've done something detrimiental to other gay people. I say, FUCK THAT. Just being famous and in the closet hurts all queers. While people around us are dying, respecting the privacy of, say, the designer who marries so he can seem heterosexual and make another $25 million, begins to wear thin.

Perhaps those sentiments will appeal to the increasingly disrespectful media. Actually, I was quite surprised by how close my story came to being the stuff of tabloid dreams. Where would it have gone 20 years ago? Five years ago? And where will it go the next time?

The message to rich and famous queers is: Come out while you can, because when you die you'll be thrown on the cover of a magazine and labeled a closet case.

I may even bring you out alive.

# | 68 |

# *Why Outing Must Stop*

## C. CARR

Born in rage and hatred, directed exclusively at gay people, outing is gay bashing at its sickest. It has to stop.

A few weeks ago, posters of celebrities labeled "Absolutely Queer" appeared on a few Manhattan walls. It's no accident that they looked like Wanted Posters. That iconography goes to the heart of the matter. Gay people who practice outing must think homosexuality is criminal or they wouldn't be so passionate about attacking those

who "get away with it." This is internalized homophobia run amok.

It used to be a given in the gay community that we had to *protect* each other from the homophobes, and while we often knew who the famous queers were, vicious gossip was as vicious as it got. Outing seems to be about *impressing* the homo-

*Village Voice*, March 19, 1990, p. 37.

phobes by showing off our famous ones at any cost. When David Geffen admitted to being bisexual (and since when is that the same thing as being gay) in a recent *Vanity Fair* piece, *OutWeek* columnist Michelangelo Signorile crowed, "Geffen has finally let America know that queers are everywhere, including the upper-upper-upper crust of this society." I can understand this obsessive need to prove that we too are rich/famous/beautiful when straight society spits on us every day. But what homophobe is going to be persuaded by this? Let's stick to the self-asserting "We're here. We're queer. Get used to it."

Ostensibly, outers want closeted homosexuals to come out for the common good—consequences to their individual lives be damned. That's totalitarian thinking, a regime I can't live in. For me, gay liberation is still about individual freedom.

The more who *do* come out, the better. But I don't want to be told how to be gay. I've been through that before, back in the days of lesbian separatism. While I was living in Chicago in the mid-'70s, a political crisis developed in the community when a lesbian opened a "feminist restaurant" and decided to serve men. In separatist thinking, she was now "giving energy to the oppressor." Separatists began boycotting the restaurant and urged everyone to stop eating there—while they themselves ate at the hot dog stand down the street. (And guess who owned that joint?) Finally the feminist restaurant closed down, so we could *all* keep eating at places run by men.

Every liberation movement seems to develop this need to recreate the Victim/Oppressor paradigm within its own ranks. That's how the closet case became our enemy, while the real foe bashes all of us and gets away with it. I find it astonishing that Signorile urged people to phone/mail/fax-zap David Geffen, and protest at events he attended, "urging him to publicly come out." We have lost thousands to an epidemic which is far from over. We live in a world of Helmses and Dannemeyers. We are officially illegal in many states. We can't marry. We can't join the military. And we're out picketing David Geffen? How can we go on trivializing our oppression this way?

How can *any* liberation movement look to Hollywood for leadership? Or even role models? Outing will bring us neither. We are the vanguard. And no one who has to be forced from the closet is going to be my role model. Neither is some sacrificial lamb whose career has been ruined by the outers.

By the twisted logic he often applies in his *OutWeek* column, Signorile has insisted that he doesn't ruin careers; homophobia and straight people do that. In other words, "I just push 'em in front of the truck. The *truck* hits 'em." Signorile is the magazine's self-appointed ayatollah, who metes out the weekly scoldings and punishments, and a world of straight homophobes richly deserves his wrath. But outing gay celebs is his real passion, and an apparently unexamined one. Anyone who thinks, for example, that a lesbian can proclaim her sexuality in an industry as male-centered as Hollywood, where even straight women have trouble getting work (and no gay male actor has ever come out) has to be out of his fucking mind.

Time for a reality check. I asked a Hollywood producer who's a personal friend whether Geffen's revelations have made it easier for others to come out: "No. David Geffen is worth two billion dollars. He's a buyer, he's not out there selling his wares. I don't think anyone cares if a writer or director or studio executive is gay, because it doesn't affect viewing the movie. There *would* be consequences for actors. They're supposed to embody our fantasies. People in Hollywood imbue Middle America with ultraconservative values. They're always going to err on the side of conservatism."

Outing celebrities is a confusion of symbolic power with real clout. Like every woman, I've been harassed on the street, but "hey, babe" is nothing compared to a couple guys running at you yelling "dyke, dyke, dyke . . . " Now the outing cadre insists that such incidents wouldn't happen if a famous actress or two would have come out. Do they think these people have magic powers? Homophobia is an irrational disease from which no celebrity can save us.

I'm still waiting for the news of Malcolm Forbes's homosexuality to improve my life.

Anyone who's out knows that closet cases are often worse than straight people—in their furtiveness and confusion, and their need to not associate with the likes of us. But who has the right to decide that they should be exposed to homophobes? It is *never* right for gay people to use homophobia to punish each other. What about those closeted comedians who tell homophobic jokes? They make me sick, and so do straight comics who target queers. But why just punish the gay ones, while the straight bigots go free? It's so typical. I say, scream at them all, and don't see their movies.

Last summer, the *New York Times* reported on a study of bias-related violence. "In 'one of the most alarming findings,' the report found that while teenagers surveyed were reluctant to advocate open bias against racial and ethnic groups, they were emphatic about disliking homosexual men and women. They are perceived 'as legitimate targets which can be openly attacked,' the report said." People have a right to protect themselves from the hatred of others without being accused of hating themselves.

Signorile has written that "being gay is not a 'privacy' issue—unless you do believe that we are all harboring some dark, dirty secret." Well, the Supreme Court certainly agrees with him, as does Jerry Falwell. When a gay man from Georgia was arrested in 1982 for having sex with another man in his own bedroom, he decided to challenge the state's sodomy law on the grounds that it violated his right to privacy. In 1986, the Supreme Court decided that the right to privacy does not extend to homosexual conduct. Chief Justice Burger's concurring opinion, with its "crimes against nature" citations and history of sodomy laws since the fall of Rome, reads like a case study in officially sanctioned homophobia.

Privacy may not be important in the world we wish for, but it is in the society we're stuck with. Everyone—gay, straight and in-between—has an absolute right to decide that their intimate lives are nobody's business. As Justice Harry Blackmun wrote, in his dissenting opinion, "Depriving individuals of the right to choose for themselves how to conduct their intimate relationships poses a far greater threat to the values most deeply rooted in our nation's history than tolerance of nonconformity could ever do."

I find the outing campaign most upsetting in its affinity with the reactionary mind-set: the idea that there are authorities (mostly male) who know what's best for all of us, who are qualified to tell us how to present ourselves to the world and how to express our sexuality. It's easy to imagine religious zealots putting up posters of people with AIDS or women who've had abortions. We would regard such an act as moral terrorism, something at which the right excels. I see no reason to follow their lead if we don't want to land in their territory.

The goal of gay liberation has always been our autonomy. Abandoning that standard now, along with privacy rights and common decency—just so we can claim a few movie stars—is the most absurd excuse for political thinking I have ever encountered.

# | 69 |

## *The Inning of Outing*

### GABRIEL ROTELLO

Five years ago, as the editor of *OutWeek* magazine, I made the decision to put Mike Signorile's article "The Secret Gay Life of Malcolm Forbes" on our cover. It was the headline heard round the gay and lesbian world, the one that started the debate over one of the most controversial gay issues ever: outing.

For many people, perhaps most, what Mike and I and publisher Kendall Morrison had done seemed a moral outrage, a tactical disaster, a frightening breach of gaydom's most coveted convention: the right to privacy. Accused of being unethical ideologues or unscrupulous self-promoters, we were vilified from coast to gay coast.

Cut to five years later and a story about a very different media mogul, *Rolling Stone* founder Jann Wenner. This article sits atop the front page of *The Wall Street Journal*, in the leading news spot in perhaps America's leading newspaper.

*Advocate*, April 18, 1995, p. 80.

JANN WENNER'S RIFT WITH WIFE SHAKES UP HIS PUBLISHING EMPIRE, reads the headline. And there in the third paragraph is this item, published expressly without the permission and against the wishes of Wenner: "The 49-year-old Mr. Wenner . . . has begun an unexpected new chapter in his life. Earlier this year, he left the home he shared with his wife and three young children and began a relationship with a young male staffer at Calvin Klein."

If *OutWeek*'s Forbes article ignited the outing war with a bang, the *Journal*'s piece on Wenner—and follow-up articles in *Newsweek, The Washington Post,* and elsewhere—symbolically ends it with a whimper. "It was relevant to a very interesting story," explained the *Journal*'s managing editor, Paul Steiger. And that, it seems, is that. Outing, once so contentious that it threatened to tear the community apart, is now so commonplace that it's hard to remember what the fuss was about.

Dozens of prominent people have been described as gay without their consent or approval in the years since the Forbes revelation, from Calvin Klein to Leonard Bernstein, from Patricia Ireland to Jodie Foster, from Steve Gunderson to Richard Chamberlain to Michael Stipe to k.d. lang to Sandra Bernhard to Greg Louganis. Most have eventually acknowledged their homosexuality. Some have ignored the allegations or denied them. Still others have come out voluntarily to avoid the exercise altogether. Yet outing is hardly mentioned anymore, much less argued about. What happened?

Essentially the media have grudgingly accepted *OutWeek*'s once-radical argument. We said it was hypocritical for journalists to routinely disclose the private lives of straight celebrities in ways those celebrities disliked or considered damaging while routinely covering up all mention of gay celebrities' gay lives. We argued that if homosexuality is a healthy facet of the human condition, the media have to stop treating it as the only unmentionable in journalism's inky sea of candor. We urged journalists to treat gay celebrities the way they treat straight ones: reporting the truth of their lives, including their romantic lives, whenever it's relevant to the story.

Journalists were intrigued by the idea, but gay leaders positively freaked. The right to privacy is the pillar of our movement, they stammered. Encouraging the media to openly discuss famous gays would undermine everything we stand for. It would destroy careers. It would produce reluctant, self-hating role models. The right wing would turn the practice against us. Lesbian and gay leaders campaigned vigorously against outing and sometimes against us personally. But since outing was essentially a journalistic endeavor, it mattered less what gay leaders thought than what journalists thought. And journalists slowly realized that gay leaders' arguments did not add up and that their dire predictions did not come true.

Outing would destroy careers? Tell that to the fabulous lang, nudged out reluctantly but now one of music's biggest stars. Or former Pentagon spokesman Pete Williams, outed on the cover of *The Advocate* and then given a fat contract as an NBC News correspondent. Or Sandra Bernhard. Or Amanda Bearse. It would create terrible, self-hating role models? Tell that to entertainment mogul David Geffen, who ended up as *The Advocate*'s 1992 Man of the Year. Or to Gunderson, now a gay leader in Congress.

It would prompt a right-wing outing campaign? No sign of that. It would violate the right to privacy? Not in the sense that people have a right to live their lives without government interference. They do, and outing doesn't threaten that. Instead, the outing debate has helped clarify the difference between the right to privacy and a celebrity's purported right to secrecy.

But perhaps the biggest thing to change people's minds about outing has been society's growing openness about all things gay. As journalists have increasingly accepted homosexuality as a natural part of life, they have increasingly questioned why there needs to be an entirely different code for gay celebrities. A dishonest code at that. And they've concluded that there's no good answer.

I don't recall the outing debate as a happy time. It's never fun to be vilified, especially by your friends and allies. It's nice to know that the debate seems finally over. It's even nicer to know that we won. It means that one pernicious "special right"—that of lesbian and gay celebrities to a separate standard—has been replaced by an equal right. The right to be treated like anybody else.

# Four

# LESBIAN AND GAY

## MEDIA

# IV. A

# IN OUR OWN VOICES: THE LESBIAN AND GAY PRESS

No one looking at the young woman who walked into a lesbian bar in Los Angeles called the If Club in the summer of 1947 would have suspected that she was witnessing a milestone in lesbian and gay history. The twenty-six-year-old secretary who called herself Lisa Ben (an anagram of lesbian) was distributing copies of a new publication that she had created and called *Vice Versa* "because in those days our kind of life was considered a vice."

The magazine Lisa Ben handed out consisted of only fifteen neatly typewritten pages carefully stapled together, but it signaled the birth of the lesbian and gay press in the United States (Marcus, "Gay Gal—Lisa Ben," this volume).

The lesbian and gay movement that seemed to appear "spontaneously" across the country shortly after the 1969 Stonewall riots in New York City was in fact the result of a process begun early in a post–World War II urban gay world that was largely invisible to heterosexual society and whose growing self-consciousness in the decades before Stonewall can be traced in large part to the lesbian and gay press.

"The pioneering effort to publish magazines about homosexuality brought the gay movement its only significant victory during the 1950s" (D'Emilio 1983:115). The magazines referred to were all, like *Vice Versa*, published in California: *ONE* was founded in Los Angeles in 1953, *Mattachine Review* and the *Ladder* were launched in San Francisco in 1955 and 1956. But unlike *Vice Versa* they reached far beyond the editors' immediate circles—they were distributed nationally and built

a combined circulation of about seven thousand. They each lasted more than a dozen years and survived attacks from government agencies and officials determined to shut them down. In the words of journalism historian Rodger Streitmatter:

> Just as the founding of the first African-American newspaper, *Freedom's Journal* in 1827, has been credited with marking the beginning of a national movement to secure black civil rights, by creating a communications medium that allowed women and men all over the country to converse with each other, *One, Mattachine Review,* and *The Ladder* began to build a national gay and lesbian community. (1995:49–50)

*ONE* was written and edited by a few gay men in Los Angeles who were frustrated by the feeling that they were just talking to themselves and the knowledge that the media wouldn't print anything about their cause. *ONE* took a more militant stand than did the Mattachine Society, which by then was adopting a strategy of achieving acceptance by conforming to heterosexual standards. The head of the Mattachine Society, former newspaperman Hal Call, founded the *Mattachine Review* in 1955 as a tool to promote the organization's philosophy that public attitudes toward homosexuals would improve as soon as "sex variants began behaving in accordance with societal norms."

Neither *ONE* nor *Mattachine* was interested in representing women, and it took a group of lesbians to fill this vacuum. In 1955 four lesbian couples living in San Francisco began an organization they called the Daughters of Bilitis (the name came from French poet Pierre Louys's *The Songs of Bilitis*), and a year later DOB leaders Phyllis Martin and Del Lyon began to publish the *Ladder*. The first issue stated,

> We enter a field already ably served by ONE and *Mattachine Review*. We offer, however, that so-called "feminine viewpoint" which they have had so much difficulty obtaining. It is to be hoped that our venture will encourage the women to take an ever-increasing part in the steadily-growing fight for understanding of the homophile minority.

The *Ladder* led the way in arguing that lesbian and gay people had to think of themselves as a political force, not merely as an oppressed minority. Their role became influential when a candidate for mayor of San Francisco in the 1959 election accused Mayor Christopher of transforming the city into "the national headquarters for sex deviants" and singled out the Daughter of Bilitis in a warning to parents to guard their daughters. The editors of the *Ladder* responded with a special issue that helped bring the gay perspective into what became a major public debate. The mainstream media condemned the antigay tactic and Mayor Christopher was reelected by a wide margin. This was a turning point in the emergence of a politically active and visible lesbian and gay community in San Francisco.

The magazines operated with minuscule budgets and volunteer labor. Very few ads were ever placed by businesses; even businesses supported by gay customers were afraid to advertise in these magazines. Despite these odds the circulation of the magazines rose throughout the 1950s, with *ONE* reaching five thousand subscribers each month, and *Mattachine Review* around one thousand. The *Ladder* had the lowest circulation—a pattern to be repeated later with other lesbian publications—but its readership was much larger than its official circulation of around seven hundred. One Washington, D.C., subscriber invited friends over every month for a "*Ladder* party" at which she would read the magazine out loud to as many as thirty or forty other lesbians. Similar gatherings were held around the country (Streitmatter 1995:28).

Gay people weren't the only ones who were paying attention to these small magazines; the FBI quickly began to investigate the publications, calling them subversive, disgusting, and shocking. In 1954 Senator Alexander Wiley (R-Wis.) protested "the use of the United States mails to transmit a so-called 'magazine' devoted to the advancement of sexual perversion." The Post Office confiscated the October 1954 issue of *ONE*, but the magazine took the matter to court. In the meantime FBI agents maintained a constant harassment of the editors of all three magazines; the editors, in turn, infuriated the FBI by claiming that "everyone knew J. Edgar Hoover was queer" (Eric Marcus, "News Hound," this volume). As Hal Call put it recently, "I told [the FBI agents] the same things forty years ago that historians are just publishing today." *ONE* pursued their appeal of the Post Office rulings through the Federal courts and, in 1958, the U.S. Supreme Court issued a landmark decision establishing that the subject of homosexuality was not, per se, obscene (Streitmatter 1995:32–36).

The 1960s ushered in an era of social activism across the United States, as the civil rights movement, followed by the antiwar movement and the women's movement, engaged thousands of citizens in grassroots politics. The lesbian and gay movement took on increased fervor as activists began appearing in the Northeast as well as the West Coast. In Washington, D.C., a government employee named Frank Kameny fought back after he was fired because of his sexuality and became one of the key figures in building the gay movement. One of the first vehicles for Kameny's arguments was the *Ladder*, which was taken over in 1963 by Philadelphia activist Barbara Gittings. Gittings proceeded to add the words "A Lesbian Review" to the front cover of the magazine. As she explained, "That subtitle said, very eloquently, I thought, that the word 'lesbian' was no longer unspeakable" (Streitmatter 1995:55). Even more daring, Gittings replaced the line drawings previously used on the cover with photographs of actual lesbians (many photographed by her lover and colleague Kay Lahusen).

In 1966 Frank Kameny and another leader of the Washington Mattachine, Jack Nichols, founded the *Homosexual Citizen,* which was edited by a lesbian named Lilli Vincenz (the magazine lasted for only eighteen issues). In the first issue Vincenz explained the juxtaposition of *homosexual* and *citizen* in the magazine's name: "These words must seem irreconcilable to the prejudiced. All we can say is that these people will be surprised—for patriotism and responsible participation in our American democracy are certainly not monopolized by white Anglo-Saxon Protestant heterosexuals."

Another new magazine was begun on the East Coast in 1964, this time in Philadelphia. *Drum*, published by the Janus Society, a homosexual rights organization founded in 1960, took its name from a famous statement by Thoreau: "If a man does not keep pace with his companions, perhaps it is because he hears the beat of a different drummer." Editor Clark Polak said that he "began *Drum* magazine as a consistently articulate, well-edited, amusing and informative publication. I envisioned a sort of sophisticated, but down-to-earth, magazine for people who dug gay life and *Drum*'s view of the world" (Streitmatter 1995:61). Polak was on to something, as *Drum*'s circulation quickly climbed to ten thousand; by far the largest for a gay publication. Like the *Homosexual Citizen* and the *Ladder* under Gittings, *Drum* took a much more militant stance than had earlier publications. Polak criticized "hyper-conformist" gay people as sell-outs for saying they had no problems as long as they didn't flaunt their homosexuality.

In 1965 these activists—Kameny, Nichols, and Vincenz in Washington, and Gittings, Lahusen, and Polak in Philadelphia—were among the small number who opened a new front in the struggle for gay liberation. Following in the footsteps of civil rights and antiwar groups who had taken their protests to the streets, these activists began marching with picket signs—in front of the White House, the Civil Service Headquarters and the State Department in Washington, the United Nations in New York, and Independence Hall in Philadelphia.

Word of the pickets was spread not through the mainstream media, which largely ignored them, but in the pages and on the covers of the lesbian and gay magazines, especially the *Ladder*. When the mainstream media began to pay attention to the growing visibility of lesbian and gay people in the 1960s, their coverage tended toward alarmist expressions. The gay publications responded by printing their own reviews of the stories appearing in the *New York Times, Time,* and *Life*, blasting them for their prejudice and superficiality (Kay Tobin, "A Rebuke for TIME's Pernicious Prejudice," this volume). After *Life* published its "Homosexuality in America" feature Polak responded with an article in *Drum* by P. Arody, on "Heterosexuality in America": "Heterosexuality shears across the spectrum of American life—the professions, the

arts, business and labor. It always has. But today, especially in big cities, heterosexuals are openly admitting, even flaunting their deviation" (Streitmatter 1995:71).

The gay press made major strides in reaching larger audiences in the mid-1960s with developments on both coasts. New York journalist Al Goldstein pushed the envelope of social tolerance by launching the sex-tabloid *Screw* in 1968. The magazine was an instant success, quickly reaching a circulation of 150,000. One of the novel features of *Screw* was a column by gay activist Jack Nichols and his lover, Lige Clarke. The column brought news of the gay liberation movement to many thousands—both gay and straight—who would never see the smaller movement magazines.

Around the same time, a Los Angeles activist who used the name Dick Michaels took over a movement newsletter, renamed it the *Los Angeles Advocate*, and turned it into the country's first commercial gay paper. By the end of its second year the *Advocate* had reached a circulation of twenty-three thousand and was distributed in cities across the country. It was becoming the first national gay news magazine—a role it continues to play today (Streitmatter, "The *Advocate*: Setting the Standard," this volume).

The decade of the 1970s was a period of explosive growth for the lesbian and gay community. Commercial, political, religious, cultural, and social institutions sprang up everywhere, cultivating a growing sense of identity and spreading the word to a new generation of young people coming out into a world turned upside down.

Newspapers and magazines were established by lesbian and gay organizations and individuals all over the United States and beyond. Particularly notable was the explosive growth in lesbian feminist activism, fueled by the dual forces of the women's and the lesbian/gay movements. The early 1970s saw the founding of such journals as *Ain' t I a Woman? Amazon Quarterly, Azalea, Dyke,* the *Furies, Lavender Woman, Lesbian Connection, Lesbian Tide, Sinister Wisdom, Sisters,* and *Tribad*. Although most did not survive the 1970s, they played a major role in the emergence of lesbian-feminist consciousness and culture and introduced readers to such powerful writers as Rita Mae Brown, Audre Lorde, and Adrienne Rich (Thistlewaite, "Representation, Liberation, and the Queer Press," this volume). At the same time, significant lesbian and gay political journals were founded, notably *Gay Community News* in Boston and the *Body Politic* (1971–1988) in Toronto (Jackson, "Flaunting It," this volume).

The lesbian and gay press facilitated the emergence of a newly self-confident and visible community that demanded its share of the American dream. The political successes of the gay liberation movement, and the defeats, were reported by the lesbian and gay press while the mainstream press continued to ignore or denigrate their efforts. But the true value of the gay press did not become fully apparent until the early 1980s, when the AIDS epidemic brought down the curtain on the "golden age" of the decade following Stonewall.

The immediate response to AIDS was a deafening silence from the mainstream mass media, but even the gay press needed time to understand the magnitude of the crisis. The relationships between the various opportunistic infections associated with AIDS would not become clear for some time. In the meantime, gay physician Dr. Lawrence Mass was writing articles in the *New York Native* that were the only accounts to convey the seriousness of the situation. In the more than fifteen years since then the gay press has been the only consistent and often the most reliable source of information on the epidemic.

The outlook for gay media remains mixed. While at least sixty-five gay and lesbian newspapers are published nationwide, with an estimated total readership of three million (Wilke 1994), the movement press of the 1960s and 1970s is largely gone, replaced by such local papers as the *Washington Blade* (D.C.), the *Windy City Times* (Chicago), and *Bay Windows* (Boston).

Until recently, the only advertisers willing to support gay publications were small lesbian- and gay-oriented businesses. Fearful of alienating other customers—and unconvinced that lesbian and gay readers constituted a profitable market "niche"—national advertisers largely kept their distance. The editorial tone and sexually explicit content of some publications also posed a barrier. For years most of the ads in the *Advocate* catered to explicit sexual interests, peddling everything from massage to phone sex. National advertisers protested that this environment was unsuitable for "mainstream" products such as soap or credit cards. The result, for gay publications, was a Catch-22: to lure major advertisers, they would first need to abandon their principal source of revenue.

In the early 1990s gay publications finally broke through the advertising barrier. A growing pool of marketing data and readership surveys showed that lesbian and gay periodicals attracted a disproportionately wealthy, educated, and brand-loyal clientele. The same studies demonstrated that these readers were relatively easy to reach through the lesbian and gay press, making an efficient and easy to identify "niche market." Advertisers took notice. Absolut Vodka, Naya Waters, and Miller Beer were among the first to design campaigns aimed specifically at the gay community. By 1994 American Express, Sony, Saab, Apple Computers, Ikea, Banana Republic, and many others began to put their money where their market was.

This atmosphere of change spawned a crop of "lifestyle" publications such as *Out*, *Genre*, *Curve*, and *Ten Percent*. Unlike the movement press that preceded them, these publications favored a *Vanity Fair*-style approach that intermingled articles on popular culture, fashion, travel, and personalities with the occasional news story or editorial; politics took a back seat. Armed with approving market research, a glossy new look, and few (if any) sex ads, these publications went after large national advertisers—and got them. Following suit, the *Advocate* spun its sex-related ads (which amounted to almost a third of revenues) off into a separate publication, and refashioned itself into a *Time*-style newsmagazine (Mathews 1992).

In the mid-1990s magazines began to emerge that could be viewed as niches within niches. *Poz* is directed at people living with HIV/AIDS, and its glossy pages tend to feature drug and viatical ads. Los Angeles-based BLK publishes separate erotic magazines for black lesbians and gay men as well as a poetry magazine for black lesbians and gay men, in addition to their flagship magazine *BLK*, published since 1988. In 1996 *XY*, a slick magazine aimed at gay teens, appeared, and, although the contents were indeed addressed to young gay men, it is possible that the sexy photo spreads also attracted an older and more affluent readership. The third issue included a letter from a Kansas fifteen year old, enthusiastic about "the great stuff and . . . all the pictures of cute guys. . . . It's about the only thing I have to let me know that there are other gay youth out there." He also noted, however, "My parents look at my mail so I would get busted if I did subscribe."

For many lesbian and gay people, locating lesbian or gay publications entails both risk and expense often beyond their means. This is especially true for young people like *XY*'s correspondent. For these reasons radio and cable television (as well as video copies of independent films) have proved to be a lifeline.

Radio programs produced for and by lesbian and gay people are available on nearly one hundred public and community radio stations in the United States and Canada. Some of these programs have aired for many years, such as weekly gay and lesbian programs on WXPN-FM in Philadelphia, broadcast since the 1970s. In the late 1980s Los Angeles radio producer Greg Gordon, recalling his isolated childhood, began *This Way Out*, a weekly half-hour show that by the mid-1990s aired on eighty-five stations in seven countries. Much of his audience consists of older gays in rural areas and young people everywhere. One seventeen year old from Missouri wrote him that the program "is like finding an oasis in the middle of the desert, the desert being a tiny Midwest town. . . . The only thing for gays here is the highway to leave this hell hole and *This Way Out*" (Price 1993).

In June 1992 WNYC originated *In the Life*, a monthly gay-themed variety program now shown on over sixty public television stations around the country. Senator Robert Dole attacked the show before it had ever been shown, falsely asserting that it had been produced with taxpayer's money (the funds were raised privately) — as if lesbian and gay citizens do not pay taxes.

With the rapid expansion of cable television it was to be expected that lesbian and gay programming would begin to appear, and several fledgling enterprises were born in the early 1990s. Gay Entertainment Television offers three weekly shows via cable outlets in Los Angeles, Chicago, New York, Miami, and San Francisco. A lesbian produced program, *Dyke TV,* is carried by cable systems in more than a dozen cities (Closs, "I Want My Gay TV," this volume).

In 1992 David Surber, an advertising executive, decided to produce a video magazine for lesbians and gay men, and that September the first installment of *Network Q* was mailed to subscribers. The video magazine covered topics such as National Coming Out Day, lesbian and gay comedians, travel and resorts, political struggles, being out on campus, and the AIDS Memorial Quilt. As one forty-year-old man wrote, "It's like our very own *60 Minutes*." Many subscribers in rural areas noted that the video magazine gives them a "feeling of being part of gay America." By 1994 there were two thousand subscribers, representing all fifty states and twelve foreign countries, and it was estimated that each program was seen by 24,000 viewers. But, with a yearly subscription cost of $199 for twelve issues, the video magazine was not yet a solution to the isolation experienced by millions of lesbian and gay people who do not see their realities or their concerns reflected in the mass media. By 1995 *Network Q* had been reconfigured for cable distribution and was struggling to reach an audience.

## References

D'Emilio, John. 1983. *Sexual Politics, Sexual Communities*. Chicago: University of Chicago.

Mathews, Jay. 1992. "From Closet to Mainstream: Upscale Gay Magazines Flood the Newstand." *Newsweek*, June 1, p. 62.

Price, Deb. 1993. "Friendly Voices: Gay Radio Eases Isolation." *Detroit News*, March 4.

Streitmatter, Rodger. 1995. *Unspeakable: The Rise of the Gay and Lesbian Press in America*. Boston: Faber and Faber.

Wilke, Michael. 1994. "Gay Newspapers Try New Paths to Growth." *New York Times*, May 30, p. D35.

# | 70 |

## "Gay Gal"—Lisa Ben

### Eric Marcus

*In 1945, Lisa Ben,\* a young secretary from north-*
*ern California, set out for Los Angeles to escape*
*her overbearing parents. It was there that she first*
*met other women like her, and it was there that she*
*first put her ideas about homosexuality down on*
*paper in her own "magazine" for lesbians, which*
*she produced using sheets of carbon paper on her*
*office typewriter. Beginning in mid-1947, Lisa Ben*
*produced nine editions of* Vice Versa, *which she*
*distributed to her friends, who, in turn, passed*
*them on to their friends. Although Lisa was able to*
*produce only ten copies of each edition, her publi-*
*cation was almost certainly read by dozens, if not*
*hundreds, before it disappeared into history. . . .*

Around this time, I started writing *Vice Versa*, a
magazine for gay gals. I published the first issue
in June 1947. I wrote *Vice Versa* mainly to keep
myself company. I called it *Vice Versa* because in
those days our kind of life was considered a vice.
It was the opposite of the lives that were being
lived—supposedly—and understood and
approved of by society. And *Vice Versa* means the
opposite. I thought it was very apropos. What else
could I have called it?

I handed out the magazine for free. I never
charged for it. I felt that that would be wrong. It
was just some writing that I wanted to get off my
chest. There was never anything in the magazine
that was sexy or suggestive. I purposely kept it that
way in case I got caught. They couldn't say that
*Vice Versa* was dirty or naughty or against the law.

I typed the magazines at work. I had a boss
who said, "You won't have a heck of a lot to do
here, but I don't want you to knit or read a book.
I want you always to took busy." He didn't care
what I did as long as I got his work done first.

I put in five copies at a time with carbon
paper, and typed it through twice and ended up
with ten copies of *Vice Versa*. That's all I could
manage. There were no duplicating machines in
those days, and, of course, I couldn't go to a
printer. I learned to be a very fast typist that way.

Then I would say to the girls as I passed the
magazine out, "When you get through with this,
don't throw it away, pass it on to another gay gal."
We didn't use the term lesbian so much then. We
just said gay gal. In that way *Vice Versa* would
pass from friend to friend.

I wrote almost everything in the magazine,
although once in a while I would get a contribution. I wrote book reviews, although there were
very few books around at the time that said anything about lesbians. Even though it had been
around since 1928, I wrote a book review on *The
Well of Loneliness*, Radclyffe Hall's lesbian novel.
If there were any movies around that had the
slightest tinge of two girls being interested in one
another, I would take that story within the movie
and play it up and say, "Such and such a movie
has a scene in it with two young ladies and they
seem to be interested in one another." And then
I wrote poetry. Not a great deal of it, but a few
things.

I was never afraid of being caught. That's the
funny part about it. I never realized how serious

In Eric Marcus, *Making History: The Struggle for
Lesbian and Gay Equal Rights*, pp. 5–15. Excerpt. New
York: HarperCollins, 1992.

\* Lisa Ben is a pseudonym. She chose not to use her
real name because she is concerned that she would
upset elderly relatives who "might not take it well if they
find out I'm gay."

it was. I blithely mailed these things out from the office with no return address, until one of my friends phoned me and said, "You know, you really shouldn't be doing that. It is against the law and it could land you in trouble." And I said, "Why? I don't mention the city it's from. I don't mention anybody's name. And it's not a dirty magazine by any stretch of the imagination." And she said, "Well, it would be dirty to the straight people because it's about girls, even though you have no cuss words or anything like that in it." So I decided I wouldn't mail it from the office anymore. But can you imagine the naïveté of me? Oh dear!

▼ ▼ ▼

There's an essay I wrote for *Vice Versa* that I wanted to read to you. I haven't looked at it in a long time. It's one of my favorites, and I think it will give you some idea of the kinds of things I was thinking about back then. I'm not sure what issue it's in. Let me see. Oh, here it is, *Vice Versa—* "America's Gayest Magazine," Volume 1, Number 4, September 1947. The essay is called "Here to Stay."

Whether the unsympathetic majority approves or not, it looks as though the third sex is here to stay. With the advancement of psychiatry and related subjects, the world is becoming more and more aware that there are those in our midst who feel no attraction for the opposite sex.

It is not an uncommon sight to observe mannishly attired women or even those dressed in more feminine garb strolling along the street hand-in-hand or even arm-in-arm, in an attitude which certainly would seem to indicate far more than mere friendliness. And bright colored shirts, chain bracelets, loud socks, and ornate sandals are increasingly in evidence on many of the fellows passing by. The war had a great deal to do with influencing the male to wear jewelry, I believe, with the introduction of dog tags, identification bracelets, etc. Whether the war by automatically causing segregation of men from female company for long periods of time has influenced fellows to become more aware of their own kind is a moot question. It is interesting to note, however, that for quite some time the majority of teenage girls seem to prefer jeans and boy's shirts to neat, feminine attire. It is doubtful that this has any vast social significance, yet might not the masculine garb influence them toward adopting boyish mannerisms more than if they had adhered to typ-

ical girlish fashions?

Nightclubs featuring male and female impersonators are becoming increasingly prevalent. Even cafés and drive-ins intended for the average customer, when repeatedly patronized by inverts, tend to reflect a gay atmosphere. Such places are ever the center of attraction for a "gay crowd" and become known as a likely rendezvous in which to meet those of similar inclinations.

Books such as *Dianna* and *The Well of Loneliness* are available in inexpensive editions at book marts and even the corner drugstores. With such knowledge being disseminated through fact and fiction to the public in general, homosexuality is becoming less and less a taboo subject, and although still considered by the general public as contemptible or treated with derision. I venture to predict that there will be a time in the future when gay folk will be accepted as part of regular society.

Just as certain subjects once considered unfit for discussion now are used as themes in many of our motion pictures, I believe that the time will come when, say, Stephen Gordon will step unrestrained from the pages of Radclyffe Hall's admirable novel, *The Well of Loneliness*, onto the silver screen. And once precedent has been broken by one such motion picture, others will be sure to follow.

Perhaps even *Vice Versa* might be the forerunner of better magazines dedicated to the third sex, which in some future time might take their rightful place on the newsstands beside other publications, to be available openly and without restriction to those who wish to read them.

Currently appearing in many popular magazines are comprehensive articles on psychological differences between the two sexes, which are enlightening many women as to the unbridgeable gaps between the opposite sexes and why most of them in this rapidly changing world are unable to come to terms with each other on a mental and emotional basis.

In days gone by, when woman's domain was restricted to the fireside, marriage and a family was her only prospect, the home was the little world around which life revolved, and in which, unless wives were fortunate enough to have help, they had to perform innumerable household chores besides assuming the responsibility of bearing children. But in these days of frozen foods, motion picture palaces, compact apartments, modern innovations, and female independence, there is no reason why a woman should have to look to a man for food and shelter in return for raising his children and keeping his house in order unless she really wants to.

Today, a woman may live independently from man if she so chooses and carve out her own career. Never before have circumstances and conditions been so suitable for those of lesbian tendencies.

It surprises me now, reading this, because I haven't read it for so long. I had to stop and think, "Did I write that?" But I wrote it. I never thought of it as being bold at the time. I was just sort of fantasizing. It all has come to pass: the magazines, the movies, women that choose to live by themselves if they so wish, even if they aren't gay. Makes me feel like a fortuneteller. Yes, that's me in there. Although, I didn't sign my name to it.

I used no names in *Vice Versa* because that was back in 1947. I assured the few people who wrote articles and poems and things that I wouldn't use their names. I never used my own name in it either and never even thought of using the pseudonym "Lisa Ben" in those days. I first started using Lisa Ben in the 1950s when I wrote a story for *The Ladder*, the Daughters of Bilitis* magazine. I was a member of Daughters of Bilitis down here in L.A. Nobody used their names in that publication. So I signed my story, "Ima Spinster." I thought that was funny, but they didn't. They put up a big argument. I don't know whether they thought it was too undignified or what, but they objected strongly. If I had been as sure of myself as I am these days, I would have said, "All right,

take it or leave it." But I wasn't. So I invented the name Lisa Ben. If you've ever played anagrams you know what it turns around into.

▼ ▼ ▼

I published nine issues of *Vice Versa* before the job where I could do a lot of personal typing on my own came to an abrupt halt. Someone else bought the company, and almost everyone was let go—bosses, secretaries, errand boys, everybody. It was a mass exodus. Out we went. At the next job, I did not have an opportunity to do the magazine because the work load was heavier and there was no privacy. I didn't have a private office as I did in the first job. I thought, "Well I'll just have to give it up, that's all. I can't attempt to do the same here, or there would be repercussions." So the magazine folded.

I always hoped that I would stay in that one job and that I could turn out one of these a month and that I would be able to meet more and more girls this way, by handing out the magazine, and that I would become known among the group. You see, I was very lonely.

I didn't suppose anything could come of *Vice Versa* because I knew that in those days such magazines could not be sent to the printers and published. So it was just a sort of a gesture of love—of women loving women, and the whole idea of it. It was an enthusiasm that boiled over into these printed pages, and I wanted to give them to as many people as possible. It was a way of dividing myself into little bits and pieces and saying, "Here you are, take me! I love you all!"

---

*An organization for lesbians founded in San Francisco in 1955.

# | 71 |

## *News Hound—Jim Kepner*

ERIC MARCUS

*During its first years of publication, the pioneering ONE magazine attracted the attention of the U.S. Post Office and the FBI. The magazine also attracted the interest of Jim Kepner, a young man who worked nights at a milk-carton-manufacturing plant south of Los Angeles. Jim first learned of the magazine in 1953, through the Mattachine Society. He eventually joined ONE's small volunteer staff, working as a news writer and columnist. . . .*

*Jim is now curator of the International Gay and Lesbian Archives in Hollywood, which he founded in 1972. He lives in a small, rundown cottage at the bottom of a steep hill in an outlying Los Angeles neighborhood. His front yard is filled with cactus plants, a longtime hobby. Inside, the house overflows with files, books, and personal records collected during three and a half decades of involvement with the gay rights movement. When he recalled the past, Jim pulled details from a mind that seemed to be as fact packed as his house.*

When I first heard about the Mattachine—in the early 1950s, when I had just moved to L.A.—I thought it might also be a fantasy because the people who ran it had allowed rumors to circulate that some very influential people were behind it. The phrase, "senators and generals," was one of the first I heard. So I was not quick to join.

But I kept hearing about Mattachine through the grapevine all over town. Everybody was buzzing about this gay group where people discussed things and where there were social activities. I would occasionally hear where a meeting was taking place, but I didn't drive at the time, and the meetings would be in some other hilly area in another part of town. Also I had to be at work at midnight about eight or nine miles southeast of L.A.

In the meantime, some friends gave me a housewarming, which turned into a regular Thursday night and Friday night party. The Friday night party sometimes lasted until Monday morning. The place was crowded with a mixture of science-fiction fans, gays, ex-radicals, and other assorted individuals. Several times I took a few people into the other room to discuss quietly starting a gay magazine or organization. A few times I got three or four people who were interested, but when I called them the next day, they would say it was party talk. They'd tell me, "The last thing I want to do is get in a room with a bunch of screaming queens. Nobody could agree on anything." I said, "Look, you're not a screaming queen. I'm not a screaming queen. Why are you bringing that up?"

They also thought that nothing would ever change. But unlike most people—due, in part, to my Marxist and science-fiction background—I did not believe that society was static. Most gays did. If you mentioned organizing, they'd say that society hated us and always would, that you couldn't change things. Well, I knew that society was changing in many ways and needed to change in lots of other ways. I instinctively took a political approach to social problems. I always said, "Let's do something." Well, that approach was alien to most people, particularly most gays, and particularly at this time. This was an enormously conservative, conformist period, probably the most conformist period in our history, or at least in our recent history. We were coming into the McCarthy era.

Nothing came of my attempts to start a group

In Eric Marcus, *Making History: The Struggle for Lesbian and Gay Equal Rights*, pp. 43–53. Excerpt. New York: HarperCollins, 1992.

of my own. Eventually, in 1952, I went to my first Mattachine meeting. My friend, Betty Perdue, took me. It was in someone's big house in Los Feliz. Betty was known as "Geraldine Jackson" in the movement. She wrote a poem, "Proud and Unashamed," in the first issue of ONE magazine, though she never managed to achieve that condition herself. A Lutheran minister also went with us. He was terribly nervous, nellie, and paranoid.

When we got to the house, we knocked at the door. It was almost a "Joe sent me" sort of thing. They knew Betty and the minister, so we went right in. There were about 180 people in the room, sitting everywhere. There was a circular stairway going up to a landing, and both of those were filled with people. I was quite shocked by the number of people. About 80 percent were men, 85 percent in their thirties or younger. No one was underage. That was verboten.

The announced topic was, "What do we do with these effeminate queens and these stalking butches who are giving us a bad name?" It was a lively discussion, but it seemed to me that the ones at this meeting who were most worried about the problem happened to be the effeminate queens and stalking butches.

It took me a while to speak up. I was pretty shy, but I finally blurted out this story about the first time I went to a gay bar in the late spring of 1943. It was the Black Cat bar in San Francisco. I told them how I was going to join my brothers and sisters for the first time. I was on a cloud of idealism, so high that I was walking down Montgomery Street four inches above the sidewalk. I got almost to the door of the bar. I think I even touched the door, when all of a sudden a whole bunch of San Francisco policemen went past me and burst into the bar. I didn't see them coming. By this time I had read eight or ten novels and had read several accounts of bar raids, so I knew what was happening.

Standing outside the bar, I had chivalric visions of mounting my white charger and going in to save my brothers and sisters, but instead, I hid in the doorway across the street, feeling like shit, feeling cowardly, feeling guilty.

The first view I got of my brothers and sisters was when 12 or 15 drag queens and about 12 or 15 butch numbers—men who would be called San Francisco clones today—were led out of the bar by the police. All the clones were looking guilty, and practically all the queens were struggling and sassing the cops. I felt so good when I heard one of the queens scream at the policeman

who was shoving her, "Don't shove, you bastard, or I'll bite your fuckin' balls off!" That queen paid in blood. They beat her and two or three of the others. I was still hiding in the doorway, wanting to do something wanting to shout something, but I wouldn't have known what to shout.

When I finished this story I said, "Look, the queens were the only ones who ever fought. If not for the queens, there wouldn't have been bars that the rest of us could sneak into. Because of them, we could go to the bars and be gay for one night; we could let our hair down"—figuratively. "But when we left the bars, we pinned up our hair and pretended we were like everyone else. And they didn't." When we left the bars, we were very careful not to go out at the same time any of the queens did. Some of them were real cute about tricking us and would walk out the door at the same time one of us more closety ones went out. There was a two-step that you used to do as you went out the door. You would take the minimum number of steps you had to in order to get into a position where you appeared to be passing by the bar.

I got very angry at this attack on the queens. I said, "They're our front line. And they're not the ones who cause prejudice. People are much more upset when they find out that their neighbor or friend who wasn't obvious is, in fact, gay." I think that causes a lot more prejudice than some obvious queen. People can relate to the queens in the same way they relate to Stepin Fetchit.

The format of the meeting was such that you couldn't tell who was running it. There were unofficial cochairs, but they were instructed not to act as if they were really running things, just to keep the discussion going. There were also people who made announcements of activities. "There's going to be a beach party" or "Why don't we have a beach party, and would some people like to volunteer for arrangements?" This secrecy about who really ran the discussion groups was intentional.

By the time I got to my second or third meeting, the gossip was getting around that some of the people in charge were Communists. That was very disturbing in this period of history, because almost all the people who came to the discussion groups were very conformist, and they loved nothing better than to say, "We're just like everybody else except for what we do in bed. We don't want any special rights. We don't want to rock the boat."

When I got more involved in the organization, I realized that the need for secrecy was exaggerated. This was due, in part, to the fact that Harry Hay, one of the founders, had been through the Party, which was a pretty secret organization. But Harry also had this idea that gays had been an underground society throughout history. He had developed a Masonic Lodge approach to running Mattachine. Some of the others, like Martin Block, thought all this secrecy was a lot of bullshit.

▼ ▼ ▼

After the changeover in leadership in 1953, when Mattachine became an open, democratic organization, the society went into decline—for two reasons. First, the new leaders, who were ultraconservatives, wanted tight control of what the different chapters of the organizations did. The result was inaction—paralysis—because a chapter would decide to do something and the ultraconservatives would veto it. Second, the mystique was gone. The mystique of the original Mattachine depended on the impression that there were some big people behind the organization. That impression made it seem safe and made it seem as if there were people who would take care of things for us, so we only had to show up at meetings and discuss things like, "Should I tell my parents?" "Can you be gay and Christian?" "If we're really gay, do we have to swish?" But that wasn't the case anymore. Suddenly, we had to do something besides talk, and lot of people weren't interested in that.

I stayed with Mattachine for a while after the changeover, but eventually I became more involved in ONE magazine, which had begun publishing in early 1953. It was not a very impressive publication, and we never sold more than a few thousand copies a month, but it was the first, and it was ours.

ONE's staff seemed a little closed at the time I tried to get involved. When I spoke to a couple of people who ran the magazine, Dorr Legg and Dale Jennings, about doing some work, I wasn't exactly snatched up. So I began coming into the office frequently and talking to Dorr about ideas for articles. I did one called "The Importance of Being Honest," which appeared in March 1954. Then I wrote an article on the British witch-hunt, which had begun in the middle of 1953. Hundreds of men were arrested on homosexual charges, including several prominent men, among them actor John Gielgud. At the same time, a similar, more limited witch-hunt began in Miami. There were other witch-hunts later in var-

ious other places, including one in South Carolina at a black college and one at the beach in Santa Monica. So I began reporting on these sorts of things. Then I started writing a regular column called "Tangents." It was concerned with gay news, censorship, conformity, civil rights, gender oddities, and other subjects that seemed to relate to our field of interest.

I got lots of complaints about the column from readers because the news was bad. Bars raided. Guys murdered by someone they had picked up or someone who saw them on the street and thought they were queer. Public officials arrested in public tearooms. I explained several times to ONE subscribers that we did not have five hundred reporters scattered around the world to provide us with independent reports. I depended on the straight press, and those were the kinds of stories they were publishing about gays. I was buying as many out of town newspapers as I could.

You could read most papers for a year without finding any gay news unless you learned how to read between the lines. They might not have mentioned the raid of a homosexual or queer bar, but they mention a "house of ill repute." And if several men were arrested and no women were mentioned as present, you assumed it was not a whorehouse. In the article they might mention one man was dressed in a "womanish" manner. When Time magazine mentioned the subject, they usually used words like epicene to describe someone. When they reviewed—holding their noses—Tennessee Williams or Carson McCullers, they would use the term decadent. You looked for those words and then read the whole thing carefully. Then you would go and investigate. So I would write to one of our subscribers in the place from where the story was reported and ask, "Is this a gay story?"

I also explained to readers who complained about the negative news, "If I should know that a gay person was made president of General Electric, do you think I could report that?" Of course, I couldn't. First, we didn't report that kind of thing because of the absolute code by which it was considered unfair to bring another person out. That was an individual decision. Second, I would not have reported that kind of thing because we would have been sued for slander. The person we identified as gay would have probably lost his position anyhow. It would have hurt everybody. There was no point to it.

I also followed conformity stories. For instance, I opened one column with the awful line, "Elvis the pelvis doesn't amuse me." But I objected to what the local authorities were doing about his concerts, raiding them or refusing permission for him to perform because of his sexy gyrations. Of course, I had to show my superiority first. Actually it wasn't until the fifth or sixth song I heard that I thought Elvis was any good.

And I also reported on the slow development of long hair and the breakaway from orthodox clothing styles. I did a story on the owner of a Beverly Hills antique store who was arrested because he had a statue of Michelangelo's David in the window. Things like that. These were censorship questions in general. Censorship hit us extra hard with a double standard. Anything that was heterosexual was considered obscene if it was extremely disgusting, provocative, or sexually explicit or had an excessive use of Anglo-Saxon language or detailed descriptions of the mechanics of sex. Anything that mentioned homosexuality was obscene simply if it did not point out how terribly, terribly disgusting and evil homosexuality was. No detail was permitted. That was what got the magazine hooked by the post office.

The August 1953 issue, which had the phrase "homosexual marriage" on the cover, was seized by the post office—using the obscenity hook—and released. ONE printed an angry article saying that ONE was not grateful to the postmaster for releasing it. Some people thought that the fact that the postmaster had released it signified that we were okay, but that wasn't the case because the post office seized another issue of the magazine, the October 1954 issue, which ironically happened to have a cover story on the law of mailable material.

I think the reason behind the post office's seizure of this second issue was an article in the previous issue suggesting that everybody knew that J. Edgar Hoover was sleeping with Clyde Tolson, his close partner. That article attracted the interest of the FBI. Much later, through the Freedom of Information Act, we found a note from Hoover to Tolson, which I have a copy of somewhere in storage, saying, " We've got to get these bastards." There was also a note to the post office from Hoover urging them to check into ONE.

At the same time as the seizure, the FBI showed up at ONE's office wanting to know who had written the article about Hoover. They also came to visit me a couple of times and visited most members of the staff. One of the FBI agents sat right there in that chair. I was nervous; it was a tense situation. They asked me if a couple of members of the staff were Communists, and I hooted and said that they were very conservative. They were. I probably shouldn't have even told them that. I did say that I had been a member of the Communist Party and that I had been kicked out for being gay. They wanted me to name people I had known in the Party and what they did. I owed no thanks to the Party for kicking me out, but I would not give information about individuals who were in the Party, whom I still respected.

The case went up through the Ninth Circuit Court of Appeals, and the courts found the magazine utterly obscene, with no redeeming social values. But for the time being, the seizure affected only the individual issue. We were only forbidden to mail out further copies of that particular issue of ONE. But then several other issues were held up for a month or two. So we began using extreme measures to mail the magazine. Each member of the staff would take several long drives. At each town we would go off the highway, find the mailbox and put in five or six copies. Nothing was on the plain brown wrapper to identify the magazine. Just the addressee and our return address. We mailed no more than fifteen or twenty copies in any one town.

We did this for three or four months before we discovered that the post office knew exactly what we were doing. About five weeks after we mailed one particular issue from towns all over southern California, I got a call from the post office to come in. The post office had virtually all of the issues we had mailed out for that month on a couple of flats. You see, they were inspecting each individual copy of the magazine we sent out for anything that they could hold it for, and some of the packages we mailed didn't have enough postage. There were different enclosures in each issue, depending on whether someone was getting a renewal notice. So a lot of issues would be right on the line as to whether they needed more postage, and because Dorr Legg, who was in charge of running the magazine, was always so much of a skinflint, he wouldn't let us use extra postage.

When I was called down by the post office, I had to weigh each magazine and put extra postage on about one out of ten copies. After that, we figured there was no point mailing the magazines from all over the state, since the post office obviously had no trouble finding each copy of the magazine we mailed, no matter where we mailed it from.

The ONE obscenity case went all the way up

to the United States Supreme Court, which reversed the lower court's ruling, clearing the magazine. That was in January 1958. Unfortunately, though, there was no written opinion from the Supreme Court. But the ruling sort of opened the floodgates to publications that discussed homosexuality. It ended the double standard over what was considered obscene, and we were never bothered again.

# I 72 I

# The Advocate: Setting the Standard for the Gay Liberation Press

## RODGER STREITMATTER

Throughout its first three centuries, American journalism responded to the taboo topic of homosexuality either by ignoring it or by denouncing it as a crime against nature. Reflecting society's dominant view of "the love that dare not speak its name," newspapers and later the broadcast news media covered gay men and lesbians largely in the context of crime stories and brief items that ridiculed effeminate men or masculine women. Only in the last decade have the news media covered gay America more fully. It is not surprising, then, that as the Gay Liberation Movement began to emerge in the second half of the twentieth century, a gay and lesbian press was created to provide a forum for issues that the establishment press refused to cover. This movement press committed itself to advocating gay rights while reporting on events, issues, and cultural trends of interest to the country's gay men and lesbians.

The first widely distributed gay publication in the United States was *ONE* magazine, produced by One, Inc., in Los Angeles from 1953 to 1969.[1] Martin Block, founding editor, recalled:

Before we began publication, there was absolutely nothing in the media about gays. From the main newspapers, you wouldn't have known there were any American homosexuals whatsoever.

We wanted to change that. We set out to show that homosexuals were very much a part of American society—and had every right to be.[2]

Block's magazine consisted mostly of fictional material, such as short stories and poems with gay themes; non-fiction material such as research findings and personal essays occupied a lesser role in the editorial mix. Like *ONE*, the next several gay and lesbian publications consisted largely of fiction. *Mattachine Review* was published by the Mattachine Society in San Francisco from 1955 to 1964;[3] The *Ladder* was published by the Daughters of Bilitis in San Francisco from 1956 to 1972;[4] and the *Homosexual Citizen* was published by the Mattachine Society of Washington, D.C., from 1966 to 1967.[5]

But it was not until the late 1960s that the first hard-hitting gay newspaper began publication. The *Los Angeles Advocate*, founded in September 1967, differed from earlier gay and lesbian publications in that it adopted a strict news orientation. Unlike its predecessors, the *Advocate* contained no fiction. Instead, its editorial mix consisted entirely of non-fiction material, including news

*Journalism History*, 19(3):93–102, 1993.

stories, editorials, and columns. It also was the first gay publication to operate as an independent business financed entirely by advertising and circulation revenue, rather than by subsidies from a membership organization.

The *Advocate* continues to be published today, having evolved into both the oldest and the largest of the country's three hundred gay and lesbian publications.[6] It boasts a bi-weekly circulation of ninety thousand and is available in urban centers from coast to coast.[7] The four-color, upscale magazine devotes most of its 100 pages to feature and entertainment material, and it carries advertisements from such major companies as Absolut vodka and Evian natural spring water.[8]

To the scholar of American journalism, however, the publication's earliest years define the most important period in its history. Because the *Advocate*'s first two years preceded the June 1969 Stonewall Rebellion, which marked the beginning of the Gay Liberation Movement in this country, the twenty-two pre-Stonewall issues of the newspaper offer a case study of the role that an advocacy press played in the embryonic stages of an important social movement.[9] Although Dick Michaels, the founder of the *Advocate*, is no longer living, statements that he made before his death in 1991 show that he perceived the newspaper as a tool of the emerging struggle for gay rights.[10] In 1975, Michaels said:

> One of the principal things any movement needs is a press of its own, a newspaper. Without that, you can't inform people of what's going on. You can't tie together widespread elements.[11]

▼ ▼ ▼

A framework for scholarly analysis of the *Los Angeles Advocate* is provided by research of other advocacy presses, such as those created by African-American, women's suffrage, and women's liberation publications. Like those forms of advocacy journalism, the *Advocate* sought to give voice to a segment of the population that had been denied access to standard mass communication outlets. Likewise, the early *Advocate*'s goal of ending discriminatory treatment of gay men and lesbians was comparable to the central goals of other advocacy presses.

Recent research, however, has shown that the benefits of these presses extended far beyond their primary goals. Scholars have suggested, for example, that black newspapers created African-American role models and developed a sense of black fraternity;[12] that the suffrage press served the movement by identifying leaders and allowing its ideology to be communicated to a much more diverse audience of women;[13] and that the women's liberation press of the 1960s initiated an open forum for feminist ideas.[14]

These concepts offer models to be kept in mind as the history and major themes of the early *Los Angeles Advocate* are considered.

The *Advocate* evolved from *PRIDE Newsletter*, an internal publication distributed to members of a gay organization in Los Angeles. In September 1967, Dick Michaels, a member of PRIDE (Personal Rights in Defense and Education), transformed the newsletter into a newspaper that he distributed to the larger community of gay readers in Los Angeles. Six months later, as PRIDE began to disband, Michaels purchased the *Advocate* from the organization for one dollar.[15]

Michaels worked full time as a technical writer for a chemistry magazine, while devoting his evenings and weekends to the *Advocate*. He later recalled his motivation for founding the newspaper: "The only way to reach the gay community in L.A. and to try to unify it was to turn the newsletter into a real newspaper and get it around to more people."[16]

Michaels and his lover, Bill Rand,[17] recruited friends to write articles and to gather around their dining room table once a month to paste up the typewritten pages. They financed the publication with personal savings of a few thousand dollars. Expenses were kept at a minimum because Rand, who worked in the mailroom at the headquarters of ABC television, surreptitiously printed the first several issues after hours on the offset printing press in the ABC office.[18]

Jim Kepner, who wrote the lead article in the first issue of the *Advocate* and continued to submit occasional articles to it for twenty-five years, recently recalled: "So ABC launched one of the most important gay publications in the history of this country—unknowingly to the top management, of course."[19]

Distributors refused to touch a gay publication. So Michaels and other volunteers took copies to the city's gay bars, which then were gay men's only refuge from a hostile society, and sold them for a quarter apiece. From the beginning,

Michaels refused to give away the paper, saying: "People don't respect anything they get for free."[20] After newsstand operators saw that there was a demand for the newspaper, they agreed to stock it.[21]

Some scholars of alternative journalism who have made passing reference to the gay press have characterized the *Advocate* as being more interested in making a financial profit than in supporting the movement.[22] Kepner insists, however, that Michaels's profit-making interests were secondary. Kepner recalled: "Dick definitely started the newspaper as a movement effort, but he also was convinced that a potential for financial success was there."[23]

An editorial in the first issue articulated the *Advocate*'s journalistic mission:

> Homosexuals, more than ever before, are out to win their legal rights, to end the injustices against them, to experience their share of happiness in their own way. If the ADVO-CATE can help in achieving these goals, all the time, sweat, and money that goes into it will be well spent.[24]

▼ ▼ ▼

The twelve pages of the 8′ by 11-inch newspaper were dominated by news stories and personal columns, all focusing on events and issues relevant to gay men. Less prominent elements included editorials, book and film reviews, an activities calendar, letters to the editor, and recipes.

Despite the broad mix of material, the *Advocate*'s forte was hard news. Michaels said: "All of our resources were directed toward what the straight press wouldn't print, and what gay people needed to know about what was happening in the world."[25]

Martin Block, who lived in Los Angeles and read the *Advocate* recalled:

> Dick wanted to create the *New York Times* of the gay press, to speak with a strong editorial voice while chronicling the events of gay America. He wanted to be a very proper newspaper—gay America's newspaper of record.[26]

Although the subtitle "Newspaper of the Homophile Movement" appeared below the *Advocate*'s flag, the newspaper was created primarily for gay men. The only editorial content directed toward lesbians was an occasional column titled "What's with the Ladies."[27] A clear definition of the newspaper's target audience came when it designed a promotional campaign titled the "Groovy Guy Contest," a beauty pageant with handsome young men taking off their shirts to win cash prizes. After publishing photographs of the contestants in advance, the *Advocate* featured the winner—wearing nothing but blue jeans and a boyish smile—on its front page.[28]

The *Advocate* boasted that all opinion expressed in its pages would be confined to editorials and columns, but in reality the *Advocate* was, as its name acknowledged, an advocacy newspaper.[29] For example, a page-one article about the California Supreme Court upholding the legality of drag shows contained the editorial statement: "The new changes in the regulations are a welcome step in the right direction—one that is long overdue in Los Angeles," and a front-page article reporting the acquittal of two PRIDE members who had been arrested at a gay bar carried the forty-two-point headline: "PRIDE WINS!!"[30]

Subjectivity did not dissuade readers from buying the paper. Indeed, it clearly spurred sales. By the *Los Angeles Advocate*'s first birthday, the original press run of 500 had jumped to 5,500 and Michaels had moved the operation into its own office.[31]

▼ ▼ ▼

Advertising soared as well. The first issue carried $27 worth of retail and classified advertising, only $12 of which was ever collected. But by the end of the first year, ads were bringing in several hundred dollars an issue.[32] The largest were from mail-order companies that specialized in homoerotic books and films. Smaller ads promoted local bars, restaurants, and bookstores that catered to gay patrons. The bar ads gradually became a major presence in the newspaper. Michaels said: "Gay bars could afford it, but they were not in the habit of advertising. We had to train them to advertise, and the training took a year."[33]

By mid-1968, advertising revenue had grown to the point that Michaels could hire a part-time advertising representative. Income easily covered the salesman's salary and the newspaper's other expenses. Michaels plowed the profits back into the newspaper, with all writers and editors continuing to donate their time.[34]

During its first year. the *Advocate* quadrupled

in size, expanding from twelve to forty-eight pages. In January 1969, Michaels transformed the newspaper into a twenty-eight-page tabloid and hired a distributor to place the papers in see-through vending machines throughout Los Angeles. Sales zoomed.[35]

The ambitious publisher's next goal was to transform his local newspaper into a national one. Although the *Advocate* always had contained some news about court cases beyond Los Angeles, it had to depend on readers to send clippings.[36] With the shift to a tabloid format, Michaels hired a professional clipping service that filled each issue with news items from cities as distant as Miami and Washington, D.C. He also added "San Francisco Scene" and "New York Scene" in which columnists summarized events in their gay meccas.[37]

▼ ▼ ▼

In June 1969, on the eve of the Stonewall Rebellion, Michaels resigned from his magazine job to work full time for the *Advocate*. And by his newspaper's second birthday that September, Michaels had increased the press run to a whopping 23,000, allowing distribution in New York, Boston, Washington, Miami, and Chicago. It was also at that point that Michaels began paying his writers for their contributions.[38] In the spring of 1970, the monthly *Los Angeles Advocate* became the bi-weekly *Advocate*.[39]

In another attempt at increasing circulation, the *Advocate* tried to advertise its existence in major metropolitan newspapers. Not a single newspaper accepted the advertisements. The *Los Angeles Times* and *Boston Globe*, among others, declined to run the ads—or to justify their refusal.[40]

Some authors who have written about the Gay Liberation Movement have criticized pre-Stonewall publications for retarding the struggle for gay and lesbian liberation. They have discounted the publications as part of the Homophile Movement of the 1950s and 1960s, during which gay men and lesbians attempted to gain acceptance by conforming to the behavioral standards of the larger society. One such writer described the early *Advocate* as "totally unlike gay liberation papers" because it adopted "a guarded position" on gay rights.[41]

But the newspaper's news and editorial content refutes such characterizations. The *Advocate*, unlike the lesbian and gay publications that preceded it, placed a great deal of emphasis on its editorial page.[42] Its editorial voice was relentless in demanding gay rights, consistently speaking both with defiance and with volume.

The *Advocate*'s most militant crusade was against the Los Angeles Police Department. An editorial in the second issue accused vice squad officers of inflating their arrest records by unjustly arresting patrons of gay bars. That editorial protested: "Is there police harassment? Hell, no! This is persecution." The editorial ended not with hysterical screams, however, but with a sense of strength and empowerment: "We do not ask for our rights on bended knee. We demand them, standing tall, as dignified beings. We will not go away."[43] Reinforcing the newspaper's position was an editorial cartoon depicting a police officer preparing to draw his gun against a muscular cowboy whose holster held a copy of the Bill of Rights.

The campaign against the police was fueled by Michaels's own arrest in a Los Angeles bar in 1966, the event that had drawn him into gay activism. Because of that raid, the bar had been forced to close and patrons had been fired from their jobs—routine events throughout the country during the 1950s and 1960s. Michaels paid $600 in legal fees before being found innocent.[44]

He later described the night of his arrest:

> Vice cops came in and arrested twelve people. I was one of those tapped on the back. I was charged with a misdemeanor, lewd conduct—and I hadn't done a damned thing!
>
> Up to that time I'd always said to friends, "What are you worried about? If you're not doing anything wrong, nothing's going to happen to you." I'd swallowed all the wonderful propaganda churned out by the Los Angeles Police Department. But after my arrest, I knew there was something radically rotten going on.
>
> There probably wouldn't be any *Advocate* if it were not for that one tap on the back.[45]

Kepner recently recalled: "Dick's intention was to get the police off our backs and get rid of discrimination. So he hit hard on the police."[46] The newspaper's aggressive attitude sometimes resulted in police harassment. Kepner said: "Police cars would park in front of the office and flash their lights at everybody who came in— intimidation."[47]

Michaels was undeterred. His crusade against the police reached a crescendo during the 1969

Los Angeles City Council campaign that pitted incumbent Paul Lamport, who supported the harsh police treatment of gays, against Jack Norman, a police critic. After two gay bars had been raided within a week, the editor's page-one editorial made a startling accusation:

Two sets of arrests in a week in the Silverlake area, one of eight people and the other involving two, lead inevitably to the question: Is the LAPD working for Councilman Lamport? If not, it is an amazing coincidence because both of the bars in which the arrests took place have been very active in the campaign of Jack Norman.[48]

▼ ▼ ▼

The *Advocate*'s charge resonated through the city, and the election provided an early example of the power of the gay voting bloc, as Councilman Lamport was defeated. The day after the election, Lamport attributed the loss to the gay community's opposition. The next issue of the movement newspaper began its lead editorial with the cocky statement: "Gay power DOES work! When homosexuals can be talked into going to the polls, they can make their power felt."[49]

The *Advocate* was eager to play a leading role in amalgamating the gay community's political power. Before the 1969 election, the newspaper sent questionnaires to all candidates for mayor and city council, publishing the responses and then editorially endorsing its preferences.[50]

As a movement newspaper, the *Advocate* also gave strong support when gays defied authority. In August 1968, for example, a Los Angeles bar raid foreshadowed the Stonewall Rebellion. When police entered the Patch and arrested two men, the other 250 customers did not cower or flee from the bar. Instead, they stood their ground and jeered at the police. Recognizing the significance of the event, Michaels labeled the event "historic," and stated: "A new era of determined resistance may be dawning for L.A.'s gay community."[51] He also lauded the men's action:

The ADVOCATE salutes the customers of the Patch for their courage, individually and collectively. By staying after the LAPD's obvious intimidation, each of them made a stand for his rights. It was a positive act. And only by a series of such positive acts will the LAPD learn once and for all that it cannot use its power to persecute people.[52]

The newspaper's most pro-active effort to mobilize its readers came in an editorial proposing that gays organize a fund-raising event to create a gay legal defense fund. After three months passed with no response, Michaels scolded his readers for ignoring him and repeated his proposal. This time it caught fire. Plans for a dance were made, and three months later the Homophile Effort for Legal Protection (HELP) was established.[53]

The *Advocate* helped unify and empower the gay community in less direct ways as well. Almost two years before the Gay Liberation Movement exploded into history with the raid in New York City, the West Coast newspaper was writing as if a revolution already were in full swing. Its editorials and news stories routinely used terms such as "the movement" and "the Cause." Indeed, the banner headline across the top of its first front page read: "U.S. Capital Turns On To Gay Power."[54]

Historians of the Gay Liberation Movement who have discussed the gay press of the early 1970s have cited its graphic language as one of the elements that separated it from the mainstream press.[55] Those scholars have ignored the fact, however, that between 1967 and 1969 the *Advocate* already had shattered the conventions of journalistic language, introducing a plethora of terms and phrases never before published in American newspapers.[56] Kepner recalled:

Gay self-respect was a primary concern Dick Michaels started the *Advocate*. He knew gays were guilt-ridden and we had to get rid of that. He knew gay men had to get comfortable with themselves and their community, and that included validating the language that we used. We knew what our words meant. Why not print them?

So he intentionally created a newspaper that spoke in the language that gay people used. He wanted to say: "We don't have to conform to the linguistic dictates of society. We have our own language which works quite well, thank you."

The *Advocate* was aggressively being who we are.[57]

▼ ▼ ▼

As it spoke in the lexicon of gay America, the *Advocate* set a standard that has been followed by the hundreds of gay and lesbian newspapers that have followed it. The vocabulary that the newspaper adopted would have been unintelligible to many readers, as gay men had developed an idio-syncratic code to allow them, as members of a repressed minority group, to identify and to com-municate with each other, while avoiding the dis-criminatory treatment that they had learned would accompany public knowledge of their homosexuality. The terms could be discounted as slang, the use of which was silly or sophomoric. Because the words were widely used among gay men, however, seeing them in print—and shar-ing a common understanding of them—served to unite readers into the emerging gay community in a process similar to the bonding that takes place when two or more people share an "inside joke."[58]

In the coverage of the male beauty contest that the *Advocate* sponsored, for example, a "groovy guy" was a code phrase for a handsome gay man.[59] A first-person article about police entrapment contained the statement: "A gor-geous vice officer in white levis and showing quite a basket came through and broke the ten-sion." Among gay men, a "basket" referred to the bulge created by a man's genitalia.[60] An article about a gay rights demonstration stated that pro-testers would be directed to the staging area by signs reading: "THIS WAY GIRLS." Gay male readers, unlike heterosexual ones, knew that many gay men refer to each other in feminine terms, a way of thumbing their noses at tradi-tional gender roles.[61]

A whimsical piece titled "We Wonder Why" contained numerous words and phrases with unique meanings to gay men. In "We wonder what it would be like to be chicken again," "chicken" referred to very young men. In "We wonder why Butches are a scarce commodity," "Butches" referred to masculine gay men. In "We wonder why hearing your last lover has the crabs makes you giggle," "crabs" referred to an uncom-fortable venereal disease that was then common among gay men. In "We wonder why everyone is on a sudden health kick, hiking through the parks in great numbers," "hiking through the parks" referred to gay men cruising wooded areas in search of sex partners, a ritual that had evolved during the decades when homosexual contacts of any type were outlawed.[62]

A reader unfamiliar with gay innuendo also missed messages in editorial cartoons. In the depiction of the police officer having a showdown with the Bill-of-Rights-wielding cowboy, for example, protruding from the cowboy's back pocket was a tube of KY jelly—a lubricant that gay men use to facilitate anal intercourse.[63]

Another venue for the gay lexicon was the pop-ular classified ad section, titled "Trader Dick's," that ran on the *Advocate*'s back page. A club exclusively for gay males grabbed the reader's attention with the opening line: "Are you getting your share?"[64] Another read: "MEXICAN HOUSEBOYS. $24.00 a month. Live-in type."[65] Another began: "Buttons won't get you laid but they do start conversations! In our line you'll find such titles as: 'Batman Loves Robin'; 'Turn On, Tune In, Turn Over.'"[66]

▼ ▼ ▼

The single design element that dramatically dis-tinguishes gay newspapers from mainstream as well as other alternative newspapers is homo-erotic images. Partly because of the homosexual repression throughout American society, appear-ance and physical attributes play a major role in the gay male culture. In concert with this value system, the bare skin of handsome young men dominates more pages of gay newspapers than do columns of gray type.[67]

Historians who have mentioned the rise of the gay press have attributed the emergence of this beefcake to the spate of tabloids—such as *Gay Flames* and *Come Out!*—that burst into existence in the wake of the Stonewall Rebellion.[68] But, as with the militant editorial voice and graphic lan-guage, this element was introduced by the *Advo-cate* during the late 1960s.[69]

Kepner recalled:

> Homoerotic images were a big part of gay men's lives. So validating them was impor-tant. The muscle magazines always pre-tended to be something else. They were, sup-posedly, for art students who couldn't afford to hire models but wanted to study the human anatomy.
>
> But the *Advocate* put it out there, saying: "This is what it is, and this is what it's for. And we're not ashamed to say it." It was saying: "Gay people are erotic people, sexual people. We're going to show that. We have a right to do it. And we're doing it with pride."[70]

Homoerotic images grew increasingly promi-nent and increasingly explicit in both the editor-ial and advertising content of the movement newspaper during its first two years. Long before the Stonewall Rebellion, the *Advocate* had estab-lished homoeroticism as a staple element of the gay press.

Initial artwork was mild and playful. The first was an in-house ad that contained a drawing of two men in bed, with one of them reading the *Advocate* as a puppy slept at their feet.[71] Paid advertising went a step further. An ad for Adonis, an adult bookstore in San Francisco, featured a sketch of a beefy blond man clothed in nothing but athletic socks and a fig leaf. Copy in the ad stated: "Very few items here for little old ladies!"[72]

During 1968, the images became more detailed. In February, a column discussing a nationwide trend toward increased nudity was accompanied by a life-like drawing of a nude man,[73] and the July issue observed Independence Day by featuring a front-page photo of a well-developed patriot wearing nothing but black leather boots and a snare drum strategically placed to cover his genital area.[74]

Kepner said the increased degree of explicitness in the images reflected Michaels's gradual understanding of his market:

> Dick learned that pretty pictures on the cover was the thing to sell the papers, to get them off the racks and into people's hands so they would read about what the police were up to.[75]

Beginning in July 1968—a full year before the riot at the Stonewall Inn—every issue of the *Advocate* featured a front-page image of a man with either his chest or his buttocks exposed. It may have been more than a coincidence that the second half of 1968 also was the period during which the newspaper tripled in size, jumping from sixteen pages in June to forty-eight pages in December. One image was a photograph of a man dressed only in undershorts; another was a bare-chested Sal Mineo from one of the actor's motion picture roles.[76] The most suggestive of the cover photos showed two male pornographic film stars, both nude.[77]

One particularly noteworthy inside photograph identified the subject as the man whom the University of California's division of fine arts had labeled a "Twentieth Century Adonis." The young man wore only undershorts as he posed for a class of sculpture students. The photograph was taken during the filming of the 1940 motion picture, "The Life of Knute Rockne." By the time the *Advocate* ran the photograph, the model/actor had become politician Ronald Reagan, the conservative governor of California. The sarcastic headline above the photograph read: "No Groovy Guy . . . But 20th Century Adonis?"[78]

The *Advocate*'s most shocking images were those in its advertisements, with many of them suggesting sadomasochistic activities. Ads for a series of books titled *Dungeon*, for example, featured a photo of a naked young man, from the rear, chained to a torture device,[79] and another photo showed a man tied spread eagle on a pool table as five men, all naked except for leather jackets, approached him menacingly.[80]

▼ ▼ ▼

When the *Los Angeles Advocate* appeared in the city's gay bars in September 1967, it broke new journalistic ground. For the first time, gay America had a newspaper of its very own. This pioneering publication was not, however, without an ancestry. For it was preceded by gay and lesbian magazines as well as by other alternative newspapers that had courageously attempted to reshape both the American media and American society, even though communication scholars have, until recently, tended to discount these other voices. It is from the scholarship relevant to alternative journalism that a researcher first should turn in an effort to suggest ways in which the *Advocate*—and, therefore, the gay and lesbian press—has benefitted the social movement that it has served.

This study does not purport to offer the definitive work on the gay and lesbian press as a genre of movement journalism. The initial findings do, however, indicate the richness of the primary sources for those interested in exploring this area of scholarship. Further, this study seeks to suggest some research themes and strategies that may be helpful as additional scholarship attempts to elucidate the evolution and contribution of this largely unexplored subject area.[81]

First, the *Advocate* gave the gay male and lesbian community a powerful voice. Although it was the country's first gay newspaper, it did not limp apologetically onto the journalistic stage. Instead, it raised a defiant editorial voice that was both strong and relentless. In speaking so boldly, the *Advocate* was reminiscent of another advocacy newspaper published 140 years earlier. It was in the spring of 1827 that the premier issue of *Freedom's Journal* announced: "We wish to plead our own cause. Too long have others spoken for us. Too long has the public been deceived by misrepresentations in the things that concern us dearly."[82] With those eloquent words, the African-American press was born. But the *Advocate* could have repeated the exact same words, for it also was demanding that an oppressed segment of American society be granted the equal rights promised by the United States Constitution. In raising that voice of militancy, the *Advocate* was fulfilling one of the most basic functions of the news media—to lead society in a new direction.

At the same time, the *Los Angeles Advocate* served what often is seen as the second, but seemingly contradictory, function of American journalism—to reflect the existing values of society. This was a particularly important role for the country's first gay newspaper, as it was speaking to a largely invisible segment of society that was only beginning to acknowledge the characteristics that distinguish it as a unique culture. By speaking in the lexicon of gay America and by publishing homoerotic images, the *Advocate* served to legitimate and to affirm gay values. Jim Kepner said: "Our way of thinking about ourselves has been formed to a large extent by the gay press. Validating who we are and what we want is a very important purpose of gay newspapers."[83]

Finally, the early *Advocate* benefitted the movement for gay rights by serving as a cohesive force for a diverse readership. Similar to the way in which women's suffrage and women's liberation publications united women from heterogeneous backgrounds, the *Advocate* unified gay men—and, to a lesser degree, lesbians—who shared a sexual orientation but varied widely with respect to age, occupation, socioeconomic level, ethnicity, and religion. As one scholar of social movements wrote:

A pressing rhetorical problem for aggregates of individuals moving towards a sense of community is the creation of a common identity. People create a common consciousness by becoming aware that they are involved in an identifiable group and that their group differs in some important respects from other groups. To come to such awareness, the members need to identify their collective self.[84]

The *Advocate* provided a venue through which gay Los Angeles, and eventually gay America, could identify its collective self. By demanding an end to police harassment and by reflecting the values of an emerging gay community, this movement newspaper served to galvanize individuals who previously had felt isolated in a society that was inhospitable to them.

## NOTES

1. One, Inc., was created specifically to publish the magazine, although the corporation's activities expanded to include conducting classes, sponsoring lectures, operating a counseling center, and participating in research projects. One, Inc., continues to exist in Los Angeles today.

2. Author's interview with Martin Block, 23 April 1993, in Washington, D.C. Block was born in New York City on 27 July 1919. After working as an editor for publishing houses in New York and Los Angeles, he and several other men founded ONE magazine in January 1953. Block served as editor for five months and continued to work with the magazine for six years.

3. The Mattachine Society was founded in Los Angeles in 1950 as the first national organization of homosexuals, dedicated to bringing about social and political change for gay men and lesbians. "Mattachines" were court jesters who performed during medieval times and who are thought to have been homosexual.

4. The Daughters of Bilitis was founded as a social club for lesbians in San Francisco in 1955 and evolved into the first national organization for gay women. "Bilitis" is the heroine of the "Songs of Bilitis," erotic poems published in 1894 by Pierre Louys; in the verses, Bilitis is portrayed as a contemporary of Sappho who lived a lesbian lifestyle on the island of Lesbos.

5. The Mattachine Society of Washington was founded in 1961, adopting the name of the national organization but functioning entirely independently of it.

6. The exact number of gay and lesbian publications is unknown. This figure is based on Margaret Cruikshank, *The Gay and Lesbian Liberation Movement* (New York: Routledge, 1992), 191, and the author's interview with Jim Kepner, 26 April 1993, in Washington, D.C. Kepner is the founder of the International Gay and Lesbian Archives in Los Angeles, the country's largest repository of gay and lesbian material.

7. Author's interview with John Knoebel, 8 July 1993, in Los Angeles. Knoebel is vice president/circulation for the *Advocate*.

8. The *Advocate* changed dramatically in 1975 after it was purchased by David B. Goodstein, a Wall Street investor, for a reported $300,000. Goodstein reduced news coverage and increased the number of feature articles and interviews. Goodstein died in 1985. See Niles Merton, "A legacy of victory," *Advo-*

*cate*, 6 October 1992, 10; Stephen J. Sansweet, "A Homosexual Paper, The Advocate Widens Readership, Influence," *Wall Street Journal*, 3 November 1975, 1.

9. The Stonewall Rebellion began the night of 27 June 1969 when New York City police raided the Stonewall Inn in Greenwich Village, and hundreds of drag queens, other gay men, and lesbians fought back, first by jeering at the police and then by throwing coins, rocks, bottles, and a parking meter or two. Several days of rioting followed the incident. On the history of the Gay Liberation Movement, see John D'Emilio, *Sexual Politics, Sexual Communities: The Making of a Homosexual Minority in the United States, 1940–1970* (Chicago: University of Chicago Press, 1983); Jonathan Katz, *Gay American History: Lesbian and Gay Men in the U.S.A.* (New York: Avon, 1976).

10. Dick Michaels was a pseudonym that the founder of the *Advocate* used. Out of respect for Michael's privacy, this article does not include his real name or identifying details about his life. Michaels was born to a middle-class family in upstate New York in 1926. He worked on high school and college newspapers before earning bachelor's and doctoral degrees in chemistry. After serving two years in the U.S. Army, Michaels conducted chemical research for private industry and then wrote for a chemical trade magazine in Los Angeles for five years, during the last three of which he simultaneously edited the *Los Angeles Advocate*.

11. Kay Tobin and Randy Wicker, *The Gay Crusaders* (New York: Arno, 1975), 80.

12. The most comprehensive examination of the goals of the early African-American press is Bernell Tripp, *Origins of the Black Press; New York, 1827–1847* (Northport, Ala.: Vision, 1992), especially 82–91.

13. The most comprehensive examination of the goals of the women's suffrage press is Martha M. Solomon, ed., *A Voice of Their Own: The Woman Suffrage Press, 1840–1910* (Tuscaloosa: University of Alabama Press, 1991), especially 27–29.

14. The goals of the women's liberation press are summarized in Maurine H. Beasley and Sheila J. Gibbons, *Taking Their Place: A Documentary History of Women and Journalism* (Washington, D.C.: American University Press, 1993), 185–204.

15. "Advocate Becomes Independent," *Los Angeles Advocate* (hereafter *LAA*), February 1968, 3. PRIDE ceased to exist in July 1968. See "PRIDE Dies After Long Illness," *LAA*, July 1968, 3.

16. Sansweet, "Advocate Widens Readership," 1.

17. Bill Rand was a pseudonym. Rand died in 1990.

18. Kepner interview.

19. *Ibid.* Jim Kepner's birthdate is unknown, as he was found abandoned in Galveston, Texas, on 19 September 1923, when he was about seven months old. After completing high school, Kepner joined the Communist Party and moved to New York City in 1945 to work as a copy boy and writer for the *Daily Worker*. After his homosexuality was discovered, he was expelled from the party in 1948. He then moved to California and worked a variety of jobs, including washing dishes and shoveling sand, while writing for *ONE* and *Mattachine Review*. Kepner began collecting gay materials in 1942 and founded the International Gay and Lesbian Archives in 1972. He continues to serve as curator of the archives today.

20. Sansweet, "Advocate Widens Readership," 1.

21. Kepner interview.

22. See David Armstrong, *A Trumpet to Arms: Alternative Media in America* (Los Angeles: J.P. Tarcher, 1981), 251; Roger Lewis, *Outlaws of America: The Underground Press and its Content* (New York: Penguin, 1972), 41; Abe Peck, *Uncovering the Sixties* (New York: Citadel, 1985), 218.

23. Kepner interview.

24. "Editorial: Happy Birthday To Us," *LAA*, September 1967, 6.

25. Sansweet, "Advocate Widens Readership," 1.

26. Block interview.

27. See, for example, Helen Sanders, "What's with the Ladies," *LAA*, October 1967, 9.

28. *LAA*, September 1968, 1.

29. "Editorial: Happy Birthday To Us," *LAA*, September 1967, 6.

30. Jack Foster, "Police OK Full Drag," *LAA*, February 1969, 1; "PRIDE WINS!!" *LAA*, November 1967, 1.

31. "Editorial: Happy Birthday to Us!" *LAA*, September 1968, 14; Tobin and Wicker, *Gay Crusaders*, 81–82.

32. Sansweet, "Advocate Widens Readership," 1.

33. Tobin and Wicker, *Gay Crusaders*, 81.

34. Tobin and Wicker, *Gay Crusaders*, 81; Dick Michaels, "Your Newspaper Gets Bigger, Bigger," *LAA*, December 1968, 2.

35. Sansweet, "Advocate Widens Readership," 1.

36. "Be a Junior Newsman," *LAA*, December 1968, 3.

37. "New Features," *LAA*, April 1969, 1.

38. Sansweet, "Advocate Widens Readership," 1; Tobin and Wicker, *Gay Crusaders*, 81–82.

39. "Editorial: Welcome, U.S.," *LAA*, August 1969, 30. With its April 29–May 12, 1970, issue, the

*Advocate* became a bi-weekly. That issue also was the last on which the flag read *Los Angeles Advocate*. With the May 13–26, 1970, issue, the flag was shortened to *Advocate*.

40. Sansweet, "Advocate Widens Readership," 1.

41. Dennis Altman, *Homosexual: Oppression and Liberation* (New York: Outerbridge and Dienstfry, 1971), 120.

42. The magazine format of *ONE, Mattachine Review, The Ladder,* and *Homosexual Citizen* precluded their having an editorial page as such, although all four contained material that could be described as opinion or interpretation.

43. "Editorial: Harassment? Hell No!" *LAA*, October 1967, 6.

44. Jeff Yarbrough, "We are born," *Advocate*, 6 October 1992, 8.

45. Tobin and Wicker, *Gay Crusaders*, 79–80.

46. Kepner interview.

47. Ibid.

48. "Is the LAPD Working for Lamport?" *LAA*, March 1969, 1.

49. "Editorials: Using Our Strength, *LAA*, August 1969, 30.

50. "Six of 21 Candidates Reply; Four Answer Advocate Questions," *LAA*, March 1969, 2.

51. Dick Michaels, "Cops Join Hoods in Harassing Bar," *LAA*, September 1968, 5.

52. "Editorial: Courage Catches On," *LAA*, September 1968, 5. See also "The Patch & the Bombshell," *LAA*, October 1968, 19.

53. "All Join Hands 'n Dance," *LAA*, May 1968, 8; "Editorial: Happy Birthday to Us!" *LAA*, September 1968, 4; "Not Hopeless Yet!" *LAA*, October 1968, 18; "Legal Defense Fund Takes Shape; Dance Put Off," *LAA*, November 1968, 3; "HELP Incorporates, Gets Off to Slow Start," *LAA*, December 1968, 3.

54. Jim Kepner, "U.S. Capital Turns On To Gay Power," *LAA*, September 1967, 1. For other examples of the use of Gay Liberation Movement terms, see "Gay Power—$$$," *LAA*, October 1967, 8; "Editorial: People Who Need People," *LAA*, November 1967, 6; Dick Michaels, "The World Is My Ashtray," *LAA*, January 1968, 4; "Editorial: Unity and Action, The Saving Grace," *LAA*, April 1968, 6.

55. Armstrong, *Trumpet to Arms*, 249–50.

56. In keeping with the assimilationist goals of the Homophile Movement of the 1950s and 1960s, the four gay magazines that preceded the *Advocate* consistently used the conventional language of mainstream journalism.

57. Kepner interview.

58. On the gay and lesbian community having a unique language, see James W. Chesebro, ed., *Gayspeak: Gay Male & Lesbian Communication* (New York: Pilgrim, 1981); Judy Grahn, *Another Mother Tongue: Gay Words, Gay Worlds* (Boston: Beacon, 1984); JoAnn Loulan, *The Lesbian Erotic Dance: Butch, Femme, Androgyny, and other Rhythms* (San Francisco: Spinsters, 1990); Bruce Rodgers, *Gay Talk: A (Sometimes Outrageous) Dictionary of Gay Slang* (New York: Putnam, 1972).

59. "Groovy Guy Pageant Scores," *LAA*, September 1968, 3.

60. Corbet Grenshire, "It's the Heat, Baby," *LAA*, March 1968, 3.

61. "1st L.A. Gay-in: Ultra High Camp," *LAA*, April 1968, 2.

62. Toni Lee, "We Wonder Why," *LAA*, March 1968, 5.

63. *LAA*, October 1967, 6.

64. *LAA*, September 1967, 12.

65. *LAA*, October 1967, 11.

66. *LAA*, June 1968, 15.

67. On the importance of homoerotic images in the gay male culture, see John D. Glenn, "Gay Fantasies in Gay Publications," in Chesebro, *Gayspeak*, 104–13; Wayne Sage, "Inside the Colossal Closet," in Martin P. Levine, ed., *Gay Men: The Sociology of Male Homosexuality* (New York: Harper & Row, 1979), 148–63.

68. Armstrong, *Trumpet to Arms*, 250–51; Lewis, *Outlaws of America*, 41; Peck, *Uncovering the Sixties*, 220–21.

69. In keeping with the conformist goals of the Homophile Movement of the 1950s and 1960s, the four gay magazines that preceded the *Advocate* assiduously avoided publishing images that could have been considered offensive to the sensibilities of heterosexual society.

70. Kepner interview.

71. *LAA*, October 1967, 8.

72. *LAA*, October 1967, 12.

73. *LAA*, February 1968, 5.

74. *LAA*, July 1968, 1.

75. Kepner interview.

76. *LAA*, March 1969, 1; February 1969, 1.

77. *LAA*, December 1968, 1.

78. *LAA*, January 1969, 20.

79. *LAA*, July 1968, 20.

80. *LAA*, October 1968, 25.

81. The lesbian and gay press is not mentioned in such standard histories of the American media as Michael Emery and Edwin Emery, *The Press and America: An Interpretive History of the Mass Media,* 7th ed. (Englewood Cliffs, N.J.: Prentice-Hall, 1992) or Jean Folkerts and Dwight Teeter, *Voices of*

a *Nation: A History of the Media in the United States* (New York: MacMillan, 1989). Nor is the gay and lesbian press considered in such histories of alternative journalism as Robert J. Glessing, *The Underground Press in America* (Bloomington: Indiana University Press, 1970); Lauren Kessler, *The Dissident Press: Alternative Journalism in American History* (Beverly Hills, Calif.: Sage, 1984); Laurence Leamer. *The Paper Revolutionaries: The Rise of the Underground Press* (New York: Simon and Schuster, 1972). It is the subject of one paragraph in Lewis, *Outlaws of America*, 41, and four pages in Armstrong, *Trumpet to Arms*, 249–53, and Peck, *Uncovering the Sixties*, 218–21. Two comprehensive studies of the gay press, both from a sociological perspective, were undertaken in the 1970s but never published. They are Harold Corzine, Jr., "The Gay Press" (Ph.D. dissertation, Washington University, St. Louis, 1977) and Alan D. Winter, "The Gay Press: A History of the Gay Community and Its Publications" (M.A. thesis, University of Texas, Austin, 1976).

82. On *Freedom's Journal*, see Tripp, *Origins of the Black Press*, 12–28.

83. Kepner interview.

84. Ernest G. Bormann, *The Force of Fantasy: Restoring the American Dream* (Carbondale: Southern Illinois University Press, 1985), 11.

# | 73 |

# Representation, Liberation, and the Queer Press

## POLLY THISTLETHWAITE

I came out in a library. It was in the "new" public library building, which was really the done-over old Sears store in my Midwestern town. The new library's whole queer section consisted of fifteen, maybe twenty books on two bottom shelves of a back wall range in a dark basement corner, no lie. I think the entire bookstack arrangement centered around those Dewey decimal queer 306.7s being tucked into the building's most out-of-the-way place. Anyhow, in there I found *Sappho Was a Right-On Woman*, *The Stone Wall*, and *Our Right to Love* nestled in with some socio-psycho trash like *Sexual Deviance* and *The Homosexual in America*. Of course I was afraid to check these books out, especially those Arno reprint series books with the burnt orange covers saying HOMOSEXUALITY all over them, so on Saturdays I would inconspicuously snatch them up along with bluff material from the nearby feminist 301s, and, flushed, take them to a table across the room to read. This was the bravest thing I'd ever done. If somebody who knew me came by, I could quick switch the books so it looked like I was reading Betty Friedan.

Lesbian and gay people lay special claim to the power of the printed word. It's through the printed word, consumed privately, anonymously, that we often first call ourselves queer, where we first find others who think what we think, do what we do, write what we feel. Coming out stories are thick with accounts of self-discovery through novels, dictionaries, magazines, libraries. The mass-mediated word, key to democracy and empire building both, also finds, unites, and empowers queer communities across regional, class, ethnic, and generational boundaries. All this is kept in check, of course, by censorship and a legion of insidious oppressive political and cultural constraints.

The lesbian and gay press has shaped and reflected the rise of gay and lesbian liberation. The proliferation of gay and lesbian newspapers, newsletters, and magazines in the U.S. has allowed us to weave a well-informed network of previously isolated individuals and insulated communities. In 1924, Chicago's Society for

In Brian Wallis, ed., *Democracy: Discussions in Contemporary Culture*, 5:209–212. Seattle: Bay Press, 1990.

Human Rights published two issues of the journal *Friendship and Freedom* before organizers were arrested and brought to trial on obscenity charges. No copies of the journal are known to exist; only photographs of the covers remain. Lisa Ben's *Vice Versa* appeared in 1947 and 1948, the earliest known lesbian periodical in the U.S. It was a carbon-copied newsletter passed hand to hand among a West Coast circle of friends—you know, the softball team and the secretarial pool, girls like that.

The national "homophile" organizations of the 1950s and 1960s (The Daughters of Bilitis, the Mattachine Society, and One) built themselves by defying the law against putting queer stuff in the mail. *One, Inc.* v. *Olesen* (355 U.S. 371, January 13, 1958) established that homophile publications were, yes, "more than cheap pornography," therefore eligible to be distributed by our postal service. The paperback porn industry began to boom postwar too, with drugstore lesbo pulp novels selling like hotcakes to dykes craving popular images of themselves. Other fringy mainstream but not specifically queer publications like physique magazines, science fiction club newsletters, grocery store scandal sheets, and eventually the *Village Voice* published queer-seeking-queer personals, like this one from the June 1, 1965 Wide World Confidential pullout section of the tabloid *Keyhole*: "MODERN MICHIGAN MODEL . . . with

understanding husband seeks uninhibited fun-loving females and couples . . . "

In the spring 1979 Lesbian Herstory Archives newsletter, Joan Nestle writes, "The roots of the Archives lie in the silenced voices, the love letters destroyed, the pronouns changed, the diaries carefully edited, the pictures never taken, the euphemized distortions that patriarchy would let pass." Self-representation is essential for liberation. We must represent ourselves to ourselves and others on our own terms. Historically, we've been the social, medical, religious, psychological, legal "other," "freak," "deviant" according to the reporter, anthropologist, physician, theologian, analyst, politician, artist. In large part, the gay, lesbian, and feminist publications of the late 1960s and 1970s, *The Advocate*, *Come Out!*, *Gay Community News*, *Lesbian Tide*, and *off our backs*, began as publications from activist organizations or collectives, steeped in radical politics. Community-sustained lesbian and gay archives cropped up across the country during the seventies and eighties, as did lesbian and gay presses and bookstores. Though not unfettered by notions of assimilation, success, and respectability, the rise of lesbian and gay publishers, distributors, and archives has allowed queers control of the way we represent ourselves to each other, fostering the rise of our liberation movement. The printed word, rendered by us for each other, allows the queer nation to build, bolster, and unify.

# | 74 |

# *Flaunting It! A Decade of Gay Journalism from The Body Politic*

### ED JACKSON

For as long as homosexuals have been visible and faintly vocal, they have been accused of being *too* visible and *too* vocal. They have been told that they are acting too flamboyantly, going too far, shoving it down people's throats. Journalists quip

that the love that dared not speak its name now

In Ed Jackson and Stan Persky, eds., *Flaunting It! A Decade of Gay Journalism from The Body Politic*, pp. 1–6. Vancouver: New Star/Toronto: Pink Triangle, 1982/95.

won't shut up. And so on. In a 1928 column in the London *Sunday Express* attacking Radclyffe Hall's lesbian novel *The Well of Loneliness*, an editor said of homosexuals, "They flaunt themselves in public places with increasing effrontery and more insolently provocative bravado." In 1981 Peter Worthington, the editor of the *Toronto Sun*, wrote, "Every literate person should know that 'flaunt' is what some homosexuals do with their preferences."

*The Body Politic*, as one of the most visible gay institutions in Canada, has often been subjected to this predictable and increasingly gay-specific accusation. *Our very existence* has been interpreted as shaking an irreverent lavender fist under the noses of an affronted citizenry. Outrage, simulated or otherwise, has been the standard response of the morality-watchers.

"When a heterosexual shows a picture of his family, it's called sharing." observed lesbian comic Robin Tyler. "When we show them a picture of our lover, it's called flaunting. Isn't it time we shared?"

The discrepancy between what *The Body Politic* has actually done or written and what the ignorant, the fearful and the cynical accuse us of doing is so wide that it becomes a significant phenomenon in itself. Given how simple it is to earn the "flaunting" brickbat, it seemed time to transform it into a sweet-smelling, book-title bouquet for the world of willing readers.

## SURVIVAL

Gay pride took a quantum leap forward throughout North America in 1969, the year the gay liberation movement marks as its symbolic birth. It was the year that street queens and other bar-goers responded in an unexpected way to an harassment visit by New York policemen to a Greenwich Village bar on Christopher Street called the Stonewall Inn. The customers fought back, demonstrated, threw things at the police, distributed flyers and experienced, for the first time, the astonishing sensation of resistance.

The match, once struck, ignited a movement. The next four years saw the burgeoning of a gay press, irrepressible, irreverent, militant, lively. Social change movements, sociologist Laud Humphreys has said, "must find a common language, develop ideology, counter the propaganda control exercised by the state and communicate both warnings and hope. . . . The role of the gay press becomes a central and decisive one in the

movement for gay freedom."

One by one the journals bloomed: *Gay Sunshine* in San Francisco (August 1970), *Gay Liberator* in Detroit (April 1970), *Fag Rag* in Boston (Summer 1970), *The Body Politic* in Toronto (November 1971), *Gay News* in London, England (June 1972), and *Gay Community News* in Boston (June 1973). Suddenly so much had to be written, so much had to be said, and finally there was an audience hungry to read and eager to listen.

*The Body Politic* began as a radical tabloid born of political conviction and a hunger for change. None of its founders paused to consider the risks. No one thought of conducting a market survey to determine if there was a readership that could sustain a gay liberation magazine in Canada. Since 1971, *The Body Politic* has evolved gradually into a Toronto-centred community service newspaper with a strong national outreach, concerned with discrimination, rights and community as the immediate and practical aspects of liberation, oppression and the gay movement. Increasingly, it is also concerned with investigating the real lives of gay people, the everyday aspects of their sexuality, loves and lives.

*The Body Politic* has made many changes over the years. It discovered, for example, that it was necessary to accept display advertising in order to maintain financial solvency and that it didn't hurt to learn a few simple techniques of traditional magazine management. It learned that serving its community also meant providing basic features like classified ads and entertainment and community event listings. That functioning in the Canadian magazine world made it useful to join in common cause with other struggling periodicals. That to maintain the right to publish a magazine for sexual liberation requires an ongoing legal defence fund and increasing familiarity with the meatgrinder of the legal system.

*The Body Politic* is a testament to survival rather than a Canadian publishing success story (or are they the same thing?).

## TOMORROW'S POCKET

Issue One of *The Body Politic* tumbled off the presses in November 1971. Hawked on the streets and inside gay bars in Toronto and sold for the modest sum of twenty-five cents, it is very much a document of a particular time and place.

A lead article called "Unmasquerade" contained musings about gender roles and oppression. It was followed by an article on coming out ("Closet door, closet door, I don't need you any more") and an article on "The power of zapping," which discussed the early gay liberation tactic of gay couples entering straight clubs to "liberate" the dance floor. Reviews of the film *Sunday, Bloody Sunday* and E. M. Forster's early gay novel *Maurice* presaged *The Body Politic*'s persistent concerns with the cultural image of the homosexual. The first Community Page contained a brave little list of all of the known gay organizations in the country. One feature was called "Sweeping statements, or the ambivalence of the universe," in which the author earnestly proclaimed: "The oath to self-actualization and to a life-affirmative unity of our species must begin by seeing through the reality games which alienate and divide us." We used to say things like that. A lot.

In 1971, to have produced this twenty-page folded newsprint tabloid with its quirky counter-cultural layout and typewritten text was the most exciting activity imaginable to the little band of pioneers who called themselves the editorial collective. Over the years, hundreds of contributors and volunteers have come and gone, some have stayed longer than others, but most of them would echo the words of long-time collective member Gerald Hannon:

"I got hooked, I guess, on empowerment, the transformation of The Helpless Queer with no history and an unlikely future into Someone, into a *group* of Someones, who uncovered a history, who found heroes, who grabbed today and shook it till tomorrow fell out of its pocket and there was a place there in it for us."

## THE PERSONAL VOICE, THE POLITICAL ACT

The personal is political. Sexual politics matter. These are two fundamental principles that the gay liberation movement has learned from the women's movement. After 1969, homosexuals found an entirely new way to view their place in the world. The gay movement provided, once again in the words of Gerald Hannon, "that quick, sharp snap with the past that lifted people out of their frightened, reflex hesitations about their sexuality." That gay is good has always been one of the shiningly simple messages of the gay movement, especially to homosexuals needlessly handicapped by doubt and shame. It is a message that *The Body Politic* has tried to communicate

over and over again, for it continues to be a fresh revelation to new generations of young lesbians and gay men emerging from the prison of social condemnation. Affirming the validity of a homosexual identity is a political act and challenging the social and institutional control of our sexual lives is a political struggle. . . .

Words are our medium. Many of these words have come from writers who are not professional in any traditional sense. Some writers first found their voice in *The Body Politic*. Some have gone on to write elsewhere. Some have written nothing since. It is a source of pride that we have helped to penetrate the silence of decades and provided a medium for the articulation of previously unspoken emotions and ideas of gay people.

## THE PINK TRIANGLE

"Part of the oppression of gay people lies in the denial of our history," wrote gay historian James Steakley in 1973. "The veiled allusions, isolated anecdotes and embarrassed admissions which occasionally crop up in standard works of history provide ample evidence of this mode of oppression, which functions by silence and distortion."

Steakley was introducing his pioneering history of the early German homosexual emancipation movement, published as a three-part series in *The Body Politic*. The series was the first discussion in English of a movement which had flourished in Germany until crushed by the Nazis in the 1930s. Steakley's account was sobering: what had once been a significant force for change for homosexuals had virtually disappeared from memory. How could it have happened? Could it happen again? That series whetted our appetite for more knowledge of the past.

*The Body Politic* has long understood the importance of history in creating a sense of gay identity, and its editors and writers actively pursued articles which popularized an understanding of our past and highlighted the lessons from early movements. In 1975 *The Body Politic* organized itself legally as a non-profit corporation and chose the name Pink Triangle Press. The pink triangle was used by the Nazis to identify homosexuals in concentration camps. *The Body Politic* helped to popularize the pink triangle both as a symbol of hope and as a reminder of oppression. We placed the words of an early German gay activist on our masthead as a guide to present and future actions: "The liberation of homosexuals can only be the work of homosexuals themselves."

## "We'll Take This Place Apart"

They came on a Friday afternoon before a long New Year's Eve weekend. They even sent out for chicken sandwiches and coffee. That was when I realized they were going to stay for awhile.

It was December 30, 1977, and "they" were five burly members of Operation P, a special joint Toronto/provincial police unit set up to investigate pornography. Operation P had arrived at *The Body Politic* office armed with a search warrant to collect information in preparation for laying charges.

I happened to be in the office during that raid. When, on the advice of our lawyer Clayton Ruby, I refused to help the policemen find certain records, the sergeant in charge said, with a menacing grade-B-movie cop stare, "All right. We'll take this place apart." Nearly four hours later, twelve cartons of office documents and material were disappearing slowly down the service elevator.

On January 5, 1978 a charge was laid, under Section 164 of the Criminal Code ("use of the mails to transmit immoral, indecent and scurrilous material"), referring to an article called "Men loving boys loving men" in the current issue of *The Body Politic*.

With the police raid and the laying of charges, the life of *The Body Politic* changed abruptly and forever. When once the worst we could expect was low-level media harassment and a bland refusal to acknowledge our existence, we now faced palpable risks. Our right to publish had become an issue. *The Body Politic* was transformed into a legal case.

The newspaper found itself fighting for its life. In order to pay legal expenses we organized a defence fund which, before the legal battle was over, had raised thousands of dollars from a generous community. We worked to turn around the frightened reaction which caused some individuals to say to us: "You deserve everything you get." We helped people to rethink their views on pedophilia and to understand that the central issue was the freedom of a community's press. We went to court in 1979 and were acquitted in the flashiest trial the gay community had ever experienced. Despite the Crown's successful appeal of this decision, the long process gained us the sup-

port of many people, both gay and straight. And we continued to publish.

## Now Obscene

Even as this introduction was being written, *The Body Politic* was confronted with a fresh legal challenge. In early May, 1982 plainclothes officers from Metro Toronto Police's Morality Squad appeared at *TBP* offices armed with a search warrant. Although they took nothing during the raid, on May 12 they charged all nine members of *The Body Politic* editorial collective with "publishing obscene material." The charge referred to an article in the April issue on the etiquette of fist-fucking entitled "Lust with a very proper stranger." At the same time, a retrial on the January 1978 charges of sending immoral, indecent and scurrilous material through the mails was less than three weeks away.

That retrial (ordered by an appeal judge in a legal system that does not prohibit double jeopardy) turned out to be a shorter, much saner version of the first event. The social climate appeared to be less hysterical, the media did not sensationalize its coverage, and the Crown attorney showed little relish for his appointed task. On June 15, 1982 a provincial court judge acquitted Pink Triangle press and its officers of the same charges a second time.

The founders of *The Body Politic* could never have foreseen that the magazine would be forced constantly into challenging the limits of press freedom in Canada. But laws which classify and criminalize writing with antiquated and vague terms like "immoral," "indecent," "scurrilous" and "obscene" are clearly a threat to our ability to talk about our lives as gay people in the language of our choosing. Likewise, laws that define and stigmatize our sexual practices as "gross indecency" and as "indecent acts," and label our sexual and social meeting places, even our homes, as "common bawdyhouses" are a threat to our ability to live and love on our own terms.

Having found our voice a mere ten years ago, *The Body Politic* is not about to shut up now. Our task couldn't be clearer: keep warning, keep hoping, keep talking, keep visible.

## Looking Back (1995)

Only five years after the *Flaunting It!* introduction appeared, *The Body Politic's* voice was abruptly stilled. Number 135, dubbed the "Farewell issue" on its cover, hit the newsstands in February 1987. The preceding issue had optimistically celebrated "our first 15 years" of publishing, and contained no hint of impending trouble. The sudden demise surprised even people close to the operation. What happened?

The immediate crisis was financial, belatedly discovered (money management was never *TBP*'s strength). The cause of dwindling revenues was simple enough: fewer people were reading the paper and fewer advertisers were buying space. The larger, and more fundamental, crisis, however, was an exhaustion of spirit and vision evident in the small core of writers and editors who had kept the magazine going since its early days. By 1987, most of these people—myself included—had left the editorial collective or were in the process of leaving. Finding and keeping committed staff to replace the weary old guard become a chronic problem for *TBP* in its final years.

There was no doubt that the protracted legal battle had taken its toll, although *TBP* could justifiably boast that the state's considerable efforts to get a conviction had failed miserably. The obscenity charge based on the fistfucking article was thrown out of court in a one-day trial in November 1982. The Crown went through the motions of appealing the second acquittal of "Men loving boys loving men," but a few months later let a crucial final deadline slip by without taking action. The seized material was returned, finally, in April 1985. And so the legal ordeal ended—seven years, two charges, three trials, six appeals, and more than $100,000 in lawyers' bills later.

In the early Eighties the editorial collective had come to realize that a single print medium was no longer adequate to carry out all of the roles *TBP* had set for itself. We began to understand that *TBP* had been trying to function simultaneously as a national news magazine and as an international theoretical journal of gay liberation. What we sometimes overlooked was that *TBP* was also rooted in a particular city and a particular community. As the lesbian and gay commercial and cultural scene in Toronto grew and diversified, the need for a local gay paper appealing to a wider audience became apparent. We were reminded by an academic called as a defence witness at one of *TBP*'s trials that a reader needed a first-year college education to read the magazine.

In 1984 Pink Triangle Press launched *Xtra*, a Toronto-based free-distribution supplement. Published bimonthly and containing mostly local cultural coverage, event listings and advertising, *Xtra* grew quickly into a separate publication. It soon was being read by far more people than the subscription-based *TBP* had ever been able to attract. *Xtra* and *The Body Politic* managed to coexist for three years, but when the budget crunch came at the end of 1986, it was clear which of the two publications had become the financial drain.

Over time Pink Triangle Press recovered its financial footing. By the mid-Nineties, *Xtra* had become the largest and most successful lesbian and gay newspaper in Canada. Recently the press launched two sister publications, *Capital Xtra* in Ottawa and *Xtra West* in Vancouver. A sign of changing economic realities, the expansion was financed in part with profits from a sideline operation employing the latest technological developments in audio-text phone sex ads. Despite *Xtra*'s success, its easy-to-digest news briefs and bite-sized features are a far cry from *The Body Politic*, which for a long time enjoyed an international reputation for the depth and consistency of its political and cultural analysis.

Several factors may have contributed to this reputation. Throughout its history, *TBP* operated as an editorial collective. Feature articles and editorials were always discussed with passion and intelligence before being published. Although there were often vehement internal disagreements, a collective viewpoint eventually resulted. For years, *TBP*'s masthead claimed its editorial efforts to be "a contribution to building a gay movement and the growth of gay consciousness." At one point in the middle of the seemingly endless court appeals, a *TBP* advertisement for donations to its legal defence fund asked rhetorically: "Why don't you people just pay the fine, get out of court, and get back to publishing?" The ad's response was clear: far from being a distraction from *TBP*'s primary task of building a political movement, the legal battle *was seen to be our work.*

*The Body Politic* was uniquely blessed with a stable core of writers and editors conscious of our pioneering role in a new social movement. Although there were strong egos in this core of writers, no one individual came to personify the magazine in the public eye. As a collective, we were unshakeable in the conviction that a different kind of lesbian and gay community was in the making, and that we were playing a key role in creating it. Over the years, the collective never wavered from our certainty in the liberatory power of sexuality. To top it off, *The Body Politic* was also remarkably well written. Its editors made the craft as well as the content of progressive journalism a significant goal.

Written early in 1982, my original *Flaunting It!* introduction made no mention of AIDS, because *TBP* had barely begun to report on what we were still calling "gay cancer." A few months later, however, in an important November 1982 article called "The case against panic," activist Michael Lynch offered a cogent analysis of the dangers of letting the medical profession dictate the community's response to AIDS. He warned against taking premature steps that would destroy our few hard-won advances in sexual liberation. At the time, *TBP*'s calm political stance stood out in sharp contrast to most of the American gay press, which was caught up in a wave of anti-promiscuity hysteria. That cautious perspective on AIDS continued for the remainder of *TBP*'s life, and exposed it to occasional accusations of recklessly downplaying the extent of the crisis.

*The Body Politic* brought a consistent sexual libertarian analysis to the topics animating the sex debates of the Eighties: man-boy love, public sex, pornography, and S/M. It also provided an editorial home for a group of lesbian writers who critiqued the strategies of the anti-porn feminists, warned against the perils of censorship, and presaged the growth of today's transgressive lesbian sex culture. A healthy scepticism of state regulation in sexual matters was a hallmark of *TBP*'s

political analysis throughout its history. It was a Left-influenced critique of state power often at odds with the increasingly vocal advocates of assimilation and respectability within the gay community.

One issue *TBP* failed to come to terms with was the growing significance of race within lesbian and gay communities. Only once, in 1985, did a vigorous debate about race appear in the pages of the magazine. It was precipitated by reactions to the publication of a classified ad from a white man looking for a black "house boy." The debate left a residue of bitterness within sectors of the Toronto community and crystallized fundamental political polarities within the collective itself.

In the end, it seemed, *The Body Politic* could not keep up with the rapid shifting terrain of lesbian and gay identities and cultures. An atmosphere of scarcity had once made its voice essential, but by 1987 the chorus of queer voices was more diverse and the available media for expression more numerous. American activists, once loyal subscribers, came to find *TBP*'s cultural and news coverage too local to interest them. A new generation of readers and writers began to view *TBP* as a dinosaur—pigheaded, single-minded, and "too political."

Eventually, *The Body Politic*'s unique history of stubborn endurance came to feel like an ideological liability. Looking back nearly a decade later, that record of passionate engagement looks very much like its greatest strength.

# | 75 |

# *I Want My Gay TV*

## LARRY CLOSS

"Have you heard about the newest cable channel?" asked Jay Leno in a recent *Tonight Show* monologue. "It's called the Gay Cable Network. What do you think talk shows are like on that channel? 'Men who sleep with *women* on the next *Randy!*' "

Leno's attempt at levity to the contrary, the Gay Cable Network (GCN) is no joke. It's also not an actual network or channel. It's a Manhattan-based TV production company responsible

*Out*, September 1994, pp. 60–66, 120–123.

for eight weekly programs aimed at gay and lesbian viewers that are seen on public-access and leased-access channels. And although one of those programs *is* a talk show, it's actually more like Leno's than Oprah's.

Lou Maletta, the bald, mustached 50-something founder of GCN, was among a group of 30 who gathered in New York earlier this year for a weekend summit on the state and fate of gay and lesbian television—TV produced by gays for gays (as opposed to network and cable shows that feature incidental gay and lesbian characters). On a Friday evening they converged on the cavernous downtown loft of Marvin Schwam—founder of another production company, Gay Entertainment Television (GET)—to meet, greet, and eat while watching five-minute clips of gay and lesbian TV shows from across the country, produced by some of those present.

For almost two hours, tapes popped in and out of the VCR in Schwam's flamboyantly furnished quarters—described by one awed visitor as "a cross between the Bat Cave and an Oriental bordello"—as highlights from gay and lesbian talk shows, game shows, fashion shows, variety shows, and even a soap opera flashed by on the screen of Schwam's 45-inch projection TV.

Hope for a future in which such viewing options are commonplace is what brought so many together, at Schwam's loft that night and at a conference room in the Pennsylvania Hotel the next day. They were there because they believe that gay and lesbian TV is approaching the critical mass that makes its move to mainstream television inevitable. The increasing volume and diversity of lesbian and gay TV shows on public-access and leased-access channels—and the fact that a few have attracted national advertisers—have created the buzz that we are on the verge of gay television's prime time. Adding fuel to the fire have been articles in *Newsweek*, *The New York Times*, the *Los Angeles Times*, *Inside Media*, and *The Village Voice*, as well as a CNN Headline News report, and the unlikely presence of GET at the 1994 TV industry program bazaar sponsored by the National Association of Television Program Executives (NATPE).

Should we believe the hype? Not necessarily. More than anything else, the New York workshop proved to be a reality check that revealed the significant obstacles still standing in the way of gay and lesbian TV. Problems with content, quality, financing, distribution, visibility, marketing, and the radical Right must be overcome if we ever

really expect to get with the program.

▼ ▼ ▼

Gay TV began in the late '70s as a reaction to the general lack of gay-oriented programming on network television. Except for the occasional made-for-TV movie (1972's *That Certain Summer* with Hal Holbrook and Martin Sheen, 1978's *A Question of Love* with Jane Alexander and Gena Rowlands), and the occasional character in a sitcom or dramatic series (Billy Crystal as Jodie on *Soap*, Al Corley and Jack Coleman as Steven Carrington on *Dynasty*), gay men and lesbians rarely saw themselves when they watched TV. To the rescue came cable, camcorders, and the Federal Communications Commission (FCC).

As cable companies spread across the country, the FCC mandated that a number of channels on each system be reserved for public access, offering free TV time to anyone inclined to play producer. Would-be TV execs could do their thing with production equipment often provided by cable companies, or with their own home-video cameras, available and affordable for the first time. Leased-access channels offered another avenue, supplying inexpensive airtime, and—unlike public access—allowing the sale of commercials.

One of the first to fully grasp the potential of this new outlet was Maletta, who, in 1982, began producing *Men & Films*, a weekly half-hour review of new male porn videos, taped in his Manhattan apartment and shown only in New York. "People were starting to buy a lot of VCRs and porn videos," says Maletta. "At that time there were no rental clubs, you had to buy videos. When you got home and put the tape in the machine, you frequently found out that the quality of the picture on the box was a hell of a lot better than the quality of the tape, and whoever was in the picture wasn't even *in* the tape."

*Men & Films* quickly evolved beyond its original premise. "This was 1982, the beginning of the AIDS epidemic," Maletta recalls. "The gay community was becoming aware that there was this new kind of cancer going around. By the eighth show, we started including short news segments about it, because nobody in the straight media was even discussing it."

Twelve years later, Maletta still produces *Men & Films*, but the short news segments have grown into an hourlong news show, *Gay USA*, seen on access channels in 22 cities. He now owns a fully equipped studio with 15 cameras, two editing suites, and a postproduction facility, with which he produces a total of eight shows. The studio itself reveals his range of interests: In one corner sits the elaborate set for the late-night talk show *Stonewall Place After Dark*, an incredibly detailed replica of a New York City subway station. In the opposite corner hangs a sling that's seen its share of action on *In the Dungeon*, a hard-core look at the leather and S/M scene.

While Maletta may have been one of gay TV's pioneers, he is no longer the only game in town. A former associate, Barry Z (as in Zabuski), has gone on to create his own slate of shows. His Alternative Television/Total Entertainment Network Plus, which rather boldly claims to be "the largest producer of gay and lesbian TV in the world," churns out eight weekly programs seen in New York, Los Angeles, and Miami, including *The Barry Z Show*, an in-studio celebrity schmooze-fest, and *Drag Talk*, which is self-explanatory. Meanwhile, Schwam's Gay Entertainment Television, available on access channels in New York, Los Angeles, San Francisco, Miami, and Chicago, as well as on satellite, produces the co-sexual *Party Talk*, a loose and loopy look at who's fierce and what's fabulous; *Makostyle*, a fashion magazine hosted by Andy Warhol protégé Christopher Makos; and *Inside/Out*, an issues-centered talk show for lesbians and gay men.

All the shows Maletta, Schwam, and Barry Z produce and distribute represent only a fraction of what's out there. Also based in New York are two news and entertainment magazines, *Dyke TV*, seen in 15 cities and on satellite, and public television's *In the Life*, seen on 70 stations. But New York doesn't have a monopoly on access shows. Originating from Fairfax, Virginia, is a similar show, *One in 10 People*, seen in 25 cities, and from Los Angeles comes *Tricks*, a gay version of *Studs* seen in five cities. In addition, there are dozens of shows locally produced and presented, from *Lavender Lounge*, a San Francisco-based variety show, to *Latinos en Acción*, a New York interview show for gay and lesbian people of color. Taking a slightly different tack, there are mail-order videotape magazines such as *Network Q*, based in Albuquerque, and *One TV*, based in Houston, which was launched in May.

Recently there have even been a few isolated examples of gay TV—or at least gay-friendly TV—shown on national television. In January a six-hour adaptation of Armistead Maupin's *Tales of the City* aired on PBS's *American Playhouse*, and last December cable's Comedy Central telecast *Out There*, a one-hour special showcasing gay standups. (A sequel was taped during Gay Games in June for broadcast October 11, National Coming Out Day.) HBO is also getting into the act, having given two of the comics featured in *Out There*—Suzanne Westenhoefer and Bob Smith—their own half-hour specials in July.

▼ ▼ ▼

Not everyone who's anyone in gay TV was on hand at the New York workshop, but a substantial number were, as well as a few interested observers. All maintained that a significant gay and lesbian presence on television will help unite a divided community and dispel longstanding stereotypes.

"We are the most disparate group of people on the planet," says NBC News producer Joe DeCola. "We have two things in common: who we fall in love with, and repression. Everything else about us is vastly different. One of the reasons we are relatively weak in what should be such a clear struggle is that we don't have a place to build consensus, a place to talk to each other, a place to find our voice. Electronic media is the solution to that."

"This is not just gay programming," adds Schwam. "This is programming that will allow straight America to make gay friends. In addition to giving gay America many intelligent, talented peers to look at every week, gay TV gives straight people a chance to see what our culture is really all about, as opposed to the tabloid talk shows that emphasize the sensational aspects of our community."

But gay TV itself sometimes emphasizes the sensational aspects of our community, raising concerns about what face we should put forward. What, for instance, would a casual channel surfer think if he or she were unexpectedly confronted by Hedda Lettuce camping it up on *Drag Talk*, or Slave Dale being bound and gagged on *In the Dungeon*?

"I think we have to stop thinking about positive images and start focusing on diverse images," says Donald Suggs, director of public affairs at the New York chapter of the Gay and Lesbian Alliance Against Defamation (GLAAD). "One of most exciting things about these shows is that they present a much more diverse view of the gay, lesbian, drag, bisexual, and transgender community than you see in the straight media. On *Party Talk*, for instance, you have someone like movie reviewer [and GLAAD membership director] Cathay Che, who is really projecting to an audience that hasn't been reached, gay Asian-Americans. *Party Talk* is also one of the few shows where you see a drag queen being taken seriously. A lot of it is tongue-in-cheek, but as the host, Linda Simpson is not there for you to laugh *at*, she's there for you to laugh *with*."

As the producer and host of *Latinos en Acción*, Carlos Cordero feels that it's imperative for any program designed to meet the needs of a particular group within the gay and lesbian community to speak to the entire community as well. "My show is definitely for people of color, but the message is universal," says Cordero, 30, program manager of Project ACHIEVE (AIDS Community Health Initiative Enroute to a Vaccine Effort). "One thing I struggle to make the gay community understand is that we're too few to fight among ourselves."

It was the lack of a unified front that led to the founding of *Dyke TV* in June 1993, by Mary Patierno, Linda Chapman, and Ana Maria Simo. "The reason we started *Dyke TV* is that a lot of the shows that bill themselves as 'gay' tend to have more to do with gay men than lesbians," says Patierno, 35, who teaches at New York's School of Visual Arts. "We feel like we're filling a void. Unless we put the programming out, the past has shown that the programming won't be sensitive to our needs and issues. Lesbians have always worked in coalition with other groups, and for years our issues were put on the back burner. I think the reason there's an emerging lesbian movement is because we've come to the realization that in order to have our issues addressed, we have to do it, because nobody else will."

John Scagliotti, executive producer of *In the Life*, supports Patierno's approach. "I wouldn't call it separatist," says Scagliotti, 45, a 25-year veteran of both radio and television who won an Emmy for his documentary *Before Stonewall*. "The movement's strength is in its diversity— sometimes we come together as individuals, and sometimes we come together as coalitions." As for the content of his show, however, he has his own agenda. "I enjoy being conservative at this point. I enjoy the challenge of creating programming that's definitely for everyone, gay or straight, and creates a link between both worlds. There are straight people who work on *In the Life*, and there are straight program managers who choose to air it. We have a lot of 'Mr. and Mrs.' who send money."

Thirty-something Barry Z also views his shows as somewhat conservative, explaining that they're a reaction to what came before. "The reason I got into this is that I was sick and damn tired of gay and lesbian TV being equated with sex," he says (though he can't resist joking that the abbreviation for his company, Total Entertainment Network Plus, is 10+—"every inch great entertainment!"). "I wanted to make gay and lesbian TV more respected and accepted by everyone—the gay and lesbian community *and* the straight community. Just because Lou Maletta was a pioneer doesn't mean he gave gay TV a good reputation."

That Maletta continues to produce *In the Dungeon*, a New York–only show that occasionally features explicit sexual content, is of some concern to others as well. But Maletta defends *Dungeon* in spite of its critics. "The number of sexual programs out there is minuscule," he says. "However, sex is so commanding, so powerful, that even showing a little bit of it gets blown out of proportion. How do we correct that? By showing that it's part of the mix."

Despite some disagreements on content, gay TV producers are not divided on quality. "Just being gay is not enough to carry a show anymore," says David Van Chaney, creator of the highly polished *Tricks*. "Production values are very important." For Coky Gray and Bill Kavanagh, co-founders of the video magazine *One TV*, production values are top priority. "When we decided to do this," says Gray, 37, "our biggest challenge was not in selling the video-magazine concept, it was overcoming the perception that most of the shows out there were done very badly. I wanted to do something that I would really enjoy watching." Gray's goal is to produce a gay *Today* show.

But there's a danger in being *too* slick, says David Sloan, the producer at ABC's *20/20* responsible for segments on gay teen suicides and AIDS in the fashion community. "The biggest mistake these programs can make is to mimic mainstream television. We don't need something that looks like *Good Morning America* or *Entertainment Tonight*, because we already have those things. It's a double-edged sword. *One TV* knocked my socks off—it's breathtakingly slick— but the down side is that [co-hosts] Bruce and Pru look and sound like the any of the couples on the morning shows. By professionalizing gay programming, it can lose its punch. You have to be daring, different, if you want to be successful, if you want viewers and advertisers."

▼ ▼ ▼

In television, of course, everyone wants viewers and advertisers. And more important than any discussion of what gay TV should be is figuring out whether anybody is actually watching it. Is gay TV the tree that falls in a forest with no one around? Determining real viewership is made difficult by several factors. Nearly all gay TV shows are distributed on public-access and leased-access channels, where the drawbacks include inconsistent scheduling, zero promotion. not being listed in *TV Guide* or local newspaper supplements, and not being monitored by the A.C. Nielsen company. Without the benefit of Nielsen ratings, or any other accepted audience-measurement system, determining just who's watching what's on the air is really up in the air.

The only gay TV show that Nielsen *does* monitor is public television's *In the Life*. But *In the Life* is a monthly half-hour that's scheduled in almost as many time slots as the 70 markets in which it airs. Ratings, therefore, also vary from city to city. One recent show, for example, earned a 1 in Los Angeles and a 3.4 in New York, with a national average of 1.65 (one rating point equals 942,000 households). Tuned in by 1.5 million households, *In the Life* has by far the largest viewership of any regularly scheduled gay or lesbian show, but, by contrast, a top-rated show such as ABC's *Home Improvement* regularly earns a 21.2 rating, for approximately 20 million households.

Most producers of gay and lesbian TV can only talk about how many *potential* viewers their shows *could* reach. Schwam, for instance, estimates that GET's *Party Talk* and other programming are available to roughly 9 million households, and *Dyke TV*'s producers say it can be viewed by 6.5 million. These totals include local cable systems around the country, as well as the millions of viewers who *could* pull the shows directly off a satellite with their own dishes. Of Schwam's 9 million potential households, 7 million are U.S. and Mexican households that would only be able to see the shows off the satellite: of *Dyke TV*'s potential viewership, 2 million are from the satellite.

The question of how many viewers actually tune in is another matter. MTV—which is monitored by Nielsen, has a set channel in cable systems, does massive promotion, and is listed in local TV guides—has a potential audience of 58.4 million households, but at any given time only 1 percent (560,000) are actually tuned in. Similarly, Comedy Central has a potential of 31

million households, but only 0.3 percent (93,000) are actually tuned in at any given time.

Very generously assuming that viewers are as likely to turn on one of GET's three programs or *Dyke TV* as they are MTV or Comedy Central, the number of households actually tuning in to any particular gay TV show would be between 23,000 and 90,000. Producers for both GET and *Dyke TV* insist their shows are likely to have more than 100,000 viewers. Schwam, most of whose potential viewers are satellite dish-owners, says, "We're very specific target-marketing, whereas other channels are playing to everyone." *Dyke TV* producer Chapman throws around a 10-percent figure, which would make her viewership 650,000—larger than MTV's.

By way of contrast, *Tales of the City* received a 4.2 national rating—the highest-rated *American Playhouse* presentation on PBS since 1989—for a national audience of close to 4 million households, which would suggest that there is a massive audience for the right programming with full access to viewers, and with the necessary promotion to let viewers know how to find it in the media morass of current television offerings.

▼ ▼ ▼

It's safe to say that viewership for most other gay and lesbian shows is somewhere in the range of GET and *Dyke TV*, and that could be a problem in luring advertisers. While there have been several recent breakthroughs—advertisers that include Dewar's, Tanqueray, Miller beer, and Nora Beverages (makers of Naya Spring Water)—accurate forecasts for the future seem impossible.

"The issue is cost," says Stuart Elliott, advertising columnist for *The New York Times*. "Given the low scale of these shows now, it makes sense for advertisers to buy them. As they go bigger, the question becomes: Can they then compete for the ad dollars against sports programming or MTV?"

For advertisers, there's also the fear of being associated with anything gay or lesbian. Mainstream advertisers aren't clamoring to place commercials on the few gay-themed shows that have occasionally popped up on the networks. ABC claims it lost $1 million when advertisers yanked their spots from a 1989 episode of *thirtysomething* that featured two gay men in bed the morning after ("I was told people don't want corn flakes associated with homosexuality," executive producer Ed Zwick told the *Chicago Sun-Times*). Likewise, NBC claims to have lost $500,000 when the network aired an episode of *Lifestories* about a gay newsman and his struggle with AIDS. Most recently, several advertisers asked that their ads not air during the notorious "lesbian kiss" episode of *Roseanne*, although there were others with no such qualms, preventing any revenue loss.

"There is still enormous societal stigma against homosexuality," says Elliott. "Marketers, in their desperate attempts to be everything to everybody, are terrified that they will alienate consumers who are everything from uncomfortable about the idea of it to vehemently against it."

So why have several mass marketers chosen to support gay and lesbian TV shows? For some, it just makes good business sense to court a community that reportedly has plenty of disposable income. "To me there is absolutely no risk at all in talking to an existing consumer who is already there and drinking our product, and that is the gay market," says Dominic Brand, vice president and group product director for Dewar's, which currently sponsors *Party Talk*. Nor is he afraid of the homophobe who is more likely to casually discover Dewar's support of the gay community on TV than in a gay magazine, which, presumably, is read only by lesbians and gay men. "There's a minority who do watch those sorts of things just to provoke, but, frankly, those sorts of people are no concern of mine, because they're not existing consumers or potential ones. They're just troublemakers."

Sophia Nieves, spokeswoman for Miller Lite beer, agrees. "Miller advertises on gay shows because they provide us with a chance to reach an appropriate audience," she says. "It's the same basic marketing judgment we apply to any advertising decision. It's not that complicated, really."

Ditto, says Stu Levitan, vice president and general manager for U.S. operations at Nora Beverages, explaining why Naya underwrites *In the Life*. "Basically," he says, "I identified the gay community as a tremendously loyal consumer that was perfect for my product. Yeah, there's a risk, and I've had some backlash, even from some of our distributors who don't understand why we're in that marketplace. But I'm able to tell people that it has been a good business decision for us and it's certainly not the entire bent of our advertising campaign."

Not all advertisers share Levitan's outlook, however, as Marvin Schwam discovered when he asked a *Party Talk* sponsor to renew its commitment recently. "This particular advertiser was

very supportive when *Party Talk* was only seen in New York," says Schwam. "Now the show is seen in several cities and it's been written up in the national press. This advertiser's support of the show has been mentioned, and that's made the company hesitant to continue with us. It's like they're saying, 'We like gays, but we don't want anyone else to know.' "

Ironically, those advertisers who have no hesitation about supporting gay TV may ultimately force the hands of those still somewhat reluctant to do so. "Most advertising is basically defensive," explains David Mulryan, director of business development at Mulryan & Nash, a New York-based advertising agency that has created campaigns for the Netherlands Board of Tourism and *Angels in America* to court the gay and lesbian community. "Absolut was the first vodka company to advertise in the gay market, and now others feel compelled to follow suit in an attempt to neutralize Absolut's position. I think you'll see the same with the beer companies. Miller has come on extremely strong in the gay market and all of the other beer companies are going to have to do the same."

▼ ▼ ▼

Even if gay TV shows manage to meet the challenge of getting sufficient advertising, there is another, possibly more imposing problem: the radical Right. Consider what happened when PBS presented *Tales of the City* last January on *American Playhouse*. Based on the first book in Maupin's six-book saga about the residents of 28 Barbary Lane in San Francisco in the '70s, the miniseries was universally praised by critics and proved so popular with viewers that its ratings were double PBS's prime-time average and the highest for any PBS drama series in five years. Although a handful of public television stations refused to air *Tales*—and some aired an edited version—because it featured drug use, nudity, profanity, and a passionate lip lock between two gay men, *American Playhouse* executive producer Lindsay Law was so pleased with *Tales*' performance that he immediately commissioned a script for *More Tales*. That's when the trouble began.

In March, radical Right ringleader Reverend Donald E. Wildmon and his Tupelo, Mississippi-based American Family Association (AFA) launched a vicious campaign, attacking *Tales* as the latest example of PBS being the "Homosexual Pride Tax-Payer Funded TV Network." U.S. Congressmen were sent 12-minute videotapes featuring *Tales* excerpts with letters urging them to use their influence to prevent tax dollars from being spent by PBS to "promote the homosexual lifestyle." Shortly afterward, *American Playhouse* announced that it would not be pursuing *More Tales*, claiming that the decision was purely financial: The original *Tales* was produced by Great Britain's Channel 4 at a cost of $8 million. PBS purchased the American broadcast rights for about $1 million. Channel 4 wanted PBS to co-finance *More Tales*, to the tune of $4 million, but PBS claimed that wasn't possible because of "programming priorities" and the network's limited budget.

Despite that rationale, accusations flew that PBS had capitulated to Wildmon, who told *The Washington Post* that he didn't claim credit, "but if credit is going to be given, I'll wear it with a mark of pride." PBS vehemently denies that Wildmon had anything to do with its decision, but *Tales* author Maupin refuses to believe it, for one very simple reason. "The question I have yet to have answered is, Would PBS run *More Tales* if we managed to finance it independently? No one will answer that. If PBS acknowledges the success of *Tales* and the enormous audience and critical response it received, why wouldn't it be easy enough to say, Well, yes, of course, we'd be delighted to take a freebie one more time?"

Maupin's take on the *Tales of the City* situation—that the radical Right will do anything in its power to prevent positive images of gays on TV—was echoed by CBS officials after Wildmon's AFA targeted the May 1 episode of *Northern Exposure*, in which Cicely's gay innkeepers, Ron and Erick, exchanged wedding vows. "[It's] simply another example of the entertainment industry's pro-homosexual propaganda," said Wildmon. When network affiliates in Louisiana and Alabama refused to air the episode, CBS released a statement saying, "Clearly, this is a matter of a coalition putting pressure on small Southern markets, attempting to censor a program they have not seen."

Gay TV producers say they too have run up against the radical Right. Last February, for example, WEYS, a commercial UHF station in Key West, had scheduled an episode of David Surber's mail-order video magazine, *Network Q*. Although most of the station's schedule is filled with religious programming from the Trinity Broadcasting Network, based in Santa Ana, California, and Spanish-language programming from the Tele-mundo network, WEYS had also been airing a locally produced gay talk show, *The Open Closet*. But *The Open Closet* was abruptly canceled, and *Network Q* never aired, prompting accusations that Trinity had pressured WEYS to pull the programs, a charge station management denies. Surber doesn't buy it.

"Everybody's talking about how gay programming is becoming a real option on mainstream television," he says. "But I think this illustrates the kind of hurdle we have waiting for us. The station was supportive. The audience was there. The advertisers were there. The Christians just had a bigger stick. Preventing real access to television is one of the best ways to ensure that our community remains a fragmented political force."

Producer Scagliotti has a similar war story. "We can't get *In the Life* on in the South, because we're not the only ones who are organized in public television," he says. "We're trying to get the gay and lesbian community to relate to public television as an institution that they're a part of. But in the South, the 700 Clubs do the same thing. They tell their members that they should become members of their local public television stations. We go to these meetings with program directors and they say, 'We'd love to carry you, but most of our members belong to the 700 Club.'"

▼ ▼ ▼

In spite of such setbacks, there is mounting evidence that gay TV may yet become an irresistible force, if for no other reason than the fact that there's definitely an audience for it out there. Although PBS has refused to finance *More Tales of the City* for inclusion in its national programming lineup, PBS station KQED in San Francisco—where a significant amount of money was raised when *Tales* was rerun during pledge drives—is attempting to raise the needed capital on its own. The reason, according to KQED station manager and director of programming Kevin Harris, is simple: "When you get something that performed as extraordinarily as *Tales*, there's obviously a big need for that kind of programming."

Executives at Comedy Central reached the same conclusion when the gay comedy special *Out There* pulled in 50 percent more viewers than usual for the show's time slot. Although *Out There* producers Trevor Hopkins and Juliet Blake point out that the program was in no way intended to be "a party to which straight viewers weren't invited," Comedy Central's senior vice-president of programming, Mitch Semel, feels that support from the gay and lesbian community had a lot of do with the show's success. "The ratings boost told me how powerful very targeted marketing and press are," says Semel. "The gay community got invested in the show, and I have to think that had a lot to do with how well we did." Equally significant was the fact that although several advertisers requested that their commercials not run during the show, several others had no problem with it, including Apple Computers, Bugle Boy clothes, and Universal Pictures.

What might the future hold for gay and lesbian TV, in the best of all possible worlds? "My particular dream is to have a 24-hour premium gay cable channel," says NBC's DeCola, voicing the hope of many gay TV producers. He estimates that investors would have to put up $20 to $30 million to make it a reality and prevent any dependency on "whimsical, sometimes homophobic" funding sources. "I think a good name for the company would be, 'Not By the Kindness of Strangers Productions.'"

According to DeCola, someone who knows a thing or two about the kindness of strangers—and the feasibility of a gay cable channel—is Scagliotti, who helms the highest-profile gay TV show in the country. "If there's anyone who's proven there's an audience out there, it's John," says DeCola. "After only two seasons, and with no national advertising and promotion, *In the Life* has 8,000 people who contribute an average of $35 a year to keep it going."

Still, it's not much to hang a $20 to $30 million investment on, and DeCola admits that an actual gay cable channel is probably a long way off. As for the immediate future of gay and lesbian TV, we can expect more of the same. "Cable access shows for gays and lesbians are not going to go away," he says. "They're a wonderful training ground for people to learn how difficult it is to put together a program and what it takes in terms of skill, talent, and money."

▼ ▼ ▼

For now, more likely than a gay cable channel or a mainstream gay TV show is an increased gay and lesbian presence on television in general. For better or worse, not a week goes by without Oprah and company tackling gay issues. Network news magazines such as *60 Minutes*, *PrimeTime Live* and *20/20* continue to offer more and more coverage of the community. Prime time itself is now home to at least six gay and lesbian characters: Nancy (Sandra Bernhard) and Leon (Martin Mull) on *Roseanne*, Matt Fielding (Doug Savant) on *Melrose Place*, Ron and Erick (Doug Ballard and Don McManus) on *Northern Exposure* and—who would have guessed?—Smithers on *The Simpsons*. And perhaps most significant of all, two gay men are featured in a new commercial for Ikea home furnishings that's running in New York, Philadelphia, and Washington, D.C.

The fact that most American viewers accept all this as part of the mix may be an indication of things to come. Even more telling, perhaps, was the reaction of TV industry types to *Party Talk* co-host, drag star (and OUT contributor) Linda Simpson at this year's NATPE convention—no one even blinked. "Just in case I happened to be someone they eventually want to associate with," says Simpson.

Will they? Armistead Maupin isn't so sure. "PBS has no problem putting on *Prime Suspect 3*, which offered a parade of rent boys, hustlers, and transvestites, because it presents a picture of gay life that fulfills all the expectations of an ignorant public," he says. "The great crime of *Tales of the City* was that it crossed over into the mainstream and that made it immensely threatening to people who want to keep fags in a nice safe little box with a warning sign on it."

As they say in TV Land, stay tuned.

# IV. B

# THE GOOD PARTS: PORNOGRAPHY

Whenever a new communications technology arrives on the scene, it can safely be predicted that among its earliest users will be the Catholic Church and the creators and purveyors of explicit sexual imagery. Those with the strongest, if not necessarily the purest, motives will be the ones to explore the possibilities inherent in each medium to capture words and images and to convey them to those hungering for their messages. In the case of pornography, sexual images and stories have generally been officially condemned while privately enjoyed. They have also offered channels for the vicarious expression and satisfaction of minority interests that are difficult, embarrassing, and occasionally illegal to indulge in reality. For lesbians and gay men, whose sexuality is officially denied and erased, pornography often provided a vital message: "For isolated gays porn can be an important means of saying 'other gays exist' " (Mercer and Julien 1994:195).

Lesbian writer Dorothy Allison recalls her first encounter with "hard-core" paperbacks she found under her parents' mattress when she was a child:

What the books did contribute was a word—the word *Lesbian*. When she finally appeared . . . I knew her immediately. . . . When she pulled the frightened girl close after thirty pages, I got damp all down my legs. That's what it was, and I wasn't the only one even if none had turned up in the neighborhood yet. Details aside, the desire matched up. She wanted women; I wanted my girlfriends. The word was Lesbian. After that, I started looking for it. (1994:187)

The pornography she found was (most likely) written by and for straight men, who have always appreciated a bit of lesbian spice in their erotic menu, an appetizer before the main course. For gay men, however, heterosexual pornography has never been a welcoming venue. Still, as Waugh (1996) has documented, since the invention of photography gay men have created, collected, and enjoyed their own pornography. Even so, only in recent decades has it become possible for most gay youth and adults to explore this narrow channel of imagery created for and by queers.

John Burger (1995) has written an account of gay male video pornography that illustrates several ways "these videos serve as history texts of the gay male experience":

First, many of them resituate gay men into past and present social conditions in which they have mostly been hidden (such as the California gold rush, the U.S. Armed Forces, and college fraternities). Second, the videos also document current gay-specific social conditions, such as bar life, nightclubs, bathhouses, and so on . . .

These videos . . . are important documents not only of the all-gay environment, real or invented, but of the gay male psyche which so desperately envisions such spaces where they can be free from the social oppressions encountered daily. . . . If we must be marginalized, let us at least create enjoyable spaces on the fringe—whether in imaginary representations or in reality, like the bathhouses. (34, 45)

Similar accounts of pornography produced for and by lesbians (certainly a more recent and limited genre) note its importance for those "for whom sexual imagery is one link in a social and cultural lifeline, a link emblematic of their refusal to accept established sexual hierarchies and their will to make their own place" (Henderson, "Lesbian Pornography," this volume). It must be acknowledged, however, that minority cultural production is not immune from contagion by the racism and sexism endemic to our culture (Fung, this volume).

The existence of these sexual images is a threat to those who guard the ramparts of the sexual reservation. Visible lesbian or gay (or any unconventional) sexuality undermines the unquestioned normalcy of the status quo and opens up the possibility of making choices that people might never have otherwise considered. The fight to keep sexuality invisible (especially in its "deviant" forms) is part of an ancient battle waged by the forces of established order against the subversive potential of powerful images and the wayward impulses they might inspire in the vulnerable. The vulnerable, it is important to recognize, are rarely if ever the holders of established power themselves but rather those over whom that power is held: children, women, and "lower classes" of all sorts.

Traditionally, the only acceptable storytellers outside the circle of family and immediate community were those certified by religious institutions. The emergence of schools intruded a new group of specialists between children and the world into which they grow up. The arrival of mass media of communications fundamentally altered the situation: children were increasingly open to influences that parents, priests, and teachers could neither monitor nor control. Beginning with the widespread availability of printed materials to the literate, increasing with media less dependent on literacy (photography, movies, radio, and even the telephone), and culminating with television's omnipresence (and, newly creeping over the horizon, the Internet), children have become more and more independent consumers of mass-produced stories.

The feared power of images—verbal or, even more powerfully, visual—seems to reside in the representation of precisely those behaviors and options the holders of power wish to deny to those they control, protect, and fear.

For reasons that extend beyond the scope of this introduction, images of violence have remained ubiquitously available, though they have been repeatedly denounced by moral authorities and endlessly studied by media researchers. Images of sexual behavior, in contrast, have been the targets of more effective attack, and their availability has generally been hedged around with legal proscriptions. While parents, preachers, and politicians have criticized violence in the movies, comic books, and television, they have succeeded in criminalizing many explicit sexual images and have prosecuted those who produce or distribute and even, on occasion, those who consume them.

The legal term for prohibited sexual representations (in words or images) is *obscenity*, and its most influential definition in Western law comes from Victorian England's Lord Chief Justice Cockburn, who ruled in 1868 (*Regina v. Hicklin*) that "the test of obscenity is this: whether the tendency of the matter charged as obscenity is to deprave and corrupt those who minds are open to such immoral influences, and into whose hands a publication of this sort may fall" (Kendrick 1987:121). Just a few years later, in the United States, Anthony Comstock successfully lobbied for the passage of "An Act for the Suppression of Trade in, and Circulation of, Obscene Literature and Articles of Immoral Use," which President Grant signed in 1873 and was widely referred to as the Comstock Law.

Comstock came to be a symbol of America's fear of uncontrolled sexuality, just as his unique position as special agent of the U.S. Post Office for over forty years made him its moral policeman. In his writing and in his crusades against immorality Comstock articulated a widespread obsession with the ubiquitous *Traps for the Young* (the title of his 1883 work) that lay in wait. "Newspapers, 'half-dime' novels, advertisements, theaters, saloons, lotteries, pool halls, postcards, photographs, even painting and sculpture—wherever the poor child turned, in Comstock's nightmarish America, something lurked, ready to debauch him" (Kendrick 1987:138).

In the 1970s North American and Western European societies witnessed an explosion in sexual expression by gay men and, to a lesser extent, lesbians, that added a new chapter to the so-called sexual revolution of the 1960s. The convergence of post-Stonewall openness and the newly available video technologies did much to facilitate the gay porn industry, just as porn was helping to popularize the VCR. In 1978 and 1979, before the major movie studios adopted the new technology, more than 75 percent of the videocassettes sold were pornographic. For gay people the opportunity to view pornography in the privacy of the home was especially welcome, even before AIDS made porn the safest form of sex (except, unfortunately, for many performers).

The same period also witnessed the emergence of the sexual and cultural counterrevolution that has come to play a large role in contemporary politics. At the same moment that lesbian and gay people joined to fight against the reactionary forces led by Anita Bryant in Florida and State Senator Briggs in California, many feminists were turning their attention to symbolic violence against women in media and advertising and its possible role in encouraging rape. By the late 1970s Women Against Violence in Pornography and the Media, in California, and Women Against Pornography, in New York, used marches through "red light" districts to "take back the night." However, despite their claims, the antiporn crusaders did not speak for all feminists, and theirs were not the only voices being raised. When the San Francisco lesbian S/M group Samois emerged in 1979 a line was drawn, and lesbian sexuality became a central battleground of what came to be called the "sex wars" (Hunter 1995).

Lesbians resisting the antiporn arguments acknowledged the "deeply erotophobic" nature of Western culture (Hollibaugh 1983:35) but argued against the choice of primary targets: "Instead of traipsing through porn districts . . . we might be demanding better contraception, self-defense classes, and decent non-judgmental sex education. Then women would be strong enough to make our 'no's' stick as well as our 'yes's' " (ibid.). Further, and equally important, they were alarmed at the essentialist view of female sexuality implicit in the antiporn ideology:

> They state that power in sex is male, because it leads to dominance and submission which are in turn defined as exclusively masculine. They suggest that any arousal which is translated through images and expressions of power originates from a masculine and sexist kind of desire. Any similar arousal felt by women is simply false consciousness. In real life this forces many feminists to give up sex as they enjoy it, and forces an even larger group to go underground with their dreams. For many women who have no idea what they might eventually want it means silencing and fearing the unknown aspects of their passions, as they begin surfacing. Silence, hiding, fear, shame—these have always been imposed on women so that we should have no knowledge, let alone control, of what we want. Will we now impose these on ourselves? (Hollibaugh 1983:35)

The sex wars loosed a flood of debate with (mostly lesbian) feminists playing leading roles on both sides (Henderson, "Lesbian Pornography"; Nestle, "My History with Censorship," "My Mother Liked to Fuck"; Tucker, "Gender, Fucking, and Utopia," this volume). But the issue moved beyond the level of even acrimonious debate when the dominant antiporn activists, Andrea Dworkin and Catherine MacKinnon, entered the political and legislative arena. In 1983 they drafted an ordinance that was subsequently adopted by the Minneapolis City Council but vetoed by the mayor. They were more successful in Indianapolis, where the mayor signed it into law. The ordinance never went into effect, however, as it was immediately challenged in the federal courts, where it was ultimately ruled unconstitutional.

The Dworkin/MacKinnon ordinance was not based on standard obscenity arguments. Pornography for Dworkin and MacKinnon is not a *representation* of harm against women, it *is* harm against women (in MacKinnon's words, "Pornography amounts to terrorism" against women). At the very least, it is the theory of which rape is the practice (to paraphrase a famous statement by Robin Morgan). Among the more striking and troublesome features of their analysis and their ordinance is the claim that women *cannot* consent to perform in porn: "A woman's decision to pose for a sexual image should be treated as the product of coercion even under circumstances where a man's decision would be treated as voluntary and consensual" (Strossen 1995:181). The logic of presumptive nonconsent makes adult women equivalent to minors.

However, these very features of the Dworkin/MacKinnon position also contained the seed of their eventual constitutional undoing. By arguing that pornography must be seen as a vehicle of sexist ideology, they confer on it the status of political thought and thus render it worthy of constitutional protection. In the end, this was a major rationale in the federal courts' decisions striking down the Indianapolis ordinance (Duggan, Hunter, and Vance 1985).

The Dworkin/MacKinnon analysis was more successful in Canada, where the Canadian Supreme Court in the 1992 *R. V. Butler* decision adopted the position "that sexually explicit materials may degrade women and present a risk of harm to society by their very existence" (Fund for Free Expression 1994:1). The *Butler* decision "interpreted the Canadian obscenity laws as embodying the MacKinnon-Dworkin concept of pornography and hence outlawed materials that are 'degrading' or 'dehumanizing' to women" (Strossen 1995:19). Although Dworkin did not support the application of their position to an obscenity statute, in contrast to the civil damages approach of their ordinance (Toobin 1994:78), MacKinnon saluted Canada as "the first place in the world that says what is obscene is what harms women, not what offends our values" (Lewin 1992). However, the first targets of prosecution following *Butler* were the lesbian magazine *Bad Attitude* and feminist and gay and lesbian bookstores. As a customs official explained things, "There is no law that says we should look at gay bookstores more than others. But there is an obvious logic to the situation" (Toobin 1994:72).

The alliance between antiporn feminists and the right wing that pushed for repressive legislation in Minneapolis and elsewhere began to crumble under the counterattack of groups like the Feminist Anti-Censorship Task Force (FACT) and the patent bias of the attorney general's Commission on Pornography (the "Meese Commission") helped alert the public to the repressive agenda of the antiporn forces.

By the mid-1990s it appears that the sex wars have died down, and it is possible to agree with Heather Findlay that "sex-positive feminists—those of us who are generally in support of the philosophy and civil rights of pornographers, S/M activists and sex workers—have won the lesbian sex wars" (1996:27). Findlay's evidence consists of the abundance of "high quality, often experimental lesbian erotics" available in print, image, and video.

Some of the credit for this might even go to the antiporn feminists. As Victoria Brownworth put it, "Lesbian erotica was born out of . . . the antipornography wave—partially because it was being born anyway, and partially in retaliation. Some lesbians had waited a long time to have sex and have fun, and didn't want to be told what kind of sex was politically correct and what kind wasn't" (1991:4). However, much of the credit must go to the commercial opportunities and technological advances that have made the production and distribution of lesbian and, especially gay male pornography financially viable. The free market *can* be a vehicle for free speech.

## REFERENCES

Allison, Dorothy. 1994. "A Personal History of Lesbian Porn." In Dorothy Allison, *Skin: Talking About Sex, Class, and Literature*. Ithaca, N.Y.: Firebrand.

Brownworth, Victoria. 1991. "Butch and Femme: Who's On Top?" *San Francisco Bay Times*, January, pp. 4–5, 9.

Burger, John. 1995. *One-Handed Histories: The Eroto-Politics of Gay Male Video Pornography*. New York: Harrington Park.

Duggan, Lisa, Nan Hunter, and Carole Vance. 1985/1995. "False Promises: Feminist Antipornography Legislation." In Lisa Duggan and Nan Hunter, eds., *Sex Wars: Sexual Dissent and Political Culture*, pp. 43–67. New York: Routledge.

Findlay, Heather. 1996. "A Winner in the Lesbian Sex Wars?" *Harvard Gay and Lesbian Review*, 3(3):27–30.

Fund for Free Expression. 1994. "Canada's Anti-Pornography Ruling." *Human Rights Watch Free Expression Project*, 6:1.

Hollibaugh, Amber. 1983. "The Erotophobic Voice of Women: Building a Movement for the Nineteenth Century." *NY Native*, September 26, pp. 32–35.

Hunter, Nan. 1995. "Contextualizing the Sexuality Debates: A Chronology." In Lisa Duggan and Nan Hunter, eds., *Sex Wars: Sexual Dissent and Political Culture*, pp. 16–29. New York: Routledge.

Kendrick, Walter. 1987. *The Secret Museum: Pornography in Modern Culture*. New York: Viking.

Lewin, Tamar. 1992. "Canada Court Says Pornography Harms Women." *New York Times*, February 28, p. B7.

Mercer, Kobena and Isaac Julien. 1994. "True Confessions." In Thelma Golden, ed., *Black: Representations of Masculinity in Contemporary American Art*, pp. 191–200. New York: Abrams.

Strossen, Nadine. 1995. *Defending Pornography: Free Speech, Sex, and the Fight for Women's Rights*. New York: Scribner.

Toobin, Jeffrey. 1994. "X-Rated." *New Yorker*, October 3, pp. 70–78.

Waugh, Thomas. 1996. *Hard To Imagine: Gay Male Eroticism in Film and Photography From Their Beginnings to Stonewall*. New York: Columbia University Press.

# | 76 |

## Coming to Terms: Gay Pornography

### RICHARD DYER

The main suggestions I'd like to make in this essay about gay male pornographic cinema are quite brief and simple. Broadly I'm going to argue that the narrative structure of gay porn[1] is analogous to aspects of the social construction of both male sexuality in general and gay male sexual practice in particular. But before getting on to that it seems necessary to say a few things by way of introduction. Pornography has recently become a Big Topic in left cultural work[2] and what I'm going to say needs to be situated in relation to this.

First, a definition—a working definition, the one I'm going to be working with here, rather than a statement of the correct definition of pornography. I want some definition that is as broadly descriptive as possible. Discussion about porn tends to start off by being either for or against all porn and to be caught up in equally dubious libertarian or puritanical ideas. I don't mean to imply that I believe in the myth of objectivity, that I start off utterly neutral. I'm a gay man, who has (unlike women) easy access to porn and can take pleasure in it,[3] but who feels a commitment to the more feminist inflections of gay male politics. I'm also a socialist who sees porn as capitalist production but does not believe all capitalist cultural production always all the time expresses capitalist ideology (cf. Lovell 1980). I'm constantly looking for moments of contradiction, instability and give in our culture, the points at which change can be effected, and want to start out with the possibility of finding it in porn as anywhere else. So the definition I'm going to use is that a pornographic film is any film that has as its aim sexual arousal in the spectator.

This definition makes porn film a familiar kind of genre, that is, one that is based on the effect that both producers and audiences know the film is supposed to have. It is not defined (or I am not asking to define it here), like the Western, gangster film, or musical, by such aesthetic, textual elements as iconography, structure, style and so on, but by what it produces in the spectator. It is like genres such as the weepie and the thriller, and also low or vulgar comedy. Like all of these, it is supposed to have an effect that is registered in the spectator's body—s/he weeps, gets goose-bumps, rolls about laughing, comes. Like these genres, porn is usually discussed in relation to a similar, but "higher" genre which doesn't have a bodily effect—weepies (melodramas and soap opera) are compared to tragedy or realist drama, thrillers to mystery/detective stories (based on intellectual, puzzle-solving narratives), low comedy (farce) to high comedy (comedy of manners), and porn to erotica.

I'd like to use porn as a neutral term, describing a particular genre. If one defines porn differently, then the kind of defence of porn as a genre (but emphatically not of most porn that is actually available) that I'm involved with here is not really possible. Current feminist critiques of pornography (e.g. Dworkin 1981, Griffin 1981, Lederer 1980) rightly stress the degradation of women that characterizes so much heterosexual porn, and these critiques in fact define pornography as woman-degrading representations of sexuality. Although feeling closer to some of those feminist articles that take issue with this hardline anti-porn position (Myers 1982, Allen and Harris 1982, Winship 1982, Rich 1982), I do not feel as

*Only Entertainment*, 121–134. New York: Routledge, 1992.

out of sympathy with, say, Andrea Dworkin's work as many people, and especially gay men, that I know. Although in relation to gay porn Dworkin is in some respects inaccurate (e.g. in stressing gay porn's use of socially inferior—young, black—men in "feminine" positions, whereas similarity between partners is more often the case) or out of date (Allen and Harris 1982: 22), her rage at what so much of porn consists of is fully justified, and especially so because she effectively defines porn as that which is degrading and out*rageous*. But I'd like all the same to hang on to a wider notion of sexual representation, and still use the word pornography precisely because of its disreputable, carnal associations. (Maybe the feminist debate means that I can't use the word like this—but I don't want to fall for the trap of substituting the word erotica.[4])

The fact that porn, like weepies, thrillers and low comedy, is realized in/through the body has given it low status in our culture. Popularity these genres have, but arbiters of cultural status still tend to value "spiritual" over "bodily" qualities, and hence relegate porn and the rest to an inferior cultural position.

One of the results of this is that culturally validated knowledge of the body, of the body's involvement in emotion, tends to be intellectual knowledge about the body, uninformed by experiential knowledge of it.[5] Let me try to be clear about this. I'm not saying that there can be a transparent, pure knowledge of the body, untouched by historical and cultural reality. On the contrary, all knowledge is culturally and historically specific, we do not transcend our material circumstances. We learn to feel our bodies in particular ways, not "naturally." But an intellectual or spiritual knowledge about the body is different from experiential knowledge of the body— both are socially constructed, but the latter is always in a dynamic material and physical relationship with the body, is always knowledge in and of the body. Intellectual or spiritual knowledge on the other hand divorces social construction from that which it constructs, divorces knowledge about the body from knowing with the body. (Certain types of discourse analysis—but by no means all—clearly fall into the same idealist trap.[6])

Moreover, the effect of the cultural status of intellectual/spiritual accounts of the body is to relegate experiential knowledge of the body to a residual category. Of course idealist discourse accounts do not allow any such category at all.[7]

Thus experiential knowledge (except when sanctified by the subjugation of the body in most forms of "physical education") is allowed to be both inferior and just a given, not socially constructed,[8] to be just "experience," not socially constructed experiential knowledge. By valuing the spiritual, the bodily is left as something natural, and sexuality as the most natural thing of all. What is in fact also socially constructed (experiential knowledge of the body, and of sexuality) is not recognized as such, and for that reason is not reflected upon, is allowed to go its supposed own way until it meets up with spiritual censors. Even gay theory and feminist theory have been notoriously reluctant to think through the social construction of the body without lapsing into the Scylla of Lacanian psychoanalysis (where social construction does not construct anything out of any material reality) and the Charybdis of both gay liberationist let-it-all-hang-out (where sexuality is a pure impulse awaiting release) and the implicit sexual essentialism of radical feminist ideas of masculine aggression and women's power (cf. Wilson 1983).

A defence of porn as a genre (which, I repeat, is not at all the same thing as defending most of what porn currently consists of) would be based on the idea that an art rooted in bodily effect can give us a knowledge of the body that other art cannot.

Even now porn does give us knowledge of the body—only it is mainly bad knowledge, reinforcing the worst aspects of the social construction of masculinity that men learn to experience in our bodies. All the same, porn can be a site for "re-educating desire" (Carter 1981) and in a way that constructs desire in the body, not merely theoretically in relation to, and often against, it.

To do that, though, means rejecting any notion of "pure sex," and particularly the defence of porn as expressing or releasing a sexuality "repressed" by bourgeois (etc.) society. This argument has gained some ground in gay male circles, and with good reason. Homosexual desire has been constructed as perverse and unspeakable; gay porn does speak/show gay sex. Gay porn asserts homosexual desire, it turns the definition of homosexual desire on its head, says bad is good, sick is healthy and so on. It thus defends the universal human practice of same sex physical contact (which our society constructs as homosexual); it has made life bearable for countless millions of gay men.

But to move from there to suggest that what we

have here is a natural sexuality bursting out of the confines of heterosexual artificial repression is much more of a problem.

This is certainly the way that Gregg Blachford's article "Looking at pornography" (1988) can be read, and seems to be the contention behind David Ehrenstein's article "Within the pleasure principle, or irresponsible homosexual propaganda" (1980). The latter[9] argues that porn movies, unlike mainstream films that imply sexuality but don't show it, give us the pure pleasure of voyeurism which lies unacknowledged behind all cinema.

The pornographic is obvious, absolute, unmistakable—no lies or omissions or evasions can hold quarter in its sphere.

Porn is the "abandon of everything to the pleasure principle" (ibid.: 65) conceptualized as pure drive (the more usual appropriation of Freudian ideas than the Lacanian version influential in academic film studies circles). Porn itself operates with this idea, and the view is clearly expressed in the introduction to *Meat* (McDonald 1981), a collection of writings from the magazine *Straight to Hell*. The magazine, like the book, consists entirely of personal accounts of gay sexual experience sent in to the magazine by gay men. I have no reason to suppose that the accounts are not genuine both in the sense of having actually been sent in (not ghost-written) and of describing real experiences. But this "genuineness" is not to be conflated, as book and magazine do, with the notion of an unconstructed sexuality—raw, pure and so on. A reading of *Meat*, or a look at gay porn, indicates really rather obviously that the sexuality described/represented is socially meaningful. Class, ethnicity and of course concepts of masculinity and gayness/straightness all clearly mark these gay pornographic productions: and indeed the very stress on sexuality as a moment of truth, and its conceptualization as raw, pure, etc., is itself historically and culturally produced (Foucault 1980).

What makes *Meat* and gay movie-house porn especially interesting and important is the extent to which they blur the line between representation and practice. *Meat* is based on (I think largely) true encounters that really happened. Watching porn in gay cinemas usually involves having sex as well—not just self-masturbation but sexual activity with others, in a scenario brilliantly evoked by Will Aitken (1981–2) in his article "Erect in the dark." In principle then gay porn is a form of representation that can be the site and

occasion for the production of bodily knowledge of the body. In this definition, porn is too important to be ignored, or to be left to the pornographers.

## NARRATIVE MANIFESTATION

I'd like now to turn to one of the ways in which the education of desire that porn is involved in is manifested, namely its use of narrative.[10]

It is often said that porn movies as a genre are characterized by their absence of narrative. The typical porn movie, hard core anyway, is held to be an endless series of people fucking, and not even, as Beatrice Faust notes, fucking in the "normal" physiological order that Masters and Johnson have "recorded" (1982: 16). Gay porn (and indeed what hetero porn I have seen), however, is full of narrative. Narrative is its very basis.

Even the simplest pornographic loops have narrative. In those quarter-in-the-slot machines where you just get a bit of a porn loop for your quarter, you are very conscious of what point (roughly) you have come into the loop, you are conscious of where the narrative has got to. Even if all that is involved is a fuck between two men, there are the following narrative elements: the arrival on the scene of the fuck, establishing contact (through greeting and recognition, or through a quickly established eye-contact agreement to fuck), undressing, exploring various parts of the body, coming, parting. The exploration of the body often involves exploring those areas less heavily codified in terms of sexuality, before "really getting down to/on with" those that are (genitals and anus). Few short porn films don't involve most or all of these narrative elements, and in that order. Usually too there is some sort of narrative detail—in *Muscle Beach*, one man (Rick Wolfmier) arrives on the scene (a beach) in a truck, the other man (Mike Betts) is already there sunbathing; Wolfmier walks by the sea for a while; there is quite a long sequence of shot: reverse shot cutting as they see each other and establish contact; self-masturbation precedes their actual physical contact with each other; after orgasm, Wolfmier and Betts drive away together in the truck. Already then minimal character elements are present, of not inconsiderable social interest—the iconography of the truck, the looks of the two men, the culture of the beach and of bodybuilding, and so on.

Even when the film is yet more minimal than this, there is still narrative—and essentially the same narrative, too. Some gay porn loops simply show one man masturbating. A rather stylish version of this is *Roger*, which just has the eponymous star masturbating. The music is a kind of echoing drumbeat; there is no set to speak of, the lighting is red, covering the screen in varieties of pulsating hue; the film cuts between long shots and medium shots in a quite rhythmic way, often dissolving rather than cutting clean. It will be clear that there is something almost abstract or avant-gardeish about the film, as the cinematic means play visually with its solo subject, Roger masturbating. Yet even here there is a basic narrative—Roger enters, masturbates, comes. (Where you put your quarter in might mean that you start with his orgasm and run on to where he comes in; but you'd know and be able to reconstruct the proper narrative order that your quarter has cut across.)

Even in so minimal and abstract a case, there is narrative—*Roger* is a classic goal-directed narrative. The desire that drives the porn narrative forward is the desire to come, to have an orgasm. And it seems to me that male sexuality, homo or hetero, is socially constructed, at the level of representation anyway, in terms of narrative; that, as it were, male sexuality is itself understood narratively.

The goal of the pornographic narrative is coming; in filmic terms, the goal is ejaculation, that is, visible coming. If the goal of the pornographic protagonist (the actor or "character") is to come, the goal of the spectator is to see him come (and, more often than not, to come at the same time as him). Partly this has to do with "proof," with the form's "literalness," as Beatrice Faust puts it, with the idea that if you don't really see semen the performer could have faked it (and so you haven't had value for money). But partly too it has to do with the importance of the visual in the way male sexuality is constructed/conceptualized. It is striking how much pornographic literature, not a visual medium, stresses the visible elements of sex. (Most remarkable perhaps is Walter, the Victorian narrator of *My Secret Life*, with his obsessive desire to see into his partner's vagina, even to the detail of seeing, for instance, what his semen looks like after he has ejaculated it into her vagina.) Men's descriptions of their own erections seldom have to do with how their penises feel, but with how they look. The emphasis on seeing orgasm is then part of the way porn (re)produces the construction of male sexuality.

Could it be otherwise, could sexuality be rep-

resented differently? So dominant are masculine-centred definitions of sexuality that it often seems as if all representations of sexuality (pornographic or otherwise) are constructed as driven narrative. But there are alternatives, and one that struck me was the lesbian sequence at the end of *Je tu il elle*, directed by Chantal Akerman. (As Margaret Mead pointed out, you need only one example of things being different to establish that things can be different in the organization of human existence and hence that things can be changed.) The sequence itself is part of a (minimalist) narrative; but taken by itself it does not have the narrative drive of male porn. It starts *in media res*— there is no arrival in the room, the women are already making love when the sequence starts (though the previous shot has, perhaps ambiguously, established that they are going to make love); there is no sense of a progression to the goal of orgasm; nor is there any attempt to find visual or even (as in hetero porn?) aural equivalents for the visible male ejaculation. In particular, there is no sense of genital activity being the last, and getting-down-to-the-real-thing, stage of the experience. It is done in three long takes—no editing cuts across a sexual narrative (as in gay porn; see below); the harsh white lighting and the women's white bodies on crumpled white sheets in a room painted white, contribute to the effect of representing the sexuality as more dissolving and ebbing than a masculine thrusting narrative. Let me stress that I am not talking about what the women are doing—for much of the time their actions are far more snatching and grabbing than, for instance, the generally smooth, wet action of fellatio in gay porn. My point is the difference in narrative organization, in the cinematic representation of sexuality.[11]

I am not suggesting that this is a better representation of sexuality, or the correct mode for representing lesbian sexuality. Also I want to bracket the question of whether the difference between the two modes of representation is based on biological differences between female and male sexuality, or on different social constructions of sexuality, or on a combination of the two.[12] All I want to get over is the difference itself, and the fact that male porn, whether homo or hetero, is ineluctably caught in the narrative model. (This is particularly significant in hetero porn in that it is predominantly constructed around a female protagonist (Giles 1976), who is attributed with this narrativized sexuality. However, I am not about to get into whether this is a gain—a recognition of female sexuality as desire—or a loss—a construction of female sexuality in male terms.)

The basis of gay porn film is a narrative sexuality, a construction of male sexuality as the desire to achieve the goal of a visual climax. In relation to gay sexual politics, it is worth signalling that this should give pause to those of us who thought/hoped that being a gay man meant that we were breaking with the gender role system. At certain levels this is true, but there seems no evidence that in the predominant form of how we represent our sexuality to ourselves (in gay porn) we in any way break from the norms of male sexuality.

Particularly significant here is the fact that although the pleasure of anal sex (that is, of being anally fucked) is represented, the narrative is never organized around the desire to be fucked, but around the desire to ejaculate (whether or not following on from anal intercourse). Thus although at the level of public representation gay men may be thought of as deviant and disruptive of masculine norms because we assert the pleasures of being fucked and the eroticism of the anus (Hocquenghem 1978), in our pornography this takes a back seat.[13]

This is why porn is politically important. Gay porn, like much of the gay male ghetto, has developed partly out of the opening up of social spaces achieved by the gay liberation movements; but porn and the ghetto have overwhelmingly developed within the terms of masculinity. The knowledge that gay porn (re)produces must be put together with the fact that gay men (like straight men but unlike women) do have this mode of public sexual expression available to them, however debased it may be. Like male homosexuality itself, gay porn is always in this very ambiguous relationship to male power and privilege, neither fully within it nor fully outside it (cf. Barrett 1980: 42–84, passim). But that ambiguity is a contradiction that can be exploited. In so far as porn is part of the experiential education of the body, it has contributed to and legitimized the masculine model of gay sexuality, a model that always implies the subordination of women. But rather than just allowing it to carry on doing so, it should be our concern to work against this pornography by working with/within pornography to change it—either by interventions within pornographic film-making itself (Siebenand 1980), or by the development of porn within the counter-cinemas (always remembering that the distinction between porn in the usual commercial sense and sexual underground/alternative/independent cin-

ema has always been blurry when you come to look at the films themselves), or by criticism that involves audiences reflecting on their experience of pornography (rather than by closing down on reflection by straight condemnation or celebration of it).

So far all I've been talking about is the most basic, minimal narrative organization of (gay) male pornography. However, gay porn is characterized as much by the elaborations of its narrative method as by its insistence on narrative itself. Though the bare narrative elements may often not go beyond those described above, they are frequently organized into really quite complex narrative wholes. Often there is a central narrative thread—two men who are in love or who want to get off with each other—but this is punctuated by almost all of the devices of narrative elaboration imaginable, most notably flashbacks (to other encounters, or previous encounters of the main characters with each other), fantasies (again, with others or each other, of what might or could be), parallelism (cutting back and forth between two or more different sexual encounters) and so on. All preserve the coming-to-visual-climax underlying narrative organization, but why this fascination with highly wrought narrative patterns? To begin with, of course, it is a way of getting more fucks in, with more people (Mele and Thirkell 1981). There is even perhaps an element of humour, as the film-makers knowingly strain their imagination to think of ways of bringing in yet more sex acts. But it is also a way of teasing the audience sexually, because it is a way of delaying climax, of extending foreplay. In parallel sequences, each fuck is effectively temporally extended, each climax is delayed. More generally, the various additional encounters delay the fulfilment of the basic narrative of the two men who are the central characters. (For example, in L.A. *Tool and Die* the underlying narrative is Wylie's journey to Los Angeles to find a job and his lover Hank; Wylie and Hank are played by the stars of the film, Will Seagers and Richard Locke, so we know that their having sex together must be the climax; but there are various encounters along Wylie's way, including memories, observation of other couples, incidental encounters with other men, and even inserted scenes with characters with whom Wylie has no connection, before arrival at Los Angeles and finally making it with Hank.)

There is a third reason for this narrative elaboration. Just as the minimal coming-to-visual-climax structure is a structural analogue for male sexuality, so the effective multiplication of sex acts through elaborate narrativity is an analogue for a (utopian) model of a gay sexual lifestyle that combines a basic romanticism with an easy acceptance of promiscuity. Thus the underlying narrative is often romantic, the ultimate goal is to make love with *the* man; but along the way a free-ranging, easy-going promiscuity is possible. While not all gay men actually operate such a model of how they wish to organize their affective lives, it is a very predominant one in gay cultural production, a utopian reconciliation of the desire for romance and promiscuity, security and freedom, making love and having sex.

It is worth stressing how strong the element of romance is, since this is perhaps less expected than the celebration of promiscuity. The plot of *L.A. Tool and Die* outlined above is a good example, as is *Navy Blue* in which two sailors on shore leave seek out other lovers because each doesn't think that the other is gay, yet each is really in love with the other (as fantasy sequences make clear)—only at the end of the film do they realize their love for each other. Or take *Wanted*, a gay porn version of *The Defiant Ones*, in which two convicts, one gay (Al Parker) and one straight (Will Seagers), escape from prison together. Despite Seagers's hostility to Parker's sexuality, they stick together, with Parker having various sexual encounters, including watching Seagers masturbate. The film is a progression from the sadistic prison sexuality at the start (also offered, I know, as pornographic pleasure), through friendly mutual sexual pleasuring between Parker and various other men, to a final encounter, by an idyllic brookside, between Parker and Seagers which is the culmination of their developing friendship. Some men I know who've seen the film find this final sequence too conventionally romantic (which it is—that's why I like it) or else too bound up with the self-oppressive fantasy of the straight man who deigns to have sex with a fag. It can certainly be taken that way, but I know when I first saw it I was really moved by what seemed to be Seagers's realization of the sexuality of his feeling for Parker. And what particularly moved me was the moment when Seagers comes in Parker's mouth, and the latter gently licks the semen off Seagers's penis, because here it seemed was an explicit and arousing moment of genital sexuality that itself expressed a tender emotional feeling—through its place in the narrative, through the romanticism of the setting, through the delicacy of Parker's performance. If porn

taught us *this* more often . . .

One of the most interesting ways of making narratives complex in gay porn is the use of films within films. Many gay porn films are about making gay porn films, and many others involve someone showing gay porn films to himself or someone else (with the film-within-the-film then becoming for a while the film we are watching). The process of watching, and also of being watched (in the case of those films about making gay porn) is thus emphasized, not in the interests of foregrounding the means of construction in order to deconstruct them, but because the pleasure of seeing sex is what motivates (gay) male pornography and can be heightened by having attention drawn to it. (There is a whole other topic, to do with the power in play in looking/being looked at, which I won't get into here.) We have in these cases a most complex set of relations between screen and auditorium. On screen someone actually having sex is watched (photographed) by a film-maker watched (photographed) by another invisible film-maker (the one who made the film on screen), and all are watched by someone in the audience who is (or generally reckons to be) himself actually having sex. Gay porn here collapses the distinction between representation and that which it is a representation of, while at the same time showing very clearly the degree to which representation is part of the pleasure to be had even in that which it is a representation of. Porn (all porn) is, for good or ill (and currently mainly for ill), part of how we live our sexuality; how we represent sexuality to ourselves is part of how we live it, and porn has rather cornered the market on the representation of sexuality. Gay porn seems to make that all the clearer, because there is greater equality between the participants (performers, filmmakers, audiences)[14] which permits a fuller exploration of the education of desire that is going on. Porn involves us bodily in that education: criticism of porn should be opening up reflection on the education we are receiving in order to change it.

## ACKNOWLEDGEMENT

I'd like to thank Jump Cut editorial collective for their helpful and also very enjoyable involvement in the editing of this article. Since first writing it I have incorporated not only many of their suggestions but also much of the useful discussion on pornography and gay macho in the Birmingham Gay Men's Socialist Group. Many thanks to all these people, then—but I'll still take the blame for the finished article.

## NOTES

1. For the rest of the article, "gay porn" will always refer to gay male porn.

2. For a general introduction to this, see Lesage (1981) and the bibliography in Marchetti (1981).

3. This access is not actually so easy outside of certain major metropolitan centres and recent police practices in Great Britain have hit gay porn far more decisively than straight.

4. "Because it is less specific, less suggestive of actual sexual activity, 'erotica' is regularly used as a euphemism for 'classy porn.' Pornography expressed in literary language or expensive photography and consumed by the upper middle class is 'erotica'; the cheap stuff, which can't pretend to any purpose but getting people off, is smut." Ellen Willis, quoted in Carter (1981: 20–38).

5. An example of this is the role of the representation of the body in Christian iconography. At one level, the body of Christ could not be a more central motif of Christianity, most notably in the image of Christ on the cross. But the tendency remains to stress what the body means at the expense of what it is, to highlight transcendence over the body. In the Christian story of Christ as the Word made flesh, it is the Word that ultimately matters, not the flesh.

6. The magazine *mlf* is the leading example of this.

7. For a critique of idealism, Lovell (1980).

8. The one area of cultural work that has been concerned with body knowledge is dance, but the leading exponents of Modern Dance such as Isadora Duncan and Ruth St Denis have been influentially committed to notions of natural movement. See Kendall (1979).

9. I am conscious that because this article, in a manner of speaking, attacks things I have written—and even attacks what it infers from them about my sexual practices—I may here treat the article rather unfairly.

10. This is only one element of any full analysis. One of the major elements not discussed here, and that needs work doing on it, is the role of iconography—of dress and setting, and especially performers, the male types that are used, porn stars' images and so on, all drenched in ideological meanings.

11. For further discussion see Martin (1980).

12. For a discussion of this difficult nature/nurture debate from a socialist feminist perspective that does not discount the contribution of biology altogether, see Sayers (1982).

13. Waugh (1985) disputes the assertion in this paragraph.

14. This is a question of degree—producers and audiences are not equal in their power of determining the form that representation takes, and especially in a field so fiercely colonized by capitalist exploitation as pornography; and at the psychological level, performers and audience members are not necessarily equal, in that performers are validated as attractive sexual beings to a degree that audience members may not be. But the point is that they are all gay men participating in a gay sub-culture, a situation that does not hold with heterosexual porn. See Siebenand (1980) and Waugh (1985).

## REFERENCES

Aitken, Will (1981–2) "Erect in the dark," *Gay News* (Winter Extra December/January): 15–20.

Allen, Deborah and Harris, Gavin (1982) "Languages of rage and revenge," *Gay Information* 9/10: 20–7.

Barrett, Michele (1980) *Women's Oppression Today*, London: Verso.

Blachford, Gregg (1978) "Looking at pornography," *Gay Left* 6: 16–20.

Carter, Mick (1981) "The re-education of desire: some thoughts on current erotic visual practices," *Art and Text* 4: 20–38.

Dworkin, Andrea (1981) *Pornography: Men Possessing Women*, New York: Putnam's.

Ehrenstein, David (1980) "Within the pleasure principle, or irresponsible homosexual propaganda," *Wide Angle* 4 (1): 62–5.

Faust, Beatrice (1982) *Women, Sex and Pornography*, Harmondsworth, Mx: Penguin.

Foucault, Michel (1980) *The History of Sexuality*, Vol. 1, trans. Robert Hurley, New York: Vintage.

Giles, Dennis (1976) "Angel on fire," *Velvet Light Trap* 16.

Griffin, Susan (1981) *Pornography and Silence*, London: Women's Press.

Hocquenghem, Guy (1978) *Homosexual Desire*, London: Allison & Busby.

Kendall, Elizabeth (1979) *Where She Danced*, New York: Alfred Knopf.

Lederer, Laura (ed.) (1980) *Take Back the Night*, New York: William Morrow.

Lesage, Julia (1981) "Women and pornography," *Jump Cut* 26: 46–7, 60.

Lovell, Terry (1980) *Pictures of Reality*, London: British Film Institute.

McDonald, Boyd (ed.) (1981) *Meat*, San Francisco, CA: Gay Sunshine Press.

Marchetti, Gina (1981) "Readings on women and pornography," *Jump Cut* 26: 56–60.

Martin, Angela (1980) "Chantal Akerman's films: a dossier," *Feminist Review* 3: 24–47.

Mele, Sam and Thirkell, Mark (1981) "Pornographic narrative," *Gay Information* 6: 10–13.

Myers, Kathy (1982) "Towards a feminist erotica," *Camerawork* 24: 14–16, 19.

Rich, B. Ruby (1982), review of the film *Not a Love Story*, *Village Voice*, 20 July.

Savers, Janet (1982) *Biological Politics*, London: Tavistock.

Siebenand, Paul Alcuin (1980) *The Beginnings of Gay Cinema in Los Angeles: The Industry and the Audience*, Ann Arbor, Mich.: Universitv of Michigan Press.

Waugh, Thomas (1985) "Men's pornography: gay vs straight," *Jump Cut* 30: 30–6.

Wilson, Elizabeth (1983) *What Is To Be Done About Violence Against Women?* Harmondsworth, Middx: Penguin.

Winship, Janice (1982), review of Andrea Dworkin (1981) *Pornography: Men Possessing Women*, *Feminist Review* 11: 97–100.

## FURTHER READING

Henderson, Lisa (1992) "Lesbian pornography: cultural transgression and sexual demystification," in Sally Munt (ed.) *Being There: New Lesbian Criticism*, London: Harvester.

Patton, Cindy (1988) "The cum shot: three takes on lesbian and gay sexuality," *Outlook* 1 (3): 72–7.

Ross, Andrew (1989) *No Respect: Intellectuals and Popular Culture*, New York and London: Routledge.

Watney, Simon (1987) *Policing Desire*, London: Comedia/Methuen.

Waugh, Thomas (1983) "A heritage of pornography," *The Body Politic* 90: 29–33.

Williams, Linda (1990) *Hard Core: The Frenzy of the Visible*, Berkeley, CA: University of California Press.

# | 77 |

# Gender, Fucking, and Utopia: An Essay in Response to John Stoltenberg's Refusing to Be a Man

## SCOTT TUCKER

## 1. PORNOGRAPHY, LIES, AND TRUTH

"Pornography," according to John Stoltenberg, "tells lies about women. But pornography tells the truth about men."

Here on my desk is the *Leatherwomen 89* calendar, created by lesbians and given to me by one of the pictured women—who happened to be a member of FACT (Feminist Anti-Censorship Task Force) while it was active. It is open to April:

a close-up photo of a leather-vested, bare-breasted woman whose hand is gloved in another woman's ass, her cunt also visible with two rings through her labia.

"*Pornography lies about women,*" so file this image under "Lies."

Does this image fit the definition of pornography spelled out in the Civil Rights Anti-Pornogra-

*Social Text*, 27(9/2):3–34, 1990. Excerpt.

phy Ordinance created by Andrea Dworkin and Catherine MacKinnon, and defended at length in Stoltenberg's book? Using terms from the Ordinance and Stoltenberg, it is "graphic" and "sexually explicit," to be sure. But does it portray "specific genital acts"? Well, no. Does it portray "sadomasochism"? If we call the act fist-fucking it may or may not be in the repertoire of certain sadomasochists; but those who enjoy the act as a form of anal yoga quite distinct from SM prefer to call it hand-balling. Is this a depiction of "the act of making subject or subservient"? Perhaps, though these women acted in mutual consent. Are these women presented "dehumanized as sexual objects, things or commodities"? Any and all image-making dehumanizes human models to some degree; and to some degree humanizes the material—film, ink, paint, paper, canvas, clay, stone, whatever it may be.

Are these women "presented as sexual objects who enjoy pain or humiliation"? Their faces aren't visible, but would their feelings be unambiguous even if we saw smiles or grimaces? Are these women "reduced" to "body parts"? The sense of sight itself is selective and reduces all bodies into parts less than wholes; the real world is always partly opaque and hidden; pure transparency would leave no visible forms. Stoltenberg argues that porn can only present partial and mediated acts, persons, feelings; but this could be said of all art as well. Dehumanization is a matter of degree; matters of degree do matter. But then we need someone able and willing to make more distinctions than Stoltenberg, including distinctions among pornographic works.

Are these women "presented as whores by nature"? Who would read that message into this image? Would Dworkin? Would Stoltenberg? Would you? If it could be proved that these women were coerced into the act and before the camera, then there would be a criminal case for a court to judge. Laws against rape and assault already exist, but the Dworkin and MacKinnon Ordinance is just specific and just vague enough to allow all images of fucking open to the interpretation that they either document such crimes, or encourage them, or both. Stoltenberg claims this Ordinance is distinct from obscenity law and distinct from censorship because it is based on injury to a person or class of people, rather than on "offense to public morals." Furthermore, the lawsuit could be initiated by any plaintiff with "cause of action," rather than by cops and the state, and would be adjudicated in civil rather than in criminal court. Penalties would include "money damages and/or injunction" against makers and distributors of porn, rather than "imprisonment, fine, censorship."

In fact, Dworkin herself argues against obscenity laws because they allow sexist "community standards" to go unchallenged, and thus "become the formula for making pornography," in Stoltenberg's words. The "civil-rights approach" against porn assumes that all social scientists worth acknowledging have concluded that porn is an almost irresistable incentive towards rape and violence. This is spectacularly untrue. According to Stoltenberg, social science experiments show that "exposure to certain types of pornography produced significant effects such as increased levels of aggression and hostility, increased callousness toward women, and increased self-reported likelihood to rape if they thought they would not get caught." This is the single instance where Stoltenberg deigns to suggest that "certain types of pornography" may differ from others—though he prefers a categorical condemnation of all kinds.

Stoltenberg's footnote to the above quote cites the research of Dolf Zillmann, whose methodology has been criticized by many social scientists; and also cites a book edited by Malamuth and Donnerstein, both of whom have distanced themselves from the use which was made of their work during the Meese Commission on Pornography. Essentially, Malamuth and Donnerstein have stressed that the real issue is violence, not explicit sexual acts as such. In fact, social scientists have noted the rarity in pornography of the kind of violence found in "slasher films," and the rarity of full nudity in such films, much less explicit sex. Sex is "soft-core" but violence is "hard-core" in "slasher films," and the message of such films often entwines titillation with erotophobia. In this sense, *Fatal Attraction* qualifies as a "slasher film," one which received the kind of respectful reviews which cruder examples of the genre never do; a film with a broader market than porn, with a much more sexist and despicable message than most porn, and one which never received the kind of protest certain activists lavishly reserve for porn.

It is disingenuous of Dworkin, MacKinnon, Stoltenberg, and others to claim that money damages and injunctions do not amount to censorship against the makers and sellers of pornography. We are all entitled to boycott anything we choose; but the Anti-Pornography Ordinance does intend to use the power of the state to take certain products off the market. It clarifies, at least, the real economics of "free" expression, about which we should have no illusions. This ordinance was designed to be legally devious, because if pornography documents and radiates the kind of crime and evil its opponents claim, then it *should* serve as evidence in criminal court, and its creators *could* be prosecuted there to the full extent of the law for conspiracy to commit kidnapping, rape, assault, and even murder. No, these anti-porn activists understand that standards of evidence in criminal court would quickly make nonsense of their charges in all too many cases. So their civil court and "civil-rights approach" resonates with a nobler tradition than that of Mrs. Grundy and Jesse Helms, and permits a fierce and unprovable rhetoric to flourish.

Also on my desk is *The Gay Desk Calendar 1989* (Alyson Publications) open to June: a photo of myself in boots, harness, and leather jock taken in 1986, the year I won the International Mr. Leather contest. No genitals in view, no fucking, but my ass is bare and the props and regalia are redolent with perversion. Playfully perverse on a rooftop at noon, no sinister cellar or shadows. Torso twisting, tit-rings glinting, hands grasping five big iron links of a dock chain, almost a joke on *leather and chains*, minimal leather, maximum chain, both beyond utility or menace. "Our moods do not believe in each other"—so wrote Emerson. That was a good mood that year, and I can smile without disdain at this somewhat camp icon. Is it pornography?

*"But pornography tells the truth about men,"* so file this image under "Truth."

Stoltenberg and like-minded others explain to their own satisfaction why some women "lie" about themselves in their own pornography: they are men trapped in women's bodies, they are brain-washed by patriarchy, they don't know better. Furthermore, such women may call themselves feminists, but John Stoltenberg will valiantly refuse them that identity at the same time as he refuses to be a man. *He* knows better. And what truth, then, would Stoltenberg find in the photo of me in a studded jock? All dress is drag, and that photo dates from the one year in which I spent more time with barbells than with books, so that my very musculature was a change of style. All great fun, but life goes on. Nowadays I still indulge in a bit of bondage and rough stuff on rare occasions, but tenderly jerking off with an acquaintance at a recent Halloween party was just as satisfying.

If Stoltenberg's theories were true, all pornography without distinction should have an evil influence, since any degree of sexual objectification leads down the slippery slope to rape and even murder. Stoltenberg quotes Robin Morgan with approval: "Pornography is the theory and rape is the practice." In *Refusing to Be a Man*, Stoltenberg reiterates one line of radical feminist thought by insisting that "the sexual domination of women in pornography" is "the jugular vein—or perhaps, more accurately, the nerve center—of male supremacy."

Cultural struggle matters as much as any other kind, and particular images, films, and documents are worth protest; but crusades against pornography in general are a dismal distraction from gaining real justice for women, and must be fought like all other attempts at censorship. John Stoltenberg, Andrea Dworkin, Catherine MacKinnon, Robin Morgan, Phyllis Schlafly, Reverend Falwell, Cardinal O'Connor, and Senator Helms all agree that pornography of any kind is a radioactive element in and of itself. Dworkin and MacKinnon drafted and promoted legislation based on the premise that pornography violates the civil rights of women, legislation which Stoltenberg explains and defends at length in his book.

Ellen Willis—herself a radical feminist—wrote this in 1982: "It is the antipornography movement that, almost unchallenged, came to dictate the terms of feminist discussion of sex, despite the fact that it has *never* spoken for all feminists." Thanks in great part to feminists such as Dorothy Allison, Pat Califia, Lisa Duggan, Kate Ellis, Amber Hollibaugh, Gayle Rubin, Anne Snitow, Carole Vance and Ellen Willis, the antipornography faction within the women's movement has been effectively challenged. All of these same feminists have quite mixed feelings and thoughts about different kinds of porn—but they do make distinctions, and they do oppose censorship. Stoltenberg deals with this feminist challenge to his own ideology very simply in his book: all these women go unnamed, and the opposition is treated as though they had long ago been excommunicated. Here Stoltenberg confuses his own sectarianism with moral seriousness.

Anyone reading his book who didn't know better might assume the anti-pornography faction had achieved hegemony in the women's movement, when in fact it has become increasingly isolated. Stoltenberg is at least honest about the history of the Dworkin/McKinnon ordinance. It was first introduced in Minneapolis in 1983, where it was twice passed by City Council and twice vetoed by Mayor Fraser. Meanwhile, the ordinance was introduced in Indianapolis, and was passed by City Council in 1984 and signed by Mayor William Hudnut. Under challenge, the Indianapolis ordinance lost two appeals on Constitutional grounds, and the Supreme Court finally upheld the second appeals court decision in February 1986. This particular ordinance seems quite dead, and so, to a great degree, are the older debates within feminism about pornography which accompanied its rise and fall.

Other attempts are now being made to silence voices and erase images which could bear the label of pornography, most recently and notably when Senator Helms, seeing the AntiChrist glorified in the work of Serrano and Mapplethorpe, sought to apply restrictions on NEA funding for any arts project which might "promote or disseminate . . . sadomasochism . . . homoeroticism," and so forth. The Helms amendment had a few of its teeth drawn at last, though his public intimidation may encourage more "quiet diplomacy"— and de facto censorship—in arts grants and funding. Helms and others have also succesfully sabotaged any national safe sex and AIDS education program.

In 1983, Stoltenberg and I both spoke on pornography at the Philadelphia Lesbian and Gay Community Center. At that time I said, "When a mainstream major motion picture appears which is sexist but soft-core, anti-porn feminists do complain but rarely mobilize their forces in protest. Apparently they have made a strategic decision that they can rouse more populist moralism against Times Square than they can against Hollywood, and they are right. Also, when fighting porn you can win symbolically satisfying victories: it is so much easier to close down a single porn shop in an urban area destined for redevelopment than it is to close down a single advertising agency on Madison Avenue."

My own aim here is to treat pornography (however broadly or narrowly defined) as only one flashpoint of culture, one mirror of gender, one magnet of power. The very fact that certain activists make porn a centerpiece of struggle does, however, reveal the power of sexuality to rouse our deepest anxieties and utopian longings.

## 2. MAGIC AND MATERIALISM

Animating Stoltenberg's critique of pornography is a critique of gender which bears a resemblance to the work of gay historians and theorists such as Michel Foucault, Jeffrey Weeks, and the whole intellectual milieu of "social constructionists." Unless or until reproduction and child-bearing are technologically altered on a planetary scale, I believe certain aspects of gender identity will remain biologically linked for most human beings. If we agree that gender is predominantly the creation of culture, not nature, then we can agree that sexual and social life can be recreated and diversified. Culture seems, in fact, to be our specifically human nature; or we might say it is in our nature to create a whole spectrum of "second natures." But acknowledging that gender is predominantly social does not lead me and many others to all of the conclusions which Stoltenberg insists are "radical feminist." For example, I want a greater diversification of sexual images and literature, and some real workers' control of the sex industries such as prostitution. Stoltenberg wants the abolition of pornography and prostitution. I would not vote him into a Ministry of Culture.

Stoltenberg quotes Andrea Dworkin: "We are, clearly, a multisexed species which has its sexuality spread along a vast continuum where the elements called male and female are not discrete." And he adds: "I first read those words a little over ten years ago—and that liberating recognition saved my life." Dworkin's influence on Stoltenberg remains pervasive and profound, which is why I've found it necessary to discuss their work together.

Dworkin's suggestion of a multisexual human species leads Stoltenberg to state, "The idea of the male sex is like the idea of the Aryan race." Blue eyes and blond hair exist without making "the Aryan race" a separate and superior species. There is little harm in using the word race to refer to certain imprecise and changing constellations of physical characteristics. The harm comes when racists seek to value or devalue people by such characteristics, to keep people separate and unequal, "pure" and "impure." In the same way, sexism creates seperate and unequal sexes. What, then, is the relation between biology and gender? According to Stoltenberg, "The penises exist; the male sex does not. The male sex is socially constructed. It is a political entity that flourishes through acts of force and sexual terrorism." The female sex—and the subordination of women—is likewise socially created. To strengthen his analogy between race and sex, and to explode both categories, Stoltenberg stresses the existence of biological exceptions to human sexual dimorphism.

The analogy has definite limits. Variation in skin coloration (to take only one racial charac6-

istic) is much more greatly distributed over a much greater population, and is much likelier to vary with further "miscegenation" (a word beloved by racists) than is the case with variation in "gross anatomy" and in the structure of genitalia. But biological variation in sex does exist, and is not so rare as we might think: "hermaphrodites" become sacred or monstrous or sacred monsters among various peoples, either as embodiments of primordial unity, or as embodiments of disorder. Whereas modern sexologists are inclined to view this degree of biological variation as a pathology, Stoltenberg is inclined to affirm the health of differences—within the bounds of his own world view. But if Stoltenberg's real concern is to destroy masculinity and femininity as socially polarized and totalitarian genders, he hardly needs to deny the evident difference between biological males and females by stressing still other kinds of biological differences. On the contrary, this dubious biologism increases his ideological intensity, but it sharply undermines the specific ethical dimension of his feminism. Stoltenberg appeals to biology only when ideologically convenient; in other words, he doesn't take biology seriously. Indeed, he and Dworkin are materialists only to the degree this serves their particular moralism.

Having questioned the very existence of males and females, Stoltenberg maintains that any fixed sexual identity and orientation whatsoever will inevitably serve to keep male supremacy and gender polarization alive and well. Since our sexual attractions are more socially malleable than our sexual organs, this would seem to be the proper point of leverage for social change. Stoltenberg is here in the company of other "social constructionists" who have proposed a diffuse, polymorphous eroticism to replace our current desires and fixations. I don't doubt our current identities are too restrictive; I also don't doubt that definable identities will emerge even in utopia. One kind of utopian impulse is, of course, to escape any and all sexual and social definitions: in the current discourse, this is the mythic place where "social constructionism" meets "deconstructionism," like matter meeting anti-matter. Boom! Or, as Stoltenberg writes, "Poof. Now you see it, now you don't."

The line between magic and materialism grows blurred here. Being a socialist myself, I am also by definition a social constructionist, but unlike many leftist and feminist folks in this diverse camp I am much less dismissive of the idea and the reality of *human nature*. There is nothing progressive in claiming the purer (because more alterable) high ground of culture for the left and feminism, while abandoning the impure low ground of nature to reactionaries. Why should we be ecologically minded only in relation to other animal, vegetable, and mineral natures, and only technocratically minded in relation to our own?

## 3. THE PHALLUS AND THE FUCK

Stoltenberg, in line with Robin Morgan's dictum that "women are the essential proletariat," believes sex roles are the root of all evil. If sexual objectification could be abolished (by abolishing porn, for example), then we are bound by this theory to believe all economic objectification of people would wither away in turn; just as the state was once supposed to wither away after the abolition of capitalism. Certain radical feminists suggest that racism, too, and all other oppressions are epiphenomenal to the original sin—sexism. I don't believe any of this, neither as a myth of Paradise Lost nor as a political strategy for Paradise Regained.

Stoltenberg would prefer a world with as many sexes as persons, and with undifferentiated eroticism rather than sexual identities. Furthermore, Stoltenberg regards this utopia as more "true" than current reality. There are forms of mysticism which dissolve the world into a play of illusions, just as there are physicists who remind us that the ultimate reality is atomic—all these fields, factories, and fleshly organs are passing clouds. But I confess that I find love among these illusions, and greatly value these relative realities—including my own sexual orientation. I'm well aware that any kind of sexuality can be forged into a weapon against women. But Stoltenberg quotes with approval this despicable piece of heterosexist rhetoric from Phyllis Chesler: "Sons or fathers, poor men or rich men, sacred or secular: all are homosexual in their worship of everything phallic. A sexual revolution might destroy what men do so well together, away from women: the making of His-story, the making of war, the triumph of phallic will."

From the great height of a materially comfortable white American intellectual, Chesler might stoop to some sympathy for at least those men who are indeed so poor that waging war gains them a foothold in the war for wages. Her vindictive use of the word homosexual to describe "all" men is the reflex action of a moralist playing to prejudice, and is detested by this particular homosexual, myself, who has been three times assaulted by gaybashers. Oh yes, in popular psychology all gaybashers are secretly gay. Tell me another one. *And Stoltenberg does* : all men who rape women might secretly *be* women—if you draw a simple conclusion from his premise that the sexes are social fictions.

It is not at all clear to me how my struggle as a radical faggot might fit in the particular milieu of "pro-feminist" men to which Stoltenberg addresses himself (to standing ovations, as he lets us know). If heterosexism among feminists is to go unchallenged, and if the submergence of sexual orientation is a point of honor among men like Stoltenberg, then I prefer the company of radical dykes and fags.

As Dworkin and Stoltenberg's critique of porn is based on a critique of gender, so their critique of gender is based on a critique of fucking. Since some of the physical motions of fucking may resemble some of the physical motions of rape, Dworkin has written a whole book called *Intercourse* which elides one into the other with great passion and eloquence. Though Dworkin repeatedly speaks of fucking in terms of violation, invasion, and occupation, she is eager to clarify: "There is no analogue in occupied countries or in dominated races or in imprisoned dissidents or in colonialized cultures or in the submission of children to adults or in the atrocities that have marked the twentieth century ranging from Auschwitz to the Gulag." Stoltenberg expresses not merely the same ambivalence about fucking in his own book, but also the same aversion.

Utopian visionaries such as Charles Fourier, Wilhelm Reich, and Shulamith Firestone have argued for profound sexual and social changes, and Firestone's book *The Dialectic of Sex* is explicitly a work of radical feminism. She describes a form of "cybernetic socialism" which allows "the freeing of women from the tyranny of their biology," in which "childbearing could be taken over by technology," and in which childrearing would be communal rather than familial. Firestone imagines a world in which labor (in all senses of the word) becomes painless for men and women, thus breaking the curse of God in Genesis: "in sorrow thou shalt bring forth children . . . in the sweat of thy face shalt thou eat bread . . . "

Dworkin and Stoltenberg have taken what they believe is simply the next logical step: in a world of technological reproduction, why fuck at all? As fucking withers away, so (they hope) will pornography and patriarchy. Again, I believe they are both all too opportunistically selective in the sexual and social evidence with which they make their case. Among women I know, one describes childbirth as "the most ecstatic experience of my life," whereas another describes it "like shitting a basketball." As for fucking, as a gay man I'm aware that cocks don't always tickle. Women do die in childbirth, and men do rape. If some radical feminists choose to equate "phallic power" with patriarchy, I can only say that not all cocks are weapons in a sex war, and not all power is oppressive.

When I take a cock in my ass, I am actively taking power and pleasure, not simply reproducing a passive "femininity"; and when I choose to give my partner the chief balance of power in sex, so that he strokes my cock with his asshole while I lie bound to a bed, then something is going on which is not reducible to the one word "patriarchy." Since certain radical feminists are fond of conflating all cocks into one patriarchal signifier named "the phallus," and likewise reducing all forms of fucking into "the fuck" (read Dworkin in particular), this makes reality so much simpler. Nevertheless, Ellen Willis spoke for more persons than herself when she stated that she "declined to glorify diffuse, romantic, non-genitally oriented sensuality as the sole criterion that sex is 'erotic', female, and good, or to stigmatize powerful, assertive desires for genital gratification as 'pornographic', male, and bad."

In a typically idealist manner, Stoltenberg writes of the drive men feel to assert "male sexual identity," which he deconstructs thus: "The drive does not originate in the anatomy. The sensations derive from the idea." The "idea" being . . . male sexual identity. Perfectly circular, perfectly unconvincing. That our biological being may include sexual drives is regarded as a retrograde notion by certain social constructionists, a point of convergence among theorists who are otherwise quite divergent. For these folks, sexual drives conjure up only an obsolete locomotive rattling and pounding on the same old tracks of gender, and the sooner we derail it the better. In utopia we shall all grow erotic wings and fins, and other organs still more conducive to transport.

These theorists usually vague out on just what they have in mind, and a degree of uncertainty is defensible and necessary: who will blue-print the future? But Stoltenberg is especially vague, both in his grasp of present material realities and in his projection of future possibilities. He writes, "Phallic eroticism is intrinsically proprietorial," "intrinsically alienating," "intrinsically hostile . . ." Intrinsic in the sense of "normally acculturated phallic eroticism," another phrase he uses, or in the sense of biologically inherited? Perhaps both? But if Stoltenberg really aims to argue that the male sex and masculinity are equally social fictions, then he can't have it both ways. He is almost driven to acknowledge some biological base in our sexual acts despite his own ideological aversion to doing so. In contradistinction to a somewhat sexist and heterosexist psychologist, Erik Erikson, who proposed "a utopia of genitality," we might say that Dworkin and Stoltenberg propose a utopia of detumescence.

Stoltenberg is correct in stating that men are often subject to great "confusion, stress, anxiety, and fear" in conforming to masculinity. But when Stoltenberg elaborates a phenomenology of erection, he is narrowly determinist in the exclusion of biological factors (other than a passing mention of "touch and warmth"), and in his inclusion only of "various conditions of risk, peril, hazard, and threat . . . " He reemphasizes the same idea and the same words in an oddly enlightening footnote: "The elective 'forbiddenness' of homosexual encounters, as for instance in public places, and the objective physical danger of many sadistic sex practices can also be seen to preserve the role of risk, peril, hazard, and threat in effectively inducing erections."

If lesbian sadomasochists practice with sufficient will over sufficient time, maybe they, too, will induce erections. Stoltenberg is, of course, driven to interpret their present sexuality as being "phallic" in origin, with or without the use of dildoes.

## 4. Pleasure and danger, private and public

Stoltenberg's footnote is worth a volume of analysis, but a few pages will suffice here on pleasure and danger, and on privacy and publicity. Stoltenberg may lack a certain range of experience, but he also lacks imagination. Gay people often have no freedom to be gay in the privacy of their homes, due to family and neighborly pressures. When they seek out sex in "public places" such as parks, beaches, or restrooms, their actions are not always accurately described as "elective."

Lacking a secure privacy, they may find an insecure privacy and a selective publicity among similar seekers in such places. In this manner sexual repression and social oppression may eroticize risk and danger in certain persons over time. When we grant this, have we exhausted all explanations for the sexual allure of strangers? Bathhouses, bars, and clubs are, of course, examples of semi-commercial, semi-communal, semi-private, and semi-public places, and often exist in legal limbo, or are subject to police raids and closure.

What about those of us who have sought, found, and enjoyed relative sexual privacy in public places even when we have been lucky enough to be freely ourselves wherever we may live? Why should the natural world be out of bounds for sexuality? And why should sex not sometimes be a sport? Why should strangers not be lovers? In my own utopia, the sport would include no risk of meeting maniacs, no risk of meeting vice cops, and no risk of disease. But even in utopia, sporting sex may still include the play of power (unless you plan to abolish all power whatsoever, perhaps by Papal decree).

Imagine a civilized erotic life, private and public. Heterosexual men are far likelier to feel safer in public from sexually related abuse and assault than either gay men or women. They are far likelier to feel entitled to public identities and public power; far likelier to demand any and every domestic service in private life. In privacy, women don't always escape public abuse; on the contrary, it may become deadlier. In privacy, gay people often feel the world contract to the space of a closet. But whereas sex often contracts the world of women precisely down to a woman's sex, sex often expands the world of gay men—only by degrees, to be sure, but any gay sex act may be an act of resistance, since gay sex is not merely driven into privacy but into secrecy, and not merely into secrecy but into non-existence. The cultural climate can be fierce even in those states where sodomy is legally tolerated.

A heterosexual man may feel all a lesbian needs is a good fuck to be a real woman, but he'd also feel that a good fuck only makes a man a queer—feminine without being quite female. Women often desire their sexuality to be *less* public, at least less subject to male demand and advertisement. But gay people often desire a public world safe enough, at least, in which to hold hands without risking attack; safe enough, at the *very* least, in which to find others like themselves. Women are expected to wear the decorations of their sex, to be decorative; gays are expected to disguise themselves as straight, or to be decorators. Gay people have often learned to protect privacy at the same time as they claim the public world by immersing themselves in disguises and dramas, in costumes and carnivals, in art of all kinds. In time this becomes an open secret, and gay people may find themselves all too dependent on the patronage of fair-weather friends, and all too exposed to the critical denigration of perennial enemies.

In such a world, a woman may well write, as Dworkin does, that intercourse is an invasion of privacy, a destruction of personhood. As if by nature. In such a world a gay person may well translate the right to privacy into the duty of sexual secrecy. Women are likelier to lose identity in sex; gay people are likelier to find an identity in sex (and sometimes nowhere else) which also permits a temporary dissolution of everyday, enforced heterosexual misidentity. In public and in private, a woman may be considered fair game for sexual baiting or even rape; in public and in private, gay people may be considered fair game for gaybashing and for legal arrest. "The personal is political," women have claimed; and gay people have learned that even our privacy can only be secured in the public world. The Supreme Court has ruled that gay people have no right to privacy; therefore seven-hundred of us chose to be arrested for civil disobedience at the Supreme Court.

## 5. ABSENCE, DARKNESS, DEATH

Some tribes live very lightly on the earth, but most humans have done significant violence to the environment in our efforts to find shelter and found communities. Even if we grow ecologically wise and practical, the disparate power of our species to alter the planet will remain absolute. And even if all people adopt vegetarianism, what will change our need to disintegrate and so to assimilate our food? Treating nature with the utmost non-violence, we may find a way to inhale our nutrients. The general pacification may finally make the friction of sex seem all too brutish, and foster a preference for telepathy. Heaven on earth, and human evolution ever more angelic.

Out of what material reality, indeed, is sexuality socially constructed? It is not shameful to acknowledge that much is simply unknown to science at this time, or even that certain realities

may be humanly inaccessible. But the unknown should give us no permission to indulge in any ideological assertion we please. Even social constructionists who are nominally Marxist become as idealist as Stoltenberg in this matter of biology, sex, and gender. As though they fear nature is reactionary . . . *by nature*, and not simply by its reactionary use and abuse. Nature has dimensions which are amoral in relation to human moralities; but human moralities have dimensions which are also natural. Sodomy, sentences, symphonies, and culture of any kind at all, tribal or technocratic, may be symptomatic of the maladjustment of our species; but in that case, our maladjustment runs so very deep as to be a "second nature" at the very least, and more likely embodied in opposable thumbs and neural webs. We are the strangest creature, and among all other creatures, even among our own kind, we are the most estranged. We often seem powerless to prevent the abuse of our own powers.

If power corrupts, it also makes possible a whole range of personal choices and social changes. Unlike some utopians and radical feminists, I believe power and struggle are permanent factors in both nature and culture. Immediately upon reading that sentence, some will leap to the conclusion that I've just come out as a Social Darwinist and patriarchal propagandist. On the contrary. We can do without rape and war, and a peaceful communal life is possible. But we won't get from here to there without power and struggle; even if we do get there, power and struggle will take still more various and diverse forms than we now imagine. And though many progressive folks regard this as heresy, count me among those who believe that any human existence will have an irreducibly tragic dimension. Tragedy, for all we know, may strike us more clearly and purely when and if present barbarism fades into the past.

So it is not only Stoltenberg's analysis of the present world I find so partial, but also his brand of optimism for the future. No, I don't like Stoltenberg's unrelievedly earnest style; his sensibility is deeply Protestant, but go back to Luther to find passion in prose, and any tract by the Jehovah's Witnesses is much more fun. So what is it, exactly, I find so instructive, so tempting on a transcendental plane, so repellent in time and space, so cautionary in Stoltenberg?

The utopian purity of spirit. Much purer than Dworkin's, because much more purified of worldliness. Both share a metaphysical bent, but Stoltenberg is the more reductive alchemist, even more intent to take the raw and messy stuff of sex and gender and to draw out the otherworldly quintessence, the pure gold of what could be if only we, too, were pure enough to extract it from a fallen world. Sometimes Stoltenberg and I plainly don't see the available evidence with the same eyes; where he insists on seeing the fallen world, I am as likely to see . . . the world.

Take his discussion of gay male sex films, for example. All in all, they must be allowed to signify only emotional disconnection and phallic power; indeed, Stoltenberg perfects the elision of signifiers, so everything he dislikes really means the same thing as everything else he dislikes. No distinctions are made between sex films, between scenes, between directors, between performers, or between the viewers. Indeed, none are so much as named. From all such pollution, Stoltenberg abstracts one message: "The values in the sex depicted in gay male sex films are very much the values in the sex that gay men tend to have; they are very much the values in the sex that straight men tend to have; they are very much the values that male supremacists tend to have; taking, using, estranging, dominating—essentially, sexual powermongering." This is an occult science in which everything runs true to formula: A = B = C = . . .

Of all gay sex films, Stoltenberg writes, "This is sex labor that is alienated, these dead faces seem to say." Anyone who has seen Brian Hawkes sit on a cock has seen the face of rapture, or of an excellent actor; whereas Jeff Stryker, for example, goes through the robotic motions as though following Stoltenberg's script. How many porn performers have any control of their careers? How many, for that matter, have anything that might be called steady work at decent pay? How many perform to advertise for prostitution? How many work to support drug habits? How many perform to pay for school? Why don't more studios require condoms? What is the real iconography of race and racism in porn? Beginning with such questions, a serious study of this industry might be written. But I know too many performers who enjoy their work to see only "dead faces," either on screen or off.

Purity requires Stoltenberg to see only dead faces and coercion in pornography, so we might wonder whether his own fiercely ideological gaze is not at least as dehumanizing as that of the pornographer. Pornographers turn persons into images; anti-pornographers turn images into demonic powers. Stoltenberg never does specify what good sexual images might look like, nor even what good sex might be—other than being the feminist antithesis to that patriarchal thesis, phallic power. At least Stoltenberg spares us yet another defence of erotica, which all decent people agree has nothing to do with porn. Bless Stoltenberg for sparing us this sleazy decency!— probably because he suspects contraband in pretty packages, the phallic beast among the porcelain nymphs. (And he wouldn't be wrong.)

Dworkin and Stoltenberg play the pedal bass of pornography throughout their work, and elaborate their themes accordingly. Dworkin is sometimes irresistibly readable, as Stoltenberg almost never is; but Stoltenberg repays patience, because he and his work more closely approach ideal types of iconoclast and iconoclasm; with him we reach real clarity about the religious calling of many anti-porn activists. Dworkin is more artistic, which means she is always compromised in her own iconoclasm, a creator and collector of worldly things, "objectifying" her thoughts more passionately into books and speeches. Stoltenberg knows no compromise. For him all graven images of sexual activity are suspect, because for him the erotic is the sacred, and therefore not to be bound in time and space. He is more thoroughly theological, as though he had learned the second language of anti-pornography, but is still thinking in a first language of a God who is Wholly Other. Now sex has become for him the Wholly Other, and in this fallen world we only approach it "through a glass, darkly," through undeserved grace (given our gender training), and through mystical apprehension. Sex, being sacred, is degraded by depiction; sexual images are therefore impure. By nature, they limit and define, no matter how suggestive they may be. Against this physical constraint, Stoltenberg makes his metaphysical protest.

However else we differ, the significant point of contact and unity between Stoltenberg and myself is the sense that sex can be a holy mystery, and that sex has a dimension of danger. If this didn't impress me so strongly in his work, I wouldn't bother with it at all. A purist understanding of God is radically disincarnate; and so, I believe, is a purist understanding of sex. Embodiment means limitation: we can recreate ourselves in the flesh, but we all die; and we can recreate ourselves in artifacts which survive us, but which have no independent life. At its most purist—I would say at its most nihilist—utopianism is hostile to all embodiment and limitation, and paradise becomes identical with pure oblivion. In Stoltenberg's work a critique of sex and gender very nearly approaches a critique of language and imagery—but always stops short.

Sensuality, eroticism—these are the words Stoltenberg prefers to words such as sex and fucking. "A transient release from gender"—these are the words he chooses to describe the Nirvana of diffuse sensuality, and why not? Stoltenberg longs for release not only from social gender, but also from sexual orientation, and even from the male and female sexes. How much simpler life would be if all sex change operations could occur in our heads, rather than being inflicted on our bodies. Plainly some people live in chronic sexual emergency, and seek resolution in surgery—and at least one person sought it not once, but twice. According to a story in *Philadelphia Gay News* (11/10/89), "A Missouri town was surprised last month when one of its two pediatricians announced that she was a man until her 1978 sex change, and that she was going under the knife to become a man again. 'I was born a male, and I was raised a male, and I feel that's the way I'll be most contented,' said Dr. Janis Ashley, 38." If a careful reading of *Refusing to Be a Man* could have spared Dr. Ashley this particular journey through sex and gender, then I might have called the book good medicine.

Stoltenberg's book is the sectarian equivalent of sex-change surgery; and here is one of his diagnostic passages: "Self-consciousness about one's 'sexual orientation' keeps the issue of gender central at precisely the moment in human experience when it needs to become profoundly peripheral. Insistence on having a sexual orientation in sex is about defending the status quo, maintaining sex differences and the sexual hierarchy; whereas *resistance* to sexual-orientation regimentation is more about where we need to be going."

Stoltenberg insists that the male and female sexes are real only as all fictions are real, yet he recognizes the necessity of a women's movement. Now within the women's movement, there have been attempts to transcend racism by adopting the attitude of "sisters under the skin"; and black women have had to say, No: first face reality, and then we may be a black woman, a white woman, and friends. Among gay men also, a recognition rather than a submergence of class and racism has been necessary, especially as certain technocrats and public relations experts prefer a movement under the benign dictatorship of (mostly) white

professionals. As cold as that vision leaves me, I also have no desire for male bonding in any old left nor in any pro-feminist men's movement where I can't be blatantly queer. Stoltenberg's specious transcendentalism precisely serves the status quo, not any genuine common humanity.

Having noted the element of nihilism in Stoltenberg's world-view, let me note a different kind of nihilism in my own. It seems an article of faith for Stoltenberg that the erotic dimension of life is dangerous only because it has been made dangerous. What has been socially constructed can be socially deconstructed. I believe that, too. To a degree. But sexual passion often promises—and threatens—a loss of self. As the Bible says, sometimes you must lose your life to gain it. And sometimes you simply lose your life or go mad. Ideally, sex is a matter of calculated risks, with plenty of social support, adequate privacy, and medical care, if necessary. It seems clear that Stoltenberg and I value selfhood in variant forms. Stoltenberg prefers an eroticism so diffuse that it sounds less vigorous than a Swedish massage; in his utopia pain and pleasure are always clearly distinct, and a diffusion of sensation implies a concentration of identity. Not sexual identity, of course! Just identity, a self with clear boundaries and borders—in Dworkin's sense, uninvaded, unoccupied, uncolonized.

Some of us, myself included, find our pleasures and selves differently. An erotic life will include many free-floating elements, but we also deliberately concentrate sensations in order to diffuse personality. During certain times of my life, I've been actively bisexual; and in certain moods, I am so in imagination even now. But men are the true north on my personal sexual compass. I don't buy Stoltenberg's dogma that my sexual orientation serves sexism; but then I don't believe men and women are purely social fictions, either. And here's a confession which sentences me to perdition in Stoltenberg's court: yes, I believe one reason so many of us like sex so much is because we can selectively entrust ourselves to annihilation, and rise with new life from our graves and beds. (Of course, not all sex is like this; not all sex should be; plenty of sex is companionable, habitual, and self-possessed.)

In the relentlessly hygienic propaganda of American sex experts, sex and death are not acquainted; but some of us suspect they are lovers. Was it only benighted morbidity which led folks in the past to describe coming as "dying"?—sensibly so, since coming often feels like a great going away. With AIDS, of course, there has been a particularly moralistic conflation of sex and death—or rather, of gay sex and death by AIDS—as though viruses represented the law and order of the universe. Much of this can be analyzed by any decent sociologist, and any sexologist will note specifically American strains of erotophobia. But I strongly suspect that it belongs to human nature to feel ambivalent about sexuality even in the best of all possible worlds. Therefore in this world, hellish as it often is, we are all the more likely to project moral and social dramas upon sex, especially upon the sex of those *others*—women, Jews, blacks, queers, these and more.

I'm writing this very early on a cold morning, the tracery of bare branches beyond my window, and Donne's poem on the winter solstice in my lap:

> Study me then, you who shall lovers be
> At the next world, that is, at the next Spring:
>    For I am every dead thing,
>    In whom love wrought new Alchemy.
>       For his art did express
> A quintessence even from nothingnesse,
> From dull privations and lean emptiness:
> He ruined me, and I am re-begot
> Of absence, darkness, death; things which
> are not.

That comes close to speaking my own nihilism—a nihilism derived in part from nature, and in great part modified and elaborated (even in such rhyme and meter) by culture. A utopianism which doesn't acknowledge absence, darkness, death is merely the Enlightenment gone mad, our up-to-date obscurantism. In conventional politics, and even in strains of radical feminism, this utopianism has often had dangerous consequences. Anyone who values reason and democracy will do best to acknowledge these three also: absence, darkness, death. They are not even always sinister.

Finally, though Stoltenberg would not likely consider me his comrade, in fact we both work against militarism, for reproductive rights, and in hope of a more humane world. In regard to sexual expression, culture, and censorship, we do indeed part company. Each of our optimisms are in opposition, and we would not like to live in each other's utopias. I disagree in great part with both his ethics and aesthetics, but I don't disregard either; and I agree as an artist and as an activist that ethics and aesthetics are deeply

related. In a world where power is shared and negotiated to a much greater degree, people may act in ways which would surprise all present utopians, including Stoltenberg and myself. In that world, Blake's words may become more widely and clearly true: "Opposition is true friendship."

▼ ▼ ▼

Postscript: *Men Confront Pornography*, an anthology edited by Michael Kimmel, was published in January 1990, and included essays by Stoltenberg and myself. The three of us were also guests on the Phil Donahue Show. Given the format of the show, ideas are limited to sound bites before Donahue is off and running through the audience, but I was glad to wear silk and leather and talk sex to millions, trashing Senator Helms as well.

On short notice, I was forewarned that Stoltenberg would come prepared with props he uses often in pro-feminist male gatherings—namely, poster enlargements of pornographic pictures showing women on all fours, with legs spread, with breasts projected, or in other postures of sexual exposure. Nipples and cunts censored, of course, with black patches. Stoltenberg selected two jocks from the audience to imitate these postures, and got the expected laughs and giggles. At which point, I pulled out a photo of bodybuilder Bob Paris and a *New York Times* Armani ad of a jock-strapped male model, both in very stylized poses, and made an impromptu attempt to deconstruct the previous message. What I really needed were enlargements of gay male porn pictures, with guys spreading their butts, their legs, their mouths.

*Just like women?*

Just like the poor sex dolls in Stoltenberg's photo props, objects of mingled pity and hilarity, not least when imitated by men to draw a presumably feminist moral. The show didn't air until weeks after taping, so I watched it for the first time with a lesbian friend who turned to me and said, "I've been in those postures." I said, "And so have I." Of course, Stoltenberg wishes his audiences to understand that postures of sexual exposure are inherently degrading; and since such postures are coded *by* men and *for* men in so much art and porn as being "feminine" in their vulnerability and enticement, they become ridiculously "effeminate" *on* men. A mischievous gay scholar at one of Stoltenberg's male gatherings did not follow the script, and grew enthusiastic about how hot he found all those pro-feminist men imitating brazen hussies. And Stoltenberg was not amused.

Who has the power to make and break sexual metaphors and images? Already women and gay people have seized means to produce their own pornography. Stoltenberg prefers to rule this out of order, to play Calvin in his feminist Geneva. But though he preaches the gospel of sexual non-differentiation, he is not above playing to sexual prejudice. Under close questioning, it might be possible to find out just how calculating and just how unconscious Stoltenberg is when he performs with his porno flashcards. But this much must be granted: he is consistent in finding all fucking not quite human, and thus any posture which might permit penetration is likewise degrading. Decide for yourself whether this transcends sexism or gives it new dimensions. I had the bright idea on the Donahue Show of asking the jocks to hold their poses so I could climb on board and show America how to do it right, but the one prop missing was a condom.

# | 78 |

# Free Speech or Hate Speech: Pornography and Its Means of Production

## CHARLES I. NERO

I would like to share an autobiographical story with you. It is about consumer culture and sex. Now, I am not telling you this story to shock you. But some of you may be shocked. Others may not be shocked because you may have had similar experiences.

I am gay and to the best of my knowledge, men were always the catalyst for my sexual desire. The sexually explicit photographs in the *Spiegel*, *Sears*, and *Montgomery Ward* mail order catalogues generated some of my earliest desires. Photographs of men modeling underwear, and occasionally wearing only a bottom, were very hot! As a child I remember staring at these pictures and imagining how nice it would be to touch one of the models. Sometimes other young male friends would come to my house and we would lay on the floor on our stomachs and look at the models. Usually during this time, we would look at the women wearing bras, girdles, and panties. Curiously, this staring is also one of my earliest memories of learning about heterosexism

and homophobia—boys do not look at naked (or semi-naked) men; boys do look at scantily-clothed women.

I tell you this snippet of autobiography because it concerns my topic in this presentation: sexually explicit material, its means of production, and free speech. Currently, an antipornography movement seeks to create legislation that will abolish the production and the distribution of sexually explicit material—so-called pornography. Creating this type of legislation is not impossible, and, perhaps, enforcing it is not impossible. Yet it seems to me that abolishing the sexually explicit can be accomplished only with extreme difficulty. For example, to the best of my knowledge, within our house my parents never had obscenity—what antipornography lawyer Catherine MacKinnon defined as material designed "to

*Law and Sexuality: A Review of Lesbian and Gay Legal Issues*, 2:3–9, 1992.

give a man an erection."[1] I am sure that my parents, who are devout Methodists, did not consider mail order catalogues even potentially obscene. But those catalogues were quite pornographic to me and they were the catalyst for some of my earliest sexual fantasies.

Clearly, I believe that my parents could not have effectively kept potentially obscene material out of our house. Such a task would require a standard working definition of pornography. This definition would have to be broad enough to cover the range of material from *Playboy* to the *Sears Wish Book*.

The dilemma of defining such a wide range of material that my parents would have faced is similar to the one that opponents of pornography face. I believe that the task is not impossible, but the result would lead to oppression and would not further anyone's aims for social justice. I wish to argue that efforts to define pornography as hate speech for the purpose of creating legislation for its abolition are not good for our society. First, I believe that these efforts perpetuate class bias. Second, they are detrimental to sexual orientation movements.

## PART I

Invariably, efforts to define pornography as hate speech for curtailment purposes focus on pictorial representation. The 1986 Attorney General's Commission on Pornography, for example, debated the relative harm of sexually explicit material in print and pictorial formats. The majority concluded that sexual explicitness was more harmful in pictorial formats than in print formats.[2] Therefore, the Commission advocated minimal and cautious curtailment of "books consisting of nothing other than descriptions of sexual activity in the most explicit terms,"[3] even though such material is "plainly patently offensive to the vast majority of people, and plainly devoid of anything that could be considered [of] literary, artistic, political, or scientific value."[4] The Commission's decision reflected perceived differences between reading a book and looking at pictures, "the special prominence"[5] of the printed work in Western societies, and the exploitation of actual persons in pictorial formats.

Recommendations, such as the Attorney General's Commission on Pornography, create hierarchies of technology. They promote policies that regulate technology, not sexually explicit material. These policies are class biased for several reasons.

First, an effect of these policies is to make sexually explicit material unavailable to a particular population, namely, illiterate people, and, probably, non-readers of English. Both groups are heavily concentrated in low-income groups. For all intents and purposes, this type of regulation is a form of class control. A message is given that some should have sexually explicit material and others should not have it. I wonder about the rationale for this anti-egalitarian reasoning. Perhaps, it is the old idea that poor and working class people are the unfit of society. Perhaps, it is a fear that poor and working class people are more dangerous than people from the middle and upper classes. Perhaps, it is a fear of immigrants. Perhaps, it is racist also since Blacks and Latinos comprise the poor and working classes at rates disproportionate to their actual populations.

Second, regulating pictorial technology changes primarily the distribution of pornography which affects people in low income groups. It eliminates access to sexually explicit materials in its cheapest forms—video and photography at the local porno shop. There, video is available for a mere twenty-five cents to view for two to three minutes in a private booth. For three to seven dollars one can purchase magazines with pictures or sketches of nude models, fiction, letters, allegedly "true" sexual encounters sent in by other readers, trivia items, and news. These magazines usually contain four to eight models posing individually. There might be four different photographs of each model. Sometimes the pictures are glossy, sometimes each model is in one glossy photograph and the rest are on regular paper. Sometimes older editions of these magazines are sold in packs of three or four at a price under ten dollars.

Regulating distribution might be important for fighting organized crime, which is alleged to control the so-called pornographic industry. But eliminating cheap forms of sexually explicit material does not eliminate pornography's means of production, which is my third point. Pornography can be produced pictorially in forms of technology that we as a society would be loathe to subject to greater regulation than what exists currently. Would we want to regulate our easy access to cameras and chemicals to develop film? Would we want to eliminate the video recorder? Would we want to regulate the transmission of information via telephone lines? Most of us would answer "no" to these questions. We would strenuously object to having to register our cameras, film development equipment, videos, and computers with the police department as Rumanian citizens under the Ceaucescu regime had to do with typewriters. Yet, these technologies make it possible for pornography to flourish outside of an industry allegedly related to organized crime. The widespread availability of these technologies means that pictorial pornography can be produced in cottage "Mom and Pop" enterprises. Fax machines can transmit pictures via the telephone wires. Computers with modems make possible countless information networks that can make distribution of pornography extremely difficult to regulate.

Making pictorial pornography illegal merely places barriers to its accessibility along class lines. Denied are those individuals who do not have either the capital or the knowledge to gain access to these types of technology. Those without computers, modems, and fax machines cannot access pornography transmitted via the telephone lines. Those who do not have a video machine at home (or a home in which to have a video) are denied access to moving-picture porn.

Moreover, making pictorial pornography illegal may actually hurt the performers and models who make a living in it. British psychologist Lynne Segal notes that "sex workers themselves have almost always objected to others' attempts to save them from such forms of 'exploitation,' knowing full well that the economic alternatives open to them are likely to be no less, indeed perhaps a very great deal more, exploitative."[6] African-American porno actress Angel Kelly made the point that making pornography illegal hurts the performers.[7] She stated in a 1989 interview on the television show *Our Voices* that driving porn underground prevents the workers from demanding better wages and working conditions. Also, the Final Report issued by the Attorney General's commission on Pornography included statements from sex workers that coercive practices most often happen in "home-made, noncommercial" pornography.[8]

Allow me to summarize this part of my presentation. Current efforts to define pornography as hate speech usually focus on the pictorial. Efforts to restrict pictorial representations of the sexual reveal class biases. These efforts affect distribution, not the means of production of pornography. Distribution laws restrict access to pornography along class lines. These laws reveal a bias against people in low income groups.

## PART II

In this half of the presentation, I would like to examine how regulating pictorial pornography can restrict cultural formation of groups based on sexual affiliation and orientation. Specifically, I would like to address the proposition that pornography is a form of hate speech and should, therefore, be abolished.

Many people have "come to regard pornography as a type of rapist's charter, teaching men to hate and abuse women."[9] Andrea Dworkin's and Catherine MacKinnon's writings remain the bedrock of this analysis. For Dworkin the penis is a "symbol of terror," a weapon "even more significant than the gun, the knife, the bomb, the fist."[10] In the 1986 *Toward a Feminist Theory of the State*, MacKinnon defines pornography as "a form of forced sex, a practice of sexual politics, an institution of gender inequality."[11] In her 1991 *Feminism Without Illusions*, Elizabeth Fox-Genovese calls for the suppression of pornography "because it offers us an unacceptable mirror of ourselves as a people"[12] and because "the public degradation of women undermines all sense of community, including the sense of a national community that the flag represents."[13]

These analyses fail to note that pornography carries many messages other then woman hating.[14] Pornography also encourages masturbation which can only undermine a society that has traditionally created laws for regulating the orifices in which a penis can be placed. Sexually explicit gay comic strips often tackle serious issues within our community. For example, Burton Clarke's "Cy Ross and S.Q. Syndrome" deals with the important issues of racism and desire across racial boundaries.[15]

Regulating hate speech also raises a few thorny issues. Individuals who are antagonistic to gays and lesbians can appropriate the concept of hate and use it against us to prevent gay and lesbian culture building. Senator Jesse Helms, who is no friend of gays and lesbians (or African-Americans, for that matter), did just that in 1989 when he objected to publicly funded art that "denigrates, debases or reviles a person, group, or class of citizens on the basis of race, creed, sex, handicap or national origin."[16] On charges of cultural offensiveness, pro-gay and pro-lesbian speech can be regulated. Conservative African-Americans and their supporters have curtailed sexually-affirming speech of Black gays and lesbians. The showing of the gay-affirmative film *Looking for Langston* was delayed in the United States for almost a year by George Bass, the executor of the Langston Hughes estate.[17] When the film was finally shown in the United States, Hughes' poems had been removed, particularly "Cafe: 3 A.M.," which was against gay bashing by the police, and "Poem for F.S.," which was about his friend Ferdinand Smith:

*Cafe: 3 A.M.*
Detectives from the vice squad
with weary sadistic eyes
spotting fairies.
Degenerates
some folks say.
But God, Nature,
or somebody
made them that way.
Police lady or Lesbian
over there?
Where18

. . .

*Poem (For F.S.)*
I loved my friend.
He went away from me.
There's nothing more to say.
The poem ends,
Soft as it began,—
I loved my friend19

Bass was concerned with making sure that Langston Hughes' image would not be tarnished. This year at the behest of conservative African-Americans, public library officials in Los Angeles forbade putting up posters announcing the Annual Gay and Lesbian Pride Week. The conservatives claimed that a quote from Langston Hughes for gay pride was offensive to the African-American community.[20] Conservative cultural forces may have led Lorraine Hansberry to censor her own lesbianism, according to the poet and essayist Adrienne Rich.[21] Marlon Riggs's Black gay-affirmative film *Tongues Untied* was censored and charged with being "too offensive" by PBS affiliates.[22]

Labeling material "hate speech" also seeks to privilege one meaning or reading over others. This attempt to fix the meaning of pornography seeks to make it content rather than form. If pornography is content, then what distinguishes it from medical photography?[23] Art critic and film maker Kobena Mercer has argued very convincingly that the meaning in sexual representations

cannot be fixed only as hate speech such as in Robert Mapplethorpe's photographs of black men in the exhibit "The Perfect Moment."[24] Mercer has argued that Mapplethorpe's photos of black men used the aesthetics of pornography to circulate the racist fantasies of white men.[25] One year later, in an essay in *Transitions*, Mercer added another reading to Mapplethorpe's photos.[26] In Mercer's new reading, he makes connections between Mapplethorpe's work and its subversion of the category of "high" culture by racializing it. In these photos, states Mercer, "the humanist model of physical beauty said to originate with the Greeks is brought to life by the grace of men who were probably too busy hustling a means of daily survival to be bothered with an appreciation of ancient sculptures in their local art museum."[27] Mercer observes that "with the tilt of the pelvis, the black man's bum becomes a Brancusi."[28]

## CONCLUSION

Allow me to summarize by saying that we should be cautious about the whole idea of censoring pornographic speech. I believe that censoring pornography can only bring about oppression. I believe it perpetuates class bias by altering the distribution of pornography, not its means of production. I ask those of you who oppose it because it is a form of misogyny to reconsider your positions. Pornography can be many things—including and excluding misogynistic. But, as Ann Snitow has argued. "If misogyny is everywhere, why target its sexual manifestation? . . . Why assume that cordoning off of particular sexual images is likely to lessen women's oppression?"[29] I also ask you to think about regulating "hate speech." I am not fully convinced that this legal category benefits gays and lesbians. It is a slippery category. It can protect us, but it can also be the basis for eradicating us, as in the past, when sodomites were burned at the stake for heresy. Their sexual activity was against God's laws, therefore it was hateful.

Finally, let us not forget that asking the state to regulate sexuality and representation has had awful consequences in the past. Birth control and abortion advice were once considered pornography and regulated by the state. Thousands of men and women have been the victims of witch hunts to ferret gays and lesbians out of the armed service. Thousands of men and women have been sterilized and have suffered clitorectomies and castrations for excessive masturbation. Let us not relinquish our sexualities to the state!

## NOTES

1. Catherine MacKinnon, *Toward a Feminist Theory of the State*, 137 (1989).

2. 2 U.S. Department of Justice, Attorney General's Commission on Pornography, Final Report 383 (1986).

3. *Id.* at 382.

4. *Id.* at 383.

5. *Id.* at 381.

6. Lynne Segal, *Slow Motion: Changing Masculinities, Changing Men* 228 (1990).

7. *Our Voices* (1989) (television program).

8. U.S. Dep't of Justice, *supra* note 2, at 869 ("Rather [actual force or threat of force] seems concentrated in the fringe areas of bondage, sadomasochism, and home-made, noncommercial pornography.").

9. Segal, *supra*, note 6, at 221.

10. *Id.*

11. MacKinnon, *supra*, note 1, at 197.

12. Elizabeth Fox-Genovese, *Feminism Without Illusions: A Critique of Individualism* 111 (1991).

13. *Id.* at 110–11.

14. Pornography also "advocates sexual adventure, sex outside of marriage, sex for no reason other then pleasure, casual sex, anonymous sex, group sex, voyeuristic sex, illegal sex, public sex." Lisa Duggan, Nan D. Hunter, and Carole S. Vance, "False Promises: Feminist Antipornography Legislation in the U.S.," in *Women Against Censorship* 130, 135 (Varda Burstyn ed., 1985).

15. Burton Clarke, *Cy Ross and the S.Q. Syndrome* 5 BGM 11<en>18 (1990).

16. Kobena Mercer, "Looking for Trouble," 51 *Transition* 184, 197 (1991).

17. Essex Hemphill, "Undressing Icons," in *Brother to Brother: New Writings by Gay Black Men*, 181–183 (Essex Hemphill ed., 1991).

18. Langston Hughes, "Cafe: 3 A.M.," in *Black Men/White Men: A Gay Anthology* 30 (Michael J. Smith ed., 1983).

19. Langston Hughes, "Poem for F.S.," in *Black Men/White Men: A Gay Anthology supra* note 18, at 31.

20. Mark Haile, "Librarians Protest Use of Langston Hughes Poetry," 3 *BLK: Nat'l Black Lesbian and Gay Newsmag*, July 1991, at 23.

21. Adrienne Rich, "The Problem with Lorraine Hansberry," 19:4 *Freedomways* 247–255 (1979).

22. *See* Janis D. Froelich, "WEDU Board Decides Against Airing Film on Gay Black Men," *St. Petersburg Times*, June 27, 1991, at 1A.

23. *See* Simon Watney, *Policing Desire: Pornography, AIDS and the Media* (1987).

24. Mercer, *supra* note 16, at 196.

25. Isaac Julien and Kobena Mercer, "True Confessions: A Discourse on Images of Black Male Sexuality," in *Brother to Brother*, *supra* note 17, at 167, 169.

26. Mercer, *supra* note 16.

27. *Id.* at 193.

28. *Id.* at 191.

29. Ann Snitow, "Retrenchment Versus Transformation: The Politics of the Antipornography Movement," in *Women Against Censorship*, *supra* note 14 at 107, 117.

# | 79 |

## My History with Censorship

### Joan Nestle

My deep despair at the new antipornography movement and the censorial atmosphere that is fed by it is the legacy of my history. I came of age in a time that has marked me for life, the McCarthy period, the America of the 1950s. I entered the decade a lonely ten-year old living with an aunt and uncle because my mother could no longer afford to keep me. By the end of the fifties and early sixties, I was a practicing Lesbian, a member of CORE and SANE Nuclear Policy, a veteran of Freedom Rides and Woolworth picket lines, of voter registration drives and the march from Selma to Montgomery. I had refused to take cover in air raid drills and was on file as a subversive on my college campus.

I was a member of a group of students who protested against the House Un-American Activities Committee. We sat in disbelief as lawyers for the Committee screamed at and badgered an exhausted JoAnn Grant and Paul Robeson, Jr. I remember to this day the chair's words as we applauded every time one of them took the Fifth Amendment to protest the Committee's right to invade their privacy. He said, "You people"—gesturing at us—"are the scum of the earth." I remember, as we huddled in the corridor during the break, a member of the Committee steering his girlfriend away from us, even brushing her dress aside to make sure it did not touch me. I remember the fifties in tones and gestures, in cadences of accusation. I will never forget the words, "Are you now or have you ever been. . .," nor the frightened or tired or courageous eyes of those who had to hear them. I watched JoAnn Grant sit solidly while a lawyer for HUAC waved a piece of paper over her head, shouting, "Did you ever attend a Pete Seeger concert?" She refused to answer. Any answer delivered her into the hands of those who had already condemned her.

I could go on and on about what it was like to get terrified students and teachers to sign petitions, what it was like to watch the hearings day after day on television, to watch Joseph McCarthy accuse, condemn, and try his victims all at the same time—but not by law. He always said, "We do not send anyone to prison. We are not a court of law," and yet, right before one's eyes and in one's neighborhoods and over the radio, imagination and discussion were struck down.

Any dissension became a heroic act. If you spoke the wrong words or supported the wrong people, you were labeled un-American. You were sent into national, and in many cases private, exile. I watched people in their forties and fifties who had been labor organizers and social activists shrink from their children, withdraw into long, slow deaths. I heard the names read over the radio of those who were to be called in front of the Committee before the Committee even reached a city. Long enough in advance for employers to fire the accused, long enough to give neighbors the time to ostracize the marked family, long enough to give the stigmatized individual time to take his or her own life. None of this was done by legal power. It was done by the power of orthodoxy, of one prevailing view of how to make the country safe. It was not trial in a court of law with a jury: it was conviction by innuendo, by association, by labeling.

This is my historical and emotional starting point on the issue of censorship. These were the years I learned about censorship, the overt kind

---

*A Restricted Country*, pp. 120–122. Ithaca, N.Y.: Firebrand, 1987.

and the more subtle kind; the years I learned about a mentality that reserves for itself the words that mean everything good, and labels dissenters with any term that will send off the alarm. These were the years I learned about anonymous telephone calls warning people about the undesirables among them; the years I learned about visits to places of employment to make sure employers knew who they had working for them. It was the time I learned about silence, enforced by the fear of losing whole communities, about words and pictures never born because difference was a curse.

But all along I had another world to sustain me, the deviant criminalized world of butch-femme Lesbians in Village bars. Here, also, my behavior was policed. Here, also, I was part of a judged community. We were moral dangers. Here I learned that vice squads existed to keep obscenities like myself from polluting the rest of society. Here I learned how to take brutal insults to personal dignity and keep wanting and loving. Here I learned first what a community of women could do even when we were called the scum of the earth.

I worked in the gay liberation movement and the Lesbian liberation movement and then the women's movement for many years before I thought I could begin to explore the meaning of my own life, before in my own mind I was sure that we had won enough ground that I could raise some visions of resistance other than the prevailing ones of the seventies. In 1981, I wrote an article called "Butch-Femme Relationships: Sexual Courage in the 1950s" and published a short story called "Esther's Story." That year marked for me the second McCarthy period in my life. Only this time, many of the holders of truth were women.

They called the organizers of conferences where I was speaking and told them I was a "sexual deviant," labeling me as a dangerous person who betrays the feminist cause. The place where I earn my living, Queens College, was visited by a member of Women Against Pornography who saw it as her duty to warn a group of students and professors about me. "Don't you know she is a Lesbian? Don't you know she practices S&M? Don't you know she engages in unequal patriarchal power sex?" (Butch and femme is what is meant here, I think.) I was told this when I was called to the Women's Center on campus and asked by the group of women students gathered there whether the accusations were correct. Only those of you who remember the cadence of those

McCarthy words — "Are you now or have you ever been . . ." — can know the rage that grew in me at this moment. These young women, so earnest in their feminism, were so set up for this sad moment. "I cannot answer you," I said, "because to do so would bring back a world I have worked my whole life to see never come again."

In the same year, I had another painful encounter with censorship that made me feel again the wounds of the past. One of the most terrible things about the McCarthy period was that friends or supporters could be severely punished for association with a "known subversive." In 1981, Susan Cavin of *Big Apple Dyke News* accepted my short story about a one-night stand with a passing woman for publication. On a May afternoon she called to tell me that the story had been called pornographic by a woman typesetter. She had received the following letter from the Addison Press management:

Dear Susan,

I have just come from a meeting with the brass of this press regarding your paper. It seems that the typesetter that set the current issue of *B.A.D. News* made such a stink about "offensive" material, that it has caused Mr. Mills, the publisher, to reconsider our business relationship. Fearing legal problems by her potentially quitting over the issue, he would like me to communicate the following to your organization:

The Addison Press will decline to print any subsequent issues of *B.A.D. News* which contains explicit sex. This is primarily in reference to "Esther's Story" and certain dream material . . .

The choice Susan had was to drop my story and keep their printer, or to drop the printer and keep "Esther's Story." I heard her voice telling me her predicament, and it all came back. *B.A.D.* did not have and does not have many resources to rely on for cushioning. My vision had gotten them into trouble. The paper was being punished for association with my ideas. Susan held the line and found a printer in New York who did not care what the words in the story said.

After the Barnard Conference on Sexuality in 1982, when *off our backs* was doing its reporting, I received a late-night call asking me if I had ever spoken out in favor of S&M relationships. That voice over the phone, my tiredness, the power on the other end, all brought home again the litany of the fifties. I had been told by a member of WAP that if I write about butch-femme relationships in the past, I am O.K., but if I am writing about them now in any positive way, I am on the "enemy list." The labels chosen for me this time around are "reactionary," "heterosexually-identified Lesbian," "believer in patriarchal sex."

I now had a sense of what I faced—the Lesbian-feminist antipornography movement on one side, and the homophobia and antisex mentality of some straight people on the other.

Recently, sexually controversial writers lost another piece of ground. Amy Hoffman and I were asked to submit poetry to the *Women's Review of Books*, which is partially funded by Wellesley College. Both of us—she formally, me through a personal letter from a dissenting editor—were told that because our poetry was sexually explicit, the *Review* could not risk publishing it without endangering its funding from the college. Here is an example of censorship coming from a different direction: women's institutions that have some power but are afraid of using it.

Another way censorship works in our community, and it is very effective, is through the closing of bookstore doors to the works of stigmatized writers or publications judged offensive by "feminist" standards, even when they are the creations of other feminists. For instance, two journals I write for, *Bad Attitude* and *On Our Backs*, have not been allowed into many women's bookstores around this country and in Canada because the contents were found to be "prosadomasochistic, antifeminist, antiwoman, anti-Semitic, and racist." Now, as you all know, these are the words that call for exile from our community, for there is no argument possible when this code is used. (As a Jewish woman, I find it ironic that Gentiles are in such a hurry to protect me from myself.) The territory I am allowed had shrunk even more. Once you close the bookstores to a writer who has chosen to write for her community publications, you make the creation of an audience almost impossible.

Sadly, as a community, we have been inventive in discovering ways to control ideas. The refusal to allow someone to speak on a panel because she represents a certain point of view, the spreading of rumors about a woman's sexual practices, the refusal of meeting places to those who embarrass us, or the little white cards that popped up for a while in feminist bookstores, warning the

potential reader of what to expect from a book, to protect the customer's sensibilities.

The latest accusation of pornography came my way last month. Now it is not my words, but a photograph of a part of my body and a dildo and a former lover's hand that has been called unacceptable. Here it is—a forty-five-year-old Lesbian's vagina being touched and opened by her lover's hand to insert a latex dildo. This photo is one of a series of my lover and I making love that appeared in *On Our Backs*. In a subsequent issue of *off our backs*, this photo and the magazine were called pornographic. If the ordinances that are being proposed were now in power, other Lesbians could get this journal banned from the stands, and this photograph would never be seen. But, you see, this image is what my life has been about. This image is what the police tried to bash out of me. This image is what I was always told to keep secret. This image puts me and my body beyond the pale.

Think of what is happening. Think of the times and the traditional relationship between the state and sexual minorities. Think of the tools of repression some are helping to put in place.

The antipornography movement is helping to create a new McCarthy period in the Lesbian community. Some Lesbians are more acceptable than others. Leather and butch and femme Lesbians, transsexuals, Lesbian prostitutes and sex workers, writers of explicit sexual stories—little by little we are being rounded up. First we are distanced and told we are not feminists, even though many of us have spent years building the Movement. Then we are told that we are patriarchal, that we are the voices of submission and dominance, that we are heterosexual lesbians. The doors close to us. Then in a Reagan America, in a Jerry Falwell America, in a family-god-nation America, there will be nothing between us and the government the antiporn movement is helping to empower. Some Lesbian-feminists will turn us in and feel they have made the world safer for women by doing so.

All I have are my words and my body, and I will use them to say and picture the truths I know. I have been homeless before and I can be homeless again, but I almost think I have lived too long when I see lesbians become members of the new vice squad.

# | 80 |

# My Mother Liked to Fuck

JOAN NESTLE

My mother, Regina, was not a matriarchal goddess or spiritual advisor. She worshipped at no altars and many times scorned the label mother. She was a Jewish working-class widowed woman who, from the age of fourteen, worked as a bookkeeper in New York's garment district. My father died before I was born, when my mother was twenty-nine, and left her with two children to raise. My mother liked sex and let me know throughout the years both the punishments and rewards she earned because she dared to be clear about enjoying fucking.

Regina was in my mind that October afternoon I sat in the front row of 1199's union auditorium to tape the panel discussion on pornography and eros. When my mother died, she left no money, no possessions, no property, no insurance policies. She left me only a sheaf of writings, scrawled letters and poems written on the back of yellow ledger sheets. I have written a longer piece about her and me incorporating these letters, but for now I only want to talk about the courage of her sexual legacy and the sexual secrets I found in her writings and how she stood in my mind, the mind of her Lesbian daughter who has loved women for over twenty years, the afternoon of the panel.

At age thirteen my mother allowed herself to be picked up on a Coney Island beach and have sex with a good-looking Jewish young man who was in his twenties; three weeks later he invited her to his apartment where she was gang-raped by three of his friends. She became pregnant and had to have an abortion at age fourteen. The year was 1924. Her German father threatened to kill her, and she left school in the ninth grade to go to work. When my mother writes of these experiences she tells of her sexual passions, of how she wanted sex.

I remember as a little girl, the impatience with my own youth. I recognized that I was someone, someone to be reckoned with. *I sensed the sexual order of life.* I felt its pull. I wanted to be quickly and passionately involved. God, so young and yet so old. I recognized my youth only in the physical sense, as when I exposed my own body to my own vision, saw the beautiful breasts, the flat stomach, the sturdy limbs, the eyes that hid sadness, needed love—a hell of a lot of grit and already acknowledging this to be one hell of a life. I was going to find the key. I knew the hunger but I did not know how to appease it.

She goes on to speak of her shock, pain, and hurt, and later of her anger at the rape, but she ends the narrative with a sexual credo: she would not let this ugliness take away her right to sexual freedom, her enjoyment of "the penis and the vagina," as she puts it.

Respectable ladies did not speak to my mother for most of her widowed life. She picked up men at the racetrack, at OTB offices, slept with them, had affairs with her bosses, and generally lived a sexualized life. Several times she was beaten by the men she brought home. In her fifties, she was beaten unconscious by a merchant seaman when she refused to hand over her paycheck. My mother, in short, was both a sexual victim and a sexual adventurer; her courage grew as the voices of condemnation and threats of violence increased against her. I watched it all, and her belief in a woman's undeniable right to enjoy sex, to actively seek it became a part of me. But I chose women. I wanted to kill the men

---

*A Restricted Country*, pp. 144–150. Ithaca: Firebrand, 1987.

who beat her, who took her week's pay. I wanted her not to need them and to come into my world of Lesbian friendship and passion, but she chose not to. We faced each other as two women for whom sex was important, and after initial skirmishes, she accepted my world of adventure as I did hers.

The week before she died, she was sexually challenging her doctor in the hospital, telling him he probably did it too quick for a woman like her. He, red-faced and young, drew the curtain around her hurriedly. At sixty-seven, my mother still wanted sex and made jokes about what she could do when she didn't have her teeth in. My mother was not a goddess, not a matriarchal figure who looms over my life big-bellied with womyn rituals. She was a working woman who liked to fuck, who believed she had the right to have a penis inside of her if she liked it, and who sought deeply for love but knew that it was much harder to find.

As Andrea Dworkin's litany against the penis rang out that afternoon, I saw my mother's small figure with her inkstained callused hands, never without a cigarette, held out toward me, and I saw her face with a slight smile.

So nu, Joan. is this the world you wanted me to have, where I should feel shame and guilt for what I like? I did for all the years of my life. I fought the rapist and the batterer and didn't give up my knowledge of what I liked. I looked at those dirty pictures, and I saw lonely people. Sometimes I did those things they do in dirty pictures, and wives would not speak to me. Their husbands fucked me first and then went home for Shabbas. I made lots of mistakes, but one thing I never did—I never allowed anyone to bully me out of my sexual needs. Just like you, Joan, when in the fifties I took you to doctors to see if you were a Lesbian, and they said you had too much hair on your face, you were a freak, and they never stopped you either. They called you freak and me whore and maybe they always will, but we fight them best when we keep on doing what they say we should not want or need for the joy we find in doing it. I fucked because I liked it, and Joan, the ugly ones, the ones who beat me or fucked me too hard, they didn't run me out of town, and neither can the women who don't walk my streets of loneliness or need. Don't scream penis at me, but help to change the world so no woman feels shame or fear because she likes to fuck.

# | 81 |

# *Lesbian Pornography: Cultural Transgression and Sexual Demystification*

## LISA HENDERSON

### INTRODUCTION

This essay comes from an uncertain position in what feminists and observers have called the "sex debates" or sometimes the "porn wars," a long international series of analyses, counter-analyses, direct-action campaigns, legislative initiatives, testimonies, disavowals, revocations and regroupings, all around the nature of gendered sexual experience and explicit sexual representation.

For close to fifteen years these debates have raised critical questions about the relationship between sexual imagery and female sexual identity and autonomy. They have also polarised antipornography and *anti*-anti-porn feminist camps.[1] Why this division emerged or expanded when it did is not certain, though as Alice Echols points out, "it

In Sally Munt, ed., *New Lesbian Criticism*, pp. 173–191. New York: Columbia University Press, 1991.

seemed in part a reaction to the sexual revolution [of the 1960s], which increased women's sense of sexual vulnerability by acknowledging their right to sexual pleasure while ignoring the risks associated with [women's] sexual exploration" (1991, p. 289).

The complex analyses put forward by both feminist groups cannot be adequately reviewed here, though it is important to understand that for anti-porn feminists, female subordination in patriarchy is both cause and effect of female degradation in pornography. Among anti-anti-porn feminists, on the other hand, suppressing pornography inevitably becomes part and parcel of a long history of female *sexual* suppression, "closing the avenues of sexual speech at a time when women are only beginning to participate in hitherto male-dominated conversations" (Ellis, O'Dair and Tallmer, 1986, p. 6).

My position in these debates is "uncertain" — not because I can't decide who to march with; since the mid-1980s I have talked, taught and marched with the feminist anti-anti-porn contingent. Uncertain, instead, because I believe that inclusiveness is essential for sexual critique and transformation, and is undermined by a pre-emptive certainty about "good" and "bad" desire, including a feminist certainty in which some women seek to save others from themselves and their dubious sexualities, and to strip still others of their claim to feminism. To say this is not to deny sexual fear and anxiety, nor rightful anger at coercion and brutality. It is to take stock of women's sexual variability and empower sexual outsiders (especially lesbian and gay people) in a selectively anti-sexual public sphere.

This essay also comes from a poststructuralist perspective in communications and cultural studies. From this perspective, the salvation motive in anti-pornography politics is reminiscent of the mass-culture critiques of the 1940s and 1950s, which claimed mass culture's damaging effects on users and on "legitimate" culture at large. As Andrew Ross points out, though the anti-porn critique proposes to reorganise cultural conflict along gender (instead of strictly class) lines, it often "reproduces the same languages of mass manipulation, systematic domination, and victimization which had been the trademark of the Cold War liberal critique of mass culture" (1989, p. 176). Women, like other helpless groups, need protection from pornography and its users. Women who use pornography need protection from themselves, from a critical inability to pierce

their (presumed) patriarchal false consciousness.

Recent studies of media and culture have contested the model of wholesale domination, in part by looking at the reception of mass culture among different audiences or interpretative communities (e.g. Radway, 1984; Ang, 1985; Morley, 1980). Those audiences' variable uses and interpretations challenge the image of monolithic and direct effects, not just because people do different things with the media (as liberal-pluralism might propose) but because the nature of meaning is interactive rather than determined by producer and text. Readers too create meanings, and in the process they may rework a text's dominant messages. In other words, meaning is not hermetically sealed by the text, and interpretation can become the site of cultural resistance or opposition (though it does not necessarily do so). The privileged approach to studying cultural reception in this alternative model is ethnography — engaging with a community through close participation and conversation and constructing theoretically informed narratives of their social and symbolic practices, including their accounts of themselves.

These stances—an uncertain sexual politics, a cultural analysis still interested in the relationship between determination and resistance, and ethnography as a fraught but fruitful research position—underwrite the study of pornography I think is needed in ongoing feminist discussions. Though this essay is not yet a properly ethnographic account, I use these perspectives in an analysis of lesbian pornography and lesbian reading. My purposes in focusing on lesbian material are to introduce it as a symbolic domain virtually overlooked in contemporary debates, even where lesbian sexuality (in some versions) has been foregrounded, and to locate it at the sexual and political nexus of women's liberation and lesbian and gay liberation.

## BUT WHAT IS "LESBIAN PORN"?

Defining pornography is tricky political business, Potter Stewart's confidence notwithstanding. (Stewart, a U.S. Supreme Court Justice, made the legal definition airtight by claiming that he couldn't say what it was but he knew it when he saw it.) For my purposes, pornography is any symbolic expression which "seeks to arouse or which represents arousal" (Smyth, 1990, p. 153). What, then, is lesbian pornography? Depictions of women together in sexual scenarios?

This definition would include those "lesbian" scenes which occur as conventional preambles to otherwise heterosexual narratives. Such scenes raise questions of authenticity in a community whose members are wary of images—particularly sexual ones—that somehow refer to us but which we perceive to be unintended for our pleasure, unmarked by other signifiers of lesbian identity (perhaps short fingernails and haircuts, or women's communities). That does not mean such images are not pleasurable to some lesbians on some occasions. If we can read "Cagney and Lacey" as a lesbian narrative (and we do), we can also make something sexual for ourselves out of "lesbian" scenes in straight porn (cf. Williams, 1989, p. 274). Lesbian "reader address"—textual elements which suggest lesbians as the intended audience—may connote authenticity and heighten the pleasure for those who want to identify as lesbians with porn models, characters and scenarios.[2] Lesbian pleasure is not restricted to such "authentic" representations, however, nor are the pleasures they offer restricted to lesbians.

Such definitional problems acknowledged, this analysis begins with texts that seem conspicuously "lesbian," those which directly address lesbian readers and solicit lesbian identifications. The first is a sex magazine called *On Our Backs*, independently produced in San Francisco since 1984, by and for lesbians.[3] With few exceptions, *On Our Backs* publishes women-only fiction, poetry, drawings and photographs. It also features sexual advice columns, editorials on lesbian sexual culture and sexual politics, book, film and video reviews, display advertising for sexual and non-sexual services and supplies, letters to the editor, reports from lesbian events, occasional readership surveys, safer-sex guidelines, and classified personal ads and announcements, among other attractions.

The second text is *Macho Sluts* (1988), Pat Califia's debut collection of erotic short fiction, most (though not all) in the leather or sadomasochistic vein. Califia is also a novelist, an occasional contributor to *On Our Backs* and a regular sex columnist for *The Advocate*, a U.S. national gay and lesbian weekly.

Despite differences in genre and form, *On Our Backs* and *Macho Sluts* accomplish some of the same ends. They challenge received sexual ideologies, and self-consciously position their words and images on the terrain of lesbian sexual politics. As I argue, they are also "culturally transgressive" and "sexually demystifying."

## *ON OUR BACKS* AND CULTURAL TRANSGRESSION

In *The Politics and Poetics of Transgression* (1986), Peter Stallybrass and Allon White debunk the notion that the transcendent and the grotesque—the "high" and the "low"—are independent in the cultural history of the European bourgeoisie. On the contrary, high and low are radically *inter*dependent, the genteel bourgeois subject officially identifying itself by reviling the "low"—the crass, the dirty, the contaminating—but constituting itself through that very process of revulsion (p. 193): "This," it proclaims, "is what we are not."

The dynamic between high and low is part of the attraction and fascination of pornography, particularly of marginal varieties. It unabashedly objectifies, while proper society dictates that subjectivity is the means to civilisation. It invokes what consciousness represses. It foregrounds a demonised body at the expense of an idealised mind. In Stallybrass and White's captivating phrase, it poses a scandal to the dignity of hegemony (p. 25).

The visual and verbal images in *On Our Backs* connote many transgressive qualities of the "low," particularly in the political context in which the magazine was established. Here was a text subtitled "entertainment for the adventurous lesbian," a coy appropriation of the *Playboy* tag which (unlike *Playboy*) positioned lesbians as sexual objects *and* sexual subjects, directed lesbian images squarely at a lesbian readership, and opposed the stereotype of asexual, lesbian high-mindedness. Indeed, where the subtitle parodied *Playboy*, the magazine title itself was an irreverent gesture to the sexually conservative feminist publication *off our backs*. So, in 1984, at the height of both Reaganism and the feminist sex debates in the USA a group of uppity women with few resources devote what they have to launching a declaration of sexual independence, appropriating, in the process, sexual stances and strategies rooted in San Francisco's gay men's community (cf. Echols, 1991, p. 52). By anti-porn feminist standards, a retrograde moment; by the heterosexist standards of a sexually retrenching society, downright *sub*cultural.

*On Our Backs* came out celebrating a range of lesbian sexual roles, practices and fantasies, among them romance, mysticism, penetration, sadomasochism, dominance-submission, sweet-touching, butch-femme, humping, cruising, leather, bestiality, bondage, cunnilingus, lace, pyrotechnics, cross-generational seduction, public sex, exhibitionism, anal fucking, biking, group sex, masturbation, courting and fisting. Some images subvert a variety of public sexual standards (at least in my academic judgement). Some are more explicit than others in denoting women's bodies and expressing sexual responses through gestures or words. Many portray temptation, seduction, charged and spontaneous scenarios in public and private places, rather than bodily friction; but all are sexually direct.

In the stories, women characters come — some of them frequently, all of them refusing to accept the notion of orgasm as peculiarly and oppressively male, ambitiously (and thus masculinely) "goal-directed." The visual images feature stylised physique poses of women body-builders, close-up photographs of open mouths and tangled tongues, multiple-frame pictorials of indoor and outdoor seduction, women on the verge of penetration by fingers, hands and dildos, frenzied, arched bodies intertwined, bare-breasted, leather-jacketed dykes astride motorbikes, pierced clitorises and nipples, lace lingerie falling from muscular shoulders, studded leather against skin, latex-sheathed hands in the throes of safe (or is it fetishistic?) fucking. Models and characters are mostly white, though also Asian, African-American, Latina and Native American;[5] mostly thin or fleshy, though also heavy; mostly young, though also old; mostly able-bodied, though sometimes with disabilities. All connote "dyke," partly through the details of style and dialogue but also because they are, sublimely, with other women.

So here is an inventory of anti-repressive lesbian sexual portrayals, which is not to say "doing what comes naturally" so much as "doing what comes pleasurably."[6] Envisioning a deeply sexual world among women, these images trade at once on liberatory imagination and subcultural cachet. Lesbians may not consciously experience their sexuality as transgressive, even as they know it to be institutionally reviled. But such fixed, public representations of lesbian sex in a declaratively lesbian context like *On Our Backs* are a potentially transgressive and transformative site. What is socially marginal becomes symbolically central (Stallybrass and White, 1986, p. 23) through a politicised appropriation of sexual taboo, a threat (in the service of lesbian desire) to the sexual codes of both straight society and anti-porn feminist orthodoxy.

## DEMYSTIFYING DESIRE

At the same time, though, the liberatory spirit is sexually demystifying in both the fictional and non-fictional contents of *On Our Backs*. In other words, the magazine brings lesbian desire above ground, affirming its legitimacy and encouraging lesbian women to find and embrace what pleases them sexually. For example, in a lesbian sex advice column perkily named "Toys for us," editor Susie Bright (under the byline "Susie Sexpert") introduces practices which, she suggests, may be arousing but also unnerving for many lesbians. Responding to one reader anxious about "residual heterosexuality" in her attraction (and her lover's) to vaginal penetration, Susie writes:

> Ladies, the discreet, complete and definitive information on dildos is this: penetration is as heterosexual as kissing! Now the truth can be known! Fucking knows no gender. Not only that, but penises can only be compared to dildos in the sense that they take up space. Aside from difference in shape and feel, the most glaring contrast is that the dildo is at your service; it knows no desire other than your own or your partner's. Too many lesbians try on a dildo and harness in the Good Vibrations dressing room and expect the device to just take off with a life of its own. That might be exciting for a couple of sessions, but the truth is that it is much more satisfying to take the time, trial and pleasant error to find out how to maneuver your own dildo for optimal pleasure. Pretty soon you'll find yourself with a whole darling collection of dongs, and will be reduced to giving them pet names: "Where is Henri?" "Has Boom-Boom been cleaned yet" and "how could you lend out Amelia?" (1984, p. 13)[7]

Here, Bright's persona is reassuringly forthright, a 1950s-style sexual naturalism transposed to *women's* sexuality,[8] a lesbian Dr. Ruth whose mission is not only to approve lesbian sexual variability and sexual practices repudiated elsewhere, but to assure her readers of the stability of their lesbian identity in the process. "You want it?" she asks. "Try it, you'll still be a lesbian in the morning."[9] She closes her opinion of penetration with an appeal to the traditionally feminine approach of "taking your time" in sexual explorations, and a domesticated, pop-cultural invocation of all things French as sexual — "Where," she asks, "is Henri?"

Elsewhere in the magazine, anti-porn feminism's disavowal of *On Our Backs*'s erotic stances is dismissively pre-empted. In a recent issue, the "Sex-tracts" department (which reports goings-on of relevance to lesbian sexual politics) observes that in an interview in *off our backs*, anti-pornography feminist Andrea Dworkin had "targeted *On Our Backs* as a prime offender" in perpetuating sexist and patriarchal sex. "Intercourse has nothing to do with lesbians or lesbian sexuality," Dworkin is quoted as saying. "Ask Good Vibrations about their dildo sales sometime, Andrea," responds Greta Christina, the Sextracts columnist, who continues:

> Frankly, Ms. Dworkin, we find your attitudes about lesbian sex restrictive, oppressive, and yes, patriarchal. . . . But thank you for sharing (1990, p. 12)

Some readers I have encountered complain that *On Our Backs* simply doesn't have enough sex. Others are perhaps indifferent to its "non-pornographic" content (like the Sextracts column) but satisfied by the porn. Still others, though, may be reassured by the framing of lesbian pornography amid commentary which reconciles sexual exploration and lesbian empowerment; to partake is not to abandon but to heighten your hard-won consciousness. Again, the message here is the power not of transgression but of sexual revelation—discovering what pleases you. To quote Scott Tucker, "it is not true that forbidden fruit is sweet simply because it is forbidden. It is sweet because it is sweet . . ." (1991, p. 19).

The tempering effect of demystification also occurs in *On Our Backs*'s fiction, through what Sara Dunn calls a "political anxiety" circumscribing lesbian pornography (1990, p. 164). Dunn describes this anxiety as too great a concern for the politics of sexual oppression in a form whose motive is—or should be—sexual fantasy. Lesbian porn writers, she says, are so concerned about preserving "good" politics that they often come between their readers and their characters—for example, inserting the phrase "But Dana did not feel degraded" just before a submissive Dana is laid on her back to take the powerful woman in her mouth. To Dunn, it is not clear that readers want to be reassured at that moment of Dana's self-esteem, whether or not they identify with Dana.

A similar quality consistently appears in *On Our Backs*'s fiction. For example, a softball player (and first-person narrator) who finds herself roughly seduced in the locker room by an opposing outfielder declares:

> I was reduced to helpless writhing. Even if Jamey hadn't been holding my wrists, I probably wouldn't have fought her off (Dellatte, 1990, p. 42).

The player is rescued from a dubious image of coercion by acknowledging her own desire to be "handled." Her acknowledgement, like the rest of the narration, comes in interior monologue, a voice which connotes subjectivity in her desire for sexual objectification at that moment. At the same time, though, it is a wary voice, speaking words like "helpless" and making the consent ambiguous with qualifiers like "probably." The ambiguity incorporates a range of reader responses. " 'Ah,' says the aficionado of rough sexual fantasy, "she 'really' is being taken." "Interesting," responds the tentative reader, "she wants it but she thinks it's tricky."

Another example which recovers an image of sexual danger, this time through a dominant narrator, comes from a story called "The Phoenix Chair" by Susan M. (1986). It is a pyrotechnic scenario, where a woman is blindfolded and bound to a chair by her lover, who contrives to douse her in gasoline then, placing a lighter in her hand, solicits her trust try asking her to roll the tumbler. The bound woman does so, and screams wildly as she senses a fiery flash igniting before her. The dominant woman is moved by the other's trust and explains, as she holds her, how the scenario had been created—with water and just a whiff of gas, and flash paper to simulate the explosion. Considerable space is devoted to this de-briefing, to describing the scene as trustworthy theatre.

This story was in the first issue of *On Our Backs* I purchased, and I read it nervously (though still I read it). Without the de-briefing (or the frequent references to "safe words" which the bound woman could speak to stop or change the scene) I might not have looked at another issue, unable to reconcile myself to such an intense image of sexual danger, though it was indeed that: an image. Perhaps anticipating that response, perhaps reiterating s/m practice as theatre and play, risk though not coercion, the story had ended with an account of the fabrication. In this example, like the softball scenario, the transgressive representation of pleasure in danger is explicated, demystified and at least partly recovered, for readers like me.

The dialectic of transgression and demystification comes through in other readers' experiences with lesbian pornography—for example, the following comment from writer and activist Joan Nestle (1990) who makes and uses lesbian porn:

> I'll tell you the one story that transformed things for me. . . . You know, written erotica, it gives permissions, for explorations. Some people say that's terrible, I think it's wonderful. There was a very important story for me in *On Our Backs*, a story with three women together, two of them butches, wearing dildos. For the first time, the first time I'd read, a woman called her dildo a cock, and another woman went down on her. All my gay life, I wanted to use my mouth. When I read it, first I was confused. I had to reread it, thinking, "but this is three women." Since then I've enjoyed doing both. Later I wrote a story about it. That's what that story enabled. What the words did was make me face a desire and see what the taboo was about it, that desire.

Earlier in our conversation, Nestle had described the legacy of sexual shame attached to coming out as a queer in New York during the mid-1950s. For her (like others), butch and femme are roles to be reclaimed as part of lesbian history and contemporary lesbian identity, not repudiated as a pathetic or falsely conscious mockery of patriarchal gender distinctions. The pornographic image exposed, affirmed—"demystified"—her desire to go down on that cock, a desire which had troubled her as taboo: transgressive, and contemptibly so.

What aroused Nestle about this and other stories was the image of sexual tension—in her words "the manipulation of desire by three powerful people, negotiating differences in language, physical or verbal, in expressing their desires, challenging their sexual fear" (1990). Unlike Susie Sexpert's perky reassurances about the benign dildo in "Toys for us," Nestle was moved by how dildos *could* be used in the story to connote subversions of conventional gender identity and the tense (if consensual) play of sexual power between or among women partners.[10]

Nestle's comment about sexual discovery reminded me of other lesbians who, they told me, had literally "come out" through pornography, affirming their sexual attraction to women before ever having the pleasure of a woman lover. In one case, *On Our Backs*'s explicit imagery had been the source, enabling a woman in her late twenties to construct for herself an image of lesbian desire and her place within it, despite her "embarrassment at buying and owning a lesbian porn rag." Here again, the dynamic was less about transgression as an end in itself than about demystification and sweet reassurance, in a sexually hostile world which volunteers few happy occasions or means for newly experiencing one's sexuality as a lesbian.

## MACHO SLUTS

In Pat Califia's sexual storytelling, gone are *On Our Backs*'s often idyllic daytime reveries of lesbian narrators who exhibit themselves and their arousal to handsome telephone linewomen just outside the bedroom window. Califia's dominance-submission scenarios in *Macho Sluts* are high-contact, otherworldly, and often deeply romantic (if never pastel). As sexual fantasies they are sequestered in cars, hotel rooms or erotic chambers, but their characters are very much connected to lesbian and gay communities. The stories are not tentative but nor, as I shall describe, are they indifferent to sexual coercion and brutality.

In Sara Dunn's reading, Califia is among the few lesbian porn writers who "moves beyond the need to apologize," whose stories exploit rather than "coyly forgive" politically troublesome sexual images and the "disparity between private pleasures and public faces" (Dunn, 1990, pp. 167–8). Indeed, in her introduction to *Macho Sluts*, Califia calls the book a "recruitment poster, as flashy and fast and seductively intimidating as I could make it" (p. 10). Here and throughout the collection, she takes on the lesbian and gay movement's nervous resistance to moral-majority demonising about homosexual conscription. "Gays can't reproduce, so they *recruit*," opined Anita Bryant in her successful 1977 campaign to repeal a gay rights ordinance in Dade County Florida. In the oppressive company of homophobes overturning stereotypes of predatory perverts seducing young innocents is important political work. But in the long struggle for the rights of lesbian and gay people, this has come at the expense of sexual cultures within the movement (especially leatherfolk and cross-dressers), who are often repudiated by others fearful of being identified with or through them. The same is true in anti-porn feminist circles, where lesbian sadomasochists have become the fetishised "Other" of anti-porn sexual politics.

Califia will have none of it—neither from the religious Right or Women Against Pornography nor from anti-*censorship* feminists or the American Civil Liberties Union. Her reasons are not meekly libertarian, and her utopia is explicitly and richly sexual, among other qualities:

> Sex may seem like a trivial part of a radical, futuristic vision, but if we are not safe to indulge in this playful, vulnerable and necessary activity, pleasure ourselves and the others who fascinate us, how safe can a society be for women? A world that guaranteed food, shelter, medical care, full employment, literacy, day care, civil rights and democracy, but denied us sexual license, would make us nothing but well-fed domestic animals with suffrage. (1988, p. 14)

Despite Califia's refusal to retreat, the eight stories in *Macho Sluts* (including one "vanilla," or non-s/m) are introduced by a substantial pro-sex critique which, assuming one reads it, positions the porn in explicitly political terms. In other words, this too is transgressive-sex-plus-consciousness. Unlike "Toys for us," there is nothing perky about Califia's introduction, though it, like the stories, is often funny. But much like the magazine comentaries, it offers readers a new understanding, an intellectual and emotional filter for separating guilt from desire.

While Califia describes the book as her own sexual chronicle, written for those who "understand what I need and value what I see" (p 10), she is no s/m supremacist. She acknowledges that lesbian sexual tastes vary. Her characters begrudgingly concede the legitimacy of "vanilla" sex: "Look, they have a right to their own version of a good time," says the manager of a women's sex emporium about the club's non-s/m crowd (p. 106). Califia also knows that the scenes she offers are rightly subject to readers' imaginations. Resisting the assumption that lesbians want only female characters in erotic fiction, she includes two stories which prominently feature gay men. "But," she says, "if fantasies about men aren't erotic at all for you, you might want to skip these stories or mentally change the male characters into women wearing strap-ons" (p. 17). Though she is seriously critical of "hackneyed" commercial porn and lobbies for "well-written obscenity," here as elsewhere Califia does not claim an artist's

privilege of suggesting that the truth or worth of a piece lies in its author's literary intention. Throughout *Macho Sluts*, readers (novice and expert) are fondly implicated.

By the public standards of official culture, the book's sexual episodes are deeply transgressive. Among Califia's characters are an aloof and hard-edged bass player in a women's rock band called The Bitch, a name which taunts feminist protest against the Rolling Stones; the club proprietor, a six-foot, stiletto-heeled topwoman with knee-length white hair who, for a fee, orchestrates a gang scene for another topwoman; and three leather-clad policemen who "abduct" a leather-woman to dominate her sexually. In ritually propped and costumed scenarios, these characters fetishise the infliction and endurance of pain, whether by hand, cane, clamp or other device. They encounter and sometimes push the limits of their own sexual experience and consciousness. For them, sadism and masochism are disciplined transformations, evocations of the body's "stamina and grace" (p. 25).

Readers who inhabit some version of *Macho Sluts*'s sexual environments may find the stories a welcome affirmation, a rare instance of a self-identified s/m dyke writing and publishing her pieces. But as Califia makes clear throughout the book, it would be a mistake to describe as "insiders" only those who do the kinds of things her characters do. Indeed, there is an organised (and controlled) community of s/m practitioners, and Califia moves among them. But pornographic *fantasies* are just that:

> a realm in which we can embrace pleasures that we may have very good reasons to deny ourselves in real life (like the fact that something might not be nearly as much fun to do as it is to think about). (Califa, 1988, p. 16)

Accepting the stories *as* fantasies, where are we to draw the line between "insider" and "outsider"? Where stands the lesbian who never wears more leather than a softball glove or a pair of sensible pumps, yet in reading Califia recognises her own desire to be sexually taken, to have her nipples pinched, if not clamped (by something as unambiguous and thus threatening as a sexual gadget); her arms pinned by another's hands, if not locked in cuffs? To know the intimacy of offering up her sentient, vulnerable body to someone who will respect her safety *and* her desire? And where is the woman who, in bed, wants nothing more of *Macho Sluts* than the book? Is she in or out of Califia's transgressive universe?

Califia herself poses this question. In the introduction she reminds the audience that "reading this won't make you an outlaw (it's not that easy, sweetheart)" (p. 21). Here she guards hardboiled distinctions between sexual "radicals" (those who publicly position themselves on or outside the margins of sexual legitimacy) and mere consumers, and addresses the latter among her readers. In the same sentence, however, she suggests that those who enjoy the book might "think about why the law is trying to get between you and your prurient interests" (*ibid.*). In this shift of focus—from social participation in "deviant' subcultures to challenging legal restrictions on obscene writing—Califia recognises continuities in lesbian sexual desire and reminds the vanilla not to be smug: you too are deviants, she cautions, and ought to choose your allies carefully.

## MACHO SLUTS AND SEXUAL CONSENT

*Macho Sluts* also addresses a range of readers through its demystifications of s/m practice, particularly around images of consent. Indeed, in her introduction Califia challenges critics who would argue that amid the sexual coercions of patriarchal society, women cannot truly consent to sadomasochism:

> If you don't believe we choose to do s/m, you aren't using the term "consent" in any meaningful way, but rather as a synonym for "mature," "socially acceptable," and "politically correct." (p. 26)

Notwithstanding an important final chapter on lesbians, AIDS and safer sex, *Macho Sluts* is not presented as a guide to sexual practice (though Califia has published two such guides, one called *Sapphistry*, the other *The Lesbian S/M Safety Manual*). Virtually all the stories, however, make pointed distinctions between sadomasochism and sexual coercion. For example, in "Jessie," about the seduction of The Bitch's bass player, a reporter for the local feminist press interviews band members about a fight that broke out between two women at one of the band's concerts. The members are contrite, agreeing that the fight was an unfortunate moment for the women's community. Only Jessie, the bassist, dissents:

She scowled and announced that it was time for women to reclaim their violence. "I just wish the stupid cunts would cut up some rapist instead of each other." Then she offered the interviewer a line of coke.

The journalist, Amazon Birdsong, was not mollified. She could afford to buy her own coke (pharmaceutical, an ounce at a time). She had wealthy parents who love TeKanawa, had never heard of Chuck Berry, collected first editions of D. H. Lawrence, but never went near an adult bookstore. After the stinging review she published ("Pornographic Attitudes Infiltrate Wimmin's Music"), The Bitch didn't get any gigs for six months. They were rescued by a women's karate school on the brink of bankruptcy. The benefit concert they did there salvaged their foundering reputation and gave the bar owners an excuse to start booking them again. (pp. 32–3)

Invoking feminist taboos against drug use, women's violence and sexual name-calling, this passage opposes "politically correct" identifications with Jessie. It also provides a terse and witty caricature of a lesbian community divided by social class (the taste for pharmaceutical versus street coke, TeKanawa versus Chuck Berry, and D. H. Lawrence versus smut), where some use traditional capitalist sanctions against a women's rock band and the band is revived, ironically, by members of the feminist anti-violence movement. Amid this ambivalent characterisation of women's communities and Jessie's identity as an s/m dyke, the dialogue is also clear about what Jessie won't stand for: rape. Here, the story presents an unambiguous distinction between rape, as sexual violence, and dominance and submission, as consensual sexual forms.

Califia makes a similar distinction in "The Surprise Party," though the story heightens the image of sexual danger by withholding implied consent until the end. A topwoman is stopped on the street by three male police officers and taken to a hotel room for a long night of sexual submission. Throughout the encounter, the woman's reflections shift between fury at her captors and desire for the glossy, muscular and leather-bound cops.

What are we to think as we read? Has the woman been abducted? Is she being raped? The title ("Surprise Party") suggests that things may not be as they seem, and this is finally confirmed when the ringleader "cop" gives the woman a ride home, where she discovers a note from her lover on the kitchen table:

"Honey, I let myself in. Don called last night and said he and a couple of his friends were taking you to a surprise party for your birthday, so I'm not surprised to find you gone. I just climbed into your bed to wait for you. Come join me and tell me about it. I brought homemade blintzes for breakfast. I love you slavishly. Fran."

What a lucky dyke I am, she thought. First I get to star in the most scary porn movie in the world, now I come home and find that my best darling girl is waiting for me . . . (p. 242)

Though the woman did not expect the encounter, through the denouement we understand her trust in the men and thus can imagine her willing participation in the scene. The story recovers her from the corrupt image of the "rape victim who wanted it" though not without playing that image as sexual fantasy. As fantasy, the story's portrayal of submissive desire is not simply an articulation of the passive feminine position conventionally inscribed in gender relations. Instead, it becomes the object (or focus) of sexual agency: unlike rape, the woman character (and the reader who identifies with her) controls the fantasy.

A final example of sexual consent, complicated further still, comes from "The Calyx of Isis." The Calyx is a lesbian sexual utopia, a commercial centre where "maybe for the first time in history, lesbians have the choice to be really promiscuous, if that's what they want to do" (p. 94). In the club are bars, baths, dance floors, restaurants and massage rooms patronised by women of all persuasions. Says Tyre, the manager:

We get couples looking for a threesome, single women looking for Ms. Right or Ms. Wrong or Ms. Right Away, black and white and Hispanic and Asian women who are bisexuals, transsexuals, homosexuals, heterosexuals and trysexuals, as in "I'll try anything." Witches and bikers and herbalists and cops and chiropractors and truck drivers and real-estate agents and drug dealers and lobbyists and martial-arts instructors and female bankers and mechanics and dentists and housepainters. (*ibid.*)

The Calyx is ensconced in feminist communities and sensibilities, providing grants to childcare centres, setting up weekday clinics for cervical smears and STD tests, and responding to curious inquiries from nearby anthropologists about the chance to do participant observation. "Only if they'll take their clothes off and stay in the maze," says Tyre. A popular place, the club protects its clientele from gaybashers who cruise the neighbourhood looking for someone to hurt. Well-equipped bouncers guard the nightly queue, dealing personally with threatening passers-by and taking licence plate numbers to track down harassing drivers. At The Calyx, the staff are serious about women's safety.

The club also caters to "specialty" scenarios—indeed the story unfolds around an extended group scene commissioned by a topwoman to witness her lover's strength and devotion. One after the other, Roxanne (the lover) wears out eight dominant women in the basement chambers. Throughout the scene the narration returns to Roxanne, whose fear and desire are elaborately voiced in the third person. The tops change, but Roxanne remains at centre stage.

In so consistently voicing Roxanne's consciousness, in describing the scene as "hers," and through frequent references to "safe words," Califia implies consent in dramatic acts of submission and the fetishising of pain and trust. Late in "The Calyx of Isis," however, she uses the rule of consent to intensify the story's transgressions. When one of the topwomen badmouths another, the offending woman's lover is infuriated and rushes at her, *rescinding* her safe word and (with the others) subjecting her to sexual domination. "This is not consensual" screams the first, a line which took me by surprise. Am I to read this, too, as a staged part of the scenario? In the ritualised codes of sadomasochism, are safe words ever rescinded? I find myself appealing for reassurance to the world beyond the book. The story has abandoned the denotation of consent and relies on the nature of representation itself to distinguish between sexual coercion and sexual fantasy. My anxiety as a reader is visceral, but emotional realism needn't reify the image as sexual coercion. It is a character, not a woman, who is seemingly rushed against her will.

## CONCLUSION

Appeals to representation, however, will satisfy neither my critics nor Califia's, and in many ways that is as it should be. Images and the practices they signify are different but not unrelated. Some critics and activists refuse the difference and argue that pornography *is* violence against women. Others say it cultivates callousness towards the sexual brutality many women suffer. Few consider the women (and men) for whom sexual imagery is one link in a social and cultural lifeline, a link emblematic of their refusal to accept established sexual hierarchies and their will to make their own place. In *On Our Backs* and *Macbo Sluts*, the refusal is dramatically public. While their images transgress anti-porn feminist orthodoxy and the heterosexual mainstream, they also expose, demystify and affirm precisely that part of lesbianism that is so threatening: we take our place among women through sexual and political desire, and in the process declare some resistance to heterosexist and patriarchal cultural scripts. That is not to say, however, that thus declared we are unencumbered. Resistance is resistance, not freedom — to wit, a concluding retrospection:

▼ ▼ ▼

Some years ago, at the meetings of an academic association, I took a taxi from the conference hotel to a lesbian bar, to attend a get-together hosted by the association's lesbian and gay caucus. A friendly and easy-going driver in his early sixties greeted me as the tourist I obviously was and asked me where to. In my caution and self-consciousness, I named the intersection rather than the lesbian establishment.

"You going to the bar?" he inquired as we pulled away from the kerb. "Yeah," I told him, smiling at the irony. The driver asked what brought me to town and I described the conference. Was I a professor? I said I was. He looked over his shoulder and shook his head, smiling an easy smile.

"You don't need anybody, do you?" he said, half asking, half stating. I laughed out loud. "I need a lot of folks" was my response, but I knew what he meant. We reached the bar, like so many others a friendly, shabby place in a treacherous and isolated part of town. The driver told me he would wait until I got inside, and gave me the taxi company's card so I could call when I was ready to leave.

"Don't wait on the street for your cab back," he cautioned, "the driver'll come in and get you." I thanked him for his hospitality.

Inside the bar, I thought for a moment about our exchange. Here I was (as the driver could tell) looking neither for men's companionship nor for economic security, yet vulnerable in this spot at this moment, a lesbian open to dykebashing by

her presence in the very place that promised some retreat. The driver had been struck by her independence, but seeing she was alone, he offered his protection. A paternal gesture? Perhaps, but also a respectful one: the danger was real and she deserved his concern.

I close with this account because it speaks to both distance and proximity between dominant and resistant cultures. The driver, a working person, was not the ruling class, but our encounter and his insight deeply and clearly reflected the structural position of women in patriarchy: even in sexual resistance, we define ourselves (and are partly defined) in relation to dominant gender and sexual orders.

As resistant texts, *On Our Backs* and *Macho Sluts* embody this contradiction. Lesbian pornography does not exist beyond sex-gender and other forms of oppression, but nor does it simply reproduce them. My anxious response to "The Phoenix Chair" or "The Calyx of Isis" comes, perhaps, from a sexual fear many women know, but it is not the same fear that keeps me off some streets at night, nor does it negate the spirit or the image of lesbian sexual self-recognition and celebration, both there for the interpreting through the lens of sexual political struggle. *On Our Backs* and *Macho Sluts* are not for everyone, but they happily imagine a world in which sexual violence and coercion are separated from the power of female sexuality, and neither poses a singular or prescriptive equation for lesbian desire.

*On Our Backs* and *Macho Sluts* are also commodity forms (though their modest profits are more equitably created and distributed among a different group of cultural producers). While it is compelling to imagine desire released from commodification as well as fear, it is not clear that certain sexual practices will disappear if and when their commodification does. Sex is embedded in capitalism, but sex and capitalism are not the same. Nor is resistance necessarily doomed to "licensed release," a ritual contestation which ultimately consolidates the established order (cf. Stallybrass and White, 1986, p. 13). While social structures are always at work in private experience, such a rigidly deterministic view misses the survival value and the political momentum of small and great subversions, refusals, irreverences, new imaginings — particularly those made in the name and experience of pleasure. Their power is often to make and keep the struggle — for self-determination — possible.

## NOTES

With thanks to the Lesbian Herstory Archives in New York City for their pornography files. The Archives is an extraordinary place to work and to keep one's faith in resistance as an essential part of culture, politics, scholarship and everyday life. Thanks as well to LHA co-founder Joan Nestle for her time and insight, and to Kathryn Furano, Larry Gross, Bette Kauffman, Sally Munt, Scott Tucker and Angharad Valdivia for their critical and editorial assistance.

1. Some of the pivotal texts in feminist anti-pornography writing include Dworkin (1981), Barry (1979, esp. Ch. 9), Lederer (1980), Cole (1989), Jeffreys (1985, 1986) and Leidholdt and Raymond (1990). For the anti-anti-porn position, see, e.g., Vance (1984), Snitow, Stansell and Thompson (1983), Burstyn (1987) and *Feminist Review* (1990).

2. The question of what media images women identify with remains open for many mainstream forms as well as for pornography. For further discussion, see Schwictenberg, 1990. On pornography, see "When girls look at boys" (1989), a group interview (which appeared in *On Our Backs*) of lesbian women who use gay men's pornography.

3. *On Our Backs* is not alone in the production of lesbian-directed pornography. *Bad Attitude* started up in Boston in 1986, joined shortly thereafter by *Outrageous Women* and *Idos*.

4. Though I do not equate anti-pornography feminism and reactionary federal politics, I do think the anti-porn position was poised for appropriation by political opportunists whose motives were and are anything but feminist (in the USA, Edwin Meese, Jerry Falwell and Jesse Helms among them).

5. In a recent issue (Nov./Dec. 1990), a reader wrote in to protest that *On Our Backs* featured too few images of Black models or stories about Black lesbian characters. In response, editor Susie Bright agreed, saying that although the magazine does publish work by Black lesbians, they don't get as many submissions as they'd like. She went on to encourage women of colour, big women, older women, "all kinds of women," to submit stories and photography. Bright's "diversity program" makes sense in terms of the reader's letter, but it doesn't address why the magazine receives so few submissions from women of colour, who may have a more complicated historical relationship than white lesbians to sexual objectification by outsiders, and to predominantly white lesbian and gay communities (including the producers of *On Our Backs*).

6. For a critique of "naturalism" in the rhetoric of

both anti-pornography feminism and sexual liberationism, see Weir and Casey (1984).

7. Good Vibrations is a sex shop in San Francisco catering predominantly for women.

8. On the ideology of sexual naturalism in the USA of the late 1950s, see Richard Dyer's chapter on Marilyn Monroe in *Heavenly Bodies* (1986). Dyer discusses the use of Monroe's image in a rhetoric rarely directed towards *women's* sexual liberation.

9. Here I am quoting from Bright's 1986 presentation at Giovanni's Room, a Philadelphia lesbian/gay/feminist bookstore.

10. A gay male friend tells me that lesbians are not the only ones who play with gender signifiers in sexual contexts. Some gay men do too, saying (for example) "I want *his* pussy" or "I want him in my pussy."

## WORKS CITED

Ang, Ien (1985) *Watching Dallas: Soap opera and the melodramatic imagination.* New York: Methuen (English transl.)

Barry, Kathleen (1979) *Female Sexual Slavery.* New York: New York University Press.

Bright, Susie (1984) "Toys for us." *On Our Backs*, 1, 1, p. 13.

Burstyn, Varda, ed. (1987) *Women Against Censorship.* Vancouver: Douglas McIntyre.

Califia, Pat (1981) *Sapphistry.* Tallahassee, FL: Naiad Press.

Califia, Pat (1988) *Macho Sluts.* Boston, MA: Alyson.

Califia, Pat (1990) (ed.) *The Lesbian S/M Safety Manual.* Boston, MA: Alyson.

Christina, Greta (1990) "Sextracts: Dworkin saves us from ourselves." *On Our Backs*, 6, 5, pp. 12–13.

Cole, Susan G. (1989) *Pornography and the Sex Crisis.* Toronto: Amanita.

Dellatte, Gina (1990) "Low and inside." *On Our Backs*, 6, 5, pp. 28–9, 42–3.

Dunn, Sara (1990) "Voyages of the valkyries: Recent lesbian pornographic writing." *Feminist Review*, 34, pp. 161–70.

Dworkin, Andrea (1981) *Pornography: Men possessing women.* New York: Perigree.

Dyer, Richard (1986) *Heavenly Bodies.* New York and London: St Martin's Press.

Echols, Alice (1989) *Daring to be Bad: Radical feminism in America, 1967–1975.* Minneapolis: University of Minnesota Press.

Echols, Alice (1991) "Justifying our love? The evolution of lesbianism through feminism and gay male politics." *The Advocate*, 573, pp. 48–53.

Ellis, Kate, Barbara O'Dair and Abby Tallmer (1986) "Introduction," in Kate Ellis, Nan D. Hunter, Beth Jaker, Barbara O'Dair and Abby Tallmer, eds, *Caught Looking: Feminism, pornography, and censorship*. New York: Caught Looking.

*Feminist Review* (1990) Perverse Politics: Lesbian issues. No. 34.

Jeffreys, Sheila (1985) *The Spinster and her Enemies: Feminism and sexuality, 1880–1930*. London: Pandora.

Jeffreys, Sheila (1986) "Sadomasochism: The erotic cult of fascism." *Lesbian Ethics*, 2, 1, pp 65–82

Lederer, Laura (ed) (1980) *Take Back the Night: Women on pornography*. New York: Morrow.

Leidholt, Dorchen and Janice G. Raymond (1990) *The Sexual Liberals and the Attack on Feminism*. New York: Pergamon Press.

M., Susan (1986) "The Phoenix Chair." *On Our Backs*, 18–19, p. 49.

Morley, David (1980) *The Nationwide Audience*. London: British Film Institute.

Nestle, Joan (1990) Personal interview. New York, 10 May, 1990.

Radway, Janice (1984) *Reading the Romance: Women, patriarchy and popular literature*. Chapel Hill: University of North Carolina Press.

Ross, Andrew (1989) "The popularity of pornography," in Ross, *No Respect: Intellectuals and Popular Culture*. New York: Routledge.

Schwictenberg, Cathy (1990) "Theorizing the feminist audience." Paper presented to the meetings of the International Communications Association, Feminist Scholarship Interest Group, Dublin, June.

Smyth, Cherry (1990) "The pleasure threshold: Looking at lesbian pornography on film." *Feminist Review*, 34, pp. 152–9.

Snitow, Ann, Christine Stansell and Sharon Thompson, eds (1983) *Powers of Desire: The politics of sexuality*. New York: New Feminist Library/Monthly Review Press.

Stallybrass, Peter and Allon White (1986) *The Politics and Poetics of Transgression*. Ithaca, NY: Cornell University Press.

Tucker, Scott (1991) "Gender, fucking and utopia: An essay in response to John Stoltenberg's *Refusing to be a Man*." *Social Text*, 27, pp. 3–34.

Vance, Carole, ed. (1984) *Pleasure and Danger: Exploring female sexuality*. London: Routledge and Kegan Paul.

Weir, Lorna and Leo Casey (1984) "Subverting power in sexuality." *Socialist Review*, 14 3–4, pp. 139–57.

"When girls look at boys." (1989) Group interview. *On Our Backs*, 5, pp. 28–31, 42–3.

Williams, Linda (1989) *Hard Core: Power, pleasure and the "frenzy of the visible."* Berkeley: University of California Press.

# | 82 |

# *Looking for My Penis: The Eroticized Asian in Gay Video Porn*

RICHARD FUNG

Several scientists have begun to examine the relation between personality and human reproductive behaviour from a gene-based evolutionary perspective. . . . In this vein we reported a study of racial difference in sexual restraint such that Orientals > whites > blacks. Restraint was indexed in numerous ways, having in common a lowered allocation of bodily energy to sexual functioning. We found the same racial pattern occurred on gamete production (dizygotic birthing frequency per 100: Mongoloids, 4; Caucasoids,

In Bad Object Choices, ed., *How Do I Look?* pp. 148–160. Seattle: Bay, 1988.

8; Negroids, 16), intercourse frequencies (premarital, marital, extramarital), developmental precocity (age at first intercourse, age at first pregnancy, number of pregnancies), primary sexual characteristics (size of penis, vagina, testis, ovaries), secondary sexual characteristics (salient voice, muscularity, buttocks, breasts), and biologic control of behaviour (periodicity of sexual response, predictability of life history from onset of puberty), as well as in androgen levels and sexual attitudes.[1]

This passage from the *Journal of Research in Personality* was written by University of Western Ontario psychologist Philippe Rushton, who enjoys considerable controversy in Canadian academic circles and in the popular media. His thesis, articulated throughout his work, appropriates biological studies of the continuum of reproductive strategies of oysters through to chimpanzees and posits that degree of "sexuality"—interpreted as penis and vagina size, frequency of intercourse, buttock and lip size—correlates positively with criminality and sociopathic behavior and inversely with intelligence, health, and longevity. Rushton sees race as the determining factor and places East Asians (Rushton uses the word *Orientals*) on one end of the spectrum and blacks on the other. Since whites fall squarely in the middle, the position of perfect balance, there is no need for analysis, and they remain free of scrutiny.

Notwithstanding its profound scientific shortcomings, Rushton's work serves as an excellent articulation of a dominant discourse on race and sexuality in Western society—a system of ideas and reciprocal practices that originated in Europe simultaneously with (some argue as a conscious justification for[2]) Colonial expansion and slavery. In the nineteenth century these ideas took on a scientific gloss with social Darwinism and eugenics. Now they reappear somewhat altered, in psychology journals from the likes of Rushton. It is important to add that these ideas have also permeated the global popular consciousness. Anyone who has been exposed to Western television or advertising images, which is much of the world, will have absorbed this particular constellation of stereotyping and racial hierarchy. In Trinidad in the 1960s, on the outer reaches of the empire, everyone in my schoolyard was thoroughly versed in these "truths" about the races.

Historically, most organizing against racism has concentrated on fighting discrimination that stems from the intelligence—social behavior variable assumed by Rushton's scale. Discrimination based on perceived intellectual ability does, after all, have direct ramifications in terms of education and employment, and therefore for survival. Until recently, issues of gender and sexuality remained a low priority for those who claimed to speak for the communities.[3] But antiracist strategies that fail to subvert the race—gender status quo are of seriously limited value. Racism cannot be narrowly defined in terms of race hatred. Race is a factor in even our most intimate relationships.

The contemporary construction of race and sex as exemplified by Rushton has endowed black people, both men and women, with a threatening hypersexuality. Asians, on the other hand, are collectively seen as undersexed.[4] But here I want to make some crucial distinctions. First, in North America, stereotyping has focused almost exclusively on what recent colonial language designates as "Orientals"—that is East and Southeast Asian peoples—as opposed to the "Orientalism" discussed by Edward Said, which concerns the Middle East. This current, popular usage is based more on a perception of similar physical features—black hair, "slanted" eyes, high cheek bones, and so on—than through a reference to common cultural traits. South Asians, people whose backgrounds are in the Indian subcontinent and Sri Lanka, hardly figure at all in North American popular representations, and those few images are ostensibly devoid of sexual connotation.[5]

Second, within the totalizing stereotype of the "Oriental," there are competing and sometimes contradictory sexual associations based on nationality. So, for example, a person could be seen as Japanese and somewhat kinky, or Filipino and "available." The very same person could also be seen as "Oriental" and therefore sexless. In addition, the racial hierarchy revamped by Rushton is itself in tension with an earlier and only partially eclipsed depiction of all Asians as having an undisciplined and dangerous libido. I am referring to the writings of the early European explorers and missionaries, but also to antimiscegenation laws and such specific legislation as the 1912 Saskatchewan law that barred white women from employment in Chinese-owned businesses.

Finally, East Asian women figure differently from men both in reality and in representation. In "Lotus Blossoms Don't Bleed," Renee Tajima points out that in Hollywood films:

There are two basic types: the Lotus Blossom Baby (a.k.a. China Doll, Geisha Girl, shy Polynesian beauty, et al.) and the Dragon Lady (Fu Manchu's various female relations, prostitutes, devious madames). . . . Asian women in film are, for the most part, passive figures who exist to serve men—as love interests for white men (re: Lotus Blossoms) or as partners in crime for men of their own kind (re: Dragon Ladies)."[6]

Further:

Dutiful creatures that they are, Asian women are often assigned the task of expendability in a situation of illicit love. . . . Noticeably lacking is the portrayal of love relationships between Asian women and Asian men, particularly as lead characters.[7]

Because of their supposed passivity and sexual compliance, Asian women have been fetishized in dominant representation, and there is a large and growing body of literature by Asian women on the oppressiveness of these images. Asian men, however—at least since Sessue Hayakawa, who made a Hollywood career in the 1920s of representing the Asian man as sexual threat[8]—have been consigned to one of two categories: the egghead/wimp, or—in what may be analogous to the lotus blossom–dragon lady dichotomy—the kung fu master/ninja/samurai. He is sometimes dangerous, sometimes friendly, but almost always characterized by a desexualized Zen asceticism. So whereas, as Fanon tells us, "the Negro is eclipsed. He is turned into a penis. He is a penis,"[9] the Asian man is defined by a striking absence down there. And if Asian men have no sexuality, how can we have homosexuality?

Even as recently as the early 1980s, I remember having to prove my queer credentials before being admitted with other Asian men into a Toronto gay club. I do not believe it was a question of a color barrier. Rather, my friends and I felt that the doorman was genuinely unsure about our sexual orientation. We also felt that had we been white and dressed similarly, our entrance would have been automatic.[10]

Although a motto for the lesbian and gay movements has been "we are everywhere," Asians are largely absent from the images produced by both the political and the commercial sectors of the mainstream gay and lesbian communities. From the earliest articulation of the Asian gay and lesbian movements, a principal concern has

therefore been visibility. In political organizing, the demand for a voice, or rather the demand to be heard, has largely been responded to by the problematic practice of "minority" representation on panels and boards.[11] But since racism is a question of power and not of numbers, this strategy has often led to a dead-end tokenistic integration, failing to address the real imbalances.

Creating a space for Asian gay and lesbian representation has meant, among other things, deepening an understanding of what is at stake for Asians in coming out publicly.[12] As is the case for many other people of color and especially immigrants, our families and our ethnic communities are a rare source of affirmation in a racist society. In coming out, we risk (or feel that we risk) losing this support, though the ever-growing organizations of lesbian and gay Asians have worked against this process of cultural exile. In my own experience, the existence of a gay Asian community broke down the cultural schizophrenia in which I related on the one hand to a heterosexual family that affirmed my ethnic culture and, on the other to a gay community that was predominantly white. Knowing that there was support also helped me come out to my family and further bridge the gap.

If we look at commercial gay sexual representation, it appears that the antiracist movements have had little impact: the images of men and male beauty are still of white men and white male beauty. These are the standards against which we compare both ourselves and often our brothers—Asian, black, native, and Latino.[13] Although other people's rejection (or fetishization) of us according to the established racial hierarchies may be experienced as oppressive, we are not necessarily moved to scrutinize our own desire and its relationship to the hegemonic image of the white man.[14]

▼ ▼ ▼

In my lifelong vocation of looking for my penis, trying to fill in the visual void, I have come across only a handful of primary and secondary references to Asian male sexuality in North American representation. Even in my own video work, the stress has been on deconstructing sexual representation and only marginally on creating erotica. So I was very excited at the discovery of a Vietnamese American working in gay porn.

Having acted in six videotapes, Sum Yung Mahn is perhaps the only Asian to qualify as a gay porn "star." Variously known as Brad Troung or

Sam or Sum Yung Mahn, he has worked for a number of different production studios. All of the tapes in which he appears are distributed through International Wavelength, a San Francisco-based mail order company whose catalog entries feature Asians in American, Thai, and Japanese productions. According to the owner of International Wavelength, about 90 percent of the Asian tapes are bought by white men, and the remaining 10 percent are purchased by Asians. But the number of Asian buyers is growing.

In examining Sum Yung Mahn's work, it is important to recognize the different strategies used for fitting an Asian actor into the traditionally white world of gay porn and how the terms of entry are determined by the perceived demands of an intended audience. Three tapes, each geared toward a specific erotic interest, illustrate these strategies.

*Below the Belt* (1985, directed by Philip St. John, California Dream Machine Productions), like most porn tapes, has an episodic structure. All the sequences involve the students and sensei of an all-male karate *dojo*. The authenticity of the setting is proclaimed with the opening shots of a gym full of *gi*-clad, serious-faced young men going through their weapons exercises. Each of the main actors is introduced in turn; with the exception of the teacher, who has dark hair, all fit into the current porn conventions of Aryan, blond, shaved, good looks.[15] Moreover, since Sum Yung Mahn is not even listed in the opening credits, we can surmise that this tape is not targeted to an audience with any particular erotic interest in Asian men. Most gay video porn exclusively uses white actors; those tapes having the least bit of racial integration are pitched to the speciality market through outlets such as International Wavelength.[16] This visual apartheid stems, I assume, from an erroneous perception that the sexual appetites of gay men are exclusive and unchangeable.

A Karate dojo offers a rich opportunity to introduce Asian actors. One might imagine it as the gay Orientalist's dream project. But given the intended audience for this video, the erotic appeal of the dojo, except for the costumes and a few misplaced props (Taiwanese and Korean flags for a Japanese art form?) are completely appropriated into a white world.

The tape's action occurs in a gym, in the students' apartments, and in a garden. The one scene with Sum Yung Mahn is a dream sequence. Two students, Robbie and Stevie, are sitting in a locker room. Robbie confesses that he has been having strange dreams about Greg, their teacher. Cut to the dream sequence, which is coded by clouds of green smoke. Robbie is wearing a red headband with black markings suggesting script (if indeed they belong to an Asian language, they are not the Japanese or Chinese characters that one would expect). He is trapped in an elaborate snare. Enter a character in a black *ninja* mask, wielding a *nanchaku*. Robbie narrates: "I knew this evil samurai would kill me." The masked figure is menacingly running the nanchaku chain under Robbie's genitals when Greg, the teacher, appears and disposes of him. Robbie explains to Stevie in the locker room: "I knew that I owed him my life, and I knew I had to please him [long pause] in any way that he wanted." During that pause we cut back to the dream. Amid more puffs of smoke, Greg, carrying a man in his arms, approaches a low platform. Although Greg's back is toward the camera, we can see that the man is wearing the red headband that identifies him as Robbie. As Greg lays him down, we see that Robbie has "turned Japanese"! It's Sum Yung Mahn.

Greg fucks Sum Yung Mahn, who is always face down. The scene constructs anal intercourse for the Asian Robbie as an act of submission, not of pleasure: unlike other scenes of anal intercourse in the tape, for example, there is no dubbed dialogue on the order of "Oh yeah . . . fuck me harder!" but merely ambiguous groans. Without coming, Greg leaves. A group of (white) men wearing Japanese outfits encircle the platform, and Asian Robbie, or "the Oriental boy," as he is listed in the final credits, turns to lie on his back. He sucks a cock, licks someone's balls. The other men come all over his body; he comes. The final shot of the sequence zooms in to a close-up of Sum Yung Mahn's headband, which dissolves to a similar close-up of Robbie wearing the same headband, emphasizing that the two actors represent one character.

We now cut back to the locker room. Robbie's story has made Stevie horny. He reaches into Robbie's pants, pulls out his penis, and sex follows. In his Asian manifestation, Robbie is fucked and sucks others off (Greek passive/French active/bottom). His passivity is pronounced, and he is never shown other than prone. As a white man, his role is completely reversed: he is at first sucked off by Stevie, and then he fucks him (Greek active/French passive/top). Neither of Robbie's manifestations veers from his prescribed role.

To a greater extent than most other gay porn tapes, *Below the Belt* is directly about power. The hierarchical dojo setting is milked for its evocation of dominance and submission. With the exception of one very romantic sequence midway through the tape, most of the actors stick to their defined roles of top or bottom. Sex, especially anal sex, as punishment is a recurrent image. In this genre of gay pornography, the role-playing in the dream sequence is perfectly apt. What is significant, however, is how race figures into the equation. In a tape that appropriates emblems of Asian power (karate), the only place for a real Asian actor is as a caricature of passivity. Sum Yung Mahn does not portray an Asian, but rather the literalization of a metaphor, so that by being passive, Robbie actually becomes "Oriental." At a more practical level, the device of the dream also allows the producers to introduce an element of the mysterious, the exotic, without disrupting the racial status quo of the rest of the rape. Even in the dream sequence, Sum Yung Mahn is at the center of the frame as spectacle, having minimal physical involvement with the men around him. Although the sequence ends with his climax, he exists for the pleasure of others.

Richard Dyer, writing about gay porn, states that

> although the pleasure of anal sex (that is, of being anally fucked) is represented, the narrative is never organized around the desire to be fucked, but around the desire to ejaculate (whether or not following from anal intercourse). Thus, although at a level of public representation gay men may be thought of as deviant and disruptive of masculine norms because we assert the pleasure of being fucked and the eroticism of the anus, in our pornography this takes a back seat.[17]

Although Tom Waugh's amendment to this argument—that anal pleasure is represented in individual sequences[18]—also holds true for *Below the Belt*, as a whole the power of the penis and the pleasure of ejaculation are clearly the narrative's organizing principles. As with the vast majority of North American tapes featuring Asians, the problem is not the representation of anal pleasure per se, but rather that the narratives privilege the penis while always assigning the Asian the role of bottom; Asian and anus are conflated. In the case of Sum Yung Mahn, being fucked may well be his personal sexual preference. But the fact remains that there are very few occasions in North American video porn in which an Asian fucks a white man, so few, in fact, that International Wavelength promotes the tape *Studio X* (1986) with the blurb "Sum Yung Mahn makes history as the first Asian who fucks a non-Asian."[19]

Although I agree with Waugh that in gay as opposed to straight porn "the spectator's positions in relation to the representations are open and in flux,"[20] this observation applies only when all the participants are white. Race introduces another dimension that may serve to close down some of this mobility. This is not to suggest that the experience of gay men of color with this kind of sexual representation is the same as that of heterosexual women with regard to the gendered gaze of straight porn. For one thing, Asian gay men are men. We can therefore physically experience the pleasures depicted on the screen, since we too have erections and ejaculations and can experience anal penetration. A shifting identification may occur despite the racially defined roles, and most gay Asian men in North America are used to obtaining pleasure from all-white pornography. This, of course, goes hand in hand with many problems of self-image and sexual identity. Still, I have been struck by the unanimity with which gay Asian men I have met, from all over this continent as well as from Asia, immediately identify and resist these representations. Whenever I mention the topic of Asian actors in American porn, the first question I am asked is whether the Asian is simply shown getting fucked.

*Asian Knights* (1985, directed by Ed Sung, William Richhe Productions), the second tape I want to consider, has an Asian producer-director and a predominantly Asian cast. In its first scenario, two Asian men, Brad and Rick, are seeing a white psychiatrist because they are unable to have sex with each other:

> Rick: We never have sex with other Asians. We usually have sex with Caucasian guys.
>
> Counselor: Have you had the opportunity to have sex together?
>
> Rick: Yes, a coupla times, but we never get going.

Homophobia, like other forms of oppression, is seldom dealt with in gay video porn. With the exception of safe sex tapes that attempt a rare blend of the pedagogical with the pornographic, social or political issues are not generally associated with the erotic. It is therefore unusual to see one of the favored discussion topics for gay Asian consciousness-raising groups employed as a sex fantasy in *Asian Knights*. The desexualized image of Asian men that I have described has seriously affected our relationships with one another, and often gay Asian men find it difficult to see each other beyond the terms of platonic friendship or competition, to consider other Asian men as lovers.

True to the conventions of porn, minimal counseling from the psychiatrist convinces Rick and Brad to shed their clothes. Immediately sprouting erections, they proceed to have sex. But what appears to be an assertion of gay Asian desire is quickly derailed. As Brad and Rick make love on the couch, the camera cross-cuts to the psychiatrist looking on from an armchair The rhetoric of the editing suggests that we are observing the two Asian men from his point of view. Soon the white man takes off his clothes and joins in. He immediately takes up a position at the center of the action—and at the center of the frame. What appeared to be a "conversion fantasy" for gay Asian desire was merely a ruse. Brad and Rick's temporary mutual absorption really occurs to establish the superior sexual draw of the white psychiatrist, a stand-in for the white male viewer, who is the real sexual subject of the tape. And the question of Asian-Asian desire, though presented as the main narrative force of the sequence, is deflected, or rather reframed from a white perspective.

Sex between the two Asian men in this sequence can be related somewhat to heterosexual sex in some gay porn films, such as those produced by the Gage brothers. In *Heatstroke* (1982), for example, sex with a woman is used to establish the authenticity of the straight man who is about to be seduced into gay sex. It dramatizes the significance of the conversion from the sanctioned object of desire, underscoring the power of the gay man to incite desire in his socially defined superior It is also tied up with the fantasies of (female) virginity and conquest in Judeo-Christian and other patriarchal societies. The therapy-session sequence of *Asian Knights* also suggests parallels to representations of lesbians in straight porn, representations that are not meant to eroticize women loving women,

but rather to titillate and empower the sexual ego of the heterosexual male viewer.

*Asian Knights* is organized to sell representations of Asians to white men. Unlike Sum Yung Mahn in *Below the Belt*, the actors are therefore more expressive and sexually assertive, as often the seducers as the seduced. But though the roles shift during the predominantly oral sex, the Asians remain passive in anal intercourse, except that they are now shown to want it! How much this assertion of agency represents a step forward remains a question.

Even in the one sequence of *Asian Knights* in which the Asian actor fucks the white man, the scenario privileges the pleasure of the white man over that of the Asian. The sequence begins with the Asian reading a magazine. When the white man (played by porn star Eric Stryker) returns home from a hard day at the office, the waiting Asian asks how his day went, undresses him (even taking off his socks), and proceeds to massage his back.[21] The Asian man acts the role of the mythologized geisha or "the good wife" as fantasized in the mail-order bride business. And, in fact, the "house boy" is one of the most persistent white fantasies about Asian men. The fantasy is also a reality in many Asian countries where economic imperialism gives foreigners, whatever their race, the pick of handsome men in financial need. The accompanying cultural imperialism grants status to those Asians with white lovers. White men who for various reasons, especially age, are deemed unattractive in their own countries, suddenly find themselves elevated and desired.

From the opening shot of painted lotus blossoms on a screen to the shot of a Japanese garden that separates the episodes, from the Chinese pop music to the chinoiserie in the apartment, there is a conscious attempt in *Asian Knights* to evoke a particular atmosphere.[22] Self-conscious "Oriental" signifiers are part and parcel of a colonial fantasy—and reality—that empowers one kind of gay man over another. Though I have known Asian men in dependent relations with older, wealthier white men, as an erotic fantasy the house boy scenario tends to work one way. I know of no scenarios of Asian men and white house boys. It is not the representation of the fantasy that offends, or even the fantasy itself, rather the uniformity with which these narratives reappear and the uncomfortable relationship they have to real social conditions.

*International Skin* (1985, directed by William

Richhe, N'wayvo Richhe Productions), as its name suggests, features a Latino, a black man, Sum Yung Mahn, and a number of white actors. Unlike the other tapes I have discussed, there are no "Oriental" devices. And although Sum Yung Mahn and all the men of color are inevitably fucked (without reciprocating), there is mutual sexual engagement between the white and non-white characters.

In this tape Sum Yung Mahn is Brad, a film student making a movie for his class. Brad is the narrator, and the film begins with a self-reflexive "head and shoulders" shot of Sum Yung Mahn explaining the scenario. The film we are watching supposedly represents Brad's point of view. But here again the tape is not targeted to black, Asian, or Latino men; though Brad introduces all of these men as his friends, no two men of color ever meet on screen. Men of color are not invited to participate in the internationalism that is being sold, except through identification with white characters. This tape illustrates how an agenda of integration becomes problematic if it frames the issue solely in terms of black-white, Asian-white mixing: it perpetuates a system of white-centeredness.

▼ ▼ ▼

The gay Asian viewer is not constructed as sexual subject in any of this work—not on the screen, not as a viewer. I may find Sum Yung Mahn attractive, I may desire his body, but I am always aware that he is not meant for me. I may lust after Eric Stryker and imagine myself as the Asian who is having sex with him, but the role the Asian plays in the scene with him is demeaning. It is not that there is anything wrong with the image of servitude per se, but rather that it is one of the few fantasy scenarios in which we figure, and we are always in the role of servant.

Are there then no pleasures for an Asian viewer? The answer to this question is extremely complex. There is first of all no essential Asian viewer. The race of the person viewing says nothing about how race figures in his or her own desires. Uniracial white representations in porn may not in themselves present a problem in addressing many gay Asian men's desires. But the issue is not simply that porn may deny pleasures to some gay Asian men. We also need to examine what role the pleasure of porn plays in securing a consensus about race and desirability that ultimately works to our disadvantage.

Though the sequences I have focused on in the preceding examples are those in which the discourses about Asian sexuality are most clearly articulated, they do not define the totality of depiction in these tapes. Much of the time the actors merely reproduce or attempt to reproduce the conventions of pornography. The fact that, with the exception of Sum Yung Mahn, they rarely succeed—because of their body type, because Midwestern-cowboy-porn dialect with Vietnamese intonation is just a bit incongruous, because they groan or gyrate just a bit too much—more than anything brings home the relative rigidity of the genre's codes. There is little seamlessness here. There are times, however when the actors appear neither as simulated whites nor as symbolic others. There are several moments in *International Skin*, for example, in which the focus shifts from the genitals to hands caressing a body; these moments feel to me more "genuine." I do not mean this in the sense of an essential Asian sexuality, but rather a moment is captured in which the actor stops pretending. He does not stop acting, but he stops pretending to be a white porn star. I find myself focusing on moments like these, in which the racist ideology of the text seems to be temporarily suspended or rather eclipsed by the erotic power of the moment.

In "Pornography and the Doubleness of Sex for Women," Joanna Russ writes

> Sex is ecstatic, autonomous and lovely for women. Sex is violent, dangerous and unpleasant for women. I don't mean a dichotomy (i.e., two kinds of women or even two kinds of sex) but rather a continuum in which no one's experience is wholly positive or negative.[23]

Gay Asian men are men and therefore not normally victims of the rape, incest, or other sexual harassment to which Russ is referring. However, there is a kind of doubleness, of ambivalence, in the way that Asian men experience contemporary North American gay communities. The "ghetto," the mainstream gay movement, can be a place of freedom and sexual identity. But it is also a site of racial, cultural, and sexual alienation sometimes more pronounced than that in straight society. For me sex is a source of pleasure, but also a site of humiliation and pain. Released from the social constraints against expressing overt racism in public, the intimacy of sex can provide my (non-Asian) partner an opening for letting me know my place—sometimes literally, as when after we come, he turns over and asks where I come from.[24] Most gay Asian men I know have similar experiences.

This is just one reality that differentiates the experiences and therefore the political priorities of gay Asians and. I think, other gay men of color from those of white men. For one thing we cannot afford to take a libertarian approach. Porn can be an active agent in representing and reproducing a sex-race status quo. We cannot attain a healthy alliance without coming to terms with these differences.

The barriers that impede pornography from providing representations of Asian men that are erotic and politically palatable (as opposed to correct) are similar to those that inhibit the Asian documentary, the Asian feature, the Asian experimental film and videotape. We are seen as too peripheral, not commercially viable—not the general audience. *Looking for Langston* (1988),[25] which is the first film I have seen that affirms rather than appropriates the sexuality of black gay men, was produced under exceptional economic circumstances that freed it from the constraints of the marketplace.[26] Should we call for an independent gay Asian pornography? Perhaps I am, in a utopian sort of way, though I feel that the problems in North America's porn conventions are manifold and go beyond the question of race. There is such a limited vision of what constitutes the erotic.

In Canada, the major debate about race and representation has shifted from an emphasis on the image to a discussion of appropriation and control of production and distribution: who gets to produce the work. But as we have seen in the case of *Asian Knights*, the race of the producer is no automatic guarantee of "consciousness" about these issues or of a different product. Much depends on who is constructed as the audience for the work. In any case, it is not surprising that under capitalism, finding my penis may ultimately be a matter of dollars and cents.

## NOTES

I would like to thank Tim McCaskell and Helen Lee for their ongoing criticism and comments, as well as Jeff Nunokawa and Douglas Crimp for their invaluable suggestions in converting the original spoken presentation into a written text. Finally, I would like to extend my gratitude to Bad Object-

Choices for inviting me to participate in "How Do I Look?"

1. J. Philippe Rushton and Anthony F. Bogaert, University of Western Ontario, "Race versus Social Class Difference in Sexual Behaviour: A Follow-up Test of r/K Dimension," *Journal of Research in Personality* 22 (1988), 259.

2. See Eric Williams, *Capitalism and Slavery* (New York: Capricorn, 1966).

3. Feminists of color have long pointed out that racism is phrased differently for men and women. Nevertheless, since it is usually heterosexual (and often middle-class) males whose voices are validated by the power structure, it is their interests that are taken up as "representing" the communities. See Barbara Smith, "Toward a Black Feminist Criticism," *All the Women Are White, All the Blacks Are Men, But Some of Us Are Brave: Black Women's Studies* (Old Westbury NY: The Feminist Press. 1982), 162.

4. The mainstream "leadership" within Asian communities often colludes with the myth of the model minority and the reassuring desexualization of Asian people.

5. In Britain, however, more race-sex stereotypes of South Asians exist. Led by artists such as Pratibha Parmar, Sunil Gupta, and Hanif Kureishi, there is also a growing and already significant body of work by South Asians themselves which takes up questions of sexuality.

6. Renee Tajima, "Lotus Blossoms Don't Bleed: Images of Asian Women," *Anthologies of Asian American Film and Video* (New York: A distribution project of Third World Newsreel, 1984), 28.

7. ibid, 29.

8. See Stephen Gong, "Zen Warrior of the Celluloid (Silent) Years: The Art of Sessue Havakawa," *Bridge* 8, no. 2 (Winter 1982–83), 37–41.

9. Frantz Fanon, *Black Skin, White Masks* (London: Paladin, 1970), 120. For a reconsideration of this statement in the light of contemporary black gay issues, see Kobena Mercer, "Imaging the Black Mans Sex," in *Photography/ Politics: Two*, ed. Pat Holland, Jo Spence, and Simon Watney (London: Comedia/ Methuen, 1987); reprinted in *Male Order: Unwrapping Masculinity*, ed. Rowena Chapman and Jonathan Rutherford (London: Lawrence and Wishart, 1988), 141.

10. I do not think that this could happen in today's Toronto, which now has the second largest Chinese community on the continent. Perhaps it would not have happened in San Francisco. But I still believe that there is an onus on gay Asians and other gay people of color to prove our homosexuality.

11. The term *minority* is misleading. Racism is not a matter of numbers but of power. This is especially clear in situations where people of color constitute actual majorities, as in most former European colonies. At the same time, I feel that none of the current terms are really satisfactory and that too much time spent on the politics of "naming" can in the end be diversionary.

12. To organize effectively with lesbian and gay Asians, we must reject self-righteous condemnation of "closetedness" and see coming out more as a process or a goal, rather than as a prerequisite for participation in the movement.

13. Racism is available to be used by anyone. The conclusion that—because racism = power + prejudice—only white people can be racist is Eurocentric and simply wrong. Individuals have varying degrees and different sources of power, depending on the given moment in a shifting context. This does not contradict the fact that, in contemporary North American society, racism is generally organized around white supremacy.

14. From simple observation, I feel safe in saying that most gay Asian men in North America hold white men as their idealized sexual partners. However, I am not trying to construct an argument for determinism, and there are a number of outstanding problems that are not easily answered by current analyses of power. What of the experience of Asians who are attracted to men of color, including other Asians! What about white men who prefer Asians sexually? How and to what extent is desire articulated in terms of race as opposed to body type or other attributes? To what extent is sexual attraction exclusive and/or changeable, and can it be consciously programmed? These questions are all politically loaded, as they parallel and impact the debates between essentialists and social constructionists on the nature of homosexuality itself. They are also emotionally charged, in that sexual choice involving race has been a basis for moral judgment.

15. See Richard Dyer, *Heavenly Bodies: Film Stars and Society* (New York: St. Martin's Press, 1986). In his chapter on Marilyn Monroe, Dyer writes extensively on the relationship between blondness, whiteness, and desirability.

16. Print porn is somewhat more racially integrated, as are the new safe sex tapes—by the Gay Men's Health Crisis, for example—produced in a political and pedagogical rather than a commercial context.

17. Richard Dyer, "Coming to Terms," *Jump Cut*, no. 30 (March 1985), 28.

18. Tom Waugh, "Men's Pornography, Gay vs. Straight," *Jump Cut*, no. 30 (March 1985), 3 1.

19. *International Wavelength News* 2, no. 1 (January 1991).

20. Tom Waugh, "Men's Pornography, Gay vs. Straight," 33.

21. It seems to me that the undressing here is organized around the pleasure of the white man in being served. This is in contrast lo the undressing scenes in, say, James Bond films, in which the narrative is organized around undressing as an act of revealing the woman's body, an indicator of sexual conquest.

22. Interestingly, the gay video porn from Japan and Thailand that I have seen has none of this Oriental coding. Asianness is not taken up as a sign but is taken for granted as a setting for the narrative.

23. Joanna Russ, "Pornography and the Doubleness of Sex for Women," *Jump Cut*, no. 32 (April 1986), 39.

24. Though this is a common enough question in our postcolonial, urban environments, when asked of Asians it often reveals two agendas: first, the assumption that all Asians are newly arrived immigrants and, second, a fascination with difference and sameness. Although we (Asians) all supposedly look alike, there are specific characteristics and stereotypes associated with each particular ethnic group. The inability to tell us apart underlies the inscrutability attributed to Asians. This "inscrutability" took on sadly ridiculous proportions when during World War II the Chinese were issued badges so that white Canadians could distinguish them from "the enemy."

25. Isaac Julien (director), *Looking for Langston* (United Kingdom: Sankofa Film and Video, 1988).

26. For more on the origins of the black film and video workshops in Britain, see Jim Pines, "The Cultural Context of Black British Cinema," in *Black-frames: Critical Perspectives on Black Independent Cinema*, ed. Mybe B. Cham and Claire Andrade-Watkins (Cambridge, Mass.: MIT Press, 1988), 26.

# IV.C
## QUEERS IN CYBERSPACE

Arguments in support of free speech generally invoke the concept of a marketplace of ideas, in which all may offer their views and all may therefore encounter diverse and possibly persuasive opinions. Following on this is the principle articulated by Supreme Court Justices Holmes and Brandeis that the "appropriate response to speech with which one disagrees is not censorship but counterspeech" (Strossen 1995:41). However, in practice, not all speech is equal, and, as A. J. Liebling famously put it, the press is free to the one who owns it. In a community defined by the boundaries of the modern nation-state—or even, say, of Peoria—the marketplace of ideas is not a physical agora or forum in which citizens assemble and debate the issues of the day. If we have a modern agora, it exists in the glow of the television screen, and most citizens are banished to the sidelines, listening perhaps but hardly contributing *counterspeech* in response to views with which they disagree. True, we can, and many do, call in to the numerous radio talk shows, but their effect on public discourse and consciousness has yet to be established—certainly it seems likely that callers are speaking to like-minded citizens, not persuading those of divergent views. Those whose lives or convictions place them outside the mainstream are not likely to find their realities reflected in the images and voices that dominate the public sphere of our society. In fact, they might deem themselves lucky if they do not find themselves the objects of ridicule and attack.

In the lesbian and gay studies course that was the stimulus for this *Reader* the first written assignment each year has asked the students to "pretend" that they are fifteen year olds (not too big a stretch for most of them) and beginning to question their sexuality. The assignment is to go to a public library and, acting the part of a timid fifteen year old, see what information is available on homosexuality. Over the years since that assignment was first given, in 1980, there has been a steady improvement in the materials discovered by those pretend teens in the public libraries in and around Philadelphia. But improvement shouldn't be interpreted as perfection—far from it. For every student who finds *One Teenager in Ten* (Heron 1983) or *Becoming Visible* (Jennings 1994) on the shelves, there is another who turns up the *Catholic Encyclopedia* or David Ruben's *Everything You Wanted to Know About Sex, But Were Afraid to Ask*. But there are new resources increasingly available to teens as well as to older lesbian, gay, bisexual, and transgendered people—in cyberspace.

*Cyberspace* is a term first introduced in 1981 by science fiction writer William Gibson to describe the newly emerging electronic frontier that now goes under such names as the Information Superhighway, the Internet, and the World Wide Web. This isn't the place to attempt an adequate description of cyberspace, were that even possible, but several basic attributes are relevant here. Cyberspace offers an electronic agora that comes close to realizing the promise of a level playing field of information and opinion and thus offers the possibility of a truly free marketplace of ideas. It also guarantees a cacophony of competing voices in which your message may suffer the fate of the tree falling in the forest with no one to hear it. As Herbert Simon put it, the scarce commodity in this new world is not information but attention. However, for all the booming, buzzing confusion of cyberspace, it is possible to navigate as well as surf, to find information, make friends, and influence people.

Queers were among the first to realize the potential of this new technology. As an Associated Press story put it, "It's the unspoken secret of the online world that gay men and lesbians are among the most avid, loyal and plentiful commercial users of the Internet" (6/24/96). Not suprisingly, it wasn't long before entrepreneurs began to develop this promising tract of electronic real estate. As Tom Rielly, the founder of *Planet Out*, an electronic media company that began on the Microsoft Network in 1995, explained, "Traditional mass media is very cost-intensive. Gays and lesbians don't have a high level of ownership of mainstream media properties. The Internet is the first medium where we can have equal footing with the big players" (Lewis 1995b). For Rielly and his financial backers the attractions of marketing to a large and underserved group were obvious. But cyberspace also provides "a gathering point for millions of lesbians, gay men, bisexuals, transvestites and others who may be reluctant to associate in public" (ibid.). For those who are, with or without good reason, afraid to visit gay establishments or subscribe to gay publications, "gay online services bring the gay community into their homes, where they're shielded from their neighbors and coworkers" (Associated Press, 6/24/96).

The queer cybernaut who sets sail guided by the many "search engines" available on the Internet will readily find a wealth of information and organizational resources. The Queer Resources Directory, for example, offers a structured map of topics and areas housing files and links to other sites. Among the national organizations that can be reached via the Internet are the National Gay and Lesbian Task Force, Gay and Lesbian Alliance Against Defamation (GLAAD), the Human Rights Campaign, Parents and Friends of Lesbians and Gays (P-FLAG), as well as several specifically electronic magazines and cyberversions of print magazines. Beyond the organizations and the electronic magazines lies the vast territory of the "chat rooms" and bulletin board discussion groups. "On any given evening, one-third of all the member-created chat rooms on America Online are devoted to gay topics" (Associated Press, 6/24/96).

Among those for whom the Internet is most valuable are teenagers, previously isolated, fearful, and scattered, who are using computer networks to declare their homosexuality, meet, and seek support from other gay youths. The stories that fly through the ether make it all too clear that the Internet can literally be a lifesaver for many queer teens trapped in enemy territory (Silberman, "We're Teen, We're Queer, and We've Got E-Mail"; Walsh, "Logging On, Coming Out," this volume). In addition to bulletin boards and one-to-one correspondence, queer youth can now locate sites specifically created for them such as *Oasis* and *YouthArts*. *Oasis* is a monthly electronic magazine for lesbian and gay teens that includes regular columns by a P-FLAG leader and a clincal psychologist specializing in working with gay youth and suicide prevention. *Oasis* also features a lineup of youth columnists that has included a sixteen-year-old high school student from Nova Scotia, a sophomore at Kansas State University, and a law student at the University of North Carolina. *YouthArts*, founded by lesbian author and activist Patricia Nell Warren, describes itself as "a contemporary museum/library of the creative works of young lesbians, gays, bisexuals, transgendered, and questioning young people. Here on the Web, WE have our own space."

The involvement of teens, gay or otherwise, in the Internet, highlights one of the most controversial aspects of this electronic frontier—its ability to transmit sexually explicit images and words. Every new communications technology has been put to work in the service of humanity's boundless interest in sex. "Sometimes the erotic has been a force driving technological innovation; virtually always, from Stone Age sculpture to computer bulletin boards, it has been one of the first uses for a new medium" (Tierney 1995). As might be expected, queers were among those using the Internet to locate sexual images and stories and to contact potential sexual partners (Tsang, "Notes on Queer 'N Asian Virtual Sex," this volume). As also might be expected, the Internet quickly attracted the attention of the censorious, and, once again, the protection of children was their rallying cry.

In 1994 Martin Rimm, an undergraduate at Carnegie Mellon University, conducted a study of the Usenet, a global network of fifteen thousand discussion groups, and concluded that "83.5 percent of all images posted on the Usenet are pornographic" (Lewis 1995). A *Time* magazine cover story on "cyberporn" based largely on Rimm's study (June 26, 1994) added fuel to a growing political bonfire. Senator Charles Grassley (R-Iowa) introduced *Time*'s story into the Congressional Record, repeating the claim that "83.5 percent of all computerized photographs available on the Internet are pornographic," in support of his proposed Protection of Children from Computer Pornography Act of 1995 (Senate, 6/26/95). Senator Grassley was not successful in his attempt to "stem this growing tide" of "vile pornography," perhaps because the Rimm study was quickly discredited once experts were consulted. Even Rimm's faculty adviser noted that the study revealed a "tendency to want to make generalizations that couldn't be made" (Lewis 1995a). But Rimm's study and the media hype were merely a symptom of a larger phenomenon, and although the 83.5 percent claim may have faded, the anticyberporn crusade continued. The May 1995 issue of *Family Voice*, the magazine of the right-wing Concerned Women for America warned readers, "The Internet has become the latest avenue for pornography to slip into the home."

When Anthony Comstock secured passage of "An Act for the Suppression of Trade in, and Circulation of, Obscene Literature and Articles of Immoral Use," which President Grant signed in 1873, he was focused on the distribution of information about abortion, contraception, or sexual activity through the mails, and in his uniquely created position as special agent of the U.S. Post Office he served as America's censor for forty years. "Spread throughout the country, indiscriminately accessible, public and private at once, the postal system had (odd as it may sound) something sexy about it. Left unpoliced, sex bred chaos; uninspected, the mails might do the same" (Kendrick 1987:145). If Comstock were still alive, he would be even more terrified of the Internet, as it far exceeds the postal system in speed (to put it mildly) and in its potential to reach those he considered susceptible to the traps laid for the young.

Fifteen-year-old Daniel Montgomery, for example. In June 1995 the Seattle papers reported that the teenager had been "lured" away from home by a stranger, but not someone "casing his neighborhood or hanging around outside his high school" (Byrnes 1995). "Instead, the mysterious character known to the Montgomerys only as 'Damien Star' was lurking in a place that proven much more ominous: cyberspace." The encounter took place in a "gay chat room" on America Online — "it was there that the man apparently enticed Daniel Montgomery with secret promises" to run away from home and join him in San Francisco. Daniel's father believed his son was the victim of "an organized attempt by adults to recruit boys like Daniel." The vice principal of his school told the paper that "we've certainly had runaways before . . . but holy cow, this makes you sick."

Within a few days, however, it seemed that things were not quite as Comstockian as earlier reports had suggested. Daniel's father is identified with the religious right and acknowledged that "there are issues between him and the teenager," presumably because "Daniel may have been sexually confused" (Weise 1995). More important, it turned out that Damien Starr wasn't the pseudonym of a dirty old man who was infiltrating the Internet to lure innocent teenagers into a life of depravity. Damien Starr is the real name of a San Francisco teenager who met Daniel Montgomery in a gay America Online chat room and apparently responded sympathetically to accounts of his difficulties with his parents.

The unmasking of Damien Starr did nothing to allay the fears of those who see in the Internet a threat to the innocent and vulnerable. The week after Daniel Montgomery returned home to his parents the United States Senate voted to impose heavy fines and prison terms on those who distribute sexually explicit material over computer networks:

> Voting 84–16 in a session rife with lurid talk about child pornography and on-line descriptions of bestiality, advocates of tough regulation easily overwhelmed objections from a handful of lawmakers who said the measure would violate constitutional rights to free speech and threaten the growth of computer networks. "Take a look at this disgusting material, pictures which were copied for free off the Internet only this week," said Sen. Jim Exon, D-Neb., the measure's chief sponsor, as he brandished a big blue binder with a bright red label: "Caution." (Andrews 1995b)

Senator Exon, like his predecessors back to Comstock, presented his role as protecting children, not as restricting expression. "I'm not trying to be a super censor. The first thing I was concerned with was kids being able to pull up pornography on their machines" (Andrews 1995a). Special Agent Comstock was present in more than spirit, however, as the U.S. Congress moved toward the inclusion of Senator Exon's Communications Decency Act (CDA) as part of the omnibus Telecommunications Reform Act signed by President Clinton on February 8, 1996. The CDA revived the provisions of the 1873 Comstock Act prohibiting mailing of abortion-related materials across state lines, which are still on the books though essentially nullified by Roe v. Wade, and added them to the prohibition against making available to minors on-line materials that "in context, depicts or describes in terms patently offensive as measured by contemporary community standards, sexual or excretory activities or organs." The CDA was the target of an immediate lawsuit filed by the ACLU in the name of a group of plaintiffs that included Planned Parenthood, Critical Path AIDS Project, and *YouthArts*.

In June 1996 a three-judge federal district court panel struck down the CDA. Judge Stewart Dalzell wrote that "the Internet may fairly be regarded as a never-ending worldwide conversation. The Government may not, through the CDA, interrupt that conversation. As the most participatory form of mass speech yet developed, the Internet deserves the highest protection from government intrusion" (*ACLU v. Reno*). The following year the U.S. Supreme Court voted seven to two to affirm the lower court's decision.

## REFERENCES

Andrews, Edmund. 1995a. "Panel Backs Smut Ban on Internet." *New York Times*, March 24.

— 1995b. "On-Line Porn May Be Illegal." *New York Times*, June 15.

Associated Press. 1996. "Gay and Lesbian Net Surfers: A Dream Market in the Online World." June 24.

Byrnes, Susan. 1995. "Parents Suspect Cyberspace 'Kidnap.'" *Seattle Times*, June 2.

Heron, Ann. 1983. *One Teenager in Ten: Writings by Gay and Lesbian Youth*. Boston: Alyson.

Jennings, Kevin. 1994. *Becoming Visible: A Reader in Gay and Lesbian History for High School and College Students*. Boston: Alyson.

Kendrick, Walter. 1987. *The Secret Museum: Pornography in Modern Culture*. New York: Viking.

Lewis, Peter. 1995a. "Pornography Study on Computers Seen as Sensationalistic." *New York Times*, July 3.

— 1995b. "Planet Out's Gay Services on Virtual Horizon." *New York Times*, August 21, p. D3.

Strossen, Nadine. 1995. *Defending Pornography: Free Speech, Sex, and the Fight for Women's Rights*. New York: Scribner.

Weise, Elizabeth. 1995. "Cyberspace Runaway." Associated Press, June 5; "Cyberspace Suspect Also a Teen." Associated Press, June 7.

# | 83 |

# Notes on Queer 'N Asian Virtual Sex

## Daniel C. Tsang

The relationship between technology and sexuality is a symbiotic one. As humankind creates new inventions, people find ways of eroticizing new technology. Today, sex shops sell sex toys for all sorts of sex acts, but in fact, virtually anything can be a turn-on to someone. Once, lacking a real dildo, my partner and I dug out a frozen carrot from the refrigerator, thawed it under running water, and tried, rather unsuccessfully to use it as an organic replacement. The role sex plays in human endeavor is an area always worth exploring, and despite the contemporary focus on matters sexual, one could argue that society has paid attention to sex throughout recorded history. Tierney even argues that the

> erotic technological impulse dates back at least to some of the earliest works of art, the so-called Venus figurines of women with exaggerated breasts and buttocks, which were made by firing clay 27,000 years ago — 15 millenniums before ceramics technology was used for anything utilitarian like pots.[1]

So it is not surprising that with the advent of the information super-highway, more and more folks are discovering the sexual underground within the virtual community in cyberspace.

Like the stereotypical computer nerd, I have sat in front of my computer, pressed some keys, and connected to a remote computer, perhaps twice daily, if not more often. But unlike the desexualized computer nerd, I have used the computer to connect to a Bulletin Board System (BBS) with a significant number of gay Asian members and used it to meet others for affection, romance, love and sex for several years. In fact, as I write, I have logged on to this board over 1,680 times, out of over 600,000 calls made by everyone to the board since its creation in September 1991. How many sexual partners I have met will remain a state secret. Of the 1,088 BBSers registered, some eighty-eight (8 percent) identify as Asian gay or bisexual males.

Initially this just seemed like the computerized, electronic version of placing or responding to a personal ad, as I had several times before. But as time went on, it dawned on me that this was something entirely different, with the potential for creativity (and mischief) largely untapped by myself and most of the others (I presumed) on the BBS.

One need not belabor the differences between pen and paper and the computer to recognize that with instantaneous communication now available, dating — and fulfilling our sexual desires — are much more immediately realizable.

Friends may bemoan months of BBSing without meeting anyone in the flesh, but they, alas, miss the point. The online experiences are ones that I cherish, not just the real live ones.

On the board, fantasy substitutes for hard reality. For a couple of years I had been chatting electronically with this college student; recently I called his college (he had given me his name and address) and found he did not exist, nor did his dormitory. Yet this was someone with whom I had even chatted "voice," i.e., on the phone. Could he have been a figment of my imagination? Or did he give me false identification? Or worse still, was an undercover government agent infiltrating the board to investigate my sex life? After all, the CIA has admitted collecting information about me and giving it away to a foreign government.[2]

*Amerasian Journal*, 20(1):117–128, 1994.

It does pay to have a sense of "healthy paranoia" online. For despite the illusion of privacy, nothing one types is really truly private. The sysop [system operator] can "tap" your electronic conversations; who knows if the recipient is not "downloading" your love notes? Sometimes, in "open chat," the forum is deliberately not private, and several people can chat at once or almost at once. All participants get to read your the messages flying back and forth. Without even the National Security Agency having its Clipper chip access, BBSing is arguably more open than chatting in public. Berlet (1985), for example, argues that today's BBS sysops "are merely the modern incarnation of the pesky and audacious colonial period pamphleteers like John Peter Zenger and Thomas Paine" and that today, "Zenger might well be a political dissident running a controversial BBS while listening to audio tapes of the 'Police' singing about surveillance," and should thus protected by privacy laws from government intrusion.[3]

But despite the best efforts of these civil libertarians to protect the privacy of BBSers, those who chat online need a wake-up call: the notion of privacy is, in the end, an illusion. Like the HIV status of your electronic mate, don't be deluded. Play safe: treat every message as public, and every sexual partner as HIV positive. The BBS challenges traditional notions of privacy and obscures the lines between private and public.

One reason BBSing is so fascinating is that the online environment truly allows one to continually reinvent one's identity, including the sexual. For once, you are in total control of your sexual identity, or identities, or at least what you decide to show the outside world.

Indeed, it is our sexualities that are on display. In real life, but more so in virtual reality, our sexualities are not fixed, but constantly in flux. In the Foucauldian sense, we re-invent our sexualities. Over time we can have more than one. And there are more than just gay or straight. And despite the protestations of the latest adherents to gay ideology that they were born gay, the online environment reminds us that our sexualities are ephemeral, to be changed with a stroke of a key. These are social constructs, not biological essentialisms.

In virtual reality, we can take on other identities than our current one, often with no one else the wiser. In time, these online identities may become more real than the physical one.

One student I know even signs on under a friend's I.D. so that he can maximize his time on the board; and he is on the board for hours daily even during exam week. Personally, I can't tell you how long it has been since I have been to a gay bar, except to pick up gay magazines; like numerous others, electronic cruising has replaced bar hopping.

The BBS I am most often on allows its members (those who pay or like me, were grandfathered in) to post not only a written biography of ourselves, answers to numerous questionnaires, but also digital portraits of ourselves. In turn, members can peruse (or "browse") these bios and questionnaire responses, as well as retrieve and down- load your digital image, and see you in the flesh, even nude.

Thus, with a keystroke, one can change one's biographical particulars, e.g., ethnicity, age, domestic partnership status, class, or even sexual orientation. This means, of course, that all the posted information should be taken with a grain of salt.

Age is one good example. This board, like many others, restricts membership to adults (eighteen and over). Hence, any minor who seeks access must lie about his age. In fact two had been kicked off the board because they were minors, according to the sysop. (The board is predominantly male, with only a handful of female, out of almost 1,100 members.) On the other end of the age scale, because of the disdain against them, some older men do not give their true age. When I went on I put my age as thirty-six; after several years, it has been changed only by one year, to thirty-seven.

Ethnicity or race is another characteristic that can be changed, almost at will. If being Vietnamese today is not what you want to be, you could pick some other category. One BBSer from Taiwan even picked "Caucasian," and found out lots more people wanted to chat with him than when he was "Chinese," a recognition that the electronic environment does not screen out racist sentiments.

Caucasians inhabit most of this virtual space, although there is significant Asian presence (on this board, as reported above, some 8 percent). Although Caucasians will describe themselves as being of various European backgrounds, depending on the person, the distinctions may not be revealing. If Caucasians see us as the "other," we admittedly often see the white race as just monolithic. Once, when I wrote about the "rice queen" phenomenon in a gay magazine, *Frontiers*, several white readers wrote in to argue that I was racist, because I lumped all whites together. It seems to be an empirical question as to whether or not white Americans really do identify as "Italian" or "German." The dominant role race plays in American society tends to obscure the diversities that exist in all cultures.

When I was growing up in Hong Kong, I definitely could tell the British colonials apart from the other *gwailos*. Ethnically Chinese, my Hong Kong I.D. card was stamped "American," because my mom was born in the U.S., but I never felt American, until years after I had lived in the States. As Dana Takagi argues [elsewhere in this volume], the study of gay Asians awakens us to the dangers of essentializing the Asian American. In fact, like sexualities, Asian American identities are not static, but in constant flux. The contemporary influx of South-east Asians and other Asian subgroups to this country makes us realize that one can no longer limit our discourse to Chinese or Japanese subcultures.

The diversity of Asian identities in the U.S. is reflected in the Asian gay or bisexual male membership of the BBS. The figures for female Asians or straight Asians on the board are too few for meaningful analysis. Although anyone can access this board by modem, given this particular BBS's location in Orange County, California, which has seen a 271 percent increase in its Vietnamese population in the decade since the 1980 census, it is surprising that only a few (thirteen) of the Asian gays or bisexuals on the board identify themselves as Vietnamese. That figure is identical to the number identifying as Japanese. In fact, the majority of the gay or bisexual Asians say they are Chinese (thirty-three in all). The 1990 census shows an increase of 191 percent in the Chinese population in the county. Filipino gay or bisexuals are also a significant number on this board, adding up to seventeen. The 1990 census shows that Filipinos have also increased in size in the county since the last census, by 178 percent. There are nine Amerasian or Eurasian gay or bisexuals and four Pacific Islander gays or bisexuals. There is only one Thai, and two East Indians. Although I have chatted with at least one Korean American on the board, he and any other apparently did not publicly identify their ethnicity.

Because this board was set up to serve gay males (in fact the sysop is a gay Vietnamese immigrant), there are few females on the board. Since some on the board specify they would only chat with other males, a female BBSer is at a disadvantage. She can continue to stay on the board as a female, or she can change her gender on her electronic biography. Whether anyone has done that remains an open question. Despite the preference of many to chat only with other males, the few hardy souls who are female have stuck it out, although one friend I know dropped out soon after, but also because she had relocated north.

One could argue that by signing up for the board, one is, in fact, taking the first step toward "coming out." Even though one can remain largely anonymous on the board with "handles" that are pseudonyms and not real names, the fact that a BBSer needs to identify his sexual orientation on the board makes it an important act of coming out. Many of the BBSers, for example, note in their biographies that they are just "coming out." Surprisingly, there are very few BBSers who identify as straight on the board. One might have thought that it would be easier, and less threatening to initially label oneself as straight. Undoubtedly a few do that, since they stay on the board quite a while and do engage in deep chats with those identifying as gay or bisexual. They are often asked why they are on a gay board. Yet the query is posed not to exclude but out of curiosity, I suspect, and out of a hope, perhaps, that the straight identity is indeed in flux, and moving toward a gay identity.

More of the Asians (like the non-Asians) identify themselves on the board as gay rather than bisexual. One might have thought that it would be less threatening to come out as bisexual. (If queried, many of the bisexuals would insist, however, that they are true bisexuals, and not just going through a phase). There are, however, differences within the various Asian groups as to the prevalence of bisexuals.

With the caveat that this is by no means a random sample, Japanese and Filipinos appear to be the two groups of Asian gays with the highest percentage identifying as bisexual, if we discount the one case of a bisexual Thai man, or the two cases of East Indian men, one of whom calls himself bisexual. Thirty percent (or four out of thirteen) of the Japanese males call themselves bisexual, the rest label themselves as gay. Twenty-nine percent or five of all seventeen Filipino males on the board identify as bisexual, with the rest calling themselves gay. One out of the four Pacific Islander males on the board identifies as bisexual. The rest identify as gay. Among Vietnamese males, only two out of thirteen (15 percent) identify as bisexual; the rest call themselves gay. Similar low percentages exist for Chinese males (almost 10 percent or three out of thirty-three). The others say they are gay. Only 11 percent or one out of the nine Amerasians or Eurasian males identifies as bisexual. The others identify as gay.

Age-wise, the Asian gay or bisexual males range from eighteen to fifty-five. Chinese gay males are generally younger (average age 24.8); with Chinese bisexual males a bit older (25.6). Among Filipinos, gay men average almost twenty-seven years old; bisexual men average over thirty-one years old. Japanese gay males are older (average thirty-two years old), although bisexual Japanese males are younger (twenty-seven years old). Vietnamese bisexual men show the reverse trend; they are older on average (thirty-two years old) than the gay Vietnamese men (twenty-eight). The one bisexual Amerasian is aged thirty-four; the average for the eight gay Amerasians is almost twenty-nine years old. Among Pacific Islanders, the age is 25.6 on average for gay men, and nineteen for the one bisexual man. Of the two East Indians, one is a bisexual eighteen-year old man, another a twenty-four year old gay man.

It should be noted, however, that identifying as gay or bisexual on a BBS is not the same as coming out to someone directly. Because of the presumed anonymity of the board, such a disclosure is made much more easily. Often, I have had prolonged chats with someone who pours out his love life online, something he would probably only do because I am a stranger. Hotline volunteers are familiar with this phenomenon.

As I write, Gay Asians have become more visible, the 1994 Lunar New Year celebrations marking the first time a gay and lesbian Asian contingent has marched in San Francisco's Chinatown. No one has done such a comparative study, yet, but one could postulate that it is harder for Asians (than Caucasians) to come out, given cultural and family traditions, and that the rate at which Asians come out varies by national origin.

Anthropologist Joseph Carrier and his colleagues have in fact studied the sexual habits of Vietnamese immigrants in Orange County, California. They have found that assimilated Vietnamese Americans are more ready to identify as "gay," whereas those who are more recent immigrants or less assimilated do not, even if they engage in homosexual behavior.[4] This supports Tomas Almaguer's observation that some Chicanos "come out" genitally but not cerebrally. In other words, they engage in gay sex, but without the self identification as gay or bisexual. Loc Minh Truong, who was almost bashed to death by two Caucasian youths later convicted of gay bashing, insists he is not gay, even though he was once convicted of lewd conduct on the same beach where the hate crime later occurred.[5]

In light of the above, it is surprising that so few on the BBS actually refuse to identify as gay or bisexual. Only a handful on the board who are Asian say they are straight.

I have also argued elsewhere that just as many homosexuals attempt to pass as straight, some Asians in North America attempt to pass as white.[6] I mentioned above the case of a college student from Taiwan who, in an apparent experiment, changed his ethnic identity from Chinese to Caucasian on the BBS, and almost immediately, received many more queries and invitations to "chat."

That there are others who are in fact uncomfortable with their ethnic identity is suggested by the several dozen, presumably of varying ethnicities, who identify as "others" in the category for ethnicity. To be sure, many may have found the categories listed inappropriate (especially those with a multiethnic heritage). But I suspect a certain percentage decline to state their ethnicity in the hopes that their chances on the board will be improved. Ethnic identity and age are the two identifying characteristics that flash on the screen whenever a BBSer tries to contact another BBSer to chat.

Online, it is of course possible to reconstruct not only one's sexual orientation, but also one's racial and ethnic identity. And indeed one's entire biography. In a racist society, it is perhaps surprising that not more do that. Fung has argued:

> Gay society in North America, organized and commercial, is framed around the young middle-class white male. He is its customer and its product. Blacks, Asians and Latin Americans are the oysters in this meat market. At best we're a quaint specialty for exotic tastes. Native people aren't even on the shelves.[7]

Exoticized and eroticized, Gay Asian males are nonetheless considered a "quaint specialty." This became quite clear with a recent mail message from a self-described "rice queen" on the board who wrote me:

> Hi, they say opposites attract, so I am looking for an unabashed snow queen with nice patties! To rest upon my snowey [sic] slopes. . . .

I have written to over fifteen Asians on this BBS but none of them has replied. Can you give me some helpful hints? Don't worry, I can take criticisms [sic].

Why are Asian males the subject of desire of so-called rice queens? A Japanese American I met on the board wrote in his short-lived print newsletter, *Daisuki-Men*, that there are three reasons: China Doll syndrome (i.e., Asian males are seen as feminine); perception that Asians are submissive; and the rice queens' obsession with things Asian (as indicated by decorating their residences with Asian knick knacks).[8]

One could go on, but the point is made. "[O]ur (presumed) racial characteristics are fetishized by the non-API gay communities as a frozen form of desirability—one that is derived from an Orientalist perspective. In this economy of desire, the trade is almost always unidirectional, where APIs are encouraged to use our 'exotic appeal,' our 'Oriental sensuousness,' to maximize our attractiveness . . . " according to Hom and Ma (1993).[9]

As Asians, we resent being treated as objects, or as the "Other," but given the mainstream definition of beauty in this society, Asians, gay or straight, are constantly reminded that we cannot hope to meet such standards. Fung writes that in commercial gay male representation, it is the image of white men that is set up as the ideal: "Although other people's rejection (or fetishization) of us according to the established racial hierarchies may be experienced as oppressive, we are not necessarily moved to scrutinize our own desire and its relationship to the hegemonic image of the white man."[10] With such lack of self-scrutiny, is it any wonder that some gravitate to the Great White Hope as their savior?[11]

For it is not just Caucasians who see Asians as a specialized taste. Asians are so specialized that for some Asians, fellow Asians are not even on the shelf.

A twenty-five-year old Japanese American sparked a recent debate on this very issue when he posted the following on a public bulletin board: "Like the stereotypical Asian, I prefer to date Caucasian men."

Now, as some subsequent BBSers pointed out, a stereotype has some basis in fact. To be sure there are Asians who feet attracted only to Caucasians. Hom and Ma have observed that since "many of us 'came out' in the Euro/American gay context, our ideals of male beauty are necessarily influenced by the dominant cultural standards of beauty and desirability."[12]

But it is probably safe to say that most Asians do not have exclusive attractions to one race. Even on this board, very few indicated publicly their attraction to their own race or strictly to another race. One suspects such a stereotype (that Asians prefer Caucasians) is based not only on self-hate and dominant beauty standards, but also because interracial couples stand out and thus are much more visible. In contrast, groups like Gay Asian Pacific Alliance (in the San Francisco Bay area) and Gay Asian Pacific Support Network (in Southern California), which provide safe spaces for Asian gays to meet each other, are largely invisible to the gay mainstream, in part because Caucasians are not in control and are in fact absent.[13] One could argue that the gay press will report the news of white gays much more than it will of nonwhite gays. It largely ignores the activities of people of color, except as they relate to HIV.

Furthermore, the online debate suffered from an implicit acceptance of a way of viewing sexuality and racial identity in dualistic terms: gay or straight, white or Asian (complementing mainstream media's black/white dichotomy). Not all Asians feel the same way, of course, nor do all Caucasians. Lumping each group together tends to obscure more than it unveils. Furthermore, there's more diversity (even on the BBS) than this white/Asian dichotomy allows. How about all the Latino Americans on the board? Or the African Americans? One can postulate, as I have argued, that our identification with the struggles of the U.S. civil rights movement draws some of us in solidarity with other people of color, so that this focus on white/Asian relationships is misleading.[14]

As I explore BBSing further, I see more transgressing of these traditional dichotomies, Asians cohabiting with Blacks or Latinos. But not just racial barriers are transgressed. Monogamy is another. On the board, romance, marriage, love and lust are redefined. One bisexual Southeast Asian (who has a steady girlfriend he plans to marry) is an occasional fuckbuddy, visiting every so often in person, or more often, engaging in cybersex or phone sex.

The sexual practices that Asians on board find desirable run the gamut, from oral to anal sex, sadomasochism, and frottage. Some BBSers specifically ask other Asians to check out their electronic bios; others ask non-Asians to browse their sexual histories. Some readily admit their penis size, others say they are too shy. They report sizes ranging from five to eight inches. Many admit they have been tested for HIV, although some say it's too personal a question to answer. Some admit to smoking pot. Detailed analysis awaits further coding of the data.

BBSers provide more evidence that campaigns against sex in the schools have failed and that the Reagan/Bush years of sexual repression are over. The proliferation of sex boards suggests that a vibrant sexual underground has spawned right under the unsuspecting eyes of parents.

Given the prevalence of Asians in computer-related careers, one would not be surprised to find BBSers to be the places where gay or bisexual Asians gain entree into the sexual communities that now span the globe. Given restrictive drinking ages that bar anyone under twenty-one from gay bars, BBSers have become an easy way for young gays of whatever ethnicities to enter the sexual underground. And this is not just a U.S. phenomenon. France is in many ways ahead of us; authorities there banished the telephone book (thereby saving many trees). Instead, every household received a computer terminal, thus in one stroke, bringing the French into the electronic age. Inevitably, the sex boards on the Minitel became the hottest venues for a newly electronically enfranchised constituency.[15] A comparative study of Vietnamese in Orange County and in Paris cruising on their respective sex boards would be an exciting contribution to the study of Asian sexualities.

The prevailing, if contradictory images of the Asian male as Kung Fu expert or computer nerd is one that also renders him desexualized. In other words, the penis is missing in the dominant representation of the Asian male. In his "lifelong" quest for his lost penis, Fung found it in a Vietnamese American, going by various names including Sum Yung Mahn, who acted in gay porn videos.[16] In fact a BBSer claimed to be the same actor, but has since left the board so it has been impossible to confirm his identity.

BBSers, then challenge prevailing notions of Asian males as asexual. They provide Asians and Pacific Islanders an anonymous forum for sexually explicit dialog and for exploring their sexualities. On these boards, APIs are truly "breaking the silence" about taboo sexualities. In the process, APIs are empowered to voice our own forbidden desires and to re-construct our own sexual identities.

## NOTES

1. John Tierney, "Porn, the Low-Slung Engine of Progress," *The New York Times*, (January 9, 1994), Section 11:9.

2. For an early account of the case, Tsang v. CIA, see G.M. Bush, "Librarian Takes on CIA: UCI Employee Wants to Know About His File," *Los Angeles Daily Journal* (February 6, 1992), Section II, 1, 18. The admission about releasing information about me to a foreign government appears in court documents. The student later explained online that because he lived in a homophobic dorm, he had given me fake identification information.

3. Chip Berlet, "Privacy and the PC: Mutually Exclusive Realities?" Paper prepared for the 1985 National Conference on Issues in Technology and Privacy," Center for Information Technology and Privacy Law, John Marshall Law School, Chicago, Illinois, June 21–23, 1985. Electronic version stored in public eye database on PeaceNet.

4. Joseph Carrier, Bang Nguyen and Sammy Su, "Vietnamese American Sexual Behaviors and HIV Infection," *The Journal of Sex Research* 29:4 (November 1992):547–560.

5. Daniel C. Tsang, "The Attack on Loc Minh Truong: The Intersection of Sexual Orientation, Race and Violence," *RicePaper* 2:7 (Winter 1993):10–11.

6. Daniel Tsang Chun-Tuen, "Gay Awareness," *Bridge* 3:4 (February 1975):44–45.

7. Cited in Daniel Tsang, "Struggling against Racism," in Tsang, *The Age Taboo* (Boston: Alyson, 1981):163.

8. Sumo, "From the Editor." *Daisuki-Men* 1 (1992):4.

9. Alice Y. Hom and Ming-Yuen S. Ma, "Premature Gestures: A Speculative Dialogue on Asian Pacific Islander Lesbian and Gay Writing," *Journal of Homosexuality*, 26:2/3 (1993):38.

10. Richard Fung, "Looking for My Penis: The Eroticized Asian in Gay Video Porn." In Bad-Object Choices, editor, *How Do I Look? Queer Film and Video* (Seattle: Bay Press, 1991):149.

11. See Daniel C. Tsang, "M. Butterfly Meets the Great White Hope," *Informasian* 6:3 (March 1992):3–4.

12. Hom and Ma, "Premature Gestures," 37–38.

13. A rare exception to usual mainstream non-coverage is when a major newspaper published my essay, "Laguna Beach Beating Opens Closed Asian Door," *Los Angeles Times* (January 18, 1993):B5, which focused on gay Vietnamese in Southern California. Cf. Daniel C. Tsang, "Asian-Americans

Come Out Actively in Orange County," *Orange County Blade* (February 1993):39.

14. Daniel Tsang, "Lesbian and Gay Asian Americans: Breaking the Silence," *A/PLG Newsletter* (October 1990):14–17.

15. See chapter 8, "Telematique and Messageries Roses" in Howard Rheingold, *The Virtual Community* (Reading, Massachusetts: Addison-Wesley, 1993):220–240.

16. Fung, "Looking for My Penis," 149–150.

# | 84 |

# We're Teen, We're Queer, and We've Got E-mail

## STEVE SILBERMAN

There's a light on in the Nerd Nook: JohnTeen ø is composing e-mail into the night. The Nerd Nook is what John's mother calls her 16-year-old's bedroom—it's more cramped than the bridge of the Enterprise, with a Roland CM-322 that makes "You've got mail" thunder like the voice of God.

John's favorite short story is "The Metamorphosis." Sure, Kafka's fable of waking up to discover you've morphed into something that makes everyone tweak speaks to every teenager. But John especially has had moments of feeling insectoid—like during one school choir trip, when, he says, the teacher booking rooms felt it necessary to inform the other students' parents of John's "orientation." When they balked at their kids sharing a room with him, John was doubled up with another teacher—a fate nearly as alienating as Gregor Samsa's.

The choir trip fiasco was but one chapter in the continuing online journal that has made JohnTeen ø—or as his parents and classmates know him, John Erwin—one of the most articulate voices in America Online's Gay and Lesbian Community Forum.

From: JohnTeen ø

My high school career has been a sudden and drastic spell of turbulence and change that has influenced every aspect of life. Once I was an automaton, obeying external, societal, and parental expectations like a dog, oblivious of who I was or what I wanted. I was the token child every parent wants—student body president, color guard, recipient of the general excellence award, and outstanding music student of the year. I conformed to society's paradigm, and I was rewarded. Yet I was miserable. Everything I did was a diversion from thinking about myself. Finally, last summer, my subconsciousness felt comfortable enough to be able to connect myself with who I really am, and I began to understand what it is to be gay.

JohnTeen ø is a new kind of gay kid, a 16-year-old not only out, but already at home in the online convergence of activists that Tom Rielly, the co-founder of Digital Queers, calls the "Queer Global Village." Just 10 years ago, most queer teens hid behind a self-imposed don't-ask-don't-tell policy until they shipped out to Oberlin or San Francisco, but the Net has given even closeted kids a place to conspire. Though the Erwins' house is in an unincorporated area of Santa Clara County in California, with goats and llamas foraging in the backyard, John's access to AOL's gay and lesbian forum enables him to follow dispatches from queer activists worldwide, hone his writing, flirt, try on disposable identities, and battle bigots—all from his home screen.

John's ambitions to recast national policy before the principal of Menlo School even palms him a diploma (John's mother refers to him as her "little mini-activist") are not unrealistic. Like the ur-narrative of every videogame, the saga of gay teens online is one of metamorphosis, of "little mini" nerds becoming warriors in a hidden Stronghold of Power. For young queers, the Magic Ring is the bond of community.

John's posts have the confidence and urgency of one who speaks for many who must keep silent:

> The struggle for equal rights has always taken place on the frontier of the legal wilderness where liberty meets power. Liberty has claimed much of that wilderness now, but the frontier always lies ahead of us. . . . The frontier of liberty may have expanded far beyond where it began, but for those without rights, it always seems on the horizon, just beyond their reach.

And the messages that stream back into John's box are mostly from kids his own age, many marooned far from urban centers for gay and lesbian youth. Such is Christopher Rempel, a witty, soft-spoken Ace of Base fan from (as he puts it) "redneck farmer hell." Christopher borrowed the principal's modem to jack into a beekeepers BBS and gopher his way to the Queer Resources Directory, a multimeg collection of text files, news items, and services listings.

> My name is Christopher and I am 15 years old. I came to terms that I was gay last summer and, aside from some depression, I'm OK. I am *not* in denial about being gay.
>
> I would like to write to someone that I can talk to about issues I can't talk about with my friends. I don't play sports very much, but I make it up in my knowledge of computers. I am interested in anybody with an open mind and big aspirations for the future.

A decade ago, the only queer info available to most teens was in a few dour psychology texts under the nose of the school librarian. Now libraries of files await them in the AOL forum and elsewhere — the Queer Resources Directory alone contains hundreds — and teens can join mailing lists like Queercampus and GayNet, or tap resources like the Bridges Project, a referral service that tells teens not only how to get in touch with queer youth groups, but how to jumpstart one themselves.

Kali is an 18-year-old lesbian at a university in Colorado. Her name means "fierce" in Swahili. Growing up in California, Kali was the leader of a young women's chapter of the Church of Jesus

Christ of Latter-day Saints. She was also the "Girl Saved by E-mail," whose story ran last spring on CNN. After mood swings plummeted her into a profound depression, Kali — like too many gay teens — considered suicide. Her access to GayNet at school gave her a place to air those feelings, and a phone call from someone she knew online saved her life.

Kali is now a regular contributor to Sappho, a women's board she most appreciates because there she is accepted as an equal. "They forgive me for being young," Kali laughs, "though women come out later than guys, so there aren't a lot of teen lesbians. But it's a high of connection. We joke that we're posting to 500 of our closest friends."

"The wonderful thing about online services is that they are an intrinsically decentralized resource," says Tom Rielly, who has solicited the hardware and imparted the skills to get dozens of queer organizations jacked in. "Kids can challenge what adults have to say and make the news. One of the best examples of teen organizing in the last year was teens working with the Massachussets legislature to pass a law requiring gay and lesbian education in the high schools. If teen organizers are successful somewhere now, everyone's gonna hear about it. This is the most powerful tool queer youth have ever had."

Another power that teenagers are now wielding online is their anger. "Teens are starting to throw their weight around," says Quirk, the leader of the AOL forum. (Quirk maintains a gender-neutral identity online, to be an equal-opportunity sounding board for young lesbians and gay men.) "They're complaining. It used to be, 'Ick — I think I'm gay, I'll sneak around the forum and see what they're doing.' With this second wave of activism, it's like, 'There's gay stuff here, but it's not right for me.' These kids are computer literate, and they're using the anger of youth to create a space for themselves."

The powers that be at AOL, however, have not yet seen fit to allow that space to be named by its users — the creation of chat rooms called "gay teen" anything is banned. "AOL has found that the word 'gay' with the word 'youth' or 'teen' in a room name becomes a lightning rod for predators," says Quirk. "I've been in teen conferences where adult cruising so overwhelmed any kind of conversation about being in high school and 'What kind of music do you like?' that I was furious. Until I can figure out a way to provide a safe space for them, I'm not going to put them at risk."

Quirk and AOL are in a tight place.

Pedophilia has become the trendy bludgeon with which to trash cyberspace in the dailies, and concerned parents invoke the P-word to justify limiting teens' access to gay forums. At the same time, however, postings in the teens-only folder of the Gay and Lesbian Community Forum flame not only the invasion of teen turf by adults trolling for sex, but also the adults claiming to "protect" them by limiting their access to one another.

One anonymous 17-year-old poster on AOL dissed the notion that queer teens are helpless victims of online "predators":

> There are procedures for dealing with perverts, which most teens (in contrast with most of the adults we've encountered) are familiar with. Flooding e-mail boxes of annoying perverts, "IGNORE"-ing them in chat rooms, and shutting off our Instant Messages are all very effective methods. We are not defenseless, nor innocent.

The issue is further complicated by the fact that the intermingling of old and young people online is good for teens. The online connection allows them to open dialogs with mentors like Deacon Maccubbin, co-owner of Lambda Rising bookstore in Washington, DC. As "DeaconMac," Maccubbin has been talking with gay kids on CompuServe and AOL for eight years. One of the young people DeaconMac corresponded with online, years ago, was Tom Rielly. "Deacon was the first openly gay man I'd ever had a conversation with, and he had a very clear idea of what his role was. He was nurturing and mentoring; he sent me articles; and he didn't come on to me," says Rielly. "I'll never forget it as long as I live."

In the past, teens often had to wait until they were old enough to get into a bar to meet other gay people — or hang around outside until someone noticed them. Online interaction gives teens a chance to unmask themselves in a safe place, in a venue where individuals make themselves known by the acuity of their thought and expression, rather than by their physical appearance.

When JohnTeen Ì logged his first post in the gay AOL forum, he expressed outrage that the concerns of queer teens — who are at a disproportionately high risk for suicide — were being shunted aside by adult organizations. His post was spotted by Sarah Gregory, a 26-year-old anarchist law student who helped get the National Gay and Lesbian Task Force wired up. "I really wanted to hit this kid between the eyes with the fact that a national organization saw what he was saying and cared that gay youth were killing themselves," Gregory recalls. A correspondence and friendship began that would have been unlikely offline — for, as Gregory says, "I don't notice 16-year-old boys in the real world."

Gregory explains: "I remember one particularly graphic letter I sent John in response to his questions. I wrote a huge disclaimer before and after it. But then I remembered how desperately I wanted to be talked to as an adult, and a sexual being, when I was 14. Thinking back, that's the point where John stopped sounding so formal, so much like a well-bred teenager talking to an authority figure, and became my friend. It's also the last time he talked about suicide. It scared me how easily his vulnerability could have been exploited, but I'd do it again in a heartbeat."

"I didn't even listen to music," moans John recalling his nerdhood, when the only thing he logged in for was shareware. Now the background thrash for his late-night e-mail sessions is Pansy Division. "To keep myself in the closet, I surrounded myself with people I'd never find attractive. I had two different parts of my life: the normal part, where I worked hard in school and got good grades, and this other part, where I was interested in guys but didn't do anything about it." For many kids, writing to John or to other posters is where a more authentic life begins:

> Dear JohnTeen:
>
> I am so frustrated with life and all of its blind turns. Am I gay? What will happen if I tell friends and my mom? . . . (I still don't 100% know that I am gay only that I am not heterosexual SO WHAT AM I) I really want to fit somewhere and also to love someone (at this point I don't care who). . . . Please EMAIL back and enlighten me. You have been very inspirational to me. I have no idea how you gained the courage to come out. Thanks, James

But John Erwin must guard against JohnTeen Ì becoming a full-time gig: he not only has the frontiers of liberty to defend and his peers to "enlighten," but like any 16-year-old, he needs space to fuck up, be a normal teenage cockroach, and figure out who he is. And he'd like to find someone to love. Does he have anyone in mind? "Yes!" he grins, pulling out his yearbook and leafing to a photo of a handsome boy who says he's straight.

Is John's dream guy online?

"No. I wish," John says. "If he was online, I could tell him how I feel."

# | 85 |

## Logging On, Coming Out

### JEFF WALSH

I was 23 when I accepted that I was gay. I remember it being such a rush to finally talk to other gay people on my home computer. At that point I thought falling in love and living a happy life were things I could never have. I'll also never forget how alone I used to feel after I shut off my computer because that was the only place my gay community existed.

I live in a conservative Catholic town and at the time didn't know anyone else here. The only media coverage of gays was about pride parades or activists screaming with queer rage about AIDS. I needed much tamer images to help me accept myself. So every night while my parents slept upstairs, I'd spend hours in the basement on my computer. Normally I spent my time attempting to write a screenplay, which was about three teenagers trying to get their lives in order. All my writings included gay characters, though I never consciously put them in to deal with my own gay feelings. They always just seemed to work well in the story.

The script I was writing featured Paul, a gay teen, as one of the main characters. Whenever I wrote a scene involving Paul, however, I got writer's block. I would normally attribute it to my not being gay. How could I know what it was like to be a gay teen in high school?

I decided to take some time off from my writing after receiving a trial membership to the America Online (AOL) computer network. I didn't plan to become a member, but a trial subscription offered ten free hours on-line. I figured I'd look around, grab some free files, and then cancel my membership. The night I planned to cancel though, I found live on-line chat rooms where up to 23 people could talk on any subject. That night a chat room existed for "hot young gay teens." *This will be great,* I thought. *I can ask these guys what it's like being a gay teen.*

I entered the room and informed everyone that I was a heterosexual screenwriter writing about a gay teen and needed to talk about what being a gay teen is like. Everyone was supportive, but the more everyone talked, the more confused I became. I'd had many of the same feelings they did growing up, so their stories didn't seem to apply only to gay teens. So much for helping Paul.

I then arranged to meet one of the teens for a private on-line chat. I was hoping it would lead to more revelations, and it certainly did. When we met the next night in a private room, he willingly answered my questions. Then he asked me a few. I told him I had wondered whether I was gay but had attributed those feelings to my desire to overcome being overweight. I merely wanted to have a nice body like some of the guys I admired, but that was where it ended. I knew I didn't want any of these guys physically because I couldn't picture anything past nudity. If I had been gay or bisexual, I figured, I would have been able to picture sexual contact.

I talked with with the teen on-line for a long time that night. He initially told me he was bisexual. Five hours and many questions later, we both typed to each other that we thought we were gay. As for my screenplay, it ended up being more catharsis than fiction and is still unfinished. I did, however, do a lot of work on what it meant to be gay that summer in 1992.

Since I still didn't have anyone local to talk with, I made on-line friends with guys all over the country. However, on-line services are not free,

*Advocate,* October 18, 1994, p. 6.

and my chats with my new friends—as well as calls to some of them on the phone—ran up large bills. Within three months I was broke, my credit card filled, and my entire paycheck going to pay my phone bills. I had to leave AOL and pay off my debt

But my time on-line had indeed been fruitful. I started coming out to my mother and my coworkers. I began making friends locally and became the cochair of my university's gay student group. And when the semester started, I wrote gay columns in the student newspaper and for a local gay 'zine.

This year I was finally able to sign back on to AOL. This time I'm 26, I'm comfortable about being gay, and I've even lost some weight. Now it's my turn to help others. I've talked to many people who are gay, some as young as 13, and I find it rewarding to be able to help them feel more comfortable about their sexuality.

The on-line world offers a lot more than just a chance to make new friends. With even the most basic computer, anyone can tap into a wide array of services. Gays on-line can E-mail President Clinton, make new friends, talk about gay issues in message boards, get support, or contact a number of national gay groups.

Just about everything you are looking for you can find on-line. In fact, within the past few weeks, I met someone who lives close to me. We've been talking for a while now, and hopefully, we'll be getting together soon. So perhaps once again my computer will help me find something that's been missing in my life.

# *Five*

# COMMUNITY

## PROSPECTS AND TACTICS

# V. A
# QUEER POSITIONS AND PERSPECTIVES

In June 1969 the riots that erupted during a routine police raid on the Stonewall Inn, a gay bar in Greenwich Village, served as the spark that ignited a new gay liberation movement. The homophile movement of the early 1950s was founded by men "who were either members of the Communist party or traveled in left-wing circles. Standing outside the political mainstream, they also broke with accepted notions of homoerotic behavior and pioneered in conceiving homosexuals as an oppressed minority" (D'Emilio 1983:58). A few years later Frank Kameny and his allies in Washington and New York crafted a public strategy modeled on the civil rights movement of the late 1950s and early 1960s, using court challenges and small-scale symbolic public actions. The movement that spread like wildfire across the country after Stonewall was inspired by the New Left, and its leaders were veterans of the civil rights and antiwar movements of the 1960s.

This new generation of gay leaders were faced with the problem of creating a 1960s-style mass movement out of a group that had long learned to hide its identity from public view. The influence of the "Black Is Beautiful" rhetoric of the civil rights movement, translated by Frank Kameny into "Gay Is Good," can be seen in the central emphasis gay liberationists placed on the affirmation of gay pride, but for this to be a political as well as a personal achievement gay identity needed to be publicly affirmed. The new movement was founded on the importance of coming out as a *public* as well as an individual act. "Coming out also posed as the key strategy for building a movement. . . . Visible lesbians and gay men also served as magnets that drew others in. Furthermore, once out of the closet, they could not easily fade back in. Coming out provided gay liberation with an army of permanent enlistees" (D'Emilio 1983:235–236).

The gay liberation movement that placed coming out at the top of its agenda was largely a young person's movement, made up at least initially of New Left activists or counterculturalists who "had already decided that American society was corrupt and oppressive" (D'Emilio 1983:246). They had relatively little to lose by coming out publicly. The theory and strategy of the post-Stonewall movement was centered on the ideology of public self-disclosure as the key to psychological health for individual gay people and to liberation from oppression for the gay community. Thus, from the start there was a rift between the openly lesbian and gay activists of the movement and the majority of homosexuals who remained, and remain today, in the closet. While understanding and sympathizing with those who would be truly vulnerable to discrimination and reprisals if they were to come out, gay activists have long expressed impatience and anger with those whose wealth and position would protect them from such dangers. Of course, these are the very people who are less likely to feel pinched by the constraints of disguise and evasion. After all, "they can make their closets as commodious as castles" (Tucker, "Our Right to the World," this volume).

One of the strongest polemics of the early years of gay liberation was a British pamphlet called *With Downcast Gays: Aspects of Homosexual*

*Self-Oppression* which asserted that the new and important contribution of the movement was the realization that "by oppressing *ourselves*, we allow homosexual oppression to maintain its overwhelming success" (Hodges and Hutter, *With Downcast Gays*, this volume).

Far more than merely challenging laws against homosexual acts, the gay liberation movement of the early 1970s saw itself as part of a vanguard of sexual and cultural change that would sweep aside the narrow boundaries of sexual orientation and repressive morality, abolishing roles and institutions defined by heterosexism and patriarchy (Wittman [1970] 1972; Firestone 1971; Altman 1971). "Once everyone was free to express her or his latent sexualities, boundaries between the homosexual and the heterosexual should fade into irrelevance and false partitions in the flow of desire give way to personal fulfillment" (Adam 1995:84).

Many factions and individuals identified with the gay liberation movement saw their destiny linked with that of other radical struggles, particularly the movement against the Vietnam War and the Black civil rights and women's movements. In a high point for this position, Black Panther leader Huey Newton urged his colleagues to "unite with [homosexuals and women] in a revolutionary fashion," because "homosexuals are not given freedom and liberty by anyone in the society. Maybe they might be the most oppressed people in the society" ([1970] 1972:195–196). At the same time, other factions and individual activists felt that such coalitions diluted and weakened the struggle for gay rights, and many groups split along this fault line (years later similar splits divided groups organized to deal with AIDS).

In addition to the discord between the liberationists and the more narrowly focused reformers, there were other significant divisions cutting through the territory of queerdom. North American lesbian and gay consciousness was heavily influenced by the model of racial and ethnic minorities and has consistently stressed the concept of a gay community. "This 'ethnic' self-characterization by gays and lesbians has a clear political utility, for it has permitted a form of group organizing that is particularly suited to the American experience, with its history of civil-rights struggles and ethnic-based, interest group-competition" (Epstein 1992:255).

The rhetoric of ethnicity adopted by the lesbian and gay movement presents an essentialist definition of an identity assumed to overlay or even supersede other categories of identification such as race or gender or traditional ethnicity. But these other aspects of personhood and social being do not conveniently fade away once a lesbian-and-gay identity has been proclaimed. Women and people of color as well as working-class people have had grounds to complain that this newly celebrated identity was largely molded in the image of white male middle-class experience and aspirations (Radicalesbians, "The Woman-Identified Woman"; Clarke, "Lesbianism"; Quintanales,"I Paid Very Hard," this volume).

An early division within the post-Stonewall gay liberation movement came about when lesbians insisted on the distinctiveness of their experience and their oppression. An influential formulation was Adrienne Rich's concept of the "lesbian continuum" of woman-identified experience that can be found throughout each woman's life and throughout history (1980). In Rich's view, lesbian existence is denied not only by the institutionalized heterosexuality of patriarchal society but also by dissolving lesbians into a generalized gay population. On the contrary, Rich insists, lesbian experience is, "like motherhood, a profoundly *female* experience, with particular oppressions, meanings and potentialities we cannot comprehend as long as we simply bracket it with other sexually stigmatized existences" (1980:81). Many lesbians who did not share Rich's essentialist belief in a transhistorical, pan-cultural lesbian continuum nevertheless agreed that lesbianism should be defined in terms of identification with women, and thus they preferred to see themselves as lesbian feminists.

The women's movement, however, could be as hostile to lesbian visibility as gay men were oblivious to feminist concerns. There were uneasy relations between some feminist leaders and the many lesbians engaged in building the women's movement, and they burst into flames when Betty Friedan denounced the "lavender menace" that threatened to discredit feminism. The lesbians fought back with guerrilla theater, taking over a conference stage dressed in "Lavender Menace" T-shirts and demanding solidarity (Klemesrud, "The Lesbian Issue and Women's Lib," this volume). The struggle led to a greater integration of many lesbian feminists within the women's movement and a corresponding separation from identification with a community that included gay men. As Jill Johnston put it, "Considering the centrality of lesbianism to the Women's Movement it should now seem absurd to persist in associating lesbian women with the male homosexual movement. Lesbians are feminists, not homosexuals" (Johnston 1975:86).

But just as lesbian feminists could rightly condemn the rhetoric of gay community as male-defined, so, too, they were criticized for painting a portrait of "woman" drawn too narrowly in their own image: "The focus on women 'as women' has addressed only one group of women—namely, white middle-class women of Western industrialized countries . . . [and treated] the difference of white middle-class women from all other women as if they were not differences" (Spelman 1988:3). Race and class presented alternative claims to be the primary basis on which identities were forged (Clarke, "Lesbianism"; Quintanales,"I Paid Very Hard," this volume). A lesbian identity based on race and class in addition to gender did not readily lend itself to the separatism urged by many lesbian feminists. As Barbara Smith put it,

You are very aware of the choice—that in being a lesbian you understand that you really don't need men to define your identity, your sexuality, to make your life meaningful or simply to have a good time. That doesn't necessarily mean that you have no comprehension of the oppressions that you share with men. And you see white women with class privilege don't share oppression with white men. They're in a critical and antagonistic position whereas Black women and other women of color definitely share oppressed situations with men of their race. What white lesbians have against lesbians of color is that they accuse us of being "male identified" because we are concerned with issues that affect our whole race. They express anger at us for not seeing the light. That is another aspect of how they carry on their racism. (1981:121–122)

By the mid-1970s activists had been successful in obtaining concessions and policy changes by the psychiatric profession and the media that, however limited, signaled the beginnings of a shift in the cultural landscape. In the realm of politics the early post-Stonewall movement racked up successes in obtaining passage of civil rights ordinances by numerous municipal and county government only to find them under fire from a newly energized right-wing opposition. In 1977, in an early preview of much that has since become familiar, singer Anita Bryant led a coalition of religious and political reactionaries to "Save Our Chil-

dren" by repealing Dade County, Florida's gay rights ordinance. Their success in Dade County was rapidly followed by similar defeats for gay rights in St. Paul, Minnesota, Wichita, Kansas, and Eugene, Oregon. The score was evened somewhat in November 1978 with the defeat of the "Briggs Initiative," which would have barred lesbian, gay, or pro-gay teachers from California schools. But within weeks of this victory the most visible gay elected official, San Francisco Supervisor Harvey Milk, was assassinated by right-wing politician Dan White. When White was given a light sentence, riots ensued that engulfed many police cars in flames (Adam 1995).

The gay movement in place in the early 1980s when AIDS first began to appear was a movement that had placed the right to privacy at the center of its agenda. In the 1960s the defense of privacy had become the primary legal and rhetorical argument liberalizing movements had used to secure the right to contraception and abortion and to force back the forces of sexual censorship. Flying the same banner, the reformist wing of the gay movement used the rhetoric of privacy rather than the more subversive language of sexual liberation. But by the mid-1980s this strategy was neither sufficient nor viable in itself. The resurgent right wing, triumphantly occupying the White House in 1981, undertook a concerted campaign to deny gay people whatever degree of social legitimacy had been gained in several decades of struggle. In all this the issue of lesbian and gay visibility played a central role; one that revealed the double-edged sword of privacy (Tucker, "Beyond the Right to Privacy," this volume).

The concept of a right to privacy arose out of nineteenth-century Victorian morality, which created an ideology of distinct public and private spheres and confined women to the private domestic sphere (cf. Wolff 1988). In the period following World War II the defense of the private realm became the primary focus of liberal efforts to reconcile the "interests of society" and the rights of the individual. The "right to privacy," first expressed in an effort to protect the sanctity of the Victorian domestic sphere, would now be invoked as a defense against the enforcement of Victorian morality. In 1954 the British government established the Wolfenden Committee on Homosexual Offences and Prostitution. The *Wolfenden Report*, issued in 1957, was a landmark in the postwar evolution of a new standard for policing sexual behavior. Although generally seen as a victory for liberalism and individual freedom, the *Report* must also be seen as a strategic retrenchment rather than an abdication of the desire to control the expression of sexuality.

The key to the *Wolfenden Report* is in the distinction between public and private. The purpose of criminal law, it argued, is to preserve *public* order and decency, not to enforce *private* morality. "There must be a realm of private morality and immorality which is in brief and crude terms not the law's business. . . . (I)t is not in our view the function of the law to intervene in the private lives of citizens or to seek to enforce any particular patterns of behaviour" (*The Wolfenden Report* 1964:23f). But there is an important corollary to the report's hands off stance toward private morality: "The logic of the distinction between private and public behaviour was that the legal penalties for *public* displays of sexuality could be strengthened at the same time as private behaviour was decriminalized" (Weeks 1981:243). The *Wolfenden Report* did much to promote the "right to privacy" as the rallying cry of liberal reformers as Western culture moved into the "permissive" sixties.

In the landmark case of *Griswold v. Connecticut* in 1965 the U.S. Supreme Court first recognized a constitutional right to privacy. The Court voided Connecticut's prohibition against the sale or use of contraceptives, because the law could only be enforced if the police were allowed to "search the sacred precincts of marital bedrooms for telltale signs."

The right to privacy extended to married couples and, in later decisions, to unmarried persons wishing to use contraceptives, unmarried women wishing to terminate a pregnancy, and people wishing to watch dirty movies in the privacy of their homes (Smith 1980:269). But, it is important to note, the Court in *Griswold* stressed that "it in no way interferes with a State's proper regulation of sexual promiscuity or misconduct." It was soon made clear that the Supreme Court was not about to interfere with the state's desire to regulate *some* expressions of sexuality: in 1976 it upheld a Virginia decision punishing sodomy between consenting male adults, and, later in the same year, it left standing another Virginia decision that punished a married couple for engaging in oral-genital sex (Tucker, "Beyond the Right to Privacy," this volume).

In 1986, in the infamous *Bowers v. Hardwick* decision, the Supreme Court stripped the right to privacy argument of its last vestige of credibility as a defense of gay sexuality: "*Hardwick* said that our sexuality makes us criminals and outlaws, that

alone in our bedrooms we have no rights, we have no freedoms. It said to us that every night we engage in acts of civil disobedience and we decided it was time to take that show on the road! . . . We've got to join the battle where it has been called, we've got to fight it in public" (Cerullo 1988:68–69). The day after the 1987 March on Washington for Lesbian and Gay Rights, over six hundred demonstrators were arrested sitting in at the Supreme Court. The temperature of activism was rising once more.

The heat of lesbian and gay anger was fueled by more than the *Hardwick* decision. The AIDS epidemic had revealed a fundamental truth that many lesbian and gay people had been able to avoid confronting: America is a deeply homophobic and racist society.

At the New York Gay and Lesbian Pride parade in June 1990, fifteen thousand copies of an anonymous broadside bearing the simple but arresting title *Queers Read This: I Hate Straights* (this volume) were distributed. The essay, which quickly spread around the city and was reprinted in *Out-Week* magazine, articulated a sense of gay rage that was widely felt, and it struck a responsive chord in communities around the country. The essay began with the writer's feelings of being marginalized in a straight world: "I have friends. Some of them are straight. . . . Year after year I continue to realize that I am only half listened to, that I am an appendage to the doings of a greater world, a world of power and privilege, of the laws of installation, a world of exclusion." The essay went on to focus on the mounting rage of those caught up in the fight against AIDS and for equal treatment of lesbians and gay men, the rage of those for whom marginality is a constant experience. The authors of the anonymous pamphlet were among those who gathered shortly afterward to found the militant but short-lived Queer Nation.

## REFERENCES

Adam, Barry. 1995. *The Rise of a Gay and Lesbian Movement.* Boston: Twayne.

Altman, Dennis. 1971. *Homosexual: Oppression and Liberation.* New York: Avon.

Cerullo, Margaret. 1988. "Night Visions: A Lesbian/Gay Politics for the Present." *Radical America,* 21(2–3):67–71.

D'Emilio, John. 1983. *Sexual Politics, Sexual Communities.* Chicago: University of Chicago Press.

Epstein, Steven. 1992 [1987]. "Gay Politics, Ethnic Identity: The Limits of Social Constructionism."

In E. Stein, ed., *Forms of Desire*, 239–294. New York: Routledge.

Firestone, Shulamith. 1971. *The Dialectic of Sex*. New York: Bantam.

Jay, Karla and Allen Young, eds. 1972. *Out of the Closets: Voices of Gay Liberation*. New York: Douglas.

Johnston, Jill. 1975. "Are Lesbians 'Gay'?" *Ms.*, June, p. 85–86.

Newton, Huey. [1970] 1972. "A Letter to the Revolutionary Brothers and Sisters About the Women's Liberation and Gay Liberation Movements." In Joseph McCaffrey, ed., *The Homosexual Dialectic*, pp. 195–197. Englewood Cliffs: Prentice-Hall.

Rich, Adrienne. 1980. "Compulsory Heterosexuality and Lesbian Existence." In Catherine Stimpson and Ethel Person, eds., *Women: Sex and Sexuality*. Chicago: University of Chicago Press.

Smith, Barbara and Beverly Smith. 1981. "Across the Kitchen Table: A Sister-to-Sister Dialogue." In Cherríe Moraga and Gloria Anzaldúa, eds., *This Bridge Called My Back: Writings by Radical Women of Color*, pp. 113–127. Watertown, Mass.: Persephone.

Smith, Robert Ellis. 1980. *Privacy: How to Protect What's Left of It*. New York: Anchor.

Spelman, Elizabeth. 1988. *The Inessential Woman: Problems of Exclusion in Feminist Thought*. Boston: Beacon.

Weeks, Jeffrey. 1981. *Sex, Politics, and Society*. London: Longman.

Wittman, Carl. [1970] 1972. "Refugees from Amerika: A Gay Manifesto." In Joseph McCaffrey, ed., *The Homosexual Dialectic*, pp. 157–171. Englewood Cliffs, N.J.: Prentice-Hall.

*Wolfenden Report: Report of the Committee on Homosexual Offences and Prostitution*. 1964. New York: Lancer.

Woolf, Janet. 1988. "The Culture of Separate Spheres." In Janet Wolff and John Seed, eds., *The Culture of Capital: Art, Power, and the Nineteenth-Century Middle Class*. Manchester: Manchester University Press.

# | 86 |

# With Downcast Gays: Aspects of Homosexual Self-Oppression

ANDREW HODGES AND DAVID HUTTER

## SELF-OPPRESSION AND SELF-PUBLICATION: A PREFACE BY ANDREW HODGES

*Between April 1973 and April 1974, when I was a maths student in London, I worked with the artist David Hutter on writing a pamphlet on the concept of Self-Oppression which had earlier been promulgated in the Gay Liberation Front Manifesto (1971). We collaborated very closely in the writing, and then we published it ourselves, under the name of Pomegranate Press. We launched it at Great Malvern, Worcestershire, where the conference of the Campaign for Homosexual Equality took place in May 1974.*

*We sold 3,000 copies at 20p, and then reprinted it in April 1975.*

*But in 1977 we passed it on to Pink Triangle Press in Toronto. About 12,000 copies were printed in all, roughly half circulating in Britain and half in North America. On the whole it got quite a welcome in the gay activist world of that time. It might even be true to say, as the Queer Resources Directory listing now does, that it was a seminal text. Thanks, QRD! (But in my mind's ear I can hear David laughing at the metaphor). It was translated into French and German, and excerpts also appeared in Swedish and Italian magazines.*

*It has been out of print since about 1981. David and I talked about the possibility of it being republished with a new introduction in 1984, but nothing came of it. The complete text can be found at http://www.TURING.ORG.UK/wdg/intro.html*

## SELF-OPPRESSION

The ultimate success of all forms of oppression is our self-oppression. Self-oppression is achieved when the gay person has adopted and internalized straight people's definition of what is good and bad.

So begins the section on self-oppression contained in the London Gay Liberation Front Manifesto. For us it summarized all that was new and important in Gay Liberation—the realization that inasmuch as we are agents of our own oppression, so we have power to overcome it.

This booklet aims to explore some of these ideas and to explain how, by oppressing ourselves, we allow homosexual oppression to maintain its overwhelming success. It begins where Psychiatry and the Homosexual left off; again it makes no attempt to identify the causes of homosexual oppression, only the means by which it gains its ends. Written by gays to be read by gays, its choice of subject means that it is critical throughout. But we hope that one thing will gleam through this criticism of our fellow homosexuals: that since self-oppression is the creature of oppression, our criticism is only a pale shadow of the anger we feel towards those who have trapped us into doing their work for them.

## PARDON US FOR LIVING

Before going on to describe how homosexuals oppress themselves, we should first explain why

In With Downcast Gays: Aspects of Homosexual Self-Oppression, pp. 1–42. Excerpt. Toronto: Pink Triangle, 1974.

they do so. It is because we learn to loathe homo-sexuality before it becomes necessary to acknowl-edge our own. As children and young people we never hear anything good said about gay life, and only see it referred to as a subject for mockery, dis-gust or pity. Moreover gays, like cuckoos, are reared in alien, heterosexual nests, and even at home the message is the same. Never having been offered positive attitudes to homosexuality, we invariably adopt negative ones, and it is from these that all our values flow.

### Self-hatred

We have been taught to hate ourselves—and how thoroughly we have learnt the lesson. Some gays deliberately keep away from teaching lest they be a corrupting influence. Others, except for brief, furtive sexual encounters, consciously avoid the company of gay people because they cannot bear to see a reflection of their own homosexuality. More typically our self-hatred is unconscious and our self-oppression automatic. . . . So ingrained is our assumption of second-class status that we fail to notice even external oppression unless we make a positive effort to root it out. We seldom recognize the queer-basher's fist in the liberal's guiding hand. "How can you be sure you are homosexual?" asks the psychiatrist. Whenever does he ask heterosexuals the converse question? This interchange of homo- and hetero-sexual is a certain test for both gay and self-oppression. Another is to compare ourselves with other minorities, who may well resent and complain of things we tolerate. Gay people say they fear the loss of non-gay "friends" if their homosexuality is revealed. What Jew would value the friendship of the anti-Semitic? Once blacks underwent the painful operation of having their hair straight-ened in an effort to resemble their white masters. This glaring act of self-oppression is nowadays repudiated by every Afro hair-style. If only an insurgent gay movement could sweep away gay people's futile and unending attempts to straighten their lives!

### Evading the issue

Once they can on longer deny their homosexual-ity, gays find ways to avoid confronting the fact that they are the people they despise. It is not easy to live with raw, undiluted self-hatred. Devious and complex are the means by which gay people come to terms with the dilemma of finding themselves

to be that which they have been taught to hate.

The G.L.F. manifesto rightly identified the final stage of self-oppression as saying—and believing—"I am not oppressed." Conscious every minute that they are seen as ridiculous and pitiable, for ever working out ways to suppress evi-dence of their homosexuality, how can gay people make such a claim? But they do. The Campaign for Homosexual Equality constantly receives let-ters imploring it to put a stop to the activities of the radical members. "We are not oppressed," the writers say, "so please don't let them rock the boat." Ironically, the metaphor aptly expresses the danger and insecurity of our oppressed situation.

Of course it is the very degree of success with which gay people can conceal their identity that makes it possible for them to shrug off their oppression. Indeed it is possible for gays, by deny-ing their homosexuality in every social situation, to imagine that they share the status of non-gay people. Their deception goes deeper: they go on to adopt the attitudes of their oppressors—even the logic and language of the non-gay people with whom they identify. Such "well-adapted" homo-sexuals have never in reality adapted to their homosexuality, only to its brutal suppression. They will never acknowledge a lifetime's subju-gation and dishonesty. "Well-adapted" homosexu-als would prefer to carry their oppression to the grave rather than admit that it exists.

### Two typical cases

Facing the superior smile of the gay psychiatrist who has grown rich and respected by writing and lecturing on the "problem" of homosexuality, and who recommends psychotherapy for "these peo-ple"; or the weary eyes of a homosexual academic who counters every assertion of the ubiquity of oppression with, say, an instance of eighteenth-century bawdry—one realizes that powerful ene-mies lie within our own ranks. Always they refute the general by the trivial. Cornered and chal-lenged to drop their pretense, these Uncle Toms retreat behind a smokescreen of bogus objectiv-ity. "If gay pride," they ask, "why not queer-bash-ers' pride?" The more masochistic their pro-nouncements, the prouder they become of their detachment. Always the onus is put upon us to prove the validity of our sexual pleasure, never on our persecutors to justify their infringement of our liberty. "You're talking about Utopia," they cry if one dares to suggest that it is society that must adapt to us, not us to society. One longs for such people to display genuine emotion, to cry out against the distortion of their lives; to admit that their social status has been paid for by a million petty deceits and the death of all spontaneity; above all to realize that the outward conformity of which they are so proud has stunted and falsified all their relationships.

The extent of our self-oppression is indicated by the fact that out of the millions of gay people in Britain only a thousand or so are actively associated with the gay movement, and out of these few only a minority are really determined to press home their demands on a society that persecutes and derides them. The majority of homosexuals, like underpaid but genteel office-workers, refuse to join the union. They prefer the imagined status that comes from identifying with the management.

## UNDER THE GREENWOOD TREE

Homosexual public speakers find three complaints against gay people cropping up with monotonous regularity. Thinly disguised as questions inevitably come the accusations that gay men are mannered and effeminate, corrupters of children, and are given to a mindless animal promiscuity that prevents their forming lasting relationships. "Responsible" gay activists respond in the appropriate apologetic, self-oppressive manner to the first two charges by pointing out the homosexual men do not necessarily look feminine and vice versa, and that few gay people are interested in the very young; but probably none claim that "only a minority of homosexuals are promiscuous."

Our spokesmen generally point out that there are many happily settled homosexual couples whose lives of quiet fidelity pass unnoticed, and correctly they go on to point out that such permanent gay relationships receive none of the recognition and support from family and social institutions that married couples take for granted. Unfortunately these facts are all too often used as excuses, the assumption that promiscuity is necessarily a bad thing remains unchallenged and we are presented with an ideal to which we should aspire, and a standard by which we may be measured. We shall explain how in effect there is imposed upon us yet one more hideous oppression.

### Heterosexual mannerisms

It is a basic mistake to accept heterosexual conventions as God-given criteria by which gay people may be judged. Instead we should use the insights that we have gained as homosexuals to criticize a sexist and hypocritical society. An example of the failure to do this can be seen when the fact that gay couples are childless is pleaded as an excuse for their relationships ending; and our spokesmen fail to point out that if married couple stay together only for what they imagine to be the benefit of their children, they are not models of permanence but of thwarted impermanence. Instead of comparing our freedom unfavorably with such unions, homosexuals should feel pity for heterosexuals who find themselves trapped in an unhappy marriage and rejoice in the liberty their own homosexuality bestows.

Gay people have no reason to envy the institutionalized sexuality available to heterosexuals, cluttered as it is with ceremonies of courtship and marriage and further poisoned by a division of roles which condemns the man to dominate and the woman to submit. A heterosexual pick-up is fraught with the implications of the man conquering ands the woman surrendering; it is unlikely to enjoy the sense of mutual agreement enjoyed by gay people. For this reason it is easier for homosexuals to make sexual contacts, and once made there is no tedious process of persuasion—no ritualized escalation of intimacy to be carried out before sexual pleasure is realized.

### More than two can play

When apologetic gay speakers mention and then disparage the accessibility of gay sex, they display a naive belief that non-gay people themselves pay more than lip-service to the value of monogamy. Heterosexuals would dearly like the availability of desirable bodies and the affectionate sharing of pleasure that gay people can enjoy. The heterosexual world has no equivalent of a gay sauna! Moreover our heterosexual detractors betray their limited vision by their mistaken assumption that promiscuity is incompatible with lasting relationships. Homosexuals are in the happy position of being able to enjoy both at once. A gay couple in the street will be admiring the same people, probably be exchanging remarks about them; already the heterosexual model is inadequate to describe what is going on. It is perfectly easy for a gay couple to enjoy all the mutual care in the world and also enjoy sex with others separately or together. These things are possible simply because homosexuals can identify with the sexual feelings of those they care for in a way logically impossible for non-gay people. For this reason it is easy for a gay partnership to develop into a non-sexual relationship in which the partners share loving companionship but find sexual pleasure outside the union—unlike many heterosexual marriages which turn into a boring embittered cohabitation in which sexual attraction has long vanished but fidelity is still rigidly enforced.

The model of heterosexual marriage often actually discourages gay people from entering into any kind of permanent relationship, since they are unwilling to accept the exclusivity which they imagine a relationship must entail; moreover partnerships which do begin often break up because one partner thinks that he ought to feel jealous, or the other is unnecessarily secretive and guilty about "extra-marital" affairs. It is not the homosexual nature of such relationships which causes trouble but the poisonous influence of the heterosexual model. An irony of which we would remind the gay apologist is the fact that heterosexuals think nothing more comic than the idea of two men cooking and ironing together, or more pathetic than two women struggling to change a wheel—such is the value which in reality is placed on the pair-bonding by means of which responsible homophiles hope to gain social acceptance.

### Positive gains

Determined as they are to overlook the positive gains enjoyed by gay people, our detractors ignore the value and meaning that promiscuous, unattached homosexuals place upon friendship, which for them has a far deeper significance than for most married people who direct what they have of love and concern into the narrow confines of the family circle. Many homosexuals have close friends to whom they turn for companionship and support while finding sexual pleasure outside this circle. The ability that gay people possess to form deep and lasting friendships gives the lie to the idea that we must inevitably face a lonely old age. Logically the reverse is true, for unless their timing is perfect, it is inevitable that one partner of even a happy marriage will be left behind to face a future without the "other half" upon whom they have developed a total dependence. Anyway why deny the eroticism of novelty in favor of the repressive dogma that sex is only satisfactory with one lifelong partner? Is there not a genuine ideal in the ability of gay people to gain immediate trust and sexual satisfaction with peo-

ple from anywhere in the world? In these respects the writer of any gay porn story offers more insight into our hearts than do the ponderous utterances of homosexual apologists who usually exclude any mention of the physical reality of our sexual lives, leaving their puzzled listeners to form a picture of unhappy gay relationships based on the heterosexual model of allowable monogamy and forbidden promiscuity.

Puritanism lies at the heart of the distrust of promiscuity. Puritanism thrives upon the universal fear than someone is getting something for nothing. If pleasure is not paid for with money, people feel that it must still be paid for in other ways: commitment, responsibility, even a lifetime's mutual incompatibility is not thought too great a price to pay for occasional moments of sexual pleasure. Even Gay Liberationists sometimes speak as though their sexuality had to pay its way by virtue of breaking down sexual roles or undermining capitalism. Gay sex, unencumbered as it is with conception and contraception, could be as free and available as sunshine and air, and yet we are encouraged to disown these benefits in favor of the dubious respect gained by mimicking the outward forms of family life.

### Ironies

Anyone looking upon the gay movement with detachment finds ironies at every turn. Not least of these is the fact that although the movement has only arisen because there exists a situation of fluidity and rapid social change our homophile spokesmen can think of nothing better to do with this new freedom of thought than to urge gay people to accept the claustrophobic restrictions of a life-long union. They are busily pushing us into the prison from which intelligent heterosexuals are trying to escape. We foresee future anthropologists turning to the pair-bonding of discreet homosexuals as the only means left available of examining the long-defunct institution of marriage.

Gay activists should stand up for the variety and freedom in sexuality that gay people can enjoy, and yet how often do we read articles in the gay press containing words to the effect that "we shall never deserve our liberation until we stop being so promiscuous." Such phrases expose two aspects of self-oppression. Not only are our moral standards being measured against those of our heterosexual oppressors, but liberation is accepted as something that must be worked for and deserved rather than a fundamental right of which we have been deprived. It would be nearer the truth to say that we shall never deserve our liberation so long as we attempt to ingratiate ourselves into heterosexual favor by adopting the standards of the non-gay world.

## FLAUNTING OURSELVES

The phrase "coming out," as used by gay people, has three meanings: to acknowledge one's homosexuality to oneself; to reveal oneself to homosexuals to other gay people; and lastly, to declare one's homosexuality to everyone and anyone.

Homosexuals are unlike any other oppressed group in that their identity is almost always invisible to others. They can even conceal their identity from themselves, for such is the disgust attached to the word "homosexual" that many people who have need of homosexual experience never acknowledge it, and sometimes even those who quite frequently seek out such experience manage to convince themselves that they are not really "one of them." Behind so much that has been expressed in the gay movement lies the awareness that there exist these people who are so oppressed that they have not come out in the first sense of "admitting" their gay feelings even to themselves. Many are married with their children and throughout their lives have been totally denied any sexual pleasure. They raise no protest at their deprivation, for they cannot admit that it exists, and they can never be reached by openly gay people, for it is openness they fear. . . . There are a number of organizations trying to end the isolation of such people, but self-oppression so profound is unlikely to be ended by a few telephone conversations or by the arguments of this booklet. This essay is only about those who identify themselves as gay among gay people, but do not come out to the outside world.

### Under plain cover

If asked, closet gays often say that, although they "don't shout about it on every street corner," their friends know and their parents "must have realized by now," but "they've never asked me about it, so I haven't brought the subject up." Pressed further, they add that they "don't see the point of telling people at work," as "what I do in bed is my own business, and anyway I might lose my job." Some gay people go to considerable lengths to fake up a heterosexual image, devising tales of suitably remote fiancees, passing appreciative or disparaging comments on women (or men), and laughing heartily at the usual stream of jokes about homosexuals.

Actually these stratagems are unnecessary, because unless there is some reason to believe otherwise, it is always taken for granted that people are heterosexual. Deception need not be a positive act; one can deceive by default. At work, camp jokes will not demonstrate that one is gay; they will be accepted just as jokes, and one kiss at the Christmas party will be sufficient to wipe out a whole year's subtle hints and innuendoes.

The fear of putting a job at risk is often deliberately exaggerated by those who need a convincing excuse for secrecy. If they really wanted to come out and were prevented only by the threat of economic deprivation, they would be bitterly angry about discrimination rather than, as is usual, passively accepting it as inevitable. Most homosexuals would suffer little loss in purely material terms by coming out. It is the loss of a protective shell which is the real barrier.

Gays expose the fact that they are merely looking for excuses for remaining in the closet when they plead their purely voluntary activities as reasons for secrecy. Apparently we are expected to see their hobbies as some inescapable, unchangeable aspect of their lives. When they say that if they came out they could not continue with their Church or youth work, one can only question the value of commitments which involve supporting organizations apparently so homophobic. It would be truer to say that their self-hatred lies so deep that they leap at any chance to hide their real nature.

### Privileged gays

Many ordinary gays respond to their oppression by gravitating to jobs where they can be fairly open with the people they work with. Women may become ambulance drivers or join the Forces; men tend to work as nurses, telephone operators, in travel agencies or department stores. The acceptance of a restricted range of employment may be self-oppressive, but how straightforward and honest it is compared with the web of deception woven by those work gives them a position of social prestige.

By a curious coincidence one of the writers of this essay has found himself on two separate occasions attended by a homosexual doctor. In neither case was he aware of this until told by a third person. In each case, by making no secret of his own homosexuality he gave every opportunity for his doctor to be frank and open, but both doctors continued to behave as though homosexuality were an abnormality they had only otherwise encountered in medical textbooks. It was an amusing but saddening experience to see a homosexual attempt the role of the detached heterosexual adviser, asserting the authority he felt would be his due were he a "normal" man talking down to a "queer." Leaving aside the wretched negative attitudes these doctors must have had to their own homosexuality, we can imagine the innumerable opportunities to help confused and anxious gay people that were allowed to slip by. Doctors have a prestigious position in our society, and it would be helpful to any young gay to find that his doctor readily and openly shared his homosexuality.

## Self-oppression or self-interest?

Passing as heterosexual is by no means a private matter, for one self-oppressive deceit generates a thousand others. Friends and lovers are all included by being told what they may say on the telephone and how to behave in the street. The selfishness of those with privileged positions to defend seeps through the whole gay community, and the demoralizing message is absorbed by the great number of ordinary gays who have no privileges whatever to protect.

Homosexuals who have access to the media and refuse to come out allow those who condemn or pity us to dominate the stage. . . .

It is not that people of status should come out in order to make a propaganda point about how important or talented gay people are. It is simply that gays in the public view are ideally placed to give society a truthful view of its homosexual component.

Privileged closet gays are traitors to the gay cause, but as yet they are never referred to as such. We so lack any sense of common identity that the notion of treachery is scarcely formed. It is almost as if our bitter oppression were merely an elaborate game of pretense, the winner being those who perpetrate the cleverest frauds.

## Borrowed plumes

Gay people who pose as heterosexuals are not just deceiving others but, if they take pride in affec-

tion or esteem which is conditional on their wearing a mask of heterosexuality, also deceive themselves. Only self-oppression could allow us to value the friendship of those who, if the cards were on the table, would be revealed as our enemies. The reply to all this is likely to be "Oh, but my sex life is so unimportant; why make an issue of it?" If it's that unimportant, why make a secret of it! "Better to be hated for what one is," said Andre Gide, "than loved for what one is not."

If, furthermore, our homosexuality is never discussed with those heterosexual friends who know us to be gay, more harm is done than if we deceive them into accepting us as heterosexuals. To share the knowledge of one's homosexuality with non-gay people but never to speak of it is to tacitly agree that, like bad breath, homosexuality is something embarrassing, best left unmentioned. Why should we discuss heterosexuals' relationships with non-gay friends while allowing our own loves and fantasies to be passed over as unsuitable for general conversation?

## Against the grain

To state explicitly that one is homosexual goes against a lifetime's conditioning. The shame we have been taught to feel is deep and real. The words "I am homosexual" stick in the throat. But coming out is essential. While the majority of gay people continue to hide their "shameful" secret, the achievements of the gay movement are bound to remain insubstantial. . . . While most gays hide their identity, the greater will be the problems of those who have come out, were prised out, or by virtue of their evident homosexual traits were always out. How often do discreet homosexuals stand by while their more obvious brothers and sisters are made the butt of heterosexual mockery.

All that we have said reflects the idea of the formation of a sense of community. Coming out is even more meaningful now that the existence of the gay movement allows us to think in terms of coming out together. Ripples of self-disclosure reinforce each other within a wave of social change. A community can only exist when we identify with each other's needs. So often identification is purely negative; gays cannot ally with those who reflect what they hate in themselves; fearing to come out they are unwilling to unite with those who have the power to expose them. Once one does regard other people as part of a genuine community demanding support, coming out becomes a meaningful way of giving that support.

By coming out with people they already know, gay people can demonstrate that homosexuals are real people whose lives cannot be trampled on. "We are the people you warned us against" captures the effect. If they can discuss their feelings and lovers when heterosexuals discuss theirs, this have far more effect than any amount of propaganda about the "validity" of homosexual relationships. By coming out indiscriminately (by wearing a badge, for instance), gays oblige everyone to see that there are people who feel no shame in being known as homosexual. "Gay Pride" is the concept formed in opposition to the shame that all gay people are conditioned to feel, a shame that society demands as the condition for its limited tolerance; to deny this shame is to demand unconditional acceptance. It is pointless to limit coming out to "those who will understand"; only by public, indiscriminate, indiscreet self-disclosure can this shame be denied.

### A conspiracy of silence

Even within the gay movement change is slow and reluctant. The many lecturers and teachers within it are invariably conceded a need for secrecy, and no-one questions the value of an educational career dependent on dishonesty. It is probably widely assumed that dismissal will follow swiftly and surely upon the self-disclosure of any schoolteacher, and certainly teachers have been dismissed or lost chances of promotion after having been "discovered." But we know of a number of teachers whose careers so far remain unprejudiced by the fact that they have disclosed their homosexuality. . . .

It might be imagined that good news such as this would pass through the gay community with the speed of fire; we can only explain its actual sluggish progress by the supposition that such examples of honesty cast too strong a light upon the grubby lies and deceits of those who might be instrumental in passing on the news. To speak of openness is to deny the need for secrecy.

The kind of news that does spread rapidly is that such-and-such a celebrity bishop/singer /M.P./tennis star — is homosexual. That this knowledge should be kept safely within the confines of the gay world points to the fact that such secrecy is not only the choice of the individual, but also that of the gay world. No homosexual can be secret without being celibate; the fact that the real nature of such people is not known to the population at large is because gay people keep each other's "guilty" secrets lest in telling them they reveal their own. Helping to shore up each others' deceits is almost the only recognition most homosexuals give to the idea of a gay community. But ironically this false support prevents the community from operating as such and enjoying any sense of genuine mutual support. So often any victimization suffered by those who come out in difficult circumstances is simply dismissed by other gays as being the inevitable reward for "exhibitionism." "What can they expect," they say, "if they insist on flaunting themselves?"

## A CASE IN POINT

Much that we have discussed in the previous essay can be seen illustrated in the life of the writer E. M. Forster. We choose Forster as an example of a public figure who did not come out, rather than equally dishonest homosexual novelists such as Somerset Maugham, Henry James and Hugh Walpole, because Forster never considered himself merely as a commercial writer, but claimed a larger reputation as a moralist and social commentator. In his novels, as in his many essays and broadcasts, he gently chipped away at conservative institutions and religious beliefs, propounding instead the value of freedom, individual commitment and above all personal honesty. But his own honesty never extended to a public acknowledgment of his homosexuality, which he kept secret throughout his life.

Perhaps Forster's most famous remark was that if he were forced to choose between betraying his country and betraying his friends, he hoped he would have the courage to betray his country. Since the choice was unlikely ever to be presented, this was an easy, if startling, claim to make. The real choice for Forster lay between damaging his reputation and betraying his fellow homosexuals. Alas, it was his reputation that he guarded and gay people whom he betrayed.

### Now you see me, now you don't

Forster's early novel The Longest Journey contains a poignant description of a young man's entrapment in a marriage whose emotional poverty is contrasted both with the male friendships he enjoyed as an undergraduate and with the vitality of Stephen, a country boy who confronts him with the news that they are half-brothers. He abandons the marriage with Stephen's help and dies saving Stephen's life. Forster must have felt that the story had been too revealing, for in his later work only a few tiny incidents (such as the men bathing together in A Room With a View) remain to expose his emotional heart. Within his published work, the existence of gay people is carefully concealed. In his novel A Passage to India, Fielding, an unmarried schoolmaster in his early forties, could easily be taken to represent a repressed or "discreet" homosexual were it not that the author cautiously provided him with a youthful heterosexual romance and (at some cost to the credibility of the plot) married him off towards the end of the book. Perhaps Forster wished to stress the character's heterosexuality because, in so far as he reflects Forster's own attitude to India, Fielding can be regarded as a self-portrait.

After 1926 Forster's output of novels came to an end, and in 1946 he relaxed into the undemanding security of a life fellowship at King's College, Cambridge, where he lived until his death in 1970. Soon after he died, appreciations of his work spoke openly of an unpublished novel, written in 1914, which had not only a homosexual theme, but a happy ending. This book, Maurice, was published in 1971.

## Maurice

Possibly in 1914 such a novel could only have had a private publication, but from the 'twenties onwards—after The Well of Loneliness and the later volumes of Remembrance of Things Past had appeared—this would no longer have been so. In any case many books with homosexual themes appeared during the 'thirties and 'forties. Forster was once asked why he never published Maurice, but was content to show the manuscript to a few select, discreet friends. He replied that its publication would destroy the public image that his other writing had created. So true—and yet his immense reputation could have ensured that the novel received serious attention and a wide readership. But, far from exploiting this prestige, Forster concealed the existence of the novel throughout his life, directing that it should only be published posthumously. Much later he wrote on the manuscript "Publishable, but is it worth it?" Certainly it was worth it, but less so in 1971 than between the wars, when only the chromium-plated rich and the intellectual elite of Cambridge and Bloomsbury remained uncorroded by

the self-hatred that came of internalizing the utter disgust that most people felt for homosexuality. These years still lay within the aftermath of the Wilde trials: the homosexual dark ages when gay people were no longer ignored, but actively persecuted.

In writing this, we are not opening up a literary controversy. The publication of Maurice could have been of real practical help to countless gay people. Reading it recently, a friend in his sixties commented: "What a difference it would have made to my life if I had been able to read it when I was twenty." He could have done.

So readily does the gay community accept that homosexuality is a secret and individual matter that Forster took it for granted that his privileged status as the Grand Old (heterosexual) Man of English Letters would never be threatened by the public revelation of his homosexuality by any of those gay people who confidentially knew of it. Even through the ten years that successive governments failed to implement the meager recommendations of the Wolfenden Report, when public opinion was waiting to be led, he remained silent, preferring to watch the drama dispassionately from the stalls rather than take his proper place on the stage. Had he been prepared to come out, it is possible that so prestigious a figure would have had influence in bringing forward homosexual law reform. Certainly the open homosexuality of such a respected figure would have given us heart when we cringed before the gloating reports of the homosexual witch-hunts that were a feature of life into the early 'sixties.

▼ ▼ ▼

E. M. Forster is a classic example of the person who is widely known within the sophisticated gay community as a homosexual, and whose name is added with pride to the list of famous names that gay people so eagerly make. Since all such lists are apologetic they are all self-oppressive, but in this case there is particular irony. Throughout his life Forster betrayed other gay people by posing as a heterosexual and thus identifying with our oppressors. The novel which could have helped us find courage and self-esteem he only allowed to be published after his death, thus confirming belief in the secret and disgraceful nature of homosexuality. What other minority is so sunk in shame and self-oppression as to be proud of a traitor?

## GRATITUDE FOR TOLERANCE

Liberals are liberation's most insidious enemy. Their deep sense of heterosexual superiority remains untouched by their concern for the "plight" of gay people. They appear to concede so much while in reality conceding nothing; leaving the underprivileged to struggle against . . . not genuinely expressed reaction and hatred, but "sympathy" and "understanding."

Talk of "tolerance" being "genuine" or "complete" is meaningless. Tolerance is extended to something regrettable. Why be grateful for it?

### Small mercies

Liberal remarks on homosexuality are only to be distinguished from reactionary ones by their being prefaced by a declaration of benevolent intention. As an example of such humbug we can do no better than quote the Archbishop of York, who having first spoken of "accepting" and "understanding" homosexual clergymen, went on to describe a "healthy heterosexuality" as the proper end-product of Christian guidance. So confusing was the gentle liberal preface that some gay people thought he was ushering a new era of morality and failed to observe that he was merely putting forward the oppressive psychiatric view of homosexuality as a sickness. . . .

Gay people often think that things are moving in their direction if they are so much as mentioned in a broadcast. We heard one gay man argue for the existence of a more tolerant attitude towards homosexuality by citing the program "If You Think You've Got Problems," which took the daring step of allowing a sixteen-year-old boy to ask the panel whether he was likely to become homosexual since he was solely attracted to his own sex. "Don't commit yourself, don't give yourself a label, be open to a variety of experience," they advised. One needs to translate: "Don't be too eager to say that you are sick; find a girl soon and it may yet be possible to smother your homosexual feelings."

Taken literally, what the "experts" said was good, but until we hear heterosexuals advised with equal vigor to make homosexuality a part of their experience, we shall not be fooled into believing such "permissive" chatter to be anything but the veiled disparagement that it is. . . .

It does not require very profound understanding of human nature to see that the boy already knew the answer to his question. What he sought was not information, but reassurance that his homosexuality was natural and good. What he

received was the raw material from which he will build a lifetime's self-oppression, and from which other gay listeners will reinforce their own. These throwaway remarks give a much better insight into the speakers' true feelings than carefully composed statements of good will and "concern" (composed more to demonstrate the nobility of mind of the liberal than to aid gay people in any practical way). . . .

Gay people have been totally conned into accepting that their way of life is so shameful as to be unmentionable. When they do find their feelings discussed or their existence recognized, no matter how patronisingly, they are amazed and delighted. It is incredible that despite our numbers, and our large representation on the staff of the BBC, gay people continue to swallow the line that, over the air, homosexuality is a subject to be treated with caution. Like maltreated but faithful dogs we lick our master's boots in gratitude for being noticed, if only by a passing kick.

Even within the gay movement it is thought to be a cause for great rejoicing if we are given a tiny interview on local radio—as though the importance of gay people's lives were on a par with stamp-collecting. In fact we should regard anything less than our full free and equal representation by the broadcasting medium as the deep oppression—deep because of the way we take it for granted—that it is. The validity of our way of life, the acknowledgment of our value as equal citizens will not be demonstrated by somber discussions at midnight, or by allowing plays with homosexual themes to end happily rather than with suicides and murders, or even by a gay half-hour a week. Genuine homosexual equality will be demonstrated when boys are seen kissing boys, and girls girls, not on programs which begin at eleven o'clock at night, but at five in the afternoon.

### We're all bisexual really

The line between integrating a minority and suppressing any manifestation of its identity is a fine one, and those intellectuals who have fallen under the spell of modish, surrealistic psychoanalytical ideas, that embrace a notion of sexuality so diffuse and all-pervasive as to become meaningless, find no difficulty in crossing it. By accepting that every commonplace act is charged with sexual implications they can easily agree that there is a latent homosexual element within all of us. It is then easy to say that everyone has a heterosexual component, and thus behind a facade of bogus equality make redundant the very concept of gay people, let alone gay rights. The existence of laws which discriminate against us, our constant awareness of social disadvantage, and our ceaseless mockery by the public at large can all be callously ignored. How can homosexual discrimination exist if there are no homosexuals?

If this bland assertion of universal bisexuality has a familiar ring, perhaps we are reminded of the fashionable cry, "We're all middle-class now." This phrase conveniently abolishes economic exploitation at a stroke—for how can working-class people be exploited if there is no working class? It salves the consciences of the well-off by suggesting that everyone shares their privileges and comforts. Proponents of belief in a universal bourgeoisie can ignore the fact that one end of this middle-class spectrum has to endure housing, employment and education that the other end would not tolerate for a minute; similarly, believers in universal bisexuality can forget that the homosexual end of the supposed bisexual spectrum is denied rights and privileges which those at the heterosexual end take for granted. Of course both of these assertions are untrue. We are neither all middle-class nor are we all bisexual, and equality cannot be created by the dishonest use of words. It is true, however, that both statements are made by those who prefer to smother unpleasant realities beneath the warm comfortable blanket of liberal cant. Only self-oppression could allow us to overlook these realities. We must never be seduced into passive acceptance of them in exchange for the dud cheque of nominal integration that the idea of universal bisexuality bestows.

But many homosexual intellectuals do cling to this notion of universal bisexuality, superficially so generous to the endless diversity of human sexual experience, yet actually so crushing towards any movement for the improvement of the lot of gay people. They see evidence of homosexuality in the most conformist heterosexual activities like rugby clubs; they rush to defend queer-bashers as repressed homosexuals (are Paki-bashers then repressed Pakistanis?) and gleefully savor the color-supplement psychology that Don Juan was a homosexual desperately trying to deny it. What these homosexuals are in fact doing it finding an easement of their guilt by bestowing a little of it upon everyone. Heterosexuals who claim "we're all bisexual really" modestly imply "We are none of us quite perfect"; homosexuals who gratefully echo them add "Let him who is without sin cast the first stone."

## Instant integration

Nominal integration is no abstract matter: gay clubs have been opposed on the grounds that homosexuals should not be creating ghettoes but should be mixing with everyone else. Liberals who talk in this facile way have grasped the notion of individuals stigmatized by the label "homosexual" but not what that label is all about.

Homosexuality is not simply a personal quirk but a matter of relationships, and as such requires social expression. What could be more natural than for homosexuals to enjoy each others' company—even in a society in which homosexuality was not stigmatized. The reactionary blimp who rumbles on about "secret societies" is in fact closer to the truth than the liberal who claims that homosexuals are no different from anyone else.

Talk of "getting homosexuals out of the ghettoes" conceals both the liberal dislike of groupings which exclude him and the fact that most gays would dearly like a ghetto to get out of. The liberal vents his displeasure by telling gay people that they are divisive if they fail to mix socially with non-gay people, saying that instead they should devote their energies to the life of the community as a whole.

Liberals so easily betray the emptiness of their calls for integration. Mary Stott in the Guardian chides lesbians for feeling like outcats, and then in next breath says that "we" should "accept" homosexuals—as though the readership of the Guardian were exclusively heterosexual! The liberal "we" invariably excludes the very minority whose integration is being urged.

If liberals do fail to grasp the physical reality of gay life, then gays themselves are partly to blame. We find it easier to announce that we are gay than to communicate what this actually means. We need only think of the extreme reluctance of homosexuals to enjoy any kind of physical contact in public. Even those gay people who like to dress or talk or behave in a way which openly signals their homosexuality are unlikely to make visible the physical attraction that is its central reality. Of course the law denies us the freedom to kiss and touch that heterosexuals take for granted, but it is not legal discrimination but homosexual shame which prevents us making an open display of the reality of our physical homosexual love.

▼ ▼ ▼

If it is really true that non-gay people are offended by the sight of gays kissing, then they must learn to overcome it. The best we can do is to show sympathy for irrational phobias which they seem quite unable to control.

The siren song of nominal integration is hard to resist, and its subtle exploitation of the language of liberation creates numerous traps for the unwary. There is the seductive argument that Gay Liberation is divisive; that it artificially splits us off from the rest of the "rich tapestry of life." We are so flattered to be counted as part of any form of life, rich or otherwise, that we are liable to overlook the fact that jackboots have worn our patch of tapestry somewhat threadbare. Intellectual gays sometimes respond to this ploy by refusing to go along with the gay movement for the noble-sounding reason that they see themselves as part of the whole human race and are unwilling to be identified with just one small part of it. "I'm not joining any liberation movement," they cry, clambering on to the nigger end of the bus. "I'm part of the wide, wide spectrum of humanity."

The easiest way of all for the liberal to deal with the intractable otherness of homosexuals, and one which requires the minimum of reorientation, is to reduce everything to the level of prejudice or discrimination. Then, confident that these twin evils have been uprooted, the heterosexual can continue to live happily in a world totally indifferent to the needs of gay people. English teachers can continue to encourage girls to write essays on "the qualities I shall require in a husband"; planners will ease us all into small communities, each with its school and shopping center—paradises for the acquiescent nuclear family, but foreign hells for gays; almost hourly we shall be reminded of the "housewife's" shopping basket. The liberal conscience will be clear, but we shall still find ourselves living in a foreign land in which every social institution has been devised for a life-style alien to our own.

This may be the best that liberal well-wishers can imagine for us, but we have no need to accept such a limited vision.

## THE POINT OF IT ALL

This booklet concentrates on how we see ourselves. We have not attempted to measure the extent to which gay people are promiscuous, but we have discussed the "ideal" of sexual exclusiveness. We have not written about the fact of bisexuality, but we have dealt with ways in which it too is distorted into an oppressive "ideal." It is the attitude of gay people to coming out, to gender roles, to the media, that has concerned us. We have not tried to formulate a political theory, but only described a state of mind in which gay people can approach one without betraying their gay experience.

There is good reason for our choice. We do not really know the facts about homosexuality; no-one does. No random sample of homosexuals has ever been, or—while most gays continue to hide their identity—ever can be made. What we have written springs from the limited experience of two urban men, who write about the only kind of gay people they really know.

No homosexual is an island. When gays say that they have to be "discreet," they support the idea that homosexuality—our homosexuality—is offensive; when they describe themselves as "a typical case," they label us as "cases." Oppression is as much the creature of self-oppression as the converse. External oppression we can only fight against; self-oppression we can tear out and destroy.

# The Woman-Identified Woman

## RADICALESBIANS

What is a lesbian? A lesbian is the rage of all women condensed to the point of explosion. She is the woman who, often beginning at an extremely early age, acts in accordance with her inner compulsion to be a more complete and freer human being than her society—perhaps then, but certainly later—cares to allow her. These needs and actions, over a period of years, bring her into painful conflict with people, situations, the accepted ways of thinking, feeling and behaving, until she is in a state of continual war with everything around her, and usually with her self. She may not be fully conscious of the political implications of what for her began as personal necessity, but on some level she has not been able to accept the limitations and oppression laid on her by the most basic role of her society—the female role. The turmoil she experiences tends to induce guilt proportional to the degree to which she feels she is not meeting social expectations, and/or eventually drives her to question and analyze what the rest of her society, more or less accepts. She is forced to evolve her own life pattern, often living much of her life alone, learning usually much earlier than her "straight" (heterosexual) sisters about the essential aloneness of life (which the myth of marriage obscures) and about the reality of illusions. To the extent that she cannot expel the heavy socialization that goes with being female, she can never truly find peace with herself. For she is caught somewhere between accepting society's view of her—in which case she cannot accept herself—and coming to understand what this sexist society has done to her and why it is functional and necessary for it to do so. Those of us who work that through find ourselves on the other side of a tortuous journey through a night that may have been decades long. The perspective gained from that journey, the liberation of self, the inner peace, the real love of self and of all women, is something to be shared with all women—because we are all women.

It should first be understood that lesbianism, like male homosexuality, is a category of behavior possible only in a sexist society characterized by rigid sex roles and dominated by male supremacy. Those sex roles dehumanize women by defining us as a supportive/serving caste in relation to the master caste of men, and emotionally cripple men by demanding that they be alienated from their own bodies and emotions in order to perform their economic/political/military functions effectively. Homosexuality is a by-product of a particular way of setting up roles (or approved patterns of behavior) on the basis of sex; as such it is an inauthentic (not consonant with "reality") category. In a society in which men do not oppress women, and sexual expression is allowed to follow feelings, the categories of homosexuality and heterosexuality would disappear.

But lesbianism is also different from male homosexuality, and serves a different function in the society. "Dyke" is a different kind of put-down from "faggot," although both imply you are not playing your socially assigned sex role—are not therefore a "real woman" or a "real man." The grudging admiration felt for the tomboy and the queasiness felt around a sissy boy point to the same thing: the contempt in which women—or those who play a female role—are held. And the investment in keeping women in that contemp-

In Karla Jay and Allen Young, eds., *Out of the Closets: Voices of Gay Liberation*, pp. 172–177. New York: Douglas, [1970] 1972.

tuous role is very great. Lesbian is the word, the label, the condition that holds women in line. When a woman hears this word tossed her way, she knows she is stepping out of line. She knows that she has crossed the terrible boundary of her sex role. She recoils, she protests, she reshapes her actions to gain approval. Lesbian is a label invented by the man to throw at any woman who dares to be his equal, who dares to challenge his prerogatives (including that of all women as part of the exchange medium among men), who dares to assert the primacy of her own needs. To have the label applied to people active in women's liberation is just the most recent instance of a long history; older women will recall that not so long ago, any woman who was successful, independent, not orienting her whole life about a man, would hear this word. For in this sexist society, for a woman to be independent means she can't be a woman—she must be a dyke. That in itself should tell us where women are at. It says as clearly as can be said: women and person are contradictory terms. For a lesbian is not considered a "real woman." And yet, in popular thinking, there is really only one essential difference between a lesbian and other women: that of sexual orientation—which is to say, when you strip off all the packaging, you must finally realize that the essence of being a "woman" is to get fucked by men.

"Lesbian" is one of the sexual categories by which men have divided up humanity. While all women are dehumanized as sex objects, as the objects of men, they are given certain compensations: identification with his power, his ego, his status, his protection (from other males), feeling like a "real woman," finding social acceptance by adhering to her role, etc. Should a woman confront herself by confronting another woman, there are fewer rationalizations, fewer buffers by which to avoid the stark horror of her dehumanized condition. Herein we find the overriding fear of many women towards exploring intimate relationships with other women: the fear of her being used as a sexual object by a woman, which not only will bring no male-connected compensations, but also will reveal the void which is woman's real situation. This dehumanization is expressed when a straight woman learns that a sister is a lesbian; she begins to relate to her lesbian sister as her potential sex object, laying a surrogate male role on the lesbian. This reveals her heterosexual conditioning to make herself into an object when sex is potentially involved in a rela-

tionship, and it denies the lesbian her full humanity. For women, especially those in the movement, to perceive their lesbian sisters through this male grid of role definitions is to accept this male cultural conditioning and to oppress their sisters much as they themselves have been oppressed by men. Are we going to continue the male classification system of defining all females in sexual relation to some other category of people? Affixing the label lesbian not only to a woman who aspires to be a person, but also to any situation of real love, real solidarity, real primacy among women is a primary form of divisiveness among women: it is the condition which keeps women within the confines of the feminine role, and it is the debunking/scare term that keeps women from forming any primary attachments, groups, or associations among ourselves.

Women in the movement have in most cases gone to great lengths to avoid discussion and confrontation with the issue of lesbianism. It puts people up-tight. They are hostile, evasive, or try to incorporate it into some "broader issue." They would rather not talk about it. If they have to, they try to dismiss it as a "lavender herring." But it is no side issue. It is absolutely essential to the success and fulfillment of the women's liberation movement that this issue be dealt with. As long as the label "dyke" can be used to frighten women into a less militant stand, keep her separate from her sisters, keep her from giving primacy to anything other than men and family—then to that extent she is controlled by the male culture. Until women see in each other the possibility of a primal commitment which includes sexual love, they will be denying themselves the love and value they readily accord to men, thus affirming their second-class status. As long as male acceptability is primary—both to individual women and to the movement as a whole—the term lesbian will be used effectively against women. Insofar as women want only more privileges within the system, they do not want to antagonize male power. They instead seek acceptability for women's liberation, and the most crucial aspect of the acceptability is to deny lesbianism—i.e., deny any fundamental challenge to the basis of the female role.

It should also be said that some younger, more radical women have honestly begun to discuss lesbianism, but so far it has been primarily as a sexual "alternative" to men. This, however, is still giving primacy to men, both because the idea of relating more completely to women occurs as a negative reaction to men, and because the lesbian relationship is being characterized simply by sex, which is divisive and sexist. On one level, which is both personal and political, women may withdraw emotional and sexual energies from men, and work out various alternatives for those energies in their own lives. On a different political/psychological level, it must be understood that what is crucial is that women begin disengaging from male-defined response patterns. In the privacy of our own psyches, we must cut those cords to the core. For irrespective of where our love and sexual energies flow, if we are male-identified in our heads, we cannot realize our autonomy as human beings.

But why is it that women have related to and through men? By virtue of having been brought up in a male society, we have internalized the male culture's definition of ourselves. That definition views us as relative beings who exist not for ourselves, but for the servicing, maintenance and comfort of men. That definition consigns us to sexual and family functions, and excludes us from defining and shaping the terms of our lives. In exchange for our psychic servicing and for performing society's non-profit-making functions, the man confers on us just one thing: the slave status which makes us legitimate in the eyes of the society in which we live. This is called "femininity" or "being a real woman" in our cultural lingo. We are authentic, legitimate, real to the extent that we are the property of some man whose name we bear. To be a woman who belongs to no man is to be invisible, pathetic, inauthentic, unreal. He confirms his image of us—of what we have to be in order to be acceptable by him—but not our real selves; he confirms our womanhood—as he defines it, in relation to him—but cannot confirm our personhood, our own selves as absolutes. As long as we are dependent on the male culture for this definition, for this approval, we cannot be free.

The consequence of internalizing this role is an enormous reservoir of self-hate. This is not to say the self-hate is recognized or accepted as such; indeed most women would deny it. It may be experienced as discomfort with her role, as feeling empty, as numbness, as restlessness, a paralyzing anxiety at the center. Alternatively, it may be expressed in shrill defensiveness of the glory and destiny of her role. But it does exist, often beneath the edge of her consciousness, poisoning her existence, keeping her alienated from herself, her own needs, and rendering her a stranger to other women. Women hate both themselves and other women. They try to escape by identifying with the oppressor, living through him, gaining status and identity from his ego, his power, his accomplishments. And by not identifying with other "empty vessels" like themselves, women resist relating on all levels to other women who will reflect their own oppression, their own secondary status, their own self-hate. For to confront another woman is finally to confront one's self— the self we have gone to such lengths to avoid. And in that mirror we know we cannot really respect and love that which we have been made to be.

As the source of self-hate and the lack of real self are rooted in our male-given identity, we must create a new sense of self. As long as we cling to the idea of "being a woman," we will sense some conflict with that incipient self, that sense of I, that sense of a whole person. It is very difficult to realize and accept that being "feminine" and being a whole person are irreconcilable. Only women can give each other a new sense of self. That identity we have to develop with reference to ourselves, and not in relation to men. This consciousness is the revolutionary force from which all else will follow, for ours is an organic revolution. For this we must be available and supportive to one another, give our commitment and our love, give the emotional support necessary to sustain this movement. Our energies must flow toward our sisters, not backwards towards our oppressors. As long as women's liberation tries to free women without facing the basic heterosexual structure that binds us in one-to-one relationship with our own oppressors, tremendous energies will continue to flow into trying to straighten up each particular relationship with a man, how to get better sex, how to turn his head around—into trying to make the "new man" out of him, in the delusion that this will allow us to be the "new woman." This obviously splits our energies and commitments, leaving us unable to be committed to the construction of the new patterns which will liberate us.

It is the primacy of women relating to women, of women creating a new consciousness of and with each other which is at the heart of women's liberation, and the basis for the cultural revolution. Together we must find, reinforce and validate our authentic selves. As we do this, we confirm in each other that struggling incipient sense of pride and strength, the divisive barriers begin to melt, we feel this growing solidarity with our sisters. We see ourselves as prime, find our centers inside of ourselves. We find receding the sense of alienation, of being cut off, of being behind a locked window, of being unable to get out what we know is inside. We feel a realness, feel at last we are coinciding with ourselves. With that real self, with that consciousness, we begin a revolution to end the imposition of all coercive identifications, and to achieve maximum autonomy in human expression.

# | 88 |

# *Lesbianism: An Act of Resistance*

## CHERYL CLARKE

For a woman to be a lesbian in a male-supremacist, capitalist, misogynist, racist, homophobic, imperialist culture, such as that of North America, is an act of resistance. (A resistance that should be championed throughout the world by all the forces struggling for liberation from the same slave master.) No matter how a woman lives out her lesbianism—in the closet, in the state legislature, in the bedroom—she has rebelled against becoming the slave master's concubine, viz. the male-dependent female, the female heterosexual. This rebellion is dangerous business in patriarchy. Men at all levels of privilege, of all classes and colors have the potential to act out legalistically, moralistically, and violently when they cannot colonize women, when they cannot circumscribe our sexual, productive, reproductive, creative prerogatives and energies. And the lesbian—that woman who, as Judy Grahn says, "has taken a woman lover"[1]—has succeeded in resisting the slave master's imperialism in that one sphere of her life. The lesbian has decolonized her body. She has rejected a life of servitude implicit in Western, heterosexual relationships and has accepted the potential of mutuality in a lesbian relationship—*roles* notwithstanding.

Historically, this culture has come to identify lesbians as women, who over time, engage in a range and variety of sexual-emotional relationships with women. I, for one, identify a woman as a lesbian who says she is. Lesbianism is a recognition, an awakening, a reawakening of our passion for each (woman) other (woman) and for same (woman). This passion will ultimately reverse the heterosexual imperialism of male culture. Women, through the ages, have fought and died rather than deny that passion. In her essay, "The Meaning of Our Love for Women Is What We Have Constantly to Expand" Adrienne Rich states:

> . . . Before any kind of feminist movement existed, or could exist, lesbians existed: women who loved women, who refused to comply with behavior demanded of women, who refused to define themselves in relation to men. Those women, our foresisters, millions whose names we do not know, were tortured and burned as witches, slandered in religious and later in "scientific" tracts, portrayed in art and literature as bizarre, amoral, destructive, decadent women. For a long time, the lesbian has been a personification of feminine evil.

> . . . Lesbians have been forced to live between two cultures, both male-dominated, each of which has denied and endangered our existence. . . . Heterosexual, patriarchal culture has driven lesbians into secrecy and guilt, often to self-hatred and suicide.[2]

In Cherríe Moraga and Gloria Anzaldúa, eds., *This Bridge Called My Back: Writings by Radical Women of Color*, pp. 128–137. Watertown, Mass.: Persephone, 1981.

The evolving synthesis of lesbianism and feminism—two women-centered and powered ideologies—is breaking that silence and secrecy. The following analysis is offered as one small cut against that stone of silence and secrecy. It is not intended to be original or all-inclusive. I dedicate this work to all the women hidden from history whose suffering and triumph have made it possible for me to call my name out loud.*

The woman who embraces lesbianism as an ideological, political, and philosophical means of liberation of all women from heterosexual tyranny must also identify with the world-wide struggle of all women to end male-supremacist tyranny at all levels. As far as I am concerned, any woman who calls herself a feminist must commit herself to the liberation of all women from coerced heterosexuality as it manifests itself in the family, the state, and on Madison Avenue. The lesbian-feminist struggles for the liberation of all people from patriarchal domination through heterosexism and for the transformation of all socio-political structures, systems, and relationships that have been degraded and corrupted under centuries of male domination.

However, there is no one kind of lesbian, no one kind of lesbian behavior, and no one kind of lesbian relationship. Also there is no one kind of response to the pressures that lesbians labor under to survive as lesbians. Not all women who are involved in sexual-emotional relationships with women call themselves lesbians or identify with any particular lesbian community. Many women are only lesbians to a particular community and pass as heterosexuals as they traffic among enemies. (This is analogous to being black and passing for white with only one's immediate family knowing one's true origins.) Yet, those who hide in the closet of heterosexual presumption are sooner or later discovered. The "nigger-in-the-woodpile" story retells itself. Many women are politically active as lesbians, but may fear holding hands with their lovers as they traverse heterosexual turf. (This response to heterosexual predominance can be likened to the reaction of the black student who integrates a predominately white dormitory and who fears leaving the door of her room open when she plays gospel music.) There is the woman who engages in sexual-emotional relationships with women and labels herself bisexual. (This is comparable to the Afro-American whose skin-color indicates her mixed ancestry

yet who calls herself "mulatto" rather than black.) Bisexual is a safer label than lesbian, for it posits the possibility of a relationship with a man, regardless of how infrequent or non-existent the female bisexual's relationships with men might be. And then there is the lesbian who is a lesbian anywhere and everywhere and who is in direct and constant confrontation with heterosexual presumption, privilege, and oppression. (Her struggle can be compared to that of the Civil Rights activist of the 1960's who was out there on the streets for freedom, while so many of us viewed the action on the television.)

Wherever we, as lesbians, fall along this very generalized political continuum, we must know that the institution of heterosexuality is a die-hard custom through which male-supremacist institutions insure their own perpetuity and control over us. Women are kept, maintained, and contained through terror, violence, and spray of semen. It is profitable for our colonizers to confine our bodies and alienate us from our own life processes as it was profitable for the European to enslave the African and destroy all memory of a prior freedom and self-determination—Alex Haley notwithstanding. And just as the foundation of Western capitalism depended upon the North Atlantic slave trade, the system of patriarchal domination is buttressed by the subjugation of women through heterosexuality. So, patriarchs must extol the boy-girl dyad as "natural" to keep us straight and compliant in the same way the European had to extol Caucasian superiority to justify the African slave trade. Against that historic backdrop, *the woman who chooses to be a lesbian lives dangerously.*

As a member of the largest and second most oppressed group of people of color, as a woman whose slave and ex-slave foresisters suffered some of the most brutal racist, male-supremacist imperialism in Western history, the black lesbian has had to survive also the psychic mutilation of heterosexual superiority. The black lesbian is coerced into the experience of institutional racism—like every other nigger in America—and must suffer as well the homophobic sexism of the black political community, some of whom seem

---

*I would like to give particular acknowledgment to the Combahee River Collective's "A Black Feminist Statement." Because this document espouses "struggling against racial, sexual, heterosexual, and class oppression," it has become a manifesto of radical feminist thought, action and practice.

to have forgotten so soon the pain of rejection, denial, and repression sanctioned by racist America. While most political black lesbians do not give a damn if white America is negrophobic, it becomes deeply problematic when the contemporary black political community (another male-dominated and male-identified institution) rejects us because of our commitment to women and women's liberation. Many black male members of that community seem still not to understand the historic connection between the oppression of African peoples in North America and the universal oppression of women. As the women's rights activist and abolitionist, Elizabeth Cady Stanton, pointed out during the 1850's, racism and sexism have been produced by the same animal, viz. "the white Saxon man."

Gender oppression (i.e. the male exploitation and control of women's productive and reproductive energies on the specious basis of a biological difference) originated from the first division of labor, viz. that between women and men, and resulted in the accumulation of private property, patriarchal usurpation of "mother right" or matrilineage, and the duplicitous, male-supremacist institution of heterosexual monogamy (for women only). Sexual politics, therefore, mirror the exploitative, class-bound relationship between the white slave master and the African slave—and the impact of both relationships (between black and white and woman and man) has been residual beyond emancipation and suffrage. The ruling class white man had a centuries-old model for his day-to-day treatment of the African slave. Before he learned to justify the African's continued enslavement and the ex-slave's continued disfranchisement with arguments of the African's divinely ordained mental and moral inferiority to himself (a smokescreen for his capitalist greed) the white man learned, within the structure of heterosexual monogamy and under the system of patriarchy, to relate to black people—slave or free—as a man relates to a woman, viz. as property, as a sexual commodity, as a servant, as a source of free or cheap labor, and as an innately inferior being.

Although counter-revolutionary, Western heterosexuality, which advances male-supremacy, continues to be upheld by many black people, especially black men, as the most desired state of affairs between men and women. This observation is borne out on the pages of our most scholarly black publications to our most commercial black publications, which view the issue of black male and female relationships through the lens of heterosexual bias. But this is to be expected, as historically heterosexuality was one of our only means of power over our condition as slaves and one of two means we had at our disposal to appease the white man.

Now, as ex-slaves, black men have more latitude to oppress black women, because the brothers no longer have to compete directly with the white man for control of black women's bodies. Now, the black man can assume the "master" role, and he can attempt to tyrannize black women. The black man may view the lesbian—who cannot be manipulated or seduced sexually by him—in much the same way the white slave master once viewed the black male slave, viz. as some perverse caricature of manhood threatening his position of dominance over the female body. This view, of course, is a "neurotic illusion" imposed on black men by the dictates of male supremacy, which the black man can never fulfill because he lacks the capital means and racial privilege.

> Historically, the myth in the Black world is that there are only two free people in the United States, the white man and the black woman. The myth was established by the Black man in the long period of his frustration when he longed to be free to have the material and social advantages of his oppressor, the white man. On examination of the myth this so-called freedom was based on the sexual prerogatives taken by the white man on the Black female. It was fantasized by the Black man that she enjoyed it.[3]

While lesbian-feminism does threaten the black man's predatory control of black women, its goal as a political ideology and philosophy is not to take the black man's or any man's position on top.

Black lesbians who do work within "by-for-about-black-people" groups or organizations either pass as "straight" or relegate our lesbianism to the so-called "private" sphere. The more male-dominated or black nationalist bourgeois the organization or group, the more resistant to change, and thus, the more homophobic and anti-feminist. In these sectors, we learn to keep a low profile.

In 1979, at the annual conference of a regional chapter of the National Black Social Workers, the national director of that body was given a standing ovation for the following remarks:

Homosexuals are even accorded minority status now. . . . And white women, too. And some of you black women who call yourselves feminists will be sitting up in meetings with the same white women who will be stealing your men on the sly.

This type of indictment of women's revolution and implicitly of lesbian liberation is voiced throughout the bourgeois black (male) movement. But this is the insidious nature of male supremacy. While the black man may consider racism his primary oppression, he is hard-put to recognize that sexism is inextricably bound up with the racism the black woman must suffer, nor can he see that no women (or men for that matter) will be liberated from the original "master-slave" relationship, viz. that between men and women, until we are all liberated from the false premise of heterosexual superiority. This corrupted, predatory relationship between men and women is the foundation of the master-slave relationship between white and black people in the United States.

The tactic many black men use to intimidate black women from embracing feminism is to reduce the conflicts between white women and black women to a "tug-o'-war" for the black penis. And since the black lesbian, as stated previously, is not interested in his penis, she undermines the black man's only source of power over her, viz. his heterosexuality. Black lesbians and all black women involved in the struggle for liberation must resist this manipulation and seduction.

The dyke, like every dyke in America, is everywhere—in the home, in the street, on the welfare, unemployment, and social security rolls, raising children, working in factories, in the armed forces, on television, in the public school system, in all the professions, going to college or graduate school, in middle-management, et. al. The black dyke, like every other non-white and working class and poor woman in America, has not suffered the luxury, privilege, or oppression of being dependent on men, even though our male counterparts have been present, have shared our lives, work, and struggle, and, in addition, have undermined our "human dignity" along the way like most men in patriarchy, the imperialist family of man. But we could never depend on them "to take care of us" on their resources alone—and, of course, it is another "neurotic illusion" imposed on our fathers, brothers, lovers, husbands that they are supposed to "take care of us" because we

are women. Translate: "to take care of us" equals "to control us." Our brothers', fathers', lovers', husbands' only power is their manhood. And unless manhood is somehow embellished by white skin and generations of private wealth, it has little currency in racist, capitalist patriarchy. The black man, for example, is accorded native elite or colonial guard or vigilante status over black women in imperialist patriarchy. He is an overseer for the slave master. Because of his maleness he is given access to certain privileges, e.g. employment, education, a car, life insurance, a house, some nice vines. He is usually a rabid heterosexual. He is, since emancipation, allowed to raise a "legitimate" family, allowed to have his piece of turf, viz. his wife and children. That is as far as his dictatorship extends for, if his wife decides that she wants to leave that home for whatever reason, he does not have the power or resources to seduce her otherwise if she is determined to throw off the benign or malicious yoke of dependency. The ruling class white man on the other hand, has always had the power to count women among his pool of low-wage labor, his means of production. Most recently, he has "allowed" women the right to sue for divorce, to apply for AFDC, and to be neocolonized.

Traditionally, poor black men and women who banded together and stayed together and raised children together did not have the luxury to cultivate dependence among the members of their families. So, the black dyke, like most black women, has been conditioned to be self sufficient, i.e. not dependent on men. For me personally, the conditioning to be self-sufficient and the predominance of female role models in my life are the roots of my lesbianism. Before I became a lesbian, I often wondered why I was expected to give up, avoid, and trivialize the recognition and encouragement I felt from women in order to pursue the tenuous business of heterosexuality . And I am not unique.

As political lesbians, i.e. lesbians who are resisting the prevailing culture's attempts to keep us invisible and powerless, we must become more visible (particularly black and other lesbians of color) to our sisters hidden in their various closets, locked in prisons of self-hate and ambiguity, afraid to take the ancient act of woman-bonding beyond the sexual, the private, the personal. I am not trying to reify lesbianism or feminism. I am trying to point out that lesbian-feminism has the potential of reversing and transforming a major component in the system of women's oppression, viz. predatory heterosexuality. If radical lesbian-feminism purports an anti-racist, anti-classist, anti-woman-hating vision of bonding as mutual, reciprocal, as infinitely negotiable, as freedom from antiquated gender prescriptions and pro-scriptions, *then all people struggling to transform the character of relationships in this culture have something to learn from lesbians.*

The woman who takes a woman lover lives dangerously in patriarchy. And woe betide her even more if she chooses as her lover a woman who is not of her race. The silence among les-bian-feminists regarding the issue of lesbian rela-tionships between black and white women in America is caused by none other than the cen-turies-old taboo and laws in the United States against relationships between people of color and those of the Caucasian race. Speaking heterosex-ually, the laws and taboos were a reflection of the patriarchal slave master's attempts to control his property via controlling his lineage through the institution of monogamy (for women only) and justified the taboos and laws with the argument that purity of the Caucasian race must by pre-served (as well as its supremacy). However, we know that his racist and racialist laws and taboos did not apply to him in terms of the black slave woman just as his classist laws and taboos regard-ing the relationship between the ruling class and the indentured servants did not apply to him in terms of the white woman servant he chose to rape. The offspring of any unions between the white ruling class slave master and the black slave woman or white woman indentured servant could not legally inherit their white or ruling class sire's property or name, just their mothers' condi-tion of servitude.

The taboo against black and white people relating at any other level than master-slave, supe-rior-inferior has been propounded in America to keep black women and men and white women and men, who share a common oppression at the hands of the ruling class white man, from orga-nizing against that common oppression. We, as black lesbians, must vehemently resist being bound by the white man's racist, sexist laws, which have endangered potential intimacy of any kind between whites and blacks.

It cannot be presumed that black lesbians involved in love, work, and social relationships with white lesbians do so out of self-hate and denial of our racial-cultural heritage, identities, and oppression. Why should a woman's commit-ment to the struggle be questioned or accepted on

the basis of her lover's or comrade's skin color? White lesbians engaged likewise with black les-bians or any lesbians of color cannot be assumed to be acting out of some perverse, guilt-ridden racialist desire.

I personally am tired of going to events, con-ferences, workshops, planning sessions that involve a coming together of black and other les-bians of color for political or even social reasons and listening to black lesbians relegate feminism to white women, castigate black women who pro-pose forming coalitions with predominantly white feminist groups, minimize the white woman's oppression and exaggerate her power, and then finally judge that a black lesbian's com-mitment to the liberation of black women is dubi-ous because she does not sleep with a black woman. All of us have to accept or reject allies on the basis of politics not on the specious basis of skin color. *Have not black people suffered betrayal from our own people?*

Yes, black women's experiences of misogyny are different from white women's. However, they all add up to how the patriarchal slave master decided to oppress us. We both fought each other for his favor, approval, and protection. Such is the effect of imperialist, heterosexist patriarchy. Shu-lamith Firestone, in the essay, "Racism: the Sex-ism of the Family of Man," purports this analysis of the relationship between white and black women:

> How do the women of this racial Triangle feet about each other? Divide and conquer: Both women have grown hostile to each other, white women feeling contempt for the "sluts" with no morals, black women feeling envy for the pampered "powder puffs." The black woman is jealous of the white woman's legiti-macy, privilege, and comfort, but she also feels deep contempt. . . . Similarly the white woman's contempt for the black woman is mixed with envy: for the black woman's greater sexual license, for her gutsiness, for her freedom from the marriage bind. For after all, the black woman is not under the thumb of a man, but is pretty much her own boss to come and go, to leave the house, to work (much as it is degrading work) or to be "shift-less." What the white woman doesn't know is that the black woman, not under the thumb of one man, can now be squashed by all. There is no alternative for either of them than the choice between being public or private property, but because each still believes that the other is getting away with something both

can be fooled into mis-channeling their frustration onto each other rather than onto the real enemy, "The Man."[4]

Though her statement of the choices black and white women have under patriarchy in America has merit, Firestone analyzes only a specific relationship i.e. between the ruling class white woman and slave or ex-slave black woman.

Because of her whiteness, the white woman of all classes has been accorded, as the black man has because of his maleness, certain privileges in racist patriarchy, e.g. indentured servitude as opposed to enslavement, exclusive right to public assistance until the 1960's, "legitimate" offspring and (if married into the middle/upper class) the luxury to live on her husband's income, etc.

The black woman, having neither maleness nor whiteness, has always had her heterosexuality, which white men and black men have manipulated by force and at will. Further, she, like all poor people, has had her labor, which the white capitalist man has also taken and exploited at will. These capabilities have allowed black women minimal access to the crumbs thrown at black men and white women. So, when the black woman and the white woman become lovers, we bring that history and all those questions to the relationship as well as other people's problems with the relationships. The taboo against intimacy between white and black people has been internalized by us and simultaneously defied by us. If we, as lesbian-feminists, defy the taboo, then we begin to transform the history of relationships between black women and white women.

In her essay, "Disloyal to Civilization: Feminism, Racism, Gynephobia," Rich calls for feminists to attend to the complexities of the relationship between black and white women in the United States. Rich queries:

What caricatures of bloodless fragility and broiling sensuality still imprint our psyches, and where did we receive these imprintings? What happened between the several thousand northern white women and southern black women who together taught in the schools founded under Reconstruction by the Freedmen's Bureau, side by side braving the Ku Klux Klan harassment, terrorism, and the hostility of white communities?*[5]

So, all of us would do well to stop fighting each other for our space at the bottom, because there ain't no more room. We have spent so much time hating ourselves. Time to love ourselves. And that, for all lesbians, as lovers, as comrades, as freedom fighters, is the final resistance.

## NOTES

1. Grahn, Judy. "The Common Woman," *The Work of a Common Woman*. Diana Press. Oakland, 1978, p. 67.

2. Rich, Adrienne, *On Lies, Secrets, and Silence: Selected Prose 1966–1978*. W. W. Norton. New York, 1979, p. 225.

3. Robinson, Pat and Group, "Poor Black Women's Study Papers by Poor Black Women of Mount Vernon, New York," in T. Cade (ed). *The Black Woman: An Anthology*. New American Library. New York, 1970. p. 194.

4. Firestone, Shulamith, *The Dialectic of Sex: The Case for Feminist Revolution*. Bantam Books, New York, 1972, p. 113.

5. Rich, op. cit., p. 298.

---

* One such example is the Port Royal Experiment (1862), the precursor of the Freedmen's Bureau. Port Royal was a program of relief for "freed men and women" in the South Carolina Sea Islands, organized under the auspices of the Boston Education Commission and the Freedmen's Relief Assoc. in New York and the Port Royal Relief Assoc. in Philadelphia, and sanctioned by the Union Army and the Federal Government. See *The Journal of Charlotte Forten* on the "Port Royal Experiment" (Beacon Press, Boston, 1969). Through her Northern bourgeois myopia, Forten recounts her experiences as a black teacher among the black freed men and women and her Northern white women peers.

# | 89 |

# I Paid Very Hard for My Immigrant Ignorance

### MIRTHA QUINTANALES

Dear Barbara (Smith), Columbus, Ohio
January, 1980

Thanks for your letter. I can appreciate your taking the time to write. It can get so difficult for busy people to keep up with correspondence . . . I only hope that you have taken some time to rest, gather your energies. I'm just beginning to emerge from a several-week period of semi-hermitdom myself. I, too, was exhausted. Too much work too many responsibilities—often the worry of not moving fast enough, or too fast to have any kind of an impact. After a brief peaceful interlude, the pressures are beginning to build again, Oh well . . .

I wanted to tell you about my visit to San Francisco, about coming together with my Latina lesbian/feminist sisters. The joy and the pain of finding each other, of realizing how long we've "done without," of how difficult it's going to be to heal ourselves, to find our voices . . . But how perfectly wonderful to finally have a family, a community. Yet I find that there is too much to tell. Cannot easily compress it all in a letter. How I wish that we could meet and talk! So much of the Black lesbian/feminist experience speaks to our own . . . I passed around all the literature you'd handed out at conferences—including Conditions 5. And the Latina sisters were amazed. Lorraine Bethel's "What Chou Mean We White Girl?" was especially telling . . . Many of our feelings given form, meaning. Please let her know that her work has been very helpful to us—particularly in sorting out what we want and don't want in our relationsips with white, mainstream American feminists. Yes, there is a lot we can learn from each other.

But Barbara, I am worried. At the moment I am in the process of organizing a roundtable for the NWSA* conference, on the topic of racial and ethnic minority lesbians in the U.S. There are two other women involved—a Greek friend of mine from Berkeley, and a Black woman from San Francisco. And I feel the tension building. The Greek woman's many attempts to "connect" with Third World lesbians and "Women of Color" (most poignantly at last year's conference) have been met with outright rejection. Unfortunately, being loud, aggressive and very Greek-identified, she has found a great deal of rejection in white, mainstream lesbian/feminist circles as well. Clearly she does not fit there either.

The Black woman's commitments, from what I can gather, are understandably with Third World women, women of color. And I am quite uncomfortably in the middle. As a Third World, Caribbean woman I understand what it means to have grown up "colonized" in a society built on slavery and the oppression of imperialist forces. As an immigrant and a cultural minority woman who happens to be white-skinned, I empathize with the pain of ethnic invisibility and the perils of passing (always a very tenuous situation—since acknowledgement of ethnic ties is inevitably accompanied by stereotyping, prejudice *and* various kinds of discrimination—the problem is not just personal, but "systemic," "political"—one more reality of American "life.") How to reconcile these different kinds of "primary emergencies": race and culture? Of

In Cherríe Moraga and Gloria Anzaldúa, eds., *This Bridge Called My Back: Writings by Radical Women of Color*, pp. 150–156. Watertown, Mass.: Persephone, 1981.

* National Women's Studies Association

course this kind of conflict tends to obscure the issue of *class* and its relationship to race and ethnicity so important for the understanding of the dilemma.

Not all Third World women are "women of color"—if by this concept we mean exclusively "non-white." I am only one example. And not all women of color are really Third World—if this term is only used in reference to underdeveloped or developing societies (especially those not allied with any superpower). Clearly then it would be difficult to justify referring to Japanese women, who are women of color, as Third World women. Yet, if we extend the concept of Third World to include internally "colonized" racial and ethnic minority groups in this country, so many different kinds of groups could be conceivably included, that the crucial issue of social and institutional racism and its historic tie to slavery in the U.S. could get diluted, lost in the shuffle. The same thing would likely happen if we extended the meaning of "women of color" to include all those women in this country who are victims of prejudice and discrimination (in many respects), but who nevertheless hold racial privileges and may even be racists.

I don't know what to think anymore. Things begin to get even more complicated when I begin to consider that many of us who identify as "Third World" or "Women of Color," have grown up as or are fast becoming "middle-class" and highly educated, and therefore more privileged than many of our white, poor and working-class sisters. Sometimes I get angry at my lover because she does not seem to relate to my being a "Cuban" lesbian. And yet, can I really relate to the fact that she grew up in a very small town, in a working-class family—with little money, few other resources, little encouragement to get an education, etc.? Yes . . . and no. There have been times in my life when my family had little money or food. There have been times in my life when I lived from day to day not knowing if I would be alive "tomorrow"—not knowing really how it felt to plan for "next month," or "next year."

Yet, even though I grew up having to heat my bathwater and sleep in a very lumpy bed, even though I grew up often being ashamed of bringing my friends home because our furniture was old and dilapidated, I went to private schools, spent summers at the beach, traveled, had plenty of toys and books to read; took music and dancing lessons, went horsebackriding—my parents being very conscious of, and being very *able* to give us

the best (if not always in terms of material comforts) that their middle-class resources gave them access to—including the services of a long string of nurse-maids (my mother worked, and in Cuba often the *maids* had maids—even if it meant putting little girls to work as servants and babytenders—economic exploitation galore!).

Yes, I have suffered in this country. I have been the victim of blatant prejudice and institutional discrimination. As an ethnic minority woman and a lesbian I have lived in the margins, in fear, isolated, disconnected, silent and in pain. Nevertheless, those early years of relatively "blissful" middle-class childhood (although I have to say that after age 7 it was *hell*—political violence and death always lurking) in my own country where I was simply part of the "mainstream" if not a little better off because of my father's professional status, have served me as a "cushion" throughout my life. Even in the United States, as an essentially middle-class (and white-skinned woman), I have had "opportunities" (or have known how to make them for myself), that my very white, working-class American lover has never had. Having managed to graduate from college (one out of three in her graduating high school class who managed to make it *to* college) against tremendous odds, she is still struggling with the fact that she may never really learn the ropes of surviving well in mainstream, middle-class American society. And need I add that mainstream white, middle-class American feminism is as insensitive to her needs as it is to mine?

I realize that I cannot fight everybody's battles. But need I create false enemies in order to wage my own? I am a bit concerned when a Latina lesbian sister generalizes about/puts down the "white woman"—especially if she herself has white skin. In the midst of this labeling, might she not dismiss the fact of her own white privileges—regardless of her identification with Black, Native American, and other Third World women of color? Might she not dismiss the fact that she may often be far better off than many white women? I cannot presume to know what it is really like to be a Black woman in America, to be racially oppressed. I cannot presume to know what it is really like to grow up American "White Trash" and destitute.

But I am also a bit concerned when a Black sister generalizes about/dismisses all non-black women, or all women who are not strict "women of color" or strictly "Third World." If you are not WASP in this country, if you or your family have known the immigrant experience or ghetto life, you are likely to be very much acquainted with the social, economic, political reality of internal colonization. Yes, racism is a BIG MONSTER we all need to contend with—regardless of our skin color and ethnic affiliation. But I think we need to keep in mind that in this country, in this world, racism is used *both* to create false differences among us *and* to mask very very significant ones—cultural economic, political . . . And yes, those who have been racially oppressed must create separatist spaces to explore the meaning of their experiences—to heal themselves, to gather their energies, their strength, to develop their own voices, to build their armies. And yes, those of us who have not been victims of racial oppression must come to terms with our own racism, our own complicity with this system that discriminates and oppresses on the basis of skin color and body features. And of course it would be irresponsible liberal folly to propose that social and institutional racism could be eliminated by simply "becoming" personally non-racist, by becoming "integrated" in our private lives . . . How ridiculous for white folk to think that a long history of slavery and every other kind of oppression, that an *ongoing* and *insidious* reality of social, economic, political exploitation could be magically transcended through a few individual choices . . . And even if everybody's skin should suddenly turn black, it would be quite impossible to truly know what it means to have grown up—generation after generation—Black and female in America. Of course our skin is not likely to "turn," and so regardless of how "conscious" we claim to be of the "Black experience" in America, we shall always be limited by our own history and the reality of our white skin and the privileges it automatically confers on us.

Ironically, when a Black American sister (or anyone for that matter) puts me, or other ethnic women of this society in the same category with the socially dominant White American Woman on the basis of lighter-than-black skin color, she is in fact denying my history, my culture, my identity, my very being my pain and my struggle. She too is being *personally* racist. When she fails to recognize that the "social privileges" of lighter-than-black ethnic-minority lesbians in this society are almost totally dependent on our denial of who we are, on our *ethnic death*, she also falls prey to the racist mythology that color differences are the end-all indications of social inequality. That those who happen to have the "right" skin color are not only all alike but all hold the same social privileges. Yes, lighter-than-black skin color *may* confer on some ethnic minority women the option of becoming "assimilated," "integrated" in mainstream American society. But is this really a privilege when it always means having to become invisible, ghost-like, identity-less, community-less, totally alienated? The perils of "passing" as white American are perils indeed. It should be easy enough at least for *lesbians* to understand the meaning of being and yet not being, of "merging" and yet remaining utterly alone and in the margins of our society.

And while it is true that a lesbian/feminist community and culture have emerged, while it is true that Black, Latina and other Third World/lesbians "of color" have begun to speak up, it is not true that we have yet engaged in a truly un-biased, un-prejudiced *dialogue*. We are still measuring each other by the yardstick of the White, Capitalist, Imperialist, Racist American Patriarch. We are still seeing radical differences when they don't exist and not seeing them when they are critical. And most disastrously, we are failing to recognize much of what we *share*. Is it not possible for us to recognize, respect and settle our differences; to validate our various groups' struggles and need for separate spaces, and yet to open our eyes to the fact that divided we are only likely to succeed at defeat?

It is pure folly to think that a small group of Latina or Black or Chinese American lesbians can, on its own, create a feminist revolution. It is pure folly to think that middle-class Wasp feminists can do so . . .

Barbara, I ache to live with and love with my Latina lesbian/feminist sisters—to speak "Spanglish," to eat arroz con frijoles, to dance to the salsa, to openly talk sex and flirt with one another; to secretly pray to Yemayá, Chango, Oshun, and the Virgen de Guadalupe. I run to them for refuge, for dear life!

But when I meet you and other Black lesbian sisters—and am moved by what we seem to share, I ache for you also. I spend time with Stacy (Anastasia) and other Southern European/North African/Mediterranean lesbian sisters—and am stirred by what we seem to have in common, I feel deep yearning for them . . . I read the words of other ethnic American lesbian sisters and I find that I understand them and want to share in these women's lives. And I live, love and work with working-class sisters. Have lived, loved and worked in the poor urban ghettos of Chicago and

Boston. Have spent some time in the poor, rural, isolated mountains of New Mexico. Have traveled to Latin American countries, to India, Thailand, Taiwan, Hong-Kong, Japan—feeling the pain of my poor and hard-working sisters—struggling against all odds to stay alive, to live with dignity. I cannot sleep sometimes—haunted by the memories of such all-encompassing poverty—the kind of poverty that even poor Americans could not begin to conceive. India. India was the unraveling. How insignificant our troubles seem in the United States . . . How ridiculously small my own struggles . . . I don't feel guilt or shame, but this nausea . . . To find us squabbling over who may or may not be called a feminist, who may or may not join or take part in this or that particular political group, etc, etc. The privilege of having feminist "groups"—most women in the world just eat shit. And lesbians—who really knows the fate of most lesbians in the world, especially the Third World?

Is it not possible for all of us here in America to turn *right now* to *all* the sisters of the world—to form a common, human-woman-lesbian bond?

I have lost some sleep lately pondering over this race/culture/class problem . . . We've got to do *something!* Many of us Latinas are non-white—as a matter of fact, most of us are racially mixed to various degrees. Ask a Black or "mulatto" Puerto Rican woman what her identity is though, and most likely she will tell you "Puerto Rican." All Chinese American women are non-white. But ask any of them what her identity is. She will not tell you "yellow," she will tell you Chinese, or Chinese American. Many African peoples are "Black," but ask a Nigerian, an Ethiopian, etc. what her identity is, and she will tell you "Nigerian," or "Ethiopian," or whatever . . . Obviously "Black Culture" is an American phenomenon. Many of us don't really understand this. I know I didn't for a long time. When I first came to this country I just assumed that Black people were simply American (for that matter I just assumed *all* Americans shared the same "American Culture"). I grew up with people of all kinds of skin-color—but we were all *Cuban* and understood each other, even though we *could* recognize the most minute "color differences," even though we could recognize class differences. How was I supposed to know—given the propaganda—that there was no such thing as a "melting pot"? How was I supposed to know that racism was so widespread and so deeply ingrained in American society? I was *shocked* in my sophomore year in college when several Black women implied that I was a racist when I said I could not figure out what was different about being Black or Yellow, or White, or Red in the United States. I could understand not knowing about a "culture," but not knowing about a "race"? Was "race" per se so important? Was it really linked to a "culture"? This was a weird notion to me indeed!

Well I paid very hard for my immigrant ignorance. I'm still paying—even though I have learned a great deal since then about American sub-cultures and about American racism. Many of my Latina sisters have had similar experiences, and the big question is always there—Will we ever really be accepted by our Black American sisters? I cannot really convey the pain—especially in those of us who *are* Afro-Hispanic-American but light skinned—of seeing so much of ourselves in, of being so drawn to African-American women, and yet feeling that we are very likely to be denied a connection, to be rejected. The fucking irony of it! Racism. It has so thoroughly poisoned Americans of all colors that many of us can simply not see beyond it. I'm sorry about this long letter Barbara—especially this last part. But I have not been able to get over this pain. I used to have this recurrent dream (for years) that I would alternately become black and white and black and white over and over and over again . . . It felt really good. But I've never quite figured out all of what it meant . . . Well, take care Barbara.

In sisterhood,
Mirtha

# Our Right to the World: Beyond the Right to Privacy

## SCOTT TUCKER

Dear camerado! I confess I have urged nward with me, and still urge you, without the least idea what is our destination, Or whether we shall be victorious, or utterly quelled and defeated.

WALT WHITMAN, "AS I LAY WITH MY HEAD IN YOUR LAP, CAMERADO"

How has the lesbian and gay movement grown and evolved since that night in June 1969 when the Stonewall Inn was raided by cops, and the patrons fought back with mockery and fury? In September of the same year, the first issue of a radical gay liberation newspaper called *Come Out!* appeared. Here is a telling passage from the first editorial: "We will not be gay bourgeoisie, searching for the sterile 'American Dream' of the ivy-covered cottage and the corporation job, but neither will we tolerate the exclusion of homosexuals from any area of American life. . . . Does society make a place for us as a man? A woman? A homosexual or a lesbian? How does the family structure affect us? What is sex? What does it mean? What is love? As homosexuals we are in a unique position to examine these questions from a fresh point of view. You'd better believe we are going to do so—that we are going to transform the society at large through the realization of our own consciousness."

Today in 1982, after years of turmoil alternating with apathy, it is too easy for seasoned gay people to smile at such words, like adults listening to baby-talk. The fact is that the questions which children raise often take whole lives to answer—perhaps the whole of human history. Society, family, sex, love—these raise questions for even the most "apolitical" gay person, questions which we are struggling to answer in our daily lives. Those who wrote that editorial back in 1969 had every right to speak for themselves and to try steering the gay movement in a radical

direction. When they insisted that they would *not* be gay bourgeoisie, they were surely aware that other gay people *would* be. True, their attack on the American Dream and the ivy-covered cottage seems facile now—some silly things were said in those early days—but those who now equate resignation with maturity are simply resigned. They claim they got wiser, but they just got tired.

A full decade after that editorial was written, Vito Russo quoted a veteran of the Stonewall Rebellion in the *Village Voice*: "When we fought back at the Stonewall ten years ago, we didn't think the benefits would be seven hundred leather bars and the right to join the army. That isn't exactly what we had in mind." At the time of Stonewall, many counter-culture gay activists believed that a new world was rising from the ashes of the old. Capitalism and patriarchy would collapse of their own weight and weakness, and society would become one great androgynous Commune. Instead of the Commune, what we got was Christopher Street and Castro Street: gay hippies became gay clones.

There are still some gays who consider gay ghettoes completely corrupt and who believe the gay movement has been completely co-opted. They share this view, in fact, with some of the most mechanical straight leftists.

The reality is more complex and hopeful. The gay ghetto is not utopia, yet the urban concentration of self-identified gays has been a great source

*Body Politic*, July/August 1982, pp. 29–33.

of power. Without gay visibility and solidarity, populist uprisings like the Stonewall, San Francisco and Toronto rebellions would have been impossible. Ghettoes of all kinds are contradictory in nature: for gays, as for many others, they serve both as a detention camp and a liberated zone. The Jewish ghettoes of Russia and Eastern Europe nourished a rich culture, but the Cossacks knew where to find many victims when they were in the mood for a pogrom. A ghetto is somewhat like a factory, where many people are gathered to be exploited, but where they also have the power to call a strike, or even kick out the boss and take over the place themselves.

Our right to the world is denied in countless ways, and by default gay ghettoes become the only place where many of us feel relatively free or safe. For that reason, gay ghettoes become lightning rods for right-wing wrath. There are people of *all* political stripes who plainly fear and resent our pleasure, freedom and strength.

And we ourselves, in the very act of casting off our chains, often see freedom through the eyes of slaves. How could it be otherwise? Much of the media maintains a fair weather liberalism, but prevailing winds of reaction alter its course. In 1980 CBS broadcast the infamous "Gay Power, Gay Politics," which focused on San Francisco as the place where gay power had advanced furthest. The CBS crew took a safari through San Francisco, and it showed the civilized world a zoo. A few gay power-brokers were presented as jackals who had sharpened their teeth on Mayor Dianne Feinstein. The leather numbers became iguanas, meant to rouse a dread of reptiles; the drag queens and Hallowe'en scenes surely roused disgust among the hawkish citizenry—all that peacock plumage!

But most significantly, a hidden camera was used to film gay men cruising half-naked in Buena Vista Park, like savages roaming the bushland, perhaps. A nuclear family living near the park was interviewed in the following segment, and the parents expressed fears that their children might be traumatized by the sight of sex.

Is it innately more traumatizing to see a cock sucked than to see an apple eaten?

## PRIVACY, AUTONOMY AND THE STATE

Sex forgotten is sex best served. . . . I look forward to a homosexual leadership that values its gains (and they have been immense) and adopts a

strategy of low public visibility to keep from losing these gains. The closet is no longer a guilt-ridden cell. Today it is, as a man's home should be, his castle.

CHARLES MCCABE, COLUMNIST FOR THE *SAN FRANCISCO CHRONICLE*, FROM A SERIES CALLED "SEX IN THE STREETS," 1979

The right of an individual to live as he or she chooses can become offensive. The gay community is going to have to face this.

SAN FRANCISCO MAYOR DIANNE FEINSTEIN, INTERVIEWED IN *LADIES HOME JOURNAL*, 1979.

Legal and "common sense" definition of public and private space, property, rights and duties evolve through history, and tell us much about the moral and material order of any given social group. In the Fall 1981 issue of *Gay Books Bulletin*, an illuminating piece by Wayne Dynes was published called "Privacy, Sexual Orientation and the Self-Sovereignty of the Individual: Continental Theories, 1762–1908." Dynes argues that privacy evolved as a complex of concepts, and he traces one branch of their evolution "to the heart of European Enlightenment." After the French Revolution, a mass of literature was printed dealing with political reform, and likewise much literature appeared dealing with sexuality. Dynes writes, "A little known but highly significant example of the mixture of sex and politics—or sexual politics, if you will—is a brochure of 1790: *Les petits bougres au manège*. The anonymous work presents itself as a plea for homosexual rights, apparently the first of its kind. The Revolution, according to the writer, has secured citizens in their right to property. Now what could be more clearly one's own property than the parts of one's body, including one's genitals? What citizens choose to do with them, either alone or in the company of other consenting citizens, is not the business of the state."

In an ambitious 1908 doctoral dissertation called "The Right over One's Self," German law student (and later gay activist) Kurt Hiller dealt with the following topics and in the following order: suicide, self-mutilation, duelling, incest, homosexuality, bestiality and abortion. "Hiller's analysis," Dynes writes, "of the various rationalizations that have accumulated in favor of criminal sanctions in the categories he considers reveals that they have almost always had a religious or mystical origin. As such they are arguments that, in a modern secular state, should not be permitted to pass unchallenged. Ultimately, however, the key to the matter lies in the fact that the criminalization of all these things interferes with the right to control one's own body."

The moral and legal order of society may require sexual secrecy at the same time as the material order makes such secrecy impossible. In colonial and rural America, for example, many large families lived, loved and died within homes consisting of a single room. Privacy, therefore, often had to be found out of doors. In his book, *Privacy: How to Protect What's Left of It*, Robert Ellis Smith points out that sex "didn't always take place in the bedroom, of course. In fact, men and women often retreated to the woods for intimate relationships. . . . Domestic relations court records of the period are filled with accounts like the one about a couple 'making love among the mustard topes and other wedes.' "

In cold weather and at night, a barn was often found suitable, but sometimes a curtain hung round a bed had to serve, and sharing beds with relatives and visiting strangers was common. Such arrangements encouraged a certain communalism, though they also encouraged sexual sneakiness, particularly in a Christian, and predominantly Puritan, culture. Making love among the mustard tops sounds charming, but this erotic idyll is to be found, after all, in court records.

According to an account of town records in David Flaherty's *Privacy in Colonial New England*, there was much commotion in Boston in 1757 because of "many persons washing themselves in publick and frequented places to the great reproach of modesty and good manners." And so the town meeting "voted and ordered that no person whosoever above the age of 12 years shall in less than an hour after sun-set undress themselves and go into the water within ten rods of any dwelling house in this town, at that time inhabited, nor shall any person being in the water, swim to such parts of the town as to be plainly within sight of any dwelling house. . . . " Town meetings seem to me a good form of democracy, but I wonder how many of those "many persons washing themselves in publick" were present to vote at *that* meeting. I suspect that the Puritan merchants found Boston's riff-raff too undisciplined. Nude beaches have provoked similar controversy and ordinances in recent years.

In 1890, writes Robert Ellis Smith, "Mrs. Samuel D. Warren was outraged at the press coverage of parties and dances in the city of Boston. This prompted her husband, a professor law at Harvard University, to join a colleague, Louis D. Brandeis, in devising 'the right of the individual to be let alone.' A Warren-Brandeis law journal article on the right to privacy became the fountainhead of later law and social policy in the United States. . . . " In that article, Warren and Brandeis expressed special concern about developing communications technology: "Instantaneous photographs and newspaper enterprise have invaded the sacred precincts of private and domestic life and numerous mechanical devices threaten to make good the prediction that 'what is whispered in the closet shall be proclaimed from the housetops.' "

We can see that the same technological advances which *profited* the well-to-do classes were also being used to expose their personal and social life to the world. There was, after all, a profit to be made from the increasing literacy of the masses. In 1890 the lower classes of Boston were largely housed in crowded and filthy slums, as they were elsewhere in the country as it became more industrialized and urbanized. Workers and poor people did not have the option of pursuing sex and privacy in the woods as did colonial and rural Americans; we can be sure that many trysts took place in the alleys and odd corners of the city, as has always been true of city life. When it came time to formulate the right to privacy in legal terms, that formulation was not prompted by any concern for the privacy of the lower classes. No, what prompted its formulation was the fact that Mrs. Samuel D. Warren was outraged at the press coverage of parties and dances in the city of Boston.

The bourgeois origin of that legal right does not mean that it should be despised as such; it does mean that bourgeois formulations of privacy serve bourgeois interests best. The economic cycles of capitalism forcibly collectivize and atomize masses of people, with little respect to the organic integrity of communities—much less personal autonomy or privacy. When state snoopers try to take a woman off welfare because she keeps "a man in the house," she may have precious few legal or financial means to defend *her* right to privacy. The very wealthy, in contrast, often protect *their* privacy with extensive perimeters of property. Fifty years after formulating the right to privacy with his colleague Warren, Louis D. Brandeis was savvy enough to say, "We can have democracy in this country, or we can have great wealth in a few hands, but we can't have both."

When the National Committee for Sexual Civil Liberties met in Detroit in May, 1981 for its twelfth annual conference, the opening discussion concerned the police harassment of gay individuals and the raids on gay bathhouses in Canada. As Paul Hardman wrote in his conference report for *Gay Books Bulletin* (Fall 1981), "What has to be understood is the fact that the law is quite different in Canada, despite our common Anglo-Saxon heritage, so that Canadians do not have Constitutional rights in the sense that we do in the United States." Canada's federal and provincial governments, with the significant exception of Québec, have recently adopted a constitution; like the U.S. Constitution, it has no provision which specifically defines and defends the right to privacy. But that right has a legal history in the U.S., as it does not in Canada. *The Body Politic* (TBP) reported last November that a provincial court judge had acquitted retired teacher Don Franco of being the keeper of a common bawdyhouse in his own home, and the defence lawyer in that case was quoted as saying, "This is the first criminal case to make the right to privacy a keystone of the judgment—it's important in American law but almost never encountered in Canada."

The Canadian gay movement is fighting on many fronts, and these battles are important not only for gays, but for all struggling sectors of Canadian society. *TBP* is waging a crucial fight for freedom of speech and of the press, as is well known. Don Franco's trial and acquittal is a groundbreaking legal event in Canada, particularly since Judge Charles stated explicitly that Section 183 of the Criminal Code, concerning "anyone found in a common bawdyhouse" "certainly makes breathtaking inroads into a person's right to privacy.... Parliament should take a look at it."

The Right to Privacy Committee is, of course, admirably embattled. All of these fights are well worth fighting, an I have great admiration for the gay Canadians in the front ranks of struggle. I hope raising questions about the right to privacy is not, therefore, taken as mean-spirited sniping. But the right to privacy is a double-edged sword. Privacy can be *enforced* as well as pursued. In a comradely spirit, I will give some examples of the unwise use of this weapon in the U.S. gay movement. From these examples it should be clear that

there is such a thing as *reckless reformism*, since we have all heard to the point of nausea about reckless radicalism.

When Charles Brydon resigned as co-director of The National Gay Task Force, he gave a speech to a group of gay professionals stressing that a key strategy in the coming years should be pursuit of the right to privacy. Brydon stressed that conservatives are great partisans of this right. Ronald Reagan, after all, opposed the anti-gay Briggs Amendment on the grounds that it constituted government intrusion into personal life. Likewise, arch-conservative Barry Goldwater blasted the Moral Majority for obscuring the separation of church and state—a strict theocracy is not ideal for business. The right is not immune to factionalism, yet all sectors of the right are free to interpret our right to privacy as being our right to the closet. Gay professionals and well-to-do gays are not necessarily averse to this interpretation if, as Charles McCabe suggested in the *San Francisco Chronicle*, they can make their closets as commodious as castles.

In a tune of reaction, more voices are being heard in the gay movement urging gays to get on the right side of power. But it is precisely with the ruling Republicans that the right to privacy strategy lands gays in trouble. Tim Drake, one of two openly gay delegates at the 1980 Republican convention, was featured in an article in the *Washington Blade*. Drake urged that conservatives who take a principled stand on privacy would be likely to repeal sodomy statutes and other discriminatory legislation. "However," the article notes, "gay Republicans admit that a Catch-22 situation arises when attempts are made to gain Republican support for gay rights legislation." Drake explained: "If you say we must make laws so that the government won't interfere in our private lives, many Republicans turn around and ask, 'Wouldn't this civil rights legislation put government control over a social issue? Isn't this more governmental intrusion?' I tend to avoid the issue altogether," Drake concluded.

Here is a classic example of the way in which folks who abandon the struggle for gay liberation are finally forced to compromise even the struggle for gay rights. We cannot be anarchist purists in this matter, disdaining the legal apparatus of the state entirely. Certainly we should have no delusions: legislation is not liberation; being legal is not being free. Yet gay liberation means waging an open fight for gay rights as one means of building a militant, grass-roots movement.

In the April 1, 1982 issue of the *Advocate*, Larry Bush writes, "There is a good case to be made for a link between gay interests and conservatives of conscience, as gay Republicans frequently tell their gay Democratic friends. . . . Some prominent anti-abortion leaders, notably Paul Brown of the Life Amendment Political Action Committee and Representative Henry Hyde have also dissociated themselves from anti-gay efforts. . . . "

The effort to deprive women of the choice of abortion is a *crime* against women. It was with good reason that Kurt Hiller included both abortion and homosexuality under the right over one's self. The conservatives of conscience Larry Bush mentions would be better known as opportunist reactionaries. A tactical and temporary retreat on the gay issue does not prevent them from advocating reactionary moralism. Gay males who pursue their own privacy at the expense of the autonomy of women will certainly lose allies. Gay male separatists may forge a fragile alliance with the gangsters in government, but this has nothing to do with gay liberation. This is merely the business-as-usual horse-trading of political hacks.

The political rationale for concentrating on the right to privacy was best explained by Jim Foster, who is a Democratic Party lieutenant. According to a recent profile in *Christopher Street* (issue 60), "Foster feels that the gay community needs a new rallying point and a new symbol. The new word is 'privacy,' and the symbol is that old favorite, the dollar sign." Civil rights, according to Foster, simply *bores* people: after all, wasn't all *that* taken care of by Martin Luther King? "Foster insists that the gay community's problems are neither economic survival (for most gay people), nor are they strictly a matter of civil rights. . . . Our issue, he claims, is the protection of our privacy. . . . Politicians, he believes, are ready to let us define our issues this way. . . . That's where the dollar sign comes in. 'The truth is that money buys you access to the political process,' explains this gay community's mercenary Machiavellian." An *endearing* epithet, no doubt.

It is due to gay leaders like Foster that gays are often perceived as being genetically programmed for affluence—and resented accordingly. In one sense, the gay movement is no different than most movements for social change in the U.S.—it is not really one movement but several, spread across the social and political spectrum. The gay movement Foster belongs to is satisfied with a political system which is more and more inacces-

sible the less and less money one makes; such a system deserves to be turned upside down. The members of Foster's movement can indeed afford to be bored with civil rights; they can indeed be satisfied with pursuing their right to privacy.

These are examples of political pitfalls which Canadian gays will certainly face, even if the right to privacy is carved in marble in every Canadian court. As things stand, the seemingly scholastic debates in Canadian courts about private and public space and behavior are, in fact, revelations of the sexual and social order. "Acts of gross indecency" are mentioned in the bawdyhouse laws, and leave much to the imagination; if they are defined to include homosexual acts as such, then *any* place where gays have sex—public or private, bathhouse or bedroom—becomes a bawdyhouse. When the first Barracks trial ended last June, Judge Rice chose not to accept this argument from the government prosecutor. Rather than judging indecency by the *kind* of acts performed, Judge Rice judged indecency by the *number of persons* participating in such acts. If the *act* is not indecent, why does the *number* of participants make it so? Does the act of eating *become* indecent when a dozen people sit down at one table? Is a murder made *less* indecent when there is no accomplice or witness?

Judge Rice found the Barracks indecent because it was not "private." It would be hard to find a judge who would come out and say that sexuality as such is indecent. This *is* the twentieth century. Yet the question arises: *How has the right to privacy become so easily translated into the duty of sexual secrecy?*

Even in the U.S., where the legal definition of privacy is more sophisticated, that particular and peculiar translation has been made by many local, state and Supreme Court decisions. In 1976, in a case involving homosexuals, the Supreme Court upheld a decision by a Virginia court that a state law punishing sodomy between consenting adults was not an unconstitutional invasion of privacy. That seems a simple case. A few months later the Supreme Court refused to consider a Fourth Circuit Court of Appeals decision that allowed Virginia to punish a married couple for committing sodomy, which in *this* case meant that the wife sucked off her husband and a male friend within the couple's home. Someone took photographs, which their daughters found and displayed at school and which were finally secured by the authorities. "Once a married couple admits strangers as onlookers, federal protection dissolves," decided the Fourth Circuit. "If the couple performs sexual acts for the excitation or gratification of welcome onlookers, they cannot selectively claim the state is an intruder."

We may expect every kink of barbarism from the state when such legalism passes for logic. Presumably the state has the right to crash any party you throw in your home or out, as long as the activities at that party—whether eating spaghetti, watching TV or reading poetry—produce an *erotic* intensity of excitation or gratification in welcome onlookers and participants.

Three members of that court dissented from that decision. Robert Ellis Smith writes, "What would not normally be punishable (sexual adventures by a married couple in private) cannot be punishable because of the presence of a third person, they said. The dissenters further recognized that sexual activity between married persons 'can never be made criminal'—even if done in public—unless it violates some other criminal offence such as lewdness, indecent exposure, or disorderly conduct."

When, we might ask, does public sex *not* violate some such criminal statute? Notice the legal nicety with which the dissenters deal with the sexual adventures of married heterosexuals; would they have taken such care with the Virginia homosexuals convicted of the same crime?

"We conclude that secrecy is not a necessary element of the right (to privacy)," said the dissenters. According to Smith, "One of the dissenters was J. Braxton Craven, Jr., a respected Harvard-educated jurist who thought that the right to privacy is not limited to what goes on in private, contrary to popular impression." The right to privacy, Craven stated, "may be termed more accurately 'the right to be let alone' or personal autonomy, or simply 'personhood.' "

A standard statement made by both gay rights advocates and anti-gay bigots is that *sexuality is a private matter*. Each side means something different: *Let us live our lives in peace*, and *Get back into the closet*. Sexual privacy is enforced in our society for the same reason that sexual privacy is invaded, precisely because, in Robert Ellis Smith's words, "*Sex is the least private of acts.*" We might say that exposing one's "private parts" to even one person is a more public act that walking in a crowd all clothed. This very stripping away of civilized garb and sexual restraint must therefore be shrouded in secrecy. Secrecy, as we have seen, was Judge Rice's definition of privacy and decency in the first Barracks trial; secrecy again

was a prime condition of privacy and decency when the U.S. Fourth Circuit Court of Appeals allowed Virginia to convict a couple of sodomy.

The pyramid of the state begins to crumble when too many slaves become too undisciplined at one time in one place. "Political repression begins with sexual repression," says historian Herman Rebel. "Sexual activity defies the state, because it is the ultimate act of anarchy. Sex is what two persons decide to do." Two persons, or three, or four, five, six. . . . It is true that the more people involved in sex or any other "private" activity, the further the boundaries of privacy must be extended. If two people make love all alone in a wilderness, we might say they had privacy. If six or a dozen people make love in one room, then we might say that privacy should include the right to choose one's own public—a right which should apply in both bedrooms and bathhouses. Or whorehouses, for that matter. The further we extend the concept of privacy, the more public and worldly it must become: here again the heart of the matter is "the right to be let alone, or personal autonomy, or simple 'personhood.' "

"The right to be let alone" takes us full circle back to the classic formulation of Warren and Brandeis in 1891. This is bourgeois jurisprudence at its most magnanimous. But in 1982 it is high time to state a plain fact and act on it: there is no true autonomy which is purely personal. Autonomy exists *between* people and *within* a world which surrounds the individual. The right to be lt alone is a poor right if we are denied the right to associate: the right to form *community*.

## POPULISM AND SOCIALISM

Pharaoh is gone, but his work remains; the master has ceased to be master, but the slaves have not ceased to be slaves. A people trained for generations in the house of bondage cannot cast off in an instant the effects of that training and become truly free, even when the chains have been struck off.

—AHAD HA-'AM, *MOSES*

When, during the November 1919 revolution, the masses were demonstrating in the Tiergarten in Berlin, most of the demonstrators took great care not to walk on the grass. This story, whether it is true or merely well-invented, sums up an important aspect of the tragedy of the revolutionary movement: the bourgeoisification of those who are to make the revolution.

—WILHELM REICH, *WHAT IS CLASS-CONSCIOUSESS?* 1934

Obviously gays today are exercising much more than their right to be let alone; they are exercising their right to create communities and their right to publicity. Because gay social life and sexuality is often so playful and so visible on the streets of urban gay ghettoes—in the very way gays dress and caress—this has drawn erotophobic damnation from conservatives, liberals, leftists and feminists alike. Richard Goldstein once wrote a superb article for the *Village Voice* (Oct. 1, 1979) called, "I left my scalp in San Francisco: The Politics of Sexuality in an American Town." Concerning Mayor Feinstein, who had authorized raids on backroom bars, Goldstein wrote, "She will encourage a new gay leadership composed of people who have stable, successful lives and want others to have the same. She will encourage homosexuals to abandon their communalism and draw upon the same restraint that animates all middle-class life."

The Right to Privacy Committee's former chairperson, George Smith, has argued in the pages of *TBP* that the right to privacy may not be very radical, but it is a working basis of unity for a coalition which fights for "our community's right to exist." I have the sincerest admiration for the work he and other RTPC members are engaged in and for the spirit they have shown. But it is precisely on those grounds—our community's right to exist—that we must question a concept and strategy which obscures as much as it clarifies. The raids on Canada's gay baths were not only an invasion of privacy, they were also an invasion of the semi-commercial, semi-communal life of the gay ghetto. It is primarily our *public* existence, and not our right to privacy, which is under assault by the right. That is why, for example, former State Senator Briggs of California tried to deny gay schoolteachers their right to teach. His main concern was to destroy the virus of gay liberation before children could catch the disease: gay liberation cannot *be* gay unless it is contagious, as contagious as freedom itself.

The original basis of unity for the gay liberation movement was, in essence, quite simple. It

remains quite revolutionary. *Gay people have a right to freedom; gay people have a right to the world.* When that world and that freedom have been won, then our right to privacy will finally be secure. The danger which concerned Warren and Brandeis in 1890 was that "what is whispered in the closet shall be proclaimed from the housetops." In 1982 we must certainly be on our guard against illegitimate surveillance of and intrusion into our personal and political lives. It helps to be a little paranoid when there is strange static on your phone and when your mail is tampered with. But the paramount concern for the gay liberation movement should remain our right to proclaim gay liberation from the housetops, and not the security of our closets. As our society stands, a lesbian president of General Motors or of the U.S. would certainly be an extraordinarily successful deviant. Every sophisticated ruling class has made room at the top for some of the very people it oppresses. Gay liberation, however, means much more than integration—or accommodation—into a society which is based on domination.

I remember a demonstration in Philadelphia which was organized by a city councilman, a closeted gay businessman and a bunch of rabbis, priests and ministers. A rally was held at a corner where gays and prostitutes often cross paths, and speeches were made calling for the cops and politicians to sweep the whores, dope dealers and muggers off the streets. There had been crime and violence in the neighborhood, and thus support was drummed up from gay business and gay neighbors, among others. Yet gays were used and abused by people who had no commitment to our freedom. We should have been the first to demand the decriminalization of prostitution, to demand the abolition of the Vice Squad, to question its relations with organized crime, to demand community-based patrols and to demand that hustlers and runaways be seen as persons, not simply as juvenile delinquents. Our economy will continue prostituting all of us until the nature of work itself changes in our society, whether we sell our brains and hands to a boss, or whether we sell our sex to a john. How many of us had our first taste of sexual, social and economic independence by hustling as young gay men? Many of us, if we look at the streets; many of us, if more of us were to tell the truth. Instead of showing gay solidarity with prostitutes and hustlers, we sold out to a pack of priests and politicians. We sold out to a Vice Squad which raided gay baths and bookstores. We built "unity" with our oppressors, and we built it on our own backs. It is this kind of populism which we must be wary of.

"Spirit," wrote the anarchist and socialist Gustav Landauer, "is something that dwells equally in the hearts and animated bodies of all individuals, which erupts out of them with a natural compulsion as a binding quality and leads them to associate together. The state is never established inside the individual. It has never become an individual quality, never been voluntary. It resides rather in the centralism of command and discipline instead of in the center that rules the world of the spirit: that is the heartbeat and free independent thinking of the living body of the person." Spirit, as Landauer uses the term, is what Wilhelm Reich would have called "the self-governing character structure," and what I have been calling "autonomy."

In a crucial sense, Landauer was mistaken when he claimed "the state is never established inside the individual." An efficient state resorts to force and violence only rarely; it relies instead on enslaving spirits, so that each person becomes a "willing" building block in the pyramid of the state. Paraphrasing Landauer, it makes more sense to say that autonomy and authoritarianism are at odds in each person. And when we examine a populist phenomenon like the Nazi movement or the Moral Majority—without making glib equations—then we must paraphrase Landauer again: slavishness, too, is something that dwells equally in the hearts and animated bodies of all individuals, which erupts out of them with a natural compulsion as a binding quality and leads them to associate together.

Populist movements in the U.S. have often been propelled by class struggle, but have blundered and broken apart when what passed for unity was, as in the case of many labor union drives, built by white men on the backs of women and blacks. A populist movement often pulls in two directions at once, revolutionary and reactionary, as in the case of the U.S. anti-nuclear movement. It is revolutionary when people rise up and demand that Reagan and Brezhnev cease their international terrorism; it is reactionary when certain anti-nuclear forces express a "back-to-Nature" philosophy which keeps women barefoot and pregnant and puts gays beyond the pale. Likewise, what passes for feminism in sectors of the women's movement is sexist and Victorian. In the socialist movement itself, a "pro-family" trend has emerged which is, in fact, anti-feminist and anti-gay; patriarchal populism has plagued the left throughout its history. The same contradictory populism operates in the U.S. gay movement, where some forces pursue gay rights in the narrowest sense, excluding gay liberation, and other forces pursue gay liberation in the fullest sense, including gay rights. Our right to privacy and our right to the world are both populist demands. But the right to privacy orients the gay movement in a conservative direction, not inconsistent with gay rights as such; whereas our right to the world is the soul of gay liberation and ultimately moves the gay movement beyond populism.

Gay liberation means creating a world in which heterosexist norms have been subverted. The social changes that involves would have revolutionary effects on every aspect of life, from child-rearing to the organization of the economy—to the very definition of sexuality itself.

Conservative and liberal figures in the gay movement do not hesitate to state their goals and tactics, but gay socialists often do. We hesitate because the very terms of public discourse must change: in the gay movement, in the left, and in society at large. This is not the place to elaborate detailed strategy. But it is urgent to put the matter of gay liberation and socialism squarely and clearly before ourselves and everyone, gay and straight, men and women, people of all races, nationalities, occupations and classes. "Unity!" gay liberals and anti-reds will cry. "Unity!" will cry the patriarchs of the left. But we, too, seek unity: We will have neither gay liberation nor socialism if we don't have both together. We must insist on a conception of unity which is not new, but which must always be fought for and renewed. Having had unity built on our backs so often—in Hitler's Germany, in Castro's Cuba, in Falwell's America—we now insist on a unity built with the greatest democracy from below. We may fall short of that ideal, but we will not even approach it if we settle for "practical politics," meaning business-as-usual.

When the Nazis were on the rise in the mid-thirties, Wilhelm Reich argued for a radical synthesis of the personal and the political. One of Reich's conclusions was quite foolish: "the more clearly developed are the natural heterosexual inclinations of a juvenile, the more open he will be to revolutionary ideas; the stronger the homosexual tendency within him and also the more repressed his awareness of sexuality in general, the more easily he will be drawn toward the right." It is more accurate to say that sexual repression in gays and straights serves both the authoritarian right and left. Gay people, like all oppressed groups, respond to oppression with various strategies: some seek to survive unobtrusively; others seek to serve the existing order; still others seek to understand and change the very structure of society. Among gay rebels and radicals, a few try turning Reich's homosexual-reactionary equation around by equating sodomy with subversion. But there is nothing inherently radical in simply being gay. We have good reason to become socialists, but building a lesbian and gay left—as well as a broader socialist movement—requires some difficult and conscious steps.

Early in the century, Rosa Luxemburg wrote, "Indeed, union makes strength—but union of firm, inner conviction, not an external mechanical coupling together of elements that oppose each other internally. Strength lies not in our numbers, but in our spirit, in the clarity and energy animating us."

This kind of spirit, clarity and energy is what animated the gay liberation movement to seek "to transform the society at large through the realization of our own consciousness." Strength, of course, lies not only in our spirit but also in our numbers. If a right-wing technocrat like Richard Viguerie can use these words of William James as a motto, then so can we: "A small force, if it never lets up, will accumulate effects more considerable than those of much greater forces if these work inconsistently."

# | 91 |

# *Chasing the Crossover Audience and Other Self-Defeating Strategies*

## MICHAEL DENNENY

The production of any writing necessarily takes place within a cultural and social context. This guarantees that the act of writing, the decision to publish and disseminate writing, and its evaluation by the critics and ultimate reception by the public (often divergent responses, at least initially) will be permeated and shaped, facilitated or distorted, by the specific social situation and the cultural politics of the moment.

It is unwise to ignore these issues of cultural politics, for their influence is utterly pervasive. It is the nature of such issues that they cannot be "solved" once and for all; rather they are like fault lines that articulate the underlying stresses of a given situation and trace the hidden geography of the cultural moment.

But, if they cannot be solved, they *can* be thought about; one can strive to reach not an answer but perhaps greater clarity about the issue, and in the process better locate oneself in the contemporary world.

The issue I would like to begin discussing is that current obsession of gay writers—and, to a lesser extent, gay editors—the fabled crossover book.[*] Having been an editor of *Christopher*

*Out/Look*, Winter 1989, pp. 16–21.

[*] In this discussion, I am referring only to gay male writers. Because of the historical connection of gay women to the (non-gay) women's movement, the crossover situation for lesbian writers is completely different, and perhaps more promising. My own impression is that gay women writers—like the remarkable surge of black women writers—can more easily find an audience for their work among non-gay women influenced by the feminist movement (though, of course, I could be mistaken). There is nothing analogous to this in the situation of gay men.

*Street Magazine*, working today as a book editor involved in the publication of gay writing, and as a gay writer myself, I have had the opportunity of watching a virtual parade of gay writers through the last decade and have followed with interest the changing fortunes of gay writing in the marketplace, as well as the changing attitudes and intentions of the writers themselves. With the recent breakthrough to national visibility in the mainstream media (both *Newsweek* and the *New York Times* have within the last year published several articles about gay writing "reaching the mainstream") and the critical and commercial success of a (small) number of gay books over the last few years, has come a new and startling ambition by many gay writers to achieve success with a wider audience.

Increasingly I hear about "the crossover audience" and "the crossover book," the book that will appeal to gay *and* straight audiences alike. Indeed, many of the younger writers resist being categorized as "merely" gay writers, that territory being a "literary ghetto" which they feel unfairly limits both their audience and their income. Considering that only a few years ago it was a struggle just to get a gay book published or to sell enough copies to break even, this is a notable development, undoubtedly a sign of the enormous and underappreciated distance we have come in a very short time. Still it raises some new and troublesome issues that can be seen more clearly in the context of our recent history.

In the beginning, that is in the mid-seventies, when gay authors as we know them began to be published, there was not much, if any, talk about crossover books or crossover audience. When Edmund White, Andrew Holleran, Larry Kramer, Felice Picano and others decided to write and publish gay fiction they were taking what was at the time a huge risk that their literary careers would be distorted or derailed, marginalized or altogether aborted by that decision. These people were not under the illusion that the straight world was eager to read about our lives. At the time it was quite clear that the straight world would rather not know we even existed, and when they were forced into that awareness their general response was hostility. And this was only to be expected. After all, the mechanism by which this society implemented the oppression of gay people was to extend a blanket of invisibility over most gay life while simultaneously promoting lurid images of marginal figures—the doomed drag queen, the sick child molester, the pathetic

sissy. This cultural manifestation of the dominant social and political power was buttressed by laws that made sodomy illegal, harassment by organs of the government (such as the Post Office and the House Un-American Activities Committee), and the occasional prosecution and jailing of deviants.

However, since it is clear that all these police measures and punishments did *not* in fact stop homosexual activity but only inhibited the assertion of a public gay identity, I think it's equally clear that the major and most effective weapon used against us by this society was the cultural war of enforced silence mixed with false images and derogatory definitions. Since this war was carried out by the cultural—and especially the literary—organs of society, it was unlikely that those same organs would suddenly welcome a new literature that attempted to free gay people from the false consciousness fostered by the dominant society, a consciousness consisting of society's hatred of homosexuals internalized into self-hatred. Gays were oppressed by society, but more important, society through use of its cultural power *got gays to oppress themselves*—not only a neat trick but perhaps the most efficient means of oppression.

What motivated White, Holleran, and the others was not a naive hope for a straight readership nor the expectation that the literary establishment would or could give them a fair hearing. What impelled them to jump into the arena of gay writing was the enormous energy that had been released by the Stonewall riots and that, to our amazement, seemed only to gain momentum in the years that followed. Stonewall was the critical point, the unpremeditated and still somewhat inexplicable event that unleashed a vast reconstitution of gay society: gay bars, baths, bookstores, and restaurants opened, gay softball teams, newspapers, political organizations, and choruses proliferated. Gay groups of all sorts popped up while gay neighborhoods emerged in our larger, and many of our smaller cities. This was and is a vast social revolution that to my mind has received nowhere near the attention it deserves: a new community came into being in an astonishingly short period of time. The excitement of those days captured the imagination of the writers, while the emergence of the gay community provided the beginning of a public as interested in reading about gay life as the writers were in writing about it.

▼ ▼ ▼

Time passed, struggles were won, and gradually, grudgingly, the literary establishment ceded some marginal room to gay books. More important *by far*, a new generation of gay writers emerged in the mid-eighties whose talent, diversity, and sheer numbers exceeded our wildest hopes—we are now in the midst of a burst of gay writing such as has never been seen before. And, of course, the social and political situation has changed. The mayor of New York now walks in the Gay Pride parade, the Gay Men's Chorus performs at Carnegie Hall, Harvey Fierstein charms everybody's mother on television talk shows, and AIDS has made us relentlessly visible to mid-America. As the situation of gay people in this country has changed, so the situation of the gay writer has changed, and almost entirely for the better.

The "second generation" of younger gay writers appearing as the eighties got under way did not share with their predecessors the initial experience of confronting a homophobic literary culture head on, when it was a victory simply to get a gay novel published or reviewed (no matter how condescendingly) in the mainstream national media. This work had been done, the situation was improved. The issue now was the age-old plaint of any writer: how to make a decent living.

And here arose a problem. A gay book is defined in the publishing industry as a book directed toward a gay readership—the gay public. And while this gay public *is* expanding (a decade ago there were some nine gay bookstores in this country; there are today thirty-two), this market is still limited. For the gay writer trying to earn a decent income, there were two possibilities: the continued growth of the gay public which would provide more readers, or the chance to sell their books to the more numerous straight audience.

So it is not surprising that more and more one hears of gay writers who bridle at being labelled gay writers, who wish their book to be marketed to the so-called general public, whose ambition is to see their books in chain stores rather than their local gay bookstore.

What could possibly be wrong with this, you might wonder—every writer, after all, wants to make as much money from his or her book as possible. This is only reasonable. They do not want to be labelled gay writers or have their books categorized as gay fiction because of commercial considerations. Like all writers, they want to reach a larger public and sell more books. Which

seems fair enough at first glance, but this position has some implications worth noticing. The premise is that a book will be more successful, a writer will make more money, if the work is not identified as gay. Now, why is this? Because, evidently, the so-called general public and the literary establishment prefer not to buy books by explicitly gay authors, books "only" about gay life, books that, in some sense, *are* gay. And, by and large, I think this is probably true. They don't. It has been true for a good long time now, in fact; there is nothing new in this analysis of the situation. What is new—and to me discouraging—is the idea that instead of facing this fact head on, and *changing* it, some members of this second generation believe the best strategy is to avoid the outright identification, the specific and glaring label: "gay."

Now I ask you: what is this except a literary version of the old strategy of "passing," or not calling undue attention to the fact that one is gay. Because to call undue attention to the fact that one is gay is to open oneself to homophobic attack, to insist that one's book is a gay novel is to risk . . . having the public label it a gay novel. And gay novels they don't rush to read. Once again the old blanket of silence.

The basic flaw with this strategy is that it would leave the homophobic response intact. It would not change the basic situation. But the basic situation is what must be changed if there is to be anything like a gay literature or a gay culture. These writers believe they can sidestep the issue, that they can ask that their books be judged from an exclusively literary point of view, as if the literary establishment had not in fact been a constituent and active part of the homophobic culture of this society.

To me this seems shortsighted and self-destructive, for homophobia still courses through the structures of this literary establishment, as it does through the culture at large. To believe that the homophobia which reached demented proportions in this country in the fifties and sixties could be eradicated in the last twenty years is simply silly. Like racism, homophobia has been endemic in the West for many centuries and like black people we must face the fact that it will not disappear soon—face the fact, live with the fact, and produce our work and structure our ways of life in the teeth of that fact.

Black authors do not get joy from the fact that they have to do their writing in what remains, both subtly and blatantly, a racist society. But they do it, and often with more grace than anybody has the right to expect. A couple of weeks ago, I watched an almost classic liberal, Bill Moyers, on his television show ask August Wilson, "Don't you ever get tired of writing about the black experience?" A question of such breathtaking stupidity that even Wilson paused. Would Moyers ask John Updike whether he ever gets tired of writing about the white experience? Would he ask Dostoevsky if he ever gets tired of writing about the Russian experience? Would he ask Sophocles whether he ever gets tired of writing about the Greek experience?

Just think for a moment about what is really being said here. The implication is that "the black experience" is somehow limited, is something one could get tired of, is not inexhaustible the way life is. After all, one can't quite imagine even Moyers asking, "Don't you ever get tired of writing about the human experience?" I mean, what else is there to write about? And unfortunately the reason one cannot imagine Moyers asking Updike, "Don't you ever get tired of writing about the white experience?" is that he probably equates "the white experience" with life itself. And this is the crux of the matter, in this case the crux of cultural racism. The idea that somebody's life is of less extent, of smaller consequence, carries less weight is at the heart of racism, or in our case, of homophobia.

Black writers have much practice dealing with this type of idiocy. Listen, for instance, to Toni Morrison in an article last year in the *New York Times*:

> Ms. Morrison said that unlike some authors who despise being labeled, she does not mind being called a black writer, or a black woman writer. "I've decided to define that, rather than having it be defined for me," she said. "In the beginning, people would say, 'Do you regard yourself as a black writer, or a black woman writer?' So at first I was glib, and said I'm a black woman writer, because I understood that they were trying to suggest that I was 'bigger' than that, or 'better' than that. I simply refused to accept their view of bigger and better. I really think the range of emotions and perceptions I have had access to as a black person and as a female person are greater than those of people who are neither. I really do. So it seems to me that my world did not shrink because I was a black female writer. It just got bigger."

Ethan Mordden makes the same point in the introduction to *Buddies*.

> Despite straights' lack of comprehension and outright intolerance, gays inevitably comprehend straights, because, whatever our sexuality, we all grow up within the straight culture as participants.... Gays understand straights; but straights don't understand gays any more than whites understand blacks or Christians understand Jews, however good their intentions.

There is much confusion about this topic of minority writers, or regional writers. This confusion stems from the insistence of those straight middle-class white men who control the organs of cultural definition in this society that the only valid, universal image of the contemporary human condition is ... the straight middle-class white man. This is pure cultural politics—the use of culture to reinforce the politically dominant position of one group within the society.

But as well as being a power struggle, this attitude has a much deeper, more insidious effect, one that would be especially deplorable if it confused the writers themselves. To demote our literature to a peripheral status, to try to make our writers "merely" gay writers is not only a classic power play, it also entails a basic and total misunderstanding of the nature of writing. As Jean Strouse pointed out recently (in the *New York Times Book Review*):

> Louise Erdrich's novels, regional in the best sense, are 'about' the experience of Native Americans the way Toni Morrison's are about black people, William Faulkner's and Eudora Welty's about the South, Philip Roth's and Bernard Malamud's about Jews: *the specificity implies nothing provincial or small* [emphasis added].

(One might note parenthetically that we don't see the words: "Edmund White's and Andrew Holleran's are about gay people" in this otherwise lucid and sane declaration.)

Specific does not mean provincial. My god, think of what Jane Austen was able to do within the narrow confines of courtship rituals in early nineteenth century England. Or, to take an example from our own day, consider how the most successful musical in all of Broadway history is described by Charlie Willard, a dance captain for that show:

white line on the stage. Dealing with the very specific milieu and ambience of chorus dancers, it somehow spoke to everyone, and from the very beginning, it cut across the gypsy story. Because of that, it's often forgotten that it was intended to be a show that celebrated a subculture.

Specific and concrete reality is indeed the origin of all great works of literature. And if Dostoevsky is not diminished because he wrote "only" about the Russians, or Synge the Irish, or Sophocles the Greeks, then gay writers are in no way diminished because they write about life as it presents itself to and is experienced by gay people. The idea that this is somehow a failing, a limitation, is simply absurd and would never have gotten into circulation if it were not a disguise for a political agenda.

Those gay authors who are so anxious to cultivate the crossover audience should realize that the task before us is rather to help bring into existence and further develop a new audience, the gay audience. And the reasoning behind this assertion is very simple. Given the fact that at the moment we live in what continues to be a homophobic society, the idea that gay writers could achieve success with the general public implies either that the general public cease being so homophobic or that the gay writer cease being . . . so gay. The first—that the general public become less homophobic—is unlikely unless we *do* something about it; for instance, publish and buy gay books, do our bit to strengthen and enrich the gay community, while making our lives and our art a more public and therefore more accepted fact. The second—that gay writers

become less gay—unfortunately is always a possibility; when I was in college it was classically known as selling out, a cliché admittedly, but a cliché that might fit the situation of someone who doesn't want to be known as a gay writer because he will sell more books, or gain a greater literary reputation that way.

▼ ▼ ▼

The task before us is to create a gay literature and a gay culture in the midst of a situation that is hostile to that literature and that culture, and to bend every effort to face up to and eradicate homophobia in this society. The way to do this is to encourage the further emergence of a literate gay public which supports and involves itself with the quite remarkable gay writing that is now being created. Once there is a sizable and substantial gay reading public, the books they buy and read and value will attract the interest and the curiosity of the so-called "general public." The way to the general audience is through the specific audience, the way to the general public is through the gay public.

The present generation of gay writers, both those who emerged in the seventies and those who appeared in the eighties, were called into existence by a remarkable social revolution, this unexpected and mighty upsurge of collective energy that started with Stonewall, *whether they know it or not*. Of course, it's better to know it. Not to know it, to ignore or forget it, means not to know where one is, means to cut yourself off from the historical roots, the cultural energy that sustains the creative act and sets it within a social and political context, that gives it not only meaning but value.

# | 92 |

## Queers Read This: I Hate Straights

How can I tell you. How can I convince you, brother, sister that your life is in danger: That everyday you wake up alive, relatively happy, and a functioning human being, you are committing a rebellious act. You as an alive and functioning queer are a revolutionary.

There is nothing on this planet that validates, protects or encourages your existence. It is a miracle you are standing here reading these words. You should by all rights be dead. Don't be fooled, straight people own the world and the only reason you have been spared is you're smart, lucky or a fighter.

Straight people have a privilege that allows them to do whatever they please and fuck without fear. But not only do they live a life free of fear; they flaunt their freedom in my face. Their images are on my TV, in the magazine I bought, in the restaurant I want to eat in, and on the street where I live. I want there to be a moratorium on straight marriage, on babies, on public displays of affection among the opposite sex and media images that promote heterosexuality. Until I can enjoy the same freedom of movement and sexuality, as straights, their privilege must stop and it must be given over to me and my queer sisters and brothers. Straight people will not do this voluntarily and so they must be forced into it. Straights must be frightened into it. Terrorized into it. Fear is the most powerful motivation. No one will give us what we deserve. Rights are not given they are taken, by force if necessary. It is easier to fight when you know who your enemy is. Straight people are your enemy. They are your enemy when they don't acknowledge your invisibility and continue to live in and contribute to a culture that kills you. Every day one of us is taken by the enemy. Whether it's an AIDS death due to homophobic government inaction or a lesbian bashing in an all-night diner (in a supposedly lesbian neighborhood).

### AN ARMY OF LOVERS CANNOT LOSE

Being queer is not about a right to privacy; it is about the freedom to be public, to just be who we are. It means everyday fighting oppression; homophobia, racism, misogyny, the bigotry of religious hypocrites and our own self-hatred. (We have been carefully taught to hate ourselves.) And now of course it means fighting a virus as well, and all those homo-haters who are using AIDS to wipe us off the face of the earth. Being queer means leading a different sort of life. It's not about the mainstream, profit-margins, patriotism, patriarchy or being assimilated. It's not about executive directors, privilege and elitism. It's about being on the margins, defining ourselves; it's about gender-fuck and secrets, what's beneath the belt and deep inside the heart; it's about the night. Being queer is "grass roots" because we know that everyone of us, everybody, every cunt, every heart and ass and dick is a world of pleasure waiting to be explored. Everyone of us is a world of infinite possibility. We are an army because we have to be. We are an army because we are so powerful. (We have so much to fight for; we are the most precious of endangered species.) And we are an army of lovers because it is we who know what love is. Desire and lust, too. We invented them. We come out of the closet, face the rejection of soci-

Leaflet distributed at annual gay pride parade, June 1990, New York City, pp. 1–2.

ety, face firing squads, just to love each other! Every time we fuck, we win. We must fight for ourselves (no one else is going to do it) and if in that process we bring greater freedom to the world at large then great. (We've given so much to that world: democracy, all the arts, the concepts of love, philosophy and the soul, to name just a few gifts from our ancient Greek Dykes, Fags.) Let's make every space a Lesbian and Gay space. Every street a part of our sexual geography. A city of yearning and then total satisfaction. A city and a country where we can be safe and free and more. We must look at our lives and see what's best in them, see what is queer and what is straight and let that straight chaff fall away! Remember there is so, so little time. And I want to be a lover of each and every one of you. Next year, we march naked.

## ANGER

"The strong sisters told the brothers that there were two important things to remember about the coming revolutions, the first is that we will get our asses kicked. The second, is that we will win."

I'm angry. I'm angry for being condemned to death by strangers saying, "You deserve to die" and "AIDS is the cure." Fury erupts when a Republican woman wearing thousands of dollars of garments and jewelry minces by the police lines shaking her head, chuckling and wagging her finger at us like we are recalcitrant children making absurd demands and throwing temper tantrum when they aren't met. Angry while Joseph agonizes over $8,000 a year for AZT which might keep him alive a little longer and which makes him sicker than the disease he is diagnosed with. Angry as I listen to a man tell me that after changing his will five times he's running out of people to leave things to. All of his best friends are dead. Angry when I stand in a sea of quilt panels, or go to a candlelight march or attend yet another memorial service. I will not march silently with a fucking candle and I want to take that goddamned quilt and wrap myself in it and furiously rend it and my hair and curse every god religion ever created. I refuse to accept a creation that cuts people down in the third decade of their life.

It is cruel and vile and meaningless and everything I have in me rails against the absurdity and I raise my face to the clouds and a ragged laugh that sounds more demonic than joyous erupts from my throat and tears stream down my face

and if this disease doesn't kill me, I may just die of frustration. My feet pound the streets and Peter's hands are chained to a pharmaceutical company's reception desk while the receptionist looks on in horror and Eric's body lies rotting in a Brooklyn cemetery and I'll never hear his flute resounding off the walls of the meeting house again. And I see the old people in Tompkins Square Park huddled in their long wool coats in June to keep out the cold they perceive is there and to cling to whatever little life has left to offer them. I'm reminded of the people who strip and stand before a mirror each night before they go to bed and search their bodies for any mark that might not have been there yesterday. A mark that this scourge has visited them.

And I'm angry when the newspapers call us "victims" and sound alarms that "it" might soon spread to the "general population." And I want to scream "Who the fuck am I?" And I want to scream at New York Hospital with its yellow plastic bags marked "isolation linen," "ropa infecciosa" and its orderlies in latex gloves and surgical masks skirting the bed as if its occupant will suddenly leap out and douse them with blood and semen giving them too the plague.

And I'm angry at straight people who sit smugly wrapped in their self-protective coat of monogamy and heterosexuality confident that this disease has nothing to do with them because "it" only happens to "them." And the teenage boys who upon spotting my Silence = Death button begin chanting "Faggot's gonna die" and I wonder, who taught them this? Enveloped in fury and fear, I remain silent while my button mocks me every step of the way. And the anger I felt when a television program on the quilt gives profiles of the dead and the list begins with a baby, a teenage girl who got a blood transfusion, an elderly Baptist minister and his wife and when they finally show a gay man, he's described as someone who knowingly infected teenage male prostitutes with the virus. What else can you expect from a faggot?

I'm angry.

## QUEER ARTISTS

Since time began, the world has been inspired by the work of queer artists. In exchange, there has been suffering, there has been pain, there has been violence. Throughout history, society has struck a bargain with its queer citizens: they may pursue creative careers, if they do it discreetly.

Through the arts queers are productive, lucrative, entertaining and even uplifting. These are the clear-cut and useful by-products of what is otherwise considered antisocial behavior. In cultured circles, queers may quietly coexist with an otherwise disapproving power elite.

At the forefront of the most recent campaign to bash queer artists is Jesse Helms, arbiter of all that is decent, moral, christian and amerikan. For Helms, queer art is quite simply a threat to the world. In his imaginings, heterosexual culture is too fragile to bear up to the admission of human or sexual diversity. Quite simply, the structure of power in the Judeo-Christian world has made procreation its cornerstone. Families having children assures consumers for the nation's products and a work force to produce them, as well as a built-in family system to care for its ill, reducing the expense of public healthcare systems.

ALL NON-PROCREATIVE BEHAVIOR IS CONSIDERED A THREAT, from homosexuality to birth control to abortion as an option. It is not enough, according to the religious right, to consistently advertise procreation and heterosexuality . . . it is also necessary to destroy any alternatives. It is not art Helms is after . . . . IT IS OUR LIVES! Art is the last safe place for lesbians and gay men to thrive. Helms knows this, and has developed a program to purge queers from the one arena they have been permitted to contribute to our shared culture.

Helms is advocating a world free from diversity or dissent. It is easy to imagine why that might feel more comfortable to those in charge of such a world. It is also easy to envision an amerikan landscape flattened by such power. Helms should just ask for what he is hinting at: State sponsored art, art of totalitarianism, art that speaks only in christian terms, art which supports the goals of those in power, art that matches the sofas in the Oval Office. Ask for what you want, Jesse, so that men and women of conscience can mobilize against it, as we do against the human rights violations of other countries, and fight to free our own country's dissidents.

## IF YOU'RE QUEER,

Queers are under siege.

Queers are being attacked on all fronts and I'm afraid it's OK with us.

In 1989, there were 50 "Queer Bashings" in the month of May alone. Violent attacks, 3,720 men, women and children died of AIDS in the same month, caused by a more violent attack—government inaction, rooted in society's growing homophobia. This is institutionalized violence, perhaps more dangerous to the existence of queers because the attackers are faceless. We allow these attacks by our own continued lack of action against them. AIDS has affected the straight world and now they're blaming us for AIDS and using it as a way to justify their violence against us. They don't want us anymore. They will beat us, rape us and kill us before they will continue to live with us. What will it take for this not to be OK? Feel some rage. If rage doesn't empower you, try fear. If that doesn't work, try panic.

## SHOUT IT!

Be proud. Do whatever you need to do to tear yourself away from your customary state of acceptance. Be free. Shout.

In 1969, Queers fought back. In 1990, Queers say OK. Next year, will we be here?

## I HATE . . .

I hate Jesse Helms. I hate Jesse Helms so much I'd rejoice if he dropped down dead. If someone killed him I'd consider it his own fault.

I hate Ronald Reagan, too, because he massmurdered my people for eight years. But to be honest, I hate him even more for eulogizing Ryan White without first admitting his guilt, without begging forgiveness for Ryan's death and for the deaths of tens of thousands of other PWA's—most of them queer. I hate him for making a mockery of our grief.

I hate the fucking Pope, and I hate John fucking Cardinal fucking O'Connor, and I hate the whole fucking Catholic Church. The same goes for the Military, and especially for Amerika's Law Enforcement Officials—the cops—state sanctioned sadists who brutalize street transvestites, prostitutes and queer prisoners. I also hate the medical and mental health establishments, particularly the psychiatrist who convinced me not to have sex with men for three years until we (meaning he) could make me bisexual rather than queer. I also hate the education profession, for its share in driving thousands of queer teens to suicide every year. I hate the "respectable" art world; and the entertainment industry, and the mainstream media, especially The New York Times. In fact, I hate every sector of the straight establishment in this country—the worst of whom actively want all queers dead, the best of whom never stick their necks out to keep us alive.

I hate straight people who think they have anything intelligent to say about "outing." I hate straight people who think stories about themselves are "universal" but stories about us are only about homosexuality. I hate straight recording artists who make their careers off of queer people, then attack us, then act hurt when we get angry and then deny having wronged us rather than apologize for it. I hate straight people who say, "I don't see why you feel the need to wear those buttons and T-shirts. I don't go around telling the whole world I'm straight."

I hate that in twelve years of public education I was never taught about queer people. I hate that I grew up thinking I was the only queer in the world, and I hate even more that most queer kids still grow up the same way. I hate that I was tormented by other kids for being a faggot, but more that I was taught to feel ashamed for being the object of their cruelty, taught to feel it was my fault. I hate that the Supreme Court of this country says it's okay to criminalize me because of how I make love. I hate that so many straight people are so concerned about my goddamned sex life. I hate that so many twisted straight people become parents, while I have to fight like hell to be allowed to be a father. I hate straights.

WHERE ARE YOU SISTERS?

I wear my pink triangle everywhere. I do not lower my voice in public when talking about lesbian love or sex. I always tell people I'm a lesbian. I don't wait to be asked about my "boyfriend." I don't say it's "no one's business."

I don't do this for straight people. Most of them don't know what the pink triangle even means. Most of them couldn't care less that my girlfriend and I are totally in love or having a fight on the street. Most of them don't notice us no matter what we do. I do what I do to reach other lesbians. I do what I do because I don't want lesbians to assume I'm a straight girl. I am out all the time, everywhere, because I WANT TO REACH YOU. Maybe you'll notice me, maybe we'll start talking, maybe we'll exchange numbers, maybe we'll become friends. Maybe we won't say a word but our eyes will meet and I will imagine you naked, sweating, openmouthed, your back arched as I am fucking you. And we'll be happy to know we aren't the only ones in the world. We'll be happy because we found each other, without saying a word, maybe just for a moment. But no.

You won't wear a pink triangle on that linen lapel. You won't meet my eyes if I flirt with you on the street. You avoid me on the job because I'm "too" out. You chastise me in bars because I'm "too political." You ignore me in public because I bring "too much" attention to "my" lesbianism. But then you want me to be your lover, you want me to be your friend, you want me to love you, support, you, fight for "OUR" right to exist.

## WHERE ARE YOU?

You talk, talk, talk about invisibility and then retreat to your homes to nest with your lovers or carouse in a bar with pals and stumble home in a cab or sit silently and politely by while your family, your boss, your neighbors, your public servants distort and disfigure us, deride us and punish us. Then home again and you feel like screaming. Then you pad your anger with a relationship or a career or a party with other dykes like you and still you wonder why we can't find each other, why you feel lonely, angry, alienated.

## GET UP, WAKE UP SISTERS!!

Your life is in your hands.

When I risk it all to be out, I risk it for both of us. When I risk it all and it works (which it often does if you would try it), I benefit and so do you. When it doesn't work, I suffer and you do not.

But girl you can't wait for other dykes to make the world safe for you. STOP waiting for a better more lesbian future! The revolution could be here if we started it.

Where are you sisters? I'm trying to find you, I'm trying to find you. How come I only see you on Gay Pride Day?

We're OUT, Where the fuck are YOU?

## WHEN ANYONE ASSAULTS YOU FOR BEING QUEER, IT IS QUEER BASHING. RIGHT?

A crowd of 50 people exit a gay bar as it closes. Across the street, some straight boys are shouting "Faggots" and throwing beer bottles at the gathering, which outnumbers them by 10 to 1. Three queers make a move to respond, getting no support from the group. Why did a group this size allow themselves to be sitting ducks?

Tompkins Square Park, Labor Day. At an annual outdoor concert/drag show, a group of gay men were harassed by teens carrying sticks. In the midst of thousands of gay men and lesbians, these straight boys beat two gay men to the ground, then stood around triumphantly laughing amongst themselves. The emcee was alerted and warned the crowd from the stage, "You girls be careful. When you dress up it drives the boys crazy," as if it were a practical joke inspired by what the victims were wearing rather than a pointed attack on anyone and everyone at that event.

What would it have taken for that crowd to stand up to its attackers?

After James Zappalorti, an openly gay man, was murdered in cold blood on Staten Island this winter, a single demonstration was held in protest. Only one hundred people came. When Yuseuf Hawkins, a black youth, was shot to death for being on "white turf" in Bensonhurst, African Americans marched through that neighborhood in large numbers again and again. A black person was killed BECAUSE HE WAS BLACK, and people of color throughout the city recognized it and acted on it. The bullet that hit Hawkins was meant for a black man, ANY black man. Do most gays and lesbians think that the knife that punctured Zappalorti's heart was meant only for him?

The straight world has us so convinced that we are helpless and deserving victims of the violence against us, that queers are immobilized when faced with a threat. BE OUTRAGED! These attacks must not be tolerated. DO SOMETHING. Recognize that any act of aggression against any member of our community is an attack on every member of the community. The more we allow homophobes to inflict violence, terror and fear on our lives, the more frequently and ferociously we will be the object of their hatred. Your body cannot be an open target for violence. Your body is worth protecting. You have a right to defend it. No matter what they tell you, your queerness must be defended and respected. You'd better learn that your life is immeasurably valuable, because unless you start believing that, it can easily be taken from you. If you know how to gently and efficiently immobilize your attacker, then by all means, do it. If you lack those skills, then think about gouging out his fucking eyes, slamming his nose back into his brain, slashing his throat with a broken bottle—do whatever you can, whatever you have to, to save your life!

reeuQ yhW
Queer!

Ah, do we really have to use that word? It's trouble. Every gay person has his or her own take on it. For some it means strange and eccentric and kind of mysterious. That's okay, we like that. But some gay girls and boys don't. They think they're more normal than strange. And for others "queer" conjures up those awful memories of adolescent suffering. Queer. It's forcibly bittersweet and quaint at best—weakening and painful at worst. Couldn't we just use "gay" instead? It's a much brighter word and isn't it synonymous with "happy?" When will you militants grow up and get over the novelty of being different?

## WHY QUEER

Well, yes, "gay" is great. It has its place. But when a lot of lesbians and gay men wake up in the morning we feel angry and disgusted, not gay. So we've chosen to call ourselves queer. Using "queer" is a way of reminding us how we are perceived by the rest of the world. It's a way of telling ourselves we don't have to be witty and charming people who keep our lives discreet and marginalized in the straight world. We use queer as gay men loving lesbians and lesbians loving being queer.

Queer, unlike GAY, doesn't mean MALE.

And when spoken to other gays and lesbians it's a way of suggesting we close ranks, and forget (temporarily) our individual differences because we face a more insidious common enemy. Yeah, QUEER can be a rough word but it is also a sly and ironic weapon we can steal from the homophobe's hands and use against him.

## NO SEX POLICE

For anyone to say that coming out is not part of the revolution is missing the point. Positive sexual images and what they manifest saves lives because they affirm those lives and make it possible for people to attempt to live as self-loving instead of self-loathing. As the famous "Black is beautiful" slogan changed many lives, so does "Read my lips" affirm queerness in the face of hatred and invisibility as displayed in a recent governmental study of suicides that states at least one third of all teen suicides are Queer kids. This is further exemplified by the rise in HIV transmission among those under 21.

We are most hated as queers for our sexualness, that is, our physical contact with the same sex. Our sexuality and sexual expression are what makes us most susceptible to physical violence. Our difference, our otherness, our uniqueness can either paralyze us or politicize us. Hopefully, the majority of us will not let it kill us.

## QUEER SPACE

Why in the world do we let heteros into queer clubs? Who gives a fuck if they like us because we "really know how to party?" WE HAVE TO IN ORDER TO BLOW OFF THE STEAM THEY MAKE US FEEL ALL THE TIME! They make out wherever they please, and take up too much room on the dance floor doing ostentatious couples dances. They wear their heterosexuality like a "Keep Out" sign, or like a deed of ownership.

Why the fuck do we tolerate them when they invade our space like it's their right? Why do we let them shove heterosexuality—a weapon their world wields against us—right in our faces in the few public spots where we can be sexy with each other and not fear attack?

It's time to stop letting the straight people make all the rules. Let's start by posting this sign outside every queer club and bar:

## RULES OF CONDUCT FOR STRAIGHT PEOPLE

1. Keep your display of affection (kissing, hand-holding, embracing) to a minimum. Your sexuality is unwanted and offensive to many here. 2. If you must slow dance, be as inconspicuous as possible. 3. Do not gawk or stare at lesbians or gay men, especially bull dykes or drag queens. We are not your entertainment. 4. If you cannot comfortably deal with someone of the same sex making a pass at you, get out. 5. Do not flaunt your heterosexuality. Be Discreet. Risk being mistaken for a lezzie or a homo. 6. If you feel these rules are unfair, go fight homophobia in straight clubs, or: 7. Go Fuck Yourself.

## I HATE STRAIGHTS

I have friends. Some of them are straight.

Year after year, I see my straight friends. I want to see them, to see how they are doing, to add newness to our long and complicated histories, to experience some continuity. Year after year I continue to realize that the facts of my life are irrelevant to them and that I am only half listened to, that I am an appendage to the doings of a greater

world, a world of power and privilege, of the laws of installation, a world of exclusion. "That's not true," argue my straight friends. There is the one certainty in the politics of power: those left out of it beg for inclusion, while the insiders claim that they already are. Men do it to women, whites do it to blacks, and everyone does it to queers. The main dividing line, both conscious and unconscious, is procreation . . . and that magic word— Family. Frequently, the ones we are born into disown us when they find out who we really are, and to make matters worse, we are prevented from having our own. We are punished, insulted, cut off, and treated like seditionaries in terms of child rearing, both damned if we try and damned if we abstain. It's as if the propagation of the species is such a fragile directive that without enforcing it as if it were an agenda, humankind would melt back into the primeval ooze.

I hate having to convince straight people that lesbians and gays live in a war zone, that we're surrounded by bomb blasts only we seem to hear, that our bodies and souls are heaped high, dead from fright or bashed or raped, dying of grief or disease, stripped of our personhood.

I hate straight people who can't listen to queer anger without saying "hey, all straight people aren't like that. I'm straight too, you know," as if their egos don't get enough stroking or protection in this arrogant, heterosexist world. Why must we take care of them, in the midst of our just anger brought on by their fucked up society?! Why add the reassurance of "Of course, I don't mean you. You don't act that way." Let them figure out for themselves whether they deserve to be included in our anger.

But of course that would mean listening to our anger, which they almost never do. They deflect it, by saying "I'm not like that" or "Now look who's generalizing" or "You'll catch more flies with honey . . . " or "If you focus on the negative you just give out more power" or "you're not the only one in the world who's suffering." They say "Don't yell at me, I'm on your side" or "I think you're overreacting" or "BOY, YOU'RE BITTER."

They've taught us that good queers don't get mad. They've taught us so well that we not only hide our anger from them, we hide it from each other. WE EVEN HIDE IT FROM OURSELVES. We hide it with substance abuse and suicide and overachieving in the hope of proving our worth. They bash us and stab us and shoot us and bomb us in ever increasing numbers and still we freak out when angry queers carry banners or signs that say BASH BACK. For the last decade they let us die in droves and still we thank President Bush for planting a fucking tree, applaud him for likening PWAs to car accident victims who refuse to wear seatbelts. LET YOURSELF BE ANGRY. Let yourself be angry that the price of our visibility is the constant threat of violence, anti-queer violence to which practically every segment of this society contributes. Let yourself feel angry that THERE IS NO PLACE IN THIS COUNTRY WHERE WE ARE SAFE, no place where we are not targeted for hatred and attack, the self-hatred, the suicide—of the closet. The next time some straight person comes down on you for being angry, tell them that until things change, you don't need any more evidence that the world turns at your expense. You don't need to see only hetero couple grocery shopping on your TV . . . You don't want any more baby pictures shoved in your face until you can have or keep your own. No more weddings, showers, anniversaries, please, unless they are our own brothers and sisters celebrating. And tell them not to dismiss you by saying "You have rights," "You have privileges," "You're overreacting," or "You have a victim's mentality." Tell them "GO AWAY FROM ME, until YOU can change." Go away and try on a world without the brave, strong queers that are its backbone, that are its guts and brains and souls. Go tell them go away until sthey have spent a month walking hand in hand in public with someone of the same sex. After they survive that, then you'll hear what they have to say about queer anger.

Otherwise, tell them to shut up and listen.

# V. B
# THE NEW RIGHT=THE OLD WRONGS

In September 1970 *Harper's* magazine published a cover essay by Joseph Epstein: "Homo/Hetero: The Struggle for Sexual Identity." Epstein's essay was later described by conservative writer Midge Decter as "an elegant and thoughtful" account of "the tangle of his feelings and attitudes towards homosexuality and towards the then new question of homosexual rights." Gay readers saw the essay rather differently: it was an unabashed proclamation of homophobia masquerading as analysis. Epstein assured his readers that he had not "accepted" homosexuality. On the contrary, "If I had the power to do so, I would wish homosexuality off the face of the earth." The essay ended with an even more chilling declaration: "There is much that my four sons can do in their lives that might cause me anguish, that might outrage me, that might make ashamed of them and of myself as their father. But nothing they could ever do would make me sadder than if any of them were to become homosexual." In response the Gay Activists Alliance occupied the offices of *Harper's* for a day and tried to explain to the editors why the Epstein essay was offensive and dangerous. Midge Decter, then *Harper's* executive editor, complained about the lack of style exhibited by the demonstrators; she expected more "dash and high taste" from the amusing fairies she preferred to these humorless activists who were "turning their condition into politics" (Decter, "The Boys on the Beach," this volume).

Decter was quite right. Lesbian and gay activists had turned to politics, refusing the role of specimens whose psychiatric condition was diagnosed and treated by doctors, whose moral condition was ministered to by clergy, whose behavior was monitored by the police and the courts, and whose public image was controlled by the mass media. Post-Stonewall activists, trained in the trenches of the civil rights and antiwar movements, were speaking out and standing up—and sitting in. The newly militant movement began to score impressive victories in several institutional arenas: in 1973 the American Psychiatric Association removed homosexuality from its list of mental disorders; the mass media began to pay more attention to feedback from gay activists, and even allow them to speak for themselves occasionally; corporations began to announce policies of nondiscrimination, and municipalities around the country began to enact antidiscrimination ordinances. The backlash was not long in coming.

As Anita Bryant's campaign to repeal Dade County's gay rights ordinance was moving toward its successful conclusion, *Newsweek* columnist George Will warned that such ordinances were more than mere civil rights legislation; rather, they were "weapons in a battle to force society formally to indicate that homosexuality is a matter of indifference . . . as morally irrelevant as skin color" (Will 1977). Looking into his crystal ball, Will laid out an entire agenda that would follow if gay rights ordinances were allowed to stand (and if the Equal Rights Amendment was ratified): next would come the right to marry, the right "to adopt children, to have homosexuality 'fairly represented' as an 'alternative' lifestyle in every child's sex-education classes, and in literature in public libraries" (ibid). And, of course, he was correct; these are all demands that lesbian and gay citizens have made and continue to make in our quest for equality and justice.

The successes of the antigay backlash efforts of the late 1970s are related to the large-scale entry of Christian evangelicals into the political arena and their alliance with the more traditional anti-Communist right-wing establishment. Stalwarts of the right, concerned that the nation's will to power had been sapped by the "Vietnam syndrome," formed the Committee on the Present Danger in 1976 (Cleaver 1993:203). In addition to cold warriors Paul Nitze and Eugene Rostow, the committee included such prominent neoconservatives as *Commentary* magazine editor Norman Podhoretz and his wife, Midge Decter. Writing in *Harper's* on the cultural costs of the post-Vietnam syndrome, Podhoretz claimed that the United States suffered from "a generalized contempt for middle-class or indeed any kind of heterosexual adult life" (Podhoretz 1977).

This theme was expanded at length by Midge Decter in her account of the tragic reverse metamorphosis of the fluttering gay butterflies into grim movement caterpillars ("The Boys on the Beach," this volume). A central part of her analysis focuses on the carefree life of "the overwhelmingly vast majority of homosexuals . . . their smooth and elegant exteriors, unmussed by traffic with the detritus of modern family existence." Taken along with Decter's confession that "the idea of homosexuals as discriminated against in housing and employment . . . seemed . . . bewildering," the essay includes elements of hostility and resentment that have characterized much of the right's attack on queers in the past two decades. Lesbians and gay men (especially gay men) are copping out on the responsibilities of life: "No households of wives and children requiring security; no entailments of school bills, doctor and dentist bills; no lifetime of acquiring the goods needed for family welfare and the goods desired for family entertainment, with a margin left over for that greatest of all heterosexual entailments: the Future." But, of course, real lesbian and gay people, unlike the figments of Decter's Fire Island fantasies, do face many of these concerns, and often do so against fierce opposition.

The attacks on gay people as irresponsible scofflaws successfully avoiding the burdens of middle-class life also resonate with earlier alarms about the consequences of women abandoning their "traditional roles" and "competing with men." In 1968 writers Peter and Barbara Wyden published *Growing Up Straight: What Every Thoughtful Parent Should Know About Homosexuality*, a veritable encyclopedia of homophobia. The book draws heavily on the theories of Irving

Bieber and other psychiatrists of the mothers-did-it school, and the recent emergence of women's liberation receives close attention:

> The modern dilemma boils down to this: a man is not less masculine if he helps with the dishes in a full-fledged man-wife partnership. But he *can* be made less masculine by a wife who insists that he wash the dishes because she is moved by competitive, domineering feelings towards him. . . . If the dishes are washed in a spirit of let's-all-pitch-in-and-get-this-over-with, everybody benefits. All too often, however, unhealthy emotions are involved. When these are sensed by a child, he may get the idea that the parent's natural roles have somehow been reversed. And *that* conclusion can then become one of the factors pre-disposing the child toward homosexuality. (Wyden and Wyden 1968:163)

As early as the mid-1970s a group of right-wing organizers had determined that "social issues" would best serve to attract funds and votes. Building on experience in the Goldwater and Wallace campaigns, Richard Vigurie pioneered the use of direct mail for political organizing and fund-raising. Howard Phillips founded the Conservative Caucus and focused on grassroots organizing. Conservative Catholic Paul Weyrich attracted funding from the Coors family to found the Heritage Foundation in 1973 and the Free Congress Foundation in 1977. In 1979 Weyrich and Phillips "engineered the Moral Majority, drafting Jerry Falwell to front the first organization that built a mass following for conservative religious politics" (Stan 1995).

The core of the New Right argument seemed to be that "welfare state expenditures have raised taxes and added to inflation, pulling the working woman into the labor force and thereby destroying the fabric of the patriarchal family and hence the moral order of society" (Eisenstein 1982:85). Falwell quickly issued a call for the renewal of patriarchy: "The progression of big government is amazing. A father's authority was lost first to the village, then to the city, next to the State, and finally to the empire" (1980:26). By the 1980s the rhetoric of "saving families" and "saving children" had become a centerpiece of right-wing antifeminist and antigay strategy, continuing to dominate American politics ever since.

After the Moral Majority claimed credit for Reagan's victory over Carter in 1980, the Christian right became increasingly focused on amassing political power. They did this both by building independent organizations, amassing enormous financial power through broadcast and cable programming, direct mail, and video cassette distribution, and by direct involvement in Republican party politics (Weir, "In God's Country," this volume). In 1989 the Moral Majority disbanded, but, at the same time, televangelist Pat Robertson used the 1.9 million names he had collected from his unsuccessful 1988 run for the Republican presidential nomination to "identify 175,000 key activists and donors, and launch the Christian Coalition [whose] stated goal was 'to build the most powerful political force in American politics' " (Hardisty 1995:96). In 1996, research by the Pew Research Center for the People and the Press indicated that one-quarter of all registered voters are white evangelical Protestants, and Pat Robertson boasts that "evangelical Christians and pro-life Catholics have the ability to elect any person to any office in any state, city or town in America" (Novosad 1996:26).

As the 1980s drew to a close the right wing broadened the political counterrevolution they were mounting against the gains of minorities and women to encompass the domain of elite culture. Although the political struggles of the 1980s had often been fought on the field of culture, it was the lowlands of mass and even marginal media—commercial television, rock and roll, pornography—that drew the attention of moral enforcers. Signaling the opening of a new front, Patrick Buchanan called for "a cultural revolution in the '90s as sweeping as the political revolution in the '80s." In terms Carole Vance analogized to Nazi cultural metaphors, Buchanan warned that "just as a poisoned land will yield up poisonous fruits, so a polluted culture, left to fester and stink, can destroy a nation's soul" (Vance 1989). In the ensuing skirmishes the forces of counterrevolution laid siege to art and public broadcasting agencies that dared to exhibit the work of uppity gays and blacks. Most notorious were the series of attacks in 1989 on the National Endowment for the Arts (NEA) for funding arts programs that included Andres Serrano's photograph, "Piss Christ," and Robert Mapplethorpe's explicitly sexual photographs of gay men. Shortly afterward, the NEA barred grants to three openly gay artists whose work was overtly political (John Fleck, Holly Hughes, Tim Miller) and to sex radical Karen Finley. The choice of targets was not random:

Conservatives certainly understood the impact that homoerotic work would have on the public. By manifesting gay and lesbian desire, they argued, such art "promotes" homosexuality, making it more acceptable. And, in a way, this is true: Gay and lesbian artists rightfully want to celebrate their sexualities just as heterosexual artists do, and public celebration will help to legitimate these sexualities. (Bolton 1991:26)

In the wake of the right's success in appealing to "family values" and demonizing feminists and queers—along with single mothers, welfare recipients, and immigrants—as the threats to the American Dream, the left began to play catch-up. In 1982 John Judis, an editor of the leftist paper *In These Times*, wrote of "the danger of ideology over politics," explaining that "society does not have the same responsibility towards homosexuality—whether as sexual behavior or as living arrangement—that it has toward the child-bearing family" (Judis 1982). Following Reagan's landslide victory over Mondale in 1984, Democratic party leaders determined to move their party to the center. "Paul Kirk, then head of the Democratic National Committee . . . stated, 'Fringe issues and life style issues such as gay rights cannot be the priority in the dialogue of a major party' " (Tucker 1989:85). By the end of the decade the Democratic Leadership Council cofounded by Governor Clinton of Arkansas had begun to lay out the strategy of rightward "centrism" that later characterized the Clinton presidency.

But if the left was moving rightward to compete with the Republicans, the right had long been busy shifting the goal posts ever farther away from the center. Disappointed with Bush's centrist compromises, the religious Right began to turn its attention to state and local issues. Christian Coalition founding director Ralph Reed noted that "the real battles of concern to Christians are in the nighborhoods, school boards, city councils, and state legislatures" (Goldin 1993:19). These new religious right-wing political initiatives have often focused directly on homosexuality, as in the many statewide initiatives and referenda to prohibit civil rights protections against discrimination—protections they have labeled "special rights" for gays. This strategy, while sometimes successful, was stymied by the Supreme Court's 1996 *Romer v. Evans* decision that Colorado's Amendment 2 was unconstitutional. But, successful or not, these battles served both to organize and raise funds for the right and to divert enormous amounts of lesbian and gay energies and resources away from the fight to obtain basic civil rights.

A favorite tactic for the Christian Coalition has been what they call "stealth campaigning," focusing on

> low-turnout school board, city council and party organization races where a motivated minority could carry the day, and then [mobilizing their] followers through churches to support coalition-backed candidates, while neutralizing potential opposition by concealing from the public the religious basis of their candidacy. When Election Day came, many of these candidates won simply by gathering 20 percent of the vote in a crowded field. (Judis 1994)

Tavares, Florida, a small town north of Orlando, learned about this strategy when Pat Hart became chair of the school board in 1992 once Christian Coalition members achieved a majority. Mrs. Hart, who "originally ran on a tax-efficiency platform, emphasizing her religious agenda only after narrowly winning election" (Rohter 1994), moved to severely limit sex education, mandate creationism in the science curriculum, and amend the state's multicultural curriculum to teach that the United States was "unquestionably superior" to any other society in human history. In Merrimack, New Hampshire, after a Christian Right majority took over the school board in 1994, that majority ruled that the school day would begin with a moment of silence, considered adding creationism to the science curriculum, and adopted a policy prohibiting "any program or activity that has the purpose or effect of encouraging or supporting homosexuality as a positive lifestyle alternative." The policy required teachers to ensure that only negative references to homosexuality occurred in their classes and forbade guidance counselors from aiding lesbian and gay students (Shea 1995). The policy alarmed many in the community who had previously paid little attention to school board policies, and in 1996 a new majority was elected that quickly repealed the policy. Similar reversals in San Diego and Vista, California, and Helena, Montana, showed that stealth campaign tactics can be defeated once that are exposed (Smolowe 1995).

The political landscape of the 1990s includes fierce struggles by the right to prevent any further erosion of the patriarchal traditions they see under attack from women, minorities, and queers. In terms reminiscent of earlier antifeminist hysteria, Pat Robertson in a 1992 fund-raising letter wrote that feminism "encourages women to leave their husbands, kill their children, practice witchcraft, destroy capitalism and become lesbians" (quoted in DeParle 1996:24). In 1991 University of Colorado football coach Bill McCartney, well-known for his antigay views, started Promise Keepers, an evangelical Christian organization dedicated to exhorting men to "reclaim authority" from women (Novosad 1996). As explained by Promise Keeper and evangelist Tony Brown, the first step is to "sit down with your wife and say something like this: 'Honey, I've made a terrible mistake. I've given you my role. I gave up leading this family, and I forced you to take my place. Now I must reclaim that role.' Don't misunderstand what I'm saying here. I'm not suggesting that you ask for your role back, I'm urging you to *take it back*" (Bellant 1995:82). Building on their links with Focus on the Family, the Christian Coalition, and other groups, Promise Keepers has sponsored mass meetings in stadiums across the country where thousands of men have been instructed to take back their roles, and to "give the country back to God" (Novosad 1996:27).

By the mid-1990s the use of "traditional family values" as a political code for attacking women, welfare, and queers echoed across a wide spectrum of American politics. At the kinder, gentler end are neoconservatives like William Kristol, former chief of staff for Dan Quayle and now editor of the *Weekly Standard*, who "scoffs at the notion that issues like gay rights are a distraction from the real business of government," saying,

> There's this notion here in Washington that everyone should spend all their time discussing individual lines of the budget, and whether the tax rate should be 34 or 35 percent for corporations. But you can make the case that, in fact, over the long term society is going to be much more shaped by the lessons we teach our kids and the public policies we pursue regarding homosexuality, the family, issues like that. (Toner 1993)

Kristol is joined by psychologist E. L. Pattullo ("Straight Talk About Gays," this volume), who believes "that those who find themselves homosexuals be treated with dignity and respect," while still guarding "against any thing which might mislead wavering children into perceiving society as indifferent to the sexual orientation they develop." The danger is acute because, "In a wholly nondiscriminatory world, the advantages of heterosexuality would not be obvious." It seems that Bill Clinton shares the views of Pattullo and Kristol, for, while he had his press secretary describe the 1996 Defense of Marriage Act as "gay baiting pure and simple," he nevertheless signed the act because "he believes, frankly, that the underlying position in the bill is right. That's consistent with his personal views" (White Housing briefing, July 13, 1996).

While the neoconservatives and "new Democrats" are compassionate in their heterosexism, the standard bearers of the religious right exhibit no such weakness. In a keynote address to the National Religious Roundtable in January 1996 Conservative Caucus founder Howard Phillips sounded the call:

> The issue in politics today is not Republican versus Democrat, or conservative vs liberal. It is rather, under what authority, and by what standard shall we live? As individuals, as families, as communities, and a civil polity, the laws of God are fixed for all generations. His law is unchanging, it cannot be altered by a two-thirds vote of Congress, by a presidential executive order, or even by a unanimous decision of the U.S. Supreme Court. . . . Homosexuality is not merely a threat to public health; it is an abomination in God's sight. If America is to be blessed by God, if our nation is to be approved by God, we must not exalt, subsidize, or accept the legalization of that which He declares to be an abomination. The judgment of God overrides the opinions of men. . . . That means capital punishment must be the policy. (Porteus 1996)

## REFERENCES

Bellant, Russ. 1995. "Promise Keepers: Christian Soldiers for Theocracy." In Chip Berlet, ed., *Eyes Right: Challenging the Right-Wing Backlash*, pp. 81–85. Boston: South End.

Bolton, Richard. 1991. "What Is to Be Un-done: Rethinking Political Art." *New Art Examiner*, June, pp. 25–28.

Cleaver, Richard. 1993. "Sexual Dissidents and the National Security State." In Richard Cleaver and Patricia Myers, eds., *A Certain Terror: Heterosexism, Militarism, Violence and Change*, pp. 171–208. Chicago: Great Lakes Region AFSC.

DeParle, Jason. 1996. "A Fundamental Problem." *New York Times Magazine*, July 14, pp. 18–25, 32, 35–44.

Eisenstein, Zillah. 1982. "The Sexual Politics of the New Right." In Nannerl O. Keohane, Michelle Z. Rosaldo, and Barbara C. Gelpi, eds., *Feminst Theory: A Critique of Ideology*, pp. 77–98. Chicago: University of Chicago Press.

Epstein, Joseph. 1970. "Homo/hetero: The Struggle for Sexual Identity." *Harper's*, September, no. 241.

Falwell, Jerry. 1980. *Listen America!* New York: Doubleday.

Goldin, Greg. 1993. "The 15 Percent Solution: How the Christian Right Is Building from Below to Take Over from Above." *Village Voice*, April 6, pp. 19–22.

Hardisty, Jean. 1995. "Constructing Homophobia." In Chip Berlet, ed., *Eyes Right: Challenging the Right-Wing Backlash*, pp. 86–104. Boston: South End.

Judis, John. 1982. "The Danger of Ideology Over Politics." *In These Times*, February 3.

Judis, John. 1994. "Crosses to Bear: The Many Faces of the Religious Right." *New Republic*, September 12, pp. 21–25.

Novosad, Nancy. 1996. "God Squad: The Promise Keepers Fight for a Man's World." *Progressive*, August, pp. 25–27.

Podhoretz, Norman. 1977. "The Culture of Appeasement." *Harper's*, October.

Porteus, Skipp. 1996. "Conservative Calls for Execution of Homosexuals: Phillips Sets Tone for Strategy Briefing." *Freedom Writer*, Institute for First Amendment Studies, March.

Rohter, Larry. 1994. "Battle Over Patriotism Curriculum." *New York Times*, May 15, p. A-22.

Shea, Lois. 1995. "Teaching on Gays Banned by Board." *Boston Globe*, August 16.

Smolowe, Jill. 1995. "Outfoxing the Right." *Time*, July 10, p. 38.

Stan, Adele. 1995. "Power Preying." *Mother Jones*, December.

Tucker, Scott. 1989. "All in the Family?" Z *Magazine*, May, pp. 85–88.

Vance, Carole. 1989. "The War on Culture." *Art in America*, September, pp. 39–45.

Will, George. 1977. "How Far Out of the Closet?" *Newsweek*, May 30, p. 92.

Wyden, Peter and Barbara Wyden. 1968. *Growing Up Straight: What Every Thoughtful Parent Should Know About Homosexuality*. New York: Stein and Day.

# | 93 |

## The Boys on the Beach

### MIDGE DECTER

When the homosexual-rights movement first burst upon the scene a little more than a decade ago, a number of people I used to know must have been—as I was myself—more than a little astonished. These were the heterosexuals (in the current parlance of homosexual heterosexual relations, the "straights") who, along with me and my family, used to spend summers in a seaside resort community called Fire Island Pines.

In the years that we all summered there, Fire Island Pines was, at a rough count, about sixty percent homosexual. Though we didn't yet have a name for the phenomenon, the community was distinctly a "new-class" enclave: on the whole young, affluent, enlightened, and breezy in both its styles and attitudes. Most of the houses there—they were high-grade beach shacks really—were informally well-appointed and by the standards of the day expensive. The snobbery of the place, which was considerable, had to do not with old notions of class but with the relative distribution of up-to-the-minute high taste in dress, decor, and opinion. And its denizens, homosexual and heterosexual alike, were predominantly professionals and people in soft, marginal businesses—lawyers, advertising executives, psychotherapists, actors, editors, writers, publishers, gallery owners, designers, decorators, etc. Since included in the estimate that put the heterosexuals at forty percent were hordes of young children and a large number of husbands who remained in the city and commuted to the beach on weekends, the dominance of the homosexuals over the general atmosphere was even greater than the numbers imply. All this was in the early 60's.

What must have been astonishing some years later to the straights of Fire Island Pines was not so much that the homosexual community had given birth to a Gay Lib movement—by the 70's movements were after all a commonplace; everyone was professing to be roused to action about something—as the particular claims this movement was making about the condition of its constituency. Like every movement inspired by the political culture of the 60's, Gay Lib had its radicals, its moderates, and its fellow travelers, each group speaking at a separate decibel level and in a slightly different tone of voice and each addressing itself to a seemingly different set of demands, ranging from the radicals' vision of nothing less than a complete rewriting of the sexual and social constitution to the fellow travelers' plea for nothing more than a new spirit of toleration. Nevertheless, through all the variations there ran the same general assertion about the status of the homosexual in American society. This was that for an altogether private preference for sexual partners of his own gender, the homosexual had been hounded from pillar to post. He was discriminated against in such areas as housing and employment; he was held up to ridicule, treated as an object of loathing; he was frequently the victim of violence at the hands of the police and other rough customers; and possibly worst of all, he was made an outcast and pariah by his own family.

Whatever the remedy held to be most essential for overcoming this state of affairs, from revolution down to the simple recognition of the homosexual's legitimacy as an alternative human possibility, the homosexual community was serving notice that it would no longer sit still for what had become its accustomed treatment from

*Commentary*, August 1980, pp. 35–48. Excerpt.

straight society. Homosexuals were no longer to be called "fags," "queers," "pansies," or (how archaic the word seemed even then) "fairies." They were to be called "gays"—a term implying admission of the unrecognized and unconfessed envy throbbing in the heart of every anxious heterosexual. They were no longer to be mocked in public entertainments. They were no longer to be deemed sick by a mental-health profession caught up in the treacherous confusion between the statistical norm and normality. They were no longer to be kept out of desirable housing or barred from employment—most particularly employment as schoolteachers.

In short, they were no longer to be forced by social and economic necessity, and above all shame, into living a life of concealment. Henceforth their homosexuality was to be deemed, by themselves as well as others, a perfectly natural inclination among all other natural inclinations. Indeed, throwing off the shackles of a dead and arbitrary if not perverted religious piety and an ugly and oppressive bourgeois sensibility, they were to bring spiritual cleansing to everybody by asserting their preference defiantly, with pride: the process now known to the world as "coming out of the closet." . . .

Fire Island is a long, narrow sandspit that serves, for a stretch of some thirty miles or so, as a kind of barrier between the rough and capricious Atlantic Ocean and the southern coast of Long Island. No cars are allowed there. It is, then, a heaven of freedom for small children, given their liberty to roam everywhere, except into the surf, from the earliest possible age. Lolling about on the great stretches of white sand that are the hallmark of the Eastern littoral, the mothers of these children are also offered an unprecedented amount of freedom to turn their thoughts elsewhere. Moreover, since time on the beach is spent by all in that state close to nakedness which is at once both erotically provocative and highly deadening to the provocation, the preoccupation with matters of gender was inescapable and yet lent itself in quality to a good deal of detached contemplation. Added to the natural detachment induced by the bikini, just then newly entrenched in fashion among women and homosexual men, was the absence for the women of any threat—or promise—of erotic charge from most of the males around for most of the time. This combination led to a good deal of easy social comfort compounded by an oddly intent watchfulness.

At least on the part of the women. On the part of the homosexual men,[1] whose turf this stretch of beach so incontestably was—anyway, until the arrival of the "daddy boats" each Friday evening somewhat redressed the balance for two days or so—all was open and heedless. I might have said, open and carefree, for the homosexuals appeared to be far less taken up with issues of propriety and social appearance than we were and far more taken up with various forms of play; but carefree was the last word that would have applied to them. Of this, more later.

But did they, too, not go off to the city to earn their livings, like the straight husbands and fathers, and return to us on Fridays? Many of them did. Yet there was always a full complement of homosexuals left behind during the week. I cannot account precisely for this fact. Some were teachers, and so at leisure in the summer. Some were engaged in free-lance professions, such as design, interior decoration, modeling, acting, and possibly they were taking the whole summer, or most of it, off. Some were young men who had recently arrived in the East from their hometowns in the Midwest and were living temporarily under the protection of an older, or anyway more established, "friend." Some were simply the homemakers, the "wives," of an enduring coupledom. And many, many were guests, members of an army of transients, arriving, leaving, staying on, making use of otherwise empty rooms, empty beds, and houses on loan while their owners or tenants had to be elsewhere. Each ferry to the island—in the height of the season there were six or seven a day—seemed to bring a full load of these, and carry another away.

In any case, they were around in full force and perfectly content to act out their lives, until bedtime or party-time, before us; and we spent a good deal of our free waking time watching them.

We? Them? Was there then no ordinary, unself-conscious individual human connection between the straights and homosexuals of Fire Island Pines? At the time, we would all certainly have said so: neighborliness beyond any question, friendship undoubtedly, and even, in some cases, intimacy. Looking back from here, however— which is, I admit, a perspective that distorts as much as it clarifies—I am not so sure. Simply in order not to wound, there had to have been much in their real attitudes toward us that they left unexpressed, as there had to have been in our real attitudes toward them.

As a rule, for instance, we were not invited to

their parties, not their real parties. There were lunches, dinners, cocktails we all enjoyed together, and large bonfire gatherings on the beach, where lobsters and ears of corn would be steamed in seaweed and vast quantities of wine consumed. But the great elaborate celebrations, costume balls really, that were the center of a fierce social competitiveness raging in the homosexual community, we did not attend; or, should a rare invitation be extended to some few of the specially privileged among us, attended only briefly and early.

There would be four or five of these occasions in a season, their hosts vying with one another for extravagance of conception and design and growing successively more "creative" in order that they might be credited with having produced the most unforgettable party of the year. . . .

We straights followed all these preparations with suitable curiosity, but I do not remember that any of us ever expressed any serious regret at being excluded or ever took offense. We knew without making any point of it that as the night wore on, the entertainment was bound to take a turn we would prefer not to witness.

So it did, in the end, always boil down to a case of us and them.

▼ ▼ ▼

We ourselves, of course, were not a monolithic group. For one thing, some of us had been better prepared by our city lives for the various modes of homosexual display. To be a member of the literary or artistic or theatrical world, for example, meant that one had come to take quite for granted most of the styles and habits of expression by which homosexuals revealed themselves. We tended to make less of these things, and by the same token to be less gingerly and exquisite in our relation to them, than others. Then too—inevitably—the women among us had a different response from the men.

Among the women, their feelings about homosexual men could often serve as a kind of litmus test of their feelings about men in general. For however the issue was approached—in terms of manners, personal qualities, style, or moral conduct—homosexuality foremost and of necessity raised the specter of sex. Certain of the women, out of a lifetime of pain about their own value as sexual providers, were unequivocally hostile (although, curiously, this did not prevent them from spending a good deal of time with the young homosexuals they went out of their way to cultivate). Others were particularly enthusiastic about the small gentle attentions, such as the holding of doors, placing of chairs, lighting of cigarettes, that homosexual men invariably plied one with and straight men rarely. "They make you feel," it was said, without any apparent consciousness of what was being betrayed by the remark, "like a real woman."

Still others professed feelings that were a confusion of private fondness and public bewilderment. Though they knew in their heads that it was the case, deep down they could not really credit the idea that homosexuality was an abiding and serious way of life: given the proper conditions, an effective course of therapy, say (or the right woman?), it would go away.

For all of us, though, whether we acknowledged it or not, being surrounded by homosexuals put our very existence as women on the line. Nobody, not even the most energetically tolerant liberals among us, claimed to be indifferent. Nor did I ever hear an expression of pity for the plight of homosexuals.

With our husbands, the matter was even more complicated. New-class men do not, at least in mixed company, tend to give voice to their feelings toward homosexuals in any of the standard primitive terms of fear, loathing, and abuse that must to this day be heard in the locker rooms and bars of the working class. They have been brought up not to do so; they are too worldly to do so; their schooling and business and professional life have put them in the way of contact with homosexuals whom they would not wish to offend; and besides, the deep influence of the psychotherapeutic world view on the educated has softened the contours of their passions about *all* forms of human conduct. Many of the straight men in the Pines pretended to be mildly amused. Many—though it was all but impossible to succeed in this—continued trying not to notice. But for the most part, the tension, while given only oblique expression, was noticeable—in a certain edge in the voice, a quick turning of the head to avert the eyes from the sight of a homosexual caress, a not-quite suppressed shudder, in the odd fixed gaze that accompanied the most casual social exchange between a straight and homosexual man, as if the two were transmitting a volume of unspoken messages beneath the ceremonial chatter.

This tension the homosexuals themselves gave a name to. They called it "H.D.," homosexual dread, or sometimes "H.P.," homosexual panic, and declared themselves to be vindicated by it.

The fact that a straight man felt noticeably uneasy with them, they said, was the sure sign that he was tempted and panicked by his temptation, thus proving that the true number of homosexuals in this world, had they all but the courage to admit it, would be as the stars in the firmament.

▼ ▼ ▼

In the case of the husbands at Fire Island Pines, the homosexuals were right about one thing. Their uneasiness did contain a large component of fear. The fear of straight men in the face of the homosexual community, however, is not that they will be tempted to join in but that they are being diminished by it, diminished in their persons and diminished in their lives. As women in a full company of homosexual men feel devalued and sexually rejected—that is the very reason certain women, they used to be called "fag hags," choose to spend their lives in such company—heterosexual men feel themselves mocked. They feel mocked in their unending thralldom to the female body and thus their unending dependence on those who possess it. They feel mocked by the longing for and vulnerability to and even humiliation from women they have since boyhood permitted themselves to endure, while others, apparently just like themselves, showily assert their escape from these things.

They feel mocked most of all for having become, in style as well as in substance, family men, caught up in getting and begetting, thinking of mortgages, schools, and the affordable, marking the passage of years in obedience to all the grubby imperatives that heterosexual manhood seems to impose. In assuming such burdens they believe themselves entitled to respect, but homosexuality paints them with the color of sheer entrapment.

In Fire Island Pines they were in fact being mocked explicitly, not so much by individual homosexuals as by the reigning homosexual fashion. The essence of that fashion was the worship of youth—youth understood not even as young manhood but rather boyhood (and indeed, the straight women among themselves always referred to the homosexuals as "the boys"). On the beach particularly, this worship became all powerful and inescapable to the eye. It was a constant source of wonder among us, and remains so to me to this day, that by far the largest number of homosexuals had hairless bodies. Chests, backs, arms, even legs, were smooth and silky, an impression strengthened by the fact that they

were in addition frequently and scrupulously unguented to catch the full advantage of the sun's ultra violet. We were never able to determine just why there should be so definite a connection between what is nowadays called their sexual "preference" and their smooth feminine skin. Was it a matter of hormones, or was there some constant special process of depilation? But smooth-skinned they were, and, like the most narcissistic of pretty young girls and women, made an absolute fetish of the dark and uniform suntan, devoting hours, days, weeks, to turning themselves carefully to the sun. Nor was this tanning flesh ever permitted to betray any of the ordinary signs of encroaching mortality, such as excess fat or flabbiness or on the other hand the kind of muscularity that suggests some activity whose end is not beauty. In short, year by year homosexuals of all ages presented a never-ending spectacle, zealously and ruthlessly monitored, of tender adolescence.

Clothed, they were slender, seamless, elegant, and utterly chic. The two shops in the Pines that, along with a grocery and meat store, a hotel and two bars, constituted its entire commercial establishment, were boutiques. They were crowded day and night with men going through racks, trying on, viewing themselves in mirrors, consulting one another with that earnest sociability that so often overtakes women on shopping sprees. Next to suntan, new clothes were the most constant tribute Narcissus paid to his ageless body. Naked or covered, then, the homosexuals offered their straight neighbors an insistent reminder of the ravages to their own persons wrought by ordinary heterosexual existence. A friend who was visiting the beach for the first time was driven to exclaim, "Look at us—even our feet are fat!"

A subsidiary worship was that of the phallus. It took the form in this mixed community of the sartorial claim, made by means of pocketless tight pants and scanty but padded bathing trunks, that the phallus was both ubiquitous in the affairs of men and central to them. Now, contrary to the theories of numerous sex experts and a few female ideologues, women are not much interested in or moved by the phallus apart from the rest of the particular individual man whose accouterment it is. Forced willy-nilly by homosexual fashion to take special prior notice of the male organ, they were inclined to a certain detached ribaldry, of the kind associated in literature with old crones who have seen their share of human foibles and no longer feel implicated. The fierce display of crotch was not in any case addressed to them but to other men, as a kind of erotic, or perhaps only dirty-boyish, promise. Undertaken in imitation of female body display—a kind of surrogate for the feminine show of breasts as a means of seduction—the homosexuals' proclaimed preoccupation with the phallus had its own mocking effect on heterosexuals.

▼ ▼ ▼

Beyond issues of body and dress, the homosexuals' mockery was outspoken and intentional, and included self-mockery as well. I am referring here to the manner of speech, gesture, and home decoration known as "camp." Camp is a phenomenon that has, as it was created to do, bred considerable confusion among the obtuse and innocent over the years. In essence, it is a style based on the making of a joke, usually a flippant or unpleasant or even macabre joke, at the expense both of the one who makes it and the one—or ones, or whole world—who witnesses it. The mode in which this joke is made is that of the gross exaggeration, to the point of transcendent ridicule or parody, of something cheap, tawdry, ugly, deficient, or painful in order to impose it as something newly acceptable. Thus it is at one and the same time an aggression and an insinuation.

Deliberate overdressing is a form of camp. As is the decoration of one's home with expensive versions of once-popular cheap mass artifacts, like calendar art and comic strips. As is, for example, the adulation of a figure like Mae West, all by herself an exemplarily ambiguous camp artifact. As are overemphatically mincing manners of speech and usages of words. In general, like the weirdly dressed mannequins in the windows of a number of the most fashionable stores or the grotesquely painted faces and misproportioned bodies of the photographers' models gracing the pages of women's fashion magazines, camp involves the transvaluation and assimilation of the aesthetically distressing. The main thing is that it is entirely a homosexual creation, a brilliant expression of homosexual aggression against the heterosexual world. Its origin was perhaps the drag queen, the creature got up and painted like a child's version of a fancy lady, doing dirt both on himself as a homosexual and on the human condition which necessitates a division into two sexes.

Like many intended insults, camp came to be naively taken over by many of its victims. Middle-class suburban audiences have for years been applauding homosexual plays for being profound statements about themselves and their lives: consider the kudos heaped on the works of Tennessee Williams, Edward Albee, and others, for presenting what could only have been homosexual relationships as the deeper truth about love in our time. Women have permitted themselves to be rendered breastless, and men to become pocketbook carriers, by homosexual designers. And trend-mongering heterosexuals have embraced camp within their repertoire of taste.

The final mockery was an unintentional one, though possibly the most keenly experienced by the straights. That was the peculiar affluence of homosexual life. As it happened, there were a large number of normally affluent people among both communities. The Pines, as I have already pointed out, was in the main a new-class settlement, and by the early 60's the members of this class were by and large making a good living and some of them were doing considerably better than that. But with only a few exceptions, the homosexuals lived, job for job and income for income, as if they had more money than we did. The difference was subtle and would be hard, especially after so many years, to pin down in detail. It had to do with the feverish shopping I have described; with the cut of their clothes; with the expensive novelty, in constant replenishment, of their furnishings; with their parties; with what must have been the impressive amplitude of their bar bills; with their more extensive and more indulgent leisure; with their ceaseless, as it is now called, "trading up" in houses and building of new ones. Those of us familiar with homosexuals and their lives in the city found the difference even more striking there . . .

The point is that even the so evidently lesser of the homosexual communities had an air of sportiness, of freedom from financial care, that the heterosexuals did not feel. This air was based in reality, of course. The money, however limited, that the homosexual had in his pocket was, all of it, for him to spend on himself. No households of wives and children requiring security; no entailments of school bills, doctor and dentist bills; no lifetime of acquiring the goods needed for family welfare and the goods desired for family entertainment, with a margin left over for that greatest of all heterosexual entailments, the Future: no such households burdened the overwhelmingly vast majority of homosexuals. Thus their smooth and elegant exteriors, unmussed by traffic with the detritus of modern family existence, constituted a kind of sniggering reproach to their striving and harried straight brothers. See what you have got yourself into, they seemed to be saying, no wonder you have so much less for yourself— and look it . . .

▼ ▼ ▼

The idea of homosexuals as discriminated against in housing and employment, then, must have taken a little getting used to by my former neighbors in the Pines. Nor, for those who lived and who worked anywhere within, or even just near to, the precincts of high-fashion society, would this idea have seemed any less bewildering in the city. Just to name the professions and industries in which they had, and still have, a significant presence is to define the boundaries of a certain kind of privilege: theater, music, letters, dance, design, architecture, the visual arts, fashion at every level—from head, as it were, to foot, and from inception to retail—advertising, journalism, interior decoration, antique dealing, publishing . . . the list could go on.

I do not suppose, but would not be certain, that homosexuals have established much of a presence in basic industry or government service or in such classic professions as doctoring and lawyering, but then for anyone acquainted with them as a group the thought suggests itself that few of them have ever made much effort in these directions. And that profession over which so much of the recent debate on homosexual rights has raged, namely teaching, may provide a convenient point for the marshaling of opposition to Gay Lib (the question of the corruption of the young), but in the real world this debate is pure abstraction. Homosexuals do in fact teach school, from the elementary grades to the universities; an open-eyed visit to just about any institution of learning, public or private, will supply verification. They always have, what is more, been teachers, and in goodly number. Some of them have indeed seduced their students, or tried to, and others, no doubt the majority, have not. (What is really behind the homosexuals' charge of discrimination in the school system is something else: the requirement that they be discreet. But that is an entirely different matter.)

Moreover, not only are they solidly ensconced in these after all interesting, and far from low-paid, areas of making a livelihood, but here again, anyone who has known them as a group cannot but be mindful of the fact that where so ensconced, they themselves have engaged in a good deal of discriminatory practice against others. There are businesses and professions in which it is less than easy for a straight, unless he make the requisite gestures of propitiation to the homosexuals in power, to get ahead.

*Known them as a group.* No doubt this will in itself seem to many of the uninitiated a bigoted formulation. Yet one cannot even begin to get at the truth about homosexuals without this kind of generalization. They are a group so readily distinguishable that, as we came to see in that summertime mingling of homosexuals and straights, they can in a single sweeping glance around a crowded room and with unerring accuracy recognize one another. More than that, whatever one's theory of the nature and origins of homosexuality, it is undeniable that the homosexual community boasts—or at least did in those years—an unaccountably high proportion of extremely talented persons. Does homosexuality have the effect of releasing talent, or is it that the talented are more inclined to be homosexual? Like the argument about the physiological versus the psychological genesis of homosexuality, the question bores. The concrete reality, however, does not.

Nor is this talent confined to work. There is such a thing, for example, as a unique and entirely characteristic homosexual form of wit. It is difficult to describe and analyze—as is any form of wit—but unmistakable. Its central characteristic is malice, but that does not describe it either, for the malice is of a special kind, brilliantly playful and startling in equal measure. I remember once discovering that a man I had met was homosexual when, in the course of our conversation, he described a certain grand lady we were gossiping about as someone who wears a tiara on her mustache. But except were one to quote from Oscar Wilde, who fashioned his witticisms to be written down and subsequently read, examples would tend to go dead on the page. Suffice it to say that, provided such malice is not trained upon oneself, intelligent homosexuals can be the most naughtily amusing company in the world.

There is also such a thing as characteristic homosexual speech, though many homosexuals I have known do not use it except for momentary effect, as a gesture of comradeship with the other homosexuals present. That mode of speech—it is something of an accent redolent of small towns in the Midwest whence so many homosexuals seemed to have migrated to the big city and something of an inflection suggesting the promise of camp—was the pervasive sound in Fire Island

Pines. To this day, even the youngest of the children who spent time there can recognize this speech and identify its user.

So no matter how well we knew them as individuals, we continued unavoidably to see them in the gross, as a collectivity. And far from being the objects of our ridicule, they were the ones who, in those days and nights on the white Atlantic sands, were doing all the ridiculing.

▼ ▼ ▼

We knew, of course, that in their other, city, life, things were not precisely the same. By the sense of great release with which some of them disembarked from the boats at the harbor landing—greeting their hosts and friends in the attitude of that Byron lady who asked, "Wherefore doth the ravishing not commence?"—one could see that for them their sojourn on the island represented an escape from the tyranny of circumspection. Why else, for that matter, would they have banded together as they had, here and elsewhere, creating summer enclaves for themselves? Even in this consciously proper community, where the gaudier forms of homosexual amusement, if any, were confined within doors, they showed signs of the feeling that they were "coming out." There on the dock, before one's very eyes, telltale gestures grew more emphatic, telltale speech grew freer, voices more raucous. Stripping down to their bikinis at once and heading for the beach where the twin kings Sun and Phallus awaited their devotions, they literally commenced to dance.

Dancing was in those days an important symbol of the hampering of homosexual freedom. Forbidden by law to dance as male couples in public, they had devised a form of group dancing—perhaps originally an adaptation of folk dance—in which they lined up side by side, ten or fifteen abreast, and executed in unison a rather elaborate pattern of steps. (By the late 60's, when people on dance floors danced by themselves only in some rough proximity to their partners, did they know that they were engaged in a borrowing from the homosexuals?) This dance, known first as the "hully gully" and later much elaborated upon, they rehearsed assiduously, instructing all newcomers, at the edge of the surf. On any afternoon, groups of them could be seen up and down the beach, going through their paces: step-kick-back-turn. Here at least they could spend their days without concern for the impression they were making. If we, arrayed on the beach with our toddlers, bottles, toys, sand pails, bags of fruit, were inclined to laugh at the deadly earnestness of those rehearsals, it mattered not the tiniest bit to them.

Their very unconcern for our opinion paradoxically attested to a life heavy with such concern elsewhere. While neither poor nor excluded, they were clearly people whose existence was normally shadowed with some degree of disquiet. Moreover, we knew—because our friends among them told us and because to live as a conscious member of enlightened society means to know such things—that they lived in a rather different relation to, say, the police than we did. Any one of them, caught in the wrong attitude in the wrong bar in the wrong neighborhood on the wrong night, might be subjected to humiliations that no record of good citizenship and no amount of high position in society would protect him from. (To people like us, especially in those years of growing political restlessness, such a position was not without its attractions.) I myself had personally known of a case of an eminent figure in his field, among the most highly respected men in the world, who had to telephone a young friend in the middle of the night and ask his assistance in securing his release from the hands of the law. He had, on a street corner in Greenwich Village, solicited a man who turned out to be a plainclothes cop.

The police were not much in evidence in Fire Island. On occasional tours of duty from the mainland, usually in response to some complaint, they might patrol the beach, picking up, or scattering, copulating couples or merely ordering the dousing of a bonfire. In the city, however, they were a presence, if only as a theoretical possibility, in the life of virtually every homosexual. As were other embodiments of authority whom we heterosexuals never thought about except to suppose that they were working for us.

The homosexuals therefore were people who, by our lights and standards, lived dangerously. But we also knew, even from the vantage point of the safe precincts of the Pines, that the danger was to some considerable extent a danger they courted. The eminent man arrested for soliciting later admitted that within the first few seconds of their encounter he had sensed that the object of his attentions was a policeman but had pursued the conversation nevertheless. He had also sometimes gone to that waterfront street in Manhattan where the truckdrivers customarily loitered outside their trucks to receive the ministrations, and the money, of the homosexuals and to mete out

brutality in return. Those less brilliantly perceptive about the waywardness of the human heart
than he no doubt plunged into whatever dangers
they put themselves to in a state of greater innocence about the meaning of their complicity.
Many no doubt plunged not at all or moved
blindly into their entrapments. Still, even on the
evidence of the unharried homosexual life in the
Pines, then so respectable as to erect barriers
against the flamboyance of a Cherry Grove, the
temptations of ugliness were never far off.

▼ ▼ ▼

There was another kind of unease, however,
having little or nothing to do with the heterosexual world at large, that hung like a cloud over
beach and bar. In this case the discomfort—if that
is the word for it—was an endogamous one,
revealed in their relations to one another. For
despite the continual partying and visiting, dancing and celebration, and despite the sense of
liberation bred in all of us at the recognition that
we were literally cut off from our ordinary lives
by a body of water, there was, if I may be forgiven
the pun, strangely little of gaiety among
the homosexuals. We, with all our domestic
trappings and woes—among a fairly wide circle
of summer friends, for instance, only three
marriages, my own included, have remained
intact and God knows how many of our children
were subsequently carried off in the hurricane
of the 60's—seemed far more open to our
pleasures. . . .

Being purely voluntary and without external
sanction, even the most enduring of homosexual
connections must bear the freight of a certain
adolescent anxiety—what has nowadays for the
same reason taken hold among the heterosexuals
and goes by the name of "the meaningful relationship." Nowadays, too, there is a heterosexual
institution, ostensibly created for social pleasure,
that must be as glum with the burden of adolescent purpose as were those gay bars in the Pines:
I mean the singles bar. But then, in any case,
nothing seemed more singular than the disjunction in homosexual gatherings between the
appearance of well-heeled good health and high
spirits and the underlying atmosphere of a potentially explosive petulance. Within seconds, fool-
ing around could turn into nastiness, and nastiness to profound gloom.

We, of course, also had our scenes and
wreaked injuries upon one another, but in a different way. Among us the aggression was more

local and more predictable, usually the result of
practiced marital squabbling in which certain
individuals could be counted on to assume their
accustomed roles. With the homosexuals, it was
general and free-floating, being by inclination
highly promiscuous—promiscuity is after all the
natural condition of young males undomesticated by women, and homosexuals are after all,
no matter how much they wish it not to be, still by
definition males undomesticated by women—
they had to view every flirtation as the possibility
of a real betrayal, even if it did not eventually go
anywhere. So jealousy and sulking were endemic.
. . .

It seemed evident to me then (and it seems to
me still, despite vociferous declarations to the
contrary) that whatever the attractions of the
homosexual life were to those who adopted it, the
simple pleasures of the bed, the pleasures awaiting those straggling homecomers, were far from
foremost.

But, it will be objected, cannot the same be
said of the attractions of heterosexual life? Is not
the history of our century, not to mention the century preceding, strewn with the human rubble of
a great battle to overcome sexual distaste, from
the devotees of the sex manual to the radicals of
the Women's Lib movement (who were in those
years gathering fury in the wings)? The answer is
that whatever disciplines it might entail, heterosexuality is not something adopted but something
accepted. Its woes—and they have, of course,
nowhere been more exaggerated than in those
areas of the culture consciously or unconsciously
influenced by the propaganda of homosexuals—
are experienced as the woes of life itself.

Particularly under the aegis of their new movement, homosexuals have spoken a great deal
about "accepting" their homosexuality. But
accept it—in the sense of acknowledging the
comedy of one's entanglement with a reasonable
amount of good humor and getting on with one's
business—is precisely what they have never done.
On the contrary, they have, during the old Fire
Island days figuratively and later literally, in every
possible way made a gigantic issue of it.

The meaning of those undeniable marks of
dread that collected around the boundaries of the
homosexuals' actual erotic life, then, is that for
many if not all of them homosexuality represented a flight from women far more than a
wholehearted embrace of men. This was understood in her bones by every heterosexual woman
on the beach. For some it was a source of comfort,

for others, of discomfort ranging from vague to acute; but that we were, to put it mildly, unwanted added a certain tone to all of our summertime experience.

The fact that the homosexuals' flight from women was accompanied by a good deal of female imitation pointed neither to sympathy with nor flattery of the female principle. For that aspect of the female being imitated through homosexuality, in dress, manner, and even in some of the attention to domestic detail, was femininity in its unformed and unrealized condition: in other words, girlishness. Now, girlishness is femaleness before it has incorporated the possibilities, and the dangers, of reproduction. Women who sustain this condition into their adult lives are expressing hatred for their destined role as the messengers of mortality—it being women who principally teach the lesson that to be human is to be born, to grow old, and to die. And men who seek to appropriate the advantages of girlishness—i.e., homosexuals—are most of all expressing their refusal to receive that message. It was homosexuality that Simone de Beauvoir succeeded in describing so brilliantly when she wrote in her famous woman-hating book, *The Second Sex*:

The little boy would like to have sprung into the world like Athena fully grown, fully armed, invulnerable. To have been conceived and then born an infant is the curse that hangs over his destiny, the impurity that contaminates his being. And, too, it is the announcement of his death.

The desire to escape from the sexual reminder of birth and death, with its threat of paternity—that is, the displacement of oneself by others—was the main underlying desire that sent those Fire Island homosexuals into the arms of other men. Had it been the opposite desire—that is, the positive attraction to the manly—at least half the boutiques would long since have been out of business, half the alcohol (and latterly, the drugs) would have remained unconsumed, and gay bars might, even under the watchful eyes of the police, have been reasonably sociable places. . . .

▼ ▼ ▼

At the end of our fifth summer in the Pines, we decided not to return there any more. There were a number of reasons for this decision, but prominent among them was the fact that the balance between the homosexuals and the straights had clearly begun to tilt. The former were growing ever more numerous and concomitantly ever less circumspect both in their public demeanor and in their private behavior toward us. It is hard to know how or why this happened; possibly the political mood that was to erupt into gay activism was already brewing beneath the surface of homosexual life, or possibly the community was simply giving way beneath the pressure of the sheer new numbers of young men opting to be homosexual.

In any case, our once friendly neighbors were beginning to indicate to us in all sorts of ways—from a new shrillness of voice to the appearance of drag costumes in the afternoon to a provocative display of social interest in our teen-age children—that the place was getting too small to contain the tastes and wishes of both communities. How the older homosexual residents of the Pines, they who had worked so hard to maintain its sense of propriety, felt about all this I was never able to discover. However they did feel, within a few years Fire Island Pines was to become a renowned center of intense and open homosexual expression, and by the end of the decade one by one the last of the remaining heterosexual families had backed off. So I lost contact with the place, and was reminded of it again only when a number of homosexual tracts and novels, part of that vast outpouring of confessional literature that seems nowadays to accompany every rights movement, persuaded me that were I to return, I would hardly recognize my old haunt.

These tracts and novels also persuaded me that I would hardly recognize my old homosexual friends as well. First of all, in their rage to "tell all"—a literary impulse that hovers uncertainly for the homosexuals, exactly as it does for the Women's Libbers, somewhere between aggressive exhibitionism and a plaintive appeal for pity—the new homosexual writings betray a great falling away from the talent and wit that were so characteristic a mark of their predecessors. Gay Lib "literature" is now characterized by an earnestness and callowness and crudity that are the very last qualities one who knew them would have associated with homosexuals.

Several years after the summers I have been describing, I was working at *Harper's* magazine and we were demonstrated against by representatives of a coalition of gay-rights organizations. We had published an elegant and thoughtful essay by Joseph Epstein discussing the tangle of his feelings and attitudes toward homosexuality and toward the then-new question of homosexual rights. In response, this coalition staged a sit-in in our office. They arrived with the inevitable platoon of TV cameras and reporters and, having had their moment in the sun of the media, settled down for a rather rude daylong visit. Two things astonished me, based upon my background of experience in Fire Island Pines, about that sit-in. One was the drab and unprepossessing appearance of the demonstrators; no gathering of homosexuals I had ever seen had been so without dash and high taste. The other was the humorless unimaginativeness with which they had adopted the political gesturing of others. The homosexuals I had known, were they ever to have engaged in so unlikely a borrowing from the repertoire of militancy as a sit-in, would have found some witty and arresting way to adapt it. (One feature of the demonstration, however, came as no surprise at all: by late afternoon, their confrontation with us had evolved into an outpouring of confidences. They spoke of their therapists and their mothers.)

In the course of the proceedings, someone hurled at us the challenge, "Are you aware of how many suicides you may be responsible for in the homosexual community?" *Suicides?* At that moment, the charge was merely an expression of inarticulate anger where argument had failed, but the cry behind it was something to be filed away for further reflecting upon. Clearly, turning their condition into politics was having some sort of profound effect on homosexuals.

The true nature of that effect would take some time to become clear, distracted as both they and the rest of us got to be by all the noise of political demand and legal argument. Before that point, however, there was the predictable literary barrage I have already mentioned. And equally predictable, the reception of this barrage on the part of all the important cultural institutions of the country grew ever more piously accepting. On both sides, naturally, the goddess of commerce quickly entered to receive her accustomed full tribute. In addition to the articles, tracts, and novels, magazines devoted to photographic genuflection before the altar of Phallus exfoliated before one's eyes on the newsstands; each week, as it seemed, produced a new one. The shops and department stores whose wares and decor had long whispered to the initiated that they were heavily under the influence of homosexual taste began now positively to shout the message—and to assume an ever more commanding position among the clientele of the fashionably aspiring new class. Homosexuality, like negritude and womanhood, had become a full-scale "market." Even TV dramas, the incomparable barometer of the winds and pressures of American liberal thought, featured episodes in which homosexual characters revealed themselves and achieved full recognition and understanding.

Where the culture goes, particularly those aspects of the culture that attain to market status, there also goes science. So it was that representatives of the psychiatric profession hastened to strike homosexuality from its official catalogue of illness; no doubt a vast body of research confirming this new omission is soon to occupy a major share of attention at scientific meetings.

In short, in less than a decade's time, homosexual activism had moved from angry defiance to the perhaps disappointing discovery that so far as American liberalism was concerned, it was beating down an open door. If that first angry defiance seemed out of keeping with the spiritual dimensions of homosexuality as one had come to think of them—somehow at once too solemn and too tacky—the spectacle of homosexuality at liberty added new depths to those dimensions. . . .

▼ ▼ ▼

What indeed has happened to the homosexual community I used to know—they who only a few short years ago were characterized by nothing so much as a tender, sweet, vain, pouting, girlish attention to the youth and beauty of their bodies? Whose obsession was adolescent play, and whose safety valve for that obsession was alcohol? Whose primary pleasure was in dress and decor and all things that covered their world with a sparkling if ambiguous surface?

They have "come out," as the saying goes, with a mighty and terrible bang. No longer allowed to hint, to insinuate, to keep private counsel—for hinting, insinuating, keeping private counsel are now politically forbidden marks of repression—they have lost their lightness of touch, and with it, whatever lightness of heart it made possible. Having been defined, or defined themselves, as political victims, they must turn their way of living into an ideology and stand four-square behind it. In other words, thanks to Gay Lib, what was once a strategy of flight, tricky and absorbing, has been transformed into a tactic of frontal assault. Homosexuals in this new time may be relieved of the old need to be vigilant and deceitful, to resort to that form of bohemian resistance described by

James Joyce as "silence, exile, and cunning." But to judge from all their current forms of self-directed violence, their new dispensation has brought them anything but relief on a number of other scores. Take San Francisco, where they have not only laid claim to but achieved a vast measure of open power; where in order to insure her election Diane Feinstein, the present mayor, was made to offer them a public apology and promise them her special friendship; where spokesmen for Gay Lib control banks and major businesses; and where the atmosphere is so hospitable that thousands of new homosexual immigrants seek haven there each year. With each succeeding level of acknowledged public influence, San Francisco homosexuals have produced an even more voluminous and active underlife. The freedom to rise, it would seem, is also very much the freedom to sink. . . .

One thing is certain. To become homosexual is a weighty act. Taking oneself out of the tides of ordinary mortal existence is not something one does from any longing to think oneself ordinary (but only following a different "lifestyle"). Gay Lib has been an effort to set the weight of that act at naught, to define homosexuality as nothing

more than a casual option among options. In accepting the movement's terms, heterosexuals have only raised to a nearly intolerable height the costs of the homosexual's flight from normality. Faced with the accelerating round of drugs, S-M, and suicide, can either the movement or its heterosexual sympathizers imagine that they have done anyone a kindness?

## NOTE

1. There were also homosexual women at the Pines, but they were, or seemed to be, far fewer in number. Nor, except for a marked tendency to hang out in the company of large and usually ferocious dogs, were they instantly recognizable as the men were. Oddly, or perhaps not oddly, once we came to know who they were, they were more likely to keep away from straight women and stay by themselves. One summer, however, one of the "mommies" was seduced by, and moved herself and her children in with, the leading lesbian of the place, a former policewoman. This was the only incident I can remember that produced general shocked disapproval among the heterosexuals.

# | 94 |

## Straight Talk About Gays

### E. L. PATTULLO

The campaign for gay rights steadily gains ground. Just this past summer, a young Eagle Scout, recently emerged from the closet, filed a suit that bids fair to overturn Scouting's ban on homosexual members. The dismissal of a full colonel in the National Guard after she publicly acknowledged her lesbianism prompted wide protest. In the first round of his presidential candidacy, Ross Perot stumbled when he seemed to suggest homosexuality would disqualify one for service in his cabinet. Bill Clinton, on the other

hand, won widespread acclaim by promising to end the prohibition against homosexuals in the military and to press the gay-rights agenda. Across the country, colleges and state and local governments which have not yet acted are pondering regulations that would prohibit discrimination on grounds of sexual orientation. Early in the fall, Cambridge, Massachusetts approved legislation

*Commentary*, December 1992, pp. 21–24.

extending "spousal rights" to partners of homosexual employees.

There are a few pockets of resistance, stemming almost entirely from religious considerations. Some years ago, when he was England's chief rabbi, Sir Immanuel Jakobovits, writing in the London *Times*, insisted that "All the authentic sources of Judaism condemn homosexual relations as a heinous offense." In mid-July of this year, the press reported a directive from the Vatican to U.S. bishops instructing them about the areas in which it is legitimate to discriminate against homosexuals. And in Oregon, Protestant evangelicals were behind the extremist move to proclaim homosexuality "abnormal, wrong, unnatural, and perverse" (in the words of Oregon's Ballot Measure 9, which was rightly defeated last month).*

But what about people who are neither extremist nor subject to religious dicta on the question, who are neither homosexual nor homophobic, and who are still uneasy about the movement to abolish all societal distinctions between heterosexual and homosexual? Is there a secular reason for such people to resist this movement? I think there is.

I begin with the fact that there is much we do not know about human sexuality, especially on the all-important issue of how sexual orientation is determined. For any to whom this is not self-evident, I invoke the conclusion of John Money, emeritus professor of psychology at Johns Hopkins, who is widely respected, by gays and straights alike, as one of the leading experts on the subject. In an April 1987 article in the *American Psychologist* (later expanded into the book *Gay, Straight, and In-Between* ), he writes:

On the issue of the determinants of sexual orientation . . . the only scholarly position is to allow that prenatal and postnatal determinants are not mutually exclusive.

Despite our ignorance, however, there is good reason to think that a very substantial number of people are born with the potential to live either straight or gay lives. But, again, just as no one knows why a person becomes straight or gay, no one knows how many people, at birth, have the potential to mature into either one of these sexual orientations.

In Alfred Kinsey's landmark study, nearly 50 years ago, 37 percent of the men and 13 percent of the women reported responding, to the point of

orgasm, to members of their own sex sometime during their lives. But we cannot be sure how representative Kinsey's sample was of the whole population. According to a 1991 NAS-NRC study which examined the results of five probability surveys (all limited to males and concerning only their adult experience), about 5 to 7 percent of the respondents admitted same-gender sexual contact. But the study warned that these "estimates might be considered lower bounds on the actual prevalence of such contact."

▼ ▼ ▼

Still, whatever the exact numbers may be, it is clear that many people have a capacity for becoming either straight or gay. In addition, it is almost certain that the social environment plays a part, though we do not know just what that part is, in determining one's primary sexual orientation.

Not for everyone. Many straights and gays insist that they have never strayed from their predominant sexual orientation in thought, word, or deed. However, there are also many others who fall somewhere in the middle of the continuum. It is these individuals with whom I am principally concerned here, and I will refer to them as "waverers."

It is the fact that there is a bit of the waverer in so many of us, I believe, which explains the stubborn persistence of some prejudice against homosexuals, even among those who abhor the mistreatment they have suffered. Often, straights are threatened not because gays are so different, but because they are so similar. Some straights are quite conscious of having homosexual proclivities and are fearful of undermining their predominant heterosexuality. Others unconsciously share the same fear. Even those wholly unthreatened recognize the existence of a temptation that could endanger the heterosexuality of loved ones—particularly children and young adults.

Whether there is ground in reality for these fears remains a question. Money, in the article mentioned earlier, asserts, without explaining, that "the concept of voluntary choice is as much in error here as in its application to handedness or to native language."

Now, few would disagree that something as basic as sexual orientation must be the result of a chain of events so complex that we are unaware of

---

* However, a less extreme initiative outlawing "protective status based on homosexual, lesbian, or bisexual orientation" passed in Colorado.

having made a choice—in the sense of preferring chocolate to vanilla. However, it seems possible that substantial numbers of youngsters do have the capacity to "choose" in the same sense they "choose" the character that will mark them as adults—that is, through a sustained, lengthy process of considered and unconsidered behaviors. Though we acknowledge some influences—social and biological—beyond their control, we do not accept the idea that people of bad character had no choice. Further, we are concerned to maintain a social climate that will steer them in the direction of the good.

Several recent research reports have suggested that, in some cases, genes may be at the root of a homosexual orientation, but none pretends to be conclusive. Many people, straight and gay, welcome such evidence, believing that society's prejudice would dissipate faster were it established that homosexuals are born, not made. But to date, evidence that genes (or hormones, which probably play a more important role) are a sufficient cause of human sexual preference is nonexistent, and no serious student of human sexuality is prepared to deny that nurture is an important factor.

Not even Money denies it. While dismissing as obsolete the old nature-nurture controversy and insisting that social learning is no less biological than genes or hormones, Money acknowledges that such learning depends upon what society teaches:

> Sheep, cattle and swine and other four-legged species are, more or less, hormonal robots insofar as a masculine or feminine mating pattern can be foreordained on the basis of regulating the prenatal hormonalization of the brain. Even among sheep, however, the final outcome will be influenced by whether the lamb grew up in a normal flock of ewes and rams or in a sex-segregated herd. Primates are even more influenced by the social conditions of growing up and are less subject to hormonal robotization.

▼ ▼ ▼

Surely decency demands that those who find themselves homosexual be treated with dignity and respect. But surely too, reason suggests that we guard against doing any thing which might mislead wavering children into perceiving society as indifferent to the sexual orientation they develop.

Not all will agree as to what reason suggests. A gay friend, wholly content with his orientation and unable to imagine being straight, nevertheless insists that the advantages of being straight are so apparent that no one, young or old, could possibly mistake them. There is no doubt that this is true at present, especially when AIDS remains rampant and when the drive toward full equality for homosexuals is still short of its goal. But the question is whether the advantages would continue to be so apparent—especially to young waverers—if, as, and when all legal and social distinctions between straights and gays have disappeared.

After all, the young are powerfully influenced—in sexual as well as in other matters—by the values of the peers with whom they associate. In a wholly nondiscriminatory world, the advantages of heterosexuality would not be obvious. It seems plausible that, in such a world, waverers who happened to fall in with predominantly homosexual peers and adults would be likely to gravitate toward the gay rather than the straight life.

All the more so when we consider how much the cultural climate in our own world has already changed with respect to homosexuality. In a growing number of schools throughout the country children are taught that the gay life is as desirable as the straight—if not indeed more desirable—and such instruction (which is often hard to distinguish from outright indoctrination) begins as early as the elementary grades. The same idea is increasingly propagated on television and in films. And it is strongly reinforced in colleges and universities.

Nor, curiously, has the appearance of AIDS affected the growing acceptance of homosexuality as a completely legitimate "alternative lifestyle." If anything, the opposite has been the case, perhaps because gay-rights activists and their straight supporters have been so successful in spreading the notion that heterosexuals are as threatened by AIDS as are homosexuals. One consequence of this may have been to remove the additional obstacle which the fear of AIDS would otherwise have placed in the way of male waverers who are tempted by homosexuality (and who, in an age of aggressive feminism, may also be even more frightened of girls than they would formerly have been).

In depicting these developments, I am not endorsing the "seduction" theory of the genesis of homosexuality. That is, I do not believe that one's sexual orientation is significantly affected simply by a traumatic, early sexual encounter, be it actual genital contact or simply an emotional attachment. However, if learning has a role in fixing sexual orientation, it is not unreasonable to suppose that the values of friends, as well as the gender of those with whom one first enjoys the raptures of erotic love, will influence the direction of future sexual preference.

Here again, I repeat there are certainly many at either end of the continuum who from earliest memory are so strongly attracted either to those of their own or to those of the other sex as to be impervious to change, whatever the environment. But it is a good bet that substantial numbers of children have the capacity to grow in either direction. Such young waverers, who until now have been raised in an environment overwhelmingly biased toward heterosexuality, might succumb to the temptations of homosexuality in a social climate that was entirely evenhanded in its treatment of the two orientations.

Hence to the extent that society has an interest both in reproducing itself and in strengthening the institution of the family—and to the extent that parents have an interest in reducing the risk that their children will become homosexual—there is warrant for resisting the movement to abolish all societal distinctions between homosexual and heterosexual.

▼ ▼ ▼

Here we confront a dilemma: how can we rid society of irrational prejudice against gays if explicit evidence of society's bias against homosexuality is an important element in the process by which many children become straight adults?

I do not know the answer, nor, I think, does anyone else. But in the absence of an answer, we proceed as if the dilemma did not exist. Already, in many circles, any who question any part of the gay-rights agenda are branded bigots and homophobes, deserving only of obloquy. Why?

A principal reason is that most straights have acquaintances and many have close friends or relatives, sometimes their own children, who are homosexual. Knowing how much these have suffered in the past; aware that in all respects other than sexual orientation they differ not at all from straights; seeing how much homosexuals have gained through the changes already accomplished, we are reluctant to acknowledge that some social distinctions may still be justified. In addition, most well-educated people, identifying

the plight of homosexuals with that of racial minorities and women, conclude that there is no more basis for discriminating between gay and straight than between men and women or between those of dark and light skin.

It is indubitable, however, that skin color and gender are genetically determined, whereas it is certain that—often, if not always—the postnatal environment influences sexual orientation. Until we know otherwise, we must assume that our conscious attitudes and behavior toward homosexuality play a part in this process. At present this is only speculation, but it is a more plausible speculation than that which posits no connection between sexual orientation and social mores.

In this state of uncertainty, there is no justification for governmental action giving homosexuals a special status and making it illegal to discriminate in any way on grounds of sexual orientation. The question is best handled by allowing individuals and institutions to act as they will—within the civil-rights boundaries that currently protect everyone, gay and straight alike. But the argument offered here—that we know too little about the genesis of sexual orientation safely to outlaw discrimination in all areas—points to a few guidelines.

Basing myself on this argument, I would deny homosexual couples the privilege of adoption and, in custody cases involving natural parents, I would discriminate in favor of a straight parent over a gay one, other things being equal. Similarly, organizations like the Boy Scouts, whose *raison d'etre* is to shape the character and psyche of growing children, should remain free to exclude avowed homosexuals from their ranks. Schools should also be able to insist that homosexual elementary- and secondary-school teachers not flaunt their sexual orientation in ways likely to influence their pupils. Nor should schools be forced to authorize the formation of gay and lesbian student organizations, let alone to propagandize their pupils. How this is to be squared with the First Amendment I leave to the courts; certainly the problem of just how and where to draw the line will fuel endless debate in many a school committee.

Though I am uneasy at the spectacle of assertively homosexual resident advisers in undergraduate dormitories, I doubt that colleges should restrict gays—some of whom are our best teachers—in any way. (My own institution, Harvard, ever at the cutting edge, has long since banned discrimination on the basis of sexual preference, as has the Commonwealth of Massachusetts.) Since sexual orientation may well be settled by college age, there is less warrant for discrimination in higher education.

On the other hand, many youngsters still become sexually active only in their late teens, so this may be a time when the waverers among them are at a critical point in the determination of their predominant orientation. The uncertainty is such that colleges should be free to adopt differing policies. (Many religious institutions, of course, regard homosexuality as sinful and will want to discriminate against gays on that ground—but that is a different question.)

▼ ▼ ▼

I believe my obvious ambivalence about the appropriate role for gays in a straight society is widely shared. For that reason, and because my main purpose is to promote the kind of reasoned discussion that has been conspicuously absent to date, let me briefly state three counter-arguments that occur to me.

Treating homosexuals differently in any way condemns youngsters, who from earliest memory know themselves to be gay, to growing up in full awareness of society's desire that they become what they cannot be—straight. An eagerly awaited result of the gay-rights movement has been the possibility of creating a better environment for such youngsters by including homosexual role models among teachers, care-givers, etc. Whether the lot of these children will be much eased in a society that is tolerant of gays, while explicit about limiting their role, is highly questionable. Children are cruel, and just as short or unathletic or homely boys and girls suffer for their state, so would those who differ in sexual preference.

More basic is the contention of my comfortably gay friend, mentioned earlier, that the advantages of being straight are so obvious that none can ever mistake them. My initial response was that this view is an artifact of cultural history, in which homophobia has long been so widespread that it is almost impossible to imagine what society would look like in its absence. But, conceivably, there is something inherent in the human psyche that prompts everyone to recognize that heterosexuality is preferable, whatever his own orientation. Like an instinct, this may be ineradicable. If so, even total success in abolishing overt discrimination would do little to increase the odds of waverers growing up to be gay rather than

straight.

Obviously, this would blow my thesis right out of the water. It is not, however, an argument that will appeal to gay activists, implying as it does that even in an entirely nondiscriminatory world a homosexual orientation would always be recognized as a misfortune. Still, in the present state of our knowledge, this is among the possibilities.

The most persuasive objection is one that will find favor especially with those, gay and straight, who have never wavered in their sexual orientation and thus have no feeling for the many who have. It is this: precisely *because* we do not understand the role of environment or nurture in the development of sexual preference, we should proceed to abolish all discrimination against homosexuals. We know success in that endeavor would make life much easier for gays, and we do not know that it would do any harm. Indeed, it may even be that the environmental factors which contribute to homosexuality are completely independent of our conscious attitudes and behaviors. If common sense seems to suggest otherwise, on scientific questions common sense is more often wrong than right. Nutrition, hormonal processes, unknown family circumstances, or social interactions that apparently have nothing to do with sexual orientation—any or all of these (sometimes, perhaps, combined with a genetic predisposition) may be responsible for the effect.

According to this line of thought, reason suggests not—as I have insisted—that we abandon the drive to abolish all distinctions between gays and straights, but that we accept some risk in order to seize the good represented by a society free of discrimination. The risk we would accept is only that a certain number of children would live gay lives when they might have lived straight ones. But in a genuinely nondiscriminatory world that should be no great tragedy; in fact, if overpopulation continues to threaten the planet, gay adults might become more socially valuable than straight ones.

▼ ▼ ▼

But be all that as it may, we must start from where we are. And where we are is that increasing numbers of straights, as well as gays, are determined to rid society of irrational hatred of homosexuals. At the same time, the heterosexual community remains firm in its conviction that it is better to be straight than gay, and few parents want to do anything that might increase the chances of their children growing up homosexual. Though our knowledge of how society and culture affect the development of sexual preference is sadly limited, we dare not risk failing to give children clear, repeated signals as to society's preference.

Even as we move to abolish gay-baiting and gay-bashing, therefore, we have good reason to resist the demand of gay-rights activists that any and every difference in the treatment of homo-sexuals be entirely outlawed. We must be sophisticated enough to change the attitudes and actions that are prompted only by irrational prejudice, while retaining distinctions that may be necessary to ensure that all children clearly understand the desirability of growing up to be heterosexual adults.

# | 95 |

# *In God's Country*

## JOHN WEIR

I am a middle-class gay white man. You may think that's no big deal, but I know plenty of people who have a problem with it. I am standing with at least a hundred of them right now. Regular suburban moms and dads and young professionals and teenage kids with hip-hop haircuts, they could be a roomful of everyone you know. But they happen to be on the cutting edge of a national political movement. They are warriors for Christ. Their hands are raised to greet the Holy Ghost, and to push homosexuality back into the closet. I am a homosexual in their antigay activist church.

In other words, I am preaching with the enemy. This is the Springs of Life Ministries, a Christian evangelical church in the high Mojave Desert an hour northeast of Los Angeles. It is the church that reordained disgraced televangelist Jim Bakker before he went to prison. And its leaders Ty and Jeannette Beeson executive-produced *The Gay Agenda*, the notorious twenty-minute video supplied to the Joint Chiefs of Staff and Congress during last year's debate on gays in the military. The tape includes, among other so-called truths about homosexuals, the claim that 17 percent of us like to roll in each other's feces and eat it, an activity identified by a Santa Cruz physician as "mudrolling."

*The Gay Agenda* started an area trend. Last summer, Reverend Lou Sheldon's Orange County-based Traditional Values Coalition, a Christian lobbying group, produced *Gay Rights/Special Rights* to generate antigay feeling in the black community. The forty-minute tape depicts homosexuals as a gang of high-income whites co-opting the civil rights movement in order to recruit the young, cow the government, mesmerize the press, and spread disease.

Both videotapes and a dozen others like them resemble Nazi propaganda that claimed that Jews are lice-infested money-lending whoremongers. The tapes are also extremely effective. They helped overturn or prevent the passage of gay rights laws in places like Colorado and Cincinnati, Ohio. And they will be used this fall to sway voters considering antigay legislation in Arizona, Idaho, Nevada, Michigan, Missouri, Oregon, and Washington, and in counties, cities, and towns across the country. The videos feign objectivity, as if to enlighten rather than prejudice viewers. But their power goes beyond reason: They tell middle Americans that I eat shit.

▼ ▼ ▼

I am standing in a fundamentalist church in Lancaster, California, on a chilly night around Christmas in order to deny this. The problem is, there is nobody here scary enough to confront. The members of Ty Beeson's congregation aren't

*Details*, May 1994, pp. 116+.

Nazis. They're nice-guy next-door neighbors. And the Springs of Life church isn't a massive Orwellian Ministry of Truth, but a long, low, flat, pink building surrounded by mountains and desert scrub. It is as modest as any other structure in town, including the gay bar. But unlike the Back Door, where patrons park behind and slip in unnoticed, Springs of Life has its name on the building, and its celebrants enter in front.

I was expecting a Klan rally, but instead I have walked into *Sing Along With Mitch.* There is a stage with a gospel rock band, six vocalists with hand mikes, and two people with overhead projectors flashing lyrics on the walls. Parishioners are clapping and smiling and raising their hands into the air, palms forward, to receive the Holy Spirit. These are people who listen regularly to sermons about Third World "heathens coming into America and beginning to rip our prosperity off," to quote their pastor, Ty Beeson. But they don't seem hateful. They seem like my high school homeroom twenty years later. We could probably get together and reminisce about the Allman Brothers.

We sing for an hour. Then the music subsides, and one of the onstage singers comes down center to a podium. It turns out to be Beeson, whose sermons include snide references not just to immigrants, but intellectuals, liberals, homosexuals, homeless people, and the media. A small effusive man in a business suit with white hair curled close to his head, he is a former realtor, with a salesman's talent for making people feel simultaneously cared for and intimidated. "Read the map, stupid," he says, scolding us to open up our moral guidebook, the Bible, and find the way.

"Hey, God!" a parishioner says cheerfully. The young married couple beside me get out their Bible and a pen and paper for notes. This is not just a church but an activist enclave, and Beeson refers to his parishioners as soldiers engaged in a war. He talks about "volunteering" for the Lord and taking America back. Looking around the room, I can see people losing themselves to the romance of becoming "empowered." I know their glassy-eyed expression intimately, for I have worn it myself at ACT UP demonstrations and at AIDS and gay activist meetings. It is the blissful, thoughtless glow of surrendering to the collective agenda.

Beeson introduces the sermon's main text, from John 10:10: "The thief cometh not, but for to steal, and to kill, and to destroy. . . ." This is an aerospace and military town suffering through a post–cold war economy in a state with the worst unemployment rate in the country. It must be comforting to have a demon. I have demons, too. So when Beeson asks us to join together in rebuking them, I willingly comply.

"Devourer, you are rebuked," I say along with everyone else in the room, happy for the moment to be part of something larger than myself. "Now point to your neighbor and say it," Beeson commands. I shoot my finger into the faces of the young couple beside me, who lent me a pen and paper for notes. "Devourer, you are rebuked," I say, thinking of evils outside my control, like AIDS. The couple says it back to me, thinking perhaps of pro-choice supporters killing their unborn children, or schoolteachers passing out condoms, or men seducing little boys, or, well, me.

After all, it's in the Bible, stupid. Leviticus 18:22: "Thou shalt not lie with mankind, as with womankind: It is abomination." Furthermore, "If a man lies with a male as with a woman . . . they must be put to death. . . ." Then there is Paul in the New Testament getting uptight about the "effeminate," who are denied the Kingdom of God, along with fornicators, idolaters, adulterers, and abusers of themselves. Suddenly I remember: I am the Devourer. Returning my pen apologetically to my neighbors, I fold my hands nervously and wait for the service to end.

▼ ▼ ▼

Evangelical christians are kind of like the guys who called me faggot in high school. Unforgiving in public, they can be tolerant, even tender, when you get them alone. But just when I start to like them okay, they remind me who their friends are, and I end up cursing myself for forgetting what I already know.

What I know is this: There are more than 60 million born-again Christians in America, including Pentecostals, Charismatics, Baptists, and some Episcopalians, Methodists, and Presbyterians. Their religious practices differ, but they all read the Bible faithfully or literally and worry that our country has strayed too far from its teachings. Along with voters who earn more than $200,000 a year, they are the Republican party's largest and most faithful constituency. The moral territory they claim is anything involving sex, the family, education, and religious expression. More and more, it is becoming their political agenda.

They are represented by lobbyists in Washington, D.C., supported by wealthy Southern Californian heirs and entrepreneurs, catered to by politicians whom they helped elect, and linked by a sophisticated communications dynasty. Their nationwide cable broadcasting networks attract millions of viewers each week. Their organizations share data banks and massive mailing lists. People contributing to one of the major evangelical Christian outlets—such as Dr. Beverly LaHaye's Concerned Women for America, the largest women's political group in the country, or televangelist Pat Robertson's popular viewer-supported TV show, the *700 Club*—are tracked by statisticians and targeted for fund-raising pleas and information circulars from numerous others. Someone buying *Gay Rights/Special Rights* may end up on mailing lists for a dozen other antigay videos, some of which are titled *Homosexuality: #1 Threat to Public Health*, *Child Molestation and Homosexuality*, and *The Gay Conspiracy*.

This is something else I know: Homosexuality is revitalizing their movement. According to *Los Angeles Times* reporter David Colker, who reported on *The Gay Agenda* in early 1993, the Beesons' Lancaster ministry was suffering from a dwindling membership and reduced capital before it got into the video business. And evangelical leaders and strategists around the country, deprived of the communist threat and unable to win massive support for the antiabortion struggle, have rediscovered a longtime adversary.

▼ ▼ ▼

It is Thursday evening at the weekly "inside the issues" seminar at the Springs of Life Ministries. Ty is out with the flu, and Jeannette Beeson is presiding alone over an audience of fifty parishioners at tables spread through the hall. Jeannette is dressed in a pretty green crushed-velvet suit, with her shoulder-length brown hair feathered to frame her heart-shaped face. Accompanied by a pianist, she is reading excerpts from recent newspapers and periodicals, reinterpreting news stories from a righteous Christian perspective.

Like many evangelical Christians, Jeannette knows more about homosexuality than I do. She combs the straight press for stories about gay politics, gender bending, and sex scandals, and her regular reading list includes mainstream gay magazines like *The Advocate*, *Out*, and *Frontiers*, as well as local gay newspapers that I have never heard of. Having written for some of the magazines she refers to, I feel an odd intimacy with her. After all, no one is as attentive as your foes.

"Now listen to this," she says, picking up a copy of *Frontiers*. "Here's a story written by a homosexual with AIDS, who says he wants to make his illness sound sexy." Her voice is piercing and bitter, like a soap opera actress going for pathos but managing only sarcastic disdain. She reads a few lines from the tongue-in-cheek story, whose irony eludes her, before putting it aside in disgust. "It isn't enough that they're diseased," she says, "but now they want to talk about how much fun it is."

Moving on to a story in *Out* about gay marriage, she makes a point of mispronouncing author Michelangelo Signorile's last name before condemning his piece. "They want the same rights as everyone else," she says, appalled by what I take for granted. But her contempt is not limited to homosexuals. She goes off on angry riffs about homeless people, cross-dressers, Michael Jackson, men who wear earrings, Madonna, and Barbra Streisand, whose support of the Gay and Lesbian Alliance Against Defamation and various AIDS charities are indecencies to keep in mind, she warns, "the next time you hear someone say what a great woman she is."

She is a parody of Christian unforgiving. I have to keep reminding myself that she's not Dana Carvey doing a routine on *Saturday Night Live*. It is hard to believe that she isn't kidding when, for instance, she launches into a tirade over a local newspaper story about Barbie and G.I. Joe. A group called the Barbie Liberation Organization had switched the dolls' voice boxes, so that Barbie said things like "Eat lead, Cobra," while G.I. Joe talked excitedly about shopping and school. The gender switching outrages Jeannette. "What is the country coming to when we can't even buy the Barbie doll we want?" she asks, fully in earnest. "This is how they advance their agenda. It starts with male rock stars wearing earrings, and then Barbie, and the next thing you know, we can't tell the difference between men and women anymore. We have to draw the line somewhere."

▼ ▼ ▼

The line between out homosexuals and born-again Christians is fuzzier than you think. We both have big martyr complexes. And our movements are based on equally vague intuitions of faith and sexuality. After all, it's just as hard to document a conversation with the Holy Ghost as it is to explain a sexual impulse. Christians find God, homosexuals find themselves, and our common battleground is cluttered with egotists immersed in self-discovery. No one in America is more confessional than gays and Holy Ghosters—our coming-out stories and their tales of miraculous conversion are tailor-made for *Oprah*. Perhaps that is why we find ourselves so often facing each other on daytime tabloid TV.

And it is hard to imagine our public confrontations occurring between other adversaries. Last September, when the Reverend Lou Sheldon appeared at a Sunday night service at San Francisco's Hamilton Square Baptist Church, he was greeted outside by a gang of pierced and depilated radical dykes and fags, dyed in war paint and ready for battle. Of course, one of them was dressed as a nun, which is mistakenly aiming at Catholics when your real target is, say, Charismatic Presbyterians. But the radical queer community doesn't bother to differentiate among its enemies.

Similarly, the evangelical movement doesn't make distinctions when it is confronted with what Sheldon calls "a bunch of half-naked savages." Sheldon acts as if all gays get crazed and rampant in public. And a Christian woman confronting a queer activist at Hamilton Square seemed to think she was polling the entire homosexual community when she asked, "What do you want from us?" Of course, the activist played into her fears and shouted, "We're coming for your children, and what we can't fuck we'll eat!"

There is an irony gap here. Bible-reading Christians don't have a sense of humor about biblical issues. When they see people outside a church dressed up like demons from hell, they seem to think life is imitating scripture. According to an eyewitness inside the church, Lou Sheldon was so overcome when queers disrupted the service that he fled to the choir. Backed into a corner by a pay phone, he dialed 911. Shortly afterward more police arrived. Now, you can see this as Sheldon acting out his Christian martyr complex, or you can see it as his getting evidence to support it. You can call it gay self-empowerment, or misbegotten faggot nonsense. All I know is, if my life were a morality play in which I cast some people as saviors and others as devourers, I know which role I would offer to Queer Nation.

▼ ▼ ▼

Christian evangelicals make so many unself-conscious references to the devil, Satan, the devourer, the thief who comes for our prosperity, our happiness, our children, that we think they have to be kidding. But they are dead serious.

They are also extremely smart. For instance, they have embarked on a shrewd campaign to convince Americans that homosexuals are guilty of everything the evangelicals are attempting. When Christians say homosexuals want to take over your schools, captivate your offspring, run your media, and irreversibly damage the quality of your life, they are really talking about themselves. Enforced school prayer, the compulsory teaching of creationism as a viable, *scientific* alternative to the theory of evolution, capital punishment for abortionists, adulterers, and homosexuals—these are just a few of the political causes that some members of the movement are seriously pursuing. In comparison, my goals are merely defensive: I want legal protection from discrimination. I want to be sure I won't get fired, or thrown out of my apartment, or denied medical care or government assistance because I'm gay.

But it's even simpler than that. Days before sitting in on Jeannette Beeson's seminar, I spend Christmas Eve at a buffet dinner party in West Hollywood, given by a gay man from Pakistan who shares a modest white stucco house with his mother. She holds court in the front room, surrounded by her son's friends—twenty or thirty neatly dressed gay men with nowhere else to go on this particular holiday. Some of them are exiled from their families, some are here because their lovers can't take them home, and one of them shows up with his mother in time to sing Christmas carols. We eat politely off paper plates, carol, and go to Christmas Mass at the Episcopal church across the street. Singing "O Holy Night" with a bunch of gay men and two of their mothers, it occurs to me that the gay agenda is just this—to be able to introduce your mom to your friends, especially at Christmas.

▼ ▼ ▼

But evangelical Christians continue to set the terms of the debate with sermons and videos and TV shows and newsletters insisting that gays want more than their fair share. And Christian strategists not only have immediate access to their audience, but seemingly unlimited tax-free funding. Churchgoers contribute anything from twenty-five dollars a year to 10 percent of their income to their church and "related ministries." Nonprofit, nondenominational political lobbying groups like the Traditional Values Coalition are wholly supported by tax-free donations from their member churches and individual contributors. The threat of the so-called homosexual agenda is an extremely lucrative resource.

"Boy, those tapes are a gold mine," says Dr. Mel White, a Dallas-based minister for the gay and lesbian Metropolitan Community Church, who describes himself in tabloid-headline fashion as "*the* ghostwriter for the religious Right." Until he came out as gay in 1987, White wrote books with Billy Graham, Pat Robertson, and Jerry Falwell. Now he is the reprobate child of the evangelical movement, trumpeting his apostasy like former goody-two-shoes daughter Patti Davis ratting on mama Nancy Reagan. He remembers one conversation with Falwell where the Reverend said, "Thank God for those gays. They get me all the publicity I need. If they didn't exist, I'd have to invent them."

Surely homosexuality has been a godsend to the Springs of Life. *The Gay Agenda*, released in October 1992 and priced at $13.95, sold over 100,000 copies in just over a year, grossing almost $1.5 million against a production cost of "in the neighborhood of $75,000," according to the tape's producer, Bill Horn. Lou Sheldon estimates that he's sold and/or distributed 20,000 copies of *Gay Rights/Special Rights*, available since July 1993 for $19.95 a piece. He claims the video, which cost at least $50,000 to produce, won't earn out for a year. But White scoffs at that. "Sheldon is giving those tapes away to people who give him contributions," White says. "And a twenty-dollar video is suddenly worth $100 or $1,000 in donations. There's no calculating how much money they're making." More than just an abomination, homosexuality is damn good business.

▼ ▼ ▼

It also makes everyone uncomfortable, which is what religious zealots count on to get antigay laws passed. I am driving very fast down Highway 5 when the Pacific Ocean suddenly opens out spectacularly on my right and the radio crackles nostalgically with an old Ten Years After song, "I'd Love to Change the World." When I was twelve, the band's lead singer, Alvin Lee, was the essence of cool. But now I am surprised by the song's opening words, "Everywhere is freaks and hairies, dykes and fairies, tell me where is sanity." Lee isn't mocking homosexuals, he's aping the way people talked about anyone who lived on the fringe. But if the line isn't overtly antigay, it reflects a society that is. Members of the religious Right aren't imposing antigay feelings on an unwilling world. They are exploiting a sentiment that aleady exists in the culture—nobody likes a homo.

▼ ▼ ▼

Lou Sheldon's son Steve is a typical strategist for the antigay religious Right. Fresh-faced in blue duck trousers, a white button-down shirt and tie, he looks like a smart errand boy for a Republican senatorial campaign—not surprising since he identifies himself as a policymaker first, a Christian second. "We're a lobbying group, not a church," he stresses when he comes out of his office to meet me. Indeed, the atmosphere at the Traditional Values Coalition, in Anaheim near Disneyland, is corporate rather than religious. A receptionist named Carol sits at her computer terminal behind a sliding glass partition, taking calls. "No speakee Spanishee," she sweetly tells a caller, in a hokey Spanish accent which is my first clue that I have passed beyond the Orange curtain, from multicultural Los Angeles to homogeneous Orange County, California.

When Steve greets me, I am sitting on a black leather couch clutching a copy of *Gay Rights/Special Rights*. We shake hands and I ask to meet his father. Prickly but polite, he explains that Lou is in Missouri today, advising voters about passing a statewide antigay law.

"Why did you want to speak to my dad?" he asks.

"I wanted to talk about his videotape," I say, holding it up. "It's a pretty impressive piece of work. And I've seen a few like it. I saw *The Gay Agenda*, and I just bought one called *The Gay Conspiracy*."

"What's that?" Steve says, finally looking interested.

"I just got it today," I say, proud of my discovery. "Just down the freeway from here in Santa Ana. At a place called the Citizens for Excellence in Education."

"Bob Simonds' group has a tape?" Steve asks, interrupting me.

"Yeah, I haven't seen it yet," I say casually. Almost winking, I add, "I'll let you know how it is."

Steve smiles, and suddenly we are on the same side. I don't tell him I'm gay. Instead I compliment him. I tell him how startled I was to see gay and lesbian leaders like former National Gay and Lesbian Task Force head Torie Osborn and playwright and AIDS activist Larry Kramer quoted in the video.

"It was smart how you used their own words against them," I say sincerely. The tape also includes footage of gay men and lesbians speaking to camera crews who never identified themselves as antigay activists. "They played right into your hands. Even some of the leadership."

"Yeah, I like to think of us as kind of like Get Smart and K.A.O.S.," he says, putting a sitcom spin on our relationship.

But his joking tone is a tease. He doesn't really think that homosexuality is anything to laugh about. I am remembering the Sheldons' videotape. The slickest of its kind, it contains the following elements, now standard in the growing antigay genre:

—testimony from doctors and nurses deploring gay sex acts

—writhing naked men and bare-chested women at gay rights marches screaming to overtake the world

—pedophiles demanding a lower age of consent

—"reformed" homosexuals testifying about the sickness of "the gay lifestyle"

—leathermen proclaiming that violent sex brings them closer together ("I like electricity," one says)

—baffled children weeping at drag queens

The images are lifted from gay and lesbian gatherings, the quotes from public interviews, the statistics from medical journals—it is all very convincing. And not all of it is a lie. Taken out of context, a lot of public celebrations look satanic. Christian dogmatists understand this. They know best how to stereotype the gay community, using their words and actions against them.

Of course, *Gay Rights/Special Rights* is ultimately a piece of soft-core titillation about what men do to each other. Its subtext is the understanding all men share about their indiscriminate sex drives. Talking to Steve Sheldon, I feel like his dark sexual double. Contemporaries, we grew up in the same culture. We both watched *Get Smart*. And to him, it seems, a gay man is just a straight guy on a dick-driven sex binge.

▼ ▼ ▼

I am thirty-five years old. I have been arrested at Act Up demonstrations. I have outed myself in print. I have worn pink triangles on my lapel. But I have never uttered the words "I am homosex-

ual" or "I'm gay" to anyone. I came out to my brother by making pointed references to Lou Reed lyrics. My mother figured it out during a conversation we had about the difference between me and George Peppard in *Breakfast at Tiffany's*. And what I told my father, haltingly, was, "My sexual preference is men," which kept me from having to mouth the sinister, reptilian word "homosexual" or the even worse "gay," which sounds like it involves lots of pastel colors and thousands of dollars in decorating fees.

But after two weeks of talking to members of the evangelical Christian movement, all across the sprawling suburban future-world of Southern California, it occurs to me that few of them have ever met a real homosexual. Perhaps they face them on TV debates, or help them seek aversion therapy, or film them gyrating naked on floats at gay pride parades. Ty Beeson took his congregation to see the AIDS quilt when it was on display in Lancaster last fall, and he must have encountered some homosexuals there. But I begin to feel, perhaps naively, that what is needed is discreet engagements over coffee—homosexuals sharing Maxwell House moments with members of the Christian Right.

So on the last day of my journey, with Patti Smith coming over my rental car radio—"Jesus died for somebody's sins, but not mine," she sings, and I admire her certainty—I head up the Golden State from Los Angeles to Highway 14 for the Antelope Valley, to tell someone at Springs of Life that I'm gay.

I choose Bill Horn. As the media spokesperson for the Report, the ministry's media production arm, he produced and promoted five antigay videos, *Sexual Orientation or Sexual Deviation: You Decide*; *The Gay Agenda*; *The Gay Agenda in Public Education*; *The Gay Agenda: The March on Washington*; and *Gay Pride '93*. He is the propaganda minister of the antigay movement, but like Steve Sheldon, he's just a regular guy. He is my age, with clear eyes and an open face anchored by a sandy-colored mustache. Like my own brother, he is devoted to his children, whose photographs decorate the walls and desk of his office. And like both my brother and my father, he has worked in television, as a sportscaster for a Bakersfield affiliate. If business is family, we are almost related.

He greets me at the door to his office in sweats and sneakers and apologizes for being in a rush. He has just been talking about homosexuality on a phone hookup to listeners of KCNR in Salt

Lake City—"not a Christian but a secular station," he assures me. After this, he has to get ready for a business trip to Iowa. He travels almost every weekend to speak out against homosexuality on radio or television programs.

Setting up my tape recorder in his crowded gray office, I am trying not to notice the autographed pictures of Colin Powell, Dan Quayle, and Pat Buchanan—high-profile leaders with antigay stances—on the wall above my head. Letting him know I'm gay would be like going back to my high school and telling the big-shouldered guys who used to call me faggot, "You're right."

I'm not sure I'm ready to take that risk. But when Bill starts spewing his prerecorded thoughts about homosexuals, I have to do something. "The average homosexual is dead by the age of forty-one," he says flatly. "We have tremendous love for the homosexual, and we want them out of the lifestyle, because"—he opens a local gay rag and turns to the death notices—"when you pick up any gay newspaper, look at the obituaries." He stabs the page with his index finger. "Thirty years old." He stabs it again, pointing to a photograph. "Look at this guy. When was he born? I'm sure he's in his thirties." Another stab. "Nineteen fifty-five to 1993. And if you really want to have compassion for people, then tell them what they're doing causes death and destruction."

I am nodding, surprised he can't hear my heart beating. "You know, Bill," I start softly, "I gotta tell you, I'm gay."

The tape recorder is running. He looks at me, not astonished, but with something like concern.

"You didn't tell me that," he says quietly.

"No, I didn't tell you that."

I don't know what to expect—whether he will get out the Lysol and fumigate the office, or embrace me in Christian forgiving, or ask me to leave the room. Maybe he is worried about how this will sound months from now, when Jeannette Beeson reads it to the congregation. "See, I knew, John." He uses my name almost tenderly as an intimacy between us. "So you're gay. I wish you weren't," he says, nodding to the obit page. "But it doesn't matter. So you're gay? So what?"

It's not exactly a Kodak moment. But it is remotely comforting. I am just beginning to trust him when he starts in on what homosexuals do, this time focusing not just on sex but money and power.

He makes a series of dubious statements about homosexuals, depicting us as primarily high-income, hypereducated, and male. The people he describes do not sound like the homosexuals I know. He says the average gay man makes more than $55,000 a year, a figure he attributes to the *Wall Street Journal*. He says 60 percent of all gay men are college graduates. He tells me that 65 percent of all gay men have traveled overseas, and when I admit that I have as well, he calls me a typical homosexual. He asks if I have produced five children, like he has. He says the problem with gay men is that men don't withhold sex from each other like women withhold it from men. He asks me flat out what homosexuals do, whether it's oral sex or anal sex or what. "There's only two holes, after all," he says.

I am a thirty-five-year-old man discussing the intricacies of anal sex with a straight guy who makes antigay videos, but in spite of ourselves, we bond. Because we are both recovered boys who had to find a way to fit the mold of masculinity, with its impossibly rigid parameters. Bill suggests that gay men come from homes with absent fathers, yet in America it seems that everybody's dad is missing or abusive (although my dad was neither). And if Bill is anything like me, he still had to figure out on his own what it means to be a man.

It occurs to me that what I call homophobia may just be Bill's way of measuring how differently we turned out as men. I don't have photographs of five children on my desk at home. I don't have a family of dependents to educate and support. I have HIV-positive friends to care for. But what Bill sees when he looks at me is promiscuity, affluence, mobility. And what he sees when he watches a group of gays and lesbians protesting antigay legislation is not an oppressed minority, but a bunch of middle-class white people demanding recognition of their entitlement.

Bill and Steve and I are just alike. We are white men living in America who have been told all our lives that we are owed the world. But now our high school roles are reversed. It looks to them like I am getting every sixteen-year-old schoolboy's dream—plenty of sex, a lot of money, and the freedom to go wherever I want. It must seem that between prom night and their thirtieth birthdays the lisping high school faggots somehow got ahead. The idea that we now want more must look like not playing fair.

▼ ▼ ▼

It isn't enough to say that the Christian Right is homophobic. If faith in God and sexual desire are ineffable, so is fear of other people.

I am driving as fast as I can down the freeway to Los Angeles, away from the biblical paradise, breaking the speed limit in order to get back to Sodom and mingle with my own. Jethro Tull is singing "Jesus saves" on the radio, and I am thinking, For what? For a utopia where every man is manly enough and doesn't have sex outside of marriage and never sleeps with other people's spouses and who worships no god but the god of Moses and who never masturbates, or anyway not without remorse—what man is that? The evangelical movement is not just about pushing a bunch of homosexuals back into the closet. It's about being so intolerant that the kingdom of God, when it comes, will look like the landscape from my window as I reach the Escondido summit—vast, Edenic, and completely uninhabited.

# V. C
# A PLACE AT WHICH TABLE?

Sexual acts between members of the same sex occur in all societies, but only in some instances have they become the organizing principle for distinctive subcultures, and only in recent times have these subcultures achieved a level of public visibility comparable to ethnic and racial communities (Weeks 1981). The emergence of modern gay and lesbian subcultures (which are not necessarily the same) was made possible by the transformation and dislocations wrought by industrialization, which "brought rapid growth to the cities, often rupturing traditional family relations" (Adam 1978:25) and creating opportunities for gays and lesbians to congregate more or less anonymously. For women, even more than for men, the movement "from the domestic sphere into the public realm in education, work and politics allowed them to function somewhat independently of their families. The availability of jobs for women was particularly important because it gave them the opportunity to support themselves" (Kennedy and Davis 1993:9).

As unprecedented numbers migrated from rural to urban areas, there grew up in these expanding cities a wide range of voluntary communities and forms of association. Not surprisingly, marginal territories were the only ones accessible to these pioneers of gay and lesbian institutions and communities. Declining working-class neighborhoods and abandoned industrial real estate offered spaces in which deviant subcultural identity could be coalesced around such institutions as bars. Lesbian archivist Joan Nestle cites the recollections of a lesbian musician about

the Moody Garden Gang, a butch-femme working-class lesbian community in Lowell, Massachusetts, in the 1950s:

> It was our Mecca, we were family, and we had found a home. . . . So many of the kids ask what's so special about Moody Gardens. To us it was our world, a small world, yes, but if you were starving you didn't refuse a slice of bread, and we were starving just for the feeling of having others around us. We were kings of the hill. We were the *Moody Gardens*. . . . If there hadn't been little Moody Gardens all over the world, we wouldn't even be allowed to get together as we do today and feel, in a small way, we are being accepted and we are not alone. (Nestle 1987:113)

Accelerated by the dislocations brought about by World War II, the migration of lesbian and gay people to large cities began to change the face of urban neighborhoods as gay communities began to emerge across North America (D'Emilio 1989). Unlike the walled-in ghettoes of some European cities or the clearly marked ethnic or racial quarters in cities around the world, North American lesbian and gay communal identity through the 1960s was centered almost exclusively on bars and, in the case of gay men, bathhouses. Beyond the city limits the remote and unfashionable real estate of Provincetown, Key West, and Fire Island sheltered the growth of lesbian and gay resort communities (Newton 1993).

The first explosion of lesbian and gay liberation after Stonewall was fashioned in the spirit of the

1960s, setting out to transform society and sweep constraining sex and gender roles into the dustheap of history. What was unleashed, however, was a furor of community building and commercialism that created an array of institutions and spaces in which lesbian and gay cultures flourished and expanded. Generally setting roots in marginal spots—whether remote rural communes or warehouse districts in big cities—where possibly hostile neighbors were few and costs were low, lesbian and gay people began to expand the infrastructure of collective existence.

Over the course of the 1970s gay men in European and North American cities developed a fairly complete set of basic social services beyond the bars. These included bookstores, churches and synagogues, travel agencies, periodicals, political clubs, historical societies, charities, a savings-and-loan association, etc. Indeed, an entire *Gay Yellow Pages* in San Francisco features myriad gay businesses and services, just as do the *Hispanic Yellow Pages* and *Chinese Yellow Pages* there (Murray 1992:111–112).

This process of urban community and institution building has come to be tagged with the often pejorative term *gentrification*. But the reality is more complex than the term suggests. The best-known example of this is the fact that "the process of urban renovation in San Francisco has been largely . . . triggered by gay people" (Castells 1983:158). Geographer Barbara Weightman noted that "about 90% of the houses involved in San Francisco's Victorian Alliance Program are being rehabilitated by gay individuals or couples" and goes on to say that, because gays are "more willing than straights to live in urban transitional areas . . . where middle-class families with children are reluctant to go," they might be viewed as "urban pioneers" (1981:109).

There is another side to this, of course. The rhetoric of gentrification tends to ignore the reality that the upgrading of "transitional" neighborhoods by "urban pioneers" frequently involves the displacement of their mostly working-class, often elderly residents and communities of color. The newcomers often rehabilitate abandoned housing stock, but the resulting rise in real estate values tends to push up rentals and taxes for those living in the vicinity.

The process begins when "relatively low-wage gay renters" move into a run-down neighborhood where, "with the landlord's permission, they engage in . . . `incumbent upgrading' " putting in what has been called sweat equity" (Lauria and Knopp 1985:160). This first wave of low-wage gay residences in an urban area may attract other, more affluent gays to the neighborhood. These gay men (and, to a lesser degree, lesbians, who often have fewer economic resources) further build up the network of renovated housing and small businesses that constitutes an urban community.

Gay neighborhoods in cities across the country serve as places to which (mostly young) men and women escape in order to come out and as the bases for the formation of community economic and political power. What is often called a gay ghetto bears many similarities to urban communities created by other marginalized groups: "The territorial boundaries of a [gay] community are required for the same reasons that Jewish people in Europe, black people in America, and oppressed minorities all over the world have always needed them—for everyday survival" (Castells 1983:158). Yet, as Castells points out with reference to San Francisco, there is also a difference:

> Unlike other oppressed communities, gay people have raised the physical standards and economic value of the space they have occupied. . . . They have intentionally located themselves, individually or collectively, to build up a new community at a financial and social cost that only "moral refugees" are ready to pay. They have paid for their identity, and in doing so have most certainly gentrified their areas. They have also survived and learned to live their real life. At the same time, they have revived the colors of the painted facades, repaired the shaken foundations of the buildings, lit up the tempo of the street and helped make the city beautiful and alive, all in an age that has been grim for most of urban America. (1983:160f)

In 1981 Michael Denneny published a "Gay Manifesto for the 80's," proclaiming the need for gay people to construct and occupy (psychologically if not geographically) independent communities.

> If society tries to destroy us by first isolating us, it follows that what is necessary to fight back is not only defiance but the acknowledgment of a community and the construction of a world. . . . The further construction and consolidation of the gay ghetto is an immediate and necessary political objective. (1981:17)

While Denneny's analysis was acute and persuasive, he was overly optimistic in his declaration that gay people have no material demands to make on society: "We do not require social programs, jobs, day-care centers, educational and professional quotas, or any of the other legitimate demands of previously exploited minority groups. Our demands will not cost the body politic one cent" (17). In addition to his apparent obliviousness to the real needs of many lesbians and some gay men for day care and other social programs, this statement can only be read as tragically ironic, published as it was just months before the first reports of "a rare cancer among gay men."

The strength of these newly elaborated lesbian and gay communities was both severely tested and magnificently demonstrated when the AIDS epidemic exploded in the midst of the largest gay ghettoes. As the institutions of mainstream society circled their wagons, leaving gay men and the other "high-risk groups" outside, gay men and lesbians organized to provide care for people with AIDS and to fight for adequate public support for research and treatment. Derided by many as a commercialized and soulless culture, and rightly criticized for the racism and class bias it shares with the rest of society, the gay ghetto was revealed at the moment of crisis as a source of solidarity and power.

The 1980s were a decade of struggle, both within the sexual minority communities as the "sex wars" raged and beyond, as the resurgent right wing continued to use attacks on gay people in their organizing and fund-raising. In 1985, in a keynote speech to an organizing conference of the religious right, "How to Win an Election," Newt Gingrich stated, "AIDS will do more to direct America back to the cost of violating traditional values, and to make America aware of the dangers of certain behaviors than anything we've seen. For us, it's a great rallying cry." AIDS and political battles also made gay people visible to America as nothing before had done, however, and by the end of the decade we were an unavoidable part of the national landscape.

In her account of gay male subcultures in Chicago and Kansas City in the mid-1960s Esther Newton described two categories of homosexuals:

> The overts live their *entire* lives within the context of the community; the coverts live their entire *nonworking* lives within it. That is, the coverts are "straight" during working hours, but most social activities are conducted with and with reference to other homosexuals. These overts and coverts

together form the core of the homosexual community. (1979:21)

Writing in the early 1970s, Newton acknowledged that the term *community* might not be appropriate to characterize gay people, though by the time she was preparing the 1979 edition she noted that "homosexuals are much closer to constituting a political force than they were in 1968," thanks to the emergence of the younger generation of gay activists (1979:23n). Indeed, the institution and community building of the 1970s and 1980s created an array of possibilities for lesbian and gay people to live in multiple worlds without the subterfuges of previous decades. The successes of the lesbian and gay movement include the expansion of opportunities for integrating the private and public spheres of people's lives. Many who would have been among Newton's coverts are now able to live less constrained working lives (Woods 1993), while others still feel compelled to hide from family or colleagues (Yang, "Out of Asia," this volume).

One notable consequence of the changes wrought by the lesbian and gay movement was that conservative closet doors began to inch open. In the early 1980s rumors of the existence of gay Republicans would be confirmed only though scandal, as when Congressman Robert Bauman, chairman of the American Conservative Union, was arrested for soliciting sex with a male minor (Gross 1993:27). Others, such as right-wing fundraiser Terry Dolan or newspaper publisher C. K. McClatchy, were revealed as gay when they died of AIDS. But by the end of the decade the ranks of openly gay conservatives began to swell (Rees, "Homocons"; Chellew, "The Naked Truth," this volume). Among those who quickly rose to prominence were Marvin Liebman, a former Jew whose conversion to Catholicism had been sponsored by his close friend and conservative ally William F. Buckley—Liebman first came out in an open letter to Buckley in the *National Review*. Liebman joined with other gay Republicans in building the Log Cabin gay Republican organization, but, unlike most of them, he split with the party over its officially homophobic policies.

Another newly hatched gay figure was cultural critic Bruce Bawer, who served for four years as movie critic for the conservative monthly the *American Spectator*, despite what he later acknowledged as its viciously homophobic articles, until they censored his review of a gay-themed film (Bawer 1993). Having straightened his spine enough to disassociate from his homophobic colleagues, Bawer wrote A *Place at the Table,* in which he celebrates the ordinariness of the "silent majority" of gay Americans, such as the gay men he sees in church, "every last one of them elegantly turned out in suit and tie and polished black shoes" (157), who would never consider marching in a gay pride parade. These are contrasted with those who do march, "unconventionally attired," leathermen and drag queens, militant activists, and all those he refers to as subculture-oriented gays.

> To look at and listen to some of the subculture-oriented gays who have presented themselves as spokespeople for the homosexual population, alas, is to be disturbed at the thought of their influence on the views of homosexuality held both by heterosexuals and by the countless young people who every day discover their own homosexuality. (43)

A third gay conservative who came to prominence in the early 1990s was British expatriate Andrew Sullivan, whose tenure as editor of the *New Republic* put an openly gay conservative at the helm of a venerable (formerly liberal) magazine. In his essays and his book, *Virtually Normal* (1995), Sullivan argued for the integration of lesbian and gay people into such central societal institutions as the military and marriage (Sullivan, "Here Comes the Groom," this volume). Indeed, the exclusion of queers from these institutions has occupied center stage in the political struggles of the "gay nineties."

Presidential candidate Bill Clinton's campaign pledge to end military discrimination received little media attention, presumably because it was carefully confined to appearances before gay audiences. But when the question was put to him in a postelection news conference, after a Federal judge reinstated a discharged gay officer, Clinton stood by his promise and set off the first firestorm of his presidency. However, faced with a Pentagon and a Senate Armed Services Committee chair determined to intimidate the first president who had never served in the armed forces—who had, in fact, avoided service and opposed the Vietnam War—Clinton capitulated. The resulting "don't ask, don't tell, don't pursue" policy was far from the "honorable compromise" Clinton declared it to be, and by many accounts lesbian and gay military personnel are worse off than before.

The military debate revived deep-seated fears of pollution and desecration. Everyone recognized the echoes of the 1948 struggle over Truman's order ending racial discrimination in the military, although General Colin Powell was quick to deny that the parallel was appropriate. However, it is difficult not to detect similarities between the near hysteria over the prospect of openly gay soldiers sharing barracks and showers with straight boys and the words of Republican Congressman Lewis of Kentucky in 1948, urging his colleagues to "imagine, if you please, a colored man sleeping in a lower berth in the same coach just opposite a white woman in easy arm's reach of each other. Does not such tend to encourage amalgamation of the races?"

Although General Powell was unwilling to acknowledge the similarity to the defining civil rights struggle of the past half-century—the fight against institutionalized racism—many civil rights leaders were less obtuse (Gates, "Blacklash?"; Smith, "Blacks and Gays," this volume). Dr. William F. Gibson, National Chairman of the Board of NAACP, issued a press release endorsing the April 25, 1993, March on Washington for Lesbian, Gay, and Bi Equal Rights and the effort to repeal the ban on gays in the military. "The alibis and excuses they're giving," he wrote, "are the same ones they tried to use to keep Black Americans out of the military. . . . No citizen should be excluded from any aspect of life because of race, religion, or sexual orientation."

Even before the military discrimination issue catapulted into the headlines lesbian and gay leaders were debating the question of marriage. Was this an important goal in our pursuit of full equality, or a misguided attempt to assimilate into a hopelessly heterosexist institution? (Sullivan, "Here Comes the Groom"; Stoddard, "Why Gay People Should Seek the Right to Marry"; Ettelbrick, "Since When Is Marriage a Path to Liberation?" this volume). Despite the fact that "the overwhelming majority of same-sex couples who have actually obtained marriage licenses in the United States have been women" (Eskridge 1993:1492), gay opposition to marriage has often been formulated in terms of feminist hostility toward an institution rooted in patriarchy (Brownworth 1999). At the same time, other feminists argued that gay marriage might "disrupt both the gendered definition of marriage and the assumption that marriage is a form of socially, if not legally, prescribed hierarchy. . . . Legalization of lesbian and gay marriage poses a threat to gender systems, not simply to antilesbian and antigay bigotry" (Hunter 1991:112—-113).

While the debate remains unresolved, individual lesbian and gay couples called the question. Just as the military's policies were challenged first by individuals who resisted being discharged by taking the issue to the Federal courts, it was couples demanding—and being denied—marriage licenses that made a legal issue of this form of discrimination. The "official" movement, like society at large, was taken by surprise when a suit by three couples led the Supreme Court of Hawaii to start that state down the road to same-sex marriage.

Same-sex marriage is an issue that engaged the passion of many lesbian and gay people, who view it as a basic human right, while at the same time it stoked the flames of bigotry ignited by the right. As early as February 1996 the Christian Coalition organized a National Campaign to Protect Marriage on the eve of the Iowa Republican Caucuses, and as the 1996 presidential campaign progressed those marching under the banner of "traditional family values" sought to make same-sex marriage an major issue. In May the "Defense of Marriage Act" (DOMA) was introduced in Congress by (thrice-wed) Rep. Bob Barr (R-Ga.) and cosponsored by Republican presidential candidate (twice-wed) Senator Bob Dole. In what a Wyoming editor called a "blatantly unconstitutional provision, DOMA says that if one state recognizes a same-sex marriage, other states do not have to recognize that marriage as legal" (Levendosky 1996).

Although judiciary subcommittee chair Charles Canaday (R-Fla.) claimed that DOMA was necessary to preserve the "essential nature of the family, the fundamental building block of society" (Yang 1996), former civil rights leader John Lewis (D-Ga.) characterized it more accurately: "I have known racism. I have known bigotry. This bill stinks of the same fear, hatred and intolerance. It should not be called the Defense of Marriage Act. It should be called the defense of mean-spirited bigots act" (House of Representatives, 7/11/96).

The latest frontier of the gay right was opened in 1996 by journalist Chandler Burr in the *Weekly Standard*. Burr wishes to persuade his readers that "a conservatism unremmitingly hostile to homosexuality and *truly* committed to the resurgence of conservative thought with real impact on public policy can, and should embrace the gay gene" (1996:23). The promise Burr lays out is twofold. "The gay gene is a remarkable vindication of conservative ideas about human nature and may offer one of the most devastating refuta-

tions of liberalism we have yet seen" (22). But, beyond demonstrating that "the brand of liberalism that now dominates public policy is futile because it ignores human nature," genetic research will offer a final solution to homosexuality: elimination through genetic surgery, a measure that Burr himself, as "an ardent assimilationist . . . would not be opposed to considering" (25).

## REFERENCES

Bawer, Bruce. 1993. A *Place at the Table: The Gay Individual in American Society*. New York: Poseidon.

Brownworth, Victoria. 1996. "Tying the Knot or the Hangman's Noose: The Case Against Marriage." In Victoria Brownworth, *Too Queer: Essays from a Radical Life*, pp. 129–136. Ithaca: Firebrand.

Burr, Chandler. 1996. "Why Conservatives Should Embrace the Gay Gene." *Weekly Standard*, December 16, pp. 22–26.

Castells, Manuel. 1983. *The City and the Grassroots: A Cross-Cultural Theory of Urban Social Movements*. Berkeley: University of California Press.

D'Emilio, John. 1989. "Gay Politics and Community in San Francisco Since World War II." In Martin Duberman, George Chauncey, and Martha Vicinus, eds., *Hidden from History*, pp. 456–473. New York: NAL.

Denneny, Michael. 1981. "A Gay Manifesto for the 80's." *Christopher Street*, January, pp. 13–21.

Eskridge, William. 1993. "A History of Same-Sex Marriage." *Virginia Law Review*, vol. 79.

Gross, Larry. 1993. *Contested Closets: The Politics and Ethics of Outing*. Minneapolis: University of Minnesota Press.

Hunter, Nan. 1995 [1991]. "Marriage, Law and Gender: A Feminist Inquiry." In Lisa Duggan and Nan Hunter, *Sex Wars*, pp. 107–122. New York: Routledge.

Jackson, Peter. 1992. *Maps of Meaning*. London: Routledge.

Kennedy, Elizabeth and Madeline Davis. 1993. *Boots of Leather, Slippers of Gold: The History of a Lesbian Community*. New York: Routledge.

Lauria, Mickey, and Lawrence Knopp. 1985. "Toward an Analysis of the Role of Gay Communities in the Urban Renaissance." *Urban Geography*, 6(2):152–169.

Levendosky, Charles. 1996. "Congressmen Promote Institutionalized Bigotry." *New York Times News Service*, May 16.

Murray, Steven. 1992. "Components of Gay Community in San Francisco." In Gilbert Herdt, ed., *Gay Culture in America*. Boston: Beacon.

Nestle, Joan. 1987. "Voice from Lesbian Herstory." In Joan Nestle, *A Restricted Country*. Ithaca: Firebrand.

Newton, Esther. 1979. *Mother Camp*. Chicago: University of Chicago Press.

——1993. *Cherry Grove, Fire Island*. Boston: Beacon.

Rouilard, Richard. 1991. "Editorial." *Advocate*, August 27.

Sullivan, Andrew. 1995. *Virtually Normal: An Argument About Homosexuality*. New York: Knopf.

Weightman, Barbara. "Toewards a Geography of the Gay Community." *Journal of Cultural Geography* (1981), 1:106–112.

Woods, James D. 1993. *The Corporate Closet: The Professional Lives of Gay Men in America*. New York: Free Press.

Yang, John. 1996. "House Bill to Stop Gay Marriages Has Stormy Start." *Washington Post*, June 13.

# | 96 |

# Here Comes the Groom: A (Conservative) Case for Gay Marriage

## Andrew Sullivan

Last month in New York, a court ruled that a gay lover had the right to stay in his deceased partner's rent-control apartment because the lover qualified as a member of the deceased's family. The ruling deftly annoyed almost everybody. Conservatives saw judicial activism in favor of gay rent control: three reasons to be appalled. Chastened liberals (such as the *New York Times* editorial page), while endorsing the recognition of gay relationships, also worried about the abuse of already stretched entitlements that the ruling threatened. What neither side quite contemplated is that they both might be right, and that the way to tackle the issue of unconventional relationships in conventional society is to try something both more radical and more conservative than putting courts in the business of deciding what is and is not a family. That alternative is the legalization of civil gay marriage.

The New York rent-control case did not go anywhere near that far, which is the problem. The rent-control regulations merely stipulated that a "family" member had the right to remain in the apartment. The judge ruled that to all intents and purposes a gay lover is part of his lover's family, inasmuch as a "family" merely means an interwoven social life, emotional commitment, and some level of financial interdependence.

It's a principle now well established around the country. Several cities have "domestic partnership" laws, which allow relationships that do not fit into the category of heterosexual marriage to be registered with the city and qualify for benefits that up till now have been reserved for straight married couples. San Francisco, Berkeley, Madison, and Los Angeles all have legislation, as does the politically correct Washington, D.C., suburb, Takoma Park. In these cities, a variety of interpersonal arrangements qualify for health insurance, bereavement leave, insurance, annuity and pension rights, housing rights (such as rent-control apartments), adoption and inheritance rights. Eventually, according to gay lobby groups, the aim is to include federal income tax and veterans' benefits as well. A recent case even involved the right to use a family member's accumulated frequent-flier points. Gays are not the only beneficiaries; heterosexual "live-togethers" also qualify.

There's an argument, of course, that the current legal advantages extended to married people unfairly discriminate against people who've shaped their lives in less conventional arrangements. But it doesn't take a genius to see that enshrining in the law a vague principle like "domestic partnership" is an invitation to qualify at little personal cost for a vast array of entitlements otherwise kept crudely under control.

To be sure, potential DPs have to prove financial interdependence, shared living arrangements, and a commitment to mutual caring. But they don't need to have a sexual relationship or even closely mirror old-style marriage. In principle, an elderly woman and her live-in nurse could qualify. A couple of uneuphemistically confirmed bachelors could be DPs. So could two close college students, a pair of seminarians, or a couple of frat buddies. Left as it is, the concept of

*New Republic*, August 28, 1989, pp. 20—22.

domestic partnership could open a Pandora's box of litigation and subjective judicial decision-making about who qualifies. You either are or are not married; it's not a complex question. Whether you are in a "domestic partnership" is not so clear.

More important, the concept of domestic partnership chips away at the prestige of traditional relationships and undermines the priority we give them. This priority is not necessarily a product of heterosexism. Consider heterosexual couples. Society has good reason to extend legal advantages to heterosexuals who choose the formal sanction of marriage over simply living together. They make a deeper commitment to one another and to society; in exchange, society extends certain benefits to them. Marriage provides an anchor, if an arbitrary and weak one, in the chaos of sex and relationships to which we are all prone. It provides a mechanism for emotional stability, economic security, and the healthy rearing of the next generation. We rig the law in its favor not because we disparage all forms of relationship other than the nuclear family, but because we recognize that not to promote marriage would be to ask too much of human virtue. In the context of the weakened family's effect upon the poor, it might also invite social disintegration. One of the worst products of the New Right's "family values" campaign is that its extremism and hatred of diversity has disguised this more measured and more convincing case for the importance of the marital bond.

The concept of domestic partnership ignores these concerns, indeed directly attacks them. This is a pity, since one of its most important objectives—providing some civil recognition for gay relationships—is a noble cause and one completely compatible with the defense of the family. But the way to go about it is not to undermine straight marriage; it is to legalize old-style marriage for gays.

▼ ▼ ▼

The gay movement has ducked this issue primarily out of fear of division. Much of the gay leadership clings to notions of gay life as essentially outsider, anti-bourgeois, radical. Marriage, for them, is co-optation into straight society. For the Stonewall generation, it is hard to see how this vision of conflict will ever fundamentally change. But for many other gays—my guess, a majority—while they don't deny the importance of rebellion 20 years ago and are grateful for what was done, there's now the sense of a new opportunity. A

need to rebel has quietly ceded to a desire to belong. To be gay and to be bourgeois no longer seems such an absurd proposition. Certainly since AIDS, to be gay and to be responsible has become a necessity.

Gay marriage squares several circles at the heart of the domestic partnership debate. Unlike domestic partnership, it allows for recognition of gay relationships, while casting no aspersions on traditional marriage. It merely asks that gays be allowed to join in. Unlike domestic partnership, it doesn't open up avenues for heterosexuals to get benefits without the responsibilities of marriage, or a nightmare of definitional litigation. And unlike domestic partnership, it harnesses to an already established social convention the yearnings for stability and acceptance among a fast-maturing gay community.

Gay marriage also places more responsibilities upon gays: it says for the first time that gay relationships are not better or worse than straight relationships, and that the same is expected of them. And it's clear and dignified. There's a legal benefit to a clear, common symbol of commitment. There's also a personal benefit. One of the ironies of domestic partnership is that it's not only more complicated than marriage, it's more demanding, requiring an elaborate statement of intent to qualify. It amounts to a substantial invasion of privacy. Why, after all, should gays be required to prove commitment before they get married in a way we would never dream of asking of straights?

Legalizing gay marriage would offer homosexuals the same deal society now offers heterosexuals: general social approval and specific legal advantages in exchange for a deeper and harder-to-extract-yourself-from commitment to another human being. Like straight marriage, it would foster social cohesion, emotional security, and economic prudence. Since there's no reason gays should not be allowed to adopt or be foster parents, it could also help nurture children. And its introduction would not be some sort of radical break with social custom. As it has become more acceptable for gay people to acknowledge their loves publicly, more and more have committed themselves to one another for life in full view of their families and their friends. A law institutionalizing gay marriage would merely reinforce a healthy social trend. It would also, in the wake of AIDS, qualify as a genuine public health measure. Those conservatives who deplore promiscuity among some homosexuals should be among the first to support it. Burke could have written a powerful case for it.

The argument that gay marriage would subtly undermine the unique legitimacy. of straight marriage is based upon a fallacy. For heterosexuals, straight marriage would remain the most significant—and only legal—social bond. Gay marriage could only delegitimize straight marriage if it were a real alternative to it, and this is clearly not true. To put it bluntly, there's precious little evidence that straights could be persuaded by any law to have sex with—let alone marry—someone of their own sex. The only possible effect of this sort would be to persuade gay men and women who force themselves into heterosexual marriage (often at appalling cost to themselves and their families) to find a focus for their family instincts in a more personally positive environment. But this is clearly a plus, not a minus: gay marriage could both avoid a lot of tortured families and create the possibility for many happier ones. It is not, in short, a denial of family values. It's an extension of them.

Of course, some would claim that any legal recognition of homosexuality is a de facto attack upon heterosexuality. But even the most hardened conservatives recognize that gays are a permanent minority and aren't likely to go away. Since persecution is not an option in a civilized society, why not coax gays into traditional values rather than rail incoherently against them?

There's a less elaborate argument for gay marriage: it's good for gays. It provides role models for young gay people who, after the exhilaration of coming out, can easily lapse into short-term relationships and insecurity with no tangible goal in sight. My own guess is that most gays would embrace such a goal with as much (if not more) commitment as straights. Even in our society as it is, many lesbian relationships are virtual textbook cases of monogamous commitment. Legal gay marriage could also help bridge the gulf often found between gays and their parents. It could bring the essence of gay life—a gay couple—into the heart of the traditional straight family in a way the family can most understand and the gay offspring can most easily acknowledge. It could do as much to heal the gay-straight rift as any amount of gay rights legislation.

If these arguments sound socially conservative, that's no accident. It's one of the richest ironies of our society's blind spot toward gays that essentially conservative social goals should have the appearance of being so radical. But gay marriage is not a radical step. It avoids the mess of domestic partnership; it is humane; it is conservative in the best sense of the word. It's also practical. Given the fact that we already allow legal gay relationships, what possible social goal is advanced by framing the law to encourage those relationships to be unfaithful, undeveloped, and insecure?

# | 97 |

# Why Gay People Should Seek the Right to Marry

## Thomas B. Stoddard

Even though, these days, few lesbians and gay men enter into marriages recognized by law, absolutely every gay person has an opinion on marriage as an "institution." (The word "institution" brings to mind, perhaps appropriately, museums.) After all, we all know quite a bit about the subject. Most of us grew up in marital households. Virtually all of us, regardless of race, creed,

Out/Look, 6:9—13, 1989.

gender, and culture, have received lectures on the propriety, if not the sanctity, of marriage—which usually suggests that those who choose not to marry are both unhappy and unhealthy. We all have been witnesses, willing or not, to a lifelong parade of other people's marriages, from Uncle Harry and Aunt Bernice to the Prince and Princess of Wales. And at one point or another, some nosy relative has inevitably inquired of every gay person when he or she will finally "tie the knot" (an intriguing and probably apt cliché).

I must confess at the outset that I am no fan of the "institution" of marriage as currently constructed and practiced. I may simply be unlucky, but I have seen preciously few marriages over the course of my forty years that invite admiration and emulation. All too often, marriage appears to petrify rather than satisfy and enrich, even for couples in their twenties and thirties who have had a chance to learn the lessons of feminism. Almost inevitably, the partners seem to fall into a "husband" role and a "wife" role, with such latter-day modifications as the wife who works in addition to raising the children and managing the household.

Let me be blunt: in its traditional form, marriage has been oppressive, especially (although not entirely) to women. Indeed, until the middle of the last century, marriage was, at its legal and social essence, an extension of the husband and his paternal family. Under the English common law, wives were among the husband's "chattel'—personal property—and could not, among other things, hold property in their own names. The common law crime of adultery demonstrates the unequal treatment accorded to husbands and wives: while a woman who slept with a man who wasn't her husband committed adultery, a man who slept with a woman not his wife committed fornication. A man was legally incapable of committing adultery, except as an accomplice to an errant wife. The underlying offense of adultery was not the sexual betrayal of one partner by the other, but the wife's engaging in conduct capable of tainting the husband's bloodlines. (I swear on my *Black's Law Dictionary* that I have not made this up!)

Nevertheless, despite the oppressive nature of marriage historically, and in spite of the general absence of edifying examples of modern heterosexual marriage, I believe very strongly that every lesbian and gay man should have the right to marry the same-sex partner of his or her choice, and that the gay rights movement should aggressively seek full legal recognition for same-sex marriages. To those who might not agree, I respectfully offer three explanations, one practical, one political and one philosophical.

## THE PRACTICAL EXPLANATION

The legal status of marriage rewards the two individuals who travel to the altar (or its secular equivalent) with substantial economic and practical advantages. Married couples may reduce their tax liability by filing a joint return. They are entitled to special government benefits, such as those given surviving spouses and dependents through the Social Security program. They can inherit from one another even when there is no will. They are immune from subpoenas requiring testimony against the other spouse. And marriage to an American citizen gives a foreigner a right to residency in the United States.

Other advantages have arisen not by law but by custom. Most employers offer health insurance to their employees, and many will include an employee's spouse in the benefits package, usually at the employer's expense. Virtually no employer will include a partner who is not married to an employee, whether of the same sex or not. Indeed, very few insurance companies even offer the possibility of a group health plan covering "domestic partners" who are not married to one another. Two years ago, I tried to find such a policy for Lambda, and discovered that not one insurance company authorized to do business in New York—the second-largest state in the country with more than 17 million residents—would accommodate us. (Lambda has tried to make do by paying for individual insurance policies for the same-sex partners of its employees who otherwise would go uninsured but these individual policies are usually narrower in scope than group policies, often require applicants to furnish individual medical information not required under most group plans, and are typically much more expensive per person.)

In short, the law generally presumes in favor of every marital relationship, and acts to preserve and foster it, and to enhance the rights of the individuals who enter into it. It is usually possible, with enough money and the right advice, to replicate some of the benefits conferred by the legal status of marriage through the use of documents like wills and power of attorney forms, but that protection will inevitably, under current circumstances, be incomplete.

The law (as I suspect will come as no surprise to the readers of this journal) still looks upon lesbians and gay men with suspicion, and this suspicion casts a shadow over the documents they execute in recognition of a same-sex relationship. If a lesbian leaves property to her lover, her will may be invalidated on the grounds that it was executed under the "undue influence" of the would-be beneficiary. A property agreement may be denied validity because the underlying relationship is "meretricious"—akin to prostitution. (Astonishingly, until the mid-seventies, the law throughout the United States deemed "meretricious" virtually *any* formal economic arrangement between two people not married to one another, on the theory that an exchange of property between them was probably payment for sexual services; the Supreme Court of California helped unravel this quaint legal fantasy in its 1976 ruling in the first famous "palimony" case, *Marvin v. Marvin*.) The law has progressed considerably beyond the uniformly oppressive state of affairs before 1969, but it is still far from enthusiastic about gay people and their relationships—to put it mildly.

Moreover, there are some barriers one simply cannot transcend outside of a formal marriage. When the Internal Revenue Code or the Immigration and Naturalization Act say "married," they mean "married" by definition of state statute. When the employer's group health plan says "spouse," it means "spouse" in the eyes of the law, not the eyes of the loving couple.

But there is another drawback. Couples seeking to protect their relationship through wills and other documents need knowledge, determination and—most importantly—money. No money, no lawyer. And no lawyer, no protection. Those who lack the sophistication or the wherewithal to retain a lawyer are simply stuck in most circumstances. Extending the right to marry to gay couples would assure that those at the bottom of the economic ladder have a chance to secure their relationship rights, too.

## THE POLITICAL EXPLANATION

The claim that gay couples ought to be able to marry is not a new one. In the seventies, same-sex couples in three states—Minnesota, Kentucky and Washington—brought constitutional challenges to the marriage statutes, and in all three instances they failed. In each of the three, the court offered two basic justifications for limiting marriage to male-female couples: history and pro-

creation. Witness this passage from the Supreme Court of Minnesota's 1971 opinion in *Baker v. Nelson*: "The institution of marriage as a union of man and woman, uniquely involving the procreation and rearing of children within a family, is as old as the book of Genesis. . . . This historic institution manifestly is more deeply founded than the asserted contemporary concept of marriage and societal interests for which petitioners contend."

Today, no American jurisdiction recognizes the right of two women or two men to marry one another, although several nations in Northern Europe do. Even more telling, until earlier this year, there was little discussion within the gay rights movement about whether such a right should exist. As far as I can tell, no gay organization of any size, local or national, has yet declared the right to marry as one of its goals.

With all due respect to my colleagues and friends who take a different view, I believe it is time to renew the effort to overturn the existing marriage laws, and to do so in earnest, with a commitment of money and energy, through both the courts and the state legislatures. I am not naive about the likelihood of imminent victory. There is none. Nonetheless—and here I will not mince words—I would like to see the issue rise to the top of the agenda of every gay organization, including my own (although that judgment is hardly mine alone).

Why give it such prominence? Why devote resources to such a distant goal? Because marriage is, I believe, the political issue that most fully tests the dedication of people who are not gay to full equality for gay people, and also the issue most likely to lead ultimately to a world free from discrimination against lesbians and gay men.

Marriage is much more than a relationship sanctioned by law. It is the centerpiece of our entire social structure, the core of the traditional notion of "family." Even in its present tarnished state, the marital relationship inspires sentiments suggesting that it is something almost suprahuman. The Supreme Court, in striking down an anti-contraception statute in 1965, called marriage "noble" and "intimate to the degree of being sacred." The Roman Catholic Church and the Moral Majority would go—and have gone—considerably further.

Lesbians and gay men are now denied entry to this "noble" and "sacred" institution. The implicit message is this: two men or two women are incapable of achieving such an exalted domestic state. Gay relationships are somehow less significant, less valuable. Such relationships may, from time to time and from couple to couple, give the appearance of a marriage, but they can never be of the same quality or importance.

I resent—indeed, I loathe—that conception of same-sex relationships. And I am convinced that ultimately the only way to overturn it is to remove the barrier to marriage that now limits the freedom of every gay man and lesbian.

That is to not to deny the value of "domestic partnership" ordinances, statutes that prohibit discrimination based on "marital status," and other legal advances that can enhance the rights (as well as the dignity) of gay couples. Without question, such advances move us further along the path to equality. But their value can only be partial. (The recently enacted San Francisco "domestic partnership" ordinance, for example, will have practical value only for gay people who happen to be employed by the City of San Francisco and want to include their non-marital spouses in part of the city's fringe benefit package; the vast majority of gay San Franciscans—those employed by someone other than the city—have only a symbolic victory to savor.) Measures of this kind can never assure full equality. Gay relationships will continue to be accorded a subsidiary status until the day that gay couples have *exactly* the same rights as their heterosexual counterparts. To my mind, that means either that the right to marry be extended to us, or that marriage be abolished in its present form for all couples, presumably to be replaced by some new legal entity—an unlikely alternative.

## THE PHILOSOPHICAL EXPLANATION

I confessed at the outset that I personally found marriage in its present avatar rather, well, unat-tractive. Nonetheless, even from a philosophical perspective, I believe the right to marry should become a stated goal of the gay rights movement.

First, and most basically, the issue is not the desirability of marriage, but rather the desirability of the *right* to marry. That I think two lesbians or two gay men should be entitled to a marriage license does not mean that I think all gay people should find appropriate partners and exercise the right, should it eventually exist. I actually rather doubt that I, myself, would want to marry, even though I share a household with another man who is exceedingly dear to me. There are others who feel differently, for economic, symbolic, or romantic reasons. They should, to my mind, unquestionably have the opportunity to marry if they wish and otherwise meet the requirements of the state (like being old enough).

Furthermore, marriage may be unattractive and even oppressive as it is currently structured and practiced, but enlarging the concept to embrace same-sex couples would necessarily transform it into something new. If two women can marry, or two men, marriage—even for heterosexuals—need not be a union of a "husband" and a "wife." Extending the right to marry to gay people—that is, abolishing the traditional gender requirements of marriage—can be one of the means, perhaps the principal one, through which the institution divests itself of the sexist trappings of the past.

Some of my colleagues disagree with me. I welcome their thoughts and the debates and discussions our different perspectives will trigger. The movement for equality for lesbians and gay men can only be enriched through this collective exploration of the question of marriage. But I do believe many thousands of gay people want the right to marry. And I think, too, they will earn that right for themselves sooner than most of us imagine.

# | 98 |

# Since When Is Marriage a Path to Liberation?

### Paula L. Ettelbrick

"Marriage is a great institution . . . if you like living in institutions," according to a bit of T-shirt philosophy I saw recently. Certainly, marriage is an institution. It is one of the most venerable, impenetrable institutions in modern society. Marriage provides the ultimate form of acceptance for personal intimate relationships in our society, and gives those who marry an insider status of the most powerful kind.

Steeped in a patriarchal system that looks to ownership, property, and dominance of men over women as its basis, the institution of marriage long has been the focus of radical feminist revulsion. Marriage defines certain relationships as more valid than all others. Lesbian and gay relationships, being neither legally sanctioned or commingled by blood, are always at the bottom of the heap of social acceptance and importance.

Given the imprimatur of social and personal approval which marriage provides, it is not surprising that some lesbians and gay men among us would look to legal marriage for self-affirmation. After all, those who marry can be instantaneously transformed from "outsiders" to "insiders,' and we have a desperate need to become insiders.

It could make us feel OK about ourselves, perhaps even relieve some of the internalized homophobia that we all know so well. Society will then celebrate the birth of our children and mourn the death of our spouses. It would be easier to get health insurance for our spouses, family memberships to the local museum, and a right to inherit our spouse's cherished collection of lesbian mystery novels even if she failed to draft a will. Never again would we have to go to a family reunion and debate about the correct term for introducing our lover / partner / significant other to Aunt Flora. Everything would be quite easy and very nice.

So why does this unlikely event so deeply disturb me? For two major reasons. First, marriage will not liberate us as lesbians and gay men. In fact, it will constrain us, make us more invisible, force our assimilation into the mainstream, and undermine the goals of gay liberation. Second, attaining the right to marry will not transform our society from one that makes narrow, but dramatic, distinctions between those who are married and those who are not married to one that respects and encourages choice of relationships and family diversity. Marriage runs contrary to two of the primary goals of the lesbian and gay movement: the affirmation of gay identity and culture; and the validation of many forms of relationships.

When analyzed from the standpoint of civil rights, certainly lesbians and gay men should have a right to marry. But obtaining a right does not always result in justice. White male firefighters in Birmingham, Alabama have been fighting for their "rights" to retain their jobs by overturning the city's affirmative action guidelines. If their "rights" prevail, the courts will have failed in rendering justice. The "right" fought for by the white male firefighters, as well as those who advocate strongly for the "rights" to legal marriage for gay people, will result, at best, in limited or narrowed "justice" for those closest to power at the expense of those who have been historically marginalized.

The fight for justice has as its goal the realignment of power imbalances among individuals and classes of people in society. A pure "rights" analysis often fails to incorporate a broader

*Out/Look*, 6:9, 14–17, 1989.

understanding of the underlying inequities that operate to deny justice to a fuller range of people and groups. In setting our priorities as a community, we must combine the concept of both rights and justice. At this point in time, making legal marriage for lesbian and gay couples a priority would set an agenda of gaining rights for a few, but would do nothing to correct the power imbalances between those who are married (whether gay of straight) and those who are not. Thus, justice would not be gained.

Justice for gay men and lesbians will be achieved only when we are accepted and supported in this society despite our differences from the dominant culture and the choices we make regarding our relationships. Being queer is more than setting up house, sleeping with a person of the same gender, and seeking state approval for doing so. It is an identity, a culture with many variations. It is a way of dealing with the world by diminishing the constraints of gender roles which have for so long kept women and gay people oppressed and invisible. Being queer means pushing the parameters of sex, sexuality, and family, and in the process transforming the very fabric of society. Gay liberation is inexorably linked to women's liberation. Each is essential to the other.

The moment we argue, as some among us insist on doing, that we should be treated as equals because we are really just like married couples and hold the same values to be true, we undermine the very purpose of our movement and begin the dangerous process of silencing our different voices. As a lesbian, I am fundamentally different from non-lesbian women. That's the point. Marriage, as it exists today, is antithetical to my liberation as a lesbian and as a woman because it mainstreams my life and voice. I do not want be known as "Mrs. Attached-To-Somebody-Else." Nor do I want to give the state the power to regulate my primary relationship.

Yet, the concept of equality in our legal system does not support differences, it only supports sameness. The very standard for equal protection is that people who are similarly situated must be treated equally. To make an argument for equal protection, we will be required to claim that gay and lesbian relationships are the same as straight relationships. To gain the right, we must compare ourselves to married couples. The law looks to the insiders as the norm, regardless of how flawed or unjust their institutions, and requires that those seeking the law's equal protection situate themselves in a similar posture to those who are already protected. In arguing for the right to legal marriage, lesbians and gay men would be forced to claim that we are just like heterosexual couples, have the same goals and purposes, and vow to structure our lives similarly. The law provides no room to argue that we are different, but are nonetheless entitled to equal protection.

The thought of emphasizing our sameness to married heterosexuals in order to obtain this "right" terrifies me. It rips away the very heart and soul of what I believe it is to be a lesbian in this world. It robs me of the opportunity to make a difference. We end up mimicking all that is bad about the institution of marriage in our effort to appear to be the same as straight couples.

By looking to our sameness and de-emphasizing our differences, we don't even place ourselves in a position of power that would allow us to transform marriage from an institution that emphasizes property and state regulation of relationships to an institution which recognizes one of many types of valid and respected relationships. Until the constitution is interpreted to respect and encourage differences, pursuing the legalization of same-sex marriage would be leading our movement into a trap; we would be demanding access to the very institution which, in its current form, would undermine our movement to recognize many different kinds of relationships. We would be perpetuating the elevation of married relationships and of "couples" in general, and further eclipsing other relationships of choice.

Ironically, gay marriage, instead of liberating gay sex and sexuality, would further outlaw all gay and lesbian sex which is not performed in a marital context. Just as sexually active non-married women face stigma and double standards around sex and sexual activity, so too would non-married gay people. The only legitimate gay sex would be that which is cloaked in and regulated by marriage. Its legitimacy would stem not from an acceptance of gay sexuality, but because the Supreme Court and society in general fiercely protect the privacy of marital relationships. Lesbians and gay men who do not seek the state's stamp of approval would clearly face increased sexual oppression.

Undoubtedly, whether we admit it or not, we all need to be accepted by the broader society. That motivation fuels our work to eliminate discrimination in the workplace and elsewhere, fight for custody of our children, create our own families, and so on. The growing discussion about the right to marry may be explained in part by this need for acceptance. Those closer to the norm or to power in this country are more likely to see marriage as a principle of freedom and equality. Those who are more acceptable to the mainstream because of race, gender, and economic status are more likely to want the right to marry. It is the final acceptance, the ultimate affirmation of identity.

On the other hand, more marginal members of the lesbian and gay community (women, people of color, working class and poor) are less likely to see marriage as having relevance to our struggles for survival. After all, what good is the affirmation of our relationships (that is, marital relationships) if we are rejected as women, black, or working class?

The path to acceptance is much more complicated for many of us. For instance, if we choose legal marriage, we may enjoy the right to add our spouse to our health insurance policy at work, since most employment policies are defined by one's marital status, not family relationship. However, that choice assumes that we have a job and that our employer provides us with health benefits. For women, particularly women of color who tend to occupy the low-paying jobs that do not provide healthcare benefits at all, it will not matter one bit if they are able to marry their woman partners. The opportunity to marry will neither get them the health benefits nor transform them from outsider to insider.

Of course, a white man who marries another white man who has a full-time job with benefits will certainly be able to share in those benefits and overcome the only obstacle left to full societal assimilation—the goal of many in his class. In other words, gay marriage will not topple the system that allows only the privileged few to obtain decent health care. Nor will it close the privilege gap between those who are married and those who are not.

Marriage creates a two-tier system that allows the state to regulate relationships. It has become a facile mechanism for employers to dole out benefits, for businesses to provide special deals and incentives, and for the law to make distinctions in distributing meager public funds. None of these entities bothers to consider the relationship among people; the love, respect, and need to protect that exists among all kinds of family members. Rather, a simple certificate of the state, regardless of whether the spouses love, respect, or even see each other on a regular basis, dominates

and is supported. None of this dynamic will change if gay men and lesbians are given the option of marriage.

Gay marriage will not help us address the systemic abuses inherent in a society that does not provide decent health care to all of its citizens, a right that should not depend on whether the individual 1) has sufficient resources to afford health care or insurance, 2) is working and receives health insurance as part of compensation, or 3) is married to a partner who is working and has health coverage which is extended to spouses. It will not address the underlying unfairness that allows businesses to provide discounted services or goods to families and couples—who are defined to include straight, married people and their children, but not domestic partners.

Nor will it address the pain and anguish of the unmarried lesbian who receives word of her partner's accident, rushes to the hospital and is prohibited from entering the intensive care unit or obtaining information about her condition solely because she is not a spouse or family member. Likewise, marriage will not help the gay victim of domestic violence who, because he chose not to marry, finds no protection under the law to keep his violent lover away.

If the laws change tomorrow and lesbians and gay men were allowed to marry, where would we find the incentive to continue the progressive movement we have started that is pushing for societal and legal recognition of all kinds of family relationships? To create other options and alternatives? To find a place in the law for the elderly couple who, for companionship and economic reasons, live together but do not marry? To recognize the right of a long-time, but unmarried, gay partner to stay in his rent-controlled apartment after the death of his lover, the only named tenant on the lease? To recognize the family relationship of the lesbian couple and the two gay men who are jointly sharing child-raising responsibilities? To get the law to acknowledge that we may have more than one relationship worthy of legal protection?

Marriage for lesbians and gay men still will not provide a real choice unless we continue the work our community has begun to spread the privilege around to other relationships. We must first break the tradition of piling benefits and privileges on to those who are married, while ignoring the real life needs of those who are not. Only when we de-institutionalize marriage and bridge the economic and privilege gap between the married and the unmarried will each of us have a true choice. Otherwise, our choice not to marry will continue to lack legal protection and societal respect.

The lesbian and gay community has laid the groundwork for revolutionizing society's views of family. The domestic partnership movement has been an important part of this progress insofar as it validates non-marital relationships. Because it is not limited to sexual or romantic relationships, domestic partnership provides an important opportunity for many who are not related by blood or marriage to claim certain minimal protections.

It is crucial, though, that we avoid the pitfall of framing the push for legal recognition of domestic partners (those who share a primary residence and financial responsibilities for each other) as a stepping stone to marriage. We must keep our eyes on the goals of providing true alternatives to marriage and of radically reordering society's view of family.

The goals of lesbian and gay liberation must simply be broader than the right to marry. Gay and lesbian marriages may minimally transform the institution of marriage by diluting its traditional patriarchal dynamic, but they will not transform society. They will not demolish the two-tier system of the "haves" and the "have nots." We must not fool ourselves into believing that marriage will make it acceptable to be gay or lesbian. We will be liberated only when we are respected and accepted for our differences and the diversity we provide to this society. Marriage is not a path to that liberation.

# 1 99 1

## *Homocons*

### MATTHEW REES

When Michael Duffy gathered his friends together at Boston's Claddagh restaurant in January 1990, he told them, "I have an important announcement to make today." They figured he was going to announce that, at 26, he was running for a state representative's seat in his South End neighborhood. "But before I continue there's something about myself I want to make clear. It's something I've told my parents about and they're comfortable with it, and I hope you will be too. The fact is," said Duffy, pausing for effect, "I'm a Republican."

Duffy is one of a growing number of openly gay Republicans: homoconservatives. What was once a simple contradiction is increasingly a complicated political stance, putting both conservatives and liberals in a tough political bind. Where once the oxymoronic lives of gay Republicans were resolved by the closet, they're now provoking querulous debate on both right and left.

The old paradigm of the homoconservative is perhaps best represented by Roy Cohn and Terry Dolan. Cohn, chief counsel to Joseph McCarthy, was both rabidly anti-gay in public and unabashedly homosexual in private. Even when dying of AIDS in 1986, he refused to be open about his sexuality. Similarly, New Right fundraiser Terry Dolan, a closeted homosexual, led the National Conservative Political Action Committee, which raised direct-mail funds by generating anti-homosexual hysteria.

Then, in the 1970s and '80s, a couple of organizations were set up to cater to uncloseted Republicans. The first, the "Log Cabin Club," was formed in San Francisco in 1977 to oppose a California state initiative that would have prevented gays from teaching in public schools. A more conservative group, Concerned Americans for Individual Rights. was formed in 1984. But when it sponsored a panel debate on gay issues at that year's GOP convention, the panelists were the only ones who showed up. The group folded the next year.

Recently a change has taken place. The

*New Republic*, June 8, 1992, pp. 30–31.

National Log Cabin Federation now boasts of 4,500 members from a dozen states and hopes to have a strong presence at the Republican convention in Houston. Duffy, who narrowly lost his race in Boston, is now head of the Massachusetts Commission Against Discrimination, and one of several openly gay Republicans serving in government-related positions around the country. In California, Governor Pete Wilson has appointed openly gay Republicans to senior positions in the Department of Motor Vehicles and the Office Consumer Affairs. Frank Bowman, a founding member of the San Francisco Log Cabin Club, is the liaison to the gay community for San Francisco Mayor Frank Jordan. In Massachusetts, Richard Tafel, president of the NLCF, is an appointee of Republican Governor William Weld in the State's Department of Public Health. Marvin Liebman, who announced his sexuality in the pages of *National Review* two years ago, is the director of special projects at the Federal Trade Commission. Deroy Murdock, a black homocon (yes, they exist too), spent three years in the mid-'80s working for Orrin Hatch on the Judiciary Committee and is now a free-lance writer in New York. The pièce de résistance is Justin Raimondo, chairman of the Libertarian Republican Organizing Committee, who runs the San Francisco Pat Buchanan campaign. No kidding.

It's small-fry compared with the Democrats, of course, who have sixty-one publicly elected gay officials, but it represents a growing response to where the votes are. A 1991 poll of 7,500 gay men and lesbians by the gay-owned, Chicago-based marketing firm Overlooked Opinions showed 11 percent identifying themselves as Republicans, 20 percent as independents, and 64 percent as Democrats. Such polls almost certainly undercount Republicans, many of whom are closeted and leery of polls. Gregory King, spokesman for the Human Rights Campaign Fund, a national gay PAC, argues that "the Democratic nature of the gay vote is exaggerated. I would estimate that nationally gays probably vote about 40 percent Republican."

It's this voting clout that has attracted Republican politicians. The Overlooked Opinions survey revealed 86 percent of gays reported voting in the 1988 presidential election. Weld was widely believed to have won a majority of the state's gay vote thanks to his pro-gay stance, a bloc he claimed was critical to his close win over Democrat John Silber. Of perhaps greater importance than gay voter turnout, however, is gay money.

HRCF doled out $518,000 in the 1990 election cycle and is projecting $1 million in contributions in 1992. That would make it one of the twenty-five largest PACs in the country. Republicans don't like to turn that kind of money down.

Gay Republicans—like black Republicans—face opposition from two quarters: their fellow minority members and the Republican establishment. Marti Goodson, a 54-year-old pro-life lesbian from Tampa, Florida, says, "Coming out of the political closet can be more difficult than coming out of the sexual closet because gay conservatives have almost nowhere to go." Duffy's 1990 race typifies the narrow stretch of ground on which homocons tread. The Massachusetts Gay and Lesbian Political Caucus endorsed Duffy's opponent, a straight black Democrat. Local gay congressman Barney Frank also opposed him. The Republican Party, apart from Weld, didn't exactly embrace him. Gay liberals get particularly incensed. Tafel has been called "Phyllis Schlafly with a jockstrap." Since affiliating with the Buchanan campaign, Raimondo has received telephoned death threats from representatives of ACT-UP. "Collaborators," "sellouts," and "self-haters" are among the milder labels thrown around. Peter Gomes, a gay, black conservative pastor at Harvard, who presided over Ronald Reagan's inauguration, describes the reaction as presumptive: "There is a kind of liberal arrogance that would make the assumption that because I am both gay and black that I would automatically be a Democrat."

To many gay (and straight) liberals, however, gay Republicans are preposterous. Frank says gay conservatives use the log cabin as their symbol "because their role model is Uncle Tom." (They say it's a reference to Abraham Lincoln.) "Any gay person who has an allegiance to the Republican Party is a co-conspirator in our oppression," says Greg Scott of Queer Nation's D.C. chapter. He believes gay Republicans "should not be welcome in our bars, our meeting places, or our beds. I would prefer it if they simply remained celibate." Gay Republicans are not surprised at this treatment. "Like other minority groups, we're challenging a power structure, and in doing so, we are challenging the legitimacy of those at the top," says Tafel.

The reaction in the GOP can be equally vehement. All the strongest opponents of gay rights are Republicans. William Dannemeyer, Republican representative from Orange County, is renowned for his gay-baiting. He wrote a 228-page book on the subject, in which he argues that "we must either defeat militant homosexuality or it will defeat us." Buchanan has called AIDS "divine retribution" against gays, and Jesse Helms's views on the subject hardly need elaboration. When Commerce Secretary Robert Mosbacher (who has an openly lesbian daughter) met with representatives of the National Gay and Lesbian Task Force in February, the Christian Life Commission of the Southern Baptist Convention fired off a letter to Bush, calling upon him to "disavow any support or sympathy for the homosexual civil rights agenda." In an April 21 meeting with evangelical leaders, Bush said he disagrees with proposals to codify "the homosexual agenda" and opposes giving legal recognition to same-sex marriages.

▼ ▼ ▼

How do gay Republicans justify their alliance with conservatives who otherwise denigrate them? Mostly they don't. Although none of the gay Republicans I spoke with said he or she had faced much personal homophobia from Republican allies, they concede that it exists. Former Mississippi Republican Representative John Hinson, who works for a gay organization in Virginia, says that "as long as the hard right remains as stridently and as shrilly opposed to gay rights and as long as they retain their control over mechanisms of the party, gays are not going to join." He says that the GOP should embrace gay rights the way the Democrats embraced civil rights at their 1948 convention. Frank Ricchiazzi, executive director of the National Log Cabin PAC, says, "We have a large group of Ayatollah Khomeinis in our party."

Homocons stay in the party partly out of pragmatism, arguing that as long as gays are beholden to the Democrats, they'll never achieve a real breakthrough. They also argue that the Democrats take gays for granted: "There's a real plantation mentality among gays when dealing with the Democratic Party," says Tafel. But the primary reason gay Republican's stay in the GOP is that philosophically they have more in common with Republicans than with Democrats. Although all of them seek the repeal of Sodomy laws and the ban on gays in the military, and favor domestic partnership laws, they tend to be skeptical of anti-discrimination laws and hate-crimes legislation. Some say they would have even vetoed the recent gay rights bill in California, as Wilson did, because government would not be in the business of mandating equality. Raimondo believes "people have the right to discriminate. This bill could have forced a lesbian bar to hire a straight door-keeper." Roy Childs, a gay libertarian who works for Lassez Faire Books in New York, also would have opposed the bill. "I am an ardent supporter of the right to discriminate as long as force is not used," says Childs, who weighs 450 pounds and made a name for himself by recently going on "20/20" and defending the right of a hospital to fire a nurse because of her obesity.

Although many of the Log Cabin Clubs are populated by libertarians, they're not devoid of right-wingers. Leonard Green, a D.C.-based black homocon, supports arresting women who have abortions, labels President Bush "a moderate Democrat in disguise," and says he is "very supportive" of Helms on issues other than race and homosexuality. When asked if he would ever support Frank, he says, "That would be equivalent to a black South African supporting apartheid." Raimondo dismisses Buchanan's comments about gays, saying that "the problem isn't the message, it's the messenger. Pat is saying the same thing the San Francisco AIDS Foundation is saying, but it's considered homophobic when he says AIDS is transmitted through anal sex." Goodson has been active in New Right politics for ten years and opposed the Equal Rights Amendment on the grounds of government intrusion. "I am very pro-family, but I also believe a family can be started by two people of the same sex."

In most cases, the delicate balance gay Republicans try to strike between their sexual orientation and their broader political philosophy doesn't cut it in today's divisive sexual politics. Their fellow homosexual activists seem increasingly radicalized by groups such as Queer Nation; their fellow Republicans are moving to the right in an attempt to deflect the threat from the Buchanan insurgency (the NLCF was rebuffed recently in its attempt to testify before the GOP platform committee). Wilson wrecked his credibility with many gay voters by vetoing the gay rights bill in California, arguing that gays were already adequately protected. Although some gay Republicans agreed with Wilson, the public relations with more liberal gays was terrible. Robert Bauman, a conservative former congressman, says the veto "was perhaps one of the most damning measures ever for the gay Republican movement." Only Weld seems to offer much substantive hope for the future. Yet his vision of a Republican Party that is economically conservative but tolerant of a wide variety of groups and lifestyles is still, for many Republicans, a distant prospect. If it ever materializes, for this generation of gay Republicans it may come just a little too late.

# | 100 |

## *The Naked Truth*

### CANDACE CHELLEW

Another summer season of gay pride parades and the gala Stonewall 25 celebration have come and gone, and once again we have presented America with a freak show. Media across the nation have shown all our drag queens, leather boys, bare-breasted women, and other displays of "gay pride." As a lesbian I am ashamed.

Ask any gay man or lesbian marching down Any Street U.S.A., why he or she is there, and most will say, "To fight for my rights." I have news: We're going about it the wrong way. The gay and lesbian movement is in desperate need of a new, improved image. Every time the TV flashes an image of a fruity queen dressed in out-rageous clothes or leather boys in practically no clothes or women with no shirts, our cause takes a giant leap backward.

We will never get our rights until Middle Americans believe we are not a threat to them or their chosen lifestyles. And we will never be able to avoid antigay legislation until we present an image that Middle America can accept and respect. Martin Luther King Jr. knew this. Watch any old film of King's marches, and you will see smartly dressed protesters presenting themselves with dignity and showing the world they were united for one purpose—their rights. There were no floats, no dancing in the streets—only serious-minded human beings looking for their fair share.

It has been said that image is everything, and it is true. Look at the religious right for the perfect example. When vehement attacks on gays and lesbians during the last presidential election cam-paign contributed to the defeat of George Bush, conservatives realized they needed to tone down their hateful rhetoric. Now they present them-selves as nonaggressive "family values" propo-nents who focus more on crime than on opposing gay rights. Oh, to be sure, they still hate us with a profound passions, but they have discovered it is not politically prudent to take such an intolerant stand publicly.

We need to become serious about winning our rights. We need to study closely the organiz-ing tactics of the right wing and adapt them to our needs. We need fundraising, not queers across America saving for the next big party or scrounging to pay the six-figure debt left by Stonewall 25. We need to get serious before our enemies prevail against us while we party our lives away.

The gay community's use of demonstrations as an attempt to change America's view of us is sort of like showing up to play a baseball game and—instead of suiting up and getting on the field—painting some signs, wearing funny clothes, building floats, and marching around the field demanding that the other side let us win or at least cough up a few unearned points. This strategy is unrealistic. To win the game you must play the game.

All the sign waving, marching, and shouting serve only to objectify the entire community. It is easy to hate us when you don't know us, and what average buttoned-down American wants to get to know a freaky-looking half-naked man or woman who enjoys flaunting and shouting in public?

When a friend of mine first came out, I took him to visit the Metropolitan Community Church that I attend, and his first remark upon seeing the congregation was, "They look like reg-ular people!" He was expecting a freak show

*Advocate*, September 6, 1994, p. 5.

because that's all he had seen on TV. And don't blame the media for this perception. As a media veteran I can tell you that television loves a show, and when the gay and lesbian community puts on a show, that's what you're going to see. Gays and lesbians who live quietly with their partners, pets, and children and are just trying to pay the bills and get ahead in a world where the odds are stacked against them don't get a lot of airtime.

For all the talk of diversity, the reality is that America is a homogeneous nation. We must realize that what we do on gay pride day affects how we are treated the other 364 days of the year. If we ostracize America, try to shout down our enemy, or make ourselves appear superior to others, we should not be surprised when those in power deny us our basic rights. As Dr. King said, "The nonviolent resister does not seek to humiliate or defeat the opponent but to win his friendship and understanding." This is what the fight for gay and lesbian rights should be about—winning over our enemies instead of trampling over them.

For a few marches in the coming years, why don't we try to look like everyday people on gay pride day? Or better yet, let's dress in our professional clothes so people will know we come from all walks of life. And for heaven's sake, no floats or bare chests—male or female. If that doesn't make a big impact on how we are perceived, then break out the chiffon, party all you want, and equal rights be damned. But I believe you'll be hearing Middle America scream, "Those can't be queers; they look like regular people!" Then we'll be on the road to winning our rights.

# | 101 |

## *Out of Asia*

### JEFF YANG

It cost $750,000 to unlock Nicky Y.'s closet. That was the budget for Ang Lee's film *The Wedding Banquet*, which debuted this summer in Nicky's native Taiwan to thundering acclaim and shocking popular appeal. Who thought that a film whose central characters were a gay couple (one of them white, no less) would be a success? Certainly not the man on whose life story the movie was based.

But the film is now the highest-grossing Taiwanese movie in history. And, though Nicky has not yet mustered the will to fully come out to his parents, he thinks it may have cracked his closet door open, just a sliver.

"I really think my parents suspect," Nicky says, still not sure whether he should feel hope or fear. "After all, my mother has seen this movie. And my friend Neil [Peng, co-writer of the film] always mentions that the film was based on a very good friend of his. But like typical Chinese parents, I don't think they *want* to know."

Nicky is, like many other gay Asian immigrants, out in America, but not in his land of birth. All his life he's been torn between being true to his identity and true to his parents' expectations; through the half-mask of film, he's finally able to tell part of his story. "Unfortunately," he sighs, "this is the most complex coming out process anyone could have possibly thought of. I wish it could have been simpler."

But fictions, cinematic or otherwise, are never as simple as they seem. The madcap humor of *Wedding Banquet* stems from the attempts of Wai Tung to hide his gay identity from his parents; he obfuscates, he lies, he bumbles desperately into a marriage of convenience. Though Nicky never had to go that far, one scene in particular sums up his life in self-imposed hiding: Wai Tung and his lover scrambling through their house, removing the casual iconography of their lifestyle—vacation photos, ACT UP posters, copies of *Out* mag-

*Village Voice*, October 12, 1994, p. 16.

azine—and replacing them with signifiers of a Good Chinese Boy: wall-scrolls of brush paintings, family pictures, *Forbes*. Out goes one culture, in comes another, never the twain to meet. And we moviegoers can watch and laugh. For gay Asians like Nicky, the laughter comes at a somewhat steeper price than $7.50 a seat.

▼ ▼ ▼

In his book *Passions of the Cut Sleeve*, Bret Hinsch tells the story of the love between the Han Emperor Ai (6 B.C.–1 A.D.) and his favorite, Dong Xian:

*Emperor Ai was sleeping in the daytime with Dong Xian stretched out across his sleeve. When the emperor wanted to get up, Dong Xian was still asleep. Because he did not want to disturb him, the emperor cut off his own sleeve and got up. His love and thoughtfulness went this far!*

A romantic, and probably apocryphal, story, but one that inspired copious literary references; in time, the "cut sleeve" came to signify a kind of perfect male same-sex relationship, eros nestled firmly in the lap of agape. It's one of many poetic metaphors—linked pieces of jade, half-eaten peaches (after the tale of the favorite who offered his king a peach that he'd found sweet, rather than finish it himself)—which attest to the existence of a gay-positive tradition in Chinese history. But Neo-Confucian austerity in the Song dynasty (10th–12th century A.D.), the legalistic stridency of the Qing (17th–20th century A.D.—punishment for consensual sodomy being a month in the stocks and "100 heavy blows"), and, of course, the arrival of Western sexual mores sealed that tradition's fate.

The Chinese Communist Party instituted a policy of prosecuting gays and lesbians under the blanket charge of "hooliganism"; as late as September 1992, 88 gays were arrested in a single village. Homosexuality, when not being treated as a crime, was seen as a mental illness, curable with electroshock, herbal medicine, and aversion therapy. In Taiwan, editorials regularly linked homosexuality to crime, and asked that "young people with homosexual tendencies . . . free themselves from abnormal feelings. By all means do not set foot in the same evil circles!"

The peach was half-uneaten. The peach is half-chewed.

▼ ▼ ▼

For Nicky, the result of unraveling of the cut sleeve was less oppression than repression. He recalls knowing he was gay as early as high school and even experimenting with same-sex classmates: "We were like any adolescents; just messing around," he says. "Most of them are leading the so-called straight life. I don't know whether it was truly just a phase for them, or if they're suppressing their sexuality."

He adds, however, that if it were indeed "just a phase," he wouldn't be too surprised. Taiwanese society's taboo against discussion of sexual matters—hetero and homo—leads to a general naïveté about labels like gay and straight. "I've noticed," he says, "that Americans put a great emphasis on machismo; there's no such thing in Taiwanese culture. In this culture, people are very conscious of body contact. In Taiwan it is quite common for boys to go out as friends, and hold hands. And certainly, that has to do with ignorance of the subject: there isn't any talk about homosexuality, so we don't think about being categorized."

Nicky knew he was different: he didn't know what it meant. He didn't meet an openly gay man until he came to the U.S. at the age of 24. "I went to my first gay bar in San Francisco," he recalls. "I still remember, I walked into this bar, and this bartender kissed me on the lips and said, 'What can I do for you?' I was shocked, in a pleasant way. It was the first time I'd been kissed by another man."

Nicky reveled in his freedom, but saw it as his last flight before returning to the filial fold. "I was trying to fool myself that I could have it all: I could go to gay bars, have a gay life, but I was still thinking at the time that I would eventually get married and have a wife and children."

▼ ▼ ▼

The idea that gay life is recreation and "real" life is procreation is a painful dichotomy that Nicky says many of his friends have been forced to accept.

"I have one Korean friend here who's very out in every aspect of his life, but not to his parents in Korea," he says. "His parents kept on going to these computer matchmaking services, and he would give them very difficult conditions: he told them, I want a very glamorous, beautiful woman who's fluent in English. Somehow they found this woman, a Korean woman who grew up in Canada, a fashion buyer, glamorous, beautiful, and of course a fluent speaker of English. And he and she were set up to meet in a café. So my friend and this woman sit down, and she says,

'You know, I don't want to be here, my parents made me come.' And he was thinking, *me too.* The woman continued: 'Besides, I'm not interested in Asian men; I prefer Caucasian men.' And my Korean friend thought, *me too.* And on top of that, she added, ' I already *have* a white boyfriend.' And he thought to himself, *me too!*"

▼ ▼ ▼

Like many of his friends and like Wai Tung in the movie, Nicky is in a long-term relationship with a white man—they celebrated their 10th anniversary this year. It's because of his boyfriend that Nicky has been leaning toward coming out to his family.

"My lover has AIDS," he says quietly. "He's a wonderful person, and I'd like my parents to get to know him. I also feel that the time left for me to get to know my parents, to reconcile my feelings and emotions with them, is getting shorter and shorter. My mother is 70 years old."

He's conscious of the complexities of white-Asian gay relationships, however. He mentions the group Asians & Friends, whose functions he and his lover occasionally attend. "I don't like the picture I see there," he says. "There are Asian-Caucasian couples, but the Caucasian guy is always an older man, who plays the role of the bread-earner. The Asian guy tends to be a recently arrived immigrant, someone in a subordinate position. My own determination not to fit into that kind of stereotype has affected my relationship: From the very beginning, I said, don't you ever expect me to be an 'obedient Oriental wife'; when we go out, I won't follow you three steps behind. I've said this so many times now, my lover jokes that, instead of me being an 'obedient Oriental wife,' he's an obedient *Occidental* wife.

He has a nicer and more patient temperament than I do. In our relationship, I tend to boss him around."

▼ ▼ ▼

Besides taking care of his lover, Nicky Y. has been spending time carving a new role for himself: leader for gay Taiwanese youth. In June, he returned to Taiwan to speak to the nation's first and only gay student group—founded as a result of the heightened dialogue raised by the movie.

"They basically said the movie had opened a whole new atmosphere in Taiwan," he says. "They had first tried to form their group as a social one, and of course the college administration thought, 'A gay social group? That means *orgies. Sex parties.* No, you *cannot* form a gay social group!' The administration even threatened to test all of the students who were going to join the club for HIV. Their defense was to leak all of this information to the media; they gave me a pile of clippings, which were, by and large, supportive. In the end, the university let them form a group—but they had to form it as a 'homosexual issues study group.' But they still hold their social functions!"

If the cultures of gay and Chinese identity have not yet met at the station, at least they're on the right track. Nicky is looking forward to the day when he can openly hang his lover's photo and his father's calligraphy side by side, but he knows as well as anyone that Taipei—and the dusty foundation of Chinese culture that it rests upon—took lifetimes to build. It certainly won't burn in a day.

# | 102 |

## *Blacklash?*

### Henry Louis Gates, Jr.

For some veterans of the civil-rights era, it's a matter of stolen prestige. "It is a misappropriation for members of the gay leadership to identify the April 25 march on Washington with the Rev. Dr. Martin Luther King Jr.'s 1963 mobilization," one such veteran, the Reverend Dennis G. Kuby, wrote in a letter to the editor that appeared in the *Times* on the day of the march. Four days later, testifying before the Senate Armed Services Committee's hearings on the issue of gays in the military, Lieutenant General Calvin Waller, United States Army (retired), was more vociferous. General Waller, who, as General Norman Schwarzkopf's second-in-command, was the highest-ranking black officer in the Gulf War's theatre of operations, contemptuously dismissed any linkage between the gay-rights and civil-rights movements. "I had no choice regarding my race when I was delivered from my mother's womb," General Waller said. "To compare my service in America's armed forces with the integration of avowed homosexuals is personally offensive to me." This sentiment—that gays are pretenders to a throne of disadvantage that properly belongs to black Americans, that their relation to the rhetoric of civil rights is one of unearned opportunism—is surprisingly widespread. "The backlash is on the streets among blacks and black pastors who do not want to be aligned with homosexuals," the Reverend Lou Sheldon, chairman of the Traditional Values Coalition, crowed to the *Times* in the aftermath of the march.

That the National Association for the Advancement of Colored People endorsed the April 25th march made the insult all the deeper for those who disparage the gay-rights movement as the politics of imposture—Liberace in Rosa Parks drag. "Gays are not subject to waterhoses or police dogs, denied access to lunch counters or prevented from voting," the Reverend Mr. Kuby asserted. On the contrary, "most gays are perceived as well educated, socially mobile and financially comfortable." Even some of those sympathetic to gay rights are unhappy with the models of oppression and victimhood which they take to be enshrined in the civil-rights discourse that many gay advocates have adopted. For those blacks and whites who viewed last month's march on Washington with skepticism, to be gay is merely an inconvenience; to be black is to inherit a legacy of hardship and inequity. For them, there's no comparison. But the reason the national conversation on the subject has reached an impasse isn't that there's simply no comparison; it's that there's no simple comparison.

Prejudices, of course, don't exist in the abstract; they all come with distinctive and distinguishing historical peculiarities. In short, they have content as well as form. Underplaying the differences blinds us to the signature traits of other forms of social hatred. Indeed, in judging other prejudices by the one you know best you may fail to recognize those other prejudices *as* prejudices.

To take a quick and fairly obvious example, it has been observed that while anti-black racism charges its object with inferiority, anti-Semitism charges its object with iniquity. The racist believes that blacks are incapable of running anything by themselves. The anti-Semite believes (in one popular bit of folklore) that thirteen rabbis rule the world.

*New Yorker*, May 17, 1993, pp. 42–43.

How do gays fit into this scheme? Uneasily. Take that hard-ridden analogy between blacks and gays. Much of the ongoing debate over gay rights has fixated, and foundered, on the vexed distinction between "status" and "behavior." The paradox here can be formulated as follows: Most people think of racial identity as a matter of (racial) status, but they respond to it as behavior. Most people think of sexual identity as a matter of (sexual) behavior, but they respond to it as status. Accordingly, people who fear and dislike blacks are typically preoccupied with the threat that they think blacks' aggressive behavior poses to them. Hence they're inclined to make exceptions for the kindly, "civilized" blacks: that's why "The Cosby Show" could be so popular among white South Africans. By contrast, the repugnance that many people feel toward gays concerns, in the first instance, the status ascribed to them. Disapproval of a sexual practice is transmuted into the demonization of a sexual species.

In other respects, too, anti-gay propaganda sounds less like anti-black rhetoric than like classical anti-Jewish rhetoric: both evoke the image of the small, cliquish minority that nevertheless commands disproportionate and sinister worldly influence. More broadly, attitudes toward homosexuals are bound up with sexism and the attitudes toward gender that feminism, with impressive, though only partial, success, asks us to reëxamine.

That doesn't mean that the race analogy is without merit, or that there are no relevant points of comparison. Just as blacks have historically been represented as sexually uncontrollable beasts, ready to pounce on an unwilling victim with little provocation, a similar vision of the predatory homosexual has been insinuated, often quite subtly, into the defense of the ban on gays in the military.

But can gays really claim anything like the "victim status" inherited by black Americans? "They admit to holding positions in the highest levels of power in education, government, business, and entertainment," Martin Mawyer, president of the Christian Action Network, complains, "yet in the same breath, they claim to be suffering discrimination in employment." Actually, the question itself is a sand trap. First, why should oppression, however it's measured, be a prerequisite for legal protection? Surely there's a consensus that it would be wrongful, and unlawful, for someone to discriminate against Unitarians in housing or employment, however secure Americans Unitarians were as a group. Granted, no one can legislate affection or approval. But the simple fact that people enjoy legal protection from religious discrimination neither confers nor requires victimization. Why is the case of sexual orientation any different?

Second, trying to establish a pecking order of oppression is generally a waste of time: that's something we learned from a long-standing dialogue in the feminist movement. People figured out that you could speak of the subordination of women without claiming, absurdly, that every woman (Margaret Thatcher, say) was subordinate to every man. Now, the single greatest predictor of people's economic success is the economic and educational level of their parents. Since gays, like women, seem to be evenly distributed among classes and races, the compounding effect of transgenerational poverty, which is the largest factor in the relative deprivation of black America, simply doesn't apply. Much of black suffering stems from historical racism; most gay suffering stems from contemporary hatred. It's also the case that the marketing surveys showing that gays have a higher than average income and education level are generally designed to impress potential advertisers in gay publications; quite possibly, the surveys reveal the characteristics only of gays who are willing to identify themselves as such in a questionnaire. Few people would be surprised to learn that secretiveness on this matter varies inversely with education and income level.

What makes the race analogy complicated is that gays, as demographic composites, do indeed "have it better" than blacks—and yet in many ways contemporary homophobia is more virulent than contemporary racism. According to one monitoring group, one in four gay men has been physically assaulted as a result of his perceived sexual orientation; about fifty per cent have been threatened with violence. (For lesbians, the incidence is lower but still disturbing.) A moral consensus now exists in this country that discriminating against blacks as teachers, priests, or tenants is simply wrong. (That doesn't mean it doesn't happen.) For much of the country, however, the moral legitimacy of homosexuals, as homosexuals, remains very much in question. When Bill Crews, for the past nine years the mayor of the well-scrubbed hamlet of Melbourne, Iowa, returned home after the April 25th march, at which he had publicly disclosed his homosexuality for the first time, he found "Melbourne Hates Gays" and "No Faggots" spray-painted on his house. What makes the closet so crowded is that gays are, as a rule, still socialized—usually by their nearest and dearest—into shame.

Mainstream religious figures—ranging from Catholic archbishops to orthodox rabbis—continue to enjoin us to "hate the sin": it has been a long time since anyone respectable urged us to, as it were, hate the skin. Jimmy Swaggart, on the other hand, could assure his millions of followers that the Bible says homosexuals are "worthy of death" and get away with it. Similar access to mass media is not available to those who voice equivalent attitudes toward blacks. In short, measured by their position in society, gays on the average seem privileged relative to blacks; measured by the acceptance of hostile attitudes toward them, gays are worse off than blacks. So are they as "oppressed"? The question presupposes a measuring rod that does not and cannot exist.

To complicate matters further, disapproval of homosexuality has been a characteristic of much of the black-nationalist ideology that has reappeared in the aftermath of the civil-rights era. "Homosexuality is a deviation from Afrocentric thought, because it makes the person evaluate his own physical needs above the teachings of national consciousness," writes Dr. Molefi Kete Asante, of Temple University, who directs the black-studies program there, one of the country's largest. Asante believes that "we can no longer allow our social lives to be controlled by European decadence," and argues that "the redemptive power of Afrocentricity" provides hope of a

cure for those so afflicted, through (the formulation has a regrettably fascist ring) "the submergence of their own wills into the collective will of our people."

In the end, the plaintive rhetoric of the Reverend Mr. Kuby and those civil-rights veterans who share his sense of unease is notable for a small but significant omission: any reference to those blacks who are also gay. And in this immediate context one particular black gay man comes to mind. Actually, it's curious that those who feel that the example of the 1963 march on Washington has been misappropriated seem to have forgotten about him, since it was he, after all, who organized that heroic march. His name, of course, was Bayard Rustin, and it's quite likely that if he had been alive he would have attended the march on Washington thirty years later.

By a poignant historical irony, it was in no small part because of his homosexuality—and the fear that it would be used to discredit the mobilization—that Rustin was prevented from being named director of the 1963 march; the title went to A. Philip Randolph, and he accepted it only on the condition that he could then deputize Rustin to do the arduous work of coördinating the mass protest. Rustin accepted the terms readily. In 1963, it was necessary to choose which of two unreasoning prejudices to resist, and Rustin chose without bitterness or recrimination. Thirty years later, people marched so his successors wouldn't have to make that costly choice.

# | 103 |

## *Blacks and Gays: Healing the Great Divide*

### BARBARA SMITH

In 1993, it has been declared that two essential aspects of my identity are at war with one another. As a person of color, a lesbian, and a feminist, I've spent a great deal of energy refusing to let others pit the various elements of who I am against each other. I always maintain that these elements only

*seem* to be in opposition in this particular time and place, under U.S. capitalism, whose functioning has always required that large groups of

*Gay Community News*, October 1993, pp. 7+.

people be economically, racially and sexually oppressed, and that these potentially dissident groups be kept divided from each other at all costs.

For the first time, however, the relationship between the African American and gay communities is being widely debated both within and outside of movement circles, and surviving as a Black lesbian or gay man has become that much harder. Catalysts for this discussion have been gay leaders' cavalier comparisons between lifting the military ban and racially desegregating the armed forces following World War II, and the decision by the NAACP and other Black civil rights organizations to speak out in favor of lesbian and gay rights and to support the March on Washington. Those decisions have met with protests from some sectors of the Black community and have also spurred the debate.

Ironically, the group of people who are least often consulted about their perspectives on this great divide are those who are most deeply affected by it: Black lesbian and gay activists. Contradictions that we have been grappling with for years, namely homophobia in the Black community, racism in the gay community, and the need for both communities to work together as allies to defeat our real enemies, are suddenly on other people's minds. Because Black lesbians and gays are not thought of as leaders in either movement, however, this debate has been largely framed by those who have frighteningly little and inaccurate information.

Thanks in part to the white gay community's own public relations campaigns, Black Americans view the gay community as uniformly wealthy, highly privileged and politically powerful, a group that has suffered nothing like the centuries of degradation caused by U.S. racism. Rev. Dennis Kuby, a civil rights activist, states in a letter to the *New York Times*. "Gays are not subject to water hoses and police dogs, denied access to lunch counters, or prevented from voting." But most Blacks have no idea that we are threatened with the loss of employment, housing and custody of our children, and are subject to verbal abuse, gay bashing, and death at the hands of homophobes. Kuby's statement also does not acknowledge Black lesbians and gays who have been subjected to all of the racist abuse he cites.

Because we are rendered invisible in both Black and gay contexts, it is that much easier for the Black community to oppose gay rights and to express homophobia without recognizing that these attacks and the lack of legal protections affects its own members.

The racism that has pervaded the mainstream gay movement only fuels the perceived divisions between Blacks and gays. Single issue politics, unlike gay organizing that is consciously and strategically connected to the overall struggle for social and economic justice, do nothing to convince Blacks that gays actually care about eradicating racial oppression. At the very same time that some gays make blanket comparisons between the gay movement and the Black civil rights movement, they also assume that Black and other people of color have won all our battles and are in terrific shape in comparison with gays.

In a December, 1992 interview in the *Dallas Voice*, lesbian publisher Barbara Grier stated: "We are the last minority group unfairly legislated against in the U.S." Grier's perception is, of course, inaccurate. Legislation negatively affecting people of color, immigrants, disabled people, and women occurs every day, especially when court decisions that undermine legal protections are taken into account.

In 1991, well before the relationship between the gay community and the Black community was a hot topic, Andrew Sullivan, editor of *The New Republic*, asserted the following in *The Advocate*.

"The truth is, our position is far worse than that of any ethnic minority or heterosexual women."

> Every fundamental civil right has already been granted to these groups. The issues that they discuss now involve nuances of affirmative action, comparable pay and racial quotas. Gay people, however, still live constitutionally in the South of the '50s. . . .

Sullivan's cynical distortions ignore that quality of life is determined by much more than legislation. Clearly, he also knows nothing about the institution of slavery. Joblessness, poverty, racist and sexist violence, and the lack of decent housing, health care and education make the lives of many "ethnic minorities" and "heterosexual women" a living hell. But Sullivan doesn't care about these folks. He just wants to make sure he gets what he thinks he deserves as a powerful white male.

Lesbians and gay men of color have been trying to push the gay movement to grasp the necessity of anti-racist practice for nigh onto 20 years. Except in the context of organizing within the women's movement with progressive white lesbian feminists, we haven't made much progress.

I'm particularly struck by the fact that, for the most part, queer theory and politics, which are so popular, offer neither substantial anti-racist analysis nor practice. Queer activists' understanding of how to deal with race is usually limited to their including a few lesbians or gay men of color in their ranks, who are expected to carry out the political agenda that the white majority has already determined, and/or sleeping with people of color.

This month Lesbian Avengers from New York City will travel to several states in the Northeast on what they are calling a "Freedom Ride." When lesbians of color from Albany, New York pointed out that the appropriation of this term is offensive because the organization has no demonstrated involvement in anti-racist organizing and has made no links with people of color, including non-lesbians and gays in the communities they plan to visit. Even when we explained that calling themselves "Freedom Riders" might negatively affect the coalitions we've been working to build with people of color in Albany, the group kept the name and really made token changes in their press prelease.

## THE RIGHT TARGETS COMMUNITIES OF COLOR

These divisions are particularly dangerous at a time when the white right wing has actually targeted people of color with their homophobic message. As white lesbian activist Suzanne Pharr points out in "Racist Politics and Homophobia" (*Transformation*, July/August 1993):

> Community by community, the religious Right works skillfully to divide us along fissures that already exist. It is as though they have a political seismograph to locate the racism and sexism in the lesbian and gay community, the sexism and homophobia in communities of color. While the Right is *united* by their racism, sexism and homophobia in their goal to dominate all of us, we are divided by our own racism, sexism, and homophobia.

The Right's divisive strategy of enlisting the Black community's support for their homophobic campaign literally hit home for me in June. A Black lesbian who lives in Cleveland, Ohio

where I grew up, called to tell me that a group of Black ministers had placed a virulently homophobic article in Cleveland's Black newspaper, *The Call and Post*.

Entitled "The Black Church Position Statement on Homosexuality," the ministers condemn "HOMOSEXUALITY (including bisexual as well as gay or lesbian sexual activity) as a lifestyle that is contrary to the teachings of the Bible." Although they claim to have tolerance and compassion for homosexuals, their ultimate goal is to bring about "restoration," i. e., changing lesbians and gays back into heterosexuals in order "to restore such individuals back into harmony with God's will." One of the several sources they cite to prove that such "restoration" is possible is the Traditional Values Foundation Talking Points, 1993, a publication of the Traditional Values Coalition.

The ministers also held a meeting and announced their goal to gather 100,00 signatures in Cleveland in opposition to the federal gay and lesbian civil rights bill, HB 431, and to take their campaign to Detroit and Pittsburgh. A major spokesperson for the ministers, Rev. Marvin McMichol, is the minister of Antioch Baptist Church, the church I was raised in and of which the women in my family were pillars. Antioch was on a number of levels one of the most progressive congregations in Cleveland, especially because of the political leadership it provided at a time when Black people were not allowed to participate in any aspect of Cleveland's civic life.

McMichol states, "It is our fundamental, reasoned belief that there is no comparison between the status of Blacks and women, and the status of gays and lesbians." He explains that being Black or female is an "ontological reality . . . a fact that cannot be hidden," whereas "homosexuality is a chosen lifestyle . . . defined by behavior not ontological reality."

By coincidence, I met Rev. McMichol in May when Naomi Jaffe, an activist friend from Albany, and I did a presentation on Black and Jewish relations at the invitation of Cleveland's New Jewish Agenda. Antioch Baptist Church and a synagogue co-sponsored the event. My cousin had informed me that McMichol had just stepped down as head of the NAACP. Naomi and I were struck by his coldness to us throughout the evening. This was in sharp contrast to the kind reception we received from both the Black and Jewish participants, most of whom were elder women. We guessed that it was because of his homophobia and sexism. Little did we know at the time how right we were.

When I first got news of what was going on in my home town I was emotionally devastated. It would have been bad enough to find out about a major Black-led homophobic campaign in any city in this country, but this place wasn't an abstraction, it was where I came from. It was while growing up in Cleveland that I first felt attracted to women and it was also in Cleveland that I grasped the impossibility of ever acting upon those feelings. Cleveland is a huge city with a small town mentality. Now I was being challenged to deal with homophobia, dead up, in the Black community at home.

I enlisted the help of NGLTF and Scot Nakagawa who runs their Fight the Right office in Portland, Oregon and of members of the Feminist Action Network (FAN), the multi-racial political group I belong to in Albany. Throughout the summer we were in constant contact with people in Cleveland. FAN drafted a counter petition for them to circulate and in early September several of us went there following NGLTF's and Stonewall Cincinnati's Fight the Right Midwest Summit. Unfortunately, by the time we arrived, the group that had been meeting in Cleveland had fallen apart.

We had several meetings, primarily with Black lesbians, but found very few people who were willing to confront the severe threat right in their midst. Most of the women we met even refused to acknowledge the seriousness of the ministers' campaign. We had been warned that remaining closeted prevented activism, but we also found a deep reluctance to deal with Black people in Cleveland's inner city, because of both closeting and class divisions. Cleveland's white lesbian and gay community had never proven itself to be particularly supportive of anti-racist work, and racial segregation seemed to characterize the gay community, just as it does the city as whole.

I cannot say that our efforts to support a visible challenge to the ministers in Cleveland was particularly successful. The right wing's ability to speak to the concerns and play upon the fears of those it wishes to recruit; the lack of visionary political leadership, locally and nationally, among both Black and white lesbians and gays;

and the difficulty of countering homophobia in a Black context, especially when it is justified by religious pronouncements, make this kind of organizing exceedingly hard. But we had better learn how to do it quickly and extremely well if we do not want the Christian right wing to end up running this country.

Since returning from Cleveland we have been exploring the possibility of launching a nationwide petition campaign to gather at least 100,000 signatures from Black people who support lesbian and gay rights. One Black woman, Janet Perkins, a heterosexual Christian who works with the Women's Project in Little Rock, Arkansas has already spoken out. In a courageous article entitled, "The Religious Right: Dividing the African American Community" (*Transformation*, September/October 1993) Perkins calls upon the ministers in Cleveland and the entire Black church to practice love instead of condemnation. She writes:

> These African-American ministers fail to understand they have been drawn into a plot that has as its mission to further separate, divide and place additional pressure on African-Americans so they are unable to come together to work on the problems of the community. . . .

What is needed in our community is a unity and bond that can't be broken by anyone. We must see every aspect of our community as valuable and worth protecting, and yes, we must give full membership to our sisters and brothers who are homosexual. For all these years we have seen them, now we must start to hear them and respect them for who they are.

This is the kind of risk-taking and integrity that makes all the difference. Perkins publicly declares herself an ally whom we can depend upon. I hope in the months to come the gay and lesbian movement in this country will likewise challenge itself to close this great divide, which it can only do by working toward an unbreakable unity, a bond across races, nationalities and classes that up until now this movement has never had.

# V. D
## PARTING GLANCES

# | 104 |

## *Why I'm Not a Revolutionary*

SARAH SCHULMAN

In the vocabulary of the old left, the reason for living was revolution. In our time, however, we comprise the first generation who does not think that the future will be better. We fear the future. We live in a profound state of nostalgia. Concepts like *revolution* just become reminders of the impossibility of change. *Revolution* has come to represent everything we can't have and can't achieve. We know we won't make a revolution and so now we have to ask ourselves if there is anything else we *can* do. In my case, I favor resistance over the concept of revolution. One act of resistance every day is something I think we can all incorporate into our lives. Because, obviously as far as lesbians and gay men go, the status quo is pretty awful for us at this time—so each of us continuing to live tomorrow exactly the way we lived this morning really just means more of the same.

One man whose act of resistance profoundly affected me is Derrick Bell. He is a black law professor who had an appointment at Harvard Law School. But Derrick Bell, having reached the most prestigious position in his profession committed a very unusual act. He refused to be contained by Harvard Law School. He announced that he would carry out a one-man strike; he would refuse to teach another day until Harvard tenured one black woman on their law faculty. Not only was Bell willing to risk all his prestige and salary and corporate power—for Harvard is a corporation—but, he was willing to do this to advocate for a group of people, black women, who had less power than he did in the academic hierarchy. Most interestingly for me, he refused to be a token. He refused to be the only one with access.

Well, in case you don't know the punch-line, Derrick Bell's teaching strike went on for four semesters and two summer sessions and finally he had to either resign from Harvard or go back to work in defeat because they had no intention of tenuring a black woman. So, he resigned. He did put those two years to good use however, by writing a book, *Faces at the Bottom of the Well*, in which he brilliantly describes what he calls "the permanence of racism."

Bell believes, as a result of his own life's experiences, that racism is a permanent institution of American life. It is an inherent characteristic of American culture and forms a crucial part of the economic. social, and political life of the nation. And, of course, this understanding can be applied as well to homophobia and to sexism, the final frontier. The permanence of these hierarchies of domination is a bitter pill to swallow—but, like substituting resistance for revolution—it can free us of many of the psychological strategies that keep us from taking concrete action on our own behalf.

In the past we believed that visibility and civil rights were the keys to transforming the lives of gay people, of people of color, and of women in this country. And that philosophy made sense because when we identify who does not have basic rights under the law, we are talking about the vast majority of Americans. We believed that if the legal system would recognize our full humanity and if people who despise us or, more importantly, resent us, could only get to know us better, our oppression would be reduced. We believed this process would improve our own lives and the many generations ahead with whom we identify.

In Sarah Schulman, *My American History: Essays, 1981–1994*, pp. 258–263. New York: Routledge, 1992.

Yet, this past summer, 24 years after Stonewall, 73 years after women got the vote, 19 years after the Civil Rights Act, this nation was subjected to the most vicious and vile public display of homophobia ever to be portrayed in the national media. Resolutions are currently pending in Oregon, Colorado, Tampa, Florida, and Portland, Maine that would significantly limit the rights of gay men and lesbians. Simultaneously, this nation continues to abandon people with AIDS and has no compassion for their survivors. Some cities have gay rights bills, but that doesn't stop gay bashings. Some cities have job protection clauses, but that doesn't stop people from being fired arbitrarily. We have huge numbers of people who are entirely open about their homosexuality, but they are ignored by the national discourse and excluded from the intellectual life of the nation. I think it should be obvious to all of us that actions directed towards convincing other people to like us have not worked as a strategy. Instead, we must focus, as Derrick Bell has done, on protecting our own community and strengthening that community's political power.

On September 26th a twenty-nine-year-old black lesbian named Hattie Mae Cohens and a forty-five-year-old white gay man named Brian Mock were at home in the apartment they shared in Salem, Oregon when a group of skinheads threw a molotov cocktail into their basement and these two members of our community were burned to death. Can you smell their burning bodies? These two martyrs were murdered five weeks before the state they died in was about to vote on the worst anti-gay legislation that has ever been seen in this nation. Even though this is the Emmet Till case of the nineties it was completely ignored by the national media. Even out gay people in major news organizations did not get this story into print. The only straight paper that reported on it was the *Oregonian*. And do you know what was on the cover that week of *QW*, New York's weekly lesbian and gay magazine? An interview with Susan Sarandon. Please *QW*, one act of resistance every day.

Lesbians, also, are under great pressure to be contained, to minimize or eliminate the lesbian content of our work, of our biographies in order to be invited into American culture. In the eighties a number of us tried to imagine a fiction in which the lesbian voice was the neutral, objective, and authoritative voice of the novel. But that is an effort that can only come from some illusion of empowerment. Today, in the midst of the devas-tation and pressure that is gay life in America, lesbian fiction across the board has become obsessed with our marginality. And those of us who are out look at the closeted and semi-closeted with more investment than ever.

One night I was hanging out with a bunch of friends flipping through the pages of *Vanity Fair* magazine. Annie Leibovitz had just published a series of full color portraits entitled "Heroes of the Gulf War," featuring a variety of killers in romantic poses. Thoroughly disgusted, we sat down and wrote her a collective letter. "We use our talents for peace," we said. "You are using yours for war." Of course she never responded.

Why do I take the actions of famous lesbians so personally? Sometimes it seems as though those of us who are out in our professions have gone as far as we will ever be allowed to go and are now standing, noses pressed against the glass wall that separates "us" from "them." Perhaps that's why I reacted so strongly to the recent *New York Times Magazine* cover story profile on Susan Sontag. The article carefully protected her closet. They didn't create fake husbands or faux boyfriends—but they collaborated with her in reinforcing the lie that brilliant and creative women must sacrifice sex and love in order to achieve.

In the *Times* profile, Sontag describes talking to her psychiatrist about her guilt over writing a romance novel instead of social criticism because she believes that fiction is not as useful a contribution to the public good. The doctor reassures her that giving people reading pleasure is also important. I wanted to scream. Why hasn't she asked these questions about her own homosexuality and the gay and lesbian community? Why isn't she concerned about the contribution she is withholding from us when she refuses—as one of the most respected women in the world—to come out as the dyke that she is? Lesbians suffer a real brain drain because so many of our great artists, leaders, and social thinkers are closeted. What does Sontag have to say about the struggle to build an integrated homosexual life? About how to build activist movements? About how to strategize to end AIDS? She did write a book, *AIDS and Its Metaphors*, but her closet kept her from addressing homophobia and its impact on the epidemic in precisely the way that her openness about having cancer *enhanced* her analysis of the stigmatization of disease in *Illness As Metaphor*. What does Sontag feel, sitting in *her* apartment when she hears about Hattie Mae

Cohens? Can anything other than the desire to be accepted by straight people be at the root of Sontag's closet?

Many people argue that an artist's homosexuality is irrelevant to their work. But the way in which submerged lesbian content distorts artistic expression was made clear to me when I saw Anna Deveare Smith's play *Fires in the Mirror*, a smash hit one-woman show that ran at the Public Theater this year. Smith's piece addresses the conflict between Hasidic Jews and blacks in Crown Heights, Brooklyn. She recites, verbatim, testimony from a wide range of black and Jewish figures on the event and adapts a variety of personae to enact each character. But what really shocked me the most was the unspoken (and unacknowledged by critics) lesbian subtext that ran throughout the play.

To be specific, encoded in Smith's piece was a very subtle but persistent series of references to black lesbians. First of all, Smith plays the whole show in male drag. But the closet made its first overt appearance on stage in a short scene, early in the piece, where she portrays Angela Davis, the revolutionary black leader and teacher who is also a lesbian. Smith plays Davis wearing a black leather jacket as she is teaching in the History of Consciousness Department at the University of California in Santa Cruz. Davis is making a statement about how race is not sufficient enough of a category for her to use as the sole basis of community. "I am interested in community that is not static." Davis says. "I'm interested in coming together in a different way." Now, if the audience knew that Davis is a lesbian, her rejection of race as the only category for identity could take on a meaning that would be very challenging for homophobes of all racial groups. But, without this knowledge, the reverse impact occurs, where the audience can come away thinking that Angela Davis has mellowed, has become a liberal, is now a humanist. The closet here distorts a very important piece of information about the political and emotional life of one of America's most heroic figures.

Throughout the play Smith graciously avoids any mention of romantic love, sexuality, masculinity, or "the family." She never portrays a woman in a traditionally seductive or "feminine" manner. Instead, she emphasizes the intellectual life of most of her female characters—both black and Jewish. She actually remains quite gender neutral throughout. Additionally when playing Jewish males—who are usually seen as less mas-

culine than dominant culture males—she essentially plays them almost as herself—with little affectation of vocal tone or body movement that would traditionally signify masculinity.

In fact, the only overt discussion of black sexuality comes from Big Mo, a rapper based in Crown Heights. Mo complains that too many other female rappers are capitulating to dehumanizing images of black women's sexuality. She acknowledges that she has been put down for taking this stance but confidently asserts that, despite the criticism, she knows that "I'm not man-bashing. I'm female-asserting." Of the two women Mo points to as heroic exceptions to this collusion with dominant images of black women, one—Queen Latifah—is also widely believed to be a lesbian.

Obviously these questions of black lesbian identity are very important in Smith's life. But, by consciously burying them so deeply in her work, she is contributing to a huge pretense about events like Crown Heights. If we continue to insist that categories like *black* and *Jewish* are closed and not mitigated by other factors such as gender, sexuality, class loyalty, etc., then we will have a harder time imagining an alternative for human relations. The closeting of the controversy of homosexuality resulted in a more manageable and streamlined discussion of relations between blacks and Jews, but that containment is ultimately false. I'm Jewish and I have relationships with black people who are both homosexual and heterosexual. My homosexuality is a very significant mitigating factor in those relationships. I could not participate in a constructive discussion of black/Jewish relationships without including it.

I understand the desire to keep one's lesbianism out of the artistic product. I sit there like the rest of you and watch closeted women or semicloseted artworks achieve a level of reward that is systematically denied the rest of us. I'm sure I'm not the only one in this room who sits home at night thinking "Should I write a straight novel under a pseudonym?" and other weird thoughts like, "Should I write for television?" because the approval is so seductive. But instead, I have to choose, every day, the path of one act of resistance. Once a day say something complicated, take on something difficult, challenge yourself, surprise the people around you, resist acting for the approval of straight people, of white people, of men. Talk about Hattie Mae Cohens at work tomorrow. Say her name.

# | 105 |

## *In an Afternoon Light*

ESSEX HEMPHILL

On a recent afternoon in Philadelphia I walked to the corner of 63rd and Malvern Streets to catch a number 10 trolley, *my* imaginary streetcar named Desire. Waiting, when I arrived at the stop was another black man, sipping a bottle of beer and smoking a cigarette. He wore sunshades and was built three sizes larger than my compact frame. I guessed him to be in his thirties though his pot-belly suggested an older age or the consumption of too much beer and soul food. A blue hand towel was tossed over his right shoulder. A base-ball jacket was draped across his left thigh. He was sitting on the wall I sit on when I wait here. Since there was no trolley in sight, I guardedly walked over and sat at the far end of the wall. He contin-ued to drink his beer as I observed him from the corner of my eye. I pretended to occupy myself with looking for an approaching trolley. He abruptly ended our brief interlude of silence. For no apparent reason he blurted out, "Man, the women's movement is ruling the world. It's turn-ing our sons into faggots and our men into punks."

"What do you mean?" I asked, raising my voice as loudly as he had raised his. Indignation and defensiveness tinged my vocal cords. I thought his remarks were directed specifically at me.

"You see all the cars going by?" he asked, ges-turing at the traffic.

"Yeah, so what about it?"

"Well, can't you see that all the drivers in the cars are women—"

"Which only means more women are driving" I interjected.

"—because women have caused major changes in society, brother. Women are ruling more things now. That's why I don't want my son to spend all his time with his mother, his grand-mother, and those aunts of his. His mother and I don't live together, but I go visit him and take him downtown or to the movies or down to the Boys' Club to watch basketball games. I think that's important, so he'll know the difference."

"The difference in what?" I asked.

"The difference between a woman and man. You know . . ."

"Which is supposed to be determined by what—how they use their sex organs? What I do know, brother, is that thirteen- and fourteen-year-old black children are breeding babies they can't care for—crack babies, AIDS babies, accidental babies, babies that will grow up and inherit their parents' poverty and powerlessness. The truth is, young people are fucking because they want to fuck. They're encouraged to fuck. Yet we don't talk to them frankly and honestly about sex, sexu-ality, or their responsibility."

"Okay, brother, hold that thought. You're mov-ing too fast. See, this is what I mean. Suppose you grow up in a home with your father being a min-ister and your mother is there all the time taking care of the house and kids. You grow up, go off to college, and get a good education. Then you decide you gonna be gay. You like men. I say you learned that. Education did that. Your folks didn't teach you that."

"That's bullshit, and you know it," I insisted. "It's stupid to suggest that women or education can make a man gay. What you fail to understand is that this is the natural diversity of human sexu-ality no matter what we call it. Also, my father is a

In Essex Hemphill, ed., *Brother to Brother: New Writings by Black Gay Men*, pp. 258–260. Boston: Alyson, 1991.

minister, my mother was at home raising us before they divorced, and I went to college. And you know what? I'm a faggot."

"No you ain't!"

"Yes I am. In fact, I'm becoming a well-known faggot."

"I don't believe you."

"Why not?"

"Because you ain't switching and stuff."

"Yeah, all you think being gay is about is men switching—but you're wrong. I'm a faggot because I love me enough to be who I am. If your son grows up to be a faggot, it won't be because of the way you or his mother raised him. It will be because he learns to trust the natural expression of his sexuality without fear or shame. If he learns anything about courage from you or his mother, then he'll grow up to be himself. You can't blame being straight or gay on a woman or education. The education that's needed should be for the purpose of bringing us all out of sexual ignorance. It's just another tactic to keep us divided—these sex wars we wage. Our sexuality is determined by the will of human nature, and nature is the will of God . . ."

He sat there for a moment staring at me, sipping his beer. He lit another cigarette. I realized then that he could beat me to a pulp if he chose to impose his bigger size, his vociferous masculinity on me. But I wasn't afraid for what I had said and revealed. On too many occasions, I have sat silently as men like him mouthed off about gays and women, and I said nothing because I was afraid. But not today. Not this afternoon. The longer I sit silently in my own community, my own home, and say nothing, I condone the ignorance and its by-products of violence and discrimination. I prolong my existence in a realm of invisibility and complicity. I prolong our mutual suffering by saying nothing.

Neither of us spoke another word. In this tense interlude, a bus and trolley approached. I was angry with having to encounter him on such a glorious spring day, but this is the kind of work social change requires. I consoled myself believing this.

When he rose I immediately rose too—a defensive strategy, a precaution.

"It's been good talking to you, brother. I'll think about what you've said." He extended his hand to me just as the bus and the trolley neared. I looked at his hand, known and unknown to me, offered tenuously, waiting to clasp my hand.

"Yeah, it was cool talking to you, too," I returned, as I hesitantly shook his hand. He swaggered to the bus and boarded with his beer hidden under the jacket he carried. I walked into the street to meet the trolley in an afternoon light devoid of shame.

# CREDITS

Martin Duberman, "A Matter of Difference," reprinted from the *Nation*, July 5, 1993, pp. 2–24. Copyright © 1993 the Nation Company, Inc.

Erica E. Goode, "Intimate Friendships," copyright, July 5, 1993, *U.S. News & World Report*, pp. 49–52.

John Boswell, "Concepts, Experience, and Sexuality," reprinted from Ed Stein, ed., *Forms of Desire*. New York: Routledge, pp. 133–74, orginally published by Garland, 1990. Copyright Estate of John Boswell.

John D'Emilio, "Capitalism and Gay Identity," copyright © 1983 by Snitow, Stansell and Thompson. Reprinted by permission of the Monthly Review Foundation.

Lillian Faderman, "A Worm in the Bud: The Early Sexologists and Love Between Women," *Odd Girls and Twilight Lovers*, 1991, pp. 37–61. Copyright © Columbia University Press, 1991.

George Chauncey, "The Bowery as Haven and Spectacle" from *Gay New York*. Copyright © George Chauncey. Reprinted by permission of Basic Books, a division of HarperCollins Publishers, Inc.

Joseph Beam, "Making Ourselves from Scratch," in Essex Hemphill, ed., *Brother to Brother: New Writings by Black Gay Men*, conceived by Joseph Beam. Boston: Alyson, pp. 261–62. Copyright © Dorothy Beam. Reprinted by permission.

Arlene Stein, "Becoming Lesbian: Identity Work and the Performance of Sexuality," *Sex and Sensibility: Stories of a Lesbian Generation*, pp. 65–90. Copyright © 1997 the Regents of the University of California.

Pat Califia, "Gay Men, Lesbians, and Sex: Doing It Together," *Advocate*, July 7, 1983, pp. 24–27. Copyright © Pat Califia.

Dana Y. Takagi, "Maiden Voyage: Excursion into Sexuality and Identity Politics in Asian America," *Amerasia Journal* 20(1), 1994, pp. 1–17. Copyright © Amerasia Journal.

Carol Queen, "Strangers at Home: Bisexuals in the Queer Movement," *Outlook* 16, 1992, pp. 23, 29–33. Copyright © Carol Queen.

Ara Wilson, "Just Add Water: Searching for the Bisexual Politic," *Outlook* 16, 1992, pp. 22, 24–28. Copyright © Ara Wilson.

Leslie Feinberg, "To Be or Not to Be," *Transgender Warriors*, Boston: Beacon Press, 1996, pp. 101–7. Copyright © 1996 Leslie Feinberg. Reprinted by permission of Beacon Press.

Walter Williams, "The Abominable Sin: The Spanish Campaign Against 'Sodomy,' " in *The Spirit and the Flesh: Sexual Diversity in American Indian Culture*, Boston: Beacon Press, 1986, pp. 131–40. Copyright © 1986 Walter Williams. Reprinted by permission of the Beacon Press.

Joseph Cardinal Ratzinger, "Letter to the Bishops of the Catholic Church on the Pastoral care of Homosexual Persons," 1986, Vatican City: Congregation for the Doctrine of the Faith.

Peter J. Gomes, "Homophobic? Re-Read Your Bible," *New York Times*, August 17, 1992, p. A:19. Copyright © 1992 the New York Times Company. Reprinted by permission.

Deb Price, "Biblical Verse: Is It a Reason or an Excuse?" *Detroit News*, August 24, 1993. Reprinted by permission.

Reprinted by permission.

Victorial Brownworth, "Pop Tune Can Comfort Teens Unsure of Their Sexuality," *Philadelphia Daily News*, July 25, 1995. Reprinted courtesy of the *Philadelphia Daily News* and the author.

Richard Dyer, "Stereotyping," in Richard Dyer, ed., *Gays and Film*, New York: Zoetrope, 1977, pp. 27–39. Copyright © Richard Dyer. Reprinted by permission.

Caroline Sheldon, "Lesbians and Film: Some Thoughts," in Richard Dyer, ed., *Gays and Film*. New York: Zoetrope, 1977. Reprinted by permission.

George Custen, "Where Is the Life That Late He Led? Hollywood's Construction of Sexuality in the Life of Cole Porter," original manuscript, 1994. Copyright © 1994 George Custen.

Marguerite Moritz, "Old Strategies for New Texts: How American Television Is Creating and Treating Lesbian Characters," in R. Jeffrey Ringer, ed., *Queer Words, Queer Images: Communication and the Construction of Homosexuality*. New York: New York University Press, 1994, pp. 122–42. Reprinted by permission.

Frank Bruni, "Culture Stays Screen Shy of Showing the Gay Kiss," *Detroit Free Press*, February 11, 1994, p. 1. Reprinted by permission.

Joshua Gamson, "Do Ask, Do Tell," *American Prospect*, Fall 1995. Copyright © 1995 New Prospect, Inc. Reprinted by permission.

David Ehrenstein, "More Than Friends," *Los Angeles Magazine*, May 1996. Copyright © 1996 David Ehrenstein.

Liz Kotz, "Anything But Idyllic: Lesbian Filmmaking in the 1980s and 1990s," in Arlene Stein, ed., *Sisters, Sexperts, Queers*. New York: Penguin, 1993, pp. 67–80. Copyright © 1993 Arlene Stein. Reprinted by permission of Dutton Signet, a division of Penguin Books USA, Inc.

"Perverts Called Government Peril" *New York Times*, April 19, 1950, p. 25. Copyright © 1950 the New York Times Company. Reprinted by permission.

"The Homosexual in America" *Time*, January 21, 1966, pp. 40–41. Copyright © 1966 Time Magazine.

Kay Tobin, "A Rebuke for *Time*'s Pernicious Prejudice," *Ladder*, April 1966, pp. 20–22. Copyright © 1966 Kay Tobin Lahusen. Reprinted by permission.

Charles Alverson, "A Minority's Plea: U.S. Homosexuals Gain in Trying to Persuade Society to Accept Them," *Wall Street Journal*, July 17, 1968. Reprinted by permission of the *Wall Street*

*Journal.* Copyright © 1993 Dow Jones and Company, Inc. All rights reserved worldwide.

Lisker, Jerry, "Homo Nest Raided!: Queen Bees are Stinging Mad," *New York Daily News*, July 6, 1969. Copyright © New York Daily News.

Lacey Fosburgh, "The 'Gay' People Demand Their Rights," *New York Times*, July 5, 1970, p. E-12. Copyright © 1970 the New York Times Company. Reprinted by permission.

Judy Klemesrud, "The Lesbian Issue and Women's Lib," *New York Times*, December 18, 1970. Copyright © 1970 the New York Times Company. Reprinted by permission.

Ransdell Pierson, "Uptight on Gay News: Can the Straight Press Get the Gay Story Right?" *Columbia Journalism Review*, March/April, 1982, pp. 25–33. Reprinted by permission.

Michelangelo Signorile, "Out at the New York Times," *Advocate*, May 5 and 19, 1992, pp. 34–42 and 38–42. Reprinted courtesy of Liberation Publications, Inc.

Edward Albert, "Illness and Deviance: The Response of the Press to AIDS," in Douglas A. Feldman and Thomas M. Johnson, eds., *Social Dimensions of AIDS*. Westport, Conn.: Praeger, 1986, pp. 163–78. Copyright © 1986 Preager Publishers. Reprinted with permission of the Greenwood Publishing Group, Inc., Westport, Conn.

James Kinsella, "The Second Wave," *Covering the Plague: AIDS and the American Media*, New Brunswick, N.J.: Rutgers University Press, 1989, pp. 242–53. Copyright © 1989 Rutgers, the State University. Reprinted by permission of Rutgers University Press.

Vito Russo, "A Test of Who We Are as a People," *Democracy: Discussions in Contemporary Culture* 5, edited by Brian Wallis. Seattle: Bay Press, 1990, pp. 299–302. Copyright © People With AIDS Coalition.

Jessea N. R. Greenman, "More to the Shilts Story," *MediaFile*, April/May, 1994, p. 3. Copyright © 1994 Jessea N. R. Greenman.

Richard Goldstein, "Big Science: What Ever Happened to Safe Sex?" *OUT*, May 1997, pp. 62–66. Copyright © 1997 Richard Goldstein. Reprinted by permission.

Larry Gross, *Contested Closets: The Politics and Ethics of Outing*. Minneapolis: University of Minnesota, 1993, pp. 1–12, 35–45, 124–132. Copyright © 1993 the Regents of the University of Minnesota.

Michelangelo Signorile, "How I Brought Out Malcolm Forbes and the Media Blinked," *Village*

*Voice*, April 3, 1990, pp. 23–24. Reprinted by permission of the author and the Village Voice.

C. Carr, "Why Outing Must Stop," *Village Voice*, March 19, 1990, p. 37. Reprinted by permission of the author and the Village Voice.

Gabriel Rotello, "The Inning of Outing," *Advocate*, April 18, 1995, p. 80. Reprinted courtesy of Liberation Publications, Inc.

Eric Marcus, " 'Gay Gal'—Lisa Ben," in *Making History: The Struggle for Lesbian and Gay Equal Rights*, New York: HarperCollins, 1992, pp. 5–15. Copyright © 1992 Eric Marcus. Reprinted by permission of HarperCollins Publishers, Inc.

Eric Marcus, "News Hound—Jim Kepner," in *Making History: The Struggle for Lesbian and Gay Equal Rights*, New York: HarperCollins, 1992, pp. 43–53. Copyright © 1992 Eric Marcus. Reprinted by permission of HarperCollins Publishers, Inc.

Rodger Streitmatter, "The *Advocate*: Setting the Standard for the Gay Liberation Press," *Journalism History* 19(3), 1993, pp. 93–102. Reprinted by permission of the author and Journalism History.

Polly Thistlethwaite, "Representation, Liberation, and the Queer Press," in Brian Wallis, ed., *Democracy: Discussions in Contemporary Culture* 5. Seattle: Bay Press, pp. 209–12. Copyright © 1990 Bay Press. Reprinted by permission.

Ed Jackson, "Introduction," in Ed Jackson and Stan Persky, eds., *Flaunting It! A Decade of Gay Journalism from The Body Politic*. Vancouver: New Star Books/Toronto: Pink Triangle Books, 1982, pp. 1–6.

Larry Closs, "I Want My Gay TV," *OUT*, September 1994, pp. 60–66, 120–23. Copyright © Larry Closs. Reprinted by permission.

Richard Dyer, "Coming to Terms: Gay Pornography," *Only Entertainment*, New York: Routledge, 1992, 121–34. Copyright © 1992 Richard Dyer. Reprinted by permission.

Scott Tucker, "Gender, Fucking and Utopia," *Social Texts* 27(9/2), 1990, pp. 3–34. Copyright © 1990 Scott Tucker. Reprinted by permission.

Charles Nero, "Free Speech or Hate Speech: Pornography and Its Means of Production," *Law and Sexuality: A Review of Lesbian and Gay Legal Issues* 2, 1992, pp. 3–9. Copyright © 1992 Law and Sexuality: A Review of Lesbian and Gay Legal Issues. All rights reserved.

Joan Nestle, "My History with Censorship," *A Restricted Country*, Ithaca: Firebrand, 1987, pp. 120–22. Copyright © 1987 Joan Nestle.

Joan Nestle, "My Mother Liked to Fuck," *A Restricted Country*, Ithaca: Firebrand, 1987, pp. 144–50. Copyright © 1987 Joan Nestle.

Lisa Henderson, "Lesbian Pornography: Cultural Transgression and Sexual Demystification," in Sally Munt, ed., *New Lesbian Criticism*, New York: Columbia University Press, 1991, pp. 173–91. Copyright © 1991 Lisa Henderson. Reprinted by permission.

Richard Fung, "Looking for My Penis: The Eroticized Asian in Gay Video Porn," in Bad Object Choices, eds., *How Do I Look?* pp. 148–60. Copyright © Bay Press. Reprinted by permission.

Daniel C. Tsang, "Notes on Queer 'N Asian Virtual Sex," *Amerasian Journal* 20(1), 1994, pp. 117–28. Copyright © 1994 Amerasia Journal.

Steve Silberman, "We're Teen, We're Queer, and We've Got E-Mail," *Wired*, November 1994, pp. 1–3. Copyright © 1994–96 Wired Magazine Group, Inc. All rights reserved.

Jeff Walsh, "Logging On, Coming Out," *Advocate*, October 18, 1994, p. 6. Reprinted courtesy of Liberation Publications, Inc.

Andrew Hodges and David Hutter, *With Downcast Gays: Aspects of Homosexual Self-Oppression*, London: Pomegranate Press, 1994. Copyright © 1994 Pomegranate Press.

Radicalesbians, "The Woman-Identified Woman," in Karla Jay and Allen Young, eds., *Out of the Closets: Voices of Gay Liberation*, New York: Jove, 1970, pp. 172–77. Reprinted by permission of the editors.

Cheryl Clarke, "Lesbianism: An Act of Resistance," in Cherríe Moraga and Gloria Anzaldúa, eds., *This Bridge Called My Back: Writings by Radical Women of Color*. Watertown, Mass.: Persephone Press, 1981, pp. 128–37. Copyright © 1983. Used by permission of the author and of Kitchen Table: Women of Color Press, P.O. Box 908, Latham, NY 12110.

Mirtha Quintanales, "I Paid Very Hard for My Immigrant Ignorance," in Cherríe Moraga and Gloria Anzaldúa, eds., *This Bridge Called My Back: Writings by Radical Women of Color*. Watertown, Mass.: Persephone Press, 1981, pp. 150–56. Copyright © 1983. Used by permission of the author and of Kitchen Table: Women of Color Press, P.O. Box 908, Latham, NY 12110.

Scott Tucker, "Our Right to the World: Beyond the Right to Privacy," *Body Politic*, July/August 1992, pp. 29–33. Copyright © 1982 Scott Tucker. Reprinted by permission.

Michael Denneny, "Chasing the Crossover Audi-

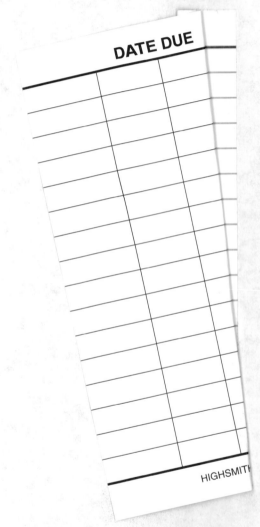

**DATE DUE**

HIGHSMITH